The

Film Cultures

Reader

Edited by

Graeme Turner

London and New York

First published 2002
by Routledge
11 New Fetter Lane, London EC4P 4EE

Simultaneously published in the USA and Canada
by Routledge
29 West 35th Street, New York, NY 10001

Typeset in Perpetua/Bell Gothic
by Florence Production Ltd, Stoodleigh, Devon
Printed and bound in Great Britain
by TJ International Ltd, Padstow, Cornwall

British Library Cataloguing in Publication Data
A catalogue record for this book is available from the British Library

Library of Congress Cataloging in Publication Data
The film cultures reader/edited by Graeme Turner.
    p. cm.
  Includes bibliographical references and index.
  1. Motion pictures.   I. Turner, Graeme.
  PN1994.F4384 2002
  791.43–dc21   2001048577

ISBN 0–415–25281–4 (hbk)
ISBN 0–415–25282–2 (pbk)

The Film Cultures Reader

This companion reader to *Film as Social Practice* brings together key writings on contemporary cinema, exploring film as a social and cultural phenomenon.

Key features of the reader include:

- Thematic sections, each with an introduction by the editor
- A general introduction by Graeme Turner
- Sections: understanding film, film technology, film industries, meanings and pleasures, identities, audiences and consumption

Contributors: Tino Balio, Sabrina Barton, Tony Bennett, Jacqueline Bobo, Stella Bruzzi, Edward Buscombe, Jim Collins, Barbara Creed, Richard Dyer, Jane Feuer, Miriam Hansen, John Hill, Marc Jancovich, Susan Jeffords, Isaac Julien, Annette Kuhn, P. David Marshall, Judith Mayne, Kobena Mercer, Tania Modleski, Steve Neale, Tom O'Regan, Stephen Prince, Thomas Schatz, Gianluca Sergi, Ella Shohat, Jackie Stacey, Janet Staiger, Robert Stam, Chris Straayer, Yvonne Tasker, Stephen Teo, Janet Woollacott, Justin Wyatt.

Editor: Graeme Turner is Professor of Cultural Studies at the University of Queensland. He is the author of *Film as Social Practice*, third edition (Routledge 1999) and *British Cultural Studies*, second edition (Routledge 1996).

Contents

List of illustrations   *ix*
Notes on contributors   *xi*
Acknowledgements   *xvi*
Preface   *xix*

Graeme Turner
EDITOR'S INTRODUCTION   1

PART ONE
Understanding film

Graeme Turner
INTRODUCTION   11

1   Tony Bennett and Janet Woollacott
    TEXTS AND THEIR READINGS   14

2   Annette Kuhn
    WOMEN'S GENRES   20

3   Judith Mayne
    PARADOXES OF SPECTATORSHIP   28

4   Janet Staiger
    RECEPTION STUDIES IN FILM AND TELEVISION   46

PART TWO
Technologies

Graeme Turner
INTRODUCTION   73

5   Edward Buscombe
SOUND AND COLOUR   77

6   Steve Neale
COLOUR AND FILM AESTHETICS   85

7   Richard Dyer
LIGHTING FOR WHITENESS   95

8   Gianluca Sergi
A CRY IN THE DARK: THE ROLE OF THE POST-CLASSICAL
FILM SOUND   107

9   Stephen Prince
TRUE LIES: PERCEPTUAL REALISM, DIGITAL IMAGES
AND FILM THEORY   115

10   Barbara Creed
THE CYBERSTAR: DIGITAL PLEASURES AND
THE END OF THE UNCONSCIOUS   129

PART THREE
Industries

Graeme Turner
INTRODUCTION   135

11   Tom O'Regan
A NATIONAL CINEMA   139

12   John Hill
BRITISH CINEMA AS NATIONAL CINEMA: PRODUCTION,
AUDIENCE AND REPRESENTATION   165

13   Stephen Teo
POSTMODERNISM AND THE END OF HONG KONG CINEMA   174

14 Thomas Schatz
    THE NEW HOLLYWOOD   184

15 Tino Balio
    'A MAJOR PRESENCE IN ALL THE WORLD'S IMPORTANT
    MARKETS': THE GLOBALIZATION OF HOLLYWOOD IN THE 1990s   206

PART FOUR
Meanings and pleasures

Graeme Turner
INTRODUCTION   219

16 Richard Dyer
    MONROE AND SEXUALITY: DESIRABILITY   223

17 P. David Marshall
    THE CINEMATIC APPARATUS AND THE CONSTRUCTION
    OF THE FILM CELEBRITY   228

18 Jane Feuer
    SPECTATORS AND SPECTACLES   240

19 Stella Bruzzi
    DESIRE AND THE COSTUME FILM: *PICNIC AT HANGING ROCK*,
    THE AGE OF INNOCENCE, THE PIANO   246

20 Tania Modleski
    THE TERROR OF PLEASURE: THE CONTEMPORARY
    HORROR FILM AND POSTMODERN THEORY   268

21 Jim Collins
    GENERICITY IN THE NINETIES: ECLECTIC IRONY AND
    THE NEW SINCERITY   276

PART FIVE
Identities

Graeme Turner
INTRODUCTION   291

22 Yvonne Tasker
    ACTION HEROINES IN THE 1980s: THE LIMITS OF 'MUSCULINITY'   295

23 Sabrina Barton
YOUR SELF STORAGE: FEMALE INVESTIGATION AND MALE
PERFORMATIVITY IN THE WOMAN'S PSYCHOTHRILLER   311

24 Chris Straayer
THE HYPOTHETICAL LESBIAN HEROINE IN
NARRATIVE FEATURE FILM   331

25 Susan Jeffords
CAN MASCULINITY BE TERMINATED?   344

26 Isaac Julien and Kobena Mercer
DE MARGIN AND DE CENTRE   355

27 Ella Shohat and Robert Stam
THE IMPERIAL IMAGINARY   366

PART SIX
Audiences and consumption

Graeme Turner
INTRODUCTION   379

28 Justin Wyatt
HIGH CONCEPT AND MARKET RESEARCH: MOVIE
MAKING BY THE NUMBERS   382

29 Miriam Hansen
CHAMELEON AND CATALYST: THE CINEMA AS AN
ALTERNATIVE PUBLIC SPHERE   390

30 Jackie Stacey
HOLLYWOOD CINEMA: THE GREAT ESCAPE   420

31 Jacqueline Bobo
WATCHING THE COLOR PURPLE: TWO INTERVIEWS   444

32 Mark Jancovich
'A REAL SHOCKER': AUTHENTICITY, GENRE AND
THE STRUGGLE FOR DISTINCTION   469

References   481
Index   511

Illustrations

Figures

Figure 7.1	*Rising Sun*: Wesley Snipes, Harvey Keitel and Sean Connery	103
Figure 9.1	Digital compositing in *Forrest Gump*	116
Figure 9.2	*Jurassic Park*: not the real T. Rex	117
Figure 9.3	*Forrest Gump*: computer-generated crowd	122
Figure 9.4	Computer imaging in *The Mask*	125
Figure 19.1	Anne Lambert in *Picnic at Hanging Rock*	255
Figure 19.2	Michelle Pfeiffer and Daniel Day Lewis in *The Age of Innocence*	259
Figure 19.3	Daniel Day Lewis as Newland in *The Age of Innocence*	261
Figure 19.4	Holly Hunter and Maori women in *The Piano*	265
Figure 23.1	Jodie Foster in *Silence of the Lambs*	314
Figure 23.2	Jodie Foster and Kasi Lemmons in *Silence of the Lambs*	317
Figure 23.3	Jill Schoelen, Shelley Hack and Terry O'Quinn in *The Stepfather*	320
Figures 24.1 and 24.2 Dominique Sanda and Geraldine Chaplin in *Voyage en Douce*		335
Figures 24.3 and 24.4 Isabelle Huppert and Miou-Miou in *Entre Nous*		337
Figures 24.5 and 24.6 *Entre Nous* (above) and *Voyage en Douce* (below)		339
Figure 30.1	Doris Day in *Calamity Jane*	422
Figure 30.2	Publicity still of Joan Crawford	434

Tables

Table 30.1 Gross box-office receipts   422

Table 30.2 Frequency of cinema-going in the UK in 1943   423

Table 30.3 Cinema admissions and net box-office takings (UK)   427

Table 30.4 Dyer's model of the appeal of entertainment forms   430

Notes on contributors

Tino Balio is Chair of the Department of Communication Arts and Executive Director of the University of Wisconsin–Madison Arts Institute. He is the author of numerous books and articles on the American film industry, including a two-volume history of United Artists Corporation and *Grand Design: Hollywood as a Modern Business Enterprise, 1930–1939* (1993).

Sabrina Barton has published articles on Hitchcock and on the woman's psychothriller. She is an Assistant Professor in the English Department at The University of Texas at Austin, where she teaches courses in film and gender studies. The title of her book-in-progress is *Look At It My Way: Competing Identities in Hitchcock, the Woman's Psychothriller* and *Feminist Film Theory*.

Tony Bennett is Professor of Sociology at the Open University where he is also Director of the Pavis Centre for Social and Cultural Research. His recent publications include the *Birth of the Museum: History, Theory, Politics* (1995), *Culture: A Reformer's Science* (1998) and, as co-author, *Accounting for Tastes: Australian Everyday Cultures* (1999).

Jacqueline Bobo is Chair and Associate Professor of Women's Studies and Associate Director of the Center for Black Studies at the University of California, Santa Barbara. She holds a PhD in Film Studies and is the author of *Black Women as Cultural Readers* (1995), the editor of *Black Women Film and Video Artists* (1998) and *Black Feminist Cultural Criticism* (2001).

Stella Bruzzi is Senior Lecturer in the Department of Media Arts, Royal Holloway, University of London. She is the author of *Undressing Cinema: Clothing and Identity in the Movies* (Routledge, 1997) and *New Documentary: A Critical Introduction* (2000). She is also co-editor with Pamela Church Gibson of *Fashion Cultures: Theories, Explorations and Analysis* (2000) and is currently writing a book on fatherhood, masculinity and Hollywood.

Edward Buscombe was formerly Head of Publishing at the British Film Institute, and is now Visiting Professor at Southampton Institute. His most recent publications include *British*

Television: A Reader, and *The Searchers*, a volume in the BFI Film Classics series. He is working on a history of the Western film genre in the 1950s.

Jim Collins is Associate Professor of Film, Television and English at the University of Notre Dame. Most recently, he has edited *High-Pop: Making Culture into Popular Entertainment* (2001). He is also the author of *Architectures of Excess: Cultural Life in the Information Age* (1995) and *Uncommon Cultures: Popular Culture and Post-Modernism* (1989). He has also co-edited *Film Theory Goes to the Movies* (1993).

Barbara Creed has spoken and published widely on film, feminism and popular culture. She is author of *The Monstrous-Feminine: Film, Feminism, Psychoanalysis* and co-editor of *Body Trade: Captivity, Cannibalism and Colonialism in the Pacific*. At present she is completing a book on sexuality and the media. She is head of the Cinema Studies programme at the University of Melbourne.

Richard Dyer is Professor of Film and Television Studies at the University of Warwick. He is the author of many books which deal with film representation and entertainment, including *Stars* (1979), *Heavenly Bodies: Film Stars and Society* (1987) and *White* (1997).

Jane Feuer is Professor of English at the University of Pittsburgh where she teaches courses in film studies. She is the author of *The Hollywood Musical* (1982) and *Seeing through the Eighties: Television and Reaganism* (1995). She has published numerous articles about television and is also working on a book about teen films.

Miriam Hansen is Ferdinand Schevill Distinguished Service Professor in the Humanities at the University of Chicago, where she teaches in the Department of English and the Committee on Cinema and Media Studies. She is the author of *Babel and Babylon: Spectatorship in American Silent Film* (1991), numerous articles on international early cinema, film aesthetics, and theories on cinema, modernity and the public sphere. She is completing a study on 'The Other Frankfurt School: Kracauer, Benjamin, and Adorno on Cinema, Mass Culture, and Modernity'.

John Hill is Professor of Media Studies at the University of Ulster. He is the author of *Sex, Class and Realism: British Cinema 1956–63* and *Cinema in the 1980s*, co-author of *Cinema and Ireland*, and co-editor of various books including *The Oxford Guide to Film Studies*.

Mark Jancovich is Senior Lecturer and Director of the Institute of Film Studies at the University of Nottingham, UK. He is the author of several books: *Horror* (1992), *The Cultural Politics of the New Criticism* (1993), *Rational Fears: American Horror in the 1950s* (1996), and *The Film Studies Reader* (co-edited with Joanne Hollows and Peter Hutchings, 2000). He is currently editing *Changing Channels: Television in the Digital Age* and *The Horror Film Reader*.

Susan Jeffords is Professor of English and Women's Studies at the University of Washington. She is author of *The Remasculinization of America: Gender and the Vietnam War* (1989), *Hard Bodies: Hollywood Masculinity in the Reagan Era* (1994), and co-editor of *Seeing through the Media: The Persian Gulf War* (1994). She is currently working on a book on rape and US national identity.

Isaac Julien is research fellow in Contemporary Arts at Oxford Brookes University, and a film-maker who works across the media of video, installation, photography and film. He lectures and writes extensively on issues of black cultural politics, film, art and sexuality.

Annette Kuhn is Professor of Film Studies at Lancaster University, England; and an editor of the journal *Screen*. Publications include: *Women's Pictures: Feminism and Cinema* (2nd edn, 1994), *Family Secrets: Acts of Memory and Imagination* (1995), and, as editor, *Queen of the 'B's: Ida Lupino Behind the Camera* (1995), *Screen Histories: A Screen Reader* (with Jackie Stacey, 1998), and *Alien Zone II: The Spaces of Science Fiction Cinema* (1999). She is currently completing a monograph on cinema and cultural memory.

P. David Marshall is currently the Chair of the Department of Communication Studies at Northeastern University in Boston. Along with many articles on the Internet, popular culture and cultural studies, he is the author of *Celebrity and Power* (Minnesota 1997), *Modes for Cultural Analysis* (Sage) and *New Media Culture* (Edward Arnold, forthcoming 2002–3), and co-author of *Fame Games: the Production of Celebrity in Australia* (Cambridge 2000 – with Graeme Turner and Frances Bonner), and *Web Theory* (Routledge, forthcoming 2001 – with Robert Burnett). He is the founding editor of the online journal *M/C – a journal of media and culture*.

Judith Mayne is Professor of French and Women's Studies at Ohio State University. She is the author of several books in film studies, including *Directed by Dorothy Arzner* (1994) and *Framed: Feminists, Lesbians & Media Culture* (2000).

Kobena Mercer writes and teaches on the visual arts of the black diaspora. He is editor of *Black Film/British Cinema* (1988), author of *Welcome to the Jungle* (1994) and has contributed exhibition catalogue essays to *Black Male* (Whitney Museum 1994), *Pictura Britannica* (Sydney 1997) and *Adrian Piper: A Retrospective* (Baltimore 1999).

Tania Modleski is Professor of English at the University of Southern California. She is author of *Old Wives' Tales, and Other Women's Stories*, and several other books on women, film and popular culture.

Steve Neale is Research Professor in Film, Media and Communication Studies at Sheffield Hallam University. He is the author of *Genre* (BFI 1980), *Cinema and Technology* (Macmillan 1985) and *Genre and Hollywood* (Routledge 2000), co-author of *Popular Film and Television Comedy* (Routledge 1990) and co-editor of *Contemporary Hollywood Cinema* (Routledge 1998). He is currently editing a book on *Genre and Contemporary Hollywood* for the BFI.

Tom O'Regan works between film and cultural criticism and policy analysis. He is Director of the Australian Key Centre for Cultural and Media Policy located at Griffith University in Brisbane. His books include *Australian National Cinema* (1996) and *Australian Television Culture* (1992). He was a founding editor of *Continuum* and was co-responsible for that journal's first sixteen issues.

Stephen Prince is Associate Professor of Communication Studies and has taught film theory, history and criticism at Virginia Tech for eleven years. He is the author or editor of seven books: *Screening Violence* (2000), *Savage Cinema: Sam Peckinpah and the Rise of Ultraviolet Movies*

(1998), *A New Pot of Gold: Hollywood Under the Electronic Rainbow* (2000), *The Warrior's Camera: The Cinema of Akira Kurosawa* (1999), *Visions of Empire: Political Imagery in Contemporary Hollywood Film* (1992), *Movies and Meaning: An Introduction to Film* (1997; 2000), and *Sam Peckinpah's The Wild Bunch* (1999).

Thomas Schatz is Professor and Chair of the Radio–Television–Film Department at the University of Texas, where he has been on the faculty since 1976. He has written four books about Hollywood films and film making, and also has written for numerous magazines, newspapers and academic journals, including the *New York Times*, *Premiere*, *The Nation*, and *Film Comment*. He is currently working on a history of MCA–Universal with co-author Thom Mount, former President of Universal Pictures.

Gianluca Sergi teaches film studies at the University of Staffordshire (UK). He is particularly interested in film sound and performance and has published articles in the *Journal of Popular Film and Television* and chapters in *Contemporary Hollywood Cinema* (1998) and *Screen Acting as Art and Performance* (1999). His most recent publication discusses the figure of the spectator as listener in *Hollywood Spectatorship* (2001). He is currently preparing a book on the working practices of contemporary Hollywood film-makers.

Ella Shohat is Professor of Film and Cultural Studies at the City University of New York (CUNY), Staten Island and at the Graduate Center of CUNY. She is the author of *Israeli Cinema* and *Unthinking Eurocentrism* (with Robert Stam) and editor of *Dangerous Liaisons* and *Talking Visions*.

Jackie Stacey is Reader in Women's Studies and Sociology in the Department of Sociology at Lancaster University. She is author of *Star Gazing: Hollywood Cinema and Female Spectatorship* (1994) and *Teratologies: A Cultural Study of Cancer* (1997), and is a co-editor of *Screen*.

Janet Staiger is author of, most recently, *Perverse Spectators: The Practices of Film Reception* and *Blockbuster TV: Must-See Sitcoms in the Network Era*. She teaches critical and cultural studies and gender and sexuality studies at the University of Texas at Austin where she is the William P. Hobby Centennial Professor in Communication.

Robert Stam is Professor of Cinema Studies at New York University, and is the author of many books on the cinema, including *Reflexivity in Film and Literature*, *Subversive Pleasures*, *Tropical Multiculturalism*, and *Film Theory: An Introduction*. *Unthinking Eurocentrism* won the Best Film Book Award in 1995.

Chris Straayer is Associate Professor and Chair of the Department of Cinema Studies at New York University. She lectures and writes on queer studies, feminist film studies, video art. She is author of *Deviant Eyes, Deviant Bodies: Sexual Re-Orientations in Film and Video* (1996). She has curated multiple programmes for television, festivals and museums, including 'Lesbian Genders' at the Whitney Museum of American Art. Currently she is writing a book on intersecting discourses on/of transsexuality.

Yvonne Tasker is Senior Lecturer in Film Studies at the University of East Anglia, UK. She is the author of *Spectacular Bodies: Gender, Genre and the Action Cinema* (1993) and *Working Girls:*

Gender and Sexuality in Popular Cinema and is currently working on a new volume of essays on action and adventure cinema.

Stephen Teo is a writer and critic, author of *Hong Kong Cinema: The Extra Dimensions* (BFI: 1997). He was born in Malaysia but migrated to Hong Kong in 1982 where he worked as a critic, writer and translator for the Hong Kong International Film Festival, and dabbled in documentary and short-film film making. His writings have appeared in many international publications, including *Film Comment*, *CinemaScope*, *Cinemaya*, and *Far Eastern Economic Review*. He is currently based in Melbourne, Australia where he is doing a postgraduate degree by research and is also teaching a course on Asian cinemas at RMIT University.

Janet Woollacott is the co-author (with Tony Bennett) of *Bond and Beyond: The career of a popular hero* (1987) and co-editor of a number of readers in the area of film and television including (with Tony Bennett *et al.*) *Popular Television and Film* (1981).

Justin Wyatt is an Associate Professor in the School of Radio, Television and Film at the University of North Texas. He is the author of *High Concept: Movies and Marketing in Hollywood* (1994).

Acknowledgements

Tony Bennett and Janet Woollacott, 'Texts and their readings' from *Bond and Beyond* (London, Palgrave and New York, Routledge Inc., 1987), pp. 59–69. Reproduced by permission of Palgrave and Routledge, Inc., part of the Taylor & Francis Group.

Annette Kuhn, 'Women's genres' in *Screen* 25(1), pp. 18–28. Reprinted by permission of *Screen*.

Judith Mayne, 'Paradoxes of spectatorship' in *Cinema and Spectatorship* (London, Routledge, 1993), pp. 77–102. Reprinted by permission of the publisher.

Janet Staiger, 'Reception studies in film and television' in *Interpreting Films* (Princeton, Princeton University Press, 1992), pp. 49–78. Reprinted by permission of Princeton University Press.

Edward Buscombe, 'Sound and Colour' from *Jump Cut* 17, 1977. Reprinted by permission of the author.

Steve Neale, 'Colour and film aesthetics' in *Cinema and Technology* (London, Palgrave, and Bloomington, Indiana University Press, 1985), pp. 154–8. Reproduced by permission of Palgrave and Indiana University Press.

Richard Dyer, 'Lighting for whiteness' in *White: Essays on Race and Culture* (London, Routledge, 1997), pp. 89–103. Reprinted by permission of the publisher.

Gianluca Sergi, 'A cry in the dark: the role of post-classical film sound' in Steve Neale and Murray Smith (eds), *Contemporary Hollywood Cinema* (London, Routledge, 1998) pp. 156–65. Reprinted by permission of the publisher.

Stephen Prince, 'True lies: perceptual realism, digital images and film theory' from *Film Quarterly* 49(3), Spring 1996, pp. 27–37. Copyright © 1995 by the regents of the University of California. Reprinted by permission.

Barbara Creed, 'The cyberstar: digital pleasures and the end of the Unconscious' from *Screen* 41(1), pp. 79–86. Reprinted by permission of *Screen*.

Tom O'Regan, 'A national cinema' from *Australian National Cinema* (London, Routledge, 1996), pp. 45–65. Reprinted by permission of the publisher.

John Hill, 'British Cinema as a national cinema: productions, audience and representation' in Pam Cook (ed.), *The British Cinema Book*, (London, BFI, 1997), pp. 244–54. Reprinted by permission of BFI Publishing.

Stephen Teo, 'Postmodernism and the end of Hong Kong Cinema' in Hong Kong Cinema (London, BFI, 1997), pp. 243–55. Reprinted by permission of BFI Publishing.

Thomas Schatz, 'The new Hollywood' in Jim Collins, Hilary Radner and Ava Preacher Collins (eds), *Film Theory Goes to the Movies* (New York, Routledge Inc., 1992), pp. 8–36. Reproduced by permission of Routledge, Inc., part of the Taylor & Francis Group.

Tino Balio, '"A major presence in all the world's important markets": the globalization of Hollywood in the 1990s' in Steve Neale and Murray Smith (eds), *Contemporary Hollywood Cinema* (London, Routledge, 1998), pp. 58–73. Reprinted by permission of the publisher.

Richard Dyer, 'Monroe and sexuality: desirability' in *Heavenly Bodies* (London, Palgrave, 1987), pp. 23–34. Reproduced by permission of Palgrave.

P. David Marshall, 'The cinematic apparatus and the construction of the film celebrity' in *Celebrity and Power* (University of Minnesota Press, 1997), pp. 79–94. Reprinted by permission of The University of Minnesota Press.

Jane Feuer, 'Spectators and spectacles' in *The Hollywood Musical* (London, Palgrave, 1992), pp. 23–34. Reproduced by permission of Palgrave.

Stella Bruzzi, 'Desire and the costume film: *Picnic at Hanging Rock*, *The Age of Innocence*, *The Piano*' in *Undressing Cinema* (London, Routledge, 1997), pp. 35–63. Reprinted by permission of the publisher.

Tania Modleski, 'The terror of pleasure: the contemporary horror film and postmodern theory' in Tania Modleski (ed.), *Studies in Entertainment* (Bloomington, Indiana University Press, 1986), pp. 155–66. Reproduced by permission of Indiana University Press.

Jim Collins, 'Genericity in the nineties: eclectic irony and the new sincerity' in Jim Collins, Hilary Radner and Ava Preacher Collins (eds), *Film Theory Goes to the Movies* (New York, Routledge Inc., 1992), pp. 242–62. Reproduced by permission of Routledge, Inc., part of the Taylor & Francis Group.

Yvonne Tasker, 'Action heroines in the 1980s: the limits of "musculinity"' in *Spectacular Bodies* (London, Routledge, 1993), pp. 132–53. Reprinted by permission of the publisher.

Sabrina Barton, 'Your self storage: female investigation and male performativity in the woman's psychothriller' in Jon Lewis (ed.), *The New American Cinema* (Durham, Duke University Press, 1998), pp. 187–216. © 1998, Duke University Press. All rights reserved. Reprinted with permission.

Chris Straayer, 'The hypothetical lesbian heroine in narrative feature film' in *Deviant Eyes, Deviant Bodies* (New York, Columbia University Press, 1996), pp. 9–22. © 1996 Chris Straayer. Reprinted by permission of the publisher.

Susan Jeffords, 'Can masculinity be terminated?' in Steven Cohan and Ina Rae Hark (eds), *Screening the Male* (London, Routledge, 1993), pp. 245–61. Reprinted by permission of the publisher.

Isaac Julien and Kobena Mercer, 'De margin and de centre' in *Screen* 29(4), pp. 2–10. Reprinted by permission of *Screen*.

Ella Shohat and Robert Stam, 'The imperial imaginary' in *Unthinking Eurocentrism* (London, Routledge, 1994), pp. 100–14 and 131–4. Reprinted by permission of the publisher.

Justin Wyatt, 'High concept and market research: movie making by numbers' in *High Concept: Movies and Marketing in Hollywood* (Austin, University of Texas Press, 1994). © 1994 Justin Wyatt. By permission of the University of Texas Press.

Miriam Hansen, 'Chameleon and catalyst: the cinema as an alternative public sphere' in *Babel and Babylon* (Cambridge, Harvard University Press, 1991), pp. 90–125.

Jackie Stacey, 'Hollywood cinema – the great escape' in *Star Gazing* (London, Routledge, 1993), pp. 80–125. Reprinted by permission of the publisher.

Jacqueline Bobo, 'Watching *The Color Purple*: two interviews' in *Black Women as Cultural Readers* (New York, Columbia University Press, 1995), pp. 91–132. © 1995 Columbia University Press. Reprinted by permission of the publisher.

Mark Jancovich, '"A real shocker": authenticity, genre and the struggle for distinction' in *Continuum*, 14:1, 2000, pp. 23–34. Reprinted by permission of the publisher. http://www.tandf.co.uk

Preface

THE FILM CULTURES READER is a collection of influential contributions to the study of film and popular culture. Most selections were published in the last decade, and deal with contemporary commercial cinema as the object of study. *The Film Cultures Reader* also deals with certain quite recent shifts in the direction of the field of film studies. These are shifts that reveal the benefit of some relatively new disciplinary influences from cultural studies, television studies, audience studies or ethnography, and social history.

There are many *Readers* currently available which will present a more conventional – perhaps, more disciplinary – account of the field than is presented here. Typically, such accounts reflect a tradition of formal analysis which is most interested in classical Hollywood cinema, European art cinema or the avant-garde; and which maintains close theoretical links with what is customarily described as screen theory: usually comprised of 'apparatus theory', semiology, psychoanalysis and feminist film theory. The value of such accounts is not denied, but there are now very many of them. The discipline they construct for film studies is, of course, firmly embedded in what follows; indeed, most of the contributions to this *Reader* deal directly with this tradition and its intellectual legacy in order to make their arguments.

However, *The Film Cultures Reader* has different priorities to pursue and different emphases to strike. In some respects a continuation of the project that resulted in my 'cultural studies' introduction to film studies, *Film as Social Practice* (1999), this *Reader* also locates film within the study of contemporary popular culture and the media. As a result, *The Film Cultures Reader* addresses itself to readers who are as likely to come from a background in media studies, communication studies or cultural studies, as in film studies. The common element, hopefully attracting this disparate and hypothetical readership, is an approach which treats the feature film – together with the audiences who consume it and the industries which produce it – as a cultural or social practice, rather than as an aesthetic object.

I would admit that drawing this dichotomy so baldly suggests a division in the field that is not nearly as clear, universal or as stable as the preceding sentence might imply. However, it is a means of unequivocally specifying the concerns of this *Reader*. I wish to draw attention to a body of work on the cultural function of the commercial feature film that has tended to be relegated to the tail-end of other collections. Articles of this kind are often recommended as examples of new and positive trends in the field, it is true, but they must take their place as the most recent event in a much longer disciplinary history. In order to find the room to give this work its due, much of that disciplinary history remains unrepresented in this *Reader*. There are no articles from Eisenstein, Bazin, Metz or any of the traditional foundational figures. They will not be invisible, because reference to their arguments will occur within the excerpts and the introductory material as well. However, examples of their work are readily available elsewhere, and more detailed accounts of their place in the history of film studies are readily available too.

The space made available by this strategy enables *The Film Cultures Reader* to concentrate on its core interests – not only recent theoretical debates about popular film, but also to develop the suggestion that the study of film has, in practice if not in theory, been redefined over the last decade. Consequently, the emphasis is not only on the film text, or on understanding the processes through which we make sense of film as a medium. It is also, perhaps even primarily, upon the cultural contexts in which the consumption of film takes place as well as the industrial contexts within which it is produced. While specific film texts certainly occupy much of the attention of the excerpts in this *Reader*, none have a canonical interest. Typically, they are interested in the meanings and pleasures popular films provide to their audiences, or in the part that movies play in the construction of social identities. The focus, then, is upon the cultures in and around the feature film as a form of popular entertainment in contemporary western societies today. In my view, that accurately reflects the nature of the interest in the medium expressed by many students and teachers of film at the moment, where it is increasingly enclosed within discussions of the media and popular culture.

This *Reader* was conceived initially as a companion text to *Film as Social Practice*, but it has grown a little beyond that, I believe. If that is the case, then some credit is due to others than myself. In particular, I should record my gratitude to Rebecca Barden at Routledge who encouraged me to develop this *Reader*, and to Alistair Daniel for seeing it through to completion. Sue Luckman and John Gunders provided invaluable assistance in searching out permissions, preparing the manuscript and compiling the bibliography. Thanks, too, are due to the contributors, of course, for generously agreeing to the reproduction of their work for this project. I also wish to thank the three anonymous readers of the original proposal for their very tactful and helpful criticisms and suggestions which, I believe, have resulted in a much more adventurous and interesting book.

Graeme Turner
Brisbane, 2001

GRAEME TURNER

EDITOR'S INTRODUCTION

I

THE HISTORY OF THE FEATURE FILM INDUSTRY is marked by the competing claims that can be made for it. To many commercial film-makers, film is an expressive art; their movies are imprinted with their own experience and points of view. To many producers, however, and certainly to the distributors and exhibitors, film is a commercial commodity most likely to return a profit if the audience finds it entertaining. To some sectors of the cinema audience, film is the premier modern art form and the object of avid attention; to another, larger, sector of the movie audience lining up for the latest blockbuster, it is an entertainment and a social event. Within the history of film studies, too, the feature film has been the subject of competing claims.

The first narrative feature films were being screened less than a decade after the Lumière brothers' demonstration of the medium in Paris in 1895. By the beginning of World War I, silent film (albeit as one component within a night's programme in vaudeville venues or theatres) was attracting a regular and substantial popular audience. As the feature film built its commercial audience, its narratives were becoming more sophisticated. Not only could it accurately reproduce the real, but it could also transform it into something else. D. W. Griffith's *Birth of a Nation* (1915) clearly invited recognition as an artistic statement, and many commentators joined Vachel Lindsay in claiming film as 'the seventh art' (1915), and a form which should be protected from the likely consequences of its populist and commercial beginnings.

The aesthetic potential of film narrative attracted more interest as understanding of the medium developed. In the 1920s, Russian film-maker Sergei Eisenstein was instrumental in developing a theory of montage, insisting that the relation between shots was the fundamental structural component in film narratives. Implicit in the theory of montage was the capacity of the film-maker to transform the real, and to employ the raw materials of the image in order to say new things – to speak about politics or the human condition. The famous Kuleshov experiments were cited as evidence of the power invested in film editing.[1] If the construction of the relations between consecutive shots determined the production of meaning, then audiences could be made to read the combination of shots in predictable ways.

Claims that editing was central to the production of meaning in film did not settle the matter. Indeed, they opened a vein of debate that continues today. This concerns the cinema's 'proper' function – whether it simply documents reality or turns it into art. The opposing positions are usually described through the labels of 'formalism' and 'realism'. Formalist approaches to cinema emphasize its ability to transform the real into a textual form that should itself be the focus of intense attention – film art. Realist approaches emphasize the cinema's capture of 'the real', and thus focus attention on those aspects of the real world the film is about – crudely, the assumptions underpinning documentary film. As the technologies used within the production industry changed – from silent to sound, and from black-and-white to colour – these debates became embedded even in discussions about production practices (the essays from Buscombe and Neale in this volume deal with this). Objections to the increasing verisimilitude generated by the introduction of sound were based primarily in a formalist aesthetic. Resistance to an increase in the feature film's 'realism' (in this context, the enhanced correspondence between the real world and its representation) was fuelled by the fear that this would circumscribe the capacity of film to work as art. Alternatively, the relatively gradual take-up of colour as the film stock of choice was influenced by the prevailing conventions through which realism was signified in the feature film. At the time, colour was the conventional choice for the representation of fantasy or spectacle: it did not then denote 'the real'.

In the context of the debate between the realists and formalists, it is conventional to deal with Andre Bazin as the counterpoint to Eisenstein. According to Bazin, the camera was there to document the real, and the fundamental mode of film construction was not editing but *mise-en-scène*, or the arrangement of elements within the frame (1967). The composition of the image is the key, and it implied a greater degree of negotiation between the spectator and the image as meaning is generated. For Bazin, it is as if the meaning of the film is finally constructed at the point of consumption, not the point of production. Since the spectator is the one who scans the frame to produce the meaning, rather than merely serving as the point at which the meanings contained in individual shots are combined, Bazin's shift in emphasis constitutes a significant shift in the location of power.

II

Although debate about the nature and function of film has been vigorous since its invention, such debates were not formalized into a programme of study or research until relatively recently. In most countries, film studies did not exist as a discipline or as an institution until well into the 1960s. At the time it came into being, of course, there was still a clear split in western societies' cultural assessments of the status and function of 'the movies'. Popular cinema, particularly the output of Hollywood, was widely regarded by intellectuals as meretricious entertainment for the masses, in ways that were roughly consonant with the line taken by the Frankfurt School's dismissal of the 'culture industries' and what has been called elsewhere the 'culture and civilisation tradition' (Turner 1996, pp. 36–43). Exempted from this blanket dismissal, however, were the productions of a European avant-garde which offered quite different fare to the American studios. Their films set out to make unique, often personal, statements and were often formally innovative or challenging. Those who valued what came to be seen as 'art film' regarded the European film-makers' refusal to be constrained by mainstream narrative genres and their resistance to classic Hollywood narrative conventions as evidence of their seriousness as artists.

We know that this set of aesthetic preferences was slightly reconfigured as a result of an intervention published in the French journal Bazin had founded, *Cahiers du Cinema*. Film-maker Francois Truffaut (1954) challenged the conservative view of mainstream film and the elitist assessment of their audiences. Among the consequences of this challenge was that interest in certain Hollywood directors became more intellectually respectable. Such directors, it was held, worked within constricting industrial conditions but nevertheless managed to imprint their own personal stamp on their films. This personal stamp, the mark of the *auteur*, recovered whole genres of films for discussion through a mode of criticism and analysis which was specifically developed to account for the conditions of production pertaining to popular film while searching for the legitimating imprint of authorship.

While there were certainly many other factors involved, it is possible to argue that this development provided a crucial enabling condition for the establishment of the film studies departments which appeared in American universities during the 1960s and 1970s, and which spread into other countries over the following years. Often offshoots of literary studies departments, early film studies departments tended to replicate the analytical protocols of their literary studies training in their teaching programs and in their choice of texts. As a result, it is not surprising that they exercised a preference for self-consciously symbolic and modernist films – very much the kind of thing being turned out by the high end of the European and Scandinavian industries at the time. As the *auteur* theory was further developed by US scholars (Sarris 1962–3), certain Hollywood directors became relatively canonical figures: Howard Hawks, John Ford and Alfred Hitchcock, for instance. The bulk of mainstream commercial cinema, however, remained outside the pale.

As a result, a central and discomforting component of the new discipline's orientation was put in place. While film studies was focused upon understanding the medium and spent the next few decades making great strides towards that objective, it was not at all enthusiastic about the most commercial dimension of that medium – popular cinema. What was to be a long and productive period of theoretical development and debate about the function of film was concerned most intensively with the processes of identification constructed through the apparatus of the medium and the possibilities of interpretation these processes provided (or denied) to the film spectator. The conclusions drawn did not encourage a reassessment of the cultural politics of the mainstream feature film. However, most of this theoretical development occurred in complete separation from any account of the actual processes of consumption employed by viewers inside the cinema. It also occurred at a considerable distance from any serious (empirical or otherwise) investigation of the appeal of popular film to its viewers. Popular film certainly received attention, but overwhelmingly it was examined as the vehicle for the reproduction of regressive ideological formations. Even the considerable volume of work on the textual features of film genres, I would argue, ultimately contributed to such a project.

The period from the 1970s through the 1990s is rightly seen as an extremely fertile period for developing our understanding of how film works. It is also widely regarded as subject to a considerably hegemonic complex of intellectual influences, which dominated the field and, some would claim, excluded alternatives. What has come to be called 'screen theory'[2] approached the cinema as a large, multi-faceted and determining institution, an 'apparatus' that inevitably produced conservative ideological effects. Theorists such as Metz (1975), Baudry (1974–5) and Mulvey (1975) drew upon combinations of Freudian and post-Freudian psychoanalysis, semiotics, and Althusserian explanations of the interpellating function of ideology. In the case of Laura Mulvey, this generated an extraordinarily influential feminist critique of the visual pleasures provided by classic Hollywood films which enforced the spectator's identification with a masculine, narratively powerful, point of view. Film, from such perspectives, always worked in a determining manner that instructed the viewer how to consume it.[3] The pay-off for those who responded appropriately was certainly pleasure, but it was scopophilic, voyeuristic, masculinist and ultimately ideologically conservative. Hence, the popular appeal of the movies was inherently regressive. Hollywood film offered us the pleasure of looking at the figures on the screen and thus possessing them; and of having a complacent version of the real ritually confirmed by the ideological closure offered at the end of the film narrative. According to such accounts, what was described as 'realist' popular cinema (and this has a highly specific meaning in this context)[4] was beyond redemption. Ideologically conservative and formally seductive, the realist film narrative positioned us as passive receptors (see Comolli and Narboni 1971). The only escape was to break with the dominant formal conventions of the commercial feature film and opt for a more progressive, avant-garde, cinematic practice.

The sophistication of this body of theory was profound. However, as with other areas of cultural theory during this period, the universality of the explanation of the medium and its ideological effects ultimately challenged assent. Somewhere in the explanation, there had to be room for variation, historical specificities, for the possibility of change. As was the case with arguments about whether television viewers were at the mercy of the television 'message' (such as the encoding–decoding discussions being held within the Birmingham Centre for Contemporary Cultural Studies at the time (see Turner 1996, pp. 83–8), the suggestion that we were all cultural dupes dismissed the experience of ordinary people and privileged the perspective of the elite critic. In the case of television, theories about the positioning of the viewer, the degree of freedom they enjoyed in constructing the meaning of the message, were eventually tested through empirical research (such as Morley's *Nationwide* studies and the many other projects which have followed this avenue of enquiry since).[5] No such avenue was explored within screen theory. Not surprisingly, many questioned the 'monolithic' nature of the theory, its invocation of a unified subjectivity that could be operated, irresistibly, by the cinematic apparatus (Carroll 1996). And some questioned whether this was good enough as an account of the pleasures of popular cinema for audiences claiming different identities, sexual orientation and class affiliation (Tasker 1993).

Shifts of position over the last decade or so have acknowledged such limitations. Laura Mulvey's original 1975 article generated an enormous amount of debate and the result has been a gradual process of qualification – a process in which she has played a significant role herself (1981). The modification of theories of what she called 'the male gaze', however, are part of a progressive renovation of the claims made by screen theory as it responded to the competing claims from other traditions of research. In particular, the recovery of a sense of agency for the individual viewer and the acceptance that the process of viewing must be historically contingent, as well as a renewed interest in the social and economic history of the commercial production industry, has displaced the universalizing implications of screen theory. The need to account for the pleasures of popular cinema audiences, in ways that acknowledge at least the theoretical possibility that they may not be ideological dupes, has become irresistible.

As a result of the hegemony described, however, film studies in the early 1990s was not particularly well equipped to address such a task. In order to do so, they had to look elsewhere, as does Annette Kuhn in her essay in this collection. Recognizing the need to look for treatments of audiences that do not take their passivity for granted, Kuhn points to the example of Janice Radway's early 'reception studies' of a group of popular fiction readers in the US (1984). Miriam Hansen (1991), drawing upon social history and archival research, examines specific film audiences and the social practices and pleasures which attended film-going at particular historical conjunctures. Responding to some of the more contextual approaches employed within cultural studies work on other forms of popular cultural texts, Yvonne Tasker's *Spectacular Bodies* (1993) examines constructions of the female body across a range of locations from film texts to body building practices in order to understand the pleasures the much maligned 1990s action film offers its audience.

As the above paragraph implies, the enabling models for work of this kind have not necessarily come from film studies. They have come from cultural studies, from television studies, from ethnography and audience studies and from social and media history. Although there is plenty of textual analysis in the examples just mentioned, its objective is neither aesthetic nor canonical. And although popular culture is taken seriously in all cases, it is not simply a recuperative exercise that is being undertaken. That is, these essays are not interested in establishing the artistic credentials of the texts in question. Rather, they are interested in establishing a more complex and nuanced understanding of the competing forces which frame the individual experience of popular culture in general, and popular film in particular.

The result, I would argue, amounts to something like a paradigm shift within film studies. Popular cinema is moving into the centre of the picture, on something a little closer to its own terms. The conception of the audience is coming under the influence of research traditions more common in television studies than in film, and often they are called audiences as well as spectators. Critiques of the hegemony of what is variously called 'grand theory', screen theory, or just plain 'theory', have become relatively commonplace.

III

David Bordwell has coined the term 'grand theory' to describe a totalizing tendency within film studies, linked to and informed by psychoanalysis, semiology and feminist film theory (1996). Like those working in 'grand theory', Bordwell, too, is interested in understanding how film audiences/spectators make meaning from the combination of sound and image in the cinema. However, Bordwell and Carroll have both argued that this is an issue of cognition, of understanding how the mind processes this information, rather than an issue for psychoanalysis (1996; 1996). This argument is made from within a competing theoretical paradigm, that of cognitivism. Since cognitivism is to some extent an empirical method and is not primarily interested in engaging with the politics of the relation between the spectator and the cinematic apparatus, Bordwell argues, 'grand theory' has discounted it. For his own part, Bordwell has maintained a consistent critique of what he sees as the dominant theoretical influences within contemporary film studies – and these include those I have previously discussed under the label of screen theory, as well as those I have suggested might constitute new and alternative influences. Therefore, Bordwell rejects psychoanalysis for its arrogant essentialism and cultural studies for its trendy relativism. Neither provide him with an acceptable means of explaining the relation between the film spectator and the film text.

It is not only cognitivists who have mounted this kind of critique. David E. James (1996), in one of the very few recent books (James and Berg 1996) to have addressed the issue of class in the cinema, also accuses screen theory of producing a legacy of essentialism. What David James means by this is slightly different to Bordwell. His complaint is provoked by the sweeping nature of the claims made from within this theoretical tradition, and by their relative insensitity to the contingencies of context and history. According to James, screen theory argued that the ideological effects of cinema were 'socially uniform because they were intrinsic to its apparatus, to the historical conditions of its invention, and to all cases of its use apart from deliberate avant-gardist ruptures of its fundamental and enabling mechanism, primary identification' (p. 16). As a consequence of the influence of Lacanian psychoanalysis, James suggests, the only specific category of social difference screen theory could properly address was sexuality – hence the virtual disappearance of the consideration of class from film studies from the late 1980s to the present (p. 17).

Judith Mayne's history of film theory's consideration of the category of the spectator, *Cinema and Spectatorship* (1993), is more or less aligned with the directions taken by the theoretical tradition she interprets. While Mayne defends the usefulness of the concept of the spectator and of psychoanalytic approaches to understanding how film works, however, she also acknowledges that there are things worth doing which are not assisted by this tradition. The assumption that the spectator passively consumes the products of the cinematic apparatus is qualified by the need to also examine 'real spectators' within specific historical contexts. While Mayne ultimately resists the claims of cognitivism to better explain the film-spectator relation, she does support the use of ethnographic methods. The distinction she appears to make regards cognitivism as irretrievably apolitical, whereas ethnography is informed 'by a desire to make scholarship more politically and ideologically involved rather than less so' (p. 61). The growth in the importance of questions of cultural identity – so-called identity politics – to film studies seems to be in the background here and, as Jaqueline Bobo's essay in this collection demonstrates, ethnography has actively participated in the development of those kinds of political claims.

Feminist film theory has been the major tradition over the last two decades, and has produced many benefits. As I mentioned earlier, there is a strong thread of internal critique within feminist film theory which has explored alternatives to the 'male gaze' argument and the essentialised notion of the female spectator. Steve Cohan and Ira Mae Hark, though, introduce their collection of essays on masculinity in the cinema (1993) by accusing this tradition of marginalizing discussion of the construction of masculinity. (Their collection is the source of Susan Jeffords' essay, reproduced in this reader.) According to them, feminist film theory has 'by and large minimized and taken for granted the complex and considerable cultural investment which classical Hollywood cinema has historically expended in the display of the male' (p. 1). There is a danger, Cohan and Hark argue, that the overwhelming amount of attention devoted to the representation of the female takes far too much for granted about how men are represented on the screen. Worse, it is possible that 'the scant attention paid to the spectacle of men ends up reinforcing the apparent effacement of the masculine as a social construction in American culture' (p. 3). However, this assymetry is being addressed, appropriately enough, from within feminism. As Yvonne Tasker's work has demonstrated, a close attention to the use of the male body in the action film produces quite different conclusions to those which might seem implicit in earlier accounts of the classical Hollywood cinema.

These, then, are among the criticisms of pre-1990s film studies, and they are representative of a broad tendency. From the responses and counter arguments indicated above, it is possible to perceive some agreement about suggestions for new directions for film studies. Bordwell and

Carroll both argue for more modest research projects that are not simply instantiations of a 'grand theory'. For Bordwell, these constitute 'middle level research' and for Carroll, 'piece-meal research'. What they actually mean by such phrases turns out to be similar: film history, film historiography, economic histories of the film industries, the exhibition networks and so on. Bordwell calls for more 'problem- rather than doctrine-driven' research which 'cuts across trad-itional boundaries among film aesthetics, institutions and audience response' (1996, p. 28).

Judith Mayne (1993, Chapter 3) also considers what she describes as 'historical models' for film studies research and argument. These are not dissimilar from those recommended by Bordwell and Carroll. Mayne acknowledges the importance of approaches which attempt to contextualize film within popular culture – territory, so far, developed by cultural studies and audience studies. Among the avenues she nominates are research into magazines as locations for evidence about actual audiences; the examination of 'stars', drawing on Richard Dyer's work which firmly situates the discussion of the star as a social and cultural question; and histories of exhibition, reception and consumption along the lines explored by Hansen, Staiger and Bobo in this collection. Mayne does not entirely surrender the territory to history or cultural studies, though. She reminds us, for instance, of one application of psychoanalytic theory that does work actively with a conception of history – Elsaesser's notion of the 'social imaginary' constructed by the German cinema, which informs so much subsequent work on national cinemas. And finally, as Mayne emphasizes, many of the shifts I have just been mapping could be said to have emerged organically from the continuing project of feminist film theory, which is where Hansen's work would legitimately be located.

All of this effectively lays out a new agenda for film studies. Prominent within this agenda, and in this reader, is research into the cultural function of popular cinema genres, into audi-ence reception and consumption of the movies, and into a version of film history that is more interested in industry economics than the formation of a canon. Such work is influenced, I would argue, most significantly by cultural studies. This is particularly the case with British cultural studies. Some of the work coming from the UK, by Yvonne Tasker and Jackie Stacey, for instance, could be as comfortably located within cultural studies as within film studies. I do not want to over-emphasize this tendency, however. It does not represent a sea change, in that it has by no means comprehensively displaced 'grand theory', nor is it discontinuous with what has gone before. Rather, we are witnessing an increasing diversification, a growing plurality of approaches to film studies.

I know the account presented here has rocketed through the details and nuances of a history of film studies in order to present its argument with some economy, and that some distinctions will be lost along the way. The argument has its polemical edge, also, and I would not expect it to be welcomed by everyone. There are good reasons for this. For a start, there are significant differences between the teaching and research going on in different national locations. Screen theory and some versions of film aesthetics probably retain much of their dominance in the US. Institutionally, the importance of a highly elaborated film theory as a means of legitimating the new discipline is not easily set aside and intra-institutional rivalries have not gone away. The competition from newer humanities fields or disciplines like media studies and cultural studies is often vigorously resisted and trade with such competitors anxiously scrutinized. However, I think that there is a now a very strong case to argue that in the UK and in Australia at least, where television has always been in a close disciplinary relation to film studies and so there is probably less at stake institutionally, and where cultural studies has been more pervasive in its influence on secondary and tertiary education curricula, the paradigm shift I describe has already occurred.

The kinds of work laid out in this collection seem to me to be what is being taught in most places in these countries now. Increasingly, too, it is being taught in the US and Canada as well. As a result, it is important that a collection with this specific focus should exist, in order to acknowledge that this is a trend currently in play, and entitled to representation.

IV

Accordingly, then, the readings in this book have been chosen to highlight recent directions in the study of film as culture, as industry, or as social practice. Included among these directions are the following:

- The influence of new technologies on our understanding of film.
- The history and political economy of national and international film industries.
- The meanings and pleasures generated in popular film texts and genres.
- The construction of film audiences and social identities.
- The influence of cultural studies and cultural history on the methodologies used to study film and popular culture.

The book is divided into six parts. *Part 1: Understanding film* presents essays or chapters from books which have proved influential in producing or responding to the shift towards cultural studies approaches. Tony Bennett and Janet Woollacott's study of the figure of James Bond introduced the notion of 'reading formations' to cultural studies, and it has been taken up by a number of film scholars, such as Barbara Klinger in *Melodrama and Meaning* (1994), as a means of contextualizing the relationship between texts and readers. Annette Kuhn's essay on women's genres also moves film studies away from the abstract theoretical category of the spectator, and towards the material historical entity of the 'social audience'. As I have argued above, questions of spectatorship and ideology lose some of their dominance in the 1990s as film is approached in different ways. In an excerpt from *Cinema and Spectatorship*, Judith Mayne represents an overview of the competing positions within film studies that have contested the metaphor of spectatorship and the psychoanalytic tradition in film analysis. In the final contribution to this section, Janet Staiger outlines three competing approaches to film – semiotics, cognitivism and cultural studies – as a preliminary to developing her argument for an historicized version of reception studies in film.

Part 2: Technology emphasizes the importance of technology for film and cultural studies. In the past, with the exception of the moment when sound was introduced to the industry, visual technologies have occupied the vast majority of scholarly attention. The interplay between sound and image constitutes an area that is really yet to be explored comprehensively, and those interested in this interplay have found the visual emphasis in film studies extremely frustrating. Shifts in film production practices now may have altered this situation slightly. As popular cinema relies increasingly upon spectacle for its appeal, the role of the specific technologies used to create these spectacles has become more interesting to film and to cultural studies. New production technologies – in particular computer-generated imagery – have challenged definitions of the form and destabilized assumptions about our perception of 'the real'. Part 2 begins with two, relatively early but important, articles on sound and colour from Ed Buscombe and Steve Neale. An excerpt from Richard Dyer's *White* (1997) raises the issue of the ideological function of cinema technologies through an analysis of film lighting. Articles by Gianluca Sergi, Stephen Prince and Barbara Creed then focus on the shifts in our theorisation of film engendered by the contemporary development of digital sound technology and computer generated imagery.

Part 3 deals with the film industries. The first group of essays examines the role of the 'national' film industry through essays from Australia, the UK and Hong Kong. Tom O'Regan presents an overview of the commercial and cultural policy debates around the concept of the national cinema in Australia and elsewhere. John Hill describes the production industry and its audience in his account of the British cinema in the mid-1990s. Stephen Teo maps current directions in the more unequivocally commercial, but highly politicized context of the Hong Kong production industry in the late 1990s. Turning to Hollywood, Thomas Schatz provides his influential account of the generic economy of the 'New Hollywood' and Tino Balio summarizes recent developments in the political economy of Hollywood as the industry continues to globalize.

The focus of *Part 4: Meanings and pleasures* is the film text — its appeal, its function for its audience, and its cultural roots and resonance. The section begins with two essays on the appeal of the star in order to approach the kinds of culturally mediated pleasures popular film provides. While Richard Dyer's work on stars is familiar and influential, David Marshall's more recent work sets out to describe the celebrity of the film star as a medium-specific phenomenon. The following articles in this part move on to discussions of the meanings and pleasures offered by particular film genres. Genres dealt with include the musical (Jane Feuer), the period film (Stella Bruzzi), the horror film (Tania Modleski) and the recent trends for highly self-reflexive genre films and nostalgic essays in 'the new sincerity' (Jim Collins).

The implied starting point in *Part 5: Identities* is the 'male gaze' debate of the 1970s and 1980s, and the series of arguments and responses it produces. These arguments are available in many other *Readers*, so Part 5 begins with relatively recent developments from this debate: Yvonne Tasker and Sabrina Barton explore new approaches to feminine identities. In a counterpoint to the focus of these two excerpts, Susan Jeffords discusses the construction of masculinity in late 1990s Hollywood. Moving away from Hollywood, Isaac Julien and Kobena Mercer analyse the relations between mainstream cinema and black or diasporan cinema, most particularly in the UK. Chris Straayer outlines a 'hypothetical' lesbian reading of two French films and, in an excerpt from *Unthinking Eurocentrism*, Ella Shohat and Robert Stam connect the development of the medium of film to the project of imperialism at the beginning of the twentieth century.

Finally, *Part 6: Audiences and consumption*. In comparison to the literature on television audiences, there is not yet a large literature (or even much in the way of a methodology) on the study of film audiences. Increasingly, as we have seen, this is nominated as an area urgently in need of development. *Part 6* foregrounds key contributions to this development — and again much of this work is influenced by cultural studies and cultural history. Beginning with Justin Wyatt's industrially oriented account of how market research determines which films get to an audience in the first place, this section goes on to foreground discussions of 'actual' audiences. Miriam Hansen studies the histories of those who actually did go to the silent cinema to determine what uses they made of it, Jaqueline Bobo interviews black female audiences of *The Color Purple*, and Jackie Stacey corresponds with groups of women whose everyday lives in post-war Britain were enriched by Hollywood's images of desire. In the final selection, Mark Jancovich examines the success of the teen-slasher horror film in order to develop a better understanding of cult readings of Hollywood texts.

Notes

1   In these it was found that viewers would interpret the same image differently if it was paired with different images; so, for instance, the expressionless face of a man followed by a shot of a piece of bread might connote hunger, but when followed by a shot of a child it might connote something else. An account of a contemporary attempt to repeat these experiments can be found in Stephen Prince and Wayne E. Hensley, 'The Kuleshov Effect: Recreating the Classic Experiment', *Cinema Journal* 31(2): Winter 1992, pp. 59–75.

2   This is largely connected, although not wholly, to the British magazine *Screen*, particularly during the 1970s and 1908s. A good account of this work, which does centre 'screen theory' in the middle of the enterprise of film studies is Lapsley and Westlake's *Film Theory: An Introduction* (1988).

3   This section is necessarily very sketchy, as it moves quickly through a very complex body of theory in order to make the argument which follows. For a full outline of the kind of arguments made, readers should consult the references cited or more developed accounts such as Lapsley and Westlake or my own *Film as Social Practice* (1999).

4   In this context, 'realism' refers to an effect of the dominant narrative conventions in film and television, which is to place the spectator in an ideologically conservative relation to the narrative. 'Realism', then, means an unproblematic acceptance of the status quo that is inscribed into the formal structures of popular narratives. That such narratives might present a radical or critical view of the world was, some argued, theoretically impossible. Hollywood cinema was the classic example of this. For an important set of debates about this issue, see Tony Bennett *et al.* (eds), *Popular Television and Film* (1981).

5   See, for instance, Morley (1980a; 1980b; 1986), Ang (1985; 1989) and the David Gauntlet and Annette Hill *TV Living* (1999) project. This work now amounts to a significant tradition in television and cultural studies.

PART ONE

Understanding film

THE SELECTIONS IN THIS PART take the view that the text is merely one, albeit crucially important, element in a complex of factors, institutions and industrial structures relevant to the study of film culture. In recent years, the study and teaching of film has become increasingly concerned with these other – particularly the cultural and industrial – factors in order to examine the social origins of audiences' readings of film texts. How films are understood by their audiences is more than a problem of film form, and this fact is increasingly reflected in the concerns of contemporary film studies. The first group of readings, while they may seem to be a slightly idiosyncratic group of readings to collect under the topic of 'Understanding Film', will nevertheless help us to chart one of the fundamental ways in which film studies has been 'reinvented' in recent years.

As I suggested in the Introduction, some of the most recent provocations for thinking about the understanding of film have come from outside film studies – from media histories, feminist studies, television studies and cultural studies. Tony Bennett and Janet Woollacott's (1987) cultural studies' analysis of 'the figure of James Bond' – that is the 'James Bond' constructed in the novels and films, their promotion, marketing and patterns of cultural circulation and consumption – has been particularly influential. New appraisals of the understanding of popular cinema (Klinger 1994; Staiger 1992) have drawn on elements of the Bennett and Woollacott argument in order to focus on how films are read or interpreted. The excerpt reproduced in this reader contains Bennett and Woollacott's influential notion of 'reading formations'. In the reading, which is taken from the chapter called 'Reading Bond', Bennett and Woollacott argue that the various 'texts' of Bond are not necessarily examples of the places where 'the business of culture is conducted'. Rather, these texts are 'sites around which the predominantly social affair of the struggle for the production of meaning is conducted'. Bennett and Woollacott are critical of approaches to understanding the figure of Bond which see the texts as the primary evidence, and which regard shifts in audience readings merely as 'different responses to "the same text"'. Instead, Bennett and Woollacott recommend attention to the social conditions that have organized these shifting readings of the figure of Bond through the films and novels. They describe these conditions as 'reading formations', defining the term as referring to 'the specific determinations which bear in upon, mould and configure the relations between texts and readers in determinant conditions of reading'.

In their opposition to an analytic focus which 'stabilizes texts as objects of study "in themselves"', Bennett and Woollacott run against the grain of much of the history of film studies – where, of course, the individual text has been studied often in precisely this way. However, their approach is consonant with the development of film historiography and the social-historical focus upon actual film audiences evident in, say, Miriam Hansen's work, as well as the increasing trade in ideas between those studying popular film and those working with other popular media forms.

Comparisons with the differing institutional and theoretical histories of other media forms (in this case, television), are productive for the author of the second selection in Part I. Annette Kuhn's essay on women's genres starts out discussing television soap opera and film melodrama through their nominated target markets – female audiences. Kuhn asks how do such forms 'address, or construct, a female or feminine spectator?' Currently, she suggests, film studies finds it very difficult to provide a comprehensive answer to such a question. Commencing with post-Freudian film theory's focus on the formal properties of these genres as the location for the construction of their spectator/audience, Kuhn makes the point that there are now (she is writing in 1984) competing theoretical perspectives onto such genres, which reveal the limitations of such orthodox assumptions. While she acknowledges psycho-analytic accounts of the gendered film spectator, she is sceptical about their universal applicability: psychoanalytic concepts of subjectivity 'seem to offer little scope', she says, 'for theorizing subjectivity in its cultural or historical specificity'. They cannot tell us very much about how particular films might be aimed at a specific female audience.

This limitation is implicit in the conventional elision between the terms 'spectator' and 'audience': the one effectively read off the text, and the other open to more empirical veri-fication, but often used interchangeably as if there were no difference between these two concepts or their sphere of application. Kuhn argues that the concepts of spectator and audi-ence are distinct, and should not be 'reduced to one another'. Like Bennett and Woollacott, Kuhn questions the implications of the gulf between the conventional practices employed within textual analysis in film and television studies, and the more contextual or institutional inquiries which might help one locate and describe the actual audience of, say, a television soap opera.

Television studies has tended to emphasize the determining nature of contextual factors more than has been the case in a film studies preoccupied with the aesthetic and the textual, but Kuhn does not argue for one tradition over the other. Rather, Kuhn recommends the usefulness of the category of 'the social audience' as 'a point of contact between text and context' in both film and television. The concept of the social audience – referring to the group of people actually seated in the auditorium watching the film – 'emphasizes the status of cinema and television as social and economic institutions' and creates a category of person who can be interviewed, counted, surveyed and so on. However, it is also the case that this social audience buy their tickets to watch films in order to become 'spectators' 'in the moment they engage in the processes and pleasures of meaning-making'. The categories flow into each other – 'in taking part in the social act of consuming representations, a group of spectators becomes a social audience' – in ways that are both continuous and distinct.

As I argued in the Introduction, the universalism implicit in the concept of the spectator developed in 1970s apparatus theory and ideological textual analysis has been largely discred-ited. In its place, those continuing to work on issues of spectatorship now focus on understanding the relation between psychic and social life and the cinema. Judith Mayne's *Cinema and Spectatorship* (1993) remains one of the most useful accounts of debates about spectatorship. After reviewing these debates in the context of criticism from competing traditions, Mayne deals directly with the totalizing effect of much of this theoretical tradition. She follows this discussion with a series of case studies – of texts, stars and audiences.

In the chapter selected for this volume, 'Paradoxes of Spectatorship', Mayne reflects on the strengths and weaknesses of this tradition of work. Mayne acknowledges the tension between theoretical accounts which project a homogeneous relation between spectator and text, and the need to acknowledge a far more heterogeneous material relation – as well as an increasingly diverse range of modes of cinematic representation and address, even in mainstream cinema. Accepting the cultural studies proposition that textual meaning is contextually negotiated rather than irresistably inscribed, Judith Mayne demonstrates the usefulness of the concept of the spectator while also canvassing the difficulties raised by new approaches to understanding film. She, too, welcomes the influence of cultural studies approaches that emphasize agency and resistance, but argues against their easy adoption as complacent accounts of the power of the spectator/viewer over the text. Like Kuhn, she also recognizes the inadequacy of solely text-based theories of readership, and the need for multiple perspectives onto this issue. Moving from cultural studies to the new historicism tradition within literary studies, her argument also takes us in the direction of a closer attention to the social and empirically grounded.

The main title of Janet Staiger's *Interpreting Films* (1992) might once have signified a discussion of the formal or textual analysis of cinema texts. In an interesting sign of the shift I have been mapping out in Part I, and as spelt out in its subtitle, the book is actually a study of the historical reception of films. It is about the audience's interpretations, not those of the critic, and about the need to provide an understanding of the historical context which has helped to generate these interpretations. In the chapter excerpted here, 'Reception Studies in Film and Television', Staiger discusses a number of contemporary approaches to film studies which contain the potential to move towards a 'context-activated historical model' for interpreting films – but which, for various reasons, have failed. All 'classical film philosophies', she argues, come up with the same model of the relations between texts and spectators: 'the cinema text works on an essentially receptive and ideal spectator'. While Staiger is admirably even-handed as she presents her schematic reading of aspects of the history of film studies, her objective is to challenge the text-activated approach to film studies which she regards as having been privileged at the expense of a spectator-activated approach.

Staiger's project, as she describes it in the Preface to *Interpreting Films*, stresses 'contextual factors rather than textual materials or reader psychologies as most important in illuminating the reading process or interpretation' (xi). Although Staiger nominates cultural studies as the field to which this book contributes, it is not the conventional formation of the field that she addresses. She does find British cultural studies work on the social production of meaning useful, and she seems particularly interested in Tony Bennett's work. However, the effect of this book is to resituate the field of film studies in a closer relation to the contextual orientations found within cultural studies generally but also within communications, television and media studies. Notably, this book is relatively unusual in film studies for the ease with which it moves across the disciplinary boundaries of literary studies, linguistics, television and communications studies as a means of criticizing the current shape of the field. As a result, not only is it a persuasive critique, but it is also a very useful overview of the many provocations from other disciplines which question film studies' traditional orientations as a disciplinary field.

Chapter 1

TONY BENNETT AND JANET WOOLLACOTT

TEXTS AND THEIR READINGS

IT IS NOT POSSIBLE TO ANALYSE a cultural phenomenon constituted in this way merely by studying the various 'texts of Bond' one by one and sequentially. To seek thus to stabilize them as objects of analysis would be to abstract them from the shifting orders of inter-textuality through which their actual functioning has been organized and reorganized. This would be to close off in advance the possibility of understanding the concrete history of their functioning in diverse social and ideological relations of reading. In order to do this, it is necessary to abandon the assumption that texts, in themselves, constitute the place where the business of culture is conducted, or that they can be construed as the sources of meanings or effects which can be deduced from an analysis of their formal properties. In place of this view, so powerfully implanted in our intellectual culture, we shall argue that texts constitute sites around which the pre-eminently social affair of the struggle for the production of meaning is conducted, principally in the form of a series of bids and counter-bids to determine which system of inter-textual coordinates should be granted an effective social role in organising reading practices.

The key question to which these considerations point concerns the relations between texts and their readers and the means whereby these might be analysed. Ordinarily, approaches to this question fall within two broad categories. First, there are those approaches concerned to analyse the formal mechanisms by which a text produces a position or positions for reading, organizing its own consumption in the implied, model or preferred reader – the terms vary, but the approach is essentially the same – it implicitly posits as a condition of its own intelligibility.[1] Attention here thus focuses on the intra-textual determinations of reading. Within the second approach, attention focuses on the extra-textual determinations of reading, particularly on the situationally determined frameworks of cultural and ideological reference which supply the grids of intelligibility through which different groups of readers read and interpret a given text. David Morley's study of the audience for *Nationwide* constitutes perhaps the most sophisticated application of this approach in its combination of both discursive and situational determinations.[2] Arguing that the ideological discourses which, in a particular context, mediate the relations between text and reader will influence the way a text is perceived and read, Morley gives such varying reading practice a social base in arguing that an individual's location within class, gender, ethnic and national relations will condition the mode of his/her access or exposure to the discourses which thus mediate his/her encounter with a text. The advantages of this approach are considerable in that it enables readings to be patterned into identifiable clusters whose distinguishing characteristics are explained by the operation of both cultural (discursive) and structural (social positionality) factors.

While work of considerable value has been done within both approaches, their inadequacies tend to complement one another inasmuch as both concur in accepting an essentially metaphysical view of texts. It is assumed, within the first approach, that the intra-textual processes through which reading is organized can be specified independently of the extra-textual determinations which mould and configure the reading practices of empirically diverse groups of readers. This is to suppose that there is an immovable frame separating the intra-textual from the extra-textual.[3] Similarly, while the second approach allows for a variability of reader response, it retains intact the virtual identity of the text in the respect that, when all is said and done, such variations are conceived as merely different responses to 'the same text'. According to the most developed variant of this approach – the encoding/decoding model – the process of textual production is conceived as one in which 'messages' (seemingly existing prior to any signification) are translated into socially conventionalized codes. The text which results from this process is construed as the container of 'fixed codes' which, although they may be variantly decoded, remain unaffected by such different decoding practices.[4]

Moreover, both approaches rest on and support a definite ordering of the relations between the study of texts and the study of readings such that the former always comes first and the latter second. This usually results in a normative approach to the history of reading such that readings which do not conform to the dictates of the 'fixed codes' proposed by the analyst are regarded as selective distortions or miscomprehensions of what are claimed to be objective properties of 'the text itself'. Furthermore, this has the added consequence that, in practice, nothing different actually happens. The supposition that the text must be analysed first and readings afterwards happily means that the empirical history of the diverse patterns of reading produced within different social and ideological relations of reading need not be allowed to complicate or muddy the analytical exchange between analyst and text. Robert Holub has thus commented that Iser's concept of the implied reader makes it possible to analyse the role of the reader without having to take account of the practices of real or empirical readers, thereby foreclosing any analytical 'integration of historical information in anything but a superficial fashion'. Holub's conclusion is a sufficient warning against merely tacking the study of reading on to the already completed textual analysis: 'A historical perspective cannot be attached *ex post facto* in the guise of illustrative material or mere content for the empty structure of a repertoire; it must be integrated into the very conceptual apparatus of the system.'[5]

The failure to do this has meant that most approaches to the problem of reading have amounted to little more than a series of no doubt well intended but none the less, largely gestural nods in the direction of the reader – a question of doing the same old thing, analysing texts, and then saying generously that, of course, interpretations may vary, even to the point of entertaining the prospect of unlimited semiosis. Such open-mindedness does not in itself, however, afford the means whereby the range of meanings that have *actually* been produced in relation to a particular text might be accounted for. The empirical study of reading practices is notoriously difficult, and for eminently practical reasons, particularly when the study of past readings is concerned in that, at the best, the evidence relating to these is usually wholly indirect and, therefore, largely inconclusive. While relying mainly on evidence of this kind, and thus falling short of real flesh and blood readers, we are concerned, at various points in this study, to open up a theoretical space within which the empirical study of reading practices might be located and given a more productive direction than the 'show and tell' orientation which, for the greater part, has characterized this area of work in the past.

It is worth noting, in this respect, that most approaches to the study of reading assume that texts are able to exert an appreciable social and cultural influence only once a meaning has been imputed to them through the operation of a system of interpretation, be it implicit or explicitly formulated. While such concerns are important, the tendency to pose questions relating to the social effectivity of texts solely within the framework of such a hermeneutic model has proved unduly restrictive. Recent work concerned with the functioning of literary texts within educational institutions suggests that the part they play in forming human apti-tudes and capacities is not reducible to an analysis of their received meanings. In other words, the position of the reader is not always and only that of an interpreter. However, we are primarily concerned to establish the fields of ideological meaning within which the reading of 'the texts of Bond' has been situated.

To do so, it will be necessary to take account of the determinations which have organized the reading of the Bond novels. (The same is true of the films, but in the interests of clarity of exposition, we shall address these problems primarily in relationship to the novels.) This entails that these texts be conceived as having no existence prior to or independently of the varying 'reading formations' in which they have been constituted as objects-to-be read. By 'reading formations' here, we have in mind not the generalized cultural determinations of reading considered by David Morley, but those specific determinations which bear in upon, mould and configure the relations between texts and readers in determinant conditions of reading. It refers, specifically, to the inter-textual relations which prevail in a particular context, thereby activating a given body of texts by ordering the relations between them in a specific way such that their reading is always-already cued in specific directions that are not given by those 'texts themselves' as entities separable from such relations.[6]

The text that is read, according to such a conception, is an always-already culturally acti-vated object just as, and for the same reasons, the reader is an always-already culturally activated subject. The encounter between them is always culturally, ideologically and – which is to say the same thing – inter-textually organized in such a way that their separation as subject and object is called into question. The reader is conceived not as a subject who stands outside the text and interprets it any more than the text is regarded as an object the reader encounters. Rather, text and reader are conceived as being co-produced within a reading formation, gridded on to one another in a determinate compact unity. Of course, such a reading formation is not self-generating. Rather, it is the product of definite social and ideo-logical relations of reading composed, in the main, of those apparatuses – schools, the press, critical reviews, fanzines – within and between which the socially dominant forms for the superintendence of reading are both constructed and contested.[7] Neither texts nor readers, according these formulations, exist prior to or independently of the processes through which the struggle for textual meanings is socially enacted. This is not to suggest that texts have no determinate properties – such as a definite order of narrative progression – which may be analysed objectively. But it is to argue that such properties cannot, in themselves, validate certain received meanings above others; they do not provide a point of 'truth' in relation to which readings may be normatively and hierarchically ranked, or discounted. Nor are we suggesting that readers do not have determinate properties. They most certainly do, but complexly varying ones which, rather than being attributable to the reader as a subject independent of the text, are the product of the orders of inter-textuality which have marked the reader's formation.

It will be useful, in order to lend some substance to these arguments, to consider the problems associated with the analytical strategies most commonly used in attempts to stabilize texts as objects of study 'in themselves'. There are, in the main, four such devices. First, as we have seen from Foucault's comments, the figure of the author may be invoked to provide a stabilising context which may serve as a warrant for particular readings. The key difficulty here is that the figure of the author is clearly a malleable construct which may be discursively related to the same set of texts in different ways within different regions of textual distribution. As itself a variable, the figure of the author thus cannot furnish the fixed point of support which such analysis requires. An examination of the functioning of the figure of Fleming in this respect reveals, as we shall see, not one or two, but several Flemings, related to the Bond novels in different ways and with different effects.

Second, analysis may focus on the originating moment of a text's existence or, as in many Marxist formulations, on the conditions of its production, seeking, in these, a point of anchorage in relation to which a given reading may be fastened down as, in some way, the true or original meaning of the text concerned. Analysis of the way in which a text functioned and was received in the historical relations of its time is thus claimed to reveal its 'original' and therefore 'true' meaning. An instance of this approach is provided by Umberto Eco's analysis of Eugene Sue's *Les Mystères de Paris*. Relying on the 'cultivated' codes that were supposedly shared by the author and his contemporary critics to establish the 'fixed codes' of Sue's novel, Eco interprets popular readings of the same period as a series of distortions and incomprehensions which abstracted only 'the most obvious meanings' from the 'total message'.[8]

A number of problems coalesce here. First, there are no good reasons for privileging the originating exchange between an author and his contemporary critics, even if these did constitute the author's intended public, as a means of establishing the 'fixed codes' of a text. Indeed, in the case of popular texts, there are good reasons for not doing so since the reactions of critics may have precious little bearing on the cultural business that is transacted around, through and by means of such texts in the socially predominant forms of their distribution and circulation. To conceive the readings produced within these as a lack or distortion in relation to the readings of the 'cultivated' public is merely to connive in the process whereby the cultural values which animate the reading practices of dominant social groups are habitually reified in being presented as the properties of 'texts themselves'. The second problem consists in Eco's assumption that there is, in the lives of texts, an originating exchange or founding moment – the 'moment of emission' – which can be fixed as singular. This may not be the case. It usually is only when there is a clearly bounded context – most often a performance of some kind – which defines a text's initial conditions of existence: the staging of Racine's tragedies at the court of Louis XIV, for example. However, it is rarely the case with texts which are produced, initially, in multiple form and circulated via the mechanisms of the market. And it is least of all the case with texts which come to be classified as popular since, from the very beginning of their lives, these may circulate in different forms for both the 'cultivated' and 'mass' publics and thus be ushered forth, simultaneously, into different social and ideological relations of reading. The social destinies of texts are thus often pluridimensional rather than singular from the very first moment of their publication, and not just subsequently. In such cases, there is no unique, founding set of text–reader relations which can serve as an analytical device with which to decipher the 'fixed code' of a text.

We need merely mention that 1,100 prints of *Goldfinger* were distributed during the first two weeks of the film's release for the force of this point to be felt. Where, given such a system of distribution, would it be possible to locate a sender–receiver exchange or a text–reader relationship which might be constituted as a privileged point of origin? The

première showing of the film in New York? Or its première in London? Or its first showings in Paris, Berlin or Tokyo or, for that matter, Wanganui? Clearly, the construct of an
originating moment of emission is impossible to sustain. Likewise, it would be both misleading
and singularly inconsequential, in studying the Bond novels, to privilege the exchange between
Fleming and his contemporary 'cultivated' public and to conceive other readings as a distortion or misrepresentation of the 'fixed codes' through which that exchange was regulated.
As we have seen, there *was* such a moment in the history of the Bond novels, a moment
marked by the critical production of a culturally knowing reader. However, little would
be served by basing our discussion of the novels on this moment when, quite clearly, they
have had their most significant impact within social and ideological relations of reading of a
different kind.

   Third, as in E. Hirsch Junior's work, a particular genre may be invoked to provide criteria
of relevance which can be used to limit the range of valid interpretations.[9] The problem here,
quite simply, is that genre frameworks prove relatively indeterminate and thus cannot fulfil
the stabilizing function assigned to them. Finally, an attempt may be made to construct a
particular figure of the reader as a means of determining the 'fixed codes' of a text. The practical consequence of this, however, is that it proves impossible to analyse the reading practices
of empirically diverse groups of readers to the degree that the role of the reader turns out
to be always-already occupied by an abstract and ideal figure of the reader of the analyst's
own construction.

   Although different in other respects, all these procedures produce, as their object, 'the
text itself' only by arbitrarily privileging one set of text–reader relations above others, sometimes contending ones. The consequence of this is to establish a hierarchical ordering of the
relations between different reading practices such that some are conceived a more valid – and
therefore more worthwhile, more objective, more deserving of analysis – than others, which
are thereby ignored, written off as marginal, aberrant, quixotic or whatever. The devices used
to stabilize texts as objects of analysis 'in themselves' thereby have the effect of disabling
analysis of the ways in which their functioning within history is incessantly modified.

   Fortunately, we may pursue these problems in greater detail and, at the same time,
commence our discussion of the Bond novels since, in his classic study of these, Umberto
Eco uses a number of the devices we have enumerated in order to determine their 'fixed
codes'.[10] Eco approaches the Bond novels as instances of what he calls 'closed texts'; that is,
texts which 'apparently aim at pulling the reader along a pre-determined path', which seem
'to be structured according to an inflexible project' (p. 8). In so far as they have been designed
for the 'average reader' and are thus 'potentially speaking to everyone', Eco argues, such
texts 'can give rise to the most unforeseeable interpretations, at least at the ideological level'
(p. 8). They are 'in the last analysis randomly open to every pragmatic accident' (p. 7).
Although internally closed, such a text is randomly opened up from without by the contingent irruptions of history.

   This would seem fine. Everything is allowed for. As Eco concludes his essay:

> Since the decoding of a message cannot be established by its author, but depends
> on the concrete circumstances of its reception, it is difficult to guess what Fleming
> is or will be for his readers. When an act of communication provokes a response
> in public opinion, the definitive verification will take place not within the ambit
> of the book but in that of the society that reads it.
>
> (p. 172)

The difficulty is that 'the society that reads it' is left with little option but to deviate marginally from the position of the 'average reader', a category which, in Eco's use, limits all possibilities in advance of their actually been taken.

Notes

1   See, for an example of this approach, W. Iser, *The Act of Reading*.
2   See D. Morley, *The 'Nationwide' Audience*, BFI, London, 1980b.
3   For a discussion of the ways in which the 'frame' separating the literary from the extra-literary may shift, see J. Frow, 'The Literary Frame', *Journal of Aesthetic Education* 16(2), 1982.
4   See, for expositions and critical discussions of the encoding/decoding model, S. Hall 'Encoding/Decoding' and D. Morley 'Texts, Readers, Subjects', both in S. Hall, D. Hobson, A Lowe and P. Willis (eds) *Culture, Media, Language*, Hutchinson, London, 1980c.
5   R. Holub, *Reception Theory: A Critical Introduction*, Methuen, London, 1983, p. 99.
6   For a fuller discussion and exemplification of the concept of 'reading formation', see T. Bennett, 'Texts, Readers, Reading Formations', *The Bulletin of the Midwest Modern Language Association* 16(1), Spring 1983. Reprinted in *Literature and History* 9(2), Autumn 1983.
7   It is in this, its material social supports, that the concept of 'reading formation' differs from the concept of 'horizon of expectations' associated with the work of H. R. Jauss. For Jauss, 'horizon of expectations' refers to the subjective associations which inform the reading practices of any individual reader. The concept of reading formation, by contrast, specifies a set of objective determinations which mould and structure the terrain of the text–reader encounter.
8   See U. Eco, *The Role of the Reader: Explorations in the Semiotics of Texts*, Hutchinson, London, 1981, pp. 140–1.
9   See E. D. Hirsch Jr, *Validity in Interpretation*, Yale University Press, New Haven, 1967.
10 See U. Eco, 'Narrative Structures in Fleming', in *The Role of the Reader* (originally published in O. Del Buono and U. Eco, *The Bond Affair*, Macdonald, London, 1961).

Chapter 2

ANNETTE KUHN

WOMEN'S GENRES

I

TELEVISION SOAP OPERA AND FILM melodrama, popular narrative forms aimed at female audiences, are currently attracting a good deal of critical and theoretical attention. Not surprisingly, most of the work on these 'gyno-centric' genres is informed by various strands of feminist thought on visual representation. Less obviously, perhaps, such work has also prompted a series of questions which relate to representation and cultural production in a more wide-ranging and thoroughgoing manner than a specifically feminist interest might suggest. Not only are film melodrama (and more particularly its subtype the 'woman's picture') and soap opera directed at female audiences, they are also actually enjoyed by millions of women. What is it that sets these genres apart from representations which possess a less gender-specific mass appeal?

One of the defining generic features of the woman's picture as a textual system is its construction of narratives motivated by female desire and processes of spectator identification governed by female point-of-view. Soap opera constructs woman-centred narratives and identifications, too, but it differs textually from its cinematic counterpart in certain other respects: not only do soaps never end, but their beginnings are soon lost sight of. And whereas in the woman's picture the narrative process is characteristically governed by the enigma-retardation-resolution structure which marks the classic narrative, soap opera narratives propose

> competing and intertwining plot lines introduced as the serial progresses. Each plot . . . develops at a different pace, thus preventing any clear resolution of conflict. The completion of one story generally leads into others, and ongoing plots often incorporate parts of semi-resolved conflicts.[1]

Recent work on soap opera and melodrama has drawn on existing theories, methods and perspectives in the study of film and television, including the structural analysis of narratives, textual semiotics and psychoanalysis, audience research and the political economy of cultural institutions. At the same time, though, some of this work has exposed the limitations of existing approaches, and in consequence been forced if not actually to abandon them, at least to challenge their characteristic problematics. Indeed, it may be contended that the most significant developments in film and television theory in general are currently taking place precisely within such areas of feminist concern as critical work on soap opera and melodrama.

In examining some of this work, I shall begin by looking at three areas in which particularly pertinent questions are being directed at theories of representation and cultural production. These are, first, the problem of gendered spectatorship; second, questions concerning the universalism as against the historical specificity of conceptualizations of gendered spectatorship; and third, the relationship between film and television texts and their social, historical and institutional contexts. Each of these concerns articulates in particular ways with what seems to me the central issue here – the question of the audience, or audiences, for certain types of cinematic and televisual representation.

II

Film theory's appropriation to its own project of Freudian and post-Freudian psychoanalysis places the question of the relationship between text and spectator firmly on the agenda. Given the preoccupation of psychoanalysis with sexuality and gender, a move from conceptualizing the spectator as a homogeneous and androgynous effect of textual operations[2] to regarding her or him as a gendered subject constituted in representation seems in retrospect inevitable. At the same time, the interests of feminist film theory and film theory in general converge at this point in a shared concern with sexual difference. Psychoanalytic accounts of the formation of gendered subjectivity raise the question, if only indirectly, of representation and feminine subjectivity. This in turn permits the spectator to be considered as a gendered subject position, masculine or feminine: and theoretical work on soap opera and the woman's picture may take this as a starting point for its inquiry into spectator–text relations. Do these 'gynocentric' forms address, or construct, a female or a feminine spectator? If so, how?

On the question of film melodrama, Laura Mulvey, commenting on King Vidor's *Duel in the Sun*,[3] argues that when, as in this film, a woman is at the centre of the narrative, the question of female desire structures the hermeneutic: 'what does *she* want?' This, says Mulvey, does not guarantee the constitution of the spectator as feminine so much as it implies a contradictory, and in the final instance impossible, 'phantasy of masculinisation' for the female spectator. This is in line with the author's earlier suggestion that cinema spectatorship involves masculine identification for spectators of either gender.[4] If cinema does thus construct a masculine subject, there can be no unproblematic feminine subject position for any spectator. Pam Cook, on the other hand, writing about a group of melodramas produced during the 1940s at the Gainsborough Studios, evinces greater optimism about the possibility of a feminine subject of classic cinema. She does acknowledge, though, that in a patriarchal society female desire and female point-of-view are highly contradictory, even if they have the potential to subvert culturally dominant modes of spectator–text relation. The characteristic 'excess' of the woman's melodrama, for example, is explained by Cook in terms of the genre's tendency to '[pose] problems for itself which it can scarcely contain'.[5]

Writers on television soap opera tend to take views on gender and spectatorship rather different from those advanced by film theorists. Tania Modleski, for example, argues with regard to soaps that their characteristic narrative patterns, their foregrounding of 'female' skills in dealing with personal and domestic crises, and the capacity of their programme formats and scheduling to key into the rhythms of women's work in the home, all address a female spectator. Furthermore, she goes so far as to argue that the textual processes of soaps are in some respects similar to those of certain 'feminine' texts which speak to a decentred subject, and so are 'not altogether at odds with . . . feminist aesthetics'.[6] Modleski's view is that soaps not only address female spectators, but in so doing construct feminine subject positions which transcend patriarchal modes of subjectivity.

Different though their respective approaches and conclusions may be, however, Mulvey, Cook and Modleski are all interested in the problem of gendered spectatorship. The fact, too, that this common concern is informed by a shared interest in assessing the progressive or transformative potential of soaps and melodramas is significant in light of the broad appeal of both genres to the mass audiences of women at which they are aimed.

But what precisely does it mean to say that certain representations are aimed at a female audience? However well theorized they may be, existing conceptualizations of gendered spectatorship are unable to deal with this question. This is because spectator and audience are distinct concepts which cannot – as they frequently are – be reduced to one another. Although I shall be considering some of its consequences more fully below, it is important to note a further problem for film and television theory, posed in this case by the distinction between spectator and audience. Critical work on the woman's picture and on soap opera has necessarily, and most productively, emphasized the question of gendered spectatorship. In doing this, film theory in particular has taken on board a conceptualization of the spectator derived from psychoanalytic accounts of the formation of human subjectivity.

Such accounts, however, have been widely criticized for this universalism. Beyond, perhaps, associating certain variants of the oedipus complex with family forms characteristic of a patriarchal society and offering a theory of the construction of gender, psychoanalysis seems to offer little scope for theorizing subjectivity in its cultural or historical specificity. Although in relation to the specific issues of spectatorship and representation there may, as I shall argue, be a way around this apparent impasse, virtually all film and television theory – its feminist variants included – is marked by the dualism of universalism and specificity.

Nowhere is this more evident than in the gulf between textual analysis and contextual inquiry. Each is done according to different rules and procedures, distinct methods of investigation and theoretical perspectives. In bringing to the fore the question of spectator–text relations, theories deriving from psychoanalysis may claim – to the extent that the spectatorial apparatus is held to be coterminous with the cinematic or televisual institution – to address the relationship between text and context. But as soon as any attempt is made to combine textual analysis with analysis of the concrete social, historical and institutional conditions of production and reception of texts, it becomes clear that the context of the spectator/subject of psychoanalytic theory is rather different from the context of production and reception constructed by conjunctural analyses of cultural institutions.

The disparity between these two 'contexts' structures Pam Cook's article on the Gainsborough melodrama, which sets out to combine an analysis of the characteristic textual operations and modes of address of a genre with an examination of the historical conditions of a particular expression of it. Gainsborough melodrama, says Cook, emerges from a complex of determinants, including certain features of the British film industry of the 1940s, the nature of the female cinema audience in the post-World War II period, and the textual characteristics of the woman's picture itself.[7] While Cook is correct in pointing to the various levels of determination at work in this instance, her lengthy preliminary discussion of spectator–text relations and the woman's picture rather outbalances her subsequent investigation of the social and industrial contexts of the Gainsborough melodrama. The fact, too, that analysis of the woman's picture in terms of its interpellation of a female/feminine spectator is simply placed alongside a conjunctural analysis tends to vitiate any attempt to reconcile the two approaches, and so to deal with the broader issue of universalism as against historical specificity. But although the initial problem remains, Cook's article constitutes an important intervention in the debate because, in tackling the text–context split head-on, it necessarily exposes a key weakness of current film theory.

In work on television soap opera as opposed to film melodrama, the dualism of text and context manifests itself rather differently, if only because – unlike film theory – theoretical work on television has tended to emphasize the determining character of the contextual level, particularly the structure and organization of television institutions. Since this has often been at the expense of attention to the operation of television texts, television theory may perhaps be regarded as innovative in the extent to which it attempts to deal specifically with texts as well as contexts. Some feminist critical work has in fact already begun to address the question of television as text, though always with characteristic emphasis on the issue of gendered spectatorship. This emphasis constitutes a common concern of work on both television soaps and the woman's picture, but a point of contact between text and context in either medium emerges only when the concept of social audience is considered in distinction from that of spectator.

III

Each term – spectator and social audience – presupposes a different set of relations to representations and to the contexts in which they are received. Looking at spectators and at audiences demands different methodologies and theoretical frameworks, distinct discourses which construct distinct subjectivities and social relations. The *spectator*, for example, is a subject constituted in signification, interpellated by the film or television text. This does not necessarily mean that the spectator is merely an effect of the text, however, because modes of subjectivity which also operate outside spectator–text relations in film or television are activated in the relationship between spectators and texts.

This model of the spectator/subject is useful in correcting more deterministic communication models which might, say, pose the spectator not as actively constructing meaning but simply as a receiver and decoder of preconstituted 'messages'. In emphasizing spectatorship as a set of psychic relations and focusing on the relationship between spectator and text, however, such a model does disregard the broader social implications of filmgoing or televiewing. It is the social act of going to the cinema, for instance, that makes the individual cinemagoer part of an audience. Viewing television may involve social relations rather different from film-going, but in its own ways television does depend on individual viewers being part of an audience, even if its members are never in one place at the same time. A group of people seated in a single auditorium looking at a film, or scattered across thousands of homes watching the same television programme, is a *social audience*. The concept of social audience, as against that of spectator, emphasizes the status of cinema and television as social and economic institutions.

Constructed by discursive practices both of cinema and television and of social science, the social audience is a group of people who buy tickets at the box office, or who switch on their television sets; people who can be surveyed, counted and categorized according to age, sex and socioeconomic status.[8] The cost of a cinema ticket or television licence fee, or a readiness to tolerate commercial breaks, earns audiences the right to look at films and television programmes, and so to be spectators. Social audiences become spectators in the moment they engage in the processes and pleasures of meaning-making attendant on watching a film or television programme. The anticipated pleasure of spectatorship is perhaps a necessary condition of existence of audiences. In taking part in the social act of consuming representations, a group of spectators becomes a social audience.

The consumer of representations as audience member and spectator is involved in a particular kind of psychic and social relationship: at this point, a conceptualization of the cinematic or televisual apparatus as a regime of pleasure intersects with sociological and economic understandings of film and television as institutions. Because each term describes a distinct set of relationships, though, it is important not to conflate social audience with spectators. At the same time, since each is necessary to the other, it is equally important to remain aware of the points of continuity between the two sets of relations.

These conceptualizations of spectator and social audience have particular implications when it comes to a consideration of popular 'gynocentric' forms such as soap opera and melodrama. Most obviously, perhaps, these centre on the issue of gender, which prompts again the question: what does 'aimed at a female audience' mean? What exactly is being signalled in this reference to a gendered audience? Are women to be understood as a subgroup of the social audience, distinguishable through discourses which construct a priori gender categories? Or does the reference to a female audience allude rather to gendered spectatorship, to sexual difference constructed in relations between spectators and texts? Most likely it condenses the two meanings; but an examination of the distinction between them may nevertheless be illuminating in relation to the broader theoretical issues of texts, contexts, social audiences and spectators.

The notion of a female social audience, certainly as it is constructed in the discursive practices through which it is investigated, presupposes a group of individuals already formed as female. For the sociologist interested in such matters as gender and lifestyles, certain people bring a pre-existent femaleness to their viewing of film and television. For the business executive interested in selling commodities, television programmes and films are marketed to individuals already constructed as female. Both, however, are interested in the same kind of woman. On one level, then, soap operas and women's melodramas address themselves to a social audience of women. But they may at the same time be regarded as speaking to a female, or a feminine, spectator. If soaps and melodramas inscribe femininity in their address, women – as well as being already formed *for* such representations – are in a sense also formed *by* them.

In making this point, however, I intend no reduction of femaleness to femininity: on the contrary, I would hold to a distinction between femaleness as social gender and femininity as subject position. For example, it is possible for a female spectator to be addressed, as it were, 'in the masculine', and the converse is presumably also true. Nevertheless, in a culturally pervasive operation of ideology, femininity is routinely identified with femaleness and masculinity with maleness. Thus, for example, an address 'in the feminine' may be regarded in ideological terms as privileging, if not necessitating, a socially constructed female gender identity.

The constitutive character of both the woman's picture and the soap opera has in fact been noted by a number of feminist commentators. Tania Modleski, for instance, suggests that the characteristic narrative structures and textual operations of soap operas both address the viewer as an 'ideal mother' – ever-understanding, ever-tolerant of the weaknesses and foibles of others – and also posit states of expectation and passivity as pleasurable: 'the narrative, by placing ever more complex obstacles between desire and fulfilment, makes anticipation of an end an end in itself'.[9] In our culture, tolerance and passivity are regarded as feminine attributes, and consequently as qualities proper in women but not in men.

Charlotte Brunsdon extends Modleski's line of argument to the extra-textual level: in constructing its viewers as competent within the ideological and moral frameworks of marriage and family life, soap opera, she implies, addresses both a feminine spectator and female audience.[10] Pointing to the centrality of intuition and emotion in the construction of the woman's point-of-view, Pam Cook regards the construction of a feminine spectator as a highly problematic and contradictory process: so that in the film melodrama's construction of female point-of-view, the validity of femininity as a subject position is necessary laid open to question.[11]

This divergence on the question of gendered spectatorship within feminist theory is significant. Does it perhaps indicate fundamental differences between film and television in the spectator–text relations privileged by each? Do soaps and melodramas really construct different relations of gendered spectatorship, with melodrama constructing contradictory identifications in ways that soap opera does not? Or do these different positions on spectatorship rather signal an unevenness of theoretical development – or, to put it less teleologically, reflect the different intellectual histories and epistemological groundings of film theory and television theory?

Any differences in the spectator–text relations proposed respectively by soap opera and by film melodrama must be contingent to some extent on more general disparities in address between television and cinema. Thus film spectatorship, it may be argued, involves the pleasures evoked by looking in a more pristine way than does watching television. Whereas in classic cinema the concentration and involvement proposed by structures of the look, identification and point-of-view tend to be paramount, television spectatorship is more likely to be characterized by distraction and diversion.[12] This would suggest that each medium constructs sexual difference through spectatorship in rather different ways: cinema through the look and spectacle, and television – perhaps less evidently – through a capacity to insert its flow, its characteristic modes of address and the textual operations of different kinds of programmes into the rhythms and routines of domestic activities and sexual divisions of labour in the household at various times of day.

It would be a mistake, however, simply to equate current thinking on spectator–text relations in each medium. This is not only because theoretical work on spectatorship as it is defined here is newer and perhaps not so highly developed for television as it has been for cinema, but also because conceptualizations of spectatorship in film theory and in television theory emerge from quite distinct perspectives. When feminist writers on soap opera and on film melodrama discuss spectatorship, therefore, they are usually talking about different things. This has partly to do with the different intellectual histories and methodological groundings of theoretical work on film and on television. Whereas most television theory has until fairly recently existed under the sociological rubric of media studies, film theory has on the whole been based in the criticism-oriented tradition of literary studies. In consequence, while the one tends to privilege contexts over texts, the other usually privileges texts over contexts.

However, some recent critical work on soap opera, notably work produced within a cultural studies context, does attempt a *rapprochement* of text and context. Charlotte Brunsdon, writing about the British soap opera *Crossroads*, draws a distinction between subject positions proposed by texts and a 'social subject' who may or may not take up these positions.[13] In considering the interplay of 'social reader and social text', Brunsdon attempts to come to terms with problems posed by the universalism of the psychoanalytic model of the spectator/subject as against the descriptiveness and limited analytical scope of studies of specific instances and conjunctures. In taking up the instance of soap opera, then, one of Brunsdon's broader objectives is to resolve the dualism of text and context.

'Successful' spectatorship of a soap like *Crossroads*, it is argued, demands a certain cultural capital: familiarity with the plots and characters of a particular serial as well as with soap opera as a genre. It also demands wider cultural competence, especially in the codes of conduct of personal and family life. For Brunsdon, then, the spectator addressed by soap opera is constructed within culture rather than by representation. This, however, would indicate that such a spectator, a 'social subject', might – rather than being a subject in process of gender positioning – belong after all to a social audience already divided by gender.

The 'social subject' of this cultural model produces meaning by decoding messages or communications, an activity which is always socially situated.[14] Thus although such a model may move some way towards reconciling text and context, the balance of Brunsdon's argument remains weighted in favour of context: spectator–text relations are apparently regarded virtu-ally as an effect of sociocultural contexts. Is there a way in which spectator/subjects of film and television texts can be thought in a historically specific manner, or indeed a way for the social audience to be rescued from social/historical determinism?

Although none of the feminist criticism of soap opera and melodrama reviewed here has come up with any solution to these problems, it all attempts, in some degree and with greater or lesser success, to engage with them. Brunsdon's essay possibly comes closest to an answer, paradoxically because its very failure to resolve the dualism which ordains that spectators are constructed by texts while audiences have their place in contexts begins to hint at a way around the problem. Although the hybrid 'social subject' may turn out to be more a social audience member than a spectator, this concept does suggest that a move into theories of discourse could prove productive.

Both spectators and social audience may accordingly be regarded as discursive constructs. Representations, contexts, audiences and spectators would then be seen as a series of inter-connected social discourses, certain discourses possessing greater constitutive authority at specific moments than others. Such a model permits relative autonomy for the operations of texts, readings and contexts, and also allows for contradictions, oppositional readings and varying degrees of discursive authority. Since the state of a discursive formation is not constant, it can be apprehended only by means of inquiry into specific instances or conjunctures. In attempting to deal with the text–context split and to address the relationship between spec-tators and social audiences, therefore, theories of representation may have to come to terms with discursive formations of the social, cultural and textual.

IV

One of the impulses generating feminist critical and theoretical work on soap opera and the woman's picture is a desire to examine genres which are popular, and popular in particular with women. The assumption is usually that such popularity has to do mainly with the social audience: television soaps attract large numbers of viewers, many of them women, and in its heyday the woman's picture also drew in a mass female audience. But when the nature of this appeal is sought in the texts themselves or in relations between spectators and texts, the argu-ment becomes rather more complex. In what specific ways do soaps and melodramas address or construct female/feminine spectators?

To some extent, they offer the spectator a position of mastery: this is certainly true as regards the hermeneutic of the melodrama's classic narrative, though perhaps less obviously so in rela-tion to the soap's infinite process of narrativity. At the same time, they also place the spectator in a masochistic position of either – in the case of the woman's picture – identifying with a female character's renunciation or, as in soap opera, forever anticipating an endlessly held-off resolu-tion. Culturally speaking, this combination of mastery and masochism in the reading competence constructed by soaps and melodramas suggests an interplay of masculine and feminine subject positions. Culturally dominant codes inscribe the masculine, while the feminine bespeaks a 'return of the repressed' in the form of codes which may well transgress culturally dominant sub-ject positions, though only at the expense of proposing a position of subjection for the spectator.

At the same time, it is sometimes argued on behalf of both soap opera and film melodrama that in a society whose representations of itself are governed by the masculine, these genres at least raise the possibility of female desire and female point-of-view. Pam Cook advances such a view in relation to the woman's picture, for example.[15] But how is the oppositional potential of this to be assessed? Tania Modleski suggests that soap opera is 'in the vanguard not just of TV art but of all popular narrative art'.[16] But such a statement begs the question: in what circumstances can popular narrative art itself be regarded as transgressive? Because texts do not operate in isolation from contexts, any answer to these questions must take into account the ways in which popular narratives are read, the conditions under which they are produced and consumed, and the ends to which they are appropriated. As most feminist writing on soap opera and the woman's melodrama implies, there is ample space in the articulation of these various instances for contradiction and for struggles over meaning.

The popularity of television soap opera and film melodrama with women raises the question of how it is that sizeable audiences of women relate to these representations and the institutional practices of which they form part. It provokes, too, a consideration of the continuity between women's interpellation as spectators and their status as a social audience. In turn, the distinction between social audience and spectator/subject, and attempts to explore the relationship between the two, are part of a broader theoretical endeavour: to deal in tandem with texts and contexts. The distinction between social audience and spectator must also inform debates and practices around cultural production, in which questions of context and reception are always paramount. For anyone interested in feminist cultural politics, such considerations will necessarily inform any assessment of the place and the political usefulness of popular genres aimed at, and consumed by, mass audiences of women.

Notes

1   Muriel G. Cantor and Suzanne Pingree, *The Soap Opera*, Beverly Hills, age Publications, 1983, p. 22. Here 'soap opera' refers to daytime (US) or early evening (UK) serials, not prime-time serials like *Dallas* and *Dynasty*.

2   See Jean-Louis Baudry, 'Ideological Effects of the Basic Cinematographic Apparatus', *Film Quarterly*, 1974–5, 28(2): 39–47; Christian Metz, 'The Imaginary Signifier', *Screen*, Summer 1975, 16(2): 14–76.

3   Laura Mulvey, 'Afterthoughts on "Visual Pleasure and Narrative Cinema" . . . Inspired by *Duel in the Sun*', *Framework*, 1981, nos. 15–17, pp. 12–15.

4   Laura Mulvey, 'Visual Pleasure and Narrative Cinema', *Screen*, Autumn 1975, 16(3): 6–18.

5   Pam Cook, 'Melodrama and the Women's Picture', in Sue Aspinall and Robert Murphy (eds), *Gainsborough Melodrama*, London, British Film Institute, 1983, p. 17.

6   Tania Modleski, *Loving with a Vengeance: Mass Produced Fantasies for Women*, Hamden Connecticut, Shoe String Press, 1982, p. 105. See also Tania Modleski, 'The Search for Tomorrow in Today's Soap Operas', *Film Quarterly*, 1979, 33(1): 12–21.

7   Cook, op. cit.

8   Methods and findings of social science research on the social audience for American daytime soap operas are discussed in Cantor and Pingree, op. cit., ch. 7.

9   Modleski, *Loving with a Vengeance*, op. cit., p. 88.

10   Charlotte Brunsdon, '*Crossroads*: Notes on Soap Opera', *Screen*, Winter 1981, 22(4): 32–7.

11   Cook, op. cit., p. 19.

12   John Ellis, *Visible Fictions*, London, Routledge & Kegan Paul, 1982.

13   Brunsdon, op. cit., p. 32.

14   A similar model is also adopted by Dorothy Hobson in *Crossroads: The Drama of a Soap Opera*, London, Methuen, 1982.

15   Cook, op. cit.; E. Ann Kaplan takes a contrary position in 'Theories of Melodrama: a Feminist Perspective', *Women and Performance: a Journal of Feminist Theory*, 1983, 1(1): 40–8.

16   Modleski, *Loving with a Vengeance*, op. cit., p. 87.

Chapter 3

JUDITH MAYNE

PARADOXES OF SPECTATORSHIP

NO MATTER HOW CONTROVERSIAL and contested theories of the cinematic institution have been, few would argue with their basic premise that the capacity of the cinema to seduce, entertain or otherwise appeal to its audiences needs to be understood in ideological and psychic terms. The trick, however, is not only in understanding the relationship between the two realms of psychic and social life – a rather large undertaking in any case – but in defining with precision the ways in which the cinema is describable in terms of ideological and psychoanalytic theory, and the extent to which different types of cinema and varied contexts articulate spectatorship in different ways. Even the cognitive approach, which departs most sharply from the assumptions of 1970s film theory, is concerned with conditions of coherence and intelligibility which relate to the kind of ideological analysis central to 1970s film theory.

Does the analysis of the cinematic institution as a staging and restaging of the crises of male oedipal desire, as a regressive plenitude, apply only to a specific historical mode of the cinema – i.e. the classical, narrative Hollywood film? Or, rather, given that the emergence of the cinema is so closely linked to the fictions of Western patriarchal culture, is the cinematic apparatus as theorized in film theory bound to be the condition of *all* cinematic representation? Even within the classical Hollywood cinema, are female spectators thus bound by the Scylla of male spectatorial desire and the Charybdis of exclusion from cinematic fantasies? Given the extent to which analysis of spectatorship has focussed on sexual difference (whether foregrounded or so blatantly ignored as to function as a symptom, as in Baudry's case), are other forms of spectator identity – race, class, sexual identity other than gendered identity, age, etc. – always built upon the model of sexual difference, or are they potentially formative in their own right? And to what extent is identity a misleading route toward understanding spectatorship, particularly if it is limited by literalist assumptions, i.e. that black audiences can only 'identify' with black characters, female audiences with female ones, etc.? If apparatus theory displaced character identification as the central dynamic in understanding spectatorship, this does not mean that questions of identity have been in any way resolved. For the displacement of identification, however necessary and valuable to the project of 1970s film theory, was nonetheless accomplished at a price – a too easy equation between the 'subject' and the attributes of dominance.

Perhaps one of the greatest ironies of contemporary film studies is that the obsessive attention devoted to the cinematic institution occurred at a time when there has perhaps existed more diversity than ever before insofar as modes of cinematic representation and address are concerned. In the US alone, independent film and video, specifically addressed to a variety of markets – gay and lesbian, feminist, black, hispanic – continues to grow. One of the largest problems confronting spectatorship studies is the simultaneous affirmation of diversity and the recognition that 'diversity' can easily function as a ploy, a way of perpetuating the illusions of mainstream cinema rather than challenging them. Put another way, there is no simple division between the cinema which functions as an instrument of dominant ideology, and the cinema which facilitates challenges to it. Now if you assume, as some theorists of the 1970s did, that there is nothing about cinema that is not saturated with ideology, then the radical or contestatory powers of the cinema were limited to those films which functioned to demonstrate the ideological complicity of film.

The most promising and influential work on spectatorship assumes the necessity for understanding cinema as ideologically influenced, but not necessarily monolithically so. Linda Gordon speaks of the necessity to hold competing claims of domination and resistance in unwavering tension, refusing to collapse one into the other (1986). In spectatorship studies, several concepts have emerged to engage with the tension between cinema as monolithic institution and cinema as heterogeneous diversity. The competing claims of homogeneity (of the cinematic apparatus) and heterogeneity (of the spectator and therefore of the different ways in which the an apparatus can be understood) frame this chapter.

If the cinematic apparatus is as fully saturated with the ideology of idealism and oedipal desire as 1970s film theory would suggest, then there can be no real history of the cinema, except as variations on a common theme. Or rather, there can be no history within the cinema, if all cinema is ideological in the same way. We have already encountered criticisms of models of the cinematic apparatus for establishing a monolithic role for the spectator, and for literalizing whatever analogy was articulated, from Plato's cave to the Lacanian imaginary. An opposition between homogeneity and heterogeneity underscores these criticisms, since most alternatives to 1970s film theory take the spectator, not as the effect of the cinema institution, but as a point of departure; and not the ideal spectator as theorized by the cinematic apparatus, but the socially defined spectator who is necessarily heterogeneous – i.e. addressed through a variety of discourses. In other words, responses to apparatus theory are founded on a gap between the ideal subject postulated by the apparatus and the spectator who is always in an imperfect relation to that ideal.

In this chapter, I will examine three terms which have emerged in spectatorship studies to conceptualize the competing claims of the homogeneous cinematic institution and heterogeneous responses to it: the gap between 'address' and 'reception;' fantasy; and negotiation. Linda Gordon speaks of the need to find a method 'in between' the claims of domination and resistance, and the terms I will examine in this chapter are precisely that, concepts meant to convey the contradictory ways in which spectatorship functions. First, the relationship between cinematic address and cinematic reception opens up a space between the 'ideal' viewer and the 'real' viewer. Address refers to the ways in which a text assumes certain responses, which may or may not be operative in different reception conditions. Central to this apparent paradox is the role of the cinematic 'text,' whether defined as the individual film or as a set of operations which situate the spectator in certain ways. If spectators can and do respond to films in ways that contradict, reject, or otherwise problematize the presumably 'ideal' spectator structured into the text, then the value of textual analysis – arguably the most significant methodological direction undertaken by 1970s film theory – needs to be seriously rethought or re-evaluated.

In the previous chapter I noted that the version of psychoanalysis promoted within theories of the cinematic subject tends toward a uniform and totalizing version of the unconscious, almost always understood as the resurgence of various crises of (male) oedipal identity. The advantage of such a view, of course, is that the psychic foundations of the cultural order are open to investigation, but the disadvantages far outnumber such advantages. For the unconscious thus defined becomes one more totalizing system, and the work of the psychoanalytically inspired critic becomes just as framed by a master code as any other application of a method. In the context of these problems with psychoanalytic theory and criticism, the notion of *fantasy* has received increasing attention and is the second concept to be discussed in this chapter. An exploration of fantasy allows a far more radical exploration of psychic investment in the cinema, and suggests as well, intersections between the psychic and the political. Yet it is not altogether clear whether the implications of fantasy for the cinema allow for an understanding of the social in terms that exceed the family romance so central to any psychoanalytic understanding of culture.

It is one thing to compare the claims that can be made for cinema as a homogeneous and homogenizing, versus a heterogeneous institution, and another thing to valorize heterogeneity as necessarily contestatory. The third concept I will discuss is the term 'negotiation,' which is used frequently to suggest that different texts can be 'used,' 'interpreted,' or 'appropriated' in a variety of ways. Sometimes the diversity thus postulated by 'negotiated' readings or viewings is assumed to challenge the power of the institution. The sheer fact that a spectator or group of spectators makes unauthorized uses of the cinema is no guarantee that such uses are contestatory. Here, the central question has less to do with the status of the text, than with the value one assigns to differing modes of response – how those responses are assessed, and how film-going is 'read' in relationship to other social, cultural, and psychic formations. Indeed, the emphasis on 'negotiation' de-emphasizes the primacy of the cinematic text, focussing rather on how different responses can be read, whether critically, symptomatically or otherwise.

Address and reception

A common characteristic of textual theories of the spectator was the assumption that the cinematic apparatus 'situates,' 'positions,' or otherwise assigns a position of coherence to the implied spectator. Now however much this implied spectator position functioned as something of a phantom, and not a person to be confused with real viewers, it nonetheless managed to marginalize any consideration of how real viewers might view films in ways considerably more various than any monolithic conception of the cinematic apparatus could imply. It is one thing to assume that cinema is determined in ideological ways, to assume that cinema is a discourse (or a variety of discourses), to assume, that is, that the various institutions of the cinema *do* project an ideal viewer, and another thing to assume that those projections *work*. One of the most significant directions in spectatorship studies has investigated the gap opened up between the ways in which texts construct viewers, and how those texts may be read or used in ways that depart from what the institution valorizes.

The operative assumption here is that apparatus theories are not completely wrong, but rather incomplete. The issue is one of flexibility, of recognizing that an apparatus can have unexpected effects, and that no apparatus can function quite so smoothly and efficiently as most film theory of the 1970s would suggest. That theory was most obviously lacking and problematic in the kinds of hypotheses it led to concerning any kind of alternative cinematic practice, particularly insofar as a deconstruction of so-called dominant modes and a presumable re-positioning of the spectator are concerned. Both assume a fairly stable, fixed, one-way, top-down model of agent and object, with a spectator still locked into a programme of representation defined romantically and mechanistically according to the agenda of the film-maker or the institution – an 'active' viewer is still one 'positioned' to be so by textual constructs.

Yet to go to the other extreme, and to define texts as only offering the positions that viewers create for them, and thereby to mediate *any* notion of the cinematic institution out of existence, substitutes one monolithic political notion for another. The challenge, then, is to understand the complicated ways in which meanings are both assigned and created. If apparatus theorists were overly zealous in defining all meanings as assigned ones, there has been considerable zeal at the other end of the spectrum as well, by virtually disavowing any power of institutions and conceptualizing readers/viewers as completely free and autonomous agents – a tendency that has been particularly marked, for instance, in some versions of reader-response theory and cultural studies (especially in the US) (see Budd *et al.* 1990). Since dominant ideology is neither a person nor a one-dimensional set of concepts, it is virtually impossible to say with certainty that a particular effect is complicit with or resistant to the force of an institution. But one can assess the different effects of cinema in relationship to other discourses in order to assess the complicated ways in which the cinema functions, for instance.

One of the great difficulties here is a fairly obvious one. Individual films lend themselves to far neater and easier hypotheses about structure and excess than individual viewers or groups of viewers do. A mistrust of sociological surveys has been one of the most ingrained features of contemporary theoretical work, and so it is perhaps something of a surprise to see the analysis of 'real viewers' return, in recent years, as a theoretically credible exercise. The influence of cultural studies, specifically as defined through the work of Stuart Hall and the Centre for Contemporary Cultural Studies at the University of Birmingham, and more generally by analyses of the ways different specific audiences respond to instances of mass culture, has been enormous.

In a series of interviews with teenage girls, for instance, Angela McRobbie concluded that their passion for a film like *Flashdance* had far more to do with their own desire for physical autonomy than with any simple notion of acculturation to a patriarchal definition of feminine desirability (1984). Now it seems to me that one can only be stunned by these tentative conclusions if the model of the cinematic institution one had in the first place corresponded to the 'conspiracy theory' view of capitalism popular in some New Left circles in the 1960s. While I find McRobbie's study intriguing, and will turn to it in more detail later in this chapter, I am not convinced that her hypotheses lead necessarily to a dismissal of the power of the cinematic institution. Unfortunately, this type of work has led to a peculiar reading of the reception of mass culture, whereby any and all responses are critical ones. Some sort of understanding of the non-coincidence of address and reception is required in which power is analyzed rather than taken for granted.

One of the most influential studies along these lines is Janice Radway's *Reading the Romance*, an analysis of romance novels as they are read by a group of devoted women fans (1984). Because many of the issues that Radway raises have equal relevance to film studies, and in particular her book has been cited many times as a model of how film researchers might rethink many of the theoretical assumptions that have been seen increasingly as limitations, her book merits examination for the questions it raises for film spectatorship (Bergstrom and Doane 1989). While Radway examines the structural and ideological features of the romance novel as a genre, she situates that analysis alongside of what is perhaps the most noteworthy achievement of the book, a complex profile of a group of eager and committed romance readers. The advantage of Radway's analysis is that she acknowledges the persuasive power of the romance novel as a genre, at the same time that she refuses to reduce the genre to a series of ideological complicities. Put another way, one senses throughout *Reading the Romance* that the textual evidence is put to the test of Radway's sample audience, and vice versa.

Radway's study focuses on a group of women fictitiously referred to as the 'Smithton women,' all of whom bought the majority of their romance-reading material from a sales clerk named Dorothy Evans ('Dot'), an expert on romance fiction. Radway's study of this group of women took the form of group and individual interviews (with sixteen women), as well as a lengthy questionnaire distributed to forty-two women. Radway describes her sample as consisting for the most part of 'married, middle-class mothers,' and she notes that while 'not representative of all women who read romances, the group appears to be demographically similar to a sizable segment of that audience as it has been mapped by several very secretive publishing houses' (12). Much of the force of Radway's analysis comes from a variety of juxtapositions of differing notions of the 'ideal' – from the ideal reader as posited in much narrative analysis, to the 'ideal romance' as postulated by the Smithton women, to a feminist ideal which seems to characterize much of how Radway approaches the women's responses to romance fiction.

Radway echoes much feminist analysis of mass cultural forms when she argues that romance novels function as 'compensatory fiction,' that is, 'the act of reading them fulfills certain basic psychological needs for women that have been induced by the culture and its social struc-tures but that often remain unmet in day-to-day existence as the result of concomitant restrictions on female activity' (112–13). Like Vladimir Propp (1968) in his famous analysis of the Russian folktale, Radway notes that romance fiction is composed of certain unchanging elements – notably patriarchy, heterosexuality and male personality (143). But within those unchanging rules, romances offer the possibility of fantasizing solutions that are otherwise unavailable. Throughout *Reading the Romance*, the reading of romance fiction is portrayed as emblematic of the ambivalence which these particular women feel about themselves, not just in relationship to patriarchy, but in relationship to feminism as well. Indeed, the emphasis on female autonomy within a passionate relationship and the simultaneity of dependence and independence suggest that – to reiterate a phrase that appears frequently in Radway's analysis – romance readers want to have it both ways.

That Radway herself is ambivalent about how to read the results of her analysis is evident, especially in her conclusion. She says, 'the question of whether the activity of romance reading does, in reality, deflect such change [i.e. the restructuring of sexual relations] by successfully defusing or recontaining this protest must remain unanswered for the moment' (213). I find it curious that such a dualistic political framework should be erected in this book, but in some ways this either/or – the either/or, that is, of a conservative status quo versus radical change, of celebration versus critique – remains as a stubborn reminder that the theoretical problem raised by the apparatus (cinematic or otherwise) has not been wished away. For the very notion of a cinematic apparatus suggests a rigid distinction between what is contaminated by dominant ideology and what is not, suggests the possibility of knowing with certainty whether an activity is contestatory or conservative. What always seems to happen with such dualisms is the harden-ing of one abstraction or another – only a deconstruction of the apparatus is genuinely revo-lutionary! Readers and viewers are always active producers of meaning! – before it has been possible to consider in more depth the complexity of the issues at hand.

The major problem in Radway's analysis is that for all of the criticism offered of theoreti-cal modes which ignore real readers in favor of the critic's own projections, there is a fair share of projection and idealization going on here, as well. For the white, heterosexual, middle-class women that Radway discusses may well be complex agents who live the contradictions of middle-class patriarchal culture in equally complex ways, but they are also projections of American, middle-class, academic feminism. This is not meant in any way as a condemnation; far from it. But the desire to name 'real readers' is neither transparent nor innocent, for the women readers who appear in Radway's analysis are mediated by her questions, her analyses, and her narrative. It is inevitable that such projections exist in this kind of analysis, and unless those projections are analyzed, then we are left with an ideal reader who seems more real because she is quoted and referred to, but who is every bit as problematic as the ideal reader constructed by abstract theories of an apparatus positioning passive vessels.

It would, of course, be presumptuous of me to hypothesize what function the Smithton women have in Radway's imagination, but I can say what her analysis suggests quite strongly to me – a desire, on the part of feminists like myself, to see my mother and by extension members of my mother's generation as not so invested in patriarchy, as pre-feminist or proto-feminist, as a figure who nurtured feminism even while she argued otherwise, as someone who was really a feminist but didn't know it yet. Lest a particularly literal-minded soul wants to remind me that not all mothers of middle-class feminists fit this bill, I would say that this is precisely the point. For regardless of whether we are talking about literal mothers (as I am here), or mothers in the sense of a generation of women from whom the contemporary feminist movement developed and against whom it reacted, or a group of women who function as a horizon against which much feminist activity operates, we are talking about a construction. I doubt seriously, for instance, if the Smithton women would agree with the necessity of understanding the reading of romance fiction in the categorical terms of critique or celebration.

If analyses such as Radway's are to be based on taking other readers seriously then they must also mean taking ourselves seriously as readers – and by 'seriously' here, I mean putting our own constructions to the test. Tania Modleski has argued that with the turn to ethnography as a revitalized strategy for the analysis of mass culture, a curious assumption has been made that critics and researchers are not valid readers or viewers of mass culture, but rather detached observers (1989). I think Modleski is correct in assuming that the analysis of spectatorship is an analysis of one's *own* fascination and passion. Unless this acknowledged, then we are left with a series of fuzzily defined 'ideal readers' in whom it is difficult to know how much of their responses are displaced representations of the critic's own.

From another perspective, it could be argued that the 'ideal reader' has not been challenged so much as displaced from one realm, that of the textual properties of address, to another, that of the empirically observable woman. One of the most important strategies of Radway's analysis is, as I've indicated, the juxtaposition of the ideal reader assumed by the romance-fiction industry with women who *do* fit that profile, who are therefore the desired audience for romance novels, but who are also at the same time irreducible to structure, formula or cliché. Unfortunately, however, this challenge to the presumed homogeneity of the ideal reader does not go quite far enough. One of Radway's most important sources is Nancy Chodorow's *The Reproduction of Mothering*, a study of the asymmetrical gender patterns whereby men learn to be mothered and nurtured and women learn to provide mothering and nurturing (1978). Whereas Chodorow argues that women are socialized into mothering precisely through the (often unfulfilled) promise that the pre-oedipal patterns so central to their own development will be recreated, Radway argues that romance fiction provides precisely the kind of nurturance otherwise absent or largely missing from these women's lives.

In the appeal to Chodorow's analysis I sense most strongly the need to specify the particular nature of the needs being fulfilled. To what extent are we talking about white women whose lives are missing the kind of community network and patterns often characteristic of the lives of black women, for instance? What kind of 'middle-class' identity is at stake – the kind of precarious middle-class life characteristic of many white-collar workers? Or rather an economic identity defined largely by life style? Is the heterosexual identity of the women as stable as they, and Radway as well, seem to take great pains to stress? I am aware that these questions will strike some readers as the kind of checklist of accountability that characterizes some holier-than-thou political criticism. But my goal here is not some kind of standard of inclusivity. Rather, it is the notion of an 'ideal' reader – no matter who defines it as 'ideal' – that I think is severely limiting.

Radway's study remains the most influential example of an analysis that attempts to account, simultaneously, for the power of institutions (what she calls an 'institutional matrix') and the complex ways in which real women accomplish the 'construction of texts' (11–12). The positive critical reception that Radway's book has received suggests at the very least enormous dissatisfaction with just those limitations of exclusive textually based theories of readership. I am wary, however, of some of this positive critical reception, since I am not convinced that the notion of the 'ideal reader' has been problematized or undone so much as it has been displaced. What this suggests to me is the need to be careful of the appeals that are made in the name of empirical audiences or ethnography as the truth that will set us free from the overly abstract theorization of the past. I suspect that it may be impossible to do away entirely with the notion of an ideal reader, since we all live this culture's fictions and institutions and participate in them to some extent. I do not say this in order to imply cynically that no alternative positions of spectatorship are possible, but rather to suggest that one of the most persistent myths of spectatorship (and of theory) that has perturbed and in many ways hindered the analysis of spectatorship is the belief that it is not only possible, but necessary, to separate the truly radical spectator from the merely complicitous one. The recognition that we are all complicitous to some extent (and the 'some' is clearly what needs to be investigated) does not mean that alternative positions are impossible. Rather, that recognition would make it possible to speak of readership or spectatorship not as the knowledge the elite academic brings to the people, nor as a coded language that can only the deciphered by experts, but as a mode of encounter – between, say, Radway and the women whose responses she collected and studied.

Fantasy

While I share many of the criticisms of psychoanalytic theory that have been made in film studies in the past twenty years, the failure to take seriously psychoanalytic investigation can only lead to spectatorship studies that posit one limited definition of the subject in place of another. It is mistaken to assume, however, that all psychoanalytic film theorists subscribe to all aspects of apparatus theory, or that psychoanalytic investigations have remained unchanged in orientation since the early to mid-1970s. Indeed, one of the most significant rethinkings of psychoanalytic film theory has been in the area of fantasy, which Constance Penley specifically claims as an alternative to the 'bachelor machines' characteristic of Metz's and Baudry's approaches to the cinema. She writes:

> The formulation of fantasy, which provides a complex and exhaustive account of *the staging and imaging of the subject and its desire*, is a model that very closely approximates the primary aims of the apparatus theory: to describe not only the subject's desire for the film image and its reproduction, but also the structure of the fantasmatic relation to that image, including the subject's belief in its reality.
>
> (1985: 54)

Two essays in particular have been extremely influential in the development of a model of spectatorship which draws upon the psychoanalytic definition of fantasy. Freud's 'A Child Is Being Beaten' (1919) has been read as offering a theory of multiple masculine and feminine positions, thereby lending itself to a definition of spectatorship as oscillation rather than 'identification' in a univocal sense (Rodowick 1982, 1991; Doane 1984; Hansen 1986). The specific definition of fantasy upon which Penley draws is located in an extremely influential essay by Jean Laplanche and Jean-Bertrand Pontalis, 'Fantasy and the Origins of Sexuality' (1964/1986). Elaborating upon their claim that 'fantasy is the fundamental object of psychoanalysis' (1967/1973: 317), in this essay the authors explore a variety of components of fantasy which suggest, even more forcefully than the dream analogy so often claimed as the basis for psychoanalytic exploration of the cinema, a situation which is embodied in the cinema.

Laplanche and Pontalis distinguish three 'original' fantasies, original in the sense that they are bound up with the individual's history and origins: 'Like myths, they claim to provide a representation of, and a solution to, the major enigmas which confront the child. Whatever appears to the subject as something needing an explanation or theory, is dramatized as a moment of emergence, the beginning of a history.' Hence, Laplanche and Pontalis define three such fantasies of origins: 'the primal scene pictures the origin of the individual; fantasies of seduction, the origin and upsurge of sexuality; fantasies of castration, the origin of the difference between the sexes' (1964/1986: 19). These fantasies are 'original' not in the sense that they always 'produce' or 'cause' a given scenario, but that they form the structure of fantasy which is activated in a variety of ways.

Three characteristics of fantasy as read by Laplanche and Pontalis are particularly crucial for an understanding of the cinema as fantasy, and toward a revision of theories of the apparatus whereby the subject of the cinematic fantasy can only always be male. First, the distinction between what is conscious and what is unconscious is less important in fantasy than the distinction between those original fantasies described above, and secondary fantasies. Laplanche and Pontalis stress what they describe as the 'profound continuity between the various fantasy scenarios – the stage-setting of desire – ranging from the daydream to the fantasies recovered or reconstructed by the analytic investigation' (1964/1986: 28). As we have seen, one of the problems with much apparatus theory is a mechanistic notion of the unconscious, due largely to the fact that the desire for regression is always postulated as the repetition of the same oedipal scenario. The three original fantasies of which Laplanche and Pontalis speak are not so regimented. And given that fantasy occupies such a distinct place in psychoanalysis insofar as it extends across the boundaries of conscious and unconscious desires, then the analysis of the cinema as a form of fantasy does not require what almost inevitably amounts to a decoding approach, a rigid distinction between manifest and latent content. The area of fantasy is one where the notion of homology operates quite differently than is the case with the cinematic apparatus, since here the homology is between different types of fantasy, of which cinematic spectatorship is one example (21). Put another way, fantasy is more useful for its implications than for its possible status as equivalent to or anticipatory of the cinema.

Second, it is the very nature of fantasy to exist for the subject across many possible positions. Noting that '"A father seduces a daughter"' is the skeletal version of the seduction fantasy, Laplanche and Pontalis describe this function as follows: 'The indication here of the primary process is not the absence of organization, as is sometimes suggested, but the peculiar character of the structure, in that it is a scenario with multiple entries, in which nothing shows whether the subject will be immediately located as *daughter*; it can as well be fixed as *father*, or even in the term *seduces*' (22–3). Despite the claims to anti-essentialism of many apparatus theorists, there is a consistent tendency to conflate literal gender and address; to assume, that is, that if the film addresses its subject as male, then it is the male viewer who is thus addressed. The reading of cinematic fantasy allows no such reduction. Indeed, the notion of fantasy gives psychoanalytic grounding not only to the possibility, but to the inevitability and necessity, of the cinema as a form of fantasy wherein the boundaries of biolog-ical sex or cultural gender, as well as sexual preference, are not fixed.

Finally, emphasis is placed throughout Laplanche and Pontalis's discussion on fantasy as the *staging* of desire, fantasy as a form of *mise-en-scène*. 'Fantasy . . . is not the object of desire, but its setting. In fantasy the subject does not pursue the object or its sign: he appears caught up himself in the sequence of images' (26). Elizabeth Cowie has noted that the importance of the emphasis on fantasy as a scene 'cannot be overestimated, for it enables the considera-tion of film as fantasy in the most fundamental sense of this term in psychoanalysis' (1984: 77). While I am somewhat suspicious of any mimetic analogy, the understanding of film as fantasy does open the door to some questions and issues about spectatorship which apparatus theory tended to shut out. In any case, I think the value of fantasy for psychoanalytic read-ings of the cinema needs to be seen less in terms of a 'better' analogy than dreams, the mirror stage, or the imaginary, and more in terms of the series of questions it can engender.

In Cowie's reading of fantasy in film which relies extensively on the Laplanche and Pontalis essay, two such questions are raised: 'if fantasy is the *mise-en-scène* of desire, whose desire is figured in the film who is the subject for an of the scenario? No longer just, if ever, the so-called 'author'. But how does the spectator come into place as desiring subject of the film? Second, what is the relation of the contingent, everyday material drawn from real life, i.e. from the *social*, to the primal or original fantasies?' (1984: 87). Cowie notes how, in *Now, Voyager*, there is an oedipal fantasy, 'but where the subject positions are not fixed or completed, Charlotte is both mother and daughter, Mrs Vale and Tina.' In partial response to her first question, then, Cowie says that it is not enough to define the fantasy as Charlotte Vale's; rather, it must be defined as the spectator's:

> This is not Charlotte's fantasy, but the 'film's' fantasy. It is an effect of its narra-tion (of its *énonciation*). If we identify simply with Charlotte's desires, that series of social and erotic successes, then the final object, the child Tina, will be unsat-isfactory. But if our identification is with the playing out of a desiring, in relation to the opposition (phallic) mother/child, the ending is very much more satisfying, I would suggest. A series of 'day-dream' fantasies enfold an Oedipal, original fantasy. The subject of this fantasy is then the spectator; inasmuch as we have been captured by the film's narration, its *énonciation*, we are the only place in which all the terms of the fantasy come to rest.
>
> (1984: 91)

Cowie's response to her second question – concerning the relationship between the psychic and the social which the analysis of fantasy can comprehend – focuses on the illicit desires which the subject's pleasure in the fantasy fulfills. In *Now, Voyager*, this concerns the evacua-tion of the father; in another film discussed by Cowie, *The Reckless Moment*, what she describes as an 'unstoppable sliding of positions' results in pairings and oppositions whereby a set of equivalences is set up, and an inference is made 'which is an attack on the family as impris-oning' (1984: 101). These claims are reminiscent of the kinds of implications in 'reading against the grain' arguments about the classical cinema – i.e. that what appears to be a smooth ideological surface is marred, rather, by rebellion, critique, or even implicit rejection of those norms. What the reading of fantasy brings to such claims, however, is the insistence that investment and pleasure in film watching involve a range of subject positions. Apparatus theory tends to pose a spectator so aligned with one subject position that anything departing from that position would have to seem radical or contestatory by definition. The exploration of the classical cinema in terms of fantasy enlarges considerably what possibilities are contained within the fantasy structures engaged by film viewing, and in so doing inflects differently the notion of a 'reading against the grain.' For from the vantage point of fantasy, the distinction between 'with' and 'against' the grain of the film becomes somewhat moot.

Constance Penley assesses the importance of Cowie's approach to fantasy in terms of its assumption that positions of sexual identification are not fixed: 'Cowie's model of identification involves a continual construction of looks, ceaselessly varied through the organization of the narrative and the work of narration. The value of such a model is that it leaves open the question of the production of sexual difference in the film rather than assuming in advance the sexuality of the character or the spectator' (1988: 11). However, while it may be a matter of indifference in psychoanalytic terms whether the spectator encouraged or enabled to adopt a variety of positions is male or female, it is a matter of crucial importance within the context of spectatorship, to the extent that spectatorship involves a spectator who always brings with her or him a history, and whose experience of spectatorship is determined in part by the ways in which spectatorship is defined outside of the movie theater.

Cowie emphasizes that whatever shifting of positions occurs in the fantasies of the cinema, they 'do so always in terms of sexual difference' (1984: 102). It is one thing to assume 'sexual difference' to refer to the way in which any definition of 'femininity' is inevitably bound to accompanying definitions of 'masculinity,' and another thing to assume that the only possible relationship between the two is in some version of heterosexuality. Put another way, the insistence upon sexual difference has had a curious history in film studies, by collapsing the shifting terms of masculinity and femininity into a heterosexual master code. Interestingly, the model of fantasy elaborated by Laplanche and Pontalis has the potential to challenge film theory's own compulsory heterosexuality. In a study of Sheila McLaughlin's film *She Must Be Seeing Things*, for instance, Teresa de Lauretis argues that the film articulates a *lesbian* version of the primal scene, where the positions of onlooker and participant are occupied by women (1989).

Barbara Creed has observed that despite the fact that the castration scenario is but one of three originary fantasies in Laplanche and Pontalis's account, it has been the near-exclusive focus of 1970s film theory (1990: 135). Creed suggests that perhaps 'the fantasy of castration *marks* all three primal fantasies to some degree' (135). The same could be said of any of the three fantasies. What might rather be the case is that the classical Hollywood cinema is made to the measure of the fantasy of sexual difference, which is of course what 1970s film theory claimed. It is unclear, in other words, just how much of a critical advantage the fantasy model offers, if it emerges as just another way of affirming the primacy of one particular configuration of desire. Alternatively, it could be argued that this is precisely where fantasy offers an understanding of the tension between the demands for regulation and homogeneity, on the one hand, and the mobility of spectatorial investment, on the other. The positions offered the spectator may be multiple, but the multiplicity finds its most cohesive articulation in the fantasy of sexual difference.

Jacqueline Rose has made a more pointed observation about the current interest in fantasy, particularly insofar as it functions as a 'saving device' against the 'depressing implications' of the psychoanalytic position that the classical cinema offers the female spectator only an impossible relation to its fictions (1990: 275).

> Unconscious fantasy can . . . be read in terms of a multiplicity of available positions for women (and men), but the way these positions work against and defensively exclude each other gets lost. . . . [W]hile we undoubtedly need to recognize the instability of unconscious fantasy and the range of identifications

offered by any one spectator of film, this can easily lead to an idealization of psychic processes and cinema at one and the same time (something for everyone both in the unconscious and on the screen).

(275)

Rose's warning echoes an earlier debate in film studies concerning the monolithic quality of film narrative, with psychoanalysis functioning as a nagging reminder that the 'resistance' of the unconscious cannot in any easy or simple way be equated with 'resistance' understood in political terms.

Fantasy does offer the possibility of engaging different desires, contradictory effect and multiple stagings. A certain version of the scenario of sexual difference emerges again and again in film theory as obsessive structure and point of return, and it is not always clear when the obsession and return are an effect of the cinema or of the theorist. In any case, it appears as though the homogeneous effects of the cinematic apparatus are understood in limited terms in the fantasy model – limited to the extent that they have only one point of reference, a notion of sexual difference which assumes the kind of essentialist quality otherwise so disavowed by psychoanalytic critics. I have no intention of reviving the political fantasy of 'integrating' Marxism and/or feminism and/or psychoanalysis; rather, it is psychoanalysis on its own terms that requires investigation, not 'rescue' by some other discourse. For it is questionable whether fantasy can engage with the complex effects of spectatorship without some understanding of how its own categories – of sexual difference, the couple, and desire – are themselves historically determined and culturally variable.

Negotiation

To put this problem a bit differently, as well as to make the transition to the next tension I want to address, the institutional models of spectatorship have been read as so rigid that there has been a real temptation to see any response that differs slightly from what is assumed to be the norm or the ideal as necessarily radical and contestatory. Such claims to alternatives require that the theory of the institution that gave rise to it be challenged simultaneously. What remains nonetheless peculiar about many theories of the cinematic institution is that they give particular and sometimes exclusive signifying possibilities to the individual film. That is to say, the individual film is taken to be a well-functioning instance of the larger effects of the cinematic institution. When other practices are taken into account, like advertising or consumer tie-ins, they are assumed to create a narrative flow every bit as seamless as that of the classical scenario itself.

Once the cinematic institution is defined and analyzed as consisting of a number of different forms of address, however, it should be possible to unpack and question the excessive monolithic quality of the apparatus. But as I suggest above, I think it is crucial to resist the temptation to see difference or multiplicity as liberatory or contestatory qualities in themselves. This attention to difference (and simultaneous inquiry into the difference that difference makes) can be understood in a variety of ways, both in terms of a single film within which a variety of not necessarily harmonious discourses collide, and in terms of the various components that define film-going in a cultural and psychic sense.

One of the key terms that has emerged in this context is *negotiation*. In an influential essay associated with cultural studies, Stuart Hall's 'Encoding/Decoding,' three decoding strategies – that is, practices of reading and making sense of cultural texts – are proposed. The dominant reading is one fully of a piece with the ideology of the text, while the negotiated reading is more ambivalent; that is, the ideological stance of a product is adjusted to specific social conditions of the viewers. The oppositional reading is, then, one totally opposed to the ideology in question (Hall 1980c).

As influential as this model has been, particularly in the foregrounding of reception contexts, it raises some problems of its own, particularly insofar as the 'dominant' and 'oppositional' readings are concerned. What is the relationship between activity and passivity in the reader/viewer, whether the reading is dominant or oppositional? If a reader/viewer occupies an oppositional stance, how does this square with the process of interpellation necessary for any response to a text? Dominant and oppositional readings may be more usefully understood, perhaps, as horizons of possibility, as tendencies rather than actual practices of reading. However, in order to foreground the activity of reading, viewing, and consuming mass culture, what Hall's model leaves relatively intact is the notion of a text's dominant ideology. This is peculiar insofar as the activity/passivity of the apparatus model appears to be reversed in favor of an active reader/viewer and a relatively stable, if not completely passive, text.

It may well be more useful to designate all readings as negotiated ones, to the extent that it is highly unlikely that one will find any 'pure' instances of dominant or oppositional readings. In other words, a purely dominant reading would presume no active intervention at all on the part of the decoder, while a purely oppositional reading would assume no identification at all with the structures of interpellation of the text. In that case, some notion of textual determination must still be necessary in order for the negotiation model to be useful.

I stress this because there is a tendency to assume that because the model of negotiation posits both the activity of the reader/viewer and the heterogeneity of the different elements of social formations, it conceives of a variety of readings, and that very heterogeneity, that very activity, is then taken to be indicative of a resistance to dominant ideology. Since I do not think that individual texts can be any more easily categorized as purely 'dominant' than spectators or readers can, I find it difficult to be quite so enthused about different or unauthorized readings as necessarily contestatory. As I suggested earlier in this chapter, one of the problems in spectatorship studies is the desire to categorize texts *and* readings/responses as either conservative or radical, as celebratory of the dominant order or critical of it. This duality forecloses the far more difficult task of questioning what is served by the continued insistence upon this either/or, and more radically, of examining what it is in conceptions of spectators' responses and film texts that produces this ambiguity in the first place.

One of the severe limitations of much apparatus theory is the assumption that certain textual strategies will necessarily produce desired reassignments of dominant subject/object relationships and subject positions. A textual strategy does not *necessarily* produce anything. But if, consequently, there is no such thing as an inherently radical technique, then there is no such thing either as an inherently conservative one. While I think most contemporary film scholars would agree with the former – would agree, that is, that this particular aspect of 1970s film theory is in need of severe revision – I am not sure that the latter will meet with such agreement, since the notion of a dominant narrative structure still appears with great regularity.

I am alluding to two extreme positions which can be sketched as follows. For many textual theorists of the 1970s, Raymond Bellour and the editors of *Camera Obscura* in particular, the value of textual analysis was to demonstrate that classical narrative produces a variety of ruptures, deviations, and crises only to recuperate them in the name of a hierarchical closure or resolution. From this point of view, any validation of those ruptures is at best naive voluntarism and at worst a refusal to acknowledge what one does not want to know –

that the cinematic apparatus works with great efficiency to channel all desire into male, oedipal desire. The apparatus works; closure and resolution are achieved. Inspired in many cases by the work of Hall and cultural studies, others, like John Fiske (1987), insist upon the social formations of audiences as the only ultimately determining factors. Both positions ascribe an unqualified power to the text, on the one hand, and social defined readers/viewers on the other. The problem in each case is that the activity of making meaning is assumed to reside in one single source – either the cinematic apparatus, or the socially contextualized viewer. To be sure, variations are allowed in either case, but they are never significant enough to challenge the basic determinism of the model in question.

While there are advantages to both of these positions, I do not want to suggest that one can take what is most appealing about two different sets of assumptions and put them together in a happy integration. Unfortunately, while the notion of negotiation is potentially quite useful, it can inspire precisely a kind of Pollyanna dialectics – the institution remains monolithic, but never *so* monolithic that readers cannot be actively oppositional. Now I do think that spectatorship studies are most useful when 'local,' that is, when examined – as I suggest in the critique of Radway's book – insofar as they problematize the ideal reader or viewer. But there still needs to be some recognition of the theoretical questions at stake. There is no necessary discontinuity between theory and local analysis. Indeed, theory becomes much more challenging when contradiction and tension, for instance, exist not as textual abstractions but as complex entities which do not always lend themselves easily to one reading or another. Film theory of the 1970s erred in attempting to account for a cinematic subject in categories that are absolute. (Even when labelled 'Western,' this usually amounts to the same thing – e.g. some will confess that they speak only of the 'Western' [white, male, etc.] subject and then proceed as if 'Western' and 'universal' were still fully commensurate terms.) But surely the conclusion is not that all theorizing is doomed to such levels of abstraction.

One particularly influential invocation of negotiation is instructive in this context, since it sets out the issues that the concept is meant to address. Indeed, in Angela McRobbie's essay 'Dance and Social Fantasy,' a study of how teenage girls respond to dance and how those responses read in relationship to the films *Flashdance* and *Fame*, negotiation seems to describe not only the teenage girls but McRobbie herself as a researcher (1984). Noting that the significance of extra-textual codes and knowledge in the reception of mass culture leads to the necessity for the researcher to 'limit strictly the range of his or her analysis,' McRobbie continues:

> It also means working with a consciously loose rather than tight relation in mind, one where an inter-discursive notion of meaning structures and textual experience leads to a different working practice or methodology. Instead of seeking direct causal links or chains, the emphasis is placed on establishing loose sets of relations, capillary actions and movement, spilling out among and between different fields: work and leisure, fact and fiction, fantasy and reality, individual and social experience.

(142)

Several negotiations form the core of McRobbie's analysis, not least of which is the juxtaposition of the responses of teenage girls to dancing as both a social and an individual activity, and the textual forms that seem to encourage such fantasies in two dance films, *Flashdance* and *Fame*. Within the two films, there are several processes of negotiation at work. In *Flashdance*, McRobbie notes that while the dance scenes are very much directed at that ubiquitous entity, the male spectator within the film, other narrative elements of the film are drawn so clearly from the woman's film that it is impossible to say with certainty that the address of the film is directed toward the woman defined unambiguously as the object of the male gaze (138). The process of negotiation here concerns, then, two different genres – the musical and the woman's film – the conventions of which may rub against each other rather than function compatibly. McRobbie also notes that in both films, there is a sometimes peculiar juxtaposition of old and new elements; the films 'place together images and moments of overwhelming conformity with those which seem to indicate a break with Hollywood's usual treatment of women' (150). In other words, the classical formulae of both films could be said to acknowledge and retreat from their own limitations insofar as representations of women are concerned.

McRobbie also insists upon the importance of understanding films like these in an intertextual network, and in the case of these two films, the expectations of dance culture can inflect the readings of the films, and vice versa. Thus the process of 'negotiation' refers to how the films are structured as cinematic texts, as well as to how the meanings of these films are 'negotiated' in relationship to one's knowledge of the dance scene outside of the movie theater. Noting that the dancehall or disco shares some similarities with the movie theater (a 'darkened space' where the spectator/dancer 'can retain some degree of anonymity or absorption'), McRobbie notes as well a significant difference: 'Where the cinema offers a one-way fantasy which is directed solely through the gaze of the spectator toward the screen, the fantasy of dancing is more social, more reciprocated' (144). Such a mapping of one context onto the other may account for a reception of these films that departs sharply from the pronouncements of film theory about the inevitability of the colonization of the female body.

Two particular points of reference recur in McRobbie's essay, and they echo some of the questions I raised in relation to Radway's *Reading the Romance*. Richard Dyer has suggested that one of the basic appeals of the movie musical is the utopian dimension, a way of providing pleasures and satisfactions that are otherwise unavailable in the culture at hand, and yet which are defined in such a way as to suggest that they can only be satisfied within capitalism (1977). Radway suggests that this utopianism – defined within the context of Nancy Chodorow's reading of women's desires for re-creation of their pre-oedipal bond – is a function of the reading of romance novels, and McRobbie's reading of dance and dance films is equally suggestive of a utopian impulse.

I do not wish to evoke a traditional and moralistic Marxism, whereby art provides us with a glimpse of the truly integrated human beings we will all become in the communist future. But I find that sometimes the utopian dimension becomes clouded by the understanding of desire as always in conflict with the dominant culture. McRobbie notes, for instance, that *Fame* presents a desire for community and family as necessarily intertwined (158), and certainly an interesting area of research is the way in which films articulate definitions which both reflect dominant ideology (the family is the basis for all community) and challenge them (communities provide what families do not, or cannot, in our culture). What makes me somewhat suspicious is the way that the discussion of utopianism seems to fall into exactly the kind of large abstractions – having to do with the 'human subject under capitalism and/or patriarchy' – that McRobbie sets out (specifically in the passage cited earlier) to challenge. In case I sound as if I am contradicting myself as far as the necessity of combining 'local' analyses with theoretical reflection is concerned, let me say that I do not think that theory means falling back into large clichés about the human subject – or the female subject.

The second recurring point of reference in McRobbie's essay is an illustration of the first. Noting that dance 'carries a range of often contradictory strands within it,' she affirms the conformity of dance with conventional definitions of femininity, but says that at the same time the pleasures of dance 'seem to suggest a displaced, shared and nebulous eroticism rather than a straightforwardly romantic, heavily heterosexual "goal-oriented" drive' (134). In another context, McRobbie describes the dance scene and suggests that as it offers a 'suspension of categories, there is not such a rigid demarcation along age, class, ethnic terms. Gender is blurred and sexual preference less homogenously heterosexual' (146). Curiously, this 'suspension of categories' is itself suspended when McRobbie reports that her sources on the pleasures of dance are 'predominantly heterosexual;' hence 'these fantasy scenarios make no claim to represent gay or lesbian experience' (145). While gay and lesbian experiences of dance may well be different, this disclaimer erects the categories of sexual preference just when the analysis of dance seems to put them into question.

I suspect that since the question of sexual preference is far more controversial than, say, the desire for a community (whether based on the family or not), and is perhaps threatening to those very viewers/participants whose desires one is attempting to take seriously, then the temptation is to shelve a consideration of it for some future analysis, or to open the question about the permeability of sexual boundaries without really pursuing it in any depth. But the deployment of gay and lesbian identities in popular culture, and the complicated responses the viewers bring to homosexuality as a moral, sexual and political issue, seem to me just the kind of *specific* area of inquiry for investigation into the utopian impulse that desires for community avoid.

Film theory has been so bound by the heterosexual symmetry that supposedly governs Hollywood cinema that it has ignored the possibility, for instance, that one of the distinct pleasures of the cinema may well be a 'safe zone' in which homosexual as well as heterosexual desires can be fantasized and acted out. I am not speaking here of an innate capacity to 'read against the grain,' but rather of the way in which desire and pleasure in the cinema may well function to problematize the categories of heterosexual versus homosexual. To be sure, this 'safety zone' can also be read as a displacement, insurance that the happy ending is a distinctly heterosexual one. But as has been noted many times, the buddy film, if it affirms any kind of sexual identity aside from a narcissistic one, is as drawn to a homosexual connection as it is repelled by it.

Taking into account the complexity of the range of responses to the stability of sexual identities and sexual categories would require an approach to negotiation that specifies the psychic stakes in such a process, rather than just stating that the psychic remains significant or important. I am not referring here to the kind of psychoanalytic theorizing typical of much 1970s film theory, where the 'unconscious' usually meant a master plot repeated again and again, an inevitable source of meaning and comprehensibility. What has been surprisingly absent from much psychoanalytic film theory is an investigation of the ways in which the unconscious refuses the stability of any categorization. The example of heterosexuality and its various 'others' seems to me a particularly crucial one to take into account, since so much of the ideology of the cinematic institution is built simultaneously on the heterosexual couple as the common denominator, on the promise of romantic fulfillment, at the same time that that couple seems constantly in crisis, constantly in need of reassurance. One would have thought this an area where the concept of negotiation would provide a useful corrective.

To take this in a somewhat different direction: The notion of negotiation is only useful if one is attentive to the problematic as well as 'utopian' uses to which negotiation can be put by both the subjects one is investigating and the researchers themselves. While I have not seen this spelled out in any detail, negotiation seems to be a variation of the Marxist notion of mediation – the notion, that is, of a variety of instances that complicate or 'mediate' in various ways the relationship between individuals and the economic structure of capitalism. Raymond Williams has noted that while the concept of mediation has the advantage of complicating significantly the cause-and-effect notion of 'reflection' so typical of a traditional Marxism, and of indicating an active process, it remains limited in its own way. Williams notes that 'it is virtually impossible to sustain the metaphor of 'mediation' . . . without some sense of separate and pre-existent areas or orders of reality. . . . Within the inheritance of idealist philosophy the process is usually, in practice, seen as a mediation between categories, which have been assumed to be distinct' (1977: 99).

Negotiation can replicate the problems that inhere in the notion of mediation by replacing the language of 'subjection' and 'imposition' with that of 'agency' and 'contradiction' but without significantly exploring how the notion of an active subject can be just as open to projections and subjections as a passive subject can. While the field of cultural studies, with its emphasis on 'negotiation' as the way readers/viewers shape mass culture to their own needs, has had an enormous impact on film studies, another direction in literary studies also makes persistent use of 'negotiation' in a rather different way. The so-called 'new historicism' has had only a limited relationship with film studies, yet some of the ways in which the concept of negotiation has emerged in new historicist studies offer a useful counterpoint to the inflection offered by cultural studies.

New historicism is most immediately associated with English Renaissance studies. But the problems new-historicist work addresses are not so different than those central to film studies, particularly insofar as a reckoning with both the advances and the limitations of 1970s film theory are concerned. Louis A. Montrose, for instance, has said that 'the terms in which the problem of ideology has been posed and is now circulating in Renaissance literacy studies – namely as an opposition between 'containment' and 'subversion' – are so reductive, polarized, and undynamic as to be of little or no conceptual value' (1989: 22). That this assessment 'applies' to film studies, particularly in relation to spectatorship, may have less to do with a striking coincidence between film studies and the new historicism, and more to do with questions central to virtually all forms of cultural analysis in the 1980s and 1990s which attempt to develop new forms of criticism and theory at the same time that they engage with their own historical legacies, particularly insofar as the 1960s and 1970s are concerned in their status as simultaneous political turning points and mythological burden.

While it is not my purpose either to align myself with a new-historicist project or to provide an extended introduction to this field, it is noteworthy that the term *negotiation* in its new historicist usage tends more toward questioning those very possibilities of radical agency that the cultural-studies approach finds in its negotiations. Stephen Greenblatt notes that capitalism 'has characteristically generated neither regimes in which all discourses seem coordinated, nor regimes in which the drive toward differentiation and the drive toward monological organization operate simultaneously, or at least oscillate so rapidly as to create the impression of simultaneity' (1989: 6). From the vantage point of this simultaneity, then, the immediate assumption that all unauthorized uses of films, and therefore spectatorial positions that depart from the presumed ideal of capitalist ideology, are virtually or potentially radical is a reading of the nature of discourse and power in our culture as more dualistic than it is.

A large part of the problem here is that the analysis of spectatorship in film studies has as a significant part of its legacy a commitment to the creation of alternative cultures and political identities which refuse to comply with dominant ideology. Phrases like 'alternative cultures' and 'refusal to comply' can of course mean a variety of things, including contradictory things. The reactions of black male spectators to the filmed popularization of Alice Walker's novel *The Color Purple* cannot be squared in any easy or even complex way with the feminist critique of the 'women as object of the male look,' yet both constitute claims to validation by marginalized groups (see Bobo 1988b). Part of the 1960s/1970s legacy of film studies is a romanticized vision of the politicized past, based on the assumption (erroneous and inaccurate) that the common denominator 'socialist' could account for any and all kind of radical and progressive social change – a utopian definition of socialism which was quickly enough put to rest by feminism and gay and lesbian liberation movements. Curiously, what seems to have persisted is a vague discourse of 'subversion' and 'alternative scenarios,' amidst conceptual confusion about just what is being subverted and for what.

Catherine Gallagher says – in what could easily function as a critique of the tendencies present in much writing about spectatorship – that new historicists have attempted to show 'that under certain historical circumstances, the display of ideological contradictions is completely consonant with the maintenance of oppressive social relations' (1989: 44). It has been crucial to spectatorship studies to understand that visions of the cinema as the inflexible apparatus of the ideological subject are as much projections of theorists' own desires as they are hypothetically interesting and useful and also historically conditioned postulates about going to the cinema. But it is equally important for such an inquiry to take place in what amounts to a new 'stage' of spectatorship studies, where the model is no longer the passive, manipulated (and inevitably white and heterosexual) spectator, but rather the contradictory, divided and fragmented subject.

The new-historicist reminder that 'negotiation' is a marketplace term tempers too quick an enthusiasm about what may ultimately be strategies of consumerism. But it is too easy to assume the cynical route (which is, after all, only the reserve of romanticism), that is, to assume in a kind of more-Foucauldian-than-thou posture that there are no alternative positions, only fictions of them. What remains vital, in the critical examination of spectatorship, is the recognition that no 'negotiation' is inherently or purely oppositional, but that the desire for anything 'inherent' or 'pure' is itself a fiction that must be contested.

What I am suggesting, in this extremely schematic encounter between new historicism and cultural studies, is that a desire for unproblematized agency – whether that of the critic or of the imaginary or real spectator(s) under investigation – persists. Even though McRobbie does question the notion of the 'ideal viewer' which, as I suggest above, is one of the limitations of Radway's analysis, there remain some echoes of an idealized female subject in her account. In an extremely provocative essay on the status of negotiation as a critical concept in studies on female spectatorship, Christine Gledhill sees negotiation as providing a possible way out of the limitations of the implications of feminist/psychoanalytic film theory and the attendant split between text and reception, particularly insofar as texts were seen as capable of situating alternative subjective positions. 'The value of "negotiations" . . . as an analytical concept is that it allows space to the subjectivities, identities and pleasures of audiences,' writes Gledhill (1988: 72). But 'subjectivity,' 'identity' and 'pleasure' are here defined in a way that acknowledges the critique of the fictions of bourgeois identity that has been central to Lacanian-inspired film theory. At the same time, those critiques are fictions, too, in supposing that any notion of identity may supposedly be 'done away with.'

In a move somewhat reminiscent of Jane Gallop's claim that 'identity must be continually assumed and immediately put into question' (1982: xii), Gledhill says that

> the concept of negotiation stops short at the dissolution of identity suggested by avant-garde aesthetics. For if arguments about the non-identity of self and language, words and meaning, desire and its objects challenge bourgeois notions of the centrality and stability of the ego and the transparency of language, the political consequence is not to abandon the search for identity. . . . The object of attack should not be identity as such but its dominant construction as total, non-contradictory and unchanging.
>
> (72)

I am suggesting, as is perhaps obvious by now, that this 'dominant construction' enters into the ways in which researchers themselves construct their audiences. This should not, of course, come as startling news to anyone familiar with the dynamics of transference and counter-transference. But in order for studies of spectatorship to engage fully with the complex dynamics that define the process of negotiation, such constructions need to be accounted for.

As Gledhill's comments suggest, one of the key issues at stake here is the competing claims of 'identity,' which have been associated with some of the most fervent debates in film studies and related fields in the past two decades. Studies of reception and negotiation are often meant to challenge the ways in which post-structuralist theorists are seen to critique any notion of the self as an agent as an inevitable fiction of bourgeois/patriarchal/idealist culture. What becomes quite difficult in that process of challenge is acknowledging the necessity of the critique of the fictions of the self without resurrecting them yourself. Somewhat curiously, the challenges to apparatus theory described in this chapter return to the problem of identification, as if to suggest that however mobile and multiple subject positions may be, spectatorship still engages some notion of identity. But then theorists of the cinematic apparatus never banished identification from film theory, but rather redefined its terms beyond those of character or a one-to-one correspondence between viewer and screen. In any case, the current visibility of identity as a problem in film studies – whether as spectre, curse, or positive value – speaks to the continued friction between subjects and viewers.

A colleague of mine once commented that much of what passes for film theory is a finger-wagging list of everything that is 'wrong' with a given position or argument. I recognize that I have indulged in some of that syndrome in this chapter, since I have focused critically on address/reception, fantasy and negotiation as important concepts for spectatorship studies; that is, I have attempted to examine the concepts closely, in a symptomatic way, without simply assigning them positive or negative marks. Two criticisms have consistently emerged in my discussion of these concepts. First, I have suggested that there is a considerable reluctance on the part of theorists to acknowledge their own investment in the process of spectatorship analysis. I do not mean by this that all critics should write in a confessional mode, or impose a first-person account in every discussion of spectatorship. I see theoretical self-consciousness, rather, as an attention to how and why certain modes of theoretical discourse, certain tropes, certain preoccupations, are foregrounded in specific critical and cultural contexts.

Second, I return frequently in this chapter to the need for more specific, local studies, where the focus would be less on large theories that can account for everything, and more on the play and variation that exist at particular junctures between the competing claims of film spectatorship – as the function of an apparatus, as a means of ideological control, on the one hand, and as a series of discontinuous, heterogeneous, and sometimes empowering responses, on the other. In the remaining chapters of the book, I turn to four such specific instances, each of which focuses on particular areas of spectatorship inquiry that have been important in film studies – textual analysis, stars, reception and 'subcultural' audiences. My aim is to approach these topics with the same attention to the tension between homogeneity and heterogeneity, between domination and resistance, that has structured this chapter, but to do so in a way more attentive to the stakes of specific, local studies. The point is not to construct yet another theory or concept of 'the' cinematic spectator, but to suggest areas of inquiry which reveal both the importance of conceptualizing spectators, and some directions these conceptualizations can now take.

Chapter 4

JANET STAIGER

RECEPTION STUDIES IN FILM AND TELEVISION

GIVEN THAT CINEMA STUDIES IN THE US has had strong ties to lit-erary traditions, it could be anticipated that reception theories in film and television[1] would tend toward the text-activated approach described in Chapter 2. This predilection has not gone unobserved, although two areas of research – feminism and recent television stud-ies – may have stimulated a recognition of the bias. For example, in 'Women's Genres,' Annette Kuhn describes the difference between thinking about a film spectator and thinking about a cinematic social audience when trying to understand gendered forms of address.[2] For the former, film studies has recently tended to consider the individual as constituted by psychic relations; in the latter case, the expectations of pleasure transform individuals into audiences in which social subjects choose whether to enter into the position offered by that experience. As Kuhn points out, the notion of the context – psychological versus social – changes the event into two different situations. 'Spectators' and 'social audiences' have dif-ferent theoretical and actual circumstances and, thus, varied relations to textual representa-tions. When the idea of what is the context changes, so do the salient determinants of the individual-as-a-subject. Consequently, also altered are what count as data to study and per-tinent methods for handling those data. For the spectator, research has focused on hypoth-esizing from textual characteristics; for the social audience, evidence is gathered and organized around predetermined categories such as sex, age, education, class and race.

In her essay, Kuhn introduces as well the historical anomaly of film scholars' focusing on spectators while early television research emphasized social audience studies. Thus, when film scholars took up television studies, one initial activity was to treat apparent formal charac-teristics of broadcast TV as determining the subject. Patrice Petro believes that certain of these textual features have been described in opposition to fictional narrative ('realist') film.[3] Television is characterized as discontinuous, direct address, self-conscious and parodic – thus, 'modernist.' Petro cautions against such a simple dichotomy. She also rejects the assumption that formal characteristics are determining for the spectator (and the social audience).

Both Kuhn and Petro include calls for research that I would consider to be reception studies. The current observation of a use-value for this type of work, however, might lead to the erroneous assumption that reception theory has only recently arrived in film studies. As I noted about the history of literary theory, questions of reader response have informed film philosophies from the inception of the medium. It seems important to me that genealogies of discourses about film and television viewers be undertaken. I will not attempt that here, but I do want to open up such a project with several thoughts about pre-1960s philosophies and current film and television research, because surprising continuities exist between them. I will then consider three dominant contemporary paradigms for studying spectators, relating them to both the considerations raised in Chapter 2 and the history of film philosophy.

Classical film philosophy and the film spectator

The neglect of the spectator in film philosophies prior to the 1960s is only apparent. It is a matter, I believe, of how classical film philosophy is ordered. This is the point that André Bazin proposed in connection to the coming of mechanically synchronized sound. Bazin argued that film history should not be split between the pre- and post-synchronized sound eras but rather between films having and not having 'faith in the image.' Bazin is suggesting that how a field of discourses is split can affect what is foregrounded to perception. Thus, perhaps the habits of our interpretive community's view that the spectator has been neglected in early film philosophy derive from classical expositions of the field, rather than from the philosophies themselves.

One of the standard expositions is Dudley Andrew's *The Major Film Theories*.[4] This book functions as a significant supplementary reading for many of the undergraduate and graduate courses in the US and is a synopsis and representation of what is regarded as a central opposition within classical film theory: formalist versus realist philosophies of cinema. Of interest is how Andrew organizes this split. He writes that formalist film philosophies arose first because of their historical situation. Cinema was not yet considered an art, so the problem was to define cinema aesthetically and thus as distinct from reality. This act followed nineteenth-century aesthetics, which also sought to make such distinctions. Thus, philosophical discourses written by Münsterberg, Arnheim, Eisenstein, Lindsay, Canudo, Delluc, Kuleshov, Pudovkin and others emphasized how cinema as an art form changed the world from chaos and meaninglessness into a self-sustaining structure and rhythm. Cinema as art was a process of transformation. Turning to the realist philosophies, which appeared later, Andrew notes that these considered how people could be brought into harmony with nature via the cinema through a reinsured perception, also the product of cinema's specificity. Kracauer, Bazin, British documentarists and Vertov provide Andrew with realist philosophies.

What is important to me in this split is that, as presented by Andrew, the same presumption regarding the spectator's relation to the object is implicit in both formalist and realist tenets. For each, the spectator is relatively passive while cinema does something. For formalist theory, cinema organizes the world; for the realist, it brings the spectator back into touch with physical reality. Both types of theoretical discourse produce text-activated approaches to the film-spectator relation.

What I would also stress here is that the question asked of the film philosophies determines the discursive field's organization. In Andrew's case, the primary question for his overall split is, what is cinema's function? It may seem trite in this day of metatheory to point out that the question the researcher elects to ask will dramatically affect the answer, but I think it does not hurt to be reminded occasionally of such truisms. Raising originating questions to consciousness helps make some assumptions explicit rather than natural. I point out the artificiality of this structure for classical film philosophy because other questions can be the originating query.[5]

Let me propose, then, that another initial question of film theories be considered. The question I ask has to do with reception studies (and has been given to me by current concerns). Let me propose that the question asked is, *What is the film philosophy's conception of what determines the spectator's relation to the cinematic text?* In some sense, this question is contained within, but not equal to, the initial question asked by Andrew. As I already pointed out, for Andrew, cinema's function has something to do with the spectator. The difference between formalist and realist philosophies is not in the possibility of affecting the spectator but in what the cinema *ought* to do, its prescriptive work. Cinema either organizes the world or duplicates the experience of perceiving of it for the spectator. Both formalist and realist propositions represent the spectator as essentially worked on by the text. The difference in philosophy is in the prescriptive work of the medium.[6]

Thus, if I ask my question (what is the spectator's relation to the cinematic text?), it seems that all classical philosophies have the same answer: the cinematic text works on an essentially receptive and ideal spectator. The reception of the film by the spectator is determined by the object, not the spectator. With a couple of exceptions that I will raise below, all classical philosophies take a text-activated position. Furthermore, as I will argue in the next section, most post-1960s theories offer the same thesis.

What I am suggesting is that in the discursive domain of film philosophy, text-activated theories far outweigh spectator-activated or context-activated ones. Perhaps this is because the writers, as in the field of literature, have used the received critical approaches discussed in Chapter 2 – formalism and phenomenology, and, later, structuralism, semiotics and post-structuralism. This does not mean that what has been must be. It seems possible that certain epistemological positions (such as some variations of phenomenology, but certainly historical and dialectical materialism) would encourage alternative theoretical emphases. In fact, the idea of 'film philosophy' itself may have limited the field's theoretical horizons – after all, it has been *film* philosophy, not *film-spectator* philosophy.

A point may be raised against this. What good is an initial question that cannot make discriminations among theories? Let me respond in two ways. For one thing, the question has already pointed out a valuable fact about film philosophies. They have been generally similar in how they address the relation of the spectator to the film. That observation may open the way to new film theorizing.

More important, despite weak attention to the spectator, film philosophies have not been all the same. For while each one posits a moderately receptive spectator, and certainly an ideal one, individual theories do not offer the same description or explanation of the relationship between spectator and film. The philosophies differ over the questions of why that spectator is as she or she is and how that spectator responds to various films. I do not intend to run through all of the dominant philosophies to prove this, but a quick examination of Eisenstein's and Münsterberg's writings is worthwhile since both of them suggest some complexity to the reception situation. Furthermore, both have interesting connections to the post-1960 paradigms.

Sergei Eisenstein

Sergei Eisenstein writes in 'The Fourth Dimension in Cinema' that 'the basic sign of the shot can be taken to be the final sum total of its effect on the cortex of the brain as a whole, irrespective of the ways in which the accumulating stimulants have come together.'[7] Eisenstein's early theory works from an assumption that the mind is matter acted upon by external stimuli. In film, montage is the source of these stimuli that produce perceptive, emotive, and cognitive responses in the spectator. Working from a mentalist view[8] of the mind, he believes that individual stimuli can be calculated and measured. Eisenstein specifically discusses the need to control the montage-material: 'Thus, where a tightly expounded fact is concerned, the work of the film director . . . requires, in addition to the mastery of production (planning and acting), a repertoire of montage-calculated angles for the camera to 'capture' these elements.'[9] The aim in his early theory is to maximize the conflict in the shot as a cell so that the tension will produce intensity and an explosion into synthesis. Since film art should consist of such a stimulation of the perceptive, emotive, and cognitive responses of the spectator, the director's selection and construction of material in the film must facilitate that threefold response. 'A *work of art . . .* is first and foremost a *tractor ploughing over the audience's psyche in a particular class context.*'[10]

As Philip Rosen has suggested, in this phase of Eisenstein's work, reception becomes pure input of ideology, which is simply equated with complexes of sensation. The problem with this is that intelligibility cannot be reduced to mere sensation; intelligibility is the organiza-tion of those sensations. As the mentalist's position acknowledges, minds can mediate those perceptions based on the individual's personal experiences, developing their own conditioned reflexes to stimuli. Thus, specificity and history could be, and ought to be, factored in.

In fact, I believe that the possibility of variant subjects troubles Eisenstein's philosophy from its start, and that through about 1932 Eisenstein grapples with the tension between wanting to control the spectator and recognizing that spectators are not ideal and tabula rasa receivers. For instance, in discussing organizing filmic material, Eisenstein parenthetically observes, "It is quite clear that for a worker and a former cavalry officer the chain of associations set off by seeing a meeting broken up and the corresponding emotional effect in contrast to the material which frames this incident, will be somewhat different."[11] As a deconstructionist would note, this parenthesis makes all the difference. Added to this is Eisenstein's extremely complicated description of the text, one that admits to contradiction as he theorizes levels of montage.

By 1932, Eisenstein seems to have reconsidered his situation. I believe he is influenced by Soviet psycho- and sociolinguistic theory, particularly the work of A. R. Luria and Lev Vygotsky, to alter his conception of the spectator.[12] His new epistemological thesis produces a change in how he will control the spectator. 'Montage form as structure' at this time 'is a reconstruction of the laws of the thought process'[13] as it was before. Only now the laws of thought change from mentalism to a dialectical materialist psycho- and sociolinguistics. In Vygotsky's theory, language is understood as a tool for thinking. As an individual develops intellectually in a social context, concepts become attached to objects and have public meaning. They also, however, accrue a per-sonal sense, a sensuality, for the specific individual.[14] Such a social and historical theory of indi-vidual language development, if applied to film spectators, demands a different textual practice, one that orders materials so that the representations the text provides fuse into images having the appropriate meanings and senses for the spectator. Eisenstein writes: 'Consequently, in the actual method of creating images, a work of art must reproduce that process whereby, *in life itself*, new images are built up in the human consciousness and feelings.'[15] For instance, the shot as a cell for conflict becomes the locus for an image association whereby '*through aggregation*, every detail is preserved in the sensations and memory *as part of the whole.*'[16] Now the shots build up a fused image with the 'chain of intervening links' condensing.[17]

Because of this shift in Eisenstein's philosophy of how the spectator's mind works, the actual montage principles change even though their functions remain the same. It is just as essential as before that the material in the film be selected and constructed by its makers. The director 'has to determine the selection of *the right people, the right faces, the right objects, the right actions, and the right sequences*, out of all the equally possible selections within the circumstances of a given situation.'[18] These choices must yield a harmonious vertical montage that reemphasizes the central dominant of the film. However, a new consideration becomes apparent: a composition should present the author's connotations. Eisenstein counsels, 'At once the question arises: with what methods and means must the filmically portrayed fact be handled so that it simultaneously shows not only *what* the fact is, and the character's attitude towards it, but also *how* the author relates to it, and how the author wishes the spectator to receive, sense, and react to the portrayed fact.'[19] This new concern develops from the 'subjective' nature of associations. Every mind can use individual bits of data to form images, but for the sensual image in the director's mind to be duplicated in the spectator's, the director must replicate the process of how that image is formed. Since the mind receives representations as images are formed, precise sequential organization of the representations that will be sent for spectatorial reception is important.

Eisenstein's later writings admit of more variation among spectators, perhaps because he has a more powerful theory of cognition and affect, one that emphasizes social and historical circumstances. His emphasis on the director's ensuring that the film's structure will construct the right impressions suggests that the spectator could easily use the representations to form alternative images, to experience the film in a manner at variance from Eisenstein's intent. Eisenstein wants to prevent errors in reading, but then he has a sociopolitical purpose in making movies. At any rate, Eisenstein seems to consider the spectator as somewhat active and able to 'misread' as well as somewhat historically grounded: the spectator's own associations already formed in social reality might interfere with those Eisenstein wishes to convey. Had Eisenstein explored film spectators more, rather than try to control them, some exciting possibilities for reception studies might have been proposed.

Hugo Münsterberg

In Hugo Münsterberg's writings a more active and historical spectator is posited, although still not without many of the presuppositions existing in most classical film philosophies. In his introduction to *The Photoplay: A Psychological Study*, Münsterberg poses two questions: 'What psychological factors are involved when we watch the happenings on the screen?' and 'What characterizes the independence of an art?'[20] For the latter question Münsterberg falls into the tradition of analyzing media specificity. For the former question, which is the foundation for his subsequent conclusions about cinema as art, Münsterberg opens the way for a spectator-response theory of cinema. Coming as he does from work in applied psychology, this might be expected.

In Part 1 of Münsterberg's text, he looks at four 'means by which the photoplay influences the mind of the spectator.' These are (1) the sensation of depth and movement; (2) attention; (3) memory and imagination; and (4) emotions. In his theory of knowledge, Münsterberg makes a distinction between 'an object of our knowledge and an object of our impression.' Sense-data input will undergo a transformation in the mind so that what is out there (the objective) may be different from an individual's experience of it (the subjective). For example, in the area of the sensation of depth and movement, Münsterberg is careful to specify that certain depth cues may give a sensation of depth, but because spectators know that the object transmitting sense-data is two-dimensional, spectators are never deceived into believing that what is seen is real depth. For the perception of movement, he takes a position surprising for his time: he notes that the impression of movement is not a result of seeing successive stages of the image but 'includes a higher mental act.' The 'motion which [*the spectator*] sees appears to be a true motion, and yet it is created by his own mind.' Thus, Münsterberg concludes, 'depth and movement . . . in the moving picture world . . . are present and yet they are not in the things. We invest the impressions with them.'[21] I am not sure that I want to go so far as to suggest that Münsterberg takes the subjective to be the real, but as an idealist, he posits a theory in which, although the mind acts as a result of sense-data, it also organizes and transforms those sense-data.

At this point, Münsterberg may still present the spectator as ideal – without variation and history, primarily because he believes these perceptual activities to be basic for human mental processes. However, when he turns to the areas of attention, memory and imagination, and emotion, he begins to suggest a more individualized and assertive spectator. As he describes the cinema's possibilities, Münsterberg writes:

> We must accompany [these filmic] sights with a wealth of ideas. They must have a meaning for us, they must be enriched by our own imagination, they must awaken the remnants of earlier experiences, they must stir up our feelings and emotions, they must play on our suggestibility, they must start ideas and thoughts, they must be linked in our mind with the continuous chain of the play, and they must draw our attention constantly to the important and essential element of the action. An abundance of such inner processes must meet the world of impressions.[22]

While the film as sense-object may supply data, Münsterberg implies that the spectator interacts on an individual basis with it. For instance, as he discusses attention factors, he argues that what creates meaning in the world is attention: 'our selection of that which is significant and of consequence.' '*The objective world*,' he writes, '*is molded by the interests of the mind*.'[23] Furthermore, personal interests, attitudes, and previous experiences will control attention. As Münsterberg works this out, he concludes that while some attention is involuntary (due to certain aspects of the sense-data, such as sudden sounds or a flash of light), other parts of attention are voluntary – people choose to what they will attend. In his analysis of the cinematic medium, then, he works to specify the particular mechanisms by which cinema controls attention (for instance, the close-up). In Münsterberg's discussion of memory, imagination and emotion, he follows the same logic. While the spectator can supply variable responses to these means of sensing, the art of the photoplay is to organize and control these responses in the most suitable way so as to achieve aesthetic effects from the experience.

What is important in Münsterberg's theory is the moderately active, self-governed and possibly historical, spectator. He assumes that personal interests, attitudes, and experiences may differ. Unfortunately, he is not interested in pursuing an analysis of those differences. Rather, he wants to determine the means to regulate or unify those responses, standards derived from his views of society and art. Indeed, although he considers censorship as interfering with freedom of expression, he also worries about 'the possibilities of psychical infliction and destruction' from the near-hypnotic effect of the flickering images. He advises 'remolding and upbuilding of the national soul.'[24]

Both Eisenstein's and Münsterberg's theories of the spectator's relation to the cinema offer potential starting points for a film-spectator philosophy. Of the pre-1960 writings about spectators, theirs are the ones edging away from a text-activated approach and toward either a spectator-activated thesis or a context-activated one. This does not mean that the other philosophies of those years are without value for elucidating a spectator-film relation. As I argued in Chapter 2, writings leaning toward a text-activated assumption still offer insights if you assume that a material world of texts exists and that the critic describes interpretative conventions that are historical.

Furthermore, even though the ideas of Eisenstein and Münsterberg are 'old,' perhaps one reason they have so much resonance with today's questions is that they are derived from theories that were predecessors to contemporary models of how humans know. Vygotsky's dialectical materialist psycho- and sociolinguistics has attracted a resurgence of scholarly interest in the last fifteen years, influencing linguistic and cognitive theories;[25] Münsterberg's psychology is a forerunner to cognitive psychology, a social science theory that informs one of the major paradigms for film reception (i.e. the work of David Bordwell).

Rereading classical film theory through asking new initial questions can be valuable in reordering the discursive field, bringing to our attention observations and propositions useful to current questions. In this case, scholars might remember that it is not just contemporary philosophies which offer theses about spectators.

Current theories of the spectator

Some research done within the past five years might be considered to belong within context-activated or reader-activated models of film and television spectators, but major competing theories still tend toward text-activated models. An example of a well-formulated statement of context-activation is an essay, 'Illicit Pleasures: Feminist Spectators and *Personal Best*,' by Elizabeth Ellsworth.[26] Ellsworth considers how lesbian feminist film critics interpreted the film *Personal Best*[27] as against how the distributing company prepared its reception as well as how dominant (male) media reviewed it. Since her hypothesis is that 'social groups use cultural forms in the process of defining themselves,' she is particularly interested in this situation, for policy-making in feminist and other progressive movements, of creating resisting readers. Ellsworth carefully establishes her model of the reception process:

> Systems of domination (economic, sexual, racial, representational) shared within particular groups (like feminists) generate specific patterns of hope, anxiety and desire. Social actors may experience these patterns initially as private, idiosyncratic, even isolated responses to cultural forms like films. But through material practices like consciousness raising groups, women's studies courses and feminist film reviewing, feminist communities collectively develop interpretative strategies for making sense of these structures of feeling, moving them into the sphere of public discourse by giving social, semantic form to anxieties and desires.[28]

Such a materialist theory assumes a complex interaction between sense-data information and a subject's transformation of those data, but the transformation is tied to specific psychological, social, and historical conditions. Interpretative strategies do not fall from the skies; they are derived in a material context. Discursive strategies for making meaning and significance have an (uneven) relation to the social formation, much as any artistic work does.

For her case example, Ellsworth describes lesbian feminists varying in four ways from dominant interpretative protocols. For one thing, 'some resisted the narrative's heterosexist closure and imagined what would happen to the characters in a lesbian future.' Additionally, most rejected large parts of the movie that could lead to a heterosexual orientation to the film's meaning. Furthermore, some readers redefined the hierarchy of actors and characters, elevating the lesbian Tory to central narrative focus and identifying with her. Such a move, Ellsworth points out, could lead to a view of the film's end as a validation of lesbianism. Finally, 'in a move that points to possibilities of strategizing for pleasure that go beyond reading films "against the grain," some reviewers named and illicitly eroticized moments of the film's inadvertent lesbian verisimilitude.' Such semic material was not what dominant media saw (e.g. '"bawdiness," "fierce combativeness" and "loyalty" (read: "clinging"),' but 'body language, facial expression, use of voice, expression of desire and strength in the face of male heterosexual dominance.'[29]

This description of one self-constructed group of readers' strategies suggests that Jonathan Culler's observations (see Chapter 2) regarding academic communities' procedures for unifying texts were not only ignored but rejected by these individuals. However, Ellsworth cautions against distorting the situation. She explicitly underlines that 'lesbian feminist reviewers stopped short of rearranging the film's chronological order, severing or rearranging cause-effect relationships in the narrative and changing who does what in the narrative.'[30] Thus, as a materialist and context-activated theory, the Ellsworth model does not give free rein to its viewing subjects. Yet, as an example of recent theorizing of reception, the model offers much for those interested in historical and materialist approaches to media interpretation.[31]

In Chapters 6 and 8, I will offer additional examples which support Ellsworth's theory that people do not reject all textual data but rather manipulate features of them in relation to what is pertinent for the individual in the specific reading context (here radical lesbian feminists viewing *Personal Best*). In this section, however, I want to compare three dominant approaches to the question of the spectator's relation to film and television: contemporary linguistic theory (derived from Saussure, informed by Lacan, often channeled through Christian Metz and the journal *Screen*); cognitive psychology theory (derived from current cognitive science, informed by Russian formalism, proposed most notably by David Bordwell); and British cultural studies (derived from Raymond Williams and Althusser, informed by Saussurean linguistics, presented most forcefully by a group of British scholars once gathered at the University of Birmingham Centre for Contemporary Cultural Studies).[32] In my opinion, all three approaches share similar goals, including wanting to propose a materialist epistemology of the subject. In some ways they are compatible, but in others they are not. For instance, as I shall note below, propositions about how the mind interacts with sense-data differ significantly between the cognitive psychology approach and the other two: cognitive psychology does not assume a linguistic base to perception.

While eventually it would be nice to resolve some of the toss-up questions such as the 'word versus thought' debate, and while such debates are significant, with real implications for models of viewing moving images, for the time being I would like to withhold judgment among the three. This is because I believe that in practice – if not theory – all three tend to present text-activated or reader-activated models of reception. I also believe that all three theoretically could offer context-activated models. The point here is to consider how the three paradigms might be useful in a historical materialist approach to the production of meaning and for interpreting moving images. I will briefly characterize each of the positions before contrasting them as well as indicating their practical bias toward the text or reader as determining.

Contemporary linguistics

The contemporary linguistic theory of relations between the spectator and moving images postulates a complicated model.[33] First of all, since the theory has historical connections to the structuralist approach that considers literary texts as sets of copresent structures (described in Chapter 2), films exhibited on screens in darkened auditoriums[34] tend to be considered similarly: they are 'read' by spectators who use codes to interpret the texts.

But viewing moving images is different from hearing words, the linguistic medium that Saussure considered when he proposed a theory of signifiers, signifieds, and signs as well as *langue* and *parole*. Since the late 1960s, writers have grappled with the difficulties of converting Saussurean linguistics from the original medium to images, with Christian Metz's attempts the most notable.[35] Metz's solution ultimately is tinged with his phenomenological heritage, but in *Film Language* he proposes that individuals learn five culturally acquired levels of codification which permit them to understand filmic narratives. These are perceptual (structuring space); denotational (recognizing and identifying objects); connotational (understanding connotations and symbolisms attached to objects); narrational (using sequencing of images to link shots temporally and spatially into narratives – the grande syntagmatique);[36] and filmic (learning medium-specific signs: e.g. in Hollywood films of the 1930s, fades denote a temporal gap).[37] Metz's epistemological philosophy at this point is partially idealist. He assumes at least one innate mental structure: people attempt to narrativize events, 'one of the great anthropological forms of *perception*.'[38] Additionally, he implicitly attributes universality to the five levels of codification. Otherwise, in a generous reading and with one exception to be noted, Metz's model permits the materialist possibility that differences as well as historical change could produce at least varieties of readings of images. The exception has to do with perceptual codes. There, by some indications, this contemporary linguistic model may offer a thesis that individuals have a universal response to viewing images, particularly in renaissance-perspective images 'positioning' the subject. That is, if perspectival and other depth codes are duplicated by the camera lenses, then a subject finds him- or herself centered in the perspectival pyramids. Such a centering offers the individual a (false) impression that he or she is producing meaning (when in fact the images are structuring the response).[39] Some writers such as Jean-Louis Baudry do seem to make such a claim. However, perception might, indeed, be cultural in a linguistic model. Since a perceiver cannot possibly process every detail that comes into his or her sensory apparatus, selection is normal and based on learned patterns.[40] Hence, context – including development of other interpretive frames, such as the knowledge of the potential effect of a 'centered' visual perspective – may be sufficient to contradict the experience. In fact, given the attention paid to the issue of the false consciousness produced by such representations, academic film critics are already resisting readers, constantly pointing out the culturally and ideologically constructed nature of the viewing experience.

Theoretically, then, the linguistic model does not imply the proposition, such as critics have charged, that 'the strategies, forms, and techniques of classical narrative cinema lock members of an audience into an epistemic position that makes it impossible for them to criticize either their own habits of perception in film viewing or the modes of perceptual intelligibility that the films themselves display.'[41] In a specific instance, the theory implies, culturally specific and competent readers will comprehend the text. But competency in reading does not imply unconsciousness in a communication event. Using culturally acquired codes to perceive and interpret a message insures neither agreement nor, most certainly, hypnotic submission. Academics at least – and likely others – refuse the position of illusion offered. This is not to say either, and on the other hand, that the subject is totally conscious in a communication event. Individuals do not have full access to *langue* or *parole*.

According to this interpretation of Metz, the variation among spectators that is sought for in a context-activated theory of reception becomes possible, although there still exists some need to work out other details. For example, given the variety within any culture, considering what is social (its *langue*) versus what is specific to an individual (*parole*), as well as *how* individual meanings could develop, would be necessary. Perhaps Vološinov's or Vygotsky's linguistics would be of assistance here, since each considers social formations as dialectical and potentially conflictual.[42] But even current sociolinguistic theory offers ideas, although the ideas are often in a functionalist model. For instance, Pierre Maranda argues that 'semantic charters condition our thoughts and emotions. They are culture-specific networks that we internalize as we undergo the process of socialization.'[43] Depending on a person's background, some semantic categories are more likely than others to be associated.

What is selected also relates to a person's 'emotion and cognitive state at the time.'[44] In fact, contemporary linguistic theory in film studies includes another thesis, one related not so much to a semiotics of interpretation as to a trajectory of pleasure. With the addition of Lacan's rewriting of Freud, cinematic linguistic theory discovered a powerful supplement that could consider affective experiences as well, particularly given its emphasis on visual perception. Stressing more of the conflictual process in psychological development than functionalist psychologies do, Lacanian psychoanalysis provides contemporary linguistics with a compatible theory of the subject. Of course, Lacanian theory also recapitulates the idealist bias of phallocentrism.

Lacanian postulates present more of a problem in developing a historical and dialectical materialist theory of understanding film than do the language aspects of the hypotheses, but I believe that returning to historical context is one solution. While Freud's particular interpretation of how individuals are constituted psychically may require revision, what remains useful is Freud's observation that social and familial circumstances are powerful determinants in constructing subjects. As a cultural proposition, Freudian theory is viable even though specific subject conditions (such as the oedipal crisis, penis envy, or sadomasochism) ought to be understood not as universals but as psychic dynamics produced historically and culturally. Revised in such a way, phallocentrism becomes a feature of a social formation, not a biological or even cultural necessity. (I also wonder if, consequently, Lacan's observation that accession to the symbolic is based on the conception of binary opposition as constituting language structuration might also be a historical rather than universal feature of language development.) The difficulty of tying together psychic dynamics with language acquisition is an essential area of continuing research, but many people believe that Freud's model is fundamentally social and historical. What pertains psychoanalytically to some individuals is not universal, and research on psychical configurations, gendering, sexuality and pleasure can continue in revised form without lapsing into idealism or text-determined propositions.

Such a revision in theories about pleasure (and affect in general) also applies to the standing hypothesis that viewing commercial broadcast television produces circumstances different from those produced by watching films. The conditions of experiencing television, it is argued, have various consequences: perceptional concentration may rely more on hearing than seeing, so people may reduce the gaze to a glance; textual information is particularly discontinuous (commercials interrupt programs or, vice versa, programs interrupt marketing), while textuality is extremely continuous (the 'flow' thesis), providing a contradictory tension for the spectator; dominant viewing circumstances in well-lighted family rooms with constant recognition of the social audience, as well as direct address by televisual narrators to the viewers, increase distanciation instead of promoting identification.[45]

Since a context-activated theory of reception posits just such local considerations as pertinent to reception (although factoring in all the variables to a model of viewing may become complicated), a context-activated approach is not theoretically at odds with the differences broadcast television might imply for reception. In fact, criticisms by feminist and television studies of earlier universalizing claims in contemporary linguistic theory have caused concern on the part of their advocates about their own tendency to universalize and idealize readers. A good instance of movements to reassert the historical foundations of the contemporary linguistic paradigm is a recent survey essay by Janet Bergstrom and Mary Ann Doane delineating the current recognition by feminists of the necessity for theorizing spectators in terms of gender, class and race. In particular, they describe the failings of earlier theorizing when spectators or audiences have been assumed to have internally consistent features. Yet the various approaches bearing on these issues do not all derive from similar premises. Bergstrom and Doane coin the term 'spectatrix' to emphasize 'the density and complexity of the matrix (or matrices)' from which scholars derive their intellectual contributions when they work beyond assumptions that the spectator can be simply hypothesized from critical assertions about the text. Again, one solution, I believe, is to reemphasize the historical possibilities of the theses about learning languages in social, public contexts.[46]

Cognitive psychology

As I mentioned in Chapter 2, various theories of reading and interpreting oral and written language have been proposed. Some function from a linguistic premise, but some take the position that perception and cognition do not require, or at least do not rely fully on, words or signs of a natural language (e.g. English, Spanish, Chinese, Arabic) for comprehension. For example, Harry Singer and Robert B. Ruddell offer four possible models of reading in their *Theoretical Models and Processes of Reading*.[47] One that I discussed in Chapter 2 is the psycholinguistic approach outlined by George L. Dillon. However, as Singer and Ruddell describe it, another model is an information processing one which proposes that readers go from print to abstract entities, but not by way of speech. Some theories go even further, arguing that natural language, is not required for thinking, that mental processing (thought) may be 'deeper' than natural language, involving mental images as distinct entities.[48] In linguistics, the debate may be described as representativism versus constitutivism, where the representativist position posits that language represents thinking, while the constitutivist holds that 'cognition is the product of propositionally based, non-visual representations,' that language *is* the information in the mind. In cognitive science the positions are labeled pictorialist and descriptionist.[49]

   Consequently, when David Bordwell argues for a constructivist cognitive psychology model of film viewing, he is overtly juxtaposing a representativist (or pictorialist) explanation of what happens when spectators watch moving images against contemporary linguistic theory, which seems to be constitutivist (or descriptionist).[50] He writes:

> It will come as no surprise that I do not treat the spectator's operations as necessarily modeled upon linguistic activities. I shall not speak of the spectator's 'enunciating' the story as the film runs along, nor shall I assume that narrative sense is made according to the principles of metaphor and metonymy. It is by no means clearly established that human perception and cognition are fundamentally determined by the processes of natural language; indeed, much psycholinguistic evidence runs the other way, toward the view that language is an instrument of and guide for mental activity. For such reasons, I do not call the spectator's comprehension 'reading' a film. It is, moreover, needlessly equivocal to speak of the spectator's activity as a 'reading' when the same word is applied to the abstract propositional arguments characteristic of critical analysis and interpretation. Viewing is synoptic, tied to the time of the text's presentation, and literal; it does not require translation into verbal terms. Interpreting (reading) is dissective, free of the text's temporality, and symbolic; it relies upon propositional language. This chapter and book try to explain viewing.[51]

As should be apparent from Chapter 2, I disagree with Bordwell's belief that viewing or perceiving can be separated, except in a most theoretical way, from interpreting or reading. I believe that interpretational propositions inform perception and viewing. However, in defence to Bordwell's representativist proposition, I do want to underscore that the vocabulary of 'reading' films should not imply a linguistic model. Regarding representativism versus constitutivism, the jury is still out for me. What matters here is that the model Bordwell proposes starts with a fundamental thesis about what spectators do when they interact with moving images: they do not process the visual images using codes and signs.

What, then, is Bordwell's model? Bordwell combines current research in cognitive sciences with a critical method that resembles the sequential text-activated approaches for literature described in Chapter 2. His epistemology of film viewing begins with the assumption that adult people think through 'organized clusters of meaning': *schemata*. While sense data are available to individuals, perception and thinking are, as Münsterberg would put it, voluntary as well as involuntary. People are 'active, goal-oriented.'[52] As children develop within a society, the routines and patterns of that social formation construct internalized sets of expectations and habits which form their schemata. Schemata continue to change through an individual's lifetime, and the cultural basis for those clusters of meaning will be crucial for a reading theory.

A standard example usually helps: the schema for the clusters of meaning associated with 'going to a restaurant in the US.'[53] Choosing to eat away from the home establishes a number of options from which derive all sorts of standard subroutines. If you select eating at a 'fast food' place, you learn that your menu is posed near a person who takes your order and your money at the same time. Your food comes later. If, however, you select dining at a 'sit-down' restaurant, you expect that a host or hostess may seat you, a busperson may offer you water, someone likely will take a predinner drink order while you peruse a booklet listing the foods, your server-for-the-meal might suggest specialties of the day as you give your selections, and only after you have enjoyed the meal will a bill arrive for payment. Of course, within either of these routines (or other 'going-out-to-eat' sequences), options exist. Yet the range of activities is delimited by social custom, and the average situation requires nearly no conscious attention to the formalities and procedures. Only if deviance occurs – your bill arrives with the predinner drink – will the schema of eating out be raised to a metaschematic level. The physiological and ecological reasons for an organism's functioning this way include reducing the number of sense variables competing for the body's attention. How could you have that stimulating conversation with your dinner partner if you had to figure out the routine every time?

This example, however, is only of one schema, and Bordwell suggests others in detail. 'The mental image of a bird is a schema for visual recognition, and the concept of a well-formed sentence functions as a schema in speech perception. Schemata may be of various kinds – prototypes (the bird image, for instance), or templates (like filing systems), or procedure patterns (a skilled behavior, such as knowing how to ride a bicycle).'[54] The complex 'going out to eat' schema includes all three types.

As indicated, the individual is goal-oriented, but sense data do not always fit into schemata. In fact, using the schemata is based on probabilities. In any actual instance, 'the perceiver in effect bets on what he or she takes to be the most likely perceptual hypothesis. Like all inferences, perceptual experience tends to be a little risky, capable of being challenged by fresh environmental situations and new schemata. After some interval, a perceptual hypothesis is confirmed or disconfirmed; if necessary, the organism shifts hypotheses or schemata.'[55]

How does this relate to watching films and television? Bordwell argues that in the analysis of viewing moving images, three things must be considered. First is the involuntary perception of image and motion (again, see Münsterberg). Thereafter, the film 'cues' the spectator to 'operate' or 'follow' various 'protocols' relating to the schemata associated with narration or other types of filmic organization. Thus, second, and assuming a knowledgeable (i.e. competent) spectator, the spectator's available schemata for viewing are pertinent. Some of these might be ideas of what story is, notions of reality and experiences or typings of related films or stylistic conventions. Then, third, and assuming a cooperative spectator, the material and structure of the film are applicable. The film 'cues and constrains' the spectator. For instance, here Bordwell offers the notions of *fabula* and *sujet* (story and plot as discussed in Chapter 2) as mental activities and textual features significant in the viewing experience. Bordwell provides a psychological explanation for what Mukařovský, Genette, and Sternberg describe ad hoc.[56]

Bordwell explicitly constructs a competent viewer as his spectator: 'a hypothetical entity executing the operations relevant to constructing a story out of the film's representations.'[57] He excludes affect, not because it is not pertinent, but because he is delimiting his field of research. He also eliminates historical and cultural differences in viewers. As he admits:

> Now there comes a methodological choice. On the one hand, the analyst could describe the various schemata that are available to a viewer at a given historical moment. . . . The alternative approach is more diachronic and text-centered. . . . I have chosen the diachronic approach because I am interested in revealing certain formal changes and alternatives within the history of narrative filmmaking.[58]

Thus, as Bordwell lays out the second half of *Narration in the Fiction Film*, he shifts focus to the last part of the triad of considerations for film viewing: the textual materials that cue, channel, and constrain spectators. Furthermore, he associates different dominant schemata activities with each of the four types of narration he describes. Classical narration calls forth detective game motifs: spectators try to guess the direction and conclusion of the narrative plot. (In terms of another system, proairetic and hermeneutic codes are privileged.) Art-cinema narration has a different 'game of form': 'The art cinema's spectator, then, grasps the film by applying conventions of objective and expressive realism and of authorial address.' (This mode emphasizes cultural and symbolic codes.) Historical-materialist narration relies on schemata related to known cultural stories as well a macrosocial theory of historical causality. Consequently, this mode emphasizes 'unusually innovative spatial and temporal construction. . . . At the barest perceptual level, narration will jolt the spectator.' The game here is stylistic, and hence perceptual, surprise and 'strain.' (Symbolic and cultural codes dominate.) Finally, in parametric narration, commonly 'the spectator's task becomes one of recognizing stylistic repetition and staying alert for more or less distinct variations.'[59] (Hermeneutic search discovering stylistic patterns tops the hierarchy of viewing activities.)

I have taken the space to describe Bordwell's model because its recent appearance makes it much less familiar to scholars of film and television than the contemporary linguistic model. Thus, its assumptions have yet to elicit a received opinion. Consequently, let me underline several propositions for which I prepared in my synopsis. For one thing, Bordwell overtly and knowingly brackets off areas that might serve as starting points for a context-activated approach to the history of viewing. These include the notion that schemata develop from cultural, social, and historical experiences. These possible starting points also involve schemata connected to affectivity. Bordwell writes that perhaps 'psychoanalytic models may be well suited for explaining emotion aspects of film viewing.'[60] Yet psycho-biological research suggests a much less distinct real separation between cognition and emotion than Bordwell makes for the purposes of his book. Bordwell is discussing these issues theoretically – i.e. as conceptual categories. I am suggesting that the research from which he draws does not prevent a linkage or even interpenetration of cognition with emotion.[61] However, because he so chooses, Bordwell does not try to supply a theory of pleasure (or other emotions or sensations).

Bordwell considers the text as 'cueing and constraining' responses of competent and cooperative viewers. The consequences of that view are descriptive discussions of 'normative' viewing, and his spectators become as ideal as those 'positioned' in contemporary linguistic theory. Sometimes, however, what is normative becomes nearly prescriptive, at least in his phrasings of ideas, if not by the terms of his theory. For example, he writes that 'the artwork is necessarily incomplete, needing to be unified and fleshed out by the active participation of the perceiver.'[62]

Finally, the motif of a game overtly appears in two of the four modes of film narration: classical and art cinema. I extended it to the other two in order to maintain consistency, but perhaps the model according to which spectators bet on probabilities in activating relevant schemata provides a primary metaphor that unconsciously appears in descriptions of the modes of narration. I wonder as well if Russian formalism's thesis of literature's autonomy and Bordwell's claim of the 'nonpractical.'[63] constituency of aesthetic activity cooperate with the game metaphor to influence an unnecessary disassociation of the process of comprehending literary or filmic texts from the very obvious fact that historical spectators do associate textual events with experiences in their everyday lives. Spectators may treat modes of narration as games, as stretching their perceptual-cognitive muscles, but is that all they do in the act of comprehension? I think not.

When proposing a field of inquiry, a scholar has every right to delimit research agendas, and Bordwell is meticulous in stating assumptions and paths-not-taken. However, as he suggests and I reinforce, cognitive psychology can be taken in several directions. One way it can go is, I believe, toward a context-activated history of spectators. As suggested above, the research itself supports this. For instance, Ulric Niesser notes that adults in Western, time-oriented cultures construct events of experience into a temporal framework of sequence; perhaps this explains why Western film viewers reorder plots into stories. Katherine Nelson finds that 'although at this point [1981], we have little systematic data, there is considerable evidence that young children's scripts [schemata of temporally and causally related actions such as 'going to the restaurant'] are initially acquired within contexts that are highly structured for them by adults.' Also some cognitive theorists who include language in their models propose that schemata are formed into 'social realities' through discussion with other individuals. In this regard a major scholar in the field, Michael Cole, believes that cognitive psychology theory is compatible with Vygotsky's psycho- and sociocultural linguistic hypotheses. Research needs to proceed on that possibility, as well as on the connections between schemata and learned *affective* (not just cognitive) responses. Finally, Niesser mentions that all thought is not goal-oriented; dreams and fantasy are 'a mode of thinking and remembering quite different from the step-by-step logic of reason.'[64]

As Bordwell summarizes, 'It is evident, though, that however much the ability to form schemata relies upon innate mental capacities, viewers acquire particular prototypes, templates, and procedures *socially*.'[65] It is that proviso which permits the possibilities of patterned historical variation among spectators.

British cultural studies

That term *social* also permits the introduction of ideology. For it is the British cultural studies researchers who emphasize that interpretations and uses of texts connect to ideologies and cultural, social, and political power. Theories of communication and cultural discourses are numerous. Some scholars assume communication is neutral – the transmittal of messages that may or may not hold ideological content (often called the 'transportation' model). Such a position is expressed in one strand of communication theory deriving from the work of Paul Lazersfeld, Kurt Lewin, Harold Lassell, Carl Hovland and Wilbur Schramm. This model also occurs when aesthetics separates form and content – a fallacy, according to much twentieth-century literary theory. Other scholars of communication and culture, such as James Carey, take the position that communication is a social or cultural ritual, 'a sharing, participation, association, fellowship.' Horace Newcomb and Paul Hirsch extend and revise that notion by proposing that at least for commercial broadcast television a 'cultural forum' provides indi-viduals not merely information but also a process for 'understanding who and what we are.'[66]

Then some theorists, such as Vygotsky and Vološinov, assume that communication is a tool. Like other means of production, communication is produced by and for its users: commu-nication transforms reality for the benefit of human beings. However, also as with other means of production, not everyone has equal access to that technology. Signs and their signifieds are not neutral but sites of power. Representations are developed in social circumstances and bear the ideological marks of their origins. The class or group that controls meanings has tremendous leverage in organizing existence for people. Thus, as Vološinov writes, the sign 'becomes an arena of the class struggle.'[67] Controlling representations and meanings is as much as part of the fight for equity as any political battle.

This notion of communication as a tool does not imply a functionalist theory of society, one that would assume a drift toward equilibrium within a social formation. Instead it posits a marxist thesis that social orders are structured in contradiction and overdetermination. Nor, however, does this notion assume conspiratorial repression by the dominant class; indeed, communication systems may function so well for the dominant class that hegemony often exists. Yet as advocates of this understanding of language caution, the very 'common sense' or 'naturalness' of discourses or meanings is a strong indicator of power at work. It is this theory of communication and cultural discourses that I shall ascribe to those individuals working in British cultural studies.

British cultural studies is a particular version of marxism developed through debates, mainly in Britain, beginning in the mid-1950s. Several histories exist, detailing a sequence of theoretical problematics from orthodox marxism through culturalist marxism (including the work of Raymond Williams and E. P. Thompson) and structuralist marxism (particularly Louis Althusser) to what Richard Johnson calls 'ideological-cultural' marxism – a label that never stuck.[68] In actuality, this last problematic is a combination of aspects of cultural and struc-tural marxism and was proposed by scholars at the Centre for Contemporary Cultural Studies at the University of Birmingham. Its tenets have gained considerable following abroad, and while many members of the original group now work elsewhere, the standard phrase 'British cultural studies' has held. I would underline that other marxist theories of cultures and their study also exist, as does nonmarxist cultural studies.

Generally, British cultural studies accepts the advancements of structuralist marxism as most notably proposed in Louis Althusser's essay 'Ideology and Ideological State Apparatuses' (and in other similar ways by other marxists).[69] The base and superstructure are theorized as distinct concepts, with elements of the superstructure having potential effect but also 'rela-tive autonomy' from other determinants. In capitalism (and perhaps other modes of production), the economic aspects of a social formation 'in the last instance' are causal, but economic structures are not sufficient to explain many specific features of a social formation. For one thing, development is uneven. The economic base (the mode of production) is contra-dictory – history moves through class struggle – and superstructural features bear the traces of that fact. Althusser splits the superstructural features into two groups. Repressive state apparatuses (RSAs) include the government, armies, police, courts, prisons. RSAs function primarily on behalf of the dominant class and often through violence or repression; they are public and generally overdetermined in an effort to repress change disadvantageous to the dominant class. Ideological state apparatuses (ISAs) are all sorts of other institutions and groups such as religions, educational systems, families, political parties, and communication and cultural media. ISAs are plural and function primarily by ideology. Consequently, contradictions and overdeterminations proliferate among the competing discourses, with all classes struggling through the ISAs.[70] Ideology is defined relationally and materially: it 'represents the imaginary relationship of individuals to their real conditions of existence.'[71] Ideology exists in the RSAs and ISAs; it exists in practices. The structured relations invite or 'interpellate' an individual to take up a position as a 'subject' in that imaginary relationship: positions of occupation, social status, gender – whatever constructed but imaginary sense of the self that is useful for the reproduction of the mode of production and the maintenance of the dominant class.

Interpellation is a tricky notion, often defined as 'hailing' the individual, calling out for the individual to recognize him- or herself as being the subject who belongs in a role. For example, reverently singing 'The Star-Spangled Banner' is taking up an ideological position of nationality, that of a US citizen. The song has interpellated, hailed its subject to position him- or herself into that constructed and, hence, imaginary identity.

This much of structuralist marxism is relatively uncontested by British cultural studies. Where disagreement develops concerns whether the human individual has volition or a consciousness that is other than 'false.' This is significant for marxists' calls for political action and change; the idea of struggle implies a need for conscious actions on the part of people, and the issues of force and consent are significant. Part of the dispute with structuralist marxism over this point derives from Althusser's use of lacanian psychoanalysis to describe interpellation. British cultural studies scholars argue that Lacan presents a transhistorical and universal theory of the subject's development; furthermore, that as Althusser argues his model, the psychoanalytical unconscious (rather than economics) becomes the primary determinant developing individuals. Such a model is unacceptable to these writers because in their view the model becomes ahistorical and change impossible to explain.[72]

As I indicated in discussing Freud and Lacan for the contemporary linguistic model, I believe that at least some Freudian-based psychologies can offer social and historical models of psychic development. I also do not think Althusser's model conflicts with such a historical reading of Freudian theories. For one thing, in Althusser, ISAs such as family relations (a major determinant in an individual's psychological development in the past century or longer) are *as ISAs* structured in contradiction; their ideologies have some (uneven) relationship to the in-the-last-instance determinant of the mode of production. Family structures are social, historical, and contradictory ideological sites, and some writers – Charlotte Perkins Gilman Stetson, for example – have made strong arguments connecting family structures such as patriarchy to economic situations such as capitalism.[73] Thus, I do not agree that Althusser's use of Freudian psychology produces a transhistorical, universal, or totally determined subject. I would also emphasize that Freudian psychology never perceived the unconscious as constituting all of the subject; in fact, in the model the ego is often in conflict with the id (or the superego) because of social and public contradictions. A somewhat more sympathetic reading of Freud is not at odds with concerns in marxism that, as historical events indicate, the individual must be represented as also having conscious intentions, understandings, and volition. Freudian psychologies just remind scholars that the consciousness is not all of what people as human organisms are and that heterogeneity and conflict are part of people's psychological dynamics. They are a historical theory of the individual as individual and social being.

In this matter, the issue of Lacan is less clear, but while Althusser's original proposition employs Lacanian language, I am not at all sure that his model's viability depends upon that language. Do the notions of 'imaginary' and 'interpellation' require the Lacanian twist? In summary, the British cultural studies position may be tossing out a powerful theory of the subject, as well as explanations of some types of affect and pleasure. In fact, some members of the group are now considering the possibilities of Freudian psychologies, particularly in relation to narration and subjectivity.[74] I shall return to this issue below.

At any rate, while temporarily eliminating psychoanalytical theory, British cultural studies theorists paid particular attention to Althusser's use of Gramsci's concept of hegemony to account for the reproduction of ideologies without repeating the universally automatic response they perceive the interpellation thesis to assert. Thus, British cultural studies attempts to synthesize Althusser and Gramsci. People are not *tabulae rasae* but exist in contradictory experiences so that while ideological hegemony often exists, opposition – or at least deviation from the dominant – does too. This can happen, they argue, because the base is contradictory and class continues to be the most significant determinant of human action.

Given these broader suppositions, what does British cultural studies offer as a theory of how readers interpret texts or view moving images? David Morley succinctly sets this out in one of the typical case studies of audiences conducted by this group of researchers. In *The 'Nationwide' Audience*, he describes, on the one side, media institutions (such as British television) as ISAs and thus not totally directed by the state. Thus, their activities are also not completely those of a dominant class. On the other side, audiences will not always read a message '"straight"': 'messages encoded one way can always be read a different way.'[75] The reasons for this are twofold. For one thing, as delineated by contemporary linguistic theory, particularly that of Vološinov and Mikhail Bakhtin, messages are complex, a 'structured polysemy.' Multiple voices, often contradictory, speak in the message, so multiple meanings exist. Polysemy, he cautions, is not equal to pluralism; discourses and codes are not equal, and dominants exist. For another thing, readers are varied.

> The audience must be conceived of as composed of clusters of socially situated individual readers, whose individual readings will be framed by shared cultural formations and practices pre-existent to the individual: shared 'orientations' which will in turn be determined by factors derived from the objective position of the individual reader in the class structure.[76]

This is not mechanistic, Morley claims, because people have consciousness. You will note that Morley brings the readings, in the last instance, down to class as determining. In fact, while he believes that 'there will always be individual private readings,' what is important is

> to investigate the extent to which these individual readings are patterned into cultural structures and clusters. What is needed here is an approach which links differential interpretations back to the socio-economic structure of society, showing how members of different groups and classes, sharing different 'cultural codes,' will interpret a given message differently, not just at the personal, idiosyncratic level, but in a way 'systematically related' to their socio-economic position.[77]

This theoretical perspective was put into a research procedure. An early task of the British cultural studies writers was to use contemporary linguistic theory and structuralist marxism to read texts ideologically. Several of the Centre people cosponsored Charlotte Brunsdon and

Morley's analysis of the British television series 'Nationwide' in the monograph *Everyday Television*. Using numerous tactics derived from Roland Barthes's work on popular culture and ideology, the writers considered the *Everyday Television* study as a 'base line . . . against which differential readings may be posed'[78] once they did fieldwork on actual audiences. The fieldwork was reported in Morley's 1980 *'Nationwide' Audience* study. Referring to F. Parkin's observations in *Class, Inequality and Political Order* that 'three broad 'ideal types' of ideological frameworks (dominant, negotiated and oppositional)' exist, Morley criticizes the simplicity of the 'number of "meaning-systems"' and the lack of multiple origins for those three frameworks.[79] Despite that, he adopts those three frameworks to describe the structured patterns of relations he finds in the responses of his audiences to 'Nationwide' and connects them to the various socioeconomic classes surveyed. Stuart Hall outlines the three frameworks: (1) the '*dominant-hegemonic position*' – reading as intended; (2) the '*negotiated code* or position' – 'decoding' via 'exceptions to the rule' of the hegemonic position; and (3) '*oppositional code*' – putting the information into 'some alternative framework of reference.'[80] Other case studies follow suit. For instance, in *Subculture* Dick Hebdige studied rock and punk groups as an oppositional production of meaning from an alienated socioeconomic class: the unemployed youth of Britain.

Fallacies in some of the initial formulations of the British cultural studies research procedure have recently produced a few modifications in their approach. One problem exists in categorizing readings into only three frameworks labeled hegemonic, negotiated, and oppositional. As Morley writes, the idea of three types of readings can become as essentialist as any text-activated notion of contemporary linguistic theory.[81] Furthermore, I would note that the terms do little to help describe what readers actually do in any instance of reading as intended, negotiated, or opposed. All the potential descriptive value of text-activated theories is lost. As work has continued, the idea of these three categories of reading strategies has given way to a continuum from hegemonic to oppositional interpretation, but the frameworks have not been altered.[82]

But more fundamental are two deeper assumptions of the Centre's research strategies. One is that despite appeals to 'polysemy,' texts are usually treated as unified, reproducing without contradiction hegemonic ideology. This is not, as I take it, a dialectical notion of textuality or the effectivity of the ideological plurality of ISAs. Produced through the class struggle, texts (and their readers) should display the features of competing and contradictory discourses, their polysemic nature. It is the case, of course, that media channels are owned and controlled for the most part by the dominant class, but that fact does not reduce textual materials into hegemonic representations. Agents of capitalism and late monopoly capitalism seek to maximize profits; a firm might choose to market products that, upon analysis, do not necessarily work toward the long-run benefit of the mode of production. Again, the tendency of textual production may appear to be toward hegemony, but cultural products are not always so monological and their contradictions should also be available for analysis. British cultural studies has produced moderately sophisticated analyses of the texts used for its audience studies, but those 'base line' texts are assumed to be entities which ought always and totally to be opposed. Thus, theoretical propositions end up essentializing capitalist-produced texts as unified.

The other deep assumption of British cultural studies that is troubling is that readers are reducible to socioeconomic categories. Such a proposition produces ideal readers. Again, *in practice*, the strategy has been, following standard positivist social scientific habits, to use preset data for categorizing audience informants. People are located as belonging to a particular class if they have particular occupations or make a certain amount of money. The obvious question of class consciousness (and possible disparities between assumed categories and consciousness) is not raised. Also not raised is the notion that a socioeconomic class member is not all that a reader might be, according to a structuralist marxist theory of the subject in a capitalist social formation. Johnson notes this: 'One of our own recurrent arguments [with Hoggart, Williams and the idea of 'a whole way of life,'] on the other hand, will be to stress the heterogeneity or complexity of 'working-class culture,' fragmented not only by geographical unevenness and parochialisms, but also by the social and sexual divisions of labour and by a whole series of divisions into spheres or sites of existence.'[83] Gender, race, ethnicity and so forth are also identities in which power differentials affect individuals. Furthermore, these identities are produced when individuals are interpellated to position themselves according to historical discursive systems. If texts are contradictory and in an uneven relation to the mode of production, identities that may be represented may be other than that of class. In fact, given the values of disguising class as pertinent, all sorts of other constructed positions may *appear* to be more significant to readers and viewers of texts: gender and race, for instance. Thus, the contextual situation of the viewer's pertinent self-identities – *as constructed historically* – may have greater salience in any specific reading instance. Analysts such as marxists may wish to discuss how those constructed identities are 'false consciousness,' but they cannot dismiss them as important causes for how people produce interpretations.

The two assumptions – (1) that media texts reproduce hegemonic ideology and (2) that readers are ideal and uncomplicated representatives of socioeconomic categories – have produced an accidental reader-activated model of reception for the Centre researchers. They imply that given the text and given the several categories of ideal and coherent readers (albeit upper- or lower-middle class or working class or unemployed), a certain type of interpretation or use will be made of the interaction with the text. Thus, the readers' class determines the experience. Where Holland and Bleich find psychological identities and Culler finds historical critical procedures, the British cultural studies scholars find socioeconomics.

As I have suggested, neither assumption is necessary in the marxist model of culture and communication that the British cultural studies theorists use. In fact, the strains of precategorizing the audience into classes are evinced by the fact that other categories of readers have recently received some attention. Morley's *Family Television* (1986) looks at fathers', mothers' and children's patterns of using television and videocassette recorders,[84] and Ien Ang's study of viewers experiencing *Dallas* raises many observations pertinent to consideration of readers from perspectives such as gender. Tamar Liebes and Elihu Katz's analysis of how five ethnic and cultural groups interpreted *Dallas* is another instance.[85] Indeed, the subject positions analyzed *may be* the most pertinent for the text(s) in question (the results are certainly fascinating), but a certain predestination in the research guides interpretations of data when categories of individuals are already constituted by the researchers.[86]

For a context-activated theory of reception, historical determinations are necessary. Not only would the specific textual address of certain subject positions seem an obvious area for research (as opposed to preconstituting the text's address and type of subject), but intertextual discourses regarding possible subjectivities for that historical time seem relevant. I note this particularly with an example. In the last twenty years, the US has witnessed an explicit constitution of variation among sexual preferences as a possible self-identity, marking out an open (if not new) regime of perception and meaning of the self. Homosexuality or bisexuality, of course, has long been a possible way of understanding one's self, but I believe that in the US the notion that heterosexuality is only one of the possible directions of sexual trajectories has just recently penetrated heterosexuals' self-imaging. It was possible to ignore this when non-heterosexuality was defined in hegemonic discourses as deviance. And many people still hold to that definition. What is different is that the sign 'homosexuality' has been and is being fought over in cultural discourses: see any number of less devastating images – still unsatisfactory, I will grant – of gays in film and television in the past ten years. Unfortunately, however, and on the other hand, the gains of Stonewall may be fleeting now that advertising statistics have indicated that gays are an excellent group to target for marketing. Capitalism may now be retaking the sign 'homosexuality' and reifying it into just another 'life-style.' A new, if more subtle, condition of repression may be appearing.

More theoretically, then, notions of the self and available subject positions are transformed in historical discursive formations and among specific contextual situations. For instance, watching *Dallas* in one's own home is different from viewing it as part of a classroom assignment. In the first case, subject positions likely to be taken up could relate to socioeconomic class, occupation, nationality, or gender. In the latter case, the subject position would involve one's role in educational institutions. Another example occurs in the case study of *Foolish Wives* (see chapter 6). The inability of readers in the early 1920s to accept female attraction to the central male figure – a male who had attributes socially, culturally and historically linked to *both* masculinity *and femininity* – was part of what made a hegemonic (if you will) reading of the text hard to achieve. Almost all the males and at least one female were moderately outraged by the film.

The idea of myself as middle-class, female, American, and so forth is a historically determined representation of an imaginary relation of myself to my real (and contradictory) existence, the terms of those subjectivities constituted through contemporary discourses about the 'self.' These 'selves' all have some near or distant relation to my real existence in terms of my material needs (and the current dominant mode of production). British cultural studies needs to foreground an observation that Hall makes an introducing Morley's *Family Television*:

> We are not 'viewers' with a single identity, a monolithic set of preferences and repetitive habits of viewing. . . . We are all, in our heads, several different audiences at once, and can be constituted as such by different programmes. We have the capacity to deploy different levels and modes of attention, to mobilise different competencies in our viewing.[87]

Not the least of these levels, modes and competencies is that logically some readers may have to hold two reading frameworks in their heads at the same time. As Richard Maltby points out, to argue about 'potentially subversive readings of Hollywood texts' requires simultaneously comprehending a hegemonic position: 'Necessarily, the subversive reading must claim knowledge of a preferred reading.'[88] Deconstructionism would counter that the opposite is true as well: to know what is preferred requires knowing what is not.

As British cultural studies proceeds, it may become more difficult to bother with the idea of a continuum of hegemonic to oppositional readings. Furthermore, as mentioned above, that continuum seems to restrict the possibilities of thinking about what readers are doing. Broadening the types of approaches that explain what readers and spectators are doing does not mean abandoning questions about political effectivity. It does make the problem of categorizing texts or readers more difficult, perhaps impossible, since some moments of the historical interaction may be progressive and others may be regressive. Such a complexity will be discussed in the historical study of the 1930s debates over *The Birth of a Nation* (see Chapter 7).

Another immediate consideration for British cultural studies may be to consider theories of affect. The tendency in this area has been to focus on the affect of pleasure (or its lack), although other affects might be considered. When dealing with this aspect of a textual experience, the researchers turn to several models, all of which are oriented toward social determinants. For example, Ang uses Pierre Bourdieu's work on the sociology of tastes. If people can identify with, or recognize, a structure of feeling, then pleasure results.[89] Such a proposition, however, does not encourage deviation from hegemonic tastes; thus it would seem that people only experience pleasure when they agree with the dominant ideology. In a call for class struggle, arguing against achieving pleasure will be difficult. Furthermore, the model, as Ang reports it, suggests isomorphic homologies between texts and preexistent, internalized structures. All sorts of pleasures and affects experienced from lack of correspondence (such as surprise or opposition) are ruled out. Finally, other affects are not addressed in her model.

Another attempt to discuss affect is in *Television Culture*, where Fiske, drawing on theories that influenced British cultural studies, offers three possible explanations of pleasure: a psychoanalytical pleasure related to desire; a physical pleasure experienced in bodily sensations (which Fiske associates with Barthes's notion of *jouissance*); and a social pleasure derived from play. The psychoanalytical pleasure is 'the product of accommodation to the dominant ideology'; the latter two 'can be associated with resistance and subversion.'[90] It is not hard to guess which explanations Fiske prefers, but to make his argument, he neglects information that might lead him to different conclusions. Regarding psychoanalysis, Fiske uses Laura Mulvey's exploratory essay 'Visual Pleasure and Narrative Cinema' to outline his thesis: a psychoanalytical theory of pleasure assumes a male spectator repeating a process that reproduces him for patriarchal cinema. Published in 1975, Mulvey's essay has been steadily revised and challenged by many individuals who promote a psychoanalytical framework for understanding aspects of desire and pleasure. To critique the psychoanalytical explanation in 1987,[91] Fiske ought to have considered the theoretical developments of the intervening years. Additionally, the psychoanalytical theory explains not only accommodation to patriarchy but also pleasure in its negotiation and opposition in moments of fantasy. In fact, it may be better at explaining deviance than conformity. What Fiske seeks (a radical politics) may also be available in the theory he rejects.

In fact, in discussing Barthe's *jouissance*, Fiske ignores that notion's grounding in just such psychoanalytical variations from normative psychology. Within *The Pleasure of the Text*, Barthes writes approvingly of Bataille and Sade, of perversions: 'Is not the most erotic portion of a body where the garment gapes? In perversion (which is the realm of textual pleasure) there are no 'erogenous zones' . . . it is intermittence, as psychoanalysis has so rightly stated, which is erotic.' And further on: 'Text of bliss [*jouissance*]: the text that imposes a state of loss, the text that discomforts . . . unsettles the reader's historical, cultural, psychological assumptions, the consistency of his tastes, values, memories, brings to a crisis his relation with language.'[92] Barthes has a theory of the pleasure and bliss of the text that is not one of a reader following the narrative of a traditional story, but his theory still has psychoanalytical roots in Julia Kristeva's work on semanalysis; *jouissance* is not just a 'physical' theory of pleasure, as Fiske would have it.

For the third of Fiske's explanations of affect, the social one of play (related to game theory), he describes pleasure derived from both empowerment and resistance. Indeed, such an approach might prove useful in the elucidation of some affective experiences, for it would be unwise to reduce all pleasure to a single determinant, such as a person's psychology. However, again, research in Britain cultural studies has tended to assume acquiescence as regressive and opposition as progressive. If the text is progressive, then opposition might be undesirable. The problem here is knowing when contradictory texts and contradictory subjects ultimately produce in a process the kind of experience that British cultural studies or Fiske seeks.

This last problem will also plague any context-activated theory of reception that also seeks to evaluate the event studied. In the next chapter, some of the possibilities for a context-activated approach will be discussed, but many of the questions that I have raised about the current three approaches to the interpretation of moving images will remain unresolved. Contemporary linguistic theory, cognitive psychology, and British cultural studies offer many ideas, but a simple meshing together of the three is theoretically unacceptable. Contemporary linguistics and British cultural studies assume a language-based reading process, but the cognitive psychology approach uses schemata that may not be represented through language. Contemporary linguistics and British cultural studies differ on how to explain the affect of pleasure: while contemporary linguistics turns to psychoanalytical theories, British cultural studies has preferred using sociological ones. Cognitive psychology indicates a willingness to allow psychoanalysis to explain affect and emotion, but its metaphor of the game also appears in one of the British cultural studies models of pleasure. Contemporary linguistic theory has recently concentrated its efforts on the issue of pleasure; British cultural studies and cognitive psychology thrive best in areas of cognitive reception.

If these are some of the dissonances among the three models, a similarity also exists. The practical bias of each has been toward a text-activated or reader-activated model. However, I have tried to suggest how each of the three might be modified into a context-activated, historical model. In trying to do this, I hope that I have not distorted the integrity of any of the approaches, each of which holds promise for furthering reception studies research.

Notes

1   I will not particularly address the issues of avant-garde film or video viewing in this book. However, I believe you could apply with little difficulty to avant-garde texts the principles developed here for studying historical spectators. The determinants of conventional reading procedures and historical discourses about avant-garde art practices would obviously be influential contextual factors. The same applies to the documentary mode.

2   Annette Kuhn, 'Women's Genres,' *Screen* 25(1) (January–February 1984): 18–28.

3   Patrice Petro, 'Television Criticism, Television History: Realism, Modernism, and Reception' (Paper delivered at the Society for Cinema Studies Conference, Madison, Wisconsin, 26–31 March 1984). Also see her 'Mass Culture and the Feminine: The "Place" of Television in Film Studies,' *Cinema Journal* 25(3) (Spring 1986): 5–21.

4   J. Dudley Andrew, *The Major Film Theories: An Introduction* (New York: Oxford University Press, 1976). Andrew's questions derive from Aristotle and are informed by Siegfried Kracauer.

5   For instance, in his lectures, David Bordwell treats classical film philosophies from another question or set of questions. He asks, What are the propositions' ontological, epistemological, and aesthetic assumptions? As he moves through the philosophies in his lectures, he tends to equate the ontological and epistemological issues with the question of whether the theories are idealist or materialist. Thus, idealist theories have been written by Arnheim and Bazin, while materialist ones come from Eisenstein and Vertov. As you can note, this produces groupings different from the ones proposed by Andrew, but the differences are not due to major changes in the reading of the philosophies so much as to a change in the initial question. It is the question that causes the difference in the splitting and subsequent categorizing of the philosophies.

I do not mean to imply that I think any one of these questions is inappropriate, invalid, or irrelevant. In fact, the advantage of having both Andrew's and Bordwell's set of queries is that each brings out certain relationships among the philosophical discourses, as well as providing means to contrast them. Optional categorizing is part of what academia considers the point of analysis – providing new information, which may require rearranging the same set of data through such new starting questions. David Bordwell, 'Lectures in Film Theory,' University of Wisconsin-Madison, Madison, Wisconsin, Spring 1978. In this, I have followed him but have revised the questions to ones of ontology, epistemology, and effectivity, with the last term stressing propositions of causality. John Fiske also defines effectivity as a 'socio-ideological term' against 'effect,' 'an individual-behavioristic one,' and this is a good distinction. *Television Culture* (London: Methuen, 1987), p. 20.

6   For Bordwell's readings classical film philosophies offer a text-activated approach to the spectator. For an idealist philosophy of cinema, the spectator has certain a priori structures that organize the sense data (as in Arnheim). While individual films may differ, the a priori structures remain static and available, determining the spectator's ability to respond to the textual features of the specific film. Bazin's writings also end up with a text-activated theory. While some films (e.g. those of Renoir, Wyler and Welles) may bring the spectator into a perceptual situation closer to that of the individual's relationship with reality, it is due to the film's formal and stylistic organization, not to any spectatorial intention or activity. When Bordwell reads the materialist philosophies of Eisenstein and Vertov, again, he discovers that the organization of the film's materials determines effects.

7   Sergei M. Eisenstein, *S. M. Eisenstein: Selected Works*, vol. 1: *Writings, 1922–34*, Richard Taylor (ed. and trans.) (London: BFI Publishing; Bloomington: Indiana University Press, 1988), p. 183. Principal influences on my interpretation of Eisenstein for this period of his writing include Andrew, *Major Film Theories*; Bordwell, 'Lectures'; Peter Wollen, *Signs and Meaning in the Cinema*, rev. ed. (Bloomington: Indiana University Press, 1972), pp. 19–73; David Bordwell, 'Eisenstein's Epistemological Shift,' *Screen* 15(4) (Winter 1974–1975): 32–46; Philip Rosen, 'Formalism, Reception and Eisenstein's Theoretical Development' (unpublished paper, March 1980); Ken Slavin, 'Generative Semiotics' (Paper delivered at the Society for Cinema Studies Conference, Madison, Wisconsin, 26–31 March 1984).

8   Slavin, 'Generative Semiotics.' A mentalist (i.e. Pavlov) in the Soviet Union in the 1920s believed that the mind was capable of mediating perceptions. The epistemological position is still, however, materialist.

9   Eisenstein, *Selected Works*, p. 47.

10   Ibid., p. 62 (italics in original).

11   Ibid., pp. 41–2.

12   Interestingly, while undergraduates are introduced to Eisenstein's early work (and not his later), scholarly debates have been most intense on the post-1930 period of Eisenstein's writings. My position in the debates rejects prior dismissals of Vygotsky as important because I believe that interpretations of Vygotsky's writings have been inadequate. I will not rehearse here my argumentation, but a valuable summary of the theory is in James V. Wertsch, *Vygotsky and the Social Formation of the Mind* (Cambridge: Harvard University Press, 1985).

13   Eisenstein, *Selected Works*, p. 236.

14   The distinction between meaning and sense appears in both Vygotsky and Eisenstein. It has a different connotation, however, from the distinction between meaning and significance described in Chapter 2. For Vygotsky and Eisenstein 'sense' has 'sensuality,' the private, psychological, affective feelings aroused by the sign.

15   Sergei M. Eisenstein, *The Film Sense*, Jay Leyda (ed. and trans.) (New York: Harcourt, Brace & World, 1942), p. 18 (italics in original).

16   Ibid., pp. 16–17 (italics in original).

17   Ibid., p. 14.

18   Ibid., p. 172 (italics in original).

19   Sergei Eisenstein, *Film Form: Essays in Film Theory*, ed. and trans. Jay Leyda (New York: Harcourt, Brace & World, 1949), p. 151 (italics in original).

20   Hugo Münsterberg, *The Photoplay: A Psychological Study* (1916; rpt. as *The Film: A Psychological Study*, New York: Dover Publications, 1970), p. 17.

21   Ibid., pp. 19, 23, 29, 30 (italics in original).

22   Ibid., p. 31.

23   Ibid., pp. 31, 46 (italics in original).

24   Ibid., pp. 95, 96.

25   See a recent extension: Barbara Rogoff, *Apprenticeship in Thinking: Cognitive Development in Social Context* (New York: Oxford University Press, 1990).

26   Elizabeth Ellsworth, 'Illicit Pleasures: Feminist Spectators and *Personal Best*,' *Wide Angle* 8, no. 2 (1986): 45–56.

27   Ellsworth quotes the film pressbook's representation of the narrative: '[Tory (Patrice Donnelly) and Chris (Mariel Hemingway)] met as strangers at the 1976 Olympic trials. They became friends, lovers, and ultimately competitors facing each other in the pentathlon at the Olympic trials in 1980' (ibid., p. 50).

28   Ibid., p. 46.

29   Ibid., pp. 53, 54.

30 Ibid., p. 55.
31 Another recent advance in this area is the work of Barbara Klinger. See her 'Digressions at the Cinema: Reception and Mass Culture,' *Cinema Journal* 28, no. 4 (Summer 1989a): 3–19, and 'Much Ado about Excess: Genre, Mise-en-Scène, and the Woman in *Written on the Wind*,' *Wide Angle* 11, no. 4 (1989b): 4–22. These essays drive from her 'Cinema and Social process: A Contextual Theory of the Cinema and Its Spectators' (PhD diss., University of Iowa, 1986). There she analyzes three reading formations for *Written on the Wind*: the academic, the industrial, and the mass cultural. See also Jacqueline Bobo, '*The Color Purple*: Black Women's Responses,' *Jump Cut* 33 (1988b), 43–51, although this article is theoretically less well-formulated.
32 This genealogy could be contested, but it is a common representation of direct influences on the individuals who were associated with one another during the 1980s at the Centre and functions at least to provide a few guideposts for those unfamiliar with the scholarship.
33 What follows is underdeveloped for the sake of concentration on the problem at hand. I assume reader familiarity with this model, but I also find helpful, particularly for the Lacanian addition, Rosalind Coward and John Ellis, *Language and Materialism: Developments in Semiology and the Theory of the Subject* (London: Routledge & Kegan Paul, 1977). Most individuals working the contemporary linguistic model also adopt structuralist marxist tenets. That, however, is not necessary to the linguistic aspect of the model, and I shall discuss the situation regarding structuralist marxism below in my coverage of British cultural studies.
34 I shall discuss the problem of commercial broadcast television below.
35 Christian Metz, *Film Language* (1968, orig. pub. 1971), Michael Taylor (trans.) (New York: Oxford University Press, 1974); Christian Metz, *Language and Cinema* (1971), Donna Jean Umiker-Sebeok (trans.) (The Hague: Mouton, 1974).
36 My phrasing may seem odd. I would argue that Metz's phenomenology underpins his linguistic theory, leading to the implication that perception and innate mental structures (the human mind as a diachronistic structure [*Film Language*, p. 47]) allow individuals to understand narratives. The grande syntagmatique is not an explanation of how people understand narratives but an after-the-fact categorization of film segments into temporal and spatial categories. See below.
37 Metz, *Film Language*, p. 62n.
38 Ibid., p. 27 (italics in original).
39 This idea also derives from structuralist marxism, which I will take up in the section on British cultural studies.
40 Ross, 'On the Concepts of Reading,' p. 95.
41 George M. Wilson, *Narration in Light: Studies in Cinematic Point of View* Baltimore: The Johns Hopkins University Press, 1986), p. 191.
42 Robert Stam makes suggestions along this line in his support of Bakhtin's and Vološinov's contributions to cultural theory. See Robert Stam, 'Film and Language: From Metz to Bakhtin,' R. Barton Palmer, 'Bakhtinian Translinguistics and Film Criticism: The Dialogical Image?' and Robert Stam, 'Bakhtinian Translinguistics: A Postscriptum,' in *The Cinematic Text: Methods and Approaches*, R. Barton Palmer (ed.) (New York: AMS Press, 1989a and 1989b), pp. 277 351.
43 Pierre Maranda, 'The Dialectic of Metaphor: An Anthropological Essay on Hermeneutics,' in *The Reader in the Text* (1980), Suleiman and Crosman (ed.), p. 185.
44 Ross, 'On the Concepts of Reading,' p. 95.
45 Rick Altman, 'Television Sound' (1987b) and Nick Browne, 'The Political Economy of the Television (Super) Text' (1984), rpt. in *Television: The Critical View*, Horace Newcomb (ed.), 4th edn (New York: Oxford University Press, 1987), pp. 566–84, 585–99 respectively; Fiske, *Television Culture*. Some interesting contradictions exist among the writers on television specificity. What I indicate in the text should be understood as an uncritical synopsis of received opinion. Additionally, this general description is held by both contemporary linguistic theory and British cultural studies since the latter agrees with many tenets of the former.
46 Janet Bergstrom and Mary Ann Doane, 'The Female Spectator: Contexts and Directions,' *Camera obscura* 20–21 (May–September 1989): 13.
47 Singer and Ruddell (ed.), *Theoretical Models and Processes of Reading* (1970), pp. 450–676.
48 William Frawley, 'Lectures in Psycholinguistics,' Newark, Delaware, University of Delaware, Spring 1983. Two recent surveys are Garnham, *Psycholinguistics*, and Danny D. Steinberg, *Psycholinguistics: Language, Mind and World* (London: Longman, 1982).

49   As I indicated above, the word-versus-thought debate seems a toss-up to me. Current neurological and language brain research concludes several things about this question, as well as about the issue of affect. A handy synopsis is Israel Rosenfield, 'A Hero of the Brain,' *New York Review of Books*, 21 November 1985, 49–55. Rosenfield gleans from the literature the following observations, which seem tome to have some interest for the issues at hand. (1) Psychological capacities such as 'recognition of objects . . . were composites of independent brain operations' (not a function of the entire brain). 'A man could see an object without recognizing it.' (2) Speech '"has as a prerequisite the ability to form cross-modal association."' That is, information such as the spoken word 'dog' can connect with the visual image of a dog. (3) It appears doubtful that writing evolved out of pictorial representation. Both notational systems and drawing developed at the same time. (4) A picture understood as a picture is deciphered by the visual system; 'a picture used in writing is ultimately deciphered by the language centers.' Apparently the brain makes distinctions depending on what it believes is the type of information desired. A related point: sign language is processed in language centers. (I wonder what happens in the case of moving images.) (5) Reading and writing, like oral language, require different and to some extent independent mechanisms. However, two recent books by Ronald A. Finke and Mark Rollins make powerful arguments for the pictorialist view; see the review by J. Michael Tarr, 'The Mind's Eye,' *Science* 249 (10 August 1990): 685.

50   David Bordwell, *Narration in the Fiction Film* (Madison: University of Wisconsin Press, 1985). As I shall describe below, Bordwell offers a constructivist cognitive psychology theory. Bordwell's model might inappropriately be combined with the work of two other individuals who do not agree with contemporary linguistic theory. These people are Noël Carroll and Edward Branigan. Carroll takes an analytical philosophy approach: while he agrees with Bordwell that the medium of the movies differs from language ('The Power of Movies,' *Daedalus* 114, no. 4 [Fall 1985]: 79–103], he describes reading in terms of propositional logic. For instance, 'The spectator is not free to make any inference he or she chooses for a given shot interpolation. Rather the induction must be constrained in terms of what is plausible to infer in virtue of the rest of the film and in terms of the cultural context of the film' ('Toward a Theory of Film Editing,' *Millennium Film Journal* 3 [1978]: 93).
      Branigan prefers a linguistic model indebted to the work of Noam Chomsky. This puts Branigan someplace between contemporary linguistic philosophy in film (with its Saussurean heritage) and a cognitive psychology position. Branigan writes: 'It is my belief that a film spectator, through exposure to a small number of films, knows how to understand a potentially infinite number of new films. The spectator is able to recognize immediately repetitions and variations among films, even though the films are entirely new, and outwardly quite distinct. . . . I believe that this ability to understand – however it is acquired – is evidence of the prior knowledge, or competence, of a spectator. The goal, then, is to explain the 'reading act' in terms of the generally unconscious methods employed in decoding texts. Not that whether or not pictures themselves are held to be symbolic in nature, the claim here is merely that a narrative arrangement of pictures is symbolic and so permits certain linguistic analogies.' *Point of View in the Cinema: A Theory of Narration and Subjectivity in Classical Film* (Berlin: Mouton Publishers, 1984), pp. 17–18.

51   Bordwell, *Narration in the Fiction Film*, p. 30.

52   Ibid., p. 31.

53   This example is derived from Katherine Nelson, 'Social Cognition in a Script Framework,' in *Social Cognitive Development*, J. H. Flavell and L. Ross (eds) (Cambridge: Cambridge University Press, 1981), pp. 101–3.

54   Bordwell, *Narration in the Fiction Film*, p. 31.

55   Ibid.

56   Jan Mukařovský does appeal to a linguistic model to explain how meanings are developed in a text. See 'On Poetic Language' (1940) in *The Word and Verbal Art*, pp. 50–3.

57   Bordwell, *Narration in the Fiction Film*, p. 30.

58   Ibid., pp. 149–50.

59   Ibid., pp. 213, 212, 242, 245, 287.

60   Ibid., p. 30.

61   As early as 1947, Jerome S. Bruner and Cecile C. Goodman argued that behavioral determinants such as 'personality dynamics,' 'quasi-tempermental characteristics like introversion and extraversion,' 'social needs, and attitudes' affected basic perception; 'Value and Need as Organizing Factors in Perception,' *Journal of Abnormal and Social Psychology* 42, no. 1 (January 1947): 33. A nice summary

of current psychochemical research on the mind is Israel Rosenfield, 'The New Brain,' *New York Review of Books*, 14 March 1985, 34–8.

62   Bordwell, *Narration in the Fiction Film*, p. 32.

63   Ibid.

64   Ulric Neisser, *Cognitive Psychology* (New York: Appleton-Century-Crofts, 1967), pp. 290, 296–99; Nelson, 'Social Cognition,' p. 105; Ragnar Rommetveit, 'Language Acquisition as Increasing Linguistic Structuring of Experience and Symbolic Behavior Control,' in *Culture, Communication, and Cognition: Vygotskian Perspectives* (1985), James V. Wertsch (ed.) (Cambridge: Cambridge University Press, 1985), pp. 193–94; Michael Cole, 'The Zone of Proximal Development: Where Culture and Cognition Create Each Other,' in *Culture, Communication, and Cognition* (1985), Wertsch (ed.), p. 154. For a recent, succinct survey of the literature in relation to an application to feminist literary theory, also see Mary Crawford and Roger Chaffin, 'The Reader's Construction of Meaning: Cognitive Research on Gender and Comprehension,' in *Gender and Reading: Essays on Readers, Texts, and Contexts*, Elizabeth A. Flynn and Patrocinio P. Schweickart (eds) (Baltimore: The John Hopkins University Press, 1986), pp. 3–30.

65   Bordwell, *Narration in the Fiction Film*, p. 149 (italics in original). Note that Bordwell says 'innate mental *capabilities*' (italics mine). He does not say innate forms or categories. What he is probably suggesting is that the biochemistry of the human body has particular preset dispositions, but this comment should not be taken to imply either idealist or copy-theory epistemologies.

66   James W. Carey, 'A Cultural Approach to Communication,' *Communications* 2 (1975): 6; Horace M. Newcomb and Paul M. Hirsch, 'Television as a Cultural Forum: Implications for Research', *Quarterly Review of Film Studies* 8, no. 3 (Summer 1983): 47. Dudley Andrew also suggests this 'social ritual' approach in 'Film and Society: Public Rituals and Private Space,' *East-West Film Journal* 1, no. 1 (December 1986): 7–22.

67   Vološinov, *Marxism and the Philosophy of Language* (1983), p. 23.

68   Descriptions of the genesis of this position with critiques of prior approaches include the following (arranged in chronological order): Johnson, 'Culture and the Historians,' pp. 41–71; Richard Johnson, 'Three Problematics: Elements of a Theory of Working-Class Culture,' in *Working-Class Culture* (1980), Clark *et al.* (eds.), pp. 201–37; David Morley, *The 'Nationwide' Audience: Structure and Decoding* (London: British Film Institute, 1980), pp. 1–21; Stuart Hall, 'Cultural Studies and the Centre: Some Problematics and Problems,' in *Culture, Media, Language: Working Papers in Cultural Studies, 1972–79*, Stuart Hall, Dorothy Hobson, Andrew Lowe, and Paul Willis (eds) (London: Hutchinson, 1980), pp. 15–47; Stuart Hall, 'The Rediscovery of "Ideology": Return of the Repressed in Media Studies,' in *Culture, Society and the Media*, ed. Michael Gurevitch, Tony Bennett, James Curran and Janet Woollacott (eds) (London: Methuen, 1982), pp. 56–90 Tamar Liebes, 'On the Convergence of Theories of Mass Communication and Literature Regarding the Role of the "Reader"' (Paper delivered at the Conference on Culture and Communication, Philadelphia, Pennsylvania, October 1986). Nonhistorical expressions of the positions and assumptions held are the following (arranged in chronological order): Iain Chambers, John Clarke, Ian Connell, Lidia Curti, Stuart Hall, and Tony Jefferson, 'Marxism and Culture,' *Screen* 18, no. 4 (Winter 1977/78): 109–19; Dick Hebdige, *Subculture: The Meaning of Style* (London: Methuen, 1979), pp. 3–19; Stuart Hall, 'Encoding/Decoding,' in *Culture, Media, Language* (1980a) Hall *et al.* (eds), pp. 128–39; Stuart Hall, 'Recent Developments in Theories of Language and Ideology: A Critical Note,' in *Culture, Media, Language* (1980e), Hall *et al.* (eds), pp. 157–62; Dave Morley, 'Texts, Readers, Subjects,' in *Culture, Media, Language* (1980a), Hall (eds) *et al.*, pp. 163–73; Stuart Hall, 'Cultural Studies: Two paradigms,' *Media, Culture and Society* 2 (1980): 57–72; James Curran, Michael Gurevitch and Janet Woollacott, 'The Study of Media: Theoretical Approaches,' in *Culture, Society and the Media* (1982), Gurevitch *et al.* (ed.), pp. 11–28; Terry Lovell, 'Marxism and Cultural Studies,' *Film Reader* 5 (1982): 184–91; Samuel L. Becker, 'marxist Approaches to Media Studies: The British Experience,' *Critical Studies in Mass Communication* 1 (1984): 66–80; (a dissenting view) Nicholas Garnham, 'Contribution to a Political Economy of Mass-communication,' in *Media, Culture and Society*, Richard Collins, James Curran, Nicholas Garnham, Paddy Scannell, Philip Schlesinger and Colin Sparks (eds) (London: Sage Publications, 1986), pp. 9–32; John Fiske, 'British Cultural Studies and Television,' in *Channels of Discourse*, Robert C. Allen (ed.) (Chapel Hill: University of North Carolina Press, 1987), pp. 254–89.

69   Louis Althusser, 'Ideology and Ideological State Apparatuses (Notes towards an Investigation)' (1970), in *Lenin and Philosophy and Other Essays*, trans. Ben Brewster (New York: Monthly Review Press, 1971), pp. 127–86.

70   I hope that this particular rewriting by me (but based on many other scholars' observations) of Althusser's Ideological State Apparatuses essay eliminates some of the valid criticisms by him and others of his original statements (specifically its 'scientificism' and 'idealism').

71   Althusser, 'Ideology,' p. 162.

72   See particularly Hall, 'Cultural Studies,' and Morley, 'Texts, Readers, Subjects.'

73   Charlotte Perkins Gilman Stetson, *Women and Economics: A Study of the Economic Relation between Men and Women as a Factor in Social Evolution* (1898; rpt. New York: Source Book Press, 1970).

74   Conversations with Richard Johnson, Austin, Texas, 20–22 September 1990.

75   Morley, *The 'Nationwide' Audience*, pp. 9, 10.

76   Ibid., p. 15.

77   Ibid., pp. 14–15.

78   Charlotte Brunsdon and David Morley, *Everyday Television: 'Nationwide,'* (London: British Film Institute, 1978), p. v.

79   Morley, *The 'Nationwide' Audience*, pp. 20, 21.

80   Hall, 'Encoding/Decoding,' pp. 136–38. What this looks like will be examined with specific examples in chapter 4.

81   Morley, 'Texts, Readers, Subjects,' p. 172.

82   Despite Morley's and others' remarks about the three frameworks' simplicity, individuals continue to use the tripartite system. See, for instance, Ien Ang, *Watching Dallas: Soap Opera and the Melodramatic Imagination* (1982), Della Couling (trans.) (London: Methuen, 1985); Fiske, 'British Cultural Studies and Television'; Fiske, *Television Culture*; Tony Bennett and Janet Woollacott, *Bond and Beyond: The Political Career of a Popular Hero* (London: Methuen, 1987); Linda Steiner, 'Oppositional Decoding as an Act of Resistance,' *Critical Studies in Mass Communication* 5, no. 1 (March 1988): 1–15.

83   Johnson, 'Culture and the Historians,' p. 62.

84   David Morley, *Family Television* (London: Comedia, 1986).

85   Tamar Liebes and Elihu Katz, 'On the Critical Ability of Television Viewers' (Paper delivered at the World Congress of Sociology, New Delhi, India, August 1986); Liebes, 'On the Convergence of Theories.' Also see Sonia M. Livingston, 'Interpreting a Television Narrative: How Different Viewers See a Story,' *Journal of Communication* 40, no. 1 (Winter 1990): 72–85.

86   Fiske, for instance, lists seven subjectivity positions (from J. Hartley): '"self, gender, age-group, family, class, nation, ethnicity"' (*Television Culture*, p. 50). Surprisingly, sexual preference is missing, something Fiske does not mention. I shall discuss this below.

87   Morley, *Family Television*, p. 10.

88   Richard Maltby, '" Baby Face" or How Joe Breen Made Barbara Stanwyck Atone for Causing the Wall Street Crash,' *Screen* 27, no. 2 (March–April 1986): 22.

89   Ang, *Watching Dallas*, pp. 20 and 47. Likewise, Morley and Hall disagree with positivist social science's 'uses and gratifications' psychology and imply that social explanations are the place to look. See Hall, 'Introduction' to Morley, *Family Television*, p. 9.

90   Fiske, *Television Culture*, p. 225.

91   The publication date of *Television Culture*. Another version of this occurs in his later *Understanding Popular Culture* (Boston: Unwin Hyman, 1989), pp. 49–68.

92   Roland Barthes, *The Pleasure of the Text* (1973), Richard Miller (trans.) (New York: Hill and Wang, 1975b), pp. 9–10, 14.

PART TWO

Technologies

DISCUSSION OF THE TECHNOLOGIES USED in the production of film has been at best patchy. There have been bursts of interest – around the introduction of sound and colour, for example – but largely this fundamental area of film studies remains undeveloped. At the moment, we are experiencing a transformation of the technical means through which films are produced. Digital technologies seem about to replace celluloid as well as many other practices once fundamental to film production. We have become accustomed to the display of computer generated imagery (CGI) in special effects sci-fi films such as the *Terminator* series. However, when a period melodrama like *Titanic* (or a sword and sandal epic like *Gladiator*), use computer-generated imagery for the background as well as the action, we have to accept that CGI has become a standard element in commercial feature film production. So much of the theoretical foundation for the discussion of film, however, assumes the performance of actors in front of a camera (Metz's semiotics of film [1978] for instance) that the incorporation of CGI as a standard production technique challenges theoretical orthodoxies. Many would argue now that the discussion of technologies needs to be moved up the batting order of film studies as technological change has not only radically altered conventional production practices in the industry but also, perhaps, the nature of the spectator's experience.

Part 2 commences with Ed Buscombe's important article, which asks what influences the uptake of technological innovation in the film industry. This is a question of particular complexity for an industry that sells unique cultural products to a mass audience whose socially constructed taste preferences determine how they choose among competing attractions. Buscombe teases out these complexities by outlining the interaction between multiple determinants – economic, aesthetic and ideological – in his comparison of two quite different histories. The introduction of sound to the cinema (which was almost immediate) is compared with the more gradual process through which colour stock replaced black and white as the dominant mode for feature film production. Buscombe emphasises the specific historical conjuncture of conditions which accompanied the introduction of these technologies in order to explain his scepticism for more schematic explanations that, for instance, privilege only the economic or industrial determinants. The economic, he says, 'can explain the necessary but not the sufficient conditions for innovation'. But a new technology 'cannot be successful unless it fulfils some kind of need', and 'the specific form' of this need will be 'ideologically determined'. Central to such determinations, in both the instances Buscombe describes, is the realist aesthetic that framed both the commercial production and reception of film.

It is with Buscombe's discussion of the realist aesthetic that Steve Neale commences the next reading, 'Colour and Film Aesthetics', taken from *Cinema and Technology* (1985). Neale shows how the disruptive potential of colour was carefully managed in Hollywood film as it was enlisted into the service of the spectacular or, later on, narrative realism. The technology was subject to the existing conventions of narrative and verisimilitude, from which colour initially represented a distraction. This was not a problem in the case of such distractions as the female body, which could be offered up as both natural and spectacular in ways that, presumably, unequivocally demonstrated the benefits of Technicolor over monochrome. However, it remains true that even today the 'symbolic organization' of colour in mainstream cinema is heavily motivated by the narrative. Neale refers to Kristeva's suggestion that such control is probably necessary because colour is capable of 'escaping, subverting and disrupting the symbolic organization to which it is subject'. As a technology, then, colour multiplies film's capacity to generate what could already be thought of as an 'overabundance of contrary meanings'.

The interest motivating both of these readings is consonant with the dominant concerns within British film studies when they were written. As suggested in the Introduction, screen theory was preoccupied at the time with critiques of the ideological work accomplished by mainstream cinema as well as with the formal character of cinematic realism. Richard Dyer's discussion of cinema lighting, although interested in the politics of conventional production practices, is more in line with a slightly later tradition that concerns itself with the examination of representations. This has less to do with issues of ideology than with the distribution and maintenance of cultural power, and the construction of erasure of identities. Taken from Dyer's *White* (1999) – which examines the valorization of the colour white in western representational traditions – 'Lighting for Whiteness' points out that 'movie lighting' is premised upon the illumination of the white face. The skin tones of white faces are the foundations for the lighting palette in mainstream cinema. To provide the same level of visibility and clarity for black faces is possible, but it requires deliberate attention. Similarly, the narrative use of light as means of drawing attention to a character, or as a means of inferring glamour or value onto an individual, carries with it a racial implication. Elsewhere in his book, Dyer goes on to argue that whiteness signifies a special cultural investment within western visual arts, that this supports and embodies an implication of racial superiority, and that the replication of this pattern in the production practices of the cinema must have political consequences.

Gianluca Sergi begins his discussion of 'post-classical' film sound (that is, post-1970s Hollywood constructions of film sound), by noting the difficulty of finding an established analytic vocabulary through which to deal with sound. He compares this situation to the analogous condition of popular music studies, where again the lack of a shared vocabulary of analysis has had an impact on the development of the field. There are other and more specific impediments to the study of film sound, however. Sergi criticizes the unconscious critical preferences that allow critics to think of a film soundtrack as principally the music track rather than, say, dialogue. In response, Sergi emphasizes the importance of understanding film sound as composed of four elements – effects, music, dialogue and silence – blended together in a complex structure which itself should be the object of analysis.

Sergi's short history of recent developments in film sound highlights the aesthetic and economic importance of the introduction of Dolby stereo systems – not so much at the point of production, but at the point of exhibition. Dolby provided the first economically viable system for sound reproduction that offered film-makers and their audiences high quality sound in the cinema. Followed in the early 1980s by the THX system and by the end of the 1980s the introduction of digital sound, the post-classical film soundtrack is very different to what preceded it. Sergi examines this difference in detail, dealing with the development of multi-layered sound, multi-directional sound, changes in industry production practices, and improved sound reproduction in the cinema. Among the results of these developments is a new role for film sound, Sergi suggests, as it 'breaks through the screen' to become an object of interest and significance in its own right. The prominence given to music soundtracks in marketing cinema to youth audiences today indicates that this new interest may also reflect their commercial importance.

Stephen Prince's article addresses a question that is now unavoidable in film studies: 'what are the implications of computer-generated imagery for representation in the cinema, particularly for concepts of photographically based realism?' 'How', he asks, 'might theory adapt to an era of digital imaging?' In an often detailed discussion of the specific techniques used in digital imaging, Prince argues that their use challenges the two most longstanding theoretical traditions in film studies. We met these in the Introduction: the realist tradition which insists on the importance of the relationship between the image and its referent in the real world, and formalist accounts which focus on film's reprocessing of its raw material into new forms. Digital imaging clearly undermines a realist account of cinema. It 'supercedes' the assumption that what we see on the screen is the product of a 'pro-filmic event', involving the camera and the real object being photographed. Similarly, it argues that accounts which suggest that 'all cinema representations are, in the end, equally artificial' as products of ideology, are perhaps too simple. After all, as Prince goes on to say, some representations 'while being referentially unreal' (i.e. they represent things we know do not exist and thus cannot be photographed, such as the dinosaurs in *Jurassic Park*), are nevertheless 'perceptually realistic' (that is, we accept the representation as corresponding with our perceptions of how a large animal such as the dinosaur might look and move).

Adopting a cognitivist perspective as the middle way between realism and formalism, Prince goes on to argue for the importance of a theory of 'perceptual correspondence' in order to understand not only how audiences view films but also the 'larger issue of how viewers see'. As we have noted earlier, cognitivism is still fighting for space within film studies internationally, so Prince's middle way – the emphasis upon perceptual correspondences – may not convince everybody. However, it is the case that once representation in film is disarticulated from an assumption that it is in some way a rendition of a 'real' object, the history of film theory has moved into new territory. Within this territory, some understanding of precisely how we make sense of computer generated imagery, and whether or now this may involve different processes (and carry different consequences) to those used to interpret photographic imagery, does need to be developed.

Barbara Creed takes up a part of this challenge in her article in *Screen*, which directly considers the ontological status of computer-generated actors or 'cyberstars'. As a result of digital technology in film, she says, 'film has been freed from its dependence on history and on the physical world'. Among the consequences of this, is 'the possibility of creating a virtual actor . . . as living actors compete with digital images for the major roles in the latest blockbuster or romantic comedy'. This does not just take us into the territory of the special effect, but also into issues around audience identification and the mysteries which surround the performance of the actor. How might we theorize the relation between the audience and the cyberstar?

Creed explores the possibility that the 'depthlessness' of the cyberstar image (its seam-less surface, on the one hand, but also our consciousness of its complete imaginariness, on the other) might affect the distance from which the spectator witnesses the behaviour on the screen. In fact, in order to identify with the image on the screen or with the character in the narrative in the manner conventionally theorized through psychoanalytic screen theory, we may need to know that the image on the screen belongs to a human being. As Creed puts it, 'it may make a significant difference if the characters on screen are played by synthespians, actors without an Unconscious'. Or, given what we know about the knowledges brought to the cinema by fans of screen stars, it might make a difference that these synthespians have no supporting and informing fabric of celebrity to provide the cultural resonance that is among the pleasures of cinema consumption. On the other hand, more cynically, contem-porary feature film's emphasis upon narrative and spectacle may make such aspects secondary for many spectators.

Creed's speculations are necessarily inconclusive but they reinforce the perception that the shifts we have seen in the technologies used to produce contemporary cinema carry with them the potential to change our relation to the medium, and to the worlds we might think of it as representing. As Creed points out, 'celluloid camera dramatically altered the rela-tionship of the individual to reality; the computer-generated image is about to change that relationship once again and in equally profound ways'.

Chapter 5

EDWARD BUSCOMBE

SOUND AND COLOUR

THE LAST ISSUE OF *FILM READER*[1] devoted half of its total space to examining the relations between industry, technology and ideology in the cinema. *Film Reader*'s initiative is a welcome sign that film theory is paying more attention to economic and technological determinants and that film history is increasingly moving out of the era of mere facts and figures towards consideration of more substantive matters.

However, an article by J. Douglas Gomery in this issue,[2] though providing valuable detailed information on the introduction of sound into Hollywood, raises some problems concerning the extent to which economics can assist our understanding of the cinema. Gomery claims that 'economic theory can explain the coming of sound.'[3] Gomery has in mind the theory of technological innovation.[4] This theory seeks to explain the factors governing the invention, innovation and diffusion of new technology in any given industry: in what circumstances new techniques or products are first invented and then introduced as practical and commercial propositions subsequently adopted by the industry as a whole. A considerable literature exists on this subject, but we may take as representative the work of one author cited by Gomery. Edwin Mansfield, in his book *Technological Change*,[5] lists several factors governing a decision to innovate once an invention has been produced:

> To being with, the firm should estimate, of course, the expected rate of return from introducing the new product or process. In the case of a new product the result will obviously depend on the capital investment that is required to introduce the innovation, the forecasted sales, the estimated costs of production, and the effects of the innovation on the costs and sales of the firm's existing product line. . . . In addition the firm should estimate, as best it can, the risks involved in innovating.[6]

Mansfield also enumerates those factors affecting the rate at which an innovation will become diffused:

> (1) the extent of the economic advantage of the innovation over older methods or products, (2) the extent of the uncertainty associated with using the innovation when it first appears, (3) the extent of the commitment required to try out the innovation, and (4) the rate of reduction of the initial uncertainty regarding the innovation's performance.

> (Mansfield, p. 88)

Mansfield also suggests that a number of factors might be expected to affect the speed of any single firm's response to a new technique: (1) the size of the firm (one would expect larger firms with more resources to be quicker at innovating); (2) the degree of expectation of profit from the new technique; (3) the rate of growth of the firm (expanding firms might innovate more easily); (4) the firm's profit level (prosperous firms would have the necessary capital or credit); (5) the age of the firm's management personnel (younger management might be more receptive to new ideas); (6) the liquidity of the firm (the more liquid the firm the better it might be able to find finance); (7) the firm's profit trend (firms with declining profits might look harder for new profits or techniques) (Mansfield, pp. 93–95).

There is nothing very profoundly 'theoretical' about Mansfield's formulations, yet they do have some explanatory power in relation to the coming of sound. Gomery has shown that Warner Brothers did pay careful attention to the question of costs and to the problem of finding the necessary capital.[7] Furthermore Mansfield's four factors affecting the rate of diffusion help to explain why the changeover to sound was so rapid. The economic performance of the new product and the speedy reduction in the uncertainty regarding that performance more than outweighed the original uncertainty itself and the high costs of installing new equipment.

The seven factors characterizing those firms most likely to innovate should provide an explanation for the fact that it was Warners, one of the smaller companies, which led the way in sound. Unfortunately, the theory of technological innovation breaks down at this point, since Mansfield can find no statistically significant correlations across a range of industries for factors 3, 4, 5, 6 and 7. The only factors known to affect a firm's willingness to innovate are its size (bigger firms do innovate faster) and the expected rate of profit. The latter point seems fairly obvious; while the former shows Warners to be an exception to the rule. Gomery is forced to look elsewhere for an explanation of Warner's actions, which were, he claims, the result of the farsightedness of Waddill Catchings, the entrepreneur who masterminded the firm's strategy. Gomery's theoretical position therefore ends up not so far as he thinks from that of the film historians he takes to task. He sets out to prove that sound was introduced as the result of an economic law which 'theory' can explain. But instead sound turns out to be the result of one man's initiative. The only substantial difference between Gomery's explanation and that of previous historians is a dispute over which individuals should get the credit, Catchings or the Warner brothers themselves.

Thus the theory of technological innovation seems of limited use, and Gomery reverts from a search for economic explanations back to a kind of 'great man' theory of history. But could a different kind of economic theory explain the coming of sound? This would depend on what kind of explanation we are looking for. The theory Gomery wants to use could only explain why it is that innovation takes the course it does. It doesn't explain why there should be innovations in the first place, a more fundamental and surely more interesting question. To answer it we cannot adopt a simple notion of supply and demand, since the public could hardly be said to have demanded sound pictures until it had seen and heard them. True, once sound had been successfully demonstrated demand affected the rate of diffusion. But the initial investment in research and development had to be made when future demand could only be guessed at.

One must start with the fundamental law that in a free market economy a firm is motivated by, to use the terms of capitalist economics, a desire to maximize profits; or, in the terms of Marxist economics, a desire to maximize the rate at which it extracts surplus value. In any given economic situation this can be done in a number of ways. For example, a firm can attempt to develop fresh markets and so achieve economies of scale. In the late 1920s the film industry had no easy way of finding fresh markets – domestic and foreign penetration of the market being near saturation point. (In 1926 US attendances ran at 100 million a week. In Britain, for example, American films had 74¼ per cent of the market at this time.)[8]

Another possibility is for a firm to lower its costs of production. Given that constant capital costs, both fixed and circulation (that is, the costs both of buildings and machinery, and of raw materials) were relatively inelastic, this could be done only be reducing the cost of variable capital, i.e. labor. (I am assuming, though I cannot prove it, that in the film industry in the late 1920s the costs of constant capital were in fact inelastic.) But in a labor-intensive industry such as filmmaking, and one in which automation had at that time gone as far as it could go (another assumption I cannot actually prove) it seems as though there was little opportunity for cutting costs. However, it is worth noting in this respect that Warners' original motive in developing sound was to use it as a means of recording vaudeville acts and musical sound tracks for silent pictures. In other words, sound was at first intended to increase the productivity of vaudeville performers and theatre musicians. Only subsequently was it seen as a means of creating an entirely new product.

Another way for a firm to increase the rate of surplus value is to increase its share of the existing market at the expense of its competitors. This can sometimes be achieved by price cutting. But the American film industry had evolved by the end of the 1920s into a mature oligopoly in which the sale of the product (i.e. exhibition) was tightly regulated by the major firms dominating the market, in cooperation with each other. Each production company needed the sales outlets (theatres) of the others in order to market its products. Thus none of the large companies could involve itself in a price war against the wishes of the others. The smaller companies, who might have had most to gain from price competition, were in the weakest position to do anything of the kind, because few of them had theatres of their own and because the majors controlled the most important theatres.

Only one way remains in such a situation for a company to secure an advantage over its competitors. It can create a new product. In a sense, of course, this happened all the time in Hollywood since every picture was unique and its uniqueness was protected by copyright. But precisely because all products were unique no company possessed a decisive advantage. This required an innovation of a different order. Such an innovation was sound, a wholly new kind of product which would make all other kinds obsolete. And the possession of this invention did indeed, for a time, give Warners a chance to increase its share of the market. (It seems likely also that it did for a while increase the absolute size of the market, bringing new customers into the theatres. And it may have helped postpone the decline in attendances brought on by the Depression.) The profits which a monopoly on a new product make possible are known in Marxist economic theory as 'technological rent'[9] and the search for this monopoly explains why innovation should be a necessary feature of the economic system even when business seems good.

From this perspective, we should not view innovation in the film industry as a rational and sought-for-outcome of attempts on the part of altruistic inventors to 'improve' film technology, nor as proof of capitalism's success in combining profit with the satisfaction of human needs. Human needs are many, but capitalism will produce only those innovations from which rent can be extracted, since the whole basis of the system is production for exchange value rather than use value. Sound would not have succeeded, admittedly, had not the public found a use for it, but the public was given 'what it wanted' only because sound offered the opportunity for a monopoly. And the same principle applies, *mutatis mutandis*, to any other technological innovation. The history of the invention of the camera itself is written largely in the patents taken out for each new modification.

Gomery argues convincingly against those film historians who claim that Warners decided to produce sound films in a desperate gamble to ward off bankruptcy; Gomery shows that the decision formed part of a carefully thought-out strategy to upgrade the company's status to that of a major.[10] But the case of sound (introduced by Warners and Fox, at that time two of the smaller studios) does not show that technological innovation in the cinema results only from a special set of circumstances. An oligopoly reduces competition in certain areas; it does not eliminate it altogether. Firms continue to compete with each other, but the main form of competition takes the shape of a search for new products. Innovation and technological rent are functions of the system as a whole, not just the result of attempts by small firms to break into the big time. The first three-component Technicolor film, for example, was released by RKO and the first CinemaScope picture by Twentieth Century Fox, both majors.

Economic theories can only partially explain technological innovations, since economics cannot say why innovations take the form they do, only why they are an essential part of the system. Economics can explain the necessary but not the sufficient conditions for innovation. No new technology can be introduced unless the economic system requires it. But a new technology cannot be successful unless it fulfills some kind of need. The specific form of this need will be ideologically determined; in the case of cinema the ideological determinant most frequently identified has been realism. Whether the search for greater realism has been welcomed, as in the case of Bazin's discussion of deep focus or Charles Barr's of CinemaScope,[11] or whether realism is subjected to a fundamental critique, as in the case of writings by Comolli and Baudry,[12] theorists appear to agree that realism indeed dictates the formation of the needs which technology satisfies.

But to define 'realism' is no simple matter; and while we may agree that realism is dominant, it may not always be the only ideological need fulfilled by technological innovations. The history of the use of color in the cinema provides an interesting test case for the precise role of realism. The scientific principles of color, like those of sound, were known long before sound or color films became technically and commercially feasible. With color, as with sound, the delay in its introduction resulted in part from technical problems in producing a system that would work under commercial operating conditions (early color films were very prone to scratching, for example). But again as with sound there was also resistance on aesthetic grounds. Douglas Fairbanks, whose picture *The Black Pirate* (1927) was produced in two-component Technicolor, complained that color had

> always met with overwhelming objections. Not only has the process of color motion picture photography never been perfected, but there has been a grave doubt whether, even if properly developed, it could be applied without detracting more than it added to motion picture technic. The argument has been that it would tire and distract the eye, take attention from acting and facial expression, blur and confuse the action. In short it has been felt that it would militate against the simplicity and directness which motion pictures derive from the unobtrusive black and white.[13]

Such objections appear rather strange if one supposes that the demand for realism in the cinema has always been merely a question of the literal rendering of appearances. We perceive the world as colored, after all, and therefore an accurate representation of it should also be colored. (Leaving aside the fact that complete accuracy is impossible since color in film only approximates the colors perceived in the real world.) But in fact it has never been a question of what *is* real but of what is *accepted* as real. And when it first became technically feasible, color, it seems, did not connote reality but the opposite.

This may in part be for historical reasons, since the very first uses of color involved the tinting of certain sequences in films shot in black and white. Such a usage was extremely conventional, a long way from a literal representation of the world. And as I suggest below, there may be more important reasons why color was not accepted as connoting reality. At any rate, the objections to which Fairbanks refers are clearly consistent with a realist aesthetic. Color would serve only to distract the audience from those elements in the film which carried forward the narrative: acting, facial expression, 'the action.' The unity of the diegesis and the primacy of the narrative are fundamental to realist cinema. If color was seen to threaten either one it could not be accommodated.

It thus becomes possible to understand why color took so much longer to take hold than sound. The technical problems were probably no greater, nor was it simply force of habit – audiences accustomed to silent pictures adapted to sound practically overnight. Color, on the other hand, has become universal only since the advent of color television, which lowered the relative resale (to television) value of theatrical features made in black and white. Color technology has taken so long to diffuse, we can conclude, partly because unlike sound it could not be instantly accommodated to the realist aesthetic.

Further evidence of color's 'unreality' for early spectators can be found in the use actually made of it. For example, in the first few years after the introduction of three-component Technicolor (originally used in the Disney cartoon *Flowers and Trees* in 1932) the great majority of films employing the process were produced within genres not notably realistic in the sense of their being accurate representations of what 'life' is 'like.' It can be argued, of course, that not many Hollywood pictures represent what life is like; but it nevertheless remains true that a kind of hierarchy ranks genres according to the extent to which the world they portray, fictional or not, is close to what the audience believes the world to be like. Thus at one end of the scale we find newsreels, documentaries, war films, crime films, etc. and at the other cartoons, musicals, westerns, costume romances, fantasies, comedies. Virtually all the early three-component Technicolor pictures are in these latter genres.[14] Thus by the 1930s the original objection to color, that it would detract from the narrative, had given way to the extent that color was permissible in *some* films, and so therefore no longer totally incompatible with audience concentration on a story. (Of course such an objection as Fairbanks describes must always have been an extreme position since certain uses of color, such as tinting, became quite common very early on.) Yet it was still considered sufficiently unrealistic to be taboo for films with 'realistic' subject matter.[15]

We must now return to the question of why color was not perceived as realistic. Why was its use during the 1930s restricted to unrealistic genres, whereas the use of sound was not? Color must surely have connoted something else. What that something else was could, I think, be demonstrated by an analysis of the color films produced. But I propose instead to take a short cut and consult an industry manual published in 1957 – *Elements of Color in Professional Motion Pictures*.[16] Written by a committee of film industry personnel, it distills the collective theory and practice of color photography in Hollywood up to the late 1950s. By this time the use of color was no longer restricted to certain genres; by the date of publication, the authors suggest, two-thirds of all features were produced in color. Nevertheless, certain of their remarks on the relation of color to realism shed some light on why for a long time color was restricted to special uses.

For the authors of this book, one should note first of all, realism is never to be equated with naturalism, strict fidelity to the world as it appears:

> This psychological factor can be of great importance in creating an atmosphere of reality or verisimilitude on the screen. With the filming of a historical or 'period' picture, for example, research is done not only on architecture and decoration, but also on the colors in use during the particular period and in the specific country.

> Yet the use of the actual colors of the period or the country are very rarely employed (sic). Because of psychological factors governing the response of a modern viewing audience, far better results are achieved by the use of a *desaturated tonality of the times*, that is, a less saturated range or 'palette' of color and pattern, but adequately punctuated with authentic identifying colors so that the end result stands to be identified as historically accurate yet believable.
>
> *(Elements*, pp. 41–2)

The colors we accept as real are therefore a compromise between what we are accustomed to and what used to be. The need to make the audience believe in what is depicted on the screen permits, indeed demands, a distortion of what actually is, or was. Such a practice can of course be observed in other aspects of Hollywood filmmaking, though the practitioners are rarely so honest about what they are doing.

The authenticity of what the producers know to be false is guaranteed by the other 'realities' of the film, principally the narrative. The authors of this textbook are in no doubt that it is to the narrative that color must ultimately be subordinate, 'the objective being to have color "act" with the story, never being a separate entity to compete with or detract from the dramatic content of the picture' (*Elements*, p. 41). Such a position is exactly what we should expect. But the book allows, interestingly, for some exceptions to this rule; other values, it seems, may conflict with the necessity of realism. First, there is the value of the star:

> The feminine star, for example, whose appearance is of paramount concern, must be given undisputed priority as to the color of make-up, hair and costume which will best complement her complexion and her figure. If her complexion limits the colors she can wear successfully, this in turn restricts the background colors which will complement her complexion and her costumes to best advantage.
>
> *(Elements*, pp. 40–1)

Thus it is not simply the appearance of the real world (modified to make it 'believable') or the requirements of the narrative which dictate the use of color. The values of stardom must have their place, even if they are in conflict with the dictates of realism (which presumably might demand background colors which did not suit the star). That the reference is to 'feminine' stars alone makes it fairly clear what kind of values are in question here.

But the authors challenge realism most strikingly in their remarks on musical and fantasy pictures. In these genres, it seems, color may escape the demands of realism; it need no longer be subordinate to plot and the appearance of the real world:

> Musicals and fantasy pictures are open to unlimited opportunities in the creative use of color. Here we are not held down by reality, past or present, and our imaginations can soar. Musicals and fantasies are usually designed to provide the eye with visual pleasure in the way that music pleases the ear.
>
> *(Elements*, p. 42)

Thus these genres are privileged; here the bonds of realism may be slipped and the audience may give itself up to 'pleasure.' The musical, interestingly, offers another means whereby the dictates of narrative can be avoided, for although musical numbers are often motivated by the plot they do sometimes succeed in cutting free of narrative altogether and functioning outside it.

Color, then, need not serve realism. It may simply provide pleasure. Yet pleasure in the cinema is never a simple matter. The pleasures cinema offers – the pleasures of realism itself or other kinds – are always within ideology. What ideological forms do the purely visual pleasures of color take? On this point the manual is silent and we must return to the films themselves.

The ideological appeal of color suggests two possibilities. First, color must signify luxury or spectacle. Whether employed in the Western to enhance the beauties of nature, in the costume drama to portray the sumptuousness of the Orient or the Old South, or in musicals to render the dazzle and glamor of showbiz, color serves to embody a world other than our own into which, for the price of a ticket, we may enter. We should not suppose, of course, that color must always signify luxury or spectacle, since such a signification depends in part upon its scarcity value and even on the mere fact of its costliness. Once color has become normal in the cinema it begins to lose these connotations. One should add, though, that in certain kinds of documentaries and even occasionally in features black and white is still used as a guarantor of truth, which would not be possible unless their opposite, color, signified something other than truth.

Second, color in early Technicolor pictures operates as a celebration of technology: 'look how marvellous the cinema is!' Color, far from providing a recognizable portrait of the real world, lifts us out of that world, above its mundane problems and unreconcilable contradictions into a new world where the limitations of the old are swept away and its difficulties transcended. (Consider, for example, the relation between the black-and-white and color sequences in *The Wizard of Oz*.) Early Technicolor functions as a form of self-reflexiveness, which instead of deconstructing the film and destroying the illusion effects a kind of reification of technology. Other forms of film technology function in the same way: Cinerama, 3D, even spectacular crane or helicopter shots all having the effect satirized in the Cole Porter song in *Silk Stockings*: 'glorious Technicolor and breathtaking CinemaScope and stereophonic sound.' So we might see color working to confirm Ernest Mandel's statement that 'Belief in the omnipotence of technology is the specific form of bourgeois ideology in late capitalism.'[17]

That color can function to signify luxury or celebrate technology does not mean that these two uses of it are necessarily subversive of the dominant cinematic ideology. Not everything which is not realism is counter-cinema. Nevertheless, color clearly did function to an extent as a contradiction of realism. Realism, though dominant, could not provide all the things which were in demand. Realist ideology held out against color first by denying its compatibility with narrative and then by confining it to certain genres. Color, however, was able to satisfy needs which realism could not. Were this not so it is hard to see how, given its unrealistic connotations, it could ever have been introduced at all. Since the 1930s, however, color has become progressively absorbed back into realism, with the result that the audience's need for spectacle and for technological wonders has had to be satisfied by a succession of further technological developments: wide screen, 3D, Sensurround and so on. Even wide screen has now (though in a form less wide than the original CinemaScope) been absorbed into conventional technique. It seems at least possible that a similar fate might have befallen 3D and other marvels had not they been too expensive for a contracting industry.

Notes

1   *Film Reader* 2 (1977b).
2   Douglas Gomery, 'Failure and Success: Vocafilm and RCA Innovate Sound,' *Film Reader* 2 (1977b): 213–21.
3   Ibid., p. 219.
4   This is outlined in some detail in Gomery's doctoral thesis: *The Coming of Sound to the American Cinema: A History of the Transformation of an Industry*, University of Wisconsin–Madison, 1975.

5   Edwin Mansfield, *Technological Change* (New York: 1971) is a shortened version of his work *The Economics of Technological Change* (New York: 1968), which Gomery cites.

6   Mansfield, *Technological Change*, pp. 77–8.

7   Douglas Gomery, 'Writing the History of the American Film Industry: Warner Brothers and Sound,' *Screen* 17, no. 1 (Spring 1976).

8   Benjamin B. Hampton, *History of the American Film Industry* (New York: 1970) pp. 362, 357.

9   Ernest Mandel in *Late Capitalism* (London: 1975) states: 'The continuous and systematic hunt for technological innovations and the corresponding surplus-profits becomes the standard hallmark of late capitalist enterprises and especially of the late capitalist large corporations' (pp. 223–4).

10 Gomery, op. cit.

11 André Bazin, 'The Evolution of the Language of Cinema' and Charles Barr, 'CinemaScope: Before and After,' both reprinted in *Film Theory and Criticism*, Gerald Mast and Marshall Cohen (eds) (New York: 1974).

12 Jean-Louis Comolli, in a series of articles 'Technique et Idéologie' beginning in *Cahiers du Cinéma* no. 231; Jean-Louis Baudry, 'Ideological Effects of the Basic Cinematographic Apparatus,' *Film Quarterly* 28, no. 2 (Winter 1974–5): 39–47.

13 Quoted in *A Technological History of Motion Pictures and Television*, ed. Raymond Fielding (Berkeley and Los Angeles: 1967), p. 54.

14 Among the early three-component Technicolor films were: *Becky Sharp* (1935), *The Garden of Allah* (1936), *Trail of the Londsome Pine* (1936), *Snow White and the Seven Dwarfs* (1937), *Nothing Sacred* (1937), *Drums* (1938), *The Adventures of Robin Hood* (1938), *Goldwyn Follies* (1938), *Sweethearts* (1938), *Dodge City* (1939), *Gone with the Wind* (1939), *Northwest Passage* (1939), *The Wizard of Oz* (1939), *Jessie James* (1939), *The Thief of Bagdad* (1939).

15 I would not wish to assert that the slow diffusion of color technology was *solely* due to ideological factors. Undoubtedly there were technical problems, possibly greater than those encountered with sound films. And because color was more expensive there was an economic rationale for reserving its use for pictures which were expensive in other ways and which could be given special treatment by exhibitors (restricted runs in large urban theatres, etc.) *Gone with the Wind* would be an example. My main point, however, is that economic factors never exist in isolation, and that in the case of color economics and ideology are mutually reinforcing. See the remarks about luxury and scarcity below.

16 *Elements of Color in Professional Motion Pictures* (New York: 1957).

17 Op. cit., p. 501.

Chapter 6

STEVE NEALE

COLOUR AND FILM AESTHETICS

Colour, realism and spectacle

IN AN ARTICLE ENTITLED 'SOUND AND COLOR', Edward Buscombe has discussed the extent to which an ideology of realism has dictated debates about technology in the cinema, not only with respect to sound and colour, but also with respect to CinemaScope, 3D and so on: 'Economic theories can only partially explain technological innovations, since economics cannot say why innovations take the form they do, only why they are an essential part of the system. Economics can explain the necessary but not the sufficient conditions for innovation. No new technology can be introduced unless the economic system requires it. But a new technology cannot be successful unless it fulfils some kind of need. The specific form of this need will be ideologically determined; in the case of cinema the ideological determinant most frequently identified has been: realism.'[1]

Buscombe then goes on, however, to note that when colour first became technically feasible, it tended to connote, not reality, but fantasy. Because colour was initially associated with fantasy and spectacle its use tended to be restricted to genres like the cartoon, the western, the costume romance and the musical rather than the war film, the documentary and the crime picture. More than that, though, colour was a *problem* for realism because colour could distract and disturb the eye. Buscombe quotes Douglas Fairbanks' comments on colour after making *The Black Pirate* in 1927: 'Not only has the process of color motion picture photography never been perfected, but there has been a grave doubt whether, even if properly developed, it could be applied, without detracting more than it added to motion picture technic. The argument has been that it would tire and distract the eye, taking attention from acting, and facial expression, blur and confuse the action. In short it has been felt that it would militate against the simplicity and directness which motion pictures derive from the unobtrusive black and white.'[2]

Colour would, or could, 'serve only to distract the audience from those elements in the film which carried forward the narrative: acting, facial expression, 'the action'. The unity of the diegesis and the primacy of the narrative are fundamental to realist cinema. If colour was seen to threaten either one it could not be accommodated'.[3] Buscombe goes on to quote from *Elements of Color in Professional Motion Pictures*, an industry manual published in 1957. The manual indeed argues that the use of colour must be carefully motivated, subordinated to the story and 'the action': 'the objective being to have color "act" with the story, never being a separate entity to compete with or detract from the dramatic content of the picture'.[4] There are exceptions to the rule of realism, however, and these include the use of colour in musicals and fantasy films: 'Musicals and fantasy pictures are open to unlimited opportunities in the creative use of color. Here we are not held down by reality, past or present, and our imaginations can soar. Musicals and fantasies are usually designed to provide the eye with visual pleasure in the way that music pleases the ear'.[5]

Colour can be used 'creatively' in those genres whose rules of verisimilitude are not tied to conventions of realism in the way that other genres, like the war film and the documentary may be. Colour can be used 'creatively' in genres 'designed to provide the eye with visual pleasure'. Colour can similarly be used in the visual presentation of the female star: 'The feminine star . . . whose appearance is of paramount importance, must be given undisputed priority as to the color of make-up, hair and costume which will best complement her complexion and her figure. If her complexion limits the colors she can wear successfully, this in turn restricts the background colours which will complement her complexion and her costumes to best advantage.[6]

The basic potential contradiction to which Buscombe refers in the use and discussion of colour during the decades which saw its gradual diffusion throughout the industry and its range of basic genres, is the contradiction between colour as an index of realism and colour as a mark of fantasy, as an element capable, therefore, of disrupting or detracting from the very realism it is otherwise held to inscribe. The contradiction is by no means absolute. It is one which is managed, contained, in a number of different ways. One of the most persistent of these has been to combine a discourse of reality with a discourse of art and artifice. Colour is valued both because it is a 'natural' ingredient of visual reality *and* because it lends itself to artistic effects. Thus alongside a discourse in which Technicolor can advertise itself with the slogan 'Technicolor *is* natural color' or in which a Kinemacolor programme can describe the Kinemacolor process as 'The GREATEST INVENTION of the CENTURY Reflecting Nature in her ACTUAL COLORS', there is a discourse which constantly invokes artifice, art and, especially, the paintings of the 'Old Masters'. The Technicolor advertisement quoted above, in addition to invoking nature, contains the claim that 'Technicolor has *painted* for the millions of motion picture "fans" a new world'. (My emphasis.) *The Gulf Between*, the early Technicolor film, was described by *Motion-Picture News* in the following terms: 'unquestionably the finest natural color picture ever produced. The process . . . results in the absence of all "fringe", absence of eye strain and produces colors that are really natural. The invitation audience . . . was moved time and again to burst into applause of the sort that lasted long. The final shot, showing the sun setting over the water is beautiful – mindful of a Japanese painting'.[7]

The *New York Times* noted that in *The Black Pirate* (1926), 'The unrivalled beauty of the different episodes is mindful of the paintings of the old masters'.[8] The *Hollywood Reporter* described the use of colour in *Ramona* as follows: 'This picture in color raises the artistic status of the screen by several degress. it will be acclaimed the most beautiful motion picture ever filmed . . . The color goes beyond anything previously achieved. Not only has the Technicolor process yielded truer values, more transparent shadows, closer uniformity, and sharper definition, but the use of color in costumes, properties, background, and make-up shows a vastly finer taste and artistry.'[9]

Much was made of pictorial references to painters like Murillo, Goya and El Greco in Rouben Mamoulian's *Blood and Sand* (1941). Mamoulian himself explained that: 'After all, in making a motion picture, and especially in making a motion picture in color, we are essentially making a series of paintings. What does it matter if we are not painting our picture with water color or oil paint, but with colored light projected on a white screen? What does it matter if our picture moves and speaks? It is still fundamentally a picture. To what better source of inspiration could we turn than to the greatest masters of painting?[10]

Meanwhile, from a different perspective, Carl Dreyer, in discussing the use of colour in film, was to bemoan the lack of genuinely 'aesthetic' colour films: 'How many of them do we remember for the aesthetic pleasure they give us? Two-three-four-five? Possibly five – but probably no more. Castellani's *Romeo and Juliet* (1953) just manages to be among them – after Olivier's *Henry V* and Kinugasa's *Gate of Hell*. Olivier got his ideas for his color schemes from the illuminated manuscripts of the period. Kinugasa got his from the classical engravings of his people'.[11]

There is a shift, then, from nature to art. But there is also a shift, evident in these quotations, from a reference to art as a means of evoking and describing some of the effects produced by colour in excess of realism, to a reference to films which reproduce certain painterly styles not only to produce those effects, but also to organize and contain them. The effects in themselves are capable of producing the kinds of irritation and disturbance to which Fairbanks refers. Once organized and contained, once composed, though, they are also capable of producing the 'aesthetic pleasure', the 'visual pleasure' to which Dreyer and the manual Buscombe quotes respectively refer. The function of organising, composing and controlling those effects was not solely provided by borrowing styles and devices direct from the visual arts. It was provided more generally by those rules and techniques devised both in theory and practice for the subordination of colour to 'the unity of the diegesis and the primacy of narrative'. It was provided too by the rules and conventions governing the relative balance between narrative, on the one hand, and spectacle, on the other, since what colour tended to provide, above all else, was spectacle.

Hence the generic variation to which Buscombe refers, where colour tended to be accommodated much more easily by the cartoon and the musical than by the war film and documentary. Hence too the ways in which colour sequences tended to be used in films early on. In von Stroheim's *The Wedding March* (1929), for instance, a two-colour process was used to film a military parade. As the parade and sequence begin the narrative comes to a halt, and spectacle takes over. A similar use of colour in sequences is apparent in the early musicals. Motivation for the abandonment of narrative in favour of spectacle is provided by the musical numbers themselves. It was generally during the course of these numbers that colour was used.

Guy Green, a cinematographer working in Britain, writing in the late 1940s, indicates the extent to which colour was identified with spectacle – and the extent to which both colour and spectacle were potentially problematic in conventional realist drama. Having discussed the properties and potentials of colour, Green proceeds as follows:

> The obvious question arising out of this is: why not use these properties of colour photography deliberately, and the answer is simple. No one has yet found a completely satisfactory method. In one field it is used with great success – the musical. The Americans with consummate technical skill exploit colour's advantages over monochrome to the full and give us a dazzling and often breathtaking eyeful, and the colour is part of the show.
>
> Photography for dramatic subjects cannot be approached in this way. It must reflect the emotional content of the screen. It must help the audience forget that

they are in a cinema at all. It must not be a glorious spectacle all on its own. Therefore in some way it must be suppressed and made to lend itself to the subject dramatically.'[12]

Similarly, Major Cornwell-Clyne, writing at the same time, notes that the one of the major factors in antagonistic public reaction to colour centres on the extent to which colour 'attracts their attention from the "story"'.[13] He goes on, like Guy Green, to discuss the use of colour, the problem of colour, in the 'dramatic film': 'In the majority of films the material is principally concerned with dramatic episodes interpreted in terms of the motion picture technique. The subject of most pictures, namely, the focus of attention is diverted from the action of the drama, or from the drama in action, by a colour incident, arrangement or phenomenon, then such colour is an intruder destroying the unity of the film and usurping the proper functioning of other more important elements of the film dynamics.'[14]

Clyne proceeds then to elaborate what he himself terms 'a law': 'Colour should never attract the attention without carrying a significance necessary for the more complete presentation to the observer of the unfoldment of the drama.

The observer should never be conscious of colour at all until it means something.'[15]

These comments highlight both the extent to which colour as a spectacle was itself, however motivated, composed and controlled, to some extent incompatible with narrative and drama, and the extent to which, in any case, such motivation, composition and control was essential: 'The observer must never be conscious of colour at all unless it means something'. Technicolor, of course, was always very much aware of the need for such control. For many years, through the agency of Natalie Kalmus, who acted as Technicolor's colour consultant, the use of colour in film was subject to a very strict and particular aesthetic regulation. Kalmus always worked very closely on the design of colour in Technicolor's films: The script of every film is sent to her beforehand, and she prepares a colour chart, scientifically planned and thoroughly detailed. Colour, material blending, types of materials, paints and floor coverings are just a few of the items dealt with at length.[16]

Her stated ideology on the place and use of colour in film, because of her position an extremely important and influential one, is the conventional mixture of realism and art: colour as an index of reality and a source of aesthetic effects:

> Motion pictures have been steadily tending towards complete realism. In the early days, pictures were a mere mechanical process of imprinting light upon film and projecting that result upon the screen. Then came the perfection of detail – more accurate sets and costumes – more perfect photography. The advent of sound brought increased realism through the auditory sense. The last step – colour, with the addition of chromatic sensations – completed the process. Now motion pictures are able to duplicate faithfully all the auditory and visual sensations.
>
> This enhanced realism enables us to portray life and nature as it really is, and in this respect we have made definite strides forward. A motion picture, however, will be merely an accurate record of certain events unless we guide this realism into the realms of art. To accomplish this it becomes necessary to augment the mechanical processes with the inspirational work of the artist. It is not enough that we put a perfect record on the screen. That record must be moulded according to the basic principles of art.[17]

She goes on to concisely delineate the principle of motivation in the use of colour and its effects in order to join together the twin poles of reality and art: 'When we receive the script for a new film, we carefully analyse each sequence and scene to ascertain what domi-

nant mood or emotion is to be expressed. When this is decided, we plan to use the appropriate colour or set of colours which will suggest that mood, thus actually fitting the colour
to the scene and augmenting its dramatic value.'[18]

Colour is 'fitted' to the scene. It 'augments' its 'dramatic value'. Like the use of tinting
and toning, colour is determined by the 'dominant mood or emotion' (though because a spectrum of colours is available the rhetoric involved in a strategy of this kind is much less evident;
it is motivated, in its turn, by the 'realism' of colour cinematography). The use of colour is
at all points aesthetically motivated. It is subordinate to the narrative, the drama, the diegesis
rather than being an autonomous element. Finally, 'Unless the dramatic aspect dictates to the
contrary, it is desirable to have all the colours in any one scene harmonious. Otherwise, we
strike an unpleasant, discordant note.'[19]

Kalmus' views were not idiosyncratic. They were perfectly consonant with the aesthetic
views and practices of Hollywood as a whole with respect to colour and its use (as the quotations cited above amply testify). With some modification they are still prevalent today. Where
her views (and those of Technicolor in general) were contravened, as for instance when John
Huston used colour filters in shooting *Moulin Rouge*, they were contravened in minor detail.
And significantly, in this particular instance, the contravention was motivated by the wish
to evoke and refer to the style of a painter, Toulouse Lautrec. We are back again with spectacle, art and the organisation of colour's effects.

Colour and the female image

Thus a constellation of terms are used to refer to and to prescribe the presence and the use of
colour in film. Nature, realism, spectacle and art recur as the key terms within a discourse about
colour, its use and its effects. This discourse and these terms function so a to negotiate in theory
(and then in practice) some of the contradictions involved in using colour and some of the effects
it can produce. These effects can exceed either nature and realism on the one hand or spectacle
and art on the other (just as spectacle and art can exceed both narrative and drama). Neither the
one set of terms nor the other seems capable, on their own, of containing fully, in descriptive
terms, some of the effects to which they refer. Moreover, there is in any case at first glance a clear
contradiction between them. It is at this point that a further element, one which is just as constant, just as persistent, enters into the ideological equation. That element is the female body.
Since women within patriarchal ideology already occupy the contradictory spaces both of nature
and culture (since they therefore evoke both the natural and the artificial) and since also they are
marked as socially sanctioned objects of erotic looking, it is no wonder that from the earliest days
of colour photography they function both as a source of the spectacle of colour in practice and as
a reference point for the use and promotion of colour in theory. The female body both bridges
the ideological gap between nature and cultural artifice while simultaneously marking and focusing the scopophilic pleasures involved in and engaged by the use of colour in film.

As evidence, one might first point to the enormous number of early colour photographs
which depict not just women, but women either in natural settings or posed in a studio
with plants and flowers: 'Old Familiar Flowers' (1919), 'Nude' (1912), 'Grecian Study'
(1913), 'The Rose Arbour' (1914), 'Girl with Flowers' (1913), 'The Two Friends' (1927),
'Portrait of a Girl' (1916), 'Lady in an Orange Dress' (1915) and 'Molly Mulligan' (1914).
(These in addition both to simple colour portraits on the one hand and to pictures like 'La
Vulgarisation' (1909) on the other.)

Moving from the field of colour photography to colour in film, one can quote Eisenstein's
description of some of the early colour films he saw in Riga: 'The coloured short films always

seemed to have a pinkish tone, whether they showed the white sails of yachts skimming over the ultramarine sea, or variously colored fruits and flowers arranged by girls with flaming red or straw-yellow hair.[20]

Or Technicolor's 1930 advertisement, 'If rainbows were black and white', which begins 'Suppose that, since the world began, rainbows had been black and white! And flowers; and trees; Alpine sunsets; the Grand Canyon and the Bay of Naples; the eyes and lips and hair of pretty girls!

Cinematographer Ray Rennahan, in giving his views about the effect of colour films on the depiction of the female body, interweaves the terms and discourses of nature and art: 'beauty', like 'woman', is both natural and artificial. Rennahan argues for a new balance between the two, a shift away from the forms of artifice marking the depiction of women in black-and-white films: 'I consider that the coming of colour will mark a return of natural-ness in screen heroines. The reason is that Technicolor requires a very light make-up. An actress appearing before a colour camera could walk off the set into the street – and if her make-up were commented on it would probably be described as insufficient! Consequently the days of painting the lily are likely to pass. Natural beauty will be at a premium. Beauty that relies on the make-up expert will be under a cloud.'[21]

What this does not acknowledge is the degree of artifice necessary for the production of 'natural beauty' and the place both of Technicolor and of the female star in the production of 'glamour'. Rennahan's remarks about make-up can be counter-pointed both with the extent to which the arrival of Technicolor required a change in make-up techniques and in the produc-tion of make-up itself (a change in part consequent upon the extent to which, as Rennahan's remarks symptomatically suggest, colour accompanied and produced a new regime of female 'beauty') and with his own subsequent remarks, which indicate the extent to which the new 'natural beauty' in combination with the qualities of Technicolor as a process excluded certain types of 'natural' colouring. During the mid-1930s, Max Factor produced a new range of make-up expressly for use in Technicolor films, basing it upon a 'cake' rather than a paste or greasepaint format. Max Factor himself pointed to the complexities (the artifice) involved: 'Previous make-ups were based on various combinations of pink, yellow and white. Well applied, they may have looked very nice to the eye but the more critical color camera unmasks it for the glaringly unnatural thing it is. In analysing the human complexion with a spectro-scope, we found that the darker pinks, or red, are present as well as certain proportions of yellow, white and blue. This is true because the skin itself is essentially a translucent covering with very little color of its own. So our new make-up had to be made to blend with not one but a number of colors.'[22]

Factor went on to note some of the changes in practice colour involved: 'In black-and-white we worked with contrasts of light and shade. When making up a blonde, for example, we sought to heighten that tonal contrast by applying a rather dark make-up which gave a positive contrast to the light hair. In color, this is not the case. A blonde or brunette would use a make-up of a color in keeping with her own complexion . . . We are no longer striving for a purely artificial contrast but seeking to imitate and enhance the subject's natural coloring.'[23]

Rennahan, meanwhile, specifies both some of the components of the new 'natural beauty' – and some of the 'natural' colours it nevertheless excluded: 'The most important quality in a color star is a perfect skin. It should be clear and delicately colored. The technicolor process is exacting; in a close-up in this process even the pores are visible.

Next in importance is a distinct shade of hair. Mid-colours are difficult. Black, though often beautiful, is difficult to light. Platinum blonde is 'out' – the most difficult shade of all to photography and useless for Technicolor. It is already going by the board in Hollywood.'[24]

'Natural beauty', for all its contradictions, was nevertheless a constant in discourses linking together Technicolor and the female body: 'Most heartening, perhaps, were the reactions to the color camera's treatment of the female lead. Wrote one critic: "Loretta Young, the most appealing of the screen's ladies, wears a black wig, photographs beautifully in natural colors."

'Another notes: "Loretta Young . . . is graced by the Technicolor camera in a mood of idyllic beauty . . . Color close-ups of Miss Young are breathtaking gems."'[25]

As mentioned above, the discourse of 'natural beauty' existed alongside, in combination with, the discourse of 'glamour'. Here the extent to which the spectacle of colour in combination with the spectacle of the female body involved an explicitly eroticised male look was perhaps much more explicitly recognized: 'To film fans, particularly during Hollywood's 'glory years', Technicolor meant glamor, spectacle and excitement.'[26]

During the filming of *Gone with the Wind*, cinematographer Ernest Haller remarked, 'Whenever an established feminine star makes her first appearance in a color film the critics almost always exclaim at great length about the new personality color gives her.

'Now that we have this fast film, which enables a cinematographer to use all the little tricks of precision lighting he has used in monochrome to glamorize his stars, I am sure that color is going to be more flattering than ever to women.'[27]

'Betty Grable in Technicolor is balm for the eyes.'[28]

'It was wartime and there were millions of American G.I.'s around the world who wanted nothing more than to have lovely, talented ladies entertain them. Movies were a touch of home, and there were few things that pleased the men in the Armed Forces more than a Technicolor movie filled with attractive females.

The timing was perfect. Technicolor had managed to glorify the leading lady just when she was about to be in big demand. The combination of Technicolor and beautiful girls was hard to resist.'[29]

Whether conceived and articulated in terms of the discourse of 'natural beauty' or the discourse of 'glamour', what was in any case both crucial and central was the inextricable interrelationship between colour (specifically Technicolor) and the image of the female body within the particular regime of representation and spectacle which the advent of colour brought to mainstream cinema: 'Arlene Dahl was called 'the girl for whom Technicolor was invented'. She had red-gold hair, bright blue eyes, a flawless complexion, and two heart-shaped beauty marks – one above the corner of her mouth, the other on her shoulder.'[30]

'Maureen O'Hara was crowned "Queen of Technicolor" after only a few appearances before the color camera. What sounds like a publicist's inspiration came instead from the Technicolor Corporation itself, which used test footage of her during the early 1940s to help sell their process to the studios.'[31]

'Try to imagine *Gone with the Wind* without Technicolor. Or *Fantasia*. Or *Ben-Hur*. Or Betty Grable.'[32]

The dimensions of colour

The role of the female body within the regime of representation inaugurated by the introduction of Technicolor was one both of focusing and motivating a set of colour effects within a system dependent upon plot and narration, thus providing a form of spectacle compatible with that system, and of making and containing the erotic component involved in the desire to look at the coloured image. Colour was capable of disturbing that system. It requires careful control and regulation. That requirement was met both by the forms of aesthetic motivation described by Natalie Kalmus and others (including those provided by styles of painting and graphic art) and by the forms of visual treatment of the female body. This is not to say that those effects were ever fully controlled or that the subjective and erotic processes involved in and engaged by looking at coloured images were ever fully contained. Precisely what those effects were or what those processes involved is difficult to specify. Colour has rarely been discussed outside the parameters of an 'objective' discourse, on the one hand, and a 'subjective' discourse on the other. The 'objective' discourse simply links colour to the objects in reality which provide its point of reference. Colour in film, or in other forms of visual representation, is seen simply as a reflection of the colour involved in the perception of those objects. The 'subjective' discourse is concerned to explore the reactions of individual subjects to various different colours. The two discourses are linked together in those various attempts which have been made to establish and to codify the 'meanings' of different colours (whose those 'meanings' are viewed as either culturally specific or as in some senses universal). The problem here tends to be the over-rigid ascription of meaning, the attempt to reduce colour or colours to specific, verbalizable phrases or words or, at best, clusters of phrases and words. Each discourse, on its own, tends to operate a form of reduction. By contrast Julia Kristeva's writings on colour in painting have attempted to recognise each of these dimensions and elements. It is worth, therefore, by way of conclusion, looking more closely at what she has to say in an attempt to map out a set of conceptual parameters within which the effects and processes involved in the use of colour in film can begin to be discussed.

Kristeva sees colour as articulated across what she calls a 'triple register'. This triple register is comprised of the pressure exerted by psychic drives in relation to external objects; that same pressure as it arises from and is articulated across the body; and signification: 'The triple register is made up of a pressure marking an outside, another linked to the body proper, and a sign'.[33] She goes on to relate this register to colour: 'Color can be defined, considering what I have just said, as being articulated on such a triple register within the domain of visual perception: an instinctual pressure linked to external objects; the same pressure causing the eroticizing of the body proper via visual perception and gesture; and the insertion of this pressure under the impact of censorship as a sign in a system of representation.'[34]

Colour then, is neither purely subjective nor purely objective. Nor are its meanings simply a matter of cultural convention. It is instead a complex phenomenon involving all three levels or factors simultaneously, the objective ('external objects'), the subjective ('an instinctual pressure . . . causing the eroticization of the body') and the cultural ('the insertion of this pressure under the impact of censorship as a sign in a system of representation'): 'Thence color, in each instance, must be deciphered according to: (1) the scale of 'natural' colors; (2) the psychology of color perception and, especially, the psychology of each perceptions's instinctual cathexis . . . and (3) the pictorial system either operative or in the process of formation.'[35]

Colour is thus – above all – a complex and composite element: 'A preeminently composite element, color condenses 'objectivity', 'subjectivity', and the intrasystematic organization of pictorial practice. It thus emerges as a grid (of differences in light, energetic charge, and systematic value) whose every element is linked with several interlocking registers.'[36]

It could be noted at this point that this 'condensation' is most acute in colour photography and cinematography. 'Objectivity' is inscribed much more markedly into the photographic and cinematic image than it is into even the most realistic of painted images. Conversely, 'subjectivity' is less heavily marked. And within mainstream cinema, at least, the symbolic organization of colour tends to be heavily motivated. All the efforts of a Natalie Kalmus were directed towards the motivation of colour system, their subordination not just to narrative, but also to the referential properties of the cinematic image. Only on the fringes of Art Cinema (in some of the films of Antonioni, Godard and Resnais) and within the field of independent and avant-garde film have the symbolic properties of colour been explored to the full. This is not to argue, though, either that the 'intrasystematic organization' of colour did not exist in mainstream cinema or that there have not historically existed a distinct set of symbolic systems into which colour has been inserted. Kalmus' job was precisely to produce colour systems, not only for each film, but also for each scene and sequence within it, matching colour to mood and atmosphere and producing a mix and balance of colours appropriate to each particular segment. And one could point beyond the level of the organization of colour that she imposed to films which involve quite complex colour systems while remaining within the aesthetic and ideological ambit of 'realism': *The Cobweb*, *She Wore a Yellow Ribbon*, *Rebel Without a Cause*, *Written on the Wind*, and so on. One could point also to the differences (as well as the similarities) between 'natural' colour films and films involving tinting and toning. The latter inevitably involved a much more heavily stylized rhetoric of colour, if only because the range of colours available within any one scene was heavily limited.

Kristeva goes on to argue that colour is capable of escaping, subverting and disrupting the symbolic organization to which it is subject. Because it touches so centrally on the drives and pressures of the psyche in general and the unconscious in particular, it is capable of shattering the rules and laws to which it may be subject in any particular pictorial or cultural system. In this sense, colour 'achieves the momentary dialectic of law – the laying down of One Meaning so that it might at once be pulverized, multiplied into plural meanings. Color is the shattering of unity.'[37]

It is this aspect of colour that Hollywood, Technicolor, Natalie Kalmus sought to control. These were the effects that required organization. The capacity of colour to produce a 'pulverisation' of meaning, a multiplicity of meanings was marked, recognised and contained through the construction of colour systems, the matching of colour to dramatic mood, on the one hand, and to the referential exigencies of landscape, décor and so on the other. Cornwell-Clyne's dictum that the observer 'should never be conscious of colour at all until it means something' should perhaps then be slightly amended. The danger was not so much meaninglessness but rather an over abundance of contrary meanings. Colour ought only to bear the 'significance necessary'. No more, no less.

Notes

1   Edward Buscombe (1977), 'Sound and Color'. *Jump Cut*, no. 17, p. 24.
2   Buscombe, op. cit., p. 24.
3   Buscombe, op. cit., p. 24.
4   Buscombe, op. cit., p. 24.
5   Buscombe, op. cit., p. 25.
6   Buscombe, op. cit., p. 25.
7   Quoted in Basten (1980), *Glorious Technicolor*, pp. 26–7.
8   Quoted in Basten, op. cit., p. 37.
9   Quoted in Basten, op. cit., p. 74.
10   Quoted in Basten, op. cit., p. 127.
11   Carl Dreyer. 'Color and Color Films', in Lewis Jacobs (ed.). *The Movies as Medium* (New York: Farrar, Strauss & Giroux, 1970) p. 197.
12   Quoted in John Huntley, *British Technicolor Films* (London: Skelton Robinson, 1949) pp. 117–8.
13   Major A. Cornwell-Clyne, 'What's Wrong With Colour?' in Huntley, *British Technicolor Films*, p. 194.
14   Cornwell-Clyne, op. cit., p. 194.
15   Cornwell-Clyne, op. cit., p. 194.

16 John K. Newman (1949), 'Profile of Natalie Kalmus', in Huntley, *British Technicolor Films*, p. 148.

17 Natalie Kalmus, 'Colour', in Stephen Watts (ed.), *Behind the Screen* (London: Arthur Barker, 1938) p. 116.

18 Kalmus, op. cit., p. 121.

19 Kalmus, op. cit., p. 123.

20 Sergei Eisenstein (1970), 'One Path to Color', in Lewis Jacobs (ed.), *The Movies as Medium*, pp. 201–2.

21 Quoted in Huntley, op. cit., p. 25.

22 Quoted in Basten, op. cit., p. 71.

23 Quoted in Basten, op. cit., p. 71.

24 Quoted in Basten, op. cit., p. 25.

25 Basten, op. cit., p. 76.

26 Robert Surtees, 'Forward' to Basten. *Glorious Technicolor*, p. 9.

27 Basten, op. cit., p. 102.

28 New York Times review of *Wabash Avenue*, plate caption in Basten, *Glorious Technicolor*, p. 111.

29 Basten, op. cit., p. 102.

30 Basten, op. cit., p. 122.

31 Basten, *Glorious Technicolor*, p. 113.

32 Surtees, op. cit., p. 9.

33 Julia Kristeva, *Desire in Language* (New York: Columbia University Press, 1980) p. 218.

34 Kristeva, op. cit., p. 219.

35 Kristeva, op. cit., p. 219.

36 Kristeva, op. cit., p. 219.

37 Kristeva, *Desire in Language*, p. 221.

Chapter 7

RICHARD DYER

LIGHTING FOR WHITENESS

T HE PHOTOGRAPHIC MEDIA AND, *A FORTIORI*, movie lighting assume, privilege and construct whiteness. The apparatus was developed with white people in mind and habitual use and instruction continue in the same vein, so much so that photographing non-white people is typically construed as a problem.

All technologies work within material parameters that cannot be wished away. Human skin does have different colours which reflect light differently. Methods of calculating this differ, but the degree of difference registered is roughly the same: Millerson (1972: 31), discussing colour television, gives light skin 43 per cent light reflectance and dark skin 29 per cent; Malkiewicz (1986: 53) states that 'a Caucasian face has about 35 per cent reflectance but a black face reflects less than 16 per cent'. This creates problems if shooting very light and very dark people in the same frame. Writing in *Scientific American* in 1921, Frederick Mills, 'electrical illuminating engineer at the Lasky Studies', noted that

> when there are two persons in [a] scene, possibly a star and a leading player, if one has a dark make-up and the other a light, much care must be exercised in so regulating the light that it neither 'burns up' the light make-up nor is of insufficient strength to light up the dark make-up.
>
> (1921: 148)

The problem is memorably attested in a racial context in school photos where either the black pupils' faces look like blobs or the white pupils have theirs bleached out.

The technology at one's disposal also sets limits. The chemistry of different stocks registers shades and colours differently. Cameras offer varying degrees of flexibility with regard to exposure (effecting their ability to take a wide lightness/darkness range). Different kinds of lighting have different colours and degrees of warmth, with concomitant effects on different skins. However, what is at one's disposal is not all that could exist. Stocks, cameras and lighting were developed taking the white face as the touchstone. The resultant apparatus came to be seen as fixed and inevitable, existing independently of the fact that it was humanly constructed. It may be – certainly was – true that photo and film apparatuses have seemed to work better with light-skinned peoples, but that is because they were made that way, not because they could be no other way.

All this is complicated still further by the habitual practices and uses of the apparatus. Certain exposures and lighting set-ups, as well as make-ups and developing processes, have become established as normal. They are constituted as the way to use the medium. Anything else becomes a departure from the norm, or even a problem. In practice, such normality is white.

The question of the relationship between the variously coloured human subject and the apparatus of photography is not simply one of accuracy. This is certainly how it is most commonly discussed, in accounts of innovation or advice to photographers and film-makers. There are indeed parameters to be recognised. If someone took a photo of me and made it look as if I had olive skin and black hair, I should be grateful but have to acknowledge that it was inaccurate. However, we also find acceptable considerable departures from how we 'really' look in what we regard as accurate photos, and this must be all the more so with photography of people whom we don't know, such as celebrities, stars and models. In the history of photography and film, getting the right image meant getting the one which conformed to prevalent ideas of humanity. This included ideas of whiteness, of what colour – what range of hue – white people wanted white people to be.

The rest of this section is concerned with the way the aesthetic technology of photography and film is involved in the production of images of whiteness. I look first at the assumption of whiteness as norm at different moments of technical innovation in film history, before looking at examples of that assumption in standard technical guides to the photographic media. The section ends with a discussion of how lighting privileges white people in the image and begins to open up the analysis of the construction of whiteness through light.

Innovation in the photographic media has generally taken the human face as its touchstone, and the white face as the norm of that. The very early experimenters did not take the face as subject at all, but once they and their followers turned to portraits, and especially once photographic portraiture replaced painted portraits in popularity (from the 1840s on), the issue of the 'right' technology (apparatus, consumables, practice) focused on the face and, given the clientele, the white face. Experiment with, for instance, the chemistry of photographic stock, aperture size, length of development and artificial light all proceeded on the assumption that what had to be got right was the look of the white face. This is where the big money lay, in the everyday practices of professional portraiture and amateur snapshots. By the time of film (some sixty years after the first photographs), technologies and practices were already well established. Film borrowed these, gradually and selectively, carrying forward the assumptions that had gone into them. In turn, film history involves many refinements, variations and innovations, always keeping the white face central as a touchstone and occasionally revealing this quite explicitly, when it is not implicit within such terms as 'beauty', 'glamour' and 'truthfulness'. Let me provide some instances of this.

The interactions of film stock, lighting and make-up illustrate the assumption of the white face at various points in film history. Film stock repeatedly failed to get the whiteness of the white face. The earliest stock, orthochromatic, was insensitive to red and yellow, rendering both colours dark. Charles Handley, looking back in 1954, noted that with orthochromatic stock, 'even a reasonably light-red object would photograph black' (1967: 121). White skin is reasonably light-red. Fashion in make-up also had to be guarded against, as noted in one of the standard manuals of the era, Carl Louis Gregory's *Condensed Course in Motion Picture Photography* (1920): 'Be very sparing in the use of lip rouge. Remember that red photographs black and that a heavy application of rouge shows an unnaturally black mouth on the screen' (316).

Yellow also posed problems. One derived from theatrical practices of make-up, against which Gregory inveighs in a passage of remarkable racial resonance:

Another myth that numerous actors entertain is the yellow greasepaint theory. Nobody can explain why a performer should make-up in chinese yellow. . . . The objections to yellow are that it is non-actinic and if the actor happens to step out of the rays of the arcs for a moment or if he is shaded from the distinct force of the light by another actor, his face photographs BLACK instantly.

(ibid.: 317; emphasis in original)

The solution to these problems was a '"dreadful" white make-up' (actress Geraldine Farrar, interviewed in Brownlow 1968: 418) worn under carbon arc lights so hot that they made the make-up run, involving endless retouching. This was unpleasant for performers and exacerbated by fine dust and ultraviolet light from the arcs, making the eyes swollen and pink (so-called 'Klieg eyes' after the Kliegl company which was the main supplier of arc lights at the time (Salt 1983: 136)). These eyes filmed big and dark, in other words, not very 'white', and involved the performers in endless 'trooping down to the infirmary' (Brownlow 1968: 418), constantly interrupting shooting for their well-being and to avoid the (racially) wrong look.

It would have been possible to use incandescent tungsten light instead of carbon arcs; this would have been easier to handle, cheaper (requiring fewer people to operate and using less power) and pleasanter to work with (much less hot). It would also have suited one of the qualities of orthochromatic stock, its preference for subtly modulated lighting rather than high contrast of the kind created by arcs. But incandescent tungsten light has a lot of red and yellow in it and thus tends to bring out those colours in all subjects, including white faces, with consequent blacking effect on orthochromatic stock. This was a reason for sticking with arcs, for all the expense and discomfort.

The insensitivity of orthochromatic stock in yellow also made fair hair look dark 'unless you specially lit it' (cinematographer Charles Rosher, interviewed in Brownlow 1968: 262). Gregory similarly advised: 'yellow blond hair photographs dark . . . the more loosely [it] is arranged the lighter it photographs, and different methods of studio lighting also affect the photographic values of hair' (1920: 317).

One of the principal benefits of the introduction of backlighting, in addition to keeping the performer clearly separate from the background, was that it ensured that blonde hair looked blonde:

The use of backlighting on blonde hair was not only spectacular but *necessary* – it was the only way film-makers could get blonde hair to look light-coloured on the yellow-insensitive orthochromatic stock.

(Bordwell *et al.* 1985: 226; my emphasis)

Backlighting became part of the basic vocabulary of movie lighting. As the cinematographer Joseph Walker put it in his memoirs:

We found [backlighting] necessary to keep the actors from blending into the background. [It] also adds a halo of highlights to the hair and brilliance to the scene.

(Walker and Walker 1984: 218)

From 1926, the introduction of panchromatic stock, more sensitive to yellow, helped with some of the problems of ensuring white people looked properly white, as well as permitting the use of incandescent tungsten, but posed its own problems of make-up. It was still not so sensitive to red, but much more to blue. Max Factor recognized this problem, developing a make-up that would 'add to the face sufficient blue coloration in proportion to red . . . in order to prevent excessive absorption of light by the face' (Factor 1937: 54); faces that absorb light 'excessively' are of course dark ones.

Colour brought with it a new set of problems, explored in Brian Winston's article on the invention of 'colour film that more readily photographs Caucasians than other human types' (1985: 106). Winston argues that at each stage the search for a colour film stock (including the development process, crucial to the subtractive systems that have proved most workable) was guided by how it rendered white flesh tones. Not long after the introduction of colour in the mid-1930s, the cinematographer Joseph Valentine commented that 'perhaps the most important single factor in dramatic cinematography is the relation between the colour sensitivity of an emulsion and the reproduction of pleasing flesh tones' (1939: 54). Winston looks at one such example of the search for 'pleasing flesh tones' in researches undertaken by Kodak in the early 1950s. A series of prints of 'a young lady' were prepared and submitted to a panel, and a report observed:

> Optimum reproduction of skin colour is not 'exact' reproduction . . . 'exact repro-
> duction' is rejected almost unanimously as 'beefy'. On the other hand, when the
> print of highest acceptance is masked and compared with the original subject, it
> seems quite pale.
>
> (David L. MacAdam 1951, quoted in Winston 1985: 120)

As noted above, white skin is taken as a norm but what that means in terms of colour is determined not by how it is but by how, as Winston puts it, it is 'preferred – whiter shade of white' (ibid.: 121). Characteristically too, it is a woman's skin which provides the litmus test.

Colour film was a possibility from 1896 (when R. W. Paul showed his hand-tinted prints), with Technicolor, the 'first entirely successful colour process used in the cinema', available from 1917 (Coe 1981: 112–39). Yet it did not become anything like a norm until the 1950s, for a complex of economic, technological and aesthetic reasons (cf. Kindem 1979), among which was a sense that colour film was not realistic. As Gorham Kindem suggests, this may have been partly due to a real limitation of the processes adopted from the late 1920s, in that they 'could not reproduce all the colours of the visible spectrum' (1979: 35) but it also had to do with an early association with musicals and spectacle. The way Kindem elaborates this point is racially suggestive:

> While flesh tones, the most important index of accuracy and consistency, might
> be carefully controlled through heavy make-up, practically dictating the overall
> colour appearance, it is quite likely that other colours in the set or location had
> to be sacrificed and appeared unnatural or 'gaudy'.
>
> (ibid.)

As noted elsewhere, accurate flesh tones are again the key issue in innovation. The tones involved here are evidently white, for it was lighting the compensatory heavy make-up with sufficient force to ensure a properly white look that was liable to make everything else excessively bright and 'gaudy'. Kindem relates a resistance to such an excess of colour with growing pessimism and cynicism through the 1930s as the weight of the Depression took a hold, to which black and white seemed more appropriate. Yet this seems to emphasise the gangster and social problem films of the 1930s over and above the comedies, musicals, fantasies and adventure films (think screwball, Fred and Ginger, Tarzan) that were, all the same, made in black and white. May it not be that what was not acceptable was escapism that was visually too loud and busy, because excess colour, and the very word 'gaudy' was associated with, indeed, coloured people?

A last example of the operation of the white face as a control on media technology comes from professional television production in the US.[1] In the late 1970s the WGBH Educational Foundation and the 3M Corporation developed a special television signal, to be recorded on videotape, for the purpose of evaluating tapes. This signal, known as 'skin', was of a pale orange colour and was intended to duplicate the appearance on a television set of white skin. The process of scanning was known as 'skinning'. Operatives would watch the blank pale orange screen produced by tapes prerecorded with the 'skin' signal, making tones whenever a visible defect appeared. The fewer defects, the greater the value of the tape (reckoned in several hundreds of dollars) and thus when and by whom it was used. The whole process centred on blank images representing nothing, and yet founded in the most explicit way on a particular human flesh colour.

The assumption that the normal face is a white face runs through most published advice given on photo- and cinematography.[2] This is carried above all by illustrations which invariably use a white face, except on those rare occasions when they are discussing the 'problem' of dark-skinned people. Kodak announces on the title page of its *How to Take Good Pictures* (1984) that it is 'The world's best-selling photography book', but all the photo examples therein imply an all-white world (with one picture of two very pink Japanese women); similarly, Willard Morgan's *Encyclopedia of Photography* (1963), billed as 'The complete photographer: the Comprehensive Guide and Reference for All Photographers' show lack of racial completeness and comprehensiveness in its illustrative examples as well as its text (even under such entries as 'Lighting in Portraiture' (Lewis Tulchin 2116–2127), 'Portrait Photography' (Edward Weston 2952–2955), 'Portraiture – Elementary Techniques' (Morris Germain 2955–2965), 'Portraiture Outdoors' (Dale Rooks 2965–2973) or 'Portraiture with the Speedlamp' (Editorial Staff 2973–2977)). Fifteen years after *John Hedgecoe's Complete Photography Course* (1979), *John Hedgecoe's New Book of Photography* (1994) is neither any more complete or new as far as face is concerned (Hedgecoe is both a bestseller and Professor of Photographic Art at the Royal College of Art in London, in other words a highly authoritative source). Even when non-white subjects are used, it is rarely randomly, to illustrate a general technical point. The only non-white subject in Lucien Lorelle's *The Colour Book of Photography* (1955) is a black woman in what is for this book a highly stylized composition (colour Plate 7). The caption reads:

> Special lighting effects are possible with coloured lamps . . . and light sources
> included in the picture. Exposure becomes more tricky, and should be based on
> a meter reading of a key highlight such as the dress.

The photo is presented as an example of an unusual use of colour, to which the model's 'colourfulness' is unwittingly appropriate. The advice to take the exposure meter reading from the dress is itself unusual: with white subjects, it is their skin that is determinant. In Lucille Khornah's *The Nude in Black and White* (1993), nine out of seventy-four illustrations feature non-white subjects – six with parts of the body painted in zebra stripes and two making an aesthetic contrast of black and white skins, all cases which play on skin colour. Only one illustration, a black mother and child, does not seem to be making a point out of the non-white subjects' colour. Some more recent guidebooks randomly do include non-white subjects,[3] but even now there is no danger of excesses of political correctness.

The texts that the illustrations accompany make the same assumption that the human subject is white. Cassell's *Cyclopaedia of Photography* (1911) is clearly destined for a world in which there are only fair faces, whose colour it is important to capture even when nature is not on one's side: 'A common defect in amateur portraits taken out of doors is the dark appearance of the sitters' faces' (Jones 1911: 428).

The most recent edition of the *Focal Encyclopedia of Photography* does at least have the grace to be upfront about the matter in the entry on 'Skin Tone':

> When used as a standard for quality control purposes, it is assumed, unless stated otherwise, that the typical subject is Caucasian with a skin reflectance of approximately 36 per cent.
>
> (Stroebel and Zakia 1993: 722)

In all this, inventors, commentators and advice-givers are not to be found stating that, if you want to capture the look of the white face correctly, you need to do so and so. They never refer to the white face as such, for to do so would immediately signal its particularity. It is rather in describing facial and skin qualities that the unpremeditated assumption of a white face is apparent. Josef von Sternberg (1955–6: 109) affirms that 'the skin should reflect and not blot light', something more readily achieved with white skin. Gerald Millerson, discussing the relative light reflectance of skin tones (1972: 35), compares 'light' skin with 'bronzed', as if dark skin is, as it is for a white norm, only sun induced. A much more racially explicit example is provided in Eric De Maré's *Photography*, a much reissued Penguin book 'designed to help and stimulate the amateur photographer' (blurb to the 1970 edition). De Maré discusses the problems of light when shooting out of doors and, inevitably, takes a young (white) woman as the subject:

> [W]e consider her complexion to be at all times of a delicious, peachy pink but, exposing on a sunny day without correction filter to adjust the blue cast from the sky, we shall be *shocked* to find that the colour film has recorded the skin as having a slight indigo tint.
>
> (1970: 295; my emphasis)

The words 'indigo' and 'tint' were widely used with a racial, even racist, meaning in British English.

A major theme in instructional writing is the elimination of shadow. This is taken as a self-evidently and absolutely desirable goal in all but those cases where the aim is a sort of 'arty' expressivity. This obsession with getting rid of shadows established itself early. Victor Fournel, writing in 1858 about contemporary portrait photography practices, noted the already elaborate apparatus to hand to eliminate shadows, observing that 'what frightens the middle classes above everything else are the model's shadows: they can only see in them a blackness which darkens [*rembrunit*] and saddens the figure' (quoted in Rouillé and Marbot 1986: 15).

Shadows on the face are one of the major *Faults in Photography* in Kurt Fritsche's 1966 book; nearly all the advice on lighting in Eugene Hanson's ideologically riveting *Glamour Guide: How to Photograph Girls* (1950) is on avoidance of shadows. In a pair of illustrations to *Photography in Colour with Kodak Films* (Bomback 1957) (colour Plate 8), the superiority of eliminated shadows is affirmed by having the model smile slightly more in the less shadowed versions and adding effects of backlighting, thus emphasizing the upbeat quality of the image. As the argument in Chapter 2 might lead one to expect, in all these – and nearly all other – examples, the model (a properly ambiguous term) is a woman, already white and in the light, not struggling towards whiteness and the light.

Elimination of shadow is partly determined by the desire for visibility. The camera lens cannot see into shadows as flexibly as can the human eye and fill lighting compensates for this. Yet even this imperative to see, and to see women, suggests a concern with the visible that has marked the white era, while shadows cut across the association of white people with the light that is explored later in this chapter.

The white-centricity of the aesthetic technology of the photographic media is rarely recognised, except when the topic of photographing non-white faces is addressed. This is habitually conceptualized in terms of non-white subjects entailing a departure from usual practice or constituting a problem. An account of the making of *The Color Purple* (1985) speaks of the 'unique photographic problems that occur when shooting a film with basically an all black cast' and goes on to detail the procedures the cinematographer, Allen Daviau, used to deal with these 'problems', in particular 'having the set interiors and set decorations darker than *normal*' (my emphasis)[4] (Harrell 1986: 54). Cicely Tyson recalled her experience of filming *The Blue Bird* in Russia in 1976, where there was little experience of filming black people. A white woman had been used during the lighting set-ups:

> They light everything for her and then I'm expected to go through the same paces with the same lighting. . . . Naturally, my black skin disappears on the screen. You can't see me at all.
>
> (quoted in Medved 1984: 128–9)

The Moscow crew (at the white centre of the multiracial USSR) assumed that there were just 'faces', which meant that they assumed a universal white face, which in turn obliged Tyson to make a fuss and become constituted as an exception or problem. In 1994, in an interview in the magazine *US* (November: 102), the African-American actor Joe Morton (whose films include *The Brother from Another Planet*, *Terminator 2* and *Speed*) was still having to consider the way he is filmed a problem: 'for black actors, if you're not lit correctly, your skin tone can look very odd. You shouldn't be lit with certain shades of green and yellow. And, lots of black men have broad noses, and that can be exaggerated.'

Such examples are not confined to mainstream Hollywood productions. Basil Wright, a leading figure in British documentary in the 1930s, gives an account of shooting in the West Indies and the difficulties of having to film at midday, with the brilliance of the sun which 'kill[ed] all detail'.

> The crux of the *problem* was encountered when negro types [i.e. the normal inhabitants] had to be shot. With bright direct sunlight coming from overhead, it was almost impossible to get a good quality negative and yet retain the negro features. Rubbing the face and arms of the subject with butter or oil only brought up a few highlights, even when aided by reflectors. Finally the problem was solved by staging scenes *in the shade* and using reflectors only.
>
> (Wright 1933: 227; first emphasis mine)

Here, what is more evidently at issue is a still rather inflexible technology, developed and adjusted for the white face; Wright's solution however is very similar to that of Daviau for *The Color Purple* fifty years later.

In Kris Malkiewicz's book *Film Lighting*, based on interviews with Hollywood cinematographers and gaffers, four of the interviewees discuss the question of lighting for black people (Malkiewicz 1986: 141). They come up with a variety of solution: 'taking light off the white person' if there are people of different colour in shot (John Alonzo), putting 'some lotion on the [black person's] skin to create reflective quality' (Conrad Hall), using 'an orange light' (Michael D. Margulies). James Plannette is robust: 'The only thing that black people need is more light. It is as simple as that.' Even this formulation implies doing something special for black people, departing from a white norm. Some of the others (lotion, orange light) imply that the 'problem' is inherent in the technology, not just its conventional use.

Elsewhere, Ernest Dickerson, Spike Lee's regular cinematographer, indicates (1988: 70) the importance of choices made at every level of light technology when filming black subjects: lighting (use of 'warmer' light, with 'bastard amber' gels, tungsten lights on dimmers 'so they [can] be dialed down to warmer temperatures', and gold instead of silver reflectors), the subject (use of reflective make-up, 'a light sheen from skin moisturizer'), exposure (basing it on 'reflected readings on Black people with a spot meter'), stock ('Eastman Kodak's 5247 with its tight grain and increased color saturation') and development (using 'printing lights in the high thirties and low forties' to ensure that 'blacks will hold up to the release prints'). Dickerson is explaining his choices against his observation that 'many cinematographers cite *problems* photographing black people because of the need to use more light on them' (my emphasis). Much of his language indicates that he is involved in correcting a white bias in the most widely available and used technology: lights are warmer (than an implied cold norm), they are dialled down (from a usual cooler temperature), they are gold not silver, and the stock has more colour saturation. The whiteness implied here is not just a norm (silver not gold) but also redolent of aspects of the conceptualization of whiteness discussed in previous chapters: coldness and the absence of colour.

The practice of taking the white face as the norm, with deleterious consequences for non-white performers (unless they are consciously taken into account), is evident in films which not only have stars of different colours but also apparently intend to treat them equally. This may be out of a liberal impulse (Sidney Poitier with Tony Curtis in *The Defiant Ones* (1958)), an expression of star power (Eddie Murphy with Nick Nolte in *48 Hours* (1982)) or identification of a box office trend (the Danny Glover–Mel Gibson *Lethal Weapon* series (1987–92)). However, it is rare that the black actor is in fact lit equally. Such films betray the assumption of the white face built into the habitual uses of the technology and have the effect of privileging the white man; they also contribute to specific perceptions of whiteness. Let me take two examples. The first, *In the Heat of the Night* (1967), makes the white man not only more visible but also more individualized. The second, *Rising Sun* (1993), goes further in privileging and constructing an idea of the white man.

The Sidney Poitier character, Virgil Tibbs, in *In the Heat* is emblematic of the Northern, educated, middle-class black man. His adversary, but fellow cop, Bill Gillespie (Rod Steiger) is, on the contrary, a contradictory character. Tibbs is identified with his home turf (Philadelphia), whereas Gillespie, on whose turf (Sparta, Mississippi) the action unfolds, is in fact from another town and not really accepted by the local force: he is in a certain way more dislocated than Tibbs. He is unthinkingly bigoted but without the obsessive racism of the (white) rest of the town and police. He has a failed marriage in his past. He is an elaborated character, not a representative figure. Much of this is conveyed by dialogue and the two performers' different acting styles: Poitier's stillness and implied intensity, Steiger's busy, exteriorised method acting. It is also conveyed by lighting.

Poitier tends to be posed in profile or near silhouette, emphasising his emblematic presence; Steiger is more often shot face on, in, rather than against the light. Poitier is thus given considerable moral and intellectual authority, but little opportunity to display the workings of individuality on the face. In one scene, Tibbs (Poitier) and Gillespie (Steiger) are sitting talking together in the latter's home. There is a degree of *rapprochement* between them, with each revealing something of himself to the other. In the establishing shot, Poitier is screen left, sitting back in a reclining chair facing screen right, and Steiger is screen right, lying on

Figure 7.1   *Rising Sun* (USA 1993): Wesley Snipes, Harvey Keitel and Sean Connery (BFI Stills, Posters and Designs).

a couch. The only visible light source is a large table lamp behind Poitier. Poitier is thus profiled and semi-silhouetted, while the light falls full on Steiger's face. As the scene proceeds, most of the shots are close-ups. The table lamp casts both their faces in half light, but this is far more marked with Poitier, whereas Steiger is given some additional fill light, removing most of the shadow from the side of his face away from the lamp. The set-ups for the shots of Poitier remain more or less side-on to camera but, after a few similar shots of Steiger, the camera takes up a frontal position for him, with backlighting and a stronger fill. As a result, not only is Steiger more fully visible to us, but he can display a range of modulations of expression that indicate the character's complex turmoil of feelings and reminiscences. Poitier, by contrast, remains the emblematic, unindividualized, albeit admirable, black man.

Rising Sun (Figure 7.1)[5] is an expensive film involving an experienced director (Philip Kaufman) and often quite elaborate and attractive lighting set-ups (cinematographer Michael Chapman). It has two major stars in it, the black star (Wesley Snipes) having at the time of the film's appearance at least as much cinema box office clout as the white star (Sean Connery).

And it is a film that knows about race: a thriller pivoting on questions of American-Japanese antagonisms, it both gives Snipes and Connery, as the detectives on the case, some (black–white) racially conscious dialogue and includes an African-American ghetto sequence to make a point about the Snipes character's roots. In other words, this is a film that has no reason not to light its central male pair so that each comes off equally well (which means, of course, not, in technical terms, lighting them the same). In separate shots they are indeed lit differently, enhancing the character and beauty of their faces to equal effect. Yet in shots featuring both of them, Connery is advantaged. A clear example occurs early on when Snipes and Connery are interviewing a security guard on a building where a corpse has been found.

The guard is the most important character in the scene in terms of narrative (what has he seen?) and emotion (he is clearly holding something back for fear of losing his job); Snipes and Connery, as the stars and the investigators, have a different kind of importance, but one is not more important than the other. however, the lighting suggests otherwise. The guard is black. The scene is mostly shot with Connery standing between the guard (screen left) and Snipes (right). The light falls on Connery and is good for his colouring. His equal partner (Snipes) and the crucial witness (the guard), on the other hand, are shrouded in darkness.[6]

This example is caused by the assumption of the white face as a norm (get Connery right and the rest will fall into place); it has the effect of privileging the white performer. It also reproduces a particular construction of whiteness. The light catches Connery's temples, while Snipes and the guard are in darkness. Connery is literally but also figuratively enlightened; the light emphasizes his forehead, or, in effect, his brain. Elsewhere, in two-shots where some kind of intermediate light setting has been chosen, not ideal for either star, Snipes' skin shines whereas Connery's disappears in the light – the surface of Snipes' flesh is evident, his corporeality, whereas Connery's flesh is dissolved into the light.

The historical construction of whiteness through light, of which *Rising Sun* is a late product, is the subject of the rest of this chapter. Before moving to that, however, I should like to look at one last recent example, which suggests both that it is not technically impossible to film black people with the same effect as for whites but that it is culturally extremely difficult.

A Few Good Men (1992) concerns two marines on trial for the murder of another. One, Lance-corporal Dawson (Wolfgang Bodison), is African-American, a point to which the film makes neither explicit nor implicit reference. At one point in the trial, it is revealed that Dawson once disobeyed an order (itself a central issue to the marine ethics on which the case turns) by taking food to a marine who was being harshly punished for a trivial mistake by being imprisoned without food; this is a turning point, because it establishes Dawson's high moral character. The shot, of him listening to his attorney Lieutenant Kaffee (Tom Cruise) drawing attention to the moral significance of his disobedience, has strong, hard side and top lighting. Dawson's (Bodison's) hair is shaved at the sides but cut to a flat top. This gives it a relatively open texture which catches the light, creating a glow atop his head, striking in a generally darkly lit scene. His fellow, white, defendant is also in the shot, but his haircut has a rounder shape and the top lighting is less full on his head, though he still benefits from the quasi-halo effect. The lighting on Dawson in more conspicuous, partly because he is the one at issue in narrative terms, but also because there is somewhat more contrast between his bright hair and dark face and because it is so unusual to see an African–American shot like this. It shows that the latter is technically possible, yet not only is the lighting unusually hard and directed, it is also called forth at an expressly ethical moment – white performers benefit habitually from such light at the head, there does not have to be a strong moral point being made.

At the end of the film, Dawson is acquitted of the murder but still dishonourably discharged: the death was the accidental result of obeying an order to rough up a weak and awkward recruit. Dawson realizes that he should have disobeyed the order in accordance with a greater moral imperative. The final shot of him is taken at the door to the trial room, as Kaffee/Cruise is telling him that he does have honour because of this realization. There is no top lighting and Dawson stands before the dark wood of the door; despite the moral accolade, there is no longer any virtuous light at his head. The film cuts back to Tom Cruise, himself dark-haired but lustrous and tinged with light from above. His character has been much more morally ambiguous throughout, and even at this point his triumph is as much a career success as a sign of moral growth, yet now the white hero has the light no longer accorded the black character. Indeed, the recognition of the latter's virtue is given to Kaffee/Cruise, who tells him that he has honour, since he (Dawson) doesn't know it for himself: the white man, with that touch of light about his head, knows and names virtue in the black man, who now blends in with the darkness of the world.

Movie lighting in effect discriminates on the basis of race. As the rest of this chapter will argue, such discrimination has much to do with the conceptualization of whiteness. There is also a rather different level at which movie lighting's discrimination may be said to operate. What is at issue here is not how white is shown and seen, so much as the assumptions at work in the way that movie lighting disposes people in space. Movie lighting relates people to each other and to setting according to notions of the human that have historically excluded non-white people.

Movie lighting focuses on the individual. Each person has lighting tailored to his or her personality (character, star image, actorly attributes). Each important person, that is. At a minimum, in a culture in which whites are the important people, in which those who have, rather than are, servants, occupy centre stage, one would expect movie lighting to discriminate against non-white people in terms of visibility, individualization and centrality. I want however to push the argument a bit further. Movie lighting valorises the notion of the unique and special character of the individuals, of the individuality of the individual. It is at the least arguable that white society has found it hard to see non-white people as individuals; the very notion of the individual, of the freely developing, autonomous human person, is only applicable to those who are seen to be free and autonomous, who are not slaves or subject peoples. Movie lighting discriminates against non-white people because it is used in a cinema and a culture that finds it hard to recognise them as appropriate subjects for such lighting, that is, as individuals.

Further, movie lighting hierarchizes. It indicates who is important and who is not. It is not just that in white racist society, those who are not white will be lit to be at the bottom of the hierarchy, but that the very process of hierarchization is an exercise of power. Other and non-white societies have hierarchies, of course; it is not innate to white nature. However, hierarchy, the aspirational structure, is one of the forms that power has taken in the era of white Western society.

Movie lighting also separates the individual, not only from all other individuals, but from her/his environment. The sense of separation from the environment, of the word as the object of a disembodied human gaze and control, runs deep in white culture. The prime reason for introducing backlighting in film was to ensure that the figures were distinguished from their ground, to make them stand out from each other and their setting. This was regarded as an obvious necessity, so clearly part of how to see life that it was an unquestionable imperative. Yet it expresses a view of humanity pioneered by white culture; it lies behind its highly successful technology and the terrible price the environment now pays for this.

People who are not white can and are lit to be individualized, arranged hierarchically and kept separate from their environment. But this is only to indicate the triumph of white culture and its readiness to allow some people in, some non-white people to be in this sense white. Yet not only is there still a high degree of control over who gets let in, but, as I want to argue in the rest of this chapter, the technology and culture of light is so constructed as to be both fundamental to the construction of the human image and yet felt to be uniquely appropriate to those who are white.

Notes

1   I am grateful to William Spurlin of the Visual and Environmental Studies Department at Harvard University for telling me of this, explaining it and commenting on drafts of this paragraph.

2   This observation is based on analysis of a random cross-section of such books published this century. See Appendix at end of chapter.

3   See Appendix at end of chapter.

4   Film stock registers contrasts less subtly than the human eye, which tends, faced with real life, to compensate for excessive lightness or darkness; a black face against a light background, of set or costume, creates a strong contrast; adequately lighting a black performer's face in such circumstances (that is, directing more light at it than one would at a white person's face) risks bleaching out the sets and costumes.

5   Note that this figure, though illustrating the general point made in this paragraph, is a production still from a different scene to that discussed here.

6   José Arroyo notes Snipes coming off badly through lighting in a more recent vehicle for him (*Money Train* 1995): 'whenever there's a white person in the frame, discerning Snipes' features becomes a matter of eye-strain' (1996: 47).

Chapter 8

GIANLUCA SERGI

A CRY IN THE DARK
The role of post-classical film sound

THE WORD 'SOUND' HAS ALWAYS HAD SEVERAL positive meanings. Indeed, expressions such as *sound* thinking, a *sound* person and *sound* judgements belong to our everyday vocabulary. However, all this stops when we reach the realm of Film Studies. Here, sound seems like an obstacle in the way of the essence of cinema: the image. This bias against sound, generated mainly by early film scholars, was partly supported by the limitations that characterized Hollywood film production and reception prior to the mid-1970s, as we shall see. However, since then, a series of technological developments and changes in production and reception have ensued, and these have modified the ways in which film sound has been constructed, and the relationship between sound and image, audience and film. It is this period, which we may define as the 'Dolby era', upon which I wish to focus here. In exploring its characteristics I shall follow two distinct 'tracks', an aesthetic one and an economic one. It is in the interaction between them that one can perhaps begin to identify the parameters of what might be called 'post-classical' film sound.

The soundtrack: a misleading notion?

Before launching into any discussion of the role – or roles – of film sound, we need to confront a major problem: the lack of a proper vocabulary with which to articulate the complexity of the subject. Although this is true of other areas of film (production design and art direction come to mind), this particular lack is an acute one. There are several reasons for it. Film sound shares the same physical medium as music, that is, sound waves, and this has often helped to reinforce the use of musical terms in discussions of sound. This is particularly evident in the insistent use of terms like pitch, tone and timbre. These terms are relevant but insufficient. They are simply not flexible enough to articulate the complexities of contemporary soundtracks (for example, musical vocabularies are concerned with sound *per se*, while film sound works in symbiosis with the image). This problem is intensified by the disparity in critical attention given to popular music as compared to the cinema. Whereas in the UK at least there are a number of TV shows which set out to discuss or to analyse films (such as *Film 98* and *Moviewatch*), equivalent programmes on pop music simply present the product or performer without ever discussing their qualities or the ways in which they work (consider, for example, *Top of the Pops* and *The Chart Show*). In short, we have an inadequate vocabulary which is in any case rarely used in popular critical contexts. Perhaps we should attempt to side-step some of these problems by turning our attention to the soundtrack itself.

Rather than being conceived as a complex combination of different elements, the term 'soundtrack' has come principally to signify the music track of a film, dialogue being confined to another – 'superior' – realm, that of the screenwriter. This is a rather convenient way of arranging perception and appreciation. First, by singling out specific portions of a soundtrack, critics can praise the contributions of individual practitioners rather than focus on the much more complicated issue of what actually becomes of these contributions once they are recorded, mixed and reproduced not as independent elements, but as elements in a complex structure. Second, this type of approach betrays a certain attitude towards the more apparently 'ordinary' elements of the soundtrack, its everyday sounds: noise and silence. Critics seem to find it easier – and worthier – to focus on the art of the spoken word or the composed note than on the unsettling noise or the 'empty' silence. Yet it is precisely the relationships between all four elements – effects, music, dialogue and silence – that require investigation, and that mark the nature of the soundtrack itself. A soundtrack is like a cake. Each ingredient has its own distinctive flavour and makes its own individual contributions. However, once blended together they cannot and should not be separated one from another. Their contribution to the final product can only be considered by referring to the other ingredients and to the cake itself as a whole.

Pre-Dolby sound

Although production during the classical period did not present sound personnel with insurmountable technical and creative barriers, reproduction did, and damagingly so. The poor conditions of sound reproduction present in the vast majority of cinemas was a key factor. Quite simply, most film theatres were incapable of coping with complex soundtracks, and often produced distracting echoes and unwanted reverberations. Loudspeakers were capable of reproducing only a very limited frequency range (they were designed principally to reproduce audible speech), and powerful sounds were in general not a feasible option because of the risks (or certainties) of sound distortion. Moreover, the (mal)practice of exhibitors in 'pumping up the volume' in order that action films had maximum impact on spectators often had the effect of wiping out the more subtle dimensions of sound design. Given these limitations, film-makers could only feasibly employ a limited number of tracks if they were to avoid a cacophony of sounds, and tended to give aural priority to music and the human voice.

This is not to underestimate the aesthetic efforts or the technological advances of the 1950s and 1960s. The differences between then and now lie largely in the combination of standards of production and reproduction. Where with a film like *Spartacus* (1960), full stereo sound reproduction was possible with only a handful of (extremely expensive) 70mm roadshow prints in a handful of first-run cinemas, the soundtrack on *Star Wars* (1977) could be reproduced to high standards in most theatres thanks to the cheaper and more flexible Dolby system. Thus where the costs of quality sound reproduction in the 1950s and 1960s and the concomitant lack of good sound facilities in most theatres tended to inhibit the development of a more positive approach to film sound, the availability of Dolby has inspired confidence, and a concomitant willingness to experiment.

In the pre-Dolby era of the 1950s and 1960s, movie soundtracks were produced in-house by the studios, limiting external influences and generating a reliance on standard practices, established techniques and old sound libraries. In order to gauge the magnitude of the problem, it is worth bearing in mind that this was a period of profound changes and developments in aural terms. The 1960s witnessed the sweeping away of established listening patterns and the introduction of increasingly sophisticated experiments in sound recording and sound reproduction in the music industry as well as a much more 'aggressive' type of sound. Rock concerts in particular, with their blend of powerfully amplified music and enhanced 'sensual' experience (literally, sex, drugs and rock 'n' roll) introduced a new type of leisure activity engaging the 'participant' (no longer merely a 'spectator') on more than just an intellectual level. In addition, squeaky transistor radios were being rapidly replaced by affordable hi-fi systems capable of reproducing good quality sound. Consumers, spectators and participants could now enjoy better quality sound at concerts and in their homes than in the vast majority of cinemas. Films and film theatres desperately lagged behind and seemed unable to respond to such changes.

The unexplored potential of the medium was embodied in the fact that sound, a three-dimensional phenomenon, the *only* three-dimensional phenomenon in the movies, was being deployed in a one-dimensional manner, and not merely in the sense that sound reproduction was generally monophonic. To put it simply, the agenda informing the use of sound was that it should fulfil one principal requirement: to match the image without attracting unwanted attention. Even when we look at one of the most obvious areas for potential aural innovation, the musical, we find further evidence of a conservative use of sound. Hugely successful films like *Gigi* (1958) and *My Fair Lady* (1964) never really threatened the established power of the characters to open their mouths and summon up rivers of melody. Contrast this with later films like *American Graffiti* (1973) and *Saturday Night Fever* (1977), where music and its sources (a pirate radio station in *Graffiti*, a discotheque in *Fever*) must be actively sought for, and where the sounds of car engines and of New York slang are given such status that they are able to interrupt the sound of the music.

However, as these examples demonstrate, the early 1970s saw some film-makers trying to use sound in new and interesting ways despite the continuing limitations of technology and studio practice. Films like *The Conversation* (1974), *Jaws* (1975), and *Taxi Driver* (1976) all evinced a willingness to experiment with the soundtrack by choosing to foreground sound (as well as music) rather than using it solely as a backdrop to the image. Moreover, this time a willingness to experiment (especially on the part of the 'movie brats'[1]) intersected with the availability of a new and important technology.

Listen, here comes Dolby

The development of sound technology from the mid-1970s on has been extensively charted in the last few years, thanks to an increasing interest in the subject. Thus it will be sufficient here to highlight the three major changes central to an understanding of what follows. First, the mid-1970s saw the introduction of the *Dolby Stereo Sound System*. This was the first economically viable stereophonic system. Employing multi-channel technology, Dolby was able to reproduce a new range of sounds (thanks to its wider frequency range) and, most importantly, it provided improved conditions of reproduction in most theatres. Second, at the beginning of the 1980s, George Lucas and his collaborators developed the *THX Sound System*. Arguably the most ambitious sound project in film history, the TXH system enables conditions of reproduction in cinemas equal to those of professional mixing stages. In principle at least, it therefore enables the standardization of sound reproduction as intended by those

at the point of production.[2] Last, but by no means least, the late 1980s have seen the introduction of digital sound in three different systems: *DTS, Dolby Digital SR-D* and *SDDS*. This
is the present and future of film sound, extending frequency range to maximum capacity and
providing discrete multi-channel recording and reproduction.[3] It allows soundtracks to reproduce extremely powerful and detailed sound at virtually zero distortion, and has generated a
number of dramatic innovations. The result of these changes is that the situation now with
regard to sound production and reproduction is almost the reverse of the situation prior to
the advent of Dolby. I should like now to explore some of these changes in more detail.

Multi-layered sound

The first major development was the introduction of multi-channel recording technology. The
use of an analogy may help us to understand the relevance of this change. Let us imagine that a
film theatre has only one access door and that it is designed to admit twenty people at any one
time. Should more than twenty people be admitted, the result would be chaos. This is akin
to the situation prior to the mid-1970s, with the dominance of monophonic sound and hence
one channel or 'door'. The introduction of stereophonic technology meant the opening of
new doors to the same auditorium, and helped remove the old limitations as to the number
of tracks those who made films could employ. The result was the use of dozens of different
tracks, which meant that film-makers had to deal with an increasingly complex, and increasingly
multi-layered, 'architecture of sound', an architecture requiring careful planning, coordination
and control.

Multi-directional sound

One of the consequences of this development was that multi-channel sound was projected
into the auditorium from a number of different directions. Pre-Dolby 'classical' sound was
overwhelmingly one-directional, and originated for the most part from the centre of the
screen.[4] This limited the potential of the soundtrack to unsettle the audiences' reception of
a film. Spectators knew exactly what to expect and where to expect it from. Contemporary
Hollywood film sound is multi-directional. Thus film-makers now are able to challenge audience assumptions as to the range, power and source of sound and sounds. Theorists like
Mary Ann Doane have argued that the new sound technology has increased the capacity of
the apparatus to 'hide' itself.[5] I would argue on the contrary that the introduction of multi-
directional sound has displaced the reproduction of sound, at least physically, from the screen
to any point in the auditorium, hence alerting the audience to its place in a constructed
environment. In other words, if it is conventional to accept that a spaceship can move towards
us frontally, on the screen, it takes a bigger leap of the imagination to accept that it is flying
over our heads and into the auditorium from a point in the cinema lobby.[6]

Larger sound budgets and increasing numbers of sound personnel

The more complex soundtracks became, the higher the budgets devoted to sound could be.
Aside from the cost implications, this meant that more people could be employed to work on
the construction of a soundtrack. Gone is the solitary credit attributing sound to one individual

department head. In has come the listing on credits of more and more people (over fifty in the case of *The Fugitive* (1993) and *Speed* (1994)), and more and more specialist functions: sound designer, supervising and sound editor, sound editor, foley artist, sound recordist, sound mixer, and so on. Moreover, sound personnel are now often involved not just in production and post-production, but in pre-production and initial planning and design as well. Crucially, the waves of sound personnel who worked in Hollywood from the 1970s on came from a variety of sonic backgrounds. They brought an awareness of sound and the possibilities of sound, bridging established patterns and contemporary innovations in both technological and cultural terms, and thus helped to spur and to enable the technological and aesthetic innovations of the post-Dolby era.

The creation of new sounds

The combination of new technologies, larger budgets and new personnel had an important effect: the creation of 'new' sounds. In an era when soundtracks were mostly created in sound studios, this was an important and significant step. Indeed, it signalled a definitive break with the sound of the past. New sounds meant new styles, and in retrospect we can pinpoint two major styles or schools: the precise and detailed Bay Area sound, influenced by the electronic and esoteric stylizations of the 1960s, and the more gutsy New York Metropolitan sound, influenced, among other things, by rap and other forms of black music. Instances of the former can be found in Spielberg's films, from the sound of Indiana Jones' cracking whip in *Raiders of the Lost Ark* (1981) to the creaking of Schindler's jacket in *Schindler's List* (1993). Examples of the latter can be found in Scorsese's films, from Jake La Motta's punches in *Raging Bull* (1980) to the editing of the fast-talking dialogue and menacing sounds in *Goodfellas* (1990).[7]

Improved sound reproduction in cinemas

Following closely on developments such as these, the quality of sound reproduction in auditoria began to improve. Sound engineers designed new auditoria and helped adapt existing ones. Sound-absorbent material was used to minimize unwanted echo and reverberation; sound insulation was improved to muffle the noise produced by projectors and air conditioning equipment, and to prevent the sounds from adjacent auditoria interfering with one another. In this context, it is significant that Lucasfilm's THX Division developed not just a sound reproduction system, but a set of criteria for sound reproduction as a whole. These developments signalled a definitive shift away from the old sound hierarchies in which speech and music were accorded unconditional priority. New auditoria were built with all four elements of the soundtrack in mind.

New sounds, new pleasures: physical sound and heightened realism

During the course of the 1970s, Hollywood's use and conception of sound underwent a fundamental change. The possibilities of multi-channel technology, a wider frequency range and improved conditions of reproduction encouraged film-makers to feel more confident about sound, and led them to rely more and more on the soundtrack. As a result, contemporary film-makers have shown an increasing awareness of the 'physical', three-dimensional qualities of sound, and audiences are encouraged not just to listen to sounds but to 'feel' them – filmgoers experience sound more sensually than ever before. The extensive use of deep bass sounds, a legacy of the new 'aggressive' sounds associated first with rock then with rap, is a mark of this new physical style. However, it is not just a matter of matching 'big' sounds with 'big' images; it is rather a matter of achieving a startling, communicative effect. Thus in the opening sequence of *Terminator 2: Judgment Day* (1991), Linda Hamilton's voice-over guides us through the devastating effects of the machines' revolt against the humans. The camera picks out a human skull. As it lingers for a moment, all sounds fade. Then as the voice-over ends, a mechanical foot appears and crushes the skull. The deep bass sound employed at this moment (a sound hardly close to the 'real' sound an action like this would produce) is used both to startle the audience and to convey the mightiness of the struggle awaiting the humans in their fight against the machines. In such cases, to use an expression dear to sound designers, the sound 'breaks through the screen' and takes centre stage.

Another development, and a further departure from classical sound, is the use of what might perhaps best be defined as 'heightened realism'. By highlighting particular sounds and softening others, film-makers can enhance sound detail in such a way as to enable audiences to hear the unhearable. An example can be found in the opening sequence of *Indiana Jones and the Temple of Doom* (1984). Three villains try to outwit Dr Jones by tricking him into drinking a glass of poisoned champagne. They reveal the nature of what it is he has drunk by showing him a bottle containing the antidote. In the struggle that ensues, the bottle is flung across the dance floor amid scenes of chaos and confusion. Yet the sound of a bottle rolling on the floor is given prominence over all the other sounds we can hear.

Thus contemporary film sound, unlike the sound in classical Hollywood cinema, is significant not just in terms of its literal meaning, but also in terms of its weight, its power, its detail and its direction. Moreover, the complexities of the contemporary soundtrack alter the relationship between sound and image. No longer content to function merely as an aural backdrop, the soundtrack takes its place as a site of interest and experiment in its own right.

The economic dimension

The need to reconsider the role and relevance of film sound in contemporary Hollywood is as much a function of economics as it is of aesthetics. This is not just a matter of production costs. Other economic factors are at stake as well.

Since the 1920s in particular, sound, and in particular musical sound, has been of great importance in marketing of films, and as an ancillary commodity or off-shoot of the industry and its product. In the form of sheet music, of stars like Eddie Cantor and Al Jolson, and in the form of radio programmes and variety shows, the cinema, music and broadcasting industries have often been interlinked through the medium of sound, and sound itself used as a vehicle for attracting audiences to films. However, sound has never been such an important marketing force as it is today. Since the introduction of Dolby, the industry has enjoyed a slow but steady revival in terms of attendances, revenues and profits. Indeed, it is worth noting that the twenty biggest money spinners in Hollywood's history have been produced in the era of Dolby sound. Emphasis has often been placed on the visual aspects and attractions of these films. But it is at least worth noting the contribution that sound has made as well, as it is a vital element in the visceral aesthetic of the contemporary blockbuster.

One of the major factors here is the extent to which audiences were now able to enjoy sound of a quality that matched, and often surpassed, that of the sound they could enjoy at home. Producers were quick to exploit the qualities of surround sound, for instance, not just in the films, but also in trailers and advertisements.[8] Film exhibitors rose to the occasion and started to advertise their theatres as being equipped with 'true stereo sound', and today all major chains make a point of advertising those theatres equipped with THX or the latest digital system. In the last few years, the ever-expanding home video industry has elected and advertised surround sound as one of its principal commercial attractions. Meanwhile the advent of a wealth of consumer magazines run by a generation of sound-sensitive media journalists has been decisive in spreading knowledge about – and an appetite for – high quality sound both at home and in the cinema.

All these developments have accompanied and been accompanied by conglomeration, particularly in the multimedia field. Large media conglomerates have invested heavily in the sites of interaction between the film and music industries – it is no accident that as I write, the three biggest selling singles in the UK in the 1990s (after 'Candle in the Wind 97') were all showcased by films, and can all be found on their soundtracks.[9] Almost inevitably, interest – financial as well as intellectual – in the new sound technologies has spilled over into the computer industry, with Dolby developing Dolby Net, a surround sound system for the Internet.

In addition, one of the bloodiest corporate battles of the last few years has been waged over digital sound. All the major companies are involved in this battle, each having developed and marketed their own particular system. MCA-Matsushita (now MCA-Seargrave) has developed DTS,[10] CBS-Sony has responded with SDDS,[11] and Dolby has collaborated with Time Warner to produce Dolby Digital SR-D.[12] What has been impressive has been the pace of acquisition of what is still a relatively new technology. When Time Warner joined forces with Dolby to launch the Dolby Stereo Digital system in 1992, there were only a handful of theatres equipped to show *Batman Returns* (1992) in digital sound. Two years later, over 2,000 systems had been installed. Even more importantly, the availability of hardware has been increasingly matched by the availability of software. Most of the majors have now pledged to produce all their new features in one or more of the digital formats, and digital is now also available in the lucrative home video and TV markets.

Agendas for further research

Vast areas still remain to be researched. The relationship between sound and censorship is one. At present, there would appear to exist an unwritten rule that 'what you can't see can't hurt you', a rule which allows spectators to hear – but not necessarily see – crushing bones, searing flesh and record-breaking sexual activity. A further issue is the issue of pleasure. A great deal of attention has been paid to visual pleasure, but little to its aural equivalent. It is significant that we tend to think of production values in visual terms, not in aural ones, despite the fact that the sound of a screeching car tyre in an elaborate chase sequence can be just as important as the close-up of the tyre itself. Another issue worth exploring is the issue of genre. Genres have frequently been defined in visual terms – in terms, for instance, of iconography – but rarely in terms of what they sound like (the musical is the obvious exception). Yet in films like *Batman Returns* we are often confronted with images that are drawn from fantasy and sci-fi, juxtaposed with sounds reminiscent of those from a 1930s gangster film.

This is a long list of topics. What is at stake is the theoretical framework that we bring to the analysis of films. The place of sound in this framework has for too long been left in the dark.

Notes

1   See Lynda Myles and Michael Pye, *The Movie Brats, How the Film Generation took over Hollywood* (London: Faber, 1979).

2   However, as Rick Altman pointed out, the concept of 'correct' sound reproduction is by no means straightforward. See 'The sound of sound', *Cineaste*, vol. 21, nos. 1–2 (1995), p. 68.

3   Six channels for DTS and Dolby SR-D, and up to eight for SDDS.

4   The only exception, as we have seen, being a handful of extremely expensive 70mm roadshow prints, prints whose soundtracks mostly – and conventionally – prioritized music and speech.

5   Mary Ann Doane, 'Ideology and the practice of sound editing and mixing', in Teresa de Lauretis and Stephen Health (eds), *The Cinematic Apparatus* (New York: St Martin's Press, 1989), pp. 47–56.

6   One of the best-known examples of directional sound occurs in the opening sequence of *Star Wars*, in which a rebel fighter and an imperial destroyer are first 'heard' at the back of the auditorium before flying over the heads of the spectators and eventually appearing on the screen.

7   Although the directors mentioned may call the shots, it is important to remember that behind these examples are the names of some of the best sound designers in Hollywood: Ben Burtt, Skip Lievsay, Frank Warner, Walter Murch and a number of others.

8   Some of these, specifically filmed for trailer presentation, employed sound in a very aggressive fashion to win viewers' attention. The sound of the earth-rumbling thumps of a terminator or of the glass-shattering force of a twister will command the attention of even the most dedicated popcorn-munching audience.

9   These are: Bryan Adams' Everything I Do, I Do It for You', from *Robin Hood: Prince of Thieves* (1991), Whitney Houston's 'I Will Always Love You', from *The Bodyguard* (1992), and Wet, Wet, Wet's 'Love Is All Around', from *Four Weddings and a Funeral* (1994).

10 DTS stands for Digital Theatre Sound, a sound-on-disc system capable of providing six discrete channels. It was launched with *Jurassic Park* in 1993.

11 SDDS stands for Sony Dynamic Digital Sound, a sound-on-film system capable of providing up to eight discrete channels. It was launched with *The Last Action Hero* in 1993.

12 SR-D stands for Spectral Recording-Digital, a sound-on-film system capable of providing six discrete channels. It was launched with *Batman Returns* in 1992.

Chapter 9

STEPHEN PRINCE

TRUE LIES
Perceptual realism, digital images and film theory

DIGITAL IMAGING TECHNOLOGIES ARE RAPIDLY transforming nearly all phases of contemporary film production. Film-makers today storyboard, shoot and edit their films in conjunction with the computer manipulation of images. For the general public, the most visible application of these technologies lies in the new wave of computer-generated and computer-enhanced special effects that are producing images – the watery creature in *The Abyss* (1989) or the shimmering, shape-shifting *Terminator 2* (1991) – unlike any seen previously.

The rapid nature of these changes is creating problems for film theory. Because the digital manipulation of images is so novel and the creative possibilities it offers are so unprecedented, its effects on cinematic representation and the viewer's response are poorly understood. Film theory has not yet come to terms with these issues. What are the implications of computer-generated imagery for representation in cinema, particularly for concepts of photographically based realism? How might theory adapt to an era of digital imaging?

Initial applications of special-effects digital imaging in feature films began more than a decade ago in productions like *Tron* (1982), *Star Trek II: The Wrath of Khan* (1982), and *The Last Starfighter* (1984). The higher-profile successes of *Terminator 2*, *Jurassic Park* (1993), and *Forrest Gump* (1994), however, dramatically demonstrated the creative and remunerative possibilities of computer-generated imagery (CGI).

Currently, two broad categories of digital imaging exist. Digital-image processing covers applications like removing unwanted elements from the frame – hiding the wires supporting the stunt performers in *Cliffhanger* (1994), or erasing the Harrier jet from shots in *True Lies* (1994) where it accidentally appears. CGI proper refers to building models and animating them in the computer. Don Shay, editor of *Cinefex*, a journal that tracks and discusses special-effects work in cinema, emphasizes these distinctions between the categories.[1]

As a consequence of digital imaging, *Forrest Gump* viewers saw photographic images of actor Gary Sinise, playing Gump's amputee friend and fellow Vietnam veteran, being lifted by a nurse from a hospital bed and carried, legless, through three-dimensional space. The film viewer is startled to realize that the representation does not depend on such old-fashioned methods as tucking or tieing the actor's limbs behind his body and concealing this with a loose-fitting costume. Instead, Sinise's legs had been digitally erased from the shot by computer.

Figure 9.1   Digital compositing in *Forrest Gump*.

Elsewhere in the same film, viewers saw photographic images of President Kennedy speaking to actor Tom Hanks, with dialogue scripted by the film's writers. In the most widely publicized applications of CGI, viewers of Steven Spielberg's *Jurassic Park* watched photographic images of moving, breathing and chomping dinosaurs, images which have no basis in any photographable reality but which nevertheless seemed realistic. In what follows, I will be assuming that viewers routinely make assessments about the perceived realism of a film's images or characters, even when these are obviously fictionalized or otherwise impossible. Spielberg's dinosaurs made such a huge impact on viewers in part because they seemed far more life-like than the miniature models and stop-motion animation of previous generations of film.

The obvious paradox here – creating credible photographic images of things which cannot be photographed – and the computer-imaging capabilities which lie behind it challenge some of the traditional assumptions about realism and the cinema which are embodied in film theory. This essay first explores the challenged posed by CGI to photographically based notions of cinematic realism. Next, it examines some of the problems and challenges of creating computer imagery in motion pictures by drawing on interviews with computer-imaging artists. Finally, it develops an alternate model, based on perceptual and social correspondences, of how the cinema communicates and is intelligible to viewers. This model may produce a better integration of the tensions between realism and formalism in film theory. As we will see, theory has construed realism solely as a matter of reference rather than as a matter of perception as well. It has neglected what I will term in this essay 'perceptual realism.' This neglect has prevented theory from understanding some of the fundamental ways in which cinema works and is judged credible by viewers.

Assumptions about realism in the cinema are frequently tied to concepts of indexicality prevailing between the photographic image and its referent. These, in turn, constitute part of the bifurcation between realism and formalism in film theory. In order to understand how theories about the nature of cinematic images may change in the era of digital-imaging practices, this bifurcation and these notions of an indexically based film realism need to be examined.

This approach to film realism – and it is, perhaps, the most basic theoretical understanding of film realism – is rooted in the view that photographic images, unlike paintings or line

Figure 9.2 *Jurassic Park*: not the real T. Rex.

drawings, are indexical signs: they are causally or existentially connected to their referents. Charles S. Peirce, who devised the triadic model of indexical, iconic, and symbolic signs, noted that 'Photographs, especially instantaneous photographs, are very instructive, because we know that in certain respects they are exactly like the objects they represent . . . they . . . correspond point by point to nature. In that respect then, they belong to the second class of signs, those by physical connection.'[2]

In his analysis of photography, Roland Barthes noted that photographs, unlike every other type of image, can never be divorced from their referents. Photograph and referent 'are glued together.'[3] For Barthes, photographs are causally connected to their referents. The former testifies to the presence of the latter. 'I call "photographic referent" not the *optionally* real thing to which an image or sign refers but the *necessarily* real thing which has been placed before the lens without which there would be no photograph.'[4] For Barthes, 'Every photograph is a certificate of presence.'[5]

Because cinema is a photographic medium, theorists of cinema developed concepts of realism in connection with the indexical status of the photographic sign. Most famously, André Bazin based his realist aesthetic on what he regarded as the 'objective' nature of photography, which bears the mechanical trace of its referents. In a well-known passage, he wrote, 'The photographic image is the object itself, the object freed from the conditions of time and space which govern it. No matter how fuzzy, distorted, or discolored, no matter how lacking in documentary value the image may be, it shares, by virtue of the very process of its becoming, the being of the model of which it is the reproduction; it *is* the model.'[6]

Other important theorists of film realism emphasized the essential attribute cinema shares with photography of being a recording medium. Siegfried Kracauer noted that his theory of cinema, which he subtitled 'the redemption of physical reality,' 'rests upon the assumption that film is essentially an extension of photography and therefore shares with that medium a marked affinity for the visible world around us. Films come into their own when they record and reveal physical reality.'[7] Like Bazin, Stanley Cavell emphasized that cinema is the screening or projection of reality because of the way that photography, whether still or in motion, mechanically (that is, automatically) reproduces the world before the lens.[8]

For reasons that are alternately obvious and subtle, digital imaging in its dual modes of image processing and CGI challenges indexically based notions of photographic realism. As Bill Nichols has noted, a digitally designed or created image can be subject to infinite manipulation.[9] Its reality is a function of complex algorithms stored in computer memory rather than a necessary mechanical resemblance to a referent. In cases like the slithery underwater creature in James Cameron's *The Abyss*, which began as a wireframe model in the computer, no profilmic referent existed to ground the indexicality of its image. Nevertheless, digital imaging can anchor pictured objects, like this watery creature, in apparent photographic reality by employing realistic lighting (shadows, highlights, reflections) and surface texture detail (the creature's rippling responses to the touch of one of the film's live actors). At the same time, digital imaging can bend, twist, stretch and contort physical objects in cartoonlike ways that mock indexicalized referentiality. In an Exxon ad, an automobile morphs into a tiger, and in a spot for Listerine, the CGI bottle of mouthwash jiggles, expands and contracts in an excited display of enthusiasm for its new formula.[10]

In these obvious ways, digital imaging operates according to a different ontology than do indexical photographs. But in less obvious ways, as well, digital imaging can depart from photographically coded realism. Objects can be co-present in computer space but not in the physical 3D space which photography records. When computer-animated objects move around in a simulated space, they can intersect one another. This is one reason why computer animators start with wireframe models which they can rotate and see through in order to determine whether the model is intersecting other points in the simulated space. Computer-simulated environments, therefore, have to be programmed to deal with the issues of collision detection and collision response.[11]

The animators who created the herd of gallimimus that chases actor Sam Neill and two children in *Jurassic Park* (Figure 9.2) were careful to animate the twenty-four gallis so they would look like they might collide and were reacting to that possibility.[12] First, they had to ensure that no gallis actually did pass into and through one another, and then they had to simulate the collision responses in the creatures' behaviors as if they were corporeal beings subject to Newtonian space.

Spielberg's dinosaurs are referentially fictional

In other subtle ways, digital imaging can fail to perform Kracauer's redemption of physical reality. Lights simulated in the computer don't need sources, and shadows can be painted in irrespective of the position of existing lights. Lighting, which in photography is responsible for creating the exposure and the resulting image, is, for computer images, strictly a matter of painting, of changing the brightness and coloration of individual pixels. As a result, lighting in computer imagery need not obey the rather fixed and rigid physical conditions which must prevail in order for photographs to be created.

One of the more spectacular digital images in *True Lies* is a long shot of a chateau nestled beside a lake and surrounded by the Swiss Alps. The image is a digital composite, blending a mansion from Newport, Rhode Island, water shot in Nevada and a digital matte painting of the Alps.[13] The compositing was done by Digital Domain, a state-of-the-art effects house created by the film's director, James Cameron. The shot is visually stunning – crisply resolved, richly saturated with color, and brightly illuminated across Alps, lake and chateau.

Kevin Mack, a digital effects supervisor at Digital Domain who worked on *True Lies* as well as *Interview with the Vampire*, points out that the image is unnaturally luminant.[14] Too much light is distributed across the shot. If a photographer exposed for the lights in the chateau, the Alps would film too dark, and, conversely, if one exposed for the Alps in, say, bright moonlight, the lights in the chateau would burn out. The chateau and the Alps could not be lit so they'd both expose as brightly as they do in the image. Mack points out that the painted light effects in the shot are a digital manipulation so subtle that most viewers probably do not notice the trickery.

Like lighting, the rendering of motion can be accomplished by computer painting. President Kennedy speaking to Tom Hanks in *Forrest Gump* resulted from two-dimensional painting, made to look like 3D, according to Pat Byrne, Technical Director at Post Effects, a Chicago effects house that specializes in digital imaging.[15] The archival footage of Kennedy, once digitized, was repainted with the proper phonetic mouth movements to match the scripted dialogue and with highlights on his face to simulate the corresponding jaw and muscle changes. Morphs were used to smooth out the different painted configurations of mouth and face.[16]

When animating motion via computer, special adjustments must be made precisely because of the differences between photographically captured reality and the synthetic realities engineered with CGI. Credible computer animation requires the addition of motion blur to simulate the look of a photographic image. The ping-pong ball swatted around by Forrest Gump and his Chinese opponents was animated on the computer from a digitally scanned photographic model of a ping-pong ball and was subsequently composited into the live-action footage of the game (the game itself was shot without any ball). The CGI ball seemed credible because, among other reasons, the animators were careful to add motion blur, which a real, rapidly moving object passing in front of a camera will possess (as seen by the camera which freezes the action as a series of still frames), but which a key-framed computer animated object does not.

In these ways, both macro and micro, digital imaging possesses a flexibility that frees it from the indexicality of photography's relationship with its referent.[17] Does this mean, then, that digital-imaging capabilities ought not be grouped under the rubric of a realist film theory? If not, what are the alternatives? What kind of realism, if any, do these images possess?

In traditional film theory, only one alternative is available: the perspective formulated in opposition to the positions staked out by realists like Kracauer, Bazin, and Cavell. This position, which might be termed the formalist outlook, stresses cinema's capability for reorganizing, and even countering and falsifying, physical reality. Early exponents of such a position include Rudolf Arnheim, Dziga Vertov and Sergei Eisenstein. In his discussion of classical film theory, Noël Carroll has pointed out this bifurcation between the camps of realism and formalism and linked it to an essentializing tendency within theory, a predilection of theorists to focus on either the cinema's capability to photographically copy physical reality or to stylistically transcend that reality.[18]

This tension in classical theory between stressing the ways film either records or reorganizes profilmic reality continues in contemporary theory, with the classical formalist emphasis upon the artificiality of cinema structure being absorbed into theories of the apparatus, of psychoanalysis, or of ideology as applied to the cinema. In these cases, cinematic realism is seen as an *effect* produced by the apparatus or by spectators positioned within the Lacanian Imaginary. Cinematic realism is viewed as a discourse *coded* for transparency such that the indexicality of photographic realism is replaced by a view of the 'reality-effect' produced by codes and discourse. Jean-Louis Baudry suggests that 'Between "objective reality" and the camera, site of inscription, and between the inscription and the projection are situated certain operations, a *work* which has as its result a finished product.'[19] Writing about the principles of realism, Colin McCabe stresses that film is 'constituted by a set of discourses which . . . produce a certain reality.'[20]

Summarizing these views, Dudley Andrew explains, 'The discovery that resemblance is coded and therefore learned was a tremendous and hard-won victory for semiotics over those upholding a notion of naive perception in cinema.'[21] Where classical film theory was organized by a dichotomy between realism and formalism, contemporary theory has preserved the dichotomy even while recasting one set of its terms. Today, indexically based notions of cinema realism exist in tension with a semiotic view of the cinema as discourse and of realism as one discourse among others.

In some of the ways just discussed, digital imaging is inconsistent with indexically based notions of film realism. Given the tensions in contemporary film theory, should we then conclude that digital-imaging technologies are necessarily illusionistic, that they construct a reality-effect which is merely discursive? They do, in fact, permit film artists to create synthetic realities that can look just like photographic realities. As Pat Byrne noted, 'The line between real and not-real will become more and more blurred.'[22] How should we understand digital imaging in theory? How should we build theory around it? When faced with digitized images, will we need to discard entirely notions of realism in the cinema?

The tensions within film theory can be surmounted by avoiding an essentializing conception of the cinema stressing unique, fundamental propeties[23] and by employing, in place of indexically based notions of film realism, a correspondence-based model of cinematic representation. Such a model will enable us to talk and think about both photographic images and computer-generated images and about the ways that cinema can create images that seem alternately real and unreal. To develop this approach, it will be necessary to indicate, first, what is meant by a correspondence-based model and, then, how digital imaging fits within it.

An extensive body of evidence indicates the many ways in which film spectatorship builds on correspondences between selected features of the cinematic display and a viewer's real-world visual and social experience.[24] These include iconic and non-iconic visual and social cues which are structured into cinematic images in ways that facilitate comprehension and invite interpretation and evaluation by viewers based on the salience of represented cues or patterned deviations from them. At a visual level, these cues include the ways that photographic images and edited sequences are isomorphic with their corresponding real-world displays (e.g. through replication of edge and contour information and of monocular distance codes; in the case of moving pictures, replication of motion parallax; and in the case of continuity editing, the creation of a screen geography with coherent coordinates through the projective geography of successive camera positions). Under such conditions, empirical evidence indicates that naive viewers readily recognize experientially familiar pictured objects and can comprehend filmed sequences, and that continuity editing enhances such comprehension.[25]

At the level of social experience, the evidence indicates that viewers draw from a common stock of moral constructs and interpersonal cues and percepts when evaluating both people in real life and represented characters in the media. Socially derived assumptions about motive, intent, and proper role-based behavior are employed when responding to real and media-based personalities and behavior.[26] As communication scholars Elizabeth Perse and Rebecca Rubin have pointed out, '" people" constitutes a construct domain that may be sufficiently permeable to include both interpersonal and [media] contexts.'[27]

Recognizing that cinematic representation operates significantly, though not exclusively, in terms of structured correspondences between the audiovisual display and a viewer's extra-filmic visual and social experience enables us to ask about the range of cues or correspondences within the images or film, how they are structured, and the ways a given film patterns its represented fictionalized reality around these cues. What kind of transformations does a given film carry out upon the correspondences it employs with viewers' visual and social experience? Attributions of realism, or the lack thereof, by viewers will inhere in the ways these correspondences are structured into and/or transformed by the image and film. Instead of asking whether a film is realistic or formalistic, we can ask about the kinds of linkages that connect the represented fictionalized reality of a given film to the visual and social coordinates of our own three-dimensional world, and this can be done for both 'realist' and 'fantasy' films alike. Such a focus need not reinstate indexicality as the ground of realism, since it can emphasize falsified correspondences and transformation of cues. Nor need such a focus turn everything about the cinema back into discourse, into an arbitrarily coded reorganization of experience. As we will see, even unreal images can be perceptually realistic. Unreal images are those which are referentially fictional. The Terminator is a represented fictional character that lacks reference to any category of being existing outside the fiction. Spielberg's dinosaurs obviously refer to creatures that once existed, but as *moving photographic images* they are referentially fictional. No dinosaurs now live which could be filmed doing things the fictionalized creatures do in *Jurassic Park*. By contrast, referentially realistic images bear indexical and iconic homologies with their referents. They resemble the referent, which, in turn, stands in a causal, existential relationship to the image.[28]

A perceptually realistic image is one which structurally corresponds to the viewer's audiovisual experience of three-dimensional space. Perceptually realistic images correspond to this experience because film-makers build them to do so. Such images display a nested hierarchy of cues which organize the display of light, color, texture, movement, and sound in ways that correspond with the viewer's own understanding of these phenomena in daily life. Perceptual realism, therefore, designates a relationship between the image or film and the spectator, and it can encompass both unreal images and those which are referentially realistic. Because of this, unreal images may be referentially fictional but perceptually realistic.

We should now return to, and connect this discussion back to, the issue of digital imaging. When lighting a scene becomes a matter of painting pixels, and capturing movement is a function

Figure 9.3   *Forrest Gump*: computer-generated crowd.

of employing the correct algorithms for mass, inertia, torque, and speed (with the appropriate motion blur added as part of the mix), indexical referencing is no longer required for the appearance of photographic realism in the digital image. Instead, Gump's ping-pong ball and Spielberg's dinosaurs look like convincing photographic realities because of the complex sets of perceptual correspondences that have been built into these images. These correspondences, which anchor the computer-generated image in apparent three-dimensional space, routinely include such variables as surface texture, color, light, shadow, reflectance, motion speed and direction.

Embedding or compositing computer imagery into live action, as occurs when Tom Hanks as Gump 'hits' the CG ping-pong ball or when Sam Neill is 'chased' by the CG gallimimus herd, requires matching both environments. The physical properties and coordinates of the computer-generated scene components must be made to correspond with those of the live-action scene. Doing this requires precise and time-consuming creation and manipulation of multiple 3D perceptual cues. Kevin Mack, at Digital Domain, and Chris Voellman, a digital modeller and animator at Century III Universal Studios, point out that light, texture and movement are among the most important cues to be manipulated in order to create a synthetic reality that looks as real as possible.[29]

To simulate light properties that match both environments, a digital animator may employ scan-line algorithms that calculate pixel coloration one scan line at a time, ray tracing methods that calculate the passage of light rays through a modelled environment, or radiosity formulations that can account for diffuse, indirect illumination by analyzing the energy transfer between surfaces.[30] Such techniques enable a successful rendering[31] of perceptual information that can work to match live-action and computer environments and lend credence and a sense of reality to the composited image such that its computerized components *seem* to fulfill the indexicalized conditions of photographic realism. When the velociraptors hunt the children inside the park's kitchen in the climax of *Jurassic Park*, the film's viewer sees their movements reflected on the gleaming metal surfaces of tables and cookware. These reflections anchor the creatures inside Cartesian space and perceptual reality and provide a bridge between live-action and computer-generated environments (Figure 9.3). In the opening sequence of *Forrest Gump*, as a CG feather drifts and tumbles through space, its physical reality is enhanced by the addition of a digitally painted reflection on an automobile windshield.

To complete this anchoring process, the provision of information about surface texture and movement is extremely important and quite difficult, because the information provided must seem credible. Currently, many of the algorithms needed for convincing movement either do not exist or are prohibitively expensive to run on today's computers. The animators and renderers at Industrial Light and Magic used innovative software to texture-map[32] skin and wrinkles onto their dinosaurs and calibrated variations in skin jostling and wrinkling with particular movements of the creatures. However, while bone and joint rotation are successfully visualized, complex information about the movement of muscles and tendons below the skin surface is lacking.

Kevin Mack describes this limit in present rendering abilities as the 'human hurdle'[33] – that is, the present inability of computers to fully capture the complexities of movement by living organisms. Hair, for example, is extremely difficult to render because of the complexities of mathematically simulating properties of mass and inertia for finely detailed strands.[34] Chris Voellmann points out that today's software can create flexors and rotators but cannot yet control veins or muscles.

Multiple levels of information capture must be successfully executed to convincingly animate and render living movement because the viewer's eye is adept at perceiving inaccurate information.[35] These levels include locomotor mechanics – the specification of forces, torques, and joint rotations. In addition, 'gait-specific rules'[36] must be specified. The *Jurassic Park* animators, for example, derived gait-specific rules for their dinosaurs by studying the movements of elephants, rhinos, komodo dragons and ostriches and then making some intelligent extrapolations. Beyond these two levels of information control is the most difficult one – capturing the expressive properties of movement. Human and animal movement cannot look mechanical and be convincing; it must be expressive of mood and affect.

As the foregoing discussion indicates, available software and the speed and economics of present computational abilities are placing limits on the complexities of digitally rendered 3D cues used to integrate synthetic and live-action objects and environments. But the more important point is that present abilities to digitally simulate perceptual cues about surface texture, reflectance, coloration, motion, and distance provide an extremely powerful means of 'gluing' together synthetic and live-action environments and of furnishing the viewer with an internally unified and coherent set of cues that establish correspondences with the properties of physical space and living systems in daily life. These correspondences in turn establish some of the most important criteria by which viewers can judge the apparent realism or credibility possessed by the digital image.

Digital imaging exposes the enduring dichotomy in film theory

Obviously paradoxes arise from these judgements. No one has seen a living dinosaur. Even paleontologists can only hazard guesses about how such creatures might have moved and how swiftly. Yet the dinosaurs created at ILM have a palpable reality about them, and this is due to the extremely detailed texture-mapping, motion animation, and integration with live action carried out via digital imaging. Indexicality cannot furnish us with the basis for understanding this apparent photographic realism, but a correspondence-based approach can. Because the computer-generated images have been rendered with such attention to 3D spatial information, they acquire a very powerful perceptual realism, despite the obvious ontological problems in calling them 'realistic.' These are falsified correspondences, yet because the perceptual information they contain is valid, the dinosaurs acquire a remarkable degree of photographic realism.

In a similar way, President Kennedy speaking in *Forrest Gump* is falsified correspondence which is nevertheless built from internally valid perceptual information. Computer modelling of synthetic visual speech and facial animation relies on existing microanalyses of human facial expression and phonetic mouth articulations. The digital-effects artist used these facial cues to animate Kennedy's image and sync his mouth movements with the scripted dialogue. At the perceptual level of phonemic articulation and facial register, the correspondences established are true and enable the viewer to accept the photographic and dramatic reality of the scene. But these correspondences also establish a falsified relationship with the historical and archival filmic records of reality. The resulting image is perceptually realistic but referentially unreal, a paradox that present film theory has a hard time accounting for.

The profound impact of digital imaging, in this respect, lies in the unprecedented ways that it permits film-makers to extend principles of perceptual realism to unreal images. The creative manipulation of photographic images is, of course, as old as the medium of photography. For example, flashing film prior to development or dodging and burning portions of the image during printing will produce lighting effects that did not exist in the scene that was photographed. The tension between perceptual realism and referential artifice clearly predates digital imaging. It has informed all fantasy and special-effects work where film-makers strive to create unreal images that nevertheless seem credible. What is new and revolutionary about digital imaging is that it increases to an extraordinary degree a film-maker's control over the informational cues that establish perceptual realism. Unreal images have never before seemed so real (Figure 9.4).

Digital imaging alters our sense of the necessary relationship involving *both* the camera and the profilmic event. The presence of either is no longer an absolute requirement for generating photographic images that correspond to spatio-temporally valid properties of the physical world. If neither a camera nor an existent referent is necessary for the digital rendition of photographic reality, the application of internally valid perceptual correspondences with the 3D world *is* necessary for establishing the credibility of the synthetic reality. These correspondences establish bridges between what can be seen and photographed and that which can be 'photographed' but not seen.

Because these correspondences between synthetic environments and real environments employ multiple cues, the induced realism of the final CG image can be extraordinarily convincing. The digital-effects artists interviewed for this essay resisted the idea that any one cue was more important than others and instead emphasized that their task was to build as much 3D information as possible into the CG image, given budgetary constraints, present computational limitations, and the stylistic demands of a given film. With respect to the latter, Kevin Mack pointed out that style coexists with the capability for making the CG images look as real as possible. The Swiss chateau composite in *True Lies* discussed earlier exemplifies this tension.

The apparent realism of digitally processed or created images, then, is a function of the way that multiple levels of perceptual correspondence are built into the image. These establish reference points with the viewer's own experientially based understanding of light, space, motion, and the behavior of objects in a three-dimensional world. The resulting images may not contain photographable events, but neither do they represent purely illusory constructions. The reliability or nonreliability of the perceptual information they contain furnishes the viewer with an important framework for evaluating the logic of the screen worlds these images help establish.

The emphasis in contemporary film theory has undeniably shifted away from the naive notions of indexical realism in favor of an attention to the constructedness of cinematic discourse. Yet indexicality remains an important point of origin even for perspectives that reincorporate it as a variant of illusionism, of the cinema's ability to produce a reality-effect.

Figure 9.4   Computer imaging in *The Mask*.

Bill Nichols notes that 'Something of reality itself seems to pass through the lens and remain embedded in the photographic emulsion,' while also recognizing that 'Digital sampling techniques destroy this claim.'[37] He concludes that the implications of this 'are only beginning to be grasped,'[38] and therefore limits his recent study of the filmic representation of reality to non-digitized images.

Digital imaging exposes the enduring dichotomy in film theory as a false boundary. It is not as if cinema either indexically records the world or stylistically transfigures it. Cinema does both. Similarly, digital-imaging practices suggest that contemporary film theory's insistence upon the constructedness and artifice of cinema's discursive properties may be less productive than is commonly thought. The problem here is the implication of discursive equivalence, the idea that all cinematic representations are, in the end, equally artificial, since all are the constructions of form or ideology. But, as this essay has suggested, some of these representations, while being referentially unreal, are perceptually realistic. Viewers use and rely upon these perceptual correspondences when responding to, and evaluating, screen experience.

These areas of correspondence coexist in any given film with narrative, formal, and generic conventions, as well as intertextual determinants of meaning. Christopher Williams has recently observed that viewers make strong demands for reference from motion pictures, but in ways that simultaneously accommodate style and creativity: 'We need films to be about life in one way or another, but we allow them latitude in how they meet this need.'[39] Thus, Williams maintains that any given film will feature 'the active interplay between the elements which can be defined as realist, and the others which function simultaneously and have either a nonrealist character (primarily formal, linguistic or conventional) or one which can be called anti-realist because the character of its formal, linguistic or conventional procedures specifically or explicitly tries to counteract the cognitive dimensions we have linked with realism.'[40] Building 3D cues inside computer-generated images enables viewers to correlate those images with their own spatio-temporal experience, even when the digitally processed image fails in other ways to obey that experience (as when the Terminator morphs out of a tiled floor to seize his victim). Satisfying the viewer's demand for reference permits, in turn, patterned or stylish deviations from reference.

Stressing correspondence-based transformational abilities enables us to maintain a link, a relationship, between the materials that are to be digitally transformed (elements of the 3D world) and their changed state, as well as providing a means for preserving a basis for concepts of realism in a digitized cinema. Before we can subject digitally animated and processed images, like the velociraptors stalking the children through the kitchens of *Jurassic Park*, to extended meta-critiques of their discursive or ideological inflections (and these critiques are necessary), we first need to develop a precise understanding of how these images work in securing for the viewer a perceptually valid experience which may even invoke, as a kind of memory trace, now historically superseded assumptions about indexical referencing as the basis of the credibility that photographic images seem to possess.

In the correspondence-based approach to cinematic representation developed here, perceptual realism, the accurate replication of valid 3D cues, becomes not only the glue cementing digitally created and live-action environments, but also the foundation upon which the uniquely transformational functions of cinema exist. Perceptual realism furnishes the basis on which digital imaging may be carried out by effects artists and understood, evaluated and interpreted by viewers. The digital replication of perceptual correspondence for the film viewer is an enormously complex undertaking and its ramifications clearly extend well beyond film theory and aesthetics to encompass ethical, legal, and social issues. Film theory will need to catch up to this rapidly evolving new category of imaging capabilities and grasp it in all of its complexity. To date, theory has tended to minimize the importance of perceptual correspondences, but the advent of digital imaging demonstrates how important they are and have been all along. Film theory needs now to pay closer attention to what viewers see on the screen, how they see it, and the relation of these processes to the larger issue of how viewers see. Doing this may mean that film theory itself will change, and this essay has suggested some ways in which that might occur. Digital imaging represents not only the new domain of cinema experiences, but a new threshold for theory as well.

Notes

1   Telephone interview with the author, 19 October 1994.
2   Quoted in Peter Wollen, *Signs and Meanings in the Cinema* (Bloomington, IN: Indiana University Press, 1976), pp. 123–4.
3   Roland Barthes, *Camera Lucida: Reflections on Photography*, Richard Howard, trans. (New York: Hill and Wang, 1981), p. 5.
4   Ibid., p. 76.
5   Ibid., p. 87.
6   André Bazin, *What Is Cinema?* vol. 1, Hugh Gray (ed. and trans.) (Berkeley, CA: University of California Press, 1967), p. 14.
7   Siegfried Kracauer, *Theory of Film: The Redemption of Physical Reality* (New York: Oxford University Press, 1960), p. ix.
8   Stanley Cavell, *The World Viewed* (Cambridge, MA: Harvard University Press, 1979), pp. 16–23.
9   Bill Nichols, *Representing Reality: Issues and Concepts in Documentary* (Bloomington, IN: Indiana University Press, 1991), note 2, p. 268.
10   The design and creation of these ads are profiled in detail in Christopher W. Baker, *How Did They Do It? Computer Illusion in Film and TV* (Indianapolis, IN: Alpha Books, 1994).

11   See Ming C. Lin and Dinesh Manocha, 'Interference Detection Between Curved Objects for Computer Animation,' in *Models and Techniques in Computer Animation*, Nadia Magnenat Thalmann and Daniel Thalmann (eds), (New York: Springer-Verlag, 1993), pp. 43–57.

12   Ron Magid, 'ILM's Digital Dinosaurs Tear Up Effects Jungle,' *American Cinematographer*, vol. 74, no. 12 (December 1993), p. 56.

13   Stephen Pizello, '*True Lies* Tests Cinema's Limits,' *American Cinematographer*, vol. 75, no. 9 (September 1994), p. 44.

14   Telephone interview with the author, October 25, 1994.

15   Telephone interview with the author, October 25, 1994.

16   Ron Magid, 'ILM Breaks New Digital Ground for *Gump*,' *American Cinematographer*, vol. 75, no. 10 (October 1994), p. 52.

17   I do not wish to imply that photography was ever a mere mechanical recording of the visual world. During shooting, printing and developing, photographers found ways of creating their own special effects. Despite this, theorists have insisted upon the medium's fundamental indexicality.

18   Noël Carroll, *Philosophical Problems of Classical Film Theory* (Princeton, NJ: Princeton University Press, 1988).

19   Jean-Louis Baudry, 'Ideological Effects of the Basic Cinematographic Apparatus,' in *Narrative, Apparatus, Ideology*, Philip Rosen (ed.) (New York: Columbia University Press, 1986), p. 287.

20   Colin McCabe, 'Theory and Film: Principles of Realism and Pleasure,' in *Narrative, Apparatus, Ideology* (1986), p. 182.

21   Dudley Andrew, *Concepts in Film Theory* (New York: Oxford University Press, 1984), p.25.

22   Telephone interview with the author, 25 October 1994.

23   Noël Carroll has urged film theory in this direction by recommending smaller scale, piece-meal theorizing about selected aspects of cinema rather than cinema in toto and on a grand scale. See *Philosophical Problems of Classical Film Theory* (1988b), p. 255, and Carroll, *Mystifying Movies: Fads and Fallacies in Contemporary Film Theory* (New York: Columbia University Press, 1988a), pp. 230–34.

24   For a fuller discussion of this literature, see my essays 'The Discourse of Pictures: Iconicity and Film Studies,' *Film Quarterly*, vol. 47, no. 1 (Fall 1993), pp. 16–28 and 'Psychoanalytic Film Theory and the Problem of the Missing Spectator,' in *Post-Theory: Reconstructing Film Studies*, David Bordwell and Noël Carroll (eds) (Madison, WI: University of Wisconsin Press, 1996).

25   See Uta Frith and Jocelyn E. Robson, 'Perceiving the Language of Films,' *Perception*, vol. 4 (1975), pp. 97–103; Renee Hobbs, Richard Frost, Arthur Davis and John Stauffer, 'How First-Time Viewers Comprehend Editing Conventions,' *Journal of Communication*, no. 38 (1988), pp. 50–60; Julian Hochberg and Virginia Brooks, 'Picture Perception as an Unlearned Ability: A Study of One Child's Performance,' *American Journal of Psychology*, vol. 74, no. 4 (December 1962), pp. 624–28; Robert N. Kraft, 'Rules and Strategies of Visual Narratives,' *Perceptual and Motor Skills* no. 64 (1987), pp. 3–14; Robert N. Kraft, Phillip Cantor and Charles Gottdiener, 'The Coherence of Visual Narratives,' *Communication Research*, vol. 18, no. 5 (October 1991), pp. 601–16; Robin Smith, Daniel R. Anderson and Catherine Fischer, 'Young Children's Comprehension of Montage,' *Child Development* no. 56 (1985), pp. 962–71.

26   See Austin S. Babrow, Barbara J. O'Keefe, David L. Swanson, Renee A. Myers and Mary A. Murphy, 'Person Perception and Children's Impression of Television and Real Peers,' *Communication Research*, vol. 15, no. 6 (December 1988), pp. 680–98; Thomas J. Berndt and Emily G. Berndt, 'Children's Use of Motives and Intentionality in Person Perception and Moral Judgement,' *Child Development* no. 46 (1975), pp. 904–12; Aimee Dorr, 'How Children Make Sense of Television,' in *Reader in Public Opinion and Mass Communication*, Morris Janowitz and Paul M. Hirsch (eds), (New York: Free Press, 1981), pp. 363–85; Cynthia Hoffner and Joanne Cantor, 'Developmental Differences in Response to a Television Character's Appearance and Behavior,' *Developmental Psychology*, vol. 21, no. 6 (1985), pp. 1065–74; Paul Messaris and Larry Gross, 'Interpretations of a Photographic Narrative by Viewers in Four Age Groups,' *Studies in the Anthropology of Visual Communication* no. 4 (1977), pp. 99–111.

27   Elizabeth M. Perse and Rebecca B. Rubin, 'Attribution in Social and Parasocial Relationships,' *Communication Research*, vol. 16, no. 1 (February 1989), pp. 59–77.

28   I am indebted to Carl Plantinga for clarification of some of these distinctions.

29   Telephone interviews with the author. October 25, 1994.

30   Stuart Feldman, 'Rendering Techniques for Computer-Aided Design,' *SMPTE Journal*, vol. 103, no. 1 (January 1994), pp. 7–12.

31   With respect to digital-imaging practices, rendering is distinct from the phases of model-building and animation and refers to the provision of texture, light, and color cues within a simulated environment.

32   Texture-mapping is a process whereby a flat surface is detailed with texture, such as skin wrinkles, and can then be wrapped around a three-dimensional model visualized in computer space. Some surfaces texture-map more easily than others. Pat Byrne, at Post Effects, points out that spherical objects are problematic because the top and bottom tend to look pinched. Telephone interview with the author, 25 October 1994.

33   Telephone interview with the author.

34   Author's interview with Kevin Mack. See also Tsuneya Kurihara, Ken-ichi Anjyo and Daniel Thalmann, 'Hair Animation with Collision Detection,' in *Models and Techniques in Computer Animation* (1993), pp. 128–38.

35   See Stephania Loizidou and Gordon J. Clapworthy, 'Legged Locomotion Using HIDDS,' in *Models and Techniques in Computer Animation* (1993), pp. 257–69.

36   Ibid., p. 258.

37   Nichols, *Representing Reality*, p. 5.

38   Ibid., p. 268.

39   Christopher Williams, 'After the Classic, the Classical and Ideology: the Differences of Realism,' *Screen*, vol. 35, no. 3 (Autumn 1994), p. 282.

40   Ibid., p. 289.

Chapter 10

BARBARA CREED

THE CYBERSTAR
Digital pleasures and the end of the Unconscious

S OMEWHERE TOWARDS THE END of the much-publicized orgy scene in Stanley Kubrick's *Eyes Wide Shut* (1999) a group of men in cloaks, accompanied by two naked women, arms linked, stroll in front of the camera. The figures are not 'real': that is, they have been digitally generated on computer. The group of seemingly casual strollers appear 'real', seem to have the same ontological status as all the other figures in the orgy scene; but they do not. These figures were inserted in all US prints of Kubrick's film to block from view an explicit, sexual scene that would have earned the film a restrictive NC-17 rating. They are not flesh-and-blood actors, paid to perform before the camera; they were most likely generated from a whole-body Cyberware scanner purchased from a special effects studio such as the Californian company, Cyberware. Like the silvery, slippery, 'liquid metal' T-1000 robot in *Terminator 2: Judgement Day* (James Cameron, 1991) or the crowd that fills the dock scene in the opening sequence of *Titanic* (James Cameron, 1997), the computer-generated figures have no referent in the real world. These are not actors playing a part: rather they are what is known in the industry as 'synthespians', 'cyberstars' or 'vactors' (virtual actors) enacting the parts of extras historically played by real actors.

When film was invented at the turn of the century it was hailed as a spectacular and uniquely modern form of entertainment. It brought together the mechanical and mystical – a new form of technology that created the illusion of living characters whose images flickered magically on the screen before the astonished gaze of the modern subject. The cinema operated on many levels: it could create a comforting illusion of the real world; a universe which did not obey the laws of time, space or movement; a surreal stream of images that seemed to match the movement of the Unconscious. The technology of camera and celluloid film stock combined with actor and director to create a world which now – at the other end of the century – is about to be transformed by another phase of technological development which should prove equally astonishing. In the future there will still be movies, but no celluloid. If there is one thing that everyone working in the industry agrees upon it is that the cinema of the future will no longer depend on film.[1] The beginning of the twentieth century saw the birth of the mechanical camera; the end of the century appears to be witnessing its death.

Digital technology has already revolutionized the cinema: firstly in relation to new modes of film production such as picture imaging, sound and editing; and secondly in relation to new modes of audience reception brought about by new film forms – the blockbuster, inter-active CD-Roms, the digital creation of virtual worlds. Celluloid cinema dramatically altered the relationship of the individual to reality; the computer-generated image is about to change that relationship once again and in equally profound ways. Through special effects (anima-tion, miniaturization) it was once possible to create objects and things which did not exist, but which did have referents in the real world – objects, drawings, clay figures. Now it is possible to create computer-generated objects, things and people that do not have referents in the real world but exist solely in the digital domain of the computer. In other words, film has been freed from its dependence on history and on the physical world. Central to these changes is the possibility of creating a virtual actor, of replacing the film star, the carbon-based actor who from the first decades of the cinema has been synonymous with cinema itself. In the future, living actors may compete with digital images for the major roles in the latest blockbuster or romantic comedy.

At the moment, computer-generated images are used either obviously and dramatically to create astonishing special effects (the T. Rex chase and creature stampede in *Jurassic Park* [Steven Spielberg, 1993]) or are used invisibly to construct particular moments (the digital crowds in the opening sequence of *Titanic*). Although a film, animation aside, has not yet been made with a computer-generated or virtual film star in the main role, this appears to be the future. A digitized film star is a studio's dream: capable of performing any task, contin-uously available, cost effective – and no scandals, unless, of course, the digital star is given an offscreen life in order to keep alive other areas of the industry such as fan magazines, merchandizing and promotions. The possibility of digital stars playing the roles of main char-acters in feature films may sound like nonsense, but the signs are there.

In 1987 the Kleiser-Walczak Construction Company commenced the Synthespian Project: its aim was to 'create life-like figures based on the digital animation of clay models'.[2] It has been possible for some time digitally to paint an actor's face onto another actor's body when the unexpected occurs, such as the death of Brandon Lee during the filming of *The Crow* (Alex Proyas, 1994): a number of scenes were finished in this way. In 1997 George Lucas's company, Industrial Light and Magic, commenced work on constructing a composite virtual actor – a synthespian made up of the bodily parts of different live actors. Prior to the Brandon Lee resurrection, the California Senate drew up what has become known as the 'Astaire' Bill. The widow of Fred Astaire, backed by the Screen Actors' Guild, sought to restrict the use of computer-generated digital images of her husband. Alarmed at the possibility of such restric-tions the studios opposed the legislation, which still has to be finalized; but it appears as if it will be legally possible to digitize dead stars in the future.[3] Companies such as Virtual Celebrity Productions have already purchased the rights to use images of a number of famous stars, including Marlene Dietrich and Vincent Price. No doubt living stars may, in their lifetime, sell the rights to digitize their images after their retirement and/or death. Arnold's famous threat, 'Ill be back', may take on new meaning.

In 1998, the first posthuman talent agency was established by Ivan Gulas, a clinical psychologist from Harvard, and Michael Rosenblatt, co-founder of the Atlantic Entertainment group. Gulas, a specialist in 'the correlation between human emotions and expression' brought Justine, the Company's first synthespian, to life using software designed 'to recreate human cells for medical imaging'. According to Gulas, they were 'even able to wrinkle skin so it behaves like real tissue'.[4] Studios are already able to purchase whole-body scanners to create synthespians for crowd and group scenes from Cyberware; and synthespians have already been used in *The Voyage Home: Star Trek IV* (Leonard Nimoy, 1986) and *Titanic*.[5] Whether or not it will ever be possible to create a synthespian capable of giving a fully convincing, nuanced, intuitive human performance is another matter and one which gives rise to differing opinions. There is no doubt, however, that the presence of cyberstars in films will significantly alter the relationship between the spectator and the image.

Eyes Wide Shut is interesting to consider in this context. Kubrick's film is based on a novel written in 1926 by Arthur Schnitzler called *Traumnovelle*, meaning 'Dream Story'. The title *Eyes Wide Shut* suggests a state of dreaming, of seeing a flow of images with one's eyes shut. The film offers an intriguing blend of the real (an actual and well-known couple playing a fictional couple); the imaginary (the narrative of sexual desire and fantasy) and the hyperreal (computer-generated characters in the orgy scene). Although the studio was responsible for the digital alterations, the 'invisible' presence of computer-generated actors in a film about a dream world invites us to speculate about the possible effects the presence of virtual stars will have on audiences. If there is a mix of living stars and synthespians, will the presence of the latter affect the way in which the spectator relates to the former? Will audiences relate differently to the synthespian because the digital star is not human but an idealized composite of those traits thought to signify star quality?

In choosing Tom Cruise and Nicole Kidman, Kubrick was perhaps playing a little with his audience. With their ideal looks, perfect bodies, star qualities, fame, wealth and exotic lifestyles, Cruise and Kidman seem to epitomize the Hollywood dream. It is not difficult to imagine the Cruise–Kidman duo as a perfect combination on which to model a synthespian couple. They are the kind of actors who could well sign a lucrative deal to sell their 'images' as the basis for creating a synthespian duo in the future – whose performances could continue well after the living actors are dead. This would not just involve the rerun of old favourites, as now happens after an actor's death, but films starring dead actors in new digitally created performances. The spectator might well feel engulfed by a sense of the uncanny as she/he watches the dead reanimated. Cruise, in fact, plays a character in *Eyes Wide Shut* who lives on the surface of things, who is in desperate need of a bad dream, a nightmare – an Unconscious, perhaps – to wake him up to the possibilities of the real world. The possibility of the flesh-and-blood actor being replaced by a virtual actor – whether based on a famous dead actor or totally computer-generated – has interesting implications for a number of areas of theoretical concern to Film and Media Studies.

In *Acting in the Cinema*, James Naremore defines acting in its 'simplest form' as 'nothing more than the transposition of everyday behaviour into a theatrical realm'.[6] It seems that computer-generated actors have already been able to enact successfully 'everyday behaviour' in a relatively convincing manner. Most audiences are blissfully unaware that they have been watching synthespians performing in films such as *The Voyage Home*, *Titanic* and *Eyes Wide Shut*.

But could cyberstars act with the emotional intensity necessary to signify a range of feelings, from the most subtle to the most powerful? We are all familiar with the mythical Kuleshov experiment in which the film director intercuts the expressionless face of an actor with different scenes (a coffin, a small child, a bowl of soup) in order to create the illusion that the actor was performing with great emotion when in fact his expression did not change from one scene to the next. Audiences praised the actor's wonderful ability to express respectively grief, tenderness and hunger. The emotional impact of each scene was created through the editing process and the willingness of the audience to read emotions into the three different scenarios. It seems clear that a virtual actor would perform exceptionally well in a similar experience. Certainly, it should not be that difficult to replicate the action performances of a blockbuster hero such as Arnold Schwarzenegger. Given that Schwarzenegger has successfully played the role of a cyborg (*The Terminator* [James Cameron, 1984]) without changing his normal acting persona, it should prove relatively easy for a cyberstar to play the action-packed blockbuster roles of a figure such as Schwarzenegger. But could cyberstars give such extraordinary performances that they could elicit total audience identification, capturing an audience and holding it spellbound? At this point in time it is impossible to answer such a question – although some theorists and film-makers do argue that such a scenario is unfeasible. According to Ross Gibson, 'acting is an extraordinarily holistic, intuitive, improvisational display of intelligence . . . not everyone can be an actor, because not everyone has that type of intelligence which is emotional, intellectual and bodily. Certainly not every digital animatronics operator is going to have that kind of intelligence . . . actorly intelligence is an extraordinary thing. . . . I don't think it's going to happen.'[7] But what if it were? In her discussion of science fiction, Michele Pierson states that 'one of the most powerful discourses' on the new technologies relates to the possibility that 'this technology might one day produce images that are so realistic it is impossible to distinguish them from objects in the real world'.[8]

Baudrillard would, of course, denounce such a possibility as another instance of the death of reality.[9] But how important is the question of 'reality' in relation to representation? The power of technology to alter reality has, after all, always been an integral part of the cinematic process. In the coming era of digitized representation the crucial questions have less to do with reality than with communication. The important thing, as Miriam Hansen has argued, is not to deny the aesthetic of the day but to try to understand it and relate it to one's own experience.[10] At the moment postmodern audiences are still fascinated with the digital special effects associated with such blockbusters as *Jurassic Park*, *Independence Day* (Roland Emmerich, 1996), *Titanic* and *The Matrix* (The Wachowski Brothers, 1999). Eventually such effects will be taken for granted, just as the appeal of special effects lost their novelty in the early decades of the cinema. However, the presence of the synthespian in film is not meant to be perceived by the audience as a 'special effect' nor to draw attention to itself: the virtual or synthetic origins of the star will have to be rendered invisible by the text in order for the character to offer a convincing, believable performance. According to Scott McQuire:

> The most noticeable change is that the credibility of CGI is now judged, not against 'reality', but 'camera-reality'. This reflects the extent to which camera based images have been internalised as a standard of true representation.[11]

But even if the new measure of assessing reality becomes that of the virtual world, the desire for realistic performances will remain a key factor.

One thing upon which all commentators agree is that digital film has a markedly different look from that of celluloid. The flow of computer-generated images has a greater potential to appear seamless. The image itself appears to lack depth; it has a plastic look. A director can touch up a virtual actor's face – remove blemishes, enhance skin colour, accentuate bone structure, deepen eye colour. What difference will it make if the spectator knows that the actor, or composite actor, who appears to be a figure of flesh and blood was 'born' in a virtual world? The cyberstar is not subject to the same experiences as the living star, experiences such as mothering, oedipal anxiety, hunger, loss, ecstasy, desire, death. The cyberstar has no repressed desires or primal traumas. In short, the synthespian does not have an Unconscious. In her discussion of computer-generated space, Vivian Sobchack argues that virtual space is marked by a new flatness or depthlessness that critics such as Fredric Jameson have argued is endemic to psotmodernism.[12] How much of the power attached to the experience of identification is derived from the spectator's awareness – conscious or not – that the star on the screen has undergone experiences common to the human subject? To what extent will the virtual nature of the star's image induce in the spectator a sense of depthlessness in his/her relationship with the figure on the screen?

In her famous essay 'Visual pleasure and narrative cinema', Laura Mulvey argues that the 'cinema satisfies a primordial wish for pleasurable looking' not just at any human figure but at the glamorous erotic star. 'Stars provide a focus or centre both to screen space and screen story where they act out a complex process of likeness and difference (the glamorous impersonates the ordinary)'.[13] In particular, Mulvey is interested in the way in which the female star is represented as a 'perfect product': her body 'stylized and fragmented by close-ups, is the content of the film and the direct recipient of the spectator's look'.[14] The potential of the new cyberstar – male or female – to be constructed as a 'perfect product' is enormous. Given the iconic qualities that Mulvey notes are associated with the closeup, the spectator may easily surrender to the hypnotic power of the 'perfect product' on the screen. But the problem of depth – in relation to the image, the origin of the synthespian and the identificatory relationship – remains. Will the spectator experience an excess of pleasure in identifying with the cyberstar, subjecting the image to her/his erotic look, or will the spectator feel removed or distanced from the image on the screen because she/he is aware that the figure is not human, that it is an image which dwells permanently in the imaginary, totally removed from the symbolic order of loss, trauma and death? Knowing that a cyberstar cannot die in the human sense must affect the way in which the spectator responds to her/his appearance, particularly the star's beauty – a quality whose meaning always invokes its opposite, the threat of loss of beauty brought about by ageing and death.

The potential for the cyberstar to epitomize a digitized form of beauty that is flawless will, combined with the seamless nature of the digital image flow, create a clean plastic cinema based on organizational modes of creativity rather than on a play of improvization and intuition. McQuire states that many 'digital effects in contemporary cinema are concerned, not to create the perfect image, but to reproduce a camera image, so they'll add flaws like edge halation, lens flare, motion blur, even grain. This suggests that our point of reference has changed. It's not the real world, but cinematic representations of the world which have become our ground of comparison.'[15] Even if digital film-makers add noise or texture to the image, the impression of one-dimensionality may remain. The emphasis on spectacle and narrative tends to render the workings of the Unconscious invisible. This tendency would become even more marked in films featuring cyberstars. If spectators relate to the screen as a site where they can play out their fantasies, it may make a significant difference if the characters onscreen are played by synthespians, actors without an Unconscious.

One of the most potentially interesting sites for employment of cyberstars is the pornographic: not because pornographic texts do not require stars with great acting potential, but because pornography is itself bound up with the question of origins. The aim of the pornographic narrative is to capture and fetishize closeup images of sexual penetration, female expressions of orgasmic pleasure and images of penile ejaculation. The pornographic text constitutes an excessive representation of the primal scene. The cyberstar is ideally suited to pornography, particularly as the cyberstar will be able to enact with great ease the bodily contortions required in order to display closeup images of the act of penetration: in the new world of computer-generated images, all bodily actions, from the simplest to the most complex, will be produced by the computer. The new world of digital images will give rise to a new primal fantasy of origins in which human (desire) and nonhuman (stars) will combine in impossible ways.

If pleasure in looking at the human form is tied to a desire to identify with idealized figures, film stars who are both ordinary and extraordinary, this desire can clearly be met by the new digital screen technology. If the moment of recognition is, as Lacan argues, a moment overlaid with misrecognition (the subject imagines its mirror image to be more perfect than it is itself) then the new digital star would, like the celluloid star, offer an idealized image as basis for identification. Identifying with the glamorous, perfect image on the screen, the spectator would be caught up in a moment of recognition and misrecognition – not between subject and an ego ideal, but between subject and non-subject which, strangely, may also function as an ego ideal. In his discussion of the 'sublime time of special effects', Sean Cubitt raises the interesting possibility of special effects generating an image of the 'impossible real'.[16] Perhaps the new viewing subject will be caught up in an 'impossible real' of the identificatory processes.

In this context, the experience of identification would be marked by a sensation of strangeness. The experience of strangeness is based on an alteration, sometimes almost imperceptible, of reality, a reconfiguration designed to create an odd, uncanny effect, one of having one's 'eyes wide shut'. In *Camera Lucida*, Roland Barthes argues that within every photograph 'is the advent of myself as other',[17] and links this other image to 'the return of the dead'.[18] Asked to identify with a cyberstar, the spectator would be haunted by a sense of uncanny: the image on the screen appears human, and yet is not human. The glamorous other is a phantom, an image without a referent in the real, an exotic chimera, familiar yet strange.

Notes

1   Scott McQuire, *Crossing the Digital Threshold* (Brisbane: Australian Key Centre for Cultural and Media Policy, 1997), p. 41.
2   Scott McQuire, 'A conversation on film, acting and multimedia: an interview with Ross Gibson'. *Practice: a Journal of Visual, Performing and Media Arts*, no. 3 (1998), p. 14.
3   Lynden Barber, 'The vision splendid', *The Weekend Australian Review*, 25–6, September 1999, pp. 16–19.
4   James Daly (ed.), 'The people who are reinventing entertainment', *Wired*, November 1997, pp. 201–5.
5   David Pescovitz, 'Starmaker', *Wired* (October 1998), p. 153.
6   James Naremore, *Acting in the Cinema*, (Berkeley, CA: University of California Press: 1988), p. 21.
7   McQuire, op. cit., p. 8.
8   Michele Pierson, 'CGI effects in Hollywood science-fiction cinema 1989–95: the wonder years', *Screen*, vol. 40, no. 2 (1999), p. 167.
9   Jean Baudrillard, 'The precession of simulacra', in *Simulations*, trans. Paul Foss (New York: Semiotext(e), 1983b), p. 8.
10   Miriam Hansen, interviewed by Laleen Jayamanne and Anne Rutherford, 'The future of cinema studies in the age of global media: aesthetics, spectatorship and public spheres', *UTS Review*, vol. 5, no. 2 (1999), pp. 94–110.
11   McQuire, op. cit., p. 5.
12   Vivian Sobchack, *Screening Space* (New York: Ungar, 1987), pp. 225–6.
13   Laura Mulvey, 'Visual pleasure and narrative cinema,' in *Visual and Other Pleasures* (London: Macmillan, 1989), p. 18.
14   Ibid., p. 22.
15   McQuire, op. cit., p. 13.
16   Sean Cubitt, 'Le Réel, c'est l'impossible: the sublime time of special effects', *Screen*, vol. 40, no. 2 (1999), pp. 123–30.
17   Roland Barthes, *Camera Lucida* (London: Fontana, 1984), p. 12.
18   Ibid., p. 9.

PART THREE

Industries

THERE HAS ALWAYS BEEN A STRONG INTEREST in writing the history of the film industry. Often, it is true, that has been very much an economic history – or perhaps a political economy of the globalizing structures of the industry. Particularly in accounts of the dominance of the American film industry, the relation between the industry and its cultural contexts or consequences has not always been a prominent consideration. It is very different for accounts of what are usually called 'national' industries. Here, the economic story is entwined with other, often cultural nationalist, objectives. The attempt to find the means for industrial survival, for instance, involves the complex and contradictory task of competing with the major producers in the marketplace while nevertheless finding ways to produce films that meet cultural as well as commercial objectives.

All national film industries require some kind of subsidy or support in order to survive. While many are able to find moments of commercial success that seem, at the time, to be on the scale of those achieved by Hollywood, reproducing those moments consistently is simply beyond the capacity of the national film industries. However, while governments would rather their film industries did turn a profit, that is not necessarily the most important objective for the industries themselves – or for their local audience. Most national film industries are founded on the premise that it is important they continue to produce their own stories for their own audience. This is regarded as a form of cultural maintenance, a means of countervailing the cultural dominance of films from multinational and globally structured media conglomerates.

A film cultures reader must necessarily provide accounts of these minor film industries and they help to problematize conventional understandings of 'the film industry'. While Hollywood is unequivocally commercial in its structures and objectives, the national industries are the hybrid products of public and private funding, commercial and cultural objectives, and the competing discourses of the national and the international. As Tom O'Regan puts it in the opening selection of this section, 'national industries are simultaneously an aesthetic and production movement, a critical technology, a civic project of state, an industrial strategy and an international project formed in response to the dominant international cinema (particularly but not exclusively Hollywood cinema)'.

O'Regan's extract is taken from his book *Australian National Cinema* (1996). The reading reproduced here presents an overview of national cinemas in general as well as a more specific discussion of the attributes Australian cinema shares with those of other countries. It also offers an incisive account of the role played by national cinemas within an internationalizing industry, the products of which are components in a popular culture increasingly shared across national (and not only Western) boundaries. As O'Regan points out, national cinemas do not represent 'alternatives to internationalization, they are one of its manifestations'. The difference between these cinemas and those with which they aim to compete, is that their project of international integration employs the tactics of the weak against the strong. Among the tactics O'Regan examines is the use of the film festival circuit – largely a circuit that privileges aesthetic or cultural aspects over commercial potential – as a means of circulating and publicizing the products of the smaller national industries. Woven throughout his account is a series of snapshots of the history of the Australian industry from the early 1970s to the mid-1990s, which highlight the commonalities and the specificities of its performance as a national cinema.

The O'Regan reading chosen here probably downplays the ways in which Australian cinema has been hooked up to discourses of, or has in some cases constituted an explicit project of, national identity. This kind of alignment is directly called up, however, in John Hill's discussion of the British cinema. Concentrating on post-1980s British cinema, but referring back to a time when the British cinema addressed an homogeneous national audience relatively unproblematically, Hill's essay maps some significant changes.

Like O'Regan, Hill notes the increasing integration between the international and local markets, even in the case of films produced by national film industries, and speculates about the consequences of this for local production strategies. Hill also underlines the slightly paradoxical importance of the 'art-cinema' networks, both in festivals and distribution circuits, for the commercial survival of much British cinema. Further, he provides a detailed analysis of shifts in the size and demographics of 'the national audience' for British film in order to make the point that although the national audience for local films may have declined, the national television audience for these same films has massively increased. Finally, he argues that while it may be hard to find the object of a singular 'national address' in what is now a highly diverse British feature film industry, this may in fact reveal a cinema 'which is more fully representative of national complexities than ever before'. The previous ideological alignment between British cinema and 'myths of national unity', an alignment that Hill's own work has charted at some length, seems to have given way to a cinema which is prepared to 're-imagine' the British nation as producing multiple articulations of national identity.

Hong Kong cinema has articulated a local narrative and visual style, and established a strong local and regional market presence. It has also exported both its styles and its personnel in sufficient numbers to exert an influence over, in particular, the generic markers of recent Hollywood action cinema. As a result, the Hong Kong film industry became a substantial entity over the 1980s and 1990s. And yet, the story to tell about this industry at this point in time is not about finding structures or cultural policy. The Hong Kong industry has had to deal with a major historical shift that has the capacity to remake the society which produces these films.

In an extract from *Hong Kong Cinema: The Extra Dimensions*, Stephen Teo writes in the shadow of Hong Kong's handover to the People's Republic of China. In so doing, he links the consequent sense of crisis and concern about the future with a radically revised sense of the past that has elsewhere been referred to as postmodernist. The term seems to have been used locally to describe Hong Kong cinema in the 1990s, despite the fact that, as Teo describes it, much of the cinema of the period is in certain ways 'also profoundly anti-postmodernist'. Nevertheless, one can see why the label might apply. It is a hybrid cinema, where personal and political concerns jostle for space alongside commercial and entertainment-industry values. Like the city which produces it, Teo says, Hong Kong cinema is 'both East (from a Western point of view) and West (from a Chinese point of view), both subaltern and hegemonic . . . both premodern and postmodern'.

Teo's account of key films locates them within a cultural context where possible and iden-tifies trends and continuities with Chinese traditions as well as with western cinema history. The theme of postmodernism is useful as means of labelling the extraordinary inventiveness and the breadth of allusion and reference within the films. Teo, however, is concerned to connect what he calls 'new wave aesthetics' with Hong Kong's complex political and cultural history. He describes it as a culture 'caught in the tension between a desire to construct a non-colonial identity by mobilizing a sense of the past' (their Chinese heritage) 'and a profound anxiety about the possibility of that identity being imposed rather than being constructed autonomously' (that is, the risks faced by a capitalist culture as it is absorbed in the politics of China). It is a condition of operation few other national cinemas have had to face.

Perhaps the most influential phrase used in recent discussions of the popular film industry has been 'the New Hollywood'. Usually seen to apply to Hollywood's production practices, marketing strategies and the pattern of commercial priorities since the 1970s, the phrase has been useful but also a little mystifying. In order to sift through the shifts variously dealt with under this term, Thomas Schatz's essay sets out an industrial and textual history of Hollywood's economic, aesthetic and technological changes since the end of World War II, but most specific-ally since 1975. Among the factors noted are the dominance of the blockbuster in Hollywood's commercial strategies since the release of *Jaws*; the marketing of individual films as the trade-mark for a range of merchandise and commodities; the challenges presented by pay TV and the VCR; and the recent generic stratification of the production industry to the US. Schatz presents an overview of the current state of the industry as well as a detailed account of the various conjunctural determinants which took it there. Fundamental to this account is the thoroughness with which the global conglomerates that now run the industry see individual films as broad commercial entities. Tied into music soundtracks, branded clothing and theme park rides, successful films have become franchise operations. As Schatz points out, in 'today's media marketplace, it has become virtually impossible to identify or isolate ''the text'' itself, or to distinguish a film's aesthetic or narrative quality from its commercial imperatives'. As a result, the study of film now requires an even broader range of disciplinary orientations and understandings than was previously the case.

This is underlined by Tino Balio's discussion of the changes that have occurred as a conse-quence of Hollywood's globalization in the 1990s. Outlining the program of mergers and corporate maneouvres which have taken place over the last decade, Balio introduces us to the new economics which now organize the international trade in feature films. What becomes clear as we go through Balio's essay is that it is no longer possible to think of the film industry as a separate sphere of economic activity. He describes an industrial environment which has been significantly affected by the importance of home video and pay television earnings and the increasing significance of the non-US market to US-based film producers as the development of shopping mall multiplexes outside the US accelerates. Also fundamentally important is the global concentration of media ownership which goes hand-in-hand with the diversification of the interests of these media proprietors. It is routine now for the major companies to pursue market dominance across the full range of media forms, as broadcast and pay television, video, film, telecommunications and information technologies converge. These shifts carry important textual consequences, of course, which Balio reveals as he describes the careers of specific films and locates their development within the commercial decision-making structures of their producers.

Balio's orientation is very much that of an economic historian; he tends not to offer critical judgements on the situation he describes – in the way that Schatz, for instance, does. Consequently, his account does not address the social or cultural consequences of the phenomenon he describes, as small indigenous industries such as those Tom O'Regan defends find themselves swamped in their own home markets by the scale of Hollywood's 'presence in all the world's major markets'.

Chapter 11

TOM O'REGAN

A NATIONAL CINEMA

Introduction

'**WHAT DOES AUSTRALIAN CINEMA** *have in common with other national cinemas* – no matter how diverse?' This chapter answers this question by establishing the characteristics of national cinemas generally through a survey of different aspects of Australian cinema. In inspecting Australian and other cinemas, I aim to generalize the shape and outlook of national cinema as a category. Like all national cinemas, the Australian cinema contends with Hollywood dominance, it is simultaneously a local and international form, it is a producer of festival cinema, it has a significant relation with the nation and the state, and it is constitutionally fuzzy. National cinemas are simultaneously an aesthetic and production movement, a critical technology, a civic project of state, an industrial strategy and an international project formed in response to the dominant international cinemas (particularly but not exclusively Hollywood cinema). Australian cinema is formed as a relation to Hollywood and other national cinemas.

National cinemas and le défi américain

> Alternative cinemas gain their significance and force partly because they seek to undermine the common equation of 'the movies' with 'Hollywood'.
> (Kristin Thompson 1985: 170)

> If you can't stand the heat, get out of the kitchen, living in the twentieth century means learning to be American.
> (Dusan Makavejev quoted in Elsaesser 1994: 24)

The American cinema looms large as a term of reference for every national cinema in the West and many beyond. Curiously, the US cinema is in many respects like other national cinemas. It relies in the first instance on the certainties of its domestic market, it is embedded in a particular industrial, policy and aesthetic milieu, it has dynamics that are simultaneously local and international, and it negotiates particular social, cultural and ethnic differences within the US. But Hollywood is not usually thought to be a 'national cinema'.

The term is reserved by critics, film-makers, policy makers, audiences and marketers for national cinemas other than the US one. For them, national cinemas provide a rubric within which cinema and television product can be differentiated from each other and from the dominant international Hollywood cinema. There is Hollywood, and there are national cinemas. Hollywood is an avowedly commercial enterprise. National cinemas are mixed-commercial and public enterprises. While the US government assists Hollywood's commercial ends, in other national cinemas there is a higher degree of formative government assistance involved in creating and sustaining them. Australian cinema, for example, is what it is today because of the ongoing governmental assistance to it since 1969. From the end of World War II to 1969 Australian feature production was sporadic and marginal because it lacked such assistance.

The American national cinema is in its reach the most international of national cinemas. It is the pre-eminent supplier of international products in various national markets. It is the closest thing we have to an audiovisual lingua franca in the world. It also has had an historical stranglehold over many of the world's cinema and more lately video markets – and this market presence is most evident in Europe, the Americas and Australasia. These countries are culturally closer to the US than those in Africa and large parts of Asia. This makes Hollywood a particularly important term of reference.

Along with India, Hollywood is one of the few cinemas that consistently dominate their domestic box offices. In the USA and India the national cinema *is* the cinema. Differences are disclosed mostly *within* the local cinema. There is, to be sure, a minor US market for the product of other national cinemas in its ethnic cinemas and its 'art cinema' circuits, indeed Elsaesser argues it was the 'US distribution practice of the art-house circuit which gave the term "art cinema" its currently accepted meaning' (Elsaesser 1994: 24). Within the US, other national cinemas occupy minor niche markets and do not threaten Hollywood's American hegemony. It makes little sense to think of these cinemas in the same 'national/international' terms that we do for national cinemas. Differentiations between the American cinema and imported product is not something US producers need to negotiate, marketers to market as 'their advantage', and American politicians to concern themselves with (unless it is to try and remove barriers to its international circulation in other national markets). Yet these are the things of central concern to film workers in other national cinemas. Rather US producers, politicians, etc. are primarily concerned with differences within the American cinema.

In most countries which have their own national cinema, cinema-going, cinema distribution, cinema viewing and cinema criticism are not primarily oriented to the local national cinema, but to the cinema more generally, and more particularly the dominant international cinema. Most national cinemas do not dominate their domestic market. American and to a lesser extent British and European cinema is central to the Australian audience's experience of the cinema, television and video. So too the local production component of the cinema, television and video industries in Australia makes up only a fraction of their total turnover. So, for example, Australian features made up between 5 per cent and 21 per cent of the local cinema box-office in the 1980s (AFC 1991: 71) which means that Australian cinema-goers saw an Australian film 'between 5 and 20% of the time depending on the films available in any particular year' (AFC 1991: 71). This situation is repeated in television drama where in 1990 local television drama comprised 16 per cent of total drama programming on the commercial television networks, 7 per cent on the foremost public service broadcaster, the ABC and a negligible proportion on the SBS (ABT 1991: 32).

The international cinemas are more naturalized parts of the cinema landscape than are the various local cinemas. Within most countries people experience the cinema more as another cinema than as their own national cinema. Andrew Higson notes that this international cinema, particularly Hollywood cinema and television, has become 'an integral and naturalized part of the national culture . . . of most countries in which cinema is an established entertainment form' (Higson 1989: 39). One of the consequences here is that, as Geoffrey Nowell-Smith writes of Britain, the American cinema is 'by now far more deeply rooted in British cultural life than is the native product' (1985: 152). Diane Collins puts this case in its strongest form for Australia (1987: 2):

> For the most of this century Australians have watched little else but American movies and America's domination of Australia's film culture extended far beyond the screen. Australians saw (and see) these films in American-style picture shows; news of the latest releases came (and comes) via the American industry's publicity methods. It was not long before locally made films were modelled on Hollywood production styles and America's movie world meant more to many Australians than homegrown celebrities.

At best, Australian films supplement the audience's and the exhibition and distribution industry's mostly Hollywood diet.

National cinemas are structurally marginal, fragile and dependent on outside help. In their own domestic market and internationally, they are often structurally dispensable in that exhibitors, distributors and audiences can make do without their product, though they cannot do without international product. The 1991 figures for Australian theatrical releases well illustrate this point: of the 238 theatrical releases, 60 per cent were sourced from the US, 10 per cent from the UK, 14 per cent from Europe (7 per cent France), 9 per cent from Australia; of the remainder 3 per cent were from the Far East, 2 per cent other, 1 per cent Canada and less than 1 per cent from New Zealand (calculated from Curtis and Spriggs 1992: 75). The lack of distributor and exhibitor interest in Australian cinema is a continuing leitmotif of Australian film history. The exhibition and distribution combine, Union Pictures, chose to consolidate itself and expand during World War I and immediately after at the expense of local production. Film activists of the 1960s regarded with justification the Australian film trade as simply an extension of the American film industry. They saw themselves as representing Australian interests, while the dominant exhibitors – Hoyts and Greater Union – represented American interests.

While most national cinema producers face difficulties in their home market, this same domestic box-office is generally crucial to all national cinemas (even Hollywood has historically relied on 45–75 per cent of its revenues from its domestic market). National cinemas generally need as good an access to their domestic box-office and to the international market as they can get to be viable. But only part of their local box-office is available – in the Australian case between 3 and 21 per cent of the box-office from 1977 to 1993 (Reid 1994: 82). Clearly they need help – and this is where government is important, as is other non-cinema backing and international involvement, whether by way of direct investment, co-productions, or simply revenues from having had a major international success.

Every national cinema activist negotiates to win ground for its national cinema in this market context. The aim of a national cinema is one of producing a local presence alongside the dominant imported presence in both the local and international markets. The task of a national cinema is to graft itself as a minor component on to the existing communication circuits and networks of cinema and television. The aim of a national cinema in this market and cultural environment is not to replace Hollywood films with say Australian films so much as to provide a viable and healthy local supplement to Hollywood cinema. National cinema producers hope, at best, for some limited import substitution and some limited overseas presence. And this is the case for all bar the largest of national cinemas – in the 1992/93 financial year, the value of

Australia's audiovisual exports were $65 million, while its import bill was a massive $437 million (Given 1994: 19). Policy-makers recognize the limits of import substitution given the cultural and economic characteristics of the Australian market; and generally the limits in export.[1] Naturalizing a local contribution to the cinema and local and international audiences to a national cinema is an unending and fraught process. A sense of the minor and subordinate role of domestic production is never far away from debates or writings on any national cinema. The local cinema needs to be worked for anew and presented to every new generation of critics, viewers, exhibitors, distributors and politicians. National cinema activists and film-makers have to think out, work at, legitimate, lobby for, self-consciously articulate and market their difference from the dominant international cinema and each other.

'[T]he cinema', Geoffrey Nowell-Smith writes, 'has always been international, both culturally and economically' (1985: 154). In this context, national cinemas routinely negotiate the extraordinary internationalism of the cinema. They do so from an unequal basis. National cinemas can expect to be no more than a junior partner to the dominant international cinemas. As Elsaesser observes '"national cinema" makes sense only as a relation, not as an essence, being dependent on other kinds of film-making, to which it supplies the other side of the coin' (1994: 25–6). A national cinema necessarily 'functions as a subordinate term' (26).

A national cinema as it is understood on everything from festival schedules to publishers lists, is a production industry operating in the context of a more significant international, usually Hollywood, market presence. For Australian and European cinema alike the 'shape' of the national cinema was partly defined by the impact of and competition provided by the North American film production and distribution industry (K. Thompson 1985: 168) and a subsidiary component of 'runaway' and 'off-shore' productions of that industry – like Stanley Kramer's *On the Beach* in 1959 or Steve Gordon's 1993 *Fortress*.

National cinemas like Australia's evolve strategies to respond to Hollywood's pre-eminent place on the cinema horizons of the Western world and beyond (I make the 'Western' qualification here to allow for the significant circulation of Indian and Hong Kong cinema in African and Asian contexts). They are thus, local film production, film policy and critical strategies designed to effectively *compete with*, *imitate*, *oppose*, *complement* and *supplement* the (dominant) international cinema. The relation between the local and the international cinema provides many 'national cinemas' with their identity and force.

Because Hollywood looms large for those cinemas culturally close to Hollywood cinema such as the English-language speaking cinemas of Canada, Australia, the UK and New Zealand, the need to imitate and oppose Hollywood is felt especially keenly. British, Australian, and Canadian film producers often tackle the competition head-on at home and abroad: with titles like *Crocodile Dundee*, *Four Weddings and a Funeral* (Newell 1994) and *The Fly* (Cronenburg 1986). These sorts of films circulated as Hollywood major product: Warner Brothers, for example, handled the international distribution of the *Mad Max* films. At times various British studios, distributors and exhibitors have sought to try to become a British Hollywood major. Being directly competitive, internationally, is an option mostly available to the English language cinemas.

This means producing films that are, if not imitative, then consonant or interchangeable with the international product. Australian film-makers are often held to 'imitate' American films, whether it be Carl Schultz's Sirkian melodrama, *Careful He Might Hear You* (1983) or Dr Miller's 'revenge/road movie' cycle of *Mad Max* (1979, 1981, 1985). As local cinema and television drama markets are dominated by imports, the local product is shaped by these imports. The prevailing international styles, techniques, technologies, programme concepts and sensibilities are used, adjusted, and transformed in their local enactment in national productions and criticism. In such circumstances of 'internationalization' and 'hybridization', it is often difficult to ascertain where the local ends and the other national or international begins (Dermody and Jacka, 1988a: 20).

Another strategy to 'counter' Hollywood competition is to compete indirectly by seeking complementarities. This market niche option can take a number of directions. It can seek local specificities in domestic social events, issues, stories and myths foregrounding the coherence of the national cultural system such as the shearers in *Sunday Too Far Away* and the famous race-horse *Phar Lap* (Wincer 1983). Elsaesser notes the 'importance of the texture of speech and voice for our idea of a national cinema' (Elsaesser, 1994: 26); there are the Australian accents in the work of script-writer and playwright, David Williamson in the 1970s with *Don's Party, Stork* (Burstall 1971), *The Removalists* (Jeffrey 1975) and *The Club* (Beresford 1976) which fore-grounded the Australian vernacular. These may draw on what Alison Butler (1992: 419) has called 'more localized approaches to cultural codification'. Alternatively it can seek an aesthetic distinction by promoting cinema product as 'Art'. Sometimes a national cinema takes on an 'avant-gardist opposition to Hollywood style' (Butler 1992: 419). Or it can do both. Doing both is central to the 'art cinema' as a strategy for a national cinema. As Elsaesser (1994: 26) notes 'one function of auteur cinema, before the advent of television, was to transcribe features of a nation's cultural tradition as figured in other art forms (the novel, theatre, opera) and to represent them in the cinema.' This can be seen in the coincidence of Australian auteurs and the literary *oeuvre*: Armstrong and Miles Franklin's *My Brilliant Career*; Weir and Joan Lindsay's *Picnic at Hanging Rock* and Weir and Christopher Koch's *The Year of Living Dangerously* (1982); Schepisi and Thomas Kenneally's *The Chant of Jimmie Blacksmith*; Beresford and Henry Handel Richardson's *The Getting of Wisdom* (1977) and Beresford and David Williamson's *Don's Party*. It can also be witnessed in the focus on the Norman Lindsay legend in John Duigan's *Sirens* (1994). Lindsay was not only a painter, novelist, poet, children's story writer and publisher but a cultural phenomenon in his own right, who scandalized Sydney society for three decades. Steve Neale (1981) argues that art and national identity are fused for the Germans in the 1920s, essentially for market niche reasons. Australia did not have this fusion until 1970 or thereabouts.[2] This doubling was first an explicit project of Australian film policy and later embodied in Peter Weir's *Picnic at Hanging Rock*. Here, for the first time, a nation's character seemed embodied in a personally idiosyncratic and poetic cinema as opposed to slick Hollywood commercial enter-tainment (and its Australian predecessors that sought to be only entertainment).

Critics and film-makers oppose Hollywood screen dominance, seeing in the local product alternatives to Hollywood norms and values. They invoke Australian film's humanist values, its black humour, its quirkiness. For Australia's festival cinema – *Breaker Morant, Sweetie* – the aim is not to directly compete so much as to complement Hollywood product. It has what Butler (1992: 418) would call its 'nationally specific styles', its 'misreadings' of Hollywood norms.

National cinemas provide a means to identify, assist, legitimate, polemicize, project and otherwise create a space nationally and internationally for non-Hollywood film-making activity. Just as 'the international' makes no sense without nations, so, in cinema terms 'national' makes no sense without 'le défi américain'.

National cinema as a local and international forum

So, national cinemas can be seen as a response to the internationalization of the cinema. They are not alternatives to internationalization, they are one of its manifestations. National cinemas, whether in the guise of a local film industry producing a variety of films or of a purveyor of the national culture or whatever, are from inception vehicles for international integration.

In Australia's case, the project of a national cinema in the multifaceted sense advanced so far, did not emerge until 1969, well after Hollywood had consolidated its international reach and control over the Australian market. At that point, formative government assistance was put into place and an Australian national cinema became a project capable of enlisting a large array of local and international actors – politicians, arts bureaucrats, voters, critics, audiences, film-makers. Before that, it was simply a struggling commercial industry, producing, or striving to produce, popular entertainment capable of intermittently enlisting government support, or it was a producer of unaffiliated product showing great promise but achieving no theatrical release like Cecil Holmes' films *Captain Thunderbolt* (1953) and *Three in One* (1957).

As one of the forms the internationalization of the cinema takes, national cinemas *localize* the cinema and explicitly *contribute* to the international cinema at one and the same time. As Kristin Thompson (1985: 168) observes:

> few national cinema industries operate in isolation; through foreign investment, competition and other types of influence, outside factors will almost invariably affect any given national cinema. Such effects have implications for most types of historical study – whether of film style, industry working, government policy, technology change or social implications.

National cinemas work to be local while streamlining themselves to be of interest to audiences outside Australia. Bruce Beresford's *The Adventures of Barry McKenzie* – a classic comedy of an 'ocker' in England – came out of a period where film policy and criticism emphasized securing a local following and gave near exclusive priority to representing Australia to itself. But the film was also from its inception international: self-consciously made for the British and Australian market it was successful in both (the Barry Humphries comic strip on which the film was based was more popular in the UK than in Australia). *Barry McKenzie* has as its erstwhile hero the monstrous Barry McKenzie who in order to acquire his inheritance must visit the 'old country', England. Apart from the opening sequence in Sydney and a brief sequence in Hong Kong immediately following, the rest of the film is concerned with Bazza's assorted English adventures. If, with his double-breasted suit, airways bag and his braggadocio, McKenzie is a camp parody of a, by then, outdated Australian masculinity (his clothes belong in the 1940s and early 1950s not the the 1960s or 1970s) he is also the Australian abroad, the colonial Candide. Episodically structured, improbably connected, the film has a farcical structure in which narrative is clearly at the service of set piece performances by Barry Crocker (Bazza), Barry Humphreys (Edna Everage and other roles), Spike Milligan and Peter Cook. In many ways the film can be regarded as a 'rewriting' of *They're a Weird Mob* (Powell 1966). It encourages not so much the 'identification' with its Australianness, but a suspending of illusionist belief, thereby producing its fantasy of the 'hyper-Australian' intersecting with an equally 'hyper-Britishness'. The film could be simultaneously, depending on where you stood: 'us sticking it up the Poms' and 'us dealing with those frightful Australians'.

This process of streamlining has a bearing on what is selected from the cultural archive – British/Australian implications in the colonial or post-colonial eras are foregrounded in many Australian films, including notable successes like *Gallipoli* and *Breaker Morant*. Michael Blakemore set his film, *Country Life* (1994) in turn-of-the-century Australia. The metropole/province relation was configured as a British/Australian relation within an Australian family. Sometimes it can be updated, as in Mark Joffe's *Spotswood* (1992) where the English efficiency expert comes to an Australian moccasin factory. The workers here are more interested in racing slot cars than working and he is eventually 'bent' towards is eccentric workers. Here again the British connection not only lies with Anthony Hopkins' presence in the lead role but in the many ways the film evokes the Ealing comedies of the 1940s and 1950s. In *Film Review 1993–4* James Cameron-Wilson described it as 'an exquisitely judged social comedy, which is written, directed and played at just the right pitch, evoking fond memories of Ealing' (in Cameron-Wilson and Speed 1993: 99).

Similarly the 'American in Australia' and, to a lesser extent, the 'Australian in America' are constant figures in the local cinema. Sometimes American 'innocents' are done down but eventually triumph over the disturbed, psychotic, murderous or rampaging monsters who happen to be Australian. Stacy Keach and Jamie Lee Curtis are the only 'normal characters' in *Roadgames* (Franklin 1981). They do battle across the Nullarbor plains with an odd assortment of weird Australians including a sex murderer, unfriendly police officers and cranky drivers. Jimmy Smits is the charismatic American University Professor in Melbourne falsely accused and imprisoned for rape in *Gross Misconduct* (George Miller 1993). He is the victim of the overheated sexual gaze of a beautiful female student who turns out to be a victim too – of incest – which retrospectively explains and justifies her actions. In *Razorback* (Mulcahy 1984), Carl (Gregory Harrison) comes to Australia to avenge the death of his wife at the hands of the eponymous wild pig, and in the process he also sorts out the malevolent local kangaroo shooters who have a symbiotic relationship with the pig.

American men provide love interests for Australian women in Chris Thomson's 1989 film *The Delinquents* – Charlie Schlatter is Kylie Minogue's love interest in this film of love on the wrong side of the tracks, and in the World War II story *Rebel* (Jenkins 1985) – Matt Dillon plays a GI deserter in Sydney hidden by a night club singer, Debbie Byrne.

Americans are often 'problematic' figures and presences which Australians need to negotiate and come to terms with – often making the Australians feel inferior. In Mora's *Death of a Soldier* (1986), James Coburn plays a senior American commander in Australia during the World War II dealing with the lines of demarcation between the American military police and the Australian civil police force over an American soldier wanted by both for a series of murders of local women. Eric Roberts in Dusan Makavejev's *The Coca-Cola Kid* (1985) is a Coca-Cola executive sent to Australia to bring Coke into the back-blocks – like the Anthony Hopkins character in *Spotswood* he achieves his goal but in the process is changed. *Dallas Doll* (Turner 1993) has Sarah Bernhardt as a morally questionable character who is simultaneously desired by and repelled by nearly every character (all Australians) in this film. She seduces nearly everyone in the family – the father, the son and the mother. Eventually the Australians turn the tables on her, or, in the case of the mother, simply assert themselves.

Finally American actors sometimes play Australian characters. Notably Meryl Streep in *Evil Angels*, Robert Mitchum and Deborah Kerr in *The Sundowners* (Zinnemann 1960), and Richard Chamberlain in *The Last Wave* (where the Chamberlain character is given as having a South American heritage).

Equally, there can at times seem to be an almost seamless web between working to be local and being internationally successful. Indeed just about every national cinema at some stage goes local in order to go international. It was an article of faith in the 1970s for the national cinema to be local in front of and behind the camera and even to be substantially locally financed. Film critics like the influential critic of *The Age* (Melbourne), Colin Bennett, in the 1970s found evidence of the wisdom of this position in Schepisi's 1970s classics – *The Devil's Playground* and *The Chant of Jimmie Blacksmith*, Armstrong's *My Brilliant Career*, Miller's *Mad Max*, and Noyce's *Newsfront*. The presence of international actors in Australian films of the decade became another, and sometimes unwanted and distracting 'noise'.

If this local orientation is now explicitly repudiated as *the* only model for a national cinema, it persists because it is a structural necessity in the Australian cinema – which like the New Zealand and German cinemas – relies so critically on the work of first and second time directors for success. Their best directors, cinematographers and actors become expatriates after a decade or less in filmmaking. Some of the most successful and high profile Australian films of the 1990s were either their director's first feature: Jocelyn Moorhouse with *Proof*, Geoffrey Wright with *Romper Stomper*, Baz Luhrmann with *Strictly Ballroom*, Paul J. Hogan with *Muriel's Wedding*, Ray Argall with *Return Home* (1990), John Ruane with *Death in Brunswick* (1991), Geoff Burton and Kevin Dowling with *The Sum of Us*, or their second feature: Stephan Elliott with *The Adventures of Priscilla: Queen of the Desert*. Additionally, many highly regarded – although not always commercially successful 1990s releases – were also the work of first-time or second-time feature directors: Jackie McKimmie (*Waiting* 1991), Tracey Moffatt (*beDevil*) and Pauline Chan (*Traps* 1994) and Alexis Vellis (*Nirvana Street Murder* 1991). By definition, first time directors are not that internationally integrated, as they are yet to prove themselves. Their locally set, locally produced and locally acted productions are their international calling cards. Australian cinema of the 1990s was – with the exception of international blockbusters set outside Australia – increasingly dependent on 'sleepers': low budget films that exceeded all expectation for success. But these were not 'sleepers' of the *Mad Max* variety. They were films from directors whose national and international careers were often established in advance through international film festival screenings of their shorts and features.

The 1990s cinema looked a lot like that of the mid- to late 1970s when there was a similar turn towards Europe and attention was being paid to gaining recognition in the international European and North American festivals. As in the earlier period, there was a shortage of Australian investors, the industry needed to rely on 'first time' directors to give the Australian industry a palpable form, and the state funding institutions played a much larger role than they did in the 1980s. It is worth noting that these 'local productions' were sometimes underwritten by state investment and subsidy in partnership with international financing, for example *Muriel's Wedding* was underwritten by French finance through CIBY Sales, with a principle involvement of Film Victoria and subsidiary involvement of the Queensland Pacific Film and Television, the NSW Film and Television Office, the AFC and the FFC.

'Going local' does not only hold out the prospect of a culturally authentic, low budget cinema just possibly able to recoup its money from the domestic market and attractive to international audiences in its Australianness (using the local to go to the universal). It also opens on to two other possibilities:

1.   The prospect of a commercially oriented exploitative cinema – a crassly commercial cinema, recycling possibly regressive notions and ideas (the 1970s 'sex comedy' classically embodied by *Alvin Purple* is often taken to be an instance here, as was the first *Mad Max* at its time of release).

2.   The prospect of a quirky, eccentric cinema to one side of the international norm as a means of establishing international attractiveness. In *Sweetie* and *Strictly Ballroom*, *Muriel's Wedding* and *The Adventures of Priscilla Queen of the Desert* a space is created for what has become an international expectation of Australian 'quirkiness', 'eccentricity' and 'individuality'.

In these features, the banality and richness of contemporary, usually urban settings and culture, are foregrounded and turned away from their usual moorings in realist social problem film-making. So Peter Castaldi praises *Strictly Ballroom* for its combination of the conventional romance fairy tale and Australian suburbia, its back streets and its dreams. This combination 'liberates the suburban from the grip of the realists and lets fantasy run free' (Castaldi 1994) as the film-makers 'took the back streets of any town and dressed them up in the most colourful, outrageous and wickedly witty way'. In making *Sweetie*, Campion took the 'short films' for which she had become internationally famous and made them longer without sacrificing their signature 'look'. As Campion reported:

> When I made them [my short films], I never thought in the future I'd have the opportunity to make such personal, off-the-wall films. But then I saw how people enjoyed them, and I thought I'd like to make a feature which went even further than they did. I decided I didn't want to ape the kind of films made by other people: I wanted to invent my own.
>
> (Quoted in Stratton 1990: 373)

In so doing, she legitimated the AFC's policy of developing talent and stylistic and plot innovation through the short film. Campion provided an example for subsequent film-makers: film-makers would be encouraged as much as possible to keep and extend the concerns and signatures of their short films into their features. In critical and marketing terms, her short films' prestigious international circulation created expectations for the director's long awaited first feature. *Sweetie's* enumeration of what Anne-Marie Crawford and Adrian Martin called 'a world defined, at a fundamentally banal and everyday level, by alienation, irresolution and incohesion' (Crawford and Martin 1989: 56–7) provided a larger statement of the work in her short films. These same characteristics are also the domain of the many everyday stories of *No Worries* (Elfick 1993), *Return Home* and *A Woman's Tale* (Cox 1991).

So to be 'wholly local' in a pure form in front of and behind the camera is not the natural condition of a national cinema – even when it looks to be doing precisely that. Most national cinemas seek to involve international players (actors, directors, distributors, festival organizers, composers, television buyers) in the creation, financing and circulation of national cinema and television texts. A feature film-maker's domestic career often hinges on getting their film into and comporting themselves appropriately at the Cannes, New York, Venice, Montreal, Toronto and London film festivals. In their choice of actors, locations, production personnel, story and dialogue, local producers routinely take into account the requirements of international circulation. Such considerations are crucial to getting films to circulate internationally, to bringing in international distributors, to securing pre-sales and co-production partners. National cinema film-makers keep abreast of contemporaneous international technical, stylistic, storytelling and organizational instruments for film-makers indigenizing them to local circumstance.

Particularly when we move to its higher budgeted form, every Western national cinema strives to be explicitly international in its textual form. No national cinema can survive on 'sleepers'. Those who make sleepers want to operate with higher budgets and a bigger scale. At some stage each national cinema has to produce expensive films and this means becoming more explicitly international. This is riskier though because more money is at stake. It also entails enlisting a lot of international allies in advance. But it is the only way of escaping the low yields and lower production values typical of the purely local product. Compared to *Crocodile Dundee* and *The Piano*, *Strictly Ballroom* and *Romper Stomper* were minor successes internationally. Half of *Strictly's* global revenues were generated in Australia; compared to 10 per cent of *The Piano's* $(US)112 million (Given 1994: 13). The sleeper *Mad Max* could never hope to compete with its high budget successor *Mad Max II* (aka *The Road Warrior*) – it was the latter, not the former, that changed international film-making, sparking many imitations, the latest of which is Kevin Costner's *Waterworld* (Reynolds 1995). Higher budget productions also benefit the local and international image of the Australian cinema. They raise the industry's infrastructure, update its domestic technological base, employ and train a large number of professionals to industry standard and drag the smaller Australian films in their wake both locally and internationally. They help create the international currency of the local cinema. (Securing an attachment on Jane Campion's *The Piano* was important to Margot Nash making the transition from documentaries to low-budget features with *Vacant Possession*.) As one Australian-based director, Werner Meyer, put it to me in 1992: what the Australian industry needed was another *Crocodile Dundee* – not because this was the sort of film he made or liked but because 'it made everything easier for everyone else in the industry'. But, of course, this is harder to achieve successfully. Sometimes the international requirements in the make up of international films change: liberal tax concessions made it possible in the 1980s to make a 'quality' blockbuster with a predominantly Australian cast, finance and explicitly foregrounded Australian connections with titles like *The Man from Snowy River*, *Mad Max II*, *Gallipoli* and *Dead Calm* being the result. But, in the 1990s, it required a project with an international setting and connection – often co-productions with Australian involvement more behind than in front of the camera, in titles like *The Piano*, *The Black Robe* (Beresford 1992) and *Green Card* (Weir 1991) which I will discuss later.

If all national cinemas are implicated internationally, Australian cinema has been remarkably implicated. This can be measured in a variety of ways, like the international financing of Australian features and television dramas (between 1988–89 and 1992–93 financial years foreign investors accounted for 39 per cent of production funding, government agencies 33 per cent and Australian private and commercial investment 28 per cent (Bean and Court 1994: 37)), or the international actors appearing in Australian cinema (some American actors not already mentioned include Tina Turner, Lee Remick, Kirk Douglas, Linda Hunt, Tom Selleck!), or, indeed the international directors working behind the camera in Australian productions. British, American, Canadian, German, Polish and Yugoslav directors have made films in Australia from Australian stories and sometimes with Australian financing. Sometimes the films of major international directors have had a lasting impact on the subsequent shape of the national cinemas they worked in, however briefly.

There can, at times, be a happy mutuality between Australia as the location for other imaginings and these imaginings as 'ours'. Some of these films became owned by Australians as theirs. The most obvious examples here are: Harry Watt's *The Overlanders* (1946), Jack Lee's *A Town Like Alice* (1956), Fred Zinnemann's *The Sundowners*, Robert Powell's *They're a Weird Mob*, Nicolas Roeg's *Walkabout* and Ted Kotcheff's *Wake in Fright*. These directors took Australian cultural artifacts – literature for Powell, Zinnemann, Kotcheff and previous 'images' of Australia for Roeg – and transformed them into films.

Some 'location' film-making projects have been crucial to Australian cinema providing models and opening out new territory for local film-makers to follow. *The Overlanders* may have been an Australian/British western but it was also a 'docu-drama' and possibly the first Australian art film. It opened the 'outback' to a different fictional emplotment and eschewed the melodramatic norms which had been essential to the 1920s and 1930s Australian cinema. Romance was downplayed. There was an absence of close-ups. The 'vast open spaces' were shot as spectacle (a repertoire still in evidence). More important was the space it created for a mutually advantageous British–Australian partnership. Through it Australia became an on-screen presence in Britain – something that was, at best, unevenly achieved in the preceding decades.

The post-1970 Australian cinema revival is particularly indebted to the Australian work of the British directors Powell (for *Weird Mob*) and Roeg (*Walkabout*); and to the Canadian, Ted Kotcheff. They prepared local and international audiences and critics for the Australian films that followed in the 1970s and beyond. Powell's *They're a Weird Mob* was a forerunner to the 'ocker' films of the 1970s and the multicultural cinema of the 1990s with its repertoires of ethnicity, ethnic mixing and cultural non-comprehension – still in evidence in *The Heartbreak Kid* and *Romper Stomper*.

Wake in Fright's prototypical middle-class male school teacher experiencing a vernacular working-class male regional culture fashioned the male ensemble film. With its dystopian view of mateship and misogyny, *Wake* introduced the idea of endemic and structural evil to Australian cinema. These rhetorical figures have persisted through to the present and have helped organize the terrain of much subsequent Australian storytelling from *Don's Party* to *Romper Stomper*. The preparedness to accept, exploit, entertain and at times exaggerate this possibility provided an important maturity to Australian film-making and undoubtedly aided its circulation in the international festival market. It helped create – after the figure of New German Cinema's 'unmastered past' – an unsavoury Australian past and present centred largely on the deeds, misogyny, limited horizons and xenophobia of white (Anglo) males. Kotcheff's film prepared the way for that mix of hyperrealism, excessive masculinity, ambiguous sexuality and misogyny so insistently present in subsequent Australian cinema.

In Roeg's *Walkabout* landscape was worked into the film as a 'character'. As the British critic Dilys Powell wrote on its release: 'it is to the eyes that *Walkabout* speaks. Mr Roeg has painted an Australian landscape, blazing, enormous; and its desert really is a red desert; the sand burns brick red' (1989: 261).

Such an emphasis on landscape as character is evident in many later films but notably Peter Weir's *Picnic at Hanging Rock*, Paul Cox's *Exile* (1993) and Robert Scholes' *The Tale of Ruby Rose* (1988). Roeg's emphasis on the uncanny and the other-worldly, the mundane and the spiritual, and the tragic clash of Aboriginal and non-Aboriginal peoples in the Australian continent opened directly on to Weir's *The Last Wave*, Schepisi's *The Chant of Jimmie Blacksmith*, Moffatt's *Night Cries – A Rural Tragedy* (1989), the children's films *Storm Boy* (Safran 1976) and *Manganinnie* (Honey 1980), and even Barron film's remake of *Bush Christmas* (Safran 1983).[3] Roeg's observations about the film are pertinent to this discussion:

> It couldn't have been made anywhere else and it was an utterly Australian film.
> . . . But it did something, I think, and I like to hope that it touched emotional
> chords that were international. I think that helped in some way to open doors for
> Australian movies.
>
> (Quoted in White 1984: 25)

Walkabout and *Wake in Fright* were seminal films for the Australian film revival to critics, audiences and film-makers alike. Actor Jack Thompson claims both films to be 'searching looks at the Australian ethos' and credits them with demonstrating 'not only to the rest of the world of film-makers but to ourselves that we were capable of making feature films' (quoted in White 1984: 27). While neither was particularly successful in Australia, Thompson notes that they were 'transitional films' signalling the transition between a feature industry marked by the 'almost totally foreign-made films being made in Australia' and an 'Australian cinema'. These two films became particularly important to the 1970s film revival, in that they created Australian cinema as an international territory in the cinema and provided directly for an Australian place. They were noticed by critics and industry figures.

National cinemas are one of the means by which the local and the international reconfigure each other. Our above example foregrounds British, American and Canadian film-makers refashioning the audiovisual representation of Australia and Australians and more than this, reconceptualizing the form, approach and stylistic means of the Australian cinema that followed

– which was largely Australian produced, directed and scripted. But such refashioning is only part of the general circulation of any national cinema as it 'travels' outside its domestic context and enters new contexts. Thomas Elsaesser (1994: 25) writes of how 'European films intended for one kind of (national) audience or made within a particular kind of aesthetic framework or ideology, for instance, undergo a sea change as they cross the Atlantic and on coming back find themselves bearing the stamp of yet another cultural currency.'

The international appreciation of national cinemas in, for example, festivals 'assign different kinds of value' to the product and in the process the films acquire a 'new cultural capital beyond the prospect of economic circulation (art cinema distribution, a television sale)'. Quite provocatively Elsaesser claims that 'the New German Cinema was discovered and even invented abroad, and had to be re-imported to be recognized as such' (1989: 300). Australian cinema from the 1970s fashioned this international process as an intrinsic part of marketing Australian cinema to local audiences. Selection at Cannes provided an imprimateur for local audiences. It also rehabilitated local directors.

When Fred Schepisi's *The Chant of Jimmie Blacksmith* came out it died at the box-office after eleven weeks. Schepisi lost a lot of his personal savings accumulated over a decade of working as a television commercial director. He was attacked from all sides. Film-maker Terry Bourke claimed this film and Weir's *Last Wave* had led Australian film-making away from commercial values and genre film-making. Veteran director and former Channel 9 boss Ken G. Hall weighed in by claiming that Schepisi should have known that films about Aborigines were box-office poison. From the other direction, James Ricketson weighed in claiming that *Jimmie Blacksmith* was a 'dinosaur, an 'ersatz Hollywood monster' and that the industry would be better funding 'four potential [low budget] *Mouth to Mouth* (Duigan 1978) than in funding one *Jimmie Blacksmith*' (Ricketson 1979, 1985: 226–7). The film's humanist values were attacked by an academic screen criticism inimical to humanism. Mudrooroo (then known as Johnson – 1987: 50) questioned the novel and the film's politics. He later wrote that the film's lingering image was that of 'a beserk boong hacking to death white ladies'. He noted the consternation among the Aboriginal family of Jimmy Governor and how they, on seeing the film, sought legal advice to try and stop its screening. It was left to Pauline Kael to salvage the film's Australian reputation somewhat. Albert Moran and I incorporated Kael's 1980 *New Yorker* review of the film into our 1985 collection *An Australian Film Reader*, partly because it provided a different view on the film as well as providing an instance of the importance to Australian cinema's international circulation of the New York critical establishment. Susan Dermody and Elizabeth Jacka (1987a: 148) noted how the republication of this review suggested that *Jimmie Blacksmith* 'may be one of the underestimated and overlooked films of the 1970s'. Through this and similar critical rethinkings, Schepisi was brought home, even though his subsequent career was now mostly in the US.

The local as much as international terrain informs perceptions and the success of the dominant, imported cinema and national cinema product in international circulation. Historically, cinema and television is international in its outlook and sensibility, while local in its national configurations. Borders – especially national borders – are significant to explaining the circulation of Hollywood and national cinemas alike. These influence the viewing of international cinema as surely as they do the local product. In answer to the question of 'what happens when a text crosses national or other borders' Alison Butler (1992: 419) answers:

> There is mounting evidence that the refunctionalization of texts is not just a mani-
> festation of occasional resistances, but the very condition of possibility of such

border crossings. Productive – and indeed unproductive – misreading is perhaps the paradigmatic operation which governs the reception of films outside – and sometimes inside – their original national contexts.

If this is the terrain of an imagined 'America' bearing sometimes a limited relation to the actual US, it is also the terrain of the 'imagined' Australia or 'Britain'. Both *Crocodile Dundee* and *Four Weddings and a Funeral* were criticized at home for providing a 'tourist's-eye view' of Australia and Britain. They both exported a view of Australian and British life 'which is more like the rest of the world wants it to be than it actually is' (Roddick 1995: 15). Here, the worry is that the 'imagined Australia' (an outback 'ocker' doing battle with crocodiles and New York escalators) or 'imagined Britain' (upper middle-class twits 'off to a smart wedding in a battered Land Rover' (15)) directly impinges and shapes domestic film production. But if Butler is right, such repositionings are an unexceptional part of the cinema landscape – and a part that film-makers are acutely aware of. Take Stephan Elliott's account of the different audience responses in France, Australia and the US to his film, *The Adventures of Priscilla, Queen of the Desert*:

> At a screening we had for an Australian audience, they laughed at all the Australianisms. The Americans laughed too, but at different jokes. There is a line where Tick says, 'Bernadette had left her cake out in the rain . . .' Last night, they [the French audience] didn't get it, whereas the Americans laughed for ten minutes.
> (Quoted in Epstein 1994: 6)

Elliott went on to observe that his film – like *Strictly Ballroom* (Luhrmann 1992) before it – was changing from 'territory to territory' to become 'a different film in different territories' (Elliott, in Epstein 1994: 6). This difference Elliott observed extended to its public meaning: it could be seen in the US gay response which saw it 'as the big one that will bring gay lifestyles into a mainstream' while Australian audiences 'embrace it as just another successful Australian film' – a musical with actors who are really recognizable' (7). And so it was for *Crocodile Dundee* too (Crofts 1992).

Such a situation leads Elsaesser (1994: 26) to declare that 'national cinemas and Hollywood are not only communicating vessels, but (to change the metaphor) exist in a space set up like a hall of mirrors in which recognition, imaginary identity and miscognition enjoy equal status.'

The local dimension of a national cinema does not only reside in the specifically local cultural codifications or domestic production traditions, but also lies in the movement of localization, the movement of indigenizing other nation's cinema product and their production models. National cinemas are one of the means by which cultural transfers are routinely accomplished in the international cinema. More than this, these cultural transfers embodied in the locally produced cinema are themselves a form of localizing and indigenizing processes. Localizing becomes the means of internationalizing; internationalizing the means of localizing. The local and the international are ineradicably mixed in the constitution of the national cinema project.

National cinemas as festival cinemas

> We [Americans] want Australian films to seem real and convincing (as if there are real films of real Australia), certainly more real and convincing that most people imagine Hollywood films to be. I suppose this is the defining characteristic – a prejudice to your advantage, really – we have towards Australian cinema, perhaps

Australia as a whole. . . . Your cinema is to us a 'specialized cinema', an art house
cinema supported by festivals, critics and filmgoers who want something different
. . . but not too different, who want a more real and convincing cinematic experience, who want to experience this sense of 'Australianicity', an Otherness that
is, in fact, not all that Other.

(29)

Tony Safford (1995) was here speaking to the Screen Producers Association of Australia conference in 1994. He was not only defining the particularity of Australian cinema to Americans
but defining as well the space of a festival cinema more generally. Like part of the output of
any national cinema, Australian cinema circulates in that principally non-Hollywood ('festival')
space of the 'foreign film' in world cinema markets. Since the 1970s film revival, there have
been a handful of internationally recognized Australian cinema auteurs (notably Peter Weir,
Bruce Beresford, Fred Schepisi from the 1970s generation; Gillian Armstrong, Phil Noyce,
George Miller of the 1980s generation; more lately, the Australian-trained Jane Campion)
and avant-garde cinema stylists (Albie Thoms in the 1960s, Tracey Moffatt in the 1990s),
internationally renowned documentarists and ethnographic film-makers (David Bradbury,
Denis O'Rourke, David and Judith MacDougall, Bob Connolly and Robin Anderson), femi-
nist experimental film-makers (Helen Grace, Laleen Jayamenne), indigenous film-makers
(Moffatt and Prattan) and a band of recognizable, adaptable actors used by accomplished mainstream and art cinema directors (Judy Davis, Jack Thompson, Sam Neil, Russell Crowe).
Their works mark out the routine Australian membership and presence at the Cannes, Berlin,
Toronto and even Singapore film festivals as something from Australia now becomes an unexceptional though minor norm at international festivals and subsequently in repertory film and
'quality' television markets.

Bill Nichols has made a number of points about the function of this film festival cinema:

The festival circuit allows the local to circulate globally, within a specific system
of institutional assumptions, priorities and constraints. Never only or purely local,
festival films nonetheless circulate, in large part, with a cachet of locally inscribed
difference and globally ascribed commonality. They both attest to the uniqueness
of different cultures and specific film-makers and affirm the underlying qualities of
an 'international cinema'.

(1994: 68)

This festival context adds 'a global overlay to more local meaning' (1994: 68) providing
'a continuous, international pattern of circulation and exchange of image-culture'. Here
Australian cinema can be seen to observe John Orr's (1993: 6) dictum that 'cinema is often
at its more powerful in film-makers who emerge from distinctive *national* traditions' and that
what he calls 'the neo-modern moment has its origin in the national cinemas of Western
Europe and the US where it engages with Western capitalist modernity'.

The different European national cinemas of the 1950s to the present and the Asian, African
and Latin American cinemas of the present provide the Australian cinema audience and local
film-makers with an important social and cultural experience of modernity, and not just in
the cinema. That Australian film-makers should want to contribute to it should come as no
surprise. Furthermore Nichols suggests that within this festival optic Hollywood occupies an
'oppositional rather than an inspirational position' (1994: 74). The film festival circuit displaces
this centre rather than 'bolstering' it (74). It provides a way of valuing its own product at
the expense of Hollywood. And therein lies its attraction for Australian film-makers and audiences alike. It naturalizes the local as internationally acceptable, just as it provides a space to

one side of the mainstream Hollywood competition. In doing so, it does not so much compete, as circulate and organize an alternative space to the common vernacular of Hollywood. As noted, an important component of this festival circuit is the art cinema, whether in its major and still dominant form of the European art cinema, or in its emergent form as films from outside the 'Western, Eurocentric centre' (Nichols 1994: 74).

Director Paul Schrader once described the difference between the European and the Hollywood film as one of attitude:

> American movies are based on the assumption that life represents you with problems, while European films are based on the conviction that life confronts you with dilemmas – and while problems are something you solve, dilemmas cannot be solved, they're merely probed or investigated.
>
> (Quoted in Elsaesser 1994: 24)

Elsaesser (1994: 24) contends that this 'might explain why a happy ending in a European art film is felt to be a cop-out, a fundamentally unserious mode of closure'. He asks: 'isn't one of the characteristics of "modern" cinema (until recently synonymous with the art film) its metaphysical doubt about master narratives of progress, preferring to be sceptical of linear time and the efficacy of action?'

Consequently the largely European derived 'art film' model and its televisual equivalent in 'quality television' has had an impact on Australian production schedules and television priorities. This poses its own obligations upon Australian cinema: a cinema created for the representation of modernist cultural themes (existentialism, the absurd, alienation, 'boundary situations') and modern political issues (class, gender, race) providing the doubling of aesthetics and politics. The best representatives of this tendency in Australian cinema usually combine fragments of all of these: from Peter Weir's *Picnic at Hanging Rock*, to Paul Cox's *Man of Flowers* (1983) to Gillian Armstrong's *The Last Days of Chez Nous* (1992), to *Sunday Too Far Away* to *Don's Party*; from *The Piano* to *The Chant of Jimmie Blacksmith*.

Not surprisingly many of Australian cinema's narrative resolutions and thematic preoccupations (though not necessarily their means of realization) are classically those of the international art cinema. As Debi Enker observes about Australian cinema's thematic preoccupations:

> Characters are repeatedly alienated and driven apart, condemned to loneliness, or at the very least to being alone. In this context, the dearth of happily resolved love stories is entirely appropriate . . . Australia's film-makers have concentrated more on the spaces that separate people, on communities that stifle the spirit and circumstances that drive lovers apart. It is a much darker and despairing vision that that of a frontier paradise promising freedom and unlimited scope for fulfilment.
>
> (1994: 224–5)

Enker goes on to note that this includes films as diverse as *Mad Max* and *Picnic at Hanging Rock*, *Caddie* and *Nirvana Street Murder*, *Breaker Morant* and *Monkey Grip* (K. Cameron 1982).

More than any other film-making project before Campion's *Sweetie* Cox's *My First Wife* (1984) fits in with European art cinema protocols. Perhaps this is why his films easily fit within local and international art film circuits. The chief interest in the film is in the break up of a relationship seen from the man's (played by John Hargreaves) perspective. The viewer is invited continually to identify with his sense of grief, remorse, betrayal. In consequence, the wife remains both a cipher and an enigma for him and for us as viewers. To realize this narrative structure, *My First Wife* entails the strategies (the feelings, intensities, excesses and neuroses) of art cinema. There is a trading in of narrative development for a vivid tableaux. It relies on an interiorizing of conflict, upon states of mind, feelings, sentiments which find their expression in repeated scenes. One such scene is the flashback to the wedding scene which provides the film's narrative image. The image here is of the Wendy Hughes character, the first wife, in her wedding dress (it's also the image used on the video dustjacket). It promises literally what is not in the present time of the film. The image of the wife at her wedding is recalled as is memory. It is insistently returned to: a counterpoint to the present of a conjugal relationship in crisis.

My First Wife invites interpretation. It is, as Bill Routt and Rick Thompson (1987: 32) would put it, a text which despite its attractive surface is not 'for everyone', as it contains, and has wrapped itself around enigmas and secrets. The enigma to be explored by viewer and film-maker alike is the meaning for the John Hargreaves character (and we viewers) of his previously unquestioned relationship with his wife. This enigma distilled in the film's narrative image – the Wendy Hughes character at her wedding happy in love with the John Hargreaves character – is the pretext and subtext of the film.

The film is built around what Horst Ruthrof (1980: 102) calls a 'boundary situation' in which 'a presented persona, a narrator, or the implied reader in a flash of insight becomes aware of meaningful as against meaningless existence'. David Bordwell (1985: 208) sees this situation as a defining characteristic of much art cinema. Certainly *My First Wife*'s impetus wholly derives from the main character's recognition that he faces a crisis of existential significance. Cox' film insists upon a degree of psychologizing as the protagonist's state of mind is visualized. This messes up the dividing line between reality and fantasy, past and present, suggesting an uneasiness with the literal present. In this Cox's bears comparison to some of Peter Weir's films – *The Last Wave* particularly – where liminal states of mind are externalized into a heightening of reality, into a literal present gone awry.

In nearly all of Cox's films there are clear moments of excess which suggest the relation of the film-maker to the apparatus. In *My First Wife* there are the sequences which are distorted, which refuse to show clearly, which derepresentationalize and thus diminish the scope for us to see anything clearly. Because they go on just a shade too long, they carry more than the existential weight of the husband's state of mind. They draw attention to themselves as play with film stock, with the form of film. They pose another disrupting enigma, that of film play. The viewer is encouraged to read different meanings into the film – not only in the end there is only the family, but also in the end there is only film and its experience.

With its invitations to psychological depth, its dislocations, its willingness to fragment, its use of the 'boundary situation' – Paul Cox's cinema is one for which readings of personal vision are appropriate, fit easily and are encouraged by the films themselves. The figure of John Hargreaves in *My First Wife* is irresistibly a stand-in for the author. If like so many 1980s films the central journey is 'His' journey, it's a journey which we are advised to speak of in personal terms.

But it's not only the kernel of interpretation at the heart of Cox's films that is refracted in their critical circulation. There is also the drive to make cinema meaningful, to reinvent it, to place oneself, one's whole being at its service. If this involves the cinematizing of the personal it also carries the megalomaniac's dream of total control and total risk. This licences his films to come stuffed with chaotic excess, prejudices, intellectual and physical obsessions, unreasonableness – thereby encouraging the reader in his or her turn to engage with them. There are few directors in Australian cinema who so insistently invite the labour of the auteurist as Paul Cox.

The festival circulation of director as auteur and the close proximity of self-expression and personal vision to national and intersubjective vision, ensures that the kind of attention the festival and related circuits confer upon a film generates a certain kind of public reputation. It gives Australian cinema generally more value, just as it permits the construction (as with all auteur-based projects) of a singular career and a star persona. As Nichols goes on to note, a transformation is involved in this passage from the local to the international:

> The entry of national cinemas and the work of individual film-makers into the international film festival circuit itself constructs new meanings, and it is these new meanings that we, as festival-goers, are most likely to discover.
>
> (71)

While this international standing and circulation may have little to tell us about what, if anything, connects any of these Australian directors, film-makers and actors it does signpost cultural estime (however liminally as birthplace or site of training) and public relations value. Both are critical to sustaining the domestic reputation of the industry on governmental and other horizons within Australia.

National cinemas and the national

> Only by being aware of its national identity can a film industry be international.
> (Volker Schlondorff 1977, quoted in Elsaesser 1989: 306)

If national cinemas are an intrinsically international form, they are also national forms. As Schlondorff's comment suggests, national cinemas do not only persist as a means to counter or accommodate Hollywood, they are sustained and shaped by local purposes of a social, economic, cultural and national nature. Moreover they need to be conscious of these. Recently, Phillip Adams reflected on his and Barry Jones' insider involvement in bringing about federal government support for a film industry in 1968–9. Here Adams explicitly brings together 'national identity' and film export – associating the former with a 'boutique industry':

> We [Phillip Adams and Barry Jones] weren't arguing for a major film industry. Just a modest effort that would allow us to explore our national identity (whatever that was) and to export it to the world's film festivals. At no stage did Jones or I believe it was either possible or useful to make more than ten or fifteen features a year, but our travels had convinced us that there was an opportunity for a boutique industry, that would make culturally specific films for up-market audiences everywhere.
>
> (Adams 1995: ix)

Every national cinema attempts at some point to turn its national distinction into an asset, not a liability. It strives at some point to be locally attached. National cinemas have to do so because the national cinema's place on the horizons of local (and international) cinema and television drama viewers is more marginal than is its international counterpart. Consequently the local connection to government, to non-cinema kinds of backing, and to international involvement whether by way of direct investment or co-productions are going to be all the more important. For this reason there is no clearer instance of this localizing moment than in the ways national cinema producers, promoters and activists call on and mobilize local resources to naturalize their films on the local industry, on local governmental, private enterprise and community horizons. These agents routinely move outside the 'film world' and call on whatever vehicles are at their disposal to bind audiences to the local product and naturalize the local cinema. They characterize the national cinema product as a story of the local people-among-themselves framing their histories, their stories, their lifeways, their locations. Going local at some point is a way of securing the resources with which to compete at home and abroad.

The vehicles drawn on are often 'outside' the typical film communicative circuits. The educational apparatus was enlisted for Peter Weir's *Gallipoli* (1981), as schools around the country organized matinée visits to the cinema during school time for its screening. This had been done before with John Heyer's *Back of Beyond* (1954) – a documentary film commissioned by the Shell Film Unit to capture the 'essence of Australia'. Schepisi drew on a dramatic local incident: the Lindy/Michael/Azaria Chamberlain story of a dingo, Uluru (Ayers Rock) and the ensuring court case which made world news in *Evil Angels/Cry in the Dark* (with Meryl Streep and Sam Neill in the lead roles). David Elfick drew on the late 1980s and early 1990s story of rural crisis, with a generation of workers on the land walking off, for his film *No Worries*. National cinemas often work to produce social purposes as a means of enlisting local audiences. Again *Gallipoli* is an instance where the film's launch and the public discussion surrounding it provided a national lesson in civics. It also provided a marketable Australian image abroad in the historical film. Elsaesser argues that countries like Australia and the UK 'without a strong and continuous tradition of film-making may have to depend on an ability to "market" the national history as spectacle for international success'. National history like the dramatic contemporary public event provides film-makers with a 'common currency' which they might otherwise lack. It 'establishes a signifying system of motifs, oppositions, antinomies and structural binarisms: the very stuff of narratives' (Elsaesser 1989: 293). Elsaesser was thinking here of historical titles like the British *Chariots of Fire* (Hudson 1981) and the Australian *We of the Never Never* (Auzins 1982). This history need not be glorious either. It can be ignominious as in *The Chant of Jimmie Blacksmith*'s insistence on white Australia's racist history (the Aboriginal survival becomes Australia's 'unmastered past' like the Holocaust for Germans); it can be about national defeat in the World War I at *Gallipoli*; and it can be about the sacrifice of principles of justice for the sake of a post-war order, as Japanese war criminals are set free and an innocent Japanese man is convicted as a scapegoat in *Blood Oath* (Wallace 1990).

These different survival options are connected to the strategies and agencies of nation-building of the state and private sector. The two dominant film-makers of 1930s and 1940s Australian cinema – Charles Chauvel and Ken G. Hall – operated in a period where there was just not the same degree of formative state support as there was after 1969. Yet these commercially minded directors were explicitly nationalist. Chauvel proclaimed his mission to be one of 'featuring Australia' as a character in his films. Later national cinema producers had outside help to survive in what Elsaesser (1989: 3) calls 'the politics of culture [support]' of the state. As Tim Rowse (1985: 67) observed, '[n]ation states promote a sense of nationhood. That is one of the functions of cultural policy.' Curiously this enabled them to be less explicitly nationalist.

A. D. Smith (1986: 129–39) distinguishes two features of the common national culture that are important to any discussion of a national cinema. There is the *national political* – the common political and civic culture involving citizenship and equality before the law; and there is the *national cultural* – the cultural core of memories, values, customs, myths, symbols, solidarities and significant landscapes shaping 'Australian' identity. For Smith no state can be workable without both a national political and national cultural sense of itself. The cinema and television matter to public policy makers, interest groups, lobbyists, film-makers and audiences as targets for their national cultural and national political projects and ambitions.

Film-making and film industry policy sustains both kinds of national definitions. The agitators for Australian cinema in the 1960s and early 1970s sought national political support for Australian cinema as a national cultural institution concerned with identity and self-expression – 'dreaming our own dreams, telling our own stories'. A measure of a self-respecting mature nation was the possession of a national cinema. Their emphasis on an open-ended national cultural ambition for the cinema helped legitimate the creation of film-making infrastructures which sustained mainstream, oppositional and peripheral cinemas. It also created a space for alternative Australian identities. If this last had been dressed up as an explicit national political project, rather than as part of a national cultural project, it might well have not got off the ground.

Film-making and film and television policy can sometimes emphasize each at the same time. In 1980 the beginnings of a fifth television network – the SBS-TV – started in Sydney and Melbourne. It was legitimated by a policy of multi-culturalism that was initially conceived as a national political project, highlighting those ethnically and culturally diverse NES background peoples in Australia. At the same time, the establishment of a generous tax concession régime encouraging private investment in film and television production (called 10BA) largely underwrote a film and mini-series boom in which the 'national cultural' was consistently foregrounded and with it the established settler culture and its Australian history. It should be noted that the 1980s was that decade in which the Australian state played the least important role in the selection of film properties and funding (reduced to 16 per cent compared to the 1990s' 39 per cent) – but it still had an indirect role through its certifying of film and mini-series as Australian to qualify for tax concession purposes. This role limited the degree of internationalization of production through the decade and inhibited the development of story properties set outside Australia. Some of the most popular Australian cinema and mini-series television of the 1980s revisited formative national moments in the national symbols-myths complex, such as the Boer War in Bruce Beresford's international 'breakthrough' film, *Breaker Morant*, the World War I in *Gallipoli*; the legend of the eponymous race-horse of the 1930s in *Phar Lap*; the bodyline cricket controversy of the 1930s between Australia and Britain in *Bodyline* (Schultz, Ogilvie, Marinos and Lawrence 1984). These productions restated and updated old myths 'dedominionizing' Australia by accentuating its 'non-English' characteristics (see Kapferer 1988: 167 and Davidson 1979 *passim*). The most popular features of the decade – *Crocodile Dundee* and *The Man from Snowy River* – revisited Australian 'bushman' archetypes and in the *Snowy River*'s case the famous poem once taught universally in Australian schools.

While this was happening some policy-makers, critics and film-makers subscribed to a different national political object. This was a reconstructed objective of a 'multicultural' Australia which was to become an increasingly important definition of Australian nationhood from the mid-1980s, culminating in the 1989 National Agenda for a Multicultural Australia. As Rowse observed in 1985 (75) it 'yields an Australianism defined by inner diversity, rather than by a homogeneous sense of being different from Britain'. It envisages an 'Australia linked in a relaxed diversity of inheritances to all the nations of Europe and Asia by the encouragement given to ethnic plurality among migrants' (75). Cathy Robinson, current Chief Executive of the AFC, observed in November 1991 that multiculturalism ensured that 'cultural policy and cultural nationalism could no longer be so easily equated' (Robinson and Given 1994: 20).

The two movements for locating a national cultural identity and a multicultural reality found some congruence in a handful of the mini-series of the late 1980s foregrounding the

NES experience of the Australian mainstream, in programmes like *The Dunera Boys* (1985, Jewish refugee experience of Australian internment), *Cowra Breakout* (1985, Japanese prisoner-of-war internment in the World War II), *Fields of Fire* (1987, 1988, 1989, Italian-Australian experience in the cane fields of north Queensland) and *Always Afternoon* (1988, a German national's experience of discrimination during the World War I).

Sometimes the two can be in conflict. With the increasing importance of multiculturalism as an official policy of state over the 1980s and a sense of the inevitability of industry internationalization by the late 1980s, film policy makers and bureaucrats certifying films as Australian for investment purposes gave policy a more national political hue. They became concerned with industrial markers – how many were involved in the making of it and in which positions. At the same time, broadcasting regulators at the then Australian Broadcasting Tribunal were concerned to evolve national cultural terminology and notions, seeking textual markers for something to be Australian (see Cunningham 1992: 56–60). For the first the issue was an employment and deployment one involving principles of equity and access. For the second it was a national cultural issue. The conflict between these two arms of government confronted a national political assessment with a national cultural one.

Both critical commentary and film industry thinking had, by the late 1980s, moved towards the notion that, in Rowse's words, 'Australianness should mean nothing more than that a number of residents of Australia were employed in the making of it' (75). This had the advantage of 'not beg[ging] the question of what people who live in Australia are concerned with' (79) and therefore living up to the promise of multiculturalism. It also had the advantage of opening the industry to what Ross Gibson (1992: 81) has called 'international contamination', in which Australian cinema could be envisaged as a large family of projects made with some Australian involvement. This entailed a significantly more commodious notion of what could be 'Australian' in order to permit some exploitation of the opportunities afforded Australia as a cultural producer in the English language, like the French–Australian co-production *Green Card* – the vehicle for Gerard Depardieu to reach a wide English-speaking audience – or Vincent Ward's remarkable *Map of the Human Heart* (1993), with its tale of an Inuit's unrequited love and Pauline Chan's *Traps* – a story of a marriage falling apart set in Vietnam of the 1950s. The preferred Australian was now what Ghassan Hage has usefully called a 'cosmopolite' – a '" mega-urban" figure, detached from strong affiliations with roots and consequently open to all forms of otherness' (Hage 1995: 76). As Deborah Jones (1992: xiv) writes in the context of *Strictly Ballroom* 'to be Australian now is to be much more like other people, anywhere, than we may have admitted in the past'. And it produces a film-making whose 'identity' is uncertain, like *The Piano* and *Sirens*.

When Elsaesser writes that 'no other European country, it seems, is as unsure of the meaning of its culture as Germany, or as obsessed with its national identity' (1989: 49) – he could just as well be writing of Australia. As with the New German Cinema, the Australian cinema since the 1970s has resolutely set about problematizing its national identity, taking on, or perhaps 'trying on' successive identities, holding together apparently incompatible national cultural and political objectives and using the nation as a means of questioning and interrogating its very national possibility and merit as such. Because of the importance of 'nations' to a national cinema, national cinemas inevitably involve questions of relative national merit.

In their own ways, Germany and Australia have problematic international identities and these influence what their cinemas can be and how they can be taken up. Both have as part of their very cinematic identity this movement of problematizing the nation, the culture, and even the society itself. Germany's Nazi history is sometimes compared to Australia's Aboriginal and Islander genocide. But mostly Australia's problem is not Germany's one of the specific kind of cultural value it musters, but rather the absence of (any) value and therefore any distinguishing culture in international circulation.

Like the German cinema, the Australian cinema has also been 'innovative and coherent' (Elsaesser 1989: 61) in its margins: its women's cinema, its films about marginal groups (the skin-heads of *Romper Stomper*, the bikers of *Stone* – Harbutt 1974), the sub-cultural lifestyles (*Monkey Grip*'s Carlton milieu, the transvestites of *The Adventures of Priscilla: Queen of the Desert*), and minority interests (the displaced persons of *Silver City*, the Greeks of *The Heartbreak Kid*, the Japanese war brides in *Aya* (Hoaas 1991), the disabled in *Struck by Lightning* (Domaradzki 1990), the Murri Aborigines of *Fringe Dwellers* (Beresford 1986) – and perhaps, most significantly, in its documentary tradition. Films produced under this logic are often seen as the true heart of Australian cinema: not only where it is at its most experimental, innovative and coherent but where it deals with the toughest issues and where it is 'most Australian'.

Yet, as with the New German Cinema, films produced under this logic also suffer a legitimation gap in that they are marginal to a significant part of the audience. At times their audiences are more virtual than actual – films to mark time, to develop talent, to get noticed to make a high budget film. But equally, as with the New German Cinema, Australian cinema in its minor streams has highly specific audiences in mind making films appealing to a small part of the audience 'from a sense of shared values and assumptions' (Elsaesser 1989: 154) but running 'the risk of being either parochial (the in-group film) or esoteric'. The cinema here 'served an audience for confirming or validating individual experience and feelings' opening on to a 'desire . . . directed at the film-maker, to represent only a "correct" political or ideologically unambiguous standpoint'. There was a constant need for self-confirmation and self-validation in the guise of criticism and *ad hoc* political theory on the part of the spectators' (159). If this is particularly true for the independent cinema in Australia with *Filmnews* until 1995, *Cantrill's Filmnotes* and *Metro* serving as vehicles to make it so; it is also true of a critical milieu seeking as a matter of some urgency to work out whether the mainstream *The Sum of Us* or *Bad Boy Bubby* or *The Piano* have got their respective sexual politics right – establishing in short whether these films can legitimately speak to 'us' in the way Campion's short films, and Ana Kokkinos' *Only the Brave* apparently do/did.

Like the New German Cinema, the search for an audience is continually foregrounded as a problem in Australian cinema. Even the villains were the same: the exhibition and distribution sector concerned with exhibiting American pictures, the local audience trained to accommodate the wrong product, the Americans who have colonized our subconscious in a thoroughly mediatized landscape – *Kings of the Road* (Wenders 1975) meets *Newsfront*! To some degree the responses are also similar: Kluge's experimentation with form in his 1970s films echoes the experimentation in distantiation found in Australian feature 'documentaries' like Cavadini and Strachen's ethnographic experimentation in the service of a political cinema in *Two Laws* (1981) or in John Hughes' Walter Benjamin inspired film *One Way Street* (1993). As in New German Cinema, there is considerable attention to getting the film processes right – ethically and politically – to obtaining the right forms of consultation particularly with respect to marginal groups. Herzog's propensity to 'test borderlines, limits and extremes' finds its Australian equivalent in Denis O'Rourke's dramatic gestures on the Pacific rim – in his documentary features *Cannibal Tours* (1988) and most extraordinarily in *The Good Woman of Bangkok* (1992). Schepisi's treatment of the media and the courts in *Evil Angels* (aka *Cry in the Dark*) as instruments of systemic harassment replicates Margarethe von Trotta's *The Lost Honour of Katharina Blum* (1975).

Elsaesser (1989: 309) notes that 'Australia . . . has seen a revival as a national cinema similar to that in West Germany'. He also notes the parallel with the new Australian cinema.

Elsaesser and Dermody and Jacka make the state central to their account. For their part, Dermody and Jacka see Australian film-makers as having three different responses as hand-maidens to the state, its reputation and its ethos. One has been to subscribe to state purposes, to the dominant national cultural purposes in a bland mainstream feature film-making, which they call the AFC-Genre; another has been to subscribe to and stress the industry and there-fore commercial purposes espousing genre film-making; and yet another – and this is by far the most dependent one on the state – is to resist both. This estimation very much consigns the mainstream product to the sidelines as either nakedly commercial or as a bland product. It certainly has been incoherent and less evidently 'innovative' in a formal and minoritarian sense. Yet this 'absent centre' at the heart of mainstream Australian features – this seeming dependence on 'other cinemas' and their norms, genres and so on – is actually one of the most fascinating aspects of Australian cinema, enabling it to speak so powerfully to local and international audiences alike in *Strictly Ballroom*, *Mad Max II* (*The Road Warrior*), *My Brilliant Career* and *Crocodile Dundee*.

The messiness of national cinemas

If there is a considerable 'local' aspect to national cinemas, there is considerable fuzziness surrounding them. At some time or other most national cinemas are not coterminous with their nation states. As we have seen, production funding is international. Formal co-production treaties between countries provide frameworks to produce films which may have little to do with either country. Peter Weir's romantic comedy, *Green Card*, is typical of the high budget strand of Australian film-making in the 1990s: it has an Australian director, it is funded by French and Australian investors and its post-production was carried out in Australia. This is a French/Australian co-production set and filmed in New York and is the story of a 'marriage of convenience' between a French man played by Gerard Depardieu and an American played by Andie MacDowell. He marries in order to gain permanent residency in the US and she to secure an apartment only available to a married woman. The comedy and the developing romance between the two evolves once they are subject of an official investigation over the status of their 'marriage'. Yet unlike the rapid-fire comedy dialogue of similar Hollywood romantic comedies casting opposites – physically, emotionally, intellectually – *Green Card* has a slower delivery of dialogue, and is consequently more muted, slow and observed. It remains true to the green card experience of the Depardieu character speaking and mastering English as a second language. This and the film's ending, where the Depardieu character is deported at the precise moment the couple realise they love each other, signifies the intrusion of the European-Australian 'reality principle' which refuses to solve the problem in a happy ending but instead substitutes a new dilemma for the old. There are no Australians in front of the camera, yet. It is, with its FFC backing, Peter Weir's 'Australian film' of the 1990s.

Many smaller national cinemas are also in product, orientation, industry and language at some stage a part of each other. Deciding where the national leaves off and another national begins is difficult in these cases because the 'national' involves both. This is particularly so for Australia and New Zealand. Close cultural, language and historical links forge an Australasian film-making and identity. Vincent Ward, Jane Campion and Cecil Homes (regarded by some as film-makers, whose promise made evident in *Three in One* and *Captain Thunderbolt* – was tragically not able to be fulfilled) are all New Zealanders. Franklyn Barrett – with Longford and McDonagh – the finest of Australian silent film-makers, came to Australia after a film-making career in New Zealand. There is a long history of Australian directors making New

Zealand films which includes Longford's *A Maori Maid's Love* 1916). Some silent films – like Beaumont Smith's *The Betrayer* (1921) – managed Australian and New Zealand locations. And New Zealand actors have always had a strong presence in Australian films from 'the clever New Zealander' Vera James (whose father secured the new Zealand distribution rights for her film *A Girl of the Bush* (Barrett 1921), to Sam Neill in *My Brilliant Career*, *Dead Calm* and *Death in Brunswick*.

Campion's explicitly Australian-based work is sometimes claimed for New Zealand cinema. *Sweetie* was screened in Sydney as part of a festival of New Zealand cinema. Is Campion a New Zealander or an Australian? Sometimes she describes herself as an Australian; just as often she associates her work – particularly her New Zealand based stories – with her Kiwi identity. This gives rise to debates over whether *The Piano* is an Australian or a New Zealand film. Does her work spanning the Tasman Sea and that of Vincent Ward (*The Navigator: A Medieval Odyssey* 1988 – the AFC and the New Zealand Film Commission's first co-production) presage the development of a more integrated 'Australasian' filmmarket to undergird an Australasian identity?

The Piano was set in New Zealand and made by a New Zealand director and of its three principals two were American and one a New Zealander. The Australian connection is solely that the AFC provided Campion with script development money and that Campion is Sydney-based, has lived in Australia for seventeen years, was trained at the AFTRS, and has used Australian film subsidy and production régimes to develop her talent and film properties. Yet *The Piano* is not simply another international production with some Australian involvement, it also represents Australasian film-making and a growing convergence and integration of the Australian and New Zealand film-making, exhibition and distribution sectors in the 1990s. This emerging situation is reminiscent of the integrated market that existed before television fractured what was a highly integrated Australasian audio-visual market.

Sweetie, *The Piano*, *Map of the Human Heart* and *An Angel at My Table* are just some of the high profile 'mixed productions' involving Australian and New Zealand collaborations of creative personnel which became an unexceptionable part of the cinema landscape in the 1990s. The 1990s also saw the return of New Zealand to the Australian imagination after so long being the 'poor relation'. Films set and shot in New Zealand gained significant audiences and acclaim from the Australian market, as *An Angel at My Table* and *The Piano* were followed up with Lee Tamahori's *Once were Warriors* (1994) and Peter Jackson's *Heavenly Creatures* (1995). Campion's films project in these terms an Australasian identity reflecting the close economic, cultural political, social and historical links between Australia and New Zealand and the significant New Zealand migrant presence in Australia. It is worth remembering in this regard that every Western national cinema is, at some stage, as a matter of national cultural policy interested in fostering international values, cooperation, mutual understanding and economic integration. The rethinking of the Australian–New Zealand relation on both sides of the Tasman at virtually every level in the late 1980s and through into the 1990s is a case in point. *The Piano* is one consequence of this rethinking. For David Robinson (1994: 125) the film becomes 'in its combination of Australasian and Hollywood practices . . . a paradigm of new international art cinema'.

Many smaller national cinemas are also at some stage part of larger national cinemas. Think of Austrian cinema with respect to German cinema; or Australian and New Zealand cinema with respect to English and American cinema. The Australian cinema of the 1930s consciously foregrounded its diasporic links to Britain – both as a means to create product suitable for sale in the UK and as a way of giving expression to a dominant (but by no means uncontested) cultural ideal of the day projecting Australia as a British-derived society. In 1930,

W. K. Hancock wrote in his authoritative work on Australians (1961: 28) 'if such a creature as the average Briton exists anywhere upon this earth, he will be found in Australia'. Ken G. Hall's *The Squatter's Daughter* (1933) set up a seamless movement from Australia to Britain and then back again. The talented musician denied opportunity within Australia in *Broken Melody* (Hall 1938) goes to England to claim his destiny as a composer of merit, to return later to Australia and reclaim his romantic love and retrieve his place in his father's affections and bail out the family farm.

The post-war Australian feature cinema up until the decisive explosion of the 1970s was significantly – and mostly – a consequence of the outreaching of other national cinemas – British, American and even French and Japanese cinemas. The 1966 film *They're a Weird Mob* is a pivotal transition film between the 'out-reaching of others' and the 'on local terms' of the 1970s. It looks back to the British and American location films of the 1950s and 1960s; and it looks forward to an 'Anglo-Australian film industry' characterized by creative partnerships like that between J. C. Williamson and Powell and Pressburger. Post-1970 Australian cinema used subsidy and television industry consolidation to forge on its own terms international partnerships in place of the off-shore productions of the 1950s and 1960s.

So too, nation states are only one among a number of organizers of films, their circulation, production and meaning. Large regional international organizations such as the European Community are taking over some of the functions of nation states and evolving film policies fostering international cooperation. So too it is a policy priority of the Australian, Canadian, English and New Zealand film organizations to pursue greater production, policy and industry links between themselves to better coordinate and integrate their markets to mutual benefit. This parallels and updates the relatively integrated 'Commonwealth' film market of the 1950s involving these same countries. *Black Robe* is an example of this increasingly formalized association between the government funding agencies of three Commonwealth countries. This film is veteran director Bruce Beresford's 'Australian film' of the 1990s. There are a host of Australians in the crew and one in the cast, in Aden Young (who grew up in Canada). It is a Canadian/Australian co-production. It is also a Canadian film set in Canada telling the story of colonization and most particularly the religious colonization of the Indian peoples of Quebec. At my local video library *Black Robe* is located on the 'festival' shelves and marketed on the dustjacket as being in continuity with the director's 1980 classic, *Breaker Morant*.

Other organizers of film production and circulation are multinational distributors, satellite television networks, international festivals, television networks and co-production arrangements. Most of this is not new. The transnational European film ideal of today had its predecessor in the Film Europe movement of the 1920s and early 1930s (K. Thompson 1987). Co-productions emerged in the 1960s to facilitate continental European film-making.

Sometimes this fuzziness in the national cinema is structural to the nation. Take for instance the language and regionally based 'national' cinemas within India and Canada. The Canadian state, for example, supports two national cinemas: an English-speaking one based in Toronto and Vancouver and a French-speaking one based in Montreal. And there are the various diasporic cinemas which in some guises have the stature of a cohesive 'national' cinema – like the 'overseas Chinese', 'Indian' and Jewish cinema which gains Australian audiences. Jewish film festivals have become a phenomenon in Australia and the US, whose product is drawn from across the world including Australia. Australian cinema's contributions to a Jewish cinema have been limited: they include Henri Safran's comedy *Norman Loves Rose* (1982) and Jackie Farkas' searing short film *The Illustrated Auschwitz* (1992) which recounts a survivor's experience of the Holocaust and how her memory of that is connected to her first post-Holocaust cultural experience of watching *The Wizard of Oz* (1939). Are the growing body of short films shot in Italian, Spanish and Greek a contribution to the Italian, Spanish and Greek 'national cinemas' or are they 'Australian cinema'? Although not part of any larger diaspora, diaspora-like structures have emerged surrounding 'first peoples' or 'Aboriginal' film-making and screening events, which bring together culturally diverse first peoples who have been marginalized in different parts of the world by processes of colonization. Is there an Aboriginal and Torres Strait Islander cinema we can call an indigenous national cinema emerging from the spaces of non-Aboriginal and Aboriginal partnerships? The AFC sponsored a touring season of films in 1995 called *Hidden Pictures*, promoting an indigenous cinema whose beginnings are located in collaborations between non-Aboriginal film-makers and Aboriginal actors and individuals – in Ned Lander's tale of an Aboriginal band on the road in *Wrong Side of the Road* (1981) and Phil Noyce's low-budget road movie *Backroads*. The openness of these film-makers to Aboriginal input and their preparedness to allow that input shape the final product prepared the way for Aboriginal film-makers like Tracey Moffatt and Anne Pratten and a greater role for Aboriginal voices.

Like many national cinemas, Australian cinema operates within the multi-ethnic context. Fourteen per cent of Australian households spoke a language other than English at home and these homes sustained 'ethnic video' and cinema outlets for screening imported, culturally appropriate product and for the screening of locally produced materials. With 22 per cent of its population born outside the country courtesy of a large post-World War II migration programme and a generous refugee programme (on a per capita basis Australia accepted more Indo-Chinese refugees than did any other country, see Lombard 1993: 18), Australian cinema may not be the natural non-Hollywood cinema of a minor but not insignificant proportion of the population. With such a multi-ethnic society the 'typical Australian' is now a product of several ancestries to the extent that Australia's cinema audience is shaped by a variety of cultural influences – which are increasingly seen in its cinema – as in the Spanish family in *Strictly Ballroom* and the Greek family in *Death in Brunswick* and *The Heartbreak Kid*.

National cinemas function within internally divided provincial contexts sustained by provincial governance and regional identities. Because many nations are, like Australia, Canada, the US and Germany federations, state or provincial authorities are also organizers of film production and circulation through, for example, various state film authorities and the local basis for censorship provisions. Elsaesser (1989: 49) notes Germany's 'long-established reflex of regionalism, and centuries of decentralization' commenting on its impact on German cinema and the politics of culture support. Australia is like Germany in this respect: regionalism is a standard reflex – the Australian states existed before 'Australia' did as a governing entity and decentralization is not only intrinsic to the European settlement of Australia but of Aboriginal and Islander society before it. Some Australian state, notably the populous New South Wales (Sydney its capital was the major centre for film production and still is) imposed film quotas in the 1930s. One of the important features of the Australian film revival was that production funding has been provided by the different states since 1972. Some Australian exhibition chains have been locality- and state-specific. And various kinds of sub-national identities provide alternative cultural materials and spaces to exploit.

A good example of this regionalism is Argall's *Return Home*. Its Adelaide setting stresses the cultural particularity of regional Australia. It foregrounds the significant migration to the metropolitan city from provincial Adelaide. It is also about diminishing living standards and downward mobility that is a marked feature of the lower middle class and working class experience over the 1980s and 1990s. One of the characters, Noel is rehabilitated by his journey home from Melbourne. The film is structured as a dialogue between two brothers, Steve (Adelaide) and Noel (metropolitan Melbourne). Each has what the other lacks. Steve owns a failing small garage business but he has family. Noel has no family but is successful and has big city Melbourne values. We are invited to read their different values in relation to the changing geographic 'landscape' of Australia. The narrative is resolved in favour of provincial Adelaide and family, as Noel returns to lend his skills to rejuvenate his brother's business. This affirmation of home has a utopian dimension, as Adelaide and South Australia have bleaker prospects compared to the booming economies of Queensland and Western Australia and the industrial heartlands of Sydney and Melbourne. Here Adelaide can be remade by the return of sons and daughters it has lost to the metropolis. Watching *Return Home* I was struck by the many parallels between it and Edgar Reitz's mini-series *Heimat* (1984). Both Australian and German cites have a deeply provincial character, with competing regional centres having different outlooks. There is the same 'rootlessness', as a post-war order was made and fashioned as a significant 'break with the past'. Both have seen significant internal migration – in Australia's case north to Queensland and west to Western Australia, and to Australia's two metropoles of Sydney and Melbourne. *Return Home*'s regionalism is achieved through its suburban characters, language, and the minute, often nostalgic descriptions of everyday life in the spacious single-storey suburbs of Adelaide. The film interweaves ideas of provincialism and homeland – giving voice to that other side of Australia life – its provincial character. here the suburban heartland is centred on the nuclear family, its local horizons, the immediate and locality-bound networks which are gently opposed to the modern city, Melbourne and its alienated vision of glass. Like *Heimat*, *Return Home* consistently exploits the tension which Kaes (1989: 168) identifies there between 'staying and leaving, between longing for distant places and homesickness'. Argall's film is a troubling objection to the changes wrought on traditional Australian communities struggling to keep their provincial lives, hopes and lifeways intact in the face of declining economic circumstance and profound structural change.

Notes

1   The only exception I can think of is the 1979 Peat Marwick, Mitchell Services report on the Australian Film Commission, which imagined unlimited horizons for Australian cinema, enacting the dream so chimerically available to the non-Hollywood English-language producers, in gaining equivalent American success. See PMM, 1979: 18–20.
2   Bill Routt, personal correspondence, August 1994.
3   The earlier film – a British location film – was directed by Ralph Smart and released in 1947.

Chapter 12

JOHN HILL

BRITISH CINEMA AS NATIONAL CINEMA
Production, audience and representation

FOLLOWING THE OSCAR-WINNING SUCCESS OF *Chariots of Fire* (1981) on 23 March 1982, the film was re-released and showed successfully across Britain in the weeks which followed. On 2 April, the Argentinians invaded the Falklands/Malvinas and, three days later, the Thatcher government despatched a naval task force from Portsmouth which successfully retook the islands in June. In a sense, the coincidence of Oscar-winning success in Los Angeles and subsequent military victory in the Falklands seemed to link the two events, and the idea of a national resurgence in both cinema ('the British are coming') and national life became intertwined. Indeed, Hugo Young reports that David Puttnam, the producer of *Chariots of Fire*, was a subsequent guest of the Prime Minister's at Chequers and that there was 'much talk in the Thatcher circle about the desirability of something similar being put on to celluloid to celebrate the Falklands victory'.[1]

There are, however, two factors which complicate this story. Despite its reputation, *Chariots of Fire* is a more complex work than is commonly suggested. Indeed, a film which is reputedly so nationalist is surprisingly conscious of the complexities of national allegiance, focusing as it does on the running careers of two 'outsiders': Harold Abrahams, a Jew of Lithuanian background, and Eric Liddell, a Scotsman born in China. If *Chariots of Fire* did become identified with renascent national sentiment, then this was probably not so much the result of the ideological outlook which the film itself manifests as of the moment at which its success was achieved. The other complicating factor is that when the film was re-released it was as part of a double bill with *Gregory's Girl* (1980). While this double bill was undoubtedly intended to showcase the range of new British cinema, there is also something a touch subversive in the way these films were coupled. For while both are British, they also represent rather different kinds of British cinema.

Chariots of Fire, at a cost of £3 million, was a comparatively expensive film for British cinema in 1980. And although it was strongly identified with 'Britishness' it was actually funded from foreign sources, including Hollywood. *Gregory's Girl*, by contrast, cost only about £200,000 and was financed from domestic sources, including the National Film Finance Corporation and Scottish Television. A clear contrast in formal approach is also apparent. Despite some play with temporal relations, *Chariots of Fire* employs a relatively straightforward narrative structure, organized around goal-oriented action and positive heroes. *Gregory's*

Girl opts for a much looser, more episodic form in which surface realism, comedy and domesticated surrealism are combined in a way which successfully fuses British comic traditions with a modernist sensibility. These differences also extend to content. While *Chariots of Fire* is focused on the past, *Gregory's Girl* is resolutely of the present. The version of the past which *Chariots of Fire* constructs, moreover, is strongly identified with the English upper classes and male achievement, while *Gregory's Girl* is set amongst the suburban middle and working classes and gently subverts conventional stereotypes of male and female roles. And if both films are 'British', *Chariots* is very much an 'English' film whereas *Gregory's Girl* is clearly 'Scottish'.

While both films are, at least partly, set in Scotland, there is a significant difference between the representations of Scotland which they provide. *Chariots of Fire* tends to look at Scotland from the outside (or rather from the metropolitan English centre), associating it with the 'natural' and the 'primitive'. *Gregory's Girl*, on the other hand, uses the 'new town' of Cumbernauld to avoid the conventional signifiers of 'Scottishness' and, in doing so, suggest an altogether more complex sense of contemporary Scottish identity. This, in turn, has links to what might be characterized as the films' different modes of cultural address. *Chariots*, with its enthusiasm for the past and links with conventional notions of English 'national heritage', offers an image of Britain which generally conforms to the expectations of an international, and especially American, audience. *Gregory's Girl* is a much more obviously local and idiomatic film. It too has an international appeal, but for an audience more likely to be European than American. And while *Chariots of Fire* is conventionally taken to be the landmark in the revival of British cinema, it may in fact be *Gregory's Girl* which provided the more reliable indicator of the way in which British film-making was developing.

Production

In the 1980s British cinema returned to the position in which it found itself in the 1920s when the government first introduced a quota for British films. In 1925 some 10 per cent of films exhibited in British cinemas were British; by 1926 this had dropped to 5 per cent.[2] The bulk of films shown were, of course, from the US. Following the abolition of the quota in 1983, the percentage of British films on British screens dwindled to similar proportions. Thus in 1992 the US had a 92.5 per cent share of the British exhibition market while British films accounted for only 4 per cent.[3]

The responses to US domination which have been available to the production sector of the British film industry in the 1980s and 1990s are, however, different from those of the 1920s. In his essay on the conceptualization of national cinemas, Stephen Crofts identifies a number of strategies available to national cinema production. For the British cinema the most important are what he describes as the imitation of Hollywood, competition with Hollywood in domestic markets and differentiation from Hollywood.[4] The imitation of Hollywood involves the attempt to beat Hollywood at its own game, a strategy which has been tried at various junctures in the history of British cinema: by Alexander Korda in the 1930s, by Rank in the 1940s, by EMI in the 1970s, and by Goldcrest in the 1980s. Given the comparative advantage which Hollywood enjoys over other national industries by virtue of its scale of production, size of domestic market and international distribution and exhibition network (amongst other factors), this has proved an economically unviable strategy and, despite some success with individual films, all such attempts have resulted in financial disaster. It is therefore the second, competitive strategy which has constituted the mainstay of British cinema.

As a result of the quota (and, later, some additional forms of state support), the existence of a commercial British cinema which did not compete with Hollywood internationally but only in the domestic market proved possible from the 1930s to – just about – the 1970s. The basis of this cinema, however, was a size of audience sufficient to sustain a domestic film industry. As cinema audiences began to decline, especially from the 1950s, the commercial viability of a cinema aimed primarily at British audiences came under threat. As a result, regular British film production (characteristically popular genre film-making) aimed at the domestic market came to a virtual halt after the 1970s when Hammer horror, the *Carry Ons* and the *Confession* films all ceased to be produced. While it had previously been possible for British films to recoup their costs on the home market, this became an exception from the 1970s onwards. Only a minority of British films achieved a domestic gross of over £1 million during the 1980s, and even an apparently popular success such as *Buster*, which grossed £3.7 million in 1988, failed to recover its production cost of £3.2 million from British box-office revenues (given that only a fraction of these actually returns to the producer).

In consequence, the place of British cinema within the international film economy has had to change. Writing in 1969, Alan Lovell argued that, unlike its European counterparts, the British cinema had failed to develop an art cinema (or at any rate that the documentary film had served in its place).[5] During the 1980s, however, it was art cinema which was to become the predominant model of British film-making. The category of 'art cinema' is not, of course, a precise one and it is used here in a relatively generous sense. David Bordwell, for example, has attempted to define 'art cinema' as a distinctive 'mode of film practice' characterized by realism, authorial expressivity and ambiguity.[6] His definition, however, is too tied to the 1960s and fails to do justice to the range of textual strategies employed by art cinema in the 1980s and 1990s. Thus, in the case of Britain, the category of art cinema may be seen to include not only the 'realism' of Ken Loach and Mike Leigh and the postmodern aesthetic experiments of Derek Jarman and Peter Greenaway, but also the aesthetically conservative 'heritage' cinema of Merchant–Ivory. In this last case, the 'art' of 'art cinema' derives not so much from the authorial presence of the director or the distance from classical narrational and stylistic techniques which such films display, as from the cachet of 'high art' which such films borrow from literary or theoretical sources.

For Crofts, art cinema is the prime example of a national cinema avoiding direct competition with Hollywood by targeting a distinct market sector. This model, he argues, aims 'to differentiate itself textually from Hollywood, to assert explicitly or implicitly an indigenous product, and to reach domestic and export markets through those specialist distribution channels and exhibition venues usually called arthouse'.[7] In this respect, the adoption of aesthetic strategies and cultural referents different from Hollywood also involves a certain foregrounding of 'national' credentials. The oft-noted irony of this, however, is that art cinema then achieves much of its status as national cinema by circulating internationally rather than nationally. While this means that art cinema (as in the case of Greenaway) may be as economically viable as ostensibly more commercial projects aimed at the 'popular' audience, it is also the case that successful British films have often done better outside Britain than within. A notorious example of this was Ken Loach's *Riff-Raff* which, at the time it won the European Film Award for Best Film in 1991, had been seen by more people in France than in the UK. Even in the case of the heritage film, it is international audiences, especially American, which have become a key source of revenues as well as prestige. As a result, it has become an attractive option to open such films in the US before a release in Britain, as was the case, for example, with both *The Madness of King George* (1995) and *Sense and Sensibility* (1995).

In both these cases – the *cinéma d'auteur* which circulates in Europe and the heritage film which appeals to the US – it can be argued that the changed economic circumstances of the British film industry have led to a certain decline of 'national' cinema, in so far as the national address which earlier commercial British cinema appeared to have is no longer so evident. In this respect, much of the lamenting of the current state of the British film industry registers a sense of loss of the connection which it is assumed the British cinema once had with a national popular audience. There is a further twist to this argument, however. For, if the decline in domestic cinema audiences has made British film production increasingly dependent upon international revenues, it has also increased its reliance on television for revenues and production finance as well. The increasing inter-relationship between film and television which was resulted has had consequences for how film is consumed, and for the way it may be judged to be 'national'.

Audience

The changing character of British cinema in the 1980s may be explained, then, in terms of the new production strategies which emerged in the wake of declining cinema audiences. In 1946, annual cinema admissions reached an all-time high of 1,635 million, but then fell steadily until 1984, when they plummeted to 58 million. There has been a subsequent increase – admissions reached over 123 million in 1994, but this is still less than for any year before 1974. It is these figures which provide the backdrop to perceptions of cinema's declining national role. For if the British cinema of World War II is still regarded as a watershed in national cinema, it is not only as a result of the films which were then made but because of the size of the cinema audience which attended them. In 1940, admissions topped 1,000 million for the first time when, partly because of a lack of alternatives, films were the most popular form of entertainment. In this respect, wartime cinema is regarded as pre-eminently 'national', because of the size and range of its audience.

Even at its peak, however, the cinema audience was never fully representative of the nation. A survey of the British cinema audience in 1943, for example, revealed that 30 per cent of the population didn't go to the cinema at all, and that certain social groups were more likely to attend the cinema than others.[8] Women went to the cinema more than men, the manual working class and lower-middle class went more frequently than managerial and professional groups, town-dwellers more than country-dwellers. Most strikingly of all, the cinema audience was characteristically made up of the young rather than the old: the under-45s accounted for 85 per cent of the cinema audience but only 68 per cent of the overall population. Cinemagoing declined significantly with age, and 60 per cent of the over-65s are reported as never going to the cinema at all. The 'national' audience for British films, even during the 'golden age' of British cinema, was neither as homogeneous nor as socially representative of the nation as is sometimes assumed.

Audience factors are also relevant when considering the subsequent decline of the cinema. If the cinema audience has become a smaller proportion of the overall population and cinemagoing no longer occupies the central place in leisure activities which it once did, the social character of the audience and its cinema-watching habits have also changed.[9] Cinemagoing has become even more heavily concentrated amongst the young, particularly the 15–34 age group, which accounted for 78 per cent of cinema attendances in 1990 (but represented only 37 per cent of the population). By comparison, only 11 per cent of the over-45s attended the cinema despite representing 46 per cent of the population. The class basis of cinemagoing has also altered. Cinemagoing is no longer a predominantly working-class activity, and in 1990 social classes ABC1 accounted for 59 per cent of cinemagoers (while representing 42 per cent of the population).[10] One explanation for this is the growth of multiplexes, which since 1985 have been responsible for reviving the cinemagoing habit, especially amongst car-owners.[11] Multiplexes have also made the cinema more attractive to women, who, following a decline in attendance in the 1950s, have accounted for about 50 per cent of the cinema audience in the 1990s. From the 1950s onwards, the working-class cinema audience has been in decline and has been replaced by an increasingly young and more affluent audience; this reflects more general trends in cinemagoing which have seen an increase in the importance of the 15–24 age group (estimated to be as much as 80 per cent of the worldwide cinema audience for English-language films).[12] This audience demography is clearly significant for national cinema: what is most popular at the cinemas is not necessarily popular with a fully representative section of the 'nation', but only with a relatively narrow segment of it.

A further complication is that, while these trends are fairly clear with regard to cinemagoing, cinemas themselves are no longer the primary site for viewing films. Despite the global decline in cinema attendances, Douglas Gomery has argued that watching films is more popular than ever.[13] People may no longer watch films in the cinemas but they do watch in increasing numbers on television and video, especially in the UK where TV and video penetration is very high by world standards. Some comparisons are appropriate. In 1994, for example, total cinema admissions in Britain were 123 million; in the same year, video rentals (which are dominated by feature films) amounted to 194 million (a considerable drop, in fact, from 328 million the previous year) and there were 66 million video retail transactions.[14] In the case of television, the contrast is even more striking. There are considerably more films on TV than in the cinemas: in 1994, 299 features were released in UK cinemas, of which 35 were 'wholly' British,[15] but in the same year 1,910 films were screened on terrestrial TV, of which 413 were British productions.[16] Films on TV are also watched by considerably more people. In 1994 the viewing figures for the top ten films on TV alone matched the total audience for all 299 films shown in the cinemas. This also means that individual films, including British films, are seen by significantly more people on television than in the cinemas. The most popular 'wholly' British film of 1992, *Peter's Friends*, was seen by approximately four times as many people when it was shown on television in 1994 than in the cinema.[17] A commercially unsuccessful film such as *Waterland* was seen by nearly 34 times as many people when it was shown on television in 1994; if its television viewing audience of 3.3 million had been converted into cinema attendances, this would have put it in the box-office top ten for 1992.

Clearly, people watch more films on television and video than they do in the cinema; and the television/video audience is more representative of the 'nation' as a whole. The group which is over-represented in the cinemas – the 16–24 year-olds – is under-represented in the television audience, and those groups which are infrequent cinemagoers – the over-45s, social groups DE, country-dwellers – are much more likely to see films on TV.[18] While there are no precise figures, it does seem that many contemporary British films which are not regarded as especially 'popular' are nonetheless seen on television by as many people as 'popular' British films of the past. To put it provocatively, it may be that a British cinema which is generally regarded as being in decline is nonetheless producing films which are often seen by as many, and sometimes more, people as films made during the 'golden age' of British cinema.

There are provisos, of course. As has often been argued, the cinema experience and the television viewing experience are dissimilar: watching films on TV or video is characteristically less concentrated than in the cinema.[19] But it is also worth noting how habitual cinemagoing was in its heyday. Browning and Sorrell report that in 1946 nearly three-quarters of those who went to the cinema more than once a month did so whatever films were being shown and without choosing between cinemas.[20] Cinemagoing was only exceptionally an 'event' and, in a number of respects, television has taken over the cinema's former function of catering to the 'regular cinemagoer'. While this is true of most television scheduling of films, however, television can also use film as an 'event', breaking up the televisual flow and offering a 'special' experience. This commonly happens with the first screening of a Hollywood blockbuster but would also be true, for example, of Channel 4's heavily trailered first screening of *Four Weddings and a Funeral* in 1996, which attracted an audience of 12.38 million.[21]

Although films can achieve very high audience figures on television, other forms of drama (especially serial drama) achieve even higher figures. In this respect, the national reach of film is generally less than that of television drama. Indeed, John Caughie has expressed an anxiety that the growth in involvement of television in film production has led to an increased investment in drama on film aimed at the international market at the expense of more local forms of television drama. He contrasts the work of Ken Loach in the 1960s and the 1990s. '*Ladybird, Ladybird*,' he argues, 'circulates within an aesthetic and a cultural sphere which is given cultural prestige (and an economic viability) by international critics' awards, whereas *Cathy Come Home* circulated as a national event and functioned as documentary evidence within the political sphere.'[22] The point is well made but it sets up too stark an opposition. For if television drama circulates less as a 'national event' in the 1990s than it did in the 1960s, this is not simply the consequence of television involvement in cinema. It has more to do with the transformations which broadcasting as a whole had undergone, especially the increase in channels (both terrestrial and non-terrestrial), the rise of video (and its opportunities for alternative viewing and time-shifting), and the fragmentation of the national audience which has resulted. If the capacity of both television drama and film to function as a national event has lessened, this is partly because the national audience for television does not exist in the same way as it did in the 1960s and partly because neither individual television programmes nor films can lay claim to the same cultural dominance within the entertainment sphere that they once could. The national audience is in fact a series of audiences which are often addressed in different ways. At the same time, the representations which British cinema then makes available to them have themselves become much more complex and varied.

Representation

There is a scene in David Hare's *Strapless* (1988) which is suggestive in this regard. A doctor, working for the NHS, addresses a group of assembled hospital workers and speaks up on behalf of 'English values'. It is a scene with loose echoes of wartime movies such as *In Which We Serve* (1942) or *Henry V* (1944) in which morale-boosting speeches upholding traditional English virtues are delivered to an assembled group (in these instances, sailors and soldiers). There are, however, significant differences. In *Strapless*, the speech is delivered not by an Englishman but by an American woman, and the group she speaks to is not the homogenous white male group of the earlier films but one which is differentiated by gender and ethnicity. By having an American defend the 'idea of Englishness', the film acknowledges the difficulty which such a speech presents for a contemporary British film and attempts to sidestep the irony which would, almost inevitably, have had to accompany its delivery by an English character (even so, there is still a hint of pastiche in the way the scene is realized). The difficulty of speaking for England is indicated, however, not only by the nationality of the speaker, but by the composition of the group she is addressing. Unlike in the earlier films, there is no confident assumption of who represents 'Englishness'.

Important works on British cinema by Jeffrey Richards on the 1930s, Charles Barr on Ealing and Raymond Durgnat on the post-war period have all uncovered in British films an effort to tell stories which invite audiences to interpret them in terms of ideas about the 'nation' and 'national identity'.[23] More recently, Andrew Higson has identified what he regards as a characteristic way of 'imagining the nation' as a 'knowable, organic community' in British films, which he links to a typically 'national style' characterized by episodic narratives involving multiple characters, a distanced observational viewpoint and a non-narrative use of space.[24] Clearly, there is a danger that such arguments underestimate the variety of British cinema and are too ready to make pronouncements about all British cinema on the basis of a selective sample of films (Higson's book deals with only five films in any detail). Nonetheless, it is equally evident that, if not all British cinema, then at least significant strands (such as wartime cinema and Ealing comedies) have evolved an aesthetic and a way of telling stories which clearly display a national-allegorical import.[25]

If this is so, then it is also apparent that the certainties concerning the nation upon which such films relied have, since the 1960s, increasingly dissolved. The strategy of national allegory, in this respect, has not so much been abandoned as refashioned to express a new sense of difference and even conflict. Films such as *My Beautiful Laundrette* (1987) and *Sammy and Rosie Get Laid* (1988) continue to employ, with a few postmodern embellishments, the stylistic features of British national cinema which Higson identifies, clearly inviting the individual stories of its characters to be read in terms of an 'allegory' of the state of the nation'. They do so, however, to project a much more fluid, hybrid and plural sense of 'Britishness' than was seen in earlier British cinema. Such films are responding to the more complex sense of national identity which has been characteristic of modern Britain. In this respect, the interests of the art film (which are often individual and subjective) may be seen to have merged with the preoccupations of public service television (which are characteristically more social and 'national' in scope). As a result, the alliance between film and television, which Caughie sees as lessening the local dimensions of *television*, may have be read as a strengthening of the local aspects of *cinema*.

Since the 1980s, it can be argued that not only has British cinema articulated a much more inclusive sense of Englishness than previously but that it has also accorded a much greater recognition to the differing nationalities and identities within Britain (including, for example, the emergence of a distinctive black British cinema). In this respect, British national cinema now clearly implies Scottish and Welsh cinema as well as just English cinema. Indeed, two of the most successful British films of the mid-1990s – *Shallow Grave* (1994) and *Trainspotting* (1995) – were very clearly Scottish. This has implications, not only for the inclusiveness of the representations of Britain which British cinema provides but also, as the example of *Gregory's Girl* indicates, for the way in which issues of national identity are then addressed.

Graeme Turner, writing of Australian cinema in the 1990s, has noted the suspicion which often accompanies discussion of both the nation and national cinema because of the socially conservative versions of national identity which these tend to imply. He argues that the post-colonial status of Australia means that its discourses of the nation are much less settled, and that it is possible for Australian films to provide 'a critical . . . body of representations within mainstream Western cinema'.[26] In the same way, the peculiar historical circumstances of Scotland and Wales – which may have gained economically from the British colonial enterprise but which, culturally, encountered subordination – provide an opening for a more complex negotiation of the discourses around the 'nation' than English/British cinema has traditionally provided. *Trainspotting* is an interesting example in this regard. One of the most commercially successful British films of 1996, it was fully financed by the public service broadcaster Channel 4, and combines an interest in social issues (drug-taking, AIDS, poverty) with a determinedly self-conscious aesthetic style reminiscent of the French and British 'new waves'. In experimenting with cinematic style, however, it also plays with the inherited imagery of England and Scotland. Thus when the film's main character, Mark Renton (Ewan McGregor), arrives in London, the film cheerfully invokes the most clichéd images of London in an ironic inversion of the touristic imagery which commonly accompanies the arrival of an English character in Scotland.[27] In a similarly iconoclastic manner, the film escorts its main characters to the Scottish countryside, not to invoke the 'romantic' beauty of the Scottish landscape but to provide Renton with the occasion for a swingeing attack on 'being Scottish' ('We're the lowest of the fucking low . . . It's a shite state of affairs and all the fresh air in the world will not make any fucking difference'). So while *Trainspotting* may speak with a voice that is decidedly Scottish, it also does so in a way which avoids simple pieties concerning Scottish, or 'British', identity.

Conclusion

I have argued elsewhere that the idea of British national cinema has often been linked, virtually by definition, to discourses of nationalism and myths of national unity.[28] However, this formulation of a national cinema underestimates the possibilities for a national cinema to re-imagine the nation, or rather nations within Britain, and also to address the specificities of a national culture in a way which does not presume a homogeneous or 'pure' national identity. Indeed, as Paul Willemen has argued, the national cinema which genuinely addresses national specificity will actually be at odds with the 'homogenising project' of nationalism in so far as this entails a critical engagement with 'the complex, multidimensional and multidirectional tensions that characterise and shape a social formation's cultural configurations'.[29] In a sense, this is one of the apparent paradoxes that this essay has been addressing: that while British cinema may depend upon international finance and audiences for its viability, this may actually strengthen its ability to probe national questions; that while cinema has apparently lost its 'national' audience in the cinemas, it may have gained a more fully 'national' audience via television; and that while the British cinema may no longer assert the myths of 'nation' with its earlier confidence, it may nonetheless be a cinema which is more fully representative of national complexities than ever before.

Notes

1   Hugo Young, *One of Us* (London: Pan, 1990), p. 277.
2   *Cinematograph Films Act, 1927: Report of a Committee Appointed by the Board of Trade* (London: HMSO, 1936), p. 5.
3   *Screen Digest*, December 1993, p. 280.
4   Stephen Crofts 'Reconceptualizing National Cinema/s', *Quarterly Review of Film and Video*, vol. 14, no. 3, 1993, p. 50.
5   Alan Lovell, *The British Cinema: The Unknown Cinema*, BFI mimeo, 1969, p. 2.
6   David Bordwell, 'The Art Cinema as a Mode of Film Practice', *Film Criticism*, vol. 4, no. 1, Fall 1979.
7   Crofts, 'Reconceptualizing National Cinema/s', p. 51.
8   Louis Moss and Kathleen Box, *The Cinema Audience: An Inquiry made by the Wartime Social Survey for the Ministry of Information* (London: Ministry of Information, 1943).
9   In 'Cinemas and Cinema-Going in Great Britain', *Journal of the Royal Statistical Society*, vol. CXVII no. 11, 1954, p. 135, Browning and Sorrell indicate that in the years 1950–52 the cinema accounted

for over 83 per cent of all taxable admissions on entertainment (including theatre, sport and other activities). In 1992, by comparison, spending on cinema admissions accounted for less than 6 per cent of household expenditure on entertainment. See Monopolies and Mergers Commission, *Films: A report on the supply of films for exhibition in cinemas in the UK* (London: HMSO, 1994), p. 90.

10   Karsten-Peter Grummitt, *Cinemagoing 4* (Leicester: Dodona Research, 1995), p. 1.

11   Between 1985, when the first multiplex was opened, and 1994 the number of multiplexes grew to 71 sites (incorporating 638 screens). By the end of 1993, about 40 per cent of all visits to the cinema were to multiplexes. See Monopolies and Mergers Commission, *Films: A report on the supply of films for exhibition in cinemas in the UK*, p. 96.

12   See the figures used by media consultant James Lee in *Movie Makars: Drama for Film and Television* (Glasgow: Scottish Film Council, 1993), p. 44.

13   Douglas Gomery, *Shared Pleasures: A History of Movie Presentation* (London: British Film Institute, 1992), p. 276.

14   These figures are taken from the *BFI Film and Television Handbook 1996* (London: British Film Institute, 1995), p. 34 and p. 47.

15   *Screen Finance*, 11 January 1995, p. 13. *Screen Finance* defines films as 'wholly' British when they were made solely by British production companies.

16   *Screen Finance*, 8 February 1995, p. 12.

17   Figures for box-office revenue come from *Screen Finance*, 24 February 1993, p. 9. I have estimated admissions for individual films by dividing 1992 box-office revenues by the average realised seat prices for that year, as identified in Monopolies and Mergers Commission, *Films: A report on the supply of films for exhibition in cinemas in the UK*, p. 102. Television viewing figures may be found in *BFI Film and Television Handbook 1996*, p. 57.

18   Patrick Barwise and Andrew Ehrenberg, *Television and Its Audience* (London: Sage, 1988), p. 29. The renting and buying of pre-recorded videos is also highest among the 'lower' social grades, especially the C2s. See BMRB International Report: CAVIAR 10, vol. 3, *Report of Findings* (February 1993), p. 21.

19   As in the cinema the bulk of films watched by British audiences on television and video are American. But it is worth noting that television not only shows more British films than the cinemas but that, as the films it shows are from different periods, the circulation of British cinema for the modern audience also involves a sense of both its past and present. Thus in 1995, to take just one example, almost as many people watched Ken Loach's *Kes* (1969) as the same director's *Raining Stones* (1993). See *Screen Finance*, 24 January 1996, pp. 16–17.

20   'Cinemas and Cinema-Going in Great Britain', p. 146.

21   These viewing figures made *Four Weddings and a Funeral* Channel 4's third most-watched broadcast ever. See *Broadcast*, 8 December 1995, p. 24.

22   John Caughie, 'The Logic of Convergence', in Hill and McLoone (eds.), *Big Picture, Small Screen* (Luton: John Libby University of Luton Press, 1996), p. 219.

23   See Jeffrey Richards, *The Age of the Dream Palace: Cinema and Society 1930–1939* (London: Routledge and Kegan Paul, 1984); Charles Barr, *Ealing Studios* (London: Cameron and Tayleur, 1977); and Raymond Durgnat, *A Mirror for England* (London: Faber and Faber, 1970).

24   Andrew Higson, *Waving the Flag: Constructing a National Cinema in Britain* (Oxford: Oxford University Press, 1995).

25   The idea of 'national allegory' has been employed, somewhat controversially, by Fredric Jameson in relation to 'third world' literature. See 'Third-World Literature in the Era of Multinational Capitalism', *Social Text*, 15, Fall 1986.

26   Graeme Turner, 'The End of the National Project? Australian Cinema in the 1990s', in Wimal Dissanayake (ed.), *Colonialism and Nationalism in Asian Cinema* (Bloomington, Indiana University Press, 1994), p. 203.

27   The script refers to this interlude as a 'contemporary retake of all those "Swinging London" montages'. See John Hodge, *Trainspotting and Shallow Grave* (London: Faber and Faber, 1996), p. 76.

28   John Hill, 'The Issue of National Cinema and British Film Production', in Duncan Petrie (ed.), *New Questions of British Cinema* (London: British Film Institute, 1992).

29   Paul Willemen, 'The National', in *Looks and Frictions: Essays in Cultural Studies and Film Theory* (London: British Film Institute, 1994), p. 212.

Chapter 13

STEPHEN TEO

POSTMODERNISM AND THE END OF
HONG KONG CINEMA

F**OR THE LAST FEW YEARS HONG KONG CINEMA** has been keeping pace with people's feverish attempts to prepare themselves for the 1997 transition. The general feeling has been of an era coming to a close. But before dynasties change, there is one last great social surge forward, like the frantic rush of a crowd at an end of year sale. The unanimous goal is to earn as much and as quickly as possible. Those who can will mitigate and invest their money overseas; those who cannot will save their money in case of an emergency. Others indulge in a consumerist binge with a sense of *fin de siècle* fatalism.

With the prospect of a future over which it will have little or no say, Hong Kong's sense of the past has undergone major changes. Instead of, as Fredric Jameson puts it, mobilizing a 'retrospective dimension indispensable to any vital reorientation of our collective future', the relation to the past has become historicist[1] in the words of postmodern architectural historians. The loss of a sense of the future together with the near-hysterical stress on the accumulation of and speculation in exchange values have triggered the current spirit of post-modernism and 'the random cannibalization of all the styles of the past', reducing that past to 'little more than a set of dusty spectacles . . . leaving us with nothing but texts to be consumed as a 'tangible symptom of an omnipresent, omnivorous and well-nigh libidinal historicism'.[2] In the 1990s, denizens of Hong Kong gobble up fads and gimmicks like fast food, moving images being no exception. Although Hong Kong confirms Linda Hutcheon's proposition that postmodernism is 'a contradictory phenomenon which uses and abuses, installs and then subverts, the very concepts it challenges',[3] it also gives the lie to postmodernism as a Western theory of development and historical periodization. Given what has been Hong Kong's predetermined scenario of time running out and its eventual assimilation into a vastly different political culture, it is important to understand the role of what may look like post-modernism and the context from which it developed. One need only look back to the 1970s and the popularity of martial arts kung fu films to see how fast Hong Kong cinema evolved. The marital arts genre was full of vigour: shots were put together with a zest that matched the actions of its characters. The 1970s were the dynamic decade in Hong Kong, and this was reflected in the energy and fevered pace of its kung fu films.

In previous chapters the point was made that the aesthetics of kung fu movies also provided the conditions for the birth of a new wave in 1979, implemented by directors born in the late

1940s and early 1950s who combined American style gusto and know-how with European aesthetics. They were followed by a second group of even younger directors who began to establish their careers in the mid-1980s, producing work of uncharacteristic maturity. One can argue over when the new wave really came of age. There was more than one possible turning point: in 1981 Tsui Hark made *All the Wrong Clues (For the Right Solution)*, or much later, with works produced by the second wave such as Stanley Kwan's *Rouge* and *Actress* or Wong Kar-wai's *Days of Being Wild*. Rather than determine a cut-off date, it is more productive to think of the new wave as an ongoing movement. The trend towards a cinema that could more easily be discussed in terms of postmodernism was first glimpsed in the mid-1980s with the increased application of special effects in the work of Tsui Hark. Content-wise, the new wave directors evolved a preoccupation with 1997 and the wider question of China and its relations with Hong Kong, Hong Kong's own 'China syndrome'. The 1997 issue was at first dealt with allegorically, but it became an open secret as film-makers faced up to China in personal attempts to examine Hong Kong's own identity. Towards the late 1990s, Hong Kong critics were already referring to a 'post-1997' sentiment. The best films at the time exerted a double impact: film-makers asserted their identity in terms of its difference from what they presented as China's, but they at the same time attempted to come to terms with China. There was an inherent contradiction in wanting to be different and yet feeling a nationalist empathy with China, a tension which increasingly became the point of reference for identity questions. Although Hong Kong is not a country, its residents possessed a form of national identity increasingly identified as Chinese even though artists expressed their Chineseness in ways that were certainly different from the way artists in China negotiated theirs.

For Hong Kong cinema, the late 1980s was also a period of social change signalled by more liberal attitudes towards film censorship and the decriminalization of homosexuality, confirmed in 1990 through a majority vote in the legislative council. The new censorship ordinance was passed in 1988 and introduced, for the first time in the territory, a ratings system. It was organized in three tiers, resulting in the rise of a new genre of soft-core pornographic films known as 'Category III films', the category reserved for those over eighteen years of age (the equivalent of the Restricted ['R'] category in Western countries). Category III films have now become such a commercial proposition that producers, distributors and exhibitors have chosen to specialize in them as a genre. Actresses such as Veronica Yip have come up through the ranks of Category III films to mainstream respectability. In political terms, however, the new censorship ordinance retained a clause to ban films that were judged to be politically sensitive and 'prejudicial to good relations with neighbouring countries'.

In the transition period to 1997, Hong Kong's relations with its future rulers remained marked by caution. In 1989, the initial outlook was one of hope and optimism, soon to be dashed by the Tiananmen massacre on 4 June. Hong Kong cinema became filled with despair and frustration, qualities expressed in John Woo's *Bullet in the Head*, released in the fall of that year. The post-Tiananmen blues also pervaded Shu Kei's documentary, *Sunless Days/Meiyou Taiyang de Rizi* (1990), which showed the film-maker's own family in transition as mother is left behind by sons who have migrated overseas. The tone was confessional, never a popular form among Hong Kong film-makers. *Bullet in the Head* failed at the box-office. *Sunless Days*, originally made for Japanese TV, was hardly shown on movie screens in the territory.

As the 1990s proceeded, a renewed optimism surfaced, tempered only by another wave of anxiety caused by Governor Chris Patten's injudicious but nevertheless popular attempts to democratize Hong Kong in the teeth of China's objections. Along with the new optimism, a new mood engulfed Hong Kong cinema in the early 1990s, characterized by local critics as postmodernism, in spite of the notorious meaninglessness of that epithet. One concrete example of 'postmodernist' restructuring in the 1990s is the virtual disappearance of the old picture palaces in the territory to make way for multiplexes and mini-theatres. In their own way, the rise of the new multiplexes shows Hong Kong succumbing to the pressure of Western-style 'uniformity'. But, as we shall see, postmodernism in Hong Kong cinema shows quite another proposition: Hong Kong society reacting against cultural uniformity, a postmodernism that is also profoundly anti-postmodernist (or postmodern).

The reason for the new optimism in the early 1990s may be found in China's own post-Tiananmen booming economy. Hong Kong film-makers seem to have outgrown the China syndrome of the mid-1980s; the easiest way Hong Kong can identify itself with China is through a booming economy. The China boom recalls Hong Kong's own experience of economic developments: it essentially leapfrogged from pre-industrial trading post to wealthy exporting, financial centre within a generation. The shift towards an economy dominated by financial speculation, skipping to a large extent the 'industrial production' phase of capitalist development, meant that Hong Kong cinema too could leap into a 'postmodern' phase without ever having been fully modern. Hong Kong's cinematic past is generally regarded as being composed of *tsaan pin*, a Cantonese term referring to dilapidated movies that are rotting away, only to be revived on TV in the graveyard hours. Cantonese opera films, melodramas, comedies, Mandarin soaps, musicals and historical epics, all these genres seeking to negotiate ways of transiting to modernism were short-circuited and prematurely relegated to the graveyard.

Most of the new wave directors were educated in film schools in the West, but they were conscious of a Chinese past. While holding the torch of an avant-garde by introducing modern aesthetics into Hong Kong cinema, they had to make themselves credible directors in the eyes of the commercial industry. They made films of a personal nature, but alternated these with commercial works; they were keen to inject generic conventions and principles of entertainment. This practice allowed them to explore the legacy of the Cantonese and Mandarin cinemas of the 1950s and 1960s and thus the history of Hong Kong itself. The one key work which, when first released, was both condemned as a sell-out and praised as an amalgamation of old and new styles was, of course, Tsui Hark's *All the Wrong Clues*.

Tsui held the key then, and holds the key now, to the new epochal shift, this time to a notion of postmodernism which can be seen as a natural outcome of the maturation of the new wave and its absorption of commercial precepts. Using Tsui as a yardstick, the postmodern phenomenon grew from a ragbag of causes and effects: new wave aesthetics mixed with Cinema City-style slapstick, anxiety over 1997 and the China syndrome, the assertion of Hong Kong's own identity as different from China, and a new sexual awakening arising from an increasing awareness of women's human rights and the decriminalization of homosexuality. But Tsui was not the only proponent of postmodernism in the 1990s. Hong Kong was also ushered into the postmodernist age by a young actor with the look of a bemused clown.[4]

Stephen Chiau Sing-chi is the ubiquitous star of the new genre of 'nonsense comedies', one manifestation in the multi-faceted grid of the postmodernist edifice. At first, he may seem a most unlikely proponent of postmodernism. In fact, he is its perfect embodiment. His screen persona mirrors the paradox that is inherent in Hong Kong's postmodernism: Chiau's characters are presented as premoderns, usually bumpkins from a Chinese village somewhere in Guangdong, who accidentally find themselves in the big city. Inevitably, these bumpkins confound everybody's lowly expectations by making big successes of themselves. Chiau's characters carry the vice of ignorance like a shining virtue and turn vulgarity into the stuff of humour. Furthermore, they are heroes of irrationality. Chiau's clowns have loose, gaping mouths whose speech patterns and dialogue are Cantonese versions of nonsense verse. In Cantonese, Chiau's brand of humour is known as *mou lei-tau* (literally, nonsense).

There is in Chiau's performances, a tone of witty self-criticism of Hong Kong people's latent prejudices against Mainlanders. His characters reflect Hong Kong's Chinese migrants as emerging from the premodern agrarian society of China into (pre/post) modern Hong Kong and, somewhat improbably, becoming an overnight success. Chiau's is, of course, a parody not only of the rags-to-riches story of Hong Kong's economic development, but also of the can-do attitudes of its entrepreneurial and gambling residents. Chiau is the archetypal postmodern (con)man, his screen persona conveying that a society has successfully side-stepped or leapt over stages of orthodox development and a new generation has come of age faster and smarter.

Chiau's rise to stardom was meteoric. A television performer who hosted a children's show and then turned to acting in drama series in the late 1980s, he first made an impact in cinema in a rather nondescript police thriller, *Final Justice/Pili Xianfent* (1988), where he played a quick-witted, street-wise kid who would go far in life while running foul of the law. Chiau repeated this characterization, with increasingly comic variations, in films such as *My Hero/Yiben Manhua Chuang Tianya* (1990) and *Curry and Pepper/Jiali Lajiao* (1990), announcing the wild and wacky heroes that would later characterize his screen image. In the summer of 1990 Chiau became 'red', as the Hong Kong saying goes, meaning 'all the rage', a household sensation. The vehicle carrying Chiau to overnight success was *All for the Winner/Du Sheng*, as Shing, a green kid from Guangzhou who comes to Hong Kong to visit his uncle (played by Ng Mang-tat, who appeared in virtually all of Chiau's movies as his sidekick). Shing possesses X-ray vision, which makes him a natural gambler. In no time, he becomes known as the 'Saint of Gamblers' and takes part in an international gambling tournament for the title King of Gamblers. He loses his X-ray vision at this crucial point because the girl he loves has been kidnapped by his opponent, only regaining his special ability when his uncle hits on the brainwave of hiring a girl to become Shing's substitute lover. That the plan works is due to Shing's discovery that the proxy lover shares one thing in common with the real one: a mole in her armpit.

All for the Winner grossed over HK $40 million, putting it among the highest-grossing movies of all time in Hong Kong cinema. Since then, four of Chiau's subsequent movies have grossed more than the magical HK $40 million mark. Three other Chiau movies are more moderate grosses, but still substantial box-office winners, bringing in over HK $30 million each. Clearly, Chiau's movies are big money-spinners, all the more phenomenal when one considers that these earnings are from Hong Kong's domestic market alone.

Western critics who have had a taste of Chiau's humour say that it will not 'translate'. Much of the humour is vulgar (toilet jokes abound in all of Chiau's films) and based on a peculiar Cantonese argot which presupposes Hong Kong residents to fully enjoy the insinuations, slang and in-jokes. The truth is that native humorists anywhere rarely do 'translate'. If they do, they have hit some kind of a nerve that transcends language. But Chiau has not confined himself to linguistic humour. One of his best films is the distinctly un-Shakespearean *All's Well, End's Well/Jia You Xi Shi* (1992, directed by Clifton Ko), a deliciously hare-brained comedy which gives the impression that Hong Kong cinema can virtually invent anything on the spot. The movie conforms to a formula of literate Cantonese humour and visual tomfoolery, with the cast (including Leslie Cheung and Maggie Cheung) sending themselves up and having great fun doing so.

Sophistication is, of course, a relative term when applied to Stephen Chiau. His next big hit, *Fight Back to School/Tao Xue Wei Long* (1992, directed by Gordon Chan), is not as unremittingly boorish or vulgar as most of Chiau's films. He plays a policeman who disguises himself as an 18-year-old juvenile and goes undercover as a student in a school in order to recover a pistol stolen from his superior. Although not departing from his standard oafish characterizations, including that of Ng Man-tat, Chiau's perennial sidekick, of more interest is the interplay between Chiau and his teachers, who are given to hurling the blackboard duster at our hero everytime he is remiss, and that between Chiau and his fellow students, who call him 'Grandpa' after he has defeated the school bully linked to the Triads.

Chiau's next mega-success, *Justice, My Foot/Shensi Guan* (which grossed just short of HK $50 million) is filled, as usual, with vulgar jokes and episodic sketches that are barely related to each other. The premise for the movie lies in a sick joke: Chiau, a successful and unscrupulous lawyer in the last century is hit by bad luck – he remains childless even though his wife (played by Anita Mui) gives birth to thirteen baby boys, all of whom die at birth. Both husband and wife are distraught, but you wouldn't know it from the feckless tone of the movie. Chiau goes on defending hopeless cases which he wins by sleight-of-mouth, and his wife, when she's not giving birth, is a part-time swordswoman fighting on the side of the oppressed.

At last count, another comedy, *Royal Tramp/Lu Ding Ji* (1992), released in two parts, took in a combined gross of HK $77 million (US $10 million), a new record. Chiau's movies prepared audiences for *mou lei-tau* parody and farce, but it is the latest 'postmodern' hits not starring Chiau which give new meaning to parody and pastiche. Improbable as it may seem, these movies with the somewhat arcane titles, *92 Legendary La Rose Noire* (1992) and *Dongcheng Xijiu* (1993), have added substance to the idea that there is a postmodernism unique to Hong Kong in the last decade of the century, before reverting to Chinese rule.

The uniqueness of Hong Kong in this respect was its existence in the modern world as a colonial outpost of the British Empire in the heart of East Asia. However, since the British Empire is itself defunct, Hong Kong, while it remained subaltern in many ways, also outstripped the Imperial power as a crucial meeting ground of East and West and, more importantly, as the base for Western capitalism's attempts to 'crack' the Chinese market. Hong Kong is both East (from a Western point of view) and West (from a Chinese point of view), both subaltern and hegemonic as a dynamic financial and trading centre, both premodern and postmodern. The Chinese have, on the whole, looked upon this blending in mock-heroic terms. Indeed, it is the very essence of parody to address such mixtures. Hong Kong film-makers in the 1990s have shown that the encounter produces strange outcomes which take the form of a kind of postmodernist high jinks which is nothing like what, for instance, American or Japanese postmodernism is supposed to be.

Hong Kong's postmodernist farces have underscored the derision in the mixing of East and West. The result is possibly to increase self-awareness – not only of what is unique about Hong Kong, but also that aspect of identity which persists in spite of the blending of cultures. Even as they join in the merry-making of mixing East and West, Hong Kong film-makers have looked increasingly into the celluloid dustbin of *tsaan pin* or 'dilapidated' cinema, which is as much a documented history of Hong Kong as any history book can be. It is a 'putative past' which belongs to Hong Kong people themselves and is the least understood and known by outsiders. This looking back into the celluloid past is best illustrated by *92 Legendary La Rose Noire*, the unexpected hit of its year which has since won a cult following among critics and audiences alike.

An off-beat pastiche of Cantonese comedy thrillers of the 1960s, the film deliberately recalls a kind of nostalgia for the pre-high tech 1960s. Outsiders may be left in the dark about its generic pedigree, but Cantonese movie buffs will pick up the nuances of the actors' speech and gestures: the jokey but not unkind allusions to *The Black Roise/Hei Meigui* (1965) directed by Chor Yuen, a black and white classic *tsaan pin* whose title character, a masked cat burglar dressed in black who steals from the rich to help the poor, re-emerges in postmodern form as the legendary *La Rose Noire*. *92 Legendary La Rose Noire* recalls Hong Kong cinema's history and analyses its shape and form. It breaks the myth that Hong Kong cinema has no history, only images. On the other hand, it suggests that Hong Kong cinema presumes to be postmodern without having been modern, implying that the 1960s was the period Hong Kong cinema should have modernized, but did not.

The trend towards pastiche has built up momentum with each new postmodern film released in the past few years. *Rose, Rose I love* You/*Meigui meigui Wo Ai Ni* (1993), the sequel to *Legendary La Rose Noire*, contains much the same zany humour as the original and similarly purports to send up (or pay tribute to) old Cantonese movies and movie stars. All the characters are named after Cantonese movie stars of the 1950s and 1960s. It tries to trump its predecessor by sending up the pop songs, styles and behaviour of the period as well. The quaintness of the old days is stressed and contrasted with changing contemporary fads and mores (karaoke and gay liberation, for instance). Erratic and eccentric like its predecessor, the parody is less fresh a second time around, but no less enjoyable.

Comedy and parody (or rather, self-parody) have always been looked upon by Hong Kong film-makers as somewhere near the summit of entertainment. In their eyes, the art of pastiche is a refinement of parody. *Dongcheng Xijiu*, a title which may literally be translated as 'The East Achieves, the West Follows', provides a summary of Hong Kong postmodernism as an exercise in the pastiching of form. Perhaps inadvertently, it has let loose formalist demons in the form of vexing questions about the real shape of Hong Kong cinema. The film is a pastiche of epic narratives inspired by the serialized martial arts novels of Jin Yong, the most popular writer in the genre whose books have been recycled into long-running TV series and movie-plus-sequels (in real life, the writer is Louis Cha, one of Hong Kong's press czars, the boss of the *Ming Pao Daily*). The actual novel parodied by the film is *The Eagle Shooting Heroes/Shediao Yingxiong Zhuan*, which features heroes with mythic powers and provided the basis for straight productions of several film versions and a TV series. The film's full title, *Shediao Yingxion Zhuan zhi Dongcheng Xijiu*, refers to a zany episode in the novel where the heroes experience adventures while saving a princess from a wicked usurper of the throne. The cast of characters includes a wicked prince, a beautiful princess, naïve young swordsmen and swordswomen, Taoist acolytes and, most memorable of all, a Buddhist devotee (played by Tony Leung Ka-fai) seeking Nirvana and reaching it only after he finds a lover who must say 'I Love You' three times. Characters are paired off and required to perform two-handed skits that recall televisual sitcoms. They congregate in an inn where the comedy becomes ever more farcical before climaxing in a Middle-Eastern palace. The incongruous set parodies *Arabian Nights* fantasies with flying boots appearing instead of flying carpets. The form is a hodgepodge, evoking Cinema City slapstick, high camp Maria Montez-Carmen Miranda comedies, Chinese episodic novels and Vaudeville sketches from Chinese opera. Eschewing linear narrative modes, the free-form has evolved not just from new wave aesthetics, but from Chinese literary and theatrical conventions as well. The title may puzzle, but the film itself should translate as postmodernist humour, Hong Kong style.

The eagerness of Hong Kong film-makers to delve into the past seems to confirm the historicist approach characterized by Jameson as one in which 'intertextuality' is the 'operator of a new connotation of "pastness" and pseudo-historical depth, in which the history of aesthetic style displaces "real" history'.[5] Nevertheless, I would argue that, contrary to the postmodern use of intertextuality as a random practice of stylistic allusions designed to efface history, there is a genuine attempt to explore history and to acknowledge, even if only grudgingly, Hong Kong's kinship with China's history, both in its glorious and tragic manifestations, while at the same time inscribing a wish to stick one's head in the sand and to efface the history that looms on the horizon by effacing the 'real' history of the past. The eclecticism that underpins Hong Kong's type of postmodernism can thus be seen as a sign of a culture caught in the tension between a desire to construct a non-colonial identity by mobilizing a sense of the past, and a profound anxiety about the possibility of that very identity being imposed rather than being constructed autonomously.

Gender-bending may be a surprising manifestation of the search for sexual identity, but it has electrified the imaginations of Hong Kong film-makers in their turn towards postmodernism. Taking its cue from older Chinese traditions of gender-bending, the Tsui Hark-produced *Swordsman II/Xiao'ao Jianghu II Dongfang Bubai* (1992) started the trend, since followed by other martial arts pictures with remote period settings, with the beautiful Dongfang Bubai or 'Asia the Invincible', the former South China tribal chief who castrated himself in order to master the arts and powers contained in a sacred scroll. The eunuch is transformed into an androgyne, a sexual state half-way towards a full sex change. Asia's plan is to dominate China, thus the world, but she fails to take into account that a woman may love a man. Asia's love object, and opponent, is the male swordsman of the title. The theme of sexual ambiguity or non-gender masks a wider sentiment of feminism and gay liberation. On the evidence of *Swordsman II* and its follow-up, *Swordsman III: The East is Red*, Tsui Hark must be considered the master of gender-bending films (although Ching Siu-tung is the actual director). Asia the Invincible is not Tsui's first character of this type: there is also the demon in *A Chinese Ghost Story*. Then as now, the motif proposes that ancient China had more liberal views towards sexuality. The central paradox of Hong Kong's post-modernism is seen working once again: the suggestion that values or attitudes to be achieved in fact stem from somewhere in the very distant past. This theme has marked other new wave works such as Eddie Fong's *An Amorous Woman of the Tang Dynasty*, a genuinely erotic work that seduces with its existentialist view of sex and liberty, perhaps Hong Kong's first mature work to offer sex as a route to existential Nirvana.

Hong Kong's postmodernism has a time dimension skewed in favour of the past and the future, skipping the present, as illustrated by the use of clocks in Wong Kar-wai's *Days of Being Wild*. It asserts that Hong Kong is what it is until a certain moment (1997), though it is anybody's guess how long after 1997 'Hong Kong' will continue to survive, not merely as an entity, but as an idea. Film-makers and other intellectuals are becoming increasingly aware that Hong Kong tradition, such as it is, will be lost and will become diluted. A fundamental contradiction arises from the adoption of a postmodern perspective. While Hong Kong intellectuals wish to ascribe Hong Kong's achievements to Chinese cultural-religious values (such as the idea that a Confucianist work ethic produced the economic miracles of East Asian countries), there is the danger that the return of 'China' may obliterate the very notion of Chineseness elaborated by the territory's artists. The loss of values which Hong Kong holds dear will correspond with its gradual assimilation into Mainland Chinese culture (more optimist pundits think that it will be the other way around). The fear is that Hong Kong's modern, unique culture which evolved from its life as a treaty port, which popular writers characterized in terms of comprador capitalism, taipans, coolies, sing-song girls, rickshaw pullers and the like, will die off. Such a fear is reflected in the postmodern cinema of the early 1990s. It acknowledges that Hong Kong culture is *also* Western and makes a last-ditch effort to assert it.

Tsui Hark's *The Wicked City/Yaoshou Dushi* (1992) conveys this post-1997 fear (the movie itself takes place after 1997). Although it is not directed by Tsui, it bears his unmistakeable stamp, being produced and scripted by him. It is an extraordinary extension of his *Once Upon a Time in China* and *Swordsman* series, all of which explore the question of East Asian malaise and rejuvenation. *The Wicked City* brings the issue home. Adapted from a Japanese animated *manga* feature of the same name, *The Wicked City* cleverly uses Hong Kong's skyline to provide a setting for an allegory about its political fate: Tsui has invoked the superstitious idea, expounded in the previous chapter, that as Hong Kong races to keep its date with destiny, demons will rise up from the nether world to control the future. The plot concerns the attempts of humans to control the activities of half-human creatures called 'Rapters' who mingle with humans in the Hong Kong (and Tokyo) of the future. Although the setting is futuristic, the mood is inescapably 'now', integrating the new Japanese–Western subculture of cyberpunk and attendant concepts such as dystopia and smart drugs: the Rapters purvey 'Happiness' potions, the basis of a new drug culture. The half-man half-monster villain climbs up to the top of Hong Kong's tallest building, the Bank of China headquarters, to drug the territory by releasing a Happiness gas in a finale unmatched since King Kong climbed the Empire State Building. The villain's father attempts to put down his son from the cockpit of a jumbo jet flying over the building. There is also a battle with a clock, signifying Hong Kong's fight against time, with the hero commenting that 'Time is a pain in the arse'. *The Wicked City* is a classic by all the standards of postmodernism: irony, parody, critical re-working of history, politics and the future. It could properly mark the end of Hong Kong cinema.

Postscript

The surge of postmodernism in Hong Kong cinema in the early 1990s coincided perfectly with the feeling that Hong Kong was pressed for time; that it was imperative for everyone to chase time in order to get the most out of their lives. Hong Kong cinema was appropriately defined by the consciousness of the impatient momentum of modern living, not to mention the consciousness of 1997 and the edgy feeling of there being no time left. However, in the two-and-a-half years since the release of *The Wicked City* and the postmodern comedies, Hong Kong cinema appears to have reacted against postmodern freneticism and the pressed-for-time mentality. It has seemed to settle down into a state of almost sublime self-reflection. The box-office 'sleeper' of 1993 was a contemporary, nostalgia-tinged re-make of the old Shaw Brothers classic *Love Without End/Bu Liao Qing* entitled *C'est la Vie, Mon Chuerie/Xin Bu Liao Qing*. The film quietly reaffirmed old-fashioned virtues as its leading man, new star Lau Ching-wan, romanced a dying Anita Yuen against a background of street-singing opera troupes. Lau and Yuen are the new icons of an intermediate generation that will bridge the 1997 transition. Similarly, the sleeper hit of 1994 was another journey into nostalgia featuring complete new stars: Clifton Ko's *I have a Date With Spring/Wo He Chun Tian You Ge Yue Hui*. Retired singer Butterfly Yiu stages a comeback in her old Kowloon nightclub and, through flashbacks, reminisces about her life with three other female singers and her unrequited love for a saxophone player. Ko successfully adapted the long-running stage play To Kowk-wai, which earned a cult following through the Urban Council theatre circuit. The film evokes a Hong Kong experiencing political instability, the action flashing back to 1967, the year of political riots inspired by China's Cultural Revolution, reflected in the uncertainty of the lives of its protagonists. Equally a backstage comedy and a sentimental but evocative melodrama, *I Have a Date With Spring* required a mature use of actors and dialogue that militated against the anarchy of postmodernism which Clifton Ko himself had previously practised in his 1990s comedies.

Gordon Chan's *The Long and Winding Road/Jinxiu Qiancheng* (1994) was perhaps the best example of the move towards a low-key restatement of humanist sentiments. A charming buddy-buddy comedy, it features Leslie Cheung as an endearing rogue, the personification of Hong Kong professionals in the 1990s with little regard for scruples and friendships in their headlong rush towards making as much money as possible. Tony Leung plays his nemesis, a drummer who works in an old folks' home. The movie deals with the ability of friendship to endure in a materialistic money-minded environment: Cheung betrays his friends by buying over the old folks home in order to earn a hefty commission, but does the right thing by his conscience in the end. Gordon Chan directs in a deliberately flat and nonchalant style that complements the two key, beautifully understated performances of Cheung and Leung.

C'est la Vie, Mon Cheri, I Have a Date With Spring and *The Long and Winding Road* encapsulated qualities of a more sedate, middle-ground consciousness tempered by a respect for old virtues while paying more than mere lip service to contemporary counter-culture conceits. The post-modernist films reaffirmed Hong Kong cinema's penchant for the cross-fertilization of genres, as shown by the films of the United Film-makers Organisation (UFO), a new production company founded in 1993 by director Peter Chan. In *Twenty Something/Wan Jiu Zhao Wu* and *He's a Woman, She's a Man/Jin Zhi Yu Ye*, both 1994 releases, uninhibited sex drives and cross-dressing were central to the plots. Although they appear consciously to discard the mantle of postmodernism, they were postmodernist in all but style. Sections of documentary-format interviews interspersed into the narratives of both films suggest that the configuration of postmodern and new wave styles was not completely obliterated. Derivative and hackneyed as they may be, they were nevertheless engaging, hugely entertaining studies of yet another generational change taking place in Hong Kong cinema.

However, even as it heads towards another chapter of generational change, all is not well within the film industry. A sense of crisis has pervaded the industry for the past two years as cinema attendances steadily fell from record levels in the late 1980s, due in large part to the rise of admission prices as cinemas upgraded facilities and transformed into multiplexes. Higher prices and more sophisticated, albeit smaller, auditoriums raised the level of expectations for quality products which were met by imported Hollywood films. For the first time, Hong Kong cinema felt threatened by Hollywood as audiences flocked to the likes of *Jurassic Park, Speed* and other foreign blockbusters. Local budgets soared accordingly, but the shrinking market, both in Hong Kong and Southeast Asia has compounded the crisis of decreased capital returns. Ironically, companies such as UFO appear to have done well by producing low-budget, quirky and personal but also commercially viable films that denote some kind of progressive momentum towards the future.

In the mid-1990s, Hong Kong was wobbling as a result of the combined effects of the bursting of economic bubbles fuelled by rising inflation rates bordering on double digits, a shrinking manufacturing sector and rising unemployment. Old Hong Kongers were starting to desert the territory, defeated by impossible rents and overcome by a conviction that standards of living have irretrievably gone down. Anxiety over 1997 and the attendant political uncertainties have undoubtedly contributed to the general sense of malaise.

Like its society, Hong Kong cinema is in a state of flux. Its present travails are the results of pondering over how to adapt to integration with China. As its transitional markets begin to shrink, the Hong Kong film industry is once again eyeing the Chinese mainland as its next great frontier. Joint ventures and co-productions with Chinese film-makers and studios are becoming the norm. It may well be that Hong Kong cinema is coming full circle. As the Shanghai cinema indisputably gave form to the Hong Kong cinema, it is now set to return to the fold of the industry in the Mainland and perhaps be brought back to the cradle of Shanghai, the original Hollywood of the East. When or if that happens, Hong Kong cinema will never be the same again.

The 1980s may well prove to be the decade in which Hong Kong achieved a full-flowering native cinema where a generation that was born and grew up in the territory came of age and took over the industry. The challenge of the future is how this generation, and the intermediate one, will adapt to integration with China and still assert the separate identity that was, briefly, theirs. In the long term, it is not even certain whether Hong Kong will be able to continue making movies in Cantonese, the dialect that has made Hong Kong cinema unique and given it its identity. As Hong Kong directors turn to making more and more films with the mainland market in mind, Mandarin will clearly replace Cantonese as the preferred screen language, although dubbing into Cantonese may remain an option to secure Hong Kong's domestic market. The rise of Mandarin films will recall the days when Cantonese-speaking audiences flocked to see Mandarin films. Then, Cantonese films faced a crisis of outmoded standards, poor quality, and a perception that Cantonese was not the language of the future. The rise of younger generations bred and born in a Hong Kong that was free to develop on its own brought Cantonese back to the screen. The conditions pertaining after 1997 will be different. Younger generations will have to live with the fact that Hong Kong is, after all, part of the Mandarin-speaking China.

What will transpire now remains to be seen, but the present economic crisis faced by Hong Kong cinema as it approaches a new century appears to signal the closing of an era and the beginning of the age of uncertainty. Hong Kong post-1997 will strive to find new cinematic paradigms as it gropes all over again to find another identity within the embrace of the great Chinese dragon.

Notes

1   Frederic Jameson, 'Postmodernism, or the Cultural Logic of Late Capitalism', *New Left Review*, no. 146, 1984, p. 66. It is worth noting that this sense of historicism is rather eccentric, since it in effect evacuates any notion of history rather than overemphasizing linear historical genealogies, which is the usual implication of the term.

2   Jameson, op. cit., pp. 65–6.

3   Linda Hutcheon, *A Poetics of Postmodernism* (London: Routledge, 1988), p. 3.

4   The look of a bemused clown could also be read as a fitting definition of or reaction to the way terms like postmodernism are bandied about, in which case Stephen Chiau Sing-chi's face represents an example of the way Hong Kong cinema simultaneously confirms and belies any notion of the postmodern.

5   Jameson, op. cit., p. 67.

Chapter 14

THOMAS SCHATZ

THE NEW HOLLYWOOD

A MONG THE MORE CURIOUS AND CONFOUNDING terms in media
studies is 'the New Hollywood.' In its broadest historical sense the term applies to the
American cinema after World War II, when Hollywood's entrenched 'studio system' collapsed
and commercial television began to sweep the newly suburbanized national landscape. That
marked the end of Hollywood's 'classical' era of the 1920s, 1930s and early 1940s, when movies
were mass produced by a cartel of studios for a virtually guaranteed market. All that changed
in the post-war decade, as motion pictures came to be produced and sold on a film-by-film
basis and as 'watching TV' rapidly replaced 'going to the movies' as America's preferred ritual
of habituated, mass-mediated narrative entertainment.[1]

Ensuing pronouncements of the 'death of Hollywood' proved to be greatly exaggerated,
however; the industry not only survived but flourished in a changing media marketplace. Among
the more remarkable developments in recent media history, in fact, is the staying power of the
major studios (Paramount, MGM, Warners, *et al.*) and of the movie itself – that is, the the-
atrically released feature film – in an increasingly vast and complex 'entertainment industry.'
This is no small feat, considering the changes Hollywood has faced since the late 1940s. The
industry adjusted to those changes, and in the process its ways of doing business and of making
movies changed as well – and thus the difficulty in defining the New Hollywood, which has
meant something different from one period of adjustment to another.

The key to Hollywood's survival and the one abiding aspect of its post-war transformation
has been the steady rise of the movie blockbuster. In terms of budgets, production values
and market strategy, Hollywood has been increasingly hit-driven since the early 1950s. This
marks a significant departure from the classical era, when the studios turned out a few 'prestige'
pictures each year and relished the occasional runaway box-office hit, but relied primarily on
routine A-class features to generate revenues. The exceptional became the rule in post-war
Hollywood, as the occasional hit gave way to the calculated blockbuster.

The most obvious measure of this blockbuster syndrome is box-office revenues, which
have indeed surged over the past forty years.[2] In 1983, *Variety* commissioned a study of the
industry's all-time commercial hits in 'constant dollars' – that is, in figures adjusted for inflation – which placed only two films made before 1950, *Gone With the Wind* (1930) and *Snow
White and the Seven Dwarfs* (1937), in the top 75.[3] In other words, of the 7,000 or so Hollywood
features released before 1950, only two enjoyed the kind of success that has become routine

since then – and particularly in the past two decades. According to *Variety's* most recent (January, 1992) update of the all-time 'film rental champs,' 90 of the top 100 hits have been produced since 1970, and all of the top 20 since *Jaws* in 1975.[4]

The blockbuster syndrome went into high gear in the mid-1970s, despite (and in some ways because of) the concurrent emergence of competing media technologies and new delivery systems, notably pay-cable TV and home video (VCRs). This was the first period of sustained economic vitality and industry stability since the classical era. Thus this post-1975 era best warrants the term 'the New Hollywood,' and for essentially the same reasons associated the 'classical' era. Both terms connote not only specific historical periods, but also characteristic qualities of the movie industry at the time – particularly its economic and institutional structure, its mode of production, and its system of narrative conventions.

This is not to say that the New Hollywood is as stable or well integrated as the classical Hollywood, however. As we will see, the government's post-war dismantling of the 'vertically integrated' studio system ensured a more competitive movie marketplace, and a more fundamentally disintegrated industry as well. The marketplace became even more fragmented and uncertain with the emergence of TV and other media industries, and with the massive changes in lifestyle accompanying suburban migration and the related family/housing/baby boom. In one sense the mid-1970s ascent of the New Hollywood marks the studios' eventual coming-to-terms with an increasingly fragmented entertainment industry – with its demographics and target audiences, its diversified 'multi-media' conglomerates, its global(ized) markets and new delivery systems. And equally fragmented, perhaps, are the movies themselves, especially the high-cost, high-tech, high-stakes blockbusters, those multi-purpose entertainment machines that breed music videos and soundtrack albums, TV series and video-cassettes, video games and theme park rides, novelizations and comic books.

Hollywood's mid-1970s restabilization came after some thirty years of uncertainty and disarray. I would suggest, in fact, that the movie industry underwent three fairly distinct decade-long phases after World War II – from 1946 to 1955, from 1956 to 1965 and from 1966 to 1975. These phases were distinguished by various developments both inside and outside the industry, and four in particular: the shift to independent motion picture production, the changing role of the studios, the emergence of commercial TV, and changes in American lifestyle and patterns of media consumption. The key markers in these phases were huge hits like *The Ten Commandments* in 1956, *The Sound of Music* in 1965 and *Jaws* in 1975 which redefined the nature, scope and profit potential of the blockbuster movie, and which lay the foundation for the films and filmmaking practices of the New Hollywood.

To understand the New Hollywood, we need to chart these post-war phases and the concurrent emergence of the blockbuster syndrome in American filmmaking. Our ultimate focus, though, will be on the post-1975 New Hollywood and its complex interplay of economic, aesthetic, and technological forces. If recent studies of classical Hollywood have taught us anything, it is that we cannot consider either the filmmaking process or films themselves in isolation from their economic, technological, and industrial context. As we will see, this interplay of forces is in many ways even more complex in the New Hollywood, especially when blockbusters are involved. In today's media marketplace, it has become virtually impossible to identify or isolate the 'text' itself, or to distinguish a film's aesthetic or narrative quality from its commercial imperatives. As Eileen Meehan suggests in a perceptive study of *Batman*, to analyze contemporary movies 'we must be able to understand them as always and simultaneously text and commodity, intertext and product line.'[5]

The goal of this essay is to situate that 'understanding' historically, tracing the emergence and the complex workings of the New Hollywood. The emphasis throughout will be on the high-cost, high-tech, high-stakes productions that have driven the post-war movie industry – and that now drive the global multimedia marketplace at large. While one crucial dimension of the New Hollywood is the 'space' that has been opened for independent and alternative cinema, the fact is that these mainstream hits are where stars, genres, and cinematic innovations invariably are established, where the 'grammar' of cinema is most likely to be refined, and where the essential qualities of the medium – its popular and commercial character – are most evident. These blockbuster hits are, for better or worse, what the New Hollywood is about, and thus are the necessary starting point for any analysis of contemporary American cinema.

Hollywood in transition

The year 1946 marked the culmination of a five-year 'war boom' for Hollywood, with record revenues of over $1.5 billion and weekly ticket sales of 90 to 100 million.[6] The two biggest hits in 1946 were 'major independent' productions: Sam Goldwyn's *The Best Years of Our Lives* and David O. Selznick's *Duel in the Sun*. Both returned $11.3 million in rentals, a huge sum at the time, and signaled important changes in the industry – through Selznick's *Duel* was the more telling of the two.[7] Like his *Gone With the Wind*, it was a prototype New Hollywood blockbuster: a 'pre-sold' spectacle (based on a popular historical novel) with top stars, an excessive budget, a sprawling story, and state-of-the-art production values. Selznick himself termed *Duel* 'an exercise in making a big-grossing film,' gambling on a nationwide promotion-and-release campaign after weak sneak previews.[8] When the gamble paid off, he proclaimed it a 'tremendous milestone in motion picture merchandizing and exhibition.'[9]

That proved to be prophetic, given Hollywood's wholesale post-war transformation, which was actually well under way in 1946. The Justice Department's pursuit of Hollywood's major powers for antitrust practices began to show results in the courts that year, and culminated in the Supreme Court's May 1948 *Paramount* decree, which forced the major studios to divest their theater chains and to cease various tactics which had enabled them to control the market. Without the cash flow from their theaters and a guaranteed outlet for their product, the established studio system was effectively finished. The studios gradually fired their contract personnel and phased out active production, and began leasing their facilities for independent projects, generally providing co-financing and distribution as well. This shift to 'one-film deals' also affected the established relations of power, with top talent (and their agents and attorneys) gaining more authority over production.[10]

The studios' new role as financing-and-distribution entities also jibed with other industry developments. The war boom had ended rather suddenly in 1947 as the economy slumped and, more importantly, as millions of couples married, settled down, and started families – many of them moving to the suburbs and away from urban centers, where movie business thrived. Declining attendance at home was complemented by a decline in international trade in 1947–48, notably in the newly reopened European markets where 'protectionist' policies were initiated to foster domestic production and to restrict the revenues that could be taken out of the country. This encouraged the studios to enter into co-financing and co-production deals overseas, which complemented the changing strategy at home and fueled the general post-war rise in motion picture imports as well as independent production.

Another crucial factor on the domestic front was, of course, television. Early on, the major studios had met the competition head on with efforts to differentiate movies from TV programs. There was a marked increase in historical spectacles, Westerns and biblical epics, invariably designed for a global market and shot on location with international casts. These were enhanced by the increased use of Technicolor and by innovations in technology, notably widescreen formats and 3D. These efforts soon began paying off despite TV's continued growth, as *Fortune's* Freeman Lincoln pointed out in a 1955 piece aptly titled, 'The Comeback of the Movies.' Lincoln noted that, traditionally, 'any picture that topped $5 million world-wide was a smash hit,' and he estimated that only about 100 Hollywood releases had ever reached that total. 'In September, 1953, Twentieth Century Fox released *The Robe*, which has since grossed better than $20 million around the world and is expected to surpass £30 million,' wrote Lincoln, and pointed out that 'in the 17 months since *The Robe* was turned loose nearly 30 pictures have grossed more than the previously magic $5 million.'[11]

As Hollywood's blockbuster mentality took hold in 1955, the majors finally ventured into television. MGM, Warners, and Fox, taking a cue from Disney and the lesser Hollywood powers already involved in 'telefilm' series production, began producing filmed series of their own in the Fall of 1955.[12] And late that year the majors also began to sell or lease their pre-1948 features to TV syndicators. In 1956 alone, some 3,000 feature films went into syndication; by 1958, all of the majors had unloaded hundreds of pre-1948 films.[13] In 1960, the studios and talent guilds agreed on residual payments for post-1948 films, leading to another wave of movie syndication and to Hollywood movies being scheduled in regular prime-time. Telefilm production was also on the rise in the late 1950s, as the studios relied increasingly on TV series to keep their facilities in constant operation, since more and more feature films were shot on location. The studios also had begun realizing sizable profits from the syndication of hit TV series, both as reruns in the US and as first-run series abroad. As the studios upgraded series production and as the preferred programming format shifted from live video to telefilm – despite the introduction of videotape in 1957 – the networks steadily shifted their production operations from New York to Los Angeles. By 1960 virtually all prime-time fictional series were produced on film in Hollywood, with the traditional studio powers dominating this trend.

Meanwhile the blockbuster mentality intensified. Lincoln had suggested in his 1955 *Fortune* piece, 'The beauty of the big picture nowadays is, of course, that there seems to be no limit to what the box office return may be.'[14] The ensuing decade bore this out with a vengeance, bracketed by two colossal hits: *The Ten Commandments* in 1956, with domestic rentals of $43 million (versus *The Robe*'s $17.5 million), and *The Sound of Music* in 1965, with rentals of $79.9 million. Other top hits from the decade included similarly 'big' all-star projects, most of them shot on location for an international market:

Around the World in 80 Days (1956; $23 million in rentals)
The Bridge on the River Kwai (1957; $17.2 million)
South Pacific (1958; $17.5 million)
Ben-Hur (1959; $36.5 million)
Lawrence of Arabia (1962; $17.7 million)
The Longest Day (1962; $17.6 million)
Cleopatra (1963; $26 million)
Goldfinger (1964; $23 million)
Thunderball (1965; $28.5 million)
Doctor Zhivago (1965; $46.5 million)

While these mega-hits dominated the high end of Hollywood's output, the studios looked for ways beyond TV series production to diversify their media interests. Besides the need to hedge their bets on high-stakes blockbusters, this impulse to diversify was a response to the post-war boom in entertainment and leisure activities, the increasing segmentation of media audiences in a period of general prosperity and population growth, and the sophisticated new advertising and marketing strategies used to measure and attract those audiences. MCA was the clear industry leader in terms of diversification, having expanded from a music booking and talent agency in the 1930s and 1940s into telefilm production and syndication in the 1950s, eventually buying Decca Records and then Universal Pictures in the early 1960s.

The 1950s and 1960s also saw diversified, segmented moviegoing trends, most of them keyed to the immense, emergent 'youth market.' With the baby boom generation reaching active consumer status and developing distinctive interests and tastes, there was a marked surge in drive-in moviegoing, itself a phenomenon directed associated with post-war suburbanization and the family boom. With the emergent youth market, drive-in viewing fare turned increasingly to low-budget 'teen-pics' and 'exploitation' films. The 'art cinema' and foreign film movements also took off in the late 1950s and early 1960s, as neighborhood movie houses and campus film societies screened alternatives to mainstream Hollywood and as film courses began springing up on college campuses. These indicated a more 'cine-literate' generation – with that literacy actually enhanced by TV, which had become a veritable archive of American film history.

While the exploitation and art cinema movements produced a few commercial hits – Hitchcock's *Psycho* and Fellini's *La Dolce Vita* in 1960, for instance – the box office was dominated well into the 1960s by much the same blockbuster mentality as in previous decades. Indeed, the biopics, historical and biblical epics, literary adaptations, and transplanted state musicals of the 1950s and 1960s differed from the prestige pictures of the classical era only in their oversized budgets, casts, running times, and screen width. If the emergent youth culture and increasingly diversified media marketplace were danger signs, they were lost on the studios – particularly after the huge commercial success of two very traditional mainstream films in 1965, *The Sound of Music* and *Doctor Zhivago*.

Actually, Hollywood was on the verge of its worse economic slump since World War II – fueled to a degree by those two 1965 hits, because they led to a cycle of expensive, heavily promoted commercial flops. Fox, for instance, went on a blockbuster musical binge in an effort to replicate its success with *The Sound of Music*, and the results were disastrous: losses of $11 million on *Dr Dolittle* in 1967, $15 million on *Star!* in 1968, and $16 million in 1969 on *Hello Dolly*, at the time the most expensive film ever made.[15] Fox then tightened its belt, avoiding bankruptcy thanks to two relatively inexpensive, offbeat films: *Butch Cassidy and the Sundance Kid* (1969; $46 million in rentals), and *MASH* (1970; $36.7 million).

Those two hits were significant for a number of reasons besides the reversal of Fox's fortunes, reasons which signaled changes of aesthetic as well as economic direction in late-1960s Hollywood. With the blockbuster strategy stalled, the industry saw a period of widespread and unprecedented innovation, due largely to a new 'generation' of Hollywood film-makers like Robert Altman, Arthur Penn, Mike Nichols, and Bob Rafelson, who were turning out films that had as much in common with the European art cinema as with classical Hollywood. There was also a growing contingent of international auteurs – Bergman, Fellini, Truffaut, Bertolucci, Polanski, Kubrick – who, in the wake of the 1966 success of Antonioni's *Blow-Up* and Claude Lelouch's *A Man and a Woman*, developed a quasi-independent rapport with Hollywood, making films for a Euro-American market and bringing art cinema into the mainstream.

Thus an 'American film renaissance' of sorts was induced by a succession of big-budget flops and successful imports. Its key constituency was the American youth, by now the most dependable segment of regular moviegoers as attendance continued to fall despite the overall increase in population. Younger viewers contributed heavily to the success of sizable hits like

Bonnie and Clyde (1967; rentals of $22.8 million), *2001: A Space Odyssey* (1968; $25.5 million), and *The Graduate* (1968; $43 million), and they were almost solely responsible for modest hits like *Easy Rider* (1969; $19 million) and *Woodstock* (1970; $16.4 million). As these films suggest, the older baby boomers were reaching critical mass as a target market and were something of a countercultural force as well, caught up in the antiwar movement, civil rights, the sexual revolution, and so on. And with the 1966 breakdown of Hollywood's Production Code and the emergence in 1968 of the new ratings system – itself a further indication of the segmented movie audiences – film-makers were experimenting with more politically subversive, sexually explicit and/or graphically violent material.

As one might suspect, Hollywood's cultivation of the youth market and penchant for innovation in the late 1960s and early 1970s scarcely indicated a favorable market climate. On the contrary, they reflected the studios' uncertainty and growing desperation. Film historian Tino Balio has written about 'the Recession of 1969' and its aftermath, when 'Hollywood nearly collapsed.'[16] *Variety* at the time pegged combined industry losses for 1969–71 at $600 million, and according to an economic study by Joseph Dominick, studio profits fell from an average of $64 million in the five-year span from 1964 to 1968, to $13 million from 1969 to 1973.[17] Market conditions rendered the studios ripe for takeover, and in fact a number of the studios were absorbed in post-1965 conglomerate wave. Paramount was taken over by Gulf Western in 1966, United Artists by Transamerica in 1967, and Warner Bros by Kinney National Services in 1969, the same year MGM was bought out by real-estate tycoon Kirk Kerkorian. This trend proved to be a mixed blessing for the studios. The cash-rich parent company relieved much of the financial pressures and spurred diversification, but the new owners knew little about the movie business and, as the market worsened, tended to view their Hollywood subsidiaries as troublesome tax write-offs.

One bright spot during this period was the surge in network prices paid for hit movies. Back in 1961, NBC had paid Fox an average of $180,000 for each feature shown on *Saturday Night at the Movies*; that year 45 features were broadcast in prime time. By 1970s, the average price tag per feature was up to $800,000, with the networks spending $65 million on a total of 166 feature films. That total jumped to 227 for the 1971–2 season, when movies comprised over one quarter of all prime-time programming. The average price went up as well, due largely to ABC's paying $50 million in the Summer of 1971 for a package of blockbusters, including $5 million for *Lawrence of Arabia*, $3 million for the 1970 hit, *Love Story*, and $2.5 million each for seven James Bond films.[18] Significantly enough, however, these big payoffs were going only to top Hollywood hits as all three networks began producing their own TV-movies. Hollywood features comprised only half of the movies shown on network TV in the 1971–2 season, and that percentage declined further in subsequent years, as made-for-TV movie production increased.

The network payoff for top movie hits scarcely reversed the late-sixties downturn, as *The Graduate* in 1968 was the only release between 1965 and 1969 to surpass even $30 million in rentals. *Butch Cassidy*, *Airport* and *Love Story* in 1969–70 all earned $45 to $50 million, carrying much of the freight in those otherwise bleak economic years. *Airport* was especially important in that it generated a cycle of successful 'disaster pictures' like *The Poseidon Adventure*, *The Towering Inferno* and *Earthquake*, all solid performers in the $40 to $50 million range, though they were fairly expensive to produce and not quite the breakaway hits that the industry so desperately needed.

The first real sign of a reversal of the industry's sagging fortunes came with *The Godfather*, a 1972 Paramount release that returned over $86 million. *The Godfather* was that rarest of movies, a critical and commercial smash with widespread appeal, drawing art cinema connoisseurs and disaffected youth as well as mainstream moviegoers. Adapted from Mario Puzo's novel while it was still in galleys, the project was scarcely mounted as a surefire hit. Director Francis Ford Coppola was a debt-ridden film school product with far more success as a writer, and star Marlon Brando hadn't had a hit in over a decade. The huge sales of the novel, published while the film was in production, generated interest, as did well-publicized stories of problems on the set, cost overruns and protests from Italian-American groups. By the time of its release, *The Godfather* had attained 'event' status, and audiences responded to Coppola's stylish and highly stylized hybrid of the gangster genre and family melodrama. Like so many 1970s films, *The Godfather* had a strong nostalgic quality, invoking the male ethos and patriarchal order of a bygone era – and putting its three male co-stars, Al Pacino, James Caan and Robert Duvall, on the industry map.

The Godfather also did well in the international market, thus spurring an upturn in the overseas as well as the domestic market. Domestic theater admissions in 1972 were up roughly 20 per cent over 1971, reversing a 7-year slide, and total box-office revenues surged from the $1 billion range, where they had stagnated for several years, to $1.64 billion. While *The Godfather* alone accounted for nearly 10 per cent of those gross proceeds, other films clearly were contributing; revenues for the top ten box-office hits of 1972 were up nearly 70 per cent over the previous year. That momentum held through 1973 and then the market surged again in 1974, nearing the $2 billion mark – and thus finally surpassing Hollywood's postwar box-office peak. Key to the upturn were the now-predictable spate of disaster films, though these were far outdistanced by three hits which, in different ways, were sure signs of a changing industry.

One was *American Graffiti*, a surprise Summer 1973 hit written and directed by Coppola protégé George Lucas. A coming-of-age film with strong commercial tie-ins to both TV and rock music, the story's 1962 setting enabled Lucas to circumvent (or rather to predate) the current socio-political climate and broadened its appeal to older viewers. Two even bigger hits were late-1973 releases, *The Sting* and *The Exorcist* ($78 million and $86 million, respectively). *The Sting* was yet another nostalgia piece, a 1930s-era gangster/buddy/caper hybrid, reprising the Newman–Redford pairing of five years earlier – something like 'Butch and Sundance meets the Godfather.' The nostalgia and studied innocence of both *The Sting* and *American Graffiti* were hardly evident in *The Exorcist*, William Friedkin's kinetic, gut-wrenching, effects-laden exercise in screen violence and horror. While *Psycho* and *Rosemary's Baby* had proved that horror thrillers could attain hit status, *The Exorcist* pushed the logic and limits of the genre (and the viewer's capacity for masochistic pleasure) to new extremes, resulting in a truly monstrous hit and perhaps the clearest indication of the emergent New Hollywood.

Jaws and the New Hollywood

If any single film marked the arrival of the New Hollywood, it was *Jaws*, the Spielberg-directed thriller that recalibrated the profit potential of the Hollywood hit, and redefined its status as a marketable commodity and cultural phenomenon as well. The film brought an emphatic end to Hollywood's five-year recession, while ushering in an era of high-cost, high-tech, high-speed thrillers. *Jaws*' release also happened to coincide with developments both inside and outside the movie industry in the mid-1970s which, while having little or nothing to do with that particular film, were equally important to the emergent New Hollywood.

Jaws, like *Love Story*, *The Godfather*, *The Exorcist* and several other recent hits, was presold via a current best-selling novel. And like *The Godfather*, movie rights to the novel were purchased before it was published, and publicity from the deal and from the subsequent production helped spur the initial book sales – of a reported 7.6 million copies before the film's release in this case – which in turn fueled public interest in the film.[19] The *Jaws* deal was packaged by International Creative Management (ICM), which represented author Peter Benchley and handled the sale of the movie rights. ICM also represented the producing team of Richard Zanuck and David Brown, whose recent hits included *Butch Cassidy* and *The Sting*, and who worked with ICM to put together the movie project with MCA/Universal and *wunderkind* director Steven Spielberg.[20]

Initially budgeted at $3.5 million, *Jaws* was expensive by contemporary standards (average production costs in 1975 were $2.5 million), but it was scarcely a big-ticket project in that age of $10 million musicals and $20 million disaster epics.[21] The budget did steadily escalate due to logistical problems and Spielberg's ever-expanding vision and confidence; in fact problems with the mechanical shark pushed the effects budget alone to over $3 million. The producers managed to parlay those problems into positive publicity, however, and continued to hype the film during post-production. The movie was planned for a Summer 1975 release due to its subject matter, even though in those years most calculated hits were released during the Christmas holidays. Zanuck and Brown compensated by spending $2.5 million on promotion, much of it invested in a media blitz during the week before the film's 464-screen opening.[22]

The print campaign featured a poster depicting a huge shark rising through the water toward an unsuspecting swimmer, while the radio and TV ads exploited John Williams's now-famous '*Jaws* theme.' The provocative poster art and Williams's pulsating, foreboding theme conveyed the essence of the film experience and worked their way into the national consciousness, setting new standards for motion picture promotion. With the public's appetite sufficiently whetted, *Jaws*' release set off a feeding frenzy as 25 million tickets were sold in the film's first 38 days of release. After this quick start, the shark proved to have 'good legs' at the box office, running strong throughout the summer en route to a record $102.5 million in rentals in 1975. In the process, *Jaws* became a veritable sub-industry unto itself via commercial tie-ins and merchandizing ploys. But hype and promotion aside, *Jaws*' success ultimately centered on the appeal of the film itself; one enduring verity in the movie business is that, whatever the marketing efforts, only positive audience response and favorable word-of-mouth can propel a film to genuine hit status.

Jaws was essentially an action film and a thriller, of course, though it effectively melded various genres and story types. It tapped into the monster movie tradition with a revenge-of-nature subtext (like *King Kong, The Birds, et al.*), and in the film's latter stages the shark begins to take on supernatural, even Satanic, qualities à la *Rosemary's Baby* and *The Exorcist*. And given the fact that the initial victims are women and children, *Jaws* also had ties to the high-gore 'slasher' film, which had been given considerable impetus a year earlier by *The Texas Chainsaw Massacre*. The seagoing chase in the latter half is also a buddy film and a male initiation story, with Brodie the cop, Hooper the scientist, and Quint the sea captain providing different strategies for dealing with the shark and different takes on male heroic behavior.

Technically, *Jaws* is an adept 'chase film' that takes the viewer on an emotional roller coaster, first in awaiting the subsequent (and increasingly graphic) shark attacks, then in the actual pursuit of the shark. The narrative is precise and effectively paced, with each stage building to a climatic peak, then dissipating, then building again until the explosive finale. The performances, camera work, and editing are all crucial to this effect, as is John Williams's score. This was in fact the breakthrough film for Williams, the first in a run of huge hits that he scored (including *Star Wars, Close Encounters of the Third Kind, Raiders of the Lost Ark* and *ET*) whose music is absolutely essential to the emotional impact of the film.

Many critics disparaged that impact, dismissing *Jaws* as an utterly mechanical (if technically flawless) exercise in viewer manipulation. James Monaco cites *Jaws* itself as the basis for the 'Bruce aesthetic' (named after the film crew's pet name for the marauding robotic shark), whose ultimate cinematic effect is 'visceral – mechanical rather than human.' More exciting than interesting, more style than substance, *Jaws* and its myriad offspring, argues Monaco, are mere 'machines of entertainment, precisely calculated to achieve their effect.'[23] Others have argued, however, that *Jaws* is redeemed by several factors, notably the political critique in the film's first half, the essential humanity of Brodie, and the growing camaraderie of the three pursuers.

Critical debate aside, *Jaws* was a social, industrial and economic phenomenon of the first order, a cinematic idea and cultural commodity whose time had come. In many ways, the film simply confirmed or consolidated various existing industry trends and practices. In terms of marketing, *Jaws*' nationwide release and concurrent ad campaign underscored the value of saturation booking and advertising, which placed increased importance on a film's box-office performance in its opening weeks of release. 'Front-loading' the audience became a widespread marketing ploy, since it maximized a movie's event status while diminishing the potential damage done to weak pictures by negative reviews and poor word of mouth. *Jaws* also confirmed the viability of the 'summer hit,' indicating an adjustment in seasonal release tactics and a few other new moviegoing trends as well. One involved the composition and industry conceptualization of the youth market, which was shifting from the politically hip, cineliterate viewers of a few years earlier to even younger viewers with more conservative tastes and sensibilities. Demographically, this trend reflected the aging of the front-end baby boomers and the ascendence not only of their younger siblings but of their children as well – a new generation with time and spending money and a penchant for wandering suburban shopping malls and for repeated viewings of their favorite films.

This signaled a crucial shift in moviegoing and exhibition that accompanied the rise of the modern 'shopping center.' Until the mid-1970s, despite suburbanization and the rise of the drive-in, movie exhibition still was dominated by a select group of so-called 'key run' bookings in major markets. According to Axel Madsen's 1975 study of the industry, over 60 per cent of box-office revenues were generated by 1,000 key-run indoor theaters – out of a total of roughly 11,500 indoor and 3,500 outdoor theaters in the US.[24] Though Madsen scarcely saw it at the time, this was about to change dramatically. Between 1965 and 1970, the number of shopping malls in the US increased from about 1,500 to 12,500; by 1980 the number would reach 22,500.[25] The number of indoor theaters, which had held remarkably steady from 1965 to 1974 at just over 10,000, began to increase sharply in 1975 and reached a total of 22,750 by 1990, due largely to the surge of mall-based 'multi-plex' theaters.[26]

With the shifting market patterns and changing conception of youth culture, the mid-1970s also saw the rapid decline of the art cinema movement as a significant industry force. A number of films in 1974–5 marked both the peak and, as it turned out, the waning of the Hollywood renaissance – Altman's *Nashville*, Penn's *Night Moves*, Polanski's *Chinatown*, and most notably perhaps, Coppola's *The Conversation*. The consummate American auteur and 'godfather' to a generation of film-makers, Coppola's own artistic bent and maverick film-making left him oddly out of step with the times. While Coppola was in the Philippines filming *Apocalypse Now*, a brilliant though self-indulgent, self-destructive venture of Wellesian proportions, his protégés Lucas and Spielberg were busy refining the New Hollywood's Bruce aesthetic (via *Star Wars* and *Close Encounters*), while replacing the director-as-author with a director-as-superstar ethos.

The emergence of star directors like Lucas and Spielberg evinced not only the growing salaries and leverage of top talent, but also the increasing influence of Hollywood's top agents and talent agencies. The kind of packaging done by ICM on *Jaws* was fast becoming the rule on high-stakes projects, with ICM and another powerful agency, Creative Artists Associates (CAA), relying on aggressive packaging to compete with the venerable William Morris Agency. Interestingly enough, both ICM and CAA were created in 1974 – ICM via merger and CAA by five young agents who bolted William Morris and, led by Michael Ovitz, set out to revamp the industry and upgrade the power and status of the agent-packager. For the most part they succeeded, and consequently top agents, most often from CAA or ICM, became even more important than studio executives in putting together movie projects. And not surprisingly, given this shift in the power structure, an increasing number of top studio executives after the mid-1970s came from the agency ranks.

Yet another significant mid-1970s industry trend was the elimination of tax loopholes and write-offs which had provided incentives for investors, especially those financing independent films. This cut down the number of innovative and offbeat films, although by now the critical mass of cinephiles and art cinema theaters was sufficient to sustain a vigorous alternative cinema. This conservative turn coincided with an upswing in defensive market tactics, notably an increase in sequels, series, reissues and remakes. From 1964 to 1968, sequels and reissues combined accounted for just under 5 per cent of all Hollywood releases. From 1974 to 1978, they comprised 17.5 per cent. *Jaws*, for instance, was reissued in 1976 (as was *The Exorcist*), generating another $16 million in rentals, and in 1978 the first of several sequels, *Jaws 2*, was released, returning $49.3 million in rentals and clearly securing the *Jaws* 'franchise.'[27]

Another crucial dimension of the New Hollywood's mid-1970s emergence was the relationship between cinema and television, which was redefined altogether by three distinct developments. The first involved TV advertising which, incredibly enough, had been an important factor in movie marketing up to that time. A breakthrough of sorts occurred in 1974 with the reissue of a low-budget independent 1971 feature, *Billy Jack*, whose director and star, Tom Laughlin, successfully sued Warner Bros. for not sufficiently promoting the film on its initial release. For the 1974 reissue, according to *Variety*, 'Laughlin compelled Warners to try what was then a revolutionary marketing tactic: 'Billy Jack' received massive amounts of TV advertising support, an unheard of practice at the time.'[28] The film went on to earn $32.5 million in rentals, after generating only $4 million in its initial release. This tactic gained further credibility with the *Jaws* campaign and others, soon becoming standard practice and taking motion picture marketing into a new era.

A second crucial development grew out of the FCC's 1972 Report and Order on Cable Television and the 1975 launch of SATCOM I, which effectively ended the three-network stranglehold over commercial television.[29] Pay-cable services started slowly after the 1972 ruling, but the launching of America's first commercially available geo-stationary orbit satellite – and the August 1975 decision by Home Box Office (HBO) to go onto SATCOM – changed all that. HBO immediately became a truly nationwide 'movie channel' and a key player in the ancillary movie market. Cable TV proved to be a boon to Hollywood in another way as well, thanks to the FCC's 'Must Carry' and 'Prime Time Access' rules which increased the demand for syndicated series and movies. That in turn sent syndication prices soaring, providing another windfall for those studios producing TV series.

An even more radical change in Hollywood's relationship with television came with the introduction in 1975 of Sony's Betamax videotape recorder, thus initiating the 'home-video revolution.' In 1977 Matsushita, the Japanese parent company of Pioneer, JVC, and other consumer electronics companies, introduced its 'video home system' (VHS), setting off a battle for the home-video market. Matsushita's VHS format prevailed for several reasons:

VHS was less expensive (though technically inferior), more flexible and efficient in off-the-air recording, and Matsushita was more savvy and aggressive in acquiring 'software' (i.e. the rights to movie titles) as a means of pushing its hardware.[30]

While Hollywood's initial response to the 'Japanese threat' was predictably (and characteristically) negative, it became increasingly evident that the key home-video commodity was the Hollywood film – and particularly the blockbuster hit with its vast multi-media potential. And there was plenty to drive these new media industries, as Hollywood's blockbuster mentality reestablished itself with a vengeance in 1977–8. Total domestic grosses, which had reached $2 billion for the first time in 1975, surged to $2.65 billion in 1977 and $2.8 billion in 1978, a 40 per cent climb in only three years, with hits like *Star Wars, Grease, Close Encounters, Superman*, and *Saturday Night Fever* doing record business. From the *Sound of Music* in 1965 through 1976, only seven pictures (including *Jaws*) had returned $50 million in rentals; in 1977–8 nine films surpassed that mark.

While *Star Wars* was the top hit of the period, doing $127 million in rentals in 1977 and then another $38 million as a reissue in 1978, *Saturday Night Fever* was, in its own way, an equally significant and symptomatic New Hollywood blockbuster. The film did well at the box office ($74 million in rentals) and signaled both the erosion of various industry barriers and also the multimedia potential of movie hits. The film starred TV sitcom star John Travolta, the first of many 'cross-over' stars of the late-1970s and 1980s. The Bee Gees soundtrack dominated the pop charts and album sales, and along with the film helped spur the 'disco craze' in the club scene and recording industry. *Saturday Night Fever* also keyed the shift from the traditional Hollywood musical to the 'music movie,' a dominant 1980s form, and was an obvious precursor to MTV.

In terms of story, *Saturday Night Fever* was yet another male coming-of-age film, centering on the Travolta character's quest for freedom, self-expression and the Big Time as a dancer on Broadway. The age-old male initiation rite had found new life in Hollywood with the success of *The Graduate* and the emergent youth market, and proved exceptionally well suited to changes in the industry and the marketplace during the 1970s. One measure of its adaptability and appeal was *Star Wars*, which charts Luke Skywalker's initiation into manhood in altogether different terms – though here too the coming-of-age story, while providing the spine of the film, is developed in remarkably superficial terms. Indeed, *Star Wars* is so fast-paced ('breathtaking,' in movie ad-speak) and resolutely plot-driven that character depth and development are scarcely on the narrative agenda.

This emphasis on plot over character marks a significant departure from classical Hollywood films, including *The Godfather* and even *Jaws*, wherein plot tended to emerge more organically as a function of the drives, desires, motivations, and goals of the central characters. In *Star Wars* and its myriad successors, however, particularly male action-adventure films, characters (even 'the hero') are essentially plot functions. *The Godfather* and *Star Wars*, for example, are in many ways quite similar but ultimately very different kinds of stories. Like *Star Wars*, *The Godfather* is itself a male action film, a drama of succession, and a coming-of-age story centering on Michael's ascension to warrior status by fighting the 'gang wars.' Both films have a mythic dimension, and are in fact variations on the Arthurian legend. But where *Star Wars* is so obviously and inexorably plot-driven, *The Godfather* develops its story in terms of character – initially Don Corleone, then sons Sonny and Michael, and finally Michael alone – whose decisions and actions define the narrative trajectory of the film.

This is not to say that *Star Wars* does not 'work' as a narrative, but that the way it works may indicate a shift in the nature of film narrative. From *The Godfather* to *Jaws* to *Star Wars*, we see films that are increasingly plot-driven, increasingly visceral, kinetic and face-paced, increasingly reliant on special effects, increasingly 'fantastic' (and thus apolitical), and increasingly targeted at younger audiences. And significantly enough, the lack of complex characters or plot in *Star Wars* opens the film to other possibilities, notably its radical amalgamation of genre conventions and its elaborate play of cinematic references. The film, as J. Hoberman has said, 'pioneered the genre pastiche – synthesizing a mythology so soulless that its most human characters were a pair of robots.'[31] The hell-bent narrative careens from one genre-coded episode to another – from Western to war film to vine-swinging adventure – and also effectively melds different styles and genres in individual sequences. The bar scene early on which introduces Han Solo's character, for instance, is an inspired amalgam of Western, film noir, hardboiled detective, and sci-fi. Thus the seemingly one-dimensional characters and ruthlessly linear chase-film plotting are offset by a purposeful incoherence which actually 'opens' the film to different readings (and readers), allowing for multiple interpretive strategies and thus broadening the potential audience appeal. This is reinforced by the film's oddly nostalgic quality, due mainly to its evocations of old movie serials and TV series (*Flash Gordon*, *Captain Video*, and so on), references that undoubtedly are lost on younger viewers but relished by their cineliterate parents and senior siblings.

Like *Jaws*, Lucas's space epic is a masterwork of narrative technique and film technology. It too features an excessive John Williams score and signature musical theme, and Lucas's general attention to sound and audio effects was as widely praised as the visuals. Indeed, while the film was shut out in its major Oscar nominations (best picture, director and screenplay), it won Academy Awards for editing, art direction, costume design, visual effects and musical score, along with a special achievement award for sound effects editing. And although *Star Wars* was the twenty-first feature to be released with a Dolby soundtrack, it was the first to induce theater owners to install Dolby sound systems.[32] There were countless commercial tie-ins, as well as a multi-billion dollar licensing and merchandizing bonanza. And strictly as a movie franchise it had tremendous legs, as this inventory of its first decade well indicates:

May 1977	*Star Wars* released
July 1978	*Star Wars* reissue #1
May 1979	*Star Wars* reissue #2
May 1980	*Star Wars* sequel #1: *The Empire Strikes Back*
April 1981	*Star Wars* reissue #3
May 1982	*Star Wars* available on videocassette
Aug 1982	*Star Wars* reissue #4
Feb 1983	*Star Wars* appears on pay-cable TV
May 1983	*Star Wars* sequel #2: *Return of the Jedi*
Feb 1984	*Star Wars* on network TV
Mar 1985	*Star Wars* trilogy screened in 8 cities
Jan 1987	'Star Tours' opens at Disneyland[33]

The promise of *Jaws* was confirmed by *Star Wars*, the only other film at the time to surpass $100 million in rentals. *Star Wars* also secured Lucas's place with Spielberg as charter member of 'Hollywood's delayed New Wave,' as J. Hoberman put it, a group of brash young filmmakers (Brian DePalma, John Landis, Lawrence Kasdan, John Carpenter, *et al.*) steeped in movie lore whose 'cult blockbusters' and genre hybrids elevated 'the most vital and disreputable genres of their youth . . . to cosmic heights.'[34] Perhaps inevitably, Lucas and Spielberg decided to join forces – a decision they made, as legend has it, while vacationing in Hawaii in May 1977, a week before the release of *Star Wars*, and during a break between the shooting and editing of *Close Encounters*. Lucas was mulling over an idea for a movie serial about the exploits of an adventurer-anthropologist; Spielberg loved the idea, and he convinced Lucas to write and produce the first instalment, and to let him direct.[35]

The result, of course, was *Raiders of the Lost Ark*, the huge 1981 hit that established the billion-dollar Indiana Jones franchise and further solidified the two film-makers in the New Hollywood pantheon. Indeed, whether working together or on their own projects – notably Spielberg on *ET* and Lucas on the *Star Wars* sequels – the two virtually rewrote the box-office record books in the late 1970s and 1980s. With the release of their third Indiana Jones collaboration in 1989, Lucas and Spielberg could claim eight of the ten biggest hits in movie history, all of them surpassing $100 million in rentals.[36] Seven of those hits came out in the decade following the release of *Jaws*, a period that Hoberman has aptly termed 'ten years that shook the world' of cinema, and that A. D. Murphy calls 'the modern era of super-blockbuster films.'[37]

Into the 1980s

The importance of the Lucas and Spielberg super-blockbusters can hardly be overstated, considering their impact on theatrical and video markets in the US, which along with the rapidly expanding global entertainment market went into overdrive in the 1980s. After surpassing $2 billion in 1975, Hollywood's domestic theatrical revenues climbed steadily from $2.75 billion in 1980 to $5 billion in both 1989 and 1990. And remarkably enough, this steady theatrical growth throughout the 1980s was outpaced rather dramatically by various 'secondary markets,' particularly pay-cable and home video. During the 1980s, the number of US households with VCRs climbed from 1.85 million (one home in 40) to 62 million (two-thirds of all homes). Pre-recorded videocassette sales rose from only three million in 1980 to 220 million in 1990 – an increase of 6,500 per cent – while the number of cable households rose from 19.6 million in 1980 to 55 million in 1990, with pay subscriptions increasing from 9 million to 42 million during the decade.[38]

This growth has been a tremendous windfall for Hollywood, since both the pay-cable and home-video industries have been driven primarily by feature films, and in fact have been as hit-driven as the theatrical market. Through all the changes during the 1980s, domestic theatrical release remained the launching pad for blockbuster hits, and it established a movie's value in virtually all other secondary or ancillary markets. Yet even with the record-setting box-office revenues throughout the 1980s, the portion of the Hollywood majors' income from theater rentals actually declined, while total revenues have soared. According to Robert Levin, president of international motion picture marketing for Disney, the domestic box office in 1978 comprised just over half (54 per cent) of the majors' overall income, with a mere 4 per cent coming from pay-cable and home video combined. By 1986, box-office revenues comprised barely one quarter (28 per cent) of the majors' total, with pay-cable and home video combining for over half (12 per cent and 40 per cent respectively).[39] Home-video revenues actually exceeded worldwide theatrical revenues that year, 1986, and by decade's end cassette revenues alone actually doubled domestic box-office revenues.[40]

Another crucial secondary market for Hollywood has been the box office overseas, particularly in Europe. While the overseas pay-TV and home-video markets are still taking shape, European theatrical began surging in 1985 and reached record levels in 1990, when a number of top hits – including *Pretty Woman*, *Total Recall*, *The Little Mermaid* and *Dances with Wolves* – actually did better box office in Europe than in the US.[41] And *Forbes* magazine has estimated that the European theatrical market will double by 1995, as multiplexing picks up in Western Europe and as new markets open in Eastern Europe.[42]

With the astounding growth of both theatrical and video markets and the continued stature of the Hollywood-produced feature, the American movie industry has become increasingly stable in the late 1980s. What's more, the blockbuster mentality seems to have leveled off somewhat. In the early 1980s, one or two huge hits tended to dominate the marketplace, doing well over $100 million and far outdistancing other top hits. From 1986–90, however, the number of super-blockbuster hits dropped while the number of mid-range hits earning $10 million or more in rentals increased significantly, as did the number returning $50 million or more – still the measure of blockbuster-hit status. From 1975 to 1985 ten films earned $100 million or more in rentals; there have been only four since. Meanwhile, the number of films earning $50 million or more has climbed considerably. From 1965 to 1975, only six reached this mark; from 1976 to 1980 there were 13; from 1981 to 1985 there were 17. From 1986 to 1990, 30 films surpassed $50 million in rentals.

As the economic stakes have risen so have production and marketing costs. The average 'negative cost' (i.e. money spent to complete the actual film) on all major studio releases climbed from $9.4 million in 1980 to $26.8 million in 1990. Over the same period, average costs for prints and advertising rose from $4.3 million per film in 1980 to $11.6 million in 1990.[43] The rise in production costs is due largely to two dominant factors: an increased reliance on special effects and the soaring salaries paid to top talent, especially stars. The rise in marketing costs reflects Hollywood's deepening commitment to saturation booking and advertising, which has grown more expensive with the continued multiplex phenomenon and the increased advertising opportunities due to cable and VCRs. The number of indoor theaters in the US increased from about 14,000 in 1980 to over 22,000 in 1990, which meant that widespread nationwide release required anywhere from 1,000 to 2,700 prints, at roughly $2,500 per print. But the primary reason for rising marketing costs is TV advertising, particularly for high-stakes blockbusters. In 1990, for example, well over $20 million was spent on TV ads alone for *Dick Tracy*, *Total Recall* and *Die Hard 2*.[44]

While this may seem like fiscal madness, there is method in it. Consider the performance of the three top hits of the 'blockbuster Summer' in 1989, Hollywood's single biggest season ever. In a four-week span beginning Memorial Day weekend, *Indiana Jones and the Last Crusade*, *Ghostbusters II* and *Batman* enjoyed successive weekend releases in at least 2,300 theaters in the US and Canada after heavy TV advertising. Each of these pre-sold entertainment machines set a new box-office record for its opening weekend, culminating in *Batman's* three-day ticket sales of $40.5 million. In an era when $100 million in gross revenues is one measure of a blockbuster hit, it took *Indiana Jones* just 19 days to reach that total; it took *Batman* 11 days. And like so many recent hits, all three underwent a 'fast burn' at the box office. Compare these week-to-week box office revenues on Hollywood's two all-time summer hits, *ET* (1982) and *Batman*, which well indicate certain crucial 1980s market trends.[45]

ET earned another $100 million at the box office, which in 1982 was its only serious source of domestic income, while *Batman* was pulled from domestic theatrical for the home-video market – where it generated another $179 million in revenues.[46] Few recent films match *Batman's* home-video performance, and for that matter, few match its box-office legs, either. In 1990, no saturation summer releases except *Ghost* and *Pretty Woman* had any real pull beyond five weeks, although a number of films (*Total Recall*, *Die Hard 2*, *Dick Tracy*) grossed over $100 million at the box office.

The three top hits of 1990, *Home Alone*, *Ghost* and *Pretty Woman*, bucked the calculated blockbuster trend and demonstrated why Hollywood relies on a steady output of 'smaller' (i.e. less expensive) films which, mainly via word of mouth rather than massive pre-selling and promotion, might emerge as surprise hits. Such 'sleepers' are most welcome, of course,

	wk 1	2	3	4	5	6	7	8	9	10
ET	$22m	22	26	24	23	23	19	19	16	15
Batman	$70m	52	30	24	18	13	11	8	5	4

even in this age of high-cost, high-tech, high-volume behemoths, and they invariably are well exploited once they begin to take off – as were those three surprise hits of 1990. And each undoubtedly will spawn a sequel of calculated blockbuster proportions, with the studio hoping not only for a profitable follow-up but for the kind of success that MGM/UA had with *Rocky*, a modest, offbeat sleeper in 1976 that became a billion-dollar entertainment franchise.

Many have touted the three 1990 hits as a return to reason in Hollywood filmmaking, including Disney production chief Jeffrey Katzenberg in a now legendary interoffice memo of January 1991. Katzenberg warned of 'the "blockbuster mentality" that has gripped our industry,' and encouraged a return to 'the kind of modest, story-driven movie we tended to make in our salad days.'[47] The memo was leaked to the press and caused quite a stir, but scarcely signaled any real change at Disney or anywhere else. *Variety* subtly underscored this point by running excerpts from the memo directly below an even more prominent story with the banner headline, 'Megabudgets Boom Despite Talk of Doom.' That story inventoried the numerous high-cost Hollywood films 'still being greenlighted,' including several at Disney.[48]

In one sense, Katzenberg's memo was a rationale for *Dick Tracy*, the 1990 Disney blockbuster that cost $46 million to produce and another $55 million to market and release, with $44 million spent on advertising and promotion alone. Those figures were disclosed some two months before Katzenberg's memo and startled many industry observers, since by then the film had run its theatrical course and returned only about $60 million to Disney in rentals. But Hollywood insiders (including Katzenberg, no doubt) well understood the logic, given today's entertainment market-place. As one competing executive told the *New York Times*, Disney had to 'build awareness' of the Tracy story and character not simply to sell the film, but to establish 'the value of a new character in the Disney family . . . so that it could be brought back in a sequel and used in Disney's theme parks.'[49]

The future of the Tracy franchise remains to be seen, but one can hardly fault Disney for making the investment. Lip service to scaled-down moviemaking aside, Hollywood's block-buster mentality is more entrenched now than ever, the industry is more secure, and certain rules of the movie marketplace are virtually set in stone. The first is William Goldman's 1983 axiom, 'nobody knows anything,' which is quoted with increasing frequency these years as it grows ever more evident that, despite all the market studies and promotional strategies, the kind of public response that generates a bona fide hit simply cannot be manufactured, calculated or predicted.[50] The studios have learned to hedge their bets and increase the odds, however, and thus these other rules – all designed not only to complement but to counter the Goldman Rule.

The most basic of these rules is that only star vehicles with solid production values have any real chance at the box office (and thus in secondary markets as well). Such films nowadays cost $20 to $30 million, and will push $50 million if top stars, special effects, and/or logistical difficulties are involved. The next rule concerns what is termed the 'reward risk' factor, and holds that reaping the potential benefits of a hit requires heavy up-front spending on marketing as well as production. A corollary to this is that risk can be minimized via pre-sold pictures, and today the most effective pre-selling involves previous movie hits or other familiar media products (TV series, pop songs, comic books). An aesthetic corollary holds that films with minimal character complexity or development and by-the-numbers plotting (especially male action pictures) are the most readily reformulated and thus the most likely to be parlayed into a full-blown franchise.

Another cardinal rule is that a film's theatrical release, with its attendant media exposure, creates a cultural commodity that might be regenerated in any number of media forms: Perhaps in pop music, and not only as a hit single or musical score; note that *Batman* had two soundtrack albums and *Dick Tracy* had three. Perhaps as an arcade game, a $7 billion industry in 1990; note that *Hook* and *Terminator 2* both were released simultaneously as movies and video games. Perhaps as a theme park ride; note that Disney earns far more on its theme parks than on motion pictures and television, and that the hottest new Disney World attraction is 'Toon Town,' adapted from *Who Framed Roger Rabbit?*[51] Perhaps as a comic book or related item; note that the Advance Comics Special Batlist offered 214 separate pieces of *Batman*-related paraphernalia.[52] Perhaps in 'novelized' form, with print (and audiocassette) versions of movie hits regularly becoming worldwide best-sellers; note that Simon and Schuster, a Paramount subdivision and the nation's largest bookseller, has devoted an entire division to its *Star Trek* publications.

These rules are evident not only in today's multimedia worldwide blockbusters, but also in the structure and operations of international corporate giants that produce and market them. Competing successfully in today's high-stakes entertainment marketplace requires an operation that is not only well financed and productive, both also diversified and well coordinated. John Mickelthwait of the *Economist* has written that an entertainment company 'needs financial muscle to produce enough software to give itself a decent chance for bringing in a hit, and marketing muscle to make the most of that hit when it happens.'[53] Thus there has been a trend toward 'tight diversification' and 'synergy' in the recent merger-and-acquisitions wave, bringing movie studios into direct play with television production companies, network and cable TV, music and recording companies, and book, magazine, and newspaper publishers, and possibly even with games, toys, theme parks and electronics hardware manufacturers as well.

So obviously enough, diversification and conglomeration remain key factors in the entertainment industry, though today's media empires are much different than those of the 1960s and 1970s like Gulf & Western, Kinney, and Transamerica. Those top-heavy, widely diversified conglomerates sold out, 'downsized' or otherwise regrouped to achieve tighter diversification. Gulf & Western, for instance, sold all but its media holdings by the late 1980s and changed its corporate name to Paramount Communications. Kinney created a media subsidiary in Warner Communications, which also downsized in the early 1980s – only to expand via a $13 billion marriage with Time in 1989 (to avoid a hostile $12 billion takeover by Paramount), thereby creating Time Warner, the world's largest multimedia company and a model of synergy, with holdings in movies, TV production, cable, records, and book and magazine publishing. Because movies drive the global multimedia marketplace, a key holding for any media conglomerate is a motion picture studio; but there is no typical media conglomerate these days due to the widening range of entertainment markets and rapid changes in media technology.

Conglomeration has taken on another new dimension in that several studios have been purchased by foreign media companies: Fox by Rupert Murdoch's News Corporation in 1985, Columbia by Sony in 1989, and MCA/Universal by Matsushita in 1990. The Fox purchase may have greater implications for TV than cinema, given the creation of a 'fourth network' in America and its expansion into Europe. The Sony and Matsushita buyouts take the cinema-television synergy in yet another direction, since this time the two consumer electronics giants are battling over domination of the multi-billion-dollar high definition television (HDTV) market. Columbia and MCA gave the two firms sizable media libraries and active production companies, which may well give them an edge in the race not only to develop but to sell HDTV.

The Sony-Columbia and Matsushita-MCA deals are significant in terms of 'talent' as well. Beyond the $3.5 billion Sony paid for Columbia, the company also spent roughly $750 million for the services of Peter Guber and Jon Peters, two successful producers (*Batman*, *Rain Man*, *et al.*) then under contact to Warners. This underscored the importance of corporate and studio management in the diversified, globalized, synergized marketplace. Indeed, the most successful companies in the mid-to-late 1980s – Paramount, Disney, Warners, and Universal – all enjoyed consistent, capable executive leadership. Successful studio management involves not only positioning movies in a global multimedia market, but also dealing effectively with top talent and their agents, which introduces other human factors into the New Hollywood equation. These factors were best indicated by the role of Michael Ovitz in both the Sony and Matsushita deals. Co-founder and chief executive of CAA, Ovitz is the most powerful agent in Hollywood's premier agency. He was a key advisor in the Sony-Columbia deal, and in fact he packaged *Rain Man* during the negotiations and later helped arrange the Guber-Peters transaction. And Ovitz quite literally brokered the Matsushita-MCA deal, acting as the sole go-between during the year-long negotiations.[54]

Ovtiz's rise to power in the New Hollywood has been due to various factors: CAA's steadily expanding client list, its packaging of top talent in highly desirable movie packages, and its capacity to secure favorable terms for its clients when cutting movie deals. In perhaps no other industry is the 'art of the deal' so important, and in that regard Ovitz is Hollywood's consummate artist. He also is a master at managing relationships – whether interpersonal, institutional, or corporate, as the Columbia and MCA deals both demonstrate. And more than any other single factor, Ovitz's and CAA's success has hinged on the increasingly hit-driven nature of the entertainment industry, and in turn on the star-driven nature of top industry products.

The 'star system' is as old as the movie industry itself, of course. 'Marquee value,' 'bankable' talent and 'star vehicles' have always been vital to Hollywood's market strategy, just as the 'star persona' has keyed both the narrative and production economies of moviemaking. In the classical era, in fact, studios built their entire production and marketing operations around a few prime star-genre formulas. In the New Hollywood, however, where fewer films carry much wider commercial and cultural impact, and where persona are prone to multimedia reincarnation, the star's commercial value, cultural cache and creative clout have increased enormously. The most obvious indication of this is the rampant escalation of star salaries during the 1980s – a phenomenon often traced to Sylvester Stallone's $15 million paycheck in 1983 for *Rocky IV*.[55] Interestingly enough, many (if not most) of the seminal New Hollywood blockbusters were not star-driven; in fact many secured stardom for their lead actors. But as the blockbuster sequels and multimedia markets coalesced in the early 1980s, both the salary scale and narrative agency of top stars rose dramatically – to a point where Stallone, Arnold Schwarzenegger, Bruce Willis, Michael Douglas, Eddie Murphy, Sean Connery and Kevin Costner earn seven- or even eight-figure sums per film, having become not only genres but franchises unto themselves, and where 'star vehicles' are often simply that: stylish, careening machines designed for their star-drivers which, in terms of plot and character development, tend to go nowhere fast.

Not surprisingly, the studios bemoan their dwindling profit margins due to increased talent costs while top talent demand – and often get – 'participation' deals on potential blockbusters.

CAA's package for *Hook* gave Dustin Hoffman, Robin Williams and Steven Spielberg a reported 40 per cent of the box-office take, and Jack Nicholson's escalating 15 to 20 per cent of the gross of *Batman* paid him upwards of $50 million.[56] While studio laments about narrowing margins are understandable, so too are agency efforts to secure a piece of the box-office take for their clients, particularly in light of the limited payoff for stars and other talent in ancillary markets and in licensing and merchandizing deals. And given the potential long-term payoff of a franchise-scale blockbuster, the stars' demands are as inevitable as the studios' grudging willingness to accommodate them. As Geraldine Fabrikant suggests in a *New York Times* piece on soaring production costs: 'Some studios can more easily justify paying higher prices for talent these days because, with the consolidation of the media industry and the rise of integrated entertainment conglomerates that distribute movies, books, recordings, television programming and magazines, they have more outlets through which to recoup their investments.'[57]

The economics and aesthetics of the new Hollywood

This brings us back, yet again, to the New Hollywood blockbuster's peculiar status as what Eileen Meehan has aptly termed a 'commercial intertext.' As Meehan suggests, today's conglomerates 'view every project as a multimedia production line,' and thus *Batman* 'is best understood as a multimedia, multimarket sales campaign.'[58] Others have noted the increased interplay of moviemaking and advertising, notably Mark Crispin Miller in a cover story for the *Atlantic*, 'Hollywood: The Ad.' Miller opens with an indictment of the 'product placement' trend in movies (a means of offsetting production costs which, as he suggests, often brings the narrative to a dead halt), and he goes on to discuss other areas where movies and advertising – especially TV advertising – have begun to merge. Like TV ads, says Miller, movies today aspire to a total 'look' and seem more designed than directed, often by filmmakers segueing from studio to ad agency. And now that movies are more likely to be seen on a VCR than a theater screen, cinematic technique is adjusted accordingly, conforming with the small screen's 'most hypnotic images,' its ads. Visual and spatial scale are downsized, action is repetitiously foregrounded and centered, pace and transitions are quicker, music and montage are more prevalent, and slick production values and special effects abound.[59]

While Miller's view of the cinema as the last bastion of high culture under siege by the twin evils of TV and advertising displays a rather limited understanding of the contemporary culture industries, there is no question but that movie and ad techniques are intermingling. In fact, one might argue that the New Hollywood's calculated blockbusters are themselves massive advertisements for their product lines – a notion that places a very different value on their one-dimensional characters, mechanical plots and high-gloss style. This evokes that New Hollywood buzzword, 'high concept,' a term best defined perhaps by its chief progenitor, Steven Spielberg, in an interview back in 1978: 'What interests me more than anything else is the idea. If a person can tell me the idea in twenty-five words of less, it's going to be a good movie.'[60] And a pretty good ad campaign as well – whether condensed into a 30-second movie trailer or as a feature-length plug for any number of multimedia reiterations.

This paradoxical reduction and reiteration of blockbuster movie narratives points up the central, governing contradiction in contemporary cinema. On the one hand, the seemingly infinite capacity for multimedia reiteration of a movie hit redefines textual boundaries, creates a dynamic commercial intertext that is more process than product, and involves the audience(s) in the creative process – not only as multimarket consumers but also as mediators in the play of narrative signification. On the other hand, the actual movie 'itself,' if indeed it can be isolated and understood as such (which is questionable at best), often has been reduced and stylized to a point where, for some observers, it scarcely even qualifies as a narrative.

Critic Richard Schickel, for instance, has stated: 'In the best of all possible marketing worlds the movie will inspire some simple summarizing graphic treatment, adaptable to all media, by which it can be instantly recognized the world over, even by subliterates.'[61] The assembly-line process in the studio era demanded that story ideas be progressively refined into a classical three-act structure of exposition, complication and resolution. But nowadays, says Schickel, 'Hollywood seems to have lost or abandoned the art of narrative. . . . [Film-makers] are generally not refining stories at all, they are spicing up "concepts" (as they like to call them), refining gimmicks, making sure there are no complexities to fur our tongues when it comes time to spread the word of mouth.' Schickel argues that all genres have merged into two meta-categories, comedies and action-adventure films, both of which offer 'a succession of undifferentiated sensations, lucky or unlucky accidents, that have little or nothing to do with whatever went before or is about to come next,' with a mere 'illusion of forward motion' created via music and editing.[62]

Schickel excuses his 'geriatric grumble' while demeaning 'youthful' moviegoers for their lack of 'very sophisticated tastes or expectations when it comes to narrative,' and his nod to audience fragmentation along generational lines raises a few important issues.[63] To begin with, younger viewers – despite 'grownup' biases about limited attention spans, depth of feeling and intellectual development – are far more likely to be active multimedia players, consumers, and semioticians, and thus to gauge a movie in intertextual terms and to appreciate in it a richness and complexity that may well be lost on middle-aged movie critics. In fact, given the penchant these years to pre-sell movies via other popular culture products (rock songs, comic books, TV series, etc.), chances are that younger, media-literate viewers encounter a movie in an already-activated narrative process. The size, scope and emotional charge of the movie and its concurrent ad campaign certainly privilege the big screen 'version' of the story, but the movie itself scarcely begins or ends the textual cycle.

This in turn raises the issue of narrative 'integrity,' which in classical Hollywood was a textual feature directly related to the integrity of both the 'art form' and the system of production. While movies during the studio era certainly had their intertextual qualities, these were incidental and rarely undermined the internal coherence of the narrative itself. While many (perhaps most) New Hollywood films still aspire to this kind of narrative integrity, the blockbuster tends to be intertextual and purposefully incoherent – virtually of necessity, given the current conditions of cultural production and consumption. Put another way, the vertical integration of classical Hollywood, which ensured a closed industrial system and coherent narrative, has given way to 'horizontal integration' of the New Hollywood's tightly diversified media conglomerates, which favors texts strategically 'open' to multiple readings and multi-media reiteration.

These calculated blockbusters utterly dominate the movie industry, but they also promote alternative films and filmmaking practices in a number of ways. Because the major's high-cost, high-stakes projects require a concentration of resources and limit overall output, they tend to foster product demand. This demand is satisfied, for the most part, by moderately priced star vehicles financed and distributed by the majors, which may emerge as surprise hits but essentially serve to keep the industry machinery running, to develop new talent, and to maintain a steady supply of dependable mainstream product. Complementing these routine features, and far more interesting from a critical and cultural perspective, are the low-cost films from independent outfits like Mirimax and New Line Cinema. In fact, the very market fragmentation which the studios' franchise projects are designed to exploit and overcome, these independents are exploiting in a very different way via their small-is-beautiful, market-niche approach.

Miramax, for instance, has carved out a niche by financing or buying and then distributing low-budget art films and imports like *sex, lies and videotape*, *My Left Foot*, *Cinema Paradiso* and *Tie Me Up, Tie Me Down* to a fairly consistent art film crowd. New Line's strategy is more wide-ranging, targeting an array of demographic groups and taste cultures from art film aficionados and environmentalists to born-again Christians and wrestling fans. If any one of New Line's products takes off at the box office, it's liable to be a teen pic like *Teenage Mutant Ninja Turtles*, which returned $67 million in rentals in 1990. While fully exploiting that hit was a real challenge for a company like New Line, an even bigger challenge, no doubt, was resisting the urge to expand their operations, upgrade their product, and compete with the majors – an impulse that proved disastrous for many independent companies during the 1980s.[64]

Thus we might see the New Hollywood as producing three different classes of movie: the calculated blockbuster designed with the multimedia marketplace and franchise status in mind, the mainstream A-class star vehicle with sleeper-hit potential, and the low-cost independent feature targeted for a specific market and with little chance of anything more than 'cult film' status. These three classes of movie have corresponding ranks of auteurs, from the superstar directors at the 'high end' like Spielberg and Lucas, whose knack for engineering hits has transformed their names into virtual trademarks, to those film-makers on the margins like Gus Van Sant, John Sayles, and the Coen brothers, whose creative control and personal style are considerably less constrained by commercial imperatives. And then there are the established genre auteurs like Jonathan Demme, Martin Scorsese, David Lynch, and Woody Allen who, like Ford and Hitchcock and the other top studio directors of old, are the most perplexing and intriguing cases – each of them part visionary cineaste and part commercial hack, whose best films flirt with hit status and critique the very genres (and audiences) they exploit.

Despite its stratification, the New Hollywood is scarcely a balkanized or rigidly class-bound system. On the contrary, these classes of films and film-makers are in a state of dynamic tension with one another and continually intermingle. Consider, for instance, the two recent forays into that most contemptible of genres, the psycho-killer/stalk-and-slash film, by Jonathan Demme in *Silence of the Lambs* and Martin Scorsese in *Cape Fear*. Each film took the genre into uncharted narrative and thematic territory; each was a cinematic tour-de-force, enhancing both the aesthetic and commercial value of the form; and each thoroughly terrified audiences, thereby reinforcing the genre's capacity to explore the dark recesses of the collective American psyche and underscoring the cinema's vital contact with its public.

Besides winning the Oscar for 'Best Picture of 1991,' *Silence of the Lambs* emerged as a solid international hit, indicating the potential global currency of the genre while raising some interesting questions about the New Hollywood's high-end products *vis-à-vis* the American cultural experience. With the rapid development of multiplex theaters and home video in Europe and the Far East, and the concurrent advances in advertising and marketing, one can readily foresee the 'global release' of calculated blockbusters far beyond the scale of a *Batman* or *Terminator 2*, let alone a surprise hit like *Silence of the Lambs*. This may require a very different kind of product, effectively segregating the calculated blockbuster from the studios' other feature output and redefining the Hollywood cinema as an American culture industry. But it's much more likely that the New Hollywood and its characteristic blockbuster product will endure, given the social and economic development in the major overseas markets, the survival instincts and overall economic stability of the Hollywood studios, and the established global appeal of its products.

Notes

1   Recent studies of 'classical' Hollywood and the 'studio system' include *The Classical Hollywood Cinema: Film Style and Mode of Production to 1960*, David Bordwell, Janet Staiger and Kristin Thompson (New York: Columbia University Press, 1985); *The Hollywood Studio System*, Douglas Gomery (New York: St. Martin, 1986); and *The Genius of the System: Hollywood Filmmaking in the Studio Era*, Thomas Schatz (New York: Pantheon, 1988).

2   Here and throughout this essay, I will be referring to '*rentals*' (or 'rental receipts') and also to '*gross revenues*' (or 'box-office revenues'). This is a crucial distinction, since the gross revenues indicate the amount of money actually spent at the box office, whereas rental receipts refer, as *Variety* puts it, to 'actual amounts received by the distributor' – i.e. to the monies returned by theaters to the company (usually a 'studio') that released the movie. Unless otherwise indicated, both the rentals and gross revenues involve only the 'domestic box office' – i.e. theatrical release in the US and Canada.

    All of the references to box-office performance and rental receipts in this article are taken from *Variety*, most of them from its most recent (11–17 January 1989; pp. 28–74) survey of 'All-Time Film Rental Champs,' which includes all motion pictures returning at least $4 million in rentals. Because this survey is continually updated, the totals include reissues and thus may be considerably higher than the rentals from initial release. In these cases I try to use figures from earlier *Variety* surveys for purposes of accuracy.

3   ' "Gone With the Wind" Again Tops All-Time List,' *Variety* (4 May 1983), p. 15.

4   'Top 100 All-Time Film Rental Champs,' *Variety* (6 January 1992), p. 86.

5   Eileen R. Meehan, ' "Holy Commodity Fetish, Batman!": The Political Economy of a Commercial Intertext,' in *The Many Lives of the Batman*, Roberta E. Pearson and William Uricchio (eds) (New York: BFI-Routledge, 1991), p. 62.

6   Christopher H. Sterling and Timothy R. Haight, *The Mass Media: Aspen Institute Guide to Communications Industry Trends* (New York: Praeger, 1978), pp. 187 and 352. Unless otherwise noted, the statistics on attendance, ticket sales, etc. are from this reliable compendium of statistical data on the movie industry.

7   'All-Time Film Champs,' *Variety* (11–17 January 1989), pp. 28–74.

8   Personal correspondence from Selznick to Louis B. Mayer, 16 September 1953; David O. Selznick Collection, Humanities Research Center, University of Texas at Austin.

9   Rudy Behlmer (ed.), *Memo from David O. Selznick* (New York: Viking, 1972), p. 373.

10 See Janet Staiger, 'Individualism Versus Collectivism,' *Screen* 24 (July–October 1983), pp. 68–79.

11 Freeman Lincoln, 'The Comeback of the Movies,' *Fortune* (February 1955), p. 127.

12 See Robert Vianello, 'The Rise of the Telefilm and the Networks' Hegemony Over the Motion Picture Industry,' *Quarterly Review of Film Studies* (Summer 1984) pp. 204–18.

13 See William Lafferty, 'Feature Films of Prime-Time Television,' in *Hollywood in the Age of Television*, Tino Balio (ed.) (Boston: Unwin Hyman, 1990), pp. 235–56.

14 Lincoln, op. cit., p. 131.

15 Stephen M. Silverman, *The Fox That Got Away* (Secaucus, NJ: Lyle Stuart Inc., 1988), pp. 323–9.

16 Tino Balio, 'Introduction to Part II' of *Hollywood in the Age of Television*, pp. 259–60.

17 Joseph R. Dominick, 'Film Economics and Film Content: 1964–83,' in *Current Research in Film* (Norwood, NJ: Ablex, 1987), p. 144.

18 Lafferty, op. cit., pp. 245–8.

19 Michael Pye and Lynda Myles, *The Movie Brats* (New York: Holt, Rinehart and Winston, 1979), p. 236.

20 Carl Gottlieb, *The Jaws Log* (New York: Dell, 1975), pp. 15–19. Note that Dell is a subdivision of MCA.

21 Gottlieb, ibid., p. 62.

22 Pye and Myles, op. cit., p. 232.

23 James Monaco, *American Film Now* (New York: New American Library, 1979), p. 50.

24 Axel Madsen, *The New Hollywood* (New York: Thomas Y. Crowell, 1975), p. 94.

25 Balio, 'Introduction to Part I,' *Hollywood in the Age of Television*, p. 29.

26 'Theatrical Data' section in '1990 US Economic Review' (New York: Motion Picture Association of America, 1991), p. 3.

27 Dominick, op. cit., p. 146.

28   Jennifer Pendleton, 'Fast Forward, Reverse,' *Daily Variety* (58th Anniversary issue, 'Focus on Entertainment Marketing,' October 1991), p. 14.
29   Michelle Hilmes, 'Breaking the Broadcast Bottleneck,' in Balio, *Hollywood*, pp. 299–300.
30   See Hilmes, ibid., and also Bruce A. Austin, 'Home Video: The Second-Run "Theater" of the 1990s,' in Balio, *Hollywood*, pp. 319–49.
31   J. Hoberman, 'Ten years That Shook the World,' *American Film* 10 (June 1985); p. 42.
32   Jim McCullaugh, '*Star Wars* Hikes Demand for Dolby,' *Billboard* (9 July 1977), p. 4.
33   '*Star Wars:* A Cultural Phenomenon,' *Box Office* (July 1987), pp. 36–8.
34   Hoberman, op. cit., pp. 36–7.
35   'Behind the Scenes on *Raiders of the Lost Ark*,' *American Cinematographer* (November 1981), p. 1096. See also Tony Crawley, *The Steven Spielberg Story* (New York: Quill, 1983), p. 90.
36   'Top 100 All-Time Film Rental Champs,' *Variety* (11–17 January 1989), p. 26.
37   Hoberman, op. cit., and A. D. Murphy, 'Twenty Years of Weekly Film Ticket Sales in U.S. Theaters,' *Variety* (15–21 March 1989), p. 26.
38   Figures from 'Theatrical Data' and 'VCR and Cable' sections in MPAA's '1990 US Economic Review.'
39   Robert B. Levin and John H. Murphy, unpublished case study of Walt Disney Pictures' 1986 marketing strategies, for use in an advertising course taught by Professor Murphy.
40   Richard Natale, 'Hollywood's New Math': Does it Still Add Up?,' *Variety* (23 September 1991), pp. 1, 95.
41   Terry Iliott, 'Yank Pix Flex Pecs in New Euro Arena,' *Variety* (19 August 1991), pp. 1, 60.
42   John Marcon, Jr., 'Dream Factory to the World,' *Forbes* (29 April 1991), p. 100.
43   Figures from 'Prints and Advertising Costs of New Features' in MPAA's '1990 US Economic Review.'
44   Charles Fleming, 'Pitching costs out of ballpark: Record pic-spending spells windfall for TV,' *Variety* (27 June 1990), p. 1.
45   'Week-by-Week Domestic B.O. Gross,' *Variety* (7 January 1991), p. 10.
46   'Video and Theatrical Revenues,' *Variety* (24 September 1990), p. 108.
47   'The Teachings of Chairman Jeff,' *Variety* (4 February 1991), p. 24. Article contains excerpts of the 11 January memo.
48   Charles Fleming, 'Megabudgets Boom Despite Talk of Doom,' *Variety* (February 1991), pp. 5ff.
49   Geraldine Fabrikant, 'In Land of Big Bucks, Even Bigger Bucks,' *New York Times* (18 October 1990b), p. C5.
50   William Goldman, *Adventures in the Screen Trade* (New York: Warner Books, 1983), p. 39.
51   'Disney's Profits in Park: Off 23%,' *The Hollywood Reporter* (15 November 1991), pp. 1, 6.
52   Meehan, op. cit., p. 47.
53   John Mickelthwait, 'A Survey of the Entertainment Industry,' *The Economist* (23 December 1989), p. 5.
54   For an excellent overview of both the Sony and Matsushita deals, and Ovitz's role in each, see Connie Bruck, 'Leap of Faith,' *New Yorker* (September 9, 1991), pp. 38–74.
55   Lawrence Cohn, 'Stars' Rocketing Salaries Keep Pushing Envelope,' *Variety* (24 September 1990), p. 3.
56   Spielberg/Hoffman/Williams deal reported in Geraldine Fabrikant, 'The Hole in Hollywood's Pocket,' *New York Times* (10 December 1990), p. C7. Nicholson deal in Ben Stein, 'Holy Bat-Debt!,' *Entertainment Weekly* (26 April 1991), p. 12.
57   Fabrikant, op. cit., p. C7.
58   Meehan, op. cit., p. 52.
59   Mark Crispin Miller, 'Hollywood: The Ad,' *Atlantic Monthly* (April 1990), pp. 49–52.
60   Quoted in Hoberman, op. cit., p. 36.
61   Richard Schickel, 'The Crisis in Movie Narrative,' *Gannett Center Journal* 3 (Summer, 1989), p. 2.
62   Schickel, ibid., pp. 3–4.
63   Schickel, ibid., p. 3.
64   See Joshua Hammer, ' "Small Is Beautiful,"' *Newsweek* (26 November 1990), pp. 52–53, and William Grimes, 'Film Maker's Secret Is Knowing What's Not for Everyone,' *New York Times* (2 December 1991), pp. B1+.

Chapter 15

TINO BALIO

'A MAJOR PRESENCE IN ALL THE WORLD'S IMPORTANT MARKETS'
The globalization of Hollywood in the 1990s

DURING THE 1990S, THE WORLDWIDE DEMAND for films increased at an unprecedented rate, the result of such factors as economic growth in Western Europe, the Pacific Rim, and Latin America, the end of the Cold War, the commercialization of state broadcasting systems and the development of new distribution technologies. To capitalize on these conditions, Hollywood entered the age of 'globalization'. As described by Time Warner, globalization dictated that the top players in the business develop long-term strategies to build on a strong base of operations at home while achieving 'a major presence in all of the world's important markets'.[1] In practice, this meant that companies upgraded international operations to a privileged position by expanding 'horizontally' to tap emerging markets world-wide, by expanding 'vertically' to form alliances with independent producers to enlarge their rosters, and by 'partnering' with foreign investors to secure new sources of financing. Achieving these goals led to a merger movement in Hollywood that has yet to run its course.

The domestic market

Home video, a fledgling technology early in the 1980s, became the fastest growing revenue stream in the business. In 1980, only around two of every 100 American homes owned a VCR; ten years later, about two-thirds did.[2] Although the theatrical box office reached a new high of $5 billion in 1989, retail video sales and rentals had surpassed that figure by a factor of two.[3] Capitalizing on the appeal of their hit pictures and film libraries, the majors were able to extract the lion's share of the revenues from the home video market; today, home video can amount for up to one-third of the total revenue of a major studio.[4]

Home video naturally stimulated demand for product. Domestic feature film production jumped from around 350 pictures a year in 1983 to nearly 600 in 1988. Surprisingly, the majors played a small role in the matter; in fact, the number of in-house productions of the majors held steady during this period, between seventy and eighty films a year.[5] The influx came from the so-called 'mini-majors' – Orion Pictures, Cannon Films and Dino De Laurentiis Entertainment – and from independents like Atlantic Release, Carolco, New World, Hemdale, Troma, Island Alive, Vestron and New Line who were eager to fill the void. These companies entered the business knowing that even a modest picture could recoup most of its costs from the pre-sale of distribution rights to pay-cable and home video.

Rather than producing more pictures, the majors exploited a new feature film format, the 'ultra-high-budget' film.[6] Popularized by Carolco Pictures, the independent production company that invested $100 million in Arnold Schwarzenegger's *Terminator 2: Judgment Day* (1991) to create a vehicle that grossed $204 million domestic and $310 million foreign, ultra-high-budget pictures started a spending spree which boosted average production budgets to new highs.[7] Contrary to common sense, pictures costing upwards of $75 million became conservative investments. Containing such elements as high concepts, big-name stars, and visual and special effects, such pictures reduced the risk of financing because (1) they consti-tuted media events; (2) they lent themselves to promotional tie-ins; (3) they became massive engines for profits in ancillary divisions like theme parks and video; (4) they stood to make a profit in foreign markets; and (5) they were easy to distribute.

Ease of distribution was linked to saturation booking. Defined as the practice of releasing new films simultaneously in every market of the country accompanied by a massive national advertis-ing campaign, saturation booking was designed to recoup production costs quickly. Standard practice at least since Universal's release of *Jaws* in 1975, saturation booking boosted print and advertising costs to over $12 million per film on the average during the 1980s; during the 1990s, studios were spending $35 million and more to promote new films.[8] The strategy generated 'ultra-high' grosses; for example, in 1989, six pictures grossed over $100 million in the US, among them *Batman* (Warner, $250 million), *Indiana Jones and The Last Crusade* (Paramount, $195 million), *Lethal Weapon 2* (Warner, $147 million) and *Honey, I Shrunk the Kids* (Disney, $130 million).[9] As *Variety* remarked, the majors 'want to knock off a bank, not a candy store'.[10]

The foreign market

The growth of the overseas market during the 1980s resulted from the upgrading of motion picture cinemas, the emancipation of state-controlled broadcasting, the spread of cable and satel-lite services, and the pent-up demand for entertainment of all types. At one time, theatrical rentals constituted nearly all of the foreign revenues of American film companies, but by 1989 they accounted for little more than a quarter. The major sources of revenue overseas for Hollywood product had become home video, theatrical exhibition and television, in that order.[11]

The largest influx came from Western European television following the liberation of the broadcast spectrum and the growth of privately owned commercial television stations and cable and satellite services. But the largest single source of overseas revenue for Hollywood was from home video. In Western Europe, the number of VCRs sold rose from around 500,000 in 1978 to 40 million, or nearly one-third of all households, ten years later. By 1990, video sales in Western Europe reached nearly $4.5 billion, with the lion's share generated by Hollywood movies.[12] More recently, the international home video market was fuelled by a surge in rev-enues from the Asia-Pacific region, which grew by more than 20 per cent in 1994 alone.[13]

Like the US, Europe's video business was fuelled by hits. Europe's theatrical market improved steadily over the decade and by 1990 yielded around $830 million in film rentals for American distributors – about half of the film rentals they collected at home.[14] The overseas market as a whole had also improved and by 1990 nearly reached parity with the US domestic market.[15] By 1994, the overseas market surpassed the domestic in film rentals for the first time.[16]

Two factors boosted the foreign box office: better cinemas and more effective marketing. Outside the US, nearly every market was under-screened. Western Europe, for example, had about one-third the number of screens per capita as the US, despite having about the same population.[17] And most of its theatres were old and worn. To resuscitate moviegoing, the American majors and their European partners launched a campaign during the 1980s to rebuild and renovate exhibition in Great Britain, Germany, Italy, Spain and other countries.

Taking advantage of the advertising opportunities created by commercial television, Hollywood pitched its wares as never before. Whole markets, such as West Germany, were opened up to television advertising. And new channels, such as MTV Europe which reached 15–20 million homes, offered opportunities for niche marketing.[18] Spending lavishly on advertising, the majors were able to bolster their ultra-high-budget pictures in theatrical and in ancillary markets and overwhelm smaller, indigenous films that could not compete in such a high-stakes environment.

Hollywood's response to globalization

The first wave of mergers

Hollywood maintained its dominant position in the worldwide entertainment market by engaging in another round of business combinations beginning in the 1980s. The new urge to merge departed significantly from the merger movement of the 1960s, which ushered the American film industry into the age of conglomerates. During the 1960s, motion picture companies were either taken over by huge multifaceted corporations, absorbed into burgeoning entertainment conglomerates, or became conglomerates through diversification. The impetus behind this merger movement was to stabilize operations by creating numerous 'profit centers' as a hedge against a business downturn in any one area.[19] The quintessential 1960s conglomerate was Gulf & Western. The parent company of Paramount Pictures as of 1966, Gulf & Western owned or had interests in a range of unrelated industries such as sugar, zinc, fertilizer, wire and cable, musical instruments, real estate and scores of others.

The merger movement of the 1980s was characterized in part by vertical integration, the desire to control the production of programming, the distribution of programming, and even the exhibition of programming. Although the trend seemed a throwback to the glorious days of the studio system, the rationale for merging was 'a faith in synergy, a belief that one plus one could equal three'. Described another way, synergy was supposed to function like a good marriage, in which 'each partner would bring qualities that when combined would magically create something better than either could achieve alone'.[20]

A prime example of the vertical integration trend was the move by film companies into exhibition. The revival of the US theatrical market, coupled with the *laissez-faire* attitude of Ronald Reagan's administration towards anti-trust issues, prompted the majors to test the terms of the Paramount decrees and 'take another fling with vertical integration'.[21] The logic seemed to be this: since only a few movies do most of the business at the box office, why not go into exhibition and profit from the hits? Columbia Pictures started the trend in 1986 by purchasing a small group of theatres in New York City. Within a year, MCA, Paramount and Warner Bros. bought or acquired stakes in important chains around the country.[22]

More significantly, the new merger movement was characterized by horizontal integration – a desire to strengthen distribution. Film industry analyst Harold Vogel described the benefits of controlling distribution as follows:

> Ownership of entertainment distribution capability is like ownership of a toll road
> or bridge. No matter how good or bad the software product (i.e. movie, record,

book, magazine, TV show or whatever) is, it must pass over or cross through a distribution pipeline in order to reach the consumer. And like at any toll road or bridge that cannot be circumvented, the distributor is a local monopolist who can extract a relatively high fee for use of his facility.[23]

Rupert Murdoch started this trend by acquiring Twentieth Century Fox in 1985. Murdoch was the head of News Corp., an Australian publishing conglomerate that owned newspapers and magazines in Sydney, London, New York and Chicago valued at over $1 billion. Acquiring a controlling interest in Twentieth Century Fox for $600 million, Murdoch embarked on a strategy 'to own every major form of programming – news, sports, films and children's shows – and beam them via satellite or TV stations to homes in the US, Europe, Asia and South America'.[24]

To strengthen Fox's presence in US television, Murdoch set out to create a full-blown fourth TV network, Fox Broadcasting, to challenge the three entrenched American TV networks, ABC, CBS and NBC. And he did so with the knowledge that the US's Federal Communications Commission (FCC) wanted to foster more competition in television broadcasting. Murdoch made his first move by acquiring Metromedia Television, the largest group of independent television stations in the country, for $2 billion.[25] Murdoch then waged a costly three-year battle to assemble a network of over 100 independent stations capable of reaching nearly all TV homes. Developing counter-programming aimed at young adults to supply those stations, Fox Broadcasting lost hundreds of millions the first three years, but in 1989 it staged a turnaround with two hit series – *America's Most Wanted* and *Married . . . with Children*.[26] More recently, Fox enhanced its reputation as a programmer by backing such series as *The Simpsons* and *The X Files* and by bidding $1.6 billion to steal away the rights to broadcast National Football League games that CBS had held for four decades.[27]

Companies such as Gulf & Western (Paramount) and Warner Communications focused on distribution by 'downsizing' their businesses. For example, Warner Communications under the direction of Steven J. Ross had evolved into a diversified entertainment conglomerate involved in a wide range of 'leisure time' businesses such as film and television, recorded music, book publishing, cable communications, toys and electronic games, and other operations. In 1982, Warner decided to restructure its operations around distribution and sold such non-essential companies as Atari, Warner Cosmetics, Franklin Mint, Panavision, the New York Cosmos soccer team and Warner's cable programming interests in MTV and Nickelodeon.

The 'downsized' Warner Communications emerged as a horizontally integrated company engaged in three areas of entertainment: (1) production and distribution of film and television programming; (2) recorded music; and (3) publishing. In addition to owning one of Hollywood's most consistently successful studios, a formidable film and television library, and the largest record company in the world, Warner had acquired the distribution systems associated with each of its product lines, including Warner Cable Communications, the nation's second biggest cable operator with 1.5 million subscribers. Warner added considerable muscle to its distribution capability when it merged with Time Inc. in 1989 to form Time Warner, the world's pre-eminent media conglomerate valued at $14 billion.[28]

Time Warner touted its merger 'as essential to the competitive survival of American enterprise in the emerging global entertainment communications marketplace'.[29] It had in mind not only the take-over of Twentieth Century Fox by Australia's News Corp., but also the anticipated acquisition of Hollywood studios by Japanese electronics giants. The first such take-over occurred in 1989, when Sony acquired Columbia Pictures Entertainment (CPE) for $3.4 billion. Sony had previously entered the US entertainment software business in 1987 when it purchased CBS Records for $2 billion. Columbia Pictures Entertainment had 'bumped along a downhill path' and experienced frequent management turnovers under its previous owner, Coca-Cola Co. But Sony considered the CPE acquisition, which included two major studios – Columbia Pictures and TriStar Pictures – home video distribution, a theatre chain and an extensive film library, as a means of creating synergies in its operations.[30] As *Variety* put it, 'The hardware company's strategists had concluded that all their fancy electronic machines would have souls of tin without a steady diet of software'.[31] To strengthen CPE as a producer of software, Sony spent lavishly to acquire and refurbish new studios and to hire Peter Guber and Jon Peters to set a course for the company.[32]

The second take-over of a Hollywood studio by a Japanese firm occurred in 1990, when Japan's Matsushita Electric Industrial Company, the largest consumer electronics manufacturer in the world, purchased MCA for $6.9 billion. Like its rival Sony, Matsushita 'thought the entertainment "software" business could provide higher profit margins than the intensely competitive, and now largely saturated, consumer electronics appliance business'.[33] And like Sony, Matsushita thought that synergies could exist between the hardware and the software business.

The parent of Universal pictures, MCA had embarked on an acquisitions binge in 1985 in an effort to offset its lagging film and television operations. In two years, the company spent $650 million to acquire toy companies, music companies, a major independent television station and a half interest in Cineplex Odeon Theaters. The diversification strategy was designed to strengthen MCA's existing positions and to extend the company into contiguous businesses. MCA's investments showing the greatest promise were the Universal Studios Tours located near the company headquarters outside of Los Angeles and near Disney World in Orlando, Florida.

International partnerships

Hollywood's second response to globalization was to seek an international base of motion picture financing. To reduce its debt load, Time Warner restructured its film and cable businesses and created Time Warner Entertainment as a joint venture with two of Japan's leading companies, electronics manufacturer Toshiba and trading giant C. Itoh. The deal netted Time Warner $1 billion and was unprecedented.[34] Following the lead of some independent producers, Twentieth Century Fox pre-sold the foreign rights to two high-profile 'event' films, Danny DeVito's *Hoffa* (1992) and Spike Lee's *Malcolm X* (1992), to reduce its exposure in these films.[35] Another common practice was to seek out co-production deals to take advantage of film subsidies in overseas markets. Studios chose this option mostly with 'unusual material' – which is to say a picture that was not a sequel, that did not have a major international star, or that did not have an 'unflaggingly high-concept' – such as Universal's *Fried Green Tomatoes at the Whistle Stop Cafe* (1991) and Paramount's *1492* (1992).[36]

To finance television programming, the majors invested in foreign media industries. When the European Union decided against removing trade barriers and tariffs on movies and television programmes in 1992 as anticipated, Time Warner, Turner, Disney, Viacom and NBC re-evaluated their relationship to this market. No longer did these companies think of Western Europe only as a programming outlet: instead they considered it as another investment source and formed partnerships with European television producers, broadcast stations, cable and satellite networks and telecommunications services. Time Warner, for example, invested in satellite broadcasting in Scandinavia, FM radio in the UK, and pay-TV in Germany and Hungary. And Disney formed joint ventures to produce children's programming in France, Germany, Italy and Spain.[37]

Domestic partnerships

Finally, Hollywood responded to globalization by competing for talent, projects and product for their distribution pipelines. The competition typically took the form of partnerships with the new breed of independent producers. Represented by the likes of Carolco, Castle Rock, Morgan Creek and Imagine Entertainment, these newcomers differed from the failed mini-majors of the 1980s – such as Orion, De Laurentiis and Cannon – in several important ways: (1) the newcomers ran 'lean machines' with only skeletal staffs rather than emulating the structure of the large studios; (2) most concentrated exclusively on filmed entertainment rather than branching out into TV; (3) most produced only a few high-quality productions each year rather than large rosters aimed at different segments of the market; (4) most distributed domestically through the majors rather than organizing their own distribution arms; and (5) most raised their production financing by keeping their eyes on the burgeoning foreign market rather than on home video deals.[38]

After the breakdown of the studio system during the 1950s, the majors regularly formed alliances with independent producers to fill out their rosters and to create relationships with budding talent. A deal might involve multiple pictures, complete financing, worldwide distribution, and a fifty-fifty profit split. Deals like these are still common, but TriStar's partnership with Carolco, Columbia Pictures' with Castle Rock and Time Warner's with Morgan Creek departed from traditional film industry practice in certain key respects: they typically involved partial financing, domestic distribution and lower distribution fees. Partnerships took this form because the majors not only needed more pictures to increase market share but also a means of sharing the risks and potential benefits of distributing ultra-high-budget pictures.[39]

Take the case of TriStar's alliance with Carolco Pictures. After aligning with TriStar, Carolco delivered three big-budget blockbusters in a row, *Total Recall* (1990), *Terminator 2: Judgment Day* (1991) and *Basic Instinct* (1992). To finance its pictures, Carolco originally made a public offering of stocks but later sold stakes in the company to Japan's Pioneer Electronics, France's Canal Plus, Britain's Carlton Communications, and Italy's Rizzoli Corriere della Sera.[40] Carolco's strategy was to cover as much of the production costs for a picture as possible by pre-selling the ancillary rights piece by piece, country by country. In this manner, Carolco was able to cover nearly all the $100 million budget, including Arnold Schwarzenegger's $12 million fee, for *Terminator 2*. TriStar Pictures paid Carolco $4 million for domestic distribution rights and had first call on the rentals until the advance was recouped, after which it levied a smaller-than-usual distribution fee. Thus the partnership lowered the risks of production financing for Carolco and enabled TriStar to share in the profits of an ultra-high-budget picture without going out on a limb.[41]

Walt Disney and Turner Broadcasting took a different tack to acquire product by moving into the specialized art film and American independent markets. In 1993, Disney linked up with Merchant–Ivory and Miramax Films, two of the most successful art film companies in the business. According to Peter Bart of *Variety*, Disney's strategy was 'to foster an eclectic slate of projects':

> While rival entertainment companies pursue the Time Warner model to become diversified, albeit debt-ridden, hardware-software conglomerates, Disney is determined to become the largest producer of intellectual property in the world. As such, the studio is committed to an astonishing sixty-films-a-year release schedule starting in 1994.[42]

Disney's deal with Merchant–Ivory, the producer of *A Room With a View* (1985), *Howard's End* (1992) and other British prestige films, was a conventional product development deal that provided partial financing in exchange for domestic distribution rights. Disney's deal with Miramax consisted of an $80 million buy-out in which Disney acquired Miramax's library of 200 art films and agreed to finance the development, production and marketing of Miramax's movies.

Founded as a distribution company by Harvey and Bob Weinstein in 1982, Miramax had 'become a logo that brings audiences in on its own'. Adopting a straight acquisition policy from the start, Miramax rose to the front ranks of the independent film market by releasing hits year in and year out that received prestigious film festival awards, including Oscars, and set box-office records. Miramax's roster included Steven Soderbergh's *sex, lies and videotape* (1989), Neil Jordan's *The Crying Game* (1992), Alfonso Arau's *Like Water for Chocolate* (1993) and Jane Campion's *The Piano* (1993). The first two pictures became big crossover hits; *Like Water for Chocolate* grossed $21 million to become 'the all-time foreign language box-office champ' in the US and *The Piano* received an incredible eight Academy Award nominations and three Oscars, including best original screenplay.

After becoming a fully autonomous division of Disney's distribution arm, Miramax continued to dominate the independent film market. In 1993, Miramax initiated a programme of production financing and expanded into the genre market through a subsidiary called Dimension Pictures. In 1994, Miramax had two big mainstream hits, Quentin Tarantino's *Pulp Fiction* and *The Crow*, which together grossed well over $100 million domestic. In 1996, Miramax maintained its cachet in the prestigious art house scene by releasing *Il Postino*, which surpassed the $21 million mark set earlier by *Like Water for Chocolate*. And by 1996, Miramax's overall track record enabled Disney to recoup its $80 million investment in the company.[43]

In an attempt to become a major motion picture producer, Turner Broadcasting moved into the independent film market by acquiring New Line Cinema and Castle Rock Entertainment in 1993 at a combined cost of $700 million.[44] Castle Rock made its reputation during the early 1990s producing top-shelf pictures such as *City Slickers* (1991), *A Few Good Men* (1992) and *In the Line of Fire* (1993). In contrast, New Line under the leadership of Robert Shay and Michael Lynne made its fortune during the 1980s producing and distributing genre pictures aimed at adolescents – for example, the *Nightmare on Elm Street* horror series and *Teenage Mutant Ninja Turtles* (1990). In 1990, New Line branched out from its traditional slate of inexpensive niche films and created a division called Fine Line Features to produce and distribute art films and offbeat fare. Within two years, Fine Line rose to the top independent ranks by backing such American ventures as Gus Van Sant's *My Own Private Idaho* (1991), James Foley's *Glengarry Glen Ross* (1992) and Robert Altman's *The Player* (1992) and by releasing such English-language imports as Derek Jarman's *Edward II* (1991) and Mile Leigh's *Naked* (1993).[45]

Acquiring New Line Cinema and Castle Rock Entertainment, Turner Broadcasting manoeuvred itself into the front ranks of Hollywood and positioned itself for global expansion.

The second wave of mergers

The merger movement entered a second phase in 1993 and involved cable and network television. Pay-TV had become a mature business by 1990.[46] Home Box Office growth levelled off at around 17 million subscribers and other large pay services, including Showtime, the Movie Channel and Cinemax, showed slight declines.[47] Home video took a toll, as did the deregulation of cable in 1984. Deregulation allowed cable operators to raise the prices of basic cable services, with the result that subscribers tended to watch basic channels such as the USA Network and Turner Network Television at the expense of the pay channels. And by 1993, basic cable services themselves had hit a plateau, the result of a static pool of viewers and market fragmentation created by added channel capacity of up to 300 channels on some services.[48]

Conditions in the cable industry prompted Viacom Inc., a leading TV syndicator and cable network company, to acquire Paramount Communications for $8.2 billion in 1993. Spearheading the second largest merger ever in the media industry after Time Warner's, Viacom's 70-year-old chairman Sumner Redstone united Viacom's MTV and Nickelodeon cable channels, Showtime pay-TV service, television syndication companies and a string of television stations with Paramount's formidable holdings in entertainment and publishing.[49] The following year, Viacom acquired Blockbuster Entertainment, the world's largest video retailer with over 3,500 video stores and various side businesses – purchase price, $7.6 billion. Like Time Warner, Viacom had become a completely integrated entertainment conglomerate.

Changes in the regulatory climate put the TV networks into play. During the 1980s, the old-line television networks – ABC, CBS and NBC – were hard hit first by independent stations, then by cable television, and then by the proliferation of cable channels. Because the number of television viewers in the country has remained static, network TV ratings declined and so did earnings.[50] Adding to the woes of the networks were restrictive FCC regulations. In place for two decades, the FCC's financial interest and syndication rules precluded ABC, CBS and NBC from producing a significant portion of the prime-time programming they broadcast, which had the effect of depriving them of the significant profits hit shows earned in syndication.

However, when the FCC voted to suspend the so-called 'finsyn' rules after 1996, the networks took on their old allure. Since the networks would likely reduce the number of programmes they ordered from outside producers and rely more on in-house projects after the expiration of the FCC rules, big suppliers like Time Warner and Disney might be hard hit. To avoid this, conventional wisdom had it that Hollywood studios would attempt to acquire the networks to 'assure themselves of a guaranteed outlet for their product'.[51]

None of the big three networks had changed hands since 1986, when the General Electric Company bought RCA, the parent company of NBC. On 31 July 1995, however, Disney announced that it would acquire Capital Cities/ABC in a deal valued at $19 billion. The merger brought together the most profitable television network and its ESPN cable service with Disney's Hollywood film and television studios, its theme parks and its vast merchandising operations.[52]

The day following the Disney deal, Westinghouse Electric, an early broadcasting pioneer, announced that it had agreed to pay $5.4 billion for CBS, the last major television network to change ownership. If the Disney deal had programme distribution as its target, the Westinghouse deal was for station market share. Michael H. Jordan, the chairman and chief executive of Westinghouse, said the deal would create a 'premiere top-notch outstanding company with 15 television stations and 39 radio stations that combined would give it direct access to more than a third of the nation's households'.[53]

The aftermath

The first mergers played themselves out with mixed results. After launching a fourth television network in the US, Rupert Murdoch's News Corp. went into direct broadcast satellite distribution. He turned his sights first on Great Britain, where he introduced Sky Television, a four-channel satellite service in 1988 at a cost of about $540 million. After spending additional millions acquiring motion picture rights to compete with his competitor, the British Satellite Corporation, Murdoch ultimately merged the two satellite services to create BSkyB that became 'the distribution gatekeeper for programmers in Britain'.[54]

Wanting to replicate his success in Britain, Murdoch bought control of Star TV, an Asian satellite business based in Hong Kong, and then either purchased or formed joint ventures to acquire or construct satellite services in Europe, Latin America and Australia. Today, Murdoch's News Corp. ranks among the world's largest communications companies with annual revenues of over $9 billion. As The Economist magazine put it:

> Nobody bestrides the global media business like Rupert Murdoch. His empire may not be the biggest. . . Yet there is no doubting . . . who is the media industry's leader. What is breathtaking about News Corp is its global reach, its sweeping ambition and the extent to which it is the creature of one man.[55]

Sony Pictures Entertainment performed reasonably well until 1993, but the following year took a $3.2 billion loss on its motion picture business, reduced the book value of its studios by $2.7 billion, and announced that 'it could never hope to recover its investment' in Hollywood.[56] Nobuyuki Idei, the Tokyo-based president of Sony Corp., took direct control of the company's Hollywood operations and installed new talent to effect a turnaround. Sony's two Hollywood studios soon returned to profitability, but not to top-tier status. The reason: Sony had neither forged connections with cable television nor had it acquired theme parks or consumer product chain stores to extend the franchises developed by its studios.[57]

The Matsushita–MCA marriage foundered as well, but for different reasons. By producing a string of hits that included two Seven Spielberg blockbusters, Jurassic Park (1993) and Schindler's List (1993), MCA become a financial bright spot in the Matsushita empire as it confronted the recession in Japan and the rising value of the yen (which would make exports more expensive). For its part, MCA hoped the merger would provide it with the financial leverage to acquire CBS and Virgin Records and the economic wherewithal to build a Universal Studios theme park in Japan. Matsushita rejected the proposals, with the result that, 'in the brave new world of vertical integration, MCA found itself alongside Sony at a competitive disadvantage compared to such rivals as News Corp. and Disney'. The rejection also created a rift with MCA's top management, chairman Lew Wasserman and president Sidney Sheinberg, who claimed that MCA's Japanese owners 'did not understand either the corporate nuances of MCA or the dynamic change of the US media business'.[58] Admitting defeat, Matsushita agreed to sell a majority interest of MCA to Seagram, the giant Canadian liquor company, for $7 billion in April 1995.[59]

Burdened with $11 billion of debt after the merger, Time Warner lost money two years in row and was plagued by clashing corporate styles among its top management following the death of Chairman Steven J. Ross in December 1992. Under the leadership of Gerald Levin, Ross's successor, Time Warner spent heavily to expand its cable television operations. Viewing 'cable as a crucial distribution technology for the so-called information highway', Levin wanted Time Warner's cable operations to become 'full-service networks', carrying not only television programming, but also telephone service, video-on-demand and home shopping services.[60]

Regaining its title as the largest media company in the world in September 1995, Time Warner bought out Turner Broadcasting System for $7.4 billion. The acquisition enlarged Time Warner's programming and distribution capacity. Among the synergies envisioned by the merger was the creation of a mammoth combined film production and distribution conglomerate that might easily dominate the business. But Turner's film companies did not live up to expectations and were awash in red ink by 1996.[61] After the merger, Time Warner took drastic action and folded Turner Pictures into Warner Brothers and put New Line Cinema up for sale. Although the measures stemmed the bleeding, Time Warner has continued to struggle under a burden of debt.

Following the merger with Paramount and Blockbuster, Viacom enjoyed the extraordinary earnings of *Forrest Gump* but in 1995, Paramount's profits dropped sharply and the studio had to write off $140 million on poorly performing pictures. To lighten its burden, Viacom took drastic action. Downsizing its operations, Viacom sold its Madison Square Garden sports and entertainment empire and its cable television systems, leaving it essentially a content company, aside from its Blockbuster Entertainment video and music stores. Redstone apparently decided that 'entertainment "content" – that is, programming – drives the entertainment business – not distribution'.[62]

Conclusion

Globalization hastened the concentration of the media by emphasizing economies of scale. Every year, a few offbeat pictures and smaller art films produced either by independents or by subsidiaries of the majors win wide critical acclaim and enjoy significant box-office success – witness *Fargo*, *The English Patient* and other Oscar nominees for best picture in 1997. Hollywood, nevertheless, remains committed to megapics and saturation booking, which have the combined effect of dominating most of the important screens around the world to the detriment of national film industries.[63]

During the 1990s, companies merged, partnered and collaborated as never before to tap all the major markets of the world. Although some of the assumptions that propelled the mergers proved false – linking electronics manufacturers (hardware) and film studios (software) did not create the synergy to stimulate VCR sales – the big got bigger. Small firms both in the US and abroad have been driven out of business or have been merged with burgeoning giants, repeating a pattern all too familiar in film industry history.

Digital compression and other new technologies will permit cable systems to transmit hundreds of channels simultaneously and allow subscribers to dial up programming on demand. But where will the new programming come from to fill all these new channels? Will cable networks simply cannibalize one another in an attempt to maintain audience share? Will pay-per-view and direct broadcast satellites with 300 channels of programming simply fragment TV audiences? In short, will the synergies of merging a Disney with a Capital Cities/ABC be worth the price?

And how much untapped potential still exists abroad? As a media industry report recently said:

> The popular notion is that there is a vast wealth of untapped potential in foreign countries for the media and entertainment industry. However, relatively few countries have disposable income per capita as high as it is in the US; cultural barriers and potential local government restrictions could be a very major problem; and competition is intense for foreign markets and making foreign inroads requires sizeable amounts of capital.[64]

Answers to questions such as these will determine the outcome of Hollywood's globalization.

Notes

1   Time Warner Inc., *1989 Annual Report* (New York: Time Warner Inc., 1990), p. 1.
2   Tom Bierbaum, 'Booming '80s behind it, vid faces uncertainty', *Variety*, 10 January 1990, pp. 31, 32.
3   Marc Berman, 'Studios miss boat on vid demographics', *Variety*, 24 September 1990, p. 15.
4   Bierbaum, op. cit., pp. 31, 32.
5   Lawrence Cohn, 'Only half of indie pics shot will see the screens in '90', *Variety*, 30 May 1990, p. 7.
6   Jeffrey B. Logsdon, *Perspectives on the Filmed Entertainment Industry* (Los Angeles: Seidler Amdec Securities Inc., 1990), p. 11.
7   Ted Johnson and Anita M. Busch, 'Mega-moolah movies multiplying', *Variety*, 29 April–5 May 1996, pp. 1, 53. Only four films besides *Terminator 2* cost $100 million or more in the period 1990–6: *Last Action Hero* (1993), *True Lies* (1994), *Batman Forever* (1995) and *Waterworld* (1995). Carrying a price tag of more than $175 million, *Waterworld* became the most expensive film ever made.
8   Gary Levin, 'Studios gamble on big bucks ad buys', *Variety*, 18–24 March 1996, pp. 11, 12.
9   'The 1980s: a reference guide to motion pictures, television, VCR, and cable', *The Velvet Light Trap*, no. 27 (Spring 1991), pp. 77–88.
10 Leonard Klady, 'Why mega-flicks click', *Variety*, 25 November–1 December 1996, pp. 1, 87.
11 From 1985 to 1989, videocassette revenues increased from $1.5 billion to $3.25 billion; theatrical film rentals rose from $800 million to $1.25 billion; and TV sales grew from $300 million to $800 million. Logsdon, 'Perspectives on the filmed entertainment industry', p. 49.
12 Geoff Watson, 'Sell-through salvation', *Variety*, 16 November 1992, p. 57.
13 Don Groves, 'Veni, video, vici', *Variety*, 3–9 April 1995, pp. 1, 46.
14 Terry Iliott, 'Yank pix flex pecs in new Euro arena', *Variety*, 19 August 1991, p. 1.
15 Geraldine Fabrikant, 'Hollywood takes more cues from overseas', *New York Times*, 25 June 1990, p. C1.
16 Leonard Klady, 'Earth to H'wood: you win', *Variety*, 13–19 February 1995, pp. 1, 63.
17 Iliott, op. cit., p. 1.
18 Don Groves, 'U.S. pix tighten global grip', *Variety*, 22 August 1990, pp. 1, 96.
19 Tino Balio *et al.* (eds.), *The American Film Industry* (Madison: University of Wisconsin Press, 1985), p. 443.
20 Calvin Sims, ' "Synergy": the unspoken word', *New York Times*, 5 October 1993, pp. C1, C18.
21 Richard Gold, 'No exit? studios itch to ditch exhib biz', *Variety*, 8 October 1990, pp. 8, 84.
22 Paul Noglows, 'Studios stuck in screen jam', *Variety*, 9 March 1992, pp. 1, 69. The move into exhibition was precipitous. Industry analysts have claimed that the majors grossly overspent to re-enter exhibition and that the timing was wrong – the reasoning being that the domestic exhibition market was heavily over-screened (unlike foreign markets) while admissions have stayed constant.
23 Harold Vogel, 'Entertainment industry', *Merrill Lynch*, 14 March 1989 (single page newsletter).
24 Geraldine Fabrikant, 'Murdoch bets heavily on a global vision', *New York Times*, 29 July 1996, pp. C1, C6–7.
25 In order to comply with FCC regulations governing the ownership of TV stations, Murdoch became a US citizen.
26 'Chernin yearning to get Fox some Hollywood respect', *Variety*, 19 August 1991, p. 21.
27 Bill Carter, 'Fox will sign up 12 new stations; takes 8 from CBS', *New York Times*, 24 May 1994, p. A1.
28 Time Warner, *1989 Annual Report*.
29 Richard Gold', Sony–CPE union reaffirms changing order of intl. showbiz', *Variety*, 27 September–3 October 1989, p. 5.
30 Charles Kipps, 'Sony and Columbia', *Variety*, 27 September–3 October 1989, p. 5.
31 Gold, op. cit., p. 5.
32 Signing the Peter Guber–Jon Peters production team alone cost Sony $700 million and was one of the most expensive management acquisitions ever.
33 Andrew Pollack, 'At MCA's parent, no move to let go', *New York Times*, 14 October 1994, p. C1.
34 Jonathan R. Laing, 'Bad scenes behind it, Time Warner is wired for growth', *Barron's*, 22 June 1992, p. 8.
35 'Newest H'wood invaders are building, not buying', *Variety*, 21 October 1991, p. 93.
36 Richard Natale, 'Risky pix get a global fix', *Variety*, 28 September 1992, p. 97.
37 Richard W. Stevenson, 'Lights! Camera! Europe!', *New York Times*, 6 February 1994, p. C1.
38 Peter Hlavacek, 'New indies on a (bank) roll', *Variety*, 24 January 1990, pp. 1, 7.

39   Hlavacek, ibid., pp. 1, 7; Richard Natale, ' "Lean" indies fatten summer boxoffice', *Variety*, 12 August 1991a, pp. 1, 61.

40   David Kissinger, 'Judgment day for Carolco', *Variety*, 2 December 1991, pp. 1, 93.

41   Richard W. Stevenson, 'Carolco flexes its muscle overseas', *New York Times*, 26 June 1991, pp. C1, C17.

42   Peter Bart, 'Mouse gears for mass prod'n', *Variety*, 19 July 1993, pp. 1, 5.

43   Greg Evans and John Brodie, 'Miramax, mouse go for seven more', *Variety*, 13–19 May 1996, pp. 13, 16.

44   J. Max Robins and Judy Brennan, 'Turner may tap Sassa to run film venture', *Variety* 23 August 1993, p. 9.

45   Bernard Weinraub, 'New Line Cinema', *New York Times*, 5 June 1994, p. F4.

46   Stated another way, the rate of growth in pay-TV subscribers declined for the first time from around 10 per cent in 1988 to 5 per cent in 1989. Geraldine Fabrikant, 'Pay cable channels are losing their momentum', *New York Times*, 28 May 1990c, p. 25.

47   Fabrikant, ibid., p. 25.

48   John Dempsey, 'Wanted: viewers for new cable channels', *Variety*, 3–9 January 1994, pp. 1, 67.

49   Geraldine Fabrikant, 'A success for dealer on a prowl', *New York Times*, 13 September 1993, p. A1.

50   Bill Carter, 'Cable networks see dimmer future', *New York Times*, 22 July 1991, pp. C1, C6.

51   Geraldine Fabrikant, 'Media giants said to be negotiating for TV networks', *New York Times*, 1 September 1994b, p. A1.

52   Geraldine Fabrikant, 'Walt Disney acquiring ABC in deal worth $19 billion', *New York Times*, 1 August 1995a, p. A1.

53   Geraldine Fabrikant, 'CBS accepts bid by Westinghouse; $5.4 billion deal', *New York Times*, 2 August 1995c, p. A1.

54   Fabrikant, op. cit., pp. C1, C6–7.

55   'Murdoch's empire: the gambler's last throw', *The Economist*, 9 March 1996, pp. 68–70.

56   James Sterngold, 'Sony, struggling, takes a huge loss on movie studios', *New York Times*, 18 September 1994, p. A1.

57   Martin Peers and Anita M. Busch, 'Sony sizes up size issue', *Variety*, 16–22 August 1996, p. 86.

58   Geraldine Fabrikant, 'At a crossroads, MCA plans a meeting with its owners', *New York Times*, 13 October 1994a, p. G13.

59   Geraldine Fabrikant, 'Seagram will by 80% of big studio from Matsushita', *New York Times*, 7 April 1995d, p. A1.

60   Geraldine Fabrikant, 'Battling for the hearts and minds at Time Warner', *New York Times*, 26 February 1995b, p. F9.

61   TBS announced that it would have to take a $60 million write-off for Castle Rock's first-quarter performance in 1996 and that New Line had a $19 million negative cash flow at the end of that period. Dan Cox, 'New Line sees red', *Variety*, 11–17 November 1996, pp. 1, 73.

62   Mark Landler with Geraldine Fabrikant, 'Sumner and his docontents', *New York Times*, 19 January 1996, p. C1.

63   The theatrical market has not become homogenized, however, because producers still must strive for novelty to capture the attention of audiences. As one media analyst dryly put it, 'poorly-produced programming compromises both content and distribution profit margins – witness how poorly produced programming has affected the asset value of Viacom or has taken Ted Turner out of play'. In 'Media mergers don't add up', *NatWest Markets*, 2 January 1996, pp. 1–5.

64   Ibid., pp. 1–5.

PART FOUR

Meanings and pleasures

THIS, OF COURSE, IS THE HEARTLAND for the discussion of film – the meanings and pleasures generated by the film text for the spectator/viewer/audience. Foremost among the questions we ask of popular texts is 'why do people want to consume them?' This enables us to think of texts as sites upon which a range of meanings might be generated and from which a range of pleasures might be sought. Further, we might think of ways in which specific reading formations might engender certain kinds of meanings, or offer certain kinds of pleasures. The emphasis here is upon what we might think of as more broadly cultural and historically specific meanings: those implicated in the choice to see a particular film text and those brought to the cinema by the audience, as well as those activated by the text as it is screened. The provocation, nevertheless, remains the film text – its appeal, its function for its audience and its cultural resonances.

The section begins with two essays which discuss the appeal of the film star from quite different perspectives in order to approach the culturally mediated pleasures the popular film provides. Richard Dyer's work on film stars has been so widely anthologized that many readers will be familiar with the more commonly used pieces – those dealing with the 'star as sign'. The short reading reproduced here is taken from *Heavenly Bodies: Film Stars and Society* (1987), and it demonstrates the kind of analysis Dyer's understanding of the star makes possible. It comes from an essay on 'Monroe and Sexuality', one of the three case studies making up the book: the other two are on Paul Robeson and Judy Garland. Chapter 16 develops a richly detailed account of mid-1950s discourses of sexuality as well as a revealing analysis of Monroe's extraordinary star appeal. Dyer outlines the publicly constructed persona of Marilyn Monroe as well as biographical details about the person 'behind' this mass-mediated image. He then analyses this representational pattern against the background of a discursive context that allocated specific meanings to 'blondness', to female sexuality and to masculine desire. His approach takes us a significant distance towards understanding Marilyn Monroe's appeal by presuming that among the factors to be understood is the specific reading formation – what her meanings 'meant' at the time they were produced and most avidly circulated.

In a chapter from his book, *Celebrity and Power*, P. David Marshall takes the next step – of examining how the film star's celebrity is produced and circulated. Beginning with a history of the film star as celebrity from the first decade of the twentieth century, Marshall points to the importance of publicity in constructing audience interest in and desire for knowledge about the individual film actor. He also points out that this necessarily takes us outside the film text. Indeed, it is crucial from the star's point of view that their publicity constructs a relation between them and their audience that is independent of the film text. Marshall's next move, though, takes us back to the film text where he presents an account of a tradition of film acting that reinforces the power of the film actor who is able to represent both themselves and their character in their performances. Drawing on Barry King's work, Marshall argues that the historical development of a connection between the actor's persona and the parts they play reinforces the audience's desire for a closer connection with the film star celebrity's authentic or private life. So, there is a specificity about the kind of celebrity produced in the cinema and in the kinds of pleasures audiences seek from it.

As a popular medium, film must work within the constraints of familiar generic structures while attempting to provide individual texts that are fresh and distinctive. There are now a number of traditions of film analysis which concern themselves with genre: as a set of formal properties to be described and (sometimes) defended, as reflections of social or cultural determinants, as a constraining factor within accounts of the production industries and so on. The second group of essays in this section develops arguments about the pleasures and meanings embedded within particular film genres: the musical, the period film, and the horror film. Jim Collins addresses the category of genre slightly differently. While nominating key patterns of 'genericity' within contemporary Hollywood, he also asks how does the category of genre 'work' in an environment saturated by entertainment options offered to multiple target audiences.

Jane Feuer's BFI monograph *The Hollywood Musical* (1982) has remained an influential study and it is one of comparatively few to focus on this genre. Musicals are popular entertainments and a body of film theory aimed at dealing with film art has found them a little intractable. Feuer's book is useful because it focuses particularly on the relationship between the audience and the film text – 'read off' the films but informed by film history and an awareness of the contexts of consumption when these films were first screened. In the short excerpt reproduced here, 'Spectators and Spectacles', Feuer investigates the unique impression of immediacy or 'liveness' that the classic Hollywood musicals produce for their cinema audiences – even to the point of eliciting applause from the cinema audience at the end of musical numbers. Techniques she discusses are employed to place 'the audience into the film' through an elimination of the separation between the audience so often pictured witnessing the performance on the screen and the audience seated in the cinema. In a detailed and careful account of identification – both with 'the audience in the film' and the subjectivities driving the narrative – she maps the shifting relations between the spectator and the spectacle that help to define the characteristic appeal of the genre.

Stella Bruzzi's first concern is not with film genre, but with costume. Her book, *Undressing Cinema* (1997) discusses film clothing as a discourse, intricately bound up with issues of race, gender, sexuality and genre. In the chapter I have taken from *Undressing Cinema*, Bruzzi focuses on the 'costume film', the period film represented by *Picnic at Hanging Rock, The Age of Innocence* and *The Piano*. What emerges is different from conventional accounts of the genre, which, as Bruzzi notes, tends to be dismissed as interesting only to the female audience (Alan Parker's reference to the 'Laura Ashley school of film making'). Rather than disregard the clothes in order to focus on the narrative – something Bruzzi suggests most critics wish, and find difficult, to do with period drama – Bruzzi focuses on the clothes them-selves as important components in the films' meanings and pleasures. Arguing that the clothes in the films she discusses set up a 'transgressive, erotic discourse', Bruzzi goes on to invest significance in the 'fetishistic attraction of the clothes themselves'. As a result, we enter the territory of Freud rather than Laura Ashley as Bruzzi argues against traditional psychoana-lytic accounts and against some historians of fashion which see the 'decorative woman' as the object only of masculine pleasure.

If the dismissal of the period film is an expression of a masculine elitism, it would not be the only popular genre to have received such treatment. Tania Modleski's essay on the horror film takes on an implicit elitism in much critical and cultural theory. This is an elitism that relegates the pleasures generated by genres of 'entertainment' to a subordinate role that is always intrinsically comforting and complacent while reserving for 'art' the capacity to discomfort and disturb. In defence of the pleasures of mass culture that, unusually, depends upon a claim for their adversarial politics, Modleski examines the pleasures offered by some 1980s horror films – *Halloween*, *Friday the Thirteenth*, *Carrie* and so on. Generic antecedents to the contemporary fashion for teen/slasher/horror pictures – *Scream, I Know What You Did Last Summer* and their sequels – these films have retained their attraction for audiences despite initial critical evaluation that saw them as simply crass and exploitative. Modleski connects their durability to the films' assault on basic bourgeois certainties – the family, the school, capitalism itself. Further, these films are notoriously open-ended in narrative terms, spawning endless sequels and reiterations of the monstrous threat that seems far from consoling. The 'sustained terror' such films create seems to be central to their appeal, and Modleski insists this requires consideration. She is not attempting to recuperate these films as art. Rather, she is attacking an elite postmodernist aesthetic that would privilege the 'adversarial' on the basis that the implied dichotomy between adversarial 'art' and complacent 'entertain-ment' misrecognises the generic characteristics as well as the political potential of both.

Prevailing critical trends are also the target of Jim Collins' study of contemporary Hollywood genres, 'Genericity in the Nineties: Eclectic irony and the new sincerity' (there is a longer version of this article in Collins' *Architectures of Excess: Cultural life in the information age*, 1995). Focusing on what he describes as a hyperconscious eclecticism in contemporary fea-ture films – where film-makers appropriate intertextual materials promiscuously across time and genres – Collins laments the failure of contemporary film criticism to 'come to terms with these very profound changes in the nature of entertainment' at the end of the century. Like Modleski, he accuses the critics of doggedly maintaining 'classical' and realist aesthetics which misrecognise the character of these popular cultural forms and their audiences. What Collins calls 'hyperconsciousness' has allowed narrative to operate at two levels simultaneously: 'in reference to character adventure and in reference to a text's adventures in the array of contemporary cul-tural production', prompting a major shift in what constitutes both entertainment and cultural literacy.

Jim Collins is particularly taken by those films which raid the array of generic texts which precede them, and turn them into self-conscious hybrids which still manage to retain 'vestiges of past significance' by 'reinscribing them into the present'. Films mentioned in this context include *Blue Velvet* and *Thelma and Louise*. These films do not simply 'camp up' the debris from other genres, exhausting their significance. Instead, they offer new kinds of significance and new kinds of audience-text relations as the appropriations 'acquire new discursive registers unfore-seen in their initial contexts'. Less exciting, and in sharp contrast to the ironic hybrids, is another genre that has also emerged since the late 1980s, which Collins labels 'the new sincerity'. These films explicitly foreclose the possibility of irony, in an attempt to recover an authenticity, purity or harmony located in an 'impossible past'. They express a profound ambivalence about modern, mass-mediated culture, and are riddled with nostalgia for a pre-modern simplicity. *Dances with Wolves, Hook* and *Field of Dreams* are the texts he focuses on here. The essay provides a review of the state of film genre at the moment, as if offers its audiences new forms of textuality, draws upon different expectations and competencies and, if Collins is correct, offers new kinds of significance.

Chapter 16

RICHARD DYER

MONROE AND SEXUALITY
Desirability

Desirability

MONROE NOT ONLY PROVIDED THE VEHICLE for expressing the playboy project of 'liberating' sexuality, she was also the epitome of what was desirable in a playmate. 'Desirability' is the equality that women in the 1950s were urged to attain in order to make men (and thereby themselves) happy. In 1953 Lelord Kordel, for instance, declared in *Coronet*:

> The smart woman will keep herself desirable. It is her duty to herself to be feminine and desirable at all times in the eyes of the opposite sex'.
>
> (quoted by Miller and Nowak 1977, p. 157)

'In the *eyes* of . . .'; the visual reference is striking despite being also so commonplace.

Monroe conforms to, and is part of the construction of, what constitutes desirability in women. This is a set of implied character traits, but before it is that it is also a social position, for the desirable woman is a white woman. The typical playmate is white, and most often blonde; and, of course, so is Monroe. Monroe could have been some sort of star had she been dark, but not the ultimate embodiment of the desirable woman.

To be the ideal Monroe had to be white, and not just white but blonde, the most unambiguously white you can get. (She was not a natural blonde; she started dyeing her hair in 1947.) This race element conflates with sexuality in (at least) two ways. First, the white woman is offered as the most highly prized possession of the white man, and the envy of all other races. Imperialist and Southern popular culture abounds in imagery playing on this theme, and this has been the major source of all race images in the twentieth century. Thus there is the notion of the universally desired 'white Goddess' (offered at the level of intellectual discourse, in 'anthropological' works such as Robert Graves' *The White Goddess*, as a general feature of all human cultures), and explicitly adumbrated in Rider Haggard's *She* and its several film versions. There is the rape motif exploited in *The Birth of a Nation* and countless films and novels before and since; and there is the most obvious playing out of this in *King Kong*, with the jungle creature ascending the pinnacle of the Western world caressingly clutching a white woman. (In the remake Jessica Lange affects a Monroe accent for the part.)

Blondeness, especially platinum (peroxide) blondeness, is the ultimate sign of whiteness. Blonde hair is frequently associated with wealth, either in the choice of the term platinum or in pin-ups where the hair colour is visually rhymed with a silver or gold dress and with jewellery. (We might remember too the title of Monroe's nude calendar pose, GOLDEN Dreams.) And blondeness is racially unambiguous. It keeps the white woman distinct from the black, brown or yellow, and at the same time it assures the viewer that the woman is the genuine article. The hysteria surrounding ambiguity on this point is astonishing. Birth of a Nation comes close to suggesting that congressman Stevens' mulatto housekeeper was a major cause of a civil war; the fact of being half-caste makes Julie into a tragic character in Show Boat; and the thought that she might be half-caste sends Elizabeth Taylor mad in Raintree County. (All these films, one might add, are based on best-selling popular novels.) The film career of Lena Horne is also instructive: as a very light-skinned black woman, she was unplaceable except as the ultimate temptress in an all-black musical, Cabin in the Sky, where the guarantee of her beauty resides in the very fact of being so light. Otherwise she could not really be given a role in a film featuring whites, because her very lightness might make her an object of desire, thus confusing the racial hierarchy of desirability.

The white woman is not only the most prized possession of white patriarchy, she is also part of the symbolism of sexuality itself. Christianity associates sin with darkness and sexuality, virtue with light and chastity. With the denial of female sexuality in the late nineteenth and early twentieth century (except as by definition a problem), sexuality also become associated with masculinity. Men are then seen as split between their baser, sexual, 'black' side and their good, spiritual side which is specifically redeemed in Victorian imagery by the chastity of woman. Thus the extreme figures in this conflation of race and gender stereotypes are the black stud/rapist and the white maiden. By the 1950s, such extremes were less current, nor did they necessarily carry with them the strict moral associations of sexual = bad, non-sexual = good; but the associations of darkness with the drives model of masculine sexuality and of fairness with female desirability remained strong. The central sexual/love relationship in Peyton Place (the original novel), between Connie Mackenzie and Michael Kyros, works very much through such an opposition. Connie's character is established through the admiration of her daughter's friend Selena (dark-haired, lower-class, soon deflowered): Selena wishes that she too had 'a wonderful blonde mother, and a pink and white bedroom of her own' like Alison, Connie's daughter (Metallious 1957, p. 39). As for Michael, the narrator explicitly defines him as 'a handsome man, in a dark-skinned, black-haired, obviously sexual way' (ibid. p. 103). The townspeople refer to the couple as 'that big, black Greek' and 'a well-built blonde' (ibid. p. 135). Their relationship is sealed when he makes love to her 'brutally, torturously' (p. 135), that is, when this desirable woman is taken by his male drive. Thus in the elaboration of light and dark imagery, the blonde woman comes to represent not only the most desired of women but also the most womanly of women.

Monroe's blondeness is remarked upon often enough in films, but only the first saloon scene in Bus Stop seems to make something of it. Beau storms in and at once sees Cherie on stage, the angel that he has said he is looking for. His words emphasize her whiteness – 'Look at her gleaming there so pale and white.' He finds in her the projection of his desires, and the song she sings might be her acknowledgement of this – 'That old black magic that you weave so well'.

Besides blondeness, Monroe also had, or seemed to have, several personality traits that together sum up female desirability in the 1950s. She looks like she's no trouble, she is vulnerable, and she appears to offer herself to the viewer, to be available. She embodies what, as quoted at the end of the last section, 'Every Husband Needs' in a wife, namely, good sex uncomplicated by worry about satisfying her. Once again, Norman Mailer articulates this way of reading Monroe – 'difficult and dangerous with the others, but ice cream with her'. Monroe, an image so overdetermined in terms of sexuality, is nevertheless not an image of the danger of sex: she is not the femme fatale of film noir and of other such hypererotic star images as Clara Bow, Marlene Dietrich, Jean Harlow and even Greta Garbo, all of whom in some measure speak trouble for the men in their films. Round about the time Monroe was becoming a major star, Twentieth Century Fox did put her in two such roles – as a psychotic baby-sitter in *Don't Bother to Knock* in 1952 and as an adultress in *Niagara* in 1953. Though commercially successful (almost any film with her in it would have been at this point), they were clearly not right for her,[1] as the reviews for *Niagara*, especially, register. Denis Myers in an article on Monroe in *Picturegoer* (9.5.53) clearly sees how her appeal is separate from any sense of her being dangerously sexual: 'In *Niagara* she has to convince us that she is desirable. Marilyn does. But – a *femme fatale*? We-ell . . .'

Several of the big Twentieth Century Fox vehicles seem, at script level, to give her a role with some castrating elements – as a gold-digger in *Gentlemen Prefer Blondes* and *How to Marry a Millionaire* she sets out to manipulate male sexual response for money, while in *There's No Business Like Show Business* she plays a showgirl who uses Tim's (Donald O'Connor) interest in her to further her career. But she's simply too incompetent, 'dumb' and, to add to it, short-sighted in *How to . . .*, winding up with a bankrupt, and in *There's No Business . . .* the plot makes it clear that she wasn't really two-timing Tim. *Gentlemen . . .* is more difficult case, but it seems to me that Monroe doesn't play the part as if she is a manipulator. (But see my discussion in *Stars*, pp. 147–8 and Pam Cook's different reading in *Star Signs*, pp. 81–2.)

In the later roles the disruption that any introduction of a highly sexual (almost the same thing as saying *any*) woman into a male character's life always involves, is defused; indeed it almost becomes the point of the films that Monroe takes the sting out of anything that her sexuality seems likely to stir up. So Richard (Tom Ewell) in *The Seven Year Itch* goes back happily to his wife, Beau (Don Murray) in *Bus Stop* gets his girl (Cherie/Monroe) and goes back to his ranch, Elsie (Monroe) in *The Prince and the Showgirl* reconciles the King (Jeremy Spenser) and his father, the Regent (Olivier), and so on. It's a standard narrative pattern – a state of equilibrium, a disruption and a return to equilibrium through resolution of the disruption; only here the cause of the disruptions (Monroe, just because she *is* sex) and the resolution are embodied in one and the same person/character (Monroe).

If Monroe's desirability has to do with her being no trouble, it also has to do with being vulnerable. Susan Brownmiller (1975, p. 333) in her study of rape, *Against Our Will*, suggests there is 'a deep belief . . . that our attractiveness to men, or sexual desirability, is in direct proportion to our ability to play the victim'. Women live 'the part of the walking wounded' and this is something that 'goes to the very core of our sexuality'. Brownmiller quotes Alfred Hitchcock saying that he looked for 'a certain vulnerability' in his leading ladies, and she points out that the dictionary definition of 'vulnerable' is 'susceptible to being wounded or hurt, or open to attack or assault' (p. 334). Thus what made Hitchcock's women stars right was that 'they managed to project the feeling that they could be wounded or "had"'. Brownmiller adds, 'And I think Hitchcock was speaking for most of his profession'. She names Monroe as perhaps 'the most famous and overworked example' of 'the beautiful victim' syndrome (p. 335).

Monroe is not generally physically abused in films. She is, rather, taken advantage of or humiliated. Very often this means little more than putting her in situations where she is exposed to the gaze of the male hero, but in two of the films that are also considered her best, *Bus Stop* and *Some Like It Hot*, this goes much further. In *Bus Stop*, she plays Cherie, a show girl who wants to get out of the cheap bar-rooms where she works, to be a success and 'get a little respect'. But even though this was the film set up for her return to Hollywood (after walking out and going to study at the Actors' Studio in New York), and she is undoubtedly the star of it, the project that carries the narrative is not Cherie's, but Beau's (Don Murray). He is looking for his 'angel' and finds her in Cherie/Monroe; the trajectory of the narrative is the defeat of her project in the name of his (getting her to marry him). One of the turning points in the film – and one we are obviously meant to find funny – occurs when Beau, an expert cowboy, lassoes Cherie as she is trying to escape him on a bus. It is not just that the narrative shows her as help-less before the male drive to conquer; the film invites us to delight in her pitiful and hopeless struggling.

Some Like It Hot is even more insidious, for its comedy depends upon plot strategies whereby Monroe/Sugar makes herself defenceless because she thinks she's safe. She is trying to escape men because of all the rotten deals they've dealt her – this is why she's joined an all woman band. Because she is trusting (and because, like any farce, *Some Like It Hot* depends upon characters in the film believing in disguises that are transparent to the audience), the film gets her into situations where she drops her guard; notably in scene with Joe (Tony Curtis), who's in drag, in the ladies' toilet on the train to Florida. Precisely because she thinks she is in the safety of woman's space, she does not protect herself from him. Before his ogling eyes (and, of course, ours), she lifts her skirt to take a brandy flask out of her garter and titi-vates her breasts in front of the mirror. Because they are actions a woman would not make in front of a man, Joe/Curtis and the assumed male audience are violating both Monroe and women's space. Moreover, she then sets up the means for further violation. She tells Joe that she wants to marry a rich man who wears glasses, and, armed with this information, he changes his disguise from drag to a short-sighted oil millionaire. In one of the most remem-bered scenes in the film, on board 'his' yacht, he also pretends to be impotent. Once again, believing she is safe, Sugar/Monroe drops any defence against his sexual harassment, drapes herself over him and kisses him long and languorously. The pleasure we are offered is not just that Marilyn Monroe is giving herself to a man (a potential surrogate for the audience), but that her defences are down, we've got her where we (supposedly) want her.

Monroe's vulnerability is also confirmed by aspects of her off-screen image, which could, indeed, be read as a never-ending series of testimonials to how easily, and frequently, she is hurt. A brief list of the main points that were so often raked over in the publicity surrounding her will suffice to indicate this, always bearing in mind that some of these never happened or are very exaggerated:

- born illegitimate to a mother who spent her daughter's childhood in and out of mental hospitals;
- fostered by several different couples;
- time spent in an orphanage (sometimes presented in Dickensian terms in the biographies, articles and interviews);
- indecently assaulted at the age of nine;
- an habitual sufferer from menstrual pains;
- three unsuccessful marriages;
- unable to bear children, having a succession of miscarriages; a nymphomaniac who was frigid (oh, the categories of 1950s' sexual theory!);
- a woman so difficult to work with Tony Curtis said kissing her was like kissing Hitler;
- a suicide, or murdered, or died of an overdose of the pills she habitually took.

It's a threnody so familiar that all retrospective articles, and references to her, invoke it, and most find quotations from Monroe to do so. Take, for instance, two books on famous people of the twentieth century who have died young. Marianne Sinclair, in *Those Who Died Young*, quotes the poem written by Monroe and published posthumously in *McCalls* in 1962:

Help! Help!
Help! I feel life coming back
When all I want is to die.

Patricia Fox Sheinwold (1980), in *Too Young to Die*, uses another quote: 'I always felt insecure and in the way – but most of all I felt scared. I guess I wanted love more than anything in the world.'

Thus the image insists that Monroe suffered, and experienced her suffering vividly throughout her life.

The appeal of this biographical vulnerability necessarily involves the power of the reader, but we need to get the emphases right here. Vulnerability may call forth any number of responses, including empathy and protectiveness as well as sadism. It is the way that the Monroe biography is ineluctably associated with sexuality that is significant – not just sexual experience itself, but the inter-relations of sexuality with menstruation, childbirth, marriage and so on. Monroe's problems are repeatedly related (often using her own words) to the need for love, meaning in the vocabulary of the (hereto) sexual love.

Unthreatening, vulnerable, Monroe always seemed to be available, on offer. At the time, and even more subsequently, many observers saw her career in terms of a series of moments in which she offered herself to the gaze of men – the *Golden Dreams* calendar, *The Seven Year Itch* subway gratings pose, shot before passing crowds in a Manhatten street, her appearances at premières in revealing and fetishistic gowns, her final nude photo session with Bert Stern and nude scene for *Something's Got to Give* . . . All these were taken as done by Monroe, the person, at her own behest. Each one a dramatic news story, they were read not as media manipulation but rather as a star's willing presentation of her sexuality to the world's gaze. Interviews could also be raided for corroborations. Maurice Zolotow (1961) quotes Monroe's words in 1950 to Sonia Wolfson, a publicity woman at Twentieth Century Fox, on the subject of the first time she put make-up on: 'This was the first time in my life I felt loved – no one had ever noticed my face or hair or me before.'

In her last interview, with *Life*, she told of the effect wearing a sweater had had on the boys at school, an effect she revelled in. So many incidents, so many remarks in interviews – if Monroe was a sex object she was not only untroublesome, vulnerable but also seemed to enjoy and promote her own objectification. She was the playboy playmate who wanted to be one.

Wanted to be . . . In the light of the women's movement and its exploration of the formation of human desire, the idea that anyone simply 'wants' to do something, out of a volition untouched by social construction, is untenable. Monroe appeared at a moment when feminism was at its lowest ebb in the twentieth century, and both her career decisions and remarks in interviews could and were read as confirming the male-serving myth of the desirable playmate. But so great an emphasis on her own purported involvement in the production of her sexy image is *also* an emphasis on the will and desire of the person who inhabits and produces the sexy image. It actually raises the question of the person who plays the fantasy, in other terms, the subject who is habitually the object of desire.

Note

1   This is not meant as a judgement of her acting capacities. Many people, both at the time and subsequently, consider her performance in *Don't Bother to Knock*, in particular, to be extremely 'good' (this is not the place to debate what criteria are in play here). What's at issue is not whether Monroe, as actress, could play 'dangerous' women, but whether her image allowed these roles to make sense if she played them. I'm arguing that on the whole it did not.

Chapter 17

P. DAVID MARSHALL

THE CINEMATIC APPARATUS AND THE CONSTRUCTION OF THE FILM CELEBRITY

THE EMERGENCE OF THE CINEMA STAR, according to Richard DeCordova, is intimately linked with the decline of the allure of the apparatus of motion picture projection. Until about 1907, the focus of attention was on the technical feat of displaying images and stories on the screen.[1] Most of early cinema was documentary in nature, with aspects of everyday life, circus performances and sporting events depicted on-screen.[2] This changed somewhat because of the constant need for new and interesting (at least previously unseen) film product. The early connection of film to the craft of illusionism and magic can be seen in the films of Georges Meliès, an illusionist turned film-maker, and in the position of the exhibition of films as a type of novelty act in vaudeville theaters.[3] In both cases, the enigmatic quality of the production was related not so much to the plot as to how the images were created and juxtaposed. Early films (pre-1907), according to DeCordova, could be characterized by their close connection to 'action' and movement. The construction of the film celebrity emerged only after an initial decade of exhibition. It is part of traditional – although now challenged – film history that the large production houses, such as Biograph, impeded the development of the star by not releasing the real names of the actors involved in any film. The impetus behind the development of stardom then was the audience's construction of intertextual continuities. According to Walker, the audience began identifying screen personalities not by their names but by nicknames that attempted to capture the face, body type or hairstyle of the performer. Designations such as 'the fat guy' and 'the girl with the curls' became a way for nickelodeon exhibitors to advertise their short features through a recognizable audience interest.[4] Hampton's *History of the American Film Industry from Its Beginnings to 1931* serves as a guide for this reading of early film and its relationship to the construction of personalities.[5] More recent scholarship has disputed the simplicity of this early account in exploring the development of the film star system. Some researchers, such as Staiger, have been able to identify forms of identification that predate previous designations of its development in the early to mid-1910s.[6] The interconnections of filmmaking to other entertainment industries, such as theater and vaudeville, which had well-developed star systems, further complicate the reasons and rationales behind the organization of a film star system. What can be safely concluded is that the reluctance to release the names of performers gradually gave way to an industry that used its performers as one of the primary forms of promotion and marketing of its product.

A more accurate way of describing the emergence of the film star is to see that the film industry was in the process of determining its categorical position in the entertainment industry. In its affiliation with vaudeville, the film industry was part of an already established and successful cultural industry that possessed its own system of fame, prestige and celebrity.[7] *Variety*, the trade newspaper for most of the vaudevillian performing arts in the early part of the twentieth century, regularly displayed large photos of vaudeville stars on the first page; the featuring of these acts became one of the central means by which the publication attached itself to the glamour of the industry. Moreover, as Allen points out, vaudeville had success- fully produced what he calls a mass audience, which included not only the working class but large segments of the middle class.[8] So the film industry had expanded its audience beyond the limited circulation of penny arcades and variations of peep shows to a national audience that encompassed both the working class and the middle class.

Film was also positioned in relationship to traditional theater, which attracted a much wealthier clientele than most vaudeville houses. The way in which the film magazine of the period, *Moving Picture World*, differentiated between the true 'acting' of the theater and the idea of performance in movies illustrates that a clear hierarchy of the arts was at work. Prior to 1907, *Moving Picture World* described movie actors usually as 'picture performers.' *To perform* was understood to connote a display of natural action. *To act* had the connotation of creating the nuances of character, the artifice of becoming the person one was playing. In the devel- opment of techniques like the close-up, in the gradual appearance of narrative structure, and in the movement to 'feature' length, one can see the attempts to build into the cinematic structure elements that would be emulative of aesthetic value perceived in theatergoing. The increasing focus on individual performers and codes of character, as opposed to the dominant code of action of early twentieth-century film, moved the film industry into an investment in a star system that at the very least emulated the theater star system. Indeed, Adolph Zukor attempted to inject the aura of the theatrical star into film by contracting with famous stage actors to appear in films. The most famous of these, Sarah Bernhardt, played the lead in the critically successful though less financially successful *Queen Elizabeth* (1912). However, the strategy contained a slightly flawed conception of the movie audience, because the most famous contract players to emerge out of Zukor's Famous Players Company were in fact known only as film stars.[9] The development of the star system thus is most indicative of a cultural industry attempting to capture a certain legitimacy and cultural space. Stars and dramas that empha- sized the psychological development of characters articulate an attempt to establish the cinema's affinity with the theater. The actual meanings of the film star of the 1910s or 1920s never achieved this aesthetic connotation because the audience's investment in the star, an audience comprising primarily working-class and middle-class individuals, expressed a distinctively filmic aura for the screen celebrity.

Edgar Morin's discussion of this aura of the film celebrity of the 1920s emphasizes the godlike quality perceived in these select few. One of the first instances of name recognition came with Nick Carter, who was still known only by his screen name. Only after playing a num- ber of different heroic roles did the star become recognizable as a hero himself.[10] By 1919, the star crystallized as an entity distinct from his or her screen personas. As an entity, the star and the industry that by this time surrounded him or her began to protect the image the star con- veyed to the public. For example, Rudolph Valentino maintained the image of the romantic and heroic lover throughout his career by actively choosing his film roles to support that construc- tion. Morin notes that Greta Garbo epitomized the separate and aloof quality of the film stars of the 1920s; she 'remained mysteriously distant from the mortals' (her audience) both in her screen presence and in her lifestyle in her grand Hollywood mansion.[11]

However, the film star aura was never so simply maintained. It was built on a dialectic of knowledge and mystery. The incomplete nature of the audience's knowledge of any screen actor became the foundation on which the film celebrity was constructed into an economic force. The staging ground from which film actors entered the world of celebrity was publicity. Publicity constitutes the extratextual movement of the screen actor into other forms of popular discourse. The staging of publicity on behalf of individual celebrities became the province of agents and specifically publicity agents. The most famous of these publicity innovators, Carl Leammle – owner of the Independent Motion Picture Company, known as Imp – was effective in separating the economic power of the individual actor as celebrity from the rest of the film industry. He staged the 'death' of the Biograph Girl, Florence Lawrence, through a press release to news outlets throughout North America. Three days later, he staged her reappearance in St. Louis, which included an exclusive feature interview and full-length photo of the star. Within that interview, certain personal details about Florence Lawrence were released that circumvented the Biograph Studios ban on the release of names or information about its film actors. Her audience learned of her love of horseback riding and of the stage, along with other details of her early life.[12] The publicity agent has continued to assume this role of enlarging the meaning of any actor in the public sphere and expanding the audience's knowledge and desire for knowledge of the celebrity's personal life.[13] Walker considers the creation of the film star as public property an industry that was very quickly '10,000' times larger than that found in the theatrical trade: there were more photos, more venues, more fan and movie magazines, and the power of simultaneous releases made the extratextual business of film star publicity central to the entire industry. Between the 1920s and the 1950s, the extratextual discourse concerning movies and their stars in Hollywood was estimated by one writer to involve 100,000 words a day. In terms of quantity, this made Hollywood the third-largest source of information, behind Washington, DC, and New York City. Also between the 1920s and the 1950s, roughly 5,000 correspondents were stationed in Hollywood to feed the world the secrets of the stars.[14]

The independence of the film celebrity

At various times in the history of film, the film star has operated as a symbol of the independent individual in modern society. This crucial symbolic value has demonstrated and reinforced the ideology of potential that is housed in all members of capitalist culture to supersede the constraints of institutions for the true expression of personal freedom. As film stars transformed into the clear economic center of film production between 1910 and 1920, they became able to determine the form and content of that production and thus began to act independently.[15] By 1919, a group of film stars that included Charlie Chaplin, Mary Pickford and Douglas Fairbanks demanded salaries and contracts that could no longer be supported by any studio. Along with director D. W. Griffith, they organized their own production and distribution company, United Artists, in order to control their own films.[16] Although the company had limited success in its early years, the existence of United Artists nevertheless underlined the top film stars' ability to express the independence of their wills and desires. It is interesting to note that the expression of independent will in the form of United Artists eventually adopted the corporate structure of the other major films companies.[17]

The economic independence of the film celebrity has always operated as a symbol of freedom within the industry and for the public. The ability to own a mansion, the opportunity to partake of prohibitively expensive forms of leisure, like yachting or polo, and the time to travel widely are some of the kinds of privileges associated with stardom. They are the rewards of an industry that is connected to a paying public through the perceived 'qualities' of its stars.

For the industry, the stars' economic value transcends the nature of their work and thus their wages far outstrip those earned by generally unionized film workers. The celebrity's independent connection to the audience permits the configuration of a separate system of value for his or her contribution to any film. This connection to the audience is on an affective or emotional level that defies clear-cut quantification of its economic import. In recent film history, the star's wage has become one of the principal costs of production. For a star of the first order, such as Arnold Schwarzenegger, Tom Cruise, Meryl Streep or Dustin Hoffman, contracts of between $2 million and $5 million are not uncommon. Over and above salary, a star may also receive a percentage of the box-office receipts.[18] In such an arrangement, not only is the star guaranteed a very high salary, he or she is also permitted to be involved in the creation of surplus value or profits, like the corporation itself. The star has become an individualized corporate entity, with recognizable brand and hoped-for audience loyalty. Kevin Costner's involvement in *Waterworld* (1995) best articulates this corporate quality of the star. As production costs soared, Costner renegotiated his fee of $12.5 million by forfeiting his 15 per cent share of the gross receipts over and above his fee in order that the film would actually be completed as planned. In this instance, through his financial stake in the film's production, the star operated in virtual partnership with Universal Studios.[19]

The capacity of the star to conform to the form of a company entails the celebrity's commitment to the organization of capital and the general operation of the film industry. The independence of the current top film celebrities is built on a long history of film studio development of their stars. From the 1920s to the 1950s, the studio system of star-making machinery was in place. By 1930, the consolidation of the industry established five major studios and three minor studios in Hollywood. The major studios not only produced films but also distributed them and owned the exhibiting theaters. Their performers, particularly the women, were often signed at young ages to long binding contracts that stipulated they could appear only in their own studios' productions. As young performers, their transcendent power and related connection to the audience, as discussed above, were virtually nonexistent. They depended on the studios to provide them with venues and film 'vehicles' in order to establish their unique economic value. Not surprisingly, the studios always had surpluses of potential stars who could be featured or relegated to the filmic version of a chorus line. The stable of actors/stars affiliated with each studio defined the dependent relationship any new Hollywood actor had to his or her studio. Once an actor was able to establish an affective relationship with the movie audience, he or she could enjoy the benefits of being an economic center of the studio system. The film actor in this process exited the private world of studio politics and entered the public world of film exhibition.

Agents representing actor/stars since Laemmle have worked at the interstices of the private and public realms of the movie industry. The agent's fundamental intention is to construct the star as a clearly separate economic entity, quite distinct from any individual film and any studio. The agent intervenes in the typical employer–employee relationship that the studio attempts to maintain to articulate the closer relationship the star has to the audience compared with either the movie or the studio. The agent actively works to shift the economic ground so that it is centered on the public construction of the star and away from the studio's original construction and investment in the star. At times, the work of the agent may be in concert with the publicity and promotional work of the film studio. However, when contracts are negotiated, the public nature of the film celebrity's power is the working space of the agent.

The centrality of the Hollywood agent in the separation of the star from the exigencies of the studio is significant. The way in which the film industry now operates with its most famous celebrities demonstrates a general industrywide consciousness of the star's independence and closer connection to an audience. Films often become centred on the star in terms of narrative and financing. For instance, if a star of the stature (i.e. audience allure) of Mel Gibson agrees to be involved in a proposed picture, then the financing of the production becomes all the more realizable. The story may also be adjusted to conform to the public's representation of the star, so that the audience's expectations are met. The film character and the star's public personality may be coordinated so that a continuity is maintained and reinforced.

The building of the public personality of the film celebrity is the work of the agent, whose job it is to forge an independent relationship between the star and the audience. The activity of creating a celebrity from film involves coordinating the reading of the star by the audience outside of the film. The character in the film may set the heroic type that the star embodies, but the relationship to the real person behind the image completes the construction of the celebrity. It is the solving by the audience of the enigma of the star's personality that helps formulate the celebrity: the audience wants to know the authentic nature of the star beyond the screen. Through reading the extratextual reports about a particular film celebrity, the audience knits together a coherent though always incomplete celebrity identity.[20]

Film celebrities' identities, which are made by the audience from the material of interviews, media reports, images, and films, are invested with conceptions of freedom, independence, and individuality. The stars' luxurious lifestyles, many depicted in a syndicated television program devoted entirely to this theme (Robin Leach's *Lifestyles of the Rich and Famous*), would seem to distance the film celebrities from the everyday experiences of their audiences. And, indeed, the stars of the 1920s had an ethereal quality that placed them quite above their audiences. However, with the institutionalization of the Hollywood press corps and the related growth in the extratextual discourse circulated about film stars, film celebrities became a blend of the everyday and the exceptional. The combination of familiarity and extraordinariness gives the celebrity its ideological power. One can see the construction of this unity in the type of acting and performing that has been central to the institution of film.

The extraordinary and the ordinary in film performance

Once the narrative film came to represent the mainstream of commercial cinema during the second decade of the twentieth century, film performance became principally a form of professional acting. The decline of the documentary, the sports film, and the newsreel as the centers of the filmic experience was furthered by the growth of radio as the preferred new medium for the discourses of news and information. Film acting, however, was perceived to represent the 'real' and the 'natural' (which are, of course, cultural constructs) to a much greater degree than stage acting. Part of this naturalistic aura surrounding film acting is derived from film's documentarian origins. The theater, with its proscenium, its staging, the clear artifice of the presentation, and the projection of the actors, is not physically present in the film. Instead, we are given an apparently less constructed scene; the camera takes us, for example, into the living room of a house after showing its exterior. In concert with this conception of the naturalness of film and the artifice of the stage, it was generally believed that a good stage actor did not necessarily make a good film actor. The stage actor had to build the believability of his or her character, had to become the character. To stage critics, acting entailed creating a temporary artifice of character, and the artifice had to be discernible. The good film actor, on the other hand, was believed to be someone who did not use the craft and artifice of acting: he or she performed naturally. Film director D. W. Griffith chose his actors more on the basis of their appearance than for their acting ability. Sergei Eisenstein searched the streets to find the faces that would typify the characters in his scenarios. Qualities of beauty, youth and stereotypical appearance became central to the profession of film acting to a degree they never achieved in stage acting. The ability to 'not act' also became a valued commodity in the search for film stars.

Attention to the naturalness of the film performer is also connected somewhat to the historical development of acting in the nineteenth and early twentieth centuries. Richard Sennett has chronicled the transformation of stage performance from the eighteenth to the nineteenth century, and he notes that in the eighteenth century, actors assumed clear-cut social positions and classes on stage, particularly in melodrama. Thus, stereotypes of performance were common; particular actors became expert at portraying particular types of classes or characters. In the nineteenth century, great acting rested on the development of a unique interpretation of the character; in other words, actors, such as Frederic Le Maitre in Paris, achieved renown for their ability to personalize their roles and transcend the text. They were thought to possess some superior quality because they could shock the audience with their ability to act naturally and therefore overcome the limitations of the characters they played.[21] The personalization of the acting profession grew gradually from the late eighteenth century throughout the nineteenth century. As Elizabeth Burns points out, the practice of linking actors' names with those of the characters they played began in the eighteenth century. As a result, audiences would see Garrick's Hamlet or Irving's Shylock; the self and the personality of the self became clear factors in the understanding of the theatrical text.[22]

In the early twentieth century, the acting techniques of Stanislavsky were gaining influence, roughly simultaneous to the narrative development of film. Although it was another three decades before Stanislavsky's techniques were formulated into the Method school of acting in the US, their investment with the construction of the self through the personalization of the character matched much of the development of Hollywood film acting. The Method technique demands that the actor internalize the psychological makeup of the character in order to achieve a more natural portrayal.[23] This technique was in opposition to the character acting tradition of the British and American stage. The theatrical tradition of the actor's observing behavior and accent from the world around him or her could be seen as developing the character from the outside in; in this technique, meticulous attention is paid to manifest signs of class and habit. Method acting, in contrast, is psychologically deep when it is taken to its extreme of character development.

The salience of Method acting for film stemmed from three factors.[24] The first is linked nominally to technological distinctions. Because film deals with faces and expressions in close-up, it made the grand and sweeping gestures of stage performance look oddly inauthentic. The close-up possibilities of film psychologized and internalized the meanings of filmic texts. With the advent of sound film, the highly developed and resonating stage voice, the very grain of that voice, also appeared unnatural and forced. New ranges and new constructions of character intimacy were possible when voice projection to a theatrical audience was no longer necessary. This relationship between technological change and the personalization of the screen performer is not simply one of cause and effect. The use of film technology is positioned around the articulation of certain kinds of powerful discourses. Film, as a type of mass media, was involved in the expression of forms of individuality that were possible within modern mass society. Film provided a channel for the proliferation of a discourse on individuality and personality. The technology of film is therefore connected to the expression of this discourse on the forms of modern individuality.[25]

The second factor leading to the relative dominance of the Method form of acting in film is that the technique allows for the expression of the personalities of the actors involved in the production. On its own, this may not seem to be a very great consideration, but if one thinks of the various interests involved in the production of a film, one can see the impetus behind constructing characterizations that transcend the individual film. As mentioned above, the film star's agent is actively working to create a unique use value and exchange value for the film actor that can be represented. Barry King has argued quite effectively that the actor as celebrity or star expresses a value that is quite separate from the individual film production.[26] Thus, the film star represents the wresting of control of the production away from the producers and the directors. If a director, like Griffith and Eisenstein, among others, chooses leads on the basis of age, beauty, or other physical features, and not on the ability of the performers to act, then the control of the production rests with the director. His or her ability to edit, to construct the scenario, to juxtapose a series of images into the story diminishes the productivity and use value of the actor to the finished product. However, if the uniqueness of the personality of the star is critical to the success of the film production, then control of the film moves toward the star's perceived interests. Method acting allows for the permutation that the internal expression of a character can also be a playing out of the psychological dimensions of the star him- or herself. According to King, this is imbricated in the control of the economics of production and the division of labor in the film industry: 'Under such circumstances, a potential politics of persona emerges insofar as the bargaining power of the actor, or more emphatically, the star, is materially affected by the *degree* of his or her reliance on the apparatus (the image), as opposed to self-located resources (the person) in the construction of persona.'[27]

King goes on to conclude that 'impersonation,' which is the ability to play a particular character, becomes less valued in the economies of film production than the capacity for 'personification' – the ability to construct a continuing personal and individual mark in each film role.[28] He explains why:

> The ramifications are complex, but basically personification serves the purposes of containing competition amongst the tele-film cartel companies by representing the star's contribution as resting on his or her private properties as a person. . . . The centrality of personae (stars) as an index of value provides a form of control – shifting or ever threatening to shift, signifiers from the actor to the apparatus – over the detail of performance in favour of those who have control over the text.[29]

The third factor leading to the interiorization of character and actor in films is connected to the audience construction of the celebrity. Method acting has deepened the significance of the mundane, the everyday lives of relatively ordinary people. In coordination with the conception that film acting does not involve the abstraction and impersonation that stage acting utilizes, the audience is positioned much closer to the enigma of the identity of the film celebrity. Moreover, the psychological identity of the film actor is more central to understanding any of the film's texts. Actors such as Marlon Brando and James Dean were able to build careers on combining the interiorization of Method acting with the search for their true selves. They were able to include the audience in this search for the ur-text of their star personalities.

The audience's pleasure and play and the construction of significance with intimacy and enigma

The relationship that the audience builds with the film celebrity is configured through a tension between the possibility and impossibility of knowing the authentic individual. The various mediated constructions of the film celebrity ensure that whatever intimacy is permitted between the audience and the star is purely at the discursive level. The desire and pleasure are derived from this clear separation of the material reality of the star as living being from the fragments of identity that are manifested in films, interviews, magazines, pinup posters, autographs and so on. Depending on the level of commitment of the audience member, certain types of fragments or traces of identity are deemed adequate. For some, the characters of the films themselves, which among them construct their own intertextual framework of the celebrity's identity, are quite sufficient. For others, those called fanatics or fans, the materiality of identity must be reinforced through the acquisition of closer representations of existence and identity. The autograph and the pinup poster epitomize the committed fan of a film celebrity. Belonging to a fan club entails an investment into the maintenance of a coherent identity, as members circulate information about the celebrity that for the members establishes a somewhat separate and distinctive episteme concerning the star's true nature. Recent work on fan culture has articulated the relative affective investment that can be part of the cultural experience of the star for the audience. Fandom can actively transform the meaning of stars well beyond the material presented in magazines and newspapers.[30]

In his book on film stars, Morin lists some of the requests that fans have made of their favorite celebrities. Some ask for locks of hair, others for small possessions that will allow the fan to enter the private sphere of the star through the fetish object. Most ask for photographs. Some are driven to ask their favorite stars' advice on their own personal matters.[31] According to Margaret Thorpe, in the 1930s and 1940s a studio typically received up to 15,000 fan letters a week. A first-class star would have received directly 300 letters a week.[32]

The range of audience participation in the construction of the film celebrity sign is wide and varied. Nevertheless, stars possess a general allure in their combination of the everyday and the extraordinary that is modalized through a discourse on intimacy and enigma. The ordinary elements of the film star are important as a marked entrance point for the audience to play with kinds of identity and identification. Since its inception, the film industry has produced stars who have emerged from apparently 'normal' backgrounds. The mythology of stardom that has been circulated in the trade literature since Laemmle's Biograph Girl media event is the possibility that anyone can be a star. Because of the sustained focus on external appearance, as opposed to acting ability, the film star appeared to be chosen quite randomly. Merit was secondary to luck and circumstance. In this way, the Hollywood film industry perpetuated a myth of democratic access. The concept of merit and ability was transposed into the language of character and the personal history of the star. Humble beginnings, hard work and honesty were the extratextual signs of the film celebrity that supported this myth of the democratic art. The extensive discourse on the stars' personal and private lives often was constructed on how fame and fortune could corrupt the ordinary human being housed in the star personality. This theme became one of the central film story lines of a progressively self-reflexive Hollywood. From *42nd Street* to three versions of *A Star Is Born*, Hollywood reinforced its anyone-can-make-it mythology.

In contradistinction to the democratic nature of access, the image of the film star expressed the inaccessibility and extraordinary quality of the celebrity lifestyle. In double senses of the word, the images of wealth were typically *classless*, and in this way were compatible with the democratic ideology that surrounded Hollywood movies, despite their oligopolistic economic structure. The mansions of the movie stars had all the signs of wealth and prestige but none of the cultural capital to reign in the appearance of excess. The swimming pools, with their unique shapes, the immodest and therefore grandiose architecture pillaged from countless traditions without cultural contextualization, and the elaborate grounds and gates were all signs of the nouveau riche, a class excluded from the dominant culture because of its inability to coordinate the signs of wealth. Movie stars' prestige was built on the signs of consumer capitalism, and their decadence and excess were celebrations of the spoils of an ultimate consumer lifestyle. Their wealth, generated through the expansion of leisure as an industry and the entertainment consumer as a widening domain of subjectivity, was cause for celebration – not cultural responsibility. To use Bourdieu's typology of taste and distinction, the movie star's ostentatious presentation of wealth exemplified an aesthetic that was obvious and overdone. In opposition, those who possessed not only capital but cultural and intellectual capital constructed their distinctive taste in terms of abstraction and distance from these more obvious and overt expressions of wealth.[33]

The power of the film celebrity's aesthetic of wealth and leisure in the twentieth century can not be seen to be static. With its close connection to the construction of consumer lifestyles, the film celebrity's forays into recreational pursuits helped define the parameters of pleasure through consumption for all segments of society. Perhaps the best example of this expansive and proliferating power to influence the entire socius has been the growing centrality of the Hollywood image of the healthy body. Tanned skin had been seen traditionally as evidence of physical labor, specifically farm labor. Although there may have been a bucolic connotation to the image of the tanned and brawny farmhand, it contained no further signification of an easy, leisurely life. To be tanned was evidence that one had engaged in hard work under the sun. Hollywood film stars helped construct a new body aesthetic as they attempted to look healthier under the intense lighting of their film shoots. The activity of suntanning achieved a glamorous connotation because it now indicated one had the time to virtually nothing but lie in the sun. The film star worked in this domain of breaking down and reconstructing conceptions of distinctions. Thus, certain expensive or class-based outdoor sports, such as yachting and tennis, provided a conduit between these new body images of health and fitness that demanded time and energy in the sun and the other moneyed classes. Leisure and wealth became in the twentieth century associated with having a tan and a well-toned body; however, these new signs, appropriated from the laboring class, had to have been achieved through sports and hobbies, and not work.[34]

The classlessness of film celebrities despite their clear wealth aligned them as a group with their audience. Their wealth, if thought of as an extrapolation of a consumer subjectivity, also aligned them with an ethos fostered in late capitalism. The construction of identity in the domains of consumption as opposed to production made the film star an image of the way in which a lifestyle/identity could be found in the domain of nonwork. The star, then, to borrow from Ewen's study of the development of a general consumer consciousness in the twentieth century through advertising and general business objectives, performed as a 'consumption ideal': a representative of the modern way of life.[35] Anyone has access to the goods of the large department stores, and therefore can play in this democratic myth of identity construction through consumption.

The chasm between the type of lifestyle constructed by the film star and that constructed by the audience is continually filled in by the rumors, gossip and stories that circulate in newspapers and magazines concerning the complex and tragic lives led in Hollywood. In early Hollywood, the reported excesses of lifestyle and success were treated in a disciplinary manner by the press. If one thinks of a film star as a consumption ideal, then failures and tragedies were the results of a consumer lifestyle that was incongruous with the personal roots of the star. Much of the writing of the personal life stories of the stars, particularly the form of gossip writing that focused on failure, emphasized the traps of success. The discourse on film star tragedy, then, was concerned with the reconciliation of the personal and the psychological with the manner and means of consumption. The root cause for the diversion of lifestyle from the person's true nature was the instant success gained by the film star. The disciplinary morals offered by these scandals of the stars for the audience concerned the need to match one's psychological personality with an appropriate lifestyle and consumption identity. The stars represented extreme constructions of lifestyle. The audience member had to work toward some kind of balance. Finally, the audience also learned about the essential human frailties and personality types of these distant stars. Despite their larger-than-life presence on screen, film stars were essentially human and covered the gamut of personality types.

Summary

The film celebrity as a general discourse occupies a central position in the development of the twentieth-century celebrity, and it is for this reason I have provided a rather lengthy genealogy of its formation. Because of cinema's history, covering the entire twentieth century, and because the cinematic apparatus's development and growth coincided with the growth and extension of consumer capitalism, the film celebrity has provided a way in which the discourses of individualism, freedom, and identity have been articulated in modern society. With the film star's relative nonattachment to material forms of production because of his or her work solely in the manufacture of images, the discourse on and about screen stars was particularly concerned with the manner of consumption and the associated construction of lifestyles. The discourse on film celebrities and their consumption was also integrated into a study of personality, character and general psychological profile. Through various extratextual sources, the celebrities provided the ground for the debate concerning the way in which new patterns of consumption could be organized to fit the innate patterns of personality.

Notes

1   Richard DeCordova, 'The Emergence of the Star System and the Bourgeoisification of the American Cinema,' in *Star Signs* (London: BFI Education, 1982), 66.

2   The exceptions to this could be seen to be Edison's films made in studios; nevertheless, the emphasis was still on the 'wonderment' of the technology and the novelty of moving images. For a thorough reading of early cinema, see Charles Musser, *History of the American Cinema*, vol. 1, *The Emergence of Cinema: The American Screen to 1907* (New York: Charles Schribner's Sons, 1990).

3   For an account of the connection of vaudeville to film, see Robert C. Allen, *Vaudeville and Film 1895–1915: A Study in Media Interaction* (New York: Arno [originally published as a PhD dissertation, University of Iowa, 1977]).

4   Alexander Walker, *Stardom: The Hollywood Phenomenon* (London: Michael Joseph, 1970).

5   Benjamin Bowles Hampton, *History of the American Film Industry from Its Beginnings to 1931* (New York: Dover, 1970[1931]).

6   Janet Staiger, 'Seeing Stars,' in Christine Gledhill (ed.), *Stardom: Industry of Desire* (London: Routledge, 1991), 6–10 (first published in *Velvet Light Trap* 20 [Summer 1983]).

7   The pervasiveness of the star system in vaudeville could have operated as the crucial limiting structure on the development of film stars in the early 1900s. Allen explains that there was an economic impetus for exhibitors to move into the showing of films, because of the escalating salaries demanded by vaudeville stars. The hybrid form to emerge out of the relative cheapness of films, in comparison to mounting an entire vaudeville show, was called 'small-time vaudeville'; fewer live acts appeared, and there was more emphasis on film. Small-time vaudeville played generally in smaller venues than traditional vaudeville shows, but 'nicer' more 'acceptable' places (to the middle classes) than the rougher and dirtier nickelodeon houses. As the power of the vaudeville stars increased, the promoters and exhibitors, and the new cultural entrepreneurs who competed with vaudeville, moved on to productions that kept the performers anonymous and cheap: films. This argument is inferred from Allen's

discussion of the development of small-time vaudeville; Allen does not specifically extend his economic argument to include this point concerning the obvious impeding of the film star system. See Allen, *Vaudeville and Film*, 230–73.

8   Ibid.

9   Walker, op. cit., 44–5.

10 Edgar Morin, *Les Stars* (Paris: Seuil, 1972), 18.

11 Ibid., 21.

12 Walker, op. cit., 36.

13 Joshua Gamson provides an insightful reading of the world of the publicity agent and the so-called team that surrounds the production of a successful celebrity. In a chapter titled 'Industrial-Strength Celebrity,' Gamson outlines the elaborate press and publicity agent machine that surrounds the successful celebrity, where up to 50 per cent of the star's income may go to these organizers of events, sitings, and so on. The goal is to make the celebrity a clear brand name. See Joshua Gamson, *Claims to Fame: Celebrity in Contemporary America* (Berkeley: University of California Press, 1994), 57–78.

14 Morin, op. cit., 11.

15 See Richard DeCordova, *Picture Personalities: The Emergence of the Star System in America* (Urbana: University of Illinois Press, 1990). DeCordova's analysis of the early star system defines quite accurately this investment of the industry and the extratextual industry in the construction of the public personality. DeCordova makes a distinction between 'picture personalities,' who were film actors between 1910 and 1919, and 'stars,' who were film actors after 1919, in terms of the relative investment in a discourse of intimacy and personal knowledge. Picture personalities, according to DeCordova, are defined publicly as homologous to their roles. Stars articulate the establishment of public personalities that literally have lives of their own in terms of extratextual (i.e. outside of their films) discourse. These classifications continue to define the way in which stars are constructed in the American film industry. See the analysis of Tom Cruise, below.

16 Douglas Gomery, *The Hollywood Studio System* (London: BFI/Macmillan, 1986), 173–80.

17 The only real difference between United Artists and the major studios was that United Artists did not become completely integrated with ownership in exhibition as well as production and distribution. Also, it should be added that most of the studios arose out of the corporate culture of exhibition and distribution.

18 In 1990, Sylvester Stallone signed a multipicture deal with Carolco for between $12 and $17 million per picture. Bruce Willis supposedly received $8 million for *The Last Boy Scout* (1991). Schwarzenegger received a jet for *Total Recall* (1990) and $12 million for *Kindergarten Cop* (1990). There is an entire hierarchy in Hollywood based on actor's pay. In 1989–90, the estimated incomes of the top nine stars were as follows: Sylvester Stallone, $63 million; Arnold Schwarzenegger, $55 million; Jack Nicholson, $50 million; Eddie Murphy, $48 million; Bruce Willis, $36 million; Michael J. Fox, $33 million; Tom Cruise, $26 million; Michael Douglas, $24 million; Harrison Ford, $22 million. Peter Bart, 'Stars to Studios: Pass the Bucks – Top Talent Seeks to Break Video Profits Barrier,' *Variety*, September 24, 1990, 1, 108.

Because of the financial clout of these artists, they are also able to fight the studios in the court for even greater returns. With 35–50 per cent of film revenues coming from video sale and rentals, the stars and their lawyers are working to negotiate even greater revenue shares from their films. Since Charlton Heston's groundbreaking deals for a percentage of the film box-office gross in the late 1950s, other stars have moved into similar financial arrangements, which have often shifted financial power to the individual stars. It is also significant that although female stars such as Whoopi Goldberg, Meryl Streep and Goldie Hawn may receive million-plus pay packages for their films, their earnings come nowhere near those of the highest-paid male stars. See also Lawrence Cohn, 'Stars' Rocketing Salaries Keep Pushing Envelope,' *Variety*, September 24, 1990, 3.

19 Costner's percentage kicks in again if and when *Waterworld*, the most expensive film (approximately $170 million) ever made, actually becomes profitable, which demonstrates the complete corporate risk involvement of a star. Jess Cagle, 'Dangerous When Wet,' *Entertainment Weekly*, July 10, 1995.

20 In a recent review of the power of publicists, Charles Fleming notes that publicists are increasingly interventionist in determining the editorial content of magazines that feature their clients on the cover: 'The balance of power between news organizations and the publicity machine that supplies them with celebrity photos and interviews has shifted . . . the publicist is now in the driver's seat.' Charles Fleming, 'Star Hungry Mags Find Flacks Flexing Muscles,' *Variety*, July 4, 1990, 1, 23.

21   Richard Sennett, *The Fall of Public Man* (New York: Random House, 1974), 204–5.

22   See Elizabeth Burns, *Theatricality* (London: Longman, 1972).

23   See Constantin Stanislavski, *Creating a Role*, Hermine I. Popper (ed.), Elizabeth Hapgood (trans.), (New York: Routledge, 1989[1961]).

24   For a fascinating account of Method acting in film, see Steve Vineberg, *Method Actors: Three Generations of an American Acting Style* (New York: Schirmer, 1991). For an account of an interpretation of the acting technique by a famous tortured celebrity, see Marlon Brando, with Robert Lindsey, *Brando: Songs My Mother Taught Me* (London: Century, 1994).

25   This could be likened to the function of the novel in the nineteenth century. The form of characterization and the investment in the personal constructed and then naturalized the conception of a kind of bourgeois individuality. Likewise film, according to Edgar Morin, actively worked to extend the bourgeois understanding of individuality to the working classes. Morin, *Les Stars*.

26   Barry King, 'Articulating Stardom,' *Screen* 26 (September–October 1985): 45–48.

27   Ibid., 45.

28   Ibid. King draws this distinction in relative value from Hortense Powdermaker, *Hollywood: The Dream Factory* (Boston: Little, Brown, 1950), 206.

29   King, op. cit., 48.

30   For an interesting survey of the work on fandom, see Lisa Lewis (ed.), *Adoring Audience: Fan Culture and Popular Media* (London: Routledge, 1992). Also see Henry Jenkins, *Textual Poachers: Television Fans and Participatory Culture* (London: Routledge, 1992).

31   Morin, op. cit., 75–83.

32   Margaret Thorpe, *America at the Movies*; cited in ibid., 66.

33   See Pierre Bourdieu, 'The Aristocracy of Culture,' in *Distinction: The Social Critique of the Judgment of Taste* (Cambridge: Harvard University Press, 1984), 11–96.

34   Richard Dyer, *Stars* (London: British Film Institute, 1979), 43–5.

35   See Stuart Ewen, *Captains of Consciousness* (New York: McGraw-Hill, 1976). Ewen speaks of youth as a 'consumption ideal,' and this idea is integrated successfully into David Buxton's critique of rock stars in *Le Rock: star système et société de consommation* (Grenoble: La Pensée Sauvage, 1985), ch. 3.

JANE FEUER

SPECTATORS AND SPECTACLES

> The personality of the dancer is missing in pictures. You're with the audiences in
> the theater. You look at them and you can embrace them and they can embrace
> you, so to speak, or you can hate each other. But you get no direct response from
> the screen. It is so remote from the empathy of live theatre.
>   Quoted in Donald Knox, *The Magic Factory* (New York: Praeger, 1973) p. 47

The proscenium and the world outside

THE HOLLYWOOD MUSICAL WORSHIPS live entertainment because live
forms seem to speak more directly to the spectator. To make a verbal analogy, live entertainment seems to be a 'first-person' form, a performance which assumes an active and present
spectator. The typical story film, on the other hand, is more like a third-person narration the
audience eavesdrops on. It is not a direct dialogue between performer and audience. Maybe
that's why so many musicals are about putting on a show rather than about making films.
Popular theater has an immediacy and flexibility that the film medium lacks. You can take a
show on the road, try it out on real live audiences; if necessary, as in *The Band Wagon*, you
can throw out a bad show and replace it with one the audience likes.

At this point, however, we are met with a contradiction. It is true that in putting on a show
the proscenium stage within the backstage musical may provide an arena for dialogue. Yet as
we have already observed, the proscenium arch may also be perceived as a barrier to direct
communication. Hence the many attempts to overcome this barrier: by turning the stage into
a nightclub, by dispensing with the stage altogether, by putting on shows in barns, and so forth.
And yet in those musicals in which 'the world is a stage', in which performances are part of the
narrative, proscenium or stage-like arenas are often *created*. In *Meet Me in St Louis*, for example,
every musical performance is either framed or placed on a stage-like platform. In 'The Boy Next
Door' and 'Have Yourself a Merry Little Christmas', Judy Garland is framed by windows. In
the cakewalk number, she and Margaret O'Brien consciously use the arch created by the passage
into the dining area as a proscenium arch. In 'The Trolley Song' the moving trolley serves as
platform. Far from wanting to eliminate stages entirely, *Meet Me in St Louis* seems to want to
put stages where there are none. And in truth, whenever a number commences in any musical,

the world does become a stage. The proscenium seems to occupy an ambiguous position in the musical film. In musicals in which the stage is a world (backstage musicals), the proscenium is perceived as a barrier and every attempt is made to bridge the distance it creates. But when performance is taken outside the theater, the proscenium is reborn out of ordinary space and the world is a stage.

Such a duality is part of the history of the genre, since musicals with performances integrated into the narrative developed alongside those with proscenium performances. Indeed many films include both types. The three major musical-producing studios of the 1930s (Warner Bros, MGM and RKO) almost always included narrative numbers in those films which featured professional entertainers, and more formal performances in those films in which the leads were non-entertainers or amateurs. Warners' backstage musicals had courtship numbers taking place outside the theater (for example 'Going Shopping with You' in *Gold Diggers of 1935*). And MGM's MacDonald–Eddy operettas, spin-offs from the earlier Paramount operettas with MacDonald and Chevalier, almost always showed at least one of the duo performing for an audience in the film. MacDonald's opening aria in *New Moon* is performed for the elegant society of first-class passengers aboard a ship. When Jeanette MacDonald at long last discovers the proper lyrics for 'Ah Sweet Mystery of Life' in *Naughty Marietta*, she trills them at another formal though amateur gathering.

It was the third of the major cycles of the 1930s, the Astaire–Rogers series at RKO, however, that contained the most complex interplay between proscenium numbers and narrative numbers. Indeed, in this series the original distinction between onstage and offstage itself begins to break down. *Top Hat* – to pick an example familiar to most – alternately creates and reduces proscenium distance. 'No Strings', the first musical number is clearly narrative, introducing the Astaire figure and initiating the conflict with Rogers. The second number, the duet 'Isn't This a Lovely Day (To Be Caught in the Rain)', brings the couple together within a stage-like space created by the bandstand under which they take shelter and upon which they dance. Astaire's 'Top Hat, White Tie and Tails' is part of musical show, yet there's some direct address to the audience; at one point Astaire 'shoots' the internal audience with his cane. 'Cheek to Cheek' and 'The Piccolino', the last two numbers in *Top Hat*, take place at the nightclub in Venice. As for Jolson, the nightclub has a more open design than does the proscenium arch and tends to create less audience distance. It's an intermediate structure, somewhere between a stage and a world. And in 'Cheek to Cheek' the night-club floor becomes a world as Astaire and Rogers whirl off into a secluded space. *Top Hat*, like so many other musicals, blends worlds and stages, reduces stages and makes stages of worlds. One might say that in *Top Hat* stages are created in order to be cancelled; distance is set up so that the film may bridge it. One needs a gap to close one. In 'Top Hat, White Tie, and Tails', the stage is quite visibly present but the staging of the number and the direct address to the audience render it impotent to create a barrier. 'Isn't It a Lovely Day' needs to create a stage for Astaire and Rogers to make a world of by falling in love. Stages appear and disappear, proving again and again that the stage is a world we needn't feel any distance from and that the world is full of the spirit of musical comedy. The performers are part of our world and we're right up there on the screen.

The audience in the film

The theatrical audience[1]

Dwight MacDonald, in his infamous attack on popular culture, bemoans the fact that 'kitsch', as he puts it, 'includes the spectator's reactions in the work of art itself instead of forcing him to make his own responses'.[2] One assumes MacDonald meant this metaphorically, but it would seem that the Hollywood musical takes him quite literally. Long before television invented the studio audience and canned laughter, the Hollywood musical was putting audiences into the film for the purpose of shaping the responses of the movie audience to the film. After 1933 it is unusual to find an onstage performance in a musical that does not include shots of applauding audiences in the theater. One could say that the internal audience in musicals, like the studio audience and canned laugher on television, are latter-day versions of the old theatrical claque. But this begs the question of the essential difference between 'stooges' in a theater and the new media derivatives of the stooge: one is live and the other isn't. Seeing the internal audience as compensation for lost liveness puts it in a new and more meaningful perspective. In order to get a direct response from the film audience, Hollywood musical-makers had to place in their path another, spectral audience. Although even today movie audiences will frequently applaud numbers in musicals, there is always an uncanny ring to it, as anyone who has witnessed this phenomenon can testify. It's just unnatural to applaud those unhearing celluloid ghosts, even though your fellow audience members can hear you. But the audience in the film makes of the movie audience a live audience.

The final show of *Summer Stock* uses the audience in the barn in this fashion. We see the folk audience responding emphatically to professional entertainment; then through the cut in to a closer view of the stage, we take the place of that folk audience. In this way our subjectivity is placed within the narrative universe of the film. Film editing has the power to help us arrive at responses the internal audience presumably came to spontaneously. In the opening sequence of *The Barkleys of Broadway*, for instance, Fred Astaire and Ginger Rogers dance 'Swing Trot', a routine designed to arouse nostalgia for the famous team, together again for the first time in ten years. The couple is preserved in a golden picture-frame proscenium as they dance one of their old routines to a choir admonishing us to 'remember *Swing Time*'. At the end of the number, a cut to a shot from the point of view of the theater's wings reveals the couple taking a bow before a live audience. And in the next shot, we see Astaire's and Rogers' curtain speech from the point of view of that live audience. The audience in the film seems to be there to express the nostalgia the number itself sought to arouse in us. For how could the theatrical audience have known that Josh and Dinah Barkley are really good old Fred and Ginger? Clearly the internal audience serves a symbolic not a realistic purpose; they are the celluloid embodiment of the film audience's subjectivity.

After watching a hundred or so of these backstage musicals, one begins to see a pattern that operates above and beyond individual variations. Through shot transitions (rather than through any particular shot) the spectator may be included in the internal audience; or he/she may replace the internal audience or both. In each case it's the intrusion of the internal audience between us and the performance which, paradoxically, gives the effect of a lived – and more significantly – a *shared* experience (for, of course, the experience of the film is lived in its own way). The conventional camera location for recording an onstage performance in a backstage musical was from an imaginary third-row-center seat within the audience. The resulting shot over the backs of the first few rows of the audience onto the stage (especially when projected upon the enormous screens of the past) gave the spectator the illusion of sitting adjacent to the internal audience, perhaps in the fourth row. We sense the spatial continuity from theater seats to movie-theater seats. Such an effect can be especially startling in musicals involving a film-within-a-film (say, the premières in *Singin' in the Rain* or *A Star is Born*, 1954) where the impression of participation this shot gives is even greater.

The shot which includes the spectator in the theatrical audience is never used alone, however, because once our subjectivity is established within the internal audience, we need to see more closely what that audience is seeing. Typically, there will be a cut to a closer view of the performance taken from the theater audience's point of view but eliminating them from the frame. In this second shot (or more properly in the effect of the cut to this shot) the spectator stands in for that of the spectral audience, rendering the performance utterly theatrical. We are, as it were, lifted out of the audience we actually belong to (the cinema audience) and transported into another audience, one at once more alive and more ghostly. And, in the cut to a closer shot, since the internal audience retreats into offscreen space, the performance can be truly 'all for us'.

This is the basic pattern, one so seemingly simple and conventional that we never stop to contemplate the perceptually quite complex sleight of hand involved. Of course there are variations on this pattern. Many musicals will dolly in and out from one shot to the next, preferring the less abrupt transition and increased subjectivity the moving camera gives. Director Vincente Minnelli liked to crane in over the backs of the audience at the start of a number so that when he craned up and all the way in at the climax, the camera movement would seem to be motivated by our subjective desires. The 1936 *Show Boat* uses long sweeping pans and even shots from over the backs of the audience in the balcony and the audience in the box seats. Whatever the technique, the effect is the same: to constantly remind the spectator that he/she is seeing from the point of view of the theatrical audience while at the same time moving in to address the performance directly to the spectator. Through a dialectic of presence and absence, inclusion and replacement, we may come to feel that we are at a live performance.

During the numbers, then, we are encouraged to identify with the audience in the film, to regain that precious live aura. yet the backstage musical is more than just onstage performances. Only the numbers attempt to achieve an illusion of live entertainment; the plots follow the pattern of traditional Hollywood narrative in which we, the film audience, look onto the story from a position outside it. The story is told to us by the camera in a more impersonal 'third-person' mode. During the stories, however, we are encouraged to identify with the performer protagonists who, after all, are the heroes of these backstage sagas. To this end, subjective camera techniques may be used (the shot-reverse shot pattern is a staple of classical narrative) but always so that we may share the point of view of the performers. During the narrative interludes, then, we are encouraged to share the point of view of the performers, but during the musical interludes, we are encouraged to actually become part of the audience in the film – a very different and much closer type of identification.

But this is not the whole story. For, since the perspective of the performers has already been established through the narrative (or through our prior acquaintance with the film's stars), it is perfectly possible for us to experience a doubled or split identification during the performance without ever experiencing this split in our consciousness as disconcerting. When, usually during the curtain calls, we see the internal audience from the point of view of the performers, we do not lose our sense of identification with the live audience. In *Show Boat* we frequently peer out over the footlights into the mirror of our 'folk' counterparts. Indeed a shot-reverse shot pattern, which alternates the point of view of the internal audience with that of the performers, is a common means of getting us back and forth from the performance to the narrative. Nor does another typical angle – from the wings of the theater onto the stage – disorient us, for we already identify with one of the performers standing in the wings, whose view we are asked to share. The opening sequence of *A Star is Born* provides a virtual glossary of all these different points of view, and we have no trouble following it. Nor does it appear odd when, in *Broadway Melody of 1940*, we watch Eleanor Powell's performance from the point of view of Astaire standing at the back of the orchestra seats; or when, in *The Band Wagon*, we get a similar Astaire perspective on ballerina Cyd Charisse.

Yet in a literal sense, these rapid shifts of viewpoints do splinter our identification during a proscenium performance. Our view of the show is like that of a Cubist painting compared to the fixed positioning and fixed identification of the audience in the film. It is the narrative that holds it all together for us. Far from being the removable connective tissue many critics imply it is, the story of a backstage musical is essential to our mode of experiencing the seeming heart of the musical – the numbers. One has only to experience an early musical with a revue format or MGM's *Ziegfeld Follies* or the compilation film *That's Entertainment* to realize how much has been lost when the backstage context is excised.

The doubled identification provided by the musical's dual registers gives a tremendous rhetorical advantage. We feel a sense of participation in the creation of entertainment (from sharing the perspective of the performers) and, at the same time, we feel part of the live audience in the theater. Only a reflexive form such as the musical can lend so much intensity to our experience of a simple song and dance. The greatest musicals knew how to transform the entire tone of a number by playing one register against the other. *An American in Paris* features Gene Kelly and Georges Guetary in a typical, happy-to-be-in-love song and dance to Gershwin's 'S'Wonderful'. At the end of the number the camera cranes majestically upward as what appears to be the entire population of Paris cheers the light-hearted performance. Only we, the audience of the film, know that the two men are singing about the same girl. Even a mediocre film can profit from the doubled identification, as when Judy Garland, swollen with unrequited live for Gene Kelly, goes out on stage to sing a poignant 'After You've Gone' in *For Me and My Gal*. The cinema takes away aura, but she also gives it back. As a reflexive form, the musical can compensate for the distance it inevitably imposes as mass art. There may be a difference between a live performance and the illusion of one, but in the Hollywood musical, we're not allowed to notice it.

The narrative audience

Despite the most valiant attempts to bring us closer to the stage, the proscenium limits our sense of participation in the performance itself. A skillful director may use the camera to animate such performances, but (with the exception of Busby Berkeley for whom the proscenium was a joke) we remain aware that the performers are up there on the stage and we are down here in the audience. We may hope that Gene or Judy will succeed; we rarely hope that 'we' will succeed. But when the performance is a spontaneous one taking place in the realm of the narrative, we may experience a strong desire to sing and dance in the rain ourselves. Spurred on by the directorial brilliance of Vincente Minnelli and the persona of Gene Kelly, MGM musicals of the 1940 began to create natural audiences that would spontaneously gather around the impromptu numbers of an Astaire or a Kelly. The entire population of a Caribbean port city gathers to watch Gene Kelly search for his 'Nina' in *The Pirate*. In *An American in Paris* the folk of Paris seem to linger in the streets in the hope that Gene Kelly will perform for them: 'By Strauss', 'I Got Rhythm' and 'S'Wonderful' are their reward. Gene Kelly likes himself as he roller skates through midtown Manhattan in *It's Always Fair Weather*; the somewhat aghast crowd that gathers to gape at him appears to like him too. When Gene Kelly dances with an old lady in 'By Strauss', or when Fred Astaire dances with the shoe-shine man in 'Shine on Your Shoes', not only does the audience appear to form spontaneously but also we are given an ordinary spectator-in-the-film, a non-dancer like us but one who's right up there performing nonetheless.

A closer look at one of these numbers – 'By Strauss' – may reveal some of the secrets buried within those spontaneously generated crowds. 'By Strauss' mocks Viennese waltzes through the clowning antics of the three major participants (Gene Kelly, Oscar Levant, Georges Guetary). The Parisian café setting provides the perfect forum for audience participation. For the first rendition of the song by the three men, Minnelli uses two basic camera set-ups, each the reverse shot of the other. In the first shot we look onto Oscar Levant at the piano in the lower right portion of the frame with Guetary and Kelly to his right. In the reverse shot we are able to see past Levant at the piano and through an open-arch doorway onto the busy Paris street. Minnelli stages and shoots in such a way that the arch assumes the guise of a natural proscenium, open in both directions. The first shot comes to represent the point of view of the street audience looking onto the performance, a point of view the spectator easily assumes. The second shot, over the performers and out through the arch, reminds us that performers and audience occupy the same space with no scenic barriers placed between them.

During a second chorus of the song, an audience consisting of the male and female proprietors of the café and the elderly proprietress of a flower shop wander in and are incorporated into the number. Until this point Minnelli has maintained a separation between performers and audience through his shot-reverse shot set-ups. Some interplay occurs when the three new observers participate in the clowning. Now significant camera movement begins to blur the division between performers and audience. As Gene Kelly rises to waltz with the elderly woman, we are able to view the street audience to the right of the frame through the open arch. Later, as the camera cranes out through the arch, the interior 'audience' remains to the rear of Kelly and his partner but the outside audience is now framed to the right of the dancing couple. The camera movement has unobtrusively created a situation whereby the couple is flanked by an 'audience' on both sides, and some members of that audience also qualify as performers. As the camera swings literally back and forth to capture the graceful pas de deux it gives us a peek at the audience surrounding the dancing couple. Inside and outside space have merged into a community celebration.

Kelly then dances with both women, his audience singing along. All take part in the finale, ending with a shout of 'By Strauss' and applause. The number fades out on the principals posing for the street audience, but the applause comes from the direction of the offscreen space the street audience now occupies. We, the spectators, are encouraged to identify with a spontaneous audience which has actually participated in the performance.

It has been said that Minnelli made the camera dance along with the performers. But that is not the only lesson directors of musicals in the 1940s and 1950s learned from Minnelli. For, when Minnelli's camera danced, it most often danced in the service of subjectivity. The camera moves to bring us closer to the dance, but also to bring us to a subjective viewpoint from within the narrative's space. The same may be said for the cuts and camera set-ups in a number such as 'By Strauss'. Minnelli rarely filmed a number in one take as was common at RKO in the 1930s; he knew this would limit the means not of showing us the dance but rather of involving us in it.

Notes

1   I shall use the terms 'internal audience' and 'theatrical audience' to refer to the audience *in* the films; the terms 'spectator' and 'film audience' to refer to the audience *of* the films.

2   'A Theory of Mass Culture', *Diogenes*, No. 3 (Summer 1953); reprinted in Bernard Rosenberg and David Manning White (eds), *Mass Culture: The Popular Arts in America*, (New York: Free Press, 1957) p. 61.

Chapter 19

STELLA BRUZZI

DESIRE AND THE COSTUME FILM: *PICNIC AT HANGING ROCK, THE AGE OF INNOCENCE, THE PIANO*

COSTUME DRAMAS, DESPITE THEIR CONTINUING popularity, have rarely elicited anything other than rather derogatory or cursory attention (although see Harper 1994; Cook 1996). A variety of reasons has been proffered for this by those, largely feminist, critics more favourably disposed to the genre, principally that the costume film is aimed at a largely female spectatorship, and so, like the melodrama, has not merited serious consideration from male writers. A charge frequently levelled at historical romances is that (unlike, presumably, comparable pieces of men's cinema) they sideline history and foreground far more trivial interests in desire, sex and clothes. Behind the genderization of the costume film lies the further implication, expanded upon by Sue Harper when she discusses costume in the Gainsborough melodrama (Harper 1987), that the films possess a covert, codified discourse that centres on the clothes themselves. It is this notion of an alternative discourse that will be explored further in this chapter and developed into a discussion of a group of modern films that focus specifically on the fetishistic value of history and historical clothes.

Recent films as diverse and distinctive as *Daughters of the Dust*, *Sommersby*, *The Piano*, *Orlando*, *The Age of Innocence* and *Sister My Sister* are symptomatic of a resurgence in costume films, a renewed interest that extends the parameters beyond the stifling daintiness of the Merchant-Ivory canon and the saccharine reworkings of Jane Austen. The latter are what Alan Parker dubbed 'the Laura Ashley school of film-making'. There are two principal charges levelled at costume films: that they lack authenticity and that they are frivolous. Pervading much of the existing critical writing given over to the costume film is a sceptical distrust of the films' motives, their prioritization of bourgeois ideals and their conservative, nostalgic view of the past. Andrew Higson and Tana Wollen, for example, talk of the British heritage films and television 'screen fictions' of the 1980s (*Chariots of Fire*, *A Room with a View*, *Brideshead Revisited*) as vacuous, uncritical and superficial, to be unfavourably compared with such interrogative contemporaneous screen ventures as *Distant Voices, Still Lives* and *Boys From the Blackstuff* (Wollen, T. 1991; Higson 1993, 1996). The strength of such arguments are obfuscated by a dogmatic lack of discernment, a refusal to acknowledge the differences as well as the similarities between films that employ period costumes, as if the costumes themselves, Delilah-like, possess a disempowering capacity to divest any film they adorn of its critical, intellectual or ironic potential. The crucial issue, and one which will be returned to in various guises throughout this book, is whether to look at or through the clothes.

Films such as *Howards End* or Ang Lee's *Sense and Sensibility* look through clothes, as the major design effort is to signal the accuracy of the costumes and to submit them to the greater framework of historical and literary authenticity. Costume films that, conversely, choose to look at clothes create an alternative discourse, and one that usually counters or complicates the ostensible strategy of the overriding narrative. When costumes are looked at rather than through, the element conventionally prioritized is their eroticism. This might be another reason for the costume film's relegation to the division of the frivolous, for it is their emphasis on sex and sexuality (such as the British costume romances of the 1940s) that appeals most to a female audience. In her discussion of the *Englishwoman's Domestic Magazine* of the 1860s, Margaret Beetham introduces a distinction of particular relevance to this examination of costume films. Beetham suggests that the *Englishwoman's Domestic Magazine* 'was caught up in several different economies and discourses', that it supported both women's growing demands for political, civil and economic rights over the decade, but nevertheless continued to publish 'sensation' fiction what focused purely on feminine desire and sexuality (Beetham 1996: 71–2). Whereas the economic discourse is no doubt perceived by most to possess intrinsic worth, the sexual discourse is more frequently dismissed as escapist fantasy. When, for example, Alison Light examines the popularity of women's historical fiction she voices her concern that a preoccupation with fantasy obscures a novel's moral, social or political message (Light 1989: 69). In a previous discussion of recent costume films I suggested a distinction could be made between the 'liberal' and the 'sexual' models adopted by women film-makers working within the genre. The 'liberal' mode (exemplified by such films as *My Brilliant Career*, *Rosa Luxemburg* and *An Angel at My Table*) seeks to map out, via the lives of emblematic or iconic historical personalities, a collective women's cultural and political history. In these films clothes are merely signifiers to carry information about country, class and period. The 'sexual' model, on the other hand, (exemplified by *The Piano* and *Sister, My Sister*, for example) foregrounds the emotional and repressed aspects of past women's lives and maps out an alternative but equally genderized territory that centres on the erotic. In these films the clothes themselves become significant components of a contrapuntal, sexualised discourse (Bruzzi 1993: 232–42).

Throughout her discussions of British costume films Sue Harper rejoices in their wilful disregard for historical accuracy in favour or a sexier escapism. In Gainsborough melodramas such as *The Wicked Lady* or *Jassy* Harper identifies a closeted 'costume narrative' in which the inauthentic period clothes are loaded with ambiguity and furtive desire, playing out 'contradictions between the verbal level of plot and scripts, and the non-verbal discourses or décor and costume' which the (largely female) audiences could 'decode' (Harper 1987: 167). At times the costumes operate metonymically, as in the 'vulval symbolism' Harper identifies in the use of fur, folds and velvet in some of the women's costumes in *The Wicked Lady* (Harper 1994: 130). Too often period costumes are presumed to signify sexual repression as opposed to the presence of an active sexual discourse. One of the intentions of this chapter is to develop previous discussions of the sexualization of costume and to propose that, through their use of historical costumes, *Picnic at Hanging Rock*, *The Age of Innocence* and *The Piano* create a transgressive, erotic discourse which exists both despite and because of the ostensible moral restrictiveness of the times in which they are set. At the heart of this dynamic ambivalence is an interest in the fetishistic attraction of clothes themselves, which is the basis for a covert dialogue between character and character and character and spectator comparable to that discovered in the use certain films have made of *haute couture*. From the moment *The Age of Innocence*, for example, represents the exclusive milieu of late 1800s New York through an exquisite, close-up montage of accessories and sartorial detail, it is apparent that it is demanding a different level of engagement from its spectators than the traditionally disengaging heritage film.[1]

Fetishism has, primarily through the application of psychoanalysis, been considered by Christian Metz, Laura Mulvey and others an influential and significant notion for understanding the eroticism of mainstream cinema. The intention of this chapter is to position costume within the debates about how gender difference and conventions of appearance inform the way in which we look by focusing on clothes and their (often implied) relationship with the body, a particularly pertinent issue when considering the supposed repressiveness of the last century. *Picnic at Hanging Rock*, *The Age of Innocence* and *The Piano* offer divergent perspectives on fetishism, and in many ways chart how approaches to sexual fetishism in general have progressed since the 1880s when the term was first applied to the 'perversion' of substituting an inanimate object for the sexual object. *Picnic at Hanging Rock*, for instance, conforms closely to Freud's hugely influential interpretation of fetishism as a male perversion through which the woman becomes a symbol of masculine desire, whilst *The Piano*, in offering a representation of the past from a clearly feminine perspective, posits the notion that fetishism is not exclusively applicable to men. Campion's film suggests that superficially restrictive clothes function as equivocal signifiers, acting both as barriers to sexual expression and as the very means of reaching sexual fulfilment. In both recent BBC Austen adaptations there were indications that female characters (and spectators) do fetishise the male body through the clothes that adorn it. In the opening episode of *Pride and Prejudice* Eliza's desire for Darcy is conveyed through a horizontal pan following the look from her eyes to Darcy's crotch, whilst in *Persuasion* the final liberation of Anne's previously repressed desire for Wentworth is described through a close-up of the Captain's stitched white gloves clasping her accepting hand. The power of clothes fetishism is that it exists on the cusp between display and denial, signalling as much a lack as a presence of sexual desire, through which it is especially relevant to films that depict a past, less ostensibly liberated age. As Louise J. Kaplan comments, '[a] fetish is designed to keep the lies hidden, to divert attention from the whole story by focusing attention on the detail' (Kaplan, L. 1993: 34), an allusion to fetish as narrative tool that is pertinent to film, as, likewise, is Robert Stoller's definition of a fetish as 'a story masquerading as an object' (Stoller 1985: 155). In all three films the fetish is, at some stage, the object or detail masking the whole story, but whereas in *Picnic at Hanging Rock* the story is left mysterious, by the time we get to *The Piano* it is unveiled.

Period clothes are not always transparent and are capable of being deeply ambiguous. To the fashion historian James Laver the crinoline, despite its 'solid and immovable' tea-cosy shape (Laver 1995: 184), is a complex and perplexing agent of seduction:

> The crinoline was in a constant state of agitation, swaying from side to side. It was like a rather restless captive balloon, and not at all, except in shape, like the igloo of the Eskimos. It swayed now to one side, now to the other, tipped up a little, swung forward and backward. Any pressure on one side of the steel hoops was communicated by the elasticity to the other side, and resulted in a sudden upward shooting of the skirt. It was probably this upward shooting which gave mid-Victorian men their complex about ankles, and it certainly resulted in a new fashion in boots.
>
> (Laver 1945: 52–3)

The more traditional view of the crinoline was as a metaphor and a metonym for women's oppression, condemned by more moralistic commentators as a garment which was 'as good a device for impeding movement as could well be devised' (Bell, Q. 1947: 90–1), and by feminists as a fashion whose 'whole style trembled with meek submissiveness' and reflected the dutiful wife's growing confinement to the bourgeois home (Wilson 1985: 30). The fundamental difference between these divergent opinions on the hooped contraption that dominated western women's fashion for over twenty years from 1856 is fetishism. Laver, for example, is not just an anti-functionalist commentator on fashion but one who, even inadvertently as above, conveys through his meticulous and excitable writing the erotic allure of garments, fabrics and accessories. He explains, in *Taste and Fashion*, how Victorian mothers like his own had to momentarily release their children's hands whilst crossing the road 'in order to gather their voluminous skirts from the ground to prevent them trailing in the mud. As they did so there was the rustle of innumerable silk petticoats underneath, and even a glimpse of lace frill' (Laver 1945: 199). The ostensible motive for the description (the mothers' sensible actions) is rapidly forgotten, and Laver's focus transferred to the underlying point of interest (the sensuality and movement of the women's clothes). A similar division between functionalism and fetishism pervades what is loosely labelled 'the costume film', where clothes usually exist as empty historical signifiers but can more imaginatively become essential components of a film's erotic language. Because the nineteenth century's fashions (for both sexes) appeared to embody what Foucault terms modern puritanism's 'triple edict of taboo, non-existence, and silence' (Foucault 1976: 5), they are fertile ground for fetishism; prohibition possessing an allure that laxity does not.

It was Krafft-Ebing in *Psychopathia Sexualis* (1886) who first used the term 'fetishism' in a sexual and criminal sense, and the term was subsequently adopted by Binet in 'Le fetishisme dans l'amour' (1888) and most notably by Freud. Foucault's reading of fetishism in *The History of Sexuality* was as 'the model perversion' which 'served as a guiding thread for analysing all other deviations' (Foucault 1976: 154), and if one turns to Freud's early writings on the subject in 'The sexual aberrations' the reason for such an assertion becomes apparent. In his first of the *Three Essays on Sexuality* written in 1905 Freud sets up a polemic, outlining what is 'aberrant' against an intentionally prescriptive and narrow sense of what constitutes 'normality', namely heterosexual, penetrative sex. Why fetishism is so important and why, therefore, 'no other variation of the sexual instinct that borders on the pathological can lay so much claim to our interest as this one' (Freud 1905: 66) is because, more clearly than the other aberrations, it simultaneously obstructs and substitutes the 'normal' sexual act. At this point Freud's emphasis is on the object choices of the fetishist, on the 'unsuitability' of the inanimate objects or the 'inappropriateness' of the part of the body substituted for the sex. Freud, like others since (for example, Gamman and Makinen 1994), identifies stages of fetishism, the situation only becoming pathological, he argues, when the fetish goes beyond being something the individual needs 'if the sexual aim is to be attained' (such as a particular hair colour, a visible naked foot, a piece of material) and actually allows the fetish to supplant that aim and become 'the sole sexual object' (Freud 1905: 66–7). Although he is already writing in terms of the fetish as symbolic (analogous to the anthropological fetish thought to embody a deity), this idea is not fully developed. By his 1909 paper 'On the genesis of fetishism' Freud has extended his argument, incorporating Krafft-Ebing's association of the fetish object with the subject's first conscious sexual impulses to explain the peculiarity of certain object-choices. It is also in this essay that Freud categorically argues for fetishism as a male perversion focused on the selection of substitutive objects that serve to repress and deny the sight of his mother's 'castration'. The essay then clearly suggests how, through an interest in fashion, women become both passive fetishists and a complete, imaginary fetish offered up for male contemplation:

> half of humanity must be classed among the clothes fetishists. All women, that is, are clothes fetishists. . . . It is a question again of the repression of the same drive, this time however in the passive form of allowing oneself to be seen, which is repressed by the clothes, and on account of which the clothes are raised to a fetish.
> (quoted in Ganman and Makinen 1994: 41)

As historians of the period have noted, fashions of the nineteenth century not only accentuated but elaborated and constructed gender difference, and, as Elizabeth Wilson puts it,
'woman and costumes together created femininity' (Wilson 1985: 29). If, therefore, this
notion of femininity is pursued, then the clothed woman mirrors the male ideal of femininity
and becomes the fetish that masks and embodies his fears of castration; a castration which,
because of how the Freudian fetish operates, is simultaneously denied and acknowledged.

This is given clarification by Freud in his 1927 essay 'Fetishism' in which he comments that
the (male) child, having 'perceived that a woman does not possess a penis', did not simply,
through fetish substitution, 'retain the belief that women have a phallus' but rather retained that
belief whilst having 'also given it up' (Freud 1927: 352–3). It is the knowingness of this ambivalent state which is most appropriate to how fetishism operates in costume films, for Freud does
not equate fetishism only with repression but introduces the more conscious, deliberate notion
of 'disavowal'; so 'yes, in his mind the woman *has* got a penis, in spite of everything; but this
penis is not the same as it was before' (Freud 1927: 353). To explain the idiosyncrasy of many
notably unphallic fetishes Freud suggests that the choice of object is dependent not on the
similarity to the penis but to the original traumatic moment of perceiving the woman (mother)
to be 'castrated'. Hence shoes, feet, underwear and substitutes for female pubic hair such as
fur or velvet are fixated on because 'it is as though the last impression before the uncanny
and traumatic one is retained as a fetish' (354). Freud understands the act of acquiring a fetish
quite unmetaphorically. The shoe, for example, can be chosen because it was the last thing the
'inquisitive boy [peering] at the woman's genitals from below, from her legs up' (354) remembers before this traumatic realization. This is obviously greatly facilitated by a wider skirt, which
is what gives Baines's action in *The Piano* of snooping up Ada's hoops as she plays her piano
such a blatant eroticism. Both disavowal and affirmation of the female 'lack', Freud concludes,
went into the construction of the fetish, which 'signified that women were castrated and
that they were not castrated' (356). To return to Foucault's comment that fetishism is the
'model perversion', it is now starkly apparent why: Freud's reading categorically defines man
as the sexual subject and the fetish-choice as driven by the fear of his own castration. Like the
perverse Chinese custom which legitimized the mutilation of the female foot so that it could be
revered as a fetish, it seems, as Freud concludes, that 'the Chinese male wants to thank the
woman for having submitted to being castrated' (357).

This fashionable foot-binding custom is more painful, perhaps, but no more contradictory
than other prevalent nineteenth-century fashions such as tight-lacing, also conventionally
understood, in that most patriarchal of times, as affirming the importance of clear gender
delineations. A significant aspect of fashion's evolution can be seen as a continuation of Darwin's
theories of difference, motivated by politics rather than necessity as J. C. Flügel suggests in his
chapter on 'The Ethics of Dress' in *The Psychology of Clothes*:

> There seems to be (especially in modern life) no essential factor in the nature,
> habits or functions of the two sexes that would necessitate a striking difference of
> costume – other than the desire to accentuate sex differences themselves.
>
> (Flügel 1930: 201)

Going against Darwin, Flügel believes that the 'logical' response to the post-industrial flaunting
of gender would be to abolish 'unnecessary sex distinctions in costume' altogether (201). He
is, however, resigned to the fact that the 'majority' desire titillation and eroticism from clothes,
and see distinctive dress as a means of stimulating sexual interests. A consistently forceful argument used to explicate the divergence between men and women's fashions is that femininity
has been emphasised for the express purpose of making women erotically appealing to men:

'for man in every age has created woman in the image of his own desire. It is false flattery of women to pretend that this is not so' (Laver 1945: 198). In a later book, *Modesty In Dress*, Laver develops this notion by identifying two polarized principles: the hierarchical and the seductive. The former is applicable to men because 'a man's clothes are a function of his relation to society' whilst the latter pertains to women because 'a woman's clothes are a function of her relation to man' (Laver 1969: 173). As Simone de Beauvoir acerbically comments in 1949, excessively feminine clothes have nothing to do with glorifying or emancipating women, but are devices of enslavement that make them prey to male desires (de Beauvoir 1949: 543).

The eroticism that dominated women's nineteenth-century fashions was perhaps more subtle and ambiguous than this implies. Flügel perceives there to be a fundamental paradox in women's clothes, that whilst they ostensibly function to emphasise morality and modesty they in effect arouse desire. As examples of this one could cite Laver's excitement at imagining the movements of the crinoline, or his equally ardent support of the small waist, corset and the deep Bertha *décolletage* which 'emphasised the impression of something very precious emerging from a complicated wrapping, as a flower emerges from the paper which encloses its stalk' (Laver 1945: 146). Perhaps unsurprisingly James Laver is neither a fan of more liberated or masculine clothes on women nor a supporter of overtly erotic fashions, maintaining that the naked body is not as appealing as the clothed one, and that a woman in suspenders is less alluring than a woman sporting a crinoline. Fetishism (as opposed to eroticism) is founded on tension, distance and imagination, and is dependent on symbolic rather than actual association between the subject and the object of (his) desire. It is precisely *because* the crinoline says 'touch me not' that Laver finds it seductive (52).

In costume films interested in sexuality (above nostalgia and history telling) the contrast between the obtainable concealed body and the means of enforcing that concealment (namely the clothes) is seen to heighten expectation and arousal. The shiny black boots in *Diary of a Chambermaid*, and Amish cap in *Witness*,[2] the lock of hair in *Golden Braid* or the scrap of dirty lace in *Picnic at Hanging Rock* are personal fetishes, inappropriate substitutes as Freud would deem them for the unobtainable woman they represent. Important to all these instances of the fetishisation of the woman and of the man's desire is the notion of difference, contrast and, most significantly, distance. Just as Christian Metz posits that distance rather than proximity is essential to the voyeuristic impulse, that 'all desire depends on the infinite pursuit of its absent object' (Metz 1975: 60), so the erotic effect of fetishised articles of clothing is essentially related to their metaphoric value. The underlying implication for fashion is that an idealized (male conceived) image of femininity acquires symbolic effect by having been constructed through costume, and that the greater the divergence between the 'natural' body and the 'unnatural', distortive clothes the greater the sexual stimulation.

This is a predominantly masculine view of the workings of clothes fetishism, and there obviously exist arguments and cinematic examples which counter it. In *Sister My Sister*, by comparison, the festishization of particularly articles of clothing, household objects and food is expressive of an exclusively female repressed sexuality. The codification of desire in this much later film uses a similar displacement tactic to Freudian male fetishism (the substitute of an inanimate object for a living object-choice) but only pertains to the sexualities of the various female characters. The strenuous affirmation of hierarchical sexual difference and the conceptualization of elaborate details and ornamentation as essential to fabricating women's attractiveness to men remain, however, the sexual mechanisms operative in a highly masculine fantasy film such as *Picnic at Hanging Rock*, an adaptation that embellishes the already insistent fetishism of Joan Lindsay's original 1968 novel.

Picnic at Hanging Rock is the story of a fictional murder mystery that took place on St Valentine's Day 1900. Most of the schoolgirls of Appleyard College go on a picnic at Hanging

Rock, a group of them want to explore the rock further and three of them (including the pivotal character Miranda) are never found, whilst Irma, who is found, cannot remember anything of what occurred. A particularly Freudian reading of fetishism, which stresses the significance of sexual difference and the importance of the 'normal' sex act, is deeply relevant to Weir's tumescent, adolescent fantasy, to its heterosexism (with its sharp gender delineations) and to its fundamental preoccupation with the transition from childhood to adulthood and thus the point of sexual awakening.

As women's exhibitionism in fashion has been understood to be for the enjoyment of men or at least as a means of ensuring their attention, so the same controlling gaze has been attributed to the male spectator looking at the fetishized, iconic female form on the screen. Whether this is through demystification or over-valuation of the woman as Laura Mulvey suggests, the fetishization relegates her to the passive role of bearer of male desires, thus dissipating the threat her very 'castrated' presence evokes. The girls in *Picnic at Hanging Rock* are subjected to both 'the investigative side of voyeurism' Mulvey identifies in Hitchcock's work and become 'the ultimate fetish' produced by von Sternberg, as often in Weir's film 'the powerful look of the male protagonist . . . is broken in favour of the image in direct rapport with the spectator' (Mulvey 1975: 311). *Picnic at Hanging Rock's* conception of fragmented, transcendent and superficial female beauty is only partially provoked by narrative necessity. Much of the film's fetishism is contained within hiatus sequences divested of any plot function in which the spectacle of beatific schoolgirl sexuality is simply offered up for display. Just as Mulvey only refers to a male spectator, so Weir only addresses a masculine erotic gaze.

Picnic opens with just such a hiatus sequence in which the pupils, preparing for their St Valentine's Day excursion, are presented to us as direct objects of fetishism. The film's mystery is sustained by elliptical dialogue, narration and image which, like Miranda's quivering opening piece of voice-over ('what we see and what we seem are but a dream – a dream within a dream') lend it a teasing, ornate vacuity. Like the expressionistic montage sequences of the classic 1930s Hollywood gangster films, the beginning of *Picnic at Hanging Rock* offers a symbolic condensation of the issues and iconography that are more conventionally enacted through the narrative, in this instance the idealization of femininity through clothes and feminine sexuality. The girls and their romanticized French teacher are dressed exclusively in frail, pristine white (with the exception of the 'deviant' Sara who has blue sleeves)[3] and are ritualistically preparing themselves not just for the day but for womanhood. Hence the dreamy reading aloud of Valentine's messages, Irma and Miranda's sensuous face-washing in front of self-scrutinising mirrors and, most fetishistically of all, lacing each other into corsets. It is the hyperbolic self-consciousness of this montage sequence that makes it so obviously symbolic, with the abundance of flowers, soft focus and golden light; an excessive fusion of the mechanics of fetishism and the fetishising potential of the cinematic apparatus. As if we needed prompting into cleaning our own glasses to further enable us to enjoy the ensuing spectacle, one girl is shown polishing *hers* immediately after the line of giggling, whispering schoolgirls has performed its corset-lacing routine. From the outset, the girls' sexuality is defined as being for an unspecified but omnipresent phallus, metonymically represented by St Valentine, but also contained within the film's masculinization of the voyeuristic and fetishistic impulses. In keeping with Lacan's notion of the phallus as something lost, forever out of reach, but nevertheless pursued as if it were attainable, there is a coalescence throughout *Picnic at Hanging Rock* between direct and indirect fetishism, between the real and the veiled. For example, before setting off on their final ascent up Hanging Rock, the girls reverentially, slowly remove their stockings and shoes: for the rock, the spectator and the unspecified phallus. There is a direct alignment at a point such as this between the active, consuming spectatorial gaze, the phallic rock (which has already been identified as such through a laboured series of low-angle shots) and the veiled phallus governing the girls' actions from the start.

The direct fetishism scenes in *Picnic at Hanging Rock* are frequently 'rites of passage' sequences in which we, the spectators, are voyeuristically engaged with the girls' progress towards maturity. There are several such rituals that have marked the transition from girlhood to womanhood through the use of clothes, most of which, like the acquisition of deforming shoes, uplifting bras and sculpting corsets or girdles, have involved extreme physical restriction. The significant ritual of *Picnic at Hanging Rock* is that of the pupils lacing each other into their corsets, an action that signals both confinement and liberation. This activity further differentiates between those who are ready for sex and those, notably the plump and uncorseted Edith, who are not.[4] Crucial to these fashions is the tension between pain and pleasure; as David Kunzle comments, 'The state of being tightly corseted is a form of erotic tension and constitutes *ipso facto* a demand for erotic release, which may be deliberately controlled, prolonged and postponed' (Kunzle 1982: 31). Kunzle, who was the first to call for a radical reassessment of the corset's relationship to female sexuality, noted that many of the advocates of tight-lacing in the mid-1800s were sexually assertive women, and that the majority of the corset's sternest critics were conservative men who felt threatened by this clandestine expression of desire. Tight-lacing (or the excessive constriction of the waist by means of corset) was a deeply ambiguous phenomenon. Whilst the corset, particularly by feminists, has been traditionally interpreted as a tyrannical garment of oppression, there are well-documented examples of tight-lacing as a popular nineteenth-century erotic pursuit. Fetishistic correspondence in innocuous sounding Victorian women's magazines such as *The Queen* and *The Englishwoman's Domestic Magazine* was rife, as readers, often vying with each other for the smallest waist, offered 'advice' on how to lace more tightly. In the correspondence pages of domestic magazines there are ample examples of women using tight-lacing for auto-erotic pleasure, describing, for instance, the light-headedness which follows the deliberate interruption of their circulation. Although it is presumed (even by Kunzle) that such tight-laced women are to be found desirable by men (Kunzle 1982: 43), it is strikingly apparent that many correspondents derive the greatest pleasure from the narcissistic contemplation of themselves in restrictive undergarments. During the 1860s–80s it was primarily men who documented the reasons why tight-lacing was reprehensible, for instance the doctors who alerted adults to the direct use of corsets for masturbatory satisfaction among pubescent girls (170–1, 218–22). A more moderate view of the 'corset controversy' than Kunzle's is offered by Valerie Steele who argues that 'most accounts of very small waists represented *fantasies*' (Steele 1985: 163), and that the vast majority of corsets in fashion museums suggest that the real average size of the Victorian and Edwardian waist was several inches wider than the 'perfect' 11 inches aspired to by readers of *Englishwoman's Domestic Magazine*. According to Steele, therefore, the idea of a tight-lacing epidemic rather than the reality of one is what excited male and female readers alike.

A preoccupation with lacing and restriction is, however, a pervasive force through *Picnic at Hanging Rock*. As if signalling its own interest in fetishism, the major departures the film makes from the original novel are the moments (such as the opening montage) which dwell on the latent perversity of the pupils' sexuality and not on the narrative. In the book there is a cursory mention of a 'padded horizontal board fitted with leather straps, on which the child Sara, continually in trouble for stooping, was to pass the gymnasium hour this afternoon' (Lindsay 1968: 131). Although bizarre, this is not presented as a sadistic instrument of torture, which is roughly in keeping with the times, as such correctional contraptions were, in 1900, considered old-fashioned but not perverse. In the film, however, the treatment of Sara is overloaded with perversity, and the shame of the teacher who has administered this punishment is likewise underlined, as she guiltily cowers behind a chair when Mademoiselle and Irma interrupt the dancing lesson. Identified from the start as the deviant pupil, she is systematically, though subtly, punished throughout the film. Because, it is insinuated, Sara is in love with Miranda, she is not allowed on the picnic, she is prevented from reading out one of her love poems and now she is strapped up.

Of persistent interest to historians has been the gender and identity of the addressee of the nineteenth-century fetish correspondences. Was it, perhaps, men who got a sexual kick out of hearing about and disapproving of women tight-lacing or whipping their horses? A similar ambiguity resides in *Picnic at Hanging Rock*. Whereas Sara can be likened to the problematic, sexually active girls who discovered devious means to practice auto-eroticism and thus implicitly deny the importance to their sexual development of the male, Irma, it is made clear, survives the tragedy of St Valentine's day to enter into an exclusively heterosexual womanhood. Whilst it is titillatingly confirmed that she, the only girl to be found alive, is sexually 'quite intact' and only superficially injured, Irma was discovered on the rock clothed but minus her corset. Kunzle quotes an Australian poem of 1890 telling of an adolescent girl who equates the pain of love with the pain of wearing a corset, and who, on the threshold of marriage, summons the 'iron-clad corset, as befits the chaste woman' asking for her companion to 'pull and heave on the laces, that the bridally enhanced body be truly ethereal'.[5] If the painful corset is a sign of virtue and maturity, it is little wonder that the fully recovered Irma (the problematic goings-on with her corset having represented her rite of passage) should return once more to Appleyard College dressed in an intensely adult scarlet cape and feathered hat, visually differentiated from the other school-girls still clothed in virginal white by colour and an ostentatiously adult hour-glass figure.

The most categorical example of the female functioning in *Picnic at Hanging Rock* to provoke both diegetic and extra-diegetic male desire is the aptly named Miranda. As she disappears up the rock she waves back at the French mistress who remarks, looking down at a reproduction in her art history book, 'now I know that Miranda is a Botticelli angel' (Figure 19.1). Thus identified with an imaginary, idealized vision of beauty, Miranda becomes the film's ultimate, mysterious fetish. The film cements this through the repeated use of a slow motion image of Miranda waving to mademoiselle (and, by implication, the adoring enraptured spectator) before turning away and disappearing forever. As *Picnic at Hanging Rock* uses clothes as one of the ways of differentiating between the girls who are on the brink of womanhood and those who are not, so it clearly demarcates the masculine and the feminine. It could be argued that, with so many women looking admiringly at Miranda, this is a film that throws into question the assertion that the active erotic gaze is necessarily male. Likewise, if one takes into account the possibility that pain can be pleasurable, there is also the subversive suggestion that women can derive fetishistic enjoyment from such oppression. It is primarily the characterization of the two adolescent males Michael and Bertie (likewise on the cusp of adulthood) that counters such a positive feminist reading. As mentioned earlier, in costume films interested in fetishism, distance and gap is significant to the relationship between clothes and desire. A film such as *Picnic at Hanging Rock* creates a mysterious, sexual world based on several enforced but never coherently explained oppositions: between clothes and bodies, spectator and narrative, people and landscape, desire and sex, male and female. Sexual difference is even represented through the use of two distinct types of music: a whimsical, feminine and indeterminate pan pipe tune for the girls, and a strident, soaring track which builds to a definite crescendo for the boys. Distance is the basis for fetishistic fantasy, perpetually denying and affirming the underlying desires through an elaborate interplay between metaphor, metonym and sexual object. The fetishist's ultimate fantasy (even if it may be Freud's) is not

Figure 19.1   Miranda (Anne Lambert) emerging from a rock in *Picnic at Hanging Rock*. Courtesy of BFI Stills, Posters and Designs.

to dispense with the fetish and unravel the mystery, but to retain (and perhaps embellish) the ambiguity. We do not wish Miranda to be explained, she is a shared fetish, the figure onto which our desires are projected. She, like the ever-veiled phallus, remains beautiful by virtue of being unfound and unexplained.

In *Picnic at Hanging Rock* such fetishistic ambiguity is expressed via the pleasure/pain dynamic as it pertains to the significant males in the film, the spectator and the eroticised clothes. Michael, an English gentleman staying with his uncle and aunt, never meets but falls deeply in love with Miranda after seeing her only once. In one of the film's 'male-bonding' scenes Michael and Bertie, a servant, watch the four girls heading for Hanging Rock cross a stream, their white dresses gleaming in the sun. Whilst Bertie makes crude comments about their legs and hour-glass figures, Michael becomes painfully smitten, haunted by the frozen image of Miranda, an image that the spectator, once again, is given in softened, slow close-up. Michael's obsession with the film's unobtainable (and hence perfect) object is for him tortuous, for us titillating, an ambivalence exemplified by his return to the rock, in a last desperate attempt to find Miranda. Throughout *Picnic at Hanging Rock* the language of desire has been the language of clothes, and in Michael's actions the transferral of attention from actual femininity to unsuitable substitutes for the sexual object is complete. In another show of male camaraderie, Bertie discovers Michael, after his night-time search of Hanging Rock for the lost girls, slumped in a catatonic trance. As the masculine music soars Michael, now transferred to the back of a buggy, holds out his trembling clenched fist towards Bertie who wrests from it a tiny scrap of lace (an exchange again not in the book). We are subsequently shown, in close-up, the frail piece of material nestling in Bertie's palm, its delicacy and white-ness symbolically contrasted with his soiled, rough skin. Without having it explained why, this improbable bit of insubstantiality is, ultimately, what propelled Michael into his catatonia, what leads Bertie to find Irma and what must suffice as the film's symbol for the impene-trable mystery of what occurred on the rock. In such a hyperbolic and hysterical film the absent object remains tantalisingly opaque, nearly sending Michael mad, but serving to preserve the spectator's fantasy of enigmatic femininity 'perfectly intact'. what has been created here is an exclusively male fantasy in which representation, symbolism and narrative converge to evoke the (adolescent) male obsession with the female sexual object. The female is both central and absent, 'the enigma the hieroglyphic, the picture, the image' (Doane 1991: 18). The only viable position for the female spectator is as an enigma-identifier; to desire to be the absented object with whom everyone is infatuated: in short, to desire to be the fetish.

Rather than being primarily an example of fetishistic behaviour as *Picnic* to a certain extent is, *The Age of Innocence*, in its treatment of the image as well as the narrative, is a total fetishis-tic experience. The absenting of particularly women's sexuality and desire is the mainstay of melodramatic romanticism, making the entire film-watching experience into a deeply fetishis-tic enterprise. Melodramas of necessity manipulate detail, visual style and music to convey emo-tions the characters are not permitted to express, thus films such as Ophuls' *Letter From an Unknown Woman*, Sirk's *All That Heaven Allows* and Scorsese's *The Age of Innocence* (which, the director readily acknowledges, is indebted to the sumptuous though claustrophobic melodra-matic tradition [Christie 1994: 10–15]) become fetish objects in themselves. *The Age of Innocence* is the clearest example to date of Scorsese's fetishisation of cinema history. Technically the film has several past reference points: there's some of the 'romance and tragedy' of Ophuls' cam-era, some 'pure Eisenstein stuff' in the editing, and the Soviet technique of using shade and light to focus on the important part of an image. There is also the conscious involvement of some of the most experienced cinematic craftspeople, such as Saul and Elaine Bass who had been design-ing title and credit sequences for over forty years, and Elmer Bernstein who wrote 'the closest to a traditional Hollywood score I have ever worked with' (Christie 1994: 14). Melodramas are narratives of allusion, Ophuls' romantic tracks, cranes and pans, for example, bearing contra-dictory functions: to create a point of identification with the characters' emotions whilst at the same time substituting for them and signalling their repression. The intensity of the desire is deflected onto the film image itself, and is eloquently understood through distance not close-ness. *The Age of Innocence* is likewise about gaps and lack. Newland Archer (the film's – although not the book's – undoubted subject) falls in love with the married but estranged Countess Ellen Olenska whilst he is engaged to her cousin May Welland. Social convention bars Newland from marrying Ellen, so he weds May. The essence of melodrama is that being in a perpetual state of loss and longing is a more delicious experience than consummation, a tantalisingly torn state preserved in *The Age of Innocence* largely through Michael Ballhaus' camera and lighting and Thelma Schoonmaker's editing; so just as Newland at the end wants to hold onto his idealised image of Ellen rather than see her again, we are fulfilled by the sensuality of the film, its roam-ing camera and slow dissolves. Because the ultimate object remains obscured and so much is left understated, fetishism also dictates that part of the enjoyment of reading or watching a piece of period romanticism is filling in the blanks. Again Scorsese uses a lush filmic style to do this, as in the instances when measured costume drama sequences dissolve into violent red or yellow that engulf the whole screen; sudden eruptions of passion and desire that, as they are flaunted, become just as rapidly repressed.

This degree of image fetishism is carried over into the narrative and *mise-en-scène*, as *The Age of Innocence* is built around detail. Most of Scorsese's films are obsessed with ritual and social codes, with how his male characters particularly perceive themselves to be defined (and confined) by their environments. It is the gap between reality and expectation that, in films like *Taxi Driver* and *Raging Bull*, prompts the extreme physical outbursts of Travis Bickle or Jake La Motta. In *The Age of Innocence* a comparable pain is evoked by an accentuation rather than diminution of the formalities and social niceties. The presentation and precision of the rituals that dominate 1870s upper-class New York society become, in Scorsese's adaptation, tempting cinematic renditions of Freud's notion of fetishistic disavowal, in particular the repeated ritual of dining. However tantalizing and excessive the food, no sooner does the ornate course appear on the table than it dissolves elegantly, effortlessly into the next, seldom to be consumed and never to be enjoyed. The one dinner that is seen be consumed (at Archer's family home) is, significantly, a badly cooked test of endurance. Whereas one's suspicions about fetishism and eroticism in *Picnic at Hanging Rock* might be that it is really a case of 'The Emperor's New Clothes' in which a fascination with costume betrays a fascination with emptiness, *The Age of Innocence* is more grandiloquently poignant in this respect, as the details are the brittle surface which both suppress and convey emotion. As Edith Wharton puts it in the original novel, 'They all lived in hieroglyphic world, where the real thing was never said or done or even thought, but only represented by a set of arbitrary signs' (Wharton 1920: 55). The pleasure in the text is being able to read those signs, to feel the intensity of the suppressed instinct conveyed through the many closely observed, ritualistic actions the adaptation focuses on such as letters being passed, cigars being clipped or hands being slipped into gloves. The potency of the metaphoric language is that the spectator is both aware that such actions and objects possess a significance beyond themselves and their immediate function, but ultimately excluded from their exact, codified meaning. This equivocal function of the imaginary sign is prominent in *The Age of Innocence*'s use of costume detail, most notably the clothes of the ostensibly transparent, straightforward May. When identifying with Newland's patronizing gaze (as we are constrained to be at the Beaufort Ball at which May announces their engagement), May is presented as an innocent cocooned in lace, muslin and organza against a complex world. There are, however, moments when costume detail is employed to suggest May's disguised strength, for example when she triumphantly manoeuvres her heavy train out of the door, having told Newland she is pregnant and thus thwarting his desire to elope with Ellen. Here, May's bustle-encased lower body, as Pam Cook implies, could be seen to function as a 'powerful image of male terror in the face of the maternal body' (Cook 1994: 46). A far less comprehensible – but more evocative and sensual – use of May's clothes as signifiers occurs when the delicate fibres of her lace-encrusted summer dress are punctured by the point of the pin she has been given for winning the archery competition. The penetration of the strands of cloth function as an abstracted image of repressed violence.

The past is made strange in *The Age of Innocence* through an obsessive attention to minutiae and authenticity, as if the spectator has been invited to observe the meticulous dissection of late nineteenth-century manners, cuisine, and clothes in order to both revel in them and recognise their role as signifiers of that society's extreme superficiality. The fetishised object thus simultaneously represses and renders visible the implied desire. As Scorsese comments about Wharton's technique, 'what seems to be description is in fact a clear picture of that culture built up block by block – through every plate and glass and piece of silverware, all the sofas and what's on them' (Christie 1994: 12). The notion of re-examining the past through the present is important to all the films being discussed in this chapter (an awareness, perhaps of differentiation is central to their fetishisation of that past), and this is the case on several levels in *The Age of Innocence*. Both Wharton and Sorcsese are outsiders looking in. Wharton had gone into exile in Europe and wrote the novel in 1920 about the 1870s New York of her childhood, and Scorsese, from a background far removed from that of the characters, had never before attempted a straight costume drama. This juxtaposition between old and new informs the film, and the primary site on which we see the tension being acted out is Gabriella Pescucci's luxurious costumes. A scene such as the one in which Newland kneels down to kiss Ellen's embroidered shoe exemplifies the film's preoccupation with making the codes of the past strange As it exists in the novel, Newland's gesture of suddenly stooping to kiss the 'tip of the satin shoe that showed under her dress' is odd but engagingly impulsive (Wharton 1920: 156). There exists, however, a chasm between imagination and realisation, and as a described passage in a book, Newland's arcane kiss can be freely imbued with whatever abstract desire the reader likes. The representation of the scene in the film is obviously less suggestive and more concrete, and the spectator is constrained to acknowledge the strangeness of the past, compelled to confront the outmoded awkwardness of the gesture rather than fantasise it into romantic abstraction.

Newland kissing Ellen's shoe offers an analysis of fetishism (its reality, its mechanics) rather than an immersion in its implied eroticism, and in its oddity the scene is illustrative of the fundamental distance between Scorsese and his subject matter. This is an audacious scene that does not comfort us with a bygone universal romanticism (where the dress is different but the language of love remains the same), but rather confronts us with a form of expression so outmoded that it is almost embarrassing to observe. Although the most obvious thing to say about *The Age of Innocence* is that it is a love story (and in that respect universal), Scorsese's adaptation focuses resolutely on the unsuitable object. The film's use of melodramatic excess highlights the painful loss and absence of what could so easily have been. Whilst the fetishism in *Picnic at Hanging Rock* is titillating and somehow a substitute for empty fantasy, in the *Age of Innocence* it is resonant with the sense that, at another time, distance would not have been necessary. In the back of a carriage from the station Newland and Ellen snatch two precious hours together; he passionately unbuttons her glove and kisses her exposed wrist, an action that is filmed with the same slow, sensuous dissolves as is much of the would-be love story (Figure 19.2). The pity is unbearable: pulling all the stops out for *this*?

Picnic at Hanging Rock and *The Piano* both imply that restrictiveness can be exciting. *The Age of Innocence* suggests that living by a strict nineteenth-century code can only be stultifying. Newland Archer is immured by the conventions that surround him, symbolised to an extent by the monotonous uniformity of his clothes. This is very much Scorsese's take on Wharton who is more resolutely critical of her protagonist, portraying him as complicit in his entrapment and not purely a victim of circumstance. At first Newland appears oblivious to the weight of convention, a lack of awareness delicately signalled during the second sequence (the Beaufort Ball) by the table of neatly laid out and labelled white evening gloves to which he blithely adds his own. Men are defined through their conformity and Newland, before he falls in love with Ellen, is quite content to comply. As the film progresses the distanciation between masculine conventionality and Archer's desire increases, until he is smothered rather than complemented by the formality of his heavy, layered clothes. One sequence evokes with particular poignancy the repression of male individuality by conformity. After Newland and Ellen have managed a brief meeting they part, the camera (carrying the inevitability of distance)

Figure 19.2 Michelle Pfeiffer and Daniel Day Lewis in *The Age of Innocence*. Courtesy of BFI Stills, Posters and Designs.

retreating cruelly from Ellen with every jump cut.[6] This snatched moment is the prelude to a scene that at first appears to possess no direct narrative function, and indeed is not in the book. In slow motion a sea of grey-suited men walk towards the camera accompanied by Michael William Both's melancholy song 'Marble Halls' ('But I also dreamt which charmed me most/That you loved me still the same'), all clutching identical bowler hats threatened by the battering wind. Although Newland then emerges from the crowd holding tightly onto his bowler, so linking this scene with the narrative proper, the potency of this image is that it can remain an abstract metaphor for fearful, unthinking male conformity, 'the conformity of men who've learnt to keep it all under their hats' (Taubin 1993: 8). Like the sudden, violent bursts of screen-drowning colour or the involuntary moan Newland emits in the previous scene as Ellen touches his hand, desire throughout *The Age of Innocence* is fleetingly permitted to surface in order to be instantly bottled up under hats and under convention

The representation of Newland Archer suggests that sartorial conformity corresponds to emotional repression, that he can be 'read' through his clothes. In one of the most influential accounts of how masculinity has been expressed through clothes, Flügel described what he termed 'The Great Masculine Renunciation', when 'Man abandoned his claim to be considered beautiful' (Flügel 1930: 111). The argument posited by Flügel for men's clothes becoming utilitarian, austere and uniform in the nineteenth century is increased democratization since the French Revolution, 'the fact that the ideal of work had now become respectable' (Flügel 1930: 112) and thus that man was, as a result, defined more by his social than his personal role. Flügel then conflates sartorial and psychological changes in a significant statement about how the masculine ideal is symbolized by physical appearance, commenting:

> It is, indeed, safe to say that, in sartorial matters, modern man has a far sterner and more rigid conscience than has modern women, and that man's morality tends to find expression in his clothes . . . modern man's clothing abounds in features which symbolize his devotion to the principles of duty, of renunciation and of self-control. The whole relatively 'fixed' system of his clothing is, in fact, an outward and visible sign of the strictness of his adherence to the social code.
>
> (Flügel 1930: 113)

Newland Archer has bought into this code of denial and fraternity: he works as a lawyer and wears his bowler hat. But just as the attention on obsessively researched surface details in *The Age of Innocence* serves to deflect attention onto what is *not* visible, so Newland's renunciatory stiffness serves to accentuate his potential for passion (Figure 19.3).

The romantic necessity of unfulfilment is expressed verbally by Countess Olenska in the shoe-kissing scene when she says 'I can't love you unless I give you up', but it is evoked filmically through the subjectification of Archer who, right at the end when he is offered the chance to see Ellen again, declines to meet her and bridge the gap between imagination and reality. As with every act of fetishism, distance preserves the mystery. So Newland would rather imagine the past Ellen than meet the present one, and as he closes his eyes a rapid montage culminating in the Ellen he remembers turning round and smiling at him flashes across the screen. Archer is playing a game with himself which he's played before: if she turns around he will go to meet her; if she does not, he will walk on by. As Amy Taubin suggests, *The Age of Innocence* is about 'the suffocating anxiety of waiting for the sign on which one believes one's life depends, wanting it to come and at the same time fearing it' (Taubin 1993: 9). Fetishism keeps the danger of change at bay.

Both *Picnic at Hanging Rock* and *The Age of Innocence* make use of the fetishistic transferral of desire for the woman onto her clothes as both the symbols and the masking agents for this fear of change. In this they are both masculine films, although *The Age of Innocence* is self-reflective in its representation of fetishism, as if offering a commentary on its peculiarity. Primarily through their portrayal of the male characters, both films emphasize the significance (if a safe conventionalism is to be maintained) of distance, the clothes and narrative separations functioning effectively as barriers. Newland Archer realizes his loss, but Michael in *Picnic at Hanging Rock* is an exemplary pathological, Freudian fetishist who keeps a voyeuristic distance between himself and Miranda.[7] Freud comments in 'Touching and Looking' that '[t]he progressive concealment of the body which goes along with civilization keeps sexual curiosity awake', and that a 'normal' endeavour would be to 'complete the sexual object by revealing its hidden parts' (Freud 1905: 69). Clearly Michael cannot go beyond scopophilia and so is exclusively confined to fetishising his fantasized object-choice.

Figure 19.3   Daniel Day Lewis as Newland in *The Age of Innocence*. Courtesy of BFI Stills, Posters and Designs.

If the man cannot (or does not want to) go beyond the level of civilised concealment, the woman inevitably becomes the passive representation of his active sexuality. A playful example of this imbalance can be found in the verses to Julia by the seventeenth-century poet and priest Robert Herrick. His poems convincingly posit the notion that distance is more erotic than closeness, and emphasise the attraction rather than the sadness of over-valuing the inappropriate substitute for the sexual object. Even in a poem such as 'The Nightpiece, To Julia', in which Herrick finally imagines a union with his ideal love, his focus are her what Freud would term 'unsuitable' feet:

> Then Julia let me woo thee,
> Thus, thus to come unto me;
> And when I shall meet
> Thy silvery feet,
> My soul I'll pour into thee.
>   (Fowler 1991: 275)

Herrick suggests that conventional consummation is not so devoutly to be wished after all, as his verse resonates with a desire for an image of woman so objectified that the mythic Julia's identity is lost beneath 'that liquefaction of her clothes' (Fowler 1991: 276). Julia's clothes are not substitutes for her absent body but signifiers of Herrick's desire. 'Delight in Disorder' conveys the intensity of Herrick's imaginatively active though repressed sexual longings through the freedom and immorality granted the clothes not the completely absented muse, as it is the dress that possesses a 'sweet disorder', the lace is 'erring', the cuff 'neglectful', the petticoat 'tempestuous' and the shoestring 'careless' (Fowler 1991: 257–8). Needless to say Herrick never gets his Julia, but the suspicion is that he is quite satisfied with observing her mischievous clothes. As he writes in 'Art above nature: To Julia' after praising again the tempting 'wild civility' of her appearance:

> I must confess, mine eye and heart
> Dote less on nature, than on art.
>   (Fowler 1991: 274)

There is a sense, therefore, that Herrick is not just making do with the glittering and the vibration of Julia's clothes, but that his erotic gaze wants to be fixed on them. It is mistaken to hold, as Steele does, that, despite everything, it is Julia and not her clothes that are Herrick's true object-choice. Steele maintains, with reference to Herrick's Julia poems, that 'the desire for the body can be partially transferred onto clothes, which then provide an additional erotic charge of their own. But ultimately it is the wearer who is 'sweet' and 'wanton' (Steele 1985: 42). Julia is a muse, an impossible, unattainable ideal, and so her clothes and not her are the substitute phallus; they are what the poet desires – and what he makes his reader desire.

Flügel concludes his section on 'The Great Masculine Renunciation and its Causes' with the observation that

> in the case of the exhibitionistic desires connected with self-display, a particularly easy form of conversion may be found in a change from (passive) exhibitionism to (active) scoptophilia (erotic pleasure in the use of vision) – the desire to be seen being transformed into the desire to see.
>
>   (Flügel 1930: 118)

And so the man does not renounce his exhibitionism at all but experiences the pleasures of 'vicarious display' (Flügel 1930: 118) through the desired woman, an active, is displaced, sexuality very apparent in Herrick's verse. In this belief, Flügel is in agreement with Darwin when he comments in *The Descent of Man* that, 'In civilised life man is largely, but by no means exclusively, influenced in the choice of his wife by external appearance' (Darwin 1871: 873). The sexual effect of display has thus been transferred to the woman. What occurs in *The Piano* in terms of fetishism (a clear indication that this film is in part a critique of both Victorian sexuality and the manner in which it has been interpreted by Flügel, Freud and others) is less to do with elaborate distanciation manoeuvres, and more to do with expressing direct desire and trying to have sex. This seems to be the intention behind the many archetypes and stereotypes that are reconsidered through the narrative in which Ada, a mute Scottish woman, has been packed off to New Zealand with her daughter Flora to marry a local landowner Stewart, but instead falls for his neighbour, George Baines. Whilst giving him piano lessons and winning back her instrument, Ada enters into an elaborate striptease whereby she exchanges and removes items of clothing in return for keys. In its re-examination of voyeurism, fetishism, striptease and hysteria, *The Piano* adopts clothes and their relationship to sexuality and the body as primary signifiers. There is a matter-of-factness in the clothes-dialogues between Ada and Baines that indicates any fetishism in this film is fetishism as a means to an end, namely intercourse. Campion herself has commented on being able to explore the physical side of a relationship in a way that Emily Brontë, for example, could not, and of being able, in the 1990s, to be 'a lot more investigative of the power of eroticism' (Campion 1993: 6). *The Piano*'s complex sensuality is informed by this eclecticism, being in several ways a re-examination of and a counter-argument to the conventional views of nineteenth-century sexuality. The film is deeply methodical in this respect, taking traditional mechanisms of desire and modes of articulation in order to question and subvert them, and, essentially, to give twentieth-century feminism a voice in situations where in the past such an intervention has not occurred.

The potential sexuality and sensuality of clothes is overtly explored in *The Piano*, as both costume and the body appear linked in this film to a complex feminist displacement of the conventionalised objectification of the woman's form via scopophilia and fetishism. It is not only Ada who is caught up in this radical exploration, although her fierce independence is essentially manifested by her repeated refusal to conform to the designated role of the pacified and distanced image of woman contained by the voyeuristic male gaze. This is where Stewart would have her, but the film strips him of this traditional power by refusing to align his look as the on-screen voyeur with ours. *The Piano* offers, in its representation of Stewart, a feminist recontextualization of Flügel. It is almost as if Stewart deliberately conforms to the ideas (or ideals) of The Great Masculine Renunciation. He is the archetypal nineteenth-century colonial husband bound by a burdensome sense of his position within patriarchal history, a character who is socially defined, obsessively aware (but not in control) of his territory, his whiteness and his role as head of the household. The problem is that Stewart inhabits a feminized not a Darwinian world to which he cannot see how to adapt because it is so manifestly correlated with Ada, his transgressive wife who creates alternative discursive strategies to counter his intended sub-jugation of her. Voyeurism, for example, as it is presented within the narrative, is not a pleasur-ably active pursuit but one born out of desperation and isolation. Stewart is forever (comically at times) portrayed as the outsider, isolated within a feminist framework by his dependency on scopophilia. He is consistently identified with an act of looking that is estranged rather than normative; squinting through a camera lens, or spying on Ada and Baines having sex through cracks in the timber and the floorboards. He is thus emasculated rather than empowered by his possession of (only) the look, as the tropes of traditional masculinity are gradually ridiculed. The misguidedness of Stewart's unthinking appropriation of convention is neatly illustrated in his costumes, which Janet Patterson deliberately made too small for Sam Neill 'to make him look uncomfortably uptight', adding that 'particularly in the scene when he first goes to meet Ada, his clothes are not a good fit' (Patterson 1993: 9). That the representation of Stewart is ironic is established in the opening sequence in which he checks his reflection and clumsily flattens his hair before meeting Ada for the first time. The would-be patriarch is the film's outsider looking in, being mimicked by his Maori helpers strutting around in top hats calling him 'dry balls'.

Stewart's masculine counterpart is Baines who, having discarded the ideology and the clothes of the European colonialist, has 'gone native'. This, again, is an example of *The Piano* intentionally bringing a 1990s consciousness to bear on a nineteenth-century narrative. Whereas Stewart is dressed in the monochrome uniform of repression, Baines formed a strong relation-ship with the Maoris and appropriated a look which closely resembles theirs. There is an easiness about Baines, illustrated by the rich blue dyes, thick weave and authentic whale-bone buttons of his costume, and the Maori-esque markings on his face.[8] Baines symbolizes the presence of the dangerous, erotic Other, the force that in the context of traditional repression narratives conventionally remains implied but concealed. A significant precursor to Baines is the man influenced by the wayward gypsy figure in several 1940s melodramas such as *Jassy*, *Blanch Fury* or the quasi-melodrama *Duel in the Sun*. The dangerous sexuality of Gregory Peck in *Duel in the Sun* or Stewart Granger in *Blanche Fury* is signalled through their ostentatious adoption of a gypsi-fied look. Thus Granger's wearing of a red polka-dot neckerchief he had brought from a gypsy woman becomes a metonym for his rebellion against social and sexual norms. These, of course, are the men both the female characters and the audience are attracted to and identify with, in part because sexual, erotic clothes are conventionally viewed as feminine. In the terms adopted by Flügel, Baines has reclaimed 'the principle of erotic exposure' (Flügel 1930: 110–11), appar-ently (by the 1850s) the sole prerogative of women, and revived male narcissism. Whereas the conventionalised interpretation of gender difference, as it has impinged on dress and physical appearance, is of the woman as object of display onto whom subjective male sexuality has been displaced, in *The Piano* the power relationship is inverted, as it is Baines who first presents himself naked to Ada thus, peacock-like, putting himself on display. In his appearance, Baines, with his Maori tattoos, hybrid clothes and unkempt hair, repeatedly functions to confront Stewart not with his supremacy but his lack.

Stewart's lack is further accentuated by his exclusion from sex, the gender conventions again being subverted to enforce this are grounded in the film's use of clothes as ambiguous signifiers for femininity. Ada's oppressive and austere Victorian costumes are made to func-tion both for and against her, and are both internal and external signifiers of her desire and her social position. The most poetic example of this is the final, perplexing image of the drowned Ada tied to her piano, encased in her billowing skirts.[9] Dressed largely in black with an austerely authentic lampshade bonnet, Ada superficially embodies the archetypal nineteenth-century wife. James Laver, for example, declares the mid-nineteenth-century bonnet to be 'a sign of submission to male authority' (Laver 1969: 123). Unlike Baines, however, who does not keep his radicalism under his hat, Ada (via her conventionality) embodies the poten-tial of clothes as an oppositional discourse not reliant for signification (even though a positive appropriation of difference) on any pre-established patriarchal models. The complexity of this situation is captured in the juxtapositional image of Ada posing for wedding photographs in a dress she has simply flung over her day clothes, without even attempting to fasten the back. The sartorial collisions here signal her clear rebellion against her designated position.

A similar duality informs the representation of clothes elsewhere in *The Piano*, for example Ada's cumbersome crinoline that both constricts her movements (as when she is negotiating the New Zealand mud) and works in support of her (as when it prevents Stewart from raping her). Clothes in *The Piano* function as discursive strategies for talking about sex, gender and the existence of desire underneath the veneer of conformity. In this the film's use of costume is reminiscent of Michel Foucault's analysis of sex and the expression of sexuality in *The History of Sexuality*. Foucault offers a revolutionary thesis for understanding the outcome of adminis-tered censorship of the articulation of desire from the eighteenth century onwards. Far from imposing censorship as the authorities had assumed, the measures that were brought in to prohibit sex and curtail the public acknowledgement of it brought into being 'an apparatus for producing an even greater quantity of discourse about sex' (Foucault 1976: 4–5). Sex was thus 'driven out of hiding and constrained to lead a discursive existence' (33), and although western laws of prohibition were enforced, they had the contradictory effect of drawing 'Western man . . . to the task of telling everything concerning his sex' (23). Silence, as Foucault maintains, is not 'the absolute limit of discourse' as there is no 'binary division to be made between what one says and what one does not say' (27). Instead, the discursive exis-tence of sex led to the teasing paradox that, in striving to consign sex 'to a shadow existence', modern societies 'dedicated themselves to speaking of it *ad infinitum*, while exploiting it as

FIGURE 19.4 Holly Hunter and Maori women in *The Piano*. Courtesy of Ronald Grant Archive.

the secret (35). The dialectic between intention and this 'putting into discourse of sex' (12) is given narrative representation in *The Piano*. Stewart, in an attempt to deny sex, attempts to repress Flora's sexuality by making her scrub down the tree trunks she (following the more expressive Maoris) has been rubbing herself against; whilst Ada and Baines, in defiance of such social regulation, evolve a sexual 'clothes language' that transgresses the presumed boundary between silence and discourse.

The eroticism of striptease, which plays on the proximity and difference between clothes and the body, has seldom been disputed; as one writer on fetishism puts it, 'the moment we invented clothing we also invented the possibility of striptease' (Brand 1970: 19). In this nineteenth-century context, the clandestine dialogue between Ada and Baines is a case of the putting into discourse of sex. Rather than repressing or camouflaging sex, the oppressive Victorian clothes become the very agents through which desire is made possible. Unlike either *Picnic at Hanging Rock* or *The Age of Innocence* in which similarly prohibitive costumes substitute the unobtainable sexual object and signal its absence, in *The Piano* (and Freud would have approved) they and their fetishistic potential act as preludes to the consummation that does occur. More so than the other films (excepting the wrist-kissing scene in *The Age of Innocence*) the fetishistic emphasis in the Ada/Baines exchanges is on the juxtaposition of clothes and body. The forbidding Victorian woman's garments become elaborate mechanisms for getting closer to her, as when Baines, crouching under the piano, raises Ada's hoops and feels with his rough fingertip the spot of flesh exposed by a hole in her worsted stocking. If such contact was simply initiated by the man this would indeed remain a rather artful but traditional striptease, but the woman's active participation in this clothes dialogue is what renders it unconventional. The striptease sequences in *The Piano* conform to how several writers have viewed female fetishism as more interested in forging links between the fetish and the desired sexual object. Brand, for example, in reference to a case from the 1890s in which a widow became fixated on her dead husband's gloves, comments that the direct association between the fetish and the desired (in this instance) man 'is typical of the female psyche which tends always to fix on one person and for whom sexual symbols are relatively unimportant save in their ability to bring the lover closer' (Brand 1970: 67).[10]

The Piano, enforcing a simple inversion of the normative process, addresses the question of what happens when the agent of the gaze is female and its object is the male body. It is in the film's representation of Ada's desire that *The Piano* adopts comparably fetishistic stylistic techniques to *The Age of Innocence*, notably the use of luscious golden light and fluid camera movements for the sequences that focus on the bodies of both Stewart and Baines. There are two such scenes in *The Piano* which most notably demonstrate female desire of the male body (for the film is unquestioningly heterosexual) and the subsequent feminisation of that body as the conventional scopophilic roles are reversed. One positions Ada as the subject of the eroticizing gaze and shows her stroking Stewart's body as he lies half asleep. The contextualization of this action emphasises, on a literal level, Ada's control over Stewart. The exchange also carries the more abstract connotation that Ada, through her relationship with Baines, has discovered an attraction for the male body. An example of the reversal of the traditional voyeuristic dynamic in which the intermediary figure of Ada is dispensed with occurs as the naked Baines is presented dusting and caressing the piano (which is, by its direct association with her, a fetish substitute for Ada). This image of the private, naked Baines who is classically unaware of being looked at, directly confronts the spectator-voyeur with an unconventional representation of masculinity as the object of the female gaze. Baines (in what is a feminist inversion of Laura Mulvey's theorisation of the voyeur/object male/female relationship) is placed 'in direct erotic rapport with the (implicitly female) spectator' (Mulvey 1975: 311). For most of the film Stewart and Baines are oppositional images constructed as the expressions of Ada's desire; the sensualization of Stewart's body is, therefore, unexpected because it uses many of the same features as the scenes between Ada and Baines, most notably the erotic play between garments and exposed flesh. Furthermore, Stewart's nakedness, like Baines's, is bathed in a lusciously sensuous orange light. *The Piano*, particularly in the two scenes in which Ada caresses Stewart,[11] has set down a radical challenge to the normative gender organisation exemplified by *Picnic at Hanging Rock*.

As Ada is demonstrably capable of fetishism and of possessing the active, scopophilic gaze the traditional paradigms with which the discussion of fetishism and *Picnic at Hanging Rock* started need to be reassessed. A demonstrable piece of women's cinema such as *The Piano* (Campion herself eschews the attribution 'feminist') challenges the conventional male assumptions about fetishism as articulated by Freud and psychologists such as Flügel and Krafft-Ebing who developed and extended his ideas. Freud's understanding of fetishism was motivated by a desire to explicate male sexuality, and as such saw women as passive fetish objects who stood for and expressed a libido which was exclusively male. Peter Weir's *Picnic at Hanging Rock* is a male fantasy which continues this patriarchal tradition in which Miranda and the other girls are the eroticised substitutes for the veiled phallus. This view of fetishism as pertaining only to the active male sexual drive is questioned by a fashion commentator such as Kunzle who, in his discussion of the secret dialogues between women concerning tight-lacing, refutes the belief that women are not fetishists. If one further links Kunzle's argument to that posited by Foucault in *A History of Sexuality*, then the possibility of clothes as sexual discourse becomes solidified. Such a discourse is predominantly aligned with a female sexuality and point of identification, as official histories of sexuality have tended to disregard active, feminine eroticism and to likewise view women's clothes as representative of a passive, repressed pattern of desire. Gamman and Makinen, for instance, question the statistical evidence (used by Freud, Krafft-Ebing and others) which suggests that women are not active fetishists, asking '[c]ould the importance that is attributed to fetishism be because it is located so firmly on the protection and valorisation of the phallus?'

(Gamman and Makinen 1994: 103). From a feminist perspective, Gamman and Makinen counter Freud's theory that a fetish is the substitute for the mother's castrated penis, although, as I have indicated, his model holds true for certain male-orientated fantasies such as *Picnic as Hanging Rock*.

The sexualization of costume, from 1940s historical melodramas to *The Piano*, similarly stems from an acknowledgement that such a pattern of female fetishism exists and can be articulated. In a broader sense, however, all three films discussed in this chapter respond positively to fetishism because of its inherent, complex ambiguity. The attraction for Wharton (and Scorsese after her), for example, is towards distance, difference and the simultaneous avowal and disavowal of eroticism. The overriding preoccupation with detail in *The Age of Innocence* derives from a fascination with the power of displacement and metaphor, and the concomitant emphasis on what is left unstated rather than what is stated. In *Harper's Bazaar* Wharton once remarked:

> I have often sighed, in looking back at my childhood, how pitiful provision was made for the life of the imagination behind those uniform brown facades, and then have concluded since, for reasons which escape us, the creative mind thrives best on a reduced diet, I probably had the fare best suited to me.
>
> (Scorsese and Cocks 1993: 183)

The clothes discourse in *The Age of Innocence* and *The Piano* is reliant on the imagination, on the power of allusion over statement. In this, the use of period costume resembles the ostensibly dissimilar function of couture designs in films. Both groups of films put in place an alternative, independent dialogue between costumes and the spectator. Subsequent chapters will examine more specific ways in which such as discourse has been continued and expanded.

Notes

1 Andrew Higson, for example, notes that in the conventional heritage film 'Camerawork generally is fluid, artful and pictorialist, editing slow and undramatic. The use of long takes and deep focus, and long and medium shots rather than close-ups, produces a restrained aesthetic of display' (Higson 1996: 233–4). This sort of style is very different from the sensuous fetishism of *The Age of Innocence*.

2 *Witness* is not strictly speaking a 'costume film' in that its setting is contemporary America. But because the strict Amish sect eschew modernity and wear traditional clothes, Kelly McGillis' costume (particularly in the eyes of the 'modernized' Harrison Ford) take on a particular, archaic eroticism.

3 Sara is consistently represented as deviant: she is, for example, an orphan, poor, solitary and is clearly in love with Miranda.

4 Later on it is Edith who, refusing to climb any further, runs back down the rock screaming; another indication (if one interprets the rock as somehow related to sexual initiation) that she lacks the maturity of the others. As they approach the rock Miranda tells her fellow schoolgirls to look up at it, but Edith the unready looks down.

5 'Brattoilette', in *Wiener Caricaturen*, 22 March 1890; quoted in Kunzle 1982: 12.

6 This is the reverse of the Truffaut three-edit sequence in *Tirez sur le Pianiste* which Scorsese has said he puts into every film.

7 Freud and others have declared, for example, that male fetishists are in fact disgusted by the sight of the female sex organs, and thus want to maintain that distance. See Freud 1927.

8 Although Janet Patterson stresses the authenticity of Baines's costume she and Campion decided that his clothes should, more generally, denote an internationalism and a desire to travel (Patterson 1993 and Campion 1993: 9).

9 This shot would not have been so ambiguous if in fact Ada had died. It is her mind's fantasy of the perfect tragic (and feminine) death.

10 Brand also discusses another case from this century of a woman who uses a pair of home-made velvet underpants as a fetish, but uses them only as foreplay (113–20). For a further discussion of female fetishism see Gamman and Makinen 1994.

11 For a further discussion of the importance of touching in *The Piano* see Bruzzi 1995.

Chapter 20

TANIA MODLESKI

THE TERROR OF PLEASURE
The contemporary horror film and postmodern theory

IN THE *GRUNDRISSE*, KARL MARX'S DESCRIPTION of the capitalist as a werewolf turns into an enthusiastic endorsement of that creature's activities. Marx tells us that the capitalist's 'werewolf hunger,' which drives him continually to replace 'living labor' with 'dead labor' (that is, human beings with machines), will lead to a mode of production in which 'labour time is no longer the sole measure and source of wealth.'[1] Thus, in the words of one commentator, 'capitalism furnishes the material basis for the eventual realization of an age-old dream of humankind: the liberation from burdensome toil.'[2] Marx's critics have tended to place him in the role of mad scientist, with his vision of the miracles to be wrought by feeding the werewolf's insatiable appetite. Writers from Jacques Ellul to Isaac Balbus have argued (to mix narratives here) that allowing the capitalist his unhindered experimentation in the 'workshops of filthy creation' – his accumulation of more and more specimens of dead labor – cannot possibly provide a blessing to humankind.

These critics claim that rather than truly liberating humanity by freeing it from burdensome toil, the proliferation of dead labor – of technology – has resulted in the invasion of people's mental, moral, and emotional lives, and thus has rendered them incapable of desiring social change. To quote Jacques Ellul, who has traced the intrusion of technique into all aspects of human existence, 'as big city life became for the most part intolerable, techniques of amusement were developed. It became indispensable to make urban suffering acceptable by furnishing amusements, a necessity which was to assure the rise, for example, of a monstrous motion picture industry.'[3] In advanced capitalism, the narrative shifts, though the genre remains the same: physical freedom – that is, increased leisure time – is brought at the price of spiritual zombieism. The masses, it is said, are offered various forms of easy, false pleasure as a way of keeping them unaware of their own desperate vacuity. And so, apparently, we are caught in the toils of the great monster, mass culture, which certain critics, including some of the members of the Frankfurt School and their followers, have equated with ideology. For the Frankfurt School, in fact, mass culture effected a major transformation in the nature of ideology from Marx's time: once 'socially necessary illusion,' it has now become 'manipulative contrivance,' and its power is such that, in the sinister view of T. W. Adorno, 'conformity has replaced consciousness.'[4]

Today many people tend to believe that other, more sophisticated approaches to the issue have superseded the Frankfurt School's conception of mass culture as a monstrous and monolithic ideological machine. The work of Roland Barthes is often cited as an example of such an advance. But when Barthes offers the converse of the proposition that mass culture (for example, the cinema) is ideology and contends rather that 'ideology is the Cinema of society,' we are entitled, I think, to question just how far this removes us from many of the premises we think we have rejected.[5] Isn't Barthes here implying that both cinema and ideology, being seamless and without gaps or contradictions, create what the Frankfurt School called the 'spurious harmony' of a conformist mass society?

According to many of the members of the Frankfurt School, high art was a subversive force capable of opposing spurious harmony. On this point especially, certain contemporary theorists have disagreed. In *The Anti-Aesthetic*, a recent collection of essays on postmodern culture, the editor, Hal Foster, suggests the need to go beyond the idea of the aesthetic as a negative category, claiming that the critical importance of the notion of the aesthetic as subversive is now, 'largely illusory.'[6] However, despite such pronouncements, which are common enough in the literature of postmodernism, I believe it can be shown that many postmodernists do in fact engage in the same kind of oppositional thinking about mass culture that characterized the work of the Frankfurt School. Take, for example, Barthes' writings on pleasure. Although it is inaccurate to maintain, as critics sometimes do, that Barthes always draws a sharp distinction between pleasure and jouissance (since in *The Pleasure of the Text* Barthes straightaway denies any such strenuous opposition), whenever Barthes touches on the subject of mass culture, he is apt to draw a fairly strict line – placing pleasure on the side of the consumer, and jouissance in contrast to pleasure. Here is a remarkable passage from *The Pleasure of the Text*, in which Barthes begins by discussing the superiority of a textual reading based on disavowal and ends by casually condemning mass culture:

> Many readings are perverse, implying a split, a cleavage. Just as the child knows its mother has no penis and simultaneously believes she has one . . . so the reader can keep saying: *I know these are only words, but all the same. . . .* Of all readings that of tragedy is the most perverse: I take pleasure in hearing myself tell a story *whose end I know*: I know and I don't know, I act toward myself as though I did not know: I know perfectly well Oedipus will be unmasked, that Danton will be guillotined, *but all the same. . . .* Compared to a dramatic story, which is one whose outcome is unknown, there is here an effacement of pleasure and a progression of *jouissance* (today, in mass culture, there is an enormous consumption of 'dramatics' and little *joussiance*).[7]

Anyone who has read Christian Metz's persuasive argument that disavowal is *constitutive* of the spectator's pleasure at the cinema will find it difficult to give ready assent to Barthes' contention that mass culture deprives the consumer of this experience.[8] And anyone who is acquainted with the standardized art products – the genre and formula stories – which proliferate in a mass society will have to admit that their import depends precisely upon our suspending our certain knowledge of their outcome – for example, the knowledge that, as the critics say, the gangster 'will eventually lie dead in the streets.' Barthes' remarks are illuminating, then, not for any direct light they shed on the high/mass culture debate, but because they vividly exemplify the tendency of critics and theorists to make mass culture into the 'other' of whatever, at any given moment, they happen to be championing – and, moreover, to denigrate that other primarily because it allegedly provides pleasure to the consumer.

While Barthes' *The Pleasure of the Text* has become one of the canonical works of postmodernism, in this respect it remains caught up in older modernist ideas about art. In an essay entitled 'The Fate of Pleasure,' written in 1963, the modernist critic Lionel Trilling speculated that high art had dedicated itself to an attack on pleasure in part because pleasure was the province of mass art: 'we are repelled by the idea of an art that is consumer-oriented and comfortable, let alone luxurious.'[9] He went on to argue that, for the modernist, pleasure is associated with the 'specious good' – with bourgeois habits, manners, and morals – and he noted, 'the destruction of what is considered to be specious good is surely one of the chief literary enterprises of our age.'[10] Hence, Trilling has famously declared, aesthetic modernity is primarily adversarial in impulse.

The 'specious good,' or 'bourgeois taste,' remains an important target of contemporary thinkers, and postmodernism continues to be theorized as its adversary. Indeed, it might be argued that post-modernism is valued by many of its proponents insofar as it is considered *more* adversarial than modernism, and is seen to wage war on a greatly expanded category of the 'specious good,' which presently includes meaning (Barthes speaks of the 'regime of meaning') and even form.[11] For example, in an essay entitled 'Answering the Question: What is Postmodernism?' Jean-François Lyotard explicitly contrasts postmodernism to modernism in terms of their relation to 'pleasure.' For Lyotard, modernism's preoccupation with form meant that it was still capable of affording the reader or viewer 'matter for solace and pleasure, [whereas the postmodern is] that which denies itself the solace of good forms, the consensus of a taste which would make it possible to share collectively the nostalgia for the unattainable.'[12] It is important to recognize the extent to which Lyotard shares the same animus as the Frankfurt School, although his concern is not merely to denounce *spurious* harmony, but to attack *all* harmony – consensus, collectivity – as spurious, that is, on the side of 'cultural policy,' the aim of which is to offer the public 'well-made' and 'comforting' works of art.[13]

Although Lyotard has elsewhere informed us that 'thinking by means of oppositions does not correspond to the liveliest modes of postmodern knowledge,' he does not seem to have extricated himself entirely from this mode.[14] Pleasure (or 'comfort' or 'solace') remains the enemy for the postmodernist thinker because it is judged to be the means by which the consumer is reconciled to the prevailing cultural policy, or the 'dominant ideology.' While this view may well provide the critic with 'matter for solace and pleasure,' it is at least debatable that mass culture today is on the side of the specious good, that it offers, in the words of Matei Calinescu, 'an ideologically manipulated illusion of taste,' that it lures its audience to a false complacency with the promise of equally false and insipid pleasures.[15] Indeed, the contemporary horror film – the so-called exploitation film or slasher film – provides an interesting counterexample to such theses. Many of these films are engaged in a unprecedented assault on all that bourgeois culture is supposed to cherish – like the ideological apparatuses of the family and the school. Consider Leonard Maltin's capsule summary of an exemplary film in the genre, *The Brood*, directed by David Cronenberg and starring Samantha Eggar: 'Eggar eats her own afterbirth while midget clones beat grandparents and lovely young school teachers to death with mallets.'[16] A few of the films, like *The Texas Chainsaw Massacre*, have already been celebrated for their adversarial relation to contemporary culture and society. In this film, a family of men, driven out of the slaughterhouse business by advanced technology, turn to cannibalism. The film deals with the slaughter of a group of young people travelling in a van and dwells at great length on the pursuit of the last survivor of the group, Sally, by the man named Leatherface, who hacks his victims to death with a chainsaw. Robin Wood has analyzed the film as embodying a critique of capitalism, since the film shows the horror both of people quite literally living off other people, and of the institution of the family, since it implies that the monster is the family.[17]

In some of the films the attack on contemporary life strikingly recapitulates the very terms adopted by many culture critics. In George Romero's *Dawn of the Dead*, the plot involves zombies taking over a shopping center, a scenario depicting the worst fears of the culture critics who have long envisioned the will-less, soul-less masses as zombie-like beings possessed by the alienating imperative to consume. And in David Cronenberg's *Videodrome*, video itself becomes the monster. The film concerns a plot, emanating from Pittsburgh, to subject human beings to massive doses of a video signal which renders its victims incapable of distinguishing hallucination from reality. One of the effects of this signal on the film's hero is to cause a gaping, vagina-like wound to open in the middle of his stomach, so that the villains can program him by inserting a video cassette into his body. The hero's situation becomes that of the new schizophrenic described by Jean Baudrillard in his discussion of the effects of mass communication:

> No more hysteria, no more projective paranoia, properly speaking, but this state of terror proper to the schizophrenic: too great a proximity of everything, the unclean promiscuity of everything which touches, invests, and penetrates without resistance, with no halo of private protection, not even his own body, to protect him anymore. . . . The schizo is bereft of every scene, open to everything in spite of himself, living in the greatest confusion.[18]

'You must open yourself completely to us,' says one of *Videodrome's* villains, as he plunges the cassette into the gaping wound. It was seem that we are here very far from the realm of what is traditionally called 'pleasure' and much nearer to so-called *jouissance*, discussions of which privilege terms like 'gaps,' 'wounds,' 'fissures,' 'splits,' 'cleavages' and so forth.

Moreover, if the text is 'an anagram for our body,' as Roland Barthes maintains, the contemporary text of horror could aptly be considered an anagram for the schizophrenic's body, which is so vividly imaged in Cronenberg's film.[19] It is a ruptured body, lacking the kind of integrity commonly attributed to popular narrative cinema. For just as Baudrillard makes us aware that terms like 'paranoia' and 'hysteria,' which film critics have used to analyze both film characters and textual mechanisms, are no longer as applicable in mass culture today as they once were, so the much more global term 'narrative pleasure' is similarly becoming outmoded.

What is always at stake in discussions of 'narrative pleasure' is what many think of as the ultimate 'spurious harmony,' the supreme ideological construct – the 'bourgeois ego.' Contemporary film theorists insist that pleasure is 'ego-reinforcing' and that narrative is the primary means by which mass culture supplies and regulates this pleasure. For Stephen Heath, Hollywood narratives are versions of the nineteenth-century 'novelistic,' or 'family romance,' and their function is to 'remember the history of the individual subject' through processes of identification, through narrative continuity, and through the mechanism of closure.[20] Julia Kristeva condemns popular cinema in similar terms in her essay on terror in film, 'Ellipsis on Dread and the Specular Seduction':

> [The] terror/seduction node . . . becomes, through cinematic commerce, a kind of cut-rate seduction. One quickly pulls the veil over the terror, and only the cathartic relief remains; in mediocre potboilers, for example, in order to remain within the range of petty bourgeois taste, film plays up to narcissistic identification, and the viewer is satisfied with 'three-buck seduction.'[21]

But just as the individual and the family are *dis*-membered in the most gruesomely literal way in many of these films, so the novelistic as family romance is also in the process of being dismantled.

First, not only do the films tend to be increasingly open-ended in order to allow for the possibility of countless sequels, but they also often delight in thwarting the audiences' expectations of closure. The most famous examples of this tendency are the surprise codas of Brian de Palma's films – for instance, the hand reaching out from the grave in *Carrie*. And in *The Evil Dead*, *Halloween* and *Friday the Thirteenth*, the monsters and slashers rise and attempt to kill over and over again each time they are presumed dead. At the end of *The Evil Dead*, the monsters, after defying myriad attempts to destroy them, appear finally to be annihilated as they are burned to death in an amazing lengthy sequence. But in the last shot of the film, when the hero steps outside into the light of day, the camera rushes toward him, and he turns and faces it with an expression of horror. In the final sequence of *Halloween*, the babysitter looks at the spot where the killer was apparently slain and, finding it vacant, says, 'It really was the bogey man.'

Second – and this is the aspect most commonly discussed and deplored by popular journalists – these films tend to dispense with or drastically minimize the plot and character and development that is thought to be essential to the construction of the novelistic. In Cronenberg's *Rabid*, the porn star Marilyn Chambers plays a woman who receives a skin transplant and begins to infect everyone around her with a kind of rabies. The symptom of her disease is a vagina-like wound in her armpit out of which a phallic-shaped weapon springs to slash and mutilate its victims. While the film does have some semblance of a plot, most of it comprises disparate scenes showing Marilyn, or her victims, or her victims' victims, on the attack. Interestingly, although metonymy has been considered to be the principle by which narrative is constructed, metonymy in this film (the contagion signified by the title) becomes the means by which narrative is *disordered*, revealing a view of a world in which the center no longer holds. Films like *Maniac* and *Friday the Thirteenth* and its sequels go even further in the reduction of plot and character. In *Friday the Thirteenth*, a group of young people are brought together to staff a summer camp and are randomly murdered whenever they go off to make love. The people in the film are practically interchangeable, since we learn nothing about them as individuals, and there is virtually no building of a climax – only variations on the theme of slashing, creating a pattern that is more or less reversible.

Finally, it should scarcely need pointing out that when villains and victims are such shadowy, undeveloped characters and are portrayed equally unsympathetically, narcissistic identification on the part of the audience becomes increasingly difficult. Indeed, it could be said that some of the films elicit a kind of *anti*-narcissistic identification, which the audience delights in indulging just as it delights in having its expectations of closure frustrated. Of *The Texas Chainsaw Massacre*, Robin Wood writes, 'Watching it recently with a large, half-stoned youth audience who cheered and applauded every one of Leatherface's outrages against their representatives on the screen was a terrifying experience.'[22] The same might be said of films like *Halloween* and *Friday the Thirteenth*, which adopt the point of view of the slasher, placing the spectator in the position of an unseen nameless presence which, to the audiences' great glee, annihilates one by one their screen surrogates. This kind of joyful self-destructiveness on the part of the masses has been discussed by Jean Baudrillard in another context – in his analysis of the Georges Pompidou Center in Paris to which tourists flock by the millions, ostensibly to consume culture, but also to hasten the collapse of the structurally flawed building.[23] There is a similar paradox in the fact that *Dawn of the Dead*, the film about zombies taking over a shopping center, has become a midnight favorite at shopping malls all over the US. In both cases the masses are revelling in the demise of the very culture they appear most enthusiastically to support. Here, it would seem, we have another variant of the split, 'perverse' response favored by Roland Barthes.

The contemporary horror film thus comes very close to being 'the other film' that Thierry Kuntzel says the classic narrative film must always work to conceal: 'a film in which the initial figure would not find a place in the flow of a narrative, in which the configuration of events contained in the formal matrix would not form a progressive order, in which the spectator/

subject would never be reassured . . . within the dominant system of production and con-sumption, this would be a film of sustained *terror*.'[24] Both in form and in content, the genre confounds the theories of those critics who adopt an adversarial attitude toward mass culture. The type of mass art I have been discussing – the kind of films which play at drive-ins and shabby downtown theaters, and are discussed on the pages of newsletters named *Trashola* and *Sleazoid Express* – is as apocalyptic and nihilistic, as hostile to meaning, form, pleasure, and the specious good as many types of high art. This is surely not accidental. Since Jean-François Lyotard insists that postmodernism is an 'aesthetic of the sublime,' as Immanuel Kant theorized the concept, it is interesting to note that Kant saw an intimate connection between the literature of the sublime and the literature of terror, and moreover saw the difference as in part a matter of audi-ence education: 'In fact, without the development of moral ideas, that which, thanks to prepara-tory culture, we call sublime, merely strikes the untutored man as terrifying.'[25] And there is certainly evidence to suggest that the converse of Kant's statement has some truth as well, since a film like *The Texas Chainsaw Massacre*, which might seem designed principally to terrify the untutored man, strikes a critic like Robin Wood as sublime – or at least as 'authentic art.' Wood writes, '*The Texas Chainsaw Massacre* . . . achieves the force of authentic art. . . . As a 'collective nightmare,' it brings to a focus a spirit of negativity, an undifferentiated lust for destruction that seems to lie not far below the surface of the modern collective consciousness.'[26] It is indeed possible for the tutored critic versed in preparatory film culture to make a convincing case for the artistic merit of a film like *The Texas Chainsaw Massacre*, as long as art continues to be theor-ized in terms of negation, as long as we demand that it be uncompromisingly oppositional.

However, instead of endorsing Wood's view, we might wish to consider what these films have to teach us about the *limits* of an adversarial position which makes a virtue of 'sustained terror.' Certainly women have important reasons for doing so. In Trilling's essay, 'The Fate of Pleasure,' he notes almost parenthetically that, according to the *Oxford English Dictionary*, 'Pleasure in the pejorative sense is sometimes personified as a female deity.'[27] Now, when pleasure has become an almost wholly pejorative term, we might expect to see an increasing tendency to incarnate it as a woman. And, indeed, in the contemporary horror film it is personified as a lovely young school teacher beaten to death by midget clones (*The Brood*), as a pretty blond teenager threatened by a maniac wielding a chainsaw (*The Texas Chainsaw Massacre*), or as a pleasant and attractive babysitter terrorized throughout the film *Halloween* by a grown-up version of the little boy killer revealed in the opening sequence. Importantly, in many of the films the female is attacked not only because, as has often been claimed, she embodies sexual pleasure, but also because she represents a great many aspects of the specious good – just as the babysitter, for example, quite literally represents familial authority. The point needs to be stressed, since feminism has occasionally made common cause with the adversarial critics on the grounds that we too have been oppressed by the specious good. But this is to overlook the fact that in some profound sense we have also been historically and physically identified with it.

Further, just as Linda Williams has argued that in the horror film woman is usually placed on the side of the monster even when she is its pre-eminent victim, so too in the scenario I out-lined at the beginning woman is frequently associated with the monster mass culture.[28] This is hardly surprising since, as we have seen, mass culture has typically been theorized as the realm of cheap and easy pleasure – 'pleasure in the pejorative sense.' Thus, in Ann Douglas's account, the 'feminization of American culture' is synonymous with the rise of mass culture.[29] And in David Cronenberg's view, mass culture – at least the video portion of it – is terrifying because of the way it feminizes its audience. In *Videodrome*, the openness and vulnerability of the media recipient are made to seem loathsome and fearful through the use of feminine imagery (the vaginal wound in the stomach) and feminine positioning: the hero is raped with a video cassette. As Baudrillard puts it, 'no halo of private protection, not even his own body . . . protect[s] him anymore.' Baudrillard himself describes mass-mediated experience in terms of rape, as when he speaks of 'the unclean promiscuity of everything which touches, invests and penetrates without resistance.' No resistance, no protection, no mastery. Or so it might seem. And yet the mastery that these popular texts no longer permit through effecting closure or eliciting narcissistic identification is often reasserted through projecting the experience of submission and defenselessness onto the female body. In this way the texts enable the male spectator to distance himself somewhat from the terror. And, as usual, it is the female specta- tor who is *truly* deprived of 'solace and pleasure.' Having been denied access to pleasure, while simultaneously being scapegoated for seeming to represent it, women are perhaps in the best position to call into question an aesthetics wholly opposed to it. At the very least, we might like to experience more of it before deciding to denounce it.

Beyond this, it remains for the postmodernist to ponder the irony of the fact that when critics condemn a 'monstrous motion picture industry' they are to a certain extent repeating the gestures of texts they repudiate. And the question then becomes: How can an adversarial attitude be maintained toward an art that is itself increasingly adversarial? In *The Anti-Aesthetic*, Hal Foster considers modernism to be postmodernism's other, and he pointedly asks, 'how can we exceed the modern? How can we break with a program that makes a value of crisis . . . or progress beyond the era of Progress . . . or *transgress the ideology of the transgressive?*'[30] Foster does not acknowledge the extent to which mass culture has also served as postmodernism's other, but his question is pertinent here too.

Part of the answer may lie in the fact that for many artists, transgression is not as impor- tant a value as it is for many theorists. A host of contemporary artistic endeavours may be cited as proof of this, despite the efforts of some critics to make these works conform to an oppositional practice. In literature, the most famous and current example of the changed, friendly attitude toward popular art is Umberto Eco's *The Name of the Rose*, which draws on the Sherlock Holms mystery tale. Manuel Puig's novels (his *Kiss of the Spider Woman*, for example) have consistently explored the pleasures of popular movies. In the visual arts, Cindy Sherman's self-portraiture involves the artist's masquerading as figures from old Hollywood films. The 'Still Life' exhibition organized by Marvin Heiferman and Diane Keaton consists of publicity stills from the files of Hollywood movie studios. In film, Rainer Werner Fassbinder continually paid homage to Hollywood melodramas; Wim Wenders and Betty Gordon return to *film noir*; Mulvey and Wollen to the fantastic; Valie Export to science fiction; and so on.

A few theorists have begun to acknowledge these developments, but usually only to denounce them. In a recent article entitled 'Post-modernism and Consumer Society,' Fredric Jameson concludes by deploring the fact that art is no longer 'explosive and subversive,' no longer 'critical, negative, contestatory . . . oppositional, and the like.'[31] Instead, says Jameson, much recent art appears to incorporate images and stereotypes garnered from our pop cultural past. However, instead of sharing Jameson's pessimistic view of this tendency, I would like to end on a small note of comfort and solace. Perhaps the contemporary artist continues to be subversive by being nonadversarial in the modernist sense, and has returned to our pop cultural past partly in order to explore the site where pleasure was last observed, before it was stoned by the gentry and the mob alike, and recreated as a monster.

Notes

1   Karl Marx, *Grundrisse: Foundations of the Critique of Political Economy* (Middlesex, England: Penguin, 1973), p. 706.

2   Isaac Balbus, *Marxism and Domination* (Princeton, NJ: Princeton University Press, 1982), p. 41.

3   Jacques Ellul, *The Technological Society*, John Wilkinson (trans.), (New York: Vintage, 1964), pp. 113–14.

4   Theodor W. Adorno, 'Culture Industry Reconsidered,' Anson G. Rabinbach (trans.), *New German Critique* 6 (Fall 1975): 17.

5   Roland Barthes, 'Upon Leaving the Movie Theater,' trans. Bertrand Augst and Susan White, *University Publishing* 6 (Winter 1979): 3.

6   Hal Foster, 'Postmodernism: A Preface,' *The Anti-Aesthetic: Essays on Postmodern Culture* Hal Foster (ed.), (Port Townsend, WA: Bay Press, 1983), p. xv.

7   Roland Barthes, *The Pleasure of the Text*, Richard Miller (trans.) (New York: Hill and Wang, 1975), pp. 47–8. Earlier Barthes remarks that 'no significance (no *jouissance*) can occur, I am convinced, in a mass culture . . . for the model of this culture is petit bourgeois' (p. 38).

8   Christian Metz, *The Imaginary Signifier: Psychoanalysis and the Cinema*, Celia Britton, Annwyl Williams, Ben Brewster, and Alfred Guzzetti (trans.), (Bloomington: Indiana University Press, 1982), pp. 99–148.

9   Lionel Trilling, 'The Fate of Pleasure: Wordsworth to Dostoevsky,' *Partisan Review* (Summer 1963): 178.

10   Ibid., p. 182.

11   Roland Barthes, *Image, Music, Text* Stephen Heath (trans.), (New York: Hill and Wang, 1977), p. 167.

12   Jean-François Lyotard, 'Answering the Question: What is Postmodernism?' Régis Durand (trans.), *Innovation/Renovation: New Perspectives on the Humanities*, Ihab Hassan and Sally Hassan (eds) (Madison: The University of Wisconsin Press, 1983), p. 340.

13   Ibid., p. 335.

14   Jean-François Lyotard, *La Condition postmoderne* (Paris: Minuit, 1979), p. 29.

15   Matei Calinescu, *Faces of Modernity: Avant-Garde, Decadence, Kitsch* (Bloomington: Indiana University Press, 1977), p. 240.

16   Leonard Maltin, *T.V. Movies*, revised edn (New York: Signet, 1981–82), p. 95.

17   Robin Wood, *American Nightmare: Essays on the Horror Film* (Toronto: Festival of Festivals, 1979), pp. 20–2.

18   Jean Baudrillard, 'The Ecstasy of Communication,' John Johnston (trans.), *The Anti-Aesthetic* (1983a), pp. 132–3.

19   Barthes, *The Pleasure of the Text*, p. 17. Barthes, however, specifies the 'erotic body.'

20   Stephen Heath, *Questions of Cinema* (Bloomington: Indiana University Press, 1981), p. 157.

21   Julia Kristeva, 'Ellipsis on Dread and the Specular Seduction,' Dolores Burdick (trans.), *Wide Angle* 3, no. 3 (1979): 46.

22   Wood, p. 22.

23   Jean Baudrillard, *L'Effet beaubourg: implosion et dissuasion* (Paris: Galilée, 1977), pp. 23–5.

24   Thierry Kuntzel, 'The Film Work 2,' Nancy Huston (trans.), *Camera Obscura* 5 (1980): 24–5.

25   Immanuel Kant, *Critique of Judgment*, trans. James Creed (Oxford: Clarendon, 1952), p. 115, quoted in Franco Moretti, *Signs Taken for Wonders* (London: Verso, 1983), p. 253 n. See his chapter on 'The Dialectic of Fear' for a very different reading of the vampire image in Marx.

26   Wood, op. cit., p. 22.

27   Trilling, op. cit., p. 168.

28   Linda Williams, 'When the Woman Looks,' *Re-vision: Essays in Feminist Film Criticism*, Mary Ann Doane, Patricia Mellencamp, and Linda Williams (eds), The American Film Institute Monograph Series, vol. III (Frederick, MD: University Publications of America, 1984), pp. 85–8.

29   Ann Douglas, *The Feminization of American Culture* (New York: Avon, 1977).

30   Foster, p. ix. My emphasis.

31   Frederic Jameson, 'Postmodernism and Consumer Society,' *The Anti-Aesthetic*, (1983), p. 125.

Chapter 21

JIM COLLINS

GENERICITY IN THE NINETIES
Eclectic irony and the new sincerity

PERHAPS THE MOST USEFUL WAY TO BEGIN discussion of 'genre film' in the early 1990s is to look at representative scenes in two quite recent Westerns, each representing in its own way how 'genericity' works in contemporary American culture. In *Back to the Future III* (1990) Marty and Doc ride through the desert in what is supposed to be 1885, charging across the landscape in their disabled DeLorean time machine, sitting side-by-side atop the car, drawn by a team of horses. This configuration of drivers, horses and desert is made to resemble not just any stagecoach in any old Western, but *the* stagecoach, namely John Ford's *Stagecoach* (1939) – a parallel made explicit by replicating one of the most famous shots of Ford's film almost exactly. The DeLorean 'stagecoach' is pulled through Monument Valley, framed in a high angle shot, moving diagonally through the frame, accompanied by soundtrack music that is remarkably similar to the 'original.' The second scene comes from *Dances With Wolves* (1990). After John Dunbar has taken part in a buffalo hunt and begun his initiation into the tribe, he contemplates the Sioux tribe moving across the horizon, silhouetted against a spectacular sunset, a picturesque vision of an unspoiled West. Dunbar says in a voice-over that he had never encountered a people so completely connected to their environment – 'The only word that came to mind was harmony' – at which point we see not the Sioux, but Dunbar framed perfectly in the midst of a magnificent sunset, situated just as heroically and just as harmoniously within that landscape.

I choose these scenes because they represent two divergent types of genre film that co-exist in current popular culture. One is founded on dissonance, on eclectic juxtapositions of elements that very obviously don't belong together, while the other is obsessed with recovering some sort of missing harmony, where everything works in unison. Where the former involves an ironic hybridization of pure classical genres in which John Ford meets Jules Verne and H. G. Wells, the latter epitomizes a 'new sincerity' that rejects any form of irony in its sanctimonious pursuit of lost purity. Despite their apparently antithetical perspectives, both types of genre films have emerged within the past decade as reactions to the same cultural milieu – namely, the media-saturated landscape of contemporary American culture. The goal of this article is to try to make sense of how these popular films make sense of our cultural existences and in so doing to explore the changing forms and functions of 'genericity' in postmodern popular culture.

I use the term 'genericity' here because I want to address not just specific genre films, but genre as a category of film production and film-viewing. Traditionally, Hollywood studios subdivided their annual production into specific genre films that, if nothing else, served as a useful way of striking a balance between product standardization and differentiation. Maintaining certain formulas that would stabilize audience expectations and, by extension, stabilize those audiences, was obviously in Hollywood's best interests. But how does the category of genre 'work' today when popular entertainment is undergoing such a massive recategorization brought on by the ever-increasing number of entertainment options and the fragmentation of what was once thought to be a mass audience into a cluster of 'target' audiences?

Genre films/genre theories: life on the new frontier

Just as generic texts have been a staple of the culture industries, genre theory has been all-pervasive within the criticism industries. Film scholars and social historians have tried to explain the cultural significance of the Western, the melodrama, and other popular genres since the 1940s, and they have employed a number of critical methodologies to explain the popularity of genres and what that popularity suggests about 'mass consciousness.' One of the most commonly used approaches once film study began to acquire a certain degree of rigor in the 1960s was myth study, i.e. reading popular narratives as the secularized myths of modern societies. This work depends on two interconnected assumptions: (1) films function as explanatory narratives told by multiple storytellers in multiple versions; and (2) out of this storytelling certain patterns emerge that reflect how the 'mass consciousness' feels about any number of issues at a given time. The genre-as-myth approach most often incorporated the work of French anthropologist Claude Lévi-Strauss, whose analysis of myth in primitive cultures provided a theoretical framework for investigating just how popular stories could be interpreted as a symbolic working-out of a given culture's core values and its most pressing social problems. The most frequently borrowed principle of Lévi-Strauss's methodology was his notion of 'structuring antinomies,' the binary oppositions around which the conflicts of any number of films were structured. This approach was used in reference to the musical and other genres (see Altman and Feuer), but it was most influential in the study of the Western. Jim Kitses, for example, in his introduction to *Horizons West* (1969), presents a table of antinomies that he believes are central to understanding the genre (Wilderness vs. Civilization, Individual vs. Community, Nature vs. Culture, etc.) and Will Wright (1975) traces the evolution of the Western by charting the changing configuration of the antinomies from the 1940s through the 1960s.

By the 1970s, however, this view that classical genres owe their success to their mythical dimensions came under closer scrutiny. John Cawelti, for example, argued that by the late 1960s–early 1970s, genre films ceased to function as pure, unalloyed myth, and that four types of what he calls 'generic transformation' appeared: the burlesque, in which the conventions of the classical genre are pushed to absurd lengths and played for laughs, e.g. *Blazing Saddles* (1974); the nostalgia film, in which the glorious myths of Hollywood's Golden Age are revisited sentimentally, e.g. *True Grit* (1978); demythologization, in which the lessons of these classical genre films are revealed to be destructive and deluding, e.g. *Little Big Man* (1970); and affirmation of the myth for its own sake, in which the original myth is seen as antiquated, but nevertheless significant in its own way, e.g. *The Wild Bunch* (1979). The chief strength of Cawelti's overview is that it recognizes that Hollywood films could not be considered 'pure myth' by the late 1960s, since all four forms of generic transformation frame the classical-genre-film-as-myth at one remove, from a self-conscious perspective in the present, clearly distanced from the imagined Golden Age. The chief limitation of Cawelti's argument is his explanation of why these transformations happened when they did. His contention that 'generic exhaustion' occurred largely because a new generation of film-makers and film-viewers (having grown up with television where older Hollywood films were ubiquitous) had acquired a degree of sophistication that made the old stories just that – old stories that failed to describe 'the imaginative landscape of the latter half of the twentieth century.' Surely this increasing sophistication, the result of a fast-developing cinematic cultural literacy, was a major factor in shaping the changes in genre films by the late 1960s–early 1970s, but that explanation doesn't really address the interconnectedness of technological and demographic changes that accompanied those changes in cinematic literacy. The advent of television didn't increase just the average film-viewer's stock of stored narrative memories, it actually changed which genres were given highest priority by Hollywood, initially by triggering the industry's move to Cinemascope, Technicolor, and stereophonic sound that resulted in the greater prominence of the Western and historical epic. But by the late 1960s, television's impact on genre films was felt in another way. The ambiguity of television in American homes by the 1960s caused a profound shift in the nature of the film-going public. Families tended to stay home and watch television and would venture forth only rarely for special event blockbusters. A new target audience emerged – namely, the youth audience, or more specifically a college-age audience – who by the late 1960s wanted a different form of entertainment, and to a certain extent received it in the form of 'counter-cultural' films like *The Graduate* (1967), *Medium Cool* (1970), *Zabriskie Point* (1970), *The Strawberry Statement* (1970), *Five Easy Pieces* (1970), which were marketed as a kind of genre unto themselves alongside the generic transformation films like *Bonnie and Clyde* (1967), *Little Big Man* (1970), etc. If genre-films-as-myth changed, it was due to the interconnectedness of social, technological, and demographic changes that gave rise to target myths for target audiences, a development that has serious ramifications for any claim that popular films reflect some sort of unitary, *mass* consciousness in some abstract sense.

If we are to understand the cultural context of genericity in the late 1980s–early 1990s, we need to examine the current set of pre-conditions formed by the interplay of cultural, technological, and demographic factors. Neither *Back to the Future III* nor *Dances With Wolves* fits any of Cawelti's categories particular well – hardly surprising given the changes that have occurred in popular entertainment since the publication of his essay in 1978. The four types of generic transformation that were simultaneously at work in the 1960s and 1970s may have differed in regard to degree of respect shown a particular genre, but in each case the transformation is one that remains within the confines of a specific genre, whereas the eclectic, hybrid genre films of the eighties and nineties, like *Road Warrior* (1981), *Blade Runner* (1982), *Blue Velvet* (1986), *Near Dark* (1988), *Who Framed Roger Rabbit?* (1988), *Batman* (1989), *Thelma and Louise* (1991), all engage in specific transformation *across* genres. Just as these eclectic films were a new development in genericity in the 1980s, so too is the 'new sincerity' of films like *Field of Dreams* (1989), *Dances With Wolves* (1990) and *Hook* (1991), all of which depend not on hybridization, but on an 'ethnographic' rewriting of the classic genre film that serves as their inspiration, all attempting, using one strategy or another, to recover a lost 'purity,' which apparently pre-existed even the Golden Age of film genre.

Just as television changed the nature of popular entertainment in the 1950s and 1960s, a whole range of technological developments had a massive impact on the shape of genre films in the 1980s and 1990s. In his essay in this collection, Tom Schatz quotes the astounding increase in VCR ownership that developed in tandem with comparable developments in cable television, premium movie channels, and further refinements in both television monitors (specifically, simultaneous display of multiple channels and remote control) and playback options with the introduction of videodiscs and CD video. These interdependent developments cannot be reduced to any one overall effect. Some of the most significant ramifications of this new media technology have been: the exponential increase in the sheer volume of images that were transmitted to/playable in the average household, a comparable increase in software (titles available on videotape, disc, etc.), and parallel developments that allow for both the faster accessing and greater manipulability of that reservoir of images. The ever-expanding number of texts and technologies is both a reflection of and a significant contribution to the 'array' – the perpetual circulation and recirculation of signs that forms the fabric of postmodern cultural life.

That a seemingly endless number of texts are subject to virtually immediate random access inevitably alters the relationship between classic and contemporary when both circulate alongside one another simultaneously. This simultaneity does not diminish the cultural 'status' of the former so much as it changes its possible functions, which has far-reaching implications for how genre, and by extension popular culture, function in contemporary culture. The evolution of genre is traditionally conceived as a three-stage pattern of development: an initial period of consolidation in which specific narratives and visual conventions begin to coalesce into a recognizable configuration of features corresponding to a stable set of audience expectations. This period is followed by a 'Golden Age,' in which the interplay of by now thoroughly stabilized sets of stylistic features and audience expectations is subject to elaborate variations and permutations. The final phase is generally described in terms of all-purpose decline, in which the played-out conventions dissolve either into self-parody or self-reflexivity (end-of-the-West Westerns from *The Man Who Shot Liberty Valance* [1962] to *The Shootist* [1976]).

This three-stage model, however, doesn't adequately explain the re-emergence of the Western, primarily because that resurgence is in many ways unprecedented. Rather than conceiving of the return of the Western as some kind of 'fourth stage,' it is perhaps more profitable to see this 'renaissance' phase in terms of technological and cultural changes that have produced a set of circumstances in which the central function of genericity is in the process of being redefined. The 'recyclability' of texts from the past, the fact that once-forgotten popular texts can now be 'accessed' almost at will changes the cultural function of genre films past *and* present. The omnipresence of what Umberto Eco has called the 'already said,' now represented and recirculated as the 'still-being-said' is not just a matter of an ever-accumulating number of texts ready to be accessed, but also involves a transformation of the 'cultural terrain' that contemporary genre films must somehow make sense of or map. If genre films of the 1930s and 1940s functioned as the myths of Depression-era and war-time American culture, how do they function when they come back around as 'classics' or just campy old movies? How does the 'cultural work' of these genre films change, especially when these mythologies of earlier periods now co-exist alongside the 'new' genre films and the mythologies they activate?

This situation is described quite effectively by Lestat, the vampire narrator of Anne Rice's *The Vampire Lestat*. As the novel opens, Lestat explains that he came back from the dead because he was awakened by the 'cacophony in the air' – the radio and television waves that penetrated even his coffin underground. Upon resurfacing, one of the things that he finds most surprising about life at the end of the twentieth century is that

> the old was not being routinely replaced by the new anymore . . . In the art and entertainment worlds all prior centuries were being 'recycled' . . . In grand florescent-lighted emporiums, you could buy tapes of medieval madrigals and play them

on your car stereo as you drove ninety miles an hour down the freeway. In the book-
stores Renaissance poetry sold side by side with the novels of Dickens or Ernest
Hemingway. Sex manuals lay on the same table with the Egyptian Book of the
Dead. . . . Countless television programs poured their ceaseless flow of images into
every air-cooled hotel room. But it was no series of hallucinations. This century had
inherited the earth in every sense.

(8–9)

The ever-expanding array to which this 'inheritance' gives rise alters not just the circumstances of *representation*, but also, just as fundamentally, the *to-be-represented*, the 'raw' experience
of daily life, which now comes to us already framed in multiple ways, *always already* so highly
mediated. The fact that the old is not replaced by the new anymore does not just change the
historical development of specific genres, it also changes the function of genre films, which, if
they can still be said to be engaged in symbolically 'mapping' the cultural landscape, must do
so now in reference to, and *through* the array that constitutes the landscape. Rice's vampire is
a case in point. Lestat's monstrosity is inseparable from his media personality – we're allegedly
reading his best-selling memoirs that he composes on his word-processor when he is not
otherwise engaged in recording his best-selling albums or making his rock videos – all of
which play globally. If the genre texts of the 1960s are distinguished by their increasing self-
reflexivity about their antecedents in the Golden Age of Hollywood, the genre texts of the late
1980s–early 1990s demonstrate an even more sophisticated hyperconsciousness concerning
not just narrative formulae, but the conditions of their own circulation and reception in the
present, which has a massive impact on the nature of popular entertainment.

When the legend becomes hyperconscious, print the . . .

Two scenes from Robert Zemeckis's *Back to the Future III* are useful examples of this emergent
type of genericity. In this film we follow the adventures of Marty and Doc on the Western frontier in the 1880s, but we are also encouraged to take simultaneous delight in the intertextual
adventures that *Back to the Future* engages in as it negotiates the array, the endless proliferation
of signs that constitutes the postmodern frontier. When the characters travel back in time to
the Old West, their trip is actually a voyage into the Old Western, a point made most explicitly in the scene where Marty attempts to drive back to the 1880s to rescue Doe from certain
death. His avenue to the past is the film screen, a metaphor literalized by his driving the time
machine through a drive-in movie screen in order to reach the past. The screen, then, is a por-
tal to a nineteenth century that can exist only in the form of images, in the form of cinematic
reconstructions, and their very materiality is overtly foregrounded by the text, a point made
especially explicit by the fact that the drive-in happens to be located within Monument Valley.
Once back in the Old Western, when the painted image of Indians gives way to the real
Indians(!) who chase the DeLorean across the desert, Marty looks into his rearview mirror to
check their location. This point of view shot is perhaps the most representative shot in the film
because it synthesizes in a single image the relationship between past and present and between
genre and postmodern culture. This image, a close-up of the mirror, taken from Marty's
perspective, frames the approaching Indians perfectly – we see 'history,' but only as an image
from the rearview mirror of the present. The literalizing of yet another metaphor concerning
the visibility of the past from the present foregrounds once again, in comedic terms, one of the
main themes of postmodern historiography – that history can exist for us now only in forms of
representation, that we construct the significance of the past only as we frame it in the present.

This, of course, has led to charges of trivialization of history (Sobchack), i.e. evil postmodern culture has 'reduced' the world to images that it then cannibalizes, as if 'History' were somehow accessible to us without the mediation of representation, and as such possesses some kind of 'sanctity' that cannot be treated ironically through such juxtapositions. In this foregrounding of time-travel as a process inseparable from the production of images, *Back to the Future III* resembles Julian Barnes' *History of the World in 10½ Chapters*, in which the narrator states, 'We cling to history as a series of salon pictures, conversation pieces whose participants we can easily reimagine back into life, when all the time it's more like a multi-media collage. . . . The history of the world? Just voices echoing in the dark; images that burn for a few centuries and then fade; stories, old stories that sometimes seem to overlap; strange links, impertinent connections' (240).

Within the Old West of *Back to the Future III*, we enter a narrative universe defined by impertinent connections, no longer containable by one set of generic conventions. We encounter, instead, different sets of generic conventions that intermingle, constituting a profoundly intertextual diegesis, nowhere more apparent than in the shot of the DeLorean time machine being pulled through the desert by a team of horses, the very co-presence of John Ford and H. G. Wells demonstrating the film's ability to access both as simultaneous narrative options, each with a set of conventions that can be recombined at will. This simultaneity of options, each subject to a kind of random access, is epitomized by the scene in which Marty prepares for his final slowdown with the villain. While practicing his draw in the mirror, dressed as Clint Eastwood in *A Fistful of Dollars* (1966), he calls up a few tough-guy lines, opting first for Eastwood's 'Make my day' from his Dirty Harry/hard-boiled incarnation (*Dirty Harry*, 1971), then Travis Bickle's 'Are you talkin' to me?' routine from *Taxi Driver* (1976). The simultaneous accessibility of the Spaghetti Westerner, the Hard-Boiled Cop, and the Urban Psychopath as potential heroic poses functions as a more sophisticated version of the print-outs that the Terminator sees before his eyes in Cameron's 1984 film, a menu of relevant lines that can be selected according to immediate need. The fact that the hero's choices are all cinematic quotations reflects not just the increasing sophistication of the cinematic literacy of *Back to the Future*'s audiences (and the profoundly intertextual nature of that literacy), but also the entertainment value that the ironic manipulation of that stored information now provides.

In contemporary popular culture, we see both the menu and its misuse; while the Terminator's options are all *appropriate* to a given situation, Marty's options are all *appropriated* from divergent contexts, all relevant insofar as they serve as macho poses, but inappropriate in that they purposely confuse time and genre. The Dirty Harry and Travis Bickle quotations are latter-day manifestations of the conventional gunfight, anachronisms in relation to the 1880s, but flashbacks in reference to the 1990s. Their co-presence in this scene reflects not the alleged 'collapse of history,' but a simultaneity that functions as a techno-palimpsest, in which earlier traces can be immediately called up, back to the surface to be replayed, or more precisely, recirculated. The act of appropriation problematizes distinctions between appropriate and inappropriate, as well as the stability of the categories of shared information that we might call cultural literacy. The categories are inappropriate only in reference to the topoi of the Old Western, but appropriate to a culture in which those topoi are one of a series of push-button options. This foregrounded, hyperconscious intertextuality reflects changes in terms of audience competence and narrative technique, as well as a fundamental shift in what constitutes both entertainment and cultural literacy in the 'Information Age.'

Contemporary film criticism has been utterly unable to come to terms with these very profound changes in the nature of entertainment because this hyperconscious eclecticism is measured against nineteenth-century notions of classical narrative and realist representation.

The indictment drawn up by critics on the 'left' and 'right,' who are always horrified by this unmanageable textuality that refuses to play by the old rules, always takes the same form – hyperconscious eclecticism is a sign of (choose one): (a) the end of 'Narrative'; (b) the end of 'the Real,' 'History,' etc.; (c) the end of art and entertainment for anyone other than over-stimulated promiscuous teenagers; (d) a sign of all-purpose moral and intellectual decay. All of this has been caused by: (a) the all-purpose postmodern malaise that is hell-bent on recycling the detrius of Western Civilization instead of presenting us with the 'really Real,' 'History,' etc.; (b) the overwhelming desire for perpetual stimulation that makes reading 'Great Books' or watching 'fine films' passé; (c) shorter attention spans caused by television, advertising, rock music, and permissive child-raising; (d) unbridled greed in people who have read neither (choose one) Aristotle or Marx; (e) technology in the hands of people described in (d). What is also left out of these pronouncements is the possibility that the nature of entertainment, narrative, art, identification may be undergoing significant reformation due to widespread changes in the nature of information distribution, access, and manipulability. That this simply doesn't exist as an option reveals the tenacity with which social critics from Allen Bloom to Jean-Louis Baudrillard still cling to notions of art, epistemology, and signification that were developed, at the very latest, in the nineteenth Century. The following quotations suggest the common concerns, as well as the hysterical tenor, or condemnations of the new *zeitgeist*.

> Picture a thirteen-year-old sitting in the living room of his family home, doing his math assignment while wearing his headphones and watching MTV. . . . A pubes-cent child whose body throbs with orgasmic rhythms, whose feelings are made articulate in hymns to the joys of onanism or the killing of parents. . . . In short, life is made into a nonstop, commercially prepackaged masturbatory fantasy.
>
> (Bloom, 74–5).

> Essentially a youthful crowd, this audience does not have very sophisticated tastes of expectations when it comes to narrative. Given that lack, they may never ask for strong, persuasive storytelling when they grow up. What we get . . . is not narrative as it has been traditionally defined, but a succession of undifferentiated sensations . . . there is in fact no *authentic* emotional build-up, consequently no catharsis at the movie's conclusion. . . . For in most movies today the traditional function has been inverted. Instead of the major dramatic incidents growing *naturally* out of the story, that is, out of the interaction of plausible characters with a recognizable moral and physical landscape, the opposite occurs. . . . [W]e are left without consoling coherences of old-fashioned movie narrative, left with anarchy, picking through the rubble it leaves in its wake, wondering what hit us.
>
> (Schickel, 3–4)

> We rarely see the kind of panoramic composition that once allowed a generous impression of quasi-global simultaneity . . . and that also, more subtly enriches the frame in most great movies, whose makers have offered *pictures*, composed of pleasurable 'touches' and legible detail. These moving tableaux often, as André Bazin argued, gave their viewers more choice, and required some (often minimal) interpretive attention. Only now and then and in films that don't come out of Hollywood – Terry Gilliam's *Brazil*, Stanley Kubrick's *Full Metal Jacket* – do we perceive such exhilarating fullness. In contrast, today's American movies work without or against the potential depth and latitude of cinema, in favor of that systematic overemphasis deployed in advertising and all other propaganda.
>
> (Miller, 52)

The all-purpose complaint about overstimulation is framed by Richard Schickel in reference to its devastating impact on narrative, but what exactly is in crisis – narrative, or just traditional notions of narrative that depend on coherence, plausibility, *authentic* emotional build-up, *natural* outgrowths and catharsis? This list of requirements grows out of conventions first developed in classical tragedy (and codified most obviously in Aristotle's *Poetics*) and then expanded in realist theater and literature of the nineteenth-century. According to this definition, virtually all modernist and postmodernist stories are deficient narratives. The only acceptable film narratives would appear to be those that are simply cinematic versions of nineteenth-century models. Cultural changes that have occurred in the twentieth-century apparently should have no impact on the well-made narrative. But even if we bracket this problem and ignore the obvious condescension in the dismissal of viewers less 'sophisticated' than Schickel, the most serious problem with his narrative complaint has to do with yet another stipulation – the 'recognizable moral and physical landscape' that characters must inhabit. This definition simply dismisses another possibility – that the popular narratives of the 1980s and 1990s present a moral and physical landscape in a state of previously unfathomable change and that these stories just might be an attempt to make the chaotic, dissonant cultures of the later decades of the twentieth century somehow more manageable through their presentation of a new mediated landscape that can be successfully mapped out only by contemporary media, and not some antiquated notion of the well-made play. The alternatives that Schickel offers – classical narrative or anarchy – are uncannily similar to the binary, either/or, all-or-nothing opposition proposed by Matthew Arnold in *Culture and Anarchy;* culture can only be 'Culture' if it imitates the culture of any time *other* than the present.

Mark Crispin Miller's condemnation of contemporary film style is cast in the same nostalgic mode, but his presuppositions regarding what films supposedly 'worked' in the good old days are even more problematic. Schickel's nostalgia is for old-fashioned storytelling that did indeed exist (and still does to a far greater extent than he is willing to allow), but Crispin Miller pines for an imaginary film-viewing state that never existed, based as it is on Bazin's now-discredited assumptions concerning the relationship among the camera, reality, and the spectator. Miller's thesis concerning the negative impact that advertising has had on filmmaking is a rhetorically powerful argument, but his grand alternative – how film used to work – is founded on a thoroughly outdated understanding of filmic representation. By invoking Bazin's idealist theory of representation, in which true cinematic geniuses allow the photographic plate to capture the 'real' in an unmediated way, thereby allowing truth to leap directly onto the celluloid strip, Miller posits an authentic or genuine form of representation against which all other types of film practice will be automatically judged deficient. The problem here, of course, is the notion of film as unmediated reality, a 'fullness' that spectators were able to contemplate, free to formulate their own interpretations out of the essential ambiguity of the filmic image. One of the main themes of film theory since the late 1960s has been the rejection of this sort of idealism, and a number of theorists have been investigating the various stylistic, institutional, and ideological apparatuses that intervene between camera and 'reality,' and then between image and spectator, all of which demonstrate that these relationships are never as unmediated as Bazin imagined them to be. Miller's sweeping rejection of Hollywood filmmaking depends on his appeal to a 'classic' film style as imagined by an antiquated film theory developed in the 1950s to describe the masterpieces of the 1930s and 1940s. It is hardly surprising that such an approach would provide only a blindered view of recent filmmaking, unable to come to terms with the highly 'mediated' nature of our contemporary cultural existence and the images needed to represent them. The 'exhilarating fullness' of this world is due to the fact that the real now comes to us always already 'imaged' in any number of ways, the 'depth and latitude' of contemporary cinema depending on the negotiation of that thickness of representation, those sedimented layers of images that define the cultural significance of any subject matter.

In all such attacks on current popular films that decry their avoidance of traditional narrative and authentic representation, one finds the same assumption – that the increasing sophistication of the media produces a sensory overload in which individual viewers are overstimulated into numbness, reachable only through blunt appeals to animal appetites. But these technophobic denunciations of media 'overload' never even begin to address the distinguishing features of recent popular narratives, namely the attempts to encounter directly that 'overload,' that semiotic excess, and turn it into a new form of narrative entertainment that necessarily involves altering the structure and function of narrative. Tim Burton's *Batman* is a useful example here, because it epitomizes these attempts to incorporate the array that now forms the 'imaginative landscape' of contemporary cultural life, and the criticism devoted to this film by Schickel and Miller epitomizes just as explicitly the failure of the antiquated paradigms they use to evaluate it. Miller dismisses *Batman* as part of the 'cartooning' of Hollywood, and Schickel cites it as one more example of deficient narrative, of visual pyrotechnics instead of plot – 'Its story – the conflict between its eponymous hero and the Joker for the soul of Gotham City – is all right, kind of fun. But that is not what the movie is primarily about. It is about – no kidding – urban design' (14). But Burton's film is about far more than urban design. It presents a decidedly 'old-fashioned' plot, but it also situates the adventures of Batman and the Joker within the mediated culture of the present and makes their manipulation of the images that surround them a crucial part of the conflicts between them.

Batman is not just vaguely symptomatic of how popular narratives try to envision the array – its main characters actively engage in different strategies of image play. Throughout the film, we see the Joker in his headquarters, producing 'cut-ups' from the photographs that surround him, and then in a later scene at the museum he defaces one painting after another either by painting over the original or writing his name over the surface. His 'hijacking' of signs is more explicit in his seizure of the television signal when he interrupts schedule programming with his own parodic advertisements. Batman's appropriation of images works according to a quite different dynamic. Like the Joker, Batman seems to spend a significant amount of time watching television, and like his adversary he is shown surrounded by images that he manipulates for his own purposes. Just as Joker is practically engulfed by the photographs he cuts up, the first sequence in the Batcave presents Batman in front of a bank of monitors, surrounded by footage of his guests that his hidden cameras have recorded, images that he 'calls up' (rather than 'cuts up') in order to summon a reality that escaped his purview the first time around. While the Joker's manipulations of images is a process of consistent deformation, Batman engages in a process of retrieval, drawing on a reservoir of images that constitutes the past. The tension between abduction and retrieval epitomizes the conflicting but complementary processes at work in the film – a text that alternately *hijacks* and *accesses* the traditional Batman topoi. German Expressionism, Gaudi's *Sagrada Familia* Cathedral, Hitchcock films, etc.

The foregrounding of disparate intertexts and the all-pervasive hyper-consciousness concerning the history of both 'high art' and popular representation has become one of the most significant features of contemporary storytelling. Narrative action now operates at two levels simultaneously – in reference to character adventure and in reference to a text's adventures in the array of contemporary cultural production. That this self-referentiality should emerge as a response to that array is comparable to parallel developments in other disciplines. Mark Poster's recent essay on modes of information is a very productive attempt to specify the impact of new technologies on the nature of information, but it also reveals the necessity of dealing with the second half of the problem – the need to specify emerging forms of textuality used to negotiate the array. He argues:

> the complex linguistic worlds of the media, the computer and the database it can access, the surveillance capabilities of the state and the corporation, and finally the discourse of science are each realms in which the representational function of language has been placed in question by different communicational patterns, each of which shift to forefront the self-referential aspect of language. In each case, the language in question is constituted as an intelligible field with a unique pattern of wrapping, whose power derives not so much from representing something else, but from its internal linguistic structure. While this feature of language is always present in its use – today, meaning increasingly sustained through mechanisms of self-referentiality and the non-linguistic thing, the referent, fades into obscurity, playing less and less of a role in the delicate process of sustaining cultural memory.
>
> (72)

While Poster wisely acknowledges that there is a plurality of discontinuous modes of information each with its own historical peculiarities, he still maintains that his self-referentiality necessarily means the loss of the 'really Real' referent – a loss which has only devastating effects on communication and subjectivity; 'instead of envisioning language as a tool of a rational autonomous subject intent on controlling a world of objects for the purpose of enhanced freedom, the new language structures refer back upon themselves, severing referentiality and thereby acting upon the subject and constituting it in new and disorienting ways' (75). But do these new structures sever referentiality or just redefine the nature of referentiality? The notion of the referent posited here presupposes that this self-referentiality necessarily replaces any other kind of referentiality, but this argument offers no compelling reason to assume that self-referentiality, *ipso facto*, cancels out other types of referentiality. The self-referentiality that is symptomatic of communication in techno-sophisticated cultures, is a recognition of the highly discursive, thoroughly institutionalized dimension of all signs. At this point these signs become doubly referential, referring to a 'really real' world, but also to the reality of the array, which forms the fabric of day-to-day experience in those very cultures. It is the individual negotiations of the array that form the delicate process of not just maintaining but constantly rearticulating cultural memories.

This 'double referentiality' is the basis of the strategies of *rearticulation* discussed in the essays by Ann Cvetkovich, Cathy Griggers, Sharon Willis and Ava Preacher Collins in Collins *et al.* (1993). The individual voguers in *Paris in Burning* (1990), Callie Khouri's screenplay for *Thelma and Louise* (1991), and Jim Jarmusch's use of Elvis in *Mystery Train* (1989), all recognize the inseparability of these two levels of referentiality in regard to notions of gender and racial difference, the nature of sexual preference, and the determination of cultural value. All such distinctions are patterns of signs, conventionalized in such a way that they are now taken to be 'real' and therefore must be exposed as such through strategies of rearticulation that change that real by foregrounding mechanisms of referentiality. *Thelma and Louise* addresses the reality of the subjugation of women through its concerted reworking of the reality of the buddy film and the Western, repeatedly emphasizing the interconnectedness of gender difference and cinematic representation. Willis states this very succinctly: 'We women were raised on the same cinematic and televisual images and stories that men were, and we were identifying, perhaps with more resistance, or more intermittence, but identifying all the same, with the same male figures and masculine scenarios as our male contemporaries. This must be the framework in which images of women raiding those nearly worn-out stories, trying on those clichéd postures might have the effect of 'newness,' and might challenge our analysis of process and the effects of identification in our histories as consumers of popular culture.' Rather than disorientation, these strategies of rearticulation that reflect a hyper-consciousness about the impact of images on social categorization are a process of fundamental *reorientation* conducted on and through that double referentiality.

The divergent, often conflicting ways in which recent narratives rearticulate conventional structures of popular genres has become a distinguishing feature of contemporary textuality, but there is no uniform politics of rearticulation anymore than there is a single aesthetic of rearticulation. The ironic, hyperconscious reworking of the array varies, from the flat-out comedic parody of *Back to the Future III* to the more unsettling, ambivalent parody of *Blue Velvet*, to the explicit hijacking of signs in a film like *Thelma and Louise*. While stakes and strategies may differ profoundly, they do have one thing in common – the recognition that the features of conventional genre films that are subjugated to such intensive rearticulation are not the mere detritus of exhausted cultures past: those icons, scenarios, visual conventions continue to carry with them some sort of cultural 'charge' or resonance that must be reworked according to the exigencies of the present. The individual generic features then, are neither detritus nor reliquaries, but *artefacts* of another cultural moment that now circulate in different arenas, retaining vestiges of past significance reinscribed in the present.

In their frustration of the homogeneity and predictability considered the prerequisite for 'genericity,' these hybrid popular narratives present a paradoxical situation in which we encounter texts composed entirely of generic 'artifacts' that contradict, as an assemblage, the function of genre as coordinator of narrative conventions and audience expectations. I use the term artifact here because the individual icon or semantic feature acquires a kind of different status, not really the same element as before, since it now comes back with a set of quotation marks that hover above it like an ironic halo. But neither is it really an exhausted piece of debris ready to be camped up. Finding an analogous sort of transformation is difficult because this transformation process is, to a great extent, unprecedented. One could point to the transformation/transportation that a tribal artifact undergoes when it is placed in the museum, when, for example, the ceremonial mask or door-lock becomes revalued as minimalist sculpture once it is solidly ensconced not just behind the glass, but with the institutional frameworks that guarantee its new value. Rather than the figural becoming merely functional, the poetic degraded to common prosaic speech, here the functional acquires a figural status, becoming marked as a special kind of expression that can no longer be taken literally. Generic artifacts, like tribal artifacts, acquire new discursive registers unforeseen in their initial contexts, but they differ in regard to stability of the rearticulation. Where the new value given to the mask is anchored within the discursive formation that is museum art, the generic artifact remains unanchored, subject to multiple transformations, multiple transportations while still retaining vestiges of the original semantic and syntactic relationships that once gave it a precise generic value.

When the legend becomes hyperconscious, print the array.

And the only words that came to mind were 'the New Sincerity'

Getting an adequate picture of contemporary genericity depends on our ability to recognize widespread changes in what constitutes narrative action and visual entertainment, but these ironic, eclectic texts are not the 'whole story,' or more appropriately, are not the *only* story. Another type of genre film has emerged since the late 1980s, which is also a response to the same media-sophisticated landscape. Rather than trying to master the array through ironic manipulation, these films attempt to reject it altogether, purposely evading the media-saturated terrain of the present in pursuit of an almost forgotten authenticity, attainable only through a sincerity that avoids any sort of irony or eclecticism. Films such as *Dances With Wolves*, *Hook* and *Field of Dreams*, all fix this recoverable purity in an impossible past – impossible because it exists not just before the advent of media corruption, but because this past is, by definition, a never-never land of pure wish-fulfillment, in which the problems of the present are symbolically resolved in a past that not only did not, but could not exist.

In *Dances With Wolves*, that lost authenticity is situated in a West before the Western 'got to it.' In other words, the narrative of *Dances* focuses on the life of Native Americans before the arrival of the white man, a period traditionally ignored by the Western film. For most of the film, the only white man on the scene is John Dunbar, and he takes on the role of proto-ethnographer, rather than that of settler. His chief activity, observing and cataloguing the Sioux way of life, respects the purity of that tribe's existence. Dunbar's journal is all-important in this regard, since it serves as a guarantee of the authenticity of his position as ethnographer and as a symbol of his difference from other white men – a point made especially obvious when his journal is literally used as toilet paper by a pair of the most repulsive cavalrymen.

But *Dances With Wolves* makes this pre-history of the Western the site of another project – beyond an ostensible desire to depict the previously undepicted – in which the problems of White America of the 1990s are first diagnosed and then solved in the imaginary of that pre-history. The film repeatedly attempts to 'demythologize' the classic Western, whether by inverting conventions or presenting what *really* happened. The manifest destiny ideology that floated implicitly or explicitly throughout virtually all classic Westerns concerned with the settling of the West is here rewritten as a ruthless imperialism. The traditional structuring antinomy, Civilization vs. Savagery, is mobilized here, but the polarities are reversed as the Sioux become the model civilization. This reversal is most apparent in the final scene in which the heroic Indian warriors recapture Dunbar, now one of their own, and kill off a few soldiers (now defined as savage) in the process. But at the same time, this rewriting of the history of the Western expansion from the perspective of Native Americans is far from an end in itself. The other major project of the narrative, John Dunbar's self-actualization, is thoroughly inter-twined with that rewriting; the virtues of the Sioux of the 1860s are expressed in terms of another ideology generated by White America, specifically a 'New Age' mentality that becomes increasingly prominent in the second half of the film, when Dunbar 'finds himself.' The Sioux language may be respected here in an unprecedented manner through the use of subtitles, but the content of their speech is remarkably similar to what my students called the 'California speak' of the present.

The complicated, conflicted agenda of the New Sincerity genre becomes apparent in the 'harmony scene' mentioned in the introduction to this essay. After Dunbar takes part in the buffalo hunt and the celebration afterward, he watches the tribe move on the next day. The scene begins with a long pan across a breathtaking sunset – a tableau shot in the tradition of the classic Western, in which the Sioux are exquisitely silhouetted as dark figures on the crest of the horizon against the purple sky. This extremely painterly composition, when combined with Dunbar's voice-over, accords the figures an almost divine status: 'It seems everyday ends with a miracle here. And whatever God may be I thank God for this day. To stay any longer would have been useless. We had all the meat we could possibly carry. We had hunted for three days, losing half-a-dozen ponies, and only three men injured. I'd never known a people so eager to laugh, so devoted to family, so dedicated to each other, and the only word that came to mind was harmony.' When we first see Dunbar, it is from the side, observing the tableau from the distance in a completely different light zone. But as the scene progresses, his point of view shots of this awe-inspiring, harmonious spectacle alternate with shots of Dunbar, now framed by exactly the same majestic purple sunset. As he waves to his companions, he has been virtu-ally united with them, set in harmony with them through the lighting and his Sioux chest-protector. Once this solidarity is established, there is a pause in the voice-over, and the last shot of the Sioux is followed by a low-angle close-up of Dunbar that monumentalizes him still further as he says, 'Many times I'd felt alone, but until this afternoon I'd never felt completely lonely.'

The progression here exemplifies the interdependency of the rewriting of history and the process of self-actualization in which the former repeatedly gives way to the latter. The voice-over praises the Sioux, but in the images they are framed as a decorative cluster of Noble Savages, with only the sympathetic White Man receiving the big close-up. Paradoxically, this scene, while it locates authenticity in the pre-history of the Golden Age of the Western, uses the Native American in a way that is remarkably similar to that employed by early nineteenth-century European fiction such as Chateaubriand's *Atala, or the Love of Two Savages in the Desert* (1801), which virtually deified the Noble Savage. The ultimate 'authenticity' here depends upon another exigency – whether the plight of the Noble Savage of the past can serve as a satisfactory site for the narcissistic projections of alienated Europeans in the present. This dimension of *Dances With Wolves* becomes particularly apparent later in the film, when Dunbar reflects on the battle with the Pawnee, a battle without a 'dark political agenda.' 'I felt a pride I'd never felt before. I'd never really known who John Dunbar was. Perhaps the name itself had no meaning, but as I heard my Sioux name being called over and over, I knew for the first time who I really was.' In *Back to the Future III*, the rearview mirror tableau of 'Indians!' emphasized the artifice of any cinematic travels into history, that all Westerns are finally nothing more than highly conventionalized representations of an imaginary West. *Dances With Wolves* avoids any such ironic constructions in its attempt to locate the authentic vision of the past; nonetheless, the seemingly unmediated tableau becomes another kind of mirror, the idealized imaginary in which the troubled hero sees himself, a mirror in which he is magi-cally healed, in harmony, although only in this unrecoverable past.

Dances With Wolves contains a number of distinguishing features of this New Sincerity genre film: the move back in time away from the corrupt sophistication of media culture toward a lost authenticity defined simultaneously as a yet-to-be-contaminated folk culture of elemental purity, and as the site of successful narcissistic projection, the hero's magic mirror; the fore-grounding not only of the intertextual, but of the 'Ur-textual,' in which an originary genre text takes on a quasi-sacred function as the guarantee of authenticity; the fetishizing of 'belief' rather than irony as the only way to resolve conflict; the introduction of a new generic imagi-nary that becomes the only site where unresolvable conflicts can be successfully resolved. While it is well beyond the scope of this essay to catalogue all the instances of this emergent config-uration or to detail its various permutations, I hope a brief analysis of two representative films, *Hook* and *Field of Dreams*, will suggest how this configuration functions in other texts.

Spielberg's continuation of the Peter Pan story foregrounds all of these emergent conven-tions, and the differences between the Disney version and the Spielberg versions of J. M. Barrie's book throw the changing stakes of the New Sincerity genre film into sharp relief. While the former establishes the opposition between childhood and adulthood, the latter adds a level of hyper-self-awareness regarding the role film plays in constructing that difference, only to provide an imaginary transgression that takes the form of an ideal synthesis of the two. The indictment of media-saturated culture is omnipresent – the portable phone and camcorder are two major obstacles between Peter (now the lawyer as pirate) and his own children. The demonization of the camcorder involves one of the most interesting contradictions within the New Sincerity – that even though the search for lost purity and authenticity may depend on dazzling special effects and the blockbuster budgets they entail, there is nevertheless a free-floating technophobia. We know that Peter is a miserable failure as a father because he sends an assistant to videotape his son's baseball game, wilfully foregoing the authentic, 'unmediated' experience of watching his son's game 'in person.' The opposition between an authentic 'live-ness' seen as superior to an artificial technology is emphasized repeatedly in the opening scenes. The family goes to a school play to see one of the children perform as Wendy in a theatrical production of *Peter Pan*, which appears to charm everyone in the diegetic audience except Peter. When the family arrives at Wendy's London townhouse, she tells the children the story of Peter Pan, the tale-telling 'primal scene' accentuated in much the same way as the reading of *Peter Pan* in a comparable scene in *ET* (1982). In the earlier Spielberg film, the transmission of the 'Ur-story' is set up in a mis-en-abîme structure – while the mother reads the 'clap your hands if you believe' passage to her daughter, the son and ET sit transfixed in the dark, listening unobserved in a closet just as the theater full of parents and children listen unobserved in the dark. The foregrounding of the Ur-text in *Hook* becomes most explicit when Wendy hands the adult Peter 'the book' – apparently the first edition of Barrie's book, which, she tells Peter, was not fiction at all, but Barrie's transcription of the children's actual adventure, made possible by the fact that Barrie was their next-door neighbor. Once back in the world of children's fantasy, Peter regains his lost purity by recovering his childish delight in the elemental among the Wild Boys – a folk culture par excellence – leading to a resolution that can be effected only in *the* never-never land. Peter succeeds as a father only by recovering the lost child within him, thereby fusing two contradictory desires in one impossible composite: the desire to become the consummate father and the desire to return to the bliss of childhood outside of any paternal control.

The determination to resolve the unresolvable in a never-never land that is available neither in the present nor the past, but in an imaginary pre-history or originary moment takes an even more fanciful form in *Field of Dreams*. The film begins with a brief family history of the main character, Ray Kinsella, accomplished through family photos and voice-over narration. The main point of this section is that Ray and his father, once close, especially in their love of baseball, broke irreconcilably during his teenage years. His father had 'died' when his beloved White Sox threw the World Series in 1920 and later died an embittered shell of a man, old before his time. Once this troubled family history is established, the action in the present begins with Ray hearing voices in his cornfield. The field, like the Western landscape, is doubly fetishized as the yet to be corrupted pre-industrial, agrarian paradise ('Is this heaven?' 'No. It's Iowa.'), and as the site of narcissistic projection, here taken to an even greater extreme as the land actually talks directly to Ray about his private psycho-drama. The Ur-text in this film is likewise taken to more elaborate lengths; the lost text becomes the lost team as the Black Sox magically reappear in the dream diamond in the midst of the cornfield. The purity of this 'text' is emphasized through explicit comparison to the corrupt present. Shoeless Joe waxes rhapsodic about the elemental joys of the game, the 'thrill of the grass,' the fact that he would have played just for meal money (unlike the soulless mercenaries of contemporary major league baseball, of course). Within this eulogizing of the game, baseball as it was played by Shoeless Joe and company becomes a folk-cultural activity – an organic and, at the same time, mystical ritual. Grafted onto this nostalgia for baseball the way it used to be is a parallel nostalgia for the 1960s, and Ray believes he must 'ease the pain' of Terence Mann, the famous counter-cultural writer who becomes a kind of proxy father-figure for Kinsella, first in the 1960s (after he reads Mann's *The Boat Rocker* he stops playing catch with his biological father), and then explicitly in the 1980s when they travel together in search of their dreams. The connection between the America of the late teens and the late 1960s is articulated by Terence Mann during his 'People Will Come' speech near the film's conclusion – both periods are collapsed into mere passing moments alongside the eternal game that represents an eternal childhood.

> Ray, people will come, Ray. They'll come to Iowa for reasons they can't even fathom. They'll turn in to your driveway not knowing for sure why they're doing it. They'll arrive at your door, as innocent as children, longing for the past. . . . They'll find they have reserved seats somewhere along the baselines where they sat when they were children and cheered their heroes, and they'll watch the game and it'll be as if they dipped themselves in magic waters. The memories will be so thick they'll have to brush them away from their faces. People will come, Ray. The one constant through all the years, Ray, has been baseball. America has rolled by like an army of steamrollers. It's been erased like a blackboard, rebuilt and erased again. But baseball has marked the time. This field, this game, it's part of our past, Ray. It reminds us of all that once was good and could be again. Oh, people will come, Ray, people will definitely come.

Mann's oration perfectly describes the appeal of the New Sincerity. Like this mythical game, these films offer the recovery of lost purity, the attempt to recapture the elemental simplicity of childhood delight in a magical state that yields its perfect resolutions of the otherwise impossible conflict. Once Kinsella's proxy father departs with the players to document their stories and what is 'out there,' Ray finally reunites with his real father – but his father as a young man, a young baseball player years before he becomes a father. Generational tensions dissolve in this imaginary realm where boys can once again play catch with their fathers before their fathers became fathers, an impossible temporality that allows boys to reconcile with their lost fathers only when they're yet to be their fathers.

The two types of genre film that I have discussed here represent contradictory perspectives on 'media culture,' an ironic eclecticism that attempts to master the array through techno-sophistication, and a new sincerity that seeks to escape it through a fantasy technophobia. That both should appear as responses to media saturation is not surprising, nor is the simultaneity of these responses; the popular narratives of the late 1980s and early 1990s articulate a profound ambivalence that reflects the lack of any sort of unitary mass consciousness. Both types of these genre films involve a meta-mythological dimension, in which the cultural terrain that must be mapped is a world already sedimented with layers of popular mythologies, some old, some recent, but all co-present and subject to rearticulation according to different ideological agendas. These emergent forms of genericity do not mark the beginning of post-postmodernism or late postmodernism, especially since the latter might turn out to be as much of a misnomer as Late Capitalism. One could just as easily argue that what we have seen of postmodernism thus far is really a first phase, perhaps Early Postmodernism, the first tentative attempts at envisioning the impact of new technologies of mass communication and information processing on the structure of narrative. If, following Marshal Berman, we might say that Modernism was a period in which all that was solid melted into air, the current period is defined by a different dynamic, in which all that is aired eventually turns solid, the transitory coming back around as the monumental with a decidedly different cultural status and cultural resonance. Contemporary popular narratives mark the beginning of the next phase, when new forms of textuality emerge to absorb the impact of these changes, and in the process turn them into new forms of entertainment.

PART FIVE

Identities

AS WE HAVE SEEN, FILM THEORY HAS MOVED from the consideration of a subjectivity that is the product of psychoanalytic processes to a new focus on a more explicitly constructed, perhaps even deliberately chosen, social identity. Changes in the political focus of cultural and critical theory in general – from a dominant interest in ideology towards an analysis of the distribution and exercise of power – have directed attention onto the specific politics of social identity within specific historical conjunctures. This attention has dwelt on, in particular, the formations of ethnicity, sexuality and gender.

The earlier debates around subjectivity can be found in other collections of readings. Rather than reproduce again the essays from Laura Mulvey, Mary Anne Doane, Linda Williams and so on, I have chosen to take their points of view as already established in order to examine examples of the legacy of, and developments from, these debates in contemporary discussions. Accordingly, while this part engages with debates about the construction of the feminine through cinema, it reflects the influence of recent critiques of the 'male gaze' tradition and its evaluation of popular cinema. There is certainly a counter-tradition of feminist analysis of popular film which does not ascribe to the avant-garde aesthetic that makes so much of the debate about 'the male gaze', and the pessimistic account of popular cinema this debate has occasioned. Instead, there is interest in recovering the positive political potential of popular forms – not so much as a recuperative aesthetic exercise as an attempt to provide analyses that more accurately account for what happens on the screen, and how that might be read by popular audiences (and the plural is significant). In the first excerpt, from *Spectacular Bodies*, Yvonne Tasker argues that women's representation in the contemporary cinema does not occur solely through the codes of femininity. Like Carol Clover in *Men, Women and Chainsaws* (1992), she chooses a critically maligned genre (action films) through which to make this argument. Much as does Modleski in the previous section, Tasker attributes some of the distaste for such films, and the consequent dismissal of the evidence they might provide for understanding the appeal of popular film, to a 'class-based, high-cultural attitude towards the popular cinema'.

The opening chapter of *Spectacular Bodies* describes the post-1980s shift that has the heroine move 'from her position as a subsidiary character within the action narrative, to the central role of *action heroine*, a figure who commands the narrative'. In Chapter 22, excerpted for this *Reader*, 'Action heroines in the 1980s: the limits of "musculinity"', Tasker narrows this down to a focus on the appearance of a muscular action heroine – such as Demi Moore's *GI Jane*. Tasker discusses the muscular heroine not only in relation to the development of 'masculine' identities for women in the cinema, but also in the context of women's increasing involvement in the sport of bodybuilding – 'health culture . . . as opposed to beauty culture'. Discussing representations of female bodybuilders, Tasker is critical of those who find the blend of standard gender signifiers ('the hardness of female muscles, the softer flesh of the breast') disturbing; feminist or not, she cautions, they are conservative responses to gendered or sexed bodily identity. Tasker coins the term 'musculinity' to describe the way that 'some of the qualities of masculinity are written over the muscular female body'. Actors she refers to here include Linda Hamilton in *The Terminator* movies, and there could be many other instances (Geena Davis in *The Long Kiss Goodnight*, for instance). The points she wishes to establish are that, on the one hand, 'signifiers of strength [i.e. muscularity] are not limited to male characters' in contemporary popular cinema and, on the other, that these 'muscu-line' action heroines are nevertheless still 'marked as women'. While musculinity, as she goes on to argue, has its limits, it constitutes a broadening of the range of representations of female identities within popular film.

Sabrina Barton's 'Your Self Storage: female investigation and male performativity in the woman's psychothriller' is also a revisionist project. Indeed, in her footnotes she says that it was Clover's discussion of the 'Final Girl' (the last, always female, victim of the monster in the slasher films Clover studies) that provoked her interest in the 'female investigator' in the films she examines. Barton's essay comes from within a more disciplinary model of film studies rather than Tasker's cultural studies inflected approach, although she acknowledges the usefulness of cultural studies' focus on 'self-centred spectatorship' and Larry Grossberg's work on rock music fans. Like Tasker, however, and despite their differences in theoretical and disciplinary orientation, Barton's study is aimed at finding a way of theoretically reclaiming the experience of the 'actual' film audience.

Paralleling the movement within cultural studies that resisted the characterisation of popular audiences of television as ideological dupes, the provocation for this is the writer's own response to the narrative function and the image of Clarice Starling in *Silence of the Lambs*. Recognizing the complications that attend her appreciation of Jody Foster's portrayal of Clarice Starling as a figure with whom female identification seems irresistible, Sabrina Barton nevertheless pursues a theorised position which more accurately reflects her own, and perhaps others', response to the film. Making use of Judith Butler's notion of the 'perfor-mativity' of gender, Barton examines a set of heroines who seem to be more 'real' (to have a coherent core self, is how Barton describes it) than Butler's argument would suppose. Further, they are narratively opposed to male monsters who are explicitly 'performative' (Buffalo Bill in *Silence of the Lambs*). Barton argues that since 'performativity tends to be negatively coded as duplicitous, fragmented, and unstable' (and traditionally, feminine), while 'real' characters are 'strong, unified and stable' (and traditionally masculine), the reversal of such a pattern within a significant number of films suggests the need to rethink the possibil-ities of female identification in contemporary cinema.

Chris Straayer's essay, 'The Hypothetical Lesbian Heroine in Narrative Feature Film', offers us a careful account of the construction of lesbian desire in response to two feature films. Straayer's discussion sets out to demonstrate a number of strategies used within the two films analysed – the French films *Entre Nous* and *Voyage en Douce* – which allow for the lesbian spectator to identify with the 'hypothetical' lesbian heroine. The argument is that lesbian desire is implicitly accommodated within these film texts. The emphasis here is not on an alternative, lesbian, reading of the meaning of the text. Rather, the emphasis is upon the structured opportunities provided in the text for lesbian identification. Among such opportunities, Straayer outlines a pattern of highly eroticised exchanges of glances between females, of female bonding, and the deployment of the male intermediary to operate as a licensing device for both heterosexual and homosexual 'viewership and desire'.

The preceding three essays demonstrate that the specificity and agency of the female spectator – as well as the pleasures of popular cinema – are now objects of study. Or, as Sabrina Barton puts it, the field has become interested in the 'valuing of spectators' potentially self-affirming relations with popular culture'. This is among the legacies of feminist film theory from the 1970s: the close attention film studies has paid to issues of representation as a result of the clear understanding that repeated patterns of representation carry material social and cultural effects. Since the 1970s, the attention paid to these patterns of representation has steadily increased. The representation of the feminine was the first area to be explored but there are now substantial literatures on the representation of various minorities, of ethnicities and on sexualities. The concerns in this literature are not with developing a canon of film texts. Indeed, it is probably true to say that their concern is not necessarily primarily with the medium of film. Rather, they are interested in uncovering what may look like disinterested operations of power – where popular media forms reproduce the exclusions and preferences of their culture – and the site they have chosen is film. They are interested in the part that the feature film plays in the social construction of identity – or as it is more widely thought of, the politics of identity: how the operation of discursive power licenses, defines and excludes specific formations of identity, and the consequences of this.

Susan Jeffords' essay 'Can Masculinity Be Terminated?' turns its attention to an identity that has been relatively ignored as criticism has concentrated on constructions of the feminine. In a sharp and witty account of the *Terminator* films, as well as a range of 1990s features which concentrate on 'new' Hollywood masculinities (*Three Men and A Baby*, *Regarding Henry* and so on), Susan Jeffords unpacks the character of this new, nurturing identity. The trend she examines does not only represent the 'warming of the male heart' and 'an improvement of father-child relations' but, less explicitly, the male replacement of women whose 'work has interfered with their ability to mother their children'. This is explicated through the example of Sarah's relationship with her son and the 'good' terminator in *Terminator 2*. This new narrative of masculinity is, Jeffords argues, 'disarmingly dangerous'. The world of the family is now offered up as an 'alternative realm' to the world of work for the exercise of masculine power and authority. (A longer version of this essay which is contained in Jeffords' book *Hard Bodies* [1994], discusses Arnold Schwarzenegger's performance in *Kindergarten Cop*.) Jeffords' essay, placed in conjunction with the three articles preceding it in this section, raises questions about what then is left for the woman in these narratives. It implies a very different politics for the 'musculine' woman represented for both sides of the argument by the figure of Sarah Connor in *Terminator 2*.

Isaac Julien and Kobena Mercer's 'De Margin and De Centre' deals with the representation of ethnicity in British cinema in the late 1980s. Originally published as the introduction to a special issue of *Screen* (29:4, 1988), called 'The Last "Special Issue" on Race?', its focus is more upon the production than the reception of film. Written at a time when a series of British films had represented themselves as being 'about' ethnicity and national identity' (*Handsworth Songs*, *My Beautiful Launderette*), Julien and Mercer's piece rejects the complacent view that this might constitute an appropriate recognition of marginalized ethnicities within the UK. Such a view accepts race and ethnicity as legitimate concerns, but still places them on the margins. Julien and Mercer call for a situation where race and ethnicity are placed in the centre of critical debates – as the proper site for the negotiation of the conflicting identities proliferating within the 'imagined community' of the British nation.

The essay provides an account of the articles contained within the special issue of *Screen*. It also provides an overview of the complicated issues involved in acknowledging the cultural construction of ethnicity, and the potential effects of defining cultural groups through their ethnicities in film funding structures as well as in the signifying practices of representation. In the UK, class has dominated film, media and cultural studies for most of their history; gender breaks through in the late 1970s and, as we have seen, exerts a powerful influence on the field. Race, however, has been a comparatively recent addition and is yet to exert anything like that level of influence. Interestingly, race is hooked up primarily to issues of identity and representation, with little interest in arguing for a progressive or avant-garde interrogation of mainstream media forms. Its interest is, as Julien and Mercer suggest, affecting debates in 'de Centre', and merely gaining representation within an avant-garde cinema simply reinforces its marginalization.

The final contribution to this part, a short section from the chapter entitled 'The Imperial Imaginary' in Ella Shohat and Robert Stam's *Unthinking Eurocentrism*, suggests yet another angle of inspection that has been under-represented within film studies. Shohat and Stam note a range of historical coincidences with the beginnings of cinema that have been recognised already – cinema and psychoanalysis, cinema and nationalism, cinema and consumerism. More importantly, though, Shohat and Stam point out that the beginnings of cinema at the end of the nineteenth century 'coincided with the giddy heights of the imperial project'. The leading film nations were also the leading imperialist countries – France, the UK, the US and Germany – and 'cinema emerged exactly at the point where the enthusiasm for the imperial project was spreading beyond the elites into the popular strata'. Imperial politics had already become mass culture. Popular tales of adventure, exploration and conquest (widely read nineteenth-century novels by Kipling, Rider Haggard and Edgar Rice Burroughs) were adapted by the cinema, as masculine romance adopted the forging of empire as the most noble of enterprises. The cinema, they go on to point out, was ideally 'suited to relay the projected narratives of nations and empires'. As we have seen in our earlier discussions of national cinemas, national culture is still 'broadly linked to cinematic fictions'. In the case they document, it was a complex of national discourses – a broadly European/American alliance of ideologies and geopolitical interests – that intersected with the spread of a popular entertainment industry that 'created a powerful hegemony of its own'. In a richly detailed account of the converging interests of science, technology, national identity, and the creation of new markets, Shohat and Stam present a powerful argument for the cinema's participation in the 'projection' and nationalization of imperial interests across the globe.

Chapter 22

YVONNE TASKER

ACTION HEROINES IN THE 1980s
The limits of 'musculinity'

I T W O U L D B E P O S S I B L E T O S E E T H E C E N T R A L I T Y of action heroines
in recent Hollywood film as posing a challenge to women's social role, and to her representation within the cinema's symbolic order. This is the terrain over which a developing
debate is currently being conducted, within feminist film criticism, as to the significance of
the action heroine. Cinematic images of women who wield guns, and who take control of
cars, computers and the other technologies that have symbolized both power and freedom
within Hollywood's world, mobilize a symbolically transgressive iconography. At the most
fundamental level, images of the active heroine disrupt the conventional notion – often
significantly present as an assumption within feminist film criticism – that women either
are, or should be, represented exclusively through the codes of femininity. The critical
suggestion that the action heroine is 'really a man', a suggestion that is addressed further
below, stems from this assumption and represents an attempt to secure the logic of a gendered
binary in which the terms 'male' and 'masculine', 'female' and 'feminine' are locked together.
As the earlier discussion of action heroines of the 1970s indicates, the female protagonists
of contemporary action films emerge from a long cinematic and literary tradition. However,
the action heroine has also, in the last twenty years, undergone a significant redefinition
in western films. Thus, although she is not a product solely of the 1980s, there is a specificity
to the appearance of recent action heroines. I characterized this in Chapter 1, in terms of
the heroine's move from her position as a subsidiary character within the action narrative,
to the central role of *action heroine*, a figure who commands the narrative. A more specific
phenomenon associated with recent cinema is the appearance of a *muscular* action heroine, a
figure who is discussed below in relation to the growth in women's involvement in bodybuilding as a sport and what this means for the development of shifting, 'masculine' identities
for women.

Frantz Fanon's analysis of the symbolic and actual limits imposed by colonialism, cited earlier, provides a useful perspective through which to think about the operation of class and race
within the muscular fantasies of empowerment that structure the action cinema. Fanon's work
also makes clear the extent to which colonial discourse positions its subject within a sexualized
rhetoric. Following on from this, Kobena Mercer has made the salient point that for critics
to talk about stereotypical representations of blackness-as-passivity in terms of the figure of

'castration', operates to once more recentre sexuality (which is fantasized as either excessive or absent) as the trope through which blackness can most usefully be spoken about and understood.[1] In criticism, as in aesthetic practice, these stereotypes cannot be simply sidestepped – this much is evident from the action films, such as *Shaft* and *Predator 2*, discussed in Chapter 2. The incorporation and working through of these stereotypes, within both contemporary criticism and the film next, makes clear the extent to which the constitution of the body as sexed and as gendered intersects with its constitution as a subject of class and racial discourse. The fantasies of a muscular physical power that Fanon speaks of – expressed in dreams of jumping, running, swimming and climbing – are also bound into images of a masculine (though not, necessarily, male) strength, that is constructed as both an expression of freedom and a form of protection. Thus he suggests that 'the native's muscles are always tensed' (Fanon 1985: 41). These images, which speak of both bodily invincibility and vulnerability, clearly accord with the kinds of operation through which the male body is constructed in the action cinema.

Metaphors of constriction and freedom, which draw from the actual limits through which lives are lived, have also been central to women's fiction. Such metaphors have been strategically mobilised by feminist writers. Maxine Hong Kingston's *The Woman Warrior* works through such an opposition in her fantastic portraits of Chinese-American womanhood thus:

> When we Chinese girls listened to the adults' talking-story, we learned that we failed if we grew up to be but wives or slaves. We could be heroines, swordswomen. Even if she had to rage across all China, a swordswoman got even with anybody who hurt her family. Perhaps women were once so dangerous that they had to have their feet bound.
>
> (Hong Kingston 1977: 25)

Here images of a fabulous power and freedom are defined against images of extreme constriction. And whilst Hong Kingston clearly refers here to a female experience, and to male experience in *China Men*, her work effectively blurs the boundaries between categories of masculinity and femininity.[2] This is a literature concerned with the history and experience of limitation and constriction as it constitutes both women and men. Both oppression and fantasised escape are, however *imaginary* they may be, in effect inscribed *over the body*. To return to the contemporary cinema, we can take the controversial film *Thelma and Louis* as a narrative of criminal women, centred on heroines who seem to delight in their transgression of both the law and of the constraints within which they have lived their lives. The film enacts a drama which is about the transgression of limits – the opening up of the American landscape of the road invokes, for example, a pioneer rhetoric. The equally controversial *Basic Instinct* orchestrates a rather different narrative of sexual investigation. The female protagonist, Catherine Tramell (Sharon Stone), is both an aggressively sexual woman and a serial killer – a criminal woman who transgresses both the law and Hollywood's conventions of female behaviour. This chapter addresses some of the issues which are posed by such films, as well as the debates which have framed their reception. What is the significance of the appearance of the female action heroine in the mainstream of Hollywood cinema production? How does this figure relate to the established Hollywood codes for representing both authority, and the populist hero's refusal of that authority? Debates concerning the political status of the active/action heroine are explored specifically in relation to *Thelma and Louise* and *Basic Instinct*. Following on from the question of 'masculinization', raised within feminist evaluations of the action heroine, the impact of women's involvement in bodybuilding is considered in terms of the transgression of bodily limits.

Sexuality, feminism and film: the controversy over *Thelma and Louise* and *Basic Instinct*

'This film is a con'. Thus ran the opening of *Spare Riob*'s review of Ridley Scott's *Alien* on its initial release back in 1979. With the exception of this film, in which Sigourney Weaver stars as Ripley, when feminist writers have addressed the action cinema at all during the 1980s, it has only been to dismiss the genre as macho and reactionary in familiar terms. However, the emergence of a series of diverse action-based films centred on female protagonists has begun to generate a debate as to the political status of these films and their heroines. *Thelma and Louis*, a road movie also directed by Ridley Scott, was the surprise hit of the summer of 1991, both in America and in European countries such as Britain and France.[3] The success of the film generated a series of articles, reviews and other commentaries which diversely praised, expressed concern or fascination at its 'gun-toting' heroines. Some saw *Thelma and Louise* as a feminist reworking of a male genre, the road movie, with women taking the place of the male buddies familiar to viewers of popular Hollywood cinema. For others, the film represented an interrogation of male myths about female sexuality, an admirable commentary on rape and sexual violence. I've already spoken of the way in which *Thelma and Louise* has been appropriated by some women as a 'lesbian film'. Elsewhere *Thelma and Louise* has been characterized as a betrayal, a narrative that cannot follow through on its own logic. Far from being about empowering women, in this view the image of women-with-guns is considered to be one which renders the protagonists *symbolically male*. Whatever view we take, *Thelma and Louse* and associated female heroines have generated, at the beginning of the 1990s, an academic and journalistic debate analogous to that sparked by the muscular male stars of the 1980s.[4] The film has also been consumed in an historical moment marked by the public re-emergence of familiar questions to do with sexuality, violence and relations of power between men and women, in the publicity surrounding the nomination of Judge Clarence Thomas to the Supreme Court and the Kennedy rape case in the US.[5]

 Thelma and Louise follows the adventures of two white southern women in the US who take off for a weekend of fun and end up on the run from the law. After an attempted rape leads to a fatal shooting and flight from the police, the theft of Louise's savings leads Thelma to armed robbery. With its outlaw heroines pushed beyond the point of no return, *Thelma and Louise* takes its place with a group of recent movies which put female protagonists at the centre of those action-based genres often reserved for men. A series of talked-about film performances from a variety of action sub-genres, all invoked the figure of the independent woman as heroine. Whilst films such as *Aliens* and *Silence of the Lambs* and the performances of their female stars have caused much critical interest, an attendant suspicion can be detected that this type of role, indeed the appearance of women in the action cinema at all, is somehow inappropriate. Critical responses are never univocal, of course, but feminist critics have responded to these films with various combinations of pleasure and disgust, enthusiasm and suspicion. These films, it seems, whilst praised and enjoyed for their centring of women, are for some potentially tainted by exploitation. Such a sense of critical unease is certainly worth exploring. For if action movies centred on men have drawn condemnation for their supposed endorsement of a hypermasculinity, how can the negative reaction to the emergence of female action heroines be contextualised and understood? The films themselves may well prove easier to understand when placed within the context of the popular cinema, and the tradition of the American action movie in particular, rather than in the context of a tradition of feminist film-making against which they are sometimes judged and, inevitably, found wanting.

Laura Mulvey concluded her well-known polemic essay of the 1970s, 'Visual Pleasure and Narrative Cinema', with the suggestion that women would have little or nothing to mourn in the passing of the Hollywood cinema.[6] While recognizing that the popular cinema of today is, in many ways, different from the popular cinema that Mulvey addresses, I want to raise a set of questions about the pleasure that both female and feminist spectators *do* take from mainstream movies, pleasures which are not dictated by any rules of same-sex identification or by heterosexual understandings of desire. The best way to express this might be in terms of a contradiction between what 'we' know and what 'we' enjoy, since the kinds of fantasy investments at work in the pleasures taken from the cinema cannot be controlled by conscious political positions in the way that some criticism seems to imply.[7] A tension between the project of legitimating women's pleasures and the desire to assess representations politically informs a good deal of feminist criticism. It is ironic then that a critical disapproval of the 1980s' and 1990s' action heroine may stem in part from a feminist cultural criticism which has, in seeking to legitimise various pleasures and pastimes, classified popular forms and genres into male and female. The notion that some forms of activity and entertainment are more appropriate to men and some to women, that some genres can be called 'masculine' whilst others are labelled 'feminine', has a long history. Such a notion has its roots in commonsense understandings of appropriate male and female behaviour as well as in the categories set up by those who produce images and fictions – such as the 'woman's film'. Ironically a desig-nation of 'inappropriate' images derived from a feminist critical tradition, coincides here with a more conventional sense of feminine decorum, a sense of knowing one's place within a gendered hierarchy. As much as anything, this critical trajectory reveals the operation within feminist criticism of a class-based, high-cultural, attitude towards the popular cinema, an atti-tude familiar from other forms of criticism. This is an important point since, as we have seen in previous chapters, class is a central term in the narratives of the popular action cinema.

Thelma and Louise charts the development of its two heroines as they move from the routines and confinement of everyday life to the freedom of the open road. In the process they move from the supposedly female space of the home to the freedom of the supposedly 'male' space that is the great outdoors. The martial-arts movie *China O'Brien* also follows this trajectory, with China resigning her job as a city cop to return to her home town, where she ultimately becomes sheriff. A montage sequence shows her driving through the countryside in an open-top car, images of her face in close-up intercut with her surroundings. Whilst there is nothing particularly unusual in this, cinematically speaking, Rothrock here occupies the role of a 'figure in a landscape', the phrase Mulvey uses to describe the narrative control assigned to the male protagonist (Mulvey 1989: 20). The film seems to coyly acknowledge this shift, including a shot of a male gas-pump attendant, his chest exposed and hair blowing in the wind. The construction of this secondary male figure as spectacle provides a counter-point to China's position as a dominating figure within the film. The road comes to signal a certain mythicised freedom.

At the outset of *Thelma and Louise*, Thelma (Geena Davies) is a shy, childlike woman, playing the role of a meek housewife to husband Darryl's macho self-centredness. Louise (Susan Sarandon) is a waitress, capable and in control, balancing the demands of customers and workmates. The two set off for the weekend, Thelma's inability to decide *anything* resulting in a jokey sequence in which she packs just about everything she owns. This confusion is intercut with the neatness of Louise's apartment, everything cleaned and in its place. These images conjure up two recognizable extremes of an inability to cope, set against a calm effi-ciency. These comic extremes in turn set up the terms within which these characters will change and develop through the course of the narrative. I've already spoken of the ways in which a rites-of-passage narrative is a key feature of the Vietnam movie, a narrative in which the (white) hero 'finds himself' in the other space of Vietnam. These narratives build on a tradition of imperialist fictions within film and literature, in which Asia and Africa are constituted as exotic spaces for adventure. This structure is seen most explicitly in *Platoon* and is parodically, if rather viciously, drawn on in the 'Asia' of *Indiana Jones and the Temple of Doom*.[8] The heroine of women's fiction is centred in a rather different rites-of-passage narrative, though one which nonetheless represents a coming to knowledge. Maria La Place discusses the operation of such a narrative trajectory in many women's novels and stories which 'centre on the heroine's process of self-discovery, on her progression from ignorance about herself (and about the world in general) to knowledge and some kind of strength' (Gledhill 1987: 152). Specifically referring to the 1940s' film and novel *Now Voyager*, La Place outlines the extent to which this transformation is both signalled and partly achieved through changes in the heroine's appearance – weight loss, new clothes, hairstyle and so on. This transformation is reminiscent of the narratives constructed around the male bodybuilder, whose physical transformation supposedly signals his changed status in the world. The rites-of-passage narrative that situates women in relation to health or body culture defines the heroine's transformation through the body. Such a transformation is enacted over the protagonists of *Thelma and Louise*, with their changing appearance seen by Kathleen Murphy as a literal shedding of skin when, in the final moments of the film, 'the Polaroid of two smiling girls on vacation that Louise shot so many miles ago blows away in the wind, as insubstantial as a snake's outgrown skin' (Murphy 1991: 29). The end credit sequence continues this theme with a series of images of the two women, taken from different points in the narrative, which trace their transformation.

There is though a further sense in which the film's drama is enacted over the bodies of the two heroines. A drunken sexual assault on Thelma propels the two women on the road. Initially it is Louise who takes control, who rebukes and then shoots Harlan dead. Thelma's response is hysteria. 'What kind of world are you living in?' cries Louise on hearing Thelma's suggestion that they hand themselves over to the police. Later, when Louise's life savings have been stolen by JD (Brad Pitt), a young man Thelma has taken a liking to, it is Thelma who begins to take charge. She robs a convenience store, a performance we see through the flickering images, filmed by the store's surveillance video, as they are replayed by the police to an astounded Darryl. By the end of the movie both Thelma and Louise are armed, literally with a gun stolen from a state trooper, and metaphorically with a powerful sense of self and of the impossibility of a return to their earlier lives. They decide to head for Mexico since, as Thelma puts it, 'Something's crossed over in me. I can't go back – I just couldn't live'. Through these later scenes, the women are no longer just running, but enjoying the journey. The film offers a series of spectacular images, visual echoes of the women's changed perception. The two women shoot up a tanker, after its driver, who has plagued them at various points along the road, has refused to apologise for his behaviour. The truck explodes in a mass of flame. Driving through the desert landscape at night, their car is lit up from within – a surreal beacon. In this quiet moment they contemplate the night sky. Exhilarating and frustrating, the now notorious final image of the film has the two women driving off a precipice rather than give themselves up.

The narrative of transformation which structures *Thelma and Louis* is analogous to the developments in Linda Hamilton's character, Sarah Connor, in *The Terminator*. Like Louise, Sarah begins the film as a harassed waitress. Told by her lover and protector, Kyle Reese, that she is destined to become a legend to the rebels of a future society, she moans that she can't even balance a cheque book. By the end of the film she has acquired military discipline, becoming well-armed and self-sufficient. The militaristic iconography is continued in the sequel, *Terminator 2*, extended and literally embodied through Hamilton's muscular frame. A turning-point for Sarah Connor in *The Terminator* comes when Kyle is wounded and she must take control. At the very moment that he looks like giving up the fight, she screams at him to move. Addressing him as 'Soldier', she takes up the role of a commanding officer who harangues a tired platoon in order to save them, a role familiar from many Hollywood war movies. It is after this proof of her transformation, and Kyle's death which follows soon after, that Sarah finally terminates the Terminator. Kyle must die since, like the male hero, it seems that the action heroine cannot be in control of an adult sexuality. At the beginning of *Aliens* Ripley refuses the offer to accompany the military on an Alien-hunting mission, telling company man Carter Burke – 'I'm not a solider'. She finally agrees to accompany the military platoon as an observer. Once there, however, despite her protestations, Ripley effectively takes control from the inexperienced military leader – like Sarah Connor she is transformed into a soldier.

It is perhaps the centrality of images of women with guns in all the films I've referred to thus far, that has caused the most concern amongst feminist critics. The phallic woman, that characters like Sarah Connor and Ripley represent, is seen as a male ruse, and a film like *Thelma and Louise* as 'little more than a masculine revenge fantasy' whose 'effect is perversely to reinforce the message that women cannot win'.[9] Here we can see the obverse process of that critical move by which the suffering of the hero has been read as a testament to his, and consequently patriarchy's, invincibility. In turn the struggles of the female protagonist seem only to reinforce her passivity and secure her ultimate failure. Disruptive narrative or representational elements exist, within such a critical view, as little more than precursors to their ultimate hegemonic incorporation. Hence these images are taken to represent a double betrayal, holding out a promise that can never be fulfilled ('This film is a con'). Though it is not the project of this book, it might well be worth exploring further the kinds of masochistic fantasies at work in such critical moves. Alternatively, situating a film like *Thelma and Louise* within the tradition of popular cinema might, as I've argued, allow us to see it differently. Within many Hollywood action narratives, access to technologies such as cars and guns (traditional symbols of power) represents a means of empowerment. These technologies are also intimately bound up with images of the masculine. The female protagonists of the films discussed above operate within an image-world in which questions of gender identity are played out through, in particular, the masculinization of the female body. Within *Thelma and Louise* the possession of guns and the possession of self are inextricably linked through the dilemmas that the film poses about freedom and self-respect. Drawing on a long history of representations of male self-sufficiency, the film traces the women's increasing ability to 'handle themselves', a tracing that follows their ability to handle a gun. Thelma can barely bring herself to handle her gun, a gift from husband Darryl, at the start of the film – picking it up with an expression of distaste, in a rather 'girlish' fashion. As the narrative progresses, she acquires both physical coordination, which denotes self-possession, and the ability to shoot straight. When the two women shoot out the tanker, they happily compliment each other on their aim.

Thelma and Louise is for the most part comic in tone. It is for this reason that, despite all the gunplay, the women only once shoot anybody, the killing which sends them on the run, through the entire course of the film – in order to keep the heroines as sympathetic figures they cannot be constructed as wantonly violent, so there is no final shootout. The carefully contained criminality represented in the figures of Thelma and Louise can be contrasted to the figure of Catherine Tramell in *Basic Instinct*, an intensely controversial film which has provoked protests in the US against its 'negative' representation of a 'lesbian' heroine. *Basic Instinct* is, by contrast to *Thelma and Louise*, a thriller, and the heroine is a monstrous but fascinating figure. We are positioned with an equally monstrous detective hero, Nick, played by Michael Douglas, who investigates a series of murders associated with Tramell. The publicity images for the film showed the two in an embrace, Douglas in profile with his back to us, Stone staring out of the image at the viewer. Because Tramell is the villain of the piece, her transgressions can be of quite a different order to the heroic women who learn about themselves, and each other, on the road in *Thelma and Louise*. The most obvious antecedent for both the narrative and characterization that *Basic Instinct* mobilizes, as well as critical models for thinking about its articulation of sexuality, is the *film noir* of the 1940s. Several critics have pointed to the power and potency of the image of the deadly *femme fatale* who is found in these films. Such critical models often direct our attention not only to the ideological implications of the narrative progression, in which the strong woman inevitably dies or is punished, but to the lasting impression that her figure leaves us with. Thus Janey Place remarks that *film noir* is 'one of the few periods of film in which women are active, not static symbols, are intelligent and powerful, if destructively so, and derive power, not weakness, from their sexuality' (Kaplan 1980: 35). Here the *femme fatale* is seen to turn around the terms within which 'woman' is defined, so that both her power, and the power against which she might be seen to resist, is constituted through the terms of sexuality.

Catherine Tramell is certainly cast as a *femme fatale*, a deadly woman who uses her sexuality against men. Tramell is a wealthy, sexually aggressive, woman who becomes involved with various men who are destined to become characters in her books, and ultimately to be killed off once they have outlived their usefulness. More controversially, Catherine is cast as bisexual – or rather polymorphously perverse. Critics who attacked the portrayal of Catherine as a lesbian, either ignored the fact that she spends a good part of the film sexually involved with men, or constructed this as a pathologizing narrative in which she is 'cured' of her lesbianism. Whilst this is certainly what Douglas's character seems to believe within the film, as he brags about his sexual performance to Catherine's girlfriend, for instance, there is also a clear sense in which the audience cannot fully accept this version of events. Indeed a sustained narrative tension stems from the ambiguity which surrounds Tramell's attitude to Douglas, particularly an uncertainty as to whether or not he will become her next victim. In the publicity poster from which Sharon Stone stares out at the viewer, her mouth (and hence her expression) remains hidden, rendering her a mysterious figure. The final image of the film itself echoes this sense, so that the ending is left deliberately sinister and uncertain. Filling the frame is the murder weapon, an ice pick, which is hidden beneath the bed that Tramell shares with Nick/Douglas. Such an ambiguity may indicate that the 'active' heroine who is associated with the figure of the *femme fatale*, as Place defines her, is quite distinct from the action heroine, who is rarely an ambiguous figure for the audience. In thinking about recent action cinema we need to pay attention not only to the ambiguity which is at stake in the gendered identity of the *active heroine*, but the redefinition of the sexed body that is worked out over the muscular female body of the *action heroine*.

Women, bodybuilding and body culture

Women are becoming increasingly involved in bodybuilding as a competitive sport. It is now also a commonplace part of the exercise programmes recommended in women's magazines, no longer perceived, as it once was, as a marginal activity associated with only a few 'fanatical' sportswomen. This involvement has led to the rapid growth of the bodybuilding industry and, as Laurie Schulze points out, shifts in the 'ideal' female body – as it is offered to women through fashion magazines, models, beauty culture and so on. The soft curves presented as defining the ideal female form in the 1950s, has shifted to an emphasis on muscle tone in images of the 1980s and early 1990s. At the same time, of course, the market for men's cosmetics has expanded, championed by several successful men's style magazines.[10] Some bodybuilding magazines now extend their promise-cum-challenge to 'build yourself a better body', to women as well as to men. Both beauty and body culture have responded then, though perhaps in contradictory ways, to the successes of the women's movement, most particularly in the repeated invocation within advertising of the figure of the (sexually) independent woman. The advent of the female bodybuilder represents a distinct part of this response. Schulze argues that the female bodybuilder 'threatens not only current socially constructed definitions of femininity and masculinity, but the system of sexual difference itself' (Gaines and Herzog 1990: 59). Bodybuilding, that is, makes explicit the extent to which both sex and gender constitute the body within culture, problematizing the boundaries of what constitutes drag (see Butler 1990; Epstein and Straub 1991). Yet Schulze is also concerned to demonstrate that the threat posed by the female bodybuilder is almost instantly allayed within a dominant culture. Her analysis thus seeks to show how the 'domestication of a potential challenge to dominant definitions of a feminine body is accomplished' (Gaines and Herzog 1990: 61). Despite this assertion of failed potential, the final pages of Schulze's essay are tentatively given over to thinking about the consumption of these images by specific audiences and within the subculture of female bodybuilding itself. Here bodybuilding is admitted as a space where the meanings attached to the sexed body are increasingly uncertain and shifting.

Given the extent to which 'woman' has been equated with nature – within both feminist and other more mainstream discourses – the muscular female body raises a different, if related, set of issues than those touched on in my discussion of the muscular male hero. Whilst the muscleman produces himself as an exaggerated version of what is conventionally taken to be masculine, the female bodybuilder takes on supposedly 'masculine' characteristics. Muscles as a signifier of *manual* labour become appropriated for the decoration of the *female* body. Both figures draw attention to and redefine a bodily understanding of gendered identity. Some of the rich connotative qualities of the muscular female body are brought out by Robert Mapplethorpe in his photographs of bodybuilder Lisa Lyons in his book *Lady: Lisa Lyons*. Published in 1983, Mapplethorpe's black and white images were the result of a sustained collaboration between the two. The photographs play with the conventional associations of the sexed body. They feature the clash of a range of 'masculine' and 'feminine' connotations, which stem not only from the presentation of the body as substance, but the ways in which it is decorated, posed and presented to the world. 'Feminine' fabrics such as lace are juxtaposed with the hard 'masculine' texture of Lyons's muscular body. At other points Lyons is dressed in fetishistic garb which is both qualified and further sexualized by her physique. This contrast is also expressed through the nudes, many of which echo classical poses associated almost exclusively with the male nude. One image focuses on a fragment of Lyons's body, isolating her arm, which is flexed to reveal biceps, and one breast. Other images frame her striking muscular poses against a natural landscape, playing off the associations of woman-as-nature against these images of woman-in-nature. Far from rendering her manly through her muscularity, these photographs emphasize both the hardness of female muscles and the softer flesh of the breasts.

Women's participation in *health* culture, bodybuilding in particular, as opposed to beauty culture, sets unconventional (for women) standards of attainment, and consequently has a series of implications for ideals of both femininity and masculinity. If the muscles of the male movie star or bodybuilder can seem either parodic or dysfunctional, then the muscles of the female bodybuilder only serve to emphasize the arbitrary qualities of these symbols of manual labour and of physical power. Conversely, the hardness of the muscles goes against a history of representation – visual and verbal – in which the female body is imagined as soft and curva-ceous. The sport of bodybuilding is thus the arena for yet another manifestation of a contradic-tion between the naturalized and the manufactured body, specifically in debates about what a female bodybuilder should look like, and how she should be *judged*. In the cinema the muscu-lar physique of Linda Hamilton as Sarah Connor in *Terminator 2* offers a distinctive visualization of the heroine. Both her physique and her tough performance is in addition to the array of weaponry with which she is endowed, making her a formidable figure. By way of contrast to her role in the earlier film, in which she needs to be taught by the male characters how to func-tion heroically, she is determined to be prepared for her second battle with the Terminator. She works out in a gym she has improvised from the iron bed in the mental institution in which she has been incarcerated following the events of the first film. This persona juxtaposes traditionally masculine and feminine characteristics – she is a butch-*femme*.

I want to discuss here the implications of the iconographic transgression at stake in recent characterizations of the action heroine generally, and the muscular female body specifically. A discussion of three quite different films may help to follow up some of these points. In *Getting Physical*, a 1984 television movie which deals with female bodybuilding, and in which Lisa Lyons herself appears, we see the protagonist discover a sense of self through bodybuilding. The semi-documentary *Pumping Iron II: The Women* (1984) follows a female bodybuilders' contest. It also received some considerable commentary from feminist critics on its release. *Perfect* (1985) casts Jamie Lee Curtis as an aerobics instructor in a California health club. Though none of these films is an action narrative, all deal with women's position within health and body culture, and all are taken from the same moment, the mid-1980s, in which the muscular male star was becom-ing a significant box-office phenomenon.

In *Getting Physical* we see women's bodybuilding through the eyes of a new recruit to the sport. The film is, on some levels, a classic makeover story in which the female protagonist, ini-tially lacking any confidence or motivation, becomes, through physical change, a confident indi-vidual in her own right who is accepted by her family, her boyfriend and the world in general as she poses on the stage of a bodybuilding contest. Kendal comes to bodybuilding by accident, has to be persuaded into it. In the film's first sequence we see her rushing to an audition for an acting role. She is clumsy and over-weight, with a tedious office job. Kendal smokes, eats a lot without any real enjoyment and does not feel comfortable with her family. Her father com-plains that she cannot 'get serious' about anything. After she is unable to defend herself from being assaulted in a parking lot Kendal goes to the police station where she meets Mickey, the man who becomes her boyfriend. He suggests she takes self-defence classes, giving her the address of a gym. On arrival at the gym Kendal is introduced to spectacular world of bodybuilding. We see the muscular bodies of women working out from Kendal's point of view. Close-ups of flexing legs and arms are intercut with her admiring face. For the first time she aspires to something, determining to look the same. Kendal is physically challenged. *Getting Physical* traces Kendall's increasing commitment to bodybuilding which ultimately leads to her decision to leave her office job and to abandon her aspirations to be an actor. Instead she enters a bodybuilding contest as a way to succeed on a public stage. Taken under the wing of a pro-fessional bodybuilder, Nadine (Sandahl Bergman), and husband/trainer, Kendal leaves home in order to train. Kendal's bodybuilding is opposed by both her boyfriend and her father, who see it as disturbing and unfeminine. Finally though they both come round, applauding her perfor-mance in the contest with which the film ends.

Whilst not a particularly sophisticated drama, *Getting Physical* poses in new terms a basic narrative that has long been a staple of women's and teenage magazines – that of acquiring confidence, independence and social/familial acceptance. The makeover is expressed through images of physical strength, which clash with a traditionally 'feminine' passivity. In the opening sequences of the film such passivity is pathologized, with Kendal presented as listless and uninterested in life. The drive for physical perfection seen in *Perfect* is, by way of contrast, constructed as pathetic and humiliating. The world of health culture is depicted through the cynical eyes of John Travolta as Adam Lawrence, a *Rolling Stone* journalist. He is interested in another, 'serious' story and follows up a piece on California health culture only as a fallback. *Perfect* deals with aerobics rather than bodybuilding. Though the film is, like *Getting Physical*, set in a gym, the connotations of aerobics emerge here as remarkably different from those of bodybuilding. Lawrence's story, which is centred on health clubs as the 'singles bars of the 1980s', is to run under the title 'Looking for Mr Goodbody'. Lawrence pretends to Jamie Lee Curtis that he is writing an in-depth piece on the club, whilst actually penning an exploitative article which mocks both the women and the men who attend the club. Their concern with the body is pathologized whilst, at the same time, Sally and Linda, two of the film's female health-club goers, are found physically wanting, photographed in 'unflattering' angles and lighting. Ironically the sexualized display of the body is one of the film's key pleasures, and was certainly central to the way in which it was marketed. Schulze criticizes *Getting Physical* for its construction of Kendal's bodybuilding as a way to 'facilitate (heterosexual) romance', despite the fact that at one point in the narrative her refusal to give up training causes her to break up with her boyfriend (Schulze 1986: 39). Further, the bodybuilding narrative of that film contrasts starkly with the obsessive reference to sexuality and the body that typifies *Perfect*, released at roughly the same time. Perhaps because of its newness, or because of the uncertainty that it seems to generate, the image of the female bodybuilder is not representable within the terms of sexualized display.

Since it is concerned exclusively with competitive bodybuilding, *Pumping Iron II: The Woman* takes on much more centrally the problems of definition that are necessarily an issue for the female bodybuilder. As various critics pointed out at the time of the film's release, its terrain is in part that of the cultural definition of femininity with which feminism has also been concerned. Here though, as with *Getting Physical*, the film has been characterized as failing to do justice to the transgressive potential of the built female body. Thus Christine Holmlund argues that:

> Far from abolishing stereotypes based on visible difference, *Pumping Iron II*, and *Pumping Iron* as well, visibly position the body as spectacle, then sell it as big business. In both films, the threat of visible difference and the threat of the abolition of visible difference are contained and marketed – as flex appeal.
>
> (Holmlund 1989: 49)

The potential of the film lies for Holmlund, as it does for most critics, in its rendering of the sexed body as artificial, self-created rather than natural. As with commentaries on the sexual politics of the muscular male stars, such an overlap between high theory and popular culture could only be a 'coincidence'. Jane Root's review picks out, for example, the moment at which 'the elderly and predominantly male judges get together to discuss the purpose of the event. Their allotted task for the evening? To "agree on a definition of femininity"'. Root suggests that this 'unselfconscious and unintentionally hilarious comment provides a neat example of the pleasures afforded by this documentary, which seems to have stumbled on some of the hottest issues around for feminism and cultural politics' (*Monthly Film Bulletin*, November 1985: 346). Root's suggestion that the film-makers and participants in female bodybuilding have 'stumbled' on a knowledge forged within feminist cultural politics is indicative of a certain intellectual arrogance in relation to popular culture. Against this we might consider that both the debates with which feminist cultural politics is engaged, and the particular forms of popular culture considered here, emerge from the same historical moment. This would involve criticism recognising its own historical location, instead of conceptualising ideas as emerging from nowhere and then being surprised that the concerns elaborated within the realm of theory might also be found in the popular.

Holmlund sees *Pumping Iron II* as voyeuristic, commercial and shallow. In a particularly telling passage, she argues, in relation to Bev Francis, the woman with the most massively built body in the film, that:

> the association of muscularity, masculinity, and lesbianism invokes these fears of a loss of love for spectators of both sexes, though in different ways. If heterosexual men see Bev as a lesbian, she is threatening: lesbians incarnate sexual indifference to men. If heterosexual women see Bev as a lesbian they must reject her: to like her would mean admitting that they might themselves be lesbian, which would in turn entail the abnegation of traditionally feminine powers and privileges.
>
> (Holmlund 1989: 43)

Apart from the construction of the audience for the film as exclusively heterosexual, we can note here how the pleasure of looking at these bodies – what Root calls the film's 'uninviting subject matter' – is erased by a feminist analysis which takes on the role of looking at and pronouncing judgement on popular culture. Holmlund's analysis depends on a clear distinction between the interdependent categories of heterosexual and homosexual. Yet might not part of the pleasure of the film be the dissolution of such rigid categories within the imaginary space of the cinema? Laurie Schulze, who initially sets out the deconstructive aspects of the female bodybuilder, produces a similar analysis in which this figure is complexly incorporated back into a patriarchal heterosexual mainstream due to an insistence on her femininity. Schulze argues that the female bodybuilder 'must be anchored to heterosexuality; if she is not, she may slip through the cracks in the hegemonic system into an oppositional sexuality that would be irrecuperable' (Gaines and Herzog 1990: 61). Yet, in terms of the problematizing of borders and boundaries, it is precisely the femininity of the female bodybuilder that destabilizes her relationship to the supposedly secure categories of sex, sexuality and gender. By existing across supposedly opposed categories, the female bodybuilder reveals the artifice of that opposition. Casting lesbianism as an irrecuperable, or even an oppositional, sexuality attempts instead to secure a binary logic. Judith Butler makes the same point when she signals the ways in which a notion of homosexuality supports and structures, is in fact necessary to, heterosexuality (Butler 1990). Indeed Schulze finds in the interviews she conducts with lesbians on the subject of female bodybuilding, a conservatism about gendered and sexed bodily identity. Schulze reports rather than analyses the responses she received, though she makes clear the extent to which the muscular-yet-feminine female body is found to be disturbing because it falls between conventional categories of sexed and gendered identity, categories which are as important to lesbian identities as they are to straight identities.[11] It is in such a way that the polymorphous perversity, which characterises Catherine Tramell in *Basic Instinct*, necessarily fails the political demands of a homosexuality defined in opposition to heterosexuality.

'Musculinity' and the action heroine

In thinking about the contemporary action heroine it would be a mistake to rely exclusively on the critical models associated with the *femme fatale* which are useful in thinking about *Basic Instinct*, since the heroines of other successful films of this period, such as *Silence of the Lambs* and *Aliens*, as well as *Fatal Beauty* or the *China O'Brien* films discussed in Chapter 1, are neither outlaws nor criminal. Their behaviour – going against the rules, going out on a limb – operates as a variant on that of the populist action hero who must break the law in order to secure some kind of justice in the world. Thus in the two *Aliens* films Ripley finds herself doing battle not only with the Alien, but with a conspiratorial company which has a ruthless disregard for human life. In *Silence of the Lambs*, trainee Clarice Starling is invited to participate in the FBI's investigation of serial killer 'Buffalo Bill' only to be systematically excluded from it. An early image frames Starling, at the FBI training centre, as the only woman in an elevator car full of men. Most of the group tower over her, whilst the pale blue of her sweatshirt contrasts to the red in which the men are dressed, emphasising her relative isolation. She ultimately aligns herself with a serial killer, Hannibal Lecter, who can provide her with clues as to the killer's identity and motivation, scraps of evidence withheld by Jack Crawford and his team. Finally it is Starling's perception that leads her to the killer's house – her quiet arrival intercut with all the blasting of Crawford and company bursting noisily into an empty house, armed to the teeth.

The position of the action heroine in relation to the institutions of the state is often as problematic as that of the hero, though this is necessarily represented in different ways. A key film in this respect is Kathryn Bigelow's *Blue Steel*, which stars Jamie Lee Curtis as a rookie New York cop. *Blue Steel* is a complex, psychological thriller which attempts to explore the role of women in the action cinema. The film both invokes and teases out the implications of the sexualized gloss that is often played out over the figure of the action heroine. Working through a sustained cinematic weapons fetish, *Blue Steel* follows through the difficult institutional location of Curtis's character, Megan Turner. At three moments, spread through the course of the narrative, Turner is asked why she became a cop. That this is insistently an issue is crucial to the rather eerie tone of the film, which has Turner play with the answers that it might be possible to give to this question: that she wanted to shoot people, or that she loves violence. Finally, she simply murmurs, 'him'. This last explanation is the most ambiguous – does 'him' refer to her father, with whom she is involved, or a more generalized 'he'? Yet an uncertainty also significantly surrounds the 'joke' explanations that Turner gives. Her deadpan assertions that she became a cop for the violence are given in response to the different attitudes, contemptuous, incredulous, fearful or patronising, that the men she meets take towards her role. Questions of status and authority are further worked through in Turner's relationship to her father and her attitude to his violent treatment of her mother. Ultimately she arrests him, cuffing him and dragging him to the car, though she can't finally turn him in.

The films discussed above all work with a variety of types of femininity, defined and redefined through the body and through the invocation and transgression of the kinds of behaviour considered appropriate for women. In *Alien*, Sigourney Weaver's Ripley is defined against a series of other female types, such as Lambert, who is weak and hysterical and, at a more metaphoric level, the ship's computer Mother. Barbara Creed has demonstrated the many ways in which the film works through monstrous images of femininity, in particular through the characterization of the Alien (Creed 1986; 1987). The spaceship, as a science-fiction microcosm of humanity, includes women within this world. The inclusion of women in both the civilian crew of the Nostromo in *Alien* and the military team of *Aliens* signals both the metaphoric status of the drama that they enact, and the fact that it is set in the future. Yet, despite her rank, the narrative makes certain that Ripley should still be seen to struggle to establish her authority with Ash in *Alien*, a struggle that reprises an earlier scene, in which Parker and Brett drown out her words with steam. These hierarchical conflicts effectively position Ripley as an outsider action heroine. As we have seen, such a marginality is crucial to the characterization of the action hero within Hollywood cinema. Similarly, as the marines in *Aliens* emerge from their 'hyper-sleep', they are reassembled into a military team of which Ripley is clearly not a part. Although Ripley is initially separated from the 'grunts' and associated with the military command, her populist allegiance to the troops quickly becomes clear.

The military coding of *Aliens* redefines the premise of the original to some extent since, as with other sequels, it must deal with the fact that the audience may already be familiar with the source of the film's horror and threat. At first Ripley is positioned on the top table with the lieutenant who, as one of the soldiers puts it, 'think's he's too good to eat with the rest of the grunts'. The hostility in *Aliens*, between an experienced crew and an inexperienced and bureaucratic officer, is familiar from a range of war and action movies. Whilst the military are in uniform and Burke, the company representative on the mission, is in civvies, Ripley's dress, with leather flying jacket and fatigues, is iconographically somewhere between the two. Early on she tells Burke that she is 'not a soldier' but as previously noted, despite being initially jumpy, Ripley is ultimately able to take command. As with any populist hero, the turning point comes when the military team find themselves defenceless against an Alien attack and the ineffectual lieutenant hesitates about pulling them out. Ripley seizes the controls of the armoured car from which they are monitoring the massacre, driving into the complex to rescue the troops. When it is revealed that the company has betrayed them all, as in the first film, it is clear whose interests Ripley defends, and she gradually emerges as the 'natural leader' of the platoon. When most of the military have been either killed or lie unconscious, Ripley suggests that Corporal Hicks take command. At this point Burke gives away his company allegiance, and his contempt for the platoon by calling Hicks a 'grunt'. We can contrast Ripley's incorporation into the military team with the isolation of Whoopi Goldberg's character in *Fatal Beauty*, discussed in Chapter 1. Goldberg/Rizzoli is repeatedly attacked by both cop colleagues and villains, assailed with verbal insults and physical violence. The film offers no supportive team to back her up, so that Goldberg is isolated within both the film frame and the narrative. Which is to say, to be a team player involves being admitted to the team in the first place.

Aliens further presents us with the striking figure of Jenette Goldstein as Private Vasquez, a muscular woman with cropped hair. Gesturing at Ripley in an early scene, Vasquez asks a fellow soldier 'Who's Snow White?', establishing something of a distance between the two, though they ultimately find themselves on the same side. Butch but not boyish, Vasquez is an iconic tough action heroine. Since Vasquez is a team player, not an outsider, she is ultimately allied with Ripley against the company and the military authorities. On waking from hyper-sleep she immediately starts doing pull-ups in front of the screen, and in a notorious scene responds to a male colleague's question 'Ever been mistaken for a man?' with the reply 'No, have you?' before slapping the hands of her buddy within the unit. Vasquez enacts the female action persona of the 'ball-busting' woman. Leona, played by Maria Conchita Alonso in *Predator 2* has a similar role, literally grabbing an annoying male cop's crotch. Later in a bar she asked him 'How are your balls?' to which he responds 'Fine – How are yours?' All this posing and verbal horseplay dwells on, and comically works over, the problems of the figure of the tough woman in the male team. In order to function effectively within the threatening, macho world of the action picture, the action heroine must be masculinised. The masculinization of the female body, which is effected most visibly through her muscles, can be understood in terms of a notion of 'musculinity'. That is, some of the qualities associated with masculinity are written over the muscular female body. 'Musculinity' indicates the way in which the signifiers of strength are not limited to male characters. These action heroines though, are still marked as women, despite the arguments advanced by some critics that figures like Ripley are merely men in drag.

In *Terminator 2* Linda Hamilton's tough physique is played off against the strength-in-fluidity of the monstrous T1000 which pursues her and her son John. The T1000 can take on any form and imitate any voice, though he spends most of the film cast as an LA cop. At times we see him turn into a mercurial liquid, reconstituting himself when damaged. His limbs can also be transformed into sharp metallic tools. I argued earlier that the T1000's fluid ability to transform his body constructs him as a feminized monster, in contrast to the solidity of Schwarzenegger as the protective cyborg, the good Terminator. The terror of the T1000 lies partly in its ability to transform its body from fluidity to a sharp metallic hardness, as when it tortures Sarah Connor by stabbing her with an arm transformed into a blade. Whilst such images obviously draw on figures of penetration, they also bring up once more themes of the vulnerability and invulnerability of the body already discussed in relation to the male hero. The significance of this motif in relation to the action heroine is discussed below.

Power and powerlessness: the body of the heroine

Whilst Sigourney Weaver's persona as Ripley has been a firm favourite with audiences, an inordinate amount of debate has been given over to the political implications of the final scenes in which, thinking she has destroyed the Alien, she undresses in preparation for sleep. Ripley's near-nakedness, her vulnerability in this sequence is not an insignificant narrative moment, but neither is it the only image in the film, or a moment only for male viewers as some critics have suggested. This much-discussed moment of the film can also be understood in terms of the extreme images of bodily vulnerability and invulnerability that are mobilized in the action cinema. As with much of the Hollywood cinema, action films operate in part to dramatize transgression – a transgression that may take the form of the breaking of official codes of the law as in *Thelma and Louise*. These codes can often be taken to stand in for symbolic codes of social behaviour. Transgression is a term resonant for feminism, implying the crossing of boundaries and the breaking of taboos. Feminist films studies has paid much attention, for example, to the figure of the *femme fatale*, a woman who destroys the hero, and ultimately herself, with her monstrous desires. Crime cinema is concerned with the delineation of normality and perversion at the obvious level of narrative content. But the cinema is also concerned to explore the exciting and often sexualized border that it thus calls into being, articulating the heroism of the gangster and his tragic demise, the sleaziness of law enforcement and the horrors of feeling trapped by the law. The establishment and transgression of limits is the stuff of Hollywood cinema rather than an occasional by-product. Thus, a politicized understanding of the image and of narrative content, such as that offered by feminism, needs to be supplemented by a sense of the image at play within a narrative dynamic which produces the cinematic experience as sensuous, rather than simply cerebral.

In James Cameron's sequel, *Aliens*, Ripley is again both a vulnerable and a powerful figure. The tension between power and powerlessness, which is that generated by the law, is also explored and exploited in action/science-fiction films such as *RoboCop* and *Total Recall* which centre on men. The body of the hero or heroine, though it may be damaged, represents almost the last certain territory of the action narrative. In *RoboCop* and *Total Recall* neither the body nor the mind is certain, both being subject to state control within a science-fiction dystopia. In *RoboCop* the figure of the cyborg plays off the metallic shell of the hero with its seeming invulnerability, against the glimpses of human flesh and the memories of a human past maintained beneath. *Total Recall* plays off the body of Schwarzenegger, famous as Mr Universe, within a narrative in which his mind has been stolen – again the hero finds himself powerless, mentally manipulated by a ruthless government agency. Similar problems of identity afflict Murphy/RoboCop, who has flashbacks of his former life, images which seem to be taken from home video since they are transmitted to us through his mechanical 'eyes'. Such images draw on the generic currency of conspiratorial science-fiction. When all else fails, the body of the hero, and not his voice, or his capacity to make a rational argument, is the place of last resort. That the body of the hero is the sole narrative space that is safe, that even this space is constantly under attack, is a theme repeatedly returned to within the action cinema.

In *Aliens* Ripley is positioned as out of place in a future world of which she knows little (she has been in hyper-sleep for fifty-seven years). Feeling like a 'fifth wheel' amongst the military team, Ripley boosts her status with the grunts by offering to take on a manual task at which she is proficient, donning a kind of mechanical skin – the loader, used to transport stores – which gives her a physical power that she is later to use in tackling the film's monstrous mother Alien. The sheer bulk of the loader gives Ripley physical stature. In this striking image the heroine directly enacts a fantasy of physical empowerment, one which is usually reserved for the hero. Her relative powerlessness, her physical vulnerability, is played with so that Weaver's femaleness additionally eroticises this fantasy of power through the transgression of gender boundaries. A much-reproduced publicity image of Weaver showed her clutching a child in one arm, weapon in another. In her confrontation with the alien the loader provides only partial protection as the monster extends its teeth inside its frame, snapping at Ripley's face.

The casting of women as the protagonists in the cop movie, the road movie, the science-fiction films and so on shifts and inflects the traditional vulnerability of the hero in such films. This is a set of genres, after all, in which the hero is constantly subject to physical violence. For women this physical vulnerability is easily mapped onto the sexualised violence of rape. The possibility of violent rape which threatens the action hero is generally only implied – though images of bodily penetration abound. Perhaps this serves to flesh out Ridley Scott's statement that *Thelma and Louise* is 'not about rape' but about 'choices and freedom'.[12] For a narrative centred on a female protagonist, rape offers one powerful way to articulate issues of freedom and choice. These issues are the substance of the road movie, as much as is the conflict between the responsibilities of home and family on the one hand, the delights of adventures and same-sex friendship on the other. Similarly, the material bond that is invoked in films such as *Aliens* and *Terminator 2* both strengthens and weakens the heroine in ways that draw on the complex history of 'woman' as a term within representation.

There is a whole range of determinants informing the production of the woman as action heroine in recent cinema. Her appearance can be seen to signal, amongst other factors, a response to feminism and the exhaustion of previous formulae. But as we have seen in relation to the problems which have surrounded the typecasting of Whoopi Goldberg as a black woman within Hollywood action pictures, images do not operate on some blank page but within cultural contexts which are crowded with competing images and stereotypes. The figure of the action hero is relentlessly pursued and punished, both mentally and physically. Beatings in back alleys and in boxing rings abound. The climactic moment of many action pictures is the final fight between the hero and the opponent who is physically stronger. The triumphal conquest over physical punishment is saturated with a different kind of coding when we are dealing with a heroine and the (almost always) already sexualised female body on the screen. Drawing on codes of chivalry, male violence against women has typically functioned within the Hollywood cinema as a signifier of evil. Feminism has proposed a rather different understanding of violence against women in relation to institutionalized male power, often expressed through metaphors of physical strength versus weakness. In thinking about women in the action film more specifically, we should consider that if women on the screen are excessively sexualized then so is the violence to which they are subject. This returns us to the frequent repetition of images and narratives associated with rape. The rape-revenge narrative is often used to provide a justification (since one is generally needed) for female violence in movies such as *I Spit on Your Grave*, *Ms 45/Angel of Vengeance* and the psychological thriller *Mortal Thoughts*. Seen against such a history, for the action heroine as much as the action hero, the development of muscles as a sort of body armour signifies physical vulnerability as well strength.

Notes

1   Kobena Mercer was speaking on 'I Want Your Sex', a documentary on images of black sexuality (broadcast on Channel 4, 12 November 1991).
2   See King-Kok Cheung's article in Marianne Hirsch and Evelyn Fox Keller (1990) for a discussion of gender, race and the critical reception of Maxine Hong Kingston's work in America.
3   Part of the discussion of *Thelma and Louise* presented in this chapter is taken from my contribution to a forthcoming volume edited by Berenice Reynaud and Ginette Vincendeau, *20 Ans De Theories Feministes Du Cinema*, Paris: CinemAction Editions du Cent.
4   See, for example, Botcherby and Garland (1991); Botcherby (1991); Murphy (1991); Dargis (1991). My discussion also draws on a paper given by Jane Arthurs, 'Thelma and Louise: On the Road to Feminism?', at a conference on Feminist Methodology (January 1992).
5   A videotape of the Kennedy-Smith rape case is now available in stores, a point which indicates both the visibility and saleability of this case in particular and rape in general.
6   Laura Mulvey (1989: 26).
7   For example, Janice Radway has suggested, in relation to the project of ethnographic research on the romance, that 'our' political project is 'one of convincing those very real people to see how their situation intersects with our own and why it will be fruitful for them to see it as we do' (1986: 107). This project, in which nothing can be taken from the popular since 'we' know best, involves the suggestion that 'fantasies can be used as a site for political intervention', a suggestion which fails to recognise the importance of a structure (to which shifting signifiers may be attached) within fantasy (ibid.: 120).

   By way of contrast we could consider the arguments made by Jacqueline Bobo in relation to *The Color Purple* in which the responses that readers make to a particular film are given a critical validity. Bobo does not approach her subject matter with the assumption that she can correct deviant readings (in Pribram 1988).
8   Jackie Chan's *The Armour of God* (Hong Kong, 1986) turns this formula around somewhat. For much of the film the Chinese adventurer heroes explore an exotic European landscape.
9   This quotation, from Joan Smith in the *Guardian*, is cited by Jane Arthurs (ibid.).
10 These comments on the form and operation of men's style magazines, draw from a paper on the subject given by Andy Medhurst at the Association for Cultural Studies Conference, Staffordshire, September 1991.
11 Similarly one of Schulze's respondents describes the image of the female bodybuilder as too 'working class', like 'Tammy Wynette with muscles' (Gaines and Herzog 1990: 77). Such a commentary makes apparent the rather obvious point that the responses made by lesbian audiences are also structured through discourses of class. To construct a lesbian audience as necessarily oppositional erases the differences existing within that supposedly simple category.
12 Interview with Ridley Scott in *Sight and Sound* (July 1991: 18-19).

Chapter 23

SABRINA BARTON

YOUR SELF STORAGE

Female investigation and male performativity in the woman's psychothriller

L ET'S BEGIN WITH AN IMAGE FROM *Pacific Heights* (1990; directed by John Schlesinger). One hand shielding her eyes from the bright Los Angeles sun, a woman wearing blue jeans and a blazer watches from shore as a man and a woman drink champagne and cavort on a small yacht, unaware that they are being watched. The woman who watches, Patty Palmer (Melanie Griffith), has followed the man on the boat, Carter Hayes (Michael Keaton), from San Francisco where he destroyed her just-bought Pacific Heights Victorian home and perhaps her relationship with her live-in boyfriend. Unhelped by the law, Patty has set out on her own to seek clues, answers, restitution, revenge. She watches as this scheming, psychotic imposter works his wiles on another victim.

Women's psychothrillers[1] unabashedly employ the larger psychothriller genre's disturbing convention of depicting women who are terrorized and attacked. However, they do so from a different perspective. The story is told predominantly from the point of view of its female protagonist who pursues, even as she is pursued by, her antagonist. In granting a more central and more active investigating role to the woman in jeopardy, these films significantly depart from most movie psychothrillers (in which women function almost solely as victimized objects).

The image of Patty voyeuristically exerting her gaze upon the unwitting villain is a useful starting point for undertaking a feminist analysis of the woman's psychothriller. As feminist film theory's single most influential article, Laura Mulvey's 'Visual Pleasure and Narrative Cinema' (1975), has argued, classical Hollywood cinema – exemplified by such Hitchcock suspense films as *Vertigo* (1958), *Rear Window* (1954) and *Marnie* (1964) – tends to equate the male with an active gaze that is associated with knowledge, power, and agency, while the female tends to be placed in a sexualized, objectified, 'to-be-looked-at' position.[2] The image from *Pacific Heights* with which I began, reverses this male-gaze/female-object gender dynamic, and signals Patty's narrative transformation from victim to investigator.

My interest, however, is not in gaze/object relations per se, but in how these and other conventionally gendered traits, actions, and associations can, potentially, be redistributed among the characters of a given film in such ways that cinema's traditional gender roles and gender meanings are revised. Since the early 1970s, feminist film theory has been grappling with (among other things) the issue of how femaleness and maleness, femininity and masculinity, are represented in narrative film, and how spectators identify (or do not identify) with such representations. In *Pacific Heights*, Patty's femininity is not of the voyeured or fetishized sort. In contrast, for example, to the meticulously made-up and elegantly costumed Tippi Hedren (an icon of blonde 1950s-style femininity) in Hitchcock's *The Birds* (1963) and *Marnie*, Patty is dressed and coiffed with deliberate casualness. This female protagonist is neither coded for visual pleasure nor portrayed as an enigma whose feminine performance mandates male investigation. Rather, Patty's subjectivity is anchored internally, in her perceptions and actions, in what the movie represents as a stable, core self. She is visually and narratively coded, I wish to argue, as 'real' rather than as 'performative.'

I am using the term 'performative' in relation to gender as described by theorist Judith Butler who argues that, however natural one's femininity or masculinity may feel or appear, gender identity is, in fact, the constituted effect of repeated poses, gestures, behaviors, positionings and articulations. Butler's influential argument builds on the poststructuralist-psychoanalytic claim that 'femininity' and 'masculinity' are not inherent and not necessarily tied to anatomy; sexual identity is psychically and linguistically based, and thus it is far more mobile and multiple than that.[3] Although some people might choose to foreground their own gender performativity (drag queens are an obvious example), socially acceptable gender identities tend to be presented as naturally emanating from an essential core self – a core self that, Butler would insist, is an illusory effect, a performance.

However illusory such a 'core self' may be, my impression from teaching film courses to undergraduates and from reading popular press film reviews (as well as from my own viewing experiences) is that many audience members seek out and value characters who are represented as possessing coherent core selves.[4] While Butler assiduously calls attention to the performative dimension of all gendered subjects, Hollywood cinema most often emphasizes and highlights the performativity of only certain categories of characters, while coding others as authentic. Through a filmic foregrounding of femininity in terms of body parts, costume, makeup, masquerade, seduction and makeover plots, women far more often than men have been explicitly aligned with the performative. This is significant from a feminist perspective because performativity tends to be negatively coded as duplicitous, fragmented and unstable, whereas the depiction of realness is coded as strong, unified and stable – in short, as the more desirable identity category.

Let me clarify by way of an example. In *Marnie*, Hedren plays a character who performs her femininity, performs her identity. Marnie constructs a series of false selves out of stories and suitcases; hard-luck tales and false identification papers; changing wardrobes, makeup and hair dyes. By contrast, the film's hero, Mark Rutland (Sean Connery), emerges as self-evidently stable, largely through his role as investigator of a mysterious and unstable woman. Marnie not only performs multiple false selves but also fundamentally does not herself know who she 'truly' is. In this manner, feminine identity comes to be defined as performative, while masculine identity is associated with authenticity. In *Pacific Heights*, as in other women's psychothrillers, the opposite dynamic is at work. It is the male who is duplicitous and unstable – a scam artist whose identity is constituted from carefully coordinated images of socially successful masculinity. When Patty looks at (and sees through) Carter's manipulative performance, she not only defines herself against the traditional to-be-looked-at version of femininity exemplified by Hedren, but, in exposing masculine masquerade, she also lays claim to a self coded as authentic.

The image from *Pacific Heights* with which I began is especially resonant for feminist film analysis and film history. Patty is played by Melanie Griffith, the real-life daughter of Tippi Hedren, who, interestingly enough, is cast as the older woman on the yacht whom Carter is drawing into his snares. In this instance, Griffith has followed her mother's footsteps into the suspense genre shaped by Hitchcock.[5] But, unlike her mother, the blonde daughter of the Hitchcock blonde watches from a critical, investigative – one might even say feminist – distance at the scenario of male manipulation and exploitation that she seeks to understand and from which she seeks to extricate herself Thus, in this brief, poignant pairing of mother and daughter, *Pacific Heights* juxtaposes two generations of women as well as two generations of the psychological suspense film genre, charting a shift in the representation of gendered subjectivity.

This essay will examine four exemplary women's psychothrillers: *Silence of the Lambs* (1990), *The Stepfather* (1987), *Sleeping with the Enemy* (1991) and *Pacific Heights*. Each of these four movies reveals the complex interplay of gendered traits and actions at stake in violent encounters between female protagonists and male antagonists. These women's psychothrillers thereby make available for analysis the implications of somewhat different arrangements of the same basic competitive economy. That is, in all four movies, a woman manages to achieve an identity that the film codes as 'real,' an identity centred in a coherent interior self. She achieves this realness at least in part through her action of resisting and, ultimately investigating a psycho-male antagonist's ostentatiously performative identity, an identity made up of formulaic poses and manipulated surfaces.

Your self storage: *Silence of the Lambs*

From the unmasking of masculine masquerade there emerges, if not a feminist role model, at least a strong woman character. Here I deliberately use what may sound like dated, 1970s feminist terms such as 'strong woman' and 'role model.' The goal of this essay is to recover a means of speaking affirmatively about cinematic representations of empowered women and so revalue the structures of viewer identification mobilized by such representations. An important motivation has been my own pleasure in watching the strong female protagonist negotiate the horrors of the woman's psychothriller, a pleasure that underscores this critical project.

Consider the realness of Clarice Starling's subjectivity in *Silence of the Lambs* (directed by Jonathan Demme), a subjectivity defined by depth rather than external props and bodily surfaces. Foster's characteristic blondeness is darkened, and she is dressed conservatively in ways that do not emphasize the body (work clothes or sweats hardly coded for Hollywood-style visual pleasure). Additional formal techniques – above all the cinematography's use of point-of-view shots – work to code the female protagonist's subjectivity as stable and active. The look and who deploys it is a powerful cinematic means to empower a character in mainstream narrative cinema: the camera looks *with* certain characters, not merely at them as visual objects.[6] Point-of-view shots are repeatedly granted to Clarice as she investigates the long series of enclosed spaces in this film, beginning with FBI supervisor Jack Crawford's (Scott Glenn) office and Hannibal Lecter's (Anthony Hopkins) cell, and concluding with Buffalo Bill's (Ted Levine) mazelike basement (Figure 23.1).

In another important strategy for establishing depth of self in its female protagonist, the film explores Clarice's own interior space of subjectivity. Two memory flashbacks to childhood, as well as the 'therapy' sessions with Hannibal Lecter (in which she candidly answers the imprisoned killer's questions about herself in exchange for information about the serial killer at large), serve to take the audience into Clarice's family history, psychic structures, feelings and motivations. Ultimately, we are brought to see her commitment to saving women as entirely coherent with her own self-rescue from childhood trauma – watching the screaming lambs being taken to slaughter, the death of her father – a coherence that serves to code her character as one in possession of a core self.

Figure 23.1   The female investigator on her own, in the dark. Jodie Foster in Jonathan Demme's *Silence of the Lambs* (Orion Pictures, 1991). Photo by Ken Regan.

The female protagonist's access to a more substantial, interior-coded identity is implicit in the remark that Hannibal offers to her early in the film: 'Look deep within yourself, Clarice.' Clarice knows that the line is, as she puts it, 'too hokey' for this genius-psychiatrist. It must be a clue, and it must point to something beyond an apparently trite call for introspection. As things turn out, it does and it doesn't. Clarice eventually tracks down evidence on the serial killer at a company in Baltimore called 'Your Self Storage.' There she investigates a space filled with a dark clutter of things that help reveal the secret self and psycho-past of (we later learn) Buffalo Bill. The psycho-killer's self is routed through a confused mass of cultural artifacts: mannequins, flags, jewelry, weaponry, costumes, makeup, the 'stored' head of a dead male lover. Penetrating this storage space filled with personal items is an important state in Clarice's attempt to understand why Buffalo Bill kills and then skins his female victims. As she later figures out, he wishes to stitch for himself an external 'suit' made from pieces of different women's skin; putting on this gruesome outfit will let him performatively inhabit the femininity that obsesses him. Along with forwarding Clarice's investigation of Bill's performativity, however, Hannibal's pun – 'Look deep within yourself' – also resonates with Clarice's growing ability to enter and explore her own self storage (which takes the internal form of memories and dreams) and thereby to find and become not just a self, but *herself*.

Because I went to see *Silence* with a gay male friend, my first reaction to the film was painfully fraught. We both heard the spectators in the row behind us mocking Buffalo Bill's cuddling of his white poodle 'Precious,' tittering 'yuck' at the sight of Bill's nipple ring, and rooting for the demise of the fag. Even so, I loved the female protagonist and therefore 'liked' the movie that brought her to me.

I later found my own conflicted viewing experience replicated in two distinct but overlapping critical debates that arose around *Silence*, both of which concerned the gender and sexual politics inherent in embracing the character of Clarice Starling. First, what did it mean for spectators to enjoy the movie and its female protagonist in view of the rampant homophobia expressed through the Buffalo Bill character? And, second, given all of the sophisticated critical work that has been done, by feminist and queer theorists among others, in deconstructing simplistic notions of identity and identification, was it theoretically and politically naive, even retrogressive, for a feminist film critic to claim Clarice as (to use another old-fashioned term) a 'positive image'?

The media's encounter with *Silence* divided along gendered lines, expressed most dramatically in the *Village Voice*'s March 1991 forum, 'Writers on the Lamb: Sorting Out the Sexual Politics of a Controversial Film.'[7] In that forum, those male contributors writing from a gay-identified political position condemned the film for adding yet another 'fag-as-psychokiller'[8] to the popular imaginary, while female contributors writing from a feminist-identified political position supported the film for its empowering representation of Clarice Starling. Amy Taubin, for example, wrote in support of the film because it portrayed 'a woman solving the perverse fiddles of patriarchy – all by herself.'

Elsewhere, film-maker Maria Maggenti offered the following formulation to three gay male anti-*Silence* co-panelists at Outwrite (the San Francisco lesbian and gay writers conference). 'You boys just don't get it . . . there is more than one way to look at a movie and women see something entirely different here than you do.'[9]

What to make of this division between the 'girls' and the 'boys'? One way to understand, and perhaps move beyond, this critical split – feminist women vs. gay men – would be to think of these two critical sides not so much as having read 'entirely different' films but as having identified with opposed characters, and as having read those characters more or less in isolation from the film's overall system of representations.

Before I continue, let me be clear: I think that responses based on how a film portrays a single character are important. Indeed, it is my argument that academic critics and theorists need to develop a more nuanced understanding of these deeply passionate responses. To do so, however, I believe that we need to grasp with more precision how films may deploy, code and gender characters as parts of a representational, psychological and ideological system of desirable realness and undesirable, dangerous performativity.

Within a particular film, certain key characters 'energize' certain psychical experiences, social concepts, and ideas. The circulation and distribution of these elements is often gender-based. In women's psychothrillers, because performativity is associated with the psychotic male antagonist, a female protagonist can emerge who is coded as having an intact, stable identity. Thus, a positive female image will come at a cost: in *Silence*, Buffalo Bill – the not exactly gay (or so claimed Jonathan Demme), not quite a transvestite, not yet a transsexual, feather-boa and makeup wearing serial killer – bears the burden of (classically feminized) performativity so that Clarice can occupy the traditionally male-identified role of investigator. In the economy of selves that the movie sets up, if one marginalized group is allowed to find a subjectivity that feels stable and authentic, another must take its place at the negative pole of performativity.[10]

In light of *Silence of the Lambs*' scapegoating of a gay character, one can understand the ambivalence registered in B. Ruby Rich's wry conclusion after she describes in the *Village Voice* forum her own warm response to Starling: 'guess I'm just a girl.' A critic with overlapping queer and feminist sympathies, Rich is not only forced to choose sides (identifying with the feminist girls), but to enter into a critical discourse that, as her use of the term 'girl' hints, some might perceive as juvenile. Rich also happens to be that rare film critic who writes for both academic and popular publications, and hence she is especially well-positioned to recognize that when a sophisticated feminist film critic these days claims a conscious identification with a positive image, she risks being construed as naive or even ignorant.

I understand her consternation. While critical theory ought not simply to line up with an untheorized, naturalized audience response, I do think it can do better at working with (not against) audience members' powerful investment in positive identity.[11] In a study of *Silence's* reception by a range of newspaper and other periodical reviewers, Janet Staiger found that 'women – both straight and lesbian – uniformly defended [Jodie Foster] (Figure 23.2) and the movie as a positive, powerful representation of a female.'[12] Staiger's study helps to render visible the second critical division that the movie provoked, which was quieter but nonetheless significant. Consider the distance between the 'I love Clarice' response that Staiger found on the part of women writing in the popular press and, for example, academic critic Judith Halberstam's Butler-influenced analysis of the performative character of Buffalo Bill. Halbertstam concludes that (what she terms) Buffalo Bill's gender trouble 'challenges' the 'heterosexist and misogynist constructions of humanness, the naturalness, the interiority of gender'; 'he rips gender apart and remakes it as a suit or a costume.'[13] I do not contest that this character indeed exemplifies performative subjectivity. But performativity is not in and of itself a subversive challenge.

Silence of the Lambs channels 'negative' performativity into what gay male critics aptly view as little more than the familiar homophobic stereotype of an effeminate psycho-killer. Moreover, it would not be going too far to say that the film associates performative versions of femininity with death. The opposition of realness and performativity as a matter of life and death for women is dramatized when Clarice visits and investigates the bedroom of a past victim, Frederika Bimmel. Most obviously, Buffalo Bill has reduced Frederika to sheer performativity by using her dead and flayed body as part of the female-suit costume he is constructing. But Frederika also has been reduced to the accoutrements of cultural femininity she has left behind: posters of glamorous women, framed family photos, romance novels, china animals, frills and chintz, and, most poignantly, a ballerina jewelry box. In this young woman's version of self storage – the ballerina figurine a perfect emblem of performed femininity – Clarice finds concealed a handful of Polaroids of Frederika, too large (for conventional beauty) in her cotton briefs, assuming a series a culturally scripted poses intended to signify feminine eroticism. In opposition to this painful instance of woman-as-failed-image – and woman as purely the static materiality of *mise-en-scène* – Clarice is defined by her investigative, analytic gaze. That gaze is inscribed by the active and mobile camera as it cuts to a point-of-view shot and pans around the spaces and surfaces of Frederika's bedroom.

The dangerous linkage of feminine performativity and death is precisely what Senator Ruth Martin, the mother of Buffalo Bill's final victim, Catherine Martin, attempts to forestall. In an effort to save her daughter, Senator Martin goes on television to plead with the serial killer for the return of her child. Her strategy is to show family snapshots of Catherine, share anecdotes and describe what her daughter must be thinking and feeling. Clarice watches the broadcast transfixed, then explains to the friend standing next to her that 'if he sees Catherine as a person and not just as an object, it's harder to tear her up.' Paradoxically, the senator's powerful enactment of Catherine through performative images and words can, at least potentially, produce a 'realness-effect' that may save her life. As this example suggests, identity at some level always involves a performance that relies on images, props, and narrative, but that does not mean that an individual is thereby reducible to that performance. Just such a threatening reduction is implicit in Hannibal's menacing compliment to Senator Martin. 'Nice suit,' he tells her. The comment links him to Buffalo Bill: both are serial killers who reduce the complexly human to its theatrical materials.[14]

Figure 23.2   The women of the FBI. Jodie Foster and Kasi Lemmons in Jonathan Demme's *Silence of the Lambs* (Orion Pictures, 1991). Photo by Michael Ginsburg.

We seem to have arrived at an impasse between many viewers' commonplace wish to feel whole, to feel real, and academic criticism's sophisticated, poststructuralist critique of identity undone. How, then, can academic feminist film criticism go about reclaiming such filmic versions of female realness as potentially empowering without repeating the mistakes of the past? The 1970s' critical approach that emphasized positive 'images of women' and surveyed and criticized negative stereotypes,'[15] alas, had some significant blind spots. Early feminist film criticism failed to acknowledge, for instance, that what counts as 'positive' or 'negative' is highly complex, situation-specific, and not self-evident. Not only are different spectators (or different genders, races, classes, sexualities, ages and so forth) likely to read images differently, but it is also simplistic to posit one-to-one correlations between and reality, or to assume one-to-one relations between, say, women viewers and women characters. After all, female spectators might just as well be identifying with images of maleness, or vice versa.[16]

Beginning in the mid-1970s and early 1980s, psychoanalytic theory, especially as reconceptualized by Jacques Lacan, seemed to many feminist film critics to offer a much richer way to think about gender identity and representation. Lacan's work emphasized the place, not of biology, but of language.[17] Butler's work on performativity, which is informed by certain key aspects of Lacan's work (although critical of certain others), also defines 'maleness' and 'femaleness' as symbolic positions that give meaning to the self, but which can never be taken for granted as fixed and unitary.

Psychoanalytic theory, especially the notion of a destabilizing division between our conscious and unconscious lives, has been especially useful in critical analyses of the horror/slasher/psychothriller genres in which the 'normal' – located in identities or social institutions – is violently disrupted by unconscious fears and desires. Starting with critic Robin Wood's groundbreaking 1979 article, 'An Introduction to the American Horror Film,' a series of psychoanalytically based, politically progressive readings of the genre have focused on and valued the ways in which figures of monstrosity transgress and subvert the norms, boundaries, and normative identity positions of patriarchal culture.[18] Rhona Berenstein continues this tradition in her 1996 *Attack of the Leading Ladies: Gender, Sexuality, and Spectatorship in Classic Horror Cinema*, and she adds a significant focus on the concepts of fantasy and performativity. Berenstein argues that horror cinema invites audiences to 'identify against themselves' and enter into 'multiple' and 'transgressive identifications and desires' that disrupt their 'day-to-day' gender and sexual positions.[19] Although Berenstein (unlike Wood) does not claim political progressiveness for the horror genre, she suggests, as does a great deal of critical work in recent years, that filmic representations of gender identity are most challenging to the status quo, and hence by implication most subversive and liberatory, when identity is exposed as performative.

In focusing on the feminist politics of the (more or less) intact identity of the strong female protagonist of the woman's psychothriller, I hope to offer an alternative to the critical emphasis on monstrosity or performativity as subversion.[20] For it seems to me that such criticism has come to rely too readily on the equation: *performative = transgressive = politically progressive*. Given such a formula it is hard to theorize, value, or even talk about our investments in representations of unified and stable selves (as if these, by definition, were retrograde).

In fact, spectatorial investments in such real and stable selves can be profitably illuminated by returning to psychoanalytic theory. Despite the overwelming attention paid to Butler's excavations into the undoing of identity, Butler's work at key junctures also concedes that identity will always, necessarily, be remade: 'constantly marshaled, consolidated, retrenched'[21] I would stress a similar point about Lacan's theory of subjectivity, that, as he argues, we are defined by a *lack-in-being*, by an incompleteness that attends ceaseless efforts to obtain a meaningful self through identifications with others. Even if such identifications – with film characters or stars, for example – are rooted in the misrecognizing of a pleasingly unified external image as one's self, such are the seeming completions of identity that make some film viewers feel *real*. Cinema offers a resource of gendered images in which spectators endlessly try (through fantasy and identification) to find or complete their selves.[22]

Domestic makeovers: *The Stepfather* and *Sleeping with the Enemy*

In *The Stepfather* (directed by Joseph Ruben) it is the sixteen-year-old stepdaughter, Stephanie (Jill Schoelen), who discovers that the role-model husband and father whom her widowed mother has married is precisely that: a man performing a scripted role, a constructed model. In their first scene together, Jerry Blake (Terry O'Quinn) comes home with a new puppy for Stephanie, prompting his wife, Susan (Shelley Hack), to declare to her husband of one year, 'you're perfect.' Stephanie is less convinced; she has been uncomfortable and suspicious from the start, resenting Jerry's efforts to substitute for and *act* like her dead father. Indeed, Stephanie is uneasily aware of the performative dimension of her stepfather's behavior. Talking to her best friend on the phone after a family supper during which she has confessed to being expelled from school, she remarks: 'It's freaky, the way he looked at me like he wanted to erase me off the face of the earth. . . . He has this whole fantasy thing, like we should be like the families on TV and grin and laugh and be having fewer cavities all the time – I swear to god, it's like having Ward Cleaver for a dad.' (Ward *Cleaver*, indeed.)

As with *Pacific Heights* and *Silence of the Lambs*, the female protagonist of this film is coded in terms of realness through her successful investigations into male performativity. The relation between the investigating woman and the performative man is illustrated by a pair of sequences that occur roughly an hour into the film. In one sequence, we watch the stepfather manufacturing a new identity for himself in the bathroom of a ferry boat as part of his elaborate preparations to, once again, murder his family, transform his identity and relocate. Then, in the sequence that immediately follows, we see the stepdaughter searching for clues to Jerry's murderous masquerade at an unoccupied house. The adjacent sequences employ a range of formal elements that help to set up an opposition between these two differently coded subject-positions-investigated (male) vs. investigating (female).

Compared to the preceding 'Jerry sequence,' for instance, the subsequent 'Stephanie sequence' employs relatively longer camera distances, longer takes and more camera mobility. As Stephanie pulls herself through a window of the locked house, the camera tracks back, thus aligning camera movement with the entering female protagonist. Stephanie constantly looks around as she walks, emphasizing her investigating impulse. We cut to a point-of-view shot as she fixes her look on what she intuitively senses is the exact location of a murder committed by her stepfather. These techniques of cinematography have the effect of producing Stephanie as an active, intact and autonomous character.

By contrast, the Jerry sequence uses more close-ups and extreme close-ups on Jerry's own face. The scene is structured with faster cuts and less camera movement. These techniques all function to foreground and fragment his bodily surfaces.[23] Perhaps most significant, the camera closes in tight on Jerry as he manipulates his contact lenses and glasses. These devices are coded as props-costume rather than corrective lenses. They grant him no clear vision or perspective. Similarly, the camera is inches from Jerry's face as he applies glue to his upper lip and then presses on a fake mustache. During this process of disguise we regularly cut to the briefcase where he stores his 'selves.' Throughout the movie, *mise-en-scène* frequently associates Jerry with suitcases, briefcases and garment bags, all of them props that allude to his externally packaged identity. In *The Stepfather* it is clearly the performative Jerry who holds the greatest visual interest for the spectator, the character who, like Buffalo Bill, plays dress-up. Visual cues continually emphasize the performative aspect of Jerry's pieced together, constructed image of respectable, middle-aged masculinity, thus reiterating his identity transformation.

In what may appear a paradox, however, the performative psycho-male of *The Stepfather* is obsessively invested in cultural images of a seamlessly real family life. He believes that the perfect makeover of self and family will finally yield a reality in line with the utterly fixed vision that he carries within himself. As Stephanie's 'Ward Cleaver' comment recognizes, the stepfather's murderous performativity is all in the service of his attempts to inhabit a particular scenario that for him fits the measure of a particular preconceived Reality with a capital 'R.' In a startling image from the film's opening scene, a wall adorned with smiling family photographs is spattered and stained with blood; the picture-perfect wife and children have been punished for falling short of the ideal image. We watch the stepfather in an upstairs bathroom as he washes the blood from his body, changes his appearance and prepares to start over with a new, carefully selected, camera-ready family. This male desperately, violently wants to be what he conceives as the real thing: the powerful, patriarchal head of a stable household. (To make even clearer that Jerry's notion of 'real' family life is based in outdated television ideals of the patriarchal family – that is, that it derives from a reiterated cultural performance – the stepfather justifies his refusal to let Stephanie go to boarding school, which would break up the family, by intoning with an eerie smile: 'Father knows best.') At a telling moment in Jerry's growing 'disappointment' (as he always put it) with his new family, we see him walking through his new neighborhood, stopping as he spots a little girl running from a happy Mom at the threshold of their home to greet Dad as he arrives home from work. The stepfather looks at this rosy image of family life with a yearning akin to that which Buffalo Bill might bring to a suitable female, whose skin he can imagine himself inhabiting because it has the right look. The visuals and narrative shape of the domestic scene evoke the fantasy of real families in which Jerry desires to find himself.

Just as Clarice finds deeper dimensions of her own self through coming to understand exactly why Buffalo Bill is so violently invested in manipulating surfaces, so Stephanie achieves more stability and coherence as a character through learning the truth of what is going on around her. The movie regularly cuts to shots of Stephanie as she reacts to or simply observes peculiarities in her stepfather's behavior, peculiarities that go unnoticed by others. When Jerry organizes a big neighborhood picnic to celebrate his new friends, his new family and his new life, Stephanie hovers on the outskirts of the gathering, watching his smooth performance of a proud family man. She can barely bring herself to pose in the family photo that Jerry engineers.

We can better appreciate the significant link between female investigation and a woman's coding as a strong and active character in the woman's psychothriller by briefly comparing this group of films with a key precursor, the 'woman's gothic' – for example, *Rebecca* (1940), *Suspicion* (1941), *Gaslight* (1944) or *The Two Mrs Carrolls* (1947) – a subset of 1940s' women's films.[24] The plots of these films revolve around a woman who discovers that she has unwittingly stepped into a dire situation by marrying a man whom she comes to suspect may be a villain. Critics Mary Ann Doane and Diane Waldman[25] have discussed the effect of contingently granting a female protagonist such an active, investigatory look and making her the locus from which the story is told. Both critics conclude that giving a woman character such narrative agency creates a crisis that can only be remedied once the female protagonist's authority is undermined, dismantled, pathologized (even if her suspicions are confirmed to be true): 'One can readily trace,' writes Doane, 'in the women's films of the 1940s, recurrent suggestions

Figure 23.3   Just like the families on TV: daughter, mother and lunatic. Jill Schoelen, Shelley Hack and Terry O'Quinn in *The Stepfather* (ITC Productions, 1986).

of [the female protagonist's] deficiency, inadequacy, and failure. . . .'[26] Or as Waldman comments, 'these films struggle with their representation of women' and, ultimately, many of them 'invalidate feminine perception, establishing a polarity between masculinity, objectivity and truth on the one hand, and femininity, subjectivity, and false judgment on the other.'[27]

By contrast to the 1940s gothics, in the woman's psychothriller of the late 1980s and 1990s the female protagonist's investigation may be challenged or uneven, but on the whole it is not pathologized or deficient. Indeed, as a rule the opposite trajectory is at work as, from the very beginning, the female protagonist's suspicions are confirmed for the audience and thus her point of view validated and aligned with objectivity, truth, and a grittily realistic understanding of the world. When she sees through the lie of masculine masquerade, that discovery, while shocking and ultimately life-threatening, helps to dislodge her from the conventionally defined storybook role of lucky daughter/wife of some perfect man, a narrative in which she does not, in the end, fit.

How do the two types of subjective realness (Jerry's and Stephanie's) that I have discussed in relation to *The Stepfather* differ from one another? The male antagonist compulsively seeks to insert himself into external scenarios that to him embody a culturally endorsed version of the real thing – 'real masculinity'; 'real family life'; a 'real marriage'; a 'real home.' By contrast, the female protagonist seeks to claim a personal and interior realness, one engaged with the vicissitudes and imperfections of her own individual history (in Stephanie's case, the loss of her father, her troubles at school, her therapy sessions). What counts for Stephanie is grappling with the dissonance between her self's authentic internal experience and the fraudulent performance of happy family that has sprung up around that self. By contrast, the stepfather is interested only in that surface simulacrum of real family relations. He wants certain roles to be played by picture-perfect actors inhabiting a seamlessly designed set. Indeed, the disjunction between these two sorts of investments, in particular the female protagonist's inability, unwillingness, and ultimately her refusal to occupy her assigned role in the man's patriarchal scenarios of Reality, emphasizes the specificity, individuality, and ultimately the realness, of her self. In showing us the violent excisions and cruel compressions necessary to sustain the male antagonist's vision of real family life (cut to the measure of 1950s domestic ideology), the movie ultimately encourages the audience to see the space or disjunction between that scenario and the female protagonist's inner self as precisely that which testifies to her realness.[28]

Sleeping with the Enemy best illustrates the space between these two sorts of investments in realness. The film opens with a married couple, Laura and Martin Burney (Julia Roberts, Patrick Bergin), summering in their spectacular modernist Cape Cod home – all white walls, black leather furniture, and gleaming reflective surfaces – located right on the ocean. We quickly discover that Martin is a maniacally controlling, psychotically perfectionistic husband who masterminds with a terrifying precision every surface of both the home and Laura's image and behavior: her clothes, sexuality, daily activities, social calendar, housekeeping, dinner menus.

A tremendous source of anxiety for Laura lies in maintaining the household's perfectly ordered arrangements of gourmet canned items. Every time that Laura opens a kitchen cabinet she fearfully encounters this performative male's external self storage. To disarrange the punctilious *mise-en-scène* of home or self is to risk being brutally beaten by its 'director' and 'designer,' Martin, whose identity seems to depend on each detail occupying its stage-managed place. 'Is everything here as it should be?' he asks with menacing composure upon finding that the bathroom hand towels have become misaligned.

Laura must meticulously inhabit Martin's stage set-home life as theatrical display is underlined by the house's huge picture windows – as well as follow the costuming and stage directions that he indicates for her, all of which contribute to maintaining his image of true conjugal bliss. In the film's second scene, Martin appears behind Laura in a mirror and, while complimenting her outfit, muses 'I wouldn't have thought of it.' In the following shot, Laura's appearance has been made over in accordance with Martin's 'thought': she now wears black instead of white, the hair is down instead of up, and even the earrings have been changed. After producing another perfect dinner one evening, Laura asks if she might work full-time at the local library, whereupon Martin asks if it is possible that she no longer cares about their home. In spite of the very 1980s' visuals of their lavish yuppie lifestyle, Martin is invested in scenarios of 'genuine' marriage and 'real' home that perhaps existed only in 1950s' pop culture, but his sense of coherent identity – and Laura's life – depend on the perfect performance of these scenarios.

From the start, however, the film provides visual cues that alert us to the fact that Laura's realness exists both outside of and beneath these frozen settings and scripts. The camera setups in front of Laura enable us to catch expressions of fear and depression as Martin comes up behind her (a recurrent pattern), such as when he returns with the (predictably selected) red roses and red lingerie after a particularly violent assault. The film's constant attention to her changing facial expressions and furtive glances speaks of the self behind the surfaces that Martin so compulsively manages. Shots of Laura gazing out the windows of their house emphasize the existence of a walled-up self. And her love of books codes the character as possessing a vivid interior life, one for which Martin has no feeling.

Although Laura does not literally investigate her male antagonist – she leaves him to start over in Cedar Falls, Iowa – *Sleeping with the Enemy's* highly compressed version of 'female investigation' can be located in two areas: the film's 'pre-plot' backstory in which, after their honeymoon, Laura discovers that she has married a monster (as in the woman's gothic), and in her hard-won education in the techniques and intricacies of performance, learned at the feet (literally) of the master, knowledge that Laura has drawn on to free herself from him and to survive on her own.

In *Sleeping with the Enemy* the assertion of the female protagonist's personal and interior realness turns out paradoxically to entail her developing her own access and relation to performative identity. Approximately fifteen minutes into the film, Laura stages her own drowning at sea. After the funeral scene, the sudden emergence of Laura's voice on the soundtrack confirms for the audience that this story is actively being told from her point of view: 'That was the night that I died and someone else was saved. Someone who was afraid of water but learned to swim. Someone who knew there would be one moment when he wouldn't be watching. . . .' The voice-over technique at once announces the rescue of a female self – its escape from an oppressive patriarchal gaze and narrative – and aligns that rescue with a woman's ability to tell her own story. The effect of Laura's voiceover is reinforced when the image track briefly shows us Laura at her secret swimming lessons, a feature of the story wholly outside Martin's 'plotting' of their life together. Although initially dissociated from the 'I' of her self – 'someone else was saved' she tells us – the process of the female protagonist's journey (metaphorized by her subsequent bus ride) is toward a space in which she can reclaim her *real* identity.

Laura masterminds her own performative 'makeover' to effect her escape. She cuts her hair and dons a wig; grabs a readied bag with costume (jeans and sneakers) and cash; flushes her wedding band in the toilet; covers her tracks; and catches a Greyhound bus to Cedar Falls where she renames herself Sara Waters, rents a house, wears simple cotton dresses and finds a job working in a library. Finally laying claim to her own self storage, Laura not only paints and decorates her house to her own taste, but she happily jumbles the contents of her own kitchen cabinets. In contrast to Martin, Laura has a more flexible and heterogeneous relation to the performative dimensions of identity.

Laura's new life includes a romantic relationship with a more benign performative male, a local drama teacher. He takes her to the school auditorium and sits in the control booth working special effects around her; later he helps her play dress-up in the costume department. These sequences show the female protagonist repeating a scene of trauma – herself as visual object of a male-orchestrated makeover – but with a non-threatening, indeed remarkably bland male (whom she nonetheless approaches with great caution). Here again, Laura is represented as mastering performativity in the form of an option and tool for accessing her own desires.[29] Her access to performativity is proven when, disguised as a man, she goes to visit her mother in a nursing home and crosses paths with Martin, who is there posing as a police detective as he tries to track down his escaped wife. If these two figures, both enacting assumed identities, seemed momentarily like duplicate images of performativity – her brown wig and thin brown mustache establish a certain resemblance with Martin (and with Jerry, the stepfather) – that mirroring only serves to foreground the female protagonist's privileged relationship with signifiers of depth and authenticity. The point is voiced most explicitly by Laura's blind mother, for whom visible surfaces are not the primary locus of reality: 'Honey, you're going to be fine. Inside you always were. There's nothing that Martin or any man can do or say to take that away: you have your self.'

The final showdown sequence of *Sleeping with the Enemy* makes clear the differing relations to realness and performativity that the movie assigns to each of the characters. When Martin finally finds Laura's new home and breaks into it, his one goal is to recreate the same scenarios he forced his wife to enact on Cape Cod. He reorders into perfect symmetry her hand towels and canned goods in an unnerving violation of her space, and he announces his return with Berlioz's *Symphonie Fantastique* (his it's-time-for-sex music) on the CD player. For Martin, the proper setting and music, speeches and gestures are all that it takes to realize the perfect conjugal reunion.

The state of Laura's interiority holds no significance for him. In response to Martin's typically theatrical bid for repossession, 'we are one – we will always be one,' a comment that would freeze his version of true love into a rigidly unchanging eternity, Laura agonizes for several painful moments . . . then shoots him. Throughout this closing sequence, as in the movie's opening sequences, the disjunction between Martin's scenarios and Laura's inner feelings testifies to the specificity of her inner self.[30]

Power tools: *Pacific Heights*

Pacific Heights begins with a woman who has mastered a number of 'power tools.' Patty and her romantic partner, Drake Goodman (Matthew Modine), share a yuppie dream: they renovate and inhabit a spectacular Victorian home whose rental units they hope will cover the mortgage. An early sequence begins with close-up shots of power tools (an electric nail gun, an electric drill), shots which then reveal that it is Patty who is doing this conventionally male-coded labor.[31] We also see her working on the plumbing and showing Drake the proper way to paint a wall. *Pacific Heights* displaces Patty's performativity by focusing on the gorgeous surfaces not of a woman but of a house (this film's object of visual pleasure), depicting a process of domestic repair and beautification in which the female protagonist plays an active role.

When psycho-tenant Carter Hayes moves in with the secret intention of appropriating the property of this naive young couple, he directs his attacks on the 'body' of the house and, more significantly, on Drake. What I find especially interesting about this women's psychothriller is its triangulation of the performativity/realness economy. Carter works his wiles on another man. He uses props, prescripted lines and false identities to manipulate Drake into a self-destructive performance of macho masculinity. Because the performative psycho-male antagonist stages his scenarios around another man, the female protagonist is able to see and critique their effects. In this regard, Patty's expertise with power tools (we see her using them two more times in the movie) signifies her resistance to becoming herself a tool of their male performativity. As a result of Carter's destructive performances on and around the house – he shifts many of its physical surface and internal borders around, just as he remodels Drake's subjectivity – the patriarchal scaffolding that supports such idealized domestic scenarios is rendered visible.

Where Patty is skeptical of Carter, Drake is his dupe. Carter gets Drake to rent him the apartment in the first place by performing an image of patriarchal masculinity that Drake cannot resist: that of the smoothtalking, Porsche-driving, $100-bill-wielding professional male. Once ensconced inside the house, the new tenant brilliantly stages scenarios that lure Drake into the role of manly protector of this family and property. For example, after Patty has a miscarriage, Carter calls the police *before* he heads upstairs with the flowers and scripted lines (about the cruelty of nature) that are calculated to elicit Drake's violent reaction. (As Carter had planned, Drake gets arrested for his macho display.) Again and again, Drake's only recourse seems to be to lapse into an aggressive, protective masculinity that lurks just beneath the ostensibly egalitarian 1990s new masculinity that he appeared to inhabit when the movie began. Drake utters such classic lines to Patty as: 'I'm on top of this, don't worry about it'; 'I'm not going to lose you, I'm not going to lose our child, and I'm not going to lose our house'; and, 'I got us into this, I'm going to get us out of it – end of discussion.'

His made-over masculinity prompts Patty to cry out: 'What is happening to you?!' What she has discovered is the conventional maleness inside Drake's self-storage. His interiority turns out to be full of cliched masculine performances that emerge once Carter pushes the right buttons. This version of maleness is represented as disempowering. By the end of the movie, Drake has been reduced to a helpless invalid lying under a quilt on a couch ingesting a series of flickering television images of performative masculinity (martial arts movies, Westerns, music videos – even the home shopping channel features a Western theme). Drake's performances of 'man of the house' disqualify him from narrative agency and action. As their lawyer says angrily, Drake's been played 'like a piano concerto.'

As is typical of the woman's psychothriller, out of the association of masculinity with per-formativity emerges the figure of the empowered female investigator. Confronted with the wreckage of her boyfriend and her house, Patty gets out the power tools and goes to work. Amid the rubble she discovers a clue – a snapshot with 'James Danforth' written on the back. It gets her out of the house, literally and figuratively. Tracking down Carter/James to a Marriott hotel in Century City, Patty gains access to his suite (by performing the role of his wife for a cham-bermaid). A quick set of eyeline-matched cuts aligns the investigating woman with the camera as she spots what is the psychothriller genre: a set of briefcases. This is the motif of carry-on luggage in which these male antagonists store their multiple selves. Going through his things, Patty finds the materials that Carter uses to construct his false identities and to manipulate other people: a social directory, newspaper clippings, financial profiles. A pile of passport-sized photos of himself, together with a family album of photos and clippings, further evoke the per-formative male's exteriorized self-storage. Patty also uncovers Carter's latest self-construction; she finds identity papers (passport, Social Security card, driver's license, credit cards) all in the (now performative) name of 'Drake Goodman' and featuring Carter's photograph.

This hotel room scene, in which Patty turns the tables and invades the victimizer's personal space, culminates her movie-long investigation of how the system of money and power actually works. From naive ignorance about capital (she is clueless about how to apply for a mortgage at the film's opening), Patty becomes a canny manipulator of the system. She concocts and directs her own script. After canceling 'Carter's/Drake's' credit cards, closing the checking account and reporting the travelers checks she finds as stolen, Patty (posing as 'Mrs Goodman') orders an elaborate dinner party for fourteen from room service (filet mignon, Caesar salad, *crème brulée* with raspberries, champagne), prompting the credit check that lands Carter temporarily in jail (and thereby disrupts the masquerade he has been using to trick the Tippi Hedren character). Patty also steals an envelope of cash and even the mint off his hotel pillow.

In the course of her maneuverings, Patty comes across a family album filled with photographs and newspapers clippings that detail the wealthy and prominent Danforth parents, the accomplishments of their two sons, and the disinheriting of the oldest son, James, from the family estate. This information hints that Carter/James's pathological invasions of other people's property and identities may be connected to the role played by money and power in the formation and dismantling of his own patriarchal identity. This perspective on her male antagonist echoes Patty's discovery of Drake's unexpected psychic investment in owning and controlling property, an investment at the core of his uncertain masculine identity.

In effect, Patty, like the other female protagonists in this genre, has come to occupy the position, and to engage in the project, that Laura Mulvey aligns with the task of feminist film criticism itself. 'As a feminist critic I could become a female spectator, searching for clues or signs with which to piece together the greater mythical narrative, beyond the screen and the story, of the social unconscious under patriarchy.'[32] The investigating woman of the woman's psychothriller traces out the 'clues' and 'signs' that will help her to expose and survive the oppressions and violences in which she, and other women, find themselves caught. I myself as a female spectator and feminist critic have been reading these women's psychothrillers for the 'clues' and 'signs' they offer with regard to one version of such a 'social unconscious under patriarchy' that casts women into rigidly scripted scenarios of gender, marriage, and family. I also have sought to explore my own investment in the figure of the female protagonist who, by way of her investigations into the performative psycho-male, achieves an empowered selfhood that feels real.

At the same time, I am not anxious blithely to champion all filmic instances of 'empowered,' 'real women' characters, nor to dismiss the performative as retrograde. It is important to examine, critically and strategically, how particular economies of both the 'real' and the 'performative' are depicted, gendered and valued or devalued within a given film, if only because, in an economy, gains are always attended by losses, and someone always pays, and sometimes it may not be the one who can best afford to. Butler writes of the 'tacit cruelties that sustain coherent identity, cruelties that include self-cruelty as well, the abasement through which coherence is fictively produced and sustained.'[33] The women's psychothriller is nothing if not a cruel genre. Its battles to construct and impose 'coherent identity' are a matter of life or death, its violence far from tacit.

Although I am arguing that there can be a feminist advantage to claiming and valuing a filmic construction of female realness, such constructions are never simply affirmative. Untroubled, unexamined identity claims have a long history of being used to exclude and abject 'difference.' The woman's psychothriller is underwritten by any number of such exclusions, marked or unmarked.

The unmarked ('natural') whiteness of the genre's investigating woman, for example, functions as an unquestioned authentic identity, implying a certain equivalence between nonwhiteness and performativity.[34] And, returning now to *Silence of the Lambs*, the emergence of Clarice Starling as a 'positive image' is contingent on the homophobic coding of Buffalo Bill as a gayish 'negative image,' a representational arrangement that displaces the question of Clarice's own sexuality. Moreover, by having the female protagonist eliminate that monstrous figure and be herself warmly welcomed into the FBI, the film deflects its critique away from dominant institutions of patriarchal power. Is this simply a case of the good daughter substituting for the good son?[35]

But the ambivalent nature of these texts ought not negate what is powerful about how structures of identity and identification work in relation to the female protagonist of the woman's psychothriller. The goal of this essay has been – without losing sight of the larger representational economy of gender – to trace out configurations of coherent female identity and the possibilities for a viewer's self-identification. As Judith Mayne observes, 'the competing claims of "identity,"' have been long 'associated with some of the most fervent debates of film studies and related fields in the past two decades.'[36] These debates persist as critics speculate about the social, psychical, and political implications of how identity is forged, dismantled and circulated.

Recent critical discussions of filmic identity have emphasized the liberatory pleasures and possibilities that may result from cinema's performative dismantlings of identity (on the screen and in the audience). But it would be a mistake to underestimate the burdens of performative identity, the plight (for some more than others) of feeling fragmented or estranged from a coherent self. I have therefore argued for the feminist importance of also laying claim to coherence, of laying claim to the stabilizing avenues of identification (with female realness, for example) that cinema can offer.

Notes

1   In addition to the films discussed in this essay, the book-length version of this project includes discussions of *What Lies Beneath* (2000), *Double Jeopardy* (1999), *Eye for an Eye* (1996); *Copycat* (1995); *True Crime* (1995); *Candyman 2* (1994) and *Candyman* (1992); *Deceived* (1991); *Love Crimes* (1991); *Defenseless* (1991); *Blue Steel* (1990); and *Positive I.D.* (1988). The woman's psychothriller is related to, but distinct from, such 1980s and 1990s movies as *Fatal Attraction* (1987), *The Hand that Rocks the Cradle* (1991) and *The Temp* (1993), which critic Julianne Pidduck calls the 'fatal femme cycle' in her article 'The 1990s Hollywood Fatal Femme: (Dis)Figuring Feminism, Family, Irony, Violence,' *Cineaction* 38 (1995): 64–72. In contrast to the female protagonists of the woman's psychothriller, these 'fatal femmes' are psychotic, destructive antagonists whom the films violently eliminate. Both film cycles, however, share an ambivalent fascination with powerful women and may perhaps be understood in part as symptoms of North American culture's ambivalence regarding feminism's advances over the past thirty years or so.

2   Laura Mulvey, 'Visual Pleasure and Narrative Cinema,' *Screen* 16, no. 3 (Autumn 1975): 6–18; rpt. in Mulvey's *Visual and Other Pleasures* (Bloomington: Indiana University Press, 1981). This essay has been critiqued in a variety of ways, not least by Mulvey herself in 'Afterthoughts on "Visual Pleasure and Narrative Cinema" inspired by *Duel in the Sun*,' *Visual and Other Pleasures*, pp. 29–38.

3   See Butler's *Gender Trouble: Feminism and the Subversion of Identity* (New York: Routledge, 1990) and *Bodies That Matter: On the Discursive Limits of Sex* (New York: Routledge, 1993). Although Butler is a philosopher rather than a film theorist, her conceptualization of gender and sexuality as performative has had a major impact on feminist and queer film analysis, enabling critics to locate the fissures and instabilities in what might otherwise look like seamless, essential identities. For discussions and examples of how poststructuralism and psychoanalysis inform film theory, see *Feminism and Film Theory*, Constance Penley (ed.) (New York: Routledge, 1988); *Film Theory: An Introduction*, Robert Lapsley and Michael Westlake (eds) (Manchester: Manchester University Press, 1988); and *New Vocabularies in Film Semiotics*, Robert Stam, Robert Burgoyne and Sandy Flitterman-Lewis (eds) (New York: Routledge, 1992).

4   One example from my teaching: it was the week before spring break, and my Hitchcock and Gender students were discussing Marnie in the context of selected readings in the feminist psychoanalytic theory of masquerade. Sophisticated observations were made about Marnie's theatrical production of an elusive subjectivity that Mark Rutland, for all his prowess, cannot entirely master. (The class had come a long way since the 'I like/dislike her' approach that had dominated at the start of the term.) With fifteen minutes of class time left, I decided, as a sort of informal overview, to ask my students which of the Hitchcock films that we had viewed seemed most challenging to the conventions of Hollywood gender representation. That question triggered an instant return to emotional connections with 'strong' stars and characters: 'I liked the two Ingrid Bergman movies the best.' 'Yeah – She was really strong and memorable.' 'It was a good strategy to start the course with Rebecca – there was nowhere to go but up from that washout wife.' 'I agree, I couldn't identify with Joan Fontaine at all.' 'But Charlie in Shadow of a Doubt was the best: she really stood up to her psycho uncle.' These responses suggested to me that my students continued to be powerfully drawn to characters whom the films explicitly coded as strong, knowledgeable, and active.

5   With his suspense films, his women's gothics and Psycho (catalyst for the slashers of the 1970s and 1980s), Hitchcock's work has been foundational to women's psychothrillers and is consistently alluded to by them in one way or another. See Tania Modleski's The Woman Who Knew Too Much: Hitchcock and Feminist Theory (New York: Methuen, 1988) for a provocative discussion of how Hollywood's traditional representation of gender is challenged by certain Hitchcock texts.

6   I am not suggesting that camera techniques have inherent meanings, nor am I implying that a character's predominance within the story depends on literal point-of-view shots, or even necessarily on the optical register. However, both because film is a visual medium and because Hollywood has consolidated a distinct narrational style, when the camera's spatial positioning is correlated with a character's positioning, that character is more likely to serve as what Seymour Chatman calls a 'filter' – optical, psychological, emotional – of the story and of the other characters. 'Filter, Center, Slant, and Interest-Focus,' in Poetics Today 7(2): 189–204. For a useful discussion of film and narrative, see 'Film-Narratology,' in New Vocabularies in Film Semiotics, Stam (ed.) et al., pp. 69–122. Unsurprisingly, women's psychothrillers feature numerous shots of the female protagonist looking. For example, in Deceived (1991, dir. Damian Harris), just after female protagonist Adrienne Saunders (Goldie Hawn) discovers that her husband is not the person she thought he was, a 55-shot sequence of female investigation begins, of which roughly half the shots could be subtitled 'Adrienne Looking.'

7   'Writers on the Lamb,' Lisa Kennedy (ed.), Village Voice, March 5, 1991, pp. 49, 56.

8   Stephen Harvey, 'Critics,' in 'Writers on the Lamb.'

9   Quoted in Michael Bronski's 'Real Politic,' Z Magazine, May 1991, p. 83.

10 An economy, in the psychoanalytic sense, refers to the organization of psychical processes in terms of 'the circulation and distribution of an energy . . . that is capable of increase, decrease and equivalence.' J. Laplanche and J.-B. Pontilis, 'Economic,' The Language of Psychoanalysis, trans. Donald Nicholson-Smith (New York: W. W. Norton), p. 127. As historians of sexuality have shown, the displacement of various threatening forces associated with femininity onto scapegoated male homosexuality is a strategy that dates back to nineteenth-century English culture: 'The supposed characteristics of homosexuality, "passion, emotional ill-discipline, and sexual looseness," were those associated with the Fallen Woman. It was the perceived feminine quality of evil attributed to the homosexual psyche which formed the link to Victorian theories of the prostitute and brought about the conception of homosexuality as a form of female sexual pathology.' Morris Meyer, 'I Dream of Jeannie: Transsexual Striptease as Scientific Display,' Drama Review 35, no. 1 (Spring 1991): 33.

11 Although cultural studies is often accused of taking untheorized audience response at face value, the field has made important headway in exploring the phenomenon of 'self-centred' spectatorship. For example, Lawrence Grossberg's work on rock-and-roll describes fandom in terms of 'mattering maps,' the mapping of one's intense affective investments across 'potential locations for [one's] self-identifications.' 'Is There a Fan in the House? The Affective Sensibility of Fandom,' in The Adoring Audience: Fan Culture and Popular Media, Lisa A. Lewis (ed.) New York: Routledge, 1992), p. 57. For a critique of cultural studies' use of audience reception, see Judith Mayne, 'Paradoxes of Spectatorship,' in her Cinema and Spectatorship (New York: Routledge, 1993), pp. 77–102.

12 Janet Staiger, 'Taboos and Totems: Cultural Meanings of Silence of the Lambs,' in Film Theory Goes to the Movies, Jim Collins, Hilary Radner and Ava Preacher Collins (eds) (New York: Routledge, 1993), p. 153.

13   Judith Halberstam, 'Skinflick: Posthuman Gender in Jonathan Demme's *Silence of the Lambs*,' *Skin Shows: Gothic Horror and the Technology of Monsters* (Durham, NC: Duke University Press, 1995), p. 177. Halberstam's essay eloquently makes the case that Buffalo Bill symbolizes a 'literal skin disease' that is shared by 'all the other characters in the film' (p. 165). Without denying that insight, I wish to point out that *Silence* nonetheless explicitly and unevenly codes and distributes identity traits.

     Silence has generated a great deal of critical commentary, not surprising given its release at a historical moment of huge cultural and critical interest in gender and sexuality. See esp. Elizabeth Young, *Silence of the Lambs* and the Flaying of Feminist Theory,' *Camera Obscura* 27 (September 1991): 5–35; Diana Fuss, 'Monsters of Perversion: Jeffrey Dahmer and *Silence of the Lambs*,' in *Media Spectacles*, Marjorie Garber, Jann Matlock and Rebecca L. Walkowitz (eds) (New York: Routledge, 1993), pp. 181–205; Julie Tharp, 'The Transvestite: Gender Horror in *Silence of the Lambs*,' *Journal of Popular Film and Television* 19, no. 3 (Fall 1991): 106–13. My own essay began as a conference talk entitled 'The Girls Against the Boys: Feminist Theory, Queer Theory, and Hollywood Cinema,' Modern Language Association, New York, December 1992. A significant number of critical responses to *Silence* cite Carol J. Clover's richly provocative study of gender in the slasher genre, *Men, Women, and Chainsaws: Gender in the Modern Horror Film* (Princeton, NJ: Princeton University Press, 1992). My thinking about the investigating woman is particularly indebted to Clover's discussion of the 'Final Girl,' that is, the masculine-coded female victim (modeled on *Psycho's* Lila Crane) who survives the attacks on the monster.

14   Clarice, like Catherine, is also associated with performative elements that help to anchor rather than to undo her character's realness. Hannibal Lecter notes Clarice's anxious efforts at elevated class performance – the good bag, the career ambitions, the laboriously improved dialect. Motivated by her deeply felt but conflicted efforts toward upward mobility, Clarice's understated artifice serves mainly to highlight the 'truth' (and transparency) of her *real* inner self. One might argue that Clarice's memory flashbacks and 'therapy' sessions with Lecter are themselves a kind of performance: an iteration of stories, images, poses and gestures, all of which produce simply the *effect* of interiority, of a core self. True enough. But that effect is effective enough, so to speak, that Clarice thereby powerfully inhabits the 'realness slot' in this film's economy of competing identities. Moreover, by bringing her own autobiography to sessions with Hannibal, Clarice comes to signify for him a real person whom later he will not be able to kill. With more space, I would argue that Hannibal Lecter functions as a hinge between Buffalo Bill, the voracious monster, and Crawford, the analytic professional, thus partially undoing another opposition: that between rabid misogyny and institutional patriarchy. Hannibal's own performativity (signaled by a blonde wig, dark glasses and costumey white suit and hat) is explicitly displayed at the end of the movie when his character gets slotted into the vacancy left by the dead Buffalo Bill.

15   An example of this approach is Sharon Smith's 'The Image of Women in Film: Some Suggestions for Future Research,' *Women and Film* 1 (1972): 13–21, followed by Marjorie Rosen's *Popcorn Venus: Women, Movies and the American Dream* (New York: Coward, McCann and Geoghegan, 1973) and Molly Haskell's *From Reverence to Rape: The Treatment of Women in the Movies* (New York: Holt, Rinehart and Winston, 1974). For an application and critique of the 'images-of-women' approach, see Linda Artel and Susan Wengraf's 'Positive Images: Screening Women's Films,' followed by Diane Waldman's 'There's More to a Positive Image Than Meets the Eye,' in *Issues in Feminist Film Criticism*, Patricia Erens (ed.) (Bloomington: Indiana University Press, 1990), pp. 9–18. Noël Carroll asks for a return to the analysis of images of women within a cognitive theory framework in 'The Image of Women in Film: A Defense of a Paradigm,' *Journal of Aesthetics and Art Criticism* 48, no. 4 (Fall 1990): 349–60. It is worth noting that cultural studies actually shares an important impulse with 1970s feminist film criticism: a valuing of spectators' potentially self-affirming relations with popular culture.

16   I want to stress that, despite the focus of this essay, potentially stabilizing identifications with the female protagonist of the woman's psychothriller are not restricted to women in the audience. Avenues of identification with realness in all forms of popular culture are variable and unpredictable, crossing lines of gender, race, ethnicity, sexuality, age and class. An example: in his aptly titled *Jackie Under My Skin: Interpreting an Icon* (New York: Farrar, Straus and Giroux, 1995), Wayne Koestenbaum (a gay Jewish man) writes eloquently of his powerful, formative identification with Jacqueline Kennedy Onassis. Koestenbaurn asserts, for example, that by emulating ordinary 'Jackie activities' ('to walk; to put on sunglasses; to swim; to reflect; to sleep; to read' and so on), one can thereby transform 'a media icon into a magical lesson in embodiment, your teacher in the art of training your "I" to feel like an "I"' (pp. 283–84).

17   Lacan theorized that we are born into a pre-existent order of meaning – what he calls the Symbolic of discourse, laws, codes, prohibitions – in which we have no choice but to assume a sexual identity (through a difficult series of unconscious repressions, identifications, and fantasies). For an explanation of Lacanian psychoanalysis and its significance for film theory, see Lapsley and Westlake's *Film Theory: An Introduction* and *New Vocabularies in Film Semiotics*, Stam (ed.) *et al.*

18   Wood, *American Nightmares: Essays on the Horror Film* (Toronto: Festival of Festivals, 1979), pp. 7–28. In her influential essay 'When the Woman Looks,' Linda Williams agrees that the horror film 'permits the expression of women's sexual potency and desire' but clarifies that 'it does so . . . only to demonstrate how monstrous female desire can be.' *Re-Vision: Essays in Feminist Film Criticism*, Mary Ann Doane, Patricia Mellencamp and Linda Williams (eds) (Frederick, Md.: AFI Monograph Series, University Publications of America, 1984), p. 97. More recently, Carol Clover's study of the slasher admires that genre's various forms of 'gender transgression,' which Clover interprets as a 'brazen tack into the psychosexual wilderness' (*Men, Women, and Chainsaws*, pp. 231, 236).

19   *Attack on the Leading Ladies* (New York: Columbia University Press, 1996), p. 58.

20   Without (as I hope is clear) rejecting critical efforts to undo the narrow ideas of normative identity perpetuated by much popular culture and some traditional academic film criticism.

21   Butler, *Bodies That Matter*, p. 105.

22   It is important to keep in mind that a person's experience of realness might also center on identifications with cultural elements explicitly coded as performative. The documentary *Unzipped* (1995), for example, explores how designer Isaac Mizrahi consolidates his identity in relation to the intensely performative images of high fashion (a message echoed by Sylvester's 'You Make Me Feel (Mighty Real)' on the soundtrack).

23   Again, though, I am not suggesting that these camera techniques have inherent meanings. The 'Adrienne Looking' sequence from *Deceived* (see n. 6 above) includes numerous close-ups of the female protagonist. However, the meaning is different from the close-ups of Jerry's face, for Adrienne, like Stephanie, is not constructed as image, reflecting back on herself, but is, rather, looking into words and images to decipher their secrets and decode their narratives.

24   Hitchcock's *Rebecca* is famous for inaugurating this cycle of women's gothics. Of the movies under discussion in this essay, *The Stepfather* is most explicit in its debt to Hitchcock, alluding to *Psycho* and *Shadow of the Doubt* in a variety of ways described by Patricia Erens in 'The Stepfather,' *Film Quarterly* 41 (Winter): 87–88. *Shadow of a Doubt* stands out for its uncompromising validation of female protagonist Charlie's (Teresa Wright) suspicions about her deadly Uncle Charlie (Joseph Cotten).

25   Mary Ann Doane, *The Desire to Desire: The Woman's Film of the 1940s* (Bloomington: Indiana University Press, 1987). Diane Waldman, 'Horror and Domesticity: The Modern Gothic Romance Film of the 1940s,' PhD diss., University of Wisconsin, Madison, 1981.

26   Doane, *The Desire to Desire*, p. 5.

27   Waldman, 'Horror and Domesticity,' p. 138.

28   Judith Butler's elucidation of the potentially dangerous (even murderous) politics of realness describes very well the stepfather's relation to what I am calling 'preconceived Reality with a capital R': 'The rules that regulate and legitimate realness (shall we call them the symbolic?) constitute the mechanism by which certain sanctioned fantasies, sanctioned imaginaries, are insidiously elevated as the parameters of realness' (*Bodies That Matter*, pp. 130–31). There is no absolute line that differentiates these 'insidiously elevated' 'sanctioned fantasies' of Reality from those experiences of realness by female protagonists that, I am arguing, feminists should learn to revalue. Indeed, to believe that we could definitively separate (what we might call, loosely speaking) 'bad' destructive scenarios of realness from 'good' empowering feelings of having a stable, real self would be ourselves to participate in the rigid absolutes fantasized by the psychotic antagonists of this genre.

29   Alternatively, one might argue that this sequence represents a woman hopelessly reimmersed in male fantasy. Both readings are available. The film certainly does not critique the status quo; moreover, it presents a nostalgic version of traditional America as its solution to female oppression. But what I am stressing is that this is the route (however unlikely) that Laura takes toward reclaiming her own identity. Indeed, this is a fantasy of a small midwestern town so embracing of people's differing realities that a gay drama teacher, misidentified by Martin as Laura's boyfriend, can cry out: 'I live with another man! ask anyone!'

30   Another way of getting at how Laura's more flexible relation to realness differs from Martin's reality would be to consider the psychological and emotional effects of the psychothriller genre. That women protagonists in this genre are by definition in jeopardy, their selves threatened, makes their feeling

real equivalent to holding onto self at an intensely individual, personal level (rather than legislating reality). In this genre, female realness is literally a form of survival.

31   Is Melanie Griffith's mastery over power tools in this woman's psychothriller a retort to *Body Double* (1984, directed by Brian De Palma), in which Griffith plays a porn star and exotic dancer whose classier female counterpart is horrifically murdered with a power drill?

32   Laura Mulvey's entry in 'The Spectatrix,' the special issue of *Camera Obscura* 20–21 (May–September 1989): 249. In this short piece, Mulvey also characterizes the critical female spectator as 'detective, semiotician and analyst' (p. 250).

33   Butler, *Bodies That Matter*, p. 115.

34   In *Pacific Heights*, two African-American male characters (a best friend and a prospective tenant) function mainly as props to – and measures of – the subjectivities of the two white protagonists. In addition, the Asian tenants are there primarily to supply 'comic' performativity, engaging in such stereotypical displays as excessive bowing and linguistic confusion. In another chapter of this project, I explore the race and performativity economies of *Candyman* (directed by Bernard Rose, 1992), which opposes (but ultimately connects) a white investigating woman – a graduate student in anthropology – to a monster-ized figure of black male performativity.

35   And in her career has Foster herself assumed the role of Hollywood's good daughter? Nonetheless, as in my discussion of the woman's psychothriller, I think that we ought not be too quick to dismiss the feminist significance of identifications with 'role model' women who survive cutthroat situations in patriarchal arenas (like Hollywood). In the course of my research I was struck by the 'strong woman' emphasis of articles on Foster in woman-targeted magazines: 'Jodie Rules: Jodie Foster Lets Loose and Takes Control' on the cover of *Vanity Fair*, May 1994; 'Wunderkind' (in a section titled 'Breaking New Ground'), *Haper's Bazaar*, November 1991, pp. 124–5; 'The Power of Women: Ten Women to Watch,' *Working Woman*, November 1991, pp. 87, 92; and 'Jodie Foster's "Best Performance": An Actress Calls Her Own Shots,' *Maclean's*, September 1991, pp. 48–9, 36.

36   Mayne, Cinema and Spectatorship, p. 101.

Chapter 24

CHRIS STRAAYER

THE HYPOTHETICAL LESBIAN HEROINE IN NARRATIVE FEATURE FILM

F EMINIST FILM THEORY BASED ON SEXUAL difference has much to gain from considering lesbian desire and sexuality. Women's desire for women deconstructs male-female sexual dichotomies, sex-gender conflation, and the universality of the oedipal narrative. Acknowledgement of the female-initiated active sexuality and sexualized activity of lesbians has the potential to reopen a space in which heterosexual women as well as lesbians can exercise self-determined pleasure.

In this chapter I am concerned mainly with films that do *not* depict lesbianism explicitly, but employ or provide sites for lesbian intervention. This decision is based on my interest in the lesbian viewer, and how her relationship to films with covert lesbian content resembles her positioning in society. In textual analyses of *Entre Nous* and *Voyage en Douce* – two French films that seemingly oblige different audiences and interpretations – I demonstrate how, rather than enforcing opposite meanings, the films allow for multiple readings which overlap. I use the term *hypothetical* here to indicate that neither the character's lesbianism nor her heroism is an obvious fact of the films. I articulate a lesbian aesthetic that is subjective but not idiosyncratic.

In particular, I examine two sites of negotiation between texts and viewers, shifts in the heterosexual structure which are vulnerable to lesbian pleasuring: the lesbian look of exchange and female bonding. I place these in contrast to the male gaze and its narrative corollary, love at first sight. I then examine the contradictions that arise when the articulation of non-heterosexual subject matter is attempted within a structure conventionally motivated by heterosexuality. Finally, the question inevitably raised by women-only interactions – 'Where is the man?' – inspires a radical disclosure of sex as historically and socially constructed and a redefinition of subjectivity.

Feminist film theory: gender, sexuality and viewership

Within the construction of narrative film sexuality, the phrase 'lesbian heroine' is a contra-diction in terms. The female position in classical narrative is a stationary site to which the male hero travels and on which he acts. The relationship between male and female is one of conquest. The processes of acting and receiving are thus genderized.[1] There can be no lesbian heroine here, for the very definition of lesbianism requires an act of defiance in relation to assumptions about sexual desire and activity. Conventional filmic discourse can only accommodate the lesbian heroine as a hero, as 'male.' Yet maleness is potentially irrelevant to lesbianism, if not to lesbians.

The lesbian heroine in narrative film must be conceived as a viewer construction, short-circuiting the very networks that attempt to forbid her energy. She is constructed from contradictions within the text and between text and viewer, who insists on assertive, even transgressive, identifications and seeing.

The Hollywood romance formula of love at first sight relies on a slippage between sexuality and love. Sexual desire pretends to be reason enough for love, and love pretends to be sexual pleasure. While sexual desire is visually available for viewers' vicarious experiences, sexual pleasure is blocked. By the time the plot reaches a symbolic climax, love has been substituted for sex, restricting sex to the realm of desire. So structured, love is unrequited sex. Since this love is hetero-love, homosexual viewers are doubly distanced from sexual pleasure.

The sexual gaze as elaborated in much feminist film theory is a male prerogative, a unidirectional gaze from male onto female, pursuing a downward slant in relation to power. In contrast, the lesbian look that I describe here requires exchange. It looks for a returning look, not just a receiving look. It sets up two-directional sexual activity.[2]

Considerable work by feminist film theorists has attempted to articulate operations of looking in narrative film texts and film spectatorship. In 'Visual Pleasure and Narrative Cinema,' Laura Mulvey describes how the patriarchal unconscious has structured classical cinema with visual and narrative pleasure specifically for the heterosexual male viewer, gratifying his narcissistic ego via a surrogate male character who condones and relays the viewer's look at the woman character, and providing him voyeuristic pleasure via a more direct, nonnarrative presentation of the woman as image (rather than character). Woman's erotic image elicits castration anxiety in the male viewer, which is eased by visual and narrative operations of fetishism and sadism. As Mulvey states, 'None of these interacting layers is intrinsic to film, but it is only in the film form that they can reach a perfect and beautiful contradiction, thanks to the possibility in the cinema of shifting the emphasis of the look.'[3]

Although Mulvey's article remains invaluable in addressing patriarchal dominance as the ideological status quo formally enforced by/in the mainstream cinema/text, it does not account for other sexual forces and experiences within society. Mulvey's arguments have been constructively elaborated, revised, and rebutted by numerous other feminist film theorists. However, much of this work has brought about an unproductive slippage between text and actuality which presses this exclusive patriarchal structure onto the world at large. This excludes the reactions of 'deviant' participants in the film event from theory's discursive event. Even though the spectator's psychology is formed within a culture that collapses sexual/anatomical difference onto gender, the same culture also contains opposing factors and configurations that generate a proliferation of discourses that instigates actual psychological diversity. It is this diversity rather than cinema's dominant ideology that we must examine in order to deconstruct the alignment of male with activity and female with passivity.

In a later article, 'Afterthoughts on "Visual Pleasure and Narrative Cinema" Inspired by *Duel in the Sun*,' Mulvey suggests that female viewers experience Freud's 'true heroic feeling' through masculine identification with active male characters, a process that allows this spectator 'to rediscover that lost aspect of her sexual identity, the never fully repressed bed-rock of feminine neurosis.' With her 'own memories' of masculinity, a certain 'regression' takes place in this deft 'trans-sex identification' and, like returning to her past daydreams of action, she experiences viewer pleasure. Nevertheless, 'the female spectator's phantasy of masculinization is always to some extent at cross purposes with itself, restless in its transvestite clothes.'[4]

Such rhetorical confusion of clothing with sex, and of both with desire for action, accepts the limitations of sex-role stereotyping in the text. True, such desire on the part of female viewers usually requires identification with male characters, but this is a limitation of mainstream cinema, not a 'regression' on the part of women.

By not addressing mechanisms of gay spectatorship, the above scheme denies gay viewing pleasure or suggests that it is achieved from the heterosexual text via transvestite ploys. Mainstream cinema's nearly total compulsory heterosexuality does require homosexual viewers to appropriate heterosexual representations for homosexual pleasure; however, the 'transvestite' viewer-text interaction, described by Mulvey and others, should not be confused with gay or bisexual viewership.

Mary Ann Doane understands this cross-gender identification by female viewers as one means of achieving distance from the text. In 'Film and the Masquerade: Theorizing the Female Spectator,' she argues that, because woman's preoedipal bond with the mother continues to be strong throughout her life (unlike man's), the female viewer – unless she utilizes artificial devices – is unable to achieve that distance from the film's textual *body* which allows man the process of voyeurism: 'For the female spectator there is a certain over-presence of the image – she *is* the image. Given the closeness of this relationship, the female spectator's desire can be described only in terms of a kind of narcissism – the female look demands a becoming.'[5] As a result, woman overidentifies with cinema's female victims, experiencing a pleasurable reconnection that is necessarily masochistic. Because her body lacks the potential for castration, 'woman is constructed differently in relation to the process of looking.'[6]

Doane goes on to describe an alternate strategy for women to overcome proximity and mimic a distance from the(ir) image – the masquerade of femininity.

> Above and beyond a simple adoption of the masculine position in relation to the cinematic sign, the female spectator is given two options: the masochism of over-identification or the narcissism entailed in becoming one's own object of desire, in assuming the image in the most radical way. The effectivity of masquerade lies precisely in its potential to manufacture a distance from the image, to generate a problematic within which the image is manipulable, producible, and readable to woman.[7]

The primary question that followed Mulvey's 'Visual Pleasure and Narrative Cinema' was: How can women's film-viewing pleasure be understood? Although subsequent feminist film theory drawing on psychoanalysis successfully opened up that field for feminist purposes and raised significant new questions, the answers it has provided – elaborations of particular processes of narcissism and transvestism – remain only partially sufficient to the original question. Much of this work has circumvented a crucial option in female spectatorship by avoiding the investigation of women viewers' erotic attraction to and visual appreciation of women characters.[8] Further work needs to examine how viewers determine films as much as how films determine viewers. And care should be taken that the theorized transvestite or bisexual viewer does not inadvertently suppress the homosexual viewer.

Eroticizing looks between women characters

Visual exchanges between same-sex characters in mainstream film typically are nonsexual. The challenge for the lesbian viewer is to eroticize these looks. She brings her desires to the heterosexual raw material and representational system of the text. Occasionally she collaborates with texts to excavate subtexts and uncover ambivalence in the patriarchal 'order.' Since the heterosexual structure of the gaze is already established as sexual, it can be built on to accomplish an erotic homosexual look.[9]

Independently structured glances between women on the screen, however, are outside convention and therefore threaten. The ultimate threat of eye contact between women, inherent in all scenes of female bonding, is the elimination of the male.[10] Any erotic exchange of glances between women requires counterefforts to disempower and de-eroticize them.

I now will focus on two films, both open to lesbian readings, that are interesting for their similarities and differences. *Voyage en Douce* (Michel Deville, 1979) is an erotic art film, bordering on 'soft porn,' about two women who take a trip to the country together. They exchange fantasies and flirtations, then return home to their male partners. *Entre Nous* (Diane Kurys, 1983) is also about the interactions between two women, but their relationship leans ostensibly toward the buddies genre. They too take a trip away from their husbands. The women demonstrate growing mutual affection and, at the film's conclusion, they are living together. Although the two films appear opposite – one pseudo-lesbian soft porn serving a male audience, the other feminist and appealing to a female audience – this dichotomy is deconstructed once viewers are actively involved.

Voyage en Douce is particularly interesting in relation to looking because, instead of resolution, it attempts sustained sexual desire. According to the conventions of pornography, the erotic involvement of two women functions as foreplay for a heterosexual climax. This does not happen in *Voyage en Douce*. Erotic looking and flirting between women is thematic in this film. The lesbian desire this stimulates is accentuated by a hierarchical looking structure that mimics the male gaze. Throughout the film, a blonde woman, Hélène (Dominique Sanda), is the more active looker and the text's primary visual narrator. It is primarily 'through her eyes' that sexual fantasies are visualized on the screen. When taking nude photographs of her brunette companion Lucie (Geraldine Chaplin), a camera prop 'equips' Hélène for this male role (Figures 24.1 and 24.2).

Hélène is also the primary pursuer in the narrative, while Lucie functions to stimulate, tease and frustrate Hélène's desire. The film's episodic structure – another convention of pornography – alternates between the women's individual sexual stories and fantasies and their erotically charged interactions. Hélène pampers Lucie, appreciates her visually and verbally reassures her about her beauty and desirability. This serves to build both a generalized sexual desire and a more specific lesbian desire. In both cases, a series of narrative denials and delays establishes an 'interruptus' motif. Early in the film, there is a point-of-view shot of a look from Lucie at Hélène's breast, which Hélène quickly covers. Later, when Hélène purposely exposes her breast to excite Lucie, Lucie is not responsive. When photographing Lucie, Hélène encourages her to remove her clothes. Lucie does so hesitantly and coquettishly, but, when Hélène attempts to take the final nude shot, she is out of film.

In several scenes Hélène and Lucie exchange unmediated glances, as do the two women characters in *Entre Nous* – Lena (Isabelle Huppert) and Madeline (Miou-Miou). Such exchanges, which occur primarily within two-person shots, gain sexual energy from the women's physical proximity and subtle body contact. The fact that two women share the film frame encourages this lesbian reading – that is, the women are consistently framed as a 'couple.' This visual motif provides a pleasurable homosexual content which is frustrated by the plot.[11] However, the absence of a short-reverse shot, reciprocal point-of-view pattern in these two-shots excludes the viewer from experiencing the looking. Thus, the viewer's identification with the women's looking is necessarily more sympathetic than empathic.

In *Entre Nous* the addition of a mirror to such a shot establishes a second, internal frame. The reciprocal point-of-view exchange achieved between these two simultaneous frames – a

Figures 24.1 and 24.2 A camera 'equips' Hélène (Dominique Sanda) for a 'male' gaze at Lucie (Geraldine Chaplin) in *Voyage en Douce* (Michel Deville, 1979).

two-shot of the women looking at each other through the mirror – allows the viewer to be sutured into the looking experience, while also experiencing the pleasure of seeing the two women together. It is notable that during this shot the women are partially nude and admiring one another's breasts (Figure 24.3).

A similar construction occurs temporally instead of spatially in another shot. Deeply depressed about the deterioration of both her marriage and her love affair, Madeline has taken her son and gone to her parents' home to recover. When Lena finds out where Madeline is, she immediately goes there and, against the mother's protests, runs to the backyard where Madeline sits in a small garden. In a subjective tracking shot, the camera first identifies our look with the look and movement of Lena approaching Madeline. Then, as the shot continues, the camera movement stops and holds steady on Madeline until Lena enters the frame. The viewer is carried into the women's space via an identification with Lena's look, then observes their embrace from an invited vantage point. This is followed by a shot of Madeline's father and son watching disapprovingly – a look from outside. Standing together, hand in hand, these two males foreground the generation missing between them – Madeline's husband. Hence their look both acknowledges and checks the dimensions of the women's visual exchange.

Voyage en Douce also contains an abundance of mirror shots, some of which similarly conduct visual exchanges between the characters, while others seem to foreground hierarchical erotic looking. In particular, several mirror shots occur in which the two women examine Lucie's image while Hélène compliments and grooms her.

Female bonding in film

What becomes evident from these examples is that, when one searches for lesbian exchange in narrative film construction, one finds a constant flux between competing forces to suggest and deny it. Because female bonding and the exchange of glances between women threaten heterosexual and patriarchal structures, when female bonding occurs in feature narrative film, its readiness for lesbian appropriation is often acknowledged by internal efforts to forbid such conclusions. As with sexuality in general, efforts to subdue lesbian connotations can stimulate innovations.

Conceptually, female bonding is a precondition for lesbianism.[12] If women are situated only in relationship to men or in antagonistic relationship to each other, the very idea of lesbianism is precluded. This partially explains the appreciation lesbian audiences have for films with female bonding. So often has female bonding stood in for lesbian content that lesbian audiences seem to find it an acceptable displacement at the conclusions of such 'lesbian romances' as *Personal Best* (Robert Towne, 1983) and *Lianna* (John Sayles, 1983).[13]

The widespread popularity of *Entre Nous* among lesbian audiences is attributable to basic narrative conditions, which are reiterated throughout the film. Most important is female bonding. The film begins with parallel editing between Lena's and Madeline's separate lives. This crosscutting constructs audience expectation and desire for the two women to meet. Once they have met, the two women spend the majority of their screen time together. Lesbian viewers experience pleasure in their physical closeness. Though lesbianism is never made explicit in the film, an erotic subtext is readily available. The specific agenda held by lesbian viewers for female bonding warrants an inside joke at the film's conclusion when Lena and Madeline are finally living together. In the 'background' a song plays: 'I wonder who's kissing her now. I wonder who's showing her how.'[14]

Figures 24.3 and 24.4 Eroticized looking and female bonding lesbianize the relationship between Lena (Isabelle Huppert, blonde) and Madeline (Miou-Miou, brunette) in *Entre Nous* (Diane Kurys, 1983).

The development of Lena and Madeline's relationship stands in sharp contrast to the development of Lena's marriage. During World War II, Lena and Michel (Guy Marchand) are prisoners in a camp. He is soon to be released and will be allowed to take his wife out with him. He is unmarried but realizes that pretending to have a wife could save someone. He selects Lena by sight alone.

In many ways, female bonding is the antithesis of love at first sight. While love at first sight necessarily de-emphasizes materiality and context, female bonding is built upon an involvement in specific personal environments. Furthermore, the relationship acquires a physical quality from the presence of personal items which, when exchanged, suggest intimacy. Women frequently wear one another's clothes in both these films. Body lotion and love letters pass between Lena and Madeline as easily as do cigarettes.

Such bonding activity between women suggests an alternate use for the feminine masquerade. This mutual appreciation of one another's feminine appearance, which achieves intimacy via an attention to personal effects, demonstrates the masquerade's potential to draw women closer together and to function as nonverbal homoerotic expression which connects image to body. This 'deviant' employment of the feminine masquerade is in contradistinction to Doane's elaboration of it as a distancing device for women.

The primary threat of female bonding is the elimination of the male. As noted, the unstated but always evident question implicit in such films – 'Where is the man?' – acknowledges defensive androcentric reactions. Its underlying presence attempts to define female bonding and lesbianism in relation to men. Publicity material accompanying a distribution print of *Voyage en Douce* from New Yorker Films describes the film as 'What women talk about when men aren't around.' In *Entre Nous*, scenes approaching physical intimacy between the two women are juxtaposed with shots signaling the lone male. Depicting female bonding as the exclusion of men moves the defining principle outside the women's own interactions. The lesbian potential, an 'unfortunate' by-product of the female bonding configuration, must be checked (Figure 24.4).

The male intermediary

One way to interfere with female bonding is to insert references to men and heterosexuality between women characters. In *Entre Nous* Madeline and Lena spend a considerable portion of their time together talking about their husbands and lovers. For example, they jointly compose a letter to Madeline's lover. Reassuring references to offscreen males, however, remain a feeble attempt to undermine the visual impact that the women together make (Figure 24.5).

To be more effective, the interference needs to be visual in order to physically separate the women's bodies and interrupt their glances. Male intermediaries are common in films with female bonding. In *Entre Nous*, when Lena and Madeline are dancing together in a Paris nightclub (the scene opens with a *male* point-of-view shot of Madeline's ass), two male onlookers become intermediaries by diverting the women's glances and easing the tension created by their physical embrace.

Voyage en Douce actually places a male body between the two women. The soft-porn approach of *Voyage en Douce* relies on titillating the male viewer with lesbian insinuations. Ultimately, however, female characters must remain available to male viewers. In one scene, Hélène and Lucie are lying in bed together in their hotel room when a young waiter from room service arrives. Together the two women flirt with him. Further teasing him, Hélène tells the boy to come and kiss Lucie (Figure 24.6). Embarrassed but aroused, he awkwardly

Figures 24.5 and 24.6 Male intermediaries both interrupt and homoeroticize female bonding in *Entre Nous* (top) and *Voyage en Douce* (below).

obliges. Hélène then verbally instructs the young male, now placed sexually between the women, on how to kiss Lucie. The inexperienced boy reinforces the male viewer's sense of superior potency – the male viewer is represented but not replaced. In this scene the boy connects the two women as much as he separates them. It is Hélène who is sensitive to Lucie's pacing and is manipulating her desire; the boy is an intermediary. Hélène's vicarious engagement, however, is confined to the realm of desire. The actual kiss excludes her.[15]

Often, as in the following example from *Entre Nous*, the connection that an intermediary provides is less obvious. Lena is on her way to meet Madeline in Paris when she has a sexual encounter with an anonymous male. A soldier who shares her train compartment kisses and caresses her. Later, while discussing this experience with Madeline, Lena 'comes to realize' that this was her first orgasmic experience. The scene on the train reasserts Lena's heterosexuality. At the same time, this experience and knowledge of sexual pleasure is more connected to her friendship with Madeline, via their exchange of intimate information, than to her heterosexual marriage of many years. In fact, it is Madeline who recognizes Lena's described experience as an orgasm and identifies it for her. Because the film cuts away from the train scene shortly after the sexual activity begins, the film viewer does not witness Lena's orgasm. Had this train scene continued, her orgasm might have approximated, in film time, the moment when Madeline names it – and Lena gasps. In a peculiar manner, then, Madeline is filmically credited for the orgasm. Likewise Lena's excited state on the train, her predisposition to sexual activity, might be read as motivated by her anticipation of being with Madeline.

A male's intrusion upon female bonding, then, is just as likely to homo-eroticize the situation as to induce corrective heterosexuality.[16] In *Entre Nous* it is Lena's jealous husband who gives language to the sexual possibilities of their friendship. By calling the women's boutique a 'whore-house,' he foregrounds the erotic symbolism that clothing provides. When he calls the women 'dykes,' he not only reveals the fears of a jealous husband but confirms the audience's perceptions.

While I would not go so far as to equate these two films, it would be naive to dismiss *Voyage en Douce* simply as a 'rip-off' of lesbianism for male voyeuristic pleasure while applauding *Entre Nous* as 'politically correct' lesbianism. In their different ways, *Entre Nous* does just as much to stimulate lesbian desire as does *Voyage en Douce*, and *Voyage en Douce* frustrates it just as much as *Entre Nous* does. The two films exhibit similar tensions and compromises. As far as any final commitment to lesbianism, *Entre Nous* is no more frank than is *Voyage en Douce*. Lesbian reading requires as much viewer initiation in one film as the other.

One could argue that any potential lesbianism in *Voyage en Douce* is undermined by heterosexual framing in early and late scenes with Hélène's male partner. Another interpretation of this framing device, however, shifts conclusions in a different direction. Early in the film, Lucie crouches outside Hélène's door. Hélène sees Lucie through the railing under the banister as she climbs the stairs to her apartment. When Lucie declares that she is leaving her male partner, Hélène takes her into her apartment where they plan a vacation together. At the film's conclusion, the two women return to Hélène's apartment. Then Lucie decides to go back to her husband, but Hélène decides to leave hers again. Inadvertently, Hélène locks herself out of the apartment without her suitcase. Instead of ringing the doorbell, she crouches in Lucie's earlier position as the camera moves down the stairs to observe her through the railing. One can read this shot as portraying the prison of heterosexuality or domesticity – as a dead end – or as indicating a cyclic structure.

Lucie's flirting and Hélène's display of lesbian desire throughout *Voyage en Douce* qualify them as hypothetical lesbian heroines as much as the women in *Entre Nous*. Ultimately, these characters' lesbianism remains hypothetical and illusory because of their isolation. The acknowledgement of lesbian desire does not, in either film, acknowledge the *condition* of lesbianism within culture.

The film opportunity

Voyage en Douce and *Entre Nous* are narrative films that exist by right of a language informed by heterosexuality. However, because they are about women's relationships, they also challenge the conventions of this language. The contradictions that result from their use of a heterosexual system for nonheterosexual narratives give rise to innovations that interact with audience expectations to create multiple and ambivalent interpretations. The focus on two women together threatens to establish both asexuality and homosexuality, both of which are outside the heterosexual desire that drives mainstream film and narrative. Therefore, simultaneous actions take place in the text to eroticize the women's interactions and to abort the resulting homoerotics. These very contradictions and opposing intentions cause the gaps and ambiguous figurations that allow lesbian readings.

I have demonstrated three such figurations: the erotic exchange of glances, which contrasts with the unidirectional, hierarchical male gaze articulated by Mulvey; eroticized female bonding, which utilizes the feminine masquerade to achieve closeness, contrasting the use and purpose of the masquerade described by Doane; and the oppositely sexed intermediary who both separates and connects the same-sexed couple, accomplishing both heterosexuality and homosexuality within the contradictory text. These structures neither replace nor compromise the heterosexual film event and text recognized and analyzed in prior feminist film theory, but rather offer additions and alternatives to account for homosexual viewership and desire.

Notes

1   See Teresa de Lauretis, *Alice Doesn't: Feminism, Semiotics, Cinema*, esp. 'Desire in Narrative,' (103–57).
2   I do not mean to essentialize a look of exchange as the only look in which lesbians partake. Of course, lesbians engage in voyeuristic looking as well as sexual exhibitionism. I am attempting here to describe a coding of lesbianism through an unconventional representation of looking.
3   Mulvey, 'Visual Pleasure and Narrative Cinema,' 17.
4   Mulvey, 'Afterthoughts on "Visual Pleasure and Narrative Cinema,"'.
5   Doane, 'Film and the Masquerade,' 22. Also see Doane's 'Masquerade Reconsidered.'
6   Doane, 'Film and the Masquerade,' 24.
7   Ibid., 31–2.
8   Such an investigation was called for nearly two decades ago by Michelle Citron, Julia Lesage, Judith Mayne, B. Ruby Rich and Anna Marie Taylor. See Citron *et al.*, 'Women and Film: A Discussion of Feminist Aesthetics.'
9   One might argue that simply substituting woman for man as owner of the gaze accomplishes an erotic lesbian look. To some extent this is true, and has been done quite successfully by Donna Deitch in *Desert Hearts* (1986), which Deitch describes in the film's publicity materials as 'just a love story, like any love story between a man and a woman.' Though certainly erotic, *Desert Hearts* 'inherits' certain problems from the traditional structure it follows (see Richard Dyer, (ed.) *Gays and Film*, 33–4). Insidious racial and class stereotypes and clichés invade the film to imply/provide the requisite power imbalance. For example, working-class women are assumed to be sexually liberated compared to the inhibited female professor. Eventually, as in countless love stories before this one, 'love' overcomes/denies class boundaries. Also, the more 'femme' partner is signified by blonde hair while the

more 'butch' is brunette. (See Dyer. *Heavenly Bodies*; Diane Hamer, ' "I Am a Woman": Ann Bannon and the Writing of Lesbian Identity in the 1950s'; and Jackie Stacey, ' "If You Don't Play, You Can't Win": *Desert Hearts* and the Lesbian Romance Film.' For a historical study of intersecting racism and heterosexism, see Siobhan Sommerville, 'Scientific Racism and the Emergence of the Homosexual Body.')

Sheer Madness (Margarethe von Trotta, 1983) initially employs a heterosexual gaze, then alters its direction. The character played by Hanna Schygulla sings the first verse of 'Will You Still Love Me Tomorrow' to her male lover, but turns to look at a woman friend during the next verse. The first direction of her glance, toward a man, both eroticizes it and distinguishes it from a male's 'downward' glance. Her ongoing song provides continuity as these characteristics carry over into the second glance, charging it with lesbian possibilities. In *The Color Purple* (Steven Spielberg, 1985). Shug (Margaret Avery) sings and dances for a sexually mixed audience in a tavern. Her suggestive use of a costume prop as a phallic object, which she pulls rhythmically towards herself, elicits appreciative sounds from the males. Thus eroticized, however, she sings her next song to another woman, Celie (Whoopi Goldberg). The men looking at Shug sufficiently confirm her sexuality, which then eroticizes her look at Celie. Such heterosexual prestructuring, however, can eroticize women's looking and counter lesbianism simultaneously.

I do not intend to imply that heterosexual presence is the only means of eroticizing women's interactions. Several examples illustrate other strategies. In *La Femme de l'hotel* (Lea Pool, 1984), the absence of heterosexuality encourages lesbian readings. Its only prominent male character is the main (female) character's brother, and he is gay. Even while precluding heterosexuality, however, this gay male foregrounds its absence. This is particularly clear in a scene where he relaxes on a bed while watching television as his sister undresses and gets into bed nude behind him. Such scenes both suggest and forbid sexuality and unhinge desire, freeing it to settle between women characters. In *Lianna* (John Sales, 1983), a lesbian 'coming-out' story, a lesbian exchange of looks is split into two separate looks. Although the two looks complement each other in relation to Lianna, the main character, each is unidirectional and maintains its sexual energy through traditional objectification. In a lesbian bar, Lianna (Linda Griffiths) feels 'looked at' by the other women. Later, on the street, Lianna is suddenly sensitized to the female population as she does the watching. In *Sheer Madness* Hanna Schygulla stands facing the film audience while a second woman watches her from window behind her. As if able to feel this look, Schygulla acknowledges it by turning away from the film audience and towards the woman, sealing a look between them. If the viewer's engagement in this scene has been primarily one of looking at Schygulla, he or she is now shut out. However, if the viewer has been identifying with Schygulla's feeling of being looked at, he or she turns with Schygulla, vicariously experiencing her visual exchange with the second woman. These two processes, of course, are not mutually exclusive.

10   Nowhere is this more explicitly played out than in Marleen Gorris's *A Question of Silence* (1982), in which eyeline matches among three women in a boutique precipitate their collaborative murder of the male boutique owner. See also my description of *Possibly in Michigan* in n. 12, below.

11   See Lucie Arbuthnot and Gail Seneca, 'Pre-Text and Text in *Gentlemen Prefer Blondes*.' Arbuthnot and Seneca describe the pleasure afforded the lesbian viewer by such framing together of women characters.

12   Something similar to female bonding might offer an 'accurate' image of lesbianism in other historical eras (see Lillian Faderman's *Surpassing the Love of Men*). However, it is important to complicate the equation of female bonding with lesbianism in contemporary representation. By standing in for lesbianism, female bonding both suggests and denies it. Female bonding in film offers lesbians many opportunities for pleasurable readings but also, by avoiding lesbian sexuality, closets them. Straight and lesbian feminists seem to constitute a homogeneous audience for female bonding films — until one focuses on readings rather than texts. In her introduction to *Between Men: English Literature and Male Homosexual Desire*, Eve Sedgwick posits a 'relatively continuous relation of female homosocial and homosexual bonds' (5). I agree that this exists, especially in contemporary representations; it is what allows 'lesbianism' to pass into the mainstream. But its denial of lesbian difference can also be homophobically interested. Within the feminism of the 1970s and 1980s, this re-presentation often served to make lesbianism acceptable to straight feminists by making it indistinguishable from 'sisterhood.' See also Katie King, 'The Situation of Lesbianism as Feminism's Magical Sign.'

On the other hand, female bonding in Cecelia Condit's experimental video *Possibly in Michigan* (1983) was read as lesbianism during the 1984 congressional debates on appropriations for the National

Endowment for the Arts (NEA). During the same year, the tape's ending scene (without its own soundtrack) was shown on Pat Robertson's *The 700 Club* on the Christian Broadcasting Network (CBN) and described not only as gay but also as antifamily and antimen. These readings were obviously against the grain of the tape. *Possibly in Michigan* is about male violence against women. A woman shoots a man who is battering her friend. There is no indication in the tape that any of the characters are gay. When he is shot, the man is wearing a comical wolf-mask. The previous battering scene, however, is constructed with realistic acting and *mise-en-scène*. Slow motion and a style of technical 'roughness' make the battering excruciating to watch. In her typical style, Condit mixes humor and the macabre on the soundtrack as well. While repeatedly hitting the woman, the man (in voice-over) both claims that he loves her and threatens to chop her up – 'all the better to eat you.' A female voice answers in singsong, 'But love shouldn't cost an arm and a leg.' After killing the man, the two women chop up his body and use his bones for a soup (thus answering the congressman's unspoken question, 'Where is the man?'). The tape ends with the women, both nude, sitting at a table sipping the broth while still another man, this time in a man-mask, stands outside the kitchen window begging for meaty tidbits.

13   This 'slippage' has been exploited in numerous lesbian film readings besides the present one. See for example Arbuthnot and Seneca's 'Pre-Text and Text in *Gentlemen Prefer Blondes*,' Jackie Stacey's 'Desperately Seeking Difference,' and Valerie Traub's 'The Ambiguities of "Lesbian" Viewing Pleasure: The (Dis)articulations of *Black Widow*.'

14   In response to a 1990 version of this essay published in *Jump Cut*, Will Harris extended my argument regarding the two-shot to uncover a greater complexity in the ending of *Entre Nous* (Harris, '*Entre Nous* and the Lesbian Heroine'). Harris argues that the scene in which Lena's husband Michel (Guy Marchand) visits the beach house where Lena, Madeline and the children are staying at the film's end 'is constructed to minimize implied lesbian/heterosexual confrontation while encouraging familiar identification' (15). Even as the dialogue and end titles in this sequence are quite explicit regarding Lena and Michel's marital breakup, the film (1) avoids further two-shots of Lena and Madeline and (2) visually unites Lena and Michel during their final conversation. The conversation is presented primarily in a short-reverse shot pattern although the camera occasionally pans between Lena and Michel, loosely connecting them. When the conversation ends, the estranged Lena and Michel are nevertheless visually 'coupled' within the shot. Just as two-shots of Lena and Madeline earlier in the film facilitated a lesbian reading against the narrative evidence of their heterosexuality, here visual 'coupling' of Lena and Michel (which actually includes one of their daughters in the background graphically situated between them) offers (perhaps subliminal) recompense or counterpleasure to those heterosexual viewers who would otherwise reject the film for its lesbian ending. Harris argues that this structure allows the film to stay within the patriarchal film conventions necessary for popular success (14–16).

15   The male intermediary is common in films that connote lesbian sexuality, for example *Black Widow* (Bob Rafelson, 1987) (see Cherry Smyth, 'The Transgressive Sexual Subject'). Such a configuration is also compatible with Lynda Hart's argument that the two female protagonists in *Basic Instinct* (Paul Verhoeven, 1992) murder together. See Hart, 'Why the Woman Did It: *Basic Instinct* and Its Vicissitudes,' in *Fatal Women*, 124–34.

16   The triangular structure here is similar to that addressed by Eve Sedgwick in *Between Men*. Following René Girard, she describes an erotic motif of rivalry between two men over a woman, noting that 'the bond that links the two rivals is as intense and potent as the bond that links either of the rivals to the beloved' (21). Although a staged rivalry informs the erotic charge between women in *Black Widow* and jealousy looms large in *Basic Instinct*, rivalry over a man is not instrumental in either *Entre Nous* or *Voyage en Douce*. For example, in *Entre Nous* Michel's sexual advance towards Madeline is extraneous to her bonding with Lena.

CHAPTER 25

SUSAN JEFFORDS

CAN MASCULINITY BE TERMINATED?

U S MASCULINITY IN HOLLYWOOD FILMS of the 1980s was largely transcribed through spectacle and bodies, with the male body itself becoming often the most fulfilling form of spectacle. Throughout this period, the male body – principally the white male body – became increasingly a vehicle of display – of musculature, of beauty, of physical feats and of a gritty toughness. External spectacle – weaponry, explosions, infernos, crashes, high-speed chases, ostentatious luxuries – offered companion evidence of both the sufficiency and the volatility of this display. That externality itself confirmed that the outer parameters of the male body were to be the focus of audience attention, desire and politics.

But there is already evidence that this emphasis on externality and the male body is shifting focus. In the 1990s, externality and spectacle have begun to give way to a presumably more internalized masculine dimension. In contrast to the physical feats of Sylvester Stallone in the *Rambo* films, the determined competitiveness of Bruce Willis's John McClane in the *Die Hard* films, the confrontations of Clint Eastwood's Dirty Harry, the whip-cracking of Harrison Ford's Indiana Jones, the steely authority of Robocop and Michael J. Fox's time-traveling dualities in *Back to the Future*, recent Hollywood male star/heroes have been constructed as more internalized versions of their historical counterparts. More film time is devoted to explorations of their ethical dilemmas, emotional traumas, and psychological goals, and less to their skill with weapons, their athletic abilities, or their gutsy showdowns of opponents.

By seeming to step back from their own spectacle, these men are presumably leaving space for Hollywood's version of 'difference,' or what it prefers to characterize as 'justice' and 'equality.' What Hollywood culture is offering, in place of the bold spectacle of male muscularity and/as violence, is a self-effacing man, one who now, instead of learning to fight, learns to love. We can include here such recent box office items as *Field of Dreams* (1989), *Robin Hood* (1991), *The Doctor* (1991), *Regarding Henry* (1991), *Switch* (1991), the new Disney *Beauty and the Beast* (1991), even *Boyz N the Hood* (1991). What I want to do here is interrogate the 'new' man of the 1990s, and find out what complications await viewers who acknowledge his existence.

As part of a widespread cultural effort to respond to perceived deteriorations in masculine forms of power, Hollywood films of the 1980s – in conjunction with the premier politician produced by that system, Ronald Reagan – highlighted masculinity (and Reagan's collaborative nationalism) as a violent spectacle that insisted on the external sufficiency of the male body/territory. Very little film time is devoted, for example, to Rambo's internal feelings. The most memorable scene here is Rambo's impassioned outburst at the end of *First Blood* (1982), in which he indicts US society for abandoning him and his fellow Vietnam veterans. But because of the fact that the speech is largely unintelligible and occurs in a brief moment at the end of the series of explosions, the focus of the scene is less on John Rambo's emotional state than upon the externalization of those emotions as violent and destructive actions, as he goes on a rampage around the gun shop where he has sought refuge from the police. And the effect of the scene is less to comment on Rambo's state of mind than to transfer guilt for his mistreatment from the small-town sheriff who harasses him to the society at large.

In the Rambo sequels, it is as if these brief moments of emotional insight have been forgotten, or consigned to what Michael Rogin has called the 'amnesia' of US political spectacle (Rogin 1990). In *Rambo: First Blood II and Rambo III* emotional expression is largely reserved for those who heroize Rambo. The most audiences see of Rambo's 'internal' workings are the times when his body is opened through wounds that he incurs. In these films, Rambo *is* externalization, so much so that his body is made indistinguishable from its surrounding environs. It is not simply that Rambo is shown principally outdoors that emphasizes his externality, but that he *is*, quite literally in *Rambo II*, that outdoors, as his body merges into mud, water and rocks to defeat his Soviet pursuers.

This pattern of internal amnesia is typical of male action film sequences of the 1980s – the *Rambos*, *Lethal Weapons* and *Die Hards* come most readily to mind. Where the first film in a sequence is likely to reveal some emotional content of its hero – Rambo's Post-Traumatic Stress Disorder, Riggs's depression about his wife's death or John McClane's distress over his wife's career – the second is likely to abandon even the momentary internal character developments that dotted these first films in favor of the externalized spectacle itself. Sequels of the 1980s offer more explosions, more killings and more outright violence. (In the most extravagant shift, Rambo expertly kills no one in *First Blood* and then turns to killing 44 people in *Rambo II* and an uncountable number in *Rambo III* (Van Biema 1985: 37).) Even the most developed emotional subplot, Riggs's suicidal guilt over his wife's death in *Lethal Weapon 1*, is not only explained but externalized in *Lethal Weapon 2* when he has sex with another woman *and* kills his wife's murderer.

The popularity and financial success of these films suggests that sequentiality itself was one of the mechanisms for Hollywood responses to crises in the representations and marketing of US masculinities in this period. It is, most directly and insistently, the question of whether and how masculinity can be reproduced successfully in a post-Vietnam, post-Civil Rights, and post-women's movement era. One of the answers that these films provide is through spectacular repetition, or, more specifically, through the repetition of the spectacles of the masculine body, a body that, in this case, includes the male hero, his weapons, and his environment.

In order to get at how this repetition works, I'd like to examine here two of the best-selling serial films of this period, James Cameron's *The Terminator* (1984) and *Terminator 2: Judgment Day* (1991), films whose narratives center on masculinity and repetition, or, more concisely, the reproduction of masculinity. But because the second of these films dips onto the 1990s, I hope to use this film sequence to comment on both the transitions and the ambiguities that are now taking place between that externalized male body and its internalized progeny.

Masculinity and/as repetition

As with so many male action films of the 1980s, and as with so much of Hollywood's altered marketing and production strategy of the same period, repetition is at the heart of both Cameron films. In writing about *The Terminator*, Karen Mann and Constance Penley argue for the importance of repetition in the film. Mann suggests that at both a structural and a thematic level, the story of the film depends upon repetition as self-reproduction, as the future steps back to re-write the past. Of the future John Connor, leader of the rebel humans fighting the machines that are out to kill them in the year 2029, she argues: 'He satisfies the fantasy of reaching back in time to control those who control him – his parents – by choosing who they are to be. . . . His choice [of his own father] provides the illusion of self-generation' (Mann 1989–90: 21). Penley takes on this same theme of re-writing the past, except that she reads it in terms of psychoanalytic categories: 'the fantasy of time travel is no more nor less than the compulsion to repeat that manifests itself in the primal scene fantasy' (Penley 1989: 47). Again, the re-writing of reproduction under the control of the male child fulfills the primal scene fantasy of being present at the moment of one's conception. In either case, both Mann and Penley recognize the importance of repetition as reproduction in these films, where the future son reaches back to the past, in effect, by choosing the father to give birth to himself (it is John Connor who decides that Kyle Reese – his father – should return to the past to 'protect' his mother, and, coincidentally, to father himself).

Much of the plot of *The Terminator* revolves around this form of repetition as self-production. *Terminator 2* takes this repetition self-consciously, knowingly re-working the plot, themes and spectacles of its predecessor. Clearly, there is a certain financial intuitiveness about repeating as much as possible about a successful film, so that the sequel can try to replicate its audience appeal and box office receipts. But Cameron does more than merely repeat in *T2*; he self-consciously reworks elements of the first plot into the second, not simply explaining or answering some of them (by finally showing us John Connor's face, for example, or narrating how Sarah Connor learned the military skills that her son was later to put to such good use against the machines), but inverting them, so that nothing in the film gets repeated *exactly*. Everything is altered, if only slightly (even Schwarzenegger's chest size is somewhat diminished), in a way that offers clues about how repetition, reproduction and self-production are working in the shift from the masculinity of the 1980s to the 1990s, how, in other words, masculinity is currently reproducing itself, i.e. through inversion rather than duplication.

T2's early trailers and commercials clued audiences in to the most obvious form of reworking in the film, the shift in the character of the Terminator: 'Once he was programmed to destroy the future. Now his mission is to save it.' The very act for which this machine got its name in the first film – the relentless hunting and killing of human targets – is the key to its changed personality in the second. In *T2*, the human-killing task is left to the newer and sleeker machine model Terminator, the liquid metal T2000, while the original Terminator, now re-programmed by the future adult John Connor to protect his 11-year-old childhood self, is instructed not to kill humans any more. (Though the plot suggests that it is young Connor who gives the Terminator this instruction, from the time of its return to the present, the Terminator has already distinguished itself from its earlier counterpart by only injuring and not killing the people it meets; it's as if not killing people was somehow now its 'nature.') Instead of being the source of humanity's annihilation, the Terminator is now the *single* guarantor of its continuation. If, in the first film, the Terminator were to kill Sarah Connor, John

Connor would not be born, and he would not be able to lead the human rebellion against the machines, leaving the machines to accomplish their goal, the extermination of all human life. Now, in the second film, the Terminator is the only one capable of protecting the young Connor from the more efficient and sophisticated T2000. And here's the biggest reworking that comes from this shift: freed from its mission of destroying humanity, the Terminator can now become not simply the protector of human life, but its generator. By 'giving' John Connor his life, the Terminator takes, in effect, Sarah Connor's place as his mother. In one of the film's most astounding inversions, the Terminator can now be said to give birth to the future of the human race.

But if the Terminator is now responsible for human futures, what has happened to Sarah Connor, the woman whose tough fighting terminated the Terminator in the first film, and whose future held out the birth of a son who would save the human race? Like the Terminator, Sarah Connor's character is repeated and inverted in the second film. Where in the first she was uncertain, frightened and weak, in her rebirth she is tough-minded, fearless and strong (the first shot is of Sarah Connor doing chin-ups in her room at the mental hospital). This 'new' Sarah Connor looks like the mercenary she has trained to be through all the intervening years, wearing military fatigues, toting heavy weapons and having a mission to perform. As final proof of her new hard character, she even forgets to love her son, chewing him out for rescuing her from the hospital: 'You can't risk yourself, even for me! You're too important. . . . I didn't need your help. I can take care of myself.' It's as if she's not a mother at all, but only a soldier for the future.

Sarah Connor does remember that she's a mother, once. When she tries to kill Miles Dyson – the man responsible for developing Skynet, the computer system that will take on the task of eliminating humans – thinking thereby to change the future, she fails. Cracking off the first few rounds of her high-powered rife, it seems that she will take the Terminator's place and do what it no longer can do – kill human beings. But when she comes face to face with Dyson lying on the floor with his wife and son crying over him, she breaks into tears and can't do it. Then, when John Connor arrives, she finally tells him that she loves him, as if her admission of failure at being a touch combatant releases her to still have the feelings of a mother.

In *The Terminator*, Sarah Connor was told that she would be, in effect, the mother of the future. That would seem, in the logic of this film, to be a pretty important job, since it's Sarah Connor who teaches her son all of the skills he will use to save humanity. Yet in the second film Sarah is effectively locked out of having any real role in the future. First, John tells the Terminator that he learned information about weapons, machines and fighting from mercenaries his mother took him to meet, not directly from her. And second, for some years, she was not present for him as a mother at all, being locked away in a mental ward where she was not allowed to see him. He was left with foster parents who taught him that every-thing his mother said about the future was a crazy illusion of her deranged and obsessed mind. Third, as an audience, we are witness to how Sarah ignores her son for most of the film. The excuse, that she's concentrating on keeping him alive, puts her in direct competition for the Terminator's role, a job – and a body – that she just can't fit. And while she's focusing on being a super-soldier, the Terminator is working on being a better mom, listening to and playing with the son that Sarah hardly notices for all the weapons she's carrying. Sarah Connor even acknowledges that the Terminator is doing a better job than she and consciously decides to leave her son in its care when she goes on what promises to be a suicide mission to kill Dyson. While John is teaching the Terminator how to give high-fives, the cinema pulls back to Sarah's point-of-view shot, and her voiceover reasons:

> Watching John with a machine. It was suddenly so clear. The Terminator would never stop. It would never hurt him. It would never leave him or get impatient with him. . . . It would die to protect him. Of all the would-be fathers who came and went over the years, this machine, this thing, was the only one who measured up. And in an insane world, it was the sanest choice.

Though Sarah refers to the Terminator as John's father here, it is apparent that, with her disappearance, it would be his sole parent, since, in the odd logic of this film, John's father was both killed in the past and hasn't even been born yet. And though Sarah calls it a father, it's clear that the Terminator doesn't do things that the mercenary father-figures did. This father doesn't teach John about weaponry or survival skills, and doesn't freak out, like the others did, about John's role in the future. And unlike Sarah, it will always stay with him. The Terminator is thus not only a father but a mother as well to John Connor – to the hope of a human future. What had been its most frightening feature in the first film – Reese tells Sarah, 'It will *never* stop!' – is now in Sarah's words its most admirable feature: it will never stop caring for John.

From the second film's outset then, Sarah Connor has been gently delegitimized in her role as the mother and protector of the human future. Though she, better than any human, understands the consequences that await unchanged human actions, and would seem as a result to be an important source of knowledge, and her survival skills and patience are admirable, she is not presented as cool and clear-thinking. Instead, as Linda Hamilton chooses to play the part, Sarah Connor is more an animal than a human, or, better yet, a human whose animal instincts have been brought out in the face of death. As one film reviewer puts it: 'She is an animal. She bares her teeth. She snarls . . . She has an animal voice. Like an animal, she does anything to protect her young. That is her strongest emotion' (Baumgold 1991: 26). So not only does Sarah not have the machine body or efficiency to compete with the Terminator as a protector for her son, her emotions as a mother are primitive, stemming more from her animal instincts than from any loving relationship between two people. When she is shown as a mother, her maternity is of the most brutish and unreflective kind.

Her final delegitimization is accomplished by none other than John Connor himself, showing how he has been able to surpass his mother's animal tendencies to remain human, even in the face of the future he knows he will confront. Importantly, the scene in which he does this succeeds all of the other deteriorations of Sarah's role as mother – her brusque treatment of her son, her mental instabilities, her emotional breakdowns, her abandoning of her son to the care of a machine – and marks the final separation of Sarah and John, or, more precisely, the termination of his final dependence on her and new alliance with the Terminator. After she has failed to kill Dyson, the Terminator sits down to narrate for Dyson the history of the future and the role he will play in it. When Dyson responds, 'How were we supposed to know?', animal Sarah attacks: 'Fucking men like you built the hydrogen bomb! Men like you thought it up. You think you're so creative. You don't know what it is to create a life, to feel something growing inside you.' But just when her feminist critique of masculine birth compensation gets rolling, John Connor calmly interrupts: 'Mom. We need to be a little more constructive here.' Seated beside the Terminator, already taking command, John's retort relegates Sarah to the crouching, chain-smoking background bundle she becomes. He and his future-self-programmed private Terminator are in control.

Masculinity as fathering

To 'flesh out,' as it were (the Terminator is a machine chassis with a flesh coating), the Terminator's change in function from killer to protector, from stranger to parent, audiences are shown not only the Terminator not killing people (its strategy now is to shoot them in the legs, *à la* the Rambo of *First Blood*), but shown as well its altered personality. It asks questions (when young John Connor tells it not to kill anyone, the Terminator asks 'Why?'; and it later asks Connor, 'Why do you cry?'), it uses slang ('No problemo'), and it plays with children (it and Connor exchange high fives).[1] Perhaps most importantly, it learns (rather than break into the starter on every stolen automobile, it learns from Connor that people usually put their keys in the car's visor). As it tells John Connor, 'The more contact I have with humans, the more I learn.' This learning is, in fact, one of the key thematic foundations of the film, since it is the Terminator's ability to learn that leads it to sacrifice itself for the survival of humanity: since humans once learned from its predecessor's computer chips how to produce the machines that would destroy the world, it must self-destruct, even though it's now a good Terminator, to prevent people from repeating that past mistake.

The Terminator offers the ostensible explanation for why men of the 1980s are changing their behavior: they learned that the old ways of violence, rationality, single-mindedness and goal-orientation (there is no one more goal-oriented than the first Terminator; as Reese says to Sarah Connor, 'He'll never stop. Not until he kills you!') were destructive, not only for individual men, but for humanity as a whole. And the solution to this dilemma? According to this film, for the 1980s man to learn from his past (future?) mistakes to produce a change in character, a 'new,' more internalized man, who thinks with his heart rather than with his head – or computer chips.

But to show that 'learning' is a non-discriminatory attitude of the 'new' masculinity, the Terminator is not the only male in *T2* to change his behavior. Miles Dyson is the African American scientist who, *T2*'s future history recalls, constructs Skynet, the computerized military defense network responsible for starting the nuclear devastation that almost ends human existence. When Sarah Connor, the Terminator and John Connor tell Dyson about how his current research will lead to a nuclear apocalypse, he volunteers to help them destroy all of his files, finally sacrificing his own life to set off the bomb that will explode the research institute he heads. (True to the new masculine ideal of non-killing, Dyson warns the police officers who have come to stop the break-in that they should leave before he sets off the bomb.) And like the Terminator, Dyson leaves behind him not only a woman and her son, but the future of the entire human race. The message here is clear: in this narrative, masculinity transcends racial difference, suggesting that the forces of change – killing to non-killing, silence to speech, indifference to love, external display to internal exploration, absent to active paternalism – not only cross racial boundaries but draw men together. What more unlikely alliance than a white-fleshed killing machine from the future and a dark-skinned benevolent scientist from the present? And yet, these 'men' work together to preserve human features; together, they give human life to the world.

The single key feature that solidifies the alliance of Dyson and the Terminator is not simply that they both believe in the Terminator's future, or that they understand the potential destructive power of Skynet, but that they are both 'fathers' – both to young male children and, by narrative implication, to the future. The scene immediately prior to Sarah Connor's attack on Dyson is the one in which she effectively turns her son over to the Terminator father. Dyson also has a son; in fact, he is the first member of the family we see besides Dyson, as the son's robot-controlled car drives into his father's computerized study. It is also the son who saves his father's life. While the wife cowers in terror at Sarah Connor's rifled commands ('Stay on the floor, bitch!'), the son cries over his father's body. It is this act which seems to draw Sarah to a halt and prevent her from terminating Dyson, as if Sarah knows that killing *any* son imperils the future. The alignment of Dyson and the Terminator is effected through the close proximity in which both men are shown as fathers. Their comparison is not, as it was between the African American police chief and the Terminator in the first film, one of human versus machine, or protector versus killer, or even black versus white, but instead one of sacrificing fathers who want to preserve a human future for their sons against the inhuman systems (mechanized or flesh) that are bent on carrying out a plan that will destroy all human life. Where humanity was the common denominator that erased racial difference in the first film, now fatherhood erases the difference between all 'new' men, whether they are machines or human.

The introduction of Dyson serves not only to show that the new masculinity transcends racial and class difference, but that the vehicle for that transformation is fathering, the link for that transformation is fathering, the link for men to 'discover' their 'new' internalized selves. Throughout the late 1980s, fathering was a key characterization and narrative device for displaying the 'new' Hollywood masculinities. In films such as *Three Men and a Baby*, *Look Who's Talking*, *One Good Cop* (1991), *Regarding Henry*, *Boyz N the Hood*, and others, fathering became the vehicle for portraying masculine emotions, ethics and commitments, and for redirecting masculine characterizations from spectacular achievements to domestic triumphs. But *Terminator 2* shows that this characterization is more than a simple warming of the individual male cold heart and an improvement of father-child relations, but instead a wholesale social patterning, in which these men become not only the replacements for women whose work has interfered with their ability to mother their children (an indictment that links otherwise diverse films like *Terminator 2* and *Boyz N the Hood*), but fathers for an entire human future. While mothers might lay claim to giving biological birth to children, these fathers insure that there will be a world for these children to life in. And they accomplish this, not with bombs and bombast, but with love and protection.

Masculinity and/as individualism

In looking at discourses about nuclear warfare, Gillian Brown focuses in on the emphasis on sequentiality in discussions of both nuclear warfare and nuclear disarmament, suggesting that this interest in sequence is an indication of the preoccupation of both factions with continuity, futures, and reproduction, or what she phrases 'the ideology of sequential self-extension.'

> When the antinuclear chain letter enjoins us to take a stake in futurity, or when the nursery rhyme reconstructs our self-extension in the world, they epitomize our familiarity with and reliance on a notion of projection in which we ourselves *are* our (possible) futures.
>
> (Brown 1989: 294)

As she astutely goes on to say, this ideology of self-extension is dependent upon a certain notion of individualism, in which the individual not only owns the narrative and therefore the sequence that it articulates, but through that narrative, owns the self as well:

> antinuclear thematics of affiliation and association share with pronuclear survivalism this desire for sequence and the narrative of possessive individualism it reprises. Thinking about the nuclear, then, is itself a sequence in the history of liberal humanism, a sequence that foregrounds the dynamic of disappearance and reappearance in the logic of self-proprietorship.
>
> (Brown 1989: 292–3)

The particular thinking about the nuclear that is narrated in *The Terminator* and *Terminator 2: Judgment Day* is equally based upon a narrative of individualism that explains the apparent contradictions between the films' seemingly left-wing antinuclear conclusions and their star's right-wing Republican endorsements. What finally resolves this narrative spectacle of violence, technology, and mechanical genocide is the even greater spectacle of male individualism in the act of self-sacrificing fathers. For what greater and more powerful act of *individual* self-determination can there be than the *rational*, willing, and determined decision to end one's own life, not in the despair of defeat but in the triumph of birth? of being the generator of the human future?

And this is what makes *T2* so disarmingly dangerous a narrative. The first film, like most Hollywood films before it, had to separate its male egos into good – Kyle Reese, Sarah Connor's protector/lover and father of John Connor, leader of the future – and evil – the Terminator, automated vehicle for the destruction of human life – largely as a result of a pattern of masculinity that necessitates defining men not by content but by opposition to an other. *T2* works by a similar pattern, with the old Terminator validating itself by protecting John Connor against the T2000 and showing itself by contrast to be more 'human.' But this second film plays with so many oppositional reversals that this familiar pattern manages to slip in a few interesting realignments.

The most obvious reversal is that of goodness and authority, represented in *T2* primarily by the police. Whereas the first film showed police officers as ineffectual but well-intentioned – they tried to protect Sarah Connor from the Terminator, but didn't believe her or Reese about its power, a failure that cost the officers their own lives – in the second, it is the police who are the greatest threat to both Connors and the Terminator. The T2000 disguises itself as a police officer, thereby not only gaining access to automated police information but also winning the confidence of unwitting citizens like John Connor's foster parents. But it is also the police who try to stop Sarah, John, Dyson, and the Terminator from destroying the Cyberdyne research lab where the computer chips and records about the first Terminator are being studied. Where in the first film the police are shown protecting people, in the second, they are shown protecting only property, principally the property of the very corporation that will decide on a path of human genocide in the future. And where the Terminator does not kill in the second film, the police do; they are responsible for the death of Dyson, and are clearly trying to kill both Connors.

It is important to look not only at what reversals take place in the depictions of the police, but what shifts these reversals imply about the oppositional definitions of masculinity in each film. In *The Terminator*, Kyle Reese was most obviously defined against the Terminator: he was human, it was a machine; he wanted to protect Sarah, it wanted to kill her; he wanted to save the human future, it wanted to prevent it; he made love to her, it hurt her; he gave her a son, it gave her a nightmare. But Reese was also opposed to the police. While they too wanted to protect Sarah, they finally could not. And against everything Sarah Connor and, by then, the audience, knew, the police did not believe Reese's story about the future. In that film, the police functioned to show that it was not enough simply not to be a machine; people had to be resourceful, have access to important information (what the future held; how to make pipe bombs; how to detect Terminators), and, most importantly, had to be able to act (the thematic anchor of masculinity in the 1980s). While the police stood around firing handguns at the Terminator (even the audience knew by this time that this was a laughable excuse for action), Reese helped Sarah escape from the Terminator. What *The Terminator* told its audiences was that if you wanted to be able to *father the future* – for this is literally what Reese did – you had to be more than good-hearted and human; you had to be strong, decisive and powerful (through knowledge) – to not only *want* to protect the mother of the future, but to be able to do it.

In the second film, the police serve again to show that being human is not enough. But here, they are opposed, not to an even more protective human (the cameras keep panning across the mottoes written on the LA police cars: 'to serve and protect'), but to a more human protector. While the Terminator is opposed to the T2000 for purposes of the thematic battle of good and evil – the survival or destruction of humanity – it is more effectively opposed to the police officers in terms of its character: the police disdain John Connor (he is a delinquent), it cares for him; they kill Dyson, it repaired his wounds after Sarah first shot him; they hide behind faceless machines, it is a machine with a face. But most importantly, in this second film, while the Terminator protects humans (not just John Connor, but through him, all humanity), the police protect machines. They amass their greatest force to protect an empty corporate building that houses the most sophisticated computer technology in the world. In contrast, the Terminator's most forceful act was re-powering itself to save Sarah and John Connor from a machine, the T2000.

These reversals of authority and oppositional presentations of police power are less a critique of institutional oppressions (the police mean well but are misinformed), and more an effort to distinguish individual actions from organized institution. By presenting the police as inefficient but well-meaning in *The Terminator* and ineffective and misguided in *Terminator 2*, individual men – Reese and the Terminator – are made to seem not only effective but *necessary*, both to the protection of women and children and to the survival of humanity. In the face of a society that is perceived as increasingly technologized, mechanized, routinized and anonymous, the power of individual decision-making and individual action is drawn as paramount in these films. Male viewers – particularly white male viewers – who may feel increasingly distanced from what they understand to be traditional male forms of power and privilege can be empowered through the assertions of the role male individualism must play in the future of humanity. *Terminator 2* can offer to these viewers not only a panacea for their feelings of disempowerment, but it can reinforce the culturally-designated culprits of that scenario in the guise of technology, machines, non-passive women, and managerial blacks as well.

Most importantly, the film accomplishes this through one of the simplest and most reassuring frameworks available to many male viewers: individualism as fathering. In a slick re-writing of the traditionally gender-marked division between public and private, the Terminator films are offering male viewers an alternative realm to that of the declining workplace and national structure as sources of masculine authority and power – the world of the family. It is here, this logic suggests, that men can regain a sense of their expected masculine power, without having to confront or suggest alterations in the economic and social system that has led to their feelings of deprivation. Throughout the 1980s, the Yankelovich Monitor of US social attitudes recorded that men's primary definitions of masculinity rested in their sense of a man being 'a good provider for his family' (Faludi 1991: 65). The Terminator films capitalize on this sensibility – one that is becoming economically and socially obsolete – by implying a relationship, not between men and the partners, but between masculinity and future generations, an abstract and inverted repetition of both the public and private realms within which many US men are sensing a deterioration of their abilities to define their identities and/as their privileges. And *T2* accomplishes this goal through the portrayal of a father's relationship with his son.

Masculinity and/as self-production

In another narrative of nuclear apocalypse, Christa Wolf speaks about the same kind of 'male rationalism' that Sarah Connor seemed to be criticizing in her attack on Dyson, saying,

> This in turn raises the question of what today could possibly still represent 'progress' . . . now that the masculine way has almost run its course – that is, the way of carrying all inventions, circumstances, and conflicts to extremes until they have reached their maximum negative point: the point at which no alternatives are left.
>
> (Wolf 1984: 244)

As if Cameron had read this book, the characters of *Terminator 2* seem to have 'learned' the lesson Wolf was trying to impart about the inevitability of warfare within the framework of a 'rational' way of thinking. Both the Terminator and Dyson seem to have understood that their forms of 'progress' – computerized technologies, advanced weaponries, enhanced defense strategies, and increasingly efficient assessments of 'life' – will lead nowhere, at least, to a human nowhere, in which the destruction of all life is the logical end-product of their programming/thinking. Wolf even anticipates the characters of these 'new' men when her protagonist, Cassandra, tells a Greek chariot driver that 'in the future there may be people who know how to turn their victory into life' (Wolf 1984: 116).

This of course seems to be the most astonishing lesson that men of the Terminator's future have learned by looking at their own futures: that the continuation of their success and powerful accomplishment of goals leads only and inevitably to the destruction of the future itself. *Terminator 2* seems to have rightly earned its label as an 'anti-nuclear' (James 1991: H9) film, one that short-circuits the nuclear nightmare by 'learning' about the limitations of male mechanization. In this way, *T2* seems more than a direct response to 1980s male characters like Rambo or Robocop, whose hardbodies imitated or integrated indestructible machines that led to the downfall of evil. Those 1980s machine-men get tossed into the steel melting pot at the end of *T2* along with the T2000 and the self-sacrificing Terminator, leaving behind the young John Connor, bearer of a new and more human future.

But what Wolf didn't anticipate was the agility of US culture to find venues for 'alternative' masculinities. Rather than acknowledge an end point at which masculinity must recognize its own negation – what seems on the surface to be the conclusion of *T2* – the film's complex reasonings supply a 'new' way for masculinity to go: not, as in the 1980s, outward into increasingly extravagant spectacles of violence and power (as Rambo and Ronald Reagan showed, these displays had become their own forms of parody), but inward, into increasingly emotive displays of masculine sensitivities, traumas, and burdens. Rather than be impressed at the size of these men's muscles and the ingenuity of their violences, audiences are to admire their emotional commitments and the ingenuity of their sacrifices, sacrifices that are being made, *T2* reminds its viewers, for their future.

T2 reveals the ways in which this link between masculinity and futures is so problematic. Donald Greiner, in his discussion of the traditions of masculine representations in the American novel, identifies the two main 'enemies' of men in these novels: space and time:

> Time is always the enemy of spaciousness for the bonded male in the American novel because, if possible immortality is associated with space, certain mortality is equated with time. . . . If men are to fulfill the destiny of America . . . then they must avoid the reality of time for the illusion of space.
>
> (Greiner 1991: 13)

What *T2* offers is an alternative way to resolve these anxieties about the ends of masculinity/territory through the manipulation of space and time via the male body. As John Connor not only chooses his own biological father in Kyle Reese (fathers himself, as it were), but also programs his mechanical father into the 'kinder and gentler' Terminator, he seems to have conquered the restrictions of time, not by expanding into external territories (the solutions of Natty Bumppo, Huck Finn or Theodore Roosevelt), but by territorializing the interior of the male body.

It is thus John Connor and not Sarah Connor or the Terminator who holds the real power of these films, and marks himself as the hero of Hollywood sequels, for it is he who survives the destruction of the 'old' masculinity, witnessing teary-eyed the Terminator's destruction. As he stands above the melting Terminators, audiences are to recognize in John Connor not only the father of his own and the human future, but the new masculinity as well.

But in one of *T2*'s most remarkable inversions, the film manages not only to reveal the 'new' masculinity/father, but to excuse the 'old' one as well. For though the Terminator must sacrifice itself in order to prevent a destructive future, the film's plot makes it clear that *it's not his fault*. Because the mechanized body from the movie's past has been shown, largely through the oppositional framework of the script, to be a 'good Terminator,' its elimination is constructed to be not vengeful but tragic. The Terminator had to sacrifice itself, not because it was 'bad' or harmful or even useless, but because others around it misused its components. Comparably, audiences can conclude that the aggressive and destructive 1980s male body that became the target for both ridicule and hatred may not have been *inherently* 'bad,' but only, in some sociologically pitiful way, misunderstood. And who, finally, does *Terminator 2* suggest *does* understand this obsolete but lovable creature? None other than John Connor, the 'new' man himself.

So, while *T2* may present John Connor as the savior of the human race, John Connor is finally saving something else, something far more immediate than a mechanized future and something far more dangerous than a personally-targeted mechanized killing machine. He is saving masculinity for itself, not only embodying the 'new' future of masculinity, but rescuing its past for revival. Because, after all, there will have to be another movie.

Note

1   This re-characterization is reinforced by one of Schwarzenegger's intervening Hollywood hits, *Kindergarten Cop*, in which viewers are treated to the spectacle of Arnold frolicking with 5-year-olds.

Chapter 26

ISAAC JULIEN AND KOBENA MERCER

DE MARGIN AND DE CENTRE

FILM CULTURE IN THE 1980S HAS BEEN MARKED by volatile recon-
figurations in the relations of 'race' and representation. Questions of cultural difference,
identity and otherness – in a word, ethnicity – have been thrown into the foreground of
contestation and debate by numerous shifts and developments. Within the British context,
these trends have underpinned controversies around recent independent films like *Handsworth
Songs, My Beautiful Launderette* and *The Passion of Remembrance* – films which have elicited critical
acclaim and angry polemic in roughly equal measure. The fragmented state of the nation
depicted from a black British point of view in the films themselves contradicts (literally, speaks
against) the remythification of the colonial past in mainstream movies such as *Gandhi* or *A
Passage to India*; yet, the wave of popular films set in imperial India or Africa also acknowledge,
in their own way, Britain's postcolonial condition in so far as they speak to contemporary
concerns. The competing versions of narrative, memory and history in this conjuncture might
be read symptomatically as a state of affairs that speaks of – articulates – conflicting identities
within the 'imagined community' of the nation.

In the international context, certain moments and trends suggest further shifts, adjustments, in the articulation of ethnicity *as* ideology. The ratings success-story of *The Cosby Show*
– 'number one' in South Africa as well as the US – has fulfilled the innocent demand for
'positive images' with a (neo-conservative) vengeance. And the very *idea* of a Hollywood
director like Steven Spielberg adapting the Alice Walker novel *The Color Purple* (in the context
of the unprecedented publication of black women writers) still seems extraordinary, however
commercially astute. In addition, the widening circulation of Third World films among western
audiences, or the televisual 'presence' of Third World spaces like Ethiopia *via* events such as
Live Aid in 1985, implies something of a shift within the boundaries that differentiated the
First and Third Worlds.

One issue at stake, we suggest, is the potential break-up or deconstruction of structures
that determine what is regarded as culturally central and what is regarded as culturally marginal.
Ethnicity has emerged as a key issue as various 'marginal' practices (black British film, for
instance) are becoming de-marginalized at a time when 'centred' discourses of cultural
authority and legitimation (such as notions of a trans-historical artistic 'canon') are becoming
increasingly de-centred and destabilized, called into question from within. This scenario,

described by Craig Owens as a crisis, 'specifically of the authority vested in western European culture and its institutions',[1] has of course already been widely discussed in terms of the characteristic aesthetic and political problems of postmodernism. However, it is ironic that while some of the loudest voices offering commentary have announced nothing less than the 'end of representation' or the 'end of history', the political possibility of the *end of ethnocentrism* has not been seized upon as a suitably exciting topic for description or inquiry.[2] We would argue, on the contrary, that critical theories are just *beginning* to recognize and reckon with the kinds of complexity inherent in the culturally constructed nature of ethnic identities, and the implications this has for the analysis of representational practices.

We chose to call this the 'last special issue' as a rejoinder to critical discourses in which the subject of race and ethnicity is still placed on the margins conceptually, despite the acknowledgement of such issues indicated by the proliferation of 'special issues' on race in film, media and literary journals.[3] The problem, paradoxically, is that as an editorial strategy and as a mode of address, the logic of the 'special issue' tends to reinforce, rather than ameliorate, the perceived otherness and marginality of the subject itself. There is nothing intrinsically different or 'special' about ethnicity in film culture, merely that it makes fresh demands on existing theories, methods and problematics. Rather than attempt to compensate the 'structured absences' of previous paradigms, it would be useful to identify the relations of power/knowledge that determine which cultural issues are intellectually prioritized in the first place. The initial stage in any deconstructive project must be to examine and undermine the force of the binary relation that produces the marginal as a consequence of the authority invested in the centre.

At a concrete level the politics of marginalization is an underlying issue in the overview of black film-making in Europe sketched by Maureen Blackwood and June Givanni. The negotiation of access to resources in training, production and distribution emerges as a common factor facing practitioners in a migrant or 'minority' situation. While highlighting the different conditions stemming from the colonial past, the comparative dimension also draws attention to the specificity of British conditions in the present, where black film-making has flourished in the state-subsidized 'independent' sector. Data compiled by June Givanni elsewhere[4] indicates some of the characteristics that constitute black British film as a 'minor' cinema: the prevalence of material of short duration, shot on video, and in the documentary genre, indicates a pattern of underfunding, or rather, taking the variety of work into consideration, a considerable cultural achievement that has been won against the odds of meagre resourcing. Moreover, shifts in the institutional framework of public funding in the UK were brought about in the 1980s as a result of a wider social and political struggle to secure black rights to representation. It was said at the time of the 1981 'riots' that this was the only way in which those excluded from positions of power and influence could make themselves heard: in any case, the events were read and widely understood as expressing protest at the structural marginalization of the black presence in British public institutions.

The consequent demand for *black representation* thus informed shifts in multicultural and 'equal opportunity' policy among institutions such as Channel Four, the British Film Institute and local authorities such as the Greater London Council. More generally, this took place in the context of a re-articulation of the category 'black' as a political term of identification among diverse minority communities of Asian, African and Caribbean origin, rather than as a biological or 'racial' category. Together, these aspects of the cultural politics of 'black representation' informed the intense debates on aesthetic and cinematic strategies within the black British independent sector. Far from homogenizing these differences, the concept has been the site of contestation, highlighted in numerous events and conferences, such as 'Third Cinema' at the Edinburgh International Film Festival in 1986 and more recently, the conference on 'Black

Film/British Cinema' at the Institute of Contemporary Arts in London.[5] It has become apparent that what is at stake in the debates on 'black representation' is not primarily a dispute over realist or modernist principles, but a broader problematic in cultural politics shaped, as Paul Gilroy suggests, by the tension between representation as a practice of depiction and representation as a practice of delegation.[6] Representational democracy, like the classic realist text, is premised on an implicitly mimetic theory of representation as correspondence with the 'real': notionally, the political character of the state is assumed to 'correspond' to the aspiration of the masses in society. However, not unlike the civil disruptions, aspects of the new wave in black British film-making have interrupted these relations of representation: in cinematic terms the challenge to documentary realism that features so prominently in more recent work, such as *Territories*, is predicated on a relational conception of representation as a practice of selection, combination and articulation. At a textual level, such shifts have contested the hegemony of documentary realism underlying the formal codification of what Jim Pines calls the master discourse of the 'race-relations narrative'.[7] This also entails awareness of extra-textual factors, such as funding, as important determinants on black film-making and its modes of enunciation, such as 'the moral imperative which usually characterizes black films, which empowers them to speak with a sense of urgency', as John Akomfrah of Black Audio Film Collective has put it.[8]

What is at issue in this problematic is the question of power, as Judith Williamson argues in her review of *The Passion of Remembrance*, 'The more power any group has to create and wield representations, the less it is required to be representative'.[9] Where access and opportunities are rationed, so that black films tend to get made only one-at-a-time, each film text is burdened with an inordinate pressure to be 'representative' and to act, like a delegate does, as a statement that 'speaks' for the black communities as a whole. Martina Attille, producer of the film, suggests that the 'sense of urgency to say it all' stems less from the artistic choices made by black film-makers and more from the material constraints in which 'sometimes we only get the one chance to make ourselves heard'.[10] Contemporary shifts have brought these problems into view, for as Williamson adds, in relation to the invisible demand to be 'representative' implicit in the rationing and rationalization of public funding, 'what is courageous in Sankofa's project is that they have chosen to speak from, but not for, black experience(s) in Britain.'

Marginality circumscribes the enunciative modalities of black film as cinematic discourse and imposes a double bind on black subjects who speak in the public sphere: if only one voice is given the 'right to speak', that voice will be heard, by the majority culture, as 'speaking for' the many who are excluded or marginalized from access to the means of representation. This of course underlines the problem of tokenism: the very idea that a single film could 'speak for' an entire community of interests reinforces the perceived secondariness of that community. The double bind of expedient inclusion as a term for the legitimation of more general forms of exclusionary practice is also the source of a range of representational problems encountered not just by black subjects, but by other groups marginalized into minority status. In the gay documentary *Word is Out* (Mariposa Film Group, 1978) the nature of this problematic is pointed out in a performative mode by a black woman who carefully describes the predicament she is placed in as a result of the editing strategy of the text:

> What I was trying to say when I asked you if I would be the only black lesbian in the film is: do you know we come in all shapes and colours and directions to our lives? Are you capturing that on the film? As a black lesbian-feminist involved in the movement, so often people try to put me in the position of speaking for all black lesbians. I happen to be *a* black lesbian among many, and I wouldn't want to be seen as *this is how all black lesbians are*.[11]

Within such a regime of representation, the restricted economy of ethnic enunciation is a political problem for at least two important reasons. First, individual subjectivity is denied because the black subject is positioned as a mouthpiece, a ventriloquist for an entire social category which is seen to be 'typified' by its representative. Acknowledgement of the diversity of black experiences and subject-positions is thereby foreclosed. Thus, second, where minority subjects are framed and contained by the monologic terms of 'majority discourse', the fixity of boundary relations between centre and margin, universal and particular, returns the speaking subject to the ideologically appointed place of the stereotype – that 'all black people are the same'.

Stuart Hall's account of the shifts taking place in contemporary black British cultural production offers a means of making sense of the 'politics of representation' at issue here. His argument that current shifts demand the recognition of the 'end of the innocent notion of the essential black subject' enables us to analyse and unpack the burden of racial representation. The recognition that 'black' is a politically and culturally constructed category, and that our metaphorical fictions of 'white' and 'black' are not fixed by Nature but by historical formations of hegemony, brings into play 'the recognition of the immense diversity and differentiation of the historical and cultural experiences of black subjects'. This has major consequences for the critical evaluation of different aesthetic and discursive strategies that articulate race at a level of language and representation.

> Films are not necessarily good because black people make them. They are not necessarily *right-on* by virtue of the fact that they deal with the black experience. Once you enter the politics of the end of the essential black subject you are plunged headlong into the maelstrom of a continuously contingent, unguaranteed, political argument and debate: a critical politics, a politics of criticism. You can no longer conduct black politics through the strategy of a simple set of reversals, putting in place of the bad old essential white subject, the new essentially good black subject.[12]

The deconstruction of binary relations thus entails the relativization and rearticulation of 'ethnicity'. This is an importantly enabling argument as it brings a range of critical issues into an explanatory structure, however tentative.

At one level, it contextualizes Salmon Rushdie's point, expressed in his polemic against *Handsworth Songs*,[13] that 'celebration makes us lazy'. Because black films have been so few and far between, up till now, there has been a tendency to 'celebrate' the fact that they ever got made at all; but this has inhibited the formulation of criticism and self-criticism and perpetuated the moral masochism of 'correctness' so pervasive in oppositional 'left' cultural politics (especially in Britain). Judith Williamson takes up this point and argues that the moralism of being ideologically 'right-on' has been conflated with aesthetic judgement and thus the formal properties of the recent 'experimental' films have been subsumed into their 'blackness' (that is, the racial identity of the authors) giving the films an 'aura of untouchability' that further pre-empts critical analysis. The problem which arises, is that such responses threaten to frame the films as merely replacing the avant-garde (as the 'latest thing') rather than as displacing the orthodoxies that have led the Euro-American vanguard (especially its formalist variant) into its current stasis. At another level, Parminder Dhillon-Kashyap argues that the debates on black British film have in turn made Asian experiences and interventions 'secondary', thus risking the replication of essentialist versions of race precisely when the re-articulation of subaltern ethnicities as 'black' seeks to undermine 'ethnic absolutism' (anchoring the culturalist terms of the 'new racism' that fixes hybridized experienced in terms of alien cultures').[14] Coco Fusco's assessment of two major conferences in the US examines the way in which two kinds of essentialist tendency, manifest in the contradictory reception of black British film, mutually forestall the politics of criticism. The impetus to 'celebrate' black cinema, on the one hand, invokes a unitary notion of blackness that precludes elucidation of 'internal' differences and diversity. The desire to 'correct' the omissions of the past within the western avant-garde, on the other hand, has led to a one-sided fixation with ethnicity as something that 'belongs' to the Other alone, thus white ethnicity is not under question and retains its 'centred' position; more to the point, the white subject remains the central reference point in the power ploys of multicultural policy. The burden of representation thus falls on the Other, because as Fusco argues, 'to ignore white ethnicity is to redouble its hegemony by naturalizing it.'

While such discursive events acknowledge contemporary shifts, their logic evades the implications of Hall's insight that the point of contestation is no longer between multiculturalism and anti-racism, but inside the concept of ethnicity itself. Within dominant discourses, 'ethnicity' is structured into a negative equivalence with essentialist versions of 'race' and 'nation' which particularize its referent, as the pejorative connotation of 'ethnic minority' implies (who, after all, constitutes the 'ethnic majority'?). On the other hand, just as it were necessary to re-appoint the category 'black', Hall argues that 'ethnicity' is a strategically necessary concept because it

> acknowledges the place of history, language and culture in the construction of subjectivity and identity, as well as the fact that all discourse is placed, positioned, situated, and all knowledge is contextual. Representation is possible only because enunciation is always produced within codes that have a history, a position within the discursive formations of a particular space and time.[15]

In this sense, 'we are all ethnically located', but the cultural specificity of white ethnicity has been rendered 'invisible' by the epistemic violence that has, historically, disavowed difference in western discourses. The rearticulation of ethnicity as an epistemological category thus involves,

> the displacement of the *centred* discourses of the West (and) entails putting into question its universalist character and its transcendental claims to speak for everyone, while being itself everywhere and nowhere.

Richard Dyer's article, 'White', inaugurates a paradigmatic shift by precisely registering the re-orientation of 'ethnicity' that Hall's argument calls for. Dyer shows how elusive white ethnicity is as a representational construct (and the difficulties this presents for constituting it as a theoretical object of analysis) and notes that, 'Black is, in the realm of categories, always marked as a colour . . . is always particularizing; whereas white is not anything really, not an identity, not a particularizing quality, because it is everything.' In other words, whiteness has secured universal consent to its hegemony as the 'norm' by masking its coercive force with the invisibility that marks off the Other (the pathologized, the disempowered, the dehumanized) as all too visible – 'coloured'.[16] Significantly, in relation to the films that Dyer discusses, whiteness only tends to become visible when its hegemony is under contestation.

The complex range of problems now coming into view in film studies around the site of ethnicity, partly as a result of developments elsewhere in literary and social theory,[17] enables a more adequate understanding of contemporary forms of contestation. The 'differences' between various black independent film practices have, to some extent, been overplayed, as the key underlying objective across each of the strategies, is to displace the binary relation of the burden of representation, most clearly pinpointed by Horace Ove:

> Here in England there is a danger, if you are black, that all you are allowed to make is films about black people and their problems. White film-makers on the other hand, have a right to make films about whatever they like.[18]

Theoretically, the displacement of binarisms has been most important in the analysis of stereotyping – the marginalization of ethnicity has been held in place by the logical impasse of the 'positive/negative' image polarity. *Screen* has contributed to the productive displacement of this stasis in a number of ways: from Steve Neale's analysis of the impossibility of the 'perfect image' sought by idealist and realist arguments, to Homi Bhabha's influential reading of colonial discourse, which emphasizes the psychic ambivalence, the fear and fascination, that informs the 'Manichean delirium' of classical regimes of racial representation.[19] However, the range of textual readings here suggests that we need to go much further towards a reflexive examination of the mutual inscription of self and other in the analysis of ethnic boundary-ness. This involves questioning the way that, during its 'centred' role in the discursive formation of film theory during the 1970s, *Screen* participated in a phase of British left culture that inadvertently marginalized race and ethnicity as a consequence of the centrifugal tendency of its 'high theory'.

During this period, one was more likely to encounter the analysis of racial stereotyping in sociology than cultural theory, where class and gender took precedence in debates on ideology and subjectivity.[20] Furthermore, without imputing maleficent intentions (because such relations are beyond the control of individual intentionality), it can be said that even within *Screen*'s important acknowledgement of ethnic differences in previous 'special issues',[21] the explanatory concept of 'Otherness' distances and particularizes ethnicity as something that happens far away, either in the US or in the Third World.[22] Space prohibits an adequate exploration of the intellectual milieu that *Screen* helped to form, but recent comments on the institutionalization of film studies have argued that '*Screen* theory', so-called, came to function as a kind of corporate 'name of the father', a 'theoretical super-ego' or even a 'phallic mother' – a centred point of reference that, like a doctrine or orthodoxy, featured a number of 'disciplinary' characteristics.[23] Jane Gaines recalls that, in the translation of '*Screen* theory' into the North American academic environment in the 1970s, leftist enthusiasm for theoretical 'correctness' was heard to speak in an unmistakably English accent.

This background is important because what emerges in the current situation is not a 'new' problematic, but a critical return to issues unwittingly 'repressed' in some of the 'old' problematics and debates. It would be useful, therefore, to tentatively draw out some of the directions in which the field is being remapped and in which the *lacunae* of previous paradigms are excavated.

First, the analysis of ethnic binarisms at the level of narrative codes returns to the question of how dominant ideologies naturalize their domination, underlying previous debates on the classic realist text. Clyde Taylor's inter-textual examination of racialized repetition that drives the reproduction of racist ideology is not simply indicative of capitalist commodification or a bourgeois world view. *Star Wars*, argues Taylor, repeats the 'blood and purity' mythology of *The Birth of a Nation*, not as a defiant assertion of WASP 'superiority' but as an embattled recoding of the master text in response to the encroaching presence of the Third World. The racial discourse sub-textualized by binary oppositions acknowledges the crises of (US) hegemony. The 'liberal' inflections in the films discussed by Richard Dyer also acknowledge the destabilization of prevailing race relations, albeit within a different set of generic and narrative conventions. Common to both readings is a concern to 'typify' textual structures that position racial and ethnic signifiers in the fixed relation of a binary opposition, whether it be one of the antagonism, accommodation or subordination.

There is, in addition, a historical emphasis that relativizes the kinds of claims once extra-polated from the formal structures of the 'CRT', as it was known. Aspects of Bhabha's theor-ization of the stereotype in colonial discourse replicate this trans-historical or de-historicized emphasis.[24] The move towards a more context-oriented view, on the other hand, indicates that although dominant discourses are characterized by closure, they are not themselves closed but constantly negotiated and restructured by the conjuncture of discourses in which they are produced. The way in which ethnic 'types' are made afresh in contemporary movies like *An Officer and a Gentleman* and *Angel Heart* – or more generally in current advertising – demands such a conjunctural approach. The theory of the stereotype cannot be abandoned as it also needs to be able to explain how and why certain ethnic stereotypes are at times recirculated, in the British context, in the work of black film and television authors.[25]

Second, there is a note of caution about reproducing binarisms at the level of theory. Cameron Bailey's reading of the accretion of 'ethnic' signifiers around the construction of (white) femininity as a source of pleasure and danger in *Something Wild* demonstrates that, rather than the familiar 'race, class, gender' mantra, analysis needs to take account of the intersections of differences, in particular of the representation of sexuality as a recurring site upon which categories of race and gender intersect. Feminist theories of the fetishistic logic inherent in the sexualization of gender-difference have provided an invaluable inventory for the reading of the eroticized othering of the black (male and female) subject. Yet, as Jane Gaines argues, the gender binarism implicit in the heterosexist presumption so often unwittingly reproduced in feminist film theory (or FFT; the acronym already indicates an orthodoxy) remains 'colour blind' to the racial hierarchies that structure mastery over the 'look'. The scenario of voyeurism, sadism and objectification played out across Diana Ross's star image in *Mahogany* enacts a patriarchal discourse of masculine 'desire', but also demands a historical understanding of the pre-textual and the contextual discourses of race that placed the black woman in the 'paradox of non-being' – a reference to the period in Afro-American history when the black female did not signify 'woman' on account of the racial ideology that made the black subject less than human.

The historical violation of black bodies in social formations structured by slavery gives rise to a discourse (encoded in both the rationalization of and resistance to such pre-modern forms of power as lynching) which has indeed the countervailing force to rival the problem-atic of castration rhetorically placed at the centre of psychoanalytic theory by the oedipal grand narrative. Just as lesbian critiques of FFT have questioned the explanatory capacity of Freudian and Lacanian theory to account for the inscription of female pleasure and desire[26] – demonstrating the contradictory subject positions occupied by different spectators – the reorientation of the spectatorship problematic in the articles by Gaines and Manthia Diawara identifies the ethnocentrism of psychoanalytic discourse as a barrier to further inquiry. Both question the universalist claims anchored in the oedipus story and imply that uncritical adher-ence to psychoanalytic theory (however enabling as a method) risks the disavowal of its Eurocentric 'authority'; Freud closes his essay on fetishism by commenting that the acknowl-edgement and disavowal of difference 'might be seen in the Chinese custom of mutilating the female foot and then revering it like a fetish after it has been multilated'[27] – surely this culture-bound aesthetic judgement is the starting-pint for a more circumspect appropriation of psychoanalytic theory.

Diawara identifies the mythic 'castration' and 'visual punishment' of the black male as a term of the 'narrative pleasures' offered by Hollywood spectacle (and also as a narratological term of closure, analogous to the 'punishment' of feminine transgression in *film noir*). By rais-ing the issue of spectatorial resistance, Diawara opens up an interesting question about the place of the black spectator in the ideological machinery of interpellation. How is the black subject sutured into a place that includes it only as a term of negation? What does the black spectator identify with when his/her mirror image is structurally absent or present only as Other? In the past, it was assumed that all social subjects acceded to the narcissistic pleasure of the 'mirror phase' in their misrecognition of themselves as the subject of enunciation, returned thus as normalized and passified 'subjects' of ideological subjection (this was the basis of Barthes' distinction between 'pleasure' and 'bliss'[28]). But what if certain social categories of spectator do not have access, as it were, to the initial moment of recognition? The question of how black subjects psychically manage to make identifications with white images is thus signposted as an important area for further inquiry.[29] Perhaps one reason why, for example, *The Cosby Show* is so popular among black audiences is that it affords the pleasure of a basic or primary narcissism even though it interpellates the minority subject, in particular, into ideological normalization.[30] A contemporary black star, like Eddie Murphy – popular with both white and black audiences – offers another source of 'bad pleasure', partly on account of the pastiche of the stereotype that he performs in his star-image as the street-credible, but ideologically unthreatening, macho loudmouth.

This is also where class comes back into the calculation of difference. An appreciation of differentiated regimes of racial representation necessitates acknowledgement of different audiences or, taken together, recognition of the different forms of ideological articulation characteristic of First and Second Cinemas, as described by the concept of Third Cinema.[31] The inscription of ethnic indeterminacy does not take place 'inside' the text, as if it were hermetically sealed, but in-between the relations of author, text and reader specific to the construction of different discursive formations. Blackness is not always a sign of racial codification (as the term *film noir* admits): its representational aura in auteurist and avant-garde traditions conventionally serves to mark off the status of the author (as white subject of enunciation) in relation to the discourse authorized in the text (as black subject of the statement). Ethnic alterity is a consistent trope of modernist differentiation in various Euro-American canons: the play of black signs that inscribe the authorial voice self-referentially in Jonathan Demme's *Something Wild* can be seen as drawing on elements of the romanticist image-reservoir, where blackness is valorized as emblematic of outsiderness and opposition-ality, that might be read off Jean Genet's *Chant d'amour* (1953), Jean-Luc Godard's *One Plus One/Sympathy for the Devil* (1960) or Laura Mulvey and Peter Wollen's *Riddles of the Sphinx* (1976). This arbitrary list (indexing disparate debates on independent film-making[32]) is made merely to point out another set of questions; namely, how to differentiate diverse appropriations of the same stock of signs and meanings built up around different discursive formations of 'race' and ethnicity? This question bears upon the broader underlying issue of the multi-accentual nature of the signs characteristic of the flashpoints of ideological contes-tation and cultural struggle.[33] It also alludes to the paradox identified in Richard Dyer's reading of Paul Robeson as a cinematic icon that meant different things to radically differentiated readers:

> Black and white discourses on blackness seem to be valuing the same things – spon-taneity, emotion, naturalness – yet giving them a different implication. Black dis-courses see them as contributions to the development of society, white as enviable qualities that only blacks have.[34]

The issue of 'envy' confirms that white identifications are as problematic (conceptually) as the ability of black readers – or readers of subaltern status – to appropriate alternative 'sub-textual' readings from the racial discourse of dominant cultural texts. *King Kong* – to cite one of the most centred mythologies of modern popular cinema – has been read as the tragic story of a heroic beast and/or the fate of a black man punished for the transgressive coupling with the white woman that he/the monster desires. These questions appear to be 'new', hence very difficult, yet we have returned, by a rather circuitous route, to the hotly contested terrain of the debates on class and culture, hegemony and subjectivity that were territorialized with such passion in the mid-1970s.[35] We must conclude that this cannot possibly be the last word on 'race' as these complicated issues are only now coming into view as a result of the critical dialogue that has engaged with the blind-spots and insights of earlier conversations. And further, that such dialogism is a necessary discursive condition for understanding contestation in film culture and other formations of cultural practice and cultural politics.

Notes

1 Craig Owens, 'The discourse of others: feminists and post-modernism' in Hal Foster (ed.), *Postmodern Culture*, London: Pluto, 1985, 57.

2 The assertion of the 'end' of everything is exemplified in Jean Baudrillard, *Simulations*, New York: Semiotext(e), 1984 and Victor Burgin, *The End of Art Theory*, London: Macmillan, 1986. More considered reflections on postmodernism, which focus on the problems of its ethnocentrism, are offered by Stuart Hall, 'On postmodernism and articulation: an interview edited by Lawrence Grossberg', in *Communications Inquiry* 10(2), 1986 (University of Iowa) and Andreas Huyssens, 'Mapping the postmodern', in *After the Great Divide*, London: Macmillan, 1987.

3 For instance, 'Black experiences', *Ten-8* 22, 1986; 'Race, writing and difference', *Critical Inquiry* 12(3), 1985 and 13(1), 1986; 'The inappropriate Other', *Discourse* 8, 1986; 'Colonialism', *Oxford Literary Review* 9, 1987 and 'The nature and context of minority discourse', I and II *Cultural Critique*, Spring and Fall, 1987.

4 *Black and Asian Film List*, compiled by June Givanni and edited by Nicky North, London, British Film Institute Education, 1988. A transatlantic comparison is offered by James A. Snead, 'Black independent film: Britain and America', in Kobena Mercer (ed.), *Black Film/British Cinema, ICA Document 7/British Film Institute Production Special*, 1988b.

5 Symposia organized by the Greater London Council in 1985 are documented in *Third Eye: Struggles for Black and Third World Cinema*, Race Equality Unit, London, GLC 1986; the Edinburgh conference is documented in Jim Pines and Paul Willemen (eds), *Third Cinema: Theories and Practices*, London, BFI (1989); and the ICA conference is documented in Kobena Mercer (ed.), op. cit.

6 'Nothing but sweat inside my hand: diaspora aesthetics and Black arts in Britain', in Kobena Mercer (ed.), op. cit. See also Pierre Bourdieu, 'Delegation and political fetishism', *Thesis Eleven* 10/11, 1984–5 (Sydney), 56–70.

7 See Jim Pines, 'The cultural context of Black British cinema', in Mbye Cham and Claire Andrade-Watkins (eds), *BlackFrames: Critical Perspectives on Black Independent Cinema*, Celebration of Black Cinema, Inc/MIT Press 1988 and Kobena Mercer, 'Diaspora culture and the dialogic imagination: the aesthetics of black independent film in Britain', ibid.

8 In Paul Gilroy and Jim Pines, 'Handsworth songs: audiences/aesthetics/independence, an interview with Black Audio Film Collective', *Framework* 35, 1988, 11.

9 *New Statesman*, 5 December 1986.

10 In 'The Passion of Remembrance: background and interview with Sankofa', *Framework* 32/33, 1986, 101.

11 In Nancy Adair and Casey Adair (eds), *Word is Out: Stories of Some of Our Lives*, New York: New Glide/Delta, 1978, 203.

12 Stuart Hall, 'New ethnicities'. Also in Kobena Mercer (ed.), *Black Film/British Cinema*, op. cit. See also Stuart Hall, 'Minimal selves', in Lisa Appignanesi (ed.), *Identity, ICA Document 6*, 1988, 44–6.

13 'Songs doesn't know the score', *Guardian*, 12 January 1987, reprinted in Kobena Mercer (ed.), *Black Film/British Cinema*, op. cit.

14 Discursive formations of British racism are discussed in Paul Gilroy, *There Ain't No Black in the Union Jack*, London: Hutchinson, 1987. Gilroy proposes the concept of syncretism to examine cultural resistance in the 'hybridized' context of black Britain, see especially chapter 5, 'Diaspora, Utopia and the critique of capitalism'.

15   Stuart Hall, 'New ethnicities', in Kobena Mercer (ed.), *Black Film/British Cinema*, op. cit.

16   The term 'people of color' operates in the US as a political term analogous to 'black' in the British context. In both instances, such terms have engendered intense semantic ambiguity and ideological anxiety as the racial mythology of 'colour' is put under erasure, cancelled out but still legible, in a deconstructive logic that depends on the same system of metaphorical equivalences and differences. Semantic indeterminacy as a condition of political contestation is discussed in Chantal Mouffe and Ernesto Laclau, *Hegemony and Socialist Strategy*, London: Verso, 1985.

17   See Stuart Hall, 'Race, articulation and societies structured in dominance', in *Sociological Theories: Race and Colonialism*, Paris: UNESCO, 1980; Edward Said, *Orientalism*, London: Routledge & Kegan Paul, 1978, and *The World, the Text and the Critic*, London: Faber, 1984l Gayatri Chakravorty. Spivak, *In Other Worlds*, London: Methuen 1987; Cornel West, 'The dilemma of a Black intellectual', *Cultural Critique* 1(1), 1986; 'Race and social theory', in M. Davis, M. Marrable, F. Pfiel and M. Sprinker (eds), *The Year Left 2*, London: Verso, 1987 and 'Marxist theory and the specificity of Afro-American oppression', in Cary Nelson and Lawrence Grossberg (eds), *Marxism and the Interpretation of Culture*, London: Macmillan, 1988.

18   Interview with Sylvia Paskin, *Monthly Film Bulletin* 54(647), December 1987.

19   Steve Neale, 'The same old story: stereotypes and difference', *Screen Education*, Autumn–Winter 1979–80, nos 32 and 33, 33–7 and Homi K. Bhabha, 'The Other question: the stereotype and colonial discourse', *Screen*, November–December 1983, 24(6), 18–36.

20   In both Weberian and marxist variants, see Charles Husband, *White Media and Black Britain*, London: Arrow, 1975 and Stuart Hall *et al.*, *Policing the Crisis*, London: Macmillan, 1978. Cultural struggles over media racism are documented in Phil Cohen and Carl Gardner (eds), *It Ain't Half Racist, Mum*, London: Comedia/Campaign Against Racism in the Media, 1982. CARM's BBC 'Open Door' programme is discussed in Stuart Hall, 'The whites of their eyes: racist ideologies and the media', in Bridges and Bunt (eds), *Silver Linings*, London: Lawrence & Wishart, 1981.

21   'Racism, colonialism and the cinema', *Screen*, March–April 1983, 24(2), and 'Other cinemas, Other criticisms', *Screen*, May–August 1985, 26(3–4).

22   Black British perspectives have rarely featured in *Screen*, but see Hazel Carby, 'Multiculture', *Screen Education*, Spring 1980, 34, 62–70; Paul Gilroy, 'C4 – Bridgehead or Bantustan?', *Screen*, July–October 1983, 24(4–5), 130–6; Robert Crusz, 'Black cinemas, film theory and dependent knowledge', *Screen*, May–August 1985, 26(3–4), 152–6.

23   The description of a 'theoretical super ego' in film studies is made by Paul Willemen in 'An avant-garde for the 80s', *Framework* 24, 1982 and in 'The Third Cinema question: notes and reflections', *Framework* 34, 1987. The characterization of orthodoxies in terms of the demands of a 'phallic mother' is made by Lesley Stern in her tribute, 'Remembering Claire Johnston', in *Film News*, 19(4), May 1988 (Sydney), reprinted in *Framework* 35, 1988. An interesting case of another translation this time in the postcolonial periphery, is provided by Felicity Collins, 'The Australian Journal of Screen Theory', in *Framework* 24, 1982.

24   Methods employed by Homi Bhabha and Gayatri Chakravorty Spivak are the subject of a critique by Benita Parry, 'Problems in current theories of colonial discourse', *Oxford Literary Review* 9, 1987.

25   An issue raised in Jim Pines' reading of sociological stereotypes in Horace Ove's *Pressure* (1975), discussed in 'Blacks in films: the British angle', *Multiracial Education* 9(2), 1981. Some of the paradoxical consequences of documentary realism in black independent film are also discussed in Kobena Mercer, 'Recoding narratives of race and nation', in *Black Film/British Cinema*, op. cit.

26   See Jackie Stacey, 'Desperately seeking difference', *Screen*, winter 1987, 28(1), 48–61; reprinted in a slightly different version in Lorraine Gamman and Margaret Marshment (eds), *The Female Gaze*, London: Women's Press, 1988.

27   Sigmund Freud, 'Fetishism', in *On Sexuality*, Harmondsworth: Pelican Freud Library 7, 1977, 357.

28   Roland Barthes, *The Pleasure of the Text*, New York: Hill & Wang, 1975.

29   This again is by no means a 'new' topic. The starting-point for James Baldwin's autobiographical reflections on cinema is his adolescent identification with Bette Davis' star image; see *The Devil Finds Work*, London: Michael Joseph, 1976, 4–7.

30   *The Cosby Show* is the subject of two conflicting readings – as a 'breakthrough' and as a 'sell out': see Mel Cummings, 'Black family interactions on television', presented at the International Television Studies Conference, London, 1986 and Pat Skinner, 'Moving way up: television's "new look" at Blacks', presented at the International Television Studies Conference, London, 1988. Both ITSC conferences sponsored by the British Film Institute and the Institute of Education, University of London.

31   The concept of 'Third Cinema' was originally proposed by Fernando Solanas and Octavio Gettino; see their 'Towards a Third Cinema', in Bill Nichols (ed.), *Movies and Methods*, London and Berkeley: University of California, 1976. It has subsequently been expanded, with particular reference to African cinema, by Teshome Gabriel, *Third Cinema in the Third World: The Aesthetics of Liberation*, Ann Arbor: UMI Research Press, 1982.

32   Jean Genet's film is the subject of intense debate in the Cultural Identities seminar on 'Sexual identities: questions of difference', in *Undercut* 17, 1988. Maxine, the black woman in *Riddles of the Sphinx*, is identified as a signifier of 'dark continent' mythology in Judith Williamson's critique of the film, 'Two or three things we know about ourselves', in *Consuming Passions*, London: Calder & Boyars, 1986, 134. Frankie Dymon Jr was involved in Godard's *One Plus One* and subsequently directed his own film, *Death May Be Your Santa Claus* (1969), described as a 'pop fantasy' by Jim Pines, in 'The cultural context of Black British cinema', op. cit.

33   Identified as indicative of class struggle, in V. N. Volosinov, *Marxism and the Philosophy of Language*, New York: Seminar Press, 1983. From another point of view, similar concepts are explored in Homi K. Bhabha's reinterpretation of Fanon's *Wretched of the Earth* (Penguin, 1970) in his essay, 'The commitment to theory', in *New Formations* 5, 1988, 20–2.

34   Richard Dyer, 'Paul Robeson: crossing over', in *Heavenly Bodies: Film Stars and Society*, London: BFI/Macmillan, 1987, 79.

35   See Rosalind Coward, 'Class, "culture" and the social formation', *Screen*, Spring 1977, 18(1) 75–105 and the response, from Ian Chambers *et al.*, 'Marxism and culture', *Screen*, Winter 1977–8, 18(4), 109–19. On authorship, enunciation and textual analysis, see Paul Willemen, 'Notes on subjectivity: on reading Edward Branigan's "Subjectivity under siege"', *Screen*, Spring (1978), 19(1), 41–69. And on critiques of '*Screen* theory' from the Centre for Contemporary Cultural Studies, see David Morley, 'Texts, readers, subjects' and Stuart Hall, 'Recent developments in theories of language and ideology: a critical note', both in Stuart Hall *et al.* (eds), *Culture, Media, Language*, London: Hutchinson, 1980.

Chapter 27

ELLA SHOHAT AND ROBERT STAM

THE IMPERIAL IMAGINARY

THE COLONIAL DOMINATION OF INDIGENOUS peoples, the scientific and esthetic disciplining of nature through classificatory schemas, the capitalist appropriation of resources, and the imperialist ordering of the globe under a panoptical regime, all formed part of a massive world historical movement that reached its apogee at the beginning of the twentieth century. Indeed, it is most significant for our discussion that the beginnings of cinema coincided with the giddy heights of the imperial project, with an epoch where Europe held sway over vast tracts of alien territory and hosts of subjugated peoples. (Of all the celebrated 'coincidences' – of the twin beginnings of cinema and psychoanalysis, cinema and nationalism, cinema and consumerism – it is this coincidence with the heights of imperialism that has been least explored.) Film was born at a moment when a poem such as Rudyard Kipling's 'White Man's Burden' could be published, as it was in 1899, to celebrate the US acquisition of Cuba and the Philippines. The first Lumière and Edison screenings in the 1890s closely followed the 'scramble for Africa' which erupted in the late 1870s; the Battle of 'Rorke's Drift' (1879) which opposed the British to the Zulus (memorialized in the film *Zulu*, 1964); the British occupation of Egypt in 1882; the Berlin Conference of 1884 which carved up Africa into European 'spheres of influence'; the massacre of the Sioux at Wounded Knee in 1890 and countless other imperial misadventures.

The most prolific film-producing countries of the silent period – Britain, France, the US, Germany – also 'happened' to be among the leading imperialist countries, in whose clear interest it was to laud the colonial enterprise. The cinema emerged exactly at the point when enthusiasm for the imperial project was spreading beyond the elites into the popular strata, partly thanks to popular fictions and exhibitions. For the working classes of Europe and Euro-America, photogenic wars in remote parts of the empire became diverting entertainments, serving to 'neutralize the class struggle and transform class solidarity into national and racial solidarity.'[1] The cinema adopted the popular fictions of colonialist writers like Kipling for India and Rider Haggard, Edgar Wallace and Edgar Rice Burroughs for Africa, and absorbed popular genres like the 'conquest fiction' of the American southwest. The cinema entered a situation where European and American readers had already devoured Livingstone's *Missionary Travels* (1857); Edgar Wallace's 'Sanders of the River' stories in the early 1900s; Rider Haggard's *King Solomon's Mines* (1885); and Henry Morton Stanley's *How I Found Livingstone* (1872), *Through the Dark Continent* (1878) and *In Darkest Africa* (1890).

English boys especially were initiated into imperial ideas through such books as Robert Baden-Powell's *Scouting for Boys* (1908), which praised:

> the frontiersmen of all parts of our Empire. The 'Trappers' of North America, hunters of Central Africa, the British pioneers, explorers, and missionaries over Asia and all the wild parts of the world . . . the constabulary of North-West Canada and of South Africa.[2]

The practical survivalist education of scouting, combined with the initiatory mechanisms of the colonial adventure story, were designed to turn boys, as Joseph Bristow puts it, into 'aggrandized subjects,' an imperial race who imagined the future of the world as resting on their shoulders.[3] While girls were domesticated as homemakers, without what Virginia Woolf called a 'room of their own,' boys could play, if only in their imaginations, in the space of empire. The fantasy of far-away regions offered 'charismatic realms of adventure'[4] free from charged heterosexual engagements. Adventure films, and the 'adventure' of going to the cinema, provided a vicarious experience of passionate fraternity, a playing field for the self-realization of European masculinity. Just as colonized space was available to empire, and colonial landscapes were available to imperial cinema, so was this psychic space available for the play of the virile spectatorial imagination as a kind of mental *Lebensraum*. Empire, as John McClure puts it in another context, provided romance with its raw materials, while romance provided empire with its 'aura of nobility.'[5]

The shaping of national identity

Beliefs about the origins and evolution of nations often crystallize in the form of stories. For Hayden White, certain narrative 'master tropes' shape our conception of history; historical discourse consists 'of the provisions of a plot structure for a sequence of events so that their nature as a comprehensible process is revealed by their figuration as a story of a particular kind.'[6] The nation of course is not a desiring person but a fictive unity imposed on an aggregate individuals, yet national histories are presented as if they displayed the continuity of the subject-writ-large.[7] The cinema, as the world's storyteller *par excellence*, was ideally suited to relay the projected narratives of nations and empires. National self-consciousness, generally seen as a precondition for nationhood – that is, the shared belief of disparate individuals that they share common origins, status, location and aspirations – became broadly linked to cinematic fictions. In the modern period, for Benedict Anderson, this collective consciousness was made possible by a common language and its expression in 'print capitalism.'[8] Prior to the cinema, the novel and the newspaper fostered imagined communities through their integrative relations to time and space. Newspapers – like TV news today – made people aware of the simultaneity and interconnectedness of events in different places, while novels provided a sense of the purposeful movement through time of fictional entities bound together in a narrative whole. As 'bourgeois epic' (in the words of Georg Lukács), the novel inherited and transformed the vocation of the classical epic (for example *The Aeneid*) to produce and heighten national identity, both accompanying and crystallizing the rise of nations by imposing a unitary topos on heterogeneous languages and diverse desires.

The fiction film also inherited the social role of the nineteenth-century realist novel in relation to national imaginaries. Like novels, films proceed temporally, their durational scope reaching from a story time ranging from the few minutes depicted by the first Lumière shorts to the many hours (and symbolic millennia) of films like *Intolerance* (1916) and *2001: A Space*

Odyssey (1968). Films communicate Anderson's 'calendrical time,' a sense of time and its passage. Just as nationalist literary fictions inscribe on to a multitude of events the notion of a linear, comprehensible destiny, so films arrange events and actions in a temporal narrative that moves toward fulfillment, and thus shape thinking about historical time and national history. Narrative models in film are not reflective microcosms of historical processes, then, they are also experiential grids or templates through which history can be written and national identity figured. Like novels, films can convey what Mikhail Bakhtin calls 'chronotopes,' materializing time in mediating between the historical and the discursive, providing fictional environments where historically specific constellations of power are made visible. In both film and novel, 'time thickens, takes on flesh,' while 'space becomes charged and responsive to the movements of time, plot and history.'[9] There is nothing inherently sinister in this process, except to the extent that it is deployed asymmetrically, to the advantage of some national and racial imaginaries and to the detriment of others.

The national situation described by Anderson becomes complicated, we would argue, in the context of an imperial ideology that was doubly transnational. First, Europeans were encouraged to identify not only with single European nations but also with the racial solidarity implied by the imperial project as a whole. Thus English audiences could identify with the heroes of French Foreign Legion films, Euro-American audiences with the heroes of the British Raj, and so forth. Second, the European empires (what Queen Victoria called the 'imperial family') were themselves conceived paternalistically as providing a 'shelter' for diverse races and groups, thus downplaying the singularities of the colonized themselves. Given the geographically discontinuous nature of empire, cinema helped cement both a national and an imperial sense of belonging among many disparate peoples. For the urban elite of the colonized lands, the pleasures of cinema-going became associated with the sense of a community of the margins of its particular European empire (especially since the first movie theaters in these countries associated with Europeans and the Europeanized local bourgeoisies).[10] The cinema encouraged an assimilated elite to identify with 'its' empire and thus against other colonized peoples.

If cinema partly inherited the function of the novel, it also transformed it. Whereas literature plays itself out within a virtual lexical space, the cinematic chronotope is literal, splayed out concretely across the screen and unfolding in the literal time of twenty-four frames per second. In this sense, the cinema can all the more efficiently mobilize desire in ways responsive to nationalized and imperialized notions of time, plot, and history. The cinema's institutional ritual of gathering a community – spectators who share a region, language and culture – homologizes, in a sense, the symbolic gathering of the nation. Anderson's sense of the nation as 'horizontal comradeship' evokes the movie audience as a provisional 'nation' forged by spectatorship. While the novel is consumed in solitude, the film is enjoyed in a gregarious space, where the ephemeral *communitas* of spectatorship can take on a national or imperial thrust. Thus the cinema can play a more assertive role in fostering group identities. Finally, unlike the novel, the cinema is not premised on literacy. As a popular entertainment it is more accessible than literature. While there was no mass reading public for imperial literary fictions in the colonies, for example, there *was* a mass viewing public for imperial filmic fictions.

The dominant European/American form of cinema not only inherited and disseminated a hegemonic colonial discourse, it also created a powerful hegemony of its own through monopolistic control of film distribution and exhibition in much of Asia, Africa, and the Americas. Eurocolonial cinema thus mapped history not only for domestic audiences but also for the world. African spectators were prodded to identify with Cecil Rhodes and Stanley and Livingstone against Africans themselves, thus engendering a battle of national imaginaries within the fissured colonial spectator. For the European spectator, the cinematic experience mobilized a rewarding sense of national and imperial belonging, on the backs, as it were, of otherized peoples. For the colonized, the cinema (in tandem with other colonial institutions such as schools) produced a sense of deep ambivalence, mingling the identification provoked by cinematic narrative with intense resentment, for it was the colonized who were being otherized.

While the novel could play with words and narrative to engender an 'aggrandized subject,' the cinema entailed a new and powerful apparatus of gaze. The cinematic 'apparatus,' that is to say the cinematic machine as including not only the instrumental base of camera, projector and screen but also the spectator as the desiring subject on whom the cinematic institution depends for its imaginary realization, not only represents the 'real' but also stimulates intense 'subject effects.' For Christian Metz, the cinematic apparatus fosters narcissism, in that the spectator identifies with him/herself as a 'kind of transcendental subject.'[11] By prosthetically extending human perception, the apparatus grants the spectator the illusory ubiquity of the 'all-perceiving subject' enjoying an exhilarating sense of visual power. From the Diorama, the Panorama and the Cosmorama up through NatureMax, the cinema has amplified and mobilized the virtual gaze of photography, bringing past into present, distant to near. It has offered the spectator a mediated relationship with imaged others from diverse cultures. We are not suggesting that imperialism was inscribed either in the apparatus or in the celluloid, only that the context of imperial power shaped the uses to which both apparatus and celluloid were put. In an imperial context the apparatus tended to be deployed in ways flattering to the imperial subject as superior and invulnerable observer, as what Mary Louise Pratt calls the 'monarch-of-all-I-survey.' The cinema's ability to 'fly' spectators around the globe gave them a subject position as film's audio-visual masters. The 'spatially-mobilized visuality'[12] of the I/eye of empire spiraled outward around the globe, creating a visceral, kinetic sense of imperial travel and conquest, transforming European spectators into armchair conquistadors, affirming their sense of power while turning the colonies into spectacle for the metropole's voyeuristic gaze.

Cinema as science and spectacle

If the culture of empire authorized the pleasure of seizing ephemeral glimpses of its 'margins' through travel and tourism, the nineteenth-century invention of the photographic and later the cinematographic camera made it possible to record such glimpses. Rather than remaining confined to its European home, the camera set out to 'explore' new geographical, ethnographic, and archeological territories. It visited natural and human 'wonders' (the Nile, the Taj Mahal) and unearthed buried civilizations (the excavations in Nubia), imbuing every sight with the wide-eyed freshness of the new machine. Yet the pioneers of the recorded image rarely questioned the constellation of power relations that allowed them to represent other lands and cultures. No one questioned how Egyptian land, history and culture should be represented, for example, or asked what Egyptian people might have to say about the matter. Thus photographers making the grand oriental tour might record their own subjective visions, but in doing so they also drew clear boundaries between the subject looking and the object being looked at, between traveler and 'traveled upon.' Photographers such as Georg Bridges, Louis de Clercq, Maxime du Camp and film-makers like Thomas Edison and the Lumière brothers did not simply document other territories; they also documented the cultural baggage they carried with them. Their subjective interpretations were deeply embedded in the discourses of their respective European empires.

The excitement generated by the camera's capacity to register the formal qualities of movement reverberated with the full-steam-ahead expansionism of imperialism itself. The camera was hired out to document the tentacular extensions of empire. Photographers and film-makers were especially attracted to trains and ships, engines of empire that delivered raw materials from the interiors of Asia, Africa and the Americas into the heart of Europe. Robert Howlett's photographs for the London *Times* of 'The Bow of the Great Eastern' (1857) not only foreshadowed subsequent homages to the futurist esthetics of the machine, but also documented the construction of an unprecedentedly large ship as a matter of national pride and a confirmation of British supremacy at sea.[13] The work of early photographers such as Felix Teynard, Maxine du Camp, Edouard-Denis Baldus, John Beasley Green, Louis de Clercq, and John Murray was supported, published and exhibited by diverse imperial institutions. De Clercq, for example, was invited to accompany the historian Emmanuel-Guillaume Rey on a French government-sponsored expedition of 1859 to the Crusader castles of Syria and Asia Minor, a trip that generated the six volumes of *Voyage en Orient, Villes, Monuments, et Vues Pittoresques de Syrie*, along with the collection of historical artifacts now housed in the Oriental Antiquities Department of the Louvre. And Murray served in the East India Company army, where, like many Englishmen in India, he took up photography as a hobby. His work, first exhibited in London in 1857 during the 'Indian Mutiny,' was encouraged by the Governor-General of India, Lord Earl Canning, the same governor who suppressed the uprising and who, together with his wife Lady Charlotte Canning, was a major patron of photography in India.

Travel photographers did not just document territories for military and governmental purposes, their photos also registered the advances of scientific activities, for example the archeological excavations of Greece and Egypt. Fascination with ancient monuments was mingled with admiration for the camera's capacity to provide a vivid sense of distant regions and remote times: a photo in Du Camp's album *Egypte, Nubie, Palestine et Syrie* (1852) – 'Westernmost Colossus of the temple of Re, Abu Simbel, 1850' – shows the photographer's assistant atop the crown of Rameses II, illustrating both relative scale and a moment of mastery and possession. If bourgeois travelers cherished photographic moments of their own exploring – as in Du Camp's photo of Flaubert in Cairo in 1850 – the colonized had to bear the weight of a generic ethnographic gaze, as in the anonymous photograph 'Women Grinding Paint, Calcultta, 1854.' The camera also played a botanical and zoological role by documenting exotic fauna and flora. Louis Pierre Théophile Dubois de Nehant's 'Another Impossible Task' (1854) shows the elephant 'Miss Betsy,' imported from India, in the Brussels Zoo, while Count de Motizon's photo (1852) captures Londoners admiring a hippopotamus captured on the banks of the White Nile. More than a servile scribe, the camera actively popularized imperial imagery, turning it into an exciting participatory activity for those in the motherland.

The social origins of the cinema were schizophrenic, traceable both to the 'high' culture of science and literature and to the 'low' culture of sideshows and nickelodeons. (At times the two cultures coalesced: the flying balloon in *Around the World in 80 Days*, designed to circle the world, is also the object of spectacle for enthusiastic Parisians.) The desire to expand the frontiers of science became inextricably linked to the desire to expand the frontiers of empire. The immediate origins of the cinema in Western science meant that filmic exhibition also entailed the exhibition of Western triumphs. The visible achievements of both cinema and science also graced the proliferating world fairs, which since the mid-nineteenth century had become the new 'international' showplaces for the spectacular fruits of industrial and scientific progress.

The visualist inclinations of Western anthropological discourse[14] prepared the way for the cinematographic representation of other territories and cultures. The 'ontologically' kinetic status of the moving image privileged the cinema not only over the written word but over still photography as well. It lent indexical credibility to anthropology, arming it with visual evidence not only of the existence of 'others' but also of their actually existing otherness. Cinema in this sense prolonged the museological project of gathering three-dimensional archeological, ethnographic, botanical and zoological objects in the metropolis. Unlike the more auratic and 'inaccessible' elite arts and sciences, a popularizing cinema could plunge spectators into the midst of non-European worlds, letting them see and feel 'strange' civilizations. It could transform the obscure *mappa mundi* into a familiar, knowable world.

Photography and the cinema represented alien topographies and cultures as aberrant in relation to Europe. Operating on a continuum with zoology, anthropology, botany, entomology,[15] biology and medicine, the camera, like the microscope, anatomized the 'other.' The new visual apparatuses demonstrated the power of science to display and even decipher otherized cultures; dissection and montage together constructed a presumably holistic portrait of the colonized. Technological inventions, in other words, mapped the globe as a disciplinary space of knowledge.[16] Topographies were documented for purposes of military and economic control, often on the literal backs of the 'natives' who carried the cinematographers and their equipment. In the colonial context, the common trope of the 'camera gun' (Marey's 'fusil cinématographique') resonated with the aggressive use of the camera by the agents of the colonial powers.[17] 'Primitive' peoples were turned into the objects of quasi-sadistic experimentation. This kind of aggression reached a paroxysm in the 1920s films of Martin and Osa Johnson, where the film-makers gleefully prodded Pygmies, whom they called 'monkeys' and 'niggers,' to get sick on European cigars. In films such as *Trailing African Wild Animals* (1922) and *Simba* (1927), the Johnsons treated African peoples as a form of wildlife. The camera penetrated a foreign and familiar zone like a predator, seizing its 'loot' of images as raw material to be reworked in the 'motherland' and sold to sensation-hungry spectators and consumers, a process later fictionalized in *King Kong* (1933). There was no clue, in such films, as to how Europeans depended for their everyday survival in the field on the knowledge, intelligence, labor and the 'enforced subordination of people the white folk insisted on seeing as perpetual children.'[18]

If cinema itself traced its parentage to popular sideshows and fairs, ethnographic cinema and Hollywoodean ethnography were the heirs of a tradition of exhibitions of 'real' human objects, a tradition going back to Columbus' importation of 'New World' natives to Europe for purposes of courtly entertainment. Exhibitions organized the world as a spectacle within an obsessively mimetic esthetic.[19] In the US, at a time roughly coincident with the beginnings of cinema, a series of fairs – the Chicago Columbian Exposition of 1893, the Omaha Trans-Mississippi Exposition in 1898, the Buffalo Pan-American Exposition in 1901, the St Louis 'Louisiana Purchase' Exposition in 1904 – introduced millions of fairgoers to evolutionary ideas about race in an atmosphere of communal good cheer. The Chicago Columbian Exposition spatialized racial hierarchies in a quasi-didactic fashion by having the Teutonic exhibits placed closest to the 'White City,' with the 'Mohammedan world' and the 'savage races' at the opposite end. Racism and 'entertainment,' as Robert W. Rydell points out, became closely intertwined.[20] The Omaha fair featured an exhibit on 'the Vanquished Races,' and in the Atlanta Exposition the Sioux were obliged to re-enact their own defeat and humiliation at Wounded Knee. The Louisiana Purchase Exposition included a Filipino exhibit that made the Pacific Islands seem as much a part of 'manifest destiny' as the conquest of the west. Such expositions gave utopian form to White supremacist ideology, legitimizing racial hierarchies abroad and muting class and gender divisions among Whites at home by stressing national agency in a global project of domination.[21]

Africans and Asians were exhibited as human figures with kinship to specific animal species, thus literalizing the colonialist zeugma yoking 'native' and 'animal,' the very fact of exhibition in cages implying that the cages' occupants were less than human. Lapps, Nubians and Ethiopians were displayed in Germany in anthropological–zoological exhibits.[22] The conjunction of 'Darwinism, Barnumism [and] pure and simple racism' resulted in the exhibition of Ota Benga, a Pygmy from the Kasai region, alongside the animals in the Bronx Zoo.[23] A precursor to Epcott's global village, the 1894 Antwerp World's Fair featured a reconstructed Congolese village with sixteen 'authentic' villagers. In many cases the people exhibited died or fell seriously ill. 'Freak shows' too paraded before the West's bemused eye a variety of 'exotic' pathologies. Saartjie Baartman, the 'Hottentot Venus,'[24] was displayed on the entertainment circuit in England and France. Although her protrusive buttocks constituted the main attraction, the rumoured peculiarities of her genitalia also drew crowds, with her racial/sexual 'anomaly' constantly being associated with animality.[25] The zoologist and anotamist George Cuvier studied her intimately and presumably dispassionately, and compared her buttocks to those of 'female mandrills, baboons . . . which assume at certain epochs of their life a truly monstrous development.'[26] After Baartman's death at the age of twenty-five, Cuvier received official permission for an even closer look at her private parts, and dissected her to produce a detailed description of her body inside out.[27] Her genitalia still rest on a shelf in the Musée de l'Homme in Paris alongside the genitalia of 'une négresse' and 'une péruvienne'[28] as monuments to a kind of imperial necrophilia. The final placement of the female parts in the patriarchally designated 'Museum of Man' provides a crowning irony.

As the product of both science and mass culture, cinema combined traveling knowledge with traveling spectacles, conveying a view of the 'world itself as an exhibition.'[29] The study of a hypersexualized 'other' in scientific discourse was paralleled by the cinema's scopophilic display of aliens as spectacle. Hollywood production abounded in 'exotic' images of moving native bodies, at times incorporating actual travelogs dug up from the archives, deployed in such films as the *Tarzan* series. Thus in a 'double standard' erotics, the Production Code of the Motion Picture Producers and Directors of America, Inc, 1930–4, which censored Jane's two-piece outfit into one in later *Tarzan* films, left intact the naked African women in the background, evoking a *National Geographic*-style prurient delight in unilateral native nudity. The portrayal of dance rituals in such films as *The Dance of Fatima* (1903), *The Sheik* (1921), *Bird of Paradise* (1932) and *Sanders of the River* (1935) displayed alien flesh to hint at the masculinist pleasures of exploration. Hiding behind a respectable figleaf of 'science' and 'authenticity,' ethnographic films focussed directly on the bouncing breasts of dancing women,[30] Hollywood films, under the surveillance of domestic moral majorities, relegated native nudity to the background, or restricted the imagery to minimal 'native' garb. Formulaic scenes of dark frenzied bodies entranced by accelerating drum rhythms relayed a fetishized image of indigenous religions. Ceremonial possession (portrayed as a kind of mass hysteria) evoked the uncontrollable id of libidinous beings. Ethnographic science, then, provided a cover for the unleashing of pornographic impulses. The cinematic exposure of the dark body nourished spectatorial desire, while marking off imaginary boundaries between 'self' and 'other,' thus mapping homologous spheres, both macro-cosmic (the globe) and microcosmic (the sphere of carnal knowledge).

Projecting the empire

The cinema combined narrative and spectacle to tell the story of colonialism from the colonizer's perspective. From the Lumière brothers' mocking portrayals of the culinary habits of North Africans in *Le Musulman Rigolo* (The Funny Muslim, 1902), through the adventure tales of *Tarzan*, to the Westerner-in-the-pot cannibal imagery of the 1980s version of *King Solomon's Mines* and the scientific missions of *Indiana Jones* (1981, 1984, 1989), dominant cinema has spoken for the 'winners' of history, in films which idealized the colonial enterprise as a philanthropic 'civilizing mission' motivated by a desire to push back the frontiers of ignorance, disease, and tyranny. Programmatically negative portrayals helped rationalize the human costs of the imperial enterprise. Thus Africa was imaged as a land inhabited by cannibals in the Ernst Lubin comedy *Rastus in Zululand* (1910), Mexicans were reduced to 'greasers' and 'bandidos' in films like *Tony the Greaser* (1911) and *The Greaser's Revenge* (1914), and Native Americans were portrayed as savage marauders in *Fighting Blood* (1911) and *The Last of the Mohicans* (1920).

Each imperial filmmaking country had its own imperial genres set in 'darkest Africa,' the 'mysterious East,' and the 'stormy Caribbean.' It was in this imperializing spirit that Thomas Alva Edison staged battles against Filipino guerillas in the fields of New Jersey (with Blacks standing in for the Filipinos) and that J. Stuart Blackton staged the Spanish–American war using scale-model battleships in local bathtubs. Indeed, many of the early American one-reelers, such as *Cuban Ambush* (1898), *Roosevelt's Rough Riders* (1898), *Troop Ships for the Philippines* (1898) and *Landing of U.S. Troops near Santiago* (1902), glorified the imperialist binge in the Caribbean and the Philippines. Even film-makers not conventionally associated with lauding imperialism betray a shared discourse of empire. Georges Méliès' filmography, for example, features a number of films related to expansionist voyages and orientalist fantasies: *Le Fakir – Mystère Indien* (1896), *Vente d'Esclaves au Harem* (1897), *Cléopatre* (1899), *La Vengeance de Bouddah* (1901), *Les Adventures de Robinson Crusoe* (1902), *Le Palais des Mille et une Nuits* (1905).[31] Similarly, in Méliès' *Le Voyage dans la Lune* (A Trip to the Moon, 1902; based on Verne's *From the Earth to the Moon*, 1865), the rocket's phallic penetration of the moon (the space frontier) recapitulates, on another level, the historical discourse of the other (imperial) 'frontier.' ('I would annex the planets if I could,' Cecil Rhodes often said.) The film is structured like a colonial captivity narrative: spear-carrying skeleton creatures burst from the moon's simulacral jungle and capture the explorers, only to be defeated by the male explorers' gunlike umbrellas, which magically eliminate the savage creatures. Such a film, not in any obvious sense 'about' colonialism, can thus be read as analogizing imperial expansion.

Many American films, for example *Beau Geste* (1930), filmed in Arizona but set in Morocco, praised the work of their imperial confrères in the French Foreign Legion. Between 1911 and 1962. France itself made over 200 feature films set in North Africa, many of them memorializing the exploits of the Legion against native rebels.[32] But the British especially became masters of the imperial epic, as in the Korda trilogy *Sanders of the River* (1935), *Drums* (1938) and *The Four Feathers* (1939) and in the films produced by Michael Balcon: *Rhodes of Africa* (1936), *The Great Barrier* (1936), and *King Solomon's Mines* (1937). At a time when roughly one-fourth of the human race lived under British rule, many films preferred a nostalgic look back at the 'pioneering' days of 'exploration' to a frontal examination of the quotidian brutality of latter-day imperialism.[33]

Cedric Hardwicke as Livingstone conducting an African choir in 'Onward Christian Soldiers' in *David Livingstone* (1936), Cecil Rhodes planning the Cape-to-Cairo railway before a map of Africa in *Rhodes of Africa*, Reginald Denny laying down imperial law to a native ruler in *Escape to Burma* (1955), Tarzan performing deeds of valor in the imperial service, such are the filmic epiphanies of empire. What Jeffrey Richards describes as the 'square-jawed, pipe-smoking, solar-topeed English sahib,' standing at the ramparts, scanning the horizon for signs of native restlessness, crystallized an ideal imperial figure for cinematic consumption. Actors such as Roland Colman, C. Aubrey Smith, Clive Brook, David Niven, Basil Rathbone, George

Sanders and Ray Milland incarnated heroic virtue in what amounted to a form of celuloid ancestor worship. *Rhodes of Africa*, for example, paints a hagiographic portrait of the imperial patriarch, constructed as an exemplum of foresight and benevolence. Both Korda and Balcon stress the austere stoic virtues and natural authority of the British on foreign strands. In *Sanders*, a film based on the popular Edgar Wallace series, a colonial District Commissioner (Sanders) puts down an uprising in Nigeria and brings British law and order to the River Territories. The usual colonial splitting pits the good Black Chief Bosambo (Paul Robeson) against the evil King Mofalaba. Colonialism, as incarnated by the authoritative and likeable Sanders, is portrayed as natural, eternal, beneficent. Africans themselves, meanwhile, were enlisted to enact their own caricatures. The exploits of figures like Sanders, Tarzan, and Quartermain brought home to the domestic public an idealized version of what abstract imperial theories meant 'on the ground.'

The imperial thrust of many of these films requires no subtle deciphering; it is right on the surface, often in the form of didactic forewords. *Sanders*, for example, is dedicated to the 'sailors, soldiers and merchant adventurers . . . who laid the foundations of the British Empire [and whose] work is carried on by the civil servants – the Keepers of the King's Peace.' The preface to *Rhodes of Africa* suggests that Africans themselves endorsed Rhodes' enterprise; the Matebele, we are told, regarded Sanders as 'a royal warrior, who tempered conquest with the gift of ruling.' Elsewhere imperial ideology is explicitly expressed through dialog. Colonel Williams in *Wee Willie Winkie* (1937) tells Shirley Temple: 'Beyond the pass, thousands of savages are waiting to sweep down and ravage India. It's England's duty, it's my duty, to see that this doesn't happen.' *Farewell Again* (1937) begins:

> All over the world, wherever the Union Jack is flown, men, from castle and cottage, city and village, are on duty . . . facing hardship, danger, death with only a brief glimpse of home. Each has his own joys and sorrows but a common purpose unites them – their country's service.

In such films, Britain's material interests in the imperialized world are masked by what Conrad's Marlowe would have called 'redeeming ideas': the battle against savagery (*Wee Willie Winkie*), the struggle to abolish slavery (*Killers of Kilimanjaro*, 1959), the fight against fascism (*The Sun Never Sets*, 1940).

A positive image of empire was also encoded into law. The British in particular imposed censorship provisions throughout their empire. In Trinidad, the censorship code forbade 'scenes intended to ridicule or criticise unfairly' British social life, 'White men in a state of degra-dation amidst native surroundings, or using violence towards natives, especially Chinese, negroes and Indians,' and 'equivocal situations between men of one race and girls of another race.'[34] In 1928 the Hong Kong censor told the American Consul-General that his duty was to uphold British prestige in 'a small settlement of white men on the fringe of a huge empire of Asiatics.' A United Artists agent in Hong Kong reported that banned subjects included 'armed conflict between Chinese and whites' and portrayals of 'white women in indecorous garb or positions or situations which would tend to discredit our womenfolk with the Chinese.'[35] The British censorship codes applied to global audiences, pressuring American producers to respect them. In 1928, Jason Joy warned production personnel that the British would not permit 'the portrayal of the white man and woman . . . in way that might degrade him or her in the eyes of the native, nor will they permit anything in films tending to incite the natives against the governing race.'[36] At the same time, colonial powers tried to prevent the development of rival 'native' cinemas. The growing power of Egyptian national cinema in the Arab world was perceived as troublesome by the French, leading them to form a special department 'responsible for setting up a production centre in Morocco whose official mission was to oppose the influence of Egyptian cinema.'[37]

Hollywood films also rendered service to empire by reconstructing colonial outposts in southern California. In Samuel Goldwyn's *The Real Glory* (1930), for example, soldiers of fortune and the American army quell a 'terrorist' uprising in the Philippines. Despite the US' own historical origins in anti-British revolt, Hollywood films often demonstrated as much enthusiasm for European colonialism as did the European films. Hollywood made more films than the French did about the French Foreign Legion,[38] and American films like W. S. Van Dyke's *Trader Horn* (1931) and *Stanley and Livingstone* (1939) glorified British colonialism in Africa. George Stevens' *Gunga Din* (1939), similarly, showed three heroic British soldiers battling savage Punjabis in nineteenth-century India.

Furthermore, the fact that American stars such as Spencer Tracy in *Stanley and Livingstone* and Charlton Heston in *Khartoum* (1966) played British colonial heroes virtually ensured the sympathetic identification of the Euro-American public, thus playing out on a thespian level the historical lap-dissolve by which the British-dominated imperialism of the nineteenth century faded into the US-dominated imperialism of the twentieth. In Henry Hathaway's *Lives of a Bengal Lancer* (1934), starring Gary Cooper, a handful of British officers hold back a native rebellion. The older officers are played by British actors, the younger by Americans, suggesting a kind of imperial succession. As Richards points out, Shirley Temple, the top box-office attraction in Britain and the US from 1935 to 1938, played a central role in the imperial films.[39] *Wee Willie Winkie*, based on a Kipling story, featured her as an American girl in India who learns about England's mission from her British grandfather, the commanding officer of a frontier fort. While the grandfather – a figure of British colonialism – is overly rigid, the American granddaughter is flexible and adept at mediation and at one point actually intervenes in a war to reconcile a rebel Khan to the British Raj. Thus the English–American family becomes enlisted in a kind of imperial allegory. Temple's diplomatic 'in-betweenness' reflects the historical in-betweenness of the US itself, as at once an anticolonial revolutionary power in relation to Native American and African peoples. Upon arriving in India, Temple confuses the Indians (natives in India) with American 'Indians' – committing Columbus' error, but in reverse. In a film released just two years later, *Susannah of the Mounties* (1939), she intervenes between the Royal Canadian Mounted Police and an 'Indian' tribe, suggesting the substitutability of the two kinds of 'Indian.' (Shirley Temple Black's later nomination as Ambassador to Ghana provides a further twist on this trope of substitutability.) Moreover, three of the epics of British India, *Lives of a Bengal Lancer, Four Men and a Prayer* (1938) and *Gunga Din*, were remade as Westerns, entitled respectively *Geronimo* (1940), *Fury at Furnace Creek* (1940) and *Soldiers Three* (1951). The imperial epic also provided the model for Westerns like *Santa Fe Trail* (1940) and *They Died with Their Boots on* (1941), while *Charge of the Light Brigade* (1938) was the model for *Khartoum*. Thus a kind of imperial circularity recycled the formulae of European supremacy *vis-à-vis* globally dispersed others, with the White European always retaining his or her 'positional superiority' (Edward Said's term).

The studios' predilection for spinning-globe logos also translated imperial ambition. The Lumières' location shootings of diverse 'Third World' sites, such as India, Mexico, Egypt, and Palestine, inaugurated this imperial mobility. The globe logo became associated with several studios (Universal, RKO), and with the British Korda brothers' productions, many of whose films, such as *Drums*, *The Four Feathers*, and *The Jungle Book* (1942), concerned imperial themes. The globe image symbolically evokes divine powers, since the created world implies a Creator. Later, TV news updated this trope of 'covering the world.' In the 1950s, John Cameron Swayze used the globe-trotting motif in his *Camel News Caravan* and

contemporary news programs call attention to it through their spherical-line globes and illuminated maps. Recent TV coverage of international crises generated further elaborations of
the trope. A Gulf War special, ABC's *A Line in the Sand*, had Peter Jennings walk on top of
a colorful political map of the Middle East as a setting for a pedagogical tour of the region's
history, in a 'covering' at once temporal and spatial. The North American TV commentator
literally steps on, sits on and looks down on the map, bestriding the narrow world 'like a
colossus.'[40]

In both cinema and TV, such overarching global points-of-view suture the spectator into
the omniscient cosmic perspective of the European master-subject. Incorporating images of
maps and globes, *Around the World in 80 Days*, (1956), for example, begins with its omniscient
narrator hailing the 'shrinking of the world' which occurred during the period that Verne was
writing his book. (The prelude to the film includes the mandatory globus prop made to spin for
the camera.) The idea of 'shrinking' materializes the confident, scientific perspective of upper-
class British men. 'Nothing is impossible,' says the David Niven character: 'when science finally
conquers the air it may be feasible to circle the globe in eighty hours.' Thus he implicitly links
the development of science to imperial control, an idea reinforced by the character's recurrent
association with the strains of 'Rule Britannia.' In recent science-fiction films such as *Return of
the Jedi* (1983), globality embraces spheres yet to be charted by NASA. The conquest of outer
space cohabits with an underlying imperial narrative in which the visualization of another planet
conforms to the representational paradigm of Third World 'underdevelopment.' A Manichean
struggle pits the hero against the new land and its natives. The exotic, teddy-bear-like 'Ewoks'
– whose language, as in most colonial films, remains unintelligible – worship the high-tech Euro-
American hero and defend him against repulsive, evil, irrational creatures. The hero's physical
and moral triumph legitimates the enemy's destruction and the paternal transformation of the
friendly 'elements' into servile allies, authorizing his right to establish new outposts (and implicitly to hold on to old ones). Like early adventure films, spectacular sci-fi and star-war video-
games visualize progress as a purposeful movement toward global ubiquity; if in the early films
traveling the ocean entailed no boundaries, in the recent ones the sky is no longer the limit.

Notes

1   See Jan Pieterse's chapter on 'Colonialism and Popular Culture' in his *White on Black: Images of Africa
     and Blacks in Western Popular Culture* (New Haven, CT: Yale University Press, 1992), p. 77.
2   Robert Baden-Powell, *Scouting for Boys*, quoted in Joseph Bristow, *Empire Boys: Adventures in a Man's
     World* (London: HarperCollins, 1991), p. 170.
3   Bristow, ibid., p. 19.
4   Patrick Brantlinger, *Rule of Darkness: British Literature and Imperialism 1830–1914* (Ithaca, NY: Cornell
     University Press, 1988), p. 11.
5   See John McClure, *Late Imperial Romance: Literature and Globalization from Conrad to Pynchon* (London:
     Verso, 1994).
6   Hayden White, *Tropics of Discourse* (Baltimore, Md.: Johns Hopkins University Press, 1978), p. 58.
7   Etienne Balibar writes: 'The histories of nations are presented to us in the form of a narrative which
     attributes these entities the continuity of a subject.' See Etienne Balibar and Immanuel Wallerstein,
     Race, Nation, Class: Ambiguous Identities(London: Verso, 1991), p. 86.
8   Benedict Anderson, *Imagined Communities* (New York: Verso, 1983), pp. 41–6.
9   For more on the extrapolation of Bakhtin's notion on the chronotope, see Robert Stam, *Subversive
     Pleasures: Bakhtin, Cultural Criticism, and Film* (Baltimore, MD: Johns Hopkins University Press, 1980);
     Kobena Mercer, 'Diaspora Culture and the Dialogic Imagination,' in Mbye Cham and Claire Andrade-
     Watkins (eds), *Blackframes* (Cambridge, MA: MIT, 1988a); and Paul Willemen, 'The Third Cinema

Question: Notes and Reflections,' in Jim Pines and Paul Willemen (eds), *Questions of Third Cinema* (London: BFI, 1989).

10   Movie theaters in the colonized world were at first built only in urban centers such as Cairo, Baghdad, Bombay. For early responses to the cinema in Baghdad, Ella Shohat has conducted a series of interviews with old Baghdadis from her own community, now dispersed in Israel/Palestine, England, and the US.

11   Christian Metz, 'The Imaginary Signifier,' in *The Imaginary Signifier: Psycho-analysis and the Cinema* (Bloomington: Indiana University Press, 1982), p. 51.

12   For more on the 'mobilized gaze' of the cinema, see Anne Friedberg's discussion in *Window Shopping: Cinema and the Postmodern* (Berkeley: University of California Press, 1993).

13   This photograph and the others discussed in this section can be found in Maria Hambourg, Pierre Apraxine, Malcolm Daniel, Jeff L. Rosenheim and Virginia Heckert, *The Waking Dream: Photography's First Century*, Selections from the Gilman Paper Company Collection (New York: Metropolitan Museum of Art, 1993).

14   For a critical study of anthropological discourse see for example, Talal Asad (ed.), *Anthropology and the Colonial Encounter* (Atlantic Highlands, NJ: Humanities Press, 1973); James Clifford and George Marcus (eds), *Writing Culture* (Berkeley: University of California Press, 1986); James Clifford, *The Predicament of Culture* (Cambridge, MA: Harvard University Press, 1988); Trinh T, Minh-ha, *Woman, Native, Other* (Bloomington: Indiana University Press, 1989); Edward Said, 'Representing the Colonized: Anthropology's Interlocutors,' *Critical Inquiry*, vol. 15, No. 2, pp. 205–25.

15   Jean Rouch in his critique of ethnographic filmmaking suggested that anthropologists should not observe their subject as if it were an insect but rather as if it were a 'stimulant for mutual under-standing.' See 'Camera and Man' in Mick Eaton (ed.), *Anthropology-Reality-Cinema*, (London: BFI, 1979), p.62. Ousmane Sembene, ironically, accused Rouch himself of filming Africans 'comme des insectes.' See special issue on Rouch, *Cinemaction*, No. 17 (1982).

16   For more on the question of science and spectacle, see Ella Shohat, 'Imaging Terra Incognita: The Disciplinary Gaze of Empire,' *Public Culture*, Vol. 3, No. 2 (Spring 1990), pp. 41–70.

17   Etienne-Jules Marey, a French physiologist interested in animal locomotion and in wildlife photog-raphy, called his 1882 camera a 'fusil cinématographique,' because of its gunlike apparatus, which made twelve rapid exposures on a circular glass plate that revolved like a bullet cylinder. The same notion was later trained against the colonial owners themselves in the Third Cinema notion of the 'camera gun' and 'guerilla cinema.'

18   Donna Haraway, *Primate Visions: Gender, Race, and Nature in the World of Modern Science* (New York: Routledge, 1989), p. 52.

19   Egyptians at an orientalist exposition were amazed to discover that the Egyptian pastries on sale were authentic. See Tim Mitchell, *Colonizing Egypt* (Berkeley: University of California Press, 1991), p. 10.

20   Robert W. Rydell, *All the World's a Fair* (Chicago: University of Chicago Press, 1984), p. 236.

21   Ibid.

22   See Pieterse, *White on Black*. On colonial safari as a kind of traveling mini-society see Donna Haraway, 'Teddy Bear Patriarch: Taxidermy in the Garden of Eden, New York City, 1908–1936,' *Social Text*, 11 (Winter 1984–5).

23   See Phillips Verner Bradford and Harvey Blume, *Ota Benga: The Pygmy in the Zoo* (New York: St Martins Press, 1992).

24   The African name of the 'Hottentot Venus' remains unknown, since it was never referred to by those who 'studied' her.

25   For further discussion on science and the racial/sexual body, see Sander Gilman, 'Black Bodies, White Bodies: Toward an Iconography of Female Sexuality in Late Nineteenth-Century Art, Medicine, and Literature,' *Critical Inquiry*, vol. 12, no. 1 (Autumn 1985); and in conjunction with early cinema, see Fatimah Tobing Rony, 'Those Who Squat and Those Who Sit: The Iconography of Race in the 1859 Films of Félix-Louis Regnault,' (*Camera Obscura* No. 28, 1992 (a special issue on 'Imaging Technologies, Inscribing Science,' Paula A. Treichler and Lisa Cartwright, eds).).

26   'Flower and Murie on the Dissection of a Bushwoman,' *Anthropological Review*, No. 5 (July 1867), p. 268.

27   Richard Altick, *The Shows of London* (Cambridge, Mass. and London: Harvard University Press, 1978), p. 272.

28   Stephen Jay Gould, *The Flamingo's Smile* (New York: W. W. Norton, 1985), p. 292. On a recent visit to the Musée de l'Homme, we found no traces of the Hottentot Venus; neither the official catalog, nor officials themselves, acknowledged her existence.

29   Mitchell, op. cit., p. 13.

30   The lure of the breast found its way even to the cover of a book on ethnographic cinema, Karl Heider's *Ethnographic Film* (Austin: University of Texas Press, 1976), which features a cartoon of a 'native' woman breast-feeding. Trinh T. Minh-ha's *Reassemblage* (1982), meanwhile, reflexively interrogates the focus on breasts in ethnographic cinema. The I-Max big-screen presentation *Secrets of the [Grand] Canyon* also reproduces the paradigm of Native American nudity/Euro-American dress.

31   Interestingly, Méliès' early fascination with spectacle dates back to his visits to the Egyptian Hall shows directed by Maskelyne and Cooke and devoted to fantastic spectacles.

32   For an analysis of the cinematic treatments of North Africa and the Arab world (especially in French films), see Pierre Boulanger, *Le Cinéma Colonial* (Paris: Seghers, 1975); Abdelghani Megherbi, *Les Algériens au Miroir du Cinema Colonial* (Algiers: Edns SNED, 1982; and also the section on 'Arabian Nights and Colonial Dreams,' in Richard Abel, *French Cinema: The First Wave 1915–1929* (Princeton, NJ: Princeton University Press, 1984).

33   For a survey of the British imperial films see Jeffrey Richards, *Visions of Yesterday* (London: Kegan and Paul, 1973).

34   From 'Trinidad Government Principles of Censorship Applied to Cinematographic Films,' internal circular in 1929, quoted in Ruth Vasey, 'Foreign Parts: Hollywood's Global Distribution and the Representation of Ethnicity,' *American Quarterly*, vol. 44, No. 4 (December 1992).

35   Memo to United Artists, 8 March, 1928, from the MPPDA (Motion Picture Producers and Directors of America, Inc) Archive, quoted in Vasey, 'Foreign Parts.'

36   A 1928 Resumé from the MPPDA Archive, cited by Vasey, 'Foreign Parts.'

37   Hala Salmane, Simon Hartog and David Wilson (eds), *Algerian Cinema* (London: BFI, 1976). See also Ella Shohat, 'Egypt: Cinema and Revolution,' *Critical Arts*, vol. 2, No. 4 (1983).

38   See Abel, op. cit., p. 151.

39   See Jeffrey Richards, 'Boys Own Empire,' in John M. Mackenzie (ed.), *Imperialism and Popular Culture* (Manchester: Manchester University Press, 1986.)

40   ABC's *A Line in the Sand* was broadcast on 14 January, 1991, a day before the US 'deadline' for Iraqi withdrawal from Kuwait.

PART SIX

Audiences and consumption

THIS IS THE AREA WHERE OTHER DISCIPLINARY traditions have most clearly influenced contemporary film studies. Most versions of film studies have not yet embraced the idea of analysing consumption – they still prefer to examine the notion of reading or the act of interpretation. Similarly, whereas television studies and areas of cultural studies have been raiding ethnographic methodologies for years, film studies has been relatively slow to use these methods to approach the analysis of Kuhn's 'social audience' – the actual spectators in the cinema. Research into audiences has developed, however, in three quite specific areas – all of which are represented in the readings for this part. First, there is the cultural history of the film audience in a specific period, such as the highly influential work of Miriam Hansen. This approach also inflects projects that have a stronger cultural studies orientation such as Jackie Stacey's study of female fans in the 1950s. Second, there is an 'audience studies' approach – which comes out of cultural studies' appropriations from ethnography, and in which interviews play a major role. Jaqueline Bobo's discussion of black women readers of *The Color Purple* belongs to this category.

The third location, where an interest in film audiences has long been established is, of course, the industry itself. It is routine for us to hear that a film has been recut in response to the comments of the test-screenings' audiences. It is also routine for recent accounts of the feature film industry to describe how the major producers have targeted a particular demographic, resulting in a burst of teen movies, teen/slasher movies, and so on. The first reading in this final part, Justin Wyatt's 'High Concept and Market Research: movie making by the numbers', is from his book, *High Concept: Movies and Marketing in Hollywood* (1994). (This extract has been edited for length and a very useful but detailed case study has been excised; interested readers are referred to the original source.) Wyatt outlines the influence of market research on feature film production since the 1980s, and in particular, the relation between market research techniques and the major companies' increasing reliance on the 'high concept' blockbuster. He describes how the techniques used to predict commercial success through the analysis of projected audience preferences inevitably privilege familiar genres employing 'bankable' stars. Innovative projects are, almost inevitably, difficult to generate within the model of the 'high concept' film. Wyatt presents a persuasive case as he suggests that the character of the mainstream feature film industry has been shaped by the conceptions of audiences in play, and consequently by the limitations of the techniques used to research these audiences.

Miriam Hansen, too, is interested in knowing more about movie audiences. She has written a social history of the audience for silent films in the US, and taken an approach which has exploded a number of myths about the nature of that audience and the pleasures and desires they pursued. Given what we know about the discussion of the female spectator in relation to classical Hollywood narrative, it is significant that her book *Babel and Babylon* (1994) sets out a very different account of the interests of the female consumer. In the extract from *Babel and Babylon*, she presents detailed research into the female audience for silent cinema. 'Chameleon and Catalyst: the cinema as an alternative public sphere' considers particular social audiences at particular historical junctures – immigrants, and, most adventurously, middle class women. As a public amusement women were free to attend, Hansen argues, the cinema 'opened up a space – a social space, as well as a perceptual, experiential horizon – in women's lives, whatever their marital status, age or background'. Importantly, these were spaces women could inhabit on their own, and where they could 'experience forms of collectivity different from those centering on the family'. Hansen also claims (and she develops a detailed case for this elsewhere in her book), the cinema actively 'catered to women as an audience'. She clearly recognizes the 'seeming paradox posed by the intersection of history and theory': the importance of the female audience to the industry, running hand in hand with the textual construction of an overwhelmingly masculine subjectivity. However, she uses this paradox as a means of arguing for the inadequacy of accounts that restrict themselves to 'textually constructed positions of subjectivity'. History enables her to examine 'the conditions of possibility' which mark this alternative public sphere, and outline the imaginative ways in which women responded to the possibilities provided.

Jackie Stacey's research reinforces Hansen's sense of the importance of the female audience to Hollywood, even though the period she examines is much later. Again, cultural and industrial history provides evidence of 'the feminization of the [film] spectator' as Hollywood seems to pitch itself repeatedly to the female audience. Like Hansen's, Jackie Stacey's study is empirically grounded in a history of the context of consumption for the images of Hollywood in 1940s and 1950s Britain. Unlike Hansen, however, she also has direct access to the written testimony of women whose lives made use of those images. From that testimony she draws the theme for this extract from a chapter in her book, *Star Gazing* (1994). 'Hollywood Cinema: the Great Escape' examines the reasons why women in wartime and immediate post-war Britain went to the movies, and finds the 'discourse of escapism' a significant factor.

Stacey's study involves examining the movie audience of the time, and their 'cinema-going practices'. In addition to more conventional sources of cultural history and cultural statistics, Stacey elicited 350 letters from women who wished to share their memories of the place cinema had played in their lives, as well as 238 responses to a more specific follow-up questionnaire. As a result, Stacey draws on an exceptionally rich array of research materials in order to explain to us what the Hollywood cinema meant to these women, the importance of Hollywood's images of identity and desire. A benefit of her work is that she has a body of discursive material through which to interrogate the familiar notion of 'escapism' as one of the reasons for cinema attendance. Stacey accepts this as a legitimate explanation from her correspondents, but then goes on to interrogate what this term seems to have meant in these specific historical circumstances and what purposes it seems to have served. Importantly, she does this by focusing on 'the whole cinema-going experience', not only the pleasures of the film text, arguing *inter alia* that 'the sensuous pleasures of the luxury of the cinema' contrasted with 'the material conditions of women's lives' at the time. 'Escapism', Stacey concludes, has many levels: 'material, sensuous, emotional, as well as psychic'. An exclusively textual focus in film studies will miss most of these levels by forgetting that, for the film audience, film-going is a material as well as a textual practice.

Jaqueline Bobo's study of black women's responses to Spielberg's film of Alice Walker's novel, *The Color Purple*, is in disciplinary terms a more conventional example of audience studies. In a chapter taken from *Black Women as Cultural Readers* (1995), Bobo describes how she used two focus groups of black women with whom she watched the film and discussed their responses to it as a representation of black women's lives. She argues that the politics of black women's status within a predominantly white society means that they must be highly skilled and sceptical readers of their culture, and that they are entirely used to adapting what bell hooks has called an 'oppositional gaze' in response to mainstream cinema. However, Bobo's discussion is aimed at a slightly more subtle problem than this might suggest. Her focus is upon black women who, despite much (both black and white) criticism of the film as denigratory of black experience, felt that the film did represent on balance a positive sign and who resented the widespread liberal assumption that their reading of the film would necessarily be negative. In particular, they resented white liberals or academics who assumed they knew how a black women might (or, even, should) read this film. Bobo points out the dangers of underestimating the sophistication and self-consciousness of the ways in which 'audiences (and a populace) negotiate their existence in a society not of their making but with some attempts at control'. How that process operates is admirably demonstrated in the chapter's recounting of the conversations between Bobo and her interviewees as they watched the film. Clearly these audiences actively negotiate their 'readings' as well, aided by a shrewd sense of the realpolitik within which the text itself was produced.

Marc Jancovich's essay, 'A Real Shocker: authenticity, genre and the struggle for distinction', takes its starting point from what he describes as 'the turn to audiences' within genre studies, a move which 'relieves the film theorist from the need to police the boundaries of what constitutes a genre'. Rather, he goes on, film audiences themselves 'can become involved in policing the boundaries of film genres' – although a great deal of the writing about genre has tended to underestimate the extent to which this occurs. Jancovich's project in this essay, then, is to examine one particular film audience – the fans of horror films – in order to find out more about the cultural construction of genre. He outlines horror fans' debates about the definition of the genre: its differentiation from sci-fi and its relation to high concept commercial 'slasher' movies (on the one hand), and low budget auteur-style horror films (on the other).

The survey more than amply demonstrates Jancovich's point. Film audiences are actively engaged in the construction and defence of these genres; they do not simply recognise them as a means of adopting the appropriate template for understanding the modalities of the narrative on the screen. Notions of authenticity and commercialism are called into play, resulting in lively debates over the genre status of a mainstream success such as *Scream*. Furthermore, Jancovich points out, to fully understand the relations between fans and genres, and to extrapolate from this understanding a wider sense of how audiences interpret the films they see, we need to examine 'the broader social activities associated with the consumption of particular genres'. Consumption is 'not simply about the engagement with a specific text, or even a group of texts, but about a series of different kinds of social events and activities': a date, a night in with a video, 'quality time' with the kids and so on. However, neither is film consumption without its patterns or its structures – including issues of taste, cultural status or values. When audiences 'struggle over differences' of classification, interpretation, or of genre definitions, these are engagements in a cultural politics we need, says Jancovich, to understand.

Chapter 28

JUSTIN WYATT

HIGH CONCEPT AND MARKET RESEARCH
Movie making by the numbers

ALTHOUGH MARKET RESEARCH IN THE FILM INDUSTRY can be traced back to forecasts of market demand for movies in 1915, market research did not become an integral part of the film industry until the late 1970s.[1] The development of more nuanced methods of audience analysis along with key changes in the institutional framework of the industry, aided the entrenchment of market research within the studios at that time. By the early 1980s, market research had become so integral to mainstream Hollywood film-making that every major studio devoted a significant portion of its marketing budget to market research.[2] At the current time, the market research managers and vice-presidents within the studios in turn coordinate their efforts with independent market research suppliers specializing in field work, tabulation, and coding. Together these forces have created a significant position for market research in the pre- and post-production life of a film. This position, however, is based upon a methodology which privileges high concept as a style of mainstream film-making within Hollywood and which cannot adequately account for many other forms of production. In this chapter, I will situate the relationship between market research and high concept in contemporary Hollywood, with an eye toward explaining factors which have contributed to the development of market research within the industry.

The growth of market research

Organized audience research has existed within Hollywood for several decades. Apart from studio sneak previews, independent companies, such as George Gallup's Audience Research Inc., Sindlinger & Company, and Leo Handel's Motion Picture Research Bureau, conducted studies for a number of studios from the late 1930s onward.[3] Bruce Austin attributes the development of independent movie market research suppliers to primary post-war factors: the introduction of television, which diminished the film audience, leaving the studios seeking methods to retain their audience, and the desire to appear economically responsible to Wall Street and the banking industry.[4] Market research during this period included audience response to sneak previews of films and more broad-based research detailing audience awareness of and interest in films, attendance patterns and recall of film advertising.[5]

Market research began to gain a great deal more prominence, however, in the 1970s. This new stature followed from the earlier attempts to make the film industry appear to be a logical, economic business. As the founding studio moguls died or retired, the studios were acquired by conglomerates: MCA acquired Universal in 1962, Gulf & Western, Paramount in 1966, Transamerica, United Artists in 1967 and Kinney National, Warner Bros in 1969.[6] With the number of film releases falling and costs rising, the conglomerates required more accountability on the part of their motion picture divisions; as Julie Salamon describes, 'They [the studios] needed to put together a seasonal string of "product" in an orderly way, and the corporate parents wanted to know that something besides somebody's seat-of-the-pants judgment was involved in the process. Research provided comfort to executives working in an industry where the average tenure in a high-ranking job was a couple of years.'[7] Consequently, the conglomerates were more receptive to market research techniques, with many executives familiar with the processes from packaged-goods marketing and merchandising.

The conglomerates further fostered ties between consumer advertising and film marketing through acquiring executives from the consumer research arena: for example, Jonas Rosenfeld, former Vice-President of Advertising, Promotion and Research at Twentieth Century Fox, was lured from the corporate division of Bristol-Meyers, while marketing vice-presidents Dana Lombardo at Disney and Richard Del Belso at Warner Bros both had extensive experience in research at advertising agencies.[8] The conglomerates' application of the market research methods traditionally used in consumer research was greeted by the creative community with skepticism at best, and hostility, at worst. Producer Keith Barish's response is representative of this hostility: 'As the larger and larger companies take over studios, they start treating film as a product no different than soda pop or potato chips. Same cost controls, same reporting structure, same market testing.'[9]

More significantly, a shift in the distribution pattern of film in the 1970s also aided the institutionalization of market research. As has already been established, with the success of 'four-wall' films, the major studios began to open films in saturation, as opposed to platform, releases centered on television advertising.[10] Universal's opening of *Jaws* in June 1975 was the starting point of this distribution trend, which soon increased so that an eagerly anticipated film in recent times, such as *Batman Returns* (1992), could open in 2,644 theaters at one time.[11] This distribution strategy depends upon a high level of awareness of film by the time of opening; if the film cannot open well in its first weekend, its chances for long-term success are extremely limited, since theaters will drop the film and the advertising support will be cut.[12] To build awareness and therefore the chances for a good opening, advertising through television, as opposed to print, became the norm. The increased cost of network and local TV buys over print advertising, along with the necessity to open a film immediately to a strong first weekend, sparked the interest of the studios in evaluating the efficacy of their advertising material.[13]

At the same time, market research as a field began to move beyond demographic profiles in predicting consumer behavior. In the 1960s, a school of research developed which sought to define consumers along psychological dimensions through discerning their needs, values, attitudes, and interests.[14] Referred to variously as psychographic or 'value and lifestyle' research, this method allowed audiences to be divided beyond sex, age, and education. With the additional information, consumers could be segmented into dimensions which cluster similar attributes or individuals, thereby allowing companies to market their products more specifically. Therefore, the studios were able to target specific groups through testing their television commercials and then arranging their media buys with television shows that would attract the desired audience. These two forces – the movement toward saturation campaigns based upon television advertising and the greater segmentation of the market through psycho-graphic research – fostered the widespread adoption of market research within the film industry. Consequently, market research has made a significant dent in the film industry, to a point where entertainment analyst Jeff Logsdon has recently estimated that at least 75 per cent of the top 200 films yearly are market researched in some form.[15]

The model of market research within the film industry

By the 1980s, a fairly uniform set of market research surveys had become common practice within the film industry. Of course, different studios chose to emphasize different market research functions, although in the press, most studio marketing executives stressed that market research played a minor role in the success of their films. The set of market research surveys which became instituted can be divided into those studies conducted pre-production and studies conducted post-production. As Thomas Simonet notes, pre-production studies are composed primarily of concept testing, casting tests, and title tests.[16] Concept testing involves breaking down a script into a short concept, which is then read to respondents so that the attractive (read 'marketable') elements might be identified. Similarly, casting tests are designed to identify marketable stars and the match between a star and a particular concept, while title tests gauge the connotations suggested by a particular title.

The majority of market research within the industry, however, occurs after the produc-tion has been completed. Recruited audience screenings are attended by those who have been selected to meet certain sex, age and lifestyle quotas. After the screening, audience members complete surveys describing the overall evaluation of the film, how strongly they would recom-mend the film to a friend, their description of the film, their media usage habits, and demographic (sex/age) characteristics. A subset of the audience may be retained for a focus group in which a moderator probes the survey questions in greater depth. In addition to recruited audience screenings, post-production market research also includes testing adver-tising material, such as print ads, trailers, and television commercials. These tests are designed to evaluate the interest and image created for the film by the advertising material.[17]

This model of market research is somewhat problematic from both a methodological and an analytical perspective. In particular, the pre-production market research has received crit-icism for being prescriptive: for dictating creative decisions based upon a quantitative score or set of scores. The post-production market research has been judged less harshly, since this research is more evaluative of a finished product for marketing purposes, rather than prescrip-tive for an evolving product.

Considering the pre-production research, perhaps the most significant methodological prob-lem is the inability to account for innovative film concepts, or as a veteran marketing consultant comments, 'anything that is innovative is hard for market research to clue in on.'[18] Consequently movies which adhere strictly to genre tend to be more attractive in concept form than films which might be described as cross-genre or outside genre. Therefore, a romantic comedy, such as *Pretty Woman*, would be easier to concept test than the comedy/family drama *Avalon*, whose cross-genre storyline would be almost impossible to reduce to a concept. The implications of this factor for high concept are clear: high concept, adhering closely to genre and previous suc-cesses offers an immediate reference point for the respondent. Therefore, high concept films would probably test higher in concept form than low concept films, other factors held constant.

In addition, another limitation in the pre-production research involves the difficulty of expressing the visual or aural nature of the medium. Films which are heavily dependent upon striking visuals, such as *Blade Runner*, *The Hunger* and *One from the Heart*, or upon their sound-tracks, such as *Purple Rain*, *Flashdance* and *Something Wild* (1986), cannot be conveyed accurately through a marketing concept. Consider for instance, a possible concept for *Purple Rain*: 'Purple Rain is a dramatic musical, starring Prince, featuring eight new Prince songs shot in music-video style.' While all these claims are true, the concept, through its form, fails to convey the music and visual style of the film. A respondent listening to the concept would indicate interest based primarily on the appeal of Prince, rather than on the film. Similarly, casting tests tend to privilege stars within their familiar genre. Concept testing responds mainly to star-driven projects, and high concept, which often relies on stars as a form of insurance, fits neatly with this paradigm.

Partly to compensate for these limitations, market researchers often resort to a rhetoric which poses another set of problems. The rhetoric of market research is centered to a certain extent around hyperbole. These concepts might link the film to be tested to past successes of the same genre. For example, the firefighter film *Backdraft* (1991) could be positioned in a concept as 'an incredibly exciting, death-defying drama in the tradition of *The Towering Inferno*.' An interest level of the film based on this concept would be biased, since the respondent would be making the equation between *Backdraft* and *The Towering Inferno*; interest in the new film would be based largely upon assuming that the two films are equivalent, which, of course, may be an incorrect assumption.

The choice of adjectives in a concept description also can affect the interest level: for example, in positioning the film as an adventure, *Backdraft* could be presented as 'suspenseful,' 'intense,' or 'the most thrilling adventure of your lifetime.' The market researchers cannot discern the extent to which interest is due to the basic storyline and, more significantly, the extent to which the wording of the concept has altered basic interest. This error in measurement has been noted by the studios: as reported in an article about leading film and television market researcher Joseph Farrell, '"Joe was off in forecasting *The Rocketeer* (1991), because, when presented to the public, it was compared to *Raiders of the Lost Ark*," recalls one marketing executive. "This summer's (1992) *Cool World* was described as continuing where *Roger Rabbit* takes off." That's "advertising," not "concept."'[19]

Although post-production research involving recruited audience screenings is more widely accepted within the industry, these surveys also remain problematic in terms of method. One of the main difficulties with audience screenings as a method to extrapolate future success involves sampling: following the basic tenet of statistical analysis, the market researchers select a sample of moviegoers to represent the general population of moviegoers.[20] One major difficulty with this process is deciding on the characteristics of the general population of movie-goers: in particular, whether this general population is, in fact, an abstract target audience which the film-makers have designed the film for, or is more representative of the spectrum of movie-goers.[21] The issue of sampling becomes even thornier considering that audience members at the screening are not just differentiated by sex and age, which target audiences are often defined by, but also by geographical location, income level, and educational background.[22] Extrapolation of the recruited audience research results beyond the limited audience sample at the screening becomes a precarious endeavor due to these inherent sampling problems.

These limitations in method historically have worked in conjunction with the increasing conglomeration of the film industry to privilege the high concept film whose economic risk is minimized through emphasizing the familiar over the original.[23] The economic appeal of the high concept film is based upon the immediate point of reference for the audience; as Tom Pollock, chairman of the MCA motion picture group, states, 'The reason studios make them [blockbusters] is because of marketing. They have instant identity.'[24] This instant identity strongly facilitates market research which, as a method, inherently favors those films which the respondent can compare to previous familiar films. Therefore, the movement toward the 'packaging' of films within the past two decades correlates with the encroachment of market research; the strong argument would be that market research has, in some sense, shaped and certainly has furthered high concept film-making. [. . .]

Factors influencing the decline of market research

[. . .] The alignment between market research and the film industry which has developed over the past two decades may be faltering, however. The adjustment in this relationship seems due to two principal factors: the movement away from the high concept syndrome and the development of the baby boom generation as an audience force. The lessening of Hollywood's emphasis on the high concept film derives in part from increasing cost in producing and marketing these films. According to the MPAA, the average film budget rose to $26.8 million in 1990, up from $18 million in 1988.[25] This increase has been driven by the escalating cost of the high concept films reliant on big starts, large-scale productions and pre-sold properties. Consider that in 1990 alone, *Total Recall* cost $60 million, with an additional $35 million in advertising costs, *Die Hard 2* also cost approximately $60 million, with $30 million in ad costs, and *Days of Thunder* was only slightly less expensive at $50 million, with $27 million in ad costs.[26] As the costs increase, these films are also rushed into distribution to save on interest payments. For example, in order to recoup its cost as soon as possible, *Days of Thunder* was released only five months after the beginning of principal photography.[27]

Just as significantly, production cost increases for the high concept films have been met with dramatic increases in advertising and marketing costs. With studios spending $50–60 million on a large-scale film, insurance for a substantial recoupment is available in advertising which establishes and reinforces the image of the film. In the past decade, television advertising has accounted for 60–70 per cent of total advertising expenditures, with key buys being commercials during primetime on the midweek evenings prior to a weekend opening.[28] Television networks have been sharply escalating rates to the studios, or as Fox marketing and distribution chairman Tom Sherak comments, 'Thursday night is a big night to spend money, if your picture comes out the next day, and the TV companies make us pay for that.'[29] Indeed, in 1990, the average movie marketing cost of major studio releases jumped 20 per cent over 1989, to an average of $26 million per film.[30]

The phenomenal increase in production and marketing costs for these commercial films has created a climate in which films such as *Dick Tracy*, grossing $104 million, and *Batman*, grossing $253 million, have failed to break even in domestic theatrical release.[31] The apparent decline of high concept became particularly evident to the studios in 1990 with the simultaneous failure of several big-budget, action-oriented sequels (*RoboCop II*, *Rocky V*, *Another 48 HRS.*) and star-power films (*Days of Thunder*, *Havana*, *Air America*). At least in the press, the studio executives have been distancing themselves from the high concept films as the staple of their production schedule. Typical of the response is Disney chairman Jeffrey Katzenberg's widely circulated memo titled 'The World is Changing: Some Thoughts on Our Business,' in which he describes the industry as facing a period of great danger and uncertainty.[32] Responding to the increasing unprofitability of the big-budget blockbusters and, in particular to *Dick Tracy* as an example of this phenomenon, Katzenberg concludes, 'We should now take a long and hard look at the blockbuster business . . . and get out of it.'[33]

As an alternative to the high concept films, Katzenberg and other executives frequently cite a need for original, inventive stories as a focus rather than large productions, stars and pre-sold properties; as Katzenberg comments, 'We must not be distracted from one fundamental concept: the idea is king.'[34] The role of market research in this process is more problematic, however. While market research can gauge the audience interest in the high concept films of identifiable stars, properties and genre allegiance, this method cannot adequately account for film narratives which lie outside existing boundaries. Therefore, in shifting the focus to 'original' stories, the industry is simultaneously decreasing the role which market research might play in the film-making process. Indeed, even in the memo, Katzenberg emphasizes that market research, which carries the aura of 'science,' should not dictate creative decisions since 'there is nothing scientific about the movie business.'[35]

To exacerbate this shift away from market research, the composition of the filmgoing audience targeted by market research has also been changing. The evolving age distribution of the population, given the growth of the baby boomers, has produced a society with increasing consumer affluence: for example, the household incomes of baby boomers will grow 56 per cent by the year 2000, compared to only 5 per cent for those under thirty-five years of age.[36] In addition, as the baby boomers and their families mature, leisure time will grow, especially as their children age and begin to leave home.[37] The effects of these demographic changes have been experienced already within the film industry. Whereas during the past two decades Hollywood focused primarily on the youth market, the filmgoing audience had been maturing during this period. Consider, from 1984 to 1989, that filmgoers aged twelve to twenty-four dropped from 54 per cent to 44 per cent as a proportion of total theatrical admissions, while filmgoers aged twenty-five to forty-nine increased from 39 per cent to 46 per cent. More significantly, in 1990, the over-forty audience jumped 24 per cent, while the under-twenty-one audience dropped 4 per cent from the previous year.[38]

This shift in audience demography has created some unexpected trends in popular films. First, as the baby boomers with children become increasingly critical to industry success, films which appeal to *both* adults and their children have become more popular: for instance, the Spielberg/Lucas adventures, *Three Men and a Baby*, *Look Who's Talking*, the new Disney cartoons (*The Little Mermaid* (1989), *Beauty and the Beast* (1991), *Aladdin* (1992)) and most strikingly *Home Alone*.[39] In addition, this adjustment in demographics has been met with a number of box office successes whose appeal has been decidedly adult: *Dangerous Liaisons* (1988), *The War of the Roses* (1989), *Parenthood* (1989), *Driving Miss Daisy* (1989) and *Thelma and Louise* (1991). These successes largely fall outside the domain of market research, however. The lack of adherence to genre, pre-sold properties, and star power creates films which cannot be encapsulized in market research concepts.

Consequently, executives have been forced to reevaluate their traditional market research approaches; as Arthur Cohen, President of Worldwide Marketing at Paramount Pictures, describes, 'Contemporary moviegoers are now a very educated populace. They're more sophisticated, so marketing becomes a more intricate task.'[40] Implicit in Cohen's statement is an understanding that the older baby boom generation filmgoers are more resistant to persuasion and therefore more resistant to film marketing as an enterprise.[41] The younger moviegoers can also be targeted with more precision. Indeed, a study by Dennis Tootelian and Ralph Gaedeke of teens across the western United States demonstrated that television was by far the most important source of information for move and entertainment choices.[42] As movie marketing consultant Ira Deutchman summarizes, '[The adult audience] is not as easy to target as a youth audience.'[43] The more mature audience segment is also less predictable in terms of film preference compared to the youth market, choosing to attend films on a situational rather than regular basis. All these qualities of the baby boom audience members – the greater sophistication in filmgoing, the higher resistance to marketing, and the unpredictability of attendance – serve to undermine further the usefulness of market research as a tool for the film industry.

The marriage between market research and the film industry may be in decline, therefore, given the shift away from the market research – ready high concept productions and the movement toward adult-oriented films which cannot be reduced effectively to the rhetoric of market research. While market research will continue to serve a certain style of mainstream Hollywood film-making, the limitations of the methods, which privilege the familiar over the original, may prove to be increasingly unsatisfactory to Hollywood. If Hollywood continues to focus attention on the adult-oriented films, for which audience demographics make a strong case, more and more studio executives may react to market research as has former Twentieth Century Fox chairman Joe Roth. In an impassioned speech, Roth vowed that his studio will completely break with a heavy reliance on research or, as he kindly referred to the market researchers, 'the voodoo makers' of the film industry.[44]

Notes

1   Bordwell, Staiger and Thompson, *The Classical Hollywood Cinema* 144.
2   Hy Hollinger, 'Hollywood's View of Research Depends on Just Who's Being Asked, What Methods are Used,' *Variety*, 12 January, 1983: 36
3   Janet Staiger, 'Announcing Wares, Winning Patrons, Voicing Ideals: Thinking about the History and Theory of Film Advertising,' *Cinema Journal 29*, no. 3 (1990): 18.
4   Bruce A. Austin, *Immediate Seating: A Look at Movie Audiences* (Belmont Calif: Wadsworth Publishing Company, 1989) 5.
5   Hollinger, op. cit., 36
6   Gregg Kilday, 'Two or Three Things We Know About . . . The Eighties,' *Film Comment*, November/December 1989: 60
7   Julie Salamon, *The Devil's Candy* (Boston: Houghton Mifflin Company, (1991) 365.
8   'Del Belso at WB,' *Variety*, 27 February, 1980: 45.
9   Peter J. Boyer, 'Risky Business,' *American Film*, January/February 1984: 14.
10   Kahn, 'The Day Film Marketing Came of Age' 38.
11   Anne Thompson, 'Reporting the Numbers,' *LA Weekly*, 24 July, 1992: 29.
12   As Thompson notes, a studio reporting box office figures to *Variety* or *The Hollywood Reporter* may actually be reporting number of theaters, not number of screens. Thompson claims, therefore, that *Batman Returns*, for example, opened on 3,600 screens in 2,644 theaters. Consequently, the necessity for a solid opening becomes even more pressing, since the studio is actually supporting more seats through playing on more than one screen in some multiplexes.
13   For an analysis of platform vs. Saturation release strategies and the accompanying advertising costs, see Lee Beaupre and Ann Thompson, 'Eighth Annual Grosses Gloss,' *Film Comment*, March/April 1983: 68.
14   Steven Knapp and Barry L. Sherman, 'Motion Picture Attendance: A Market Segmentation Approach,' *Current Research in Film: Audiences, Economics, and Law*, vol. 2, Bruce A. Austin (ed.) (Norwood, NJ: Ablex Publishing Corporation, (1986) 35–6.
15   Neal Koch, 'She Lives! She Dies! Let the Audience Decide,' *New York Times*, April 19, 1992: H11.
16   Thomas Simonet, 'Market Research: Beyond the Fanny of the Cohn,' *Film Comment*, January/February 1980: 68.
17   Ibid., 69.
18   Hollinger, op. cit., 36.
19   Elaine Dutka, 'The Man Who Makes You King,' *Los Angeles Times*, 12 July, 1992: Calendar section, 86.
20   Caryn James, 'Test Screenings of new Movies Put Demographics over Creativity,' *New York Times*, 9 March, 1988: C17.

21   As a perfect example of this problem, James describes a sneak preview of *Made in Heaven* in which the market researchers told director Alan Rudolph, 'Remember, you have to reach every dummy in the audience.' To which Rudolph replied, 'Why not get a more intelligent audience?'

22   In addition, there is a certain bias introduced by showing the movie free of charge; the audience has an incentive to be more forgiving than if they had paid for the film.

23   Thomas Simonet, 'Conglomerates and Content: Remakes Sequels, and Series in the New Hollywood.' *Current Research in Film: Audiences, Economics, and Law*, vol. 3, Bruce A. Austin (ed.) (Norwood, NJ: Ablex Publishing Corporation, 1987) 154.

24   Pat H. Broeske, 'Hollywood's '91 Focus: A Good Story,' *Los Angeles Times*, 8 January, 1991: F12.

25   Broeske, op. cit., F12.

26   Charles Fleming, 'Pitching Costs out of Control,' *Variety*, 27 June, 1990: 1

27   Lawrence Cohn, 'MegaPix for '91 Late to Gate,' *Variety*, 11 July 1990: 85.

28   Fleming, 'Pitching Costs' 29.

29   Ibid.

30   Marcy Magiera, 'Disney Adds to Tie-ins,' *Advertising Age*, February 11, 1991: 5.

31   Claudia Eller, '"Tracy" Cost Put at $101mil,' *Variety*, 22 October, 1990: 3.

32   Jeffrey Katzenberg, 'The World is Changing: Some Thoughts on Our Business,' reprinted in *Variety*, 31 January, 1991: 18+.

33   Ibid. 19.

34   Ibid.

35   Ibid.

36   Leo Bogart, 'What Forces Shape the Future of Advertising Research?' *Journal of Advertising Research*, February/March 1986: 100.

37   Judith Waldrop, 'The Baby Boom Turns 45,' *American Demographics*, January 1991: 2.

38   Betsy Sharkey, 'Spotlight on Entertainment,' *Adweek*, 18 March, 1991: 33.

39   Joseph Helgot, Michael Shwartz, Frank Romo and Jaime Korman, 'Aging Baby Boomers and Declining Leisure-Time: Strategic Implications for the Movie Industry,' MarketCast Reports, 1988.

40   Sharkey, op. cit., 32.

41   Marcy Magiera, 'Madison Avenue Hits Hollywood,' *Advertising Age*, 10 December, 1990: 24.

42   Dennis H. Tootelian and Ralph M. Gaedeke, 'The Teen Market: An Exploratory Analysis of Income, Spending, and Shopping Patterns,' *Journal of Consumer Marketing* 9.4 (Fall 1992): 38.

43   Gold, op. cit., 4.

44   Robert March, 'Roth: Instincts, Not Voodoo, Key to Future Fox Films,' *Hollywood Reporter* 21 February, 1990: 1.

Chapter 29

MIRIAM HANSEN

CHAMELEON AND CATALYST
The cinema as an alternative public sphere

IN THE PREVIOUS CHAPTER I TRACED the emergence of spectatorship as a *normative process* – in the codification of a mode of narration that absorbs empirical viewers into textually constructed positions of subjectivity, in the historical convergence of social and economic objectives and stylistic strategies. In the following, I will turn around and trace a countercurrent, emphasizing a margin that remains between the *ideal* of spectatorship operative in production and the social and cultural forms of reception. Accordingly, I will resume an argument suggested in Chapter 1 [of original publication]: that early cinema, because of its paradigmatically different organization of the relations of reception, provided the *formal* conditions for an alternative public sphere, a *structural* possibility of articulating experience in a communicative, relatively autonomous form. I believe that something of that order persisted even after the classical codes were elaborated and the textual inscription of the spectator had become standard practice – that there remained a significant margin between textually constructed molds of subjectivity and their actualization on the part of the historical viewers.

The first section of this chapter explores the conditions of cinematic reception in terms of theater experience, as a category that has been neglected by the theoretical preoccupation with the ways in which spectatorial subject is positioned through both textual strategies and the psycho-perceptual parameters of the cinema as apparatus. Although my discussion focuses on the transitional period – the decade between 1907 and 1917 – occasionally it slips beyond that historical boundary, when, in terms of the filmic text, classical modes of narration and address were more or less fully in place. Similarly, the last two sections consider particular social audiences at particular historical junctures, yet my argument has theoretical implications for other formations of spectatorship as well, and perhaps for an alternative conception of spectatorship in general. The slippage between historical and theoretical considerations, however, is not just a methodological problem, it marks the heuristic advantage, indeed the critical edge of conceptualizing the cinema in terms of the transformation of the public sphere.

The argument about early cinema as an alternative public sphere remains to some extent a theoretical construct, derived from the formal parameters of the film-viewing experience and a critical stance toward later, dominant forms of reception. To recall Negt and Kluge, even if there were no empirical traces of autonomous public formations, they could be inferred from the force of negation, from hegemonic efforts to suppress or assimilate any conditions that might allow for an alternative (self-regulated, locally, and socially specific) organization of experience. Such efforts are amply documented for the cinema – in the industrial strate-gies aimed at standardizing reception, such as the elimination and subordination of nonfilmic activities and the stylistic integration of narratorial agency into the film as finished product and mass-marketed commodity.

Yet in what sense can the relations of reception thus negated be called *alternative* – especially if the spectators of early cinema (in the context of vaudeville shows) were predom-inantly middle class? For one thing, as indicated at the end of Chapter 1, that assumption is itself questionable, since it is based on an economic definition of class and ignores the social and ideological dynamic of vaudeville as an institution. While the more advanced entrepreneurs promoted middle-class standards of propriety, vaudeville might still have offered a public horizon for the psychic and cultural scars of upward mobility and Americanization.[1] The ques-tion therefore needs to be modified: alternative *for whom* and at which historical juncture, in relation to which configurations of experience? Which social groups were likely to benefit from the type of public sphere that opened up with the cinema and, by the same token, became the occasion for its containment and transformation?

I share the perspective of social historians such as Roy Rosenzweig, Elizabeth Ewen and Kathy Peiss, who have explored the significance of the cinema for social groups whose experience was repressed, fragmented or alienated in systematic ways – the recently urbanized working class, new immigrants, and, overlapping with terms of class and ethnicity, women.[2] These groups had either no access to existing institutions of public life or, in the case of women, only in a highly regulated and dependent form, they had not previously been considered an audience in the sense of a 'viewing public.' The significance of the cinema for these groups emerges in relation to their exclusion from dominant formations of public discourse and their displacement – whether by migration, industrialization, urbanization or the growing cult of consumption – from older traditions of working-class, ethnic or gender-specific culture. At less expense than the main-stream commercial entertainments, the cinema offered an horizon that made it possible to nego-tiate the historical experience of displacement in a new social form – even though its own institutional development enhanced the very process of displacement.

If, as I think, the cinema allowed for the public recognition of concrete needs, conflicts, anxieties, memories and fantasies on the part of particular social groups, this does not mean to assume an identity of interests between the industry and those groups, let alone impute an inherently democratic quality to the capitalist market model. Rather, if an alternative forma-tion of spectatorship can be claimed, it existed both *because of* and *despite* the economic mechanisms upon which the cinema was founded, its status as an industrial-commercial public sphere. To resume Negt and Kluge's argument, as an immediate branch of capitalist produc-tion and consumption, this new type of public sphere no longer pretended, like the bourgeois model, to a separate sphere above the marketplace. Unlike the latter, which tended toward exclusion and abstraction of large parts of social experience, the industrial-commercial public spheres were, above all, indiscriminately *inclusive*. They seized upon hitherto unrepresented discourses of experience as their raw material, if only to appropriate them – as commodity – and render them politically ineffective. Yet, with neither a legitimation ideology nor experi-ential substance of their own, the industrial-commercial public spheres grafted themselves onto older forms of cultural practice, creating an unstable mixture which, for particular constituencies under particular circumstances, could produce the conditions of an alternative public sphere.

If such conditions took shape during the founding phase of the cinema, it was because of it voracious intertextuality, its dependence – for subject matter, genres, and modes of repre-sentation – upon popular entertainments and the fragments of bourgeois culture, and because of its indiscriminate appeal to as yet untapped audiences. A graphic example of this opportunistic mixture is *The Corbett–Fitzsimmons Fight*, described in my Introduction. The film's amazing success with women was to a large extent accidental, resulting from the temporary overlap of different types of public sphere: the homosocial world of late-nineteenth-century popular entertainments, and the maximally inclusive and homogenizing, specularized world of mass culture. As a moment in the history of consumer culture the incident is ambiguous, considering that less than three decades later the display of Valentino's naked torso was to become a calculated ingredient in packaging the star for his female fans. As a moment in the history of the public sphere, however, the accidental transgression of the homosocial taboo functions as a critique of the gendered delimitations of public and private, suggesting that women might be able to organize their experience in other matters as well.

Whatever autonomous formations emerged in the cinema in the following decades, they did so as a historical by-product of retrospectively more systematic processes – in the seams and fissures of institutional development. This argument seems particularly relevant with regard to the political quandary surrounding the nickelodeon. Rather than pinning the question on the class make-up of its audiences or the thematic and representational make-up of the films, the alternative potential of the nickelodeon could be described as an accidental effect of overlapping types of public sphere, of 'nonsynchronous' layers of cultural organization.[3] This nonsynchronism seems to characterize both the cinema's parasitic relationship to existing cultural traditions and, within the emerging institution, the uneven development of modes of production, distribution and exhibition.

Thus, while new methods of distribution (through a rental system of exchanges) provided the bases for circulating films on a mass-market scale, film-making during the first few years of the nickelodeon boom 'remained a cottage industry.'[4] More important, while the product could be multiplied like other mass-manufactured goods, the mode of exhibition predominant in the nickelodeons lagged behind this technological-economic standard by continuing the presentational practices of early cinema and a concomitant organisation of the relations of reception.

Theater experience versus film experience

Early film-viewers relations differed from the classical model on the stylistic level and in the mode of exhibition. It is a mark of early cinema's specificity that its effects on the viewer were determined less by the film itself than by the particular act of exhibition, the situation of reception. The variety format not only inhibited any prolonged absorption into the fictional world on screen, but the alternation of films and non-filmic acts preserved a perceptual continuum between fictional space and theater space. A sense of theatrical presence was also maintained by non-filmic activities that accompanied the projected moving image and were essential to its meaning and effect upon the viewer – lectures, sound effects, and, above all, live music. Such exhibition practices lent the show the immediacy and singularity of a one-time performance, as opposed to an event that was repeated in more or less the same fashion everywhere and whenever the films were shown. Hence the meanings transacted were contingent upon *local* conditions and constellations, leaving reception at the mercy of relatively *unpredictable*, aleatory processes.

Likewise, early film-spectator relations were characterized by a *social* dimension found later only in a diminished form. Obviously certain conventions, such as sing-alongs and amateur nights, encouraged a display of collectivity which, in retrospective accounts, became a nostalgic counterimage to the isolation endemic to the classical apparatus. Yet the term 'social' here refers not merely to the ad hoc viewing collective but also to the relation between the films and a particular social horizon of reception. This horizon was mobilized, for instance, by narrative films that depended on the audience's familiarity with the story (see *Uncle Tom's Cabin*) or, as in the case of *The 'Teddy' Bears*, invoked such familiarity only to defamiliarize it, thus drawing attention to the contradictory construction of the public sphere. Whether by virtue of its pronounced intertextuality or its greater dependence upon the situation of exhibition, early cinema advanced a more open relationship with the arena of public discourse surrounding it; this in turn allowed that discourse to be contested and interpreted in alternative ways.

The paradigmatically different organization of early cinema's relations of reception, its emphasis on theatrical presence and local variability, persisted well into the nickelodeon period. It thus briefly came to serve a more class-specific clientele than it had in the vaudeville theaters – audiences who were economically excluded from the mainstream culture of leisure and consumption and who brought their own traditions, needs and configurations of experience to the motion picture shows. Without the middle-class veneer it had acquired in vaudeville (at least in the institutionally most advanced, gentrified type of vaudeville), the variety format, in tendency, reverted to its plebeian lineage, notably in the variety theater, the circus and the road show. In this nonsynchronous mixture, the nickelodeon offered structural conditions around which older forms of working-class and ethnic culture could crystallize and responses to social pressures, individual displacement, and alienation could be articulated in a communal setting.

The relative autonomy of the nickelodeon from both a genteel high culture and the 'big-time' entertainment market was short-lived and precarious. This could be seen, on the level of filmic representation, in the dynamic of recognition and appropriation of immigrant working-class experience in the Ghetto films, in the dual address of both nickelodeon and 'new' audiences. Film production soon began to catch up with the demands of mass-cultural distribution. It adopted industrial methods of production and developed strategies of narration and address designed to reach the widest possible audience.[5] Exhibition practices, however, remained an area of considerable conflict, testifying to the potential of the cinema as an alternative public sphere. The first major attack of the antifilm forces in New York in December 1908 did not resort to confiscating reels of film but to closing the theaters, denying the physical space of the social and cultural formation that eluded hegemonic control. Subsequent campaigns by the trade press to eliminate non-filmic activities like 'cheap' vaudeville and sing-alongs were unmistakably directed against manifestations of class and ethnicity. The problem with such activities was not just their content but that they encouraged modes of spectatorial behavior which deviated from middle-class standards of reception – a more participatory, sound-intensive form of response, an active sociability, a connection with the other viewer.

The struggle over the way films were to be received echoed the wide-scale transformation of audience behavior that had been promoted since the mid-nineteenth century – in theaters, opera houses, concert halls, and museums. Prior to this transformation, audiences in both Europe and the US had a sense of themselves as a public gathering, an 'active force' (Richard Sennett) witnessing and participating in the performance. By the beginning of the twentieth century, Lawrence Levine writes, audiences in all areas (with the exception of sports and religion) 'had become less interactive, less of a public and more of a group of mute receptors', they had been privatized, converted 'into a collection of people reacting *individually* rather than collectively.' Throughout the process of transformation, the 'discipline of silence' functioned as an instrument of class segregation. As Richard Sennett observes, 'restraint of emotion in the theater became a way for middle-class audiences to mark the line between themselves and the working-class.'[6] The same principle can be seen at work in the very institutions of popular entertainment that had been segregated in the name of high culture. For the pioneers of vaudeville gentrification in the 1880s and 1890s, subduing the 'gallery gods' was a major step toward middle-class propriety. Nonetheless, working-class norms of conviviality and expressivity persisted in cheap commercial entertainments such as ethnic theater and ethnic vaudeville and, with much of the same clientele, in the nickelodeons.[7] The implementation of the rule of silence in the motion picture shows not only imposed a middle-class standard of spectatorship, by suppressing a locally and regionally specific linguistic environment – foreign languages, accents, dialects – it contributed to the cultural homogenization of a mass audience.

It could be argued that the guiding interest in eliminating non-filmic activities was the logic of classical codification, whether in the name of narrative clarity and compositional unity (Bordwell, Thompson) or the 'linearization of the visual signifier' (Burch), and that the suppression of these activities was directed not so much *against* a public sphere of class and ethnic specificity but rather *toward* the creation of a larger mass-cultural audience that submerged all social distinctions under the banner of middle-class values and standards of respectability. From the perspective of institutional development this argument is no doubt cogent, but in terms of the politics of the public sphere the development appears somewhat less providential. For not all nonfilmic activities were of the same class, as it were, nor did they all disappear at the same time and for the same reasons. On the contrary, while 'cheap' vaudeville acts and sing-alongs were ostracized for their plebeian implications, other devices were claimed by the discourse of uplift, and even became part of the ambition to create more complex yet generally accessible narratives.[8]

A case in point is the revival of the on-stage film lecturer around 1908–9. A direct descendent of the lanternist and initially identical with the film exhibitor, the lecturer was a staple of early film shows. In this tradition the lecturer was associated with genres like travelogues, scenics, topicals, and actualities, which by 1907 had sharply declined in favor of fictional narratives. Similarly, the lecturer had become a somewhat rare asset with the rise of the story film and the beginning of the nickelodeon boom. Yet, at the same time, the lecturer came to symbolize claims asserting the educational value of the medium, in keeping with a middle-class discourse of uplift. The reintroduction of the lecturer toward the end of 1908 thus served as a strategy in the fight against censorship and for respectability, most notably after the Mayor of new York made Sunday film showings contingent upon *their* 'illustrating lectures of an instructional or educational character.'[9]

There were other reasons for the revival of the lecturer, of which the bid for respectability was only one facet. The live commentary accompanying the projection of a film actually became part of the elaboration of classical narrative, a temporary solution to problems eventually resolved in a more stable and efficient manner by classical codification. Like other sound devices that supplemented the dramatic illusion on screen (such as the dubbing in of dialogue by actors behind the screen), the lecturer was considered an important means to accomplish fundamentally classical goals: narrative clarity and legibility, 'totality of effect,' absorption of the spectator. This supplementary function of the lecturer, Tom Gunning points out, was quite different from his earlier incarnation. 'The lecturer's new role consisted in aiding spectator comprehension of, and involvement with, the more complex stories,' a complexity that came with production aspiring to the status of the bourgeois drama and novel. His role was 'to *narrate* rather than hype the film as the first lecturers had done.'[10] In this proto-classical conception, the lecturer not only integrated the narration but, by the same logic, was supposed to integrate audience response as well. W. Stephen Bush, a professional lecturer writing for *The Moving Picture World*, recommends the use of 'The Human Voice' as a strategy of crowd control, as a means to suppress and channel the very discourse that made the nickelodeon an alternative public sphere:

> As the story progresses, and even at its very beginning, those gifted with a little imagi-
> nation and the power of speech will begin to comment, to talk more or less excit-
> edly and try to explain and tell their friends or neighbors. This current of mental
> electricity will run up and down, *wild, irregular, uncontrollable*. The gifted lecturer
> will gather up and *harness* this current of expressed thought. He has seen the picture
> before, and convincing the audience from the start that he has the subject well in hand,
> all these *errant sparks* will fly toward him, the *buzz and idle comment* will cease, and he
> finds himself without an effort, the spokesman for the particular crowd of human
> beings that make up his audience.[11]

While Bush's emphasis on the lecturer's cultural authority resonates with the discourse of uplift, the metaphor of electric energy points forward to the classical construction of the spectator – as a process in which the empirical viewer surrenders his or her experience to the homogenized subjectivity on screen, as if it were merely a more efficient expression of the same energy.

Yet, Noël Burch argues that, even though the lecturer was temporarily claimed by the forces of linearization, his function remained that of a supplement, adding a layer of signifi-cation external to the visual representation. Paradoxically, while aiming to clarify the narrative and enhance the viewer's absorption, the lecturer effectively undermined an emerging sense of dietetic illusion; the presence of a human voice invited closure of the fictional world on screen and thus the perceptual segregation from theater space essential to the diegetic effect.[12] It is no coincidence that Frank Woods, the first theorist of the classical diegesis, had no use for the lecturer in his recommendations toward greater 'realism.' Woods anticipated a mode of narration in which the lecturer's function would be integrated with the diegetic process in the film itself.

If the lecturer eventually followed other nonfilmic activities into oblivion, it was not just because of an undoubtedly operative tendency of linearization, but because he remained adjunct to a particular show, a live performance, the local sphere of exhibition. Whether he sailed under the flag of uplift or that of narrative effect, the lecturer represented an *interpretive agency* that was both more influential and less predictable than the piano player or sound-effects personnel. During the early teens attempts were made to circumscribe this agency. Marcus Loew's theater chain set up a staff of lecturers to cover the country, to circulate with partic-ular films; production companies sent out copy to standardize the commentary as much as possible. But such efforts were soon abandoned – as was the lecturer. By definition, the lecturer eluded the methods of mass distribution because his success depended upon inter-action with local and particular audiences – upon rhetorical skills and personal involvement, upon professional experience and familiarity with the situation of reception. It is in this tradi-tion of individual showmanship that the institution survived in certain pockets of film culture. As late as 1920 the *New York Times Magazine* reports on five 'professors' still active on the Lower East Side, in theaters catering to audiences on the threshold of Americanization. Delivered in the 'Yankee' language, the address of these lectures seems to have been as Janus-faced as that of the Ghetto films – promoting integration, while thriving on memories of ethnic difference: 'Now and then the voice coming through the megaphone drops a Yiddish phrase, and then there are wide manifestations of delight.'[13]

The ambiguous reappearances of the lecturer have to be understood in a larger context – that of the struggle for control over the film's reception between national production and distribution companies on the one hand and local exhibitors on the other. As Charles Musser has shown, early exhibitors exerted considerable influence over the meaning of films by determining the selection and sequence of scenes and the general shape of their program. The influence was curtailed with the downgrading of the exhibitor's function to that of a projectionist and the differentiation between projectionist and theater owner. The industry's growth and stabilization seemed to mandate a concentration of meaning within the film as product and commodity, and thus its increased independence from the sphere of exhibition. Developments concurrent with the elaboration of classical codes, such as the reduction of a primitive diversity of genres, the gentrification of exhibition and the introduction of the feature film, were not simply aimed at upgrading and homogenizing the audience but became issues of control between centrally organized production companies and locally based exhibitors, in the context of the Motion Picture Patents Company's efforts to impose licensing requirements on theater owners and exchanges. With the cinema's emancipation from other entertainment outlets, exhibitors had become a dynamic force in the industry, moving into production via distribution (notably the Independents) or expanding their theaters into chains. Exhibitors cultivating the local market, however, whether as managers or independent entrepreneurs, maintained a strong sense of their contribution to the product, especially as increased competition demanded that they distinguish their presentations from those of other theaters. Many local exhibitors shared their customers' ethnic and social background, an affinity that seems more likely to have created the conditions of an alternative public sphere than the often cited affinity between audiences and producers.[14]

Exhibition practices during the transitional period continued to emphasize the value of 'the show' over that of the film as circulating product. As Richard Koszarski argues, the priority of the show continued throughout the silent era, which calls into question the efficacy of the classical objective of a textually centered spectator, even at a time when classical strategies of narration and address were already fully elaborated. Thus nonfilmic activities were considered not merely as auxiliary but rather as 'added attractions' advertised along with an orchestra here and a $30,000 organ there, with powder rooms, ushers and architectural design. Roughly one-fourth to one-third of a two-hour program would be devoted to items outside the feature (which, if necessary, was cut down or projected at faster speed) – to live acts, musical performances (such as orchestral overtures or illustrated songs), news weeklies, comedy shorts or animated cartoons. More important than the textual integrity or even narrative consistency of the feature film was the overall appeal of the entertainment mix, the 'balanced program.' In Koszarski's words, 'the belief in a "balanced program" was almost mystical among silent picture palace managers, who clearly saw this part of their business as closer to the work of vaudeville managers than operators of legitimate houses.' This concept of the show enjoyed enormous popularity with audiences. Surveys throughout most of the 1920s suggest that only a small fraction (10 per cent in one survey) of moviegoers had come to see the feature, the overwhelming majority (68 per cent) had come for the 'event.' 'Going to the movies' during the silent era, Koszarski concludes, 'remained essentially a theater experience, not a film experience.'[15]

The advent of synchronized sound drastically curtailed the initiative of the individual exhibitor. The addition of a prefabricated soundtrack was yet another step toward making the film a more 'complete' product which could be distributed and consumed in more or less the same manner everywhere, and the standardized speed of projection prohibited tampering with ('improving') the feature, which had been standard practice before. Moreover, the activities surrounding the film increasingly became a promotional ritual organized from above, culminating in the 1930s with commodity tie-ups, fashion shows, give-aways, and other advertising schemes.[16] The tendency toward standardizing theater experience, however, already can be observed in the early 1920s, within the very tradition of showmanship that emphasized the exhibitor's autonomy.

For the notion of a 'balanced program' could go either way: continuing the emphasis on diversity inherited from the variety format, the 'cinema of attractions,' or streamlining the presentations to give the impression of an 'organic' whole thematically centered on the weekly feature – a distinction first analyzed by Kracauer in his 1926 essay on 'distraction.' Whatever formula was applied (the 'prologue,' the 'headliner' or 'pure,' theme-oriented spectacle), the ideal of a unified presentation raised the stakes of exhibition. As investment costs for the live aspects of the program soared, lavish presentations increasingly became the trademark of particular theater chains, either replicated locally or packaged to tour a circuit of theaters.[17]

The size and quality of the 'show' depended on the size and type of theater. The picture palaces soon 'became the flagships, the most profitable theatres in large regional chains,' but they represented only a small portion of American movie theaters – 1 per cent in 1915, 5 per cent between 1915 and 1933.[18] Neighborhood theaters charging lower prices continued in business, and continued to attract ethnic and working-class crowds. To be sure, on special occasions these audiences also visited the downtown theaters mingling there with the middle class and being treated as 'ladies and gentlemen', but the middle class did not reciprocate. Like the picture palaces, the smaller houses cultivated a belief in the 'show,' and their status among neighbourhood theaters depended upon the 'added attractions' that could be afforded. In contrast with the more expensive shows, the live portions of the program were often geared to particular ethnic and racial constituencies. In Chicago, for instance, Polish plays were performed side by side with cinematic entertainment, and, in Lizabeth Cohen's words, 'Italian music shared the stage with American Films.' Furthermore, as Mary Carbine has shown, theaters catering to black audiences included jazz performances as well as acts from the black, particularly Southern, entertainment tradition.[19] While these live portions were attractions in their own right, they also shaped the way mainstream films could be received – and reinterpreted – by nonmainstream audiences.

As long as an exhibitor catered to such audiences, the show was likely to maintain a locally specific, potentially interactive and aleatory dimension. If it did so, this was not because the individual exhibitor believed in defending communal culture against the onslaught of monopolization, but because the format was profitable and competitive. Yet that same economic principle created a kind of scissors effect: the more ambitious and costly the show, the larger and less specific its intended audience.

Spaces of transition, pockets of time

In what follows, I will discuss the question of an alternative public sphere from a less systematic perspective, focusing on the cinema's function for particular social groups at particular historical junctures, specifically, new immigrants and a recently urbanized working class as well as women both within these groups and across class and ethnic boundaries. Such a perspective must remain speculative, since it is difficult to know how these groups – or, for that matter, any group – received the films they saw and what significance moviegoing had in relation to their lives. Still, we can try to reconstruct the configurations of experience that shaped their horizon of reception, and ask how the cinema as an institution, as a social and aesthetic experience, might have interacted with that horizon.

The immigrant and working class have traditionally been singled out for their 'symbiotic relationship' with the movies, a relationship that almost instantaneously spawned a powerful mythology. It is necessary to denaturalize that 'symbiosis,' by situating the cinema's appearance in immigrant life in a particular historical constellation, broadly defined by the experience of modernization and the emergence of consumerism. In doing so, I am not presuming to offer a general theory of 'the immigrant experience'; I wish to suggest certain patterns and possibilities that may help explain the cinema's ambiguous ascendancy over other institutions of immigrant culture. Nor do I mean to obliterate significant distinctions among immigrant groups, especially with regard to moviegoing habits, or to underrate the importance of local and regional variations in immigrant culture and the demographics of film consumption.[20] Yet, despite such variations, and despite the separatism that governed relations among diverse ethnic groups, basic patterns of experience were shared by immigrant working-class communities across the board. This common experience was defined by the discrepancy between the types of society and economy the immigrants had left behind and the conditions they confronted in America (conditions themselves in rapid transformation) as well as by the particular strategies mobilized in dealing with that discrepancy.

Social historians have discussed the immigrant experience of that period (1893–1919) primarily under two overlapping aspects: modernization and, more recently, the emergence of a consumer economy. The former points back to earlier phases of industrial capitalism, the latter describes a development concurrent with – and in crucial ways dependent upon – the new wave of mass immigration. In his influential 1973 essay Herbert Gutman describes the encounter of immigrants from premodern societies with industrial modes of production as a kind of déjà vu of the experience of first-generation factory workers during the early decades of the nineteenth century: 'American society, of course, had changed greatly, but in some ways it is as if a film – run at a much faster speed – is being viewed for a second time.'[21] By the end of the century this experience entailed not only an encounter with steam, machinery and electricity, with low wages, long hours and a punitive system of work discipline, but also a more refined regime of the clock, linked to an increasing division and hierarchy of labor, standardization, and the elaboration of methods of mass production.[22] Modern factory practices were as alien to the work habits of East-European artisans and peddlers as to those of Italian or Slavic peasants. Like earlier instances of mass industrialization, they provoked forms of protest that drew strength from the very subcultures that were being negated.

Immigrants experienced the effects of accelerated industrialization not only in the factory but in all areas of everyday life – as violent displacement and deprivation, as disorientation, alienation, shock and loss. Whether they came from the small-town environment of the East-European *shtetl* or the rural *mezzogiorno*, arrival in urban America catapulted them into a world without nature, a grey concrete jungle of overcrowded tenements and filthy streets, of artificial lighting, noise and speed. The loss of preindustrial nature went hand in hand with the loss of a communal cultural and linguistic environment, a framework of traditional norms and values. The world the immigrants had left behind was one of poverty and oppression but it was a familiar one, bounded within a closed religious worldview and a hierarchic social order. The new world had promised a liberation from oppressive conditions and unlimited possibilities, instead it entailed, for first-generation immigrants at least, a reduction of space and time, a curtailment of their sphere of interaction, expression, and interpretation.[23]

The loss of that horizon of experience was superimposed with new demarcations of public and private (which themselves were undergoing a major transformation). In a society of extended families and kinship networks, the boundaries between public and private had hardly been as pronounced and were fluid at best. Transplanted into an industrial-capitalist economy, the immigrant family lost its role in the production process (similar to what had happened to the American family more than half a century earlier) and was reduced to a unit of reproduction and consumption. While the immigrant family was thus abruptly privatized, work pressures and overcrowded living conditions rendered any real privacy a luxury, purring immense strain on marital relations and relations between parents and children. At the same time immigrants were barred from most institutions of the dominant public sphere, whether by reason of language, custom, class, or lack of means and leisure time.

Yet, as Gutman admonished historians in 1973, it would be a mistake to perpetuate the notion 'that the large-scale uprooting and exploitative processes that accompanied industrialization caused little more than cultural breakdown and social anomie. Family, class and ethnic ties did not dissolve easily.'[24] And, as social historians have amply documented since, the very conditions of alienation not only mobilized a web of familial, social, and personal relationships but also gave rise to new forms of public life that mediated the loss of the old culture with the challenges of the new.[25] Speaking of the secular culture that emerged among Jewish immigrants from Eastern Europe, Irving Howe asserts that it 'was different from the one they had left behind, despite major links of continuity,' and that 'it struggled fiercely to keep itself different from the one they found in America, despite the pressures of assimiliation.'[26] The institutions of immigrant public life ranged from the traditional and in their own way exclusive voluntary societies and lodges (like the Jewish *landsmanshaftn*), through social clubs and educational centers to labor-related and political activities, from ethnic theaters, such as the Yiddish theater, the Italian opera and marionette theater and ethnic vaudeville through the more casual (though no less regular) gatherings in candy stores, soda fountains and saloons to the more anonymous and potentially dangerous encounters at the dance halls. As Roy Rosenzweig argues with regard to working-class leisure culture in Worcester, Massachusetts, such institutions constituted a local, separate, and relatively autonomous sphere which, although not overtly *oppositional*, still presented an *alternative* to dominant social norms.[27]

It is part of the cinema's ambiguous record that its success destroyed many of these institutions, especially the whole spectrum of ethnic theatrical entertainments, along with public gathering places like the candy store and the saloon.[28] As the cinema prevailed over its live competitors by virtue of the greater profit margin, it both absorbed and in crucial ways surpassed the appeal of other entertainments to immigrant audiences. The nickelodeon permitted a continuation of class and ethnically specific habits of reception because of its neighborhood character, low admission fee, and egalitarian seating structure (uniform ticket price), its informal atmosphere and interactive mode of exhibition. At the same time, moviegoing marked a departure from this tradition, opening up a less traditionally defined, qualitatively different type of public sphere.

The relation of the cinema to existing forms of immigrant public life was not just that of another institution but that of a chameleonlike creature grafting itself onto these formations. 'Despite the standardized product,' Kathy Peiss writes, 'the experience of the movies took on the flavor of the surrounding neighborhood.'[29] This observation cuts both ways. It accounts for the survival of working-class sociability and familiarity in neighborhood theaters, but it also explains the lack of these dimensions in other locations. In 1911 Mary Heaton Vorse, a Greenwich Village radical, compares motion picture audiences in Jewish and Italian areas of New York and finds a contrasting experience in a Bowery theater: 'In the Bowery you get a different kind of audience. None of your neighborhood spirit here. Even in what is called the 'dago show' – that is, the show where the occasional vaudeville numbers are Italian singers – the people seem chance-met, the audience is almost entirely composed of men, only an occasional woman.'[30] In this passage, as throughout her article, Vorse emphasizes the role of the audience as a productive force, crucial to supplying the films and numbers with an interpretive, intersubjective dimension. But the distinction she observes in the Bowery theater also describes an important difference between the cinematic institution and the more traditional ethnic entertainments: 'the people seem chance-met.'

Most institutions of immigrant public life were defined by quite strict standards of inclusion (hence also exclusion) – by origin, craft or religious affiliation – as well as particular conventions of access, especially in terms of gender and generation. Women were excluded from traditionally male working-class entertainments such as the burlesque, concert-saloons, dime museums or sports. Many other leisure activities, like a promenade in the park or a trip to more upwardly mobile entertainments like vaudeville and amusement parks, were available to them only in the company of men or the whole family. Although the tightly knit web of kinship relations and ethnic coherence may have provided a buffer against alienation and the pressures of adaptation, it also drove the younger generation to seek escape, particularly toward encounters with members of the other sex outside the narrow pale of family connections and ethnic community. One such escape was the visit to the dance hall, a new kind of social space, less personal but free of family surveillance, which for many served as a rehearsal ground for the styles of a heterosocial modernity.[31]

Because of its chameleonlike quality, the cinema seems to have assumed a certain threshold function, oscillating between the tradition of family-centered ethnic entertainment and the more anonymous, more modern forms of commercialized leisure. Cheaper than vaudeville or Coney Island and safer than the dance halls (and therefore less subject to parental censure), the cinema allowed for the mixing with friends, acquaintances and even strangers. Discussing the emergence of the audience as public in eighteenth-century Paris, Sennett distinguishes two kinds of strangers: the stranger as outsider, as in the 'categorizable strangeness of immigrants from another land,' and 'the stranger as an unknown, rather than an alien.' Although he refers to ethnic stereotyping in Boston and New York around 1900 as an example of the former, the following description seems nonetheless apt for the less clearly defined gathering of strangers in American movie theaters: 'the stranger as an unknown can dominate . . . the perceptions of people who are unclear about their own identities, losing traditional images of themselves, or belonging to a new social group that as yet has no clear label.' The farther the theater from the neighborhood centers and the less associated with a particular immigrant constituency, the more likely it was to assemble strangers of diverse ethnic backgrounds who were not only displaced in relation to dominant forms of identity but had that displacement in common with each other – 'materially alike but not cognizant of their similiarities.'[32] Like the new public spaces of the eighteenth-century cosmopolitan city, the cinema offered a site for experiencing diversity, for civil interaction among strangers. Yet the same conditions that enabled this public dimension also entailed its opposite, both with the increased privatization of viewing behavior and the textual homogenization of positions of subjectivity.

Neither a primeval paradise of viewer participation nor merely a site for the consumption of standardized products, the cinema rehearsed new, specifically modern forms of subjectivity and intersubjectivity at the same time that it addressed older needs and more recent experiences of displacement and deprivation. If it assumed both of these functions, it did so not only because of the liminal situation of its audiences and its own threshold status among commercial entertainments but also because of the particular kind of collectivity actualized in the individual viewing experience. Vorse describes in great detail a woman watching an Indian-trapper melodrama in a Lower East Side theater. Accompanied by a man, she was 'so rapt and entranced' with the events on screen 'that her voice accompanied all that happened – a little unconscious and lilting *obbligato*.' Significantly, the running commentary was in German, with an Austrian accent, rendered by Vorse in English punctuated with foreign phrases. The writer's own fascination seems divide between the heteroglossic transaction behind her and the spectacle that was prompting it: 'a guileless and sentimental dime novel, most ingeniously performed, a work of art, beautiful too, because one had glimpses of stately forests, sunlight shifting through leaves, wild, dancing forms of Indians, the beautiful swift rushing of horses.' But, as Vorse hastens to add, 'to the woman behind it was reality at its highest. She was there in a fabled country full of painted savages. The rapidly unfolding drama was to her no make-believe arrangement ingeniously fitted together by actors and picturemakers. It had happened, it was happening for her now.[33]

Whatever we make of the radical intellectual's own kind of disavowal, she describes a spectatorial disposition that is at once absorbed and active, at once self-abandoning and very much part of the situation of exhibition. The woman's expressive behavior, in particular its linguistic distinctiveness, runs counter to the middle-class standards of silence and passivity that were becoming the mark of the cinema's respectability, yet her engagement with the narrative seems consistent with the tenets of classical illusionism. The combination challenges the conceptual coupling (notably in Brechtian film theory of the 1970s) of narrative identification with spectorial passivity and, conversely, of an active mode of reception with a distanced awareness of the film's discursive operations.[34] What upsets these formalist oppositions as well is the trajectory Vorse draws between the woman's dialogue with the film and the spatial and symbolic relationship of the show with a particular social environment.

> Outside the iron city roared, before the door of the show the push-cart vendors bargained and trafficked with customers. Who in that audience remembered it? They had found the door of escape. For the moment they were in the depths of the forest following the loves of Yellow Wing and Dick. The woman's voice, so like the voice of a spirit talking to itself, unconscious of time and place, was their voice. There they were, a strange company of aliens – Jews, almost all, haggard and battered and bearded men, young girls with their beaus, spruce and dapper youngsters beginning to make their way.

The image of a female voice divorced from the body, abstracted from time and place yet speaking for a particular group or mode of being is a Romantic topos, reminiscent of Wordsworth's 'Solitary Reaper.' The woman's voice becomes the voice of the Ghetto, as it were, because it speaks from the unconscious, because it is fueled by a common need for escape. What barely saves this rhetoric from the pitfalls of the 'collective unconscious' is the configuration of the world inside and outside the movie theater, the separate yet interrelated spaces of fantasy and reality. The cinematic fantasy compensates for the deficiencies of the outside world: the pressures of survival and success, the experience of aliens, the loss of familiar surroundings. But the space of fantasy is no less alien, no more continuous with the traditions from which they had been dispossessed. It is no coincidence that the melodramatic conflict on screen revolves around terms of racial difference whether advancing an identification with the white hero at the expense of the exotic, barbaric other ('*wildes und grausames Volk*') or allowing for a fictional reconciliation of the opposition by way of an interracial romance. To whatever degree such scenarios might have served to inculcate dominant racist ideology in ethnic but white immigrants,[35] they also provide symbolic parallels with the experiential horizon of those immigrants, their own confrontation with new terms of strangeness and identity. In that sense the type of identification described by Vorse could be read as a form of reappropriation, an imaginative assimilation of foreign images to the collective experience of alienation and displacement.

In its spatial and symbolic configurations of inside and outside, of familiarity and strangeness, the cinema belongs to the social sites that Michel Foucault has characterized as 'heterotopias' – 'places [that[are absolutely different from all the sites that they reflect and speak about.' In their irreducible heterogeneity in relation to the surrounding spaces, heterotopias are 'something like counter-sites, a kind of effectively enacted utopia in which the real sites, all the other real sites that can be found within the culture, are simultaneously represented, contested, and inverted.' Foucault himself lists the cinema among a number of such sites – sites of transportation such as trains or sites of temporary relaxation such as cafes and beaches. He discusses it as an example of one particular principle of the heterotopia, the capability 'of juxtaposing in a single real place several spaces, several sites that are in themselves incompatible.' The cinema obviously qualifies as such in the very basic sense that it is 'a very odd rectangular room, at the end of which, on a two-dimensional screen, one sees the projection of a three-dimensional space.'[36]

While this spatial configuration is as old as the magic lantern show and more or less typical of the cinema throughout its history, Foucault's notion of heterotopia can be taken further to describe a more specific historical experience, during the transition from early to classical cinema, on the part of particular social groups. For over half a century urban populations in Europe and the US had been adapting to the effects of modern technology on human perception, a fundamental transformation of spatio-temporal coordinates.[37] The vast majority of immigrants arriving in American cities around the run of the century confronted this transformation from one day to the next without preparation – a shock which, according to autobiographical statements and social worker reports, left many stunned, disoriented, literally dis-placed.[38] Although the cinema no doubt participated in the historical upheaval of traditional coordinates of space and time, it also offered a refuge in which the violence of the transition could be negotiated in a less threatening, playful, and intersubjective manner.

The nickelodeon was a real place, located in the center or at the margin of the immigrants' world, ordinary and easily accessible. At the same time it opened up into a fantastic space, giving pleasure in the juxtaposition of diverse, often incompatible and at times impossible sites or sights – in the very principle of disjunction that informed the variety format. The jumble of strange and familiar, of old and new, or ordinary and exotic, made the movies an objective correlative of the immigrant experience. As a writer for the *Jewish Daily Forward* observed, 'our Jews feel very much at home with the detectives, oceans, horses, dogs and cars that run about on the screen.'[39] The significance of such a series is less in its individual referents than its cheerfully avowed randomness, a surrealistic equality among its elements. This aesthetics of disjunction not only contested the presumed homogeneity of dominant culture and society in the name of which immigrants were marginalized and alienated; more important it lent the experience of disorientation and displacement the objectivity of collective expression. It is in this sense that the notion of the cinema as a heterotopia converges with the concept of an alternative public sphere – as a medium that allows people to organize their experience on the basis of their own context of living, its specific needs, conflicts and anxieties.

The 'despatialization of subjectivity' (Mary Ann Doane) that marked the immigrants' entry into American modernity was just as much an experience of violent detemporalization. It is thus that the cinema might have functions as a 'time-place' (*Zeitort*) in Kluge's sense, a site for the actualization of different temporalities.[40] Foucault attributes this capability to heterotopias in general when he notes that they 'are most often linked to slices of time.' The experience of different temporalities is possible only at a certain stage of historical development: 'The heterotopia begins to function at full capacity when men arrive at a sort of absolute break with their traditional time.' Foucault contrasts sites concerned with the accumulation of time with a view to eternity (archives, museums, libraries) with ones that are linked 'to time in its most fleeting, transitory, precarious aspect, to time in the mode of festival.' As an example of the latter he cites the fairgrounds, 'these marvellous empty sites on the outskirts of cities that teem once or twice a year with stands, displays, heteroclite objects, wrestlers, snakewomen, fortune-tellers and so forth'; but he might as well have included preclassical cinema, the 'cinema of attractions.'[41]

Again, Foucault has to be read somewhat against the grain, read backwards through more contemporaneous historians of modernity such as Kracauer and Benjamin. Foucault tended to celebrate the ascendancy of categories of space over those of time in a somewhat ahistorical manner. Kracauer and Benjamin, however, saw in the spatialization of time a crucial moment in the historical process, itself a sign of the times. They wrote about urban spaces – streets, squares, hotel lobbies, movie theaters, arcades – as sites of a temporal crossing, as thresholds of social and political change. Thus they turned the German word for arcade, '*Passage*,' into a complex historical metaphor.[42] For both, film and photography assumed a pivotal function in the crisis that pervaded all areas of modern life, in what Kracauer called 'the all-out gamble of history.'[43] For Benjamin this crisis was linked to the general decline of the capability of experience, the disassociation of collective memory and individual recollection; by the same token, the emancipation of experience from cultural tradition and privilege, epitomized by film and photography, offered the historical chance to reshuffle the spatialized fragments of time, to make them 'quotable' and collectively accessible.[44]

As with the transformation of spiritual perception, the break with traditional temporality was exacerbated for immigrant men and women who brought preindustrial, agricultural, or artisanal rhythms of time to a country increasingly run by train schedules and the discipline of the factory clock. The enforced adaptation to the latter entailed a detemporalization, a quantification, and reification of time; it also reduced the play of memory (for Kracauer and Benjamin synonymous with the capability of experience.) While immigrant organizations and personal and kinship networks worked to keep memories of the old world alive, the pressures of Americanization demanded precisely the opposite. In a study published in 1921, Chicago sociologist William Isaac Thomas condemns the prevailing concept of 'quick and complete Americanization' for promoting the 'destruction of memories,' for preventing immigrants from living 'in the light of the past' and making constructive changes on the basis of their experience.[45]

To people under the assault of the present both on their jobs and by the institutions of dominant culture, the cinema offered a 'time-place' in a number of ways. With its lack of a fixed schedule and continuous admission, Rosenzweig contends, the nickelodeon provided a 'refuge from the time discipline of the factory.'[46] Mothers for whom family leisure activities usually meant a continuation of housework on different premises could disappear in the darkness of the movie theater for a few hours, with or without children, to vary on Horkheimer and Adorno's notorious phrase, 'just as [they] used to gaze out of the window, when there were still homes and the hour after a day's work [*Feierabend*].'[47] The dimness of the theater set the stage for the viewer's surrender to the manipulations of time on screen – the duration of a panorama shot, the thrills of fast and reverse motion, the simultaneity of parallel editing – at least until filmic temporality became more firmly subordinated to the linear momentum of narrative.

If the cinema could help immigrants come to terms with competing temporalities, it also lent itself to the unceremonious actualization of memories. This capability seems linked to the affinity of film with mimetic traces in the historical experience of nature. In journalistic discourse of the period, the cinema is often ascribed a compensatory function for people who could not afford to travel. A 1908 article for instance, emphasizes a German exhibitor's efforts to procure 'scenes from the Rocky Mountains, forest views, and flowing cascades': 'He would bring to the heart of the Ghetto the heart of Nature itself, and even though devoid of color and freshness and odor, he would at least suggest something of that flowering world which is farthest away from asphalt and brick.'[48] But for first-generation immigrants this spatial distance translated into a temporal one: it was not that they had never seen the beauties of nature, they had lost them. As Elizabeth Ewen observes, 'New York had abolished the forests for-ever, leaving them retrievable only in memory or in the pictorial reproductions that hung on the walls of tenement apartments as reminders of a world lost but not forgotten.'[49] To be sure, such reminders border on the pathetic, more likely perhaps to diminish memory than to preserve it. But the mnemonic powers of the cinema go beyond those of pictorial reproductions on the wall. If the spurious miracles of second nature succeeded in stirring up memories of the first, they did so not necessarily on the basis of literal correspondences but by way of figurative and unconscious processes. The 'sunlight shifting through leaves' that captured Vorse's imagination might not have been lost on the naive spectator entranced by the narrative; on the contrary, the emotional absorption into the latter might have fed on such ephemeral details, images charged with a different past, with memories of loss.

Benjamin described this aspect of filmic reception with the metaphor of the 'optical uncon-scious' insisting on the hidden, figurative dimension of film's 'mimetic faculty.'[50] The memory mobilized by the optical unconscious differs from any form of premeditated, discursive remem-bering or reminiscing; it belongs to the side of Proust's, *mémoire involuntaire* or the Surrealists' exercises in 'profane illumination' (and thus, by implication, to the realm of psychoanalysis). Generally, Benjamin is better known for placing the cinema on the other side of that distinc-tion, since the cinema epitomized the expansion of the archive of voluntary memory at the expense of involuntary recollection, the destruction of spatio-temporal distance, and hence of the conditions of experience – the disintegration of the 'aura.' But he was above all concerned with redeeming the possibility of experience in an irrevocably transformed world, seeking it in the track of the very agencies of transformation – technology, fashion, consumer culture – in the accumulated debris of second nature. If the cinema has a place in this project, it is through the back door of the optical unconscious, through the camera's exploration of an 'unconsciously permeated space,' whether that space pertains to preindustrial nature or the naturalized settings of urban life: 'Our taverns and city streets, our offices and furnished rooms, our train stations and factories appeared to have us locked up beyond hope. Then came film and exploded this prison-world with the dynamite of one-tenth seconds, so that now, in the midst of its far-flung ruins and debris, we calmly embark on adventurous travels.'[51] Revealing the 'natural' appearance of the capitalist everyday as an allegorical landscape, the cinema thus parallels the investigations of the Surrealists or the flaneur who seek in that landscape a mode of experience traditionally reserved for phenomena of an ostensibly more primary nature: 'the metamorphosis of the object into a counterpart [*Gegenüber*].' In this process, as Habermas paraphrases Benjamin, 'a whole field of surprising correspondences between animate and inanimate nature is opened up, wherein even *things* encounter us in the structures of frail inter-subjectivity.'[52]

If Benjamin's speculations bear on the question of the cinema's function as a public sphere, they do so in a twofold way. As an aesthetic category, the optical unconscious is more likely to erupt in some films or some genres, and during certain periods of film history rather than others. Thus, it would seem to be more germane to the cinema of attractions, to a mode of exhibition that allows for a more centrifugal, less textually predetermined reception of filmic images. As a category based on the history of human interaction with nature (*Naturgeschichte*), the optical unconscious would have had a heightened significance for groups like the new immigrants who encountered the impact of industrialization, urbanization and commodifica-tion in an accelerated, telescoped form – by lending expression to traumatic disjunctions in the social experience of nature.

If the cinema helped immigrants organize their experience on their own terms, then, not only by creating a space for the actualization of involuntary memory, of disjunctive layers of time and subjectivity, it also offered a collective forum for the production of fantasy, the capability of envisioning a different future. More than any entertainment of the period, the cinema figured as the site of magical transformation – of things, people, settings and situations. To transpose Howe's remark, it was 'something of a joke' *and* 'something of a miracle.'[53] As utopian images of 'America,' fostered by oppression and deprivation in the Old Country, crumbled under the realities of immigrant life, the cinema to some extent absorbed the functions of the utopian imagination, albeit in a diminished, alienated, and depoliticized form. Immigrant testimonies suggest that fantasies of a better life mingled older hopes with more specifically modern dreams, promises of abundance with scenarios of mobility and self-transformation.[54] While advertising was promoting such scenarios with cynical hyperbole, the cinema rehearsed them in a more structural manner – with its peculiar form of perceptual identification, its dispersal of subjectivity across a multiplicity of objects. Kracauer describes the disposition of one who 'lets himself be polymorphously projected in a movie theater': 'As a fake Chinaman he sits in a fake opium den, turns into a well-trained dog who performs ridiculously clever acts to please a female star, gathers himself into an alpine storm, gets to be circus artist and lion at once.'[55] The mobilization of the gaze that transcends physical laws as well as distinctions between subject and object, human and nonhuman nature, promises nothing less than the mobilization of the self, the transformation of seemingly fixed positions of social identity.

The mobilization, however, is promise and delusion in one. The projection of subjectivity onto the world of things, or their reflections, does not automatically open up correspondences, 'structures of frail intersubjectivity.' For Kracauer, who was both more familiar with and more skeptical vis-à-vis the cinema than Benjamin, this mode of reception entails just as much a sense of de-realization, isolation and loss: 'One forgets oneself gazing, and the big dark hole is animated with the semblance of a life that belongs to no one and consumes everyone.' The subject consumed is of course the consumer, who adapts to the object of his or her desire mimetically, by the logic of reification.

We return here to the question raised toward the end of the previous chapter, concerning the intersection of cinema and consumer culture, particularly in view of the tensions, contradictions, and ambiguities in the development of the latter. I have discussed some aspects of this question under the general heading of the industrial-commercial public spheres – their simultaneous recognition and appropriation of hitherto unrepresented discourses of social experience, their initial instability and non-synchronicity. What remains difficult to ascertain is the pace at which these new structures and media of publicity were effective in implementing the ideological and economic tenets of consumer capitalism, or, conversely, the extent to which they were used in ways that enabled and prolonged an autonomous organization of ethnic working-class experience. Lizabeth Cohen, writing on Chicago during the 1920s, argues against the critical historians who assume that mass culture instantaneously 'succeeded in integrating American workers into a mainstream, middle-class culture.' Instead, she claims, the immigrants' encounter with new commodities and technologies of reproduction took on shapes that resisted that kind of homogenization and actually helped preserve older forms of collective identity, at least for some time. The phonograph, for instance, often accused of plugging the immigrant family into a national network of standardized taste, was put to quite different uses by Chicago workers. 'In story after story they related how buying a victrola helped keep Polish or Italian culture alive by allowing people to play foreign-language records, often at ethnic gatherings.' Thus, Cohen concludes, 'owning a phonograph might bring a worker closer to mainstream culture, but it did not have to. A commodity could just as easily help a person reinforce ethnic or working class culture as lose it.'[56]

The analogy between phonograph and cinema carries only so far, considering basic differences between the apparatuses, in particular the listener's greater degree of control over the process of reception (closer in kind to today's consumption of films on videotape). After all, phonographic recording, especially of foreign or ethnically specific music, still presumed the existence of a tradition independent of the product, and thus a community of listeners and potential participants. Yet early cinema depended crucially on familiarity with extra-textual sources as well, at least until the final implementation of the classical paradigm. Furthermore, while record buyers might have had a wider choice among products, the emphasis on cinematic diversity persisted throughout the nickelodeon period, notwithstanding the dominance of the narrative film after 1907. As exhibitors reported in the trade press, scenics remained a favorite with audiences, and slapstick comedy, with its antisentimental, anti-authoritarian and anticonsumerist appeal, survived the protests of gentrifiers and guardians of culture for many years.

Most important, unlike the victrola, the cinema was predicated on collective reception; it mandated reception in a public space. Even films designed to link the cinema to mainstream culture could be received differently depending on environment, audience composition, programming, and mode of exhibition; Vitagraph's *The Life of Moses* (1909–10), for instance, provoked a hardly mainstream response among Russian Jewish audiences.[57] To go further, I believe that even explicitly Christian films, like the Italian import *Quo Vadis?* (1912), could have been reclaimed by such audiences. The relatively confused, elliptical narrative foregrounds the spectacle of religious persecutions, graphic images of people huddling together against the onslaught of absolute and irrational power, making these images available for projective identification and reappropriation into the viewers' own memories.

The question of consumerism and public life, or industrially appropriated experience and the possibility of its reclamation, cannot be approached exclusively in terms of class and ethnic background. So far I have situated the cinema in relation to the historical dynamics of three distinct though overlapping types of public life: the remnants of a bourgeois public sphere (high culture, the Genteel Tradition); the new industrial-commercial public spheres (the modern entertainment market with its new middle-class, upwardly mobile, maximally inclusive clientele); and the ethnically segregated public spheres drawing on older traditions of working class and peasant culture. The rest of this chapter focuses on a discourse that both overlays and interacts with these different types of organization: the definition of the demarcations between public and private along the lines of gender.

Women's 'craving for the cinema': the erosion of the separate spheres

The cinema's role in changing the boundaries and possibilities of public life was perhaps most pivotal for women, across – though related to – distinctions of class, racial and ethnic background, marital status, and generation.[58] Women's relations to the public sphere were governed by specific patterns of exclusion and abstraction, and the transformation of these patterns made a major difference in the conditions under which women could articulate and organize their experience. As outlined in the Introduction, the delimitation of public and private in terms of gender and sexuality was a central feature of the bourgeois public sphere in its European and American variants. From the 1820s and 1830s on, public life in the US was a predominantly masculine arena to which women had access only in a highly controlled and dependent form. Accordingly, the private realm of the family came to be identified as the domain of an idealized femininity, defined by domesticity, motherhood, sexual purity and moral guardianship. Throughout the nineteenth century the doctrine of separate spheres, the hierarchy of public/male over private/female, not only shaped – and maimed – relations between the sexes, but crucially determined the mappings of social life, of cultural institutions, itineraries of everyday life and leisure activities.[59]

The gender hierarchy of public and private structure the lives of middle-class and working-class women alike, though in different ways. Toward the end of the century, for instance, middle-class forms of leisure increasingly were becoming family-centered, that is, they encouraged women's patronage as long as they were contained within the family. At the same time, popular entertainments maintained strong segregation along gender lines: most institutions of working-class culture, such as ethnic saloons, burlesque shows, or sports events, remained exclusively male affairs; a woman could join only at the risk of her reputation. Certainly there were significant variations among immigrant groups (Germans, for instance, had no problem with women drinking in beer gardens), and many women, especially married ones, attended ethnic theaters, church-sponsored events, or the annual balls, picnics and entertainments of their husbands' fraternal organizations.[60] By and large, however, the higher the social status of the commercial entertainment form, the more acceptable it became for mixed company, conversely, the ability of an establishment to attract reputable women emerged as the touchstone of middle-class respectability.

Authorized by middle-class observers and reformers, this syllogism was employed by entertainment entrepreneurs eager to attract a more affluent upwardly mobile, and inclusive clientele. Vaudeville, in so many respects a model for the institution of cinema, is an excellent example of the dialectic of gender and status that was transforming the outlines of the public sphere. Pioneers of vaudeville gentrification, notably Tony Pastor, began to upgrade the reputation of the male-oriented variety shows by introducing 'refined' matinees for 'ladies' on weekday afternoons. By the 1880s and 1890s, evening shows too were refashioned to meet (middle-class) standards of feminine taste – by efforts to suppress working-class audience behavior, such as the ban on boisterous response, talking, drinking and smoking, and to eradicate sexual innuendo and bawdy humor from the performance. As a back-up strategy, however, Pastor is reported to have hired prostitutes to dress up as 'respectable' women and attend the shows so as to lure patrons 'seeking a refined atmosphere.' This ploy seems to have worked as well as the others. In the long run, Robert Allen writes, 'vaudeville achieved its economic success by bringing women into its audience.'[61]

That the appearance of respectability could be purchased, and that it was supplied by women who physically and ideologically figured as the repressed other of an idealized femininity, makes this anecdote symptomatic of the contradictions at work in the transformation of the public sphere. The invocation of middle-class notions of gentility in the effort to legitimize female participation in commercial entertainments testified to the erosion of the very demarcations these notions were founded upon, the gendered segregation of public and private spheres. This erosion was not happening in vaudeville alone. It was initiated, on a much larger scale, by the emergence of a consumer economy and attendant forms of culture and ideology.[62]

The new culture of consumption blurred class and ethnic divisions in an illusive community of abundance; it also undermined bourgeois divisions of public and private, above all the hierarchy of male and female spheres. Crucial to the shift from a production-centered economy to one of mass consumption was the female shopper whose numbers had increased ever since the Civil War. By 1915 'women were doing between 80 and 85 per cent of the consumer purchasing in the US.'[63] For middle-class women this meant a liberation from the narrow confines of domestic space, but also, in the long run, the surrender of a traditionally female sphere of influence to the corporately organized empire of mass consumption. For working-class women, especially recent immigrants from Southern and Eastern Europe, consumerist styles and fashions – to the extent they could afford them – promised access to a modern, American world of freedom, romance and upward mobility. At the same time, it was *their* cheap labor that enabled the mass manufacturing and sale of consumer goods.[64]

Although the rise of consumerism changed women's relationship to the public sphere fundamentally, it would be a mistake to consider consumer culture in itself as 'public' in the emphatic sense of the word. It was, and continues to be, a direct function of the capitalist market place, of private property relations; and no doubt it aimed to transform social processes of identification and interaction into private acts of acquisition. But because of its industrial-commercial basis, consumer culture introduced a different principle of publicity than that governing traditional institutions, a more direct appeal to the customers' experience, to concrete needs, desires, fantasies. In catering to aspects of female experience that hitherto had been denied any public dimension, the media of consumption offered and intersubjective horizon for the articulation of that experience. Such a horizon was precarious and at best temporary, since the appeal to women as consumers fluctuated between experimental differentiation (to satisfy as many diverse constituencies as possible) and long-term homogenization (predicated on a notion of 'woman' as white, heterosexual and middle-class).

The emerging culture of consumption, centering on advertising and the department store, was flanked by the mushrooming commercial entertainments already mentioned – amusement parks like Coney Island, vaudeville, cabarets, dance halls and, of course, the cinema. What distinguished these new forms of leisure from the traditions of both high culture and popular amusements, indeed the mark of their modernity, was that they encouraged the mingling of classes and genders. Despite the ideological character of such (self-)displays of equality, the mingling of genders must have had a greater significance for women, as a group whose movements and mode of social existence had been severely restricted by the homosocial arrangements of the traditional public spheres. Moreover, the styles of a heterosocial modernity promoted with the new leisure culture changed the definitions of female identity in relation to the family, superimposing the values of motherhood and domesticity with the appeals of pleasure, glamour, and eroticism. This shift in the social construction of femininity, generally associated with the discourse on the New Woman, exacerbated the rift between the generations, especially between immigrant mothers and their American-born or American-raised daughters. Yet it also loosened the circumscriptions of the domestic maternal role and self-image, not least because the same young working women who sought diversion outside the family and kinship networks tended to take up that role as soon as they married.[65]

More than any other entertainment form, the cinema opened up a space – as well as a perceptual, experiential horizon – in women's lives, whatever their marital status, age or background. As Kathy Peiss observes in her study of working women and leisure in turn-of-the century New York, the cinema most strikingly 'altered women's participation in the world of public, commercial amusements.' With the rise of the nickelodeon, 'women's attendance soared, women comprised 40 per cent of the working-class movie audience in 1910.'[66] Unlike vaudeville, even cheap or 'family vaudeville,' the movies offered women a more casual participation in the world of entertainments, an experience that could easily be incorporated into a variety of everyday itineraries and, at the same time, a relief from the monotony of housework. Thus, married women would drop into a movie theater on their way home from a shopping trip, a pleasure indulged in just as much by women of the more affluent classes. Schoolgirls filled the theaters during much of the afternoon, before returning to the folds of familial discipline. And young working women would find in the cinema an hour of diversion after work, as well as an opportunity to meet men. As a reporter for the *Chicago Daily Tribune* observed in 1907,

> Around 6 o'clock or just before that hour the character of the audiences in the lower State street shifted again. This time they were composed largely of girls from the big department stores, who came in with their bundles under their arms . . . They remain . . . as late as 7 o'clock with the excuse that they have no other recreation and that the street cars are uncomfortably crowded at that time of the day . . . It is certain they frequently are found talking with men of mature years, whom they could not have met before going to the theaters.[67]

Although such encounters were precisely what the middle-class opponents of the nickelodeons objected to, within the working-class community, moviegoing was considered quite innocuous, certainly in comparison with dance halls and other heterosocial amusements. Especially among recent immigrants, the movements of daughters were highly circumscribed – not only by economic necessity but even more so by the behavioral double standard of the old-world patriarchal family. For young Italian women, as for the daughters of relatively more liberal East-European Jewish families, going to the movies several times a week was often the only unsupervised leisure activity they were permitted and could afford. Though less prestigious than the more expensive and permissive entertainments in the eyes of their peer group, movie-going allowed even well-guarded immigrant daughters an opening into the emerging subculture of dating and treating.[68]

The cinema was a place women could frequent on their own, as independent customers, where they could experience forms of collectivity different from those centering on the family. Unlike mass-market fiction, which, much as it constituted a social horizon of experience, was still predicated on individual consumption in a private space, the cinema catered to women as an audience, as the subject of collective reception and public interaction. It thus functioned as a particularly female heterotopia, because, in addition to the heterotopic qualities already discussed, it 'simultaneously represented, contested and inverted' the gendered demarcations of private and public spheres. The cinema provided for women, as it did for immigrants and recently urbanized working class of all sexes and ages, a space apart and a space in between. It was a site for the imaginative negotiation of the gaps between family, school and work-place, between traditional standards of sexual behavior and modern dreams of romance and sexual expression, between freedom and anxiety. Bounded by familiar surroundings and cultur-ally accepted, within the working-class community at least, the movie theater opened up an arena in which a new discourse on femininity could be articulated and the norms and codes of sexual conduct could be redefined.[69]

This arena consisted not merely of the theater's physical space and the social environ-ment it assimilated, but crucially involved the phantasmagoric space on the screen, and the multiple and dynamic transactions between these spaces. Again, it is difficult to know how female viewers received and interpreted the films they saw, and although there are contem-porary accounts of individual women's viewing habits (like the one by Vorse), it would be premature to generalize on the basis of such accounts.[70] But we can trace some of the ways in which the industry responded to the historically unprecedented formation of women as an audience, both in terms of the logic of supply and demand and in terms of strategies designed to contain the threat this new female audience posed to the patriarchal organization of the public sphere.

The problem confronted by the industry resulted from the overlap of different types of public sphere that we saw operating in the case of *The Corbett–Fitzsimmons Fight*. On the one hand, film production drew heavily on the subject matter, genres, and performance conventions of the popular entertainment tradition, including such male-oriented spectacles as the burlesque and the peep shows; on the other hand, the establishment of the cinema as an institution hinged upon its appeal to an inclusive, heterosocial mass audience. In the eyes of middle-class reformers and advocates of censorship this overlap was at the very core of the nickelodeon problem – in the unruly conjunction of previously restricted sexually suggestive material on the screen and the large number of women in front of the screen, along with the permissive behavior that might be going on during the screening. The problem was compounded by the high proportion of juveniles in motion picture audiences: in a New York survey of 1911, 33 per cent of all moviegoers were boys and girls under eighteen (as compared to 19 per cent in vaudeville audiences). The writer in the *Chicago Tribune* cited earlier complaints about the popularity of *The Unwritten Law* (Lubin, 1907), a reenactment of the notorious Thaw-White Murder case (involving seduction and scandal), with the schoolgirl crowd: 'A good many grown women got up and went out before the completion of the series. It shocked them. But the girls remained.'

Following the model of vaudeville, the gentrifiers of cinema sought to make the shows acceptable to middle-class standards of feminine taste – at the same time as they promoted female patronage as an indicator of middle-class respectability. But the industry's efforts were not merely defensive, aimed at pacifying public opinion. Rather, both exhibitors and producers began to cater to female audiences more aggressively, appealing to women on the basis of particular intertexts and ideological discourses, with particular genres, stars and sentiments. Throughout the 1910s these attempts to respond to and expand an existing market betray an experimental quality and thus register both the upheaval of public and private in terms of gender and sexuality and the generation gap resulting from it. A well-known example of films addressing a new type of female audience, specifically young working women, were the serials, such as *The Hazards of Helen* (Kalem, 1914 on), which featured adventurous, physically active heroines. Drawing on successful columns in women's magazines, fashion journals and news-papers, the serials located pleasure in images of female competence, courage and physical movement (often involving triumphant transactions between women and technology, espe-cially trains) that marked a striking distance from Victorian ideals of femininity.[71]

Alongside this more modern, egalitarian discourse the appeal to women on the basis of domestic ideology – sexual purity, passivity, emotional superiority and moral guardianship – persisted in various guises and blends: in genres like melodrama, which tried to manage the breakdown of the separate spheres; in virginal stars like Lillian Gish and Mary Pickford; and even in the work of women directors like Alice Guy Blaché, Ida May Park and Lois Weber who used the rhetoric of domesticity to justify their position in a predominantly male industry. The appeal to women viewers in terms of essential feminine virtues also structured films of an ostensibly gender-neutral, political concern, like the films debating the US entry into the war, whether their message was pacifist (as in Ince's *Civilization* and Brenon's *War Brides*) or prointerventionist (as in Blackton's *The Battle Cry of Peace*).[72] Yet, in other genres, such as films dramatizing the fate of the fallen woman, the cult of true womanhood was invoked ideo-logically only to be challenged by strategies of representation and address: the appeal to the viewer to sympathize with the victims of social circumstance – or even to identify with the morally condemned exercise of female sexual power – necessarily 'blurred the distinction between true women and their fallen counterparts.'[73]

In the long run, the contradictions between the New Woman and the old, like tensions within the ideology of domesticity itself, were submerged in the consumerist discourse that had enabled the public articulation of competing models of female identity in the first place.

No longer grounded in the topography of separate spheres, domesticity was updated for an age of technology and consumption. As Mary Ryan observes with regard to 1920s films, the 'mischievous vivacity' of the flapper, the vitality of stars like Clara Bow, Madge Bellamy or Gloria Swanson, increasingly served to instruct the female viewer 'on how to become *correctly* modern, . . . to train the female audience in fashionable femininity.'[74] And the accidental transgressions of the homosocial taboo that had troubled the arbiters of early cinema came to inspire the more systematic appropriation of female desire at work in the marketing of stars like Valentino or the films of Cecil B. DeMille. The integration of the female address with the culture of consumption not only seems to have leveled generational differences among various types of address, but also caused the dialectic of domesticity and consumerism that had propelled the transformation of public and private spheres to collapse.

That the cinema came to function as a powerful catalyst for this transformation, that films could effectively determine the way they were received on a mass-cultural scale, hinges upon the paradigmatic shift from early to classical cinema – and the concomitant differentiation of the spectator as a hypothetical term of the film's discourse from the empirical viewer as a member of a plural, social audience. The creation of such a spectator involved the stylistic elaboration of a consistent yet *indirect* mode of address that granted the viewer access to the diegesis from a position of voyeuristic immunity and fetishistic distance. From a feminist perspective, however, the imbrication of the cinematic apparatus with psychic mechanisms of voyeurism and fetishism means yoking the spectator position to traditionally masculine perversions; these epitomize the patriarchal hierarchy of vision that constitutes the man as agent and the woman as prime object and challenge of the gaze.[75] If this scopic economy is inscribed in the *structural* organization of classical cinema, in the spectator's interaction with the film on both conscious and unconscious levels, it must have been operative, in tendency at least, during the transitional period, at the same time that the cinema was assuming a major social function for women across class and ethnic boundaries.

How do we account for this seeming paradox, posed by the intersection of history and theory, of, on the one hand, women's increased significance for the film industry as fans and consumers and, on the other, the systematic imposition, on the textual level, of masculine forms of subjectivity, of a patriarchal choreography of vision? In her study of the 1940s woman's film Mary Ann Doane argues that the paradox of women's simultaneous agency and subjection turns upon the logic of reification, the consumer's mimetic empathy with the commodity. Like Kracauer before her, Doane sees the specific link between consumerism and film spectatorship in a 'curiously passive desiring subjectivity,' a desire defined by narcissism and a fixation on appearances. More explicitly than Kracauer, she relates this form of subjectivity to the cultural construction of the feminine, traditionally aligned with the affects of empathy and over-identification. In its simultaneous appeal to the female consumer and assertion of a patriarchal hierarchy of vision, she concludes, classical cinema reduces female desire to positions of narcissism and masochism, making her the subject of a transaction designed to turn her into a commodity.[76]

This analysis undoubtedly pinpoints a powerful ideological mechanism, but its historical implementation complicates the issue. There has been a tendency in feminist film theory, especially approaches indebted to Lacanian psychoanalysis, to take the imposition of patriarchal structures of vision and desire as an expression of an essential and ostensibly timeless symbolic order (and thus, on the methodological level, as a somewhat predictable and ultimately inevitable conclusion). I consider the codification of such structures a defensive symptom, a reaction against the historical challenge the cinema presented to the gendered hierarchy of private and public spheres. The force of this reaction testifies to the power of the patriarchal tradition, but it also indicates the extent of the crisis unleashed by women's massive ascendance to a new horizon of experience.

The challenge to the gendered hierarchy of the public sphere violated a taboo that predated bourgeois sexual arrangements; the taboo on the active female gaze that pervaded traditions of representation in art, mythology and everyday life. If modern advertising and the department store had mobilized the female gaze in the service of consumption, the cinema seemed to have institutionalized women's scopophilic consumption as an end in itself, thus posing a commercially fostered threat to the male monopoly of the gaze. The conflict between economic opportunism and patriarchal ideology provoked and profound ambivalence toward the female spectator – as a subjectivity simultaneously solicited and feared, all the more so because of its collective dimensions.

The ambivalence toward the female gaze – as a manifestation of the power clustering around the female consumer – was especially acute in men like Griffith, whose own relationship with the mass market was fairly problematic (even when he seemed to have conquered it). Griffith's obsession with a sense of femininity in crisis is at the heart of *Intolerance*, a film that dramatizes the fate – and fatal power – of unmarried female characters throughout the ages. This crisis of femininity not only precipitates the multiple catastrophes in the diegesis, increasingly so as the film gets closer to the modern era; it also destabilizes the film's textual system, unraveling its self-consciously ingenious architectonic structure. The very deployment of the gaze as the medium of cinematic subjectivity is contaminated with the power of the perverted female look. This hampers the film's effectivity in engaging the spectator – or creating a coherent spectator position at all – at least by the standards of the emerging paradigm.

Throughout the transitional period and beyond, the implementation of classical codes was accompanied by allegories rehearsing at once the empowerment and containment of the female gaze, of female desire in general. This dynamic can be observed through a variety of textual figurations, ranging from Porter's Goldilocks through the figure of the Vamp epitomized by the marvelous Theda Bara, from the spinster and prostitute in *Intolerance* through the flapper of the 1920s. The drama played out in the field of cinematic vision echoes the chiasmus effect Jackson Lears discerns in the shifting gender connotations of advertising. If nineteenth-century advertising had attracted the consumer with images of abundance envisioned as feminine and maternal, the spirit that presided over twentieth-century consumption was the male genius of mass production.[77] Similarly, one could argue, the alternative public sphere that began to crystallize around the abundance of female moviegoing was harnessed by the structural masculinization of the spectator position endemic to classical cinema. However, as the cinema sought to align its appeal to women audiences with a prevailing patriarchal order of vision, it both recognized and absorbed discourses of experience that conflicted with the latter, thus reproducing the conditions for the articulation of female subjectivity along with the strategies for its containment.

Most important, the alignment of female spectatorship with a gendered hierarchy of vision was as complex and contradictory a process as the implementation of the classical system in general, neither as instantaneously effective nor ever as complete as film theorists have made it seem. If, in the fissures and detours of this process, the cinema assumed the function of an alternative horizon of experience for a large number of women, it was enabled by the same conditions that were working in favor of working-class and immigrant audiences: the instability of the cinema as an industrial-commercial public sphere, conflicts between short-term economic and long-range ideological interests, and the uneven development of modes of production, representation and exhibition. Thus, the discrepancy between film experience and theater experience I have elaborated must have played as much a part for women audiences as for other groups, if not more so, given the structural problematic of a textually anchored female address, its incompatibility with the masculine inscription of the gaze.

The industry's catering to the female consumer seems to have focused more unequivocally on 'the discursive apparatus surrounding the film than the text itself,' as, for instance, fan magazines devoted to 'the purportedly female obsession with stars, glamour, gossip and fashionability.'[78] While such discourses were designed to enhance the consumption of films on a national scale, they still belonged to the sphere of exhibition – to the side of locally specific, socially and culturally differentiated audiences and to the side of the 'show,' of singular and to some extent unpredictable performances. The star system in particular harbored this bifurcation, since it was predicted on the oscillation between filmic and extrafilmic discourses. As we shall see in the case of Valentino, the female address was lodged on two levels – the publicity surrounding the star as well as textual strategies which thematized the contradictions of female spectatorship. Although these two sets of discourses were crucially intertwined, the cult they had spawned took on a momentum of its own, eluding the control of its industrial promoters. Thus, the historical reception of Valentino opened up a public horizon for women's experience, marked by the contradictory dynamic of entrenched sexual and racial hierarchies and the consumerist appropriation of female desire.

Finally, if we accept the hypothesis of feminist film theory that the classical apparatus renders the place of the female spectator a 'locus of impossibility,'[79] there is yet another turn to the argument about the cinema as an alternative public sphere. The mismatch between the female spectator and the subject of classical cinema, her notorious over-identification with the image and structural alienation from the symbolic order rehearsed by the narrative, makes way for a mode of reception that is potentially in excess of textually constructed positions of subjectivity. It is no coincidence that, even at this early point in film history, female spectators were depicted as excessive, whether on account of their obstreperous headgear (*Those Awful Hats* [Griffith/Biograph, 1908]) or their unsuitable hysterical behavior, as in *Rosalie et Léonce à théâtre* (Gaumont, 1910).[80]

Doane sees this peculiarly female mode of reception predicated on the consumerist glance, which 'hovers over the surface of the image, isolating details which may be entirely peripheral in relation to the narrative. It is a fixating, obsessive gaze which wanders in and out of the narrative and has a more intimate relation to space – the space of rooms and of bodies – than with the temporal dimension.'[81] I share her observation, but I do not think that this type of gaze is entirely rationalized by the subsidiary strategies surrounding the film (the purpose of consumption), nor would I emphasize its diminished sense of time. As I have argued, the cinema allowed for the experience of competing temporalities, especially on the part of people who bore the brunt of modernization. The gaze distracted by the lure of consumption may not keep up with the pace of linear narrative, but it may feed on other registers of time and experience, linked to involuntary memory and associational processes in the spectator's head – the register of the 'optical unconscious.'

In her 1914 dissertation on motion picture audiences, German sociologist Emilie Altenloh found that women viewers of all classes and ages responded more strongly to the synaesthetic and kinetic aspects of films, and that they were more likely than men to forget the plot or title of a film but vividly remembered sentimental situations as well as images of waterfalls, ocean waves, and drifting ice floes. Similarly, Iris Barry defends her own passion for the cinema, asserting in 1926 that 'even in the crudest films something is provided for the imagination, and emotion is stirred by the simplest things – moonlight playing in a bare room, the flicker of a hand against a window.'[82] And Virginia Woolf, in an essay published in the same year, speaks of those rare moments, when, 'at the cinema in the midst of its immense dexterity and enormous technical proficiency, the curtain parts and we behold, far off, some unknown and unexpected beauty.'[83] The gaze that is captured by such ephemeral images is certainly not of an essentially female, let alone feminine quality, nor are these images untouched by social meaning, even and especially in their distance from a social reality that exerted increasing control over the production of experience. But if this mode of reception was more typical of female audiences, it should be theorized as a historically significant formation of spectatorship.

Just as the imposition of patriarchal structures of vision and narration appears as a response to the unprecedented mobilization of the female gaze, so is female spectatorship inevitably constituted in relation to dominant subject positions, compensating for its structural impossibility with a greater mobility and multiplicity of identifications. Yet the gap confronted by women – or, for that matter, other groups alienated from dominant positions of subjectivity – is neither accidental nor merely personal, nor just another variant of the general dynamic of misrecognition that constitutes the subject in Lacanian theory. It is part of their historical and social experience as women, contingent on sexual preference, class, race and ethnic background. Whether it can be interpreted as such – and thus be reclaimed by the experiencing subjects – depends upon, or is a measure of the extent to which the cinema functions as an alternative public sphere. Although this alternative function cannot be measured in any empirical sense, the conditions of its possibility can be reconstructed. At the same time, a tradition of female spectatorship can be traced through concrete historical manifestations – such as fan cults surrounding stars of both sexes, women's clubs engaged in film-cultural activities, or the numerous women playing the piano in movie theaters as well as women writing on film – in short, a variety of configurations, often ambiguous and contradictory, in which women not only experienced the misfit of the female spectator in relation to patriarchal positions of subjectivity but also developed imaginative strategies in response to it.

Notes

1   See Chapter 1; Robert William Snyder, 'The Voice of the City: Vaudeville and the Formation of Mass Culture in New York Neighbourhoods, 1880–1930,' PhD, diss, New York University, 1986; and Albert F. McLean, Jr., *American Vaudeville as Ritual* (Lexington: University of Kentucky Press, 1965).

2   Roy Rosenzweig, *Eight Hours for What Will: Workers and Leisure in an Industrial City, 1870–1920* (Cambridge and New York: Cambridge University Press, 1983); Elizabeth Ewen, *Immigrant Women in the Land of Dollars: Life and Culture on the Lower East Side, 1890–1925* (New York: Monthly Review Press, 1985); Kathy Peiss, *Cheap Amusements: Working Women and Leisure in Turn-of-the Century New York* (Philadelphia Temple University Press, 1986). Also see Lizabeth Cohen, 'Encountering Mass Culture at the Grassroots: The Experience of Chicago Workers in the 1920s,' *American Quarterly* 41(1) (March 1989): 6–33. Robert Sklar discusses the challenge of the new social history in his essay, '*Oh! Althusser!*: Histiography and the Rise of Cinema Studies,' *Radical History Review* 41 (1988): 10–35. Also see Judith Mayne, *Private Novels, Public Films* (Athens: University of Georgia Press, 1988), ch. 3, 'The Two Spheres of Early Cinema.'

     Only marginal in these studies, and neglected here as well, is the perspective of children and youth which, although often claimed by social workers, reformers, and advocates of censorship, has not been the subject of the kind of historical analysis devoted to the formations of class, gender, race, and ethnicity in which they partake.

3   Oskar Negt and Alexander Kluge, *Öffentlichkeit und Erfahrung: Zur Oganisationsanalyse von bügerlicher und proletarischer Öffentlichkeit* (Frankfurt A.M: Suhrkamp, 1972). The term 'nonsynchronous' was first used in a specific sense, that is toward and explanation of German fascism, by Ernst Bloch in a chapter of *Erbshaft dieser Zeit* (1935), 'Nonsynchronism and the Obligation to Its Dialectics,' trans. Mark Ritter, *New German Critique* 11 (Spring 1977): 22–38, but the notion of uneven developments in social

relations and cultural organization has a wider currency in Marxist thought, from Marx himself (*Grundrisse*, p. 26) through Walter Benjamin and Raymond Williams.

4　Charles Musser, 'The Nickelodeon Era Begins: Establishing the Framework for Hollywood's Mode of Representation,' *Framework* 22–3 (Autumn 1983): 4.

5　Janet Staiger, Part 2 of David Bordwell, Janet Staiger, and Kristin Tompson, *The Classical Hollywood Cinema: Film Style and Mode of Production to 1960* (New York: Columbia University Press, 1985).

6　Lawrence Levine, *Highbrow Lowbrow: The Emergence of Cultural Hierarchy in America* (Cambridge, Mass: Harvard University Press, 1988), p. 195; Richard Sennett, *The Fall of Public Man* (New York: Random House, 1978), p. 206.

7　Snyder, 'Voice of the City,' pp. 48–51; Rosenzweig, *Eight Hours*, pp. 199–201. On audience behavior in the ethnic theater, cf. John Corbin, 'How the Other Half Laughs,' *Harper's New Monthly Magazine* (December 1898), rpt in Neil Harris, ed. *The Land of Contrasts 1880–1901* (New York: Braziller, 1970), pp. 160–79, on Yiddish theater in particular, see Irving Howe, *The World of Our Fathers: The journey of the East European Jews to America and the Life They Found and Made* (New York: Simon & Schuster, 1976), pp. 460ff., 484, 494.

8　Although not as controversial as vaudeville acts, slide shows were seen as either conducive to gentrification (especially travelogues) or a plebeian legacy to be reformed (as in the case of song slides; see, for instance, *New York Dramatic Mirror* 61 (14 Aug. 1909): 15; *NYDM* 63 1 Jan. 1910): 16; 63 5 Feb. 1910): 16; *Moving Picture World* 4.3 (16 Jan. 1909) 70; *MPW* 5.18 (30 Oct. 1909): 597. On the competing status of nonfilmic activities, see W. Stephen Bush, 'The Added Attraction (1),' *MPW* 10.7 (18 Nov. 1911): 533–4.

9　Quoted by Tom Gunning, *D. W. Griffith and the Origins of American Narrative Film* (Urbana: University of Illinois Press, 1991), ch. 6. For the association of the lecturer with genres that were increasingly marginalized see Van C. Lee, 'The Value of a Lecture,' *MPW* 2(8) (February 1908): 93–4; H. F. Hoffman, 'What People Want.' *MPW* 7.2 (9 July 1910): 77; 'Where They Perform Shakespeare for Five Cents,' *Theatre Magazine* 8.92 (October 1908): 264–5, xi.

10　Gunning, *D. W. Griffith*, ch. 4.

11　W. Stephen Bush, 'The Human Voice as a Factor in the Moving Picture Show,' *MPW* 4.4 (23 Jan. 1909): 86 (emphasis added).

12　Noël Burch, 'Primitivism and the Avant-Gardes: A Dialectical approach,' in Philip Rosen (ed.), *Narrative, Apparatus, Ideology* (New York: Columbia University Press, 1986), pp. 488–9; and his discussion of the role of *benshi* in Japanese film history in *To the Distant Observer: Form and Meaning in Japanese Cinema* (Berkeley: University of California Press, 1979), pp. 75–85, 95–7. Also see Joseph L. Anderson, 'Spoken Silents in the Japanese Cinema, Essays on the Necessity of Katsuben,' *Journal of Film and Video* 40(1) (Winter 1988): 13–33. A similar paradox of greater realism and supplemental fragmentation can be found in the more expensive – and less common – practice of having actors supply dialogue from behind the screen.

13　'Survivors of a Vanishing Race in the Movie World,' *The New York Times Magazine* (18 January 1920): 4.

14　Ralph Cassady, 'Monopoly in Motion Picture Production and Distribution, 1908–1915,' *South California Law Review* (Summer 1959); Rosenzweig, *Eight Hours* pp. 199, 204, 216; Cohen, 'Encountering Mass Culture,' p. 14.

15　Richard Koszarski, 'Going to the Movies,' *An Evening's Entertainment: The Age of the Silent Feature Picture, 1915–1928* (New York: Scribner's, Macmillan, 1990); draft presented at the Columbia Seminar on Cinema and Interdisciplinary Interpretation, December 1986.

16　Charles Eckert, 'The Carole Lombard in Macy's Window,' *Quarterly Review of Film Studies* 3.1 (Winter 1978): 14–21; Jeanne Allen, 'The Film Viewer as a Consumer,' *Quarterly Review of Film Studies* 5(4) (Fall 1980): 48–50; Jane Gaines, 'the Queen Christina Tie-ups: Convergence of Show Window and Screen,' *Quarterly Review of Film and Video* 11(1): 35–30. For further references, see Lynn Spigel and Denise Mann, 'Women and Consumer Culture: A Selective Bibliography,' ibid., pp. 85–105.

17　Douglas Gomery, 'Toward a History of Film Exhibition: The Case of the Picture Palace,' *Film: Historical-Theoretical Speculations*, pt. 2 (Pleasantville, NY: Redgrave, 1977), p. 19; Robert Allen and Douglas Gomery, *Film History: Theory and Practice* (New York: Knopf, 1985), pp. 199–201; Kosarzski; 'Going to the Movies.' Also see Siegfried Kracauer, 'Cult of Distraction: On Berlin's Picture Palaces' (1926), trans. Thomas Y. Levin, *New German Critique* 40 (Winter 1987): 91–6.

18　Gomery, 'History of Film Exhibition,' p. 18; Koszarski, 'Going to the Movies.' Also see Douglas Gomery, 'US Film Exhibition: The Formation of a Big Business,' in Tino Balio (ed.) *The American Film Industry*, rev. edn (Madison: University of Wisconsin Press, 1985), pp. 218–28.

19   Rosenzweig, *Eight Hours* pp. 212–13; Cohen, 'Encountering Mass Culture,' p. 16; Mary Carbine, 'The Finest Outside the Loop: Motion Picture Exhibition in Chicago's Black Metropolis, 1909–28,' paper delivered at the SCS conference Iowa City, April 1989.

20   Inevitably, as with many other aspects of early film history, New York City, particularly the Lower East Side, figures as a privileged site of interpretation. Not only was it the port through which the largest number of immigrants arrived, it was also a city that was highly self-conscious about its ongoing history, producing an extraordinary wealth of sources (Peiss, *Cheap Amusements*, p. 9): Likewise, by focusing on turn-of-the-century New York, studies of immigrant culture tend to center on two major ethnic constituencies. Southern Italians and Jews from Eastern Europe. Of these two, East-European Jews have commanded a somewhat special status in relation to the cinema, because (a) Jewish immigration was primarily a family movement, with almost twice the proportion of female immigrants (43 per cent for 1899–1910) and a much lower repatriation rate than the Italian group (22 per cent); and (b) a proportionally larger number of Jews went into the entertainment business and represented a vocal force among the exhibitors (Ewen, *Immigrant Women*, pp. 51ff.; Thomas Kessner, *The Golden Door: Italian and Jewish Immigrant Mobility in New York City* [New York: Oxford University Press, 1977], p. 31).

      Recent studies in both social and film history (such as Rosenzweig on Worcester, Merritt on Boston, or Gomery on Milwaukee; see Chapter 2, note 3) have cautioned us persuasively against generalizing from the New York situation. By the same token, the injunction against positing that situation as *typical* should not prevent us from suggesting *significant* patterns and sets of problems shared by New York and other cities with large immigrant populations such as Chicago, Philadelphia or Baltimore.

21   Herbert Gutman, *Work, Culture and Society in Industrializing America* (new York Vintage, 1977), p. 22. Also see Howe, *World of Our Fathers*, p. 115. As Howe points out, for a number of East-European Jews, urbanization and proletarianization had already begun in the old country (p. 21).

22   Harry Braveman, *Labor and Monopoly Capital: The Degradation of Work in the Twentieth Century* (New York: Monthly Review Press, 1974).

23   Ewen, *Immigrant Women*, pp. 60ff.; Howe, *World of Our Fathers* pp. 69–118.

24   Gutman, *Work, Culture and Society*, p. 41.

25   Rosenzweig, *Eight Hours*, Ewen, *Immigrant Women*, pp. 14ff., and p. 271 for further references to the new immigrant history.

26   Howe, *World of Our Fathers*, p. 169.

27   Rosenzweig, *Eight Hours*, pp. 223–4. The distinction between 'oppositional' and 'alternative' is discussed by Raymond Williams, 'Base and Superstructure in Marxist Cultural Theory,' *New Left Review* 82 (December 1973): 11.

28   Howe, *World of Our Fathers*, p. 213; Ewen *Immigrant Women*, p. 216.

29   Peiss, *Cheap Amusements*, p. 149.

30   Mary Heaton Vorse, 'Some Picture Show Audiences,' *The Outlook* 98 (24 June, 1911): 446. The dependency of the mode of reception on theater location might explain the discrepancy in contemporary descriptions of audience behavior as either remarkably sociable and interactive or totally autistic, passive and mechanical; for instances of the former, see Lewis E. Palmer, 'The World in Motion,' *Survey* 22 (5 June 2909): 356, or Michael M. Davis, *The Exploitation of Pleasure* (new York: Russel Sage Foundation, 1911), p. 24; for a graphic example of the latter, see Olivia Howard Dunbar, 'The Lure of the Films,' *Harper's Weekly* 57 (18 Jan. 1913): 20, 22. Also see Levine, *Highbrow Lowbrow*, pp. 197–98.

31   Peiss, *Cheap Amusements*, ch. 4; Ewen, *Immigrant Women*, pp. 209–10; Howe, *World of Our Fathers*, pp. 208ff.

32   Sennett, *Fall of Public Man*, pp. 52, 48, 49, 87.

33   Vorse, 'Some Picture Show Audiences,' pp. 442–44.

34   For an example of this pervasive tendency, see Peter Wollen, 'Godard and Counter Cinema: *Vent d'Est*,' *Readings and Writings* (London: Verso, 1982), pp. 79–91. Patrice Petro elaborates an alternative to the male-modernist privileging of categories of distance and detachment in what she calls, with recourse to Heideger, a 'contemplative aesthetics' in her *Joyless Streets: Women and Melodramatic Representation in Weimar Germany* (Princeton: Princeton University Press, 1989), pp. 76–7, and passim. For a critique of 1970s film theory along similar lines, see D.N. Rodowick, *The Crisis of Political Modernism* (Urbana: University of Illinois Press, 1988).

35   Lauren Rabinovitz, 'The Air of Respectability: Hale's Tours at Riverview Amusement Park in 1907,' paper delivered at the SCS conference, Iowa City, April 1989.

36   Michel Foucault, 'Of Other Spaces,' *Diacritics* 16(1) (Spring 1986): 22–27; 24, 23–24, 25.

37   Stephen Kern, *The Culture of Time and Space 1880–1918* (Cambridge, MA: Harvard University Press, 1983); Walter Benjamin, 'The Work of Art in the Age of Mechanical Reproduction' (1935–36) and 'On Some Motifs in Baudelaire' (1939), trans. Harry Zohn, *Illuminations* (New York: Schocken, 1969); Wolfgang Schivelbusch, *The Railway Journey: Trains and Travel in the 19th Century*, trans. Anselm Hollo (New York: Urizen, 1979).

38   Howe, *World of Our Fathers*, pp. 69–77, 96ff.; Ewen, *Immigrant Women*, chs. 4, 7.

39   *Jewish Daily Forward* (28 July 1914), quoted in Howe, *World of Our Fathers*, p. 213.

40   Mary Ann Doane, 'When the Direction of the Force Acting on the Body Is Changed: The Moving Image,' *Wide Angle* 7.1–2 (1985): 44. Alexander Kluge, 'Die Macht des Bewußtseinsindustrie und das Schiksal unserer Öffentlichkeit,' in Klaus von Bismarck *et al.*, *Industrialisierung des Bewußtseins* (Munich: piper, 1985), p. 105. The historical significant – and imminent loss – of the cinema as a site of different temporalities is a topic of Kluge's 1985 film, *The Present's Assault on the Rest of Time (Der Angriff der Gegenwart auf den Rest der Zeit*, shown at the New York film festival under the title *The Blind Director)*; screenplay and commentary (Frankfurt: Syndikat, 1985), excerpts trans. In *New German Critique* 49 (Winter 1989). For a more systematic focus on questions of cinema and temporality, see Gilles Deleuze, *L'image temps: Cinéma 2* (Paris: Editions de Minuit, 1985).

41   Foucault, 'Of other Spaces,' p. 26; Tom Gunning elaborates on the connection between early cinema and the aesthetics of the fairground in his path-breaking essay, 'The Cinema of Attraction[s]: Early Film, Its Spectator and the Avant-Garde,' *Wide Angle* 8(3), 4 (1986): 63–70

42   See Kracauer's essays of the 1920s and early 1930s, collected in *Das Ornament der Masse* (Frankfurt: Suhrkamp, 1963) and *Straßen in Berlin und anderswo* (Frankfurt Suhrkamp, 1964); on the arcade in particular, 'Abschied von der Lindenpassage' (1930), rpt. In both volumes, trans. in Johann Friedrich Geist, *Arcades: The History of a Building Type* (Cambridge, MA: MIT Press, 1983), pp. 158–60; Benjamin, *Das Passagen-Werk* Rolf Tiedemann (ed.) (Frankfurt: Suhrkamp, 1983) as well as earlier writings such as 'A Berlin Chronicle,' *Reflections*, trans. Edmund Jephcott (New York: Harcourt Brace Jovanovich, 1978).

43   Kracauer, 'Die Photographie' (1927), *Ornament der Masse*, pp. 37ff.

44   Benjamin, 'Work of Art,' 'On Some Motifs,' 'The Storyteller,' and other essays in *Illuminations*, also see Jürgen Habermas, 'Consciousness-Raising or Redemptive Criticism' (1972), *New German Critique* 17 (Spring 1979): 30–59; Susan Buck-Morss, 'Benjamin's Passagen-Werk: Redeeming Mass Culture for the Revolution,' *New German Critique* 29 (Spring-Summer 1983): 211–40; and Miriam Hansen, 'Benjamin, Cinema and Experience: 'The Blue Flower in the Land of Technology,' *New German Critique* 40 (Winter 1987): 179–224.

45   William I. Thomas, with Robert E. Park and Herbert A. Miller, *Old World Traits Transplanted* (1921), repr. with a new introduction by Donald R. Young (Montclair, NJ: Patterson Smith, 1971), pp. 281–82.

46   Rosenzweig, *Eight Hours*, pp. 201, 217.

47   Max Horkheimer and Theodor W. Adorno, *Dialectic of Enlightenment* (1947) Trans. John Cumming (New York: Seabury, 1969), p. 139.

48   'Where They Perform Shakespeare for Five Cents,' *Theatre Magazine* 8. 92 (October 1908): 265.

49   Ewen, *Immigrant Women*, p. 61,; Howe, *World of Our Fathers*, pp. 71–2, 214–15.

50   'Work of Art,' sec. xiii; 'On the Mimetic Faculty,' first version (1935), trans. Krut Tarnowski, *New German Critique* 17 (Spring 1979): 65–9. The attribution of psychic, physiognomic and even psychoanalytic faculties to film is a topos of 1920s film theory, notably in Jean Epstein and Béla Balázs; also see Theodor W. Adorno's later comparison of film with the 'images of the interior monologue.' 'Transparencies on Film' (1966), *New German Critique* 24–5 (Fall–Winter 1981–82): 199–205.

51   *Illuminations*, p. 236, translation modified.

52   Habermas, 'Consciousness-Raising or Redemptive Criticism,' pp. 45–6.

53   Howe, *World of Our Fathers*, p. 165.

54   Ewen, *Immigrant Women*, pp. 66–7. Also see T.J. Jackson Lears, 'From Salvation to Self-Realization: Advertising and the Therapeutic Roots of the Consumer Culture, 1880–1930,' in Richard Wightman Fox and F.J. Jackson Lears (eds.) *The Culture of Consumption* (New York: Pantheon), pp. 1–38.

55   Kracauer, 'Langeweile' ('Boredom' (1924), *Ornament der Masse*, pp. 322.

56   Cohen, 'Encountering Mass Culture,' pp. 7, 9.

57   As late as two years after the film's release a trade journal reports that during screenings in a Minneapolis theater 'the very appearance of Moses on the canvas is the signal for wild applause that often continues

for several minutes' (*Molography* 6.6 [December 1911]: 8). Quoted and discussed by William Uricchio and Roberta E. Pearson, *Invisible Viewers, Inaudible Voices: Intertextuality and Conditions of Reception in the Early Cinema*, forthcoming (Princeton University Press).

58   The term 'craving for the cinema' ('*Kinosucht*') in my subheading is used by a woman interviewed by Emilie Altenloh for her 1914 dissertation on (German) cinema as a social institution, *Zur Soziologie des Kino: Die Kino-Unternehmung und die Soziaolen Schichten*, PhD, diss. Heidelberg (Leipzig: Spamersche Buchdruckerei, 1914). Also see Miriam Hansen, 'Early Silent Cinema: Whose Public Sphere?' *New German Critique* 29 (Spring–Summer 1983): 176ff., and Petro, *Joyless Streets*, pp. 3–4, 18–20.

59   Barbara Welter, 'The Cult of True Womanhood,' *American Quarterly* 18 (Summer 1966): 151–74; Nancy F. Cott, *The Bonds of womanhood: 'Woman's Sphere' in New England, 1780–1835* (New Haven: Yale University Press, 1977); Linda Kerber, 'Separate Spheres, Female Worlds, Woman's Place. The Rhetoric of Women's History.' *Journal of American History* 75 (June 1988): 9–39.

60   Peiss, *Cheap Amusements*, p. 26–30, 140–41.

61   Robert C. Allen, *Vaudeville and Film 1895–1915: A Study in Media Interaction* (New York: Arno Press, 1980), p. 30, Snyder, 'Voice of the City,' p. 41. Pastor's play is described in Albert E. Smith, *Two Reels and a Crank* (Garden City, NY: Doubleday, 1952), p. 46.

62   Although consumerism effectively destroyed the social topography of the separate spheres, its relation with domestic ideology is a dialectical one. As Ann Douglas argues with regard to the sentimentalist tradition in women's fiction, the cult of domesticity might have constituted a proto-consumer mentality to begin with; see *The Feminization of American Culture* (New York: Alfred Knopf, 1977). Douglas' argument seems confirmed for later decades by the facile adaptation of corresponding ideals of femininity into the Hollywood repertoire.

63   William Leach, 'Transformations in a Culture of Consumption: Women and Department Stores, 1890–1925,' *Journal of American History* 71(2) (September 1984): 333. For further references, see Spigel and Mann, 'Women and Consumer Culture.'

64   Ewen, *Immigrant Women*, pp. 23ff., 64ff.

65   James McGovern analyzes the break with Victorian notions of female domesticity as a simultaneous shift toward greater sexual permissiveness and desexualization, suggesting that the price of an increased equality was a 'diminished femininity'; 'The American Woman's Pre-World War I Freedom in Manners and Morals,' *Journal of American History* 55(2) (September 1968): 314–33. On the heterosocial appeal of the new commercial entertainments, see John F. Kasson, *Amusing the Million: Coney Island at the Turn of the Century* (New York: Hill & Wang, 1978), pp. 42–3, 94; Lewis A. Erenberg, *Steppin' Out: New York Nightlife and the Transformation of American Culture, 1890–1930* (Chicago: University of Chicago Press, 1981), ch. 3.

66   Peiss, *Cheap Amusements*, p. 148. For a more detailed breakdown by age, gender, and occupation an in relation to other entertainment forms, see Davis, *Exploitation of Pleasure*, pp. 30ff.

67   'Nickel Theaters Crime Breeders,' *The Chicago Daily Tribune* (13 April 1907): 3. I am indebted to Lauren Rabinowitz for this reference.

68   Ewen, *Immigrant Women*, p. 212. On different standards of respectability among working-class women, see Kathy Peiss, 'Charity Girls' and City Pleasures: Historical Notes on Working-Class Sexuality,' in Ann Snitow *et al.* (eds.), *Powers of Desire* (New York: Monthly Review Press, 1983), pp. 74–87.

69   Peiss, *Cheap Amusements*, pp. 152ff.

70   To my knowledge, there are no empirical studies singling out women's viewing habits and preferences comparable to Altenloh's 1914 dissertation (see note 58) – at least not until the Payne Fund studies undertaken between 1929 and 1932 – and even if there were, the social science methods of interrogation used tend to limit the value of such studies for reconstructing a historical horizon of reception.

71   On early serials, see Ben Singer, 'The Perils of Empowerment: Agency, Vengeance and Violation in the Serial-Queen Melodrama,' longer version of a paper delivered at the SCS conference, Iowa City, April 1989.

72   Sumiko Higashi, *Virgins, Vamps, and Flappers: The American Silent Movie Heroine* (Montreal: Eden Press Women's Publications, 1978); Alice Guy Blaché, 'Woman's Place in Photoplay Production,' *MPW* (11 July, 1914), rpt. in Karyn Kay and Gerald Peary, eds., *Women and the Cinema* (New York: Dutton, 1977), pp. 337–40. On the World War I films, see Kevin Brownlow, *The War, the West, and the Wilderness* (New York: Knopf, 1979), pp. 33, 76, 145–6.

73   Leslie Fishbein, 'The Fallen Woman as Victim in Early American Film: Soma Versus Psyche,' *Film & History* 17(3) (September 1987): 51; also see 'The Harlot's Progress in American Fiction and Film, 1900–1930,' *Women's Studies* 16 (1988).

74 Mary P. Ryan, 'The Projection of a New Womanhood: The Movie Moderns in the 1920s,' in Jean E. Friedman and William G. Shade, eds., *Our American Sisters, Women in American Life and Thought* (Boston: Allyn and Bacon, 1976), pp. 370–71.

75 See Chapter 1 at note 39 and Part III of this book.

76 Mary Ann Doane, *The Desire to Desire: The Woman's Film of the 1940s* (Bloomington: Indiana University Press, 1987), pp. 32–3 and passim. On Kracauer and female spectatorship, see Heide Schlüpmann, Patrice Petro, and Sabine Hake in *New German Critique* 40 (Winter 1987).

78 Doane, *Desire*, p. 26.

79 Mary Ann Doane, 'Misrecognition and Identity,' *Ciné-Tracts* 3.3 (Fall 1980): 29.

80 In the French comedy two women provoke the wrath of the male viewers seated in front of them by first talking and then getting wrapped up in the (theatrical) presentation to the point of a cascade of tears. The film is reproduced – though misdated – in Noël Burch's film, *Correction Please, or How We Got into Pictures* (1979).

81 Doane, *Desire*, p. 31.

82 Altenloh, *Sociologie des Kino*, pp. 79, 88, 94, Iris Barry, *Let's Go To The Movies* (New York: Payson & Clarke, 1926), p. ix.

83 Virginia Woolf, 'The Movies and Reality,' *New Republic* 47 (4 Aug. 1926): 310. Woolf's contemporary and friend Dorothy Richardson goes so far as to align the epiphantic quality of silent film with an essentially female quality, when she asserts that the coming of sound brought film closer to its 'masculine destiny' ('The Film Gone Male,' *Close-Up* [March 1932]). As Anne Friedberg concludes in her introduction to the reprint of Richardson's essay, 'for the film to have 'gone male' there had to be a *film once female*' (*Framework* 20 [1982]: 6–8).

Chapter 30

JACKIE STACEY

HOLLYWOOD CINEMA: THE GREAT ESCAPE

THIS IS THE FIRST OF THREE CHAPTERS which analyse the letters and questionnaires I received concerning Hollywood cinema and stars in Britain during the 1940s and 1950s. Each chapter deals with one of the three central discourses of spectatorship to emerge from the material I received from my respondents: escapism, identification and consumption respectively. Thus the first investigates the question of escapism and looks at the reasons why women went to the cinema; the second analyses the processes of spectatorship in terms of a range of spectator/star identifications; finally, a key consequence of film viewing, namely commodity consumption, is analysed further in the last of these chapters. The differing historical foci of each of these chapters result from the varying emphases found in the material: significantly, the discourse of escapism is most closely articulated with wartime Britain and the discourse of consumption most closely associated with post-war Britain. However, this applies only at the most general level and there are numerous examples of overlap and of the blurring of these periodic boundaries.

Before moving on to analyse spectators' memories of Hollywood cinema, it is important to set out some of the features of cinema-going in Britain during this period. This will serve first to specify more clearly the cinema-going practices of audiences in Britain during this period; second, to analyse more closely the audience composition at this time; and finally, to include some discussion of my respondents in relation to audiences more generally. Thus the following section acts as an introduction to all three subsequent chapters by offering an analysis of cinema-going practices and their significance in terms of specific groups of spectators in Britain during the 1940s and 1950s. However, the introductory section is also especially relevant to an analysis of escapism in so far as it gives some general indications of Hollywood's mass appeal in Britain at this time. The statisitics offer some of the quantitative details necessary to convey the centrality of Hollywood cinema in women's lives in Britain during the 1940s and 1950s.

Hollywood cinema in 1940s' and 1950s' Britain

The significance of the cinema

> Going to the pictures was not just an entertainment, but a way of life.
>
> (Sonja Robinson)

> The cinema meant so much to us in those days. We would rather have gone without food, and often did, than miss our weekly visits.
>
> (Pat Robinson)

> I loved all the stars of Hollywood in the 1940s and 1950s. I was a teenager in the '40s and the cinema was my world.
>
> (Anon)

The significance of the cinema in women's lives in the 1940s and 1950s cannot be over-estimated. The considerable response I received from my advertisement (350 letters) and the high return rate of the follow-up questionnaires (238 out of 258) attest to the value women continue to place on the subject of Hollywood and its stars in their lives forty and fifty years later. The pleasures of recollection, remembering and reminiscing were constantly referred to in the replies I received: I was frequently thanked for offering the opportunity for a 'a trip down memory lane'. Hollywood stars during this period, it would seem, provide an abundance of 'treasured memories' which demonstrate their lasting significance for female spectators at this time. My advertisement signified to respondents a recognition of important experiences many feared were no longer relevant, and catalysed a powerful expression of renewed enthusiasm and passion for Hollywood cinema:

> I saw *Calamity Jane* 88 times . . . My favourite star of all time, even now, is Doris Day. To me she was my idol, I loved every film she ever did, and watched most of them several times. . . . I belonged to her fan club, collected all her photos and kept a scrap book, which sad to say was stolen in the 1970s. *Calamity Jane* was my all time favourite.
>
> (Veronica Millen)

Spectators' enthusiasm for particular stars and particular films is striking. A high percentage of respondents remembered going to the cinema two or three times a week during this period. Although the women responding to an advertisement for 'keen cinema-goers' are likely to have gone more frequently than many audiences at that time, cinema attendance *was* very high during this period, especially during the 1940s. Statistics of cinema attendance during the 1940s and 1950s are sporadic and partial. There are, in fact, very few sources for such information.[1] However, piecing together what is available indicates high attendance rates, high frequency of attendance and huge profits made by motion picture industries, suggesting something of the role cinema played in people's lives at this time.

A table of the gross box-office receipts, for example, between 1935 and 1980 offers some indication of the enormous popularity of the cinema in the 1940s and 1950s (see Table 30.1).

As Table 30.1 makes clear, the gross box-office receipts totalled £114.2 million in 1945, which is nearly three times the equivalent figure in 1940, and about nine times the figure for 1980 based on the 1980 prices scale. In 1946, when cinema attendance in Britain was at its peak, cinema admissions takings totalled £121,000,000 (1946 prices) which was 'roughly one-fifth of the nation's annual clothing bill, one-seventh of its yearly outlay on rent and light, or

Figure 30.1 'I saw *Calamity Jane* 88 times . . . My favourite star of all time, even now, is Doris Day.'

Table 30.1 Gross box-office receipts

Year	£ millions (at then current prices)	£ millions (at 1980 prices)[1]
1935	38.7	
1940	44.9	(485.4)
1945	114.2	(1,027.8)
1950	105.2	(779.5)
1955	105.8	(632.7)
1960	63.6	(338.4)
1965	61.7	(278.9)
1970	59.0	(213.0)
1975	71.2	(139.6)
1980	135.7	(135.7)

Note: 1 This column, in which the purchasing power of the pound in 1980 has been reckoned as a constant 100p, shows the comparable figures for box-office receipts from 1940 onwards; VAT is included where relevant.
Source: The statistics are issued by the Department of Trade (Pirelli, 1983: 382).

one-thirteenth of its expenditure on food' (Swann 1987: 36). Even in 1955, when cinema-going had become less popular, the net takings were £105.8 million (£632.7 million by 1980s prices).

Cinema-going was the main form of leisure activity in Britain in the 1940s and 1950s. In the early 1950s, twice as much money was spent on going to the cinema as on 'going to theatres, concert halls, music halls, skating rinks, sporting events and all other places of popular entertainment' (Swann 1987: 150). Indeed, figures for 1950 highlight the popularity of the cinema over other leisure activities: in 1950 the number of cinema admissions totalled 1,611 million, compared with theatres and music halls, or football matches, each totalling 84 million (Corrigan 1983: 24). The number of cinemas in Britain in 1940 was 4,671 and this rose to a peak of 4,703 in 1945.

Cinema admissions peaked at 1,635 million in 1946 in Britain, and did not drop below 1,000 million between 1940 and 1955. According to Corrigan, cinema attendance in England, Scotland and Wales was higher than in any other country: it 'averaged twenty-eight admissions per head in 1950, compared with twenty-three in the United States' (Corrigan 1983: 25). As well as the extremely high numbers of people going to the cinema each week in Britain during this period, the frequency of attendance is also striking (see Table 30.2). The results of the Wartime Social Survey 1943, *The Cinema Audience* (Box and Moss 1943), show a high percentage of audience members attended the cinema more than once a week, especially within the younger age ranges, and that a slightly higher percentage of women attended more frequently than men.

Although the statistics in Table 30.2 do not distinguish between Hollywood and British films, a large proportion of the films seen were American. In 1939, for example, 80 per cent of films shown in Britain were American (Lant 1991), and in 1945 a total of seventy-six British films (over thirty-three-and-a-half minutes) were registered with the Department of Trade, compared with 374 'foreign' films (of over thirty-three-and-a-half minutes). Indeed, Hollywood found its most important export market in Britain. 'In 1946, for example, between them, the United States and Great Britain accounted for 120 million out of the 235 million worldwide cinema admissions each week, 30 million of these being in Britain' (Swann 1987: 9).

Table 30.2 suggests that my respondents would have been amongst those attending the cinema most often, since the combination of being young and female puts them in the highest

Table 30.2   Frequency of cinema-going in the UK in 1943

		Age				
Frequency	*Sex*	*14–17 (%)*	*18–40 (%)*	*41–5 (%)*	*46–65 (%)*	*Over 65 (%)*
Once a week or more	M	76	38	24	15	5
	W	81	45	28	119	5
Less than once a week	M	21	43	48	40	26
	W	15	36	43	42	25
Not at all	M	2	19	27	43	69
	W	2	18	28	38	70
Sample	M	151	841	378	897	193
	W	153	1,527	336	795	261

Source: Box and Moss (1943), Mass Observation File 1871.

attendance category. Most respondents are women who are now over 50-years-old and thus most of them would be included in the first two age brackets in this particular survey.

The feminization of the spectator

There has been a great deal of work investigating the masculinization of the cinema spectator within a psychoanalytic approach to the pleasures of Hollywood cinema (see Chapter 2). However, historically, it has been the female spectator who has been of most interest to the cinema and other related industries. Leo Handel (1950) argues that Hollywood studios believed women made up the highest proportion of cinema audiences and thus went to great lengths to produce films which appealed to women. Handel's summary of Hollywood's own market research reveals that gender-differentiated surveys were conducted to find out what female spectators wanted to see.

This 'feminization' of the cinema spectator is also identified in Maria La Place's illuminating analysis of the 1930s and 1940s 'woman's film' as the embodiment of many of the criteria found to be particularly desirable by female spectators:

> a set of criteria were [sic] developed for attracting women to the movies; it was concluded that women favoured female stars over male, and preferred, in order of preference, serious dramas, love stories, and musicals. Furthermore, women were said to want 'good character development', and stories with 'human interest'. In one sense, the woman's film can be viewed as the attempt to cover as much of this territory as possible.
>
> (La Place 1987: 138)

A further reason Hollywood marketing strategies paid particular attention to female spectators related to consumerism. The coincidence of the development of Hollywood cinema with the rise of consumerism more generally, in which women played a key role as consumers, has led to a consideration of the specific relationship between female spectators and Hollywood cinema. Although the theme of Hollywood cinema and consumerism is more relevant to the 1950s, when markets expanded in Britain and commodities became more widely available, it has been argued that the cinema industry (linked as it was with other consumer industries) has always addressed its female spectators as consumers more generally. Some critics have made the argument that because of the central role of the spectator as a consumer, and because it was women who were primarily addressed as consumers, a case can be made that the cinema spectator was increasingly envisaged as female:

> In the 1920s, theatre managers' trade journals described the motion picture theater not only as a temple of secular religion, but as an environment designed to stimulate the adoration of the female spectator in particular. A 1927 article in *Theater Management*, for example, stressed the importance of women as the primary component and motivators of film attendance and argued that both the appeal of the film and the theater must be geared to pleasing women's sensibilities.
>
> (Allen 1980: 486)

This is not to deny the fact that men attended the cinema regularly too. Indeed, many women remember the cinema as the main place for the pursuit of heterosexual romances and 'courtships', and thus men's presence was a necessary component of much cinema-going during this period. Ironically, this public place offered the only opportunity for the necessary privacy for many heterosexual couples before marriage. 'It seems that most of our courting was done in the pictures. It was the nearest thing to privacy any of us had in those days' (Jean Sheppard). However, men's attendance does not necessarily undermine the fact that it was women who were seen as the key *motivators* of cinema-going, and thus a crucial audience to target in Hollywood's marketing strategies.

In addition to the popularity of Hollywood films in Britain, there were many other cultural forms, associated with Hollywood, which attest to its significance in women's lives at this time. For example, in the late 1940s there were at least twenty-seven magazines about the cinema on sale to the general public. There were also several film journals aimed at more specialized audiences. Women were seen as a particularly receptive market for stories on Hollywood cinema in magazines generally (Swann 1987: 41). Fan newsletters were also prolific at this time and had high circulation figures among female spectators: 'It was possible for a fan newsletter such as the *International Jean Kent Fan Club* to have a circulation rivalling that of the *Spectator*' (ibid.: 42). As well as specialist publications, the purchasing of daily newspapers was also related to the cinema: 'in a post-war survey, a majority of newspaper readers said that local film listings were the second most important reason for buying a newspaper, whilst fully a fifth of the respondents in this survey said cinema listings were their most important reason for buying a newspaper' (ibid.: 42).

Class differences

Another important factor in determining the composition of cinema audiences was class difference. According to *The Cinema Audience* (Box and Moss 1943: 8), the highest proportion of cinema-goers who visited the cinema more than once a week in 1943 were those who worked in light munitions and other manufacturing and in clerical work. Only a small proportion of people in these groups did not go to the cinema. Agricultural workers and the retired and 'unoccupied' had the lowest cinema attenance. Those belonging to the managerial and professional classes represented a high proportion of the group who went less than once a week. Under the rather problematically general category 'housewives', a rather lower-than-average proportion went to the cinema once a week or more often. But the researchers point out that, compared with other groups, there is a high proportion of older people in this group and that younger women would more often be wage earners.

One source of research on class difference and cinema audience composition and frequency of attendance is the findings of Mark Abrams' Research Services Company. This research was produced for the Rank Organization with a view to using films to market other consumer goods. Drawing heavily on the results of the Hulton Surveys, Abrams highlighted the extent to which the cinema audience was drawn from working-class people and from younger sections of the population. In an article written for the *Hollywood Reporter*, Abrams claims that: '[t]he Working Classes flock to the movies with such avidity that they account for more than 70 per cent of the audience' (quoted in Swann 1987: 46). As Paul Swann goes on to comment, there are many competing claims about the demographies of British cinema audiences in the post-war period, but all suggest this kind of class difference in its composition.

Class position, as I have already stated, is notoriously difficult to ascertain for women, since a woman's class position is frequently defined through her husband's paid employment, and the category 'housewife' that many women use to describe themselves is one which does not explicitly indicate class position. The readers' profiles of the two magazines in which I advertised, *Woman's Realm* and *Woman's Weekly*, show that over 50 per cent of their readership come from classes C1 and C2: clerical and skilled workers. Based upon information about respondents' backgrounds, such as ownership of accommodation, educational qualifications and employment of the respondents and their spouses, my respondents typically come from similar class backgrounds. This is also consistent with the statistics available on the composition of the cinema audience during this period. However, although most of my respondents tended to come from similar class backgrounds in the 1940s and 1950s, many of them have since shifted class positions through marriage or changes in education, training and employment.

Ethnicity

To my knowledge there are no comparable surveys about the different ethnicities of cinema audiences at this time. The Hollywood audience in Britain during the 1940s and 1950s has been perceived as predominantly white, despite the fact that its ethnic composition changed considerably, particularly during the 1950s when Britain's black population grew with the need for labour from Britain's colonies (The Runnymede Trust and the Radical Statistics Group 1980). The so-called age of affluence in 1950s Britain was heavily dependent upon the importation of black workers from Britain's colonies (Fryer 1984). The cinema was also a central source for the dissemination of government 'lines' to white audiences about the new workers from the colonies. Afro-Caribbean and Asian workers were sought out by British companies and encouraged to come to Britain with the promise of employment and prosperity. In fact, they were mainly employed at low wages to do the work which many white workers were unwilling to do. The ethnic composition of Britain thus changed greatly during this period of economic expansion (Fryer 1984: 373–81). However, details about changes in the ethnic composition of British cinema audiences remain unresearched.

Furthermore, there has been very little research into the question of black audiences and their relationship to dominant white Hollywood. Until recently Elizabeth Ewen (1980) and Judith Mayne (1982) were two of the few to consider the issue of ethnicity and audiences. However, there is an increasing amount of textual criticism of Hollywood cinema in terms of its traditions of racist representations and, indeed, two recent collections on female spectatorship have included some new work on black female spectatorship. Jacqueline Bobo (1988) examines black women's readings of the film *The Color Purple* and Jacqui Roach and Petal Felix (1988) analyse questions of the black look in popular culture.

The respondents to my advertisement were all white women. This is not surprising because of the readership and orientation of the magazines which agreed to print my request. Both *Woman's Weekly* and *Woman's Realm* appeal predominantly to a white readership. Many of my respondents expressed surprise, irritation and confusion at being asked to describe their ethnicity. Some felt the question was irrelevant; others felt indignation at being asked; others still expressed anger at the categories I had chosen and crossed them out altogether. In particular, the respondents resented the category 'white European' and asserted instead their 'Englishness' or 'Britishness' which they assumed to be a white identity.

Given the predominant whiteness of Hollywood and its stars, the question of ethnicity and the appeal of Hollywood cinema at this time is a pressing one. Black female spectators have yet to be asked about their feelings about white Hollywood cinema. Certainly, in some black writing, Hollywood stars have signified desirable white femininity, producing fantasies of glamour, power and status for those women denied such 'privileges', as the opening to the novel *I Know Why The Caged Bird Sings* demonstrates:

The dress I wore was lavender taffeta, and each time I breathed it rustled, and now that I was sucking air to breathe out shame it sounded like crepe paper on the back of hearses.

As I'd watched Momma put ruffles on the hem and cute little tucks around the waist, I knew that once I put it on I'd look like a movie star. (It was silk and that made up for the awful color.) I was going to look like one of the sweet little white girls who were everybody's dream of what was right with the world. Hanging softly over the black Singer sewing machine, it looked like magic, and when people saw me wearing it they were going to run up to me and say, 'Marguerite (sometimes it was "dear Marguerite"), forgive us, please, we didn't know who you were,' and I would answer generously, 'No, you couldn't have known. Of course I forgive you.'

. . . Wouldn't they be surprised when one day I woke out of my black ugly dream, and my real hair, which was long and blond, would take the place of the kinky mass that Momma wouldn't let me straighten? My light-blue eyes were going to hypnotize them. . . . Because really I was white and because a cruel fairy step-mother, who was jealous of my beauty, had turned me into a too-big Negro girl with nappy black hair, broad feet and a space between her teeth that would hold a number two pencil.

(Angelou 1984: 3–5)

As Maya Angelou highlights, Hollywood stars produce cultural ideals of whiteness. The 'difference' between 'Marguerite' and the white movie star she fantasizes resembling can be seen to intensify the appeal in a racist society where ideals of beauty and glamour have always been white. Indeed, in the 1950s this is especially the case, when Marilyn Monroe's blondeness, for example, was a key signifier of her glamour (Dyer 1986).

The decline of the cinema in the 1950s

It is important to highlight the fact that cinema attendance was by no means consistent during the 1940s and 1950s. In fact, attendance fell considerably during the late 1940s and the 1950s

Table 30.3   Cinema admissions and net box-office takings (UK)

Year	Admissions (millions)	Net takings (£ millions)
1945	1,585	73
1947	1,462	68
1949	1,430	67
1951	1,365	71
1953	1,285	72
1955	1,182	73
1957	915	65
1959	581	69

Source: Adapted from Board of Trade Statistics (Kelly, quoted in Jarvie 1970: 116).

as Table 30.3 indicates. Reasons for this are too numerous to discuss in detail here, but tend to be attributed to changes in the Hollywood industry, especially the break-up of the studio system, the diversification of leisure markets, particularly the emergence of television, and finally to the restructuring of housing in post-war Britain, moving people away from areas with accessible local cinemas. Hollywood feature films also began to be shown on television from 1953–4 onwards.

However, whilst it is important not to treat the 1940s and 1950s as a unified time period during which the popularity of the cinema was constant, it is also true that cinema-going was an immensely popular practice that produced an enormous revenue throughout both decades in Britain. During this period, cinema attendance averaged over 1,000 million per year and net takings were over £68 million. Similarly, despite this decline in cinema attendance,[2] a 1961 survey, *The Cinema Audience*, carried out by the Screen Advertising Association, found the frequency of cinema attendance still significantly high: 30 per cent of the sample attended twice a week and another 33 per cent once a week (Jarvie 1970: 112).

Theorizing escapism

> The cinema was a night out, an escape into a more glamorous world.
>
> (Jean Johnson)

It is a truism to assert that escapism is one of the most important pleasures of Hollywood cinema. But what exactly is meant by 'escapism'? A term often meant pejoratively, 'escapism' has been applied to forms of popular culture in order to dismiss them as insignificant and unworthy of critical or academic attention. Indeed, this has been particularly true of forms of popular culture enjoyed by women – soap operas or romance fiction and films. In the light of such attacks, feminist critics have insisted on taking women's pleasures in popular culture seriously and understanding exactly what is at stake in their consumption of these particular popular forms.

In this study my request for accounts of such pleasures contradicted the assumption that women's pleasures in popular culture are unworthy of academic attention. The overwhelming and enthusiastic response I received may partly be accounted for by the feelings of validation and recognition prompted by such a request. However, some women wrote about their enthusiasm for Hollywood stars with a kind of embarrassment or self-consciousness about their pleasure, acknowledging its escapist roots which they feared might be perceived as 'trivial' or 'silly'. Respondents frequently questioned the importance of their contributions with comments such as: 'I hope this is helpful, though I fail to see how my scribblings are of interest'; or 'yes, please do quote me if you really want to, but I doubt if my memories will be of much use'. Thus, whilst keen to share their memories, some women simultaneously guarded against disparagement by building in their own auto-critique of the 'escapist' nature of their love of Hollywood and its stars. One respondent offers a retrospective analysis of her own pleasures in Hollywood's 'dreams':

> In retrospect it's easy to see Hollywood stars for what they really were. This was pretty packaged commodities . . . the property of a particular studio.
>
> At the time I did most of my film-going, while I was always aware that stars were really too good to be true, I fell as completely under the spell of the Hollywood 'Dream Factory' as any other girl of my age.
>
> (Kathleen Lucas)

The reappraisal of the pleasures offered by Hollywood stars continues:

> Looking back, I can see much of what I took as authenicity was really technical skill . . . Later on I realized just how much money and expertise went into creating the 'natural' beauties the female stars appeared to be.
>
> (Kathleen Lucas)

Other respondents articulated a strong nostalgia for Hollywood cinema of the 1940s and 1950s precisely because of the escapist pleasures they longed to recapture. When contrasting their memories of Hollywood with the cinema of today it is escapism which recurringly characterizes the pleasures many respondents feel they have lost:

> I think in those eras, we were most inclined to put stars on a pedestal. They were so far removed from everyday life, they were magical. . . . These days stars are so ordinary – the magic has gone. Hollywood will never be the same again!
>
> (Kathleen Simes)

Whether reappraised with critical hindsight, or longed for nostalgically, 'escapism' was one of the most frequent reasons given by these female spectators for their cinema-going enthusiasm in the 1940s and 1950s. There are few studies, however, that analyse what is involved in this cultural process so loosely dubbed 'escapism'.[3] Most studies fail to move beyond the level of generalization in their discussion of escapism. Those that do have not considered the gendered dimensions of escapist pleasures which are of particular relevance to this study. This chapter therefore offers both an analysis of the meanings of escapism in relation to the cinema and an investigation of the relationship between escapism and the cultural construction of femininity.

Richard Dyer's article 'Entertainment and utopia' (1985) is one of the very few attempts to deconstruct the notion of 'escapism' in relation to Hollywood cinema. He argues that two of the taken-for-granted descriptions of entertainment:

> as 'escape' and as 'wish-fulfilment', point to its central thrust, namely, utopianism. Entertainment offers the image of 'something better' to escape into, or something we want deeply that our day-to-day lives don't provide. Alternatives, hopes, wishes – these are the stuff of utopia, the sense that things could be better, that something other than what is can be imagined and maybe realised.
>
> (Dyer 1985: 222)

Dyer's article develops an analysis of what he calls 'entertainment's utopian sensibility'. Contradicting the usual exclusively textual focus of many film studies, Dyer argues that these signs work through a cultural code which can be related to a particular set of historical circumstances:

> it is important to grasp that modes of experiential art and entertainment correspond to different culturally and historically determined sensibilities. This becomes clear when one examines how entertainment forms come to have the emotional signification they do: that is, by acquiring their signification in relation to a complex of meanings in the social-cultural situation in which they are produced.
>
> (Dyer 1985: 223)

Importantly for my argument, then, Dyer highlights here the connections between pleasure and the historical and cultural locations which produce particular forms of utopian sensibility. Additionally, by focusing on utopian *sensibility*, Dyer highlights another rather neglected question within film studies – the emotional dimensions of the cinema. Despite the preoccupation with the question of (visual) pleasure in film studies generally, an understanding of the emotional significance of the cinema to its audience has remained absent.

In order to develop an understanding of utopian sensibility, Dyer constructs a series of categories through which entertainment forms can be understood: abundance, energy, intensity, transparency and community. He then relates these categories to the inadequacies of society from which people may be seeking temporary relief through the utopian sensibilities of entertainment forms. Thus, attempting to construct a framework for how entertainment works, Dyer suggests the model shown in Table 30.4.

However, although Dyer's model provides one of the few analyses of the pleasures of escapism offered by popular entertainment forms, a number of questions need further elaboration. First, the audience is, in a sense, the structuring absence in Dyer's argument. The missing link between the social tension outside the cinema and the utopian solution offered on the screen in Dyer's model is, in fact, the cinema spectator. With its emphasis on the significance of context to the pleasures of escapism, Dyer's analysis demonstrates the necessity of situating the pleasures of the text within specific locations. Thus, different audiences might bring different needs and desires to the cinema depending on their historical and cultural circumstances, Second, as Dyer himself acknowledges, these categories work at the general level and need to be explored in terms of social divisions such as gender, ethnicity and class.

Table 30.4   Dyer's model of the appeal of entertainment forms

Social tension / inadequacy / absence	Utopian solution
Scarcity (actual poverty in the society; poverty observable in the surrounding societies, e.g. Third World; unequal distribution of weath)	Abundance (enjoyment of sensuous material reality, conquest of scarcity for self and others)
Exhaustion (work as a grind, alienated labour, pressures of urban life)	Energy (capacity to act vigorously; human power, activity, potential)
Dreariness (monotony, predicability, instrumentality of the daily round)	Intensity (experiencing of emotion directly, fully, unambiguously, 'authentically', without holding back)
Manipulation (advertising, bourgeois democracy, sex roles)	Transparency (open, spontaneous, honest communications and relationships, sincerity)
Fragmentation (job mobility, rehousing and development, high-rise flats, legislation against collective action)	Community (togetherness, a sense of belonging, communal interests and activites)

Source: Dyer 1985: 224–8.

It therefore remains for this model to be reworked and adapted in relation to particular audiences in specific contexts. The rest of this chapter thus extends Dyer's argument through an analysis of the escapist pleasures of Hollywood cinema in wartime and post-war Britain remembered by the female spectators in this study.

The cinema as dream palace

Previously, the question of cinematic plreasure has been primarily analysed in terms of the visual and narrative conventions of Hollywood films. Menories of the pleasures of the cinema in wartime and post-war Britain, however, are not limited to the film text. In order to understand how the cinema offered female spectators the pleasures of escapism at this time it is necessary to analyse the whole cinema-going experience, rather than simply focusing on the details of the film text.[4] Indeed, as Rachel Low has argued, the cinema audience during this period largely consisted of habitual cinema-goers for whom the cinema was 'an institutionalized night out independent of the artistic value of the entertainment' (Low, quoted in Swann 1987: 36). It was often this ritualized night out which was remembered as particularly enjoyable by female spectators in my study: 'I loved the whole atmosphere from queueing outside, right through to the national anthem – after which it was a rush to catch the last bus home' (Kathleen Lucas).

The focus on the whole event, it might be argued, could be partly explained by the retrospective nature of these accounts. For example, the details of particular films might have been forgotten, and these 'ritualized nights out' might be more easily remembered fifty years later. However, many of my respondents also remember surprisingly detailed aspects of costume, gesture and dialogue from particular films. Instead, I would argue that what emerges from these repeated accounts of the pleasures of cinema-going practices generally is the importance of moving beyond the pleasures of the text to include the pleasures of the ritualized event.

A second issue to emerge from respondents' memories of cinema-going in Britain at this time was the material pleasure of the cinema itself. My respondents repeatedly offered vivid memories of the cinema as a physical space in which to escape the discomforts of their everyday lives. Shortages of fuel, clothes, food and other basic needs were frequently mentioned as contrasts to the environment of the cinema:

> Cinemas were warm, comfortable, attractive places, relaxing after a day's work. Sometimes one went to keep warm if coal was short.
>
> (Anon)

> For a few hours it made you forget about the war in the 1940s and after the war the drabness of everything in post war Britain. . . . We went more often during the war because you could forget the war for a few hours and the air raids that were often going on at the same time, also it was a place to be warm in the winter months, as coal was in short supply.
>
> (Joan Draper)

Cinematic pleasure, then, is remembered as having an important material dimension. Cinemas offered women a physical escape from the hardships of their lives at this time.

But cinemas were not merely recalled as warm, cosy buildings where films were screened. They were also remembered for their plush interiors, which offered a unique opportunity to enjoy the feelings associated with certain 'luxuries' rare in 1940s Britain:

> Like so many others, my life in the 1940s was pretty drab. We lived in a London flat. No electricity, no bath, no luxuries like refrigerators, telephones or cars, and of course no TV. All we had to brighten up our lives were the radio and the cinema. For 1s. 9d. we could enter another world. Oh the luxury of it, the red carpet, the wonderful portraits adorning the walls. The chandeliers hanging in the foyer and the smell!

> (Patricia Robinson)

Here, attention is drawn to the physical luxuries of the cinema in contrast to the very specific hardships of the domestic environment.

Remembering the 1940s from the vantage point of the late 1980s these contrasts between the luxuries of the cinema and the hardships of the home may have seemed particularly stark. Having lived through more prosperous years since, when many of these 'luxuries' became 'necessities' for women in Britain, the retrospective assessment of this period no doubt makes it seem even bleaker. For many women in this study the availability of mass market consumer goods, especially domestic ones, from the 1940s onwards highlights the relative hardships of the war years.

Many women included details of the cinema buildings themselves in their favourite memories of cinema-going. Cinemas in wartime and post war Britain were remembered as very particular kinds of material spaces for the consumption of Hollywood films. Thus the architecture, design and interior decor can be seen as an integral and important part of the escapist pleasures of cinema-going. A favourite cinema experience of this time, for example, was remembered as:

> visiting an exotic cinema out of my usual district with a friend. The cinema was decorated like a Moorish palace with fountains, star spangled ceiling, etc.

> (Anon)

Cinema designs at this time encouraged the feelings of entering another world;[5] in this example, the imitation of an architectural style from an 'exotic' culture is constructed as 'other' and thus provides an exciting context for the consumption of Hollywood film. One kind of otherness, provided by the style of the cinema interior, offered the context for the enjoyment of another kind of otherness, the representations of American culture in Hollywood films. Escapism, then, was experienced not only in terms of the fictional narrative viewed on the screen, but also through a feeling of 'other worldliness' produced by the design of the cinema interior.

According to Allen (1980) cinema interiors were designed and furnished in ways intended to appeal to female spectators:

> Art works in the lobbies, attractive fabrics and designs for interior decoration, and the subdued and flattering lighting were important appeals to women's tastes and to their desire for comfort and relaxation.

> (Allen 1980: 486)

Responsible for the domestic space at home, and thus acutely aware of its limitations, women could thus be relied upon to respond to the promise of luxury offered by many cinemas. The fact that women were typically reponsible for the domestic organization of households at the time meant that their desire for escape from such hardships may have been especially intense.

One aspect of this appeal remembered by many of my respondents is the sensuousness of cinematic pleasures:

> Particularly in wartime, the cinema was an escape from shortages and restrictions. I revelled in the special effects – perfumed air spray, the exotic (to me) decor,

the fancy lighting which was dimmed, then faded and finally turned off. The feel
of the plush seats and the reaction of the audience.

(Kathleen Lucas)

This quotation emphasizes the luscious nature of the cinema-going experience, for four out
of the five senses are mentioned: smell – the perfumed air spray; sight – the fancy lighting;
touch – the feel of the plush seat; and sound – the reaction of the audience.

The pleasures of wartime cinema-going, then, did not involve only the sense of sight, as is so
often assumed in analyses of visual pleasure which focus on the film text to the exclusion of other
aspects of the cinema. The debates about pleasure within film studies have concentrated on the
'visual', rather than the 'other pleasures' of the cinema (Mulvey 1989). These other 'pleasures'
are analogous, to some extent, to Dyer's non-representational signs in films, such as lighting,
colour and rhythm, which, he argues, have tended to be ignored in film analysis. Both have
crucial roles in creating atmosphere and mood and thus contribute to the pleasures of the
consumption of the film, but have remained relatively hidden within film studies analysis.

Whereas Dyer's categories of utopian sensibility work primarily at an emotional level,
the factors I have identified so far work at a more sensuous, physical level, although these
clearly have an emotional dimension. It is the sensuous pleasures of the luxury of the cinema
that provide a contrast here with the material conditions of women's lives in wartime and
post-war Britain. The cinema itself, then, not only functioned as the physical environment
for screening Hollywood films, but through its architecture, style, decor and layout, it
contributed to the pleasures of escapism remembered by these female spectators.

Moreover, these pleasures (scented smells, softness, visual attractiveness) associated with
the cinema interiors were ones which have been culturally ascribed to femininity; perfumed air,
the plush texture of the curtains and seats, the glistening chandeliers all contribute to what could
be seen as a feminized environment for consumption. The emphasis on the sensuous pleasures
of the interior, as a spectacle to be marvelled at, inviting touch and offering sweet smells, all
connote femininity and echo the feminine qualities so admired in the female stars of Hollywood.

This analysis questions the distinction between 'popular' and 'bourgeois' aesthetics formulated by Pierre Bourdieu in his study of cultural taste and class differences (see Bourdieu 1980,
1984). He argues that whereas popular aesthetics are characterized by an immediate emotional
and sensual pleasure, bourgeois aesthetics are based upon formal and universalized criteria
devoid of passion and pleasure. This distinction ignores the ways in which the pleasures of
the cinema, for example, operate at a sensual and emotional level for female spectators.
Clearly, these are also gendered pleasures at a number of levels. Indeed, it could be argued
that the cinematic space in which Hollywood films were consumed was a feminized one.[6] It
is precisely this feminization of the context of cultural consumption which contributed to the
pleasures of cinema-going at a time when such 'expressions' of femininity remained relatively
unavailable to many women in everyday life in Britain.

The centrality of material pleasure to women's memories of cinema-going at this time is
particularly important in understanding the appeal of *Hollywood* cinema and *Hollywood* stars
(Figure 30.2). associated as it was with luxury and glamour, in contrast to British drabness at
this time, Hollywood was remembered as offering an escape to a materially better world. Thus
the specific association of the luxury of Hollywood with the luxury of the cinema interiors at
this time clearly contributed to the multi-layered meanings of escapism for female spectators.

One central difference which my respondents frequently remembered as significant between
British and American cinema confirms this agument. Hollywood differed from British cinema in
numerous ways, but one crucial difference perceived by audiences at the time was the 'glamour'

Figure 30.2   'Coming down [the cinema staircase] one always felt like a Hollywood heroine descending into a ballroom.' (Publicity still of Joan Crawford.)

of Hollywood and its *stars* in contrast to the seriousness of British cinema and its *actors*.[7] Thus the palatial surroundings of cinemas in the 1940s anticipated in a very particular way the pleasures which followed in the screening of Hollywood films.

Besides anticipating the glamour associated with Hollywood, British cinemas replicated the atmosphere many women associated with Hollywood films and indeed the kinds of roles female stars might play: 'Our favourite cinema was the Ritz – with its deep pile carpet and double sweeping staircase. Coming down one always felt like a Hollywood heroine descending into a ballroom' (Anon).

The glamorous interiors of British cinemas, then, provided the cultural space for the consumption of Hollywood's glamorous femininity. Their luxurious interiors enabled the audience to begin their 'escape' before the films had begun:

> The moment I took my seat it was a different world, plush and exciting, the world outside was forgotten. I felt grown up and sophisticated.
>
> (Betty Cruse)

The physical space of the cinema provided a transitional space between everyday life outside the cinema and the fantasy world of the Hollywood film about to be shown. Its design and decor facilitated the processes of escapism enjoyed by these female spectators. As such, cinemas were dream palaces not only in so far as they housed the screening of Hollywood fantasies, but also because of their own design and decor which provided a feminized and glamorized space suitable for the cultural consumption of Hollywood films.

The material pleasures of cinema-going discussed so far fall within Dyer's utopian category of abundance. Indeed the physical pleasures of the cinema environment, such as the thick pile carpets, the texture of the seating and the perfumed air, accord perfectly with Dyer's definition of abundance as 'enjoyment of sensuous material reality, conquest of scarcity'. However, my analysis here extends Dyer's model to include an account of the ways in which such escapist pleasures are historically and culturally located. Life outside the cinema is repeatedly used in these accounts as a point of contrast with the pleasures offered inside it. Thus the fulfilment of utopian fantasies of luxury and glamour can only be fully understood when situated in relation to the hardship of wartime and post-war Britain which intensified such pleasures for these female spectators. Moreover, memories of the pleasures of abundance offered by the cinema at this time demonstrate the centrality of the construction of femininity to such pleasures. This is true both in terms of the feminization of the cinematic space and in terms of the connections between this space and the glamour of the female Hollywood stars remembered by these spectators.

A sense of belonging

In addition to the importance of the physical space cinemas provided, the shared experience of escaping into that space was remembered as significant. Here again, the focus was not specifically on the films themselves, but rather on the many contributing elements of the cinema-going experience:

> The atmosphere in those days in the cinema was wonderful. Crowds of people queueing to go in, the music playing, the rustling of sweet papers, with usherettes darting up and down the aisles shining their torches.
>
> (June Kelly)

The feeling of a shared group identity was a central component of the 'atmosphere' referred to repeatedly in descriptions of the appeal of the cinema:

> The cinema was a night out, as escape into a more exciting more glamorous world. The watching of a film with a lot of other people heightened my enjoyment of it. . . . I particularly enjoyed the company of the audience around me, the comfortable surroundings, the ice creams and the getting away from everyday life for a few hours.
>
> (Jean Johnson)

This sense of belonging to an audience is an interesting extension of Dyer's category of community which he uses to describe one aspect of utopian sensibility in film texts: 'all together in one place, communal interests, collective activity' (Dyer 1985: 228). One of the pleasures of escapism, then, was remembered as the collective sense of being part of another world:

> The cinema was a wonderful few hours of warmth, companionship and escape to a dream world, and we were part of it.
>
> (Joyce Lewis)

Indeed, sharing the appreciation of particular aspects of Hollywood was felt to connect members of the audience to each other: for example, the collective anticipation of the appearance of the favourite star was one of the unifying practices associated with being part of the cinema audience:

> What I particularly enjoyed about going to the pictures was the expectation of the shared intimacy, the waiting for the favourite star of the moment to appear.
>
> (Dawn Hellmann)

The connectedness to others through shared cultural consumption extends beyond the cinema itself and into everyday practices associated with cinema-going. Discussion of Hollywood and its stars at work and at home was one of the pleasures of the cinema frequently recalled:

> What I really enjoyed about going to the pictures was the atmosphere in the cinema – warm and friendly. It was something to look forward to and plan and then to talk about afterwards.
>
> (Mrs H. Cox)

This sense of community and of togetherness clearly broke down feelings of isolation and offered a sense of self with a collective meaning. The 'shared intimacy' and 'heightened enjoyment' of collective consumption could be read as further contributing to the feminization of cultural consumption: femininity being culturally constructed as relational and masculinity as more individuated.

The notion of femininity as more relational than masculinity has been developed by some feminist theorists, such as Nancy Chodorow (1978), using object relations theory to analyse the social construction of gender inequality.[8] Chodorow argues that the mother/boy-child relationship can be characterized by separation: mothers relate to boys from the time they are born as separate and different from themselves, thus encouraging boys' individuation/separation from their mothers, and boys in their turn negate their early sense of merging with their mothers on the basis of their difference from them. Mothers and girl children, on the other hand, do not relate through such a degree of individuation/separation: girls do not negate their early feelings of oneness with their mothers since they recognize themselves in their mothers; mothers regard their girl children as similar to themselves and identify with them, thus encouraging girls to develop a more relational sense of self.

Although there are limits to this model of gender differences between men and women, not least of which is the fixed version of masculinity and femininity which results, object relations theory nevertheless offers an interesting lens through which to analyse the pleasures of the utopian feelings of 'community' remembered by these female spectators. Indeed, it is the relational aspects of cinematic consumption that are emphasized in these aspects of collective consumption in cinemas in the 1940s. Thus escapism is not merely an individualized process, but rather involves a submergence of self into a more collective identity which could be seen to have a gendered specificity. In other words, the appeal of a utopian sense of community may be especially strong given the ways in which femininity is culturally constructed as generally more relational.

Escaping the war

> Unless you have experienced a totally blacked-out town, limited food and shops that were almost empty, you cannot comprehend the part films played in our lives.
>
> (Gwyneth Wathen)

One of Dyer's central arguments in relation to utopian sensibility is that as well as investigating the pleasurable feelings the audience escapes *into*, it is also important to analyse what it is they are escaping *from*. World War II was, not surprisingly, a constant reference point in many accounts of cinema-going during the 1940s. Hollywood films were remembered as an important contrast to the hardships and strain of wartime Britain. This extreme and dramatic context in which fear, anxiety, loss and confusion became the emotions of everyday life produced a heightened desire to 'escape into another world'. Thus the specificity of the consumption of Hollywood in Britain during the war, and during the continuing austerity of the post-war years, necessitates careful consideration in understanding the pleasures of escapism during this period.

The sense of belonging discussed above, for example, took on a particular meaning during the 1940s in relation to the war: 'the war highlighted the sense of pleasure, the cinema was a warm, communal place to go in an air-raid' (Dawn Hellmann). In this context feelings of togetherness and community took on a special significance. The sense of community was enhanced because there was a common crisis from which to escape. One of the most popular memories of World War II has been an image of people 'pulling together' in a crisis. Togetherness, then, is a predictable recollection to be associated with this time. However, the cinema provided a feeling of togetherness with a difference: unlike the sense of community found in air-raid shelters and food queues, the feelings of community recalled in relation to cinema were linked to pleasurable forms of cultural consumption. Thus, although a feeling of community might have been stronger during the war than would generally be found in many parts of British society, this feeling had particularly pleasurable connotations in relation to Hollywood cinema.

Women's lives in Britain were constantly being fragmented and disrupted by death, destruction and dislocation:

> Women all over Britain were obliged to billet the odd assortment of war workers which included miners, mothers, professors, ex-convicts, students, salesmen and labourers. . . . They were paid a 'government guinea' a week (unless it was a private arrangement) to accommodate, feed and launder for the unnerving intrusion into their already disrupted lives. In September 1939 a third of all Britons changed address and in the course of the war sixty million changes of address in a population of thirty-five million were registered. Normal life ceased as schools, homes, places of work, pubs and cinemas closed or were filled with strangers.
>
> (Minns 1980: 17)

Women were separated from relatives and friends by the war in several ways: most men were absent fighting the war, relatives and friends were under constant threat of being killed by the bombing, and children were evacuated to the country away from their mothers after severe bombing attacks. Throughout these stressful and traumatic times, the cinema was remembered as offering 'a prime source of escapism from the prevalent stresses and anxieties about my husband's serving abroad and all my young friends also serving' (Elizabeth Allan).

One of the key factors dominating life in Britain during World War II was the air-raids. For women in cities particularly, air-raids meant constantly living in fear of death, loss of family and friends and destruction of homes, workplaces and shops. Each new phase of bombing brought new grief and anxiety: 'the Blitz of September 1940 to June 1941, the 1942 Baedecker raids on historic towns, the renewed air attacks on London and other big cities in 1943 to 1944, and the V2 flying bombs and rockets of 1944 to 1945' (Braybon and Summerfield 1987: 160). Women in Britain were all subject to the horrors of the air-raids, and the cinema provided one of the only forms of relief:

> It was lovely to go to see the films – to see the lovely clothes and hear the music. It made the war seem further away, although we often had to go to the shelters during the raids, and come back and finish the film afterwards.
>
> (Kathleen March)

> It was a way of escaping from the blackout and going into a different world of the cinema, especially the musicals, as a young girl I enjoyed the music and clothes and make-believe.
>
> (Anon)

Although cinemas did close down in the first three months of the war, they were quickly reopened, and they provided a much needed feeling of continuity during a time of unpredictability, loss and change. The relocation of people and of activities meant that few previously relied-upon daily routines and/or rituals could be counted upon. Despite the occasional disruption to cinema-going during air-raids, as mentioned above, most respondents remembered little change in their cinema-going habits as a result of the war. Cinema-going, then, proved to be an important and reassuring ritual during the war, offering a brief escape from the pressures on women of wartime life.

Changes were introduced very quickly into many areas of everyday consumption, and it was women who typically had to negotiate these new circumstances. Domestic consumption in particular underwent radical transformations due to shortages and the different requirements of a wartime economy. Contrary to popular memories of the state's intervention into unpaid domestic labour, Braybon and Summerfield argue:

> It is sometimes thought that the government stepped in like a beneficent uncle during the Second World War to take over many of the domestic jobs traditionally ascribed to women, in order to release them for war work. In fact government records and women's own experiences suggest that state intervention into the domestic sphere was limited.
>
> (Braybon and Summerfield 1987: 253)

In fact, rather than releasing women from their domestic burdens, they go on to argue, government campaigns actually encouraged women to increase their domestic activities in order to meet the challenge of the demands of the wartime situation:

> the government was actively encouraging women to enlarge their domestic role through the 'make do and mend' propaganda directed at the 'housewife'. Shortages were even more acute than in the First World War, and the state depended on

women to make up the deficiencies in diet, clothing and comfort, an extra load
for already burdened women to bear.

> (Braybon and Summerfield 1987: 235)

Shortages and rationing were time-consuming and frustrating for women who had to put up with
long queues at the shops and invent new recipes to make limited food go further. Food rationing
of basics like butter, cheese, sugar, meat, tea and preserves was introduced during 1940–1.
Making food stretch to feed everyone was not easy for women on such limited restrictions:

> In 1943 the basic weekly ration per person was 4 ounces of bacon, 1s. 2d. worth of
> meat (this was about the price of a leg of mutton), 3 ounces of cheese, 2 ounces
> of tea, 8 ounces of sugar, 4 ounces preserves, and a total of 8 ounces of fats (2 oz
> cooking fat, 2 oz butter and 4 oz margarine).
>
> (Braybon and Summerfield 1987: 247)

In contrast to such difficulties many women remembered the cinema as providing a longed-
for escape. Wartime restrictions, then, provided a very particular context for the pleasures
of 'abundance' discussed above:

> I wanted to forget, just for a short time, about being cold, lonely and yes, some-
> times hungry . . . to think there was a world out there with no blackout, no
> rationing of food or essential clothing.
>
> (Elizabeth Allan)

> For a few glamorous hours, I could escape from the rationing, the queues and all
> the frustrations of wartime Britain.
>
> (Anon)

> What I enjoyed about going to the pictures most was the glamour. Escape from
> the worries of the war and its austerity. I enjoyed the walk home afterwards, my
> head full of the film I had seen.
>
> (Anon)

American culture in general, and Hollywood films in particular, were associated with glamour,
extravagance and luxury, and watching American films in wartime Britain was associated with
a temporary participation in a more affluent culture:

> The wonderful escape of wallowing in a lifestyle I would have liked for myself.
> . . . Cinema was one of the entertainment sources that kept me going throughout
> the war years – and took one's mind off the anxieties, fears and austerity of that
> time, particularly for a teenager/early twenties girl who could not get the clothes
> she wanted and sometimes not even the make-up.
>
> (Mabel Stringfellow)

What is evident in these memories of Hollywood is the perceived difference between British
and American culture in relation to material scarcity as opposed to material comfort and security, and the pleasures of the temporary escape into another world which offers these 'utopian
feelings'. This may have had a specific significance for women on two counts: first, as I have
suggested, it was women who primarily dealt with the shortages and rationing on a day-to-day
basis. For women, the escape from austerity had particular significance, since it was their
primary responsibility to provide for others. Even though so many women worked during and
after the war, 'running the home' and catering for people's material well-being continued to

be principally their responsibility. In other words, shortages and rationing affected everyone, but women had a particular responsibility for dealing with these problems and negotiating other people's relationships to them.

Second, since one crucial aspect of successful femininity has conventionally been defined through physical attractiveness, the contrast between American 'abundance' and British austerity would be remembered as especially appealing. American culture was remembered as offering 'abundant femininity', which was in turn associated with glamour and desirability, and which was unavailable to women in wartime Britain. What is important here is that the process of escapism involves the reproduction and consumption of highly gendered and historically specific forms of identity. Thus the utopian feelings experienced through Hollywood cinema in 1940s Britain need to be situated within this specific cultural context in order to understand fully their significance to female spectators.

The circulation of Hollywood stars

> Stars were – and are – what the American film was about, what the world went to see American films for, in preference to those from all other countries, including their own . . . the film star was the American industry's contribution to film as a rapturous art.
>
> (Kobal, quoted in Swann 1987: 67)

Stars were as important for cinema spectators as the narrative of the film in which they appeared. They offered one of the key sources of pleasure to the cinema audience. Stars were the most common reason given for the choice of film made in the 1940s by cinema-goers in my research, although this is hardly surprising, given the wording of my advertisement which foregrounded Hollywood stars.

Hollywood's movie star system emerged as a 'business strategy designed to generate large audiences and differentiate entertainment programs and products, and has been used for over seventy years to provide increasing returns on production investments' (Kindem 1982: 79). The rise of the star system in Hollywood, however, was not motivated solely by economic competition between movie companies, but also by 'the intense demand of movie audiences for specific performers' (ibid.: 80). The audience–star axis, then, has always been a crucial one to the success of Hollywood cinema.

Hollywood stars were controlled by studios during the 1930s and 1940s. An increasing concentration of the movie industry into the hands of the 'Big Five' (Warner Bros, Loews/MGM, Paramount, RKO and Twentieth Century Fox) and the 'Little Three' (Universal, Columbia and United Artists) during this period meant that the American movie industry became an oligopoly: in other words, all the power in the industry was concentrated in the hands of these few companies. As this concentration of power in vertically integrated major studios increased, so the control over Hollywood stars tightened.[9] In contrast to the 1920s, stars had less independence, lower salaries and little artistic control over production decisions. Increasingly they were offered restricted contracts with one company for a fixed time period and were disciplined for breaking contracts and trying to work elsewhere. It was not until the gradual break-up of the studio system in the 1950s that stars regained some independence in Hollywood. This proved a mixed blessing, however: whilst the more popular stars turned this to their advantage, the less successful ones found little work in the film industry (Kindem 1982: 88).

Hollywood stars were not simply sold to audiences through the films in which they appeared, but were surrounded by a huge publicity machine which offered audiences information about their lives and activities. Their careers were carefully planned and orchestrated to feed into popular demands and to create new ones. Audiences obtained information about stars from the huge publicity apparatus which was developed by the various studios to promote their stars and protect their investments in them. Stars made personal appearances arranged by studios to encourage their followers; they also circulated regular press releases to ensure fans kept up on the details of the careers and lives of their favourite stars. In addition, fan clubs encouraged audience interests in particular stars. Cinema-goers wrote off for signed photos to the studio or the fan club and used them as 'pin-ups' in their own domestic environments. Some fan clubs had newsletters with wide circulation. The consumption of Hollywood stars, then, was by no means limited to the viewing of the films they appeared in; an extensive publicity apparatus existed which also constructed star images for audiences at this time.

There were, too, numerous publications about the cinema which were read regularly by cinema-goers during the 1940s. *Picturegoer*, the most prestigious film magazine in Britain, was started in 1911, although it took on its more familiar format from 1931 onwards. There were numerous other magazines about the cinema during this time, including: *Film Fantasy and Fact* (formerly *Film-Fan Fare*), *Film Post* (1947–51; *Film Forecast* (1948–51); and *Screen Stories* (1948–9) (Swann 1987: 72). Certainly a very high percentage of the respondents to my research read *Picturegoer* regularly, and many of them mentioned reading at least two or three film publications at this time.

These magazines were devoted to representing the lives of stars, as well as to other features on topics such as new releases, fashion tips and results of audience polls. But women cinema-goers in my study read them to find out about the stars. They featured photographs of stars and a mixture of press releases and inside gossip. The material possessions, wealth and leisure time of individual stars were a source of constant fascination for readers: their cars, houses, swimming pools, holidays, clothes and extravagant American lifestyles were described in detail in film magazines at this time. Audiences in Britain during the 1940s were thus connected to consumption through regular information about the luxuries enjoyed by their idols.

The popularity of stars was continually evaluated by the Hollywood studios. This was hard to gauge and there continue to be competing estimations of the popularity of particular stars at any given time (Kindem 1982: 84–6). Fan clubs and fan magazines were used by studios to monitor the popularity of different stars. Fan mail was another indication of this, giving studios some idea of star popularity. Throughout the 1940s the film industry also used research carried out by George Gallup, who founded Audience Research, Inc. in 1938. This research, the 'Continuing Audit of Marquee Values', aimed not only to analyse the popularity of Hollywood stars, but also to ascertain their relevant importance in relation to other aspects of the cinema.

National identity and Hollywood stars

The star system it has been argued, is particularly characteristic of American cinema:

> This emphasis on screen talent, and the cinematic codes which evolved to render screen talent, such as the use of close-up, and 'glamour' lighting, made American film significantly different from that which evolved in much of the rest of the world. although it should be acknowledged that subsequently many other countries, such as India, have adopted star systems based on the American model of

spectacle, stardom has always been a characteristic closely tied to the American feature film.

(Swann 1987: 69)

For audiences in Britain, the Hollywood star system was in another league from the British film industry. Whilst stars did exist and were used to sell films in the British industry, they did not function on the same scale as Hollywood stars. British stars featured frequently in British film magazines and the British studio, Rank, put extensive resources into building a British star system. However, whilst British stars were extremely popular during the 1940s, and stars such as James Mason and Margaret Lockwood were often among the top-rankers in polls at the time, 'there was nothing really comparable to the big centralized industrial and marketing machinery of Hollywood' (Swann 1987:74). Furthermore, it is also important to note that, as Swann argues, 'British screen stars were never rooted in the ideology of consumerism in quite the way that American stars were as a matter of course' (ibid.: 6–70).

American stars acquired substantial and devoted followings in Britain during the 1940s and 1950s. Although it has proved impossible to find any figures for fan club membership for this period, the strength of the response to my advertisements and the passion with which women wrote about Hollywood stars both give some indication of the importance of American stars in British women's lives.

The appeal of Hollywood stars to British female spectators in particular needs to be understood in the context of the relationship between British and American cultures during this period.[10] In attempting to account for the specific appeal of Hollywood in post-war Britain, Paul Swann argues that the reasons cannot be entirely attributed to the economic imperialism of the Hollywood industry, since there were restrictions on the import of American films during this period when 'the British government pursued a vigorous campaign against the American feature film' (Swann 1987: 31). Continuing a long-standing historical battle between the British and American film industries, the British government took steps to restrict the number of American films shown in Britain in an attempt to encourage the comeback of British film onto the entertainment market (Lant 1991).

More important for understanding Hollywood's appeal, Swann argues, is the significance of American culture in Britain during this period. Daily life in Britain during the war and during the post-war period was dominated by hardship, rationing and loss of family and friends. Rationing did not stop when the war ended, in fact many items began to be rationed which had not previously been: for example, bread rationing was introduced in 1946. Generally there was a shortage of products available for purchase: food, fuel and clothes were all in short supply. Magazines advertised products that were not yet available on the British market.

In 1946 the 'Britain Can Make It' exhibition at the Victoria and Albert Museum was renamed by the popular press 'Britain Can't Have It', since so many of the new consumer products proudly exhibited were marked for export only (Swann 1987: 35). One American magazine reported about life in Britain in 1948: 'Until recently, bananas, lemons, nylon stockings, potato chips, foreign travel for pleasure, a variety of sports equipment . . . were completely unavailable' (Dawson 1948, quoted in Swann 1987: 32). Indeed in 1947, only 3.3 per cent of people in Britain went on holiday abroad, and 43 per cent had no holiday at all (Swann 1987: 45).

All in all, there were few escapes from the hardships of everyday life in Britain at this time. In this context Hollywood cinema had a particular significance in British culture:

the cinema figures prominently in most people's lives as one of the few affordable luxuries which did not require a ration book. The authorities were very conscious of the manner in which films functioned as an important release from austerity, especially for the working class filmgoer. The British worker was on the front line in the export war and Hollywood regularly came up in discussions about schemes to maintain his, or more often her, morale and productivity.

(Swann 1987: 33)

Hollywood cinema offered audiences the possibility to be part of another world far away from the difficulties of everyday life in Britain. America was frequently represented as 'the land flowing with milk and honey' (Eileen Jenkins) in Hollywood films, and the pleasures of escaping from the drabness of life in Britain during the 1940s into the luxurious and glamorous worlds of Hollywood were considerable.

Notes

1   For a useful collection of the 'facts and figures' of cinema-going in Britain, see Pirelli (1983).
2   See Philip Corrigan (1983).
3   There is some sociological work on the concept of 'escapism' (see Katz and Foulkes 1962).
4   The exclusively textual emphasis of much film studies work on the pleasures of spectatorship has meant that such questions have been ignored (see Chapter 2). Some attention has been paid to the whole cinema-going expeerience within film history (see for example Corrigan 1983).
5   For a discussion of the history of cinema architecture, see Alloway (1961) and Furnham (1972).
6   For an analysis of the relationship between mass culture and femininity, see Tania Modleski (1986a), and between the cinema in particular and femininity, see Miriam Hansen (1991), Heide Schlüpman (1980), Andreas Huyssen (1986).
7   This association of British stars with 'acting' and Hollywood stars with 'glamour' was a recurrent theme in the letters pages of *Picturegoer* during the 1940s and 1950s (see Chapter 3).
8   For a discussion of feminist uses of object relations theory, see Sayers (1986).
9   See Gomery (1986) and Balio (1976) on the studio system; see also Part 11 in Gledhill's *Stardom: Industry of Desire* (1991) for analysis of stars and the studio system.
10   For an analysis of the impact of Americanness on post-war British culture, see 'Towards a cartography of taste', in Hebdige (1988).

Chapter 31

JACQUELINE BOBO

WATCHING *THE COLOR PURPLE*
Two interviews

GIVEN THE SIMILARITIES OF *THE COLOR PURPLE* to past films that
have portrayed black people disparagingly, the fact that a large number of black women
have demonstrated positive responses appears to defy explanation. Certainly my analysis of
the film's ideological and formal construction by Steven Spielberg shows the subtle manipulations by which black people are indeed depicted in ways that have been harmful in the past.
However, there are significant differences in this specific instance, emanating from black female
history and cultural experience that have induced a positive reading or a much more suitable
reconstruction of a mainstream cultural product that needs to be considered.

It should also be noted that my examination of black women's responses to *The Color
Purple* cannot be used in a one-size-fits-all manner. It would be a mistake to assume that any
film or mainstream cultural product is without harmful effects simply because of audiences'
ability to read around the text. That so many black women were vocal about their reactions
to the film and defended it strongly and, more important, undertook a spirited defense against
the attacks on Alice Walker would have gone unnoticed if other black women had not joined
with them in a spontaneous, unorganized alliance to preserve their collective character. As
black women cultivated resistance strategies during enslavement and fought against all manner
of inequities and injustices during the early parts of this century, so too did they use the
moment of the entrance of the film *The Color Purple* to advance a better understanding and
knowledge of black women's historical and cultural legacy.

The oppositional impulse that has fueled black women's history of resistance if evident
in their reactions to *The Color Purple*. The reactions are oppositional in two respects. First,
the reactions contradict cohesive reactions by black people to past negative films such as *The
Birth of a Nation* (1915), *The Green Pastures* (1936), *Gone with the Wind* and *Porgy and Bess* (1959).
In the case of *The Color Purple* the outrage against the film is not unanimous, for black people,
and especially a vocal contingent of black men, are split and at times at odds over the film's
effect on the condition of black people in this country.

The second way in which black women's reception of *The Color Purple* is oppositional is
that it is a challenge to the mandate, given dominant media coverage, that black people should
not have positive responses to the film. Two instances in particular stand out. The first
concerned four black male panelists on *Tony Brown's Journal* who debated the effect of the

film. Three of the men were united in agreement with Brown that the film was 'the most racist depiction of black men since *The Birth of a Nation* and the most antiblack family film of the modern film era.' When the fourth panelist, Armond White, spoke in favor of the film, declaring that something worthwhile could come from it, one of the others replied derisively that if White liked the film then he may as well be white.[1]

In another instance a clip of Whoopi Goldberg was shown on *The Phil Donahue Show* while Tony Brown was a panelist. Goldberg said that those who criticize *The Color Purple* as showing negative images of black men should also criticize the singer Prince for the disturbing images he showed of black women being dumped in garbage cans in *Purple Rain*. Brown responded that there were those who practiced the art of saying what white people wanted them to say.[2]

The stakes were high in the discussions concerning the effect of the film, and anyone who did not stand with those who criticized it were at risk of having their allegiance to black people challenged. That many black women clung tightly to their positive feelings about *The Color Purple* was significant in that it allowed them to extract meaningful elements when others were issuing decrees that there should be a wholesale rejection of the film. Although the women's reactions were severely condemned and little understood, these reactions can be seen in the tradition of black women's resistant history. Again, we can go back to Toni Morrison's *Beloved* for an explanation of the motivations behind black women's seemingly outrageous actions. Morrison talks of Sethe's courageous act of going against what society said she should do. As Morrison relates not just about Sethe but about other enslaved black women protecting their children in any way they could from the devastation of enslavement, 'It was the right thing to do, but she had no right to do it.'[3] Morrison explains what it meant for black women to take control of their family's lives in a society where the laws, institutions and prevailing codes of behavior were intended to govern the women's actions:

> These women were not parents. People insisted that they have children. But they could not be mothers because they had no say about the future of those children, where they went; they could make no decisions. They frequently couldn't even name them. They were denied humanity in a number of ways . . . so she [Sethe] claimed something she had no right to claim, which was the property, her property. And claimed it so finally that she decided that she could not only dictate their lives, but end them. And when one knows what their future would be, her decision is not that difficult to understand.

Admittedly, the reactions of a group of viewers to a cultural product is not the same as someone resisting years of brutalization and the prospect that her children would suffer the same fate. However, if we consider the cumulative effect of decades of derogatory representations of black women in mainstream culture and the subsequent transfer of the images as justification for debilitating institutional and social policies, then the symbolism of black women in resistance is more congruent. It is the same spirit manifested by black women during enslavement that impelled black women viewers of the contemporary film to speak out in support of their rights as audience and in defiance of how others felt they should respond.

An additional consideration is that as cultural consumers black women, along with everyone else in consumer culture, have been constantly enjoined to attend films, to watch television programs, to consume all manner of cultural forms in which their history, experiences, and bodies were characterized in a variety of demeaning ways. There is no evidence, however, that black women as a group ever exhibited the same response to previous main-stream works as that given *The Color Purple*. A partial explanation for this lies in the way in which black women were presented in the film. For the first time black women were seen in dominant media as a major focus of the work. Although, as my analysis detailed, black women were moved aside as the center of the story and a black man's experiences were priv-ileged, black women were, nonetheless, constantly on the screen and were seen in ways not displayed before.

As an example, for a major motion picture, technicians took care in lighting, costume and set design so that black performers did not fade into the background. Allen Daviau, director of photography for *The Color Purple*, explains that he and production designer Michael Riva and set decorator Linda DeScenna discovered a way of photographing black people that had not been attempted before. Darkening the set in addition to having the performers wear dark-colored costumes appeared to be a paradox, but it allowed more subtlety of lighting. This in turn separated the black performers from the background so that there was greater clarity in the images rather than a flattening out and competition with the background elements.[4]

This technical aspect contributed to black women's incentive to identify with the women in the film, because the characters did not appear *photographically* as caricatures – although the women I interviewed were not in agreement about the effect of the 'look' of the film. One of the women expressed a feeling that was similar to one of the predominant criticisms by mainstream reviewers – that the novel was more 'gritty,' and Spielberg obscured its message by making the film look too nice. The woman who agreed with this sentiment stated that this offended her immediately when she first watched the film:

> I thought, Damn, this man [Spielberg] is trying to say, 'Oh, look, they had a rough life, but wasn't it pretty.' I mean, look at all the purple flowers. And he's saying, 'yeah, they had nappy heads and they had a hard life, but wasn't it pretty how the sun is coming in in all those shots.' He romanticized it all they way through – and the music, it was that stereotypical old white romanticized music.

When I asked her if she wanted a grittier depiction of the characters' lives, the woman replied that she wanted a more realistic film.

It is interesting that those reviewers who criticized the 'prettiness' of the film as being antithetical to the novel seem to be unaware of Alice Walker's often-expressed statement that the people she characterized in the novel were not poor, that they owned land, prop-erty and dealt in commerce. So the presumed dark and somber ambience of *The Color Purple* would have to come from the minds of the viewers, because the characters written by Walker were not in fact impoverished. It also speaks to many people's store of associations that when-ever black people are rendered in a widely circulated work, if they are not presented as poor and downtrodden they appear 'unreal' because there had been, up to that time, a scarcity of images in dominant media of well-to-do black people.

Another woman I interviewed had a contrasting view on the look of the film:

> I like the fact that it wasn't gritty. I think that if it had been gritty it would have been too much to handle. It was difficult to handle as it was; it was just real powerful. It was a lot to handle at one time. Sometimes you felt like someone had [here she makes a cutting motion across her chest] really exposed me. If it had been grittier, it might have made that even more uncomfortable, or it might have made me back away from it so much that I couldn't feel it. It would have

been too ugly. Because that's ugly; that behavior is very ugly. And I think if it had been realistic, it would have been too ugly for me to watch. And I wouldn't have seen it.

Yet another woman I interviewed spoke about the technical aspects of the film. This woman, however, talked about the subtle differences in the way in which the characters were presented. As the woman stated, Celie is photographed lovingly, whereas the character who plays Nettie, although just as dark and just as photogenic, is not. The contrast is a significant one because it illustrates two things. The first is that a director who is of the culture being portrayed is more likely to present all the characters in compatible ways, such as was the case with Dash and *Daughters of the Dust*. As director she took care and consideration in photographing not just the central character but all the people in the film, including the men.

The second part of the woman's comment relates to the way in which viewers can perceive the differences take note of them yet still find elements in the film they could enjoy and iden- tify with. It is only when audience members are asked about their reactions that these perceptions come to light. Rather than castigate the women for their engagement with the film, I asked them to explain it, and they were able to do so. Consequently, the women can be seen as much more than 'cultural dupes' – they are viewers who understand that they do not have control over image creation in mainstream media but that they do have control over how they will exhibit their responses. Thus the value of interviewing the women allows analysts to understand that audiences are not always the unthinking receivers of media messages but have the ability to manipulate their reactions in very distinctive ways. The issue then becomes what the women identified with and how that identification either was or could potentially be utilized, for progressive purposes.

For my research on *The Color Purple* I conducted two separate group interviews with black women who had seen the film. The first was conducted in December 1987 in northern California; the second was conducted in October 1988 in the Pacific Northwest. There were nine women in the first group and six in the second, for a total of fifteen women interviewed. Before the interviews I did a comprehensive review of the literature in an effort to chart black women's responses in newspapers, magazines, and journals and on radio programs. I also watched many of the nationwide television programs on which the film was discussed. These included two programs on *Tony Brown's Journal*, one of which was set up as a debate between black feminist Barbara Smith and black writer Ishmael Reed. I also watched *The Phil Donahue Show*, which presented black film historian Donald Bogle and Tony Brown as well as the one woman on the panel, Michele Wallace.

I also had discussions with several of the black female scholars who were publicly defending Alice Walker's novel and black women's reactions to the film. A key person was Barbara Christian, who traveled extensively at the time of the initial release of the film in 1986, speaking to groups of black women in a variety of settings.[5] From this research and from conversations I was able to confirm my impressions that many black women had had an over- whelmingly positive reaction to the film.

At the beginning of the interviews I questioned the women in both groups about whether they were religious, because I needed to be able to gauge their reactions to aspects of the novel and the film that dealt with religious issues, such as when Shug, in the novel, talks to Celie about her feelings about God. When Shug asks Celie what her God looks like, Celie replies that she thinks of God as 'big and old and tall and graybearded and white.' Shug tells her that her description is the one that white folks use to describe their God, the one that is written about in their bible. That is why their God looks like them. Celie tells Shug that her sister, Nettie, had written to her from Africa that Jesus's hair was like lamb's wool. Shug, referring to a much-noted hair and color bias among black people,[6] says to Celie about the texture of Jesus's hair: 'If he came to any of these churches we talking bout he'd have to have it conked before anybody paid him any attention. The last things niggers want to think about they God is that his hair kinky.'[7]

Curiously, no one expressed a particular feeling about the religious parts of the novel. This is surprising, because it is evident that Walker is presenting a critique of pervasive religious attitude among black people, and Walker's view of religion appears to be more one of pantheism than a belief in a great white deity in heaven. The women I interviewed had no reaction to Walker's representation of religion. There were, however, comments about religious moments in the film. A woman in each group mentioned the scene in which Shug leads the people who were at the juke joint down the road to the church, singing. Both the women thought the scene looked fake and was out of place in the film. In the second group two of the women disagreed that the scene was misplaced. They said that it reminded them of being in church, where people would come from outside and become part of the congregation. This drew comments from the other women: 'I didn't ever think I would feel that way when I was in church. I noticed that when I was going through my deepest, hardest time, if I would go to church and get involved in the service, and they would start singing like that, I could feel the spirit.'

To this statement another woman added that it was 'God's spirit or somebody else's, but it was some spirit.' The first woman responded that she did believe in a creator: 'I have a difficulty believing in the kind of God that I see lots of people worship. But I know there's a Creator. But my view is probably different from what they would say the Creator is supposed to be.'

Another woman joined in the sentiments expressed by the women about their feelings about a God: 'Nobody can have as many good things happen to them as have happened to me (without a whole lot of effort on my part) without something, some single spirit, some collective spirit, providing some support and guidance. I don't know if I believe in – what is it? The one, the two, and the three? The Trinity and all that, or a real, literal interpretation of the Bible, but I do believe there is something.'

The women's expressed views about the religious parts of the film are important, because they indicate the complexities involved in audience studies, especially with groups in which there are few previous studies. There are no precedents or set guidelines, and the researcher runs into others' predetermined attitudes about how the participants' comments should be assessed. With groups who have been ignored in any analysis of media responses there is a tendency for outsiders to rush into judgement rather than consider the groups' background, histories, and social and cultural experiences. Thus when the women respond in unexpected ways their statements are dismissed rather than considered within the specifics of their lives. This is illustrated especially in the women's comments about the religious elements of the film. In considering their statements it is important to understand how religion has been an integral part of black history, even though it is contested terrain for radical scholars. As Stuart Hall reminds us, religion has been used to maintain ideological control over many societies in numerous epochs.[8] However, research data shows that religion is very important in black people's lives, with over 65,000 black churches in the country with a collective membership of over 24 million people.[9] Although radical scholars question the viability of black churches and black religious attitudes, with so many black people involved in some kind of religious activity it is necessary to examine the historical evolution of their religious bonds rather than continually to condemn them. Cornel West, writing about the ways in which black people have fought against an array of forces aligned to thwart their progress and, more important, about how black people have constructed 'cultural armor' to maintain a sense of hope and meaning in their lives, notes that the creation of black religious institutions was one of the 'cultural structures of meaning and feeling that created and sustained' black communities.[10]

What this means in examining the comments from the women I interviewed is that it is important to go beyond a quick and superficial analysis of their statements and to consider their responses within the totality of their lives and within the full range of black women's past. Their statements may contradict radical sentiments, but there is no guarantee that those who claim to speak for the multitudes have any greater purchase on 'truth' than the women I interviewed. As the earlier reference from John Fiske indicated, radical scholars are not always in step with those whom they are trying to engage. If more contact was made with those who participate in a range of everyday activities and who watch and view a variety of cultural forms, then there would be a greater understanding of the ways in which audiences (and a populace) negotiate their existence in a society not of their making but with some attempts at control.

The ages of the women in the first group I interviewed ranged from early forties to late fifties. All were employed or had worked at some point in their lives. One was retired. All except two had children. Three were born in the south and had moved away when they were young. One was born and raised in the Northeast, three in the Midwest, and one in the Southwest. All but two of the women had had some college education; four held advanced degrees.

The six women in the second group ranged in age from thirty to thirty-seven. Two of the women, along with their husbands, were best friends who socialized together frequently. All four were born and raised in the South, specifically in Georgia and South Carolina. Another woman in attendance was born in the rural South and had recently lived for a time in Atlanta, Georgia. One of the women had grown up in predominantly white neighborhoods in California, one was from Chicago, and another was raised in various cities in northern California and Oregon.

Three of the women in the second group were married, two were divorced and one had never been married. Two had children. All had attended or were, at the time of the interview, attending college. One was a graduate student and another an undergraduate. Three had advanced degrees. All the women were employed, including those who were attending school. Two of the women worked at a large electronics firm in midlevel positions; one was a substitute elementary school teacher who had just moved to the area. One of the women worked as a manager of a small, community-based public service organization.

For my analysis of both sets of interviews I have changed the names of the women to preserve anonymity. The names given to the women in the first group are Christine, Stephanie, Cecelia, Lucille, Charlotte, Margaret, Danielle, Paige and Constance. The names of the women in the second group are Morgan, Phyllis, Marilyn, Anne, Grace and Whitney.

All of the women in the second group had read the book before seeing the film. In the first group about half the women had read the book first. All the women in both groups had read the novel and seen the film before the interviews. Six of the women in the first group had seen the film more than once while it was still in the theaters, and several had seen it again on video. Three of the women in the second group had seen the film twice.

Both groups were assembled for the specific purpose of discussing *The Color Purple* and other matters related to the status of black women in society. The responses from the women in the second group are especially informative because of the unique nature of the interview, which was conducted while the women were watching the videotape of *The Color Purple*. The discussion continued beyond the video as well, but their immediate, visceral responses were significant to my research because the women reacted to moments in the film that they may not have been able to recall later. Also, because all of us were watching the film together the women became comfortable enough with me present as researcher to make comments that they may have censored otherwise had the researcher not also been a black woman.

The setting for the first group of interviews was a metropolitan city with a markedly diverse economic and racial population. The location for the second set of interviews was a predominantly, almost monolithically, white city of about 40,000 people, located in the Pacific Northwest. The two major employers are a university and an electronics firm. It is an insulated community located some distance from two major metropolitan cities.

From the outset the women found moments in the film that resonated with elements in their lives. As the film opens Celie and Nettie, both young girls, play in a field of flowers. Fonso, their mother's husband, who they think is their father, approaches ominously and tells them to come in to supper. Celie smiles nervously as Nettie circles around her protectively. Fonso, looking at Celie, who is young, pregnant and self-conscious, folds his arms across his chest and tells her: 'Celie, you got the ugliest smile this side of Creation.' Celie puts her hand up to hide her smile. Nettie looks at Fonso with anger and disgust and pulls Celie's hand down from her face.

The women react strongly to this scene. When Fonso tells Celie that she has an unattractive smile there were murmurings of disapproval from the women with whom I watched the film, and in the later discussions this was seen as a significant part of the several of them. Morgan related that this scene made her realize that feelings she had about herself were also shared by others. She conveyed that it and other seemingly inconsequential parts of the film, 'the little things,' added up to her feeling as though she were looking in a mirror. Morgan noted that after Fonso commented to Celie about her smile she never smiled again without covering up her face. Morgan recalled observations that were made about her by important people in her life, such as her mother and her husband, that affected how she thought of herself. Relating this to *The Color Purple*, Morgan said that as she watched the film she realized that those attitudes belonged to her mother and her husband and weren't necessarily shared by other significant people in her life. Summing up the way in which the film affected her perceptions, she said that it was not a big moment that changed her life but 'a lot of little issues coming from a lot of different places in the film.'

Paige, from the first group, related this portion of the film to a later segment in which Shug tells Celie that she has a beautiful smile and should stop covering up her face. Paige said that she could relate to that part because the exchange with Shug made Celie's transformation at the end of the film so much more powerful. Paige recalled that everyone who loved Celie – Shug and Nettie – kept telling her to put her hand down: 'That last time that Celie put her hand down nobody told her to put her hand down. She had started coming into her own. So when she grabbed that knife, she was ready to use it.'

This comment refers to a scene near the end of the film when Mister and his family are sitting around the dinner table as Celie and Shug are preparing to leave for Memphis. Mister begins to chastise Celie, telling her that she will be back: 'You ugly, you skinny, you shaped funny, and you scared to open your mouth to people.' Celie at first sits quietly and takes Mister's verbal abuse. Then she asks him, 'Any more letters come?' She is referring to letters that Nettie has written to her from Africa, which Mister has been hiding and Celie has recently found. Mister replies nonchalantly, 'Could be, could be not. Who's to say?' Celie jumps up at that point, grabs a knife, and sticks it to Mister's throat.

In Paige's assessment of the significance of this scene, she says about Celie: 'But had she not got to that point, built up to that point [of feeling that she was worthwhile], she could have grabbed the knife and turned it the other way for all that it mattered to her. She wouldn't have been any worse off. But she saw herself getting better. So when she grabbed that knife, she was getting ready to use it, and it wasn't on herself.'

For many of the women in both groups this was considered a powerful moment in the film, because it marks a turning point for Celie, from someone who continually accepts abuse to a person who fights back against oppressive conditions. Comment from the women in the first group revealed the variety of emotions the women experienced while watching the film, as well as their view that if Celie had not changed, they would have had different responses. That she did was seen as empowering for the women because they felt she took charge of her life – as they saw that they had to do in the face of overwhelming odds. The women I interviewed did not consider themselves to be losers or in any way defeated by their life circumstances, and they liked the fact that a black woman was shown in a way they felt was similar to the way in which they dealt with adversities in their lives. Constance, in the first group, said that if Celie had not changed she would have been disgusted: 'That just gets to me, about the roles of females. If they don't change, I don't want to watch it.' Lucille added this observation:

> I had different feelings all the way through the film, because first I was very angry, then I started to feel so sad I wanted to cry because of the way Celie was being treated. It just upset me, the way she was being treated and the way she was so totally dominated. But gradually, as time went on, she began to realize that she could do something for herself, that she could start moving and progressing, that she could start reasoning and thinking things out for herself. In the end I felt a little proud of her from the way she began and the way she grew.

To this statement Margaret commented that she was proud of Celie for her growth: 'The lady was a strong lady, like I am. And she hung in there and overcame.'

As their statements indicate, the display of Celie's strength, especially during the scene at the dinner table, was impressive and significant for the women. It was also a key indication of the ways in which the women reconstructed the film, because this scene was among those that had been altered from the novel. Additionally, this part was a graphic example of Spielberg's ambivalent structure for the film. Once again, moments of power were juxtaposed with comic and severely caricatured segments. This was especially true of the way in which Old Mister's antics and those of Harpo and Sofia were constantly interspersed with the women's actions.

In this scene all the women – Celie, Shug, Sofia and Squeak – speak and exhibit power. For the first time in the film, in fact, Squeak insists on being called by her name, Mary Agnes, rather than 'Squeak,' as she has been called throughout the film. In the novel, this was actually the second time Squeak demanded to be called Mary Agnes. The first was after she was raped by her uncle, the white sheriff, after she went to the jail in a ruse concocted by the family to get Sofia released on parole. If a viewer could physically edit the film and remove the comic routines, as it appears that the women I interviewed did mentally, then the sequence featuring the women at the dinner table becomes a pivotal and empowering moment of the film.

Shug speaks first, informing Mister that Celie is going to Memphis with her and Grady. Mister replies that Celie's departure will be over his dead body. Shug answers, 'You satisfied? That's what you want?' Celie then delivers her message that Mister is 'a low-down, dirty dog. It's time for me to get away from you and into Creation. Yo'dead body be just the welcome mat I need.' Her next declaration is the spark that wakes Sofia from her somnambulate 'confused' state. Celie tells Mister that he is no better than 'some dead horse shit' and that his kids made her life there hell. She refers to them as 'these fools you never tried to raise.' Speaking over Harpo's objections, Celie informs him and everyone else at the table that if Harpo had not tried so hard to 'rule over Sofia, white folks never woulda got her.' She then tells Mister when he continues to berate her that until he does right by her everything he even thinks about is destined to fail. Mister sees this as a curse, so he yells at Celie: 'Who do you think you is? You can't cuss nobody. Look at you. You black, you poor, you ugly, you a woman. You nothing at all.' As Celie, Shug, Grady and Mary Agnes begin to drive away. Celie raises her hand and issues the final warning to Mister: 'Everything you done to me is already done to you.' She finishes with an affirmation of her knowledge that she has indeed become a worthwhile person: 'I'm poor, black; I may even be ugly. But, dear God, I'm here. I'm here.'

As the women in the second group watched the film they analyzed Celie's transformation. They compared it to black women who tap into their resources to survive, and compared Celie to those who are so abused that they do not survive.

In the film when Nettie comes to live with Celie and Mister because Fonso continues to force himself upon her, she sees Mister's kids running wild over Celie. She tells Celie not to let the kids take advantage of her and that she should stand up for herself. Nettie, however, is hotly pursued by Mister. When she rebuffs him he gets angry and forces her to leave. Celie is distraught that Nettie must leave her and attempts to hold on as Mister tries to force the two of them apart. Nettie eventually runs down the road, but not without telling Celie that nothing but death will keep them apart.

As Mister orders Nettie to leave his property and Celie clings to her, some of the women felt that Celie needed to be stronger. Grace said that Celie needed to fight back; Morgan said that back then the women had a different kind of behavior. Phyllis said that Celie did not know that she could fight back, that she had low self-esteem.

> *Grace* [observing Nettie leaving]: See she is going someplace else.
> *Whitney*: If you are confronted with a situation like that, in my mind, Celie *needs* to go someplace else.
> *Morgan*: But Celie doesn't have the same spirit. Celie has no self-esteem. Zero.
> *Phyllis*: Celie's already been beaten to the ground.
> *Whitney*: I understand than. I also understand the bond between two sisters too . . . I would not leave that property without my sister. [She repeats her statement.] I would not leave that property without my sister.
> *Phyllis*: It's easy to say you understand it, but if you haven't been there – see, I've been there.
> *Whitney*: Well, none of us have been there.
> *Phyllis*: Yeah, I've been there. I've been *there*. I've been in that very same situation. But it is a situation in which you can say something is supposed to occur, this is a survival situation. The women are trying to survive, see. They have no place to go. They don't have anything to look forward to. I mean, we do have options now. But they didn't have any options. They were somebody's chattel.
> *Morgan*: I'm not saying that Celie would have gone anyway, but you always have an option.

Grace: I'm afraid I don't understand that, because I've never been in that situation; but don't you, even if you have been beaten to the ground long enough, say, 'I'm better than this'?

Whitney: Yeah.

Phyllis: No, girlfriend, it don't work like that.

Morgan: After a point Celie gets there – where she knows that she's better. But how long does it take her?

Phyllis: But everybody doesn't do that, either. Look around you at the women who are continually abused. All their lives they *look* for abuse. They actually *seek* abuse, because that's the way they define themselves. You can't see it because – I don't know – I think sometimes that some of us are very naive. And there's nothing wrong with that. There's nothing wrong with being naive. Celie doesn't think that if she cuts his throat, he can't kill her.

In the film the young Celie prepares to shave Mister because he thinks Shug is coming. As the scene begins we see the rocking chair on an otherwise empty porch. Celie enters the frame with the straight razor, and Mister enters from the other side with the towel, saying to himself, 'My Shug is coming, and everything gonna be the way it should be. Come on girl. I'm waiting.' Mister puts the towel around his neck, and Celie moves the razor toward his neck to shave him. Suddenly he grabs her arm and warns her, 'You cut me, and I'll kill you!'

Whitney: She does think about it.

Phyllis: She thinks about cutting his throat, but she also thinks about the consequences of not killing him, which is another beating. Which is more abuse.

Morgan: I don't think that in this particular scene she even really thought about cutting his throat.

Phyllis: She's thinking about it; she's thinking about it now. But she's a young girl. She doesn't realize that if she cuts his throat bad enough he's not going to be able to hurt her. All she's thinking is that if she cuts his throat and he survives she's gonna have to suffer the consequences

Whitney: She's thinking about it now.

Phyllis: Even if she nicks the man. [She pauses.] It takes a lot to come out of low self-esteem. It takes a lot.

Whitney: But not a whole lot to get in it.

Phyllis: Not a whole lot to get in it, you're right. All it takes is one word, one person, somebody that you think is supposed to be caring about you, somebody that you have the impression that they define who you are. And if they tell you enough times and they treat you enough like you don't mean anything, you begin to actually believe that.

Morgan: If people you value don't value you –

Phyllis: And I think, in a way, that's the way black people have been in the past. Because somebody told them that they were not worthy, and we believed that for so long that it kept us from doing some of the things we needed to do to progress out of that stage. Sometimes it means that you gotta die, but you have to have enough pride, enough self-esteem to say, 'I'd rather die than live in this.'

Whitney: I understand her situation, and I understand as much as I can understand what's going on, but I still believe we always have choices.
Phyllis: Of course we do, but the thing is learning how to make those choices. Everybody doesn't learn how to make those choices.
Morgan: Some people don't even recognize that they had a choice.

While watching the scenes involving Harpo and his attempts to dominate Sofia, the women continue discussing black women who are survivors. In the film, after Sofia and Harpo fight, Sofia's family packs up her belongings and takes her and her kids away in the back of a wagon. Whitney says, 'Celie ought to be right on the back of that thing. She needs to go on with that woman. Break camp.'

Phyllis: You folks be talking about she should have gone with her, but you have to remember, girlfriend's mouth got her in jail for a while.
Whitney: That's true. Well, you gotta do what you gotta do. It's all about integrity.
Phyllis: First, it's about survival. Then it's about integrity.

When Sofia's troubles with the authorities were portrayed the women became upset and made very pointed comments. In the film Sofia and her boyfriend, the prizefighter Buster Broadnax, are in town with Sofia's kids. The mayor and his wife walk over to Sofia and her kids, and the wife begins to make a fuss over them. In the background the mayor is heard drawing the attention of some white townspeople passing by to 'Miss Millie, always going on over the coloreds.'

Marilyn: Those who work with white folk.
[Someone says, 'Lord have mercy.' Someone else says, 'Kissing all on his face' (the scene in which one of Sofia's kids wipes the kiss off).]
Phyllis: But you know what – if you kiss their kids, they just be wiping that shit off.
[Everybody laughs and agrees.]
Whitney: Thing is, don't do it, you hear?

When the mayor's wife says of Sofia's kids, 'Y'all so clean,' Grace parrots her by saying 'So clean.' Everyone is angry at the mayor's wife for thinking that they would not be clean.

Morgan: At least she had sense enough to know she was totally out of control.
JB: Yeah. With her kids?
Morgan: Yeah [suggesting that Sofia at least understood her temper enough to know to make sure her kids were safe].

The action of the film shows the mayor's wife asking Sofia if she would like to work for her as her maid. Sofia replies, 'Hell, no.' The mayor's wife asks her what she said, and Sofia repeats her statement. The mayor becomes angry and walks over to Sofia, questioning her about what she said to his wife. When Sofia repeats, 'hell, no,' he slaps her. Sofia, in turn, punches the mayor, who falls down. At that point all the townspeople run over and surround Sofia. She calls to Buster and Swain to get her children away as the townspeople yell and call her names. One white woman taunts, 'You black slut. Who do you think you are?' When a white man says to Sofia, 'Who do you think you are, you fat nigga?' the women watching are visibly upset.

Whitney: He enjoyed that.

Phyllis: You know, we didn't get no respect [i.e. when the sheriff knocks Sofia to
the ground with his gun butt].

Whitney: Whew, Lord.

Marilyn: His fist would have been enough.

[Everyone is upset. Phyllis and Morgan start crying.]

Whitney: This is what broke me up.

[Morgan and Marilyn agree.]

Marilyn: Then to put her in jail – and she ended up working for them anyway.

At this point in the film it is Christmas, and Sofia has been released from jail on probation
and is in the custody of the mayor and his wife. One of her jobs is to teach the wife how to
drive. The mayor's wife drives wildly and recklessly, and as she and Sofia careen through the
town the people on the street scatter out of the way. As they approach the store to do their
Christmas shopping the mayor's wife is chatting gaily and weaving from one side of the street
to the other. Sofia sits in the car with her head down and looks totally defeated. Marilyn is
angry about what is happening in this scene.

Marilyn: Why would she choose to have Sofia in her life?

Grace: As punishment. That's the ultimate punishment – you've got to wait on me
for the rest of your life. That's the ultimate punishment.

Marilyn: But would you want someone –

Whitney: – but, see you're thinking the way you would think.

Marilyn: That's all I can do.

Morgan: You're just not that sadistic.

As Sofia and the Mayor's wife enter the store, the mayor's wife hands Sofia her shopping list
and directs her to get the items listed. Sofia only has one good eye; the other was smashed
by the sheriff when he hit her with the butt of his gun. As Sofia tries to read the list, Celie,
who has been silently observing the mayor's wife ordering Sofia around, approaches her
quietly. She takes the list from Sofia and begins to place the groceries in a shopping bag.
While this takes place the mayor's wife is talking nonsense to the owner of the store about
Mars and how she would like to know what it's like to live there.

Phyllis: Fool.

Whitney: God forgive me, but I'd kill that woman. I'd kill that woman dead. You
hear me?

[Grace starts laughing.]

Marilyn: The film made her look like an asshole.

JB: Well, you know, one of the criticisms about that part is that they made it
seem like the white woman was the exception – just a silly little white
woman. Her comment about Mars, and stuff like that, rather than that was
routine treatment. What do you think?

Marilyn: Well, I certainly know better. I certainly know that she probably represents the majority. No, I don't think they make her less exceptional.

Anne: I think they do. Because all of a sudden you see the town. You see all the
white folk in town. You didn't see all the white people in town before. And
all of a sudden they're there. And she's the one who's the center of this
whole thing. On the whole you don't see them.

Whitney: There are certain black neighborhoods like mine [i.e. where she grew up in South Carolina] – you can stay there today and not see white people.

Grace: In my neighborhood [i.e. where she grew up] we never saw white people. I lived in an all-black neighborhood. I didn't really see white people, even when we went to town. This section in Atlanta was black in the sixties when I grew up.

Whitney: And it's still 95 per cent.

Grace: So my only real interaction with whites was when I went to college. And I think that was black parents' way of protecting their children from all the racism. It was not quite as severe as this.

[Whitney is agreeing throughout.]

Grace: I think that was their unconscious way of protecting us from all the things that would come along.

JB: Where did you go to college?

Grace: At Georgia State, which is predominantly white.

JB: How was it? Going from an all-black neighborhood –

Grace: It was more of a shock than coming out here.

[Whitney, Phyllis and I react to this.]

Whitney: You betta take that back –

Grace: Yeah. Let me change that. It was different because I had a support group.

Whitney: You could go home.

Grace: Yeah. When it would get three o'clock I was back in the black community, so all the changes I went through at Georgia State were like, Okay, I can do this for six hours, and get my support, and go back.

Whitney: That's right.

At another point in the discussion Whitney elaborated on Grace's point.

Whitney: You talking about integration, I happen to think personally, that *Brown vs. the Board* was probably the worst thing that ever happened to our people.

Phyllis: I agree. I went to segregated schools in elementary school. I started out at a Catholic school with white students, and yeah, I was speaking French and doing little Catholic things and all that stuff, but there was something about going to an all-black school . . . the teachers –

Grace: – they cared –

Phyllis: Everybody cared. If I screwed up in school –

Grace: Before you would get home they would tell your mamma.

Phyllis: Everybody would. And that is that carryover from Africa; we have lost that. And that is so sad. Because the kids now, they have no respect for life experiences. They have no understanding of what it takes to struggle. We give our children everything, we put them in these upper middle-class houses, we buy them cars. My son got mad because he asked me for a car and I told him I wasn't buying him doodley-squat 'til I saw some grades coming in. It is expected that we give them everything; they expect us to go out and buy the Guess jeans, the Swatch watches, the Reeboks, and all that stuff. They don't know how to wait for anything – it's instant gratification; everybody wants it right now. And these white kids, the way they talk to their parents – if they were my children, they would not have teeth in their mouths. They might not even be living now.

At this point Whitney makes a comment that seems not to relate to what Phyllis is saying; however, the tape is still playing, showing what is happening with Sofia and her probation with the mayor, his wife and family.

> *Whitney*: You know another thing – part of me is grateful that she [Sofia] slugged that man [after he slapped her].
> *Whitney*: That she had the courage –
> *Grace*: – to release the tension.

Although the majority of the women in both groups had talked more about Celie's growth and Sofia's strength, Danielle in the first group, felt that Shug was a better 'role model' in the film. She insisted that the other women were off the mark in characterizing Celie and Sofia as the major catalysts for the other women in the story coming into their own, because she felt Shug provided the incentive for all the other characters to change. As Danielle declared: 'She [Shug] was the catalyst for everything. I really don't think Celie would have risen above her situation or recovered from it had it not been for the power of this other woman. So I identified very much with the sisterhood.'

Danielle was also angry with those critics of the film who characterized the bond between Shug and Celie as a homosexual relationship. As she spoke there was strong agreement from the other women, especially from Danielle's mother, Margaret. Danielle stated

> I was very offended by things people were saying about this movie. When people started talking about homosexuality and lesbianism, that really offended me. As I read the book both times, I really didn't have any reaction that 'this was a lesbian situation.' [There is continual agreement from the others in the group. Margaret states several times as Danielle is speaking, 'Sisters, sisters.'] As I read it and as I felt it, the woman [Shug] was actually showing her how to love and how it feels to be loved. [Margaret underscores Danielle's sentiments by saying again, 'Sisters, sisters.'] Because she [Celie] had no self-concept, her self-esteem was zero. She's just mentally put down. And so I think Shug had enough love in her to share with this other woman. I think Shug made the supreme effort to show her how to love. And I really didn't think it was lesbianism or homosexuality. I like it because I like to see black women reach out to other black women, lift each other up, hold each other up, be there when we need each other.

When the scenes in which Shug kisses Celie were shown, it was helpful to watch them in the presence of the women in the second group. Their reactions were important to observe as the scenes were taking place. When Shug first appears in the film after coming to live with Mister and Celie, Whitney, in the second group, declares: 'She's the only one to really control him.' Phyllis states, 'Naw, he fool enough to be pussy-whipped. He controls himself. She just says the words that pull the string.' When Shug first sees Celie and tells her that she is indeed ugly, Whitney and Grace consider this a mean put down. Grace replies, 'She must be from Atlanta.' As Celie is helping Shug in the bath when she is recovering from her illness the women begin to discuss their feelings about Celie's and Shug's relationship.

> *Whitney*: The book played a little bit more on the relationship between those two women. [Everyone agrees.]
> *Morgan*: I think that would have been hard for them to bring to the film.
> *Whitney*: I think they little bit they did bring was pretty hard for a lot of people to accept.

Morgan: Shoot, it was hard for me.

JB: To watch?

Morgan: Yeah.

JB: Why?

Morgan: I'm just not real comfortable with that.

Grace: But she needed that.

Whitney Yeah.

JB: Was it hard for you to read it in the book?

Morgan: Not as much in the book.

Whitney: Because you didn't see it so graphically?

Morgan: Yes.

Grace: But she need that, she did.

Whitney: Yeah. Like Phyllis was saying. Regardless of where it's coming from.

Morgan: It wasn't that I thought it was a bad thing.

Whitney: You weren't prepared for it.

Morgan: I just wasn't prepared for it, and it was not *my* thing. And it's so different from *my* thing that it was hard for me to relate to it.

Whitney: I found it really difficult to deal with when that white man hit what's-her-name, Harpo's wife, than I did that part. That was difficult for me to deal with, sitting in a theater surrounded by white men. It was difficult.

Phyllis: I guess the reason why I didn't find it offensive was that there was some actual caring there.

[Whitney and Grace agree.]

Whitney: I didn't find it offensive. Not at all. I was just uncomfortable. Just awkward.

Phyllis: I didn't find it uncomfortable.

JB: To watch it?

Morgan: Yes.

Whitney: I would probably.

Phyllis: That's something that's private.

Morgan: Yes. I guess that's it. The only reason that I don't find it uncomfortable with men and women is that I've seen it so much. When I first started seeing women and men on television and in the movies involved in very intimate behavior I found that uncomfortable, too, because I felt like I was peeking in somebody's window, where I had no business being. And I guess I saw that as being similar, and I wasn't accustomed to it.

After Shug sings in the juke joint and everyone begins to fight, Shug leads Celie away from the fight and into her dressing room. Celie emerges shyly from another room, wearing the red dress in which Shug performed. Shug tries to get her to loosen up by playing some lively music and showing Celie how to move her body. Celie giggles self-consciously and keeps putting her hand up to her mouth. Shug asks her why she's always covering up her smile and tells Celie to show her some 'teef.' Celie begins to smile shyly and again puts her hands up to her mouth. Shug comes behind Celie and puts her arms around her, holding Celie's hands to prevent her from bringing them up to her mouth. As Celie begins to laugh freely, Shug tells her, 'See, Miss Celie, you got a beautiful smile.'

Shug next tells Celie that it's time for her to leave, time for her to start traveling again. Celie grows quiet and sad, and Shug wants to know what's disturbing her. Celie hesitates, then says, 'He beat me when you ain't here.' Although Shug admits that Albert is a bully, she wants to know why he would beat Celie. Celie replies, 'He beat me for not being you.' Shug wants to know if Celie minds her sleeping with Albert, and Celie asks her incredulously if she enjoys it. Shug tells her she has a passion for Albert and wants to know if Celie doesn't also enjoy it. Celie tells her that during sex with Mister she just pretends that she isn't even there. Mister pays no attention; he just climbs on top of her and does his 'business.' Shug says that seems like someone is just going to the toilet on her, and she tells Celie that she is still a virgin. Celie tells her she is because no one loves her, and Shug lets her know that she loves Celie. Shug then begins to kiss Celie, first on the cheek, then on the forehead, then gently all over her face, then on her mouth. Celie smiles and begins to cover her mouth, then brings her hands down to her lap. She smiles broadly and kisses Shug back. Then Celie and Shug kiss and touch each other. During this segment of the film the women comment throughout.

> *Phyllis* [in response to a statement about Celie's lack of confidence and Shug's abun-
>   dance of it]: No, girlfriend, that ain't true. Shug may have had low
>   self-esteem, too, and demonstrated it a different way.
> *Grace*: By being arrogant.

Whitney and Grace find the part of the film when Shug says to Celie, 'Show me some teef' amusing.

> *Whitney*: Show me some teef. *Teef*, honey. [Everyone laughs.]
> *Marilyn* [in response to Celie's laughing]: There you go.

During Shug's and Celie's scene in Shug's dressing room the women watching become very quiet. Most of their reactions are when Celie says something poignant like, 'He beat me when you ain't here . . . He beat me for not being you.' When Shug tells Celie she is still a virgin, Celie replies that it is true, ''cause don't nobody love me.' Morgan begins to cry. After Shug and Celie kiss, no one says anything for a while, then Phyllis and Grace comment.

> *Phyllis*: I think that's really as far as she thought it was going to go [referring to
>   the kiss].
> *Grace*: I don't think she knew what was going on.
> *Whitney*: I don't think she realized the magnitude.
> *Phyllis*: I don't think she was ready for what happened next.
> *JB*: Who wasn't, Celie?
> *Phyllis*: Yes. I don't think she was ready.
> *Morgan*: I don't think she had any concept of having that kind of relationship with
>   anyone.
> *JB*: Not that it was female or anything?
> *Morgan*: I don't think that probably played any part with her . . . and Lord knows,
>   with her I can see where she would not get excited about a man.
> [Whitney, Grace, and Phyllis agree.]
> *JB*: Do you see this as a lesbian relationship either in the book or in the film?
> *Morgan*: In the book I did, not in the film.
> *JB*: You did in the film?
> *Morgan*: In the book I did. In the film I did not.

> *Whitney*: I agree. I see it in the book and not in the film.
> *Marilyn*: I agree.
> *Morgan*: Because it wasn't enough in the film to make me necessarily feel that way.
> It was just suggested. If you had not read the book, it's possible that you
> missed the point.

Later, as we were approaching the end of the interview, when I asked the women if there was a particular scene in the film that they felt was especially significant, both Grace and Whitney referred back to the moment when Shug kisses Celie. Grace said, 'Even though it was an intimate scene between her [Celie] and Shug, I liked that because she began to feel, "I'm somebody special – I'm not like everybody has been treating me."'

Still later, when I was interviewing another group of women about their reactions to *Daughters of the Dust*, the issue of the relationship between Celie and Shug was again discussed, and one of the women made an observation that had not been considered during the incendiary environment of the film's first release: 'I think that all those people who made such a big deal out of Shug and Celie, you have got to wonder what their motivation was. If some black people didn't want to label the relationship as homosexuality, then it doesn't become an issue. I think if other people want to make it an issue, they should just go right ahead. But I don't think they should make the whole film be about that if other people saw different things in the film.'

This woman's assessment of the attempts to categorize *The Color Purple* as a lesbian work is similar to the analysis that black lesbian feminist Barbara Smith gives of the work. Smith ascribes the mass acceptance of the relationship between Shug and Celie by a heterosexual audience to the form in which Alice Walker presents the story. Smith commends Walker for addressing the issue in the first place but sees the novel as a fable rather than a 'realistic' portrayal of the lives of lesbians in a culture that would react with hostility to two women having the kind of relationship that Shug and Celie openly display. In a society where homophobia is so rampant, if two women were to interact as they do in the fictionalized story, Smith feels there would be drastic repercussions. She also refuses to categorize the relationship between Shug and Celie as a lesbian one because she feels that is not a designation they would give themselves. As she concludes about the women, 'As a black lesbian feminist reader, I have questions about how accurate it is to identify Walker's characters as lesbians at the same time I am moved by the vision of a world unlike this one, where black women are not forced to lose their families, their community, or their lives, because of whom they love.'[11]

In the extended and prolonged public discussions about *The Color Purple* questions were raised about whether the black women who were emotionally attached to the film were able to distinguish between the film and the novel. I asked the women in the second group to talk about their reactions to both the novel and the film.

> *Morgan*: I didn't really want to see this movie at first. I had enjoyed the book so
> much, I was afraid I was going to see the movie and have that experience
> ruined. And I was really, *really*, reluctant to see it. So when I did, I felt it
> complemented the book, and it didn't detract from it. I think they did a
> really good job. I still can't understand how someone can watch this movie
> without reading the book. I can't imagine what kind of perspective they
> would have. To me the book without the movie would be okay, it's hard
> for me to see how they could see the movie without the book.

JB: A lot of people didn't read the book.

Morgan: I know. I couldn't watch this movie in the state of mind of a person who hadn't read the book. When I watched the movie for the first time, it's like if you had some favorite song from when you were a kid and heard it again many, many years later, something that you associated with something very special. Reading the book was like that for me. With the book, it was an original event, and the movie was like kind of a reminder, of revisiting or reliving it.

JB: Did you feel that most black women or most black women that you talked to liked the film?

[General agreement.]

Phyllis: Overwhelmingly.

Morgan: Yes. In fact, I had to beg, plead, plead with my mother to go see it – she was afraid to see it because she felt there were too many things, from what she heard about the movie, that were too closely related to her experiences. She just didn't want to relive that. And so I pleaded and I begged and I said, Mother, go. Just go by yourself. And she finally went and saw it and had a real positive feeling about it. I kind of felt sometimes like it was mine. Not that it was mine such that nobody else could have any of it. It wasn't an exclusive ownership in that way, but it was mine.

Phyllis: I think it was a catharsis for me. Because it was some of those things I had actually lived, some of those things I had actually seen other people live. I liked being able to sit there and see it on the big screen. It was important for other people to view that, to make them aware that this is really happening, folks. For critics to say that this is a fantasy – I had a real problem with that, because it's just like saying that the 'Cosby Show' is a fantasy. I know that just like the things that have occurred in this movie are real, the things that happened in the 'Cosby Show,' I know families like that – who kid around, joke around, have all that love. Even considering black college life; there's a lot of stuff that goes on in 'A Different World' that actually happens on black campuses. It's almost as if people are negating some part of my existence when they say that this movie [*The Color Purple*] isn't real. It opened up a lot of wounds for me, it made me go inward, it made me do a lot of thinking.

Anne: I got angry that Spielberg, white man . . .

Phyllis: . . . had to do it . . .

Anne: . . . did it. I got really upset with that. I felt violated in that sense.

Phyllis: I was just glad somebody did it.

Grace: I didn't feel angry. I'm glad somebody did it. It he had not done it, I don't know too many other people who would have even tried –

Whitney: – or who would have had the money or the financial backing.

I asked Anne to elaborate on her point about Spielberg mishandling the film.

JB: You didn't like *The Color Purple*?

Anne: I didn't like it the first time I saw it. I saw it, and then I rented it this summer, and I looked at it, and I liked it. I thought, Now why didn't I like it the first time? The first time I didn't like it, I think, was because I was offended so much by this white man portraying these black people. There're

> black directors out there, there're black people out there. Damn it, let them
> get through.
>
> *Marilyn*: But who was the movie made for?
>
> *Anne*: It was made for white audiences.
>
> *Marilyn*: Okay.
>
> *Anne*: And that really made me angry, because here I was sitting in an audience of
> white people, except for one row . . .
>
> *Phyllis*: Who controls the movie money?
>
> *Anne*: White people, but . . .
>
> *Morgan*: She's not talking about the intellectual aspects of it – I mean we can all
> intellectualize things and still get pissed off.

Much of the criticism of the film revolved around white people's perceptions of black people and the feeling that black people's progress would be stymied because of the supposed harmful images presented in the film, such as those about black people's physical characteristics, skin color, hair texture and so on. I asked the women their feelings about this aspect of the film.

> *JB*: What were your feelings about any of the things that the film dealt with that
> was unique to black people? They kept saying that Shug's hair was nappy,
> [that she was] black as tar; when Celie was combing the children's hair. Did
> that –
>
> *Whitney*: Did that bother me?
>
> *JB*: Bother you watching it [in the company of a predominantly white audience]?
>
> *Grace*: That to me is the thing that makes me proud, that makes us different. It
> always has; I guess that's the way my mom brought us up. That it's all right
> to be dark and your hair is nappy; that's a good thing. So, it doesn't [bother
> me] – I'm proud of that.
>
> *Whitney*: Yes, I am to. I didn't even think about it.
>
> *Morgan*: When I watched it [here], I just tuned all that out. Just tuned out the rest
> of the audience. And I left; I went to my car, and I went home. I think
> maybe when I got out there was a sense of . . . might have been different
> if I had been watching it with a black audience. I wouldn't have felt that I
> needed to rush and get home if I didn't want to interface. I didn't want to
> see *all* those people, probably that I would have seen from work and would
> have had to interface and deal with those kinds of issues.
>
> *Whitney* [agreeing throughout]: Yes, yes.
>
> *Phyllis*: You felt like you wanted somebody you could talk to, that you could share
> it with?
>
> *Morgan*: That would have been nice. I would have been afraid [seeing the white
> people that she knew] that I would have had to explain something, where I
> would have been expected to explain something. I didn't feel like explaining
> shit to nobody.
>
> *Whitney*: Right, right.
>
> *Morgan*: You don't get it, that's your problem, not mine.
>
> *Phyllis*: Right, right.
>
> *JB*: I'm not Encyclopaedia Britannica.
>
> *Morgan*: Right. I just didn't feel like being this week's representative for all black
> America.

Phyllis: Of the black race.

Whitney: [They would ask] 'What did you think about it?'

Morgan: Yes.

Grace: Sometimes that gets real old.

I asked the women to respond to the prolonged discussions about the effect of the film.

Whitney: You mean the male–female thing? . . . Well, I talked to Howard [her husband] afterward, and he didn't feel threatened by it. I really didn't see the big deal.

Grace: I didn't, either.

Whitney: I think it was much ado about nothing.

Phyllis: I heard a lot of guys say this portrayed black men as very negative creatures, not questioning if the shoe fits, you got to wear it. If it was not a threat to you and you did not feel that's the way you are, then it should not have bothered you. But they still felt that the greater society would view them as wife-beaters and philanderers and what have you. To be absolutely honest with you, having been in Atlanta for the amount of time that I was there, 70 per cent population [that is black], I have to admit that there were a number of brothers who lived up to that.

Whitney: Well, the greater population, if you talking about whites, believe we got tails and horns, too. So they are going to think what they want to think.

Phyllis: That's true, but I guess that's why I feel comfortable with the portrayal – because I've seen black men in my own life who reacted to adversities and to a lack of feeling power the very same way that these men in this movie acted.

Morgan: In my mind it just seemed like this was one set of people and their circumstances. And that it didn't reflect on anybody else.

Whitney: We see bad [people in] movies all the time. Everybody is not like *The Godfather*, it's just a movie.

JB: But did you feel that controversy itself affected the film or the way people saw it? Did you feel – even though you didn't think the controversy was worthwhile, was it a very large issue, do you think?

Phyllis: It was blown out of proportion.

Whitney: I felt violated that we let it get out of the family.

I asked the women in the first group to respond the disparaging statements made about the film. Margaret said that she felt white people were behind the disputes and that they were putting words in the black men's mouths. Someone said that the NAACP (National Association for the Advancement of Colored People) was behind a lot of the protests against the film. Margaret replied that there were white people in the NAACP and that black men had sold out with their protests: 'You know, a piece of silver . . . they'll sell us out. People will sell us out for money.'

Danielle added: 'Why don't they protest what's on television every week? Fred Sanford and all of them.' She said that many people who did not like the film felt it was an airing of black people's dirty laundry. Paige said that there was nothing wrong with that. 'We don't always have to pretend that everything is hunky-dory. It could be that if I tell somebody and they tell somebody else, then maybe I can get some answers to some problems I have.'

Danielle followed up on her charge that *The Color Purple* was selected for criticism while other more detrimental films were not: 'Where was all this hue and cry when the Blaxpoitation films came out?' She also questioned films such as *Sounder*, which did not generate any protests and in which the black man is also depicted as a loser:

> Listening to us talk here. I'm beginning to see that it's [the protest over *The Color Purple*] a sexist thing, and that upsets me because black people in general are oppressed. We're in this together. We worked in the same fields together, we walked in the same chain coffle together. It's just sad, because we all know that we wouldn't be here without the black woman having strength.

Constance discussed the charge by some critics that neither the book nor the film was realistic. She said that someone who had seen the film declared to her that no man would allow a woman to take a razor to his neck after he had treated her so badly. Margaret replied with some heat: 'They will beat you up, black both your eyes, and then go get right in the bed and go to sleep.' This remark prompted Paige to add: 'And then will have the nerve to want you to cook them something to eat.' Danielle talked about why some black men abused black women. She referred to incidents that her mother, Margaret, had related about her father:

> My mother asked my dad how come he would jump on her. Sometimes when she hadn't done anything he would just jump on her, for GP.[12] She asked him some years after they split up, and he told her he didn't know any better. That when he sat around with the guys . . . the guys would talk about how you had to keep a woman in line, you had to whip her ass every so often. And so he told Mamma that's what he thought he was supposed to do to make sure he could be the man around the house.

Anne in the second group, referred to the contentious discussions when she talked about seeing the film in the local theater with most of the black males from the college basketball team seated behind her.

> It was also crowded, and I thought it would be really interesting to see what their reactions [would be]. There was a lot of shouting [when she saw the film], and I had just read about the controversy a couple of days before I had seen it. I thought that the guys would get real quiet and timid because of the way that the males were being portrayed. I thought that perhaps this would happen, because I heard that big mass thing going on and all these men getting angry. But they seemed to get into it, and I thought I could understand why. How often are black people recognized in this community.

Marilyn followed up on Anne's statement about why black audiences react differently to films featuring black characters than do other audiences. She also made a critical observation about how black audiences watch films in contrast to other groups of viewers.

> *Marilyn*: That's right. I got the same impression from seeing *She's Gotta Have it* and *School Daze*. I thought that *School Daze* was a really extremely silly film, but it's the kind of thing that does great things for the morale of young black people. I saw it in Seattle, and there were maybe four whites in the theater. It was like the difference between going to a white Catholic mass and going to a black Baptist church. You know how you go into a theater, and folks

> sit there quietly – well this theater was live. Everyone was just yelling and
> screaming and laughing and dancing in their chairs. But it just does great
> things for our morale.
> *JB*: To see us in films?
> *Marilyn*: Yes, it's just fun.

Because of the pervasive absence of black people in mainstream media there is a tendency to
enjoy seeing black people in television programs and films rather than critically evaluate the
works. The concern for many critics of *The Color Purple* was that this was the trap, 'the trick
bag,' into which black women fell – that they became so enamored of seeing black women
on the screen that they could not distinguish a harmful image from just the pleasure of seeing
black women in roles other than comics or domestic workers. I asked the women about this
perception.

> *JB*: To see yourself, to read about yourself [in media] is exciting, but how about
> if you see yourself negatively? Are you ever conscious that when a film is
> made by a white film-maker that there is going to be something in it that
> will portray us negatively?
> *Morgan*: You see it on TV all the time. Like, what's that silly show that's set in
> Boston? 'Spencer' – the black character on that – Hawk – is a joke. And
> it's insulting. I mean, every time I watch it, I think, Oh, God. When I see
> things like that that are very negative or stereotypical, and or incredibly one-
> dimensional, then I'm insulted.

A strongly contested dimension of the claims made about the effect of *The Color Purple* was
that it altered the way many black women perceived their lives and their relationships with
others. Although the women I interviewed were ambivalent about the long-term effects of
the film, Phyllis felt strongly that it had indeed changed many black women's outlook: 'I was
in Atlanta when the movie came out. I noticed that the movie started women doing a lot of
talking, a lot of reevaluating of how they dealt with the men in their lives – if they were
going to either buckle under or stand up. And I noticed that a lot of women began looking
at what direction they wanted to take.' Marilyn picked up on Phyllis's sentiments and expressed
her thoughts about another part of the discussion that was also challenged – that after seeing
The Color Purple many black women sought out other books by black women writers. 'In a
way it was a validation. I think it was a validation for the way . . . our lives had to be lived.
The book was the main incentive for me to want to read more, and see more of black writers.
I know a lot of black women who didn't read the book, and they had to rely on the movie.
And the movie was very validating of our lifestyle.' Morgan related her own experiences of
how, although she had not previously read many works by black women, once she read *The
Color Purple* she was motivated to read more. Morgan also made a connection with other books
she had read but had not considered their impact on her. The significance of her comments
is that it underscores the claim that the impact of the novel and the widespread coverage of
the film was so great that it provided an atmosphere that enabled the women to listen to
black female activists who placed the issues that the novel addressed within a broader context
of their past.

> *Morgan*: It's funny, I found *The Color Purple* by accident. I read the book probably
> two years before I saw the movie. I had never heard of Alice Walker. I was
> in the bookstore, I saw this book, it looked kind of interesting, so I picked
> it up.

JB: You had never heard of Alice Walker? Had you heard of any other black woman writer?

Morgan: Maya Angelou and –

Marilyn: Toni Morrison.

Anne: Shange.

JB: *Colored girls*?

Phyllis: Now that moved me too.

JB [to Morgan]: Can I ask you if both your parents are black?

Morgan: Yeah, they both are black . . . I had to think about that a second. Last time I looked they both were. [She continues her comments about reading the novel.] I mean, I just picked up this thing that I thought was going to be an interesting novel and got *sucked* in.

Marilyn: That's what happened to me. After that I read *In Search of Our Mothers' Gardens* and other books.

JB: After you read *The Color Purple*, you went out and sought out other books by [black female writers]?

Marilyn: Yes, I did.

Morgan: I did after reading that one because I had read other black stories. Now that I think about it, those were some of the ones that I really did like the best.

Marilyn: Have you read *In Search of Our Mothers' Gardens*?

Morgan: I read parts of it.

Marilyn: That was a wonderful book.

Morgan: I read a little thing here [by other black female writers] and a little thing there, and some of it I didn't like because it was so hard. It was so . . . angry. Some of it just seemed real angry.

Phyllis: Who was the woman who wrote back in the forties.

JB: Zora Neale Hurston. *Their Eyes Were Watching God*.

Morgan: Yes. I liked that story.

I asked the women in the second group to sum up their feelings about the film.

JB: If you could describe the film in one word, or just a couple of words, what would you say?

Marilyn: It's about time.

Anne: Sorry it had to be a white man. I'm sorry it had to be a white man to do it.

Phyllis: I'm just grateful that it came out.

Morgan: Personal I guess.

Anne: I guess I'm really bitter that way. I'll have to think about it.

Anne's sentiments were shared by many critics of the film who would have preferred a black film-maker translating Alice Walker's novel. As much as that may have made a significant difference, the effects of the existence of the film were still important. And black women's reactions to it were a crucial part of that effect even though their reactions were themselves criticized. However, this again emphasizes that the ability of an audience to negotiate their responses is as important as the acknowledgement of their skill in doing so, as the following example illustrates.

One of the strongest criticisms of the film concerned the metamorphosis of Shug as she was in the novel, strong and self-reliant, into the insecure, oversexed daughter of a minister, as she was portrayed in the film. I asked the women in the second group about Shug's having, in the film, a father who was a preacher. Phyllis felt that it deepened her character, and Morgan felt that it made her more well-rounded. Grace added that it revealed a vulnerable side to her, because, even though she was strong, there was a part of her that was really hurting. I asked if they felt that Shug was too strong in the novel. They did not feel that, but they reiterated that Shug was someone who had been hurt deeply and felt rejected and that her lasciviousness was her way of dealing with it. I asked if they liked her better in the film. Whitney replied: 'We like her the same either way.'

In the first group I asked the women to respond to the charge from some radical critics that Shug was deliberately changed in the film to neutralize her power by having her constantly seek a reconciliation with her father. The other women fervently agreed with the comment made by Christine: 'It didn't have that effect on me. Shug was still a strong woman. It didn't neutralize her to me. Now, if that's what they [the producers] wanted to do, they missed the boat, because it didn't do that to me. You go back and tell the critics they missed their point.'

During the course of the later interviews about the groups' reactions to *Waiting to Exhale* and *Daughters of the Dust* I shared with the women some of the criticisms asserting that because the black women who participated in my study of the film were articulate they could not possibly be representative of the majority of black women in this country. Once again the women displayed a shrewdness about their status in society and the way black women are viewed by others. One of the women wondered if the critics knew that a person could be intelligent but not necessarily well educated. Another stated that she knew of too many people who had an abundance of academic degrees, yet when they speak they say nothing. Still another commented that many people react with surprise when they hear black people speak sensibly because, too often, that is not what is allowed to be presented in a public forum. She then asked a rhetorical question toward which the other women responded with spirited agreement: 'Don't you think we would have come off sounding stupid if someone other than another black person was doing research on us?'

Notes

1   *Tony Brown's Journal*, PBS, 6 April, 1986.
2   *The Phil Donahue Show*, 25 April, 1986.
3   In an interview with Charlayne Hunter-Gault on the *MacNeil/Lehrer NewsHour*, PBS, 31 March, 1988.
4   Explanation given by Daviau in the article by Al Harrell, 'The Look of *The Color Purple*,' *American Cinematographer* (February 1986): 50–56.
5   Christian's views were also expressed in two public lectures: 'De-Visioning Spielberg and Walker: *The Color Purple*: The Novel and the Film' (Eugene, OR: Center for the Study of Women in Society, University of Oregon, May 1986); and 'Black Women's Literature and the Canon,' seminar, University of Oregon, 7 December, 1987. See also Christian's extensive examination in the Monarch Notes study guide *Alice Walker's 'The Color Purple'* (New York: Simon and Schuster, 1987). Another black female who wrote about black women's reactions to the film was Dorothy Gilliam, in '*The Color Purple* Not as Simple as Black and White,' *Washington Post*, 23 December 1985, p. B3, and 'After the "Purple" Shutout,' *Washington Post*, 27 March 1986, p. B3.
6   See, e.g. two early works written by black women that examined this issue: Zora Neale Hurston, *Their Eyes Were Watching God* (Philadelphia: J.B. Lippincott, 1937; reprint, New York: Negro Universities Press, 1969) and Gwendolyn Brooks, *Maud Martha* (New York: Harper, 1953). Toni

Morrison takes up the subject again in her first novel, *The Bluest Eye* (New York: Holt, Rinehart, and Winston, 1970: reprint, New York: Simon and Schuster, 1972). Also, the topic is given provocative examination in a recently released independently produced film, *A Question of Color* (1992), by Kathe Sandler, a black female director.

7   Alice Walker, *The Color Purple* (San Diego: Harcourt, Brace, Jovanovich, 1982), p. 202.

8   Statement made in Lawrence Grossberg (ed.), 'On Postmodernism and Articulation: An Interview with Stuart Hall,' *Journal of Communication Inquiry* 10, no. 2 1986: 45–60.

9   Figures given in 'The Black Church in America,' *Progressions: A Lilly Endowment Occasional Report* 4, no. 1 (February 1992).

10   Cornel West, 'Nihilism in Black America,' *Dissent* (Spring 1991); reprinted in Gina Dent (ed.), *Black Popular Culture* (Seattle: Bay Press, 1992), p. 40.

11   See her article 'The Truth That Never Hurts: Black Lesbians in Fiction in the 1980s,' in Joanne M. Braxton and Andrée Nicola McLaughlin (eds.) *Wild Women in the Whirlwind: Afra-American Culture and the Contemporary Literary Renaissance* (New Brunswick, N.J.: Rutgers University Press, 1990, pp. 213–45.

12   Colloquial expression that means 'general principles.'

Chapter 32

MARK JANCOVICH

'A REAL SHOCKER'
Authenticity, genre and the struggle for distinction

A familiar history

TRADITIONALLY, FILM GENRE CRITICISM has been obsessed with tying down the 'essence' of film genres: identifying the fundamental characteristics of a genre, the boundaries between genres, deciding which films belonged to which (single) genre (Altman 1999, pp. 14–24). More recently, it has become apparent that such a project is not only impossible, but also fundamentally ill-conceived. It suffers from the traditional 'empiricist dilemma': pre-selecting a group of films for study, the study of which then supposedly identifies the appropriate criteria for their selection.

It has become commonplace to suggest that the way out of this dilemma is to turn away from idealist accounts of genre to an approach whereby we accept that: 'Genre is what we collectively believe it to be' (Tudor 1986, pp. 6–7). The need to identify the single 'truth' of a genre is removed, and we can continue with historical analysis of what genres have been.

This is a familiar history – but it is also a problematic one. This article enters the debate at the point at which the turn to contextual factors in the analysis of genre is now largely accepted: but it identifies a problem in this discursive move. While the turn to audiences relieves the film theorist from the need to police the boundaries of what constitutes a genre, we find that – in ways which have simply not been sufficiently acknowledged by cultural theorists – this practice is alive and well outside the academy. In public discourse, audiences still struggle over the definitions of genres and seek to police the boundaries between them. However, this article is not an attempt to ridicule audiences for continuing to do that which academics have supposedly grown out of. It is not an attempt to berate them for their 'essentialism' or 'naivety', but rather to examine the reasons for such practices and to explore their implications for theories of genre.

Genre, consensus and audience

As suggested above, Andrew Tudor's suggestion that 'Genre is what we collectively believe it to be' has been widely influential in film theory. However, it has also been critiqued. As Rick

Altman has pointed out, such 'collective belief' or consensual agreement cannot actually be identified. As genre criticism itself shows, there may be very different conceptions of whether particular films are, say, horror or not. Tudor himself acknowledges this but simply argues: 'To research genre history, then it is necessary to include as wide a range of films as possible, while trying not to misinterpret the spectrum of audience conceptions' (Tudor 1989, p. 6)

Indeed, Altman argues that the very nature of genre makes the task of identifying collective agreement impossible. Like Tudor, he argues that the genres are not simply located in the textual features of the films themselves, and that we must 'recognize the extent to which genres appear to be initiated, stabilized and protected by a series of institutions essential to the very existence of genres' (Altman 1999, p. 85). However, he argues, genre terms are used by a whole series of 'user-groups', who use genre terms for different purposes and, hence, in different ways. Genre terms are therefore fundamentally unstable and ambiguous and resistant to any essential definition (pp. 123–4).

However, while this acknowledges that different users may hold deeply contradictory conceptions of a genre (and that even the same person may hold deeply contradictory conceptions at different moments), Altman only addresses these differences neutrally as if all were in some sense equal. However, as Ien Ang has put it, it is not the *fact* of differences but 'the meanings of differences that matter – something that can only be grasped, interpretatively, by looking at their contexts, social and cultural bases, and impacts' (1989, p. 107).

Indeed, despite his discussion of pragmatics and of the necessary indeterminacy of genre definitions, Altman shows little interest in the consumption of genres, compared with his interest in their production and mediation. For example, in his chapter, 'What role do genres play in the viewing process?', his discussion remains highly abstract from the activities of hypothetical spectators. In this way, his work is little different from those forms of genre criticism of which Hutchings says:

> Clearly audiences were important . . . but did they bring anything to genres other than the particular knowledge and competence (to do with familiarity with generic conventions) which enabled them to interpret genre films 'correctly'?
>
> Hutchings 1995, p. 66

This is not to imply that audience classifications are the only key to understanding genre – Altman brilliantly draws our attention to the important of the generic classifications of film-makers, publicists and critics – but it does seem that audience classifications tend to get lost in his study.

Indeed, the supposed turn to the audience as a means of understanding genres has often taken a less than radical form. For example, Richard Maltby and Ian Craven recognize the importance of the audience in these debates: but on a relatively superficial level that allows essential definitions in through the back door (Maltby and Craven 1995). Indeed, this manoeuvre allows Maltby and Craven, for example, to restabilize genres so that they seem to exist as stable and familiar entities that audiences simply *recognize*, rather than as constructs that are permanently indeterminate. It also enables them to refocus attention back onto the films themselves, rather than the discourses through which they are produced, mediated and consumed, as though it were here that genres and their meanings were really located after all.[1] Even more interesting, it is at this point that they return to Altman's 'semantic/syntactic approach to film genre,' a move that allows them to bring back essentialist definitions:

> Rick Altman has distinguished between what he calls the 'semantic' approach to genre – a cataloguing of common traits, characters, attitudes, locations, sets, or shots – and a 'syntactic' approach that defines genre in terms of the structural

relationships between elements that carry its thematic and social meaning. Just as the semantic approach has been most often applied to the iconography of the Western, the structure of the Western has frequently been the subject of syntactic analysis . . . [One] instance of the fruitful application of a structural approach to what Altman calls 'the genre's fundamental syntax' is Jim Kitses' highly suggestive tabulation of 'the shifting ideological play' between what he identifies as the genre's central opposition between civilisation and the wilderness.

Maltby and Craven 1995, p. 121

By simply defining the audiences' role as being to 'recognize' genres and the appropriate ways of viewing them, Maltby and Craven lose a sense of the indeterminacy of genre classifications and return once more to a sense of genres as largely stable entities defined by fundamental characteristics that are located within the formal features of film texts.

Even Altman's turn to audiences is limited. The audience that he constructs for himself in order to understand genre is, if not homogeneous, at least quite placid. It is not that Altman is oblivious to questions of taste and their relationship to consumption. He discusses, for example, the ways in which genres are not just 'good objects' but also 'bad objects'. In other words, he acknowledges that people do not just form positive identifications with genres, but negative ones: 'It would appear that genre's capacity for positive identification is matched by a tendency to view certain genres, and thus genre production in general as bad objects' (Altman 1999, p. 113). The problem with Altman's understanding of the audience is that he does not pay enough attention to the ways in which film audiences themselves can become involved in policing the boundaries of film genres: and to the important ways that questions of taste and value are caught up in this process. The previous attempts to move genre criticism away from the idealized essence, and to the culturally constructed category, have thus too often fallen back into simply using the idealized categories in ways that are rhetorically authorized by audiences. An analysis of one particular film audience – the fans of horror films – suggests that this is not a useful way to proceed in the discussion of genre film.

Genre and the production of cultural distinctions

There is no simple, single 'collective belief' as to what constitutes the horror genre, even among self-identified fans of that genre. Indeed, when we turn to that audience in order to try to understand how we might understand what a 'horror' film is, we come across a number of competing definitions. In analysing these definitions, and how they are constructed and circulated, we can see that questions of subcultural capital, taste and authenticity are an important part of the ways in which genres are formulated by horror audiences. It is these questions which genre theory has previously elided in its turn to audiences.

For example, while I have frequently argued that blood and guts *do not* define the genre and that there are many horror films which are not gory in any sense at all (see Jancovich 1992, 1996), I have often been accused, in discussions with both my students and members of the general public, of not really talking about horror (or at least not 'real' horror), but rather about mainstream commercial horror. To put it another way, they claim that what I discuss is not 'real' horror but rather the commercialized, sanitized tripe which is consumed by moronic victims of mass culture. As a result, many of these horror fans privilege as 'real' and 'authentic' those films of violent 'excess' whose circulation is usually restricted (and often secret and/or illegal), and they do so specifically to define their own opposition to, or distinction from, what they define as inauthentic commercial products of mainstream culture. They adopt the stance of a radicalized subculture or underground to distance themselves from, and define themselves as superior to, others who they construct as inferior and threatening, a mindless and conformist horde associated with mass, middlebrow and legitimate culture.[2]

In other words, struggles over the definition of horror as a genre take place *between* horror fans as much as they do between those who define themselves as pro- and anti-horror. Indeed, one can argue that there are at least three levels at which struggles over genre distinctions take place (although it is important to note that the very nature of these struggles means that these are only points in a complex and shifting continuum in which different individuals and groups seek to place themselves in relation to others).

First, there is the distinction that is often constructed by those who wish to distinguish themselves from the consumers of genre films. Hence there is the distinction between mainstream cinema, which is defined as a genre cinema, and art-cinema, which is somehow seen as a cinema which is anti-genre: a cinema which is either free from genre or else subverts the genres of mainstream culture.[3] A similar strategy is also employed at more legitimate and middlebrow levels in which supposedly 'non-generic' genres such as the 'drama' are used to distinguish specific classes of films from 'generic' genres such as westerns, romances, SF or horror.

These kinds of distinction can be clearly seen in the introduction to Barry Keith Grant's edited collection, *Film Genre Reader II* where he writes: 'Simply stated, genre movies are those commercial feature films which, through repetition and variation, tell familiar stories with familiar characters in familiar situations.' Of course such a statement is only meaningful if it is defined against something which is therefore defined as not a genre movie. While Grant concedes that 'Genre movies have comprised the bulk of film practice, the iceberg of film history', he still presupposes something that is distinct from the genre movie – 'the visible tip' of his metaphorical iceberg that he argues 'has commonly been understood as film art' (Grant 1995, p. xv). Of course, Grant wants to argue against the dismissal of the genre movie in favour of 'film art' but, in doing so, he simply calls for genre to be taken seriously as an object of study, rather than to reject the distinction between genre cinema and art cinema.

Nor is this kind of opposition simply restricted to academic writing, as can be seen in Jim Shelley's assessment of Kathryn Bigelow's *Strange Days*. For Shelley, the film 'looks like the work of one of independent cinema's most dynamic . . . challenging talents who believed she was subverting some of Hollywood's most closely-held and well established conventions [the science fiction action movie] when, in fact, all along, it was the other way around' (Shelley 1995). Here, Shelley opposes the independent cinema to Hollywood specifically around the issue of genre. Hollywood, as is often claimed, is presented as a genre cinema, while the independent cinema is seen as somehow outside genre and, in this case, as surreptitiously subverting it. Indeed, this opposition between genre cinema (which is presented as formulaic, conservative and repetitive) and the subversion of it by creative, radical and innovative auteurs goes back to auteur theory and the very origins of contemporary film studies (see Jancovich, forthcoming).

Second, there are the distinctions between fans of different genres. While it is quite possible to like both horror and SF, there are many SF fans who struggle to distinguish themselves from horror fans onto whom are deflected a series of negative associations. For example, certain SF fans seek to emphasize the seriousness of their own genre, and their investment in it, at the expense of the horror fan who comes to represent the epitome of the consumer of mass culture as moronic, threatening Other. In this way, these SF fans seek to disassociate themselves from this problematic image, an image which others impose on both horror and SF fans as a uniform mass. It is for this reason that there is so often disagreement between horror and SF fans over particular films. For example, *Alien* is often appropriated as a SF film by certain SF fans but it is also disavowed as not *real* SF by other SF fans who see it as an inauthentic SF movie, a moronic slasher movie in outer space. The same is also true the other way around with certain horror fans appropriating it as a horror movie and others dismissing it for its 'soulless' SF special effects. In both cases the fans of one genre construct fans of a different genre as the Other from which they establish their own distinction and superiority.

For example, some science fiction 'purists' claim that SF is distinguished from horror and fantasy by its relationships to scientific theory. As a result, as one science fiction fan complained in a letter to the magazine *Fear*: 'Since you added the words "Science Fiction" to the cover legend "The World of Fantasy, Horror and . . ." may I ask if there are any plans to feature either interviews or FEAR fiction from Issac Asimov, Arthur C. Clarke, Bob Shaw or Clifford D. Simak? Science-fiction is, in my opinion, lacking in your otherwise magnificent magazine.' The issue here is not that *Fear* has ignored science fiction, but rather a challenge to its very definition of science fiction. The choice of authors listed is often referred to as 'the golden age of science fiction': a period that not only tried to distinguish the term 'science fiction' from the 'space operas' of earlier periods, but also to legitimate it through the presentation of it as a forum for scientific theorization and extrapolation. For this reason, the letter is not only placed under the headline 'put science into fiction', but is roundly rebuffed by the statement that 'we don't think dry articles on theoretical space travel or planetary ecology would go down very well' (*Fear*, May–June 1989, p. 12).

None the less, this kind of definition of science fiction not only leads readers to dispute generic definitions in the magazine, but also leads to confusion and indecision within the feature writer's own articles. One reader therefore writes:

> In Issue 13, your 'Top 60 Horror Films' chart included *Alien* and *Aliens*, positioned 8th and 55th respectively . . . I may be wrong, but shouldn't these two films have been classified as science fiction? Sure there are horror elements in the form of tense atmosphere and the hideous alien creatures, but I think that such elements are more than equalled by the science fiction parts and overall feeling of the films. I may be moaning about nothing, but I've found that the term 'horror', as often referred to by you and other people in the magazine, tends to swallow up all other genres. There are distinctive characteristics, aren't there.
>
> *Fear*, August 1990, p. 82

However, while the magazine justifies the placing of these films within its 'Top 60 Horror Films' with the claim that they define horror loosely 'as anything that evokes unease' (p. 82), their own generic definitions are nowhere near as simple as this implies. In an interview with Renny Harlin, for example, there is a discussion of his involvement with a proposed *Alien III*. Here *Alien* is referred to as the 'ultimate implacable extra-terrestrial horror', while at other points it is not only defined as science fiction, but consequently distinguished from *Aliens* which is seen as not 'real' science fiction. In contrast, *Aliens* is described as 'Vietnam-in-outer-space' and Renny Harlin is approvingly quoted as calling it 'an action vehicle that only happened to take place in space' (*Fear*, May–June 1989, p. 33).

However, these contradictions do not mean that the magazine dispenses with the practice of drawing distinctions but, on the contrary, they emerge out of the specific practice of doing so. Indeed, the magazine repeatedly runs up against the problem of genre definitions specifically because it refuses to dispense with them. In his comments on the 'Top 60 Horror Movies', for example, Mark Salisbury notes the presence of films that 'sit precariously on the fringe of the horror genre (*Blue Velvet*, *Night of the Hunter*, *Apocalypse Now*, *Taxi Driver*).'

However, rather than acknowledge the ways in which the presence of these films in the list call into question the definitions of horror used by those making the selection, Salisbury claims; 'I was eventually persuaded to include the latter as they all certainly contain horrific moments, albeit unconventional ones.' As he notes: 'One of the main difficulties in compiling any list of horror films is deciding just where to draw the line.' However, rather than simply dispense with the category, he fudges: 'As you can see, my criteria for inclusion are fairly loose. Perhaps it is better that way, I'm not sure. After all, if you want to be pedantic, would you class *Alien* as a horror film, or is it science fiction?' (*Fear*, January 1990, p. 21).

However, if *Fear* seems uncomfortable with the arbitrariness of some of its definitions, *The Dark Side* can be positively perverse. For example, when asked by one reader 'Why is *Shogun Assassins* always classed as a horror film?', the response is simply: '*Shogun Assassins* tends to be thought of as a horror film because it briefly made the video nasties list.' (*The Dark Side*, June–July 1998, p. 12).

However, not all positions are quite so wilful. In *Fangoria* one letter writer praises the magazine for its coverage of *The Lost World*, but acknowledges that many readers would 'think that movies like *Jurassic Park* and *The Lost World* have no place in a horror mag'. In answer to these objections, he therefore refutes the generic classification of the films that are responsible for such objections: 'These people are missing out on a very popular and exciting subgenre of monster movies that is as old as cinema itself, yet always fresh.' (*Fangoria*, September 1997, p. 6). Here the terms are shifted from horror to monster movies and the films are thereby generically relocated from science fiction into a subgenre of the 'monster movie', a category which is legitimated through a sense of its tradition and heritage.

These debates, however, also reveal a third level of conflict: that is intrageneric conflicts between fans of a particular genre. Thus, while some horror fans embrace Freddy Kruger, of the *Nightmare on Elm Street* series, as a cult hero, others seek to disassociate themselves from these fans through an association with cult 'auteurs' such as Dario Argento. However, for other horror fans, Argento's films are too mainstream and, in distinction, they privilege more 'subversive' and 'excessive' underground films. These conflicts between those who define themselves as horror fans do not stop here, but even within the 'underground' fan culture there are continual conflicts and distinctions in operation (see, for example, Black 1996, 1998; McDonough 1994; Martin 1993; Vale *et al.*, 1986; Weldon 1983, 1996; and magazines such as *Uncut*, *Gorezone* and *Fangoria*).

For example, in *Incredibly Strange Films*, while writing about *The Wizard of Gore*, Mark Spainhower claims 'the average moviegoer will certainly be mortified by *The Wizard of Gore's* extreme sadism, as well as the "seedy" quality which pervades all of Lewis's films. Absent are the sophisticated latex prosthetics of Tom Savani or Dick Smith, which, while technically virtuosic, appear merely slick and facile next to the crude and vicious carnage of the animal innards school which Lewis himself pioneered to hideous extremes' (Spainhower 1986; p. 176). Tom Savani and Dick Smith are themselves, in publications such as *Fangoria*, *Gorezone*, *Fear* and *The Dark Side*, the subject of great adoration, but they are hardly figures who would be familiar to the majority of moviegoers. The term 'average movie goer' is therefore an extremely slippery one that the writer uses to conflate those horror fans from whom he seeks to distance himself with the notion of the 'conformist mass'. In so doing, it operates to produce a clear sense of distinction between that which is defined as the authentic subcultural self and that which is presented as the inauthentic mass cultural other.

Indeed, this process of Othering can be seen particularly clearly in the comments of one *Fear* reader who complains: 'I fear that *Fear* may well degenerate into a *Fangoria* clone . . . If I see one more letter like: "Dear *Fear*, I am a spotty, emotionally retarded teenager who wants to work in the prosthetics industry" then I shall scream (and scream!).' This writer not only seeks to present himself as serious and sophisticated in distinction to the 'spotty emotionally retarded teenagers' who are invading his domain, but the reference to 'the prosthetics industry' associates the teenagers with those sections of horror fandom that are centered around special effects figures such as Savani and around the *Friday the Thirteenth*, *Nightmare on Elm Street* and *Hellraiser*, series, an association that is emphasized by his suggestion that these teenage fans are ones 'whose bedroom walls are plastered with posters of Pinhead' (*Fear*, September 1989, p. 80).

Refusing to *Scream*

One film that has particularly provoked such struggles between horror audiences is *Scream*, and this is due to its extraordinary commercial success and the cycle that this has established. On the Web, for example, one can find a wealth of fan materials that discuss the film, and while some are clearly positive, others are more guarded and even outright hostile. The guarded responses often praise the film through its association with horror 'auteur' Wes Craven, who is seen as legtimating it, while they are also clearly troubled by the film's commercial success. As Sarah Thornton has argued, subcultural capital depends on its rarity and distinction from the supposedly mainstream audiences (Thornton 1995). The success of the film therefore threatens this sense of rarity and distinction and this situation requires these fans to distinguish between the *real* horror fans and the inauthentic interloper.

This strategy is even more pointed in the more violent attacks on the film. For example one site (arachnia.com) contains a mock political manifesto: 'Boycott Trendy Horror'.[4] The page starts with a call to arms: 'Hurry, quick – Before *they* come up with *another* sequel to *Scream*' (my emphasis). The page therefore not only presents the movement (humorously) as a form of radical political activism but also clearly invokes a sense of distinction between 'them' and 'us', between the outsider and the insider. It then calls for horror fans to 'let the makers of these horrendous, high budget "Horror" films know that you're not going to stand for it anymore'. In this way, the page repeats a familiar distinction within fan cultures between authentic 'low budget' and the inauthentic 'high budget' movie, a distinction which, as I have argued elsewhere, goes back at least as far as 1950s mass culture theory (Jancovich, forthcoming). It also places the word horror in quotation marks in order qualify this term; to suggest that it is not *real* horror.

This is made still clearer in the next sentence where it is claimed: 'They've demeaned you enough, slapping the label of the genre you love on epic tales featuring scantily clad, barely legal teen starlets.' The reference to labels again implies the distinction between authentic and inauthentic horror, but this passage also raises another issue. As Thornton points out, subcultural capital is usually gendered as masculine, and the reference to 'scantily clad, barely legal teen starlets' once again associates the films with inauthenticity through the familiar trope of 'mass culture as woman' (Huyssen 1986). Indeed, this reference to the female stars of these films covertly raises issues about the basis for the film's success, which has been directly associated with an audience of teenage females (see, for example, Cherry 1999). These films, it is implied, are not just inauthentic horror but they are made for, and consumed by, inauthentic fans: young girls who cannot have the subcultural capital to define what is hip! Of course, the irony here is that scantily clad female characters feature strongly in cycles such as the 1970s slasher film. But in this reference, the fact that female audiences are enjoying these films is being projected here onto the female characters and the female stars within the films. Indeed the site makes the female stars the target of considerable hostility, given their associations with femininity, the teenage audience and also network television.

In the process, these films are not just seen as inauthentic horror, but also as moronic entertainment for morons: 'They've insulted your intelligence by hoping you won't notice that the acting is terrible, the stories are regurgitated and the soundtracks are just hurled up Top 40 hits and a marketing ploy to further line their pockets. Isn't enough enough?' Here many of the terms usually directed against horror are deflected onto 'inauthentic' horror: it is not horror that is unintelligent, badly acted or displays formulaic storylines but inauthentic horror; and the proof of this is its audience: the consumers of Top 40 hits.[5]

These issues are made even more overt later on when the writer explains why these films are 'that big a deal':

> this new rash of movies masquerading as Horror flicks are driving classics off the shelves and good movies out of the theatres. Above all else they are giving the genre a bad name. Do you want your kids to grow up thinking a Horror movie is only possible if Neve Campbell, Jennifer Love Hewitt or Sarah Michelle Geller stars in it? I don't think so.

Again this passage uses a humorous tone – the reference to 'your kids' parodies the rhetoric of anti-horror campaigners – but it should none the less be taken seriously. The problem, this passage suggests, is that while it is only the authentic horror fan who has the right to make distinctions, their judgements are being threatened. *Their* movies are being driven off selves and out of the movie theatres, and it is not just horror that is being given a bad name, but those who would be associated with it.

The strategy is therefore to boycott these films, 'unless you promise to make fun of them the whole time'. The next is to place a link to the boycott page on your own Web site ('the one with the bondage-babe image map'.[6] In response, your page will be added to the list on the arachnia site, 'so that others who want to help bash the Hell out of New Horror can "stick together"'.

Of course, as has been stressed, this page is to some extent humorous. It is not (I believe) a real call to action, and clearly makes knowing parodic references to campaigns against horror. However, this is not to imply that it is entirely innocent. It is founded on a series of fairly familiar subcultural ideologies that reproduce existing cultural distinctions. If it is humorous, this is because the page is addressing like-minded fans but, in the process, it denigrates and Others those fans that it defines as inauthentic and so presents its tastes as inherently superior to them.

However, as the arachnia pages illustrate, these struggles for distinction are frequently posed in terms of authenticity. It is here that I have to be critical of my own work in the field which has frequently criticized other academic accounts of horror on the basis that they do not share the competences and dispositions of the popular audiences by whom horror films are 'ordinarily' consumed. This strategy has required me to speak *as* a horror fan, rather than *for* the horror fan. But it has also frequently led me to make an implicit distinction between the *real* horror fan, and the usurpation of horror by 'inauthentic others'. This can be seen, for example, in my account of *The Exorcist* and *Fatal Attraction*, both of which I have criticized as 'horror films for people who don't like horror' (Jancovich 1992). Indeed, I have long been planning to write something about the spate of 'horror films for people who don't like horror' which appeared in the early 1990s after the success of *Silence of the Lambs*, films such as Francis Ford Coppola's *Bram Stoker's Dracula*, Kenneth Branagh's *Mary Shelley's Frankenstein*, and Mike Nichol's *Wolf*. There is still something I want to say about these films, some of which

I have discussed elsewhere in relation to *Silence of the Lambs* (Jancovich 2000). However, I am now troubled by the ease with which, or even the inevitability with which, speaking *as* a horror fan transforms itself into speaking as a *real* horror fan, implicitly constructing anyone 'naïve', 'foolhardy' or 'ignorant' enough to construct the film differently as a 'phoney' horror fan. Certainly, I have partly been alerted to this by challenges to my own status as a horror fan by those who consider themselves to be more authentic, radical or whatever than myself, but this in no way diminishes the seriousness of these problems: it only emphasizes their significance.

Conclusions and conjectures

I would like to conclude this paper by suggesting ways in which this approach to audiences' construction of genres might be useful in other areas of work on genre; and to call attention to some important methodological issues which must be borne in mind as such work proceeds.

Such an approach could be applied to the study of a whole series of questions from film production, through mediation, to consumption, to say nothing of an analysis of individual films or groups of films. As Lawrence Alloway, Peter Hutchings and Rick Altman have all argued (Alloway 1971; Hutchings 1995; Altman 1999), in terms of production, it might be better to analyse films in terms of cycles, rather than genres. For example, one might examine the slasher movie, or more recent cycles such as 'from hell' movies (*The Hand that Rocks the Cradle*, *Single White Female*, etc.), 'serial killer' movies (*Silence of the Lambs*, *Seven*, *Copycat*, *Kiss the Girls*) or erotic thrillers (*Basic Instinct*, *Body of Evidence*, *Sexual Response*).

However, such broad production trends need to be understood both internally and externally, both in terms of the ways in which individual films are positioned in relation to the cycle so that a sense of familiarity and variation is established, but also the ways in which both individual films and the cycle as a whole are related to, and construct a sense of, a generic history. Films such as *Halloween*, *Hand that Rocks the Cradle*, *Silence of the Lambs*, and *Basic Instinct*, all clearly emphasize debts to the past and so *construct* a sense of their generic heritage.

These processes also need to be understood at three different levels. The first is the broad industry, or more limited studio-based, sense of economic planning in which specific cycles/genres are seen as part of an overall cultural repertoire or production strategy. The second is concerned with the specific personnel associated with the making of individual films such as writers, directors, designers, and even special effects teams. The third and final level is therefore that of marketing, distribution and exhibition in which films and groups of films are presented to the public and a sense of their identity is established.

At all these levels, however, one finds entirely contradictory and conflicting conceptions of genre definition and of the generic classification of individual films. Not only, as Berenstein has shown (Berenstein 1996), have films often been marketed in different ways to different sections of the audience (and made with these different audiences in mind), but different people within the industry may also have very different conceptions of the genre and very different investments within it. In the case of horror or action, for example, the film-makers' sense of the low cultural status of these products have often led them to conceive and present the films differently from, say, marketing personnel. Alternatively, it is also frequently the case that a specific film-maker, as John Carpenter experienced while making *The Fog*, may have a very different sense of the sort of film that they are making from that of the industry management'.[7] Indeed, these issues are often highly significant within the careers of Hollywood personnel, who are often forced to deny or suppress early work (in, for example, pornography, horror, or the exploitation cinema more generally), because it carries the wrong connotations and associations and therefore threatens the legitimacy of their later careers. Nor is this simply a threat to their 'images'. It can also threaten their position within the industry, both economically and politically.

The issue of marketing, however, often feeds into other processes of mediation over which the industry had less control, and these range from articles on films, stars, directors, etc., through reviews, to fan writing. All of these, as I have already suggested, are crucially bound up with producing different senses of genre, and even within any one publication, article or review, as I have shown elsewhere, one finds very different and usually entirely contradictory definitions of genres (Jancovich 2000).

However, one must be careful with such materials because they do not give automatic or unproblematic access to the ways in which audiences read and interpret films, but rather give a sense of the very different ways in which people are supposed to 'talk' about films. Indeed, it is important to distinguish between the activities of consuming films and the activities of talking about them. This is clearly shown in Ien Ang's work on *Dallas* where she found that many of those who wrote to her were fully aware of the ways in which their consumption of the show could be judged by others, and hence were constantly positioning what they said about the show, and their enjoyment of it, in relation to what Ang calls 'the ideology of mass culture'. Thus, she found that it was common for people simply to dismiss their engagement with the show through statements such as 'I know its rubbish but I like it', or engage in even more complex ways of talking about their relationship to the show (Ang 1985).

Alternatively, for example, horror fans often deny that horror films frighten them. Within certain circles, the very value of watching these films, or at least the value of saying certain things about that viewing experience, is to assert that they don't frighten but only amuse. I am not saying that certain people are not frightened, or that they do not enjoy specific films because they are viewed as ludicrous, but rather than within certain contexts, it would be inappropriate (other than in exceptional circumstances) to admit to being frightened by horror films. In other words, when people talk about their cultural consumption, they do so in the knowledge that what they say classifies them in the eyes of others.

In analysing these materials, it is also useful to draw upon Sara Thornton's distinction between mass, niche and micro media, 'each of which have markedly different connotations' (Thornton 1995, p. 122). Hence we might study not only the mainstream press, but also specialist film publications such as *Premiere*, *Empire*, or even *Sight and Sound*. Even then there are the more specialist film publications such as *Fangoria*, *The Dark Side*, and *Starburst*; and beyond these: fanzines, Internet discussion groups, fan club newsletters, etc. Each of these have very different (and internally contradictory) conceptions of genre, but, as Thornton points out, we must be wary of viewing the mass media as a simple threat to authentic subcultures. It may be the case that 'their diverse audience sizes and compositions and their distinct processes of circulation have different consequences' (p.122), but in contrast to much recent work, it is necessary that we neither idealize fans, nor ignore more 'ordinary' viewers.

For example, we need to be aware of the often vicious struggles for distinction within fan cultures and the power relations involved in the ways in which fan cultures construct the figure of their Other: the 'ordinary' viewer (Jancovich, forthcoming). Rather than simply accepting the fan's construction of the authentic subcultural self and the inauthentic mass cultural other, we must examine the extremely contradictory and conflicting relations between fans as well as challenging their homogenization of the 'ordinary' viewer. We must also be wary of the tendency to authorize, and present as more authentic, the tastes and definitions of fans, and we need to study and understand the ways in which other sections of the viewing public consume films. For example, it is quite clear that certain sections of the audience do not even watch horror films, but it is just as important that we analyse how these audiences construct and understand this category, and why they see it as 'not for the likes of us', as it is for us to understand why fans do see it as 'their sort of thing'.

However, in studying audiences, we need to not only examine how they make sense of specific films, and how they understand generic categories more generally, but also to move beyond questions of interpretation to examine the broader social activities associated with the consumption of particular genres. It is commonly assumed, for example, that romantic comedies are often used as date movies, or that teenage males use horror films as a rite of passage. Not only do we need to test these assumptions, but also to study *how and why* specific categories of films are seen as appropriate or inappropriate for specific social activities.

In other words, it is important to remember that film consumption is not simply about the engagement with a specific text, or even a group of texts, but a series of different kinds of social events and activities: a night out or a night in; a date; a night out with the boys or the girls; an opportunity for self-indulgence; an opportunity to interact with one's children or even to avoid such interaction; etc. These events may be ones in which the actual encounter with a specific film may be one of the least significant issues, but in which understandings of genre are none the less significant. Certain genres are understood as being appropriate or inappropriate for different kinds of social events, and the question is why and how these understandings are constructed and to what effect.

However, as has been argued, the recognition that different people interpret genres in different ways should not simply lead us to a pluralist acceptance of these differences. Differences in taste are never neutral but are always a distaste, a rejection of the tastes of others. It is the politics involved in such taste formations to which we need to address our future research. As Charlotte Brunsdon has argued, only 'the inheritors of legitimate culture . . . can afford' to withhold judgements of taste, and perhaps more worryingly 'this very avoidance of judgement seems somehow to recreate the old patterns of aesthetic domination and subordination, and to pathologize the audience' who cannot afford the luxury of such an avoidance (pp. 122–123).

When audiences struggle over the definition of genres and seek to police the boundaries between them, they are not being 'naïve' but are engaged in cultural struggles the politics of which we need to understand rather than simply ridicule as ignorant or outmoded.

Notes

1   One of the strengths of historical reception studies, particularly in the work of Barbara Klinger, has been to illustrate that such a manoeuvre does not work, and that the features of a text can be given very different meanings and generic identities in different contexts (Klinger 1994).

2   These kinds of distinction can be clearly seen, for example, in fan publications such as *Uncut*, *Fangoria* and *Gorezone*.

3   It is, however, interesting to note that certain critics have argued that the art-cinema itself can be studied as a genre (see, for example, Tudor 1973; Neale 1981).

4   I am grateful to Tim Noble for attracting my attention to these pages.

5   As Joanne Hollows has pointed out, within popular music subcultures and criticism, the authentic and subcultural is usually defined in opposition to 'chart music' which is explicitly defined as feminine, superficial and trivial (see Hollows n.d., 2000. See also Thornton 1995).

6   Women, it seems, can be the object of these fan cultures but not their subject, unless of course they are able to somehow renounce an association with femininity. This is a point not only raised by

Thornton (1995) and Hollows (2000), but also by Cherry (1999) who details the ways in which female horror fans are excluded from fan cultures that are clearly dominated not only by males, but also by the values of masculinity. This is not to deny that women can be active in fan cultures (arachnia herself is actually female) but that in order to do so they must become, as Thornton puts it, 'culturally one of the boys' (Thornton 1995, p. 104).

7   Carpenter wanted to make a Gothic ghost story but kept running into conflicts with the producers who wanted something closer to his previous hit, *Halloween*.

References

Abel, R. (1984) *French Cinema: The First Wave 1915–1929*, Princeton: Princeton University Press.

Adair, N. and C. Adair (eds), (1978) *Word is Out: Stories of Some of Our Lives*, New York: New Glide Delta.

Adams, P. (1955) 'Introduction', in Sabine, J. (ed.), *A Century of Australian Cinema*, Port Melbourne: Reed Books: vii–xi.

Adorno, T. W. (1975) 'Culture Industry Reconsidered', Rabinbach, A. G. (trans.), *New German Critique*, 6: 12–19.

—— (1981–2) 'Transparencies on Film', *New German Critique*, 24(25): 199–205.

Alberts, W. (1991) 'Prayer as an Instrument of War', *Z Magazine*, April.

Allen, J. (1980) 'The Film Viewer as Consumer', *Quarterly Review of Film Studies*, 5(4): 481–501.

Allen, R. C. (1980) *Vaudeville and Film 1895–1915: A Study in Media Interaction*, New York: Arno.

Allen, R. and Gomery, D. (1985) *Film History: Theory and Practice*, New York: Knopf.

Alloway, L. (1961) 'Architecture and the Modern Cinema', *The Listener*, 22: 1085–6.

—— (1971) *Violent America: The Movies 1946–64*, New York: Museum of Modern Art.

Altenloh, E. (1914) *Zur Soziologie des Kino: Die Kino-Unternehmung und die sozialen Schichten*, Ph.D. thesis, Heidelberg, Leipzig: Spamersche Buchdruckerei.

Althusser, L. (1971) 'Ideology and Ideological State Apparatuses (Notes Towards an Investigation), in Brewster, B. (trans.) *Lenin and Philosophy and Other Essays*, New York: Monthly Review Press, pp. 127–86.

Altick, R. (1978) *The Shows of London*, Cambridge, Mass. and London: Harvard University Press.

Altman, R. (1984) 'Towards a Theory of the History of Representational Technologies', *Iris*, 2(2): 111–24.

—— (1987a) *The American Film Musical*, Bloomington: Indiana University Press.

—— (1987b) 'Television Sound', in Newcomb, H. (ed.), *Television: The Critical View*, New York: Oxford University Press, pp. 566–84.

—— (1995) 'The Sound of Sound', *Cineaste*, 21(1–2): 68–72.

—— (1999) *Film/Genre*, London: British Film Institute.

Alton, J. (1949) *Painting with Light*, New York: Macmillan.

Amis, K. (1965) *The James Bond Dossier*, London: Jonathan Cape.

Anderson, B. (1983) 'Spoken Silents in the Japanese Cinema: Essay on the Necessity of Katsuben', *Journal of Film and Video*, 40(1): 13–33.

Andrew, D. (1984) *Concepts in Film Theory*, New York: Oxford University Press.

—— (1986) 'Film and Society: Public Rituals and Private Space', *East–West Film Journal*, 1(1): 7–22.

Andrew, J. D. (1976) *The Major Film Theories: An Introduction*, New York: Oxford University Press.

Ang, I. (1985) *Watching Dallas: Soap Opera and the Melodramatic Imagination*, Couling, D. (trans.), London: Methuen.

—— (1989) 'Wanted: audiences. On the Politics of Empirical Audience Studies', in Seiter, E. *et al.* (eds), *Remote Control: Television Audiences and Cultural Power*, London: Routledge, 96–115.

Angelou, M. (1984) *I Know Why the Caged Bird Sings*, London: Virago.

Ansen, D. (1986) 'The Big Hustle', *Newsweek*, 13 October, 68–74.

Arbuthnot, L. and Seneca, G. (1982) 'Pre-Text and Text in *Gentlemen Prefer Blondes*', *Film Reader*, 5:13–23.

Aristotle (1951) 'The Poetics', in Butcher, S. H. (ed.), *Aristotle's Theory of Poetry and Fine Art, with a Critical Text and Translation of The Poetics*, New York: Dover.

Arnold, M. (1963) *Culture and Anarchy*, Cambridge: Cambridge University Press.

Arroyo, J. (1996) 'Money Train', *Sight and Sound*, 6(6): 46–7.

Artel, L. and Wengraf, S. (1976) *Positive Images: A Guide to Non-Sexist Films for Young People*, San Francisco: Booklegger Press.

Asad, T. (1973) *Anthropology and the Colonial Encounter*, Atlantic Highlands: Humanities Press.

Attille, M. (1986) '*The Passion of Remembrance*: Background', *Framework*, 32/33, 100–3.

Austin, B. A. (1983a) 'Do Movie Ratings Affect a Film's Performance at the Ticket Window?', *Boxoffice*, March, 40–2.

—— (1983b) 'A Longitudinal Test of the Taste Culture and Elitist Hypotheses', *Journal of Popular Film and Television*, 4: 156–65.

—— (1984) 'But Why This Movie?', *Boxoffice*, February, 16–18.

—— (1989) *Immediate Seating: A Look at Movie Audiences*, Belmont: Wadsworth Publishing Company.

—— (1990) 'Home Video: The Second-Run "Theatre" of the 1990s', in Balio, T. (ed.), *Hollywood in the Age of Television*, Boston: Unwin Hyman, 319–49.

Austin, B. A., Nicolichm, A. M. J. and Simonet, T. (1981) 'MPAA Ratings and the Box Office: Some Tantalizing Statistics', *Film Quarterly*, 35: 28–30.

Australian Broadcasting Tribunal (1991) *Broadcasting in Australia*, Sydney: Australian Broadcasting Tribunal.

Australian Film Commission (1991) 'Analysis of the Performance of Australian Films Since 1980', a paper for the House of Representatives Standing Committee on Environment, Recreation and the Arts Inquiry into the Performance of Australian Film – 'The Moving Pictures Inquiry', Sydney: AFC, October.

Babrow, A. S. *et al.* (1988) 'Person Perception and Children's Impression of Television and Real Peers', *Communication Research*, 15(6), 680–98.

Bach, S. (1985) *Final Cut: Dreams and Disasters*, New York: William Morrow.

Baker, C. W. (1994) *How Did They Do It? Computer Illusion in Film and TV*, Indianapolis: Alpha Books.

Baker, R. W. (1991) 'Putting the Cult Back in Culture', *Village Voice*, 12 November, 41.

Balbus, I. (1982) *Marxism and Domination*, Princeton: Princeton University Press.

Baldwin, J. (1976) *The Devil Finds Work*, London: Michael Joseph.

Balibar, E. and Wallerstein, I. (1991) *Race, Nation, Class: Ambiguous Identities*, London: Verso.

Balio, T. (ed.) (1990) *Hollywood in the Age of Television*, Boston: Unwin Hyman.

—— (1998) 'A Major Presence in All the World's Important Markets' in Steve Neale and Murray Smith (eds), *Contemporary Hollywood Cinema*, London: Routledge.

—— Merritt, R. and Randall, R. S. (eds) (1976) *The American Film Industry*, Madison: University of Wisconsin Press.

Barber, L. (1999) 'The Vision Splendid', *The Weekend Australian*, 25–6 September, Review 16–19.

Barnes, J. (1989) *History of the World in 10½ Chapters*, New York: Knopf.

Barnouw, E. (1984) 'Torrentius and His Camera', *Studies in Visual Communication*, 10(3): 22–9.

Barr, C. (1977) *Ealing Studios*, London: Cameron and Tayleur.

—— (1985) 'CinemaScope: Before and After', in Mast, G. and Cohen, M. (eds), *Film Theory and Criticism: Introductory Readings*, 3rd edn, New York: Oxford University Press, pp. 139–63.

Barrie, J. M. (1906) *Peter Pan in Kensington Gardens*, London: Hodder and Stoughton.

Barrowclough, S. (1982) Review of *Not a Love Story*, Screen, 23: 26–36.

Barry, I. (1926) *Let's Go to the Movies*, New York: Payson and Clarke.

Bart, P. (1990) 'Stars to Studios: Pass the Bucks – Top Talent Seeks to Break Video Profits Barrier', *Variety*, 24 September, 1: 108.

—— (1993) 'Mouse Gears for Mass Prod'n', *Variety*, 19 July, 1: 5.

Barthes, R. (1975a) *Image, Music, Text*, Miller, R. (trans.) New York: Hill and Wang.

—— (1975b) *The Pleasure of Text*, Miller, R. (trans.), New York: Hill and Wang.

—— (1979) 'Upon Leaving the Movie Theater', Augst, B. and White, S. (trans.) *University Publishing*, 6.

—— (1981) *Camera Lucida: Reflections on Photography*, Howard, R. (trans.) New York: Hill and Wang; and (1984) London: Fontana.

Barton, S. (1992) 'The Girls Against the Boys: Feminist Theory, Queer Theory and Hollywood Cinema', paper presented at the Modern Language Association Conference, December.

—— (1998) 'Your Self Storage: Female Investigation and Male Performativity in the Woman's Psycho-thriller' in Jon Lewis (ed.), *The New American Cinema*, Durham: Duke University Press.

Barwise, P. and Ehrenberg, A. (1988) *Television and Its Audience*, London: Sage.

Basten, F. E. (1980) *Glorious Technicolor: The Movies' Magic Rainbow*, Cranbury: A. S. Barnes.

Bastide, R. (1967) 'Colour, Racism and Christianity', *Daedalus*, 96(2): 312–27.

Battersby, C. (1989) 'The Idea of Genius', Lecture at the National Portrait Gallery, London, 20 October, unpublished.

Baudrillard, J. (1977) *L'Effet beaubourg: implosion et dissuasion*, Paris: Galilée.

—— (1980) 'The Implosion of Meaning in the Media and the Information of the Social in the Masses', in Woodward, K. (ed.), *Myths of Information: Technology and Postindustrial Culture*, Madison: Coda Press, 137–48.

—— (1983a) 'the Ecstasy of Communication', in Foster, H. (ed.), *The Anti-Aesthetic: Essays on Postmodern Culture*, Seattle: Bay Press, pp. 126–34.

—— (1983b) 'The Precession of Simulacra', *Art and Text*, 3–47.

—— (1984) *Simulations*, New York: Semiotext(e).

—— (1991a) 'La Guerre du Golfe n'a pas eu lieu', *Libération*, 29 March.

—— (1991b) 'The Reality Gulf', *Guardian*, UK, January 11.

Baudry, J.-L. (1974–5) 'Ideological Effects of the Basic Cinematographic Apparatus'. *Film Quarterly*, 28(2): 39–47; and (1986) in Rosen, P. (ed.), *Narrative, Apparatus, Ideology*, New York: Columbia University Press.

Baumgold, J. (1996) 'Killer Women', *New York*, 29 July, 24–30.

Baxter, P. (1975) 'On the History and Ideology of Film Lighting', *Screen*, 16(3): 83–106.

Bazin, A. (1967) *What is Cinema?* Vols I and II, Gray, H. (ed. and trans.), Berkeley: University of California Press.

—— (1974) 'The Evolution of the Language of Cinema', in Mast, G. and Cohen, M. (eds), *Film Theory and Criticism: Introductory Readings*, New York: Oxford University Press.

Bean, J. and Court, D. (1994) 'Production', in Curtis, R. and Spriggs, S. (eds), *Get the Picture: Essential Data on Australian Film, Television and Video*, 3rd edn, Sydney: Australian Film Commission, pp. 30–67.

Beaupre, L. and Thompson, A. (1983) 'Eighth Annual Grosses Gloss', *Film Comment*, March/April, 68.

Becker, S. L. (1984) 'Marxist Approaches to Media Studies: The British Experience', *Critical Studies in Mass Communication*, 1: 66–80.

Beetham, M. (1996) *A Magazine of Her Own? Domesticity and Desire in the Women's Magazine 1800–1914*, London and New York: Routledge.

Behlmer, R. (ed.) (1972) *Memo from David O. Selznick*, New York: Viking.

Bell, Q. (1947) *On Human Finery*, London: Hogarth Press.

Belloni, G. and Codelli, L. (1974) 'Conversation avec Francis Ford Coppola', *Positif*, 161: 51.

Benjamin, W. (1935/1979) 'On the Mimetic Faculty', Tarnowski, K. (trans.), *New German Critique*, 17: 65–9.

—— (1969a) 'On Some Motifs in Baudelaire', in: Zohn, H. (trans.), *Illuminations*, New York: Harcourt, Brace and World, pp. 157–202.

—— (1969b) 'The Work of Art in the Age of Mechanical Reproduction', in Zohn, H. (trans.), *Illuminations*, New York: Harcourt, Brace and World, pp. 219–53.

—— (1983) *Das Passagen-Werk*, Tiedemann, R. (ed.), Frankfurt: Suhrkamp.

Bennett, T. (1982) 'Texts and Social Process: The Case of James Bond', *Screen Education*, 41.

—— (1983a) 'The Bond Phenomenon: Theorizing a Popular Hero', *Southern Review*, 16(2): 195–225.

—— (1983b) 'Texts, Readers, Text Formations', *The Bulletin of the Midwest Modern Language Association*, 16(1).

—— and Woollacott, J. (1987) *Bond and Beyond: The Political Career of a Popular Hero*, London: Methuen.

—— Boyd-Bowman, S., Mercer, C. and Woollacott, J. (1981) (eds), *Popular Television and Film*, London: BFI.

Berenstein, R. (1996) *Attack of the Leading Ladies: Gender, Sexuality, and Spectatorship in Classic Horror Cinema*, New York: Columbia University Press.

Bergman, G. M. (1977) *Lighting in the Theatre*, Stockholm: Almqvist and Wiksell International.

Bergstrom, J. and Doane, M. A. (1989) *Camera Obscura*, 20–1. Special issue on the Spectatrix.

Berman, M. (1982) *All That is Solid Melts into Air: The Experience of Modernity*, New York: Simon and Schuster.
—— (1990) 'Studios Miss Boat on Vid Demographics', *Variety*, 24 September, 15.
Berman, N. (1992) 'Nationalism Legal and Linguistic: The Teachings of European Jurisprudence', *New York University Journal of International Law and Politics*, 24(10): 1515–78.
Bernal, M. (1987) *Black Athena: The Afroasiatic Roots of Classical Civilisation*, vol. I, London: Free Association Books.
Berndt, T. J. and Berndt, E. G. (1975) 'Children's Use of Motives and Intentionality in Person Perception and Moral Judgement', *Child Development*, 46: 904–12.
Berryman, K. (1990) '*A Girl of the Bush*', in Berryman, K. (ed.), *Focus on Reel Australia*, Hendon, SA: Australian Council of Government Film Libraries in association with the National Film and Sound Archive.
Bhabha, H. K. (1983) 'The Other Question: The Stereotype and Colonial Discourse', *Screen*, 24(6): 18–36.
—— (1988) 'The Commitment to Theory', *New Formations*, 5: 5–23.
Bierbaum, T. (1990) 'Booming '80s Behind it, Vid Faces Uncertainty', *Variety*, 10 January, 31–2.
Blaché, A. G. (1977) 'Woman's Place in Photoplay Production', in Kay, K. and Peary, G. (eds), *Women and the Cinema*, New York: Dutton, pp. 337–40.
Black, A. (ed.) (1996) *Necronomicon*, Bk 1, London: Creation.
—— (ed.) (1998) *Necronomicon*, Bk 2, London: Creation.
Bloch, E. (1977) 'Nonsynchronism and the Obligation to its Dialectics', *New German Critique*, 11: 22–38.
Bloom, A. (1987) *The Closing of the American Mind: How Higher Education has Failed Democracy and Impoverished the Souls of Today's Students*, New York: Simon and Schuster.
Board of Trade, UK (1936) *Cinematograph Films Act, 1927: Report of a Committee Appointed by the Board of Trade*, London: HMSO.
Bobo, J. (1988a) '*The Color Purple*: Black Women as Cultural Readers', in Pribram, D. (ed.), *Female Spectators*, London and New York: Verso, 90–109.
—— (1988b) '*The Color Purple*: Black Women's Responses', *Jump Cut*, 33: 43–51.
—— (1995) *Black Woman as Cultural Readers*. New York: Columbia University Press.
Bogart, L. (1986) 'What Forces Shape the Future of Advertising Research?', *Journal of Advertising Research*, February/March.
Bordwell, D. (1974–5) 'Eisenstein's Epistemological Shift', *Screen*, 15(4): 32–46.
—— (1978) 'Lectures in Film Theory', University of Wisconsin-Madison. Unpublished.
—— (1979) 'The Art of Cinema as a Mode of Film Practice', *Film Criticism*, 4(1).
—— (1985) *Narration in the Fiction Film*, London: Methuen.
—— (1996) 'Contemporary Film Studies and the Vicissitudes of Grand Theory', in David Bordwell and Noel Carroll (eds), *Post-Theory: Reconstructing Film Studies*, Madison and London: University of Wisconsin Press.
—— Staiger, J. and Thompson, K. (1985) *The Classical Hollywood Cinema: Film Style and Mode of Production to 1960*, New York: Columbia University Press.
Botcherby, S. (1991) 'Thelma and Louise Go Shooting', *Trouble and Strife*, 22: 15–18.
—— and Garland, R. (1991) 'Hardware Heroines', *Trouble and Strife*, 21: 40–6.
Boulanger, P. (1975) *Le Cinéma Colonial*, Paris: Seghers.
Bourdieu, P. (1980) 'The Aristocracy of Culture', *Media, Culture and Society*, 2(3), 225–54.
—— (1984) *Distinction: The Social Critique of the Judgement of Taste*, Nice, R. (trans.), London: Routledge and Kegan Paul.
—— (1984–5) 'Delegation and Political Fetishism', *Thesis Eleven*, 10/11, 56–70.
Bovenschen, S. (1977) 'Is there a Feminine Aesthetic?', *New German Critique*, 10, 444–69.
Box, K. and Moss, L. (1943) *The Cinema Audience*, Wartime Social Survey FR 1871. Mass Observation Archive, Sussex University.
Box Office (1987) '*Star Wars*: A Cultural Phenomenon', *Box Office*, July, 36–8.
Boyd, A. S. (1967) *The Devil with James Bond*, Richmond: John Knox.
Boyer, P. J. (1984) 'Risky Business', *American Film*, January/February, 14.
Bradford, P. V. and Blume, H. (1992) *Ota Benga: The Pygmy in the Zoo*, New York: St Martin's Press.
Brand, C. (1970) *Fetish*, London: Luxor Press.
Brando, M. with Lindsey, R. (1994) *Brando: Songs My Mother Taught Me*, London: Century.
Branigan, E. (1984) *Point of View in the Cinema: A Theory of Narration and Subjectivity in Classical Film*, Berlin: Mouton.

Brantlinger, P. (1988) *Rule of Darkness: British Literature and Imperialism 1830–1914*, Ithaca: Cornell University Press.

Braverman, H. (1974) *Labor and Monopoly Capital: The Degradation of Work in the Twentieth Century*, New York: Monthly Review Press.

Braxton, J. M. and McLaughlin, A. N. (eds) (1990) *Wild Women in the Whirlwind: Afro-American Culture and the Contemporary Literary Renaissance*, New Brunswick: Rutgers University Press.

Braybon, G. and Summerfield, P. (1987) *Out of the Cage: Women's Experiences in Two World Wars*, London: Pandora.

Brewster, B. (1976–7) 'Brecht and the Film Industry', *Screen*, 16: 16–33.

Briller, B. R. (1990) 'The Globalisation of American TV', *Television Quarterly*, 24(3): 71–9.

Brinkmann, P. D. (1971) *Dr Alfred C. Kinsey and the Press*, Ph.D. thesis, Department of Mass Communications. University of Indiana.

Bristow, J. (1991) *Empire Boys: Adventure in a Man's World*, London: HarperCollins.

Britton, A. (1986) 'Blissing Out: The Politics of Reaganite Entertainment', *Movie*, 31(32): 1–42.

Broeske, P. H. (1991) 'Hollywood's '91 Focus: A Good Story', *Los Angeles Times*, 8 January, F12.

Bronski, M. (1991) 'Reel Politic', *Z Magazine*, May.

Brooks, D. (1994) 'Never for GATT', *American Spectator*, 27(1): 34–7.

Brooks, G. (1953) *Maud Martha*, New York: Harper.

Brown, G. (1989) 'Nuclear Domesticity: Sequence and Survival', in Cooper, H. M., Munich, A. A. and Squier, S. M. (eds), *Arms and the Woman: War, Gender and Literary Representation*, Chapel Hill: University of North Carolina Press, 283–302.

Browne, N. (1987) 'The Political Economy of the Television (Super) Text,' in Newcomb, H. (ed.), *Television: The Critical View*, New York: Oxford University Press, 585–99.

Browning, H. E. and Sorrel, A. A. (1954) 'Cinemas and Cinema-Going in Great Britain', *Journal of the Royal Statistical Society*, 177(2): 133–70.

Brownlow, K. (1968) *The Parade's Gone By*, London: Secker and Warburg.

—— (1979) *The War, the West and the Wilderness*, New York: Knopf.

Brownmiller, S. (1975) *Against Our Will*, London: Secker and Warburg.

Brownstein, R. (1990) *The Power and the Glitter: The Hollywood–Washington Connection*, New York: Random House.

Bruck, C. (1991) 'Leaf of Faith', *New Yorker*, 9 September, 38–74.

Bruner, J. S. and Goodman, C. C. (1947) 'Value and Need as Organizing Factors in Perception', *Journal of Abnormal and Social Psychology*, 42(10).

Brunsdon, C. (1981) '*Crossroads*: Notes on Soap Opera', *Screen*, 22(4): 32–7.

—— (1997) *Screen Tastes: Soap Operas to Satellite Dishes*, London: Routledge.

—— and Morley, D. (1978) *Everyday Television: Nationwide*, London: BFI.

Bruzzi, S. (1993) 'Jane Campion: Costume Drama and Reclaiming Women's Pasts', in Cook, P. and Dodd, P. (eds), *Women and Film: A Sight and Sound Reader*, London: Scarlet Press.

—— (1995) 'Tempestuous Petticoats: Costume and Desire in *The Piano*', *Screen*, 36: 3.

—— (1997) *Undressing Cinema: Clothing and Identity in the Movies*, London: Routledge.

Bryce, I. (1975) *You Only Live Once: Memories of Ian Fleming*, London: Weidenfeld.

Buck, E. B. (1992) 'Asia and the Global Film Industry', *East–West Film Journal*, 6(20): 116–33.

Buck-Morss, S. (1983) 'Benjamin's Passagen-Werk: Redeeming Mass Culture for the Revolution', *New German Critique*, 29: 211–40.

Budd, M., Entman, R. M. and Steinman, C. (1990) 'The Affirmative Character of US Cultural Studies', *Critical Studies in Mass Communication*, 7(2): 169–84.

Burch, N. (1979) *To the Distant Observer: Form and Meaning in Japanese Cinema*, Berkeley: University of California Press.

—— (1986) 'Primitivism and the Avant-Gardes: A Dialectical Approach, in Rosen, P. (ed.), *Narrative, Apparatus, Ideology*, New York: Columbia University Press, pp. 488–9.

Burgelman, J.-C. and Pauwels, C. (1992) 'Audiovisual Policy and Cultural Identity in Small European States: The Challenger of a Unified Market', *Media, Culture and Society*, 14(2): 169–83.

Burgin, V. (1986) *The End of Art Theory*, London: Macmillan.

Burns, E. (1972) *Theatricality*, London: Longman.

Burton, J. (1992) 'Don (Juanito) Duck and the Imperial-Patriarchal Unconscious: Disney Studios, the Good Neighbor Policy, and the Packaging of Latin America', in Parker, A., Russo, M., Sommer, D. and Yaeger, P. (eds), *Nationlisms and Sexualities*, New York: Routledge, 21–41.

Buscombe, E. (1977) 'Sound and Color', *Jump Cut*, 17.

—— (1988) *The BFI Companion to the Western*, New York: DaCapo.

Bush, W. S. (1909) 'The Human Voice as a Factor in the Moving Picture Show', *MPW*, 4(4): 86.

—— (1911) 'The Added Attraction (I)', *MPW* 10(7): 533–4.

Butler, A. (1992) 'New Film Histories and the Politics of Location', *Screen*, 33(4): 413–26.

Butler, J. (1990) *Gender Trouble: Feminism and the Subversion of Identity*, New York: Routledge.

—— (1993) *Bodies That Matter: On the Discursive Limits of Sex*, New York: Routledge.

Buxton, D. (1985) *Le Rock: star système et société de consommation*, Grenoble: La Pensée Sauvage.

Cagin, S. and Dray, P. (1984) *Hollywood Films of the Seventies: Sex, Drugs, Violence, Rock 'n' Roll and Politics*, New York: Harper and Row.

Cagle, J. (1995) 'Dangerous When Wet', *Entertainment Weekly*, 10 July.

Calinescu, M. (1977) *Faces of Modernity: Avant-Garde, Decadence, Kitsch*, Bloomington: Indiana University Press.

Callan, M. F. (1983) *Sean Connery: His Life and Times*, London: W. H. Allen.

Cameron-Wilson, J. and Speed, F. M. (1993) *Film Review 1993–94 Including Video Releases*, London: Virgin Books.

Campion, J. (1993) No Title, *Sight and Sound*, October, 3: 10.

Canby, V. (1988) 'Brotherly Love of Sorts', *New York Times*, 16 December, C12.

Cannadine, D. (1979) 'James Bond and the Decline of England', *Encounter* 53(3): 46–55.

Cantor, M. G. and Pingree, S. (1983) *The Soap Opera*, Beverley Hills: Sage.

Carbine, M. (1989) 'The Finest Outside the Loop: Motion Picture Exhibition in Chicago's Black Metropolis, 1909–1928', paper presented at the SCS Conference, Iowa City, April.

Carby, H. (1980) 'Multiculture', *Screen Education*, 34: 62–70.

Carey, J. W. (1975) 'A Cultural Approach to Communication', *Communications*, 2.

Carroll, N. (1978) 'Toward a Theory of Film Editing', *Millennium Film Journal*, 3: 92.

—— (1985) 'The Power of Movies', *Daedalus*, (114(4): 79–103.

—— (1988a) *Mystifying Movies: Fads and Fallacies in Contemporary Film Theory*, New York: Columbia University Press.

—— (1988b) *Philosophical Problems of Classical Film Theory*, Princeton: Princeton University Press.

—— (1990a) 'The Image of Women in Film: A Defense of a Paradigm', *Journal of Aesthetics and Art Criticism*, 48(4): 349–60.

—— (1990b) *The Philosophy of Horror: Or, Paradoxes of the Heart*, New York: Routledge.

—— (1996) 'Prospects for Film Theory: A personal assessment', in David Bordwell and Noel Carroll (eds), *Post-Theory: Reconstructing Film Studies*, Madison and London: University of Wisconsin Press.

Carter, B. (1991) 'Cable Networks see Dimmer Future', *New York Times*, 22 July, C1, C6.

—— (1994) 'Fox Will Sign Up 12 New Stations; Takes 8 From CBS', *New York Times*, 24 May, A1.

Cassady, R. (1959) 'Monopoly in Motion Picture Production and Distribution, 1908–1915', *South California Law Review* (Summer).

Castaldi, P. (1994) 'Movie of the Week', *The Sunday Herald Sun*, TV Extra (23 October), in *Cinedossier*, 656, 25 October 1994, 52.

Caughie, J. (ed.) (1981) *Theories of Authorship*, London: Routledge.

Caughie, J. (1996) 'The Logic of Convergence', in Hill, J. and McLoone, M. (eds), *Big Picture, Small Screen: The Relations Between Film and Television*, Luton: John Libbey/University of Luton Press.

Cavell, S. (1979) *The World Viewed*, Cambridge, Mass.: Harvard University Press.

Cawelti, J. (1976) *Adventure, Mystery and Romance: Formula Stories as Art and Popular Culture*, Chicago: University of Chicago Press.

—— (1978) '*Chinatown* and Generic Transformation in Recent American Film', in Mast, G. and Cohen, M. (eds), *Film Theory and Criticism*, New York: Oxford University Press, pp. 498–511.

Chambers, I., *et al.* (1977–8) 'Marxism and Culture', *Screen*, 18(4): 109–19.

Chanan, M. (1980) *The Dream that Kicks: The Prehistory and Early Years of Cinema in Britain*, London: Routledge and Kegan Paul.

Chateaubriand, F. R., Vicomte de (1950) *Atala*, Paris: J. Corti.

Chatman, S. (1986) 'Filter, Center, Slant, and Interest-Focus', *Poetics Today*, 7(2): 189–204.

Cherry, B. (1999) *The Female Horror Film Audience: Viewing Pleasures and Fan Practices*, Ph.D. thesis, University of Sterling.

Childers, E. (1994) 'Old-Boying', *London Review of Books*, 16(16): 3–5.

Chodorow, N. (1978) *The Reproduction of Mothering: Psychoanalysis and the Sociology of Gender*, Berkeley and Los Angeles: University of California Press.

Chomsky, N. (1993) *Year 501: The Conquest Continues*, Boston: South End Press.

Chown, J. (1981) *Hollywood Auteur: Francis Coppola*, New York: UMI Research Press.

Christian, B. (1986) 'Devisioning Spielberg and Walker: *The Color Purple*: The Novel and the Film', paper presented at the Center for the Study of Women in Society, University of Oregon, May.

—— (1987) 'Black Women's Literature and the Canon', Seminar presented at the University of Oregon, 7 December.

Christie, I. (1994) 'Interview with Martin Scorsese', *Sight and Sound*, 4(2).

Christopherson, S. and Storper, M. (1986) 'The City as Studio: The World as Back Lot: The Impact of Vertical Disintegration on the Location of the Motion Picture Industry', *Environment and Planning D: Society and Space*, 4(3): 305–20.

Churchill, W. (1992), in Jaimes, M. A. (ed.), *Fantasies of the Master Race: Literature, Cinema and the Colonization of American Indians*, Monroe, Maine: Common Courage Press.

Citron, M. *et al.* (1978) 'Women and Film: A Discussion of Feminist Aesthetics', *New German Critique*, 13: 83–107.

Clifford, J. (1988) *The Predicament of Culture*, Cambridge, Mass.: Harvard University Press.

—— and Marcus, G. (eds) (1986) *Writing Culture*, Berkeley: University of California Press.

Clover, C. J. (1989) 'Her Body Himself: Gender in the Slasher Film', in Donald, J. (ed.), *Fantasy and the Cinema*, London: British Film Institute Publishing, 91–133.

—— (1992) *Men, Women and Chainsaws: Gender in the Modern Horror Film*, Princeton: Princeton University Press.

Coe, B. (1981) *The History of the Movie Photograph*, London: Ash and Grant.

Cohan, S. and Hark, I. R. (1993) *Screening the Male: Exploring Masculinities in Hollywood Cinema*, London and New York: Routledge.

Cohen, L. (1989) 'Encountering Mass Culture at the Grassroots: The Experience of Chicago Workers in the 1920s', *American Quarterly*, 41(1): 6–33.

Cohen, P. and Gardner, C. (eds) (1982) *It Ain't Half Racist, Mum*, London: Comedia/Campaign Against Racism in the Media.

Cohen, R. (1994) 'Aux armes! France Rallies to Battle Sly and T. Rex', *New York Times*, 2 January, H1, 22–3.

Cohn, L. (1990a) 'MegaPix for '91 Late to Gate', *Variety*, 11 July, 85.

—— (1990b) 'Only Half of Indie Pics Shot Will See the Screens in '90', *Variety*, 30 May, 7.

—— (1990c) 'Star's Rocketing Salaries Keep Pushing Envelope', *Variety*, 24 September, 3.

Cole, M. (1985) 'The Zone of Proximal Development: Where Culture and Cognition Create Each Other', in Wertsch, J. V. (ed.), *Culture, Communication and Cognition: Vygotskian Perspectives*, Cambridge: Cambridge University Press.

Collins, D. (1987) *Hollywood Down Under – Australians at the Movies: 1886 to the Present Day*, North Ryde, Sydney: Angus and Robertson.

Collins, F. (1982) 'The Australian Journal of Screen Theory', *Framework*, 24: 114–19.

Collins, J. (1993) 'Genericity in the Nineties: Eclectic Irony and the New Sincerity' in Collins, J., Radner, H. and Collins, A. (eds), *Film Theory Goes to the Movies*, New York: Routledge.

—— (1995) *Architectures of Excess: Cultural Life in the Information Age*, New York: Routledge.

Collins, R. (1994) 'Unity in Diversity?' The European Single Market in Broadcasting and the Audiovisual, 1982–92', *Journal of Common Market Studies*, 32(10): 89–102.

Comolli, J.-L. and Narboni, J. (1971) 'Cinema/Ideology/Criticism', *Screen*, 12: 1.

Conant, J. (1994) 'Lestat C'est Moi', *Esquire*, March, 70–6.

Connolly, C. (1986) 'Winging It', *Rolling Stone*, 19 June, 36–8: 89.

Conway, M. and Ricci, M. (1964) *The Films of Marilyn Monroe*, Secaucus: Citadel.

Cook, P. (1979/80) 'Star Signs', *Screen*, 20(3/4): 80–8.

—— (1983) 'Melodrama and the Women's Picture', in Aspinall, S. and Murphy, R. (eds), *Gainsborough Melodrama*, London: British Film Institute.

—— (1987) *The Cinema Book*, London: British Film Institute.

—— (1994) 'Review of *The Age of Innocence*', *Sight and Sound*, 4(2).

—— (1996) *Fashioning the Nation: Costume and Identity in British Cinema*, London: British Film Institute.

Coppola, F. (1982) 'The Director on Content', *Washington Post*, August 29, 3D.

Corbin, J. (1970) 'How the Other Half Laughs', in Harris, N. (ed.), *The Land of Contrasts 1880–1901*, New York: Braziller: 160–79.

Cornwell-Clyne, A. (1949) 'What's Wrong with Colour?', in Huntley, J. (ed.), *British Technicolor Films*, London: Skelton Robinson.

Corrigan, P. (1983) 'Film Entertainment as Ideology and Pleasure: A Preliminary Approach to a History of Audiences', in Curran, J. and Porter, V. (eds), *British Cinema History*, London: Weidenfeld and Nicolson, 24–35.

Cott, N. F. (1977) *The Bonds of Womanhood: 'Woman's Sphere' in New England, 1780–1835*, New Haven: Yale University Press.

Coward, R. (1977) 'Class, "Culture" and the Social Formation', *Screen*, 18(1): 75–105.

—— and Ellis, J. (1977) *Language and Materialism: Developments in Semiology and the Theory of Subject*, London: Routledge and Kegan Paul.

Cowie, E. (1984) 'Fantasia', *m/f*, 9: 70–105.

Cox, D. (1996) 'New Line Sees Red', *Variety*, 11–17 November, 1, 73.

Crawford, A.-M. and Martin, A. (1989) 'Review of *Sweetie*', *Cinema Papers*, 73 (May), 56–7.

Crawford, M. and Chaffin, R. (1986) 'The Reader's Construction of Meaning: Cognitive Research on Gender and Comprehension', in Flynn, E. A. and Schweickart, P. P. (eds), *Gender and Reading: Essays on Readers, Texts, and Contexts*, Baltimore: Johns Hopkins University Press, pp. 3–30.

Crawley, T. (1983) *The Steven Spielberg Story*, New York: Quill.

Creed, B. (1986) 'Horror and the Monstrous-Feminine: An Imaginary Abjection', *Screen*, 27(1): 44–70.

—— (1987) 'From Here to Modernity: Feminism and Postmodernism', *Screen*, 28(2): 47–65.

—— (1990) 'Response', *Camera Obscura*, (20(21): 132–6.

—— (2000) 'The Cyberstar: Digital Pleasures and the End of the Unconscious', *Screen*, 41: 1.

Crofts, S. (1992) 'Cross-Cultural Reception: Variant Readings of *Crocodile Dundee*', *Continuum*, 5(2): 213–27.

—— (1993) 'Reconceptualizing National Cinema/s', *Quarterly Review of Film and Video*, 14(3): 49–67.

Crusz, R. (1985) 'Black Cinemas, Film Theory and Dependent Knowledge', *Screen*, 26(3–4): 152–6.

Cubitt, S. (1999) 'Le réel, c'est l'impossible: The Sublime Time of Special Effects', *Screen*, 40(2): 123–30.

Cummings, M. (1986) 'Black Family Interactions on Television', paper presented at the International Television Studies Conference, London.

Cunningham, S. (1992) *Framing Culture: Criticism and Policy in Australia*, Sydney: Allen and Unwin.

Curran, J., Curevitch, M. and Woollacott, J. (1982) 'The Study of Media: Theoretical Approaches', in Gurevitch, M., Bennett, T., Curran, J. and Woollacott, J. (eds), *Culture, Society and the Media*, London: Methuen, pp. 11–28.

Curtis, R. and Spriggs, S. (eds) (1992) *Get the Picture: Essential Data on Australian Film, Television and Video* 2nd edn, Sydney: Australian Film Commission.

Daily Variety (1994) 'After GATT Pique, Pix Pax Promoted', *Daily Variety*, 8 June, 1, 16.

Daly, J. (ed.) (1997) 'The People Who are Reinventing Entertainment', *Wired*, November: 201–5.

Daney, S. (1991) 'Maid que fait la Police', *Libération*, 15 February, 16.

Dargis, M. (1991) 'Roads to Freedom', *Sight and Sound*, July, 15–18.

The Dark Side: A Magazine of the Macabre and Fantastic (1998), June–July.

Darwin, C. (1871) *The Descent of Man and Selection in Relation to Sex*, London: John Murray.

Davidson, J. (1979) 'The de-dominionisation of Australia', *Meanjin*, 38(2): 139–53.

Davis, M. M. (1911) *The Exploitation of Pleasure*, New York: Russell Sage Foundation.

Dawtrey, A. (1994) 'Playing Hollywood's Game: Eurobucks Back Megabiz', *Variety*, 7–13 March, 1, 75.

de Beauvoir, S. (1949) *The Second Sex*, London: Picador.

DeCordova, R. (1982 and 1990) *Picture Personalities: The Emergence of the Star System in America*, Urbana: University of Illinois Press.

de Lauretis, T. (1984) *Alice Doesn't: Feminism, Semiotics, Cinema*, London: Macmillan.

—— (1989) 'Film and the Visible', paper presented at the 'How Do I Look?' Conference, New York City, October.

—— and Heath, S. (eds) (1989) *The Cinematic Apparatus*, New York: St Martins Press, and Basingstoke: Macmillan.

Deleuze, G. (1985) *L'image temps: Cinéma 2*, Paris: Editions de Minuit.

Dellar, F. (1981) *NME Guide to Rock Cinema*, Middlesex: Hamlyn.

De Maré, E. (1970) *Photography*, Harmondsworth: Penguin.

Dempsey, J. (1994) 'Wanted: Viewers for New Cable Channels', *Variety*, 3–9 January, 1: 67.

Denning, M. (1987) *Cover Stories: Narrative and Ideology in the British Spy Thriller*, London: Routledge and Kegan Paul.

Dennis, N., Henriques, F. and Slaughter, C. (1969) *Coal is Our Life*, London: Tavistock.

Dermody, S. and Jacka, E. (1987) '*An Australian Film Reader* in Question', *Continuum*, 1(1): 140–55.

—— (1988) *The Screening of Australia: Volume 2: Anatomy of a National Cinema*, Sydney: Currency Press.

Doane, M. A. (1980a) 'Ideology and the Practice of Sound Editing and Mixing', in de Lauretis, T. and Heath, S. (eds), *The Cinematic Apparatus*, Basingstoke: Macmillan, pp. 47–56.

—— (1980b) 'Misrecognition and Identity', *Ciné-Tracts*, 3(3): 25–32.

—— (1982) 'Film and the Masquerade: Theorising the Female Spectator', *Screen*, 23(3/4): 74–87.

—— (1984) 'The "Woman's Film": Possession and Address', in Doane, M. A., Mellencamp, P. and Williams, L. (eds), *Re-vision: Essays in Feminist Film Criticism*, Fredrick, Maryland: American Film Institute/University Publications of America, pp. 67–80.

—— (1985) ' "When the Direction of the Force Acting on the Body is Changed". The Moving Image', *Wide Angle*, 7(1–2).

—— (1987) *The Desire to Desire: The Woman's Film of the 1940s*, Bloomington: Indiana University Press.

—— (1991) *Femmes Fatales. Feminism, Film Theory and Psychoanalysis*, London: Routledge.

Doherty, T. (1988) *Teenagers and Teenpics: The Juvenilization of American Movies in the 1950s*, Boston: Unwin Hyman.

Dominick, J. R. (1987) 'Film Economics and Film Content: 1964–1983', in Austin, B. A. (ed.), *Current Research in Film: Audiences, Economics, and Law*, Norwood: Ablex.

Dorfman, A. and Mattelart, A. (1975) *How to Read Donald Duck: Imperialist Ideology in the Disney Comic*, New York: International General.

Dorr, A. (1981) 'How Children Make Sense of Television', in Janowitz, M. and Hirsch, P. M. (eds), *Reader in Public Opinion and Mass Communication*, New York: Free Press, 363–85.

Douglas, A. (1977) *The Feminization of American Culture*, New York: Avon.

Dreyer, C. (1970) 'Color and Color Films', in Jacobs, L. (ed.), *The Movies as Medium*, New York: Farra, Strauss and Giroux.

Drinnon, R. (1980) *Facing West: The Metaphysics of Indian-Hating and Empire-Building*, New York: Schocken.

Dudley, A. (1981) '*Broken Blossoms*: The Art and the Eros of a Perverse Text', *Quarterly Review of Film Studies*, 6(1): 81–90.

Dunbar, O. H. (1913) 'The Lure of Films', *Harper's Weekly*, 57(20): 22.

Durgnat, R. (1967) *Films and Feelings*, Cambridge, Mass.: MIT Press.

Dutka, E. (1992) 'The Man Who Makes You King', *Los Angeles Times*, 12 July, Calender Section 86.

Dyer, R. (1979a) *The Dumb Blonde Stereotype*, London: British Film Institute.

—— (1979b) *Stars*, London: British Film Institute.

—— (1980) *Gays and Films*, London: BFI.

—— (1981) 'Stars as Signs', in Bennett, T., Boyd-Bowman, S., Mercer, C. and Woollacott, J. (eds), *Popular Television and Film*, London: British Film Institute, pp. 236–69.

—— (1985) 'Entertainment and Utopia', in Nichols, B. (ed.), *Movies and Methods: Volume II*, Berkeley and London: University of California Press, pp. 220–32.

—— (1986) *Heavenly Bodies: Film Stars and Society*, Basingstoke: British Film Institute/Macmillan.

—— (1993) 'A White Star', *Sight and Sound*, 3(8): 22–5.

—— (1997) *White*, London and New York: Routledge.

Dyson, L. (1996) 'The Return of the Repressed? Whiteness, Femininity and Colonialism in *The Piano*', *Screen*, 36(3): 267–76.

Eckert, C. (1978) 'The Carole Lombard in Macy's Window', *Quarterly Review of Film Studies*, 3(1): 1–21.

Eco, U. (1966) 'Narrative Structures in Fleming', in Del Buono, O. and Eco, U. *The Bond Affair*, London: Macdonald.

—— (1981) *The Role of the Reader: Explorations in the Semiotics of Texts*, London: Hutchinson.

—— (1984) 'Postmodernism, Irony and the Enjoyable', in *Postscript to the Name of the Rose*, New York: Harcourt Brace Jovanovich, 65–7.

Economist (1994) 'A Disquieting New Agenda for Trade', *The Economist*, 332(7872): 55–6.

—— (1996) 'Murdoch's Empire: The Gambler's Last Throw', *The Economist*, 9 March, 68–70.

Ehrenstein, D. (1992) 'Two Snaps Down', *Advocate*, 3 November, 78.

Eisenstein, S. M. (1942) *The Film Sense*, Leyda, J. (ed. and trans.), New York: Harcourt, Brace and World.

—— (1949) *Film Form: Essays in Film Theory*, Leyda, J. (ed. and trans.), New York: Harcourt, Brace and World.

—— (1970) 'One Path to Color', in Jacobs, L. (ed.), *The Movies as Medium*, New York: Farra, Strauss and Giroux, pp. 201–9.

—— (1988) *S. M. Eisenstein: Selected Works, Volume One: Writings, 1922–34*, Taylor, R. (ed. and trans.), London: British Film Institute; Bloomington, Indiana University Press.

Eller, C. (1990) '"Tracy" Cost Put at $100 mil', *Variety*, 22 October, 3.

Ellis, J. (1982) *Visible Fictions*, London: Routledge and Kegan Paul.

Ellman, M. (1970) *Thinking About Women*, New York: Harcourt, Brace Jovanovich.

Ellsworth, E. (1986) 'Illicit Pleasures: Feminist Spectators and *Personal Best*', *Wide Angle*, 8(2): 45–56.

Ellul, J. (1964) *The Technological Society*, Wilkinson, J. (trans.), New York: Vintage.

Elsaesser, T. (1989) *New German Cinema: A History*, London: British Film Institute and Macmillan.

—— (1994) 'Putting on a Show: The European Art Movie', *Sight and Sound*, 4, 22–7.

Emmy (1994) 'Superhighway Summit', *Emmy*, 16(2): A1–69.

Englehardt, T. (1971) 'Ambush at Kamikaze Pass', *Bulletin of Concerned Asian Scholars*, 3(1).

Enker, D. (1994) 'Australia and Australians', in Murray, S. (ed.), *Australian Cinema*, St Leonards, Sydney: Allen and Unwin, in association with the Australian Film Commission, 211–25.

Epstein, J. (1994) 'Stephan Elliot: *The Adventures of Priscilla, Queen of the Desert*, Interview', *Cinema Papers* 101(4–10): 86.

—— and Straub, K. (eds), *Body Guards: The Cultural Politics of Gender Ambiguity*, London: Routledge.

Erenberg, L. A. (1981) *Steppin' Out: New York Night Life and the Transformation of American Culture, 1890–1930)*, Chicago: Chicago University Press.

Erens, P. (1988) 'The Stepfather', *Film Quarterly*, 41(2): 48–55.

Evans, G. and Brodie, J. (1996) 'Miramax, Mouse go for Seven More', *Variety*, May 13–19, 13, 16.

Ewen, E. (1980 'City Lights: Immigrant Women and the Rise of the Movies', *Signs*, 5(3): supplement: 45–66.

—— (1985) *Immigrant Women in the Land of Dollars: Life and Culture in the Lower East Side, 1890–1925*, New York: Monthly Review Press.

Ewen, S. (1976) *Captains of Consciousness*, New York: McGraw-Hill.

Fabrikant, G. (1990a) 'Hollywood Takes More Cues from Overseas', *New York Times*, 25 June, C1.

—— (1990b) 'In Land of Big Bucks, Even Bigger Bucks', *New York Times*, 18 October, C5.

—— (1990c) 'Pay Cable Channels are Losing their Momentum', *New York Times*, 28 May, 25.

—— (1990d) 'The Hole in Hollywood's Pocket', *New York Times*, 13 September, C7.

—— (1993) 'A Success for Dealer on a Prowl', *New York Times*, 13 September, A1.

—— (1994a) 'At a Crossroads, MCA Plans a Meeting with its Owners', *New York Times*, 13 October, G13.

—— (1994b) 'Media Giants Said to be Negotiating for TV Networks', *New York Times*, 1 September, A1.

—— (1995a) 'Walt Disney Acquiring ABC in Deal Worth £19 Billion', *New York Times*, 1 August, A1.

—— (1995b) 'Battling for the Hearts and Minds at Time Warner', *New York Times*, 26 February, F9.

—— (1995c) 'CBS Accepts Bid by Westinghouse; $5.4 Billion Deal', *New York Times*, 2 August, A1.

—— (1995d) 'Segram will Buy 80% of Big Studio from Matasushita', *New York Times*, 7 August, A1.

—— (1996) 'Murdoch Bets Heavily on a Global Vision', *New York Times*, 29 July, C1 C6–7.

Faderman, L. (1981) *Surpassing the Love of Men: Romantic Friendships and Love Between Women from the Renaissance to the Present*, New York: Morrow.

Faludi, S. (1991) *Backlash: The Undeclared War Against American Women*, New York: Crown Publishers.

Fanon, F. (1985) *The Wretched of the Earth*, Harmondsworth: Penguin.

Farnham, M. and Lundberg, F. (1947) *Modern Woman: The Lost Sex*, New York: Harper and Brothers.

Fear: Fantasy, Horror and Science Fiction, May–June 1989; September 1989; January 1990; August 1990.

Feldman, S. (1994) 'Rendering Techniques for Computer-Aided Design', *SMPTE Journal*, 103(1): 7–12.

Ferguson, M. (1992) 'The Mythology about Globalisation', *European Journal of Communication*, 7(10): 69–93.

Fetterley, J. (1978) *The Resisting Reader: A Feminist Approach to American Fiction*, Bloomington: University of Indiana Press.

Feuer, J. (1981) 'The Self-Reflexive Musical and the Myth of Entertainment', in Altman, R. (ed.), *Genre: The Musical*, London: Routledge and Kegan Paul, pp. 208–15.

Feuer, J. (1982) *The Hollywood Musical*, London: BFI.

Fielding, R. (ed.) (1967) *A Technological History of Motion Pictures and Television*, Berkeley and Los Angeles: University of California Press.

Film Journal (1994) 'Déja Vu', *Film Journal*, 97(6): 3.

Fishbein, L. (1987) 'The Fallen Woman as Victim in Early American Film: Soma versus Psyche', *Film and History*, 17(3).
—— (1988) 'The Harlot's Progress in American Fiction and Film, 1900–1930', *Women's Studies*, 16: 409–27.
Fiske, J. (1987a) *Television Culture*, London: Methuen.
—— (1987b) 'British Cultural Studies and Television', in Allen, R.C. (ed.), *Channels of Discourse: Television and Contemporary Culture*, Chapel Hill: University of North Carolina Press, 254–89.
—— (1989) *Understanding Popular Culture*, Boston: Unwin Hyman.
Fitzgerald, F. (1973) *Fire in the Lake: The Vietnamese and the Americans in Vietnam*, New York: Vintage.
Fleming, C. (1990a) 'Pitching Costs Out of Ballpark: Record Pic-Spending Spells Windfall for TV', *Variety*, 27 June, 1, 29.
—— (1990b) 'Star Hungry Mags Find Flacks Flexing Muscles', *Variety*, 4 July, 1, 23.
—— (1991) 'Megabudgets Boom Despite Talk of Doom', *Variety*, 4 February, 5.
Fleming, I. (1963) 'How to Write a Thriller', *Books and Bookmen*, May.
Flügel, J. C. (1930) *The Psychology of Clothes*, London: Hogarth.
Foster, H. (1983) 'Postmodernism: A Preface', in Foster, H. (ed.), *The Anti-Aesthetic: Essays on Postmodern Culture*, Seattle: Bay Press, ix–xvi.
Foucault, M. (1976 and 1980) *The History of Sexuality*, Harmondsworth: Penguin and New York: Vintage Books.
—— (1979) 'What is an Author?', *Screen*, 29(1): 13–29.
—— (1986) 'Of Other Spaces', *Diacritics*, 16(1): 22–7.
Fowler, A. (ed.) (1991) *The New Oxford Book of Seventeenth Century Verse*, Oxford: Oxford University Press.
Fox, D. J. (1991) 'Unraveling a Hollywood Mystery', *Los Angeles Times*, 21 August, C1.
Frawley, W. (1983) 'Lectures in Psycholinguistics', Newark: University of Delaware, unpublished.
French, B. (1978) *On the Verge of Revolt*, New York: Frederick Ungar.
French, M. (1978) *The Women's Room*, London: André Deutsch.
Freud, S. (1905) 'The Sexual Alternatives', *On Sexuality*, Penguin Freud Library, vol. 7, London: Pennguin.
—— (1927) 'Fetishism', *On Sexuality*, Penguin Freud Library, vol. 7, London: Penguin, pp. 345–57.
—— (1966) *Standard Edition of the Complete Psychological Works*, vol. 19, London: Hogarth.
—— (1991) 'The "Uncanny" ', *Standard Edition of the Complete Psychological Works*, vol. 17, London: Hogarth, pp. 219–52.
Friar, R. and Friar, N. (1972) *The Only Good Indian: The Hollywood Gospel*, New York: Drama Book Specialists.
Friedan, B. (1963) *The Feminine Mystique*, New York: W. W. Norton.
Friedberg, A. (1993) *Window Shopping: Cinema and the Postmodern*, Berkeley: University of California Press.
Frith, G. (1989) *The Intimacy Which is Knowledge: Female Friendship in the Novels of Women Writers*, Ph.D. thesis, Department of English and Comparative Literature, University of Warwick.
Frith U. and Robson, J. E. (1975) 'Perceiving the Language of Films', *Perception*, 4: 97–103.
Frow, J. (1982) 'The Literary Frame', *Journal of Aesthetic Education*, 16(2): 25–30.
Fryer, P. (1984) *Staying Power: The History of Black People in Britain*, London: Pluto Press.
Fuller, P. (1980) *Art and Psychoanalysis*, London: Writers and Readers.
Furnham, D. (1972) 'Garden of Dreams', *New Society*, 10: 279–98.
Fuss, D. (1993) 'Monsters of Perversion: Jeffrey Dahmer and *The Silence of the Lambs*', in Garber, M., Matlock, J. and Walkowitz, R. L. (eds), *Media Spectacles*, New York: Routledge, pp. 181–205.
Gabriel, T. (1982) *Third Cinema in the Third World: The Aesthetics of Liberation*, Ann Arbor: UMI Research Press.
Gagnon, J. H. and Simon, W. (1974) *Sexual Conduct*, London: Hutchinson.
Gaines, J. (1989) 'The Queen Christina Tie-Ups: Convergence of Show Window and Screen', *Quarterly Review of Film and Video*, 11(1): 35–60.
—— (1991) *Contested Culture: The Image, the Voice and the Law*, Chapel Hill: University of North Carolina.
—— and Herzog, C. (eds), (1990) *Fabrications: Costume and the Female Body*, London: Routledge/AFI.
Gallagher, C. (1989) 'Marxism and the New Historicism', in Aram Veeser, H. (ed.), *The New Historicism*, New York and London: Routledge, pp. 37–48.
Gallop, J. (1982)*The Daughter's Seduction: Feminism and Psychoanalysis*, London: Macmillan.
Gamman, L. and Makinen, M. (1994) *Female Fetishism: A New Look*, London: Lawrence and Wishart.
—— and Marshment, M. (eds) (1988) *The Female Gaze: Women as Viewers of Popular Culture*, London: The Women's Press.
Gamson, J. (1994) *Claims to Fame: Celebrity in Contemporary America*, Berkeley: University of California Press.
Garnham, A. (1985) *Psycholinguistics: Central Topics*, London and New York: Methuen.

Garnham, N. (1986) 'Contribution to a Political Economy of Mass-Communication', in Collins, R. *et al.* (eds), *Media, Culture and Society*, London: Sage Publications.

Gauntlett, D. and Hill, A. (1999) *TV Living: Television Culture and Everyday Life*, London and New York: Routledge.

Gelmis, J. (1970) *The Film Director as Superstar*, Garden City, NY: Doubleday.

Giannetti, L. (1987) *Understanding Movies*, 4th edn, Englewood Cliffs: Prentice Hall.

Gibson, R. (1992) *South of the West*, Bloomington and Indianapolis: Indiana University Press.

Gilliam, D. (1985) '*The Color Purple* Not as Simple as Black and White', *Washington Post*, 23 December, B3.

—— (1986) 'After the "Purple" Shutout', *Washington Post*, 27 March, B3.

Gilman, S. (1985) 'Black Bodies, White Bodies: Toward an Iconography of Female Sexuality in Late Nineteenth-Century Art, Medicine and Literature', *Critical Inquiry*, 12(1): 204–42.

Gilroy, P. (1983) 'C4 – Bridgehead or Bantustan?', *Screen*, 24(4–5): 130–6.

—— (1987) *There Ain't No Black in the Union Jack*, London: Hutchinson.

—— (1988) 'Nothing But Sweat Inside My Hand: Diaspora Aesthetics and Black Arts in Britain', in Mercer, K. (ed.), *Black Film/British Cinema, ICA Document 7*, London: British Film Institute Production Special.

—— and Pines, J. (1988) 'Handsworth Songs: Audiences/Aesthetics/Independence: Interview with the Black Audio Collective', *Framework*, 35: 9–18.

Givanni, J. (compiler), and North, N. (ed.) (1988) *Black and Asian Film List*, London: British Film Institute Education.

Given, J. (1994) 'Review: 1992–93', in Curtis, R. and Spriggs, S. (eds), *Get the Picture: Essential Data on Australian Film, Television and Video*, 3rd edn, Sydney: Australian Film Commission, 12–28.

Gledhill, C. (1988) 'Pleasurable Negotiations', in Pribram, E. D. (ed.), *Female Spectators*, New York and London: Verso, pp. 12–27.

—— (1991) *Stardom: Industry of Desire*, London: Routledge.

—— (ed.) (1987) *Home is Where the Heart Is*, London: British Film Institute.

—— and Williams, L. (2000) *Reinventing Film Studies*, London and New York: Arnold.

Gold, R. (1989) 'Sony-CPE Union Reaffirms Changing Order of International Showbiz', *Variety*, 27 September–3 October, 5.

—— (1990) 'No Exit? Studios Itch to Ditch Exhib Biz', *Variety*, 8 October, 8, 84.

Goldman, W. (1983) *Adventures in the Screen Trade*, New York: Warner Books.

Golodner, J. (1994) 'The Downside of Protectionism', *New York Times*, 27 February, H6.

Gomery, D. (1975) *The Coming of Sound to the American Cinema: A History of the Transformation of an Industry*, Ph.D. thesis. University of Wisconsin–Madison.

—— (1976) 'Writing the History of the American Film Industry: Warner Brothers and Sound', *Screen*, 17(10).

—— (1977a) 'Failure and Success: Vocafilm and RCA Innovate Sound', *Film Reader*, 2: 213–21.

—— (1977b) 'Toward a History of Film Exhibition: The Case of the Picture Palace'. *Film: Historical–Theoretical Speculations*, part 2, Pleasantville: Redgrave.

—— (1985) 'U.S. Film Exhibition: The Formation of a Big Business', in Balio, T. (ed.), *The American Film Industry*, revised edn, Madison: University of Wisconsin Press, pp. 218–28.

—— (1986) *The Hollywood Studio System*, New York: St Martin's.

—— (1992) *Shared Pleasures: A History of Movie Presentation*, London: British Film Institute.

Gordon, L. (1986) 'What's New in Women's History', in de Lauretis, T. (ed.), *Feminist Studies/Critical Studies*, Bloomington: Indiana University Press, 20–30.

Gornick, V. and Moran, B. K. (eds) (1971) *Woman in Sexist Society*, New York: Basic Books.

Gottlieb, C. (1975) *The Jaws Log*, New York: Dell.

Gould, S. (1985) *The Flamingo's Smile*, New York: W. W. Norton.

Grant, B. K. (1995) 'Introduction', in *Film Genre Reader II*, Austin: University of Texas Press, pp. xv–xx.

Grant, R. (1966) *Ian Fleming: The Man with the Golden Pen*, New York: Mayflower/Dell.

Greenblatt, S. (1989) 'Towards a Poetics of Culture', in Aram Veeser, H. (ed.), *The New Historicism*, New York and London: Routledge, pp. 1–14.

Gregory, C. L. (1920) *Condensed Course in Motion Picture Photography*, New York: New York Institute of Photography.

Greiner, D. J. (1991) *Women Enter the Wilderness: Male Bonding and the American Novel of the 1980s*, Columbia: University of South Carolina Press.

Grey, R. de C. (1990) *Concepts of Trade Diplomacy and Trade in Services*, Hemel Hempstead: Harvester Wheatsheaf.

Grimes, W. (1991) 'Film Maker's Secret is Knowing What's Not for Everyone', *New York Times*, 2 December, B1.

Grossberg, L. (1986) 'On Postmodernism and Articulation: An Interview with Stuart Hall', *Journal of Communication Inquiry*, 10(2): 45–60.

—— (1992) 'Is There a Fan in the House? The Affective Sensibility of Fandom', in Lewis, L. A. (ed.), *The Adoring Audience: Fan Culture and Popular Media*, London and New York: Routledge, pp. 50–65.

—— (1993) 'The Media Economy of Rock Culture: Cinema, Post-modernity and Authenticity' in Frith, S., Goodwin, A. and Grossberg, L. (eds), *Sound and Vision: The Music Video Reader*, London and New York: Routledge.

Grove, M. A. (1991) 'Hollywood Report: Future Films and Future Focus', *Hollywood Reporter*, 19–20 August, 2.

Grover, J. Z. (1995) 'Visible Lesions: Images of the PWA', in Creekmur, C. and Doty, A. (eds), *Out in Culture: Gay, Lesbian, and Queer Essays on Popular Culture*, Durham: Duke University Press, pp. 355–81.

Grover, R. and Lewyn, M. with Javetski, B. (1994) 'Sunset Boulevard for Jack Valenti?', *Business Week*, 3354, 35.

Groves, D. (1990) 'U.S. Pics Tighten Global Grip', *Variety*, 22 August, 1: 96.

—— (1994) 'O'seas B. O. Power Saluted at Confab', *Variety*, 3–9 April, 1, 46.

—— (1995) 'Vini, Video, Vici', *Variety*, 3–9 April, 1, 46.

Grumet, R. S. (1981) *Native American Place Names in New York City*, New York: Museum of the City of New York.

Grummitt, K.-P. (1995) *Cinemagoing 4*, Leicester: Dodona Research.

Guattari, F. (1984) *Molecular Revolution: Psychiatry and Politics*, Sheed, R. (trans.), New York: Penguin.

Gubernick, L. and Millman, J. (1994) 'El Sur is the Promised Land', *Forbes*, 153(7): 94–5.

Guiles, F. L. (1969) *Norma Jean*, New York: McGraw-Hill.

Gunning, T. (1986) 'The Cinema of Attraction[s]: Early Film, Its Spectator and the Avant-Garde', *Wide Angle*, 8(3–4): 630–70.

—— (1991) *D. W. Griffith and the Origins of American Narrative Film*, Urbana: University of Illinois Press.

Gutman, H. (1977) *Work, Culture and Society in Industrializing America*, New York: Vintage.

Habermas, J. (1972/1979) 'Consciousness-Raising or Redemptive Criticism', *New German Critique*, 17: 30–59.

Hage, G. (1995) 'The Limits of "Anti-Racist Sociology"', *UTS Review*, 1(1): 59–82.

Hainsworth, P. (1994) 'Politics, Culture and Cinema in the New Europe', in Hill, J., McLoone, M. and Hainsworth, P. (eds), *Border Crossing: Film in Ireland, Britain and Europe*, Belfast: Institute of Irish Studies.

Halberstam, J. (1995) 'Skinflick: Posthuman Gender in Jonathan Demme's *The Silence of the Lambs*', in *Skin Shows: Gothic Horror and the Technology of Monsters*, Durham: Duke University Press.

Hall, S. (1980a) 'Cultural Studies and the Centre: Some Problematics and Problems', in Hall, S., Hobson, D. Lowe, A. and Willis, P. (eds), *Culture, Media, Language: Working Papers in Cultural Studies, 1972–79*, London: Hutchinson, pp. 15–47.

—— (1980b) 'Cultural Studies: Two Paradigms', *Media, Culture and Society*, 2: 57–72.

—— (1980c) 'Encoding/Decoding', in Hall, S., Hobson, D., Lowe, A. and Willis, P. (eds), *Culture, Media, Language: Working Papers in Cultural Studies, 1972–79*, London: Hutchinson, 128–39.

—— (1980d) 'Race, Articulation and Societies Structured in Dominance', in *Sociological Theories: Race and Colonialism*, Paris: UNESCO.

—— (1980e) 'Recent Development in Theories of Language and Ideology: A Critical Note', in Hall, S., Hobson, D., Lowe, A. and Willis, P. (eds), *Culture, Media, Language: Working Papers in Cultural Studies, 1972–79*, London: Hutchinson, pp. 157–62.

—— (1981) 'The Whites of their Eyes: Racist Ideologies and the Media', in Bridges, G. and Brunt, R. (eds), *Silver Linings: Some Strategies for the Eighties: Contributions to the Communist University of London*, London: Lawrence and Wishart.

—— (1982) 'The Rediscovery of "Ideology": Return of the Repressed in Media Studies', in Gurevitch, M., Bennett, T., Curran, J. and Woollacott, J. (eds), *Culture, Society and the Media*, London: Methuen, pp. 56–90.

—— (1986) 'On Postmodernism and Articulation: An Interview Edited by Lawrence Grossberg', *Communications Inquiry*, 10.

—— (1988) 'Minimal Selves', in Appignanesui, L. (ed.), *Identity, ICA Document*, 6: 44–6.

—— (1996) 'New Ethnicities', in Morley, D. and Chen, K.-H. (eds), *Stuart Hall: Critical Dialogues in Cultural Studies*, London and New York: Routledge, pp. 441–9.

—— *et al.* (1978) *Policing the Crisis: Mugging, the State and Law and Order*, London: Macmillan.

Hambourg, M. *et al.* (1993) *The Waking Dream: Photography's First Century*, Selections from the Gilman Paper Company Collection, New York: Metropolitan Museum of Art.

Hamer, D. (1990) 'I Am a Woman: Ann Bannon and the Writing of Lesbian Identity in the 1950s', in Willy, M. (ed.), *Lesbian and Gay Writing: An Anthology of Critical Essays*, New York: Macmillan.

Hammer, J. (1990) 'Small is Beautiful', *Newsweek*, 26 November, 52–3.

Hampton, B. B. (19770) *History of the American Film Industry from its Beginnings to 1931*, New York: Dover Publications.

Hancock, W. K. (1961) *Australia*, Brisbane: Jacaranda Press.

Handel, L. (1950) *Hollywood Looks at its Audience*, Urbana: University of Illinois Press.

Handley, C. W. (1967) 'History of Motion-Picture Studio Lighting', in Fielding, R. (ed.), *A Technological History of Motion Pictures and Televsion*, Berkeley: University of California Press, pp. 120–4.

Handzo, S. (1995) 'The Golden Age of Film Music', *Cineaste*, 21(1–2): 46–56.

Hansen, M. (1983) 'Early Silent Cinema: Whose Public Sphere?', *New German Critique*, 29, 147–84.

—— (1986) 'Pleasure, Ambivalence, Identification: Valentino and Female Spectatorship', *Cinema Journal*, 25(4): 6–32.

—— (1987) 'Benjamin, Cinema and Experience: "The Blue Flower in the Land of Technology"', *New German Critique*, 40: 179–224.

—— (1991) *Babel and Babylon: Spectatorship in American Silent Film*, Cambridge, Mass.: Harvard University Press.

—— (1999) 'The Future of Cinema Studies in the Age of Global Media: Aesthetics, Spectatorship and Public Spheres', *UTS Review*, 5(2): 94–100.

Haraway, D. (1989a) *Primate Visions: Gender, Race and Nature in the World of Modern Science*, New York: Routledge.

—— (1989b) 'Teddy Bear Patriarch: Taxidermy in the Garden of Eden, New York City, 1908–1936', *Primate Visions: Gender, Race, and Nature in the World of Modern Science*, New York: Routledge, pp. 26–58.

Harper, S. (1987) 'Historical Pleasures: Gainsborough Costume Melodrama', in Gledhill, C. (ed.), *Home is Where the Heart Is: Studies in Melodrama and the Woman's Film*, London: BFI.

—— (1994) *Picturing the Past: The Rise and Fall of the British Costume Film*, London: BFI.

Harper's Bazaar (1991) 'Wunderkind', *Harper's Bazaar*, November, 124–5.

Harrell, A. (1986) 'The Look of *The Color Purple*', *American Cinematographer*, February, 50–6.

Harris, T. B. (1957) 'The Building of Popular Images: Grace Kelly and Marilyn Monroe', *Studies in Public Communication*, 1.

Harris, W. (1990) '*Entre Nous* and the Lesbian Heroine', unpublished paper, University of Illinois, Urbana–Champaign.

Hart, L. (1994) *Fatal Women: Lesbian Sexuality and the Mark of Aggression*, Princeton, Princeton University Press.

Harvey, S. (1991) 'Critics', in Kennedy, L. (ed.), 'Writers on the Lamb', *Village Voice*, 5 March, 49: 56.

Haskell, M. (1974) *From Reverence to Rape: The Treatment of Women in the Movies*, New York: Holt, Rinehart and Winston.

Hayward, S. (1993) 'State, Culture and the Cinema: Jack Lang's Strategies for the French Film Industry', *Screen* 34(4): 382–91.

Heath, S. (1981) *Questions of Cinema*, Bloomington: Indiana University Press.

Hebdige, D. (1979) *Subculture: The Meaning of Style*, London: Methuen.

—— (1988) 'Towards a Cartography of Taste 1935–1962', in *Hiding in the Light: On Images and Things*, London: Comedia.

Heider, K. (1976) *Ethnographic Film*, Austin: University of Texas Press.

Helgot, J., Schwartz, M., Romo, F. and Korman, J. (1988) 'Aging Baby-Boomers and Declining Leisure-Time: Strategic Implications for the Movie Industry', Marketcast Reports.

Hess, T. B. (1972) 'Pinup and Icon', in Hess, T. B. and Nochlin, L. (eds), *Woman as Sex Object*, New York: Newsweek.

Higashi, S. (1978) *Virgins, Vamps and Flappers: The American Silent Movie Heroine*, Montreal: Eden Press.

Higson, A. (1989) 'The Concept of National Cinema', *Screen*, 30(4): 36–46.

—— (1993) 'Re-Presenting the National Past: Nostalgia and Pastiche in the Heritage Film', in Friedman, L. (ed.), *British Cinema and Thatcherism: Fires Were Started*, London: UCL Press.

—— (1995) *Waving the Flag: Constructing a National Cinema in Britain*, Oxford: Oxford University Press.

—— (1996) 'The Heritage Film and British Cinema', in Higson, A. (ed.), *Dissolving Views: Key Writings on British Cinema*, London: Cassell, pp. 232–48.

Hill, J. (1992) 'The Issue of National Cinema and British Film Production', in Petrie, D. (ed.), *New Questions of British Cinema*, London: British Film Institute, pp. 10–21.

—— (1994) 'The Future of European Cinema: The Economics and Culture of Pan-European Strategies', in Hill, J., McLoone, M. and Hainsworth, P. (eds), *Border Crossing: Film in Ireland, Britain and Europe*, Belfast: Institute of Irish Studies.

—— (1997) 'British Cinema as National Cinema: Production, Audience and Representation' in Murphy, R. (ed.), *The British Cinema Book*, London: BFI.

—— and McLoone, M. (eds) (1996) *Big Picture, Small Screen: The Relations Between Film and Television*, Luton: John Libbey/University of Luton Press.

—— McLoone, M. and Hainsworth, P. (eds) (1994) *Border Crossing: Film in Ireland, Britain and Europe*, Belfast, Institute of Irish Studies/London: British Film Institute.

Hillier, J. (1985) 'Introduction', in Hillier, J. (ed.), *Cahiers du Cinema: The 1950s*, Cambridge, Mass.: Harvard University Press, pp. 1–17.

Hills, P. (1987) *The Light of Early Italian Painting*, New Haven: Yale University Press.

Hilmes, M. (1990) 'Breaking the Broadcast Bottleneck', in Balio, T. (ed.), *Hollywood in the Age of Television*, Boston: Unwin Hyman, 299–300.

Hirsch, E. D. Jr (1967) *Validity in Interpretation*, New Haven: Yale University Press.

Hirsch, M. and Keller, E. F. (eds) (1990) *Conflicts in Feminism*, London: Routledge.

Hlavacek, P. (1990) 'New Indies on a (Bank) Roll', *Variety*, 24 January, 1, 7.

Hobbs, R. *et al.* (1988) 'How First-Time Viewers Comprehend Editing Conventions', *Journal of Communication*, 38: 50–60.

Hoberman, J. (1985) 'Ten Years that Shook the World', *American Film*, 10: 34–59.

Hobson, D. (1982) *Crossroads: The Drama of a Soap Opera*, London: Methuen.

Hochberg, J. and Brooks, V. (1962) 'Picture Perception as an Unlearned Ability: A Study of One Child's Performance', *American Journal of Psychology*, 74(4): 624–8.

Hodge, J. (1996) *Trainspotting and Shallow Grave*, London: Faber and Faber.

Hoffman, H. F. (1908) 'Where They Perform Shakespeare for Five Cents', *Theatre Magazine*, 8(92): 264–5.

—— (1910) 'What People Want', *MPW*, 7(2): 77.

Hoffner, C. and Cantor, J. (1985) 'Developmental Differences in Response to a Television Character's Appearance and Behavior', *Developmental Psychology*, 21(6): 1065–74.

Holland, N. N. (1986) 'I-ing Film', *Critical Inquiry*, 12, 654–71.

Hollinger, H. (1983) 'Hollywood's View of Research Depends on Just Who's Being Asked, What Methods are Used', *Variety*, 12 January, 36.

Hollows, J. (2000) *Feminism, Femininity and Popular Culture*, Manchester: Manchester University Press.

—— (n.d.) 'Between Rock and a Hard Place: Femininity in the Popular Music Classroom', unpublished.

Hollywood Reporter 1991) 'Disney's Profits in Park: Off 23%', *The Hollywood Reporter*, 15 November, 1, 6.

Holmlund, C. A. (1989) 'Visible Difference and Flex Appeal: The Body, Sex, Sexuality, and Race in the *Pumping Iron* Films', *Cinema Journal*, 28(4): 38–51.

Holub, R. (1983) *Reception Theory: A Critical Introduction*, London: Methuen.

Hong Kingston, M. (1977) *The Woman Warrior*, London: Picador.

—— (1981) *China Men*, London: Picador.

hooks, b. (1996) *Reel to Real*, New York and London: Routledge.

Horkheimer, M. and Adorno, T. W. (1969) *Dialectic of Enlightenment*, Cumming, J. (trans.), New York: Seabury.

Horn, J. (1991) 'Audiences Make the Final Cut', *Dallas Morning News*, 13 September, C10.

Howe, I. (1976) *The World of Our Fathers: The Journey of the East European Jews to America and the Life They Found and Made*, New York: Simon and Schuster.

Huntley, J. (ed.) (1949) *British Technicolor Films*, London: Skelton Robinson.

Hurston, Z. N. (1969) *Their Eyes Were Watching God*, New York: Negro Universities Press.

Husband, C. (1975) *White Media and Black Britain*, London: Arrow.

Hutcheon, L. (1988) *A Poetics of Postmodernism*, London: Routledge.

Hutchings, D. (1983) 'No Wonder Tom Cruise is Sitting Pretty – Risky Business has paid off in Stardom', *People*, 5 September, 107–8.

Hutchings, P. (1995) 'Genre Theory and Criticism', in Hollows, J. and Jancovich, M. (eds), *Approaches to Popular Film*, Manchester: Manchester University Press, pp. 59–77.

Huyssen, A. (1986) 'Mass Culture as Woman: Modernism's Other', in Modleski, T. (ed.), *Studies in Entertainment: Critical Approaches to Mass Culture*, Bloomington: Indiana University Press, pp. 188–207.

—— (1987) 'Mapping the Post-Modern', *After the Great Divide*', London: Macmillan.

Iliott, T. (1991) 'Yank Pix Flex Pecs in New Euro Arena', *Variety*, 19 August, 1, 60.

Iser, W. (1978) *The Act of Reading: A Theory of Aesthetic Response*, London: Routledge and Kegan Paul.

Jackson Lears, T. J. (1983) 'From Salvation to Self-Realization: Advertising and the Therapeutic Roots of the Consumer Culture, 1880–1930', in Fox, R. W. and Jackson Lears, T. J. (eds), *The Culture of Consumption*, New York: Pantheon.

Jackson, R. (1981) *Fantasy: The Literature of Subversion*, London: Methuen.

James, C. (1988) 'Test Screenings of New Movies put Demographics over Creativity', *New York Times*, 9 March, C17.

—— (1991) 'A Warmer, Fuzzier Arnold', *The New York Times*, 14 July, H9.

James, D. E. (1996) 'Introduction: Is There Class in this Text?' in James, D. E. and Berg, R. (1996) (eds), *The Hidden Foundation: Cinema and the Question of Class*, Minneapolis and London: University of Minnesota Press.

—— and Berg, R. (eds) (1996) *The Hidden Foundation: Cinema and the Question of Class*, Minneapolis and London: University of Minnesota Press.

Jameson, F. (1970) 'On Raymond Chandler', *Southern Review*, 6(3): 624–50.

—— (1983) 'Postmodernism and Consumer Society', in Foster, H. (ed.), *The Anti-Aesthetic: Essays on Postmodern Culture*, Seattle: Bay Press, pp. 111–25.

—— (1984) 'Postmodernism, or the Cultural Logic of Late Capitalism', *New Left Review*, 146: 53–92.

—— (1986) 'Third-World Literature in the Era of Multinational Capitalism', *Social Text*, 15.

Jancovich, M. (1992) *Horror*, London: Batsford.

—— (1996) *Rational Fears: American Horror in the 1950s*, Manchester: Manchester University Press.

—— (2000a) 'Genre and the Problem of the Audience: Genre Classifications and Cultural Distinctions in the Promotion of *The Silence of the Lambs*', in Maltby, R. and Stokes, M. (eds), *Hollywood and Cultural Identity*, London: British Film Institute.

—— (2000b) 'A Real Shocker: Authenticity, Genre and the Struggle for Distinction', *Continuum*, 14:1.

—— (forthcoming) *Cult Fictions: Cult Movies, Subcultural Capital and the Production of Cultural Distinction*.

Jarvie, I. C. (1970) *Towards a Sociology of the Cinema*, London: Routledge and Kegan Paul.

Jeffords, S. (1993) 'Can Masculinity Be Terminated?' in Cohan, S. and Hark, I. R. (eds), *Screening the Male*, London: Routledge.

—— (1994) *Hard Bodies: Hollywood Masculinity in the Reagan Era*, New Brunswick: Rutgers University Press.

Jenkins, H. (1992) *Textual Poachers: Television Fans and Participatory Culture*, London: Routledge.

Jennings, R. (1995) 'Desire and Design – Ripley Undressed', in Wilton, T. (ed.), *Immortal, Invisible: Lesbians and the Moving Image*, London and New York: Routledge.

Johnson, C. (Mudrooroo) (1987) 'Chauvel and the Centering of the Aboriginal Male in Australian Film', *Continuum*, 1(1): 1, 47–56.

Johnson, R. (1980) 'Three Problematics: Elements of a Theory of Working-Class Culture', in Clarke, J., Critcher, C. and Johnson, R. (eds), *Working-Class Culture: Studies in History and Theory*, New York: St Martin's Press, pp. 201–37.

Johnson, T. and Busch, A. M. (1996) 'Mega-moolah Movies Multiplying', *Variety*, 29 April–5 May, 1, 53.

Johnston, S. (1982–82) 'A Star is Born: Fassbinder and the New German Cinema', *New German Critique*, 24(25): 57–72.

Jones, B. E. (1911) *Cassell's Cyclopedia of Photography*, London: Cassell.

Jones, D. (1992) 'Waltzing out of the Outback into the Ballroom', in Luhrmann, B. and Pearce, C. (eds), *Strictly Ballroom. From a Screenplay by Baz Lurhmann and Andrew Bovell*, Sydney: Currency Press, xii–xiv.

Julien, I. and Mercer, K. (1996) 'De Margin and De Centre', in Morley, D. and Chen, K.-H. (eds), *Stuart Hall, Critical Dialogues*, London and New York: Routledge.

Kaes, A. (1989) *From Hitler to Heimat: The Return of History as Film*, Cambridge, Mass.: Harvard University Press.

Kalmus, N. (1938) 'Colour', in Watts, S. (ed.), *Behind the Screen*, London: Arthur Baker.

Kant, I. (1952) *Critique of Judgement*, Creed, J. (trans.), Oxford: Clarendon Press.

Kapferer, B. (1988) *Legends of People, Myths of State*, Washington: Smithsonian Institution Press.

Kaplan, E. A. (ed.) (1980) *Women in Film Noir*, London: British Film Institute.

—— (1983) 'Theories of Melodrama: A Feminist Perspective', *Women and Performance: A Journal of Feminist Theory*, 1(1): 40–8.

—— (1983) *Women and Film: Both Sides of the Camera*, London: Methuen.

Kaplan, L. (1993) *Female Perversions: The Temptations of Madame Bovary*, London: Penguin.

Kasson, J. F. (1978) *Amusing the Million: Coney Island at the Turn of the Century*, New York: Hill and Wang.

Katz, E. and Foulkes, D. (1962) 'On the use of the Mass Media as "Escape": Clarification of a Concept', *Public Opinion Quarterly*, 26: 377–88.

Katzenberg, J. (1991) 'The World is Changing: Some Thoughts on Our Business', *Variety*, 31 January, 18.

Keane, J. (1991) *The Media and Democracy*, Cambridge: Polity Press.

Kennedy, L. (ed.) (1991) 'Writers on the Lamb', *Village Voice*, 5 March, 49: 56.

Kerber, L. (1988) 'Separate Spheres, Female Worlds, Woman's Place: The Rhetoric of Women's History', *Journal of American History*, 75: 9–39.

Kern, S. (1983) *The Culture of Time and Space 1880–1918*, Cambridge, Mass.: Harvard University Press.

Kessner, T. (1977) *The Golden Door: Italian and Jewish Immigrant Mobility in New York City*, New York: Oxford University Press.

Kilday, G. and Marcus, G. (1989) 'Two or Three Things We Know About . . . The Eighties', *Film Comment*, November/December, 60–7.

Kindem, G. (ed.) (1982) *The American Movie Industry: The Business of Motion Pictures*, Carbondale: Southern Illinois University Press.

—— (1982) 'Hollywood's Movie Star System: A Historical Overview', in Kindem, G. (ed.), *The American Movie Industry: The Business of Motion Pictures*, Carbondale: Southern Illinois University Press.

King, B. (1985) 'Articulating Stardom', *Screen*, 26: 45–8.

King, K. (1986) 'The Situation of Lesbianism as Feminism's Magical Sign: Contexts for Meaning and the US Women's Movement, 1968–1972', *Communication*, 9: 65–91.

Kipps, C. (1989) 'Sony and Columbia', *Variety*, 27 September, 5.

Kissinger, D. (1991) 'Judgement Day for Carolco', *Variety*, 2 December, 1: 93.

Kitses, J. (1969) *Horizons West: Anthony Mann, Budd Boetticher, Sam Peckinpah: Studies of Authorship within the Western*, Bloomington: Indiana University Press.

Klady, L,. (1995) 'Earth to H'wood: You Win', *Variety*, 13–19 February, 1: 63.

—— (1996) 'Why Mega-Flicks Click', *Variety*, 25 November–1 December, 1: 87.

Klinger, B. (1986) *Cinema and Social Process: A Contextual Theory of the Cinema and its Spectators*, Ph.D. thesis, University of Iowa.

—— (1989a) 'Digressions at the Cinema: Reception and Mass Culture', *Cinema Journal*, 28(4): 3–19.

—— (1989b) 'Much Ado about Excess: Genre, Mise-en-Scene, and the Woman in *Written on the Wind*', *Wide Angle* 11(4): 4–22.

—— (1994) *Melodrama and Meaning: History, Culture and the Films of Douglas Sirk*, Bloomington: Indiana University Press.

Kluge, A. (1985) 'Die Macht der Bewußtseinsindustrie und das Schicksal unserer Öffentlichkeit', in von Bismarch, K. *et al. Industrialisierung des Bewußtseins*, Munich: Piper.

Knapp, S. and Sherman, B. L. (1986) 'Motion Picture Attendance: A Market Segmentation Approach', in Austin, B. A. (ed.), *Current Research in Film: Audiences, Econonmics, and Law*, vol. 2, Norwood, New Jersey, Ablex.

Koch, N. (1992) 'She Lives! She Dies! Let the Audience Decide', *New York Times*, 19 April, H11.

Koestenbaum, W. (1995) *Jackie Under My Skin: Interpreting an Icon*, New York: Farrar, Straus and Giroux.

Koszarski, R. (1990) 'Going to the Movies', in *An Evening's Entertainment: The Age of the Silent Feature Picture, 1915–1928,* New York: Scribner's/Macmillan.

Kracauer, S. (1960) *Theory of Film: The Redemption of Physical Reality*, New York: Oxford University Press.

—— (1963) *Das Ornament der Masse*, Frankfurt: Suhrkamp.

—— (1964) *Straßen in Berlin und anderswo*, Frankfurt: Suhrkamp.

—— (1983) 'Abschied von der Lindenpassage', in Geist, J. F. (trans.), *Arcades: The History of a Building Type*, Cambridge, Mass.: MIT Press, 158–60.

—— (1987) 'Cult of Distraction: On Berlin's Picture Palaces', Levin, T. Y. (trans.), *New German Critique*, 40: 91–6.

Krafft-Ebing, R. von (1899) *Psychopathia Sexualis: With Especial Reference to the Antipathetic Sexual Instinct, a Medico-Forensic Study*, London: Redman.

Kraft, R. N. (1987) 'Rules and Strategies of Visual Narratives', *Perceptual and Motor Skills*, 64: 3–14.

–––––– Cantor, P. and Gottdiener, C. (1991) 'The Coherence of Visual Narratives', *Communication Research*, 18(5): 601–16.

Kristeva, J. (1979) 'Ellipsis on Dread and the Specular Seduction', Burdick, D. (trans.), *Wide Angle*, 3(3).

–––––– (1980) *Desire in Language*, New York: University of Columbia Press.

Kuhn, A. (1984) 'Women's Genres', *Screen*, 25(1): 18–28.

–––––– (1988) *Cinema, Censorship and Sexuality, 1909–1925*, London: Routledge.

Kuntzel, T. (1980) 'The Film Work 2', Huston, N. (trans.), *Camera Obscura*, 5: 7–68.

Kunzle, D. (1982) *Fashion and Fetishism: A Social History of the Corset, Tight-Lacing and Other Forms of Body-Sculpture in the West*, New Jersey: Rowman and Littlefield.

Kurihara, T., Anjyo, K. and Thalmann, D. (1993) 'Hair Animation with Collision Detection', in Thalmann, N. M. and Thalmann, D. (eds), *Models and Techniques in Computer Animation*, New York: Springer-Verlag, pp. 128–38.

Lacan, J. (1978) *The Four Fundamental Concepts of Psycho-Analysis*, Sheridan, A. (trans), New York: W. W. Norton.

Lafferty, W. (1990) 'Feature Films on Prime-Time Television', in Balio, T. (ed.), *Hollywood in the Age of Television*, Boston: Unwin Hyman, pp. 235–56.

Laing, J. R. (1992) 'Bad Scenes Behind it, Time Warner is Wired for Growth', *Barron's*, 22 June, 8.

Lammers, D. (1977) 'Nevil Shute and the Decline of the "Imperial Idea" in Literature', *Journal of British Studies*, 16(2): 121–42.

Landler, M. with Fabrikant, G. (1996) 'Sumner and his Discontents', *New York Times*, 19 January, C1.

Lane, S. (1965) *For Bond Lovers Only*, London: Panther.

–––––– (1965) *James Bond in Thunderball*, London: Sackville Publications.

Lant, A. (1991) *Blackout: Reinventing Women for Wartime British Cinema*, Princeton: Princeton University Press.

La Place, M. (1987) 'Producing and Consuming the Woman's Film: Discursive Struggle in *Now, Voyager*', in Gledhill, C. (ed.), *Home is Where the Heart Is: Studies in Melodrama and the Woman's Film*, London: British Film Institute, 138–66.

Laplanche, J. and Pontalis, J.-B. (1964) 'Fantasy and the Origins of Sexuality', in Burgin, V., Donald, J. and Kaplan, C. (eds), *Formations of Fantasy*, London and New York: Methuen, 5–34.

–––––– (1967) *The Language of Psychoanalysis*, Nicholson-Smith, D. (trans.), London: Hogarth Press.

Lapsley, R. and Westlake, M. (eds) (1988) *Film Theory: An Introduction*, Manchester: Manchester University Press.

Laskas, J. M. (1990) 'Car Crazy: What's Driving Tom Cruise', *Life*, June, 71.

Laver, J. (1945) *Taste and Fashion: From the French Revolution to the Present Day*, London: George Harrap.

–––––– (1969) *Modesty in Dress: An Inquiry into the Fundamentals of Fashion*, London: Heinemann.

–––––– (1995) *Costume and Fashion*, London: Thames and Hudson.

Leach, W. (1984) 'Transformations in a Culture of Consumption: Women and Department Stores, 1890–1925', *Journal of American History*, 71(2), 319–42.

Lee, J. (1993) *Movie Makers: Drama for Film and Television*, Glasgow: Scottish Film Council.

Lee, V. C. (1908) 'The Value of a Lecture', *MPW*, 2(8), 93–4.

Lev, P. (1993) *The Euro-American Cinema*, Austin: University of Texas Press.

Levin, G. (1996) 'Studios Gamble on Big Bucks Ad Buys', *Variety*, 18–24 March, 11–12.

Levin, R. B. and Murphy, J. H. (n.d.) Case Study of Walt Disney Pictures' 1986 Marketing Strategies, unpublished.

Levine, L. (1988) *Highbrow Lowbrow: The Emergence of Cultural Hierarchy in America*, Cambridge, Mass.: Harvard University Press.

Lévi-Strauss, C. (1963) *Structural Anthropology*, Jacobson, C. and Grunfest Schoept, B. (trans.), New York: Basic Books.

Lewis, J. (1993) *Whom God Wishes to Destroy*, Durham: Duke University Press.

–––––– (ed.) (1992) *The Adoring Audience: Fan Culture and Popular Media*, London: Routledge.

Liebes, T. (1986) 'On the Convergence of Theories of Mass Communication and Literature Regarding the Role of the "Reader"', paper delivered at the Conference on Culture and Communication, Philadelphia, Pennsylvania, October.

–––––– and Katz, E. (1986) 'On the Critical Ability of Television Viewers', paper delivered at the World Congress of Sociology, New Delhi, India, August.

Light, A. (1989) '"Young Bess": Historical Novels and Growing Up', *Feminist Review* 33.

Lin, M. C. and Manocha, D. (1993) 'Interference Detection Between Curved Objects for Computer Animation', in Thalmann, N. M. and Thalmann, D. (eds), *Models and Techniques in Computer Animation*, New York: Springer-Verlag, pp. 43–57.

Lincoln, F. (1955) 'The Comeback of the Movies', *Fortune*, February.

Lindsay, J. (1968) *Picnic at Hanging Rock*, Harlow: Penguin.

Lindsay, R. (1988) 'Francis Ford Coppola: Promises to Keep, *New York Times Magazine*, 24 July, 23–7.

Lindsay, V. (1915) *The Art of the Moving Picture*, New York: Macmillan.

Litman, B. R. (1980) 'Predicting Success of Theatrical Movies: New Empirical Evidence', paper presented at the National Convention of the Association for Education in Journalism, Boston, 13 August.

Livingston, S. M. (1990) 'Interpreting a Television Narrative: How Different Viewers See a Story', *Journal of Communication*, 40(1): 72–85.

Logsdon, J. B. (1990) *Perspectives on the Filmed Entertainment Industry*, Los Angeles: Seidler Amdec Securities.

Loizidou, S. and Clapworthy, G. J. (1993) 'Legged Locomotion Using HIDDS', in Thalmann, N. M. and Thalmann, D. (eds), *Models and Techniques in Computer Animation*, New York: Springer-Verlag, pp. 257–69.

Lombard, G. (1993) 'The Australian Example', *Refugees*, 93: 18–19.

Lovell, A. (1969) *The British Cinema: The Unknown Cinema*, BFI Mimeo.

Lovell, T. (1982) 'Marxism and Cultural Studies', *Film Reader*, 5: 184–91.

Lyotard, J.-F. (1979) *La condition postmoderne*, Paris: Minuit.

—— (1983) 'Answering the Question: What is Postmodernism?' in Durand, R. (trans.), Hassan, I. and Hassan, S. (eds), *Innovation/Renovation: New Perspectives on the Humanities*, Madison: University of Wisconsin Press, 325–41.

McArthur, C. (ed.) (1982) *Scotch Reels: Scotland in Cinema and Television*, London: British Film Institute.

McBride-Melinger, M. (1993) *The Wedding Dress*, New York: Random House.

McCabe, C. (1986) 'Theory and Film: Principles of Realism and Pleasure', in Rosen, P. (ed.), *Narrative, Apparatus, Ideology: A Film Theory Reader*, New York: Columbia University Press, pp. 179–97.

McCarthy, T. (1980) 'Trick or Treat', *Film Comment*, 16: 17–24.

McClure, J. (1994) *Late Imperial Romance: Literature and Globalization from Conrad to Pynchon*, London: Verso.

McCullaugh, J. (1977) '*Star Wars* Hikes Demand for Dolby', *Billboard*, 9 July, 4.

McDonagh, M. (1994) *Broken Mirrors/Broken Minds: The Dark Dreams of Dario Argento*, New York: Carol Publishing.

McDonald, D. (1953) 'A Theory of Mass Culture', in Rosenberg, B. and Manning White, D. (eds), *Mass Culture: The Popular Arts in America*, New York: Free Press, pp. 59–73.

McGovern, J. (1968) 'The American Woman's Pre-World War I Freedom in Manners and Morals', *Journal of American History* 55(2): 314–33.

McIntosh, M. (1976) 'Sexuality', *Papers on Patriarchy*, Lewes: Women's Publishing Collective.

McLean, A. F. Jr (1965) *American Vaudeville as Ritual*, Lexington: University of Kentucky Press.

Maclean's (1991) 'Jodie Foster's "Best Performance". An Actress Calls Her Own Shots', *Maclean's*, September, 48–9.

McLeod, D. K. (1987) 'Bankability Reconsidered', *Movieline*, 25 September, 23.

McNeile, C. (n.d.) *Bull-Dog Drummond*, London: Hodder and Stoughton.

McQuire, S. (1997) *Crossing the Digital Threshold*, Brisbane: Australian Key Centre for Cultural and Media Policy.

—— (1998) 'A Conversation on Film, Acting and Multimedia: An Interview with Ross Gibson', *Practice: A Journal of Visual, Performing and Media Arts*, 3.

McRobbie, A. (1984) 'Dance and Social Fantasy', in McRobbie, A. and Nava, M. (eds), *Gender and Generation*, London: Macmillan, pp. 130–61.

Madsen, A. (1975) *The New Hollywood*, New York: Thomas Y. Crowell.

Magid, R. (1993) 'ILM's Digital Dinosaurs Tear Up Effects Jungle', *American Cinematographer*, 74(12).

—— (1994) 'ILM Breaks New Digital Ground for *Gump*', *American Cinematographer*, 75(10).

Magiera, M. (1990) 'Madison Avenue Hits Hollywood', *Advertising Age*, 10 December, 24.

—— (1991) 'Disney Adds to Tie-ins', *Advertising Age*, 11 February, 5.

Mailer, N. (1973) *Marilyn*, London: Hodder and Stoughton.

Malkiewicz, K. (1986) *Film Lighting*, New York: Prentice-Hall.

Maltby, R. (1986) '"Baby Face" or How Joe Breen Made Barbara Stanwyck Atone for Causing the Wall Street Crash', *Screen*, 27(2): 222–45.

—— and Craven, I. (1995) *Hollywood Cinema: An Introduction*, Oxford: Blackwell.

Maltin, L. (1981–82) *T.V. Movies*, revised edn, New York: Signet.

Mandel, E. (1978) *Late Capitalism*, London: Verso.

Mann, K. B. (1989–90) 'Narrative Entanglements: *The Terminator*', *Film Quarterly*, 43(2): 17–27.

Mansfield, E. (1968) *The Economics of Technological Change*, New York: Longmans.

—— (1971) *Technological Change: An Introduction to a Vital Area of Modern Economics*, New York: Norton.

Mapplethorpe, R. (1983) *Lady: Lisa Lyons*, New York: Viking Press.

Maranda, P. (1980) 'The Dialectic of Metaphor: An Anthropological Essay on Hermeneutics', in Suleiman, S. and Crosman, I. (eds), *The Reader in the Text: Essays on Audience and Interpretation*, Princeton: Princeton University Press, pp. 183–204.

March, R. (1990) 'Roth: Instincts, Not Voodoo, Key to Future Fox Films', *Hollywood Reporter*, 21 February, 1.

Marcon, J. Jr (1991) 'Dream Factory to the World', *Forbes*, 29 April, 100.

Marcus, S. (1964) *The Other Victorians: A Study of Sexuality and Pornography in Mid-Nineteenth-Century England*, New York: Basic Books.

Marcuse, H. (1966) *One-Dimensional Man: Studies in the Ideology of Advanced Industrial Society*, Boston: Beacon Press.

Marshall, P. D. (1989) 'The Construction of Difference and Distinction in Contemporary Cultural Forms: An Analysis of the Magazines of Popular Music', unpublished Ph.D. project (April).

—— (1997) *Celebrity and Power*, Minneapolis: University of Minnesota Press.

Marshment, M. (1988) 'Substantial Women', in Gamman, L. and Marshment, M. (eds), *The Female Gaze: Women as Viewers of Popular Culture*, London: The Women's Press, 27–43.

Martin, J. (1993) *Seduction of the Gullible: The Curious History of the British 'Video Nasties' Phenomenon*, Nottingham: Procrustes.

Marx, K. (1973) *Grundrisse: Foundations of the Critique of Political Economy*, Harmondsworth: Penguin.

Maskosky, D. R. (1966) *The Portrayal of Women in Wide Circulation Magazine Short Stories 1905–1955*, Ph.D. thesis, University of Pennsylvania.

Maslin, J. (1993) ' "Paradise Lost" Inspires Meditation on Vampires', *New York Times*, 28 October, C15, C20.

Mayne, J. (1982) 'Immigrants and Spectators', *Wide Angle*, 5(2): 32–41.

—— (1988) *Private Novels, Public Films*, Athens: University of Georgia Press.

—— (1993) *Cinema and Spectatorship*, London and New York: Routledge.

Medved, H. and Medved, M. (1984) *The Hollywood Hall of Shame: The Most Expensive Flops in Movie History*, New York: Putnam.

Meehan, E. R. (1991) ' "Holy Commodity Fetish, Batman!". The Political Economy of a Commercial Intertext', in Pearson, R. E. and Uricchio, W. (eds), *The Many Lives of the Batman: Critical Approaches to a Superhero and his Media*, New York: British Film Institute/Routledge, pp. 47–65.

Megherbi, A. (1982) *Les Algériens au Miroir du Cinema Colonial*, Algiers: Editions SNED.

Meltzer, F. (1982) 'The Uncanny Rendered Canny: Freud's Blind Spot in Reading Hoffman's "Sandman" ', in Gilman, S. L. (ed.), *Introducing Psychoanalytic Theory*, New York: Brunner/Mazel, pp. 218–39.

Mercer, K. (1988a) 'Diaspora Culture and the Dialogic Imagination: The Aesthetics of Black Independent Film in Britain', in Cham, M. and Andrade-Watkins, C. (eds), *Black Frames: Critical Perspectives on Black Independent Cinema*, Cambridge, Mass.: Celebration of Black Cinema Inc/MIT Press, 50–61.

—— (1988b) 'Recoding Narratives of Race and Nation', in Mercer, K. (ed.), *Black Film/British Cinema*, ICA Document 7, London: British Film Institute Production Special.

—— (1988c) 'Sexual Identities: Questions of Difference', *Undercut*, 17.

Messaris, P. and Gross, L. (1977) 'Interpretations of a Photographic Narrative by Viewers in Four Age Groups', *Studies in the Anthropology of Visual Communication*, 4: 99–111.

Metallious, G. (1957) *Peyton Place*, New York: Frederick Muller.

—— (1960) *Return to Peyton Place*, New York: Frederick Muller.

Metz, C. (1971) *Language and Cinema*, Umiker-Sebeok, D. J. (trans.), The Hague: Mouton.

—— (1975) 'The Imaginary Signifier', *Screen*, 16(2): 14–76.

—— (1982) *The Imaginary Signifier: Psychoanalysis and the Cinema*, Britton, C., Williams, A. Brewster, B. and Guzzetti, A. (trans.), Bloomington: Indiana University Press.

Meyer, M. (1991) 'I Dream of Jeannie: Transexual Striptease as Scientific Display', *Drama Review*, 35(1): 25–43.

Mickelthwait, J. (1989) 'A Survey of the Entertainment Industry', *The Economist*, 23 December, 5.

Miller, D. T. and Nowak, M. (1977) *The Fifties: The Way We Really Were*, New York: Doubleday.

Miller, J. (1980) *The Rolling Stone Illustrated History of Rock & Roll*, New York: Random House/Rolling Stone Press.

Miller, M. C. (1990) 'Hollywood: the Ad', *Atlantic Monthly*, April, 49–52.

Millerson, G. (1972) *The Technique for Lighting for Television and Motion Pictures*, London: Focal Press.

Mills, F. S. (1921) 'Film Lighting as Fine Art: Explaining Why the Fireplace Glows and Why Film Stars Wear Halos', *Scientific American*, 124: 148, 157–8.

Minns, R. (1980) *Bombers and Mash: The Domestic Front 1939–45*, London: Virago.

Mitchell, T. (1991) *Colonizing Egypt*, Berkeley: University of California Press.

Modleski, T. (1979) 'Search for Tomorrow in Today's Soap Operas', *Film Quarterly*, 33(1): 12–2.

—— (1982) *Loving with a Vengeance: Mass Produced Fantasies for Women*, London: Methuen.

—— (1986a) 'Femininity as Mas[s]querade: A Feminist Approach to Mass Culture', in MacCabe, C. (ed.), *High Theory, Low Culture: Analysing Popular Televsion and Film*, Manchester: Manchester University Press, pp. 37–52.

—— (1986b) 'The Terror of Pleasure: the Contemporary Horror Film and Postmodern Theory' in Modleski, T. (ed.), *Studies in Entertainment*, Bloomington: University of Indiana Press.

—— (1988) *The Women Who Knew Too Much: Hitchcock and Feminist Theory*, New York: Methuen.

—— (1989) 'Some Functions of Feminist Criticism, or The Scandal of the Mute Body', *October*, 49: 3–24.

Monaco, J. (1979) *American Film Now*, New York: New American Library.

Monopolies and Mergers Commission. (1966) *Films: A Report on the Supply of Films for Exhibition in Cinemas in the UK*, London: HMSO.

Monthly Film Bulletin (1985) 52.

Montrose, L. A. (1989) 'Professing the Renaissance: The Poetics and Politics of Culture', in Aram Veeser, H. (ed.), *The New Historicism*, New York and London: Routledge, pp. 15–36.

Moore, K. (1990) 'Cruise Control', *Sports Illustrated*, 11 June, 50–3.

Morantz, R. C. (1977) 'The Scientist as Sex Crusader: Alfred C. Kinsey and American Culture', *American Quarterly*, 29(5): 563–89.

Moretti, F. (1982) 'The Dialectic of Fear', *New Left Review*, 136: 67–85.

Morin, E. (1972) *Les Stars*, Paris: Seuil.

Morley, D. (1980a) 'Texts, Readers, Subjects', in Hall, S., Hobson, D., Lowe, A. and Willis, P. (eds), *Culture, Media, Language: Working Papers in Cultural Studies, 1972–79*, London: Hutchinson, pp. 163–73.

—— (1980b) *The 'Nationwide' Audience: Structure and Decoding*, London: British Film Institute.

—— (1986) *Family Television*, London: Comedia.

Morris, M. (1988) 'Tooth and Claw: Tales of Survival and *Crocodile Dundee*', in Ross, A. (ed.), *Universal Abandon?: The Politics of Postmodernism*, Minneapolis: University of Minnesota Press, pp. 105–27.

Morrison, T. (1972) *The Bluest Eyes*, New York: Simon and Schuster.

Moss, L. and Box, K. (1943) *The Cinema Audience: An Inquiry made by the Wartime Social Survey for the Ministry of Information*, London: Ministry of Information.

Mouffe, C. and Laclau, E. (1985) *Hegemony and Socialist Strategy*, London: Verso.

Mukařovský, J. (1977) 'On Poetic Language', in Burbank, J. and Steiner, P. (trans. and ed.), *The Word and Verbal Art: Selected Essays by Jan Mukařovský*, New Haven: Yale University Press, 1–64.

Mulvey, L. (1975) 'Visual Pleasure and Narrative Cinema', *Screen*, 16: 6–18.

—— (1981) 'Afterthoughts on "Visual Pleasure and Narrative Cinema": . . . Inspired by *Duel in the Sun*', *Framework*, 15–17, 13–15.

—— (1989a) *Visual and Other Pleasures*, London: Macmillan.

—— (1989b) 'The Spectatrix', *Camera Obscura*, 20–1: 249.

Münsterberg, H. (1970) *The Film: A Psychological Study*, New York: Dover Publications. First published 1916 as *The Photoplay: A Psychological Study*.

Murphy, A. D. (1989) 'Twenty Years of Weekly Film Ticket Sales in U.S. Theaters', *Variety*, 15–21 March, 26.

Murphy, K. (1991) 'Only Angels Have Wings', *Film Comment*, 24(4): 26–9.

Murray, W. (1975) '*Playboy* Interview: Francis Ford Coppola', *Playboy*, July, 65–8.

Musser, C. (1983) 'The Nickelodeon Era Begins: Establishing the Framework for Hollywood's Mode of Representation', *Framework*, 22–3, 4.

—— (1990) *History of the American Cinema, Volume 1, The Emergence of Cinema: The American Screen to 1907*, New York: Charles Scribner's Sons.

Myles, L. and Pye, M. (1979) *The Movie Brats: How the Film Generation Took Over Hollywood*, London: Faber.

Naremore, J. (1988) *Acting in the Cinema*, Berkeley: University of California Press.

Nash, M. 1976) '*Vampyr* and the Fantastic', *Screen*, 17: 29–67.

Natale, R. (1991a) ' "Lean Indies" Fatten Summer Boxoffice', *Variety*, 12 August 12, 1: 61.

—— (1991b) 'Hollywood's "New Math": Does it Still Add Up?', *Variety*, 19 August, 1: 95.

—— (1992a) 'Ricky Pix get a Global Fix', *Variety*, 28 September, 97.

—— (1992b) 'Summer Plugs Clog P&A Pipe Dreams', *Variety*, 1 June, 88.

Nat West Markets (1996) 'Media Mergers Don't Add Up', *Nat West Markets*, 2 January, 1–5.

Neale, S. (1979–80) 'The Same Old Story: Stereotypes and Difference', *Screen Education*, 32(33): 33–7.

—— (1980) *Genre*, London: British Film Institute.

—— (1981) 'Art Cinema as Institution', *Screen*, 22(1): 11–40.

—— (1985) *Cinema and Technology Image, Sound, Colour*, London: BFI.

Negt, O. and Kluge, A. (1972) *Öffentlichkeit und Erfahrung: Zur Organisations-analyse von bügerlicher und proletarischer Öffentlichkeit*, Frankfurt: Suhrkamp.

Neisser, U. (1967) *Cognitive Psychology*, New York: Appleton-Century-Crofts.

Nelson, K. (1981) 'Social Cognition on a Script Framework', in Flavell, J. H. and Ross, L. (eds), *Social Cognitive Development*, Cambridge: Cambridge University Press, pp. 101–3.

Newcomb, H. M. and Hirsch, P. M. (1983) 'Television as a Cultural Forum: Implications for Research', *Quarterly Review of Film Studies*, 8(3).

Newman, J. K. (1940) 'Profile of Natalie Kalmus', in: Huntley, J. (ed.), *British Technicolor Films*, London: Skelton Robinson.

Newman, K. (1992) 'Loving the Alien', *Empire*.

New York Times Magazine (1920) 'Survivors of a Vanishing Race in the Movie World', *The New York Times Magazine*, 18 January, 4.

Nichols, B. (1991) *Representing Reality: Issues and Concepts in Documentary*, Bloomington: Indiana University Press.

—— (1994) 'Global Image Consumption in the Age of Late Capitalism', *East-West Film Journal*, 8(1): 68–85.

Noglows, P. (1992) 'Studios Stuck in Screen Jam', *Variety*, 9 March, 1: 69.

Norris, C. (1992) *Uncritical Theory: Postmodernism, Intellectuals and the Gulf War*, Amherst: University of Massachussetts Press.

Nowell-Smith, G. (1985) 'But Do We Need It?', in Auty, M. and Roddick, N. (eds), *British Cinema Now*, London: British Film Institute.

O'Dea, W. T. (1958) *The Social History of Lighting*, London: Routledge and Kegan Paul.

Ogilvy, D. (1978) 'Ogilvy Comes to New York, Ogilvy Goes to Hollywood', *New York*, 6 February, 58.

O'Regan, T. (1996) *Australian National Cinema*, London: Routledge.

Ormerod, D. and Ward, D. (1965) 'The Bond Game', *The London Magazine*, 5(2): 41–55.

Orr, J. (1993) *Cinema and Modernity*, Cambridge and Oxford: Polity Press.

Ove, H. (1987) Interview with S. Paskin, *Monthly Film Bulletin*, 54.

Owens, C. (1985) 'The Discourse of Others: Feminists and Postmodernism', in Foster, H. (ed.), *Postmodern Culture*, London: Pluto Press, pp. 57–82.

Palmer, L. E. (1909) 'The World in Motion', *Survey*, 22: 356.

Palmer, R. B. (1989) 'Bakhtinian Translinguistics and Film Criticism: The Dialogical Image?', in Palmer, R. B. (ed.), *The Cinematic Text: Methods and Approaches*, New York: AMS Press, pp. 303–41.

Parker, R. A. (1991) 'The Guise of the Propangandist: Governmental Classification of Foreign Political Films', in Austin, B. A. (ed.), *Current Research in Film: Audiences, Economics and Law*, vol. 5, Norwood: Ablex.

Parry, B. (1987) 'Problems in Current Theories of Colonial Discourse', *Oxford Literary Review*, 9: 27–58.

Passingham, K. (1975) 'James Bond', *TV Times*, 15 October.

Patterson, J. (1993) No title, *Sight and Sound*, October, 3: 10.

Pearce, G. (1992) 'Return to the Forbidden Planet', *Empire*.

Pearce, R. H. (1988) *Savagism and Civilization*, Berkeley: University of California Press.

Pearson, J. (1973) *James Bond: The Authorized Biography of 007*, London: Sidgwick and Jackson.

Peat, Marwick, Mitchell Services (1979) *Towards a More Effective Commission: The AFC in the 1980s*, Sydney: Peat, Marwick, Mitchell Services.

Peers, M. and Busch, A. M. (1996) 'Sony Sizes up Size Issue', *Variety*, 16–22 August, 86.

Peiss, K. (1983) ' "Charity Girls" and City Pleasures: Historical Notes on Working-Class Sexuality', in Snitow, A. *et al.* (eds), *Powers of Desire*, New York: Monthly Review Press, 74–87.

—— (1986) *Cheap Amusements: Working Women and Leisure in Turn-of-the-Century New York*, Philadelphia: Temple University Press.

Pendleton, J. (1991) 'Fast Forward, Reverse', *Daily Variety*, October.

Penley, C. (1985) 'Feminism, Film Theory and the Bachelor Machines', *m/f*, 10: 39–59.

—— (1988a) 'Introduction: The Lady Doesn't Vanish: Feminism and Film Theory', in Penley, C. (ed.), *Feminism and Film Theory*, New York and London: Routledge, pp. 1–24.

—— (ed.) (1988b) *Feminism and Film Theory*, New York and London: Routledge.

—— (1989) 'Time Travel, Primal Scene and the Critical Dystopia', in Donald, J. (ed.), *Fantasy and the Cinema*, London: British Film Institute Publishing, 197–212.

Perse, E. M. and Rubin, R. B. (1989) 'Attribution in Social and Parasocial Relationships', *Communication Research*, 16(1): 59–77.

Pescovitz, D. (1998) 'Starmaker', *Wired*, October.

Petro, P. (1984) 'Television Criticism, Television History: Realism, Modernism and Reception', paper delivered at the Society for Cinema Studies Conference, Madison, Wisconsin, 26–31 March.

—— (1986) 'Mass Culture and the Feminine: The "Place" of Television in Film Studies', *Cinema Journal*, 25(3): 5–21.

—— (1989) *Joyless Streets: Women and Melodramatic Representation in Weimar Germany*, Princeton: Princeton University Press.

Pidduck, J. (1995) 'The 1990s Hollywood Fatal Femme: (Dis)Figuring Feminism, Family, Irony, Violence', *Cineaction*, 38: 64–72.

Pierson, M. (1999) 'GCI Effects in Hollywood Science-Fiction Cinema 1989–95: The Wonder Years', *Screen*, 40(2): 158–76.

Pieterse, J. (1992) *White on Black: Images of Africa and Blacks in Western Popular Culture*, New Haven: Yale University Press.

Pines, J. (1981) 'Blacks in Films: The British Angle', *Multiracial Education*, 9(2).

—— (1986) '*The Passion of Remembrance*: Interview with SANKOFA', *Framework*, 32(33): 92–9.

—— (1988) 'The Cultural Context of Black British Cinema', in Cham, M. and Andrade-Watkins, C. (eds), *BlackFrames: Critical Perspectives on Black Independent Cinema*, Cambridge, Mass.: Celebration of Black Cinema Inc/MIT Press, 26–36.

—— and Willemen, P. (eds) (1989) *Questions of Third Cinema*, London: British Film Institute.

Pirelli, P. (1983) 'Statistical Survey of the British Film Industry', in Curran, J. and Porter, V. (eds), *British Cinema History*, London: Weidenfeld and Nicolson, pp. 372–82.

Pizzello, S. (1994) '*True Lies* Tests Cinema's Limits', *American Cinematographer*, 75(9).

Poe, E. A. (1883) 'The Philosophy of Composition', in Ingram, J. H. (ed.), *The Works of Edgar Allan Poe*, vol. 3, Edinburgh: Adam and Charles Black, pp. 266–78.

Pollack, A. (1994) 'At MCA's Parent, No Move to Let Go', *New York Times*, 14 October, C1.

Porter, D. (1981) *The Pursuit of Crime: Art and Ideology in Detective Fiction*, New Haven and London: Yale University Press.

Poster, M. (1990) 'Words Without Thing: The Mode of Information', *October*, 53, 63–77.

Powdermaker, H. (1950) *Hollywood: The Dream Factory*, Boston: Little, Brown.

Powell, D. (1989) *The Golden Screen: Fifty Years of Films*, Perry, G. (ed.), London: Pavilion Books.

Pribram, E. D. (ed.) (1988) *Female Spectators*, London: Verso.

Prince, S. (1993) 'The Discourse of Pictures: Iconography and Film Studies', *Film Quarterly*, 47(1): 16–28.

—— (1996a) 'Psychoanalytic Film Theory and the Problem of the Missing Spectator', in Bordwell, D. and Carroll, N. (eds), *Post-Theory: Reconstructing Film Studies*, Madison: University of Wisconsin Press, 71–86.

—— (1996b) 'True Lies: Perceptual Realism, Digital Images and Film Theory', *Film Quarterly*, 49(3): pp. 27–37.

Progressions (n.d.) 'The Black Church in America', *Progressions: A Lilly Endowment Occasional Report*, 4(1).

Propp, V. (1968) *Morphology of the Folk Tale*, Houston: University of Texas Press.

Pye, M. and Myles, L. (1979) *The Movie Brats*, New York: Holt, Rinehart and Winston.

Quester, G. H. (1990) *The International Politics of Television*, Lexington: Lexington.

Rabinovitz, L. (1989) 'The Air of Respectability: Hale's tours at Riverview Amusement Park in 1907', paper presented at the SCS Conference, Iowa City, April.

Race Equality Unit, Greater London Council (1986) *Third Eye: Struggles for Black and Third World Cinema*, London: Greater London Council.

Radway, J. (1984) *Reading the Romance: Women, Patriarchy and Popular Literature*, Chapel Hill and London: University of North Carolina Press.

Reid, M. A. (1994) 'Distribution', in Curtis, R. and Spriggs, (eds), *Get the Picture: Essential Data on Australian Film, Television and Video*, 3rd edn, Sydney: Australian Film Commission, 67–129.

Revault d'Allones, F. (1991) *la Lumière au cinéma*, Paris: Seuil/Cahiers du cinéma.

Rice, A. (1984) *The Vampire Lestat*, New York: Ballantine.

Richards, J. (1973) *Visions of Yesterday*, London: Kegan and Paul.

—— (1984) *The Age of the Dream Palace: Cinema and Society 1930–1939*, London: Routledge and Kegan Paul.

—— (1986) 'Boy's Own Empire: Feature Films and Imperialism in the 1930s', in Mackenzie, J. M. (ed.), *Imperialism and Popular Culture*, Manchester: Manchester University Press, 140–64.

—— (1988) 'National Identity in British Wartime Films', in Taylor, P. M. (ed.), *Britain and the Cinema in the Second World War*, New York: St Martin's Press, 42–61.

Richardson, D. (1932/1982) 'The Film Gone Male', *Framework*, 20: 6–8.

Ricketson, J. (1979) 'Poor Movies, Rich Movies', *Filmnews*, 9(1). Reprinted in Moran, A. and O'Regan, T. (eds), (1985) *Australian Film Reader*, Sydney: Currency Press, 223–7.

Roach, J. and Felix, P. (1988) 'Black Looks', in Gamman, L. and Marshment, M. (eds), *The Female Gaze: Women as Viewers of Popular Culture*, London: The Women's Press, pp. 130–42.

Robbins, I. A. (ed.) (1985) *The Rolling Stone Review 1985*, New York: Rolling Stone Press and Charles Scribner's Sons.

Robins, J. M. and Brennan, J. (1993) 'Turner May Tap Sassa to Run Film Venture', *Variety*, 23 August, 9.

Robinson, C. and Given, J. (1994) 'Films, Policies, Audiences and Australia', in Moran, A. (ed.), *Film Policy: An Australian Reader*, Nathan: Institute for Cultural Policy Studies, Griffith University, pp. 17–26.

Robinson, D. (1994) *Chronicle of the Cinema 1895–1995: No. 5 1980–1994*, London: British Film Institute.

Roddick, N. (1995) '*Four Weddings* and a Final Reckoning', *Sight and Sound*, January, 12–15.

Rodowick, D. N. (1982) 'The Difficulty of Difference', *Wide Angle*, 5(1): 4–15.

—— (1988) *The Crisis of Political Modernism*, Urbana: University of Illinois Press.

—— (1991) *The Difficulty of Difference*, New York and London: Routledge.

Rogin, M. (1987) *Ronald Reagan: The Movie*, Berkeley: University of California Press.

—— (1990) '"Make My Day!": Spectacle as Amnesia in Imperial Politics', *Representations*, 29: 99–124.

Rogoff, B. (1990) *Apprenticeship in Thinking: Cognitive Development in Social Context*, New York: Oxford University Press.

Rommetveit, R. (1985) 'Language Acquisition as Increasing Linguistic Structuring of Experience and Symbolic Behavior Control', in Wertsch, J. V. (ed.), *Culture, Communication and Cognition: Vygotskian Perspectives*, Cambridge: Cambridge University Press.

Rony, F. T. (1992) 'Those who Squat and Those who Sit: The Iconography of Race in the 1859 Films of Félix-Louis Regnault', *Camera Obscura*, 28: 263–89.

Rose, J. (1990) 'Response', *Camera Obscura*, 20(21):? 274–79.

Rosen, M. (1974) *Popcorn Venus: Women, Movies and the American Dream*, New York: Avon Books.

Rosen, P. (1980) 'Formalism, Reception and Eisenstein's Theoretical Development', unpublished.

Rosenfield, I. (1985a) 'The New Brain', *New York Review of Books*, 14 March, pp. 34–8.

—— (1985b) 'A Hero of the Brain', *New York Review of Books*, 21 November, 49–53.

Rosenzweig, R. (1983) *Eight Hours for What We Will: Workers and Leisure in an Industrial City, 1870–1920*, Cambridge and New York: Cambridge University Press.

Ross, A. (1989) *No Respect: Intellectual and Popular Culture*, New York: Routledge.

Rothman, W. (1982) *Hitchcock: The Murderous Gaze*, Cambridge, Mass.: Harvard University Press.

Rouch, J. (1979) 'Camera and Man', in Eaton, M. (ed.), *Anthropology–Reality–Cinema*, London: British Film Institute.

Rouillé, A. and Marbot, B. (1986) *Le Corps et son Image: Photographies du Dix-neuvième Siècle*, Paris: Contrejour.

Routt, W. and Thompson, R. (1987) '"Keep Young and Beautiful" – Surplus and Subversion in *Roman Scandals*', in O'Regan, T. and Shoesmith, B. (eds), *History on/an/in Film*, Perth: History and Film Association, pp. 31–44.

Rowse, T. (1985) *Arguing the Arts*, Ringwood: Penguin.

Runnymeade Trust and the Radical Statistics Race Group (1980) *Britain's Black Population*, London: Heinemann Educational Books.

Rushdie, S. (1987) 'Songs Doesn't Know the Score', *Guardian*, UK, 12 January.

—— (1992) *Imaginary Homelands*, London: Penguin.

Ruthrof, H. (1980) *The Reader's Construction of Narrative*, London: Routledge and Kegan Paul.

Ryan, M. P. (1975) *Womanhood in America*, New York: Franklin Watts.

—— (1976) 'The Projection of a New Womanhood: The Move Moderns in the 1920s', in Friedman, J. E. and Shade, W. G. (eds), *Our American Sisters: Women in American Life and Thought*, Boston: Allyn and Bacon.

Rydell, R. W. (1984) *All the World's a Fair*, Chicago: University of Chicago Press.

Safford, T. (1995) 'Two or Three Things I Know about Australian Cinema', *Media International Australia*, 27–9.

Said, E. (1989) 'Representing the Colonized: Anthropology's Interlocuters', *Critical Inquiry*, 15(2): 205–25.

—— (1978) *Orientalism*, London: Routledge and Kegan Paul.

—— (1984) *The World, the Text and the Critic*, London: Faber.

Salamon, J. (1991) *The Devil's Candy*, Boston: Houghton Mifflin.

Salmane, H., Hartog, S. and Wilson, D. (eds) (1976) *Algerian Cinema*, London: British Film Institute.

Salt, B. (1983) *Film Style and Technology: History and Analysis*, London: Starwood.

Sarris, A. (1962–3) 'Notes on the *Auteur* Theory', *Film Culture*, Winter.

—— (1985) 'O Hollywood!, Oh Mores', *Village Voice*, 5 March, 5.

Saxton, M. (1975) *Jayne Mansfield and the American Fifties*, Boston: Houghton Mifflin.

Sayers, J. (1986) *Sexual Contradictions: Psychology, Psychoanalysis and Feminism*, London: Tavistock Publications.

Schatz, T. (1981) *Hollywood Genres*, New York: Random House.

—— (1988) *The Genius of the System: Hollywood Filmmaking in the Studio Era*, New York: Pantheon.

—— (1993) 'The Hollywood', in Collins, J., Radner, H. and Collins, A. (eds), *Film Theory Goes to the Movies*, New York: Routledge, pp. 8–36.

Schell, J. (1991) 'Modern Might, Ancient Arrogance', *Newsday*, 12 February.

Schickel, R. (1989) 'The Crisis in Movie Narrative', *Gannett Centre Journal*, 3: 1–15.

Schivelbusch, W. (1979) *The Railway Journey: Trains and Travel in the 19th Century*, Hollo, A. (trans.), New York: Urizen.

Schlüpmann, H. (1982) 'Kinosucht', *Frauen und Film*, 33: 45–52.

Schoell, W. (1985) *Stay Out of the Shower: Twenty-Five Years of Shocker Films Beginning with Psycho*, New York: Dembner.

Schulze, L. J. (1986) '*Getting Physical*: Text/Context/Reading and the Made-for-Television Movie', *Cinema Journal*, 25(2): 35–50.

Scorsese, M. and Cocks, J. (1993) *The Age of Innocence: A Portrait of the Film Based on the Novel by Edith Wharton*, New York: Newmarket Press.

Sedgwick, E. K. (1985) *Between Men: English Literature and Male Homosocial Desire*, New York: Columbia University Press.

Sergi, G. (1998) 'A Cry in the Dark: the Role of Post-Classical Film Sound' in Neale, S. and Smith, M. (eds), *Contemporary Hollywood Cinema*, London: Routledge, pp. 156–65.

Sellors, P. (n.d.) 'Selling Paranoia: *Gilligan's Island* and the Television Medium', unpublished.

Sennett, R. (1974) *The Fall of Public Man*, New York: Random House.

Sessum, K. (1994) 'Cruise Speed', *Vanity Fair*, October.

Sharkey, B. (1991) 'Spotlight on Entertainment', *Adweek*, 18 March, 33.

Sheinwold, P. F. (1980) *Too Young to Die*, London: Cathay.

Sheldon, C. (1980) 'Lesbians and Film: Some Thoughts', in Dyer, R. (ed.), *Gays and Film*, London: British Film Institute Publishing, pp. 5–26.

Shelley, J. (1995) 'LA is Burning', *Guardian*, UK, 23 December.

Shohat, E. (1983) 'Egypt: Cinema and Revolution', *Critical Arts*, 2(4).

—— (1990) 'Imagining Terra Incognita: The Disciplinary Gaze of Empire', *Public Culture*, 3(2): 41–70.

—— (1991) 'The Media's War', *Social Text*, 28: 135–41.

—— and Stam, R. (1994) *Unthinking Eurocentrism: Multiculturalism and the Media*, New York: Routledge.

Showalter, E. (1983 4) 'Critical Cross-Dressing: Male Feminists and the Woman of the Year', *Raritan*, 3: 130–49.

Silverman, K. (1980) 'Masochism and Subjectivity', *Framework*, 12: 2–9.

—— (1986) 'Fragments of a Fashionable Discourse', in Modleski, T. (ed.), *Studies in Entertainment: Critical Approaches to Mass Entertainment*, Bloomington: Indiana University Press, pp. 139–52.

—— (1988) *The Acoustic Mirror: The Female Voice in Psychoanalysis and Cinema*, Bloomington: Indiana University Press.

Silverman, S. M. (1988) *The Fox that Got Away*, Secaucus: Lyle Stuart.

Simonet, T. (1980) 'Market Research: Beyond the Fanny of the Cohn', *Film Comment*, January/February.

—— (1987) 'Conglomerates and Content: Remakes, Sequels, and Series in the New Hollywood', in Austin, B. A. (ed.), *Current Research in Film: Audiences, Economics, and Law*, Norwood: Ablex.

—— and Harwood, K. (1976) 'Identified Auteurs Among Top-Grossing American Film Directors, 1945–1969', paper presented at the Society for Cinema Studies Conference, University of Vermont.

—— (1977) 'Popular Favorites and Critics' Darlings Among Film Directors in American Release', paper presented at the Society for Cinema Studies Conference, Northwestern University.

Sims, C. (1993) ' "Synergy". The Unspoken Word', *New York Times*, 5 October, C1, C18.

Sinclair, M. (1979) *Those Who Died Young*, London: Plexus.

Singer, B. (1989) 'The Perils of Empowerment: Agency, Vengeance and Violation in the Serial-Queen Melodrama', paper presented at the SCS Conference, Iowa City, April.

Singer, H. and Ruddell, R. (eds) (1970) *Theoretical Models and Processes of Reading*, Newark: International Reading Association.

Skinner, P. (1988) 'Moving Way Up: Television's "New Look" at Blacks', paper presented at the International Television Studies Conference, London.

Sklar, R. (1987) 'Homevideo', *Cineaste* 14(4): 29.

—— (1988) 'Oh! Althusser!: Historiography and the Rise of Cinema Studies', *Radical History Review*, 41: 10–35.

Slavin, K. (1984) 'Generative Semiotics', paper delivered at the Society for Cinema Studies Conference, Madison, Wisconsin, 26–30 March.

Slotkin, R. (1992) *Gunfighter Nation: The Myth of the Frontier in Twentieth-Century America*, New York: Atheneum.

Smith, A. D. (1986) *The Ethnic Origins of Nations*, Oxford: Basil Blackwell.

Smith, A. E. (1952) *Two Reels and a Crank*, Garden City: Doubleday.

Smith, B. (1990) 'The Truth that Never Hurts: Black Lesbians in Fiction in the 1980s', in Braxton, J. M. and McLaughlin, A. N. (eds), *Wild Women in the Whirlwind: Afra-American Culture and the Contemporary Literary Renaissance*, New Brunswick: Rutgers University Press, pp. 213–45.

Smith, R., Anderson, D. R. and Fischer, C. (1985) 'Young Children's Comprehension of Montage', *Child Development*, 56: 962–71.

Smith, S. (1972) 'The Image of Women in Film: Some Suggestions for Future Research', *Women and Film*, 1: 13–21.

Smyth, C. (1995) 'The Transgressive Sexual Subject', in Burston, P. and Richardson, C. (eds), *A Queer Romance: Lesbians, Gay Men and Popular Culture*, New York: Routledge, pp. 123–43.

Snead, J. A. (1988) 'Black Independent Film: Britain and America', in Mercer, K. (ed.), *Black Film/British Cinema, ICA Document 7*, London: British Film Institute Production Special.

Snelling, O. F. (1954) *Double O Seven, James Bond: A Report*, London: Neville Spearman Holland.

Snyder, R. W. (1986) *The Voice of the City: Vaudeville and the formation of Mass Culture in New York Neighborhoods, 1880–1930*, Ph.D. thesis, New York University.

Sobchack, V. (1980) *Screening Space: The American Science Fiction Film*, New York: Ungar.

Sobel, A. (1986) *Pornography: Marxism, Feminism and the Future of Sexuality*, New Haven: Yale University Press.

Solanas, F. and Gettino, O. (1976) 'Towards a Third Cinema', in Nichols, B. (ed.), *Movies and Methods*, London and Berkeley: University of California Press, 44–64.

Somerville, S. (1994) 'Scientific Racism and the Emergence of the Homosexual Body', *Journal of the History of Sexuality*, 5: 243–66.

Sorlin, P. (1991) *European Cinemas, European Societies 1939–1990*, London: Routledge.

Spainhower, M. (1986) 'The Wizard of Gore', in Vale, V., Juno, A. and Morton, J. (eds), *Incredibly Strange Films*, San Francisco: Research.

Spence, J. (1978/79) 'What do People Do all Day?' *Screen Education*, 29: 29–45.

Spigel, L. and Mann, D. (1989) 'Women and Consumer Culture: A Selective Bibliography', *Quarterly Review of Film and Video*, 11(1): 85–105.

Spivak, G. C. (1987) *In Other Worlds*, London: Methuen.

Spoto, D. (1983) *The Dark Side of Genius: The Life of Alfred Hitchcock*, New York: Ballentine.

Stacey, J. (1987) 'Desperately Seeking Difference', *Screen* 28(10): 48–61.

—— (1994) *Star Gazing: Hollywood Cinema and Female Spectatorship*, London and New York: Routledge.

—— (1995) '"If You Don't Play, You Can't Win": Desert Hearts and the Lesbian Romance Film', in Wilton, T. (ed.), *Immortal, Invisible: Lesbians and the Moving Image*, New York: Routledge, pp. 92–114.

Stafford, D. A. (1981) 'Spies and Gentlemen: The Birth of the British Spy Novel 1853–1914', *Victorian Studies*, 24(4): 489–509.

Staiger, J. (1983) 'Individualism Versus Collectivism', *Screen*, 23: 68–79.

—— (1990) 'Announcing Wares, Winning Patrons, Voicing Ideals: Thinking About the History of Theory of Film Advertising', *Cinema Journal*, 29(3).

—— (1991) 'Seeing Stars', in Gledhill, C. (ed.), *Stardom: Industry of Desire*, London: Routledge, pp. 6–10.

—— (1992) *Interpreting Films: Studies in the Historical Reception of American Cinema*, Princeton: Princeton University Press.

—— (1993) 'Taboos and Totems: Cultural Meanings of *The Silence of the Lambs*', in Collins, J., Radner, H. and Collins, A. (eds), *Film Theory Goes to the Movies*, New York: Routledge, pp. 142–54.

Stam, R. (1983) 'Television News and Its Spectator', in Kaplan, A. (ed.), *Regarding Television*, Fredricksburg: AFI.

—— (1989a) 'Bakhtinian Translinguistics: A Postscriptum', in Palmer, R. B. (ed.), *The Cinematic Text: Methods and Approaches*, New York: AMS Press, pp. 343–51.

—— (1989b) 'Film and Language: From Metz to Bakhtin;, in Palmer, R. B. (ed.), *The Cinematic Text: Methods and Approaches*, New York: AMS Press, pp. 277–301.

—— (1989c) *Subversive Pleasures: Bakhtin, Cultural Criticism and film*, Baltimore: Johns Hopkins University Press.

—— (1992) 'Mobilizing Fictions: The Gulf War, the Media, and the Recruitment of the Spectator', *Public Culture*, 4(2): 101–26.

—— Burgoyne, R. and Flitterman-Lewis, S. (eds) (1992) *New Vocabularies in Film Semiotics: Structuralism, Post-structuralism, and Beyond*, New York: Routledge.

Stanislavski, C. (1989) *Creating a Role*, Popper, H. I. (ed.), Hapgood, E. (trans.), New York, Routledge.

Stanley, L. (1977) *The Problematic Nature of Sexual Meanings*, Manchester: British Sociological Association Sexuality Study Group.

Steele, V. (1985) *Fashion and Eroticism: Ideals of Feminine Beauty from the Victorian Era to the Jazz Age*, New York and Oxford: Oxford University Press.

Stein, B. (1991) 'Holy Bat-Debt!', *Entertainment Weekly*, 26 April, 12.

Steinberg, D. D. (1982) *Psycholinguistics: Language Mind and World*, London: Longman.

Steinem, G. (1973) 'Marilyn: The Woman Who Died Too Soon', in Klagsbrun, F. (ed.), *The First Ms. Reader*, New York: Warner, pp. 200–12.

Steiner, L. (1988) 'Oppositional Decoding as an Act of Resistance', *Critical Studies in Mass Communication*, 4(1): 1–15.

Sterling, C. H. and Haight, T. R. (1978) *The Mass Media: Aspen Institute Guide to Communication Industry Trends*, New York: Praeger.

Stern, L. (1988) 'Remembering Claire Johnston', *Film News*, 19(4).

Sterngold, J. (1994) 'Sony, Struggling, Takes a Huge Loss on Movie Studios', *New York Times*, 18 September, A1.

Stetson, C. P. G. (1970) *Women and Economics: A Study of the Economic Relation Between Men and Women as a Factor in Social Evolution*, New York: Source Book Press.

Stevenson, R. W. (1991) 'Carolco Flexes its Muscle Overseas', *New York Times*, 26 June, C1, C17.

—— (1994) 'Lights! Camera! Europe!' *New York Times*, 6 February, C1.

Stoller, R. (1985) *Observing the Erotic Imagination*, New Haven and London: Yale University Press.

Straayer, C. (1996) *Deviant Eyes, Deviant Bodies: Sexual Reorientations in Film and Video*, New York: Columbia University Press.

Stratton, D. (1990) *The Avocado Plantation: Boom and Bust in the Australian Film Industry*, Sydney: Pan Macmillan.

Stroebel, L. and Zakia, R. (eds) (1993) *The Focal Encyclopedia of Photography*, Boston: Focal Press.

Studlar, G. (1988) *In the Realm of Pleasure: Von Sternberg, Dietrich and the Masochistic Aesthetic*, Urbana: University of Illinois Press.

Swann, P. (1987) *The Hollywood Feature Film in Postwar Britain*, Kent: Croom Helm.

Swanson, G. (1986) 'Representation', *Screen*, 27: 16–28.

Tarr, J. M. (1990) 'The Mind's Eye', *Science*, 249, 10 August: 685.

Tasker, Y. (1993) *Spectacular Bodies: Gender, Genre and the Action Cinema*, London and New York: Routledge.

Taubin, A. (1992) 'Invading Bodies: *Alien 3* and the Trilogy', *Sight and Sound*, 2(3): 8–10.

—— (1993) 'Dread and Desire', *Sight and Sound*, 3(12).

Taylor, C. (1985) *Human Agency and Language: Philosophical Papers*, Cambridge: Cambridge University Press.

Teen (1983) 'Tom Cruise Makes all the Right Moves', *Teen*, December, pp. 54–5.

Teo, S. (1997) *Hong Kong Cinema: The extra dimensions*, London: BFI.

Tey, J. (1980) 'Silent Screen Heroines: Idealisations on Film', *American Classic Screen*, 5(10): 6–8.

Tharp, J. (1991) 'The Transvestite: Gender Horror in *The Silence of the Lambs*', *Journal of Popular Film and Television*, 19(3): 106–13.

Thomas, W. I. with Park, R. E. and Miller, H. A. (1971) *Old World Traits Transplanted*, Montclair: Patterson Smith.

Thompson, A. (1992) 'Reporting the Numbers', *LA Weekly*, 24 July, 29.

Thompson, K. (1985) *Exporting Entertainment: America in the World Film Market 1907–1934*, London: British Film Institute.

Thornton, S. (1995) *Club Cultures: Music, Media and Subcultural Capital*, Oxford: Blackwell.

Thorpe, M. (1939) *America at the Movies*, New Haven, Yale University Press.

Tickner, L. (1978) 'The Body Politic: Female Sexuality and Women Artists Since 1970', *Art History*, 1(2): 236–41.

Tomaševskij, B. (1971) 'Literature and Biography', in Matejka, L. and Pomorska, K. (eds), *Readings in Russian Poetics: Formalist and Structuralist Views*, Cambridge, Mass.: MIT Press, pp. 47–55.

Tootelian, D. H. and Gaedeke, R. M. (1992) 'The Teen Market: An Exploratory Analysis of Income, Spending, and Shopping Patterns', *Journal of Consumer Marketing*, 9(4): 35–44.

Traub, V. (1991) 'The Ambiguities of "Lesbian" Viewing Pleasure: The (Dis)articulations of *Black Widow*', in Epstein, J. and Straub, K. (eds), *Body Guards: The Cultural Politics of Gender Ambiguity*, New York: Routledge.

Trilling, D. (1963) 'The Death of Marilyn Monroe', *Claremont Essays*, New York: Harcourt, Brace Jovanovich.

Trilling, L. (1963) 'The Fate of Pleasure: Wordsworth to Dostoevsky', *Partisan Review*, 30: 167–91.

Trinh, T. M.-H. (1989) *Women, Native, Other*, Bloomington: Indiana University Press.

Truffaut, F. (1954) 'A Certain Tendency of the French Cinema', *Cahiers du Cinema*, No. 31.

Tudor, A. (1973) *Theories of Film*, London: Secker and Warburg.

—— (1986) 'Genre', in Grant, B. K. (ed.), *The Film Genre Reader*, Austin: University of Texas Press.

—— (1989) *Monsters and Mad Scientists: A Cultural History of the Horror Movie*, Oxford: Blackwell.

Tulloch, J. and Alvarado, M. (1983) *Doctor Who: The Unfolding Text*, London: Macmillan.

Turner, G. (1994) 'The End of the National Project? Australian Cinema in the 1990s', in Dissanayake, W. (ed.), *Colonialism and Nationalism in Asian Cinema*, Bloomington: Indiana University Press, pp. 202–16.

—— (1996) *British Cultural Studies: An Introduction*, 2nd edn, London: Routledge.

—— (1999) *Film as Social Practice*, 3rd edn, London: Routledge.

Turner, S. (1976) *Boys Will be Boys*, Harmondsworth: Penguin.

Twitchell, J. B. (1985) *Dreadful Pleasures: An Anatomy of Modern Horror*, New York and Oxford: Oxford University Press.

Ukadike, N. F. (1994) *Black African Cinema*, Berkeley and Los Angeles: University of California Press.

Us (1990) 'Tom Cruise and His Movie Machine', *Us*, 6 August, 25.

Vale, V., Juno, A. and Morton, J. (eds) (1986) *Incredibly Strange Films*, San Francisco: Research.

Van Biema, D. H. (1985) 'With a $100 Million Gross(out), Sly Stallone Fends off *Rambo*'s Army of Adversaries', *People*, 24(2): 34–8.

Vardac, A. N. (1968) *Stage to Screen: Theatrical Method from Garrick to Griffith*, New York: Benjamin Blom.

Variety (1980) 'Del Belso at WB', *Variety*, 27 February, 45.

—— (1983) '*Gone With the Wind* Again Tops All-Time List', *Variety*, 4 May, 15.

—— (1989) 'Top 100 All-Time Film Rental Champs', *Variety*, 11–17 January, 26.

—— (1990) 'Video and Theatrical Revenues', *Variety*, 24 September, 108.

—— (1991a) 'Week-by-Week Domestic B.O. Gross', *Variety*, 7 January, 10.

—— (1991b) 'The Teachings of Chairman Jeff', *Variety*, 4 February, 24.

—— (1991c) 'Chernin Yearning to Get Fox Some Hollywood Respect', *Variety*, 19 August, 21.

—— (1991d) 'Newest H'wood Invaders are Building, Not Buying', *Variety*, 21 October, 93.

Vasey, R. (1992) 'Foreign Parts: Hollywood's Global Distribution and the Representation of Ethnicity', *American Quarterly*, 44(4): 617–42.

Velvet Light Trap (1991) 'The 1980s: A Reference Guide to Motion Pictures, Television, VCR and Cable', *The Velvet Light Trap*, 27 (Spring), pp. 77–88.

Vianello, R. (1984) 'The Rise of the Telefilm and the Networks' Hegemony Over the Motion Picture Industry', *Quarterly Review of Film Studies* (Summer): 204–18.

Vineberg, S. (1991) *Method Actors: Three Generations of an American Acting Style*, New York: Schirmer.

Virilio, P. (1989) *War and Cinema: The Logistics of Perception*, London: Verso.

Vogel, H. (1989) 'Entertainment Industry', *Merrill Lynch*, 14 March.

Vološinov, V. N. (1983) *Marxism and the Philosophy of Language*, New York: Seminar Press.

Vorse, M. H. (1911) 'Some Picture Show Audiences', *The Outlook*, 98: 446.

Waldman, D. (1981) *Horror and Domesticity: The Modern Gothic Romance Film of the 1940s*, Ph.D. thesis, University of Wisconsin, Madison.

—— (1990) 'There's More to a Positive Image than Meets the Eye', in Erens, P. (ed.), *Issues in Feminist Film Criticism*, Bloomington: Indiana University Press, pp. 9–18.

Waldrop, J. (1991) 'The Baby Boom Turns 45', *American Demographics*, January, 22–7.

Walker, A. (1974) *Hollywood England: The British Film Industry in the Sixties*, London: Michael Joseph.

—— (1970) *Stardom: The Hollywood Phenomenon*, London: Michael Joseph.

Walker, J. B. and Walker, J. (1984) *The Light on Her Face*, Hollywood: ASC Press.

Walters, M. (1978) *The Nude Male*, New York and London: Paddington Press.

Warpole, K. (1983) *Dockers and Detectives. Popular Reading: Popular Writing*, London: New Left Books.

Watson, J. (1992) 'Sell-through Salvation', *Variety*, 16 November, 57.

Weatherford, J. (1991) *Native Roots: How the Indians Enriched America*, New York: Ballantine.

Weeks, J. (1981) *Sex, Politics and Society*, London and New York: Longman.

Weiner, R. (1994) 'AFMA Welcomes Non-Film Media', *Variety*, 356(4): 18.

Weinraub, B. (1994) 'New Line Cinema', *New York Times*, 5 June, F4.

Weiss, A. (1992) *Vampires and Violets: Lesbians in the Cinema*, London: Jonathan Cape.

Weldon, M. (1983) *the Psychotronic Encyclopedia of Film*, New York: Ballantine.

—— (1996) *The Psychotronic Encyclopedia of Video*, London: Titan.

Welter, B. (1966) 'The Cult of True Womanhood', *American Quarterly*, 18: 151–74.

Wertsch, J. V. (1985) *Vygotsky and the Social Formation of the Mind*, Cambridge, Mass.: Harvard University Press.

West, C. (1986) 'The Dilemma of a Black Intellectual', *Cultural Critique*, 1(1).

—— (1987) 'Race and Social Theory', in Davis, M., Marrable, M., Pfiel, F. and Sprinker, M. (eds), *The Year Left 2*, London: Verso.

—— (1988) 'Marxist Theory and the Specificity of Afro-American Oppression', in Nelson, C. and Grossberg, L. (eds), *Marxism and the Interpretation of Culture*, London: Macmillan, pp. 17–29.

—— (1992) 'Nihilism in Black America', in Dent, G. (ed.), *Black Popular Performance*, Princeton: Princeton University Press.

Wexman, V. W. (1993) *Creating the Couple, Love, Marriage and Hollywood Performance*, Princeton: Princeton University Press.

Wharton, E. (1920) *The Age of Innocence*, London: Virago.

White, D. (1984) *Australian Movies to the World*, Sydney: Fontana and Cinema Papers.

White, H. (1978) *Tropics of Discourse*, Baltimore: Johns Hopkins University Press.

White, P. (1991) 'Female Spectator, Lesbian Spector: *The Haunting*', in Fuss, D. (ed.), *Inside/Out: Lesbian Theories, Gay Theories*, London: Routledge, pp. 142–72.

Whitman, H. (1962) *The Sex Age*, Indianapolis: Bobbs Merrill.

Willemen, P. (1978) 'Notes on Subjectivity: On Reading Edward Branigan's "Subjectivity Under Siege"', *Screen*, 19(1): 41–69.

—— (1982) 'An Avant-Garde for the '80s', *Framework*, 24: 53–73.

—— (1987) 'The Third Cinema Question: Notes and Reflections', *Framework*, 34: 4–38.

—— (1994) 'The National', in *Looks and Friction: Essays in Cultural Studies and Film Theory*, London: British Film Institute/Indiana University Press, 206–19.

Williams, C. (1994) 'After the Classic, the Classical and Ideology: The Differences of Realism', *Screen*, 34: 275–92.

Williams, L. (1984) 'When the Woman Looks', in Doane, M. A., Mellencamp, P. and Williams, L. (eds), *Re-Vision: Essays in Feminist Film Criticism*, The American Film Institute Monograph Series, vol. 3, Frederick: University Publications of America, pp. 83–99.

—— (1989) *Hard Core: Power, Pleasure and the 'Frenzy of the Visible'*, Berkeley and Los Angeles: University of California Press.

Williams, M. (1994) 'Euros Bury Dinos, Fete "List" Auteur', *Variety*, 7–13 March, 55–6.

Williams, R. (1965) *The Long Revolution*, Harmondsworth: Penguin.

—— (1973) 'Base and Superstructure in Marxist Cultural Theory', *New Left Review*, 82: 3–16.

—— (1977) *Marxism and Literature*, New York and Oxford: Oxford University Press.

Williamson, J. (1986) 'Review of *The Passion of Remembrance*', *New Statesman*, 5 December.

—— (1986) 'Two or Three Things We Know About Ourselves', *Consuming Passions: The Dynamics of Popular Culture*, London: Calder and Boyars, 131–44.

Wilson, E. (1985) *Adorned in Dreams: Fashion and Modernity*, Berkeley and Los Angeles: University of California Press.

Wilson, G. M. (1986) *Narration in Light: Studies in Cinematic Point of View*, Baltimore: Johns Hopkins University Press.

Wilton, R. H. (ed.) (1957) *Elements of Color in Professional Motion Pictures*, New York: Society of Motion Picture and Television Engineers.

Winston, B. (1985) 'A Whole Technology of Dyeing: A Note on Ideology and the Apparatus of the Chromatic Moving Image', *Daedalus*, 114(4): 105–23.

Wolf, C. (1984) *Cassandra*, Van Heurch, J. (trans.) New York: Farrar, Straus and Giroux.

Wollen, P. (1976) *Signs and Meanings in the Cinema*, Bloomington: Indiana University Press.

—— (1982) 'Godard and Counter Cinema: *Vent d'Est*', *Readings and Writings*, London: Verso, 79–91.

Wollen, T. (1991) 'Over Our Shoulders: Nostalgic Screen Fictions for the 1980s', in Corner, J. and Harvey, S. (eds), *Enterprise and Heritage: Crosscurrents of National Culture*, London and New York: Routledge.

Wood, R. (1978) 'Return of the Repressed', *Film Comment*, 14: 25–32.

—— (ed.) (1979) *American Nightmare: Essays on the Horror Film*, Toronto: Festival of Festivals.

—— (1983) 'Beauty Bests the Beast', *American Film*, 8: 63–5.

Woolf, V. (1926) 'The Movies and Reality', *New Republic*, 47: 310.

Working Woman (1991) 'The Power of Women: Ten Women to Watch', *Working Woman*, November, 87, 92.

Wright, B. (1933) 'Shooting in the Tropics', *Cinema Quarterly*, 1(4): 227–8.

Wright, W. (1975) *Six Guns and Society: A Structural Study of the Western*, Berkeley: University of California Press.

Wyatt, J. (1994) *High Concept: Movies and Marketing in Hollywood*, Austin: University of Texas Press.

—— and Rutsky, R. L. (1988) 'High Concept: Abstracting the Postmodern', *Wide Angle*, 10(4).

Young, E. (1991) '*The Silence of the Lambs* and the Flaying of Feminist Theory', *Camera Obscura*, 27: 5–35.

Young, H. (1990) *One of Us*, London: Pan.

Zolotow, M. (1961) *Marilyn Monroe: An Uncensored Biography*, London: W. H. Allen.

Index

Pages containing illustrations are indicated by italics.

92 Legendary La Rose Noire (1992) 178–9
2001: A Space Odyssey (1968) 189, 367–8
Abrams, Mark 425
The Abyss (1989) 115, 118
acting, celebrity 232–4
action films 291–2, 295–310, 344–54
action heroines 291–2, 295–310
actors/actresses: digitally-created 75–6, 129–34; female image and colour 82, 86, 89–91; film/stage acting distinction 229, 232–3; *see also* stars
Adams, Philip 155
address 29, 30–4
The Adventures of Barry McKenzie 144
The Adventures of Priscilla: Queen of the Desert 146, 151, 159
advertising: blockbusters 201; costs 386; market research on 384; postmodernism 282, 283; television 201, 383–4, 386
Africa 368–9, 372, 373
The Age of Innocence 246–67, *259*, *261*
agency 5, 192–3, 200, 230, 231–2
Airport 189
Akomfrah, John 357
Alien (1979) 297, 306–7, 308, 472–3, 474
Aliens 297, 300, 306–7, 308, 309, 473
All for the Winner/Du Sheng (1990) 177
All the Wrong Clues (For the Right Solution) (1981) 175, 176
Allan, Elizabeth 438, 439
Allen, J. 424, 432
Allen, Robert 407
All's Well, End's Well/Jia You Xi Shi (1992) 177
Alonzo, John 101
Altenloh, Emilie 413
Althusser, Louis 60–2
Altman, Rick 470–1
Altman, Robert 188
American Graffiti (1973) 109, 190
An American in Paris 244–5
An Amorous Woman of the Tang Dynasty 180
Anderson, Benedict 367–8
Andrew, Dudley 47–8, 120
Ang, Ien 64, 66, 478
An Angel at My Table 247
Angel Heart 361

Angelou, Maya 426–7
anthropology, colonialism 370–1
antitrust practices 186, 208
apparatus theory 28–45
applause, in cinemas 242
Argento, Dario 474
Arnheim, Rudolf 120
Around the World in 80 Days (1956) 187, 370, 376
art, colour 86–7, 88–9
art cinema 2–3; Britain 167, 171; genres 472; national cinemas 140, 143, 153–5; partnerships 211–12; US 1970s 192, 193; youth market 188
artifacts, genericity 286
Asia, colonialism 372
Astaire, Fred 130, 241, 242, 243, 244
attention, spectators 50, 51
Attille, Martina 357
Audience Research, Inc. 441
audiences 10, 379–81; British cinema 168–70; celebrity 234–7; *The Color Purple* 444–67; early silent films 390–414; genres 469–1; market research 382–8; musicals 220; in musicals 241–5; readings 11–13, 14–19; reception studies 13; spectator distinction 12, 22, 23–4; women 12, 24, 380–1, 406–14; *see also* social audience
Austin, Bruce 382
Australia 136, 139–64, 171
auteurs 3, 152–5
authenticity 287–90, 312, 372, 475–9
avant-garde 2–3

Baartman, Saartjie 372
Back to the Future III (1990) 276, 278, 280–1, 286
backlighting 97, 105
Bailey, Cameron 361
Bakhtin, Mikhail 368
Balcon, Michael 373, 374
Balio, Tino 137–8, 189, 206–15
Ballhaus, Michael 256
The Band Wagon 240, 243
Barish, Keith 383
The Barkleys of Broadway 242
Barnes, Julian 281
Barr, Charles 171

Barrett, Franklyn 160
Barrie, J. M. 288–9
Barry, Iris 413
Bart, Peter 211
Barthes, Roland 66, 118, 134, 268–71
Barton, Sabrina 292, 311–26
baseball movies 289–90
Basic Instinct (1992) 211, 296, 300–1, 305–6, 477
Bass, Saul and Elaine 256
Batman (1989) 197–9, 201, 207, 278, 284, 386
Batman Returns (1992) 113, 383
Baudrillard, Jean 271, 272, 274
Baudry, Jean-Louis 54, 120
Bazin, André 2, 3, 47, 118, 283
Beau Geste (1930) 373
beauty; actors 233; cyberstars 133; escapism 428–9; race
    223–4, 426–7; tans 236; women and colour film 90
Beauty and the Beast (1991) 344
Beetham, Margaret 247
Bellamy, Madge 411
Bellour, Raymond 39–40
Beloved 445
Ben-Hur (1959) 187
Benjamin, W. 403, 404
Bennett, Colin 145
Bennett, Tony 8, 11–12, 14–19
Berenstein, Rhona 318, 477
Beresford, Bruce 157, 162
Bergstrom, Janet 55–6
Berman, Marshal 290
Bernhardt, Sarah 145, 229
Bernstein, Elmer 256
The Best Years of Our Lives (1946) 186
Bhabha, Homi 360, 361
Bigelow, Kathryn 306, 472
Billy Jack (1971) 193
Biograph Studios 230
The Birth of a Nation (1915) 1, 223, 224, 360, 444
Blaché, Alice Guy 410
The Black Pirate (1927) 80, 85, 86
The Black Robe (1992) 148, 162
The Black Rose/Hei Meigui (1965) 178
Blackton, J. Stuart 373
Blackwood, Maureen 356
Blade Runner (1982) 278
Blanche Fury 264
Blazing Saddles (1974) 277
Blockbuster Entertainment 213, 215
blockbusters 188, 194–200; globalization 203; market
    research 379–80, 382–8; multimedia 201–2; New
    Hollywood 184–5, 186; postwar Hollywood 187–8;
    'ultra-high-budget' films 207
Blood Oath (1990) 156
Blood and Sand (1941) 86–7
Bloom, Allen 282
The Blue Bird (1976) 101
Blue Steel 306
Blue Velvet (1986) 221, 278, 286
Bobo, Jacqueline 6, 379, 381, 426, 444–67
Bodison, Wolfgang 104–5
body: male 344–54; muscular women 292, 300, 301–10;
    rites-of-passage narrative 299
bodybuilding 301–5
Bogle, Donald 447
Bond, James 11, 14–19
Bonnie and Clyde (1967) 189, 278
Bordwell, David 5, 6–7, 56–9, 154, 167

boundary situations 154
Bourdieu, Pierre 433
Bourke, Terry 150
Bow, Clara 225, 411
Box, K. 425
box-office receipts 184, 196–7, 421–3, 427–8
Boyz N the Hood (1991) 344, 350
Brand, C. 265–6
Brando, Marlon 190, 234
Braybon, G. 438–9
Breaker Morant 144, 153, 157
The Bridge on the River Kwai (1957) 187
Bristow, Joseph 367
British cinema 136, 165–72
British cultural studies 59–67
British Film Institute 356
Broadway Melody of 1940 (1940) 243
Broken Melody (1938) 162
The Brood 270, 273
Brook, Clive 373–4
Brown, David 191
Brown, Gillian 350
Brown, Tony 444–5, 447
Browning, H. E. 169–70
Brownmiller, Susan 225
'Bruce aesthetic' 192
Brunsdon, Charlotte 24, 25–6, 62–3, 479
Bruzzi, Stella 220–1, 246–67
BSkyB 214
buddy movies 42, 334
Bullet in the Head (1989) 175
Burch, Noël 395
burlesque, Westerns 277
Burns, Elizabeth 233
Burton, Tim 284
Bus Stop 224, 225–6
Buscombe, Edward 73–4, 77–83, 85–6, 87
Bush, W. Stephen 394–5
Buster (1988) 167
Butch Cassidy and the Sundance Kid (1969) 188, 189
Butler, Alison 143, 150–1
Butler, Judith 292, 305, 312, 317
Byrne, Pat 119, 120

C. Itoh 210
CAA *see* Creative Artists Associates
Cabin in the Sky 224
cable television 193, 196, 212–13, 215
Cahiers du Cinema 3
Calamity Jane 421, *422*
Calinescu, Matei 270
camera techniques 95–6, 242–3, 245
Cameron, James 118, 119, 345–6, 353
Cameron-Wilson, James 145
Campion, Jane 147, 160, 161, 248, 263, 266
Canada 142, 162
Cannibal Tours (1988) 159
Cape Fear 203
capitalism 78–9, 236, 268, 270–1
Carbine, Mary 397
Careful He Might Hear You (1983) 142
Carey, James 60
Carolco Pictures 207, 211
Carpenter, John 477
Carrie 272
Carroll, Noël 5, 7, 120
Carter, Nick 229

Castaldi, Peter 146–7
casting tests 384, 385
Castle Rock Entertainment 211, 212
castration scenario 35, 37
Catchings, Waddill 78
catharsis 282, 283
Cathy Come Home 170
Caughie, John 170, 171
Cavell, Stanley 118
Cawelti, John 277–8
celebrity 76, 219–20, 228–37
censorship: colonialism 372; desire 264; Hong Kong cinema 175; imperialism 374; sound 113
centre and margin 355–63
Centre for Contemporary Cultural Studies, University of Birmingham 60, 62–4
C'est la Vie, Mon Cherie/Xin Bu Liao Qing (1993) 181, 182
CGI *see* computer-generated imagery
Chamberlain, Richard 145
Chambers, Marilyn 272
Chan, Gordon 181–2
Chan, Peter 182
Channel 4 171–2, 356
The Chant of Jimmie Blacksmith 149, 150, 153, 156
Chaplin, Charlie 230
Charge of the Light Brigade (1938) 375
Chariots of Fire (1981) 165–6
Chauvel, Charles 156
Chiau Sing-chi, Stephen 176–8
China 136–7, 175–6, 178, 180, 182–3
China O'Brien 298, 306
Chodorow, Nancy 33, 436
Chor Yuen 178
Christian, Barbara 447
Christianity 224
chronotopes 368
cinemas: architecture 432–5; escapsim 431–5; experience of 392–7; *Jaws* 192; sound reproduction 75, 108–11, 113; *see also* multiplexes; nickelodeon
Cinemascope, genres 278
cinematography 95–105
class: action films 295–6; British audiences 168–9, 425–6; cultural studies 60, 62, 63–4; feminist criticism 298; imperialism 366; race 362; spectatorship of early films 391, 393–4, 397–8, 399, 407–9; stars 235–6
classical film philosophy 47–52
Cleopatra (1963) 187
Cliffhanger (1994) 115
closure, horror films 271–2
The Club (1976) 143
co-production deals 162, 210
Coburn, James 145
The Coca-Cola Kid (1985) 145
codes, spectators 53–4
cognitivism 5, 28, 53, 56–9, 67, 75
Cohan, Steve 7
Cohen, Arthur 387
Cohen, Lizabeth 397, 405
Cole, Michael 59
Collins, Ava Preacher 285
Collins, Diane 141
Collins, Jim 220, 221, 276–90
collision detection 118–19
colonialism 294, 299, 355, 366–76; ethnicity and sexuality 295–6; race 361
The Color Purple (1985) 43, 101, 355, 381, 444–67

colour 2, 73–4, 80–3, 85–93, 98–9
Columbia Pictures Entertainment (CPE) 199–200, 208, 209–10, 211
computer-generated imagery (CGI) 73, 75, 115–26
concept testing 384, 385
conglomerates 199–200, 206, 208–10, 212–13, 383, 385–6
Connery, Sean 103–4, *103*
constitutivism 56–9
consumerism 379–81; escapism 432; female spectators 407–8, 410–13, 424, 433; spectatorship of early films 398, 405–6, 407–8, 410–13; stars 236
context, spectatorship 14–19, 22–3, 25–7, 46
The Conversation (1974) 109
Cook, Pam 21, 22, 24, 26
Cool World (1992) 385
Cooper, Gary 375
Coppola, Francis Ford 190, 192
The Corbett–Fitzsimmons Fight 392, 409–10
Cornwell-Clyne, Major 88
correspondence-based model of representation 120–6
Corrigan, Philip 423
Costner, Kevin 231
costs: high concept films 386; innovation 77, 79; production 1980s 197; stars' salaries 200–1; 'ultra-high-budget' films 207
costume film 220–1, 246–67, 446
Country Life (1994) 144
Cowie, Elizabeth 36–7
Cox, Mrs H. 436
Cox, Paul 153–4
Craven, Ian 470–1
Craven, Wes 475
Crawford, Joan *434*
Creative Artists Associates (CAA) 193, 200, 201
Creed, Barbara 37, 75–6, 129–34, 306
critics, genres 221
Crocodile Dundee 142, 147, 151, 157
Crofts, Stephen 166, 167
Cronenberg, David 270–1, 272, 273–4
The Crow (1994) 130, 212
Cruise, Tom 104–5, 131
Cry in the Dark see Evil Angels
Cubitt, Sean 134
Culler, Jonathan 53
cultural identity 6, 166
cultural literacy 281
cultural studies: audiences 379; gender identity 292; history of film studies 7; race 360; reception studies 53, 59–67; spectatorship 31
culture: horror films 270–1, 272; national cinemas 135, 143, 156–60; reading formations 14–19; spectatorship 25–6
Curtis, Jamie Lee 145, 303, 304, 306
Cuvier, George 372
Cvetkovich, Ann 285
cyberpunk 181
cyberstars 75–6, 129–34
cycles, horror films 477

Dahl, Arlene 91
Dallas 64, 478
Dallas Doll (1993) 145
dance 40–2
Dances With Wolves (1990) 222, 276, 278, 287–8
The Dark Side 474
Darwin, Charles 262
Daviau, Allen 101
David Livingstone (1936) 373

Dawn of the Dead 270–1, 272
Day, Doris 421, *422*
Day Lewis, Daniel *259, 261*
Days of Being Wild 175, 180
Days of Thunder (1990) 386
de Beauvoir, Simone 251
de Clercq, Louis 370
De Maré, Eric 100
de Lauretis, Teresa 37
de Palma, Brian 272
Dead Calm 148
Dean, James 234
Death of a Soldier (1986) 145
DeCordova, Richard 228
Del Belso, Richard 383
The Delinquents (1989) 145
DeMille, Cecil B. 411
Demme, Jonathan 203
demographics 379, 383, 384, 387, 425
demythologization, Westerns 277, 287–8
Denny, Reginald 373
depth, perception of 50
Dermody, Susan 150, 160
DeScenna, Linda 446
descriptionism 56–9
desire: celebrity 234–7; censorship 264; costume film
      246–67; fantasy 34–8; female 412; lesbian 292–3,
      331–41; Monroe 223–7; negotiation 41; pleasure 66;
      race 361; spectatorship 28–9
Deutchman, Ira 387
Diary of a Chambermaid 251
Diawara, Manthia 361–2
Dick Tracy (1990) 198, 199, 386
Dickerson, Ernest 102
Die Hard (1988) 345
Die Hard 2 (1990) 386
Dietrich, Marlene 225
diffusion of innovation theory 77–80
Digital Domain 119, 122
digital imaging 73, 75, 115–26, 129–34
digital sound 75, 110, 113
Dillon, Matt 145
Dimension Pictures 212
directors 192–3, 203
Dirty Harry (1971) 281
disaster movies 189
Disney 196, 198, 210, 211–12, 213
dissonance 276
distribution 141, 208–9, 383–4, 395–6
diversification 199, 208–10
Doane, Mary Ann 55–6, 110, 320, 333, 338, 341, 411, 413
The Doctor (1991) 344
Dr Dolittle (1967) 188
Doctor Zhivago (1965) 187, 188
documentary 159
Dolby Stereo Sound System 75, 108, 109–11, 112–13, 195
Dominick, Joseph 189
Dongcheng Xijiu (1993) 178, 179
Don's Party 143, 153
Don't Bother to Knock (1952) 225
Douglas, Ann 273
Douglas, Michael 301
Draper, Joan 431
Dreyer, Carl, colour 87
drive-in theatres 188
Drums (1938) 373, 375
Du Camp, Maxine 370

Duel in the Sun (1946) 21, 186, 264
Durgnat, Raymond 171
Dyer, Richard 7, 8, 223–7; cinema lighting 74; Monroe 219;
      musicals 41; race 359, 360, 362; utopian sensibility
      429–31, 433, 435, 437; whiteness 95–105

Eastwood, Clint 344
Easy Rider (1969) 189
eclecticism 276–90
Eco, Umberto 17, 18–19, 279
economics: diffusion of innovation 77–83, 85; new 137–8;
      sound 112–13
Edison, Thomas Alva 373
editing 1–2, 242–3
Egypt 374–5
Eisenstein, Sergei 1, 48–50, 51–2, 89, 120, 233
Elements of Color in Professional Motion Pictures (1957) 81, 85–6
Elfick, David 156
Elliott, Stephen 151
Ellsworth, Elizabeth 52–3
Ellul, Jacques 268
Elsaesser, T. 7, 140, 142–3, 150–1, 153, 156, 158, 159–60,
      163
England 165–6
The Englishwoman's Domestic Magazine 247, 253
Enker, Debi 153
Entre Nous 293, 331, 334–41, *337, 339*
eroticism 247, 247–8, 250–1, 333–6
Escape to Burma (1955) 373
escapism 380–1, 420–43
ET (1982) 197–8, 289
ethnicity 293–4, 355–63; Australian cinema 163; British
      audiences 426–7; cultural studies 64; desirability of
      women 223–4; lighting 74, 95–105; public and private
      spheres 407; spectatorship 381, 391, 393–4, 395,
      397–406
ethnography 6, 371–2, 379
Europe: avant-garde 2–3; globalization of Hollywood 207–8;
      imperialism 366–76; international partnerships 210;
      market for Hollywood 196; national cinemas 153
European Community 162
Evil Angels (aka *Cry in the Dark*) 145, 156
The Evil Dead (1980) 272
Ewen, Elizabeth 391, 404, 426
exhibition: diversification in 1980s 208; escapism 431–3;
      national cinema 141; spectatorship of early films 392–7;
      US 1970s 192; *see also* cinemas
The Exorcist (1973) 190, 193, 476
exploitation films 188, 270–4
Eyes Wide Shut (1999) 129, 131

Fabrikant, Geraldine 201
Factor, Max 90, 97–8
Fairbanks, Douglas 80, 81, 85, 230
Falklands/Malvinas 165
Fame 40–1
fan clubs 235
Fangoria 474
Fanon, Frantz 295–6
fans: Britain 425, 441, 442; celebrity 235; horror 471–9
fantasy 34–8; colour 82–3, 85, 86; costume films 247;
      immigrants to US and spectatorship 405; performativity
      318; spectatorship 30; time travel 346
Farewell Again (1937) 374
Farrar, Geraldine 97
Farrell, Joseph 385
Fatal Attraction 476

Fatal Beauty 306, 307
fathering, masculinity 348–50, 351–2, 354
FCC *see* Federal Communications Commission
Fear 473–5
Federal Communications Commission (FCC) 209, 213
Felix, Petal 426
female bonding 336–40
female gaze 266, 311, 412–14
femininity 24; action heroines 291–2, 295, 296, 306;
    bodybuilding 301–5; cinema design 433–5; costume
    250–1; dance 41–2; early films 410–11; fantasy 37;
    masquerade of 333, 337; object relations theory 436–7;
    performativity 312; public and private spheres 406–8;
    woman's psychothriller 311–12
feminism: action heroines 295, 297–301; bodybuilding
    204–5, 303; costume film 246; gender identity 311–12;
    gendered spectatorship 20–7; history 4–5, 6, 7; horror
    films 273–4; identity 291, 293; linguistic theory and
    reception studies 55–6; Monroe 227; *The Piano* 263;
    Picnic at Hanging Rock 254; race 361; reception studies
    52–3; romance novels 31–4; sexuality 331–3; violence
    309–10; woman's psychothriller 311–26; women's
    genres 20–7
femme fatale 301, 305–6, 308
festival cinemas 136, 147, 150, 151–5
fetishism: colonialism 372; costume films 246, 247–57; New
    Sincerity 288–9; race 361; spectatorship of early films
    411–12
Feuer, Jane 220, 240–5
A Few Good Men 104–5
Field of Dreams (1989) 222, 278, 287, 288, 289–90, 344
Fight Back to School/Tao Xue Wei Long (1992) 177–8
Fighting Blood (1911) 373
figure in a landscape 298
film festivals 136, 147, 150, 151–5
film journals, Britain 425
film noir, femme fatale 300
film philosophy, spectators 47–52
Film Reader 77
film stocks 95–8
film studies, history 2–7
Final Justice/Pili Xianfent (1988) 177
finance 148, 155–6, 160, 232
Fine line Features 212
First Blood (1982) 344, 345, 353
Fiske, John 40, 66
A Fistful of Dollars (1966) 281
Five Easy Pieces (1970) 278
Flashdance 31, 40
Fleming, Ian 17–19
Flügel, J. C. 250–1, 260, 262, 263, 264, 266
The Fly (1986) 142
The Fog (1979) 477
folk culture 289–90
Fong, Eddie 180
Foolish Wives 65
For Me and My Gal 244
Ford, Harrison 344
Ford, John 276
formalism 2, 47–8, 75, 116, 120–1, 125
Forrest Gump (1994) 115–16, *116*, 119, 122, *122*, 124, 215
Foster, Hal 269, 274
Foster, Jodie 313–18, *314*, *317*
Foucault, Michel 249, 264, 266, 401–3
The Four Feathers (1939) 373, 375
Four Men and a Prayer (1938) 375
Four Weddings and a Funeral (1994) 142, 151, 170

Fournel, Victor 100
Fox 187, 188, 199–200
Fox, Michael J. 344
France 373, 374–5
franchises 193, 195, 196, 198, 199
Francis, Bev 305
Frankfurt School 2, 268–70
freak shows 372
Freud, S.: cultural studies 61–2; fantasy 34–5; fetishism
    249–50, 260, 266; race 361; spectators 55
Friday the Thirteenth (1980) 272
Fried Green Tomatoes at the Whistle Stop Café (1991) 210
Fritsche, Kurt 100
Fury at Furnace Creek (1940) 375
Fusco, Coco 358–9

Gaedeke, Ralph 387
Gaines, Jane 360, 361
Gainsborough Studios 21, 22, 246, 247
Gallagher, Catherine 44
Gallipoli (1981) 144, 148, 156, 157
Gallup, George 441
Gamman, L. 266–7
Gandhi 355
Garbo, Greta 225, 229
Garland, Judy 240, 244
Gaslight (1944) 320
gaze: between same-sex characters 333–6, 338, 341;
    colonialism 369, 370; lesbian spectators 332–3;
    spectatorship of early films 411–14; *see also* female gaze;
    male gaze
gender: action heroines 291–2, 295–310; costume film
    246–67; Hong Kong cinema 180; horror 475–6; identity
    311–26; lesbian heroines 292–3; object relations theory
    436–7; performativity 292, 311–26; public and private
    spheres 406–14; rearticulation 285–6; spectatorship
    21–7, 28, 406–14; subject and address 35–6; *see also*
    feminism; women
genres 276–90; audiences 381; blockbusters 202; concept
    testing 384; horror 471–9; identification 469–71;
    pleasures and meanings 220–1; reading formations 18;
    sound 113; women 20–7
Gentlemen Prefer Blondes 225
Germany 163
Geronimo (1940) 375
Getting Physical (1984) 303–4
The Getting of Wisdom (1977) 143
Ghost (1990) 197–8
Ghostbusters II (1989) 197
GI Jane (1997) 292
Gibson, Ross 132, 158
Gigi (1958) 109
Gilroy, Paul 357
Givanni, June 356
glamour 90–1, 426–7, 433–4, 439–40
Gledhill, Christine 44–5
globalization 203, 206–15
The Godfather (1972) 189–90, 194–5
Gold Diggers of 1935 (1935) 241
Goldberg, Whoopi 445
Golden Braid (1990) 251
Goldfinger (1964) 17–18, 187
Goldman, William 198
Goldstein, Jenette 307
Goldwyn, Samuel 186, 375
Gomery, J. Douglas 77–8, 79–80, 169
Gone with the Wind (1930) 184, 444

The Good Woman of Bangkok (1992) 159
Goodfellas (1990) 111
Gordon, Linda 29
gossip 236–7
government funding 144, 146, 155–6, 157, 160, 162, 163
Grable, Betty 91
The Graduate (1967) 189, 278
grand theory 5–7
Grant, Barry Keith 472
Graves, Robert 223
The Greaser's Revenge (1914) 373
The Great Barrier (1936) 373
Great Britain: Australian cinema 144–5, 148, 161–2; colonialism 373–4; ethnicity 293–4, 355–63; Hollywood cinema 1940s and 1950s 420–43; imperialism 375; national cinema 141, 142, 151, 165–72; women 380–1
Green Card (1991) 148, 158, 160
Green, Guy 87
The Green Pastures 444
Greenaway, Peter 167
Greenblatt, Stephen 43
Gregory, Carl Louis 96–7
Gregory's Girl (1980) 165–6
Greiner, Donald 353
Griffith, D. W. 1, 230, 233, 412
Griffiths, Melanie 311–13
Griggers, Cathy 285
Gross Misconduct (1993) 145
Guber, Peter 200, 210
Gulas, Ivan 130
Gulf & Western 208, 209
The Gulf Between 86
Gunga Din (1939) 375
Gunning, Tom 394
Gutman, Herbert 398, 399

Hage, Ghassan 158
Haggard, Rider 223
Halberstam, Judith 316
Hall, Conrad 101
Hall, Ken G. 150, 156, 162
Hall, Stuart 38–9, 63, 65, 358, 359, 448
Haller, Ernest 91
Halloween 272, 273
Hamilton, Linda 112, 299–300, 303, 348
Hampton, Benjamin Bowles 228
Hancock, W. K. 162
Handel, Leo 424
Handley, Charles 96
Handsworth Songs 355, 358
Hansen, Miriam 5, 132, 379, 380, 390–414
Hanson, Eugene 100
Hardwicke, Cedric 373
Hare, David 170
Hark, Ira Mae 7
Harlin, Renny 473
Harlow, Jean 225
harmony, genres 276, 287–8
Harper, Sue 246, 247
Hathaway, Henry 375
The Hazards of Helen (1914) 410
HBO *see* Home Box Office (HBO)
Heath, Stephen 271
Heavenly Creatures (1995) 161
Hebdige, Dick 63
Hedgecoe, John 99
Hedren, Tippi 312–13

hegemony 62, 63–5, 294, 359, 360, 368–9
heightened realism 112
Heimat (1984) 164
Hellmann, Dawn 436
heritage films 167–8, 246
Herrick, Robert 261–2
He's a Woman, She's a Man / Jin Zhi Yu Ye (1994) 182
Heston, Charlton 375
heterotopias 401–2
Heyer, John 156
Hidden Pictures (1995) 163
high art, pleasure 269–70
high concept 201, 207, 379–80, 382–8
Higson, Andrew 140–1, 171, 246
Hill, John 136, 165–72
Hirsch, E. Jr 18
Hirsch, Paul 60
historical materialism 53
history: costume films 246, 247; national identity 367–8
Hitchcock, Alfred 225
Hoberman, J. 195
Hoffa (1992) 210
Hoffman, Dustin 201
Hollywood: antitrust practices 186; British cinema 165, 166–7; films in Britain 1940s–1950s 420–43; genres 472; globalization 137–8, 206–15; history of film studies 3; Hong Kong cinema 182; masculinity 344–54; national cinemas 139–43, 152–3; national film industries 135; New Hollywood 137, 184–203; postwar 184–203
The Hollywood Reporter 86, 425
Holmlund, Christine 304, 305
Holub, Robert 15
Home Alone (1990) 197–8
Home Box Office (HBO) 193, 212–13
Homes, Cecil 160
homosexuality: cultural studies 64–5; hypothetical lesbian heroines 331–41; negotiation 42; representation 357–8; *Silence of the Lambs* 315–16, 326; *see also* lesbianism
Honey, I Shrunk the Kids (1989) 207
Hong Kingston, Maxine 296
Hong Kong 136–7, 174–83, 374
Hook (1991) 199, 201, 222, 278, 287, 288–9
Hopkins, Anthony 144–5
horizontal integration 208–9
Horne, Lena 224
horror films 190, 221, 268–74, 317–18, 381, 469–79; *see also* slasher films
Hovland, Carl 60
How to Marry a Millionaire (1953) 225
Howards End (1992) 247
Howe, Irving 399
Howlett, Robert 370
Hunter, Holly 265
Huston, John 89
Hutchings, P. 470
Hutcheon, Linda 174
hybrid genre films 278
hyperconscious eclecticism 280–6
hyperconsciousness 221

I Have a Date with Spring / Wo He Chun Tian You Ge Yue Hui (1994) 181, 182
ICM 193
ideal readers 32–4, 44, 63–4
idealism, theory of representation 283

identity: British audiences 1940s–1950s 426–7; celebrity 232, 234, 235; cultural studies 64; ethnicity 355–63; gender 311–26; history of film studies 6; Hong Kong cinema 175; immigrants 400; national 155–60, 367–9; national cinemas 136, 170–2; spectatorship 28
ideological state apparatuses (ISAs) 61, 62, 63
ideology: colour 83; cultural studies 60–1, 62, 63; innovation 73–4, 80; mass culture 268–9; reception studies 59–60
ideology of self-extension 350
The Illustrated Auschwitz (1992) 162
imagination, spectators 50, 51
Imagine Entertainment 211
immigrants, spectatorship of early films 397–406, 408–9
imperialism 294, 295–6, 299, 361, 366–76
In the Heat of the Night (1967) 102–3
Independent Motion Picture Company (Imp) 230
independent production 186, 202–3, 211–12, 472
India 140
Indiana Jones and the Last Crusade (1989) 197, 207, 373
Indiana Jones and the Temple of Doom (1984) 112, 299, 373
individualism, masculinity 350–3
Industrial Light and Magic 123, 130
industrialization 398–9, 404
industries 135–8; Australia 139–64; Britain 165–72; Hong Kong 174–83
information, modes of 284–5
innovation 73–4, 77–83, 85
institutional matrix 34
International Creative Management (ICM) 191
international partnerships 210
interpellation 61, 62, 362
intertextuality 14–19, 179, 201–2, 280–6, 391–2
Intolerance (1916) 367–8, 412
irony 221–2, 276–90
It's Always Fair Weather 244

Jacka, Elizabeth 150, 160
Jackson, Peter 161
James, David E. 5–6
James, Vera 161
Jameson, Fredric 132, 274
Jancovich, Mark 381, 469–79
Jarman, Derek 167
Jarmusch, Jim 285
Jassy 247, 264
Jaws (1975) 109, 185, 190–6, 383
Jeffords, Susan 293, 344–54
Jenkins, Eileen 443
Jennings, Peter 376
Jewish cinema, Australia 162
Johnson, Jean 428, 435
Johnson, Martin and Osa 371
Jones, Barry 155
Jones, Deborah 158
Jordan, Michael H. 213
jouissance 269, 271
Joy, Jason 374
Julien, Isaac 293–4, 355–63
The Jungle Book (1942) 375
Jurassic Park (1993) 116, *117*, 118–19, 121–2, 123, 474
Justice, My Foot / Shensi Guan 178

Kael, Pauline 150
Kalmus, Natalie 88–9, 91, 92–3
Kant, Immanuel 273
Kaplan, Louise J. 248

Kashyap, Parminder Dhillon 358
Katz, Elihu 64
Katzenberg, Jeffrey 198, 386–7
Keach, Stacy 145
Keaton, Michael 311
Keitel, Harvey 103–4, *103*
Kelly, Gene 244–5
Kelly, June 435
Kennedy, President J. F. 119, 124
Kerr, Deborah 145
Khartoum (1966) 375
Khornah, Lucille 99
Khouri, Callie 285
Kidman, Nicole 131
Killers of Kilimanjaro (1959) 374
Kindem, Gorham 98
Kinemacolor 86
King, Barry 234
King Kong (1933) 223, 362–3, 371
King Solomon's Mines (1937) 373
King Solomon's Mines (1985) 373
Kinney 199
Kipling, Rudyard 366, 375
Kitses, Jim 277
Kleiser-Walczak Construction Company 130
Klinger, Barbara 8
Kluge, Alexander 390, 391, 402
Ko, Clifton 181
Kodak 98, 99
Korda brothers 373, 374, 375
Kordel, Lelord 223
Koszarski, Richard 396
Kotcheff, Ted 148–9
Kracauer, Siegfried 118, 403, 405
Krafft-Ebing 249, 266
Kristeva, Julia 92–3, 271
Kubrick, Stanley 129, 131
Kuhn, Annette 4–5, 8–9, 12, 20–7, 46
Kuleshov experiment 1, 131
kung fu films 174–5
Kuntzel, Thierry 272–3
Kunzle, David 253, 254, 266
Kwan, Stanley 175

La Dolce Vita (1960) 188
La Place, Maria 299, 424
Lacan, Jacques 55, 61, 62, 317, 318
Ladybird, Ladybird 170
Lambert, Ann *255*
Lange, Jessica 223
language: cognitive psychology 56; Hong Kong cinema 182–3; montage 49; national cinemas 143; reception studies 54–6
langue 54
Laplanche, Jean 35–6, 37
Lassell, Harold 60
The Last of the Mohicans (1920) 373
The Last Wave 145, 149, 150, 154
Laughlin, Tom 193
Laver, James 248–9, 251, 264
Lawrence, Florence 230
Lawrence of Arabia (1962) 187
Lazersfelf, Paul 60
Le Musulman Rigolo (1902) 373
Le Voyage dans la Lune (A Trip to the Moon, 1902) 373
Leammle, Carl 230
Lears, Jackson 412

lecturers 394–5
Lee, Ang 247
Lee, Brandon 130
Leigh, Mike 167
leisure, stars 230–1, 236
Lemmons, Kasi *317*
lesbianism: *Basic Instinct* 301; *The Color Purple* 457–60; female
    bodybuilding 305; hypothetical lesbian heroines 331–40;
    lesbian heroines 292–3; *Personal Best* 52–3
Lethal Weapon (1987) 345
Lethal Weapon 2 (1989) 207, 345
Lévi-Strauss, Claude 277
Levin, Gerald 214
Levin, Robert 196
Levine, Lawrence 393
Lewin, Kurt 60
Lewis, Joyce 436
Liebes, Tamar 64
The Life of Moses (1909–10) 406
Light, Alison 247
lighting 74, 95–105, 119, 122, 446
Like Water for Chocolate (1993) 212
Lincoln, Freeman 187
Lindsay, Norman 143
Lindsay, Vachel 1
linguistics 53–6, 67
Little Big Man (1970) 277, 278
Lives of a Bengal Lancer (1934) 375
Loach, Ken 167, 170
Loew, Marcus 395
Logsdon, Jeff 384
Lomardo, Dana 383
The Long and Winding Road/Jinxiu Qiancheng (1994)
    181–2
The Longest Day 187
Look Who's Talking 350
Lorelle, Lucien 99
The Lost World 474
love at first sight 332, 337
Love Story 189
Lovell, Alan 167
Low, Rachel 431
Lubin, Ernst 373
Lucas, George 109, 190, 192–3, 195–6, 203
Lucas, Kathleen 428, 429, 431, 433
Lumière brothers 372–3, 375
Luria, A. R. 49
Lynne, Michael 212
Lyons, Lisa 302, 303
Lyotard, Jean-François 270, 273

McCabe, Colin 120
McClure, John 367
MacDonald, Dwight 241–2
MacDonald, Jeanette 241
Mack, Kevin 119, 122, 123, 124
McQuire, Scott 132, 133
McRobbie, Angela 31, 40–2, 44
Mad Max (1979) 142, 146, 147, 153
Mad Max 2 (*The Road Warrior*) 142, 147, 148, 278
Mad Max beyond Thunderdome (1985) 142
made-for-TV movies 189
The Madness of King George (1995) 167
Madsen, Axel 192
magazines, Britain 425, 441
Maggenti, Maria 315
Mahogany 361

Mailer, Norman 224
Makavejev, Dusan 139
make-up 90, 96–8
Makinen, M. 266–7
Malcolm X (1992) 210
male body 344–54
male gaze 4, 9, 332; history of film studies 6; identity 291;
    negotiation 41; *Picnic at Hanging Rock* 252, 254; woman's
    psychothriller 311
Malkiewicz, Kris 101
Maltby, Richard 65, 470–1
Maltin, Leonard 270
Mamoulian, Rouben 86–7
The Man from Snowy River 148, 157
Mann, Karen 346
Mansfield, Edwin 77–8
A Maori Maid's Love (1916) 161
Map of the Human Heart (1993) 158, 161
Mapplethorpe, Robert 302
Maranda, Pierre 54–5
March, Kathleen 438
margin and centre 355–63
Margulies, Michael D. 101
market research 379–80, 382–8, 425, 441
marketing: 1980s 197; audiences 379; blockbusters 198–9,
    201–2; costs 386; franchises 137; horror 477; *Jaws* 191,
    192; sound 112–13; on television 193
markets, innovation 78–9
Marloe, Conrad 374
Marnie 311, 312
Marshall, P. David 9, 219–20, 228–37
martial arts 174–5
Marx, Karl 268
Marxism 42–3, 60–7, 78
masculinity 24, 296, 344–54; action heroines 292, 295,
    301–10; clothes 258–60, 263–4; fantasy 37; female gaze
    266; history of film studies 7; identity 293; imperialism
    294, 367; performativity 312, 318–21, 323–5; racial
    stereotypes 224
MASH (1970) 188
The Mask 125
masquerade of femininity 333, 338
materialism, reception studies 53–67
Matsushita Electric Industrial Company 193–4, 199–200,
    210, 214
Mayne, Judith 6, 7, 8, 12–13, 28–45, 326, 426
MCA/Universal 188, 199–200, 208, 210, 214
meaning 11–13, 92–3, 219–22, 270
mediation, negotiation 42
Medium Cool (1970) 278
Meehan, Eileen 185, 201
Meet Me in St Louis 240
Méliès, George 373
melodrama 20–7, 256, 410
memory 50, 51, 403–4
Mercer, Kobena 293–4, 355–63
merchandising 191, 195, 199
Merchant–Ivory 211–12
mergers 199–200, 208–10, 212–13
Method school 233–4
Metz, Christian 54, 269, 369
Meyer, Werner 148
MGM 187, 189, 241
Mickelthwait, John 199
Milland, Ray 374
Millen, Veronica 421
Miller, Mark Crispin 201, 282, 283–4

Millerson, Gerald 100
Mills, Frederick 95
Minnelli, Vincente 243, 244–5
Minns, R. 437
Minogue, Kylie 145
Miramax Films 202–3, 211–12
mise-en-scène 2
Mitchum, Robert 145
modernism, pleasure 269–70, 274
modernization, immigration to US 398–9
Modleski, Tania 21–2, 24, 27, 33, 221, 268–74
Moffatt, Tracey 163
Monaco, James, *Jaws* 192
Monroe, Marilyn 219, 223–7
montage 1, 48–50
Montrose, Louis A. 43
Moore, Demi 292
morality 236–7
Morgan Creek 211
Morgan, Willard 99
Morin, Edgar 229, 235
Morley, David 14–15, 16, 62–3, 64
Morrison, Toni 445
Morton, Joe 101
Moss, L. 425
mothering 347–8, 350
Motizon, Count de 370
Moulin Rouge (Huston) 89
movement 50–1, 119, 121–3
Moving Picture World 229
multi-directional sound 110
multi-layered sound 110
multiculturalism, national cinemas 157–8, 163
multimedia 199, 200, 201–2
multiplexes 176, 182, 192
Mulvey, Laura 3–4, 5, 298; fetishism 252; film criticism
    325; gendered spectatorship 21, 22; male gaze 332, 341;
    pleasure 66, 133; voyeurism 311
Münsterberg, Hugo 50–2
Murdoch, Rupert 209, 214
Muriel's Wedding 146
Murphy, A. D. 196
Murphy, Eddie 362
Murphy, Kathleen 299
Murray, John 370
'musculinity' 292, 293, 295–310
music soundtracks 74, 75, 107–8, 113, 191, 194, 195
musicals 40–1, 82, 86, 87, 109, 220, 240–5
Musser, Charles 395–6
My Beautiful Laundrette (1987) 171, 355
My Brilliant Career 143, 247
My Fair Lady (1964) 109
My First Wife (1984) 153–4
Myers, Denis 225
Mystery Train (1989) 285
myth study 277–8, 279

narcissism 272, 333, 362
Naremore, James 131
narration, early films 394–5
narrative: blockbusters 194–5, 201–2; colour 82, 85–6,
    87–8; hyperconsciousness 221; musicals 241, 243, 244;
    postmodernism 282–6
Nash, Margot 148
national cinema 9, 135–8; Australia 139–64; Great Britain
    165–72; Hong Kong 174–83
national identity 136, 155–60, 170–2, 175, 367–9, 441–3

nationalism 156–7, 165, 172
'Nationwide' 14, 63
Native Americans 373
Naughty Marietta 241
Neale, Steve 74, 85–93, 360
Near Dark (1988) 278
negotiated code 63
negotiation, spectatorship 30, 38–45
Negt, Oskar 390, 391
Nehant, Louis Pierre Théohile Dubois 370
Neill, Sam 118–19, 161
Neissor, Ulric 59
Nelson, Katherine 59
new economics 137–8
New German Cinema 159
new historicism 43–4
New Hollywood 184–203
New Line Cinema 202, 212, 215
New Sincerity 278, 286–90
New Zealand 142, 160–1
Newcomb, Horace 60
News Corporation 199–200, 209, 213–14
newspapers 425
Niagara (1953) 225
Nichols, Bill 118, 125, 152, 155
Nichols, Mike 188
Nicholson, Jack 201
nickelodeon 392, 393–5, 399, 403, 408–9
Nightmare on Elm Street 474
Niven, David 373–4, 376
No Worries 156
Norman Loves Rose (1982) 162
nostalgia 277, 289–90
novelistic 271–2
novelizations of films 199
novels, movie rights 189–91
Now Voyager 36, 299
Nowell-Smith, Geoffrey 141, 142
nuclear warfare 350–1, 353

object relations theory 436–7
objectivity, colour 92
O'Brien, Margaret 240
oedipal scenario 29, 30, 35, 36, 361
An Officer and a Gentleman 361
O'Hara, Maureen 91
oligopoly 79, 80
Once were Warriors (1994) 161
One Good Cop 350
oppositional code 63–5
optical unconscious 404
O'Regan, Tom 135–6, 139–64
O'Rourke, Denis 159
Orr, John 152
orthochromatic film stock 96–7
Other: colonialism 369, 371, 372; genres 478–9; horror
    474–6; imperialism 373; masculinity 351–2; racial
    representation 359
Ove, Horace 359–60
The Overlanders (1946) 148
Ovitz, Michael 193, 200
Owen, Craig 356

Pacific Heights (1990) 311–13, 323–6
panchromatic stock 97–8
Paramount 186, 189, 208, 215
Paramount Communications 199, 213

Paris in Burning (1990) 285
Park, Ida May 410
Parkin, F. 63
parody 178–9
parole 54
participation deals 200–1
partnerships 210–12
A Passage to India 355
The Passion of Remembrance 355, 357
pastiche 178–9, 195
Pastor, Tony 407
patriarchy: female gaze 411–14; psychoanalysis 66; romance novels 32–3; spectatorship 28
Patten, Chris 175
Patterson, Janet 263
Paul, R. W. 98
Peirce, Charles S. 117
Peiss, Kathy 391, 399, 408
Penley, Constance 34–5, 37, 346
Penn, Arthur 188
perception 50–1, 54–5; cognitive psychology 57–8; colour 92; digital imaging technologies 116; immigrants to US and early spectatorship 402–3; realism 116, 120
perceptual correspondence 75
Perfect (1985) 303, 304
performativity 292, 311–26
period film 220–1, 246–67
Perse, Elizabeth 121
Personal Best 52–3
Pescucci, Gabriella 258
Peter's Friends (1992) 169
Peters, Jon 200, 210
Petro, Patrice 46
Pfeiffer, Michelle *259*
Phar Lap 143, 157
phonograph 405–6
photography 95–105, 117–18, 369–70
The Piano 147, 148, 153, 158, 161, 212, 246–67, *265*
Pickford, Mary 230
Picnic at Hanging Rock 143, 149, 153, 246–67, *255*
pictorialism 56–9
Picturegoer 441
Pierson, Michele 132
Pines, Jim 357
The Pirate 244
Place, Janey 300
Plannette, James 101–2
platform releases 383
Platoon 299
pleasure 219–22; celebrity 220, 234–7; colour 82–3, 85; cultural studies 66; escapism 428–43; history of film studies 4; horror films 268–74; hypothetical lesbian heroine 332; pain 253, 254; reception studies 55; sound 113; stars 133–4; women 298, 428–31
point-of-view shots 313, 334–6
Poitier, Sidney 102–3
Pollock, Tom 385
polysemy 62, 63
Pontalis, Jean-Bertrand 35–6, 37
Porgy and Bess (1959) 444
pornography 133, 175, 334, 372
The Poseidon Adventure 189
Post Effects 119
post-production market research 385
Poster, Mark 284–5
posters 191, 235

postmodernism: centre and margin 356; genres 280–90; Hong Kong 174–83; Hong Kong film 137; horror films 268–74; pleasure 270; virtual space 132
power 59–60, 60–1, 308–10
Pratt, Mary Louise 369
Pratten, Anne 163
pre-production market research 384–5
pre-selling 190–1, 199, 202, 210, 211
Predator 2 307
Pretty Woman (1990) 197–8
primal scene 35, 37
The Prince and the Showgirl 225
Prince, Stephen 75, 115–26
print capitalism 367
private sphere 352, 397–406
product placement 201
production companies 395–6
Propp, Vladimir 32
proscenium arch, musicals 240–1, 242, 244, 245
Psycho 188
psychoanalysis: computer-generated actors 76; cultural studies 61–2; fantasy 30, 34–8; fetishism 248; gender 21, 22, 317; history of film studies 3–4, 5–6; negotiation 42; pleasure 66; race 361; reception studies 55, 67; spectatorship 21, 22, 28–30
psychographic research 383
psychology, spectators 50–2
psychothrillers, woman's 311–26
public sphere 352, 380, 390–414
publicity 220, 230, 440–1
publicity agents 230, 231–2
Pulp Fiction (1994) 212
Pumping Iron II: The Women (1984) 303
Purple Rain 385
Puttnam, David 165

Queen Elizabeth (1912) 229
Quo Vardis (1912) 406

Rabid 272
race 293–4, 355–63; action films 295–6; British audiences 1940s–1950s 426–7; colonialism 371–2; *The Color Purple* 444–67; desirability 223–4; early film audiences 397; lighting 74, 95–105; spectatorship 381; *Terminator 2: Judgment Day* 349–50, 352
Radway, Janice 5, 31–4, 41
Rafelson, Bob 188
Raging Bull (1980) 111, 257
Raiders of the Lost Ark (1981) 111, 196, 373
Rain Man 200
Raintree County 224
Rambo: First Blood II (1985) 344, 345, 353
Rambo III (1988) 344, 345
Ramona 86
rape 309–10
Rastus in Zululand (1910) 373
Rathbone, Basil 373–4
Razorback (1984) 145
reading against the grain 36–7
reading formations 11–12, 16–19
readings 14–19, 38–45
Reagan, Ronald 344–5, 353
The Real Glory (1930) 375
realism: colour 74, 80–3, 85–9, 93; computer-generated imagery 75; digital imaging technologies 116–26; history of film studies 2, 4; narration 395; sound 112; spectators 47–8

realness 312–13, 317, 319–23
rearticulation 285–6
Rebecca (1940) 320
Rebel (1985) 145
reception 5, 13, 29–34, 46–67, 390–414
The Reckless Moment 36
recruited audience screenings 384, 385
recycling, genres 279–80
Redstone, Sumner 213, 215
Reed, Ishmael 447
referentiality 284–6
referents, digital imaging 118–23, 130
Regarding Henry (1991) 344, 350
reissues 193
Reitz, Edgar 164
religion 447–9
remakes 193
The Removalists (1975) 143
Rennahan, Ray 90
repetition, masculinity 346–8
representation 356–63, 369
representativism 56–9
repressive state apparatuses (RSAs) 61
reproduction, masculinity 346–8
Research Services Company 425
Return Home 163–4
Return of the Jedi (1983) 376
reward risk 198
Rhodes of Africa (1936) 373, 374
Rice, Anne 279–80
Rich, B. Ruby 315–16
Richards, Jeffrey 171, 373, 375
Ricketson, James 150
Riff-Raff 167
Rising Sun (1993) 102, 103–4, *103*
rites-of-passage narrative 299
Riva, Michael 446
RKO 241
Roach, Jacqui 426
road movies 298
Road Warrior (1981) *see Mad Max 2*
Roadgames (1981) 145
The Robe (1953) 187
Roberts, Eric 145
Robeson, Paul 362, 374
Robin Hood (1991) 344
Robinson, Cathy 157
Robinson, David 161
Robinson, Patricia 421, 432
Robinson, Sonja 421
RoboCop 308
The Rocketeer (1991) 385
Rogers, Ginger 241, 242
Rogin, Michael 345
romance novels 31–4
Romero, George 270–1
Romper Stomper 147, 149, 159
Root, Jane 304–5
Rosa Luxemburg 247
Rose, Jacqueline 37–8
Rose, Rose I Love You/Meigui Meigui Wo Ai Ni (1993) 179
Rosen, Philip 49
Rosenblatt, Michael 130
Rosenfeld, Jonas 383
Rosenzweig, Roy 391, 399, 403
Rosher, Charles 97
Ross, Steven J. 209, 214

Roth, Joe 388
Rowse, Tim 156, 157, 158
Royal Tramp/Lu Ding Ji (1992) 178
Rubin, Rebecca 121
Ruddell, Robert B. 56
Rushdie, Salmon 358
Ruthrof, Horst 154
Ryan, Mary 411
Rydell, Robert W. 371

Safford, Tony 152
Safran, Henri 162
Salamon, Julie 383
Salisbury, Mark 473–4
Sammy and Rosie Get Laid (1988) 171
Sanders, George 374
Sanders of the River (1935) 372, 373, 374
Santa Fe Trail (1940) 375
saturation booking 197, 207, 383–4
Saturday Night Fever (1977) 109, 194
Saussure 53–4
Savani, Tom 474
Schatz, Thomas 137, 184–203, 278–9
schemata 57–9, 67
Schepisi, Fred 150, 156, 159
Schickel, Richard 202, 282, 283, 284
Schindler's List (1993) 111
Schlatter, Charlie 145
Schlondorff, Volker 155
School Daze 464–5
Schoonmaker, Thelma 256
Schrader, Paul 153
Schramm, Wilbur 60
Schulze, Laurie 301–2, 305
Schwarzenegger, Arnold 131–2
science, colonialism 369–72, 376
science fiction 472–5
Scorsese, Martin 111, 203, 256–60
Scotland 165–6, 171–2
Scott, Ridley 297
Scream 475
Screen 360
Screen Actors' Guild 130
screen theory 3–6, 74, 360
scripts, concept testing 384
Seagram 214
self, gender performativity 311–26
self-extension, ideology of 350
self-identity, cultural studies 64–5
self-production, masculinity 353–4
self-referentiality 284–6
Selznick, David O. 186
semiotics, formalism 120
Sennett, Richard 233, 393 4, 400
Sense and Sensibility (1995) 167, 247
sequels 193
Sergi, Gianluca 74–5, 107–13
The Seven Year Itch 225
sexual difference 37–8
sexual identity 180
sexuality 64–5; action heroines 300; costume films 247–67;
      dance 42; ethnicity and action films 295–6; fantasy 37;
      female bodybuilding 303–5; feminist film theory 331–3;
      femme fatale 300; Hong Kong cinema 180, 182;
      hypothetical lesbian heroine 331–41; Monroe 223–7;
      see also homosexuality; lesbianism
shadow 100–1

Shallow Grave (1994) 171
Shay, Don 115
Shay, Robert 212
She Must Be Seeing Things 37
Sheinwold, Patricia Fox 227
Shelley, Jim 472
Sheppard, Jean 425
Sherak, Tom 386
Shogun Assassins 474
Shohat, Ella 294, 366–76
shopping malls 192
Show Boat (1936) 224, 243
signs 60, 92, 117–18
Silence of the Lambs (1990) 203, 297, *314*, *317*; action
    heroines 305–6; gender identity 313–18; horror films
    476–7; performativity of gender 292, 326
silent films, audiences 380, 390–414
Simba (1927) 371
Simes, Kathleen 429
Simonet, Thomas 384
Sinclair, Marianne 226–7
sing-alongs 393–4
Singer, Harry 56
Singin' in the Rain 242
Sinise, Gary 115
Sirens (1994) 143, 158
Sister My Sister 247, 251
Sky Television 213–14
slasher films 270–4, 292, 317–18, 381
Sleeping with the Enemy (1991) 313, 321–3
Smith, A. D. 156–7
Smith, Barbara 447, 460
Smith, Beaumont 161
Smith, C. Aubrey 373–4
Smith, Dick 474
Smits, Jimmy 145
Snipes, Wesley 103–4, *103*
Snow White and the Seven Dwarfs (1937) 184
soap operas, women 20–7
Sobchack, Vivian 132
social audience 12, 23, 24, 25–6, 46, 379–81
social identity 291–4
social imaginary 7
social subject, spectatorship 25–6
sociolinguistics, reception studies 54–5
Soldiers Three (1951) 375
Some Like It Hot 225–6
Something Wild 361, 362
Sony 199–200, 209–10, 214
Sorrel, A. A. 169–70
sound 74–5, 107–13; effect on exhibition 396; introduction
    of 73, 77–80; realism 2; *Star Wars* 195; voices 233
The Sound of Music (1965) 185, 187, 188
soundtracks 107–8, 194, 199
South Pacific (1958) 187
space 402–3
Spainhower, Mark 474
Spartacus (1960) 108
specious good 270, 273
spectacle: colonialism 369–72; colour 87–8, 89, 91; musicals
    220, 240–5
spectators 12–13, 28–45; audience distinction 12, 22, 23–4;
    black women 426–7, 444–67; colonialism 368–9; of *The
    Color Purple* 444–67; costume films 247; early silent films
    390–414; escapism 420–43; female 292–3, 298, 332–3,
    380–1; female realness 317; feminist film theory 331–3;
    fetishism 254–6; gender 21–7, 28, 311–12; history of

film studies 5, 6; Hollywood cinema in Britain 1940s and
    1950s 420–43; homosexuality 333; horror films 274;
    musicals 220, 240–5; national identity 368; positioning
    of 30–1; race 361–2; reception studies 13, 47–67;
    shared experience 435–7; social audience distinction 46;
    woman's psychothriller 325; women 420–43
Spielberg, Steven 192–3, 195–6, 203; *The Color Purple* 355,
    381, 444, 446, 451, 461–2; digital imaging technologies
    116; high concept 201; *Jaws* (1975) 190, 191; New
    Sincerity 288–9; participation deals 201; sound 111
Spotswood (1992) 144
The Squatter's Daughter (1933) 162
Stacey, Jackie 379, 380–1, 420–43
Stagecoach (1939) 276
Staiger, Janet 8, 13, 46–67, 228, 316
Stallone, Sylvester 200–1, 344
Stam, Robert 294, 366–76
standardization 390–1, 392–7, 399
Stanislavsky 233
Stanley and Livingstone (1939) 375
Star! (1968) 188
A Star is Born 242, 243
star system 200–1, 228–9, 413
star vehicles 200, 203
Star Wars (1977) 108, 194–5, 360
stars 7, 9; blockbusters 198; casting tests 384, 385; celebrity
    219–20, 228–37; colour 82, 86; escapism 428–9,
    440–1; Hollywood cinema in Britain 1940–50s 434,
    440–3; meanings 219; national identity 441–3; pleasure
    133–4; salaries 200–1, 231
Steele, Valerie 253
Steiger, Rod 102–3
The Stepfather (1987) 313, 318–21, *320*
stereo sound 109–11, 278
stereotypes 358, 360–1
Sternberg, Josef von 100
The Sting (1973) 190
Stoller, Robert 248
Stone, Sharon 300–1
stories, national identity 367–8
Stork (1971) 143
Straayer, Chris 292–3, 331–40
Strange Days 472
Strapless (1988) 170
The Strawberry Statement (1970) 278
Streep, Meryl 145
Strictly Ballroom (1992) 146–7, 151, 158, 163
Stringfellow, Mabel 439
structuring antinomies 277
studio management 200
studio system 184, 185, 186, 231–2, 440–1
subalterns, Hong Kong 178
subculture, genres 471–7, 478–9
subjectivity: colour 92; fantasy 34–8; gendered spectatorship
    21–2; horror films 272; identity 291; musicals 242–5;
    race and representation 358; spectatorship 23, 25–6,
    28–30, 390, 400–1, 402–3, 405, 411; woman's
    psychothriller 313, 315
Sue, Eugene 17
Summer Stock 242
Summerfield, P. 438–9
The Sun Never Sets (1940) 374
Sunday Too Far Away 143, 153
The Sundowners (1960) 145, 148
Sunless Days/Meiyou Taiyang de Rizi (1990) 175
Susannah of the Mounties (1939) 375
Suspicion (1941) 320

Swann, Paul 425, 442–3
Swanson, Gloria 411
Swayze, John Cameron 375–6
Sweetie 146, 147, 161
Switch (1991) 344
Swordsman II/Xiao'ao Jianghu II Dongfang Bubai (1992) 180
syndication 187, 189, 213
synergy 199, 208, 215
Synthespian Project 130

talent agencies 193
Tamahori, Lee 161
Tarantino, Quentin 212
Tarzan series 372, 373
Tasker, Yvonne 5, 6, 291–2, 295–310
Taubin, Amy 260, 315
Taxi Driver (1976) 109, 257, 281
Taylor, Clyde 360
Technicolor 81, 83, 86, 88–91, 93, 278
technological rent 79–80
technology 8–9, 73–6; acting 233; colonialism 371;
     colour 77–83; digital imaging 115–26; genres of films
     278–9; horror films 268; innovation 77–83, 85; lighting
     95–105; modes of information 284–5; sound 77–83,
     107–13
Teenage Mutant Ninja Turtles 203
telefilms 187
television: advertising 201, 383–4, 386; Australia 153,
     157–8; Britain 168, 169–70, 171; conglomerates 209;
     female audience 12; film marketing 193; genres of
     films 278; globalization of Hollywood 207–8;
     imperialism 375–6; international partnerships 210;
     market research 382; mergers 212–14; postwar
     Hollywood 186–7; reception studies 46–67; soap
     operas 20–7; spectator-text relationship 25; syndication
     of movies 189
Temple, Shirley 374, 375
The Ten Commandments (1956) 185, 187
Teo, Stephen 136–7, 174–83
The Terminator (1984) 281, 292, 299–300, 345–54
Terminator 2: Judgment Day (1991) 199, 207, 211; action
     heroines 300, 303, 308; computer-generated images 115,
     129; masculinity 293, 345–54; sound 112
test screenings 379, 385
The Texas Chainsaw Massacre (1974) 191, 270, 272, 273
theatre (traditional) 229, 232–3
Thelma and Louise (1991) 221, 278, 285–6, 296, 297–301,
     308
There's No Business Like Show Business 225
They Died with Their Boots on (1941) 375
They're a Weird Mob 148–9, 162
Thomas, William Isaac 403
Thompson, Jack 149
Thompson, Kristin 139, 144
Thornton, S. 475, 478
Thorpe, Margaret 235
Three Men and a Baby 350
Thunderball (1965) 187
THX Sound System 75, 109, 111, 113
tight diversification 199
time 367–8, 402–3
time travel, fantasy 346
Time Warner 113, 206, 209, 210, 211, 214–15
Time Warner Entertainment 210
Titanic (1997) 73, 129, 130
title tests 384
tokenism 357

Tony the Greaser (1911) 373
Tootelian, Dennis 387
Top Hat 241
Total Recall (1990) 211, 308–9, 386
The Towering Inferno 189
A Town Like Alice (1956) 148
Tracy, Spencer 375
Trader Horn (1931) 375
Trailing African Wild Animals (1922) 371
Trainspotting (1995) 171
trangression, feminism 308
transportation model 60
Traps 158
Travolta, John 194, 304
Trilling, Lionel 269–70, 273
TriStar 210, 211
True Grit (1978) 277
True Lies (1993) 115, 119
Truffaut, Francois 3
tsaan pin ('dilapidated' cinema) 176, 178
Tsui Hark 175, 176, 180–1
Tudor, Andrew 469–70
tungsten light 97
Turner, Graeme 1–10, 135–8; audiences and consumption
     379–81; Australian cinema 171; identities 291–4;
     industries 135–8; meanings and pleasures 219–22;
     technologies 73–6; understanding film 11–13
Twentieth Century Fox 209, 210
Twenty Something/Wan Jiu Zhao Wu (1994) 182
The Two Mrs Carrolls (1947) 320
Tyson, Cicely 101

'ultra-high-budget' films 207
uncertainty, innovation 77–8
unconscious 30, 35, 37–8, 132–3
Union Pictures 141
United Artists 189, 230
United Film-makers Organisation (UFO) 182
United States: Australian cinema 144–5, 151–2;
     imperialism 373, 375; masculinity 344–54; national
     cinemas 139–40; spectatorship of early films 390–414;
     see also Hollywood
The Unwritten Law (1907) 410
Ur-text, New Sincerity 288–9
utopian sensibilities, escapism 429–43
utopianism, musicals 41–2

Valentine, Joseph 98
Valentino, Rudolph 229, 411, 413
value and lifestyle research 383
Variety 198, 210, 229
vaudeville 228–9, 391, 393–4, 399, 407, 408
vertical integration 208, 214
Vertov, Dziga, formalism 120
Viacom Inc. 213, 215
video 169, 193–4, 196, 206, 207–8, 278–9
video games 199
video retailers 213
Videodrome 271, 273–4
Vietnam moveis 299
violence 309–10, 345, 349, 353
Virtual Celebrity Productions 130
Voellman, Chris 122, 123
Vogel, Harold 208–9
Vorse, Mary Heaton 399, 400–1
Voyage en Douce 293, 331, 334–6, *335*, 337–41, *339*
The Voyage Home: Star Trek IV (1986) 130

voyeurism: colonialism 369, 372; costume films 252–3, 260, 262–6; female spectators 333; race 361; spectatorship of early films 411–12; woman's psychothriller 311
Vygotsky, Lev 49, 52, 59

Wake in Fright 148, 149
Waldman, Diane 320
Wales 171
Walkabout 148, 149
Walker, Alexander 228, 230
Walker, Alice 355, 444, 446, 448, 460, 465–6
Walker, Joseph 97
Wallace, Michele 447
Ward, Vincent 160, 161
Warner Brothers 78, 79–80, 187, 189, 208, 241
Warner Communications 199, 209
Wasserman, Lew 214
Waterland 169
Waterworld (1995) 231
Wathen, Gwyneth 437
Weaver, Sigourney 297, 306, 308
Weber, Lois 410
Wee Willie Winkie (1937) 374, 375
Weinstein, Harvey and Bob 212
Weir, Peter 143, 149, 154, 156, 160, 252
West, Cornel 448–9
Westerns 276, 277–8, 279, 287–8, 375, 471
Westinghouse Electric 213
Wharton, Edith 257, 258, 267
White, Armond 445
White, Hayden 367
whiteness 95–105, 223–4, 359
Who Framed Roger Rabbit? (1988) 199, 278
The Wicked City/Yaoshou Dushi (1992) 180–1
The Wicked Lady 247
The Wild Bunch (1979) 277
William Morris Agency 193
William, Robin 201
Williams, Christopher 125
Williams, John 191, 195
Williams, Linda 273
Williams, Raymond 42–3
Williamson, David 143
Williamson, Judith 357, 358
Willis, Bruce 344

Willis, Sharon 285
Winston, Brian 98
Witness 251
The Wizard of Gore 474
The Wizard of Oz 83
Wolf, Christa 353
Wolfson, Sonia 227
Wollen, Tana 246
woman's gothic 320, 322
women: action heroines 291–2, 295–310; bodybuilding 301–5; costume film 246–67; desirability 223–7; female image and colour 82, 86, 89–91; genres 20–7; Hollywood cinema in Britain 1940s and 1950s 420–43; horror 273–4, 475–6; lighting 100–1; masculine bodies 292; Monroe 223–7; pleasure 298, 428–31; psychothrillers 311–26; spectatorship 12, 380–1, 391, 400, 406–14; as victims 225–6; whiteness 223
women's films 320, 424; negotiation 40–1; rites-of-passage narrative 299; spectatorship 20–7
Wong Kar-wai 175, 180
Woo, John 175
Wood, Robin 270, 272, 273, 317–18
Woods, Frank 395
Woodstock (1970) 189
Woolf, Virginia 367, 413–14
Woollacott, Janet 8, 11–12, 14–19
Word is Out 357
World War II 437–40
Wright, Basil 101
Wright, Will 277
Wrong Side of the Road (1981) 163
Wyatt, Justin 379–80, 382–8

The Year of Living Dangerously (1982) 143
Yip, Veronica 175
Young, Hugo 165
Young, Loretta 91
youth audience 188–9, 192, 202, 278, 387

Zabriskie Point (1970) 278
Zanuck, Richard, *Jaws* 191
Zemeckis, Robert 280–1
Zolotow, Maurice 227
Zukor, Adolph, stars 229